MOON

# CAROLINAS
# & GEORGIA

JIM MOREKIS

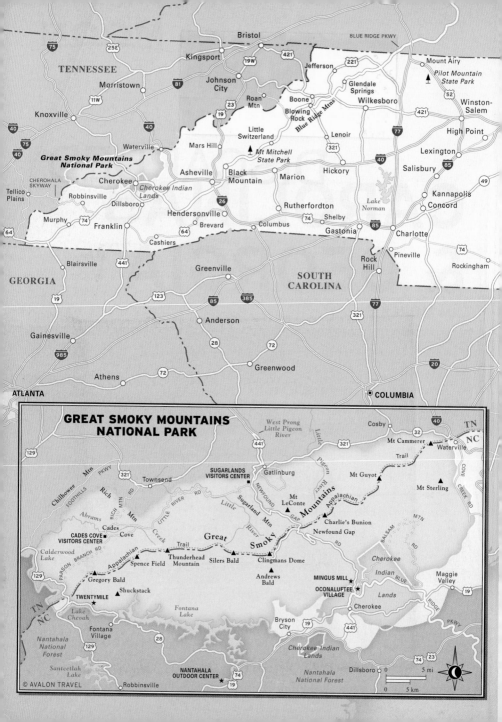

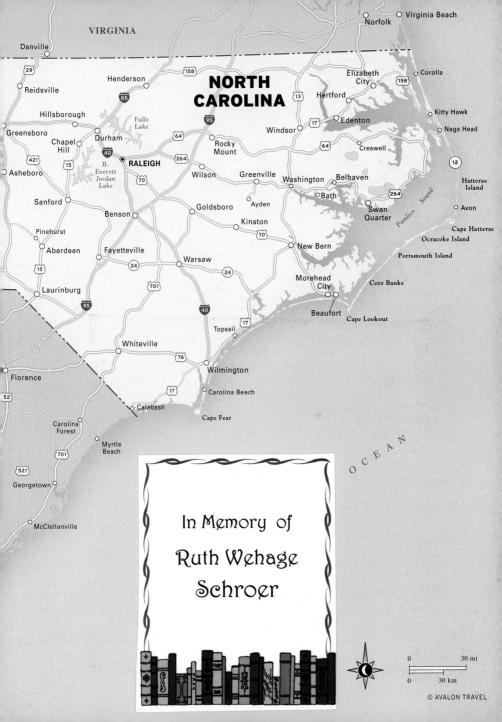

In Memory of

Ruth Wehage

Schroer

© AVALON TRAVEL

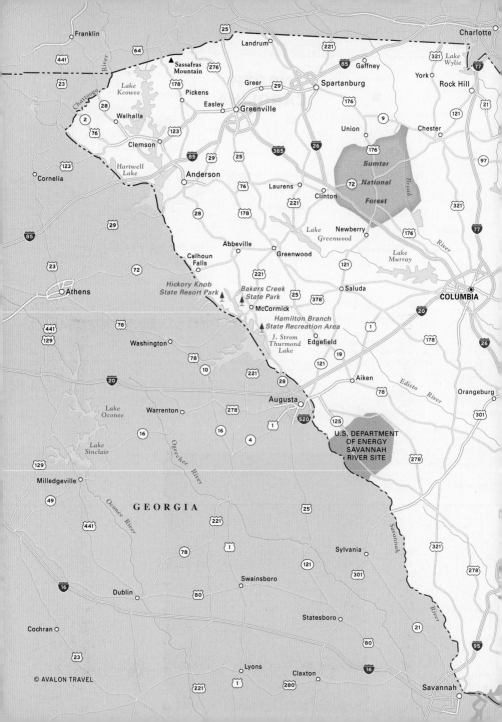
© AVALON TRAVEL

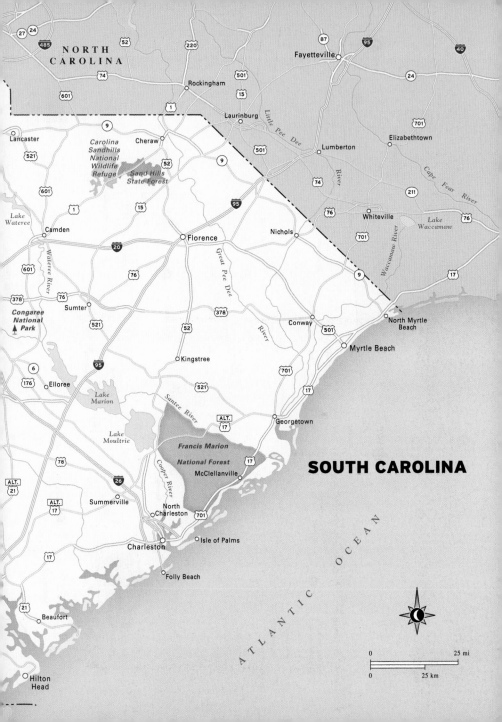

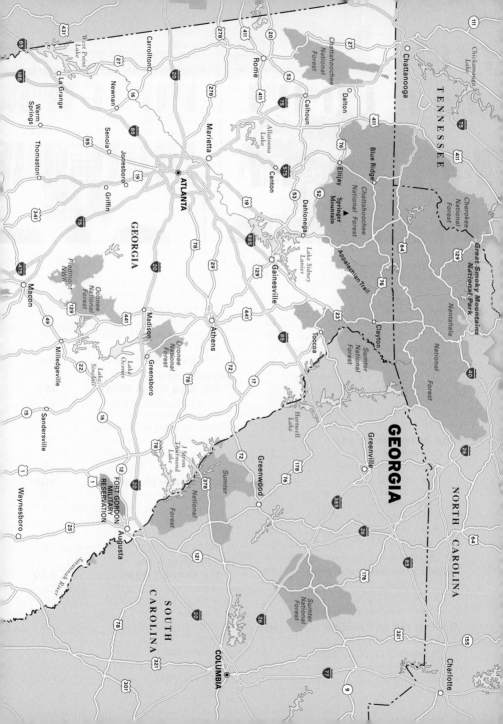

# Contents

# DISCOVER THE
# Carolinas & Georgia

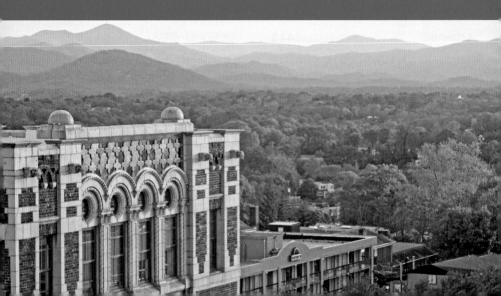

**W**hen people around the world think of the American South, it's some archetypal image from the Carolinas and Georgia that comes to mind, whether they know it or not. Spanish moss hanging from a live oak, a tangy pulled-pork barbecue sandwich, hiking the Appalachian Trail, classic lines from *Gone with the Wind*, the robust smell of a tobacco field, enjoying a cold Coca-Cola while listening to bluegrass music…This is the vivid, iconic backdrop of a real or imagined experience of the South, both for the people who've always yearned to visit as well as for those who call it home.

This is a huge area with a huge history to match. These three states encompass about 150,000 square miles and contain nearly 10 percent of the American population, living in enormous metropolitan areas, tiny crossroads hamlets, and everything in between. The Carolinas and Georgia have been the birthplace of four U.S. presidents and seminal American figures like Martin Luther King Jr.

**Clockwise from top left:** Charleston's Pineapple Fountain in Waterfront Park; Bonaventure Cemetery in Savannah; Myrtle Beach; sea oats; Cathedral of St. John the Baptist in Savannah; Asheville.

In the enormous swath of America between the Blue Ridge and the Atlantic Ocean you'll find a marvelously diverse geography, with peat-filled swamps and Appalachian balds, salty ocean waves and bass-rich lakes, sandhills and deep forest, slow-moving blackwater rivers and rushing mountain streams.

There's a lot to see and do here, whether your taste runs to rock climbing, fishing, beachcombing, kayaking, or following Southern Gothic literature. Or even just enjoying good food and drink—many of the nation's best chefs practice their trade in restaurants in Atlanta and Charleston. You could make an entire vacation of exploring down-home barbecue joints and comparing the various regional sauces that even today inspire impassioned, good-natured debate.

It may seem folly to attempt to try and tie it all together, but one common thread does run through the Carolinas and Georgia: that fabled Southern hospitality and the easy, welcoming laughter that comes with it.

**Clockwise from top left:** an alligator in Okefenokee Swamp; Drayton Hall near Charleston; birds on an Outer Banks beach; freshly picked Georgia peaches.

# 10 TOP EXPERIENCES

**1** **Driving the Blue Ridge Parkway:** With mountains, waterfalls, and historic detours, this spectacular drive is one of the most scenic in the country, especially during the fall (page 169).

**2** **Historic Charleston:** Enjoy this historic city's well-preserved sights with a walking tour of its charming, winding streets (page 279).

**3** **Historic Savannah:**
The nation's largest contiguous historic district is epitomized by nearly two dozen verdant squares, each with its own character (page 593).

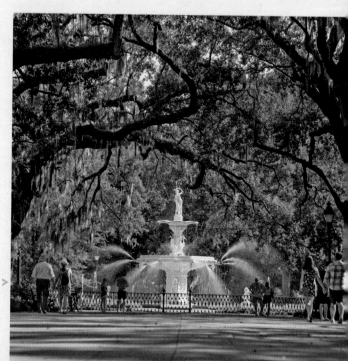

**4** **Atlanta's New South:** The still-growing economic engine of Georgia and indeed most of the southeastern U.S., "the city too busy to hate" defies stereotypes and offers cutting-edge cultural experiences (page 472).

## 5 Outer Banks Odyssey:

An utterly unique experience awaits in this chain of remote barrier islands, dotted with fishing villages, old folkways, and beachfront recreation (pages 41, 52, and 57).

>>>

## 6 Myrtle Beach:

This family-friendly getaway is designed for maximum convenience and enjoyment, with enough kitsch factor to keep things interesting. Oh, and the beaches are among the best (page 236)!

>>>

**7 Golf Galore:** Tee up a links-centric vacation at top-ranked, public courses, especially around Charlotte, Myrtle Beach, and Hilton Head Island (page 377).

>>>

**8 Great Smoky Mountains:** The Smokies offer ease of access along with stunning natural beauty and intriguing Appalachian culture (page 214).

<<<

**9 Southern BBQ:** No trip to the South is complete without partaking of the pork goodness, whether it's prepared Lexington style or with a South Carolina mustard-based sauce (page 25)!

>>>

MARTIN LUTHER KING, JR.
WAS BORN IN THIS HOUSE
JANUARY 15, 1929

**10** **African American Heritage:** This region has shaped the history of African Americans since before the nation's inception (page 31).

# The Best of the Carolinas & Georgia

This three-week circle route begins and ends in the centrally located airport hub of Charlotte. Explore the scenic Blue Ridge and Smoky Mountains, see the highlights of Georgia, soak up the history and beaches of the Atlantic coast, and experience the Outer Banks.

## Charlotte

### DAY 1

Start in **Charlotte** with a day of exploring museums. Visit the **Levine Museum of the New South** for an engaging introduction to North Carolina and Southern history, and then stop in at the **Mint Museums** to see their stellar collections of art and modern craft. Dine at any of Charlotte's hundreds of delicious international restaurants, and spend a night of Old South luxury at the **Duke Mansion** or the **VanLandingham Estate.**

the Mint Museum Uptown in Charlotte

## Blue Ridge Parkway

### DAY 2

Begin your two-day trek down the **Blue Ridge Parkway** with a visit to fun little **Boone,** two hours north of Charlotte. From Boone head down to **Blowing Rock,** then visit the **Linville Caverns,** and spend the night at **Eseeola Lodge.**

## Asheville

### DAY 3

Continue south on the Blue Ridge Parkway, with stops at the **Folk Art Center,** the **Museum of North Carolina Minerals,** and **Mount Mitchell.** This should take about 4-5 hours. This afternoon, take a walk around downtown **Asheville,** before dining at **Salsa's** and settling in for the night at one of the city's bed-and-breakfasts.

## Great Smoky Mountains National Park

### DAY 4

Get an early start and hit Highway 28, winding along **Fontana Lake** (don't miss the dam!) into Tennessee. Spend all day touring **Great Smoky Mountains National Park,** making sure to see Cades Cove, Clingmans Dome, and the elk at Cataloochee. Spend the night in **Bryson City** (at the edge of the park), or at the **Pisgah Inn** near Waynesville (about an hour away).

## Greenville and Athens

### DAY 5

Take the 90-minute drive down to **Greenville** and have lunch in the restored downtown area. Head another 90 minutes west to **Athens,** Georgia, taking a stroll on the scenic North Campus of the **University of Georgia.** After dinner at **The National,** take in a rock 'n' roll show at the **40 Watt Club.** Stay the evening at **Hotel Indigo.**

## Atlanta

### DAY 6

Take the quick drive west into **Atlanta** and go to **Centennial Olympic Park** to visit the **Georgia Aquarium** and **World of Coca-Cola.** Take in a Braves game, if they're in town, or maybe a show at the **Fox Theatre.** Settle into a night in your room across Peachtree Street from the Fox in the **Georgian Terrace Hotel.**

## FDR Country

### DAY 7

Head a couple of hours southwest to the Warm Springs-Pine Mountain area and **FDR's Little White House,** where you can explore the legacy of the president's time in Georgia. Stay the night in a historic lodge at nearby **Franklin D. Roosevelt State Park.**

## Plains

### DAY 8

Today, head southeast a short ways into little **Plains** and visit the several sites dedicated to native son **Jimmy Carter.** Make the short drive to the site of the notorious Civil War POW camp at **Andersonville** and tour the adjacent **National Prisoner of War Museum.** Spend the night in the ornate Victorian **Windsor Hotel** in nearby Americus.

## Okefenokee and Jekyll Island

### DAY 9

Get up early and make the three-hour drive to the **Okefenokee Swamp** to spend the day paddling, hiking, and bird- and alligator-watching. This evening, head up to **Jekyll Island** and stay at the legendary **Jekyll Island Club.**

## Savannah

### DAY 10

After a walk on the beach, head an hour north to **Savannah** and stroll the downtown squares, maybe adding a tour of the historic **Owens-Thomas House.** Enjoy your night's stay at a B&B like **The Gastonian** or in a boutique room at the **Bohemian Hotel.**

### DAY 11

Ride out to **Bonaventure Cemetery** to enjoy its calming beauty, and then visit **Fort Pulaski** to take in both the history and the scenic grounds. For dinner, splurge on a meal at **Elizabeth on 37th.**

## Charleston

### DAY 12

Before leaving Savannah, do some shopping on **Broughton Street.** Head an hour north to **Beaufort,** South Carolina, to walk around the charming waterfront for a while. This evening, make another one-hour journey into **Charleston** and a night at a historic B&B like the **John Rutledge House** or an evocative hotel like **The Vendue.**

### DAY 13

Stroll the streets of Charleston's **French Quarter, Rainbow Row,** and **The Battery.** Do some shopping on **King Street.** In the

Driftwood Beach on Jekyll Island

afternoon, head across the Ashley River to historic **Drayton Hall.**

## Myrtle Beach
### DAY 14
Head two hours north to the surf-and-sun playground of **Myrtle Beach** for a day on the sand and kitschy, family-friendly activities like **Ripley's Believe It or Not!** Enjoy the view from your balcony at the **Tilghman Beach and Golf Resort.**

## Wilmington
### DAY 15
After a morning swim, make the short trip into North Carolina to visit historic **Wilmington.** Take a walking tour of the gorgeous **historic district.** At night, attend a concert at **Thalian Hall,** and take your pick of beautiful bed-and-breakfasts for your night's lodging.

## The Outer Banks
### DAY 16
Head up to **New Bern** for lunch, allowing a couple of hours for travel time. Spend the afternoon touring historic **Beaufort,** making sure to leave time for a visit to the **Maritime Museum** and the **Old Burying Ground.** For supper, visit a legend, **Morehead City's Sanitary Fish Market.**

### DAY 17
Explore Down East in the morning, visiting **Harkers Island's Core Sound Waterfowl Museum.** Wend your way up to **Cedar Island,** and catch the ferry to **Ocracoke,** a 2.5-hour voyage. Stay the night at the **Captain's Landing** in Ocracoke.

### DAY 18
Explore Ocracoke in the morning, and then, early in the day, catch the ferry to **Hatteras** (40 minutes on the water). From there, head up Highway 12, tracing the Outer Banks northward. Cross onto **Roanoke Island,** visiting the **aquarium** or **Fort Raleigh National Historic Site,** and staying at the **White Doe Inn;** or keep driving north to **Nags Head,** and spend the night at the **First Colony Inn.**

# Southern BBQ

The importance of barbecue in the South cannot be overstated. It's a noun down here, something you eat rather than a verb that you do. To the Southerner, barbecue is both delicacy and staple: one of life's greatest luxuries, but one without which a person cannot be said to be truly living.

Eastern North Carolina has a vinegar and pepper sauce, and Western North Carolina takes that and adds a tomato base and brown sugar (also called Lexington style). South Carolina has a polarizing mustard-based sauce, which is found mostly in the central Midlands area of the state from Newberry almost to Charleston. Georgia features all of the above and more, but a sweeter, ketchupy sauce is the trend along the Savannah River.

As for the meat itself, in all regions there's no question about what kind you mean when you say barbecue. It's always pork, period. And connoisseurs agree that if it isn't cooked whole over an open wood fire, it isn't authentic barbecue, merely a pale—if still tasty—imitation. Sides are important, especially the item known as hash, made from pork byproducts served over rice. In any genuine barbecue place you'll also encounter cracklin's (fried pork skin), whole loaves of white bread, and, of course, sweet iced tea (called simply "sweet tea").

Aficionados further insist that a real barbecue place is open only on Friday and Saturday (some generously extend the definition to include Thursday), chops its own wood, and proffers its pig not à la carte but in a distinctive "all you care to eat" buffet style, which generally means one huge pass at the buffet line.

Key purveyors of the culinary art form include:

## EASTERN NORTH CAROLINA

- **Stamey's Old Fashioned Barbecue** in Greensboro (page 138)
- **Allen & Son BBQ** in Chapel Hill (page 128)

## WESTERN NORTH CAROLINA

- **Lexington Barbecue** in Lexington (page 139)

## SOUTH CAROLINA

- **Sweatman's Bar-b-que** in Holly Hill (page 411)
- **Fiery Ron's Home Team BBQ** in Charleston (page 333)

## GEORGIA

- **Sandfly BBQ** in Savannah (page 635)

## The Triangle

### DAY 19

Take a three-hour drive west on U.S. 64 to visit the state museums of **Raleigh:** the **North Carolina Museums of History, Natural Sciences, and Art.** Pick up a hot dog for lunch at the **Roast Grill**—don't ask for condiments!—or have a more elegant lunch inside the Museum of Art. This evening, make the quick jaunt over to **Chapel Hill,** spending a luxurious night at the **Carolina Inn.**

### DAY 20

Take a morning tour of the campus of the **University of North Carolina,** and if you're a sports fan, visit the **Carolina Basketball Museum.** Mosey the nine miles over to **Durham** for lunch at the **Thai Café** or one of the city's great taco stands. Check out campuses at **North Carolina Central University** and **Duke University.** In the evening, catch a **Durham Bulls** game, or head back to Chapel Hill for some live music at **Cat's Cradle** or **Local 506.**

## Lexington and back to Charlotte

### DAY 21

Get on I-85 for the drive back down to Charlotte—but budget time to stop for some of **Lexington**'s amazing barbecue along the way!

# The Paths of the Civil War

This itinerary for Civil War buffs, customized for those flying into and leaving from Atlanta, hits the conflict's historical highlights in Georgia and South Carolina. Because the CSS *Hunley* exhibit in Charleston toward the end of the trip is only open on weekends, ideally you should begin this trip on a Sunday or Monday.

## Day 1

Head to the **Atlanta History Center** to see exhibits on local Civil War history, as well as the **Cyclorama,** a unique Victorian-era portrayal of the Battle of Atlanta. This afternoon drive a bit east to **Stone Mountain Park** to see the huge relief sculpture of Robert E. Lee, Stonewall Jackson, and Jefferson Davis on the granite outcropping that gives the park its name.

## Day 2

Take a road trip in your rental car to North Georgia. See the burgeoning **Kennesaw Mountain National Battlefield.** Spend the rest of the day touring the expansive **Chickamauga battlefield** near the Tennessee border.

## Day 3

Drive down I-85 to I-185 and head into **Columbus** for a visit to the **National Civil War Naval Museum,** chronicling the lesser-known maritime aspect of the conflict. After lunch drive southeast on Highway 26 and spend the afternoon at the site of the notorious **Andersonville POW camp** and adjacent **National Prisoner of War Museum.** Spend the night in nearby Americus at the **Windsor Hotel.**

## Day 4

Head east to Macon for lunch at **H & H Restaurant** and a visit to the **Cannonball House,** a house museum bearing the marks of Union artillery in 1864. Afterwards, head into **Savannah** for a stay at an antebellum B&B like the **Foley House.**

battlefield at Chickamauga & Chattanooga National Military Park

Andersonville Prison

Savannah's picturesque downtown

## Day 5

Tour Savannah's downtown squares, including a stop at the **Green-Meldrim House,** General Sherman's headquarters while he was in town. Stroll along **River Street,** focal point of Savannah's huge antebellum cotton shipping industry.

## Day 6

Head east along the road to **Tybee Island** for a long visit to the scenic grounds at **Fort Pulaski,** which Robert E. Lee helped construct before the war. Once considered the most impregnable fortress in the world, Fort Pulaski's Confederate garrison was forced to surrender by the first use of rifled cannons in warfare. Close the day with the two-hour drive to **Charleston** and a night at the **Mills House Hotel,** which once hosted Lee himself.

## Day 7

Take the ferry and spend the morning at **Fort Sumter** in Charleston Harbor, where the Civil War began in April 1861. This afternoon visit the **CSS** _Hunley_ facility in North Charleston, where

the first submarine ever to attack an enemy vessel is being painstakingly restored (book tickets well in advance). Tomorrow you drive back in time to catch your flight out of Atlanta.

cannon at Fort Sumter

# Water Recreation

The Carolinas and Georgia provide a wealth of water-based enjoyment, whether by kayak, canoe, fishing boat, or just plain enjoying the beach.

## WHITE-WATER RAFTING

- The **U.S. National Whitewater Center** in Charlotte offers a variety of well-supervised activities, including rafting, paddling, and kayaking, as well as dry-land activities like zip-lining.

- **Nantahala Outdoor Center** offers rafting and tubing opportunities on the scenic Nantahala River in North Carolina.

- The **Chattooga River** at the border of the Carolinas and Georgia was the setting of the movie *Deliverance* and provides a range of rafting opportunities along Sections III and IV, designated Wild and Scenic.

- Columbus, Georgia, is tearing down obsolete earthen dams on the **Chattahoochee River** to make white-water rafting an ecotourism attraction.

Kure Beach

## BLACKWATER KAYAKING

- The Cape Fear River of North Carolina is rife with kayaking and canoeing possibilities. The 147-mile **Cape Fear River Trail** starts in J. Bayard Clark Park in Fayetteville and takes you all the way to the mouth of the river in Southport.

- **Cape Romain National Wildlife Refuge,** north of Charleston, has hundreds of square miles of sheltered and ecologically significant wetland for your paddling enjoyment.

- The **Edisto River** in coastal South Carolina is the world's longest blackwater river. Kayaking and canoeing opportunities abound, whether on your own or through numerous chartered trips.

- The **Congaree River** running through Columbia, South Carolina, is a friendly and fun place to kayak. Nearby you can paddle through the ancient wetland of **Congaree National Park,** one of the last old-growth forests left in the United States.

- The **Altamaha River Canoe Trail** in southeast Georgia takes you down one of the East Coast's largest and most protected rivers.

## FISHING AND BOATING

- **Little River,** North Carolina, seemingly offers as many fishing charters as there are people in this little town.

- **Hilton Head,** South Carolina, is optimized for the boating and fishing experience both in infrastructure and in the beautiful setting of Calibogue Sound.

- To explore Georgia's barrier islands—many of which are only accessible by boat—use **Shellman Bluff** near Darien as a convenient and charming base of operations for your maritime adventures.

## BEACHES

- The beaches on the North Carolina coast near Wilmington—**Wrightsville Beach** and **Kure Beach**—are a perfect blend of beauty and family friendliness.

- There may not be a better beach to ride your bike on than **Hilton Head,** South Carolina.

- At **Myrtle Beach,** South Carolina, you can enjoy a water park or a banana-boat ride or a Jet Ski—all in one afternoon.

- The **Outer Banks** present some amazing beach opportunities. Check out **Ocracoke Island, Cape Lookout National Seashore,** and **Jockey's Ridge State Park** for amazing coastal activities.

# Literary Lights

This week-plus driving tour takes you from the Appalachians to the ocean, following in the footsteps of legendary authors.

## Day 1

Your first stop is in **Asheville,** North Carolina. Enjoy a relaxing walk through the vibrant downtown, capped by a visit at the centrally located **Thomas Wolfe** home. A short drive away in **Flat Rock** is the home of poet **Carl Sandburg.** Retire to your swank room at the **Grove Park Inn.**

## Day 2

Get up bright and early for a drive down to **Nantahala Outdoor Center** on the Georgia-Carolinas border for some white-water rafting on the scenic Chattooga River, setting of the 1972 film adapted from **James Dickey's** novel *Deliverance.* Tonight, camp nearby at scenic **Black Rock Mountain State Park** or **Moccasin Creek State Park.**

## Day 3

Make the short drive to **Atlanta** for a visit to the **Margaret Mitchell House,** aka "the Dump," where the former newspaper reporter wrote the novel *Gone with the Wind* over a 10-year period. After a Southern comfort food lunch at nearby **Mary Mac's Tea Room,** venture into west Atlanta to visit the **Wren's Nest,** home of **Joel Chandler Harris,** author of the tales of Uncle Remus. Enjoy your night's stay at the **Georgian Terrace** hotel, where Clark Gable and Vivien Leigh stayed while in town for the *Gone with the Wind* premiere.

## Day 4

Visit **Milledgeville,** former state capital and stately town where **Flannery O'Connor** wrote all her most important works. Visit her family farm at **Andalusia** and see the room where she worked, and then head downtown to see the O'Connor collection of memorabilia at her alma mater, **Georgia College & State University.**

Andalusia, the family farm of Flannery O'Connor in Milledgeville

## Day 5

On the way out of town, head to nearby **Eatonton** and visit the re-created boyhood home of **Joel Chandler Harris,** author of the Uncle Remus stories. Take the **Alice Walker Driving Trail,** highlighting important local sites in the life of the great African American author who also called Eatonton home. Tonight, you spend the night in **Savannah,** at the **Hamilton-Turner Inn,** once owned by "Mandy," a character in **John Berendt**'s *Midnight in the Garden of Good and Evil.*

## Day 6

Tour the squares of downtown Savannah, including a stop at the **Flannery O'Connor Childhood Home** and the ornate **Cathedral of St. John the Baptist,** where she and her family attended mass. Enjoy lunch at **Mrs. Wilkes' Dining Room,** mentioned prominently in *Midnight in the Garden of Good and Evil.*

## Day 7

An hour away, walk around charming little **Beaufort,** South Carolina, which inspired so much of the work of novelist **Pat Conroy.** The grave of his father, James, aka "the Great Santini," is in the **National Cemetery** near downtown. Stay the night in the historic **Cuthbert House Inn,** which hosted cast members such as Barbra Streisand during the filming of *Prince of Tides.*

## Day 8

For an optional additional day, head to the "Holy City" of **Charleston** for a visit to **Fort Moultrie** on Sullivan's Island, where a young **Edgar Allan Poe** was stationed as a U.S. Army officer and inspired to write *The Gold Bug.* Eat a pub lunch at nearby **Poe's Tavern.** Spend the rest of the day and evening in downtown Charleston, soaking up the atmosphere that inspired the tale *Porgy and Bess,* first novelized by native son **DuBose Heyward** and then popularized by **George Gershwin**'s opera.

restored slave quarters at Boone Hall Plantation

# African American Heritage

The Carolinas and Georgia were critical not only in the U.S. civil rights movement but also in the history of African Americans since before the nation's inception. Here are some black history highlights:

## NORTH CAROLINA

- **Greensboro:** Visit the **International Civil Rights Center and Museum** in the former F. W. Woolworth retail store, site of a 1960 sit-in to protest segregation.

- **Wilmington:** This coastal city was the site of notorious race riots in 1898.

- **Rodanthe:** At the **Chicamacomico Life-Saving Station,** learn about the exploits of the African American crew at the Pea Island Life-Saving Station.

## SOUTH CAROLINA

- **St. Helena Island:** This Gullah community features the **Penn Center,** where Martin Luther King Jr. once organized civil rights activists.

- **Beaufort:** African American Civil War hero Robert Smalls has a memorial at the **Tabernacle Baptist Church.** See his former home on Prince Street. View the **Berners Barnwell Sams House,** where Harriet Tubman once worked as a nurse.

- **Daufuskie Island:** The **Mary Field School** is where author Pat Conroy once taught a group of African American schoolchildren. The experience gave him new insight into African American culture.

- **Walterboro:** The **Tuskegee Airmen Memorial** pays tribute to the World War II heroes.

- **Charleston:** Explore history at the **Old Slave Mart Museum.** The **Avery Research Center for African American History and Culture** is at the College of Charleston. **Boone Hall Plantation** has 10 of the best-restored antebellum slave quarters in the country. The **Bench by the Road** is a monument to the million or so enslaved people who first arrived in the New World at Sullivan's Island.

## GEORGIA

- **Albany:** The **Albany Civil Rights Institute** explores the Albany Movement of the early 1960s, a critical early phase of civil rights and of Martin Luther King Jr.'s legacy.

- **Atlanta:** The centerpiece of study of the civil rights movement's greatest hero, the **Martin Luther King Jr. National Historic Site** comprises his birth home, the King Center for Nonviolent Social Change, the tomb of King and his wife, Coretta Scott King, the central visitors center, and Historic Ebenezer Baptist Church. The site is within **Sweet Auburn,** the most influential traditionally black neighborhood in Atlanta. The **Center for Civil and Human Rights** is the pride of Centennial Park.

- **Sapelo Island:** This Sea Island retains ancestral African American communities with direct links to General Sherman's "40 acres and a mule" order.

- **Savannah:** The oldest black congregation in the United States worships at **First African Baptist Church,** in a historic downtown building built by enslaved people. Formerly a black-owned bank, the **Ralph Mark Gilbert Civil Rights Museum** interprets Savannah's key role in civil rights in Georgia. The **Pin Point Heritage Museum** outside Savannah chronicles the oystering community where Supreme Court justice Clarence Thomas grew up.

# Planning Your Trip

## Where to Go

### The Outer Banks and Coastal Sounds

Probably the most **culturally unique** area in this guide, the **Outer Banks** of North Carolina still harbor charming pockets of a centuries-old seafaring tradition all along their wave- and wind-battered **beach strands.** The nearby **Coastal Sounds** provide a relaxing, sheltered counterpart to the Outer Banks' heavy traffic during the high season.

### Wilmington and Cape Fear

The northernmost outpost of the **antebellum rice plantation** culture, classy little **Wilmington** has been featured in many **motion pictures** due to its nostalgically scenic character. The surrounding Cape Fear region features several **beautiful, accessible beaches** for family enjoyment.

### Central North Carolina

This culturally and politically diverse area isn't only a big golf getaway and **center of the stock-car racing universe;** it features the region's second-largest city, the financial powerhouse and ethnic melting pot of **Charlotte,** as well as the highly progressive, **university-dominated** "Triangle" of **Chapel Hill, Durham,** and **Raleigh.**

### Asheville and the Blue Ridge Parkway

A left-of-center bastion in conservative Appalachia, **Asheville** nestles a surprisingly large amount of **progressive culture,** great food, and live music into the foothills. The **Blue Ridge Parkway** is a pleasant, peaceful meander amid mountains, wildflowers, and various **state parks and campgrounds** along its 250-mile length in North Carolina, and it borders thousands of acres of **national forest.**

### Great Smoky Mountains

America's most visited national park, these **deep mountains** along the Tennessee border combine the culture of old Appalachia with friendly, **kitschy** tourist attractions. **Skiers** will enjoy the slopes available in winter, and the warmer months offer plenty of **camping, hiking,** and nature-loving activities.

### Myrtle Beach and the Grand Strand

The 60-mile Grand Strand focuses on the resort activity of **Myrtle Beach** and the adjacent, faster-growing North Myrtle Beach. Down the strand are the more peaceful areas of **Pawleys Island** and **Murrells Inlet,** with **historic Georgetown** anchoring the bottom portion of the long, skinny peninsula.

downtown Asheville

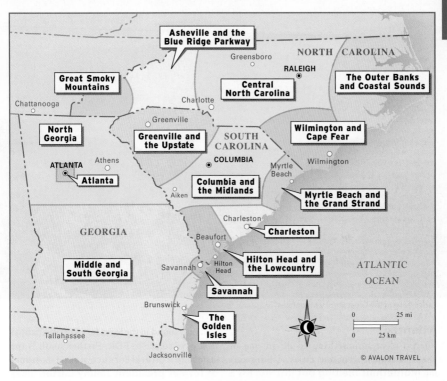

## Charleston

One of America's oldest cities and an early national center of **arts and culture,** Charleston's legendary taste for the high life is matched by its forward-thinking outlook. The birthplace of the **Civil War** is not just a city of museums resting on its historic laurels; the "Holy City" is now a **vibrant, creative hub** of the New South.

## Hilton Head and the Lowcountry

The Lowcountry's **mossy, laid-back pace** belies its former status as the heart of American plantation culture and the original cradle of secession. Today it is a mix of **history** (Beaufort and Bluffton), **natural beauty** (the ACE Basin), **resort development** (Hilton Head), **military bases** (Parris Island), and **relaxed beaches** (Edisto and Hunting Islands).

## Columbia and the Midlands

The state capital and home of South Carolina's largest university, Columbia is still a very manageable, fun place. The surrounding area, the "real" South Carolina, offers a look at a **small-town way of life** usually seen in Norman Rockwell paintings. A resurgent polo scene is bringing affluent but accessible Aiken back to its full **equestrian glory.**

## Greenville and the Upstate

Fast-growing Greenville could teach many other cities a lesson in tasteful, efficient renovation. A short drive away are the treats and treasures of South Carolina's **Blue Ridge** region—a more user-friendly, less expensive version of the trendy **mountain towns** over the border in North Carolina.

Cades Cove in the Great Smoky Mountains

## Atlanta

There's always something to do in one of America's most dynamic cities, a burgeoning **multiethnic melting pot** that also has a friendly flavor of the Old South beneath the surface. For every snarled intersection, a delightfully bucolic neighborhood tantalizes with **cafés, shops,** and **green space.** Adventurous **restaurants** and quirky **nightlife** venues are Atlanta's specialties.

## North Georgia

The Blue Ridge Mountains are the backdrop for this inspiring, scenic area full of **waterfalls, state parks,** and **outdoor adventures** for the whole family. The influence of the enormous **University of Georgia** in Athens pervades the rolling green **Piedmont** region.

## Middle and South Georgia

From **Macon** to **Columbus,** the rhythmic heart of Georgia is the soulful cradle of the state's rich **musical tradition**—and where its **best barbecue** is located. The region's therapeutic value isn't only found in the legendary **Warm Springs** that gave solace to FDR. Farther south is the state's **agricultural cornucopia** and the **home of former president Jimmy Carter,** along with the mighty and mysterious **Okefenokee Swamp.**

## Savannah

Georgia's grand old city isn't just **full of history,** though that aspect remains very much worth exploring. Savannah has found new life as an **arts and culture mecca,** with as many or more things to do on any given day than cities two or three times its size. Come prepared for high tea or a rowdy party; either way, Savannah's got you covered.

## The Golden Isles

History and salt-kissed air meet in the marshes of Georgia's chains of relatively undeveloped barrier islands. The feeling is timeless and tranquil. The Golden Isles are one of the country's **hidden vacation gems** and one of the most **unique ecosystems** in North America.

# When to Go

First things first: Most portions of the Carolinas and Georgia can get scorching hot in the **summer.** For heat-prone areas, August is the month you probably don't want to be here. Obvious exceptions are the mountainous areas along and in the Blue Ridge, and beach and resort areas such as the Outer Banks, the Cape Fear region, Myrtle Beach, and Hilton Head, all of which see their highest visitor traffic during late summer.

**Winter** tends to be quite mild in South Carolina and Georgia. However, in the deep Blue Ridge and much of the interior portion of North Carolina, winters can be cold, and in the upper mountainous regions, snowy. If you do venture into the mountains in the colder months, keep in mind that many businesses there are seasonal and might be closed during your visit.

**Autumn** leaf-watching season throughout the Blue Ridge Mountains area, from North Georgia all the way up to the Virginia border, is extremely popular. While there are plenty of picturesque and practical state parks in the Carolinas and Georgia, they fill up very quickly during the colorful leaf-turning season. Book well in advance.

The **hurricane** threat along the mid-Atlantic and Southeast coast is highest in **August and September.** Obviously, there's no way to plan in advance to avoid a hurricane, but that is when trips, especially by plane, are most likely to be disrupted.

In **Savannah** hotel rooms are difficult to get around St. Patrick's Day in the middle of March. Same goes for **Charleston** during Spoleto in late May-early June. The Masters golf tournament in **Augusta** in April fills lodging for many miles around, spilling into South Carolina. In metropolitan areas like Atlanta and Charlotte, you'll have no problem finding the lodging you need.

In the many **college towns** throughout the Carolinas and Georgia—such as Chapel Hill

Asheville's Biltmore Estate in winter

Masters golf tournament in Augusta

and Durham in North Carolina, Columbia and Clemson in South Carolina, and Athens in Georgia—lodging is at a premium during home football weekends (basketball in North Carolina). Expect a dearth of available lodging and high prices for the lodging that is available.

# Before You Go

Because of the expansive size of the region covered in this guide, and its generally blasé attitude toward public transportation, a **car** is a must for travel throughout the Carolinas and Georgia. **Atlanta** is an exception; its **public transit system,** MARTA, is extensive and reasonably priced.

While the weather tends to be on the hot-to-mild side, anywhere near the mountainous regions the weather can change on a minute-to-minute basis, from uncomfortably warm to bitingly cold and wet in a flash. If you're camping anywhere in the mountains, keep in mind that the Blue Ridge region has some of the highest rainfall totals in the country. Plan and pack your gear accordingly.

Many people flying into the region do so through **Hartsfield-Jackson International Airport** in Atlanta, Delta Airlines' headquarters and the busiest airport in the world. When there is a delay there, there's a delay pretty much everywhere. Other key airports are in Charlotte, Columbia, Savannah/Hilton Head, Charleston, and Raleigh/Durham.

# The Outer Banks and Coastal Sounds

Look for ★ to find recommended sights, activities, dining, and lodging.

# Highlights

★ **Wright Brothers National Memorial:** Visit this historic site for a fun, educational, and ultimately stirring chronicle of one of the greatest achievements in history—powered flight (page 41).

★ **Jockey's Ridge State Park:** The largest sand dune in the eastern United States is a great place to relax, enjoy the view, or fly a kite (page 42).

★ **Fort Raleigh National Historic Site:** The mysterious first chapter of English settlement in the New World unfolded here, at the site of the Lost Colony, in the 1580s (page 47).

★ **Ocracoke Island:** On this remote island, you'll find a historic village that houses one of America's most unique local communities, as well as some serious water sports and walking opportunities (page 55).

★ **Cape Lookout National Seashore:** More than 50 miles of coastline along four barrier islands are home to wild horses, dolphins, and turtle nests (page 57).

★ **North Carolina Maritime Museum:** North Carolina's seafaring heritage is represented in fascinating exhibits and activities at this great museum (page 60).

★ **Beaufort's Old Burying Ground:** In addition to being the final resting place of the "Little Girl Buried in a Barrel of Rum," this little churchyard has one of the prettiest cemeteries in the South (page 61).

★ **North Carolina Aquarium:** Sharks, jellyfish, and a myriad of other sea creatures show

their true beauty in these underwater habitats (page 65).

★ **The Great Dismal Swamp:** This natural wonder straddling the Virginia-North Carolina line is an amazing place for canoeing, kayaking, bird-watching, and sightseeing (page 66).

★ **Tryon Palace:** The splendid and, in its day, controversial seat of colonial government in North Carolina is reconstructed in New Bern's historic district (page 71).

The Outer Banks are like a great seine net set along the northeastern corner of North Carolina, holding the Sounds and inner coast apart from the open ocean, yet shimmying obligingly with the forces of water and wind.

The Outer Banks can be—and on many occasions have been—profoundly transformed by a single storm. A powerful hurricane can fill in a centuries-old inlet in one night, and open a new channel wherever it pleases. As recently as 2003, Hatteras Island was cut in half (by Hurricane Isabel), though the channel has since been artificially filled. This evanescent landscape poses challenges to the life that it supports, and creates adaptable and hardy plants, animals, and people.

The Sounds are often overlooked by travelers, but they are an enormously important part of the state and the region. Collectively known as the Albemarle-Pamlico Estuary, North Carolina's Sounds—Albemarle, Pamlico, Core, Croatan, Roanoke, and Currituck—form the second-largest estuarine system in the country after the Chesapeake Bay.

Sheltered from the Atlantic, the Inner Banks are much more accommodating, ecologically speaking, than the Outer Banks. Wetlands along the Sounds invite migratory birds by the hundreds of thousands to shelter and rest, while pocosins (a special kind of bog found in the region) and maritime forests have nurtured a great variety of life for eons. Here is where North Carolina's oldest towns—Bath, New Bern, and Edenton—set down roots, from which the rest of the state grew and bloomed.

You may hear folks in North Carolina refer to any point on the coast, be it Wilmington or Nags Head, as "Down East." In the most authentic, local usage of the term, Down East really refers to northeastern Carteret County, to the islands and marsh towns in a confined region along the banks of Core Sound, north of Beaufort.

## PLANNING YOUR TIME

The standard beach-season rules apply to the coastal areas covered in this chapter. Lodging

---

**Previous:** Outer Banks beach; Tryon Palace in New Bern. **Above:** Wright Brothers National Memorial.

# The Outer Banks and Coastal Sounds

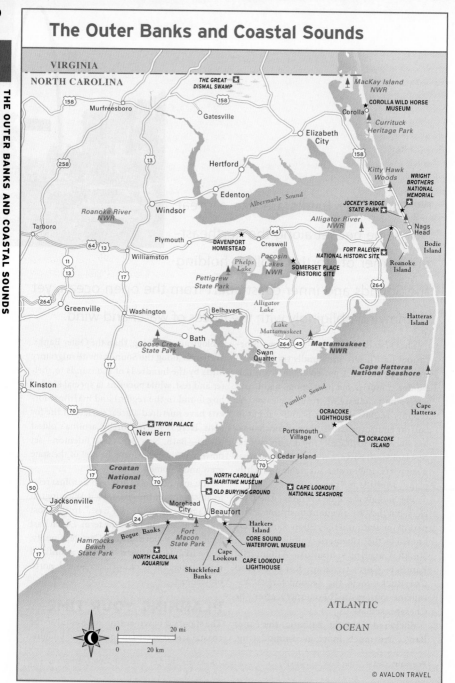

VIRGINIA
NORTH CAROLINA

THE GREAT
DISMAL SWAMP

MacKay Island
NWR

COROLLA WILD HORSE
MUSEUM

158

Murfreesboro

Gatesville

Corolla

Currituck
Heritage Park

Elizabeth
City

258

13

Hertford

158

Kitty Hawk
Woods

WRIGHT
BROTHERS
NATIONAL
MEMORIAL

Roanoke River
NWR

Windsor

Edenton

Albermarle Sound

JOCKEY'S RIDGE
STATE PARK

Tarboro

Plymouth

64

Alligator River
NWR

Nags
Head

64 13

Williamston

DAVENPORT
HOMESTEAD

Creswell

FORT RALEIGH
NATIONAL HISTORIC SITE

Bodie
Island

11

Pocosin
Lakes
NWR

Phelps
Lake

SOMERSET PLACE
HISTORIC SITE

Roanoke
Island

13

17

Pettigrew
State Park

264

264

Greenville

Washington

Belhaven

Alligator
Lake

Hatteras
Island

Goose Creek
State Park

Bath

Lake
Mattamuskeet

264 45

Mattamuskeet
NWR

17

Swan
Quarter

Cape Hatteras
National Seashore

Kinston

Pamlico Sound

Cape
Hatteras

70

OCRACOKE
LIGHTHOUSE

TRYON PALACE

New Bern

Portsmouth
Village

OCRACOKE
ISLAND

Croatan
National
Forest

70

Cedar Island

17

70

NORTH CAROLINA
MARITIME MUSEUM

CAPE LOOKOUT
NATIONAL SEASHORE

50

OLD BURYING GROUND

Jacksonville

Morehead
City

Beaufort

24

Harkers
Island

17

Bogue Banks

Fort
Macon
State Park

Cape
Lookout

CORE SOUND
WATERFOWL MUSEUM

Hammocks
Beach
State Park

NORTH CAROLINA
AQUARIUM

Shackleford
Banks

CAPE LOOKOUT
LIGHTHOUSE

17

ATLANTIC

OCEAN

0          20 mi

0          20 km

prices go up dramatically between Memorial Day and Labor Day, and though you might score a rock-bottom price if you visit on a mild weekend off-season, you might also find that some of the destinations you'd like to visit are closed.

Coastal North Carolina is beautiful four seasons of the year, and for many people fall and winter are favorite times to visit. These are wonderful times for canoeing and kayaking on eastern North Carolina's rivers, creeks, and swamps.

Late summer and early autumn are hurricane season all through the Southeast. Hurricane paths are unpredictable, so if you're planning a week on the beach and know that a hurricane is hovering over Cuba, it won't necessarily hit North Carolina, although the central Carolina coast is always an odds-on favorite for landfall.

## INFORMATION AND SERVICES

The **Aycock Brown Welcome Center** (milepost 1.5, U.S. 158, 877/629-4386, www.outerbanks.org, Dec.-Feb. daily 9am-5pm, Mar.-May and Sept.-Nov. daily 9am-5:30pm, June-Aug. daily 9am-6pm) at Kitty Hawk, the **Outer Banks Welcome Center** (1 Visitors Center Circle, Manteo), and the **Cape Hatteras National Seashore Visitors Center** (Cape Hatteras Lighthouse, Memorial Day-Labor Day daily 9am-6pm, Labor Day-Memorial Day daily 9am-5pm) on Ocracoke are all clearinghouses for regional travel information. The **Outer Banks Visitors Bureau** (www.outerbanks.org) can be reached directly at 877/629-4386. Extensive travel information is also available from the **Crystal Coast Tourism Authority** (3409 Arendell St., Morehead City, 877/206-0929, www.crystalcoastnc.org).

# Nags Head and Vicinity

TOP EXPERIENCE

The Outer Banks comprise a long sandbar, constantly eroding and amassing, slip-sliding into new configurations with every storm. The wind is the invisible player in this process, the man behind the curtain giving orders to the water and the sand. The enormous dune known as Jockey's Ridge was a landmark to early mariners, visible from miles out to sea.

According to legend, Nags Head was a sinister place of peril to those seafarers. Islanders, it's said, would walk a nag or mule, carrying a lantern around its neck, slowly back and forth along the beach, trying to lure ships into the shallows where they might founder or wreck, making their cargo easy pickings for the land pirates.

## SIGHTS
### ★ Wright Brothers National Memorial

Although they are remembered for a 12-second flight on a December morning in 1903,

Wilbur and Orville Wright actually spent more than three years coming and going between their home in Dayton, Ohio, and Kitty Hawk, North Carolina. As they tested their gliders on Kill Devil Hill, the tallest sand dune on the Outer Banks, the Wright brothers were helped by many locals, who fed and housed them, built hangars, and assisted with countless practicalities that helped make the brothers' experiment a success. On the morning of December 17, 1903, several local people were present to help that famous first powered flight get off the ground. That flight is honored at the **Wright Brothers National Memorial** (milepost 7.5, U.S. 158, Kill Devil Hills, 252/441-7430, www.nps.gov/wrbr, park year-round daily, visitors center June-Aug. daily 9am-6pm, Sept.-May daily 9am-5pm, free). At the visitors center, replica gliders are on display, along with artifacts from the original gliders and changing displays sponsored by NASA. You can also climb Kill Devil Hill to get a glimpse of what that first aviator saw.

marking the historic first flight of the Wright Brothers

## ★ Jockey's Ridge State Park

**Jockey's Ridge State Park** (Carolista Dr., off milepost 12, U.S. 158, Nags Head, 252/441-7132, www.jockeysridgestatepark.com, Nov.-Feb. daily 8am-6pm, Mar. and Oct. daily 8am-7pm, Apr.-May and Sept. daily 8am-8pm, June-Aug. daily 8am-9pm) contains 420 acres of a strange and amazing environment, the largest active sand dune system in the eastern United States. Ever-changing, this ocean-side desert is maintained by the constant action of the northeast and southwest winds. Visitors can walk on and among the dunes. It's a famously great place to fly kites, go sand-boarding, and hang glide (hang gliding requires a valid USHGA rating and a permit supplied by the park office).

## Nags Head Woods Ecological Preserve

Bordering Jockey's Ridge is another unique natural area, The Nature Conservancy's **Nags Head Woods Ecological Preserve** (701 W. Ocean Acres Dr., about 1 mile from milepost 9.5, U.S. 158, 252/441-2525, www.nature.org, daily dawn-dusk). Nags Head Woods is over 1,000 acres of deciduous maritime forest, dunes, wetlands, and interdune ponds. More than 50 species of birds nest here in season, including ruby-throated hummingbirds, green herons, and red-shouldered hawks, and it is also home to a host of other animals and unusual plants.

## Kitty Hawk Woods

Slightly smaller but no less important is The Nature Conservancy's **Kitty Hawk Woods** (south of U.S. 158 at Kitty Hawk, trail access from Woods Rd. and Birch Lane, off Treasure St., 252/261-8891, www.nature.org, daily dawn-dusk). These maritime forests harbor the unusual species of flora and fauna of the maritime swale ecosystem, a swampy forest sheltered between coastal ridges. Kitty Hawk Woods is open to the public for hiking and birding, and can be explored from the water as well. A canoe and kayak put-in is next to the parking lot of **Kitty Hawk Kayaks** (6150 N. Croatan Rd./U.S. 158, 252/261-0145, www. khkss.com).

## Currituck Heritage Park

The shore of Currituck Sound is an unexpected place to find the art deco home of a 1920s industrial magnate. The **Whalehead Club** (1100 Club Rd., off milepost 11, Hwy. 12, 252/453-9040, www.whaleheadclub.com, visitors center 11am-5pm daily, standard

# Nags Head and Vicinity

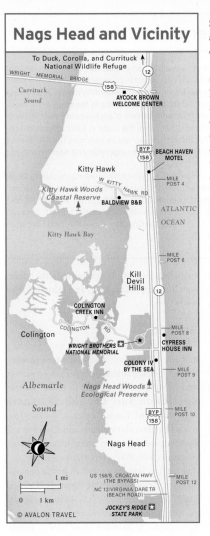

Sound, the center also has a huge collection of antique decoys—an important folk tradition of the Carolina coast.

The 1875 **Currituck Beach Lighthouse** (Currituck Heritage Park, 252/453-4939, Apr.-Nov. daily 9am-5pm, closed in rough weather, $8, free under age 7) stands on the other side of the Center for Wildlife Education. It is one of the few historic lighthouses that visitors can climb. The 214-step spiral staircase leads to the huge Fresnel lens and a panoramic view of Currituck Sound.

## Corolla Wild Horse Museum

In the town of Corolla, the circa-1900 Corolla Schoolhouse has been transformed into a museum honoring the wild horses of the Outer Banks. The **Corolla Wild Horse Museum** (1126 Old Schoolhouse Lane, Corolla, 252/453-8002, summer Mon.-Sat. 10am-4pm, off-season hours vary, free) tells of the history of the herd, which once roamed all over Corolla but now lives in a preserve north of the town.

## ENTERTAINMENT AND EVENTS

The **Outer Banks Brewing Station** (milepost 8.5, Croatan Hwy./U.S. 158, Kill Devil Hills, 252/449-2739, www.obbrewing.com) was founded in the early 1990s by a group of friends who met in the Peace Corps. The brewery-restaurant they built here was designed and constructed by Outer Bankers, modeled on the design of the old lifesaving stations so important in the region's history. The pub serves several very gourmet home-brews at $4.50 for a pint, $6 for four five-ounce samplers.

**Bacu Grill** (Outer Banks Mall, milepost 14, U.S. 158, Nags Head, 252/480-1892), a Cuban-fusion restaurant, features live jazz and blues music, and serves good beer, wine, and snacks into the wee hours of the morning. **Kelly's Outer Banks Restaurant and Tavern** (milepost 10.5. U.S. 158, Nags Head, 252/441-4116, www.kellysrestaurant.com, Sun.-Thurs. 4:30pm-midnight, Fri.-Sat. 4:30pm-2am) is

tours 9am-4pm daily, specialty tours require 24 hours advance notice, $5-15) was built as a summer cottage by Edward Collings Knight Jr., an industrialist whose fortune was in railroads and sugar.

Next to the Whalehead Club is the **Outer Banks Center for Wildlife Education** (Currituck Heritage Park, Corolla, 252/453-0221, www.ncwildlife.org, daily 9am-5pm, free). With exhibits focusing on the native birds, fish, and other creatures of Currituck

# Pronunciation Primer

The Outer Banks are a garland of peculiar names, as well as names that look straightforward but are in fact pronounced in unexpectedly quirky ways. If you make reference publicly to the town of **Corolla,** and pronounce it like the Toyota model, you'll be recognized right away as someone "from off." It's pronounced "ker-AH-luh." Similarly, **Bodie Island,** site of the stripy lighthouse, is pronounced "body," as in one's earthly shell. That same pattern of pronouncing o as "ah," as in "stick out your tongue and say 'ah,'" is repeated farther down the coast at **Chicamacomico,** which comes out "chick-uh-muh-CAH-muh-co." But just to keep you on your toes, the rule doesn't apply to **Ocracoke,** which is pronounced like the Southern vegetable and Southern drink: "OH-kruh-coke."

Farther south along the banks is the town of **Rodanthe,** which has an elongated last syllable, "ro-DANTH-ee." On Roanoke Island, **Manteo** calls out for a Spanish emphasis, but is in fact front-loaded, like so many Carolina words and names. It's pronounced "MAN-tee-oh" or "MANNY-oh." Next door is the town of **Wanchese.** This sounds like a pallid dairy product, "WAN-cheese." Inland, the **Cashie River** is pronounced "cuh-SHY," **Bertie County** is "ber-TEE," and **Chowan County** is "chuh-WON."

also a good bet for live music and has a long wine list with some lovely vintages. **Lucky 12 Tavern** (3308 S. Virginia Dare Tr., Nags Head, 252/255-5825, www.lucky12tavern.com, daily 11:30am-2am) is a traditional sports bar with TVs, foosball, and New York-style pizza.

## SPORTS AND RECREATION

### Diving

The **Outer Banks Dive Center** (3917 S. Croatan Hwy., 252/449-8349, www.obxdive. com) offers instruction and guided tours of wrecks off the coast of the Outer Banks. Guided wreck dives are only available April-November. All levels of divers are welcome.

### Hiking and Touring

The **Currituck Banks National Estuarine Preserve** (Hwy. 12, 252/261-8891, www.nc-coastalreserve.net) protects nearly 1,000 acres of woods and water extending into Currituck Sound. A 0.3-mile boardwalk runs from the parking lot to the sound, and a primitive trail runs from the parking lot 1.5 miles through the maritime forest.

**Back Country Outfitters and Guides** (107-C Corolla Light Town Center, Corolla, 252/453-0877, http://outerbankstours.com) leads a variety of tours in the Corolla region,

including Segway beach tours, wild horse-watching trips, kayaking, and other off-road tours.

### Surfing

The North Carolina coast has a strong surfing culture, not to mention strong waves, making this a top destination for experienced surfers and those who would like to learn. **Island Revolution Surf Co. and Skatepark** (Corolla Light Town Center, 252/453-9484, www.islandrevolution.com, must be over age 8 and a good swimmer, group lessons $60 pp, private lessons $75) offers private and one-on-one surfing lessons as well as board rentals. So does **Ocean Atlantic Rentals** (Corolla Light Town Center, 252/453-2440, www.oar-nc.com, group lessons $50 pp, private lessons $75, couples $120, must know how to swim), which also has locations in Duck, Nags Head, and Avon, and **Corolla Surf Shop** (several locations, 252/453-9283, www.corollasurf-shop.com, age 9 and up).

### Kayaking

The Outer Banks combine two very different possible kayaking experiences—the challenge of ocean kayaking and the leisurely drifting zones of the salt marshes and back creeks. **Kitty Hawk Sports** (798 Sunset Blvd.,

252/453-6900, www.kittyhawksports.com) is an old and established outdoors outfitter that leads kayaking and other expeditions. Another good bet is **Kitty Hawk Kayaks** (6150 N. Croatan Hwy., Kitty Hawk, 866/702-5061, www.khkss.com), which teaches kayaking and canoeing, rents equipment for paddling and surfing, and, in cooperation with The Nature Conservancy, leads tours, including overnight expeditions, through gorgeous waterways in pristine habitats.

**Kitty Hawk Kites** (877/359-8447, www.kittyhawk.com), which *National Geographic Adventure* magazine calls one of the "Best Adventure Travel Companies on Earth," has locations throughout the Outer Banks, including at Corolla.

**Coastal Kayak** (make reservations at North Beach Outfitters, 1240 Duck Rd., Duck, 252/261-6262, www.coastalkayak.org) offers tours throughout the northern Outer Banks, including guided trips through the Alligator River National Wildlife Refuge and the Pea Island National Wildlife Refuge, as well as the Pine Island Audubon Sanctuary and Kitty Hawk Woods. Tours last 2 to 3.5 hours and cost $35-50.

## FOOD

**Sam & Omie's** (7728 S. Virginia Dare Tr., Nags Head, 252/441-7366, www.samandomies.net, Mar.-mid-Dec. daily 7am-10pm, $10-25) was opened during the summer of 1937, a place for charter fishing customers and guides to catch a spot of breakfast before setting sail. It still serves breakfast, with lots of options in the eggs and hotcakes department, including a few specialties like crab and eggs Benedict. It also has a dinner menu starring seasonal steamed and fried oysters, Delmonico steaks, and barbecue.

**Tale of the Whale** (7575 S. Virginia Dare Tr., Nags Head, 252/441-7332, www.taleofthewhalenagshead.com, spring-fall daily 4pm-9pm, closed winter, $15-50) sits at a beautiful location, at the very edge of the water with a pier jutting into Roanoke Sound. There's outdoor music from a pier-side gazebo and a dining room with such a great view of the water that it feels like the inside of a ship—but the real draw is the incredibly extensive menu of seafood, steak, and pasta specials. They also have an imaginative cocktail menu.

**Grits Grill and Bakery** (5000 S. Croatan Hwy., Nags Head, 252/449-2888, daily 6am-3pm, $7-12) is a favorite for breakfast, famous for its biscuits, Krispy Kreme doughnuts, eggs, and, of course, grits.

The ★ **Blue Point** (1240 Duck Rd., Duck, 252/261-8090, www.goodfoodgoodwine.com, lunch Tues.-Sun.11:30am-2:30pm, dinner daily 5pm-9:30pm, closed Mon. in winter, $20-35) has a nouveau Southern menu, with staples like catfish and trout done up in creative ways. Among the specialties, fresh Carolina shrimp is presented on "barley risotto," with broccolini, wine-soaked raisins, and lemon arugula pesto. After-dinner drinks (among them espresso martinis and special dessert wines) complement an amazing wine list that is, if anything, even more impressive than the menu. Reservations are very necessary.

**Owens' Restaurant** (milepost 16.5, Beach Rd., Nags Head, 252/441-7309, www.owensrestaurant.com, daily 5pm-9pm, $12-25) has been in operation at Nags Head for more than 60 years, and in addition to its good seafood menu, visitors enjoy looking over the owners' collection of historical artifacts from Outer Banks maritime life. **Blue Moon Beach Grill** (4104 S. Virginia Dare Tr., Nags Head, 252/261-2583, www.bluemoonbeachgrill.com, daily 11:30am-9pm, $12-25) is a local favorite known for its seafood dishes, and it's also a popular place to grab a draft beer after work. **Tortuga's Lie** (milepost 11.5, U.S. 158/Beach Rd., 252/441-7299, www.tortugaslie.com, Sun.-Thurs. 11:30am-9:30pm, Fri.-Sat. 11:30am-10pm, $10-20) has a good and varied menu specializing in seafood (some of it local) with Caribbean-inspired preparations, with some good vegetarian options.

For casual and on-the-go chow options at Nags Head, try **Maxximuss Pizza** (5205 S. Croatan Hwy., Nags Head, 252/441-2377,

Sun.-Thurs. noon-9pm, Fri.-Sat. noon-11pm, $12-20), which specializes in calzones, subs, and panini, in addition to pizza; **Yellow Submarine** (milepost 14, U.S. 158 Bypass, Nags Head, 252/441-3511, May-Sept. Mon.-Sat. 11am-9pm, Sun. noon-9pm, Mar.-Apr., Oct.-Nov. Tues.-Sat. 11:30am-8pm, Sun. 1pm-8pm, $7-16), a super-casual sub and pizza shop; or **Majik Beanz** (4104 S. Virginia Dare Tr., Nags Head, 252/255-2700, Sun.-Wed. 7am-3pm, Thurs.-Sat. 7am-10pm) for coffee and shakes.

## ACCOMMODATIONS
### Under $150

The ★ **First Colony Inn** (6720 Virginia Dare Tr., Nags Head, 800/368-9390, www.firstcolonyinn.com, $69-299, depending on season) is a wonderful 1932 beachfront hotel. This regional landmark has won historic preservation and landscaping awards for its 1988 renovation, which involved moving the entire building, in three pieces, three miles south of its original location. The pretty and luxurious guest rooms are surprisingly affordable.

Bed-and-breakfasts include the sound-front **Cypress Moon Inn** (1206 Harbor Ct., Kitty Hawk, 877/905-5060, www.cypressmoon-inn.com, age 18 and over, $200 summer, $175 spring and fall, $135 winter), with three pretty guest rooms. The **Baldview B&B** (3805 Elijah Baum Rd., Kitty Hawk, 252/255-2829, www.baldview.com, no children or pets, $125-200) is a modern residence located on a beautiful property along the sound, with four nicely appointed guest rooms and a carriage house.

The **Cypress House Inn** (milepost 8, Beach Rd., Kill Devil Hills, 800/554-2764, www.cypresshouseinn.com, $99-199, depending on season) is a very traditional coastal Carolina-style house, built in the 1940s and an easy walk to the beach. Its hurricane shutters and cypress-paneled guest rooms will give you a taste of Outer Banks life in the days before the motels and resorts.

In Kitty Hawk and Nags Head, you'll find an abundance of motels, from chains to classic 1950s mom-and-pops. The **Surf Side Hotel**

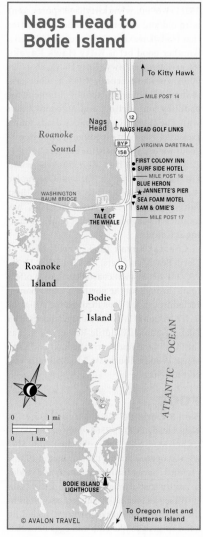

# Nags Head to Bodie Island

↑ To Kitty Hawk

MILE POST 14

Roanoke Sound

Nags Head

NAGS HEAD GOLF LINKS

BYP
158

VIRGINIA DARE TRAIL

FIRST COLONY INN
SURF SIDE HOTEL
MILE POST 16
BLUE HERON
JANNETTE'S PIER
SEA FOAM MOTEL
SAM & OMIE'S

WASHINGTON BAUM BRIDGE

TALE OF THE WHALE

MILE POST 17

Roanoke Island

Bodie Island

ATLANTIC OCEAN

0       1 mi
0    1 km

BODIE ISLAND LIGHTHOUSE

To Oregon Inlet and Hatteras Island

© AVALON TRAVEL

(6701 Virginia Dare Tr., Nags Head, www.surfsideobx.com, 800/552-7873, from $55 off-season, from $165 high season) is a favorite for simple and comfortable accommodations, with standard rooms and efficiencies in a location right on the dunes. All guest rooms at the **Blue Heron** (6811 Virginia Dare Tr., Nags Head, 252/441-7447, www.blueheronnc.com, from $50 off-season, from $130 high season) face the ocean. The Blue Heron has a heated indoor pool as a consolation on rainy days. Super-affordable is the **Sea Foam Motel** (7111 Virginia Dare Tr., Nags Head, 252/441-7320, www.outer-banks.nc.us, from $62 off-season, from $110 high season), an old-timer with a lot of retro appeal. Other good choices in the area include the **Colony IV by the Sea** (405 S. Virginia Tr., Kill Devil Hills, 252/441-5581, www.motelbythesea.com, $68-163, depending on season) and **Beach Haven Motel** (milepost 4, Ocean Rd., Kitty Hawk, 888/559-0506, www.beachhavenmotel.com, from $65 off-season, from $105 high season).

## $150-300

The **Colington Creek Inn** (1293 Colington Rd., Kill Devil Hills, 252/449-4124, www.colingtoncreekinn.com, no children or pets, $168-198, depending on season) is a large outfit with a great view of the sound and its namesake creek.

The **Sanderling Resort and Spa** (1461 Duck Rd., near Duck, 877/650-4812, www.thesanderling.com, $130-450) is a conventional full-size resort, with three lodges, a spa, and three restaurants that include the Lifesaving Station, housed in an 1899 maritime rescue station. There are various sports and recreational rental options.

## TRANSPORTATION

The closest major airport to this region is the **Norfolk International Airport** (ORF, 2200 Norview Ave., Norfolk, VA, 757/857-3351, www.norfolkairport.com), approximately one hour's drive from the northern Outer Banks. **Raleigh-Durham International Airport** (RDU, 2600 W. Terminal Blvd., Morrisville, NC, 919/840-2123, www.rdu.com) is 3 to 5 hours' drive from most Outer Banks destinations.

Only two bridges exist between the mainland and the northern Outer Banks. U.S. 64/264 crosses over Roanoke Island to Whalebone, just south of Nags Head. Not too far north of there, U.S. 158 crosses from Point Harbor to Southern Shores. Highway 12 is the main road all along the northern Outer Banks.

# Roanoke Island

Roanoke Island was the site of the Lost Colony, one of the strangest mysteries in all of American history. Its sheltered location—nestled between the Albemarle, Roanoke, and Croatan Sounds, and protected from the ocean by Bodie Island—made Roanoke Island a welcoming spot for that party of ocean-weary English people in the 1580s. Unhappily, they lacked the ability to make one of the bed-and-breakfast inns in Manteo or Wanchese their home base. Instead they cast their lots in the wilderness, and what befell them may never be known.

At the northern end of Roanoke Island is the town of Manteo and the Fort Raleigh National Historic Site. This is where most of the attractions and visitor services are concentrated. At the southern end is Wanchese, where some of Dare County's oldest families carry on their ancestral trades of fishing and boatbuilding.

## ★ FORT RALEIGH NATIONAL HISTORIC SITE

**Fort Raleigh National Historic Site** (1401 National Park Dr., Manteo, 252/473-5772, www.nps.gov/fora, park daily dawn-dusk except Christmas Day, visitors center Sept.-May daily 9am-5pm, June-Aug. daily 9am-6pm, park admission free, admission charged for Elizabethan Gardens and *The Lost Colony*) covers much of the original site of the first English settlement in the New World. Some of the earthworks associated with the original 1580s fort remain and have been preserved.

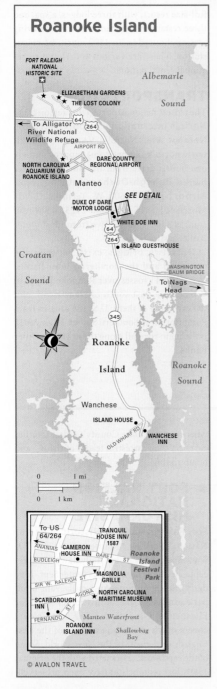

The visitors center displays some of the artifacts discovered during this restoration effort. Two nature trails in the park explore the island's natural landscape and the location of a Civil War battle.

Within the National Historic Site, two of Manteo's most famous attractions operate autonomously. About 60 years ago, Manteo's **Elizabethan Gardens** (252/473-3234, www.elizabethangardens.org, hours vary, $9 adults, $6 children) was conceived by the Garden Club of North Carolina as a memorial to the settlers of Roanoke Island. Much of the beautifully landscaped park re-creates the horticulture of the colonists' native England in the 16th century.

Also within the park boundaries is the Waterside Theater. North Carolina has a long history of outdoor drama celebrating regional heritage, and the best known of the many productions across the state is Roanoke Island's **_The Lost Colony_** (Fort Raleigh National Historic Site, Roanoke, 252/473-3414, www.thelostcolony.org, $30 adults, $28 seniors, $10 children). Chapel Hill playwright Paul Green was commissioned to write the drama in 1937 to celebrate the 350th anniversary of Virginia Dare's birth. What was expected to be a single-season production has returned almost every year for over 80 years, interrupted only occasionally for emergencies such as prowling German U-boats.

## OTHER SIGHTS

The **North Carolina Maritime Museum** (104 Fernando St., Manteo, 252/475-1750, www.obxmaritime.org, hours vary, free), whose mother venue is located in Beaufort, operates a branch here on Roanoke Island. In addition to the many traditional Outer Banks working watercraft on display, the museum holds boatbuilding and handling courses at its George Washington Creef Boathouse. Visitors not enrolled in classes can still come in and watch traditional boatbuilders at work in the shop.

The **North Carolina Aquarium on Roanoke Island** (374 Airport Rd., 3 miles north of Manteo, 866/332-3475, www. ncaquariums.com, daily 9am-5pm, $10.95 adults, $8.95 children) is one of three state aquariums on the North Carolina coast. It's a great place to visit and see all sorts of marine fauna: sharks and other less ferocious fish, crustaceans, octopuses, turtles, and more. Like its sister aquariums, it's also a research station where marine biologists track and work to conserve the native creatures of the coast.

**Roanoke Island Festival Park** (1 Festival Park, Manteo, 252/475-1500, www.roanokeisland.com, Feb. 19-Mar. and Nov.-Dec. daily 9am-5pm, Apr.-Oct. daily 9am-6pm, $8 adults, $5 ages 6-17, free under age 6) is a state-operated living history site. The highlight is the *Elizabeth II,* a reconstruction of a 16th-century ship like the ones that brought Walter Raleigh's colonists to the New World. There is also a museum, a reconstructed settlement site, and several other places where costumed interpreters will tell you about daily life in the Roanoke colony.

## TOURS

The **Downeast Rover** (sails from Manteo waterfront, 252/473-4866, www.downeastrover.com, daytime cruises $30 adults, $15 ages 2-12, sunset cruises $40) is a reproduction 19th-century 55-foot schooner that sails from Manteo on daytime and sunset cruises. Cruises last two hours and depart three times daily at 11am, 2pm, and sunset. To see the Outer Banks from the air, your options include a World War II biplane or a closed-cockpit Cessna through **Fly the Outer Banks** (410 Airport Rd., Manteo, 252/202-7433, $38-98), or a biplane through **Barrier Island Aviation** (407 Airport Rd., 252/473-4247, www.barrierislandaviation.com, $40-150).

## SHOPPING

**Manteo Booksellers** (105 Sir Walter Raleigh St., 252/473-1221 or 866/473-1222, www.manteobooksellers.com, daily 10am-6pm) is a great independent bookstore, specializing in Outer Banks history and nature, but with a wide selection for all tastes.

**Endless Possibilities** (105 Budleigh St., 252/475-1575, www.ragweavers.com, Mon.-Sat. 10am-5pm) is an unusual sort of a shop where you can buy purses, boas, rugs, and other adornments of home and body made from recycled secondhand clothes. All the profits go to support the Outer Banks Hotline Crisis Intervention and Prevention Center, a regional help line for victims of rape and

See *The Lost Colony* at Waterside Theater at Fort Raleigh National Historic Site.

# The Lost Colony

On July 4, 1584, an expedition of Englishmen commissioned by Walter Raleigh dropped anchor near Hatteras Island. Within a couple of days, local Native Americans were coming and going from the English ships, scoping out trade goods and offering hospitality. They got on famously, and when the English sailed back to Europe to tell Raleigh and the queen of the land they had found, two Indian men, Manteo and Wanchese, came along as guests. It seems that Wanchese was somewhat taciturn and found London to be no great shakes, but Manteo got a kick out of everything he saw and took to the English.

In 1585 a new expedition set out for Roanoke, this time intending to settle in earnest. When they reached the Pamlico Sound, their bad luck began. Most of their store of food was soaked and ruined when seawater breached the ship, so from the moment they arrived on shore they were dependent on the goodwill of the indigenous people. Manteo and Wanchese went to Roanoke chief Wingina to discuss the plight of the English. Wanchese, a man of superior insight, tried to convince Wingina to withhold help, but Manteo pled the colonists' case convincingly, and the English were made welcome. Winter came, and the colonists, having grown fat and happy on the local people's food, were doing precious little to attain self-sufficiency. Then a silver cup disappeared from the English compound. It was posited that the thief came from a nearby village, which was promptly burned to the ground. Worried about his own people, Wingina cut off food aid, hoping the English would either starve or go away. Instead, they killed him. Three weeks later, an English supply ship arrived with reinforcements of men and material, but they found the colony deserted.

Yet another attempt was made, this time with whole families rather than gangs of rowdy single men. A young couple named Eleanor and Ananais Dare was expecting a child when they landed at Roanoke, and soon Virginia Dare was born, the first English child born in the New World. Relations with the Native Americans grew worse, though, when the Roanoke people, now under the leadership of Wanchese, were unwilling to aid a new wave of colonists. Manteo, still a friend, tried to enlist the help of his kinfolk, but they were facing lean times as well. John White, leader of the expedition and grandfather of Virginia Dare, set out on what he planned would be a fast voyage back to England for supplies and food. Through no fault of his own, it was three years before he was able to return. When he did, he found no sign of the settlers, except "CRO" carved on a tree, and "CROATOAN" on a rail.

Thus began 400 years of unanswered questions and speculation that will probably never be resolved. Some believe that the English colonists were killed by the local people, others claim that they were captured and sold into slavery among Native Americans farther inland. Several communities in the South of uncertain or mixed racial heritage believe themselves to be descendants of the lost colonists, and some evidence suggests that this might in fact be possible. The answers may never be found, and for the foreseeable future, the mystery will still hang heavily over Roanoke Island and its two towns: Manteo and Wanchese.

domestic violence, as well as an HIV/AIDS information center. And if you happen to be in Manteo long enough, you can even take weaving lessons here.

## FOOD

Located in the Tranquil House Inn, with a great view of Shallowbag Bay, ★ **1587** (405 Queen Elizabeth Ave., 252/473-1587, www.1587.com, June-Aug. daily 5pm-9pm, Sept.-Oct. Wed.-Sun. 5pm-9pm, Jan.-Feb. Fri.-Sat. 5pm-9pm, closed Nov.-Dec., $18-29)

is widely regarded as one of the best restaurants in this part of the state. The menu is of hearty chops and seafood, with local ingredients in season, and a full vegetarian menu is also available on request. The wine list is a mile long.

**Basnight's Lone Cedar Café** (Nags Head-Manteo Causeway, 252/441-5405, www. lonecedarcafe.com, spring-fall Mon.-Wed. 5pm-close, Thurs.-Sat. 11:30am-3pm and 5pm-close, Sun. 11am-close, lunch entrées $6-18, dinner entrées $18-31) is a water-view bistro that specializes in local food—oysters from Hyde and Dare Counties, fresh-caught local fish, and North Carolina chicken, pork, and vegetables. It's one of the most popular restaurants on the Outer Banks, and they don't take reservations, so be sure to arrive early.

The **Full Moon Café** (208 Queen Elizabeth St., 252/473-6666, www.thefullmooncafe.com, high season daily 11:30am-9pm, call for off-season hours, $10-30) is simple and affordable, specializing in quesadillas and enchiladas, wraps, sandwiches, a variety of seafood and chicken bakes, and quiches.

The **Magnolia Grille** (408 Queen Elizabeth St., 252/475-9787, www.roanokeisland.net, Sun.-Mon. 7am-4pm, Tues.-Sat. 7am-8pm) is a super-inexpensive place for all three meals and snacks in between. It has a great selection of breakfast omelets, burgers, salads, soups, and deli sandwiches, with nothing more than $7.

## ACCOMMODATIONS
### Under $150

The **Island Guesthouse** (706 U.S. 64, 252/473-2434, www.theislandmotel.com, rooms from $60 off-season, from $85 high season, cottages from $125 off-season, from $200 high season, pets welcome for a fee) offers simple and comfortable accommodations in its guesthouse, with two double beds, air-conditioning, and cable TV in each room. They also rent out three tiny, cute cottages. Another affordable option is the **Duke of Dare Motor Lodge** (100 S. U.S. 64, 252/473-2175, from $42 high season). It's a 1960s motel, not at all fancy, but a fine choice when you need an inexpensive place to lay your head.

A top hotel in Manteo is the **Tranquil House Inn** (405 Queen Elizabeth Ave., 800/458-7069, www.1587.com, $109-239). It's in a beautiful location (though it's hard not to be on this island), and downstairs is one of the best restaurants in town, 1587. The **Scarborough Inn** (524 U.S. 64, 252/473-3979, www.scarborough-inn.com, $75-125,

depending on season) is a small hotel with 12 guest rooms and great rates, the sort of old-time hotel that's hard to find these days.

Over in Wanchese, the **Wanchese Inn** (85 Jovers Lane, 252/475-1166, www.wancheseinn.com, from $69 off-season, from $129 high season) is a simple and inexpensive bed-and-breakfast. It's a nice Victorian house with modern guest rooms, and there is a boat slip and available on-site parking for a boat and trailer. The **Island House** (104 Old Wharf Rd., 866/473-5619, www.islandhouse-bb.com, $85-175) was built in the early 1900s for a local coastguardsman, with wood cut from the property and nails forged on-site. It's very comfortable and quiet, and a big country breakfast is served every day.

### $150-300

The ★ **White Doe Inn** (319 Sir Walter Raleigh St., 800/473-6091, www.whitedoeinn.com, from $175 off-season, from $350 high season) is one of North Carolina's premier inns. The 1910 Queen Anne is the largest house on the island and is in the National Register of Historic Places. Guest rooms are exquisitely furnished in turn-of-the-century finery. Guests enjoy a four-course breakfast, evening sherry, espresso and cappuccino any time, and a 24-hour wine cellar. Spa services are available on-site.

The **Cameron House Inn** (300 Budleigh St., Manteo, 800/279-8178, http://cameronhouseinn.com, $130-210) is a cozy 1919 arts and crafts-style bungalow. All of the guest rooms are furnished in a lovely and understated craftsman style, but the nicest room in the house is the porch, which has an outdoor fireplace, fans, and flowery trellises.

The **Roanoke Island Inn** (305 Fernando St., 877/473-5511, www.roanokeislandinn.com, $150-200) has been in the present owner's family since the 1860s. It's a beautiful old place with a big porch that overlooks the marsh. They also rent a single cottage on a private island, five minutes away by boat, and a nice cypress-shingled bungalow in town.

# Cape Hatteras National Seashore

To many Americans, Cape Hatteras is probably familiar as a name often repeated during hurricane season. Hatteras protrudes farther to the east than any part of North America, a landmark for centuries of mariners and a prime target for storms. Cape Hatteras, the "Graveyard of the Atlantic," lies near Diamond Shoals, a treacherous zone of shifting sandbars between the beach and the Gulf Stream.

In 2003 Hurricane Isabel inflicted tremendous damage and even opened a new channel right across Hatteras Island, a 2,000-foot-wide swash that was called Isabel Inlet. It separated the towns of Hatteras and Frisco, washing out a large portion of the highway that links the Outer Banks. For some weeks afterward, Hatteras residents had to live as their forebears had, riding ferries to school and to the mainland. The inlet has since been filled in and Highway 12 reconnected, but Isabel Inlet's brief reign of inconvenience highlighted the vulnerability of life on the Outer Banks.

## BODIE ISLAND

The 156-foot **Bodie Island Lighthouse** (6 miles south of Whalebone Junction), whose huge Fresnel lens first beamed in 1872, was the third to guard this stretch of coast. The first light was built in the 1830s, but it leaned like the Tower of Pisa. The next stood straight but promised to be such a tempting target for the Union Navy during the Civil War that the Confederates blew it up themselves. An unfortunate flock of geese nearly put the third lighthouse out of commission soon after its first lighting, when they collided with and damaged the lens. The lighthouse is not open to the public, but the keeper's house has been converted into a **visitors center** (252/441-5711, call for hours).

The **Oregon Inlet Campground** (Hwy. 12, 877/444-6777, $20), operated by the National Park Service, offers camping behind the sand dunes, with cold showers, potable water, and restrooms.

## HATTERAS ISLAND

Cape Hatteras makes a dramatic arch along the North Carolina coast, sheltering the Pamlico Sound from the ocean as if in a giant cradling arm. The cape itself is the point of the elbow, a totally exposed and vulnerable spit of land that's irresistible to hurricanes because it juts so far to the southeast. Along the Cape Hatteras National Seashore, Hatteras Island is just barely wide enough to support a series of small towns—Rodanthe, Waves, Salvo, Avon, Buxton, Frisco, and the village of Hatteras—and a great deal of dramatic scenery on all sides.

### Sights

Lifesaving operations are an important part of North Carolina's maritime heritage. Corps of brave men once occupied remote stations along the coast, ready at a moment's notice to risk—and sometimes to give—their lives to save foundering sailors in the relentlessly dangerous waters off the Outer Banks. In Rodanthe, the **Chicamacomico Life Saving Station** (milepost 39.5, Hwy. 12, Rodanthe, 252/987-1552, www.chicamacomico.net, mid-Apr.-Nov. Mon.-Fri. noon-5pm, $6, $5 over age 62 and under age 17) preserves the original station building, a handsome gray-shingled 1874 structure, as well as the 1911 building that replaced it—and which now houses a museum of fascinating artifacts from maritime rescue operations.

**Cape Hatteras Lighthouse** (near Buxton, 252/473-2111, www.nps.gov/caha, mid-Apr.-May and Labor Day-mid-Oct. daily 9am-4:30pm, June-Labor Day daily 9am-5:30pm, $8 adults, $4 children, children smaller than 3 foot 5 not permitted), at 208 feet tall, is the tallest brick lighthouse in the

Cape Hatteras Lighthouse

climbing tours run every 10 minutes starting at 9am.

## Sports and Recreation

### Pea Island National Wildlife Refuge

(Hwy. 12, 10 miles south of Nags Head, 252/987-2394, www.fws.gov/peaisland) occupies the northern reach of Hatteras Island. Much of the island is covered by ponds, making this an exceptional place to see migratory waterfowl. Two nature trails link some of the best bird-watching spots, and one, the 0.5-mile North Pond Wildlife Trail, is fully wheelchair accessible.

The Outer Banks owe their existence to the volatile action of the tides. The same forces that created this habitable sandbar also make this an incredible place for water sports. **Canadian Hole,** a spot in the sound between Avon and Buxton, is one of the most famous windsurfing and sailboarding places in the world, and it goes without saying that it's also perfect for kite flying. The island is extraordinarily narrow here, so it's easy to tote your board from the sound side over to the ocean for a change of scene.

As with any sport, it's important to know your own skill level and choose activities accordingly. Beginners and experts alike can

United States. It was built in 1870 to protect ships at sea from coming onto the shoals unaware. It still stands on the cape and is open for climbing during the warm months. Tickets are sold on the premises beginning at 8:15am;

Pea Island National Wildlife Refuge

benefit from the guidance of serious water sports instructors. **Real Kiteboarding** (Cape Hatteras, 866/732-5548, www.realkiteboarding.com) is the largest kiteboarding school in the world. They offer kiteboarding camps and classes for all skill levels. **Outer Banks Kiting** (Avon, 252/305-6838, www.outerbankskiting.com) also teaches lessons and two-day camps, and carries boarders out on charter excursions to find the best spots.

There are all manner of exotic ways to tour Hatteras. **Equine Adventures** (252/995-4897, www.equineadventures.com) leads two-hour horseback tours through the maritime forests and along the beaches of Cape Hatteras. With **Hatteras Parasail** (Hatteras, 252/986-2627, www.hatterasparasail.com, parasail ride $60, kayak tour $35), you can ride 400 feet in the air over the coast, or even higher with **Burrus Flightseeing Tours** (Frisco, 252/986-2679, www.hatterasisland-flightseeing.com, $35-63 pp).

## Food

Though the **Restaurant at the Inn on Pamlico Sound** (Hwy. 12, Buxton, 252/995-7030, www.innonpamlicosound.com, $15) is primarily for guests of the inn, if you call in advance you might be able to get a reservation for dinner even if you're staying elsewhere. The chef likes to use fresh-caught seafood, sometimes caught by the guests themselves earlier in the day. Vegetarian dishes and other special requests are served.

For breakfast, try the **Gingerbread House** (52715 Hwy. 12, Frisco, 252/995-5204), which serves great baked goods made on the premises.

## Accommodations

### UNDER $150

Among the lodging choices on Hatteras Island is the **Cape Hatteras Bed and Breakfast** (46223 Old Lighthouse Rd./Cape Point Way, Buxton, 800/252-3316, $119-159), which is only a few hundred feet from the ocean. Guests rave about the breakfasts.

Simpler motel accommodations include

the clean, comfortable, and pet-friendly **Cape Pines Motel** (47497 Hwy. 12, Buxton, 866/456-9983, www.capepinesmotel.com, $49-159, depending on season, $20 pets); the **Outer Banks Motel** (47000 Hwy. 12, Buxton, 252/995-5601 or 800/995-1233, www.outerbanksmotel.com, $49-120), with both motel rooms and cottages; and the **Avon Motel** (Avon, 252/995-5774, www.avonmotel.com, $43-131, $10 pets), a pet-friendly motel that has been in business for more than 50 years.

### $150-300

Another good choice on Hatteras Island is the very fine **Inn on Pamlico Sound** (49684 Hwy. 12, Buxton, 252/995-7030 or 866/995-7030, www.innonpamlicosound.com, $120-320, depending on season). The inn is right on the sound, with a private dock and easy waterfront access. The dozen suites are sumptuous and relaxing, many with their own decks or private porches.

### CAMPING

**Rodanthe Watersports and Campground** (24170 Hwy. 12, 252/987-1431, www.watersportsandcampground.com) has a sound-front campground for tents and RVs under 25 feet, with water and electrical hookups and hot-water showers. Rates are $19.25 per night for two people, $4.75 for each additional adult, $3 for children and dogs, and an extra $4.75 per night for electrical hookups.

The National Park Service operates two campgrounds ($20) in this stretch of the national seashore: The **Frisco Campground** (53415 Billy Mitchell Rd., Frisco, 877/444-6777) opens in early April, and **Cape Point Campground** (46700 Lighthouse Rd., Buxton, 877/444-6777) opens in late May. At Frisco, you actually camp in the dunes, while at Cape Point, like the other National Park Service campgrounds in the area, the campsites are level and located behind the dunes. Both have cold showers, restrooms, and potable water.

**Frisco Woods Campground** (Hwy. 12, Frisco, 800/948-3942, www.outer-banks.com/

friscowoods, $30-90) has a full spectrum of camping options, from no-utilities tent sites and RV sites with partial or full hookups to one- and two-bedroom cabins. The campground has wireless Internet access, hot showers, and a coin laundry.

## ★ OCRACOKE ISLAND

Sixteen miles long, Ocracoke Island is the southernmost reach of the Cape Hatteras National Seashore. One of the most geographically isolated places in North Carolina, it's only accessible today by water and air. Regular ferry service didn't start until 1960, and it was only three years before that that Ocracokers had their first paved highway. In 1585, it was one of the first places in North America seen by Europeans, when the future lost colonists ran aground here. It may have been during the time they were waylaid at Ocracoke ("Wococon," they called it) that the

ancestors of today's wild ponies first set hoof on the Outer Banks. Theirs was not the last shipwreck at Ocracoke, and in fact, flotsam and goods that would wash up from offshore wrecks were among the sources of sustenance for generations of Ocracokers.

In the early 18th century, Ocracoke was a favorite haunt of Edward Teach, better known as the pirate Blackbeard. He lived here at times, married his 14th wife here, and died here. Teach's Hole, a spot just off the island, is where a force hired by Virginia lieutenant governor Alexander Spotswood finally cornered and killed him, dumping his decapitated body overboard (it's said to have swum around the ship seven times before going under), and sailing away with the trophy of his head on the bowsprit.

All of **Ocracoke Village,** near the southern end of the island, is in the National Register of Historic Places. While the

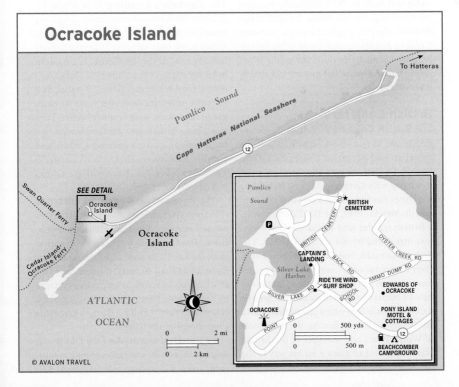

historical sites of the island are distinctive, the unique thing about the island and its people is the culture that has developed here over the centuries. Ocracokers have a "brogue" all their own, similar to those of other Outer Banks communities, but so distinctive that, in the unlikely event that there were two native Ocracokers who didn't know each other already, and they happened to cross paths somewhere out in the world, they would recognize each other right away as neighbors (and probably cousins) by the cadences of their speech.

## Ocracoke Lighthouse

A lighthouse has stood on Ocracoke since at least 1798, but due to constantly shifting sands, the inlet that it protected kept sneaking away. Barely 20 years after that first tower was built, almost a mile stretched between it and the water. The current **Ocracoke Lighthouse** (village of Ocracoke, 888/493-3826) was built in 1823, originally burning whale oil to power the beam. It is still in operation—the oldest operating light in North Carolina and the second oldest in the nation. Because it's on active duty, the public is not able to tour the inside, but a boardwalk nearby gives nice views.

## British Cemetery

The **British Cemetery** (British Cemetery Rd.) is not, as one might suppose, a colonial burial ground but rather a vestige of World War II. During the war, the Carolina coast was lousy with German U-boats. Defending the Outer Banks became a pressing concern, and on May 11, 1942, the HMS *Bedfordshire,* a British trawler sent to aid the U.S. Navy, was torpedoed by the German *U-558.* The *Bedfordshire* sank, and all 37 men aboard died. Over the course of the next week, four bodies washed up on Ocracoke. An island family donated a burial plot, and there the four men lie today, memorialized with a plaque that bears a lovely verse by Rupert Brooke, the young poet of World War I and member of the British Navy, who died of disease on his way to the battle of Gallipoli.

## Sports and Recreation

**Ride the Wind Surf Shop** (486 Irvin Garrish Hwy., 252/928-6311) gives individual and group surfing lessons, for adults and children, covering ocean safety and surfing etiquette in addition to board handling. A three-day surf camp ($200, or $75 per day) for kids ages 9 to 17 gives an even more in-depth tutorial. Ride the Wind also leads sunrise, sunset, and full-moon kayak tours around the marshes of Ocracoke ($35).

The **Schooner *Windfall*** (departs from Community Store Dock, Ocracoke, 252/928-7245, www.schoonerwindfall.com, tours $40), a beautiful 57-foot old-fashioned schooner, sails on three one-hour tours a day around Pamlico Sound. Passengers are allowed, and even encouraged, to try their hand at the wheel or trimming the sails.

## Accommodations

The **Captain's Landing** (324 Hwy. 12, 252/928-1999, www.thecaptainslanding.com, from $200 high season, from $100 off-season), with a perch right on Silver Lake (the harbor) looking toward the lighthouse, is a modern hotel owned by a descendant of Ocracoke's oldest families. Suites have 1.5 baths, full kitchens, comfortable sleeper sofas for extra guests, and decks with beautiful views. They also have a bright, airy penthouse with two bedrooms, an office, a gourmet kitchen, and even a laundry room. The Captain's Cottage is a private two-bedroom house with great decks and its own courtyard.

The **Pony Island Motel and Cottages** (785 Irvin Garrish Hwy., 866/928-4411, www.ponyislandmotel.com, from $108 high season, from $60 off-season) has been in operation since the late 1950s and run by the same family for more than 40 years. It has regular and efficiency motel rooms as well as four cottages on the grounds. Clean guest rooms, a good location, and year-round good prices make this a top choice on the island.

**Edwards of Ocracoke** (226 Old Beach Rd., 800/254-1359, www.edwardsofocracoke.com, from $53 spring and fall, from $90 summer) has several cozy bungalows typical of coastal Carolina, referred to here as "vintage accommodations." The mid-20th-century vacation ambience is very pleasant, the cabins are clean and well kept, and the prices are great.

The **Island Inn** (25 Lighthouse Rd., 252/928-4351, www.ocracokeislandinn.com, from $60 off-season, from $100 high season, no children) is in the National Register of Historic Places and bills itself as the oldest operating business on the Outer Banks. It was built in 1901 and first used as an Odd Fellows Hall; during World War II it was used as a barracks. The building is made of salvaged shipwreck wood.

### CAMPING

At **Ocracoke Campground** (4352 Irvin Garrish Hwy., Ocracoke, 877/444-6777, $23), campsites are right by the beach, behind the dunes. Remember to bring extra-long stakes to anchor your tent in the sand.

## TRANSPORTATION

The northern part of Cape Hatteras National Seashore can be reached by car via Highway 12 south from Nags Head. Following Highway 12, you'll go through the towns of Rodanthe,

Waves, Salvo, and Avon, then around the tip of the cape to Buxton, Frisco, and Hatteras, where the highway ends. From there, you have two choices: backtrack or hop a ferry.

Ocracoke can only be reached by ferry. The **Hatteras-Ocracoke Ferry** (800/368-8949, May 13-Oct. 5 5am-midnight on the half-hour, Apr. 1-May 12 and Oct. 7-Dec. 31 5am-midnight on the hour, Jan. 1-Mar. 31 4:30am-12:30am alternating half-hours, 40 minutes, free) is the shortest route to Ocracoke. If you look at a map, Highway 12 is shown crossing from Ocracoke to Cedar Island, as if there's an impossibly long bridge over Pamlico Sound. In fact, that stretch of Highway 12 is a ferry route too. The **Cedar Island-Ocracoke Ferry** (800/856-0343, www.ncdot.org/transit/ferry, May 20-Sept. 29 7am-8pm every 90 minutes, Mar.18-May 19 and Sept. 30-Oct. 27 7am-4:30pm every 3.5 hours, Jan. 1-Mar. 17 and Oct. 28-Dec. 31 7am-4:30pm every 3.5 hours), which is a 2.25-hour ride, regular-size vehicle $15 one-way. There's also a ferry between **Ocracoke and Swan Quarter** (800/345-1665, May 20-Sept. 29 6:30am-4:30pm every 3 hours, Jan. 1-May 19 and Sept. 30-Dec. 31 7am-4:30pm every 6.5 hours, 2.5 hours, regular-size vehicle $15 one-way).

# Lower Outer Banks

**TOP** EXPERIENCE

The southern reaches of the Outer Banks of North Carolina have some of the region's most diverse destinations. Core and Shackleford Banks lie within the Cape Lookout National Seashore, a wild maritime environment populated by plenty of wild ponies but not a single human. On the other hand, the towns of Bogue Banks—Atlantic Beach, Salter Path, Pine Knoll Shores, Indian Beach, and Emerald Isle—are classic beach towns. Both areas are great fun, Cape Lookout especially so for ecotourists and history buffs, and Bogue Banks for those looking for a day on the beach

followed by an evening chowing down on good fried seafood.

## ★ CAPE LOOKOUT NATIONAL SEASHORE

**Cape Lookout National Seashore** (office 131 Charles St., Harkers Island, 252/728-2250, www.nps.gov/calo) is an otherworldly place, with 56 miles of beach on four barrier islands, a long tape of sand so seemingly vulnerable to nature that it's hard to believe there were once several busy towns on its banks. Settled in the early 1700s, the townspeople of the south Core Banks made their living in fisheries that

# Lower Outer Banks

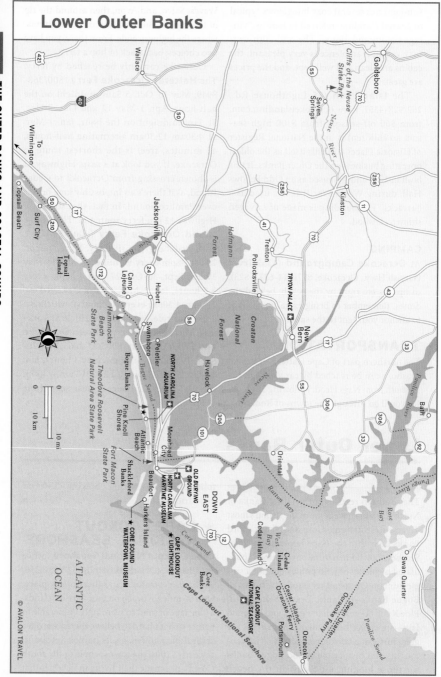

© AVALON TRAVEL

might seem brutal to today's seafood eaters—whaling and catching dolphins and sea turtles, among the more mundane species.

Wild horses roam the beaches and dunes, and dolphins frequent both the ocean and sound sides of the islands. Pets are allowed on leashes. The wild ponies on Shackleford Banks can pose a threat to dogs that get among them, and the dogs, of course, can frighten the horses, so be careful not to let them mingle.

## Cape Lookout Lighthouse

By the time you arrive at the 1859 **Cape Lookout Lighthouse** (visitors center, 252/728-2250), you'll probably already have seen it portrayed on dozens of brochures, menus, business signs, and souvenirs. With its striking diamond pattern, it looks like a rattlesnake standing at attention. Because it is still a working lighthouse, visitors are allowed in on only four days each year. Visit Cape Lookout National Seashore's website (www.nps.gov/calo) for open house dates and reservation information. The allotted times fill up almost immediately.

## Accommodations

**Morris Marina** (877/956-5688, www.cape-lookoutconcessions, $65-100) rents cabins at Great Island and Long Point. Cabins have hot and cold water, gas stoves, and furniture, but in some cases visitors must bring their own generators for lights as well as linens and utensils. Rentals are available only April-November. Book well in advance.

### CAMPING

Camping is permitted within Cape Lookout National Seashore, though there are no designated campsites or services. Everything you bring must be carried back out when you leave. Campers can stay for up to 14 days.

## Transportation

Except for the visitors center at Harkers Island, Cape Lookout National Seashore can only be reached by ferry. Portsmouth, at the northern end of the park, is a short ferry ride from Ocracoke, but Ocracoke is a very long ferry ride from Cedar Island. The **Cedar Island-Ocracoke Ferry** (800/856-0343, regular-size vehicle $15 one-way) is part of the state ferry system, and pets are allowed. It takes 2.25 hours to cross Pamlico Sound, but the ride is fun, and embarking from Cedar Island feels like sailing off the edge of the earth. The **Ocracoke-Portsmouth Ferry** (252/928-4361) is a passenger-only commercial route, licensed to Captain Rudy Austin. Phone to ensure a seat. There's also a vehicle and passenger ferry **from Atlantic to Long Point,** Morris Marina Kabin Kamps and Ferry Service (877/956-6568), on the North Core Banks; leashed or in-vehicle pets are allowed. Most ferries operate between April and November.

Commercial ferries cross every day **from mainland Carteret County** to the southern parts of the national seashore. There is generally a ferry route between Davis and Great Island, but service can be variable; check the Cape Lookout National Seashore website (www.nps.gov/calo) for updates.

**From Harkers Island,** passenger ferries to Cape Lookout Lighthouse and Shackleford Banks include Calico Jacks (252/728-3575), Harkers Island Fishing Center (252/728-3907), Local Yokel (252/728-2759), and Island Ferry Adventures (252/728-6181) at Barbour's Marina.

**From Beaufort,** passenger ferries include Outer Banks Ferry Service (252/728-4129), which goes to both Shackleford Banks and to Cape Lookout Lighthouse; Island Ferry Adventures (252/728-7555) and Mystery Tours (252/728-7827) run to Shackleford Banks. Morehead City's passenger-only Waterfront Ferry Service (252/726-7678) goes to Shackleford Banks as well. On-leash pets are generally allowed, but call ahead to confirm for Local Yokel, Island Ferry Adventures, and Waterfront Ferry Service.

# Beaufort and Vicinity

It's an oft-cited case of the perversity of Southern speech that Beaufort, North Carolina, receives the French treatment of "eau"—so it's pronounced "BO-furt"—whereas Beaufort, South Carolina, a similar Lowcountry port town south of Charleston, is pronounced "BYEW-furt."

The third-oldest town in North Carolina, Beaufort holds its own with its elders, Bath and New Bern, in the prettiness department. The little port was once North Carolina's window on the world, a rather cosmopolitan place that sometimes received news from London or Barbados sooner than from Raleigh. The streets are crowded with beautiful old houses, many built in a double-porch, steep-roofed style that shows off the early citizenry's cultural ties to the wider Caribbean and Atlantic world.

In the late 1990s a shipwreck was found in Beaufort Inlet that is believed to be that of the *Queen Anne's Revenge,* a French slaver captured by the pirate Blackbeard in 1717 to be the flagship of his unsavory fleet. He increased its arsenal to 40 cannons, but it was nevertheless sunk in the summer of 1718. Blackbeard was killed at Ocracoke Inlet a few months later, and it took five musket balls and 40 sword wounds to finish him off. Incredibly cool artifacts from the *QAR* keep emerging from the waters of the inlet. Beaufort had been a favorite haunt of Blackbeard's, and you can find out all about him at the North Carolina Maritime Museum.

## SIGHTS
### ★ North Carolina Maritime Museum

The **North Carolina Maritime Museum** (315 Front St., 252/728-7317, www.ah.dcr. state.nc.us/sections/maritime, Mon.-Fri. 9am-5pm, Sat. 10am-5pm, Sun. 1pm-5pm, free) is among the best museums in the state. Even if you don't think you're interested in boatbuilding or maritime history, you'll get caught up in the exhibits. Historic watercraft, reconstructions, and models of boats are on display, well presented in rich historical and cultural context.

Across the street from the museum's main

North Carolina Maritime Museum

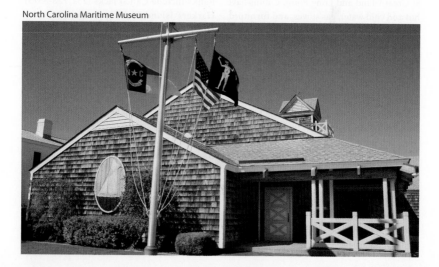

building, perched on the dock, is the **Harvey W. Smith Watercraft Center.** For many generations, North Carolina mariners had an international reputation as expert shipbuilders, and even today, some builders continue to construct large seaworthy vessels in their own backyards. Their exceptional expertise is beautifully demonstrated by the craft in the museum and by boats still working the waters today.

## ★ Old Burying Ground

One of the most beautiful places in all of North Carolina, Beaufort's **Old Burying Ground** (Anne St., daily dawn-dusk) is as picturesque a cemetery as you'd ever want to be buried in. Huge old live oaks, Spanish moss, wisteria, and resurrection ferns, which unfurl and turn green after a rainstorm, give the Burying Ground an irresistibly Gothic feel. Many of the headstones reflect the maritime heritage of this town.

One of the graveyard's famous burials is the "Little Girl Buried in a Barrel of Rum." This unfortunate waif is said to have died at sea and been placed in a cask of rum to preserve her body for burial. Visitors often bring toys and trinkets to leave on her grave, which is marked by a simple wooden plank.

## Beaufort Historic Site

The **Beaufort Historic Site** (130 Turner St., 252/728-5225, www.beauforthistoricsite.org, Dec.-Feb. Mon.-Sat. 10am-4pm, Mar.-Nov. Mon.-Sat. 9:30am-5pm, $8 adults, $4 children) re-creates life in late 18th- and early 19th-century Beaufort in several restored historic buildings. The 1770s "jump-and-a-half" (1.5-story) Leffers Cottage reflects middle-class life in its day. The Josiah Bell and John Manson Houses, both from the 1820s, reflect the graceful Caribbean-influenced architecture prevalent in the early days of the coastal South.

# SPORTS AND RECREATION
## Diving

North Carolina's coast is a surprisingly good place for diving. The **Discovery Diving Company** (414 Orange St., 252/728-2265, www.discoverydiving.com, $65-110 per excursion) leads half- and full-day diving trips to explore the reefs and dozens of fascinating shipwrecks that lie at the bottom of the sounds and ocean near Beaufort.

## Cruises and Wildlife Tours

**Coastal Ecology Tours** (252/247-3860, www.goodfortunesails.com, prices vary)

Old Burying Ground

# Blackbeard and Bonnet: The Boys of 1718

In the 18th century the Carolina coast was positively verminous with pirates. For the most part they hung out around Charleston Harbor, like a bunch of rowdies on a frat house balcony, causing headaches for passersby. Some liked to venture up the coast, however, into the inlets and sounds of North Carolina. The most famous local pirates were Blackbeard, whose real name was **Edward Teach,** and **Stede Bonnet.** They did most of their misbehaving in our waters during 1718.

Blackbeard is said never to have killed a man except in self-defense, but clearly he was so bad he didn't need to kill to make his badness known. He was a huge man with a beard that covered most of his face, and his hair is usually depicted twisted up into ferocious dreadlocks. He wore a bright red coat and festooned himself with every weapon small enough to carry; as if all that didn't make him scary enough, he liked to wear burning cannon fuses tucked under the brim of his hat. He caused trouble from the Bahamas to Virginia, taking ships, treasure, and child brides as fancy led him.

Poor Stede Bonnet. With a name like that, he should have known better than to try to make a living intimidating people. He is said to have been something of a fancy-pants, a man with wealth, education, and a nagging wife. To get away from his better half, he bought a ship, hired a crew, and set sail for a life of crime. Though never quite as tough as Blackbeard, with whom he was briefly partners, Bonnet caused enough trouble along the Southern coast that the gentry of Charleston saw to it that he was captured and hanged. Meanwhile, the Virginia nabobs had also had it with Blackbeard's interference in coastal commerce, and Lieutenant Governor Alexander Spotswood dispatched his men to kill him. This they did at Ocracoke, but it wasn't easy; even after they shot, stabbed, and beheaded Blackbeard, his body taunted them by swimming laps around the ship before finally giving up the ghost.

Blackbeard has in effect surfaced again. In 1996 a ship was found off the North Carolina coast that was identified as Blackbeard's flagship, the *Queen Anne's Revenge*. All manner of intriguing artifacts have been brought up from the ocean floor: cannons and blunderbuss parts, early hand grenades, even a penis syringe supposed to have been used by the syphilitic pirates to inject themselves with mercury. (During one standoff in Charleston Harbor, Blackbeard and his men took hostages to ransom for medical supplies. Perhaps this explains why they were so desperate.) To view artifacts and learn more about Blackbeard, Stede Bonnet, and their lowdown ways, visit the North Carolina Maritime Museum in Beaufort and in Southport, as well as the websites of the *Queen Anne's Revenge* (www.qaronline.com) and the Office of State Archaeology (www. arch.dcr.state.nc.us).

runs very special tours on the *Good Fortune* of the Cape Lookout National Seashore and other island locations in the area, as well as a variety of half-day, daylong, overnight, and short trips to snorkel, shell, kayak, and watch birds, as well as cruises to Morehead City restaurants and other educational and fun trips. Prices range from $40 per person for a 2.5-hour dolphin-watching tour to $600 per night plus meals for an off-season overnight boat rental.

**Lookout Cruises** (600 Front St., 252/504-7245, www.lookoutcruises.com) carries sightseers on lovely catamaran rides in the Beaufort and Core Sound region, out to Cape Lookout, and on morning dolphin-watching trips. **Island Ferry Adventures** (610 Front St., 252/728-7555, www.islandferryadventures.com, $10-15 adults, $5-8 children) runs dolphin-watching tours, trips to collect shells at Cape Lookout, and trips to see the wild ponies of Shackleford Banks. **Mystery Tours** (600 Front St., 252/728-7827 or 866/230-2628, www.mysteryboattours.com, $15-50 adults, free-$25 children, some cruises adults only) offers harbor tours and dolphin-watching trips as well as a variety of brunch, lunch, and dinner cruises and trips to wild islands where children can hunt for treasure.

## Food

Among the Beaufort eateries certified by Carteret Catch as serving local seafood are the **Blue Moon Bistro** (119 Queen St., 252/728-5800, www.bluemoonbistro.biz, Tues.-Sat. 5:30pm-10pm, $17-35) and **Aqua Restaurant** (114 Middle Lane, "behind Clawsons," 252/728-7777, www.aquaexperience.com, Tues.-Sat. 5:30pm-9:30pm, $15-25).

If you're traveling with a cooler and want to buy some local seafood to take home, try the **Fishtowne Seafood Center** (100 Wellons Dr., 252/728-6644) or **Tripps Seafood** (1224 Harkers Island Rd., 252/447-7700).

★ **Beaufort Grocery** (117 Queen St., 252/728-3899, www.beaufortgrocery.com, lunch and dinner Wed.-Mon., brunch Sun., $20-36), despite its humble name, is a sophisticated little eatery. At lunch it serves salads and crusty sandwiches along with "Damn Good Gumbo" and specialty soups. In the evening the café atmosphere gives way to that of a more formal gourmet dining room. Some of the best entrées include boneless chicken breast sautéed with pecans in a hazelnut cream sauce; Thai-rubbed roast half duckling; and whole baby rack of lamb, served with garlic mashed potatoes, tortillas, and a margarita-chipotle sauce. Try the cheesecake for dessert.

The waterfront **Front Street Grill** (300 Front St., 252/728-4956, www.frontstreetgrillatstillwater.com, Tues.-Sat. lunch 11:30am-2:30pm, dinner 5:30pm-9:30pm, Sunday brunch 11:30am-2:30pm, $15-22) is popular with boaters drifting through the area, as well as diners who arrive by land. The emphasis is on seafood and fresh regional ingredients. Front Street Grill's wine list is extensive, and they have repeatedly won *Wine Spectator* magazine's Award of Excellence.

## Accommodations

★ **Outer Banks Houseboats** (324 Front St., 252/728-4129, www.outerbankshouseboats.com) will rent you your own floating vacation home, sail it for you to a scenic spot, anchor it, and then come and check in on you every day during your stay. You'll have a skiff for your own use, but you may just want to lie on the deck all day and soak up the peacefulness. Rates run from $1,200 per weekend for the smaller houseboat to $3,000 per week for the luxury boat, with plenty of rental options in between.

The **Inlet Inn** (601 Front St., 800/554-5466, www.inlet-inn.com, $110-170) has one of the best locations in town, right on the water, near the docks where many of the ferry and tour boats land. If you're planning to go dolphin-watching or hop the ferry to Cape Lookout, you can get ready at a leisurely pace, and just step outside to the docks. Even in high season, rates are quite reasonable.

The **Beaufort Inn** (101 Ann St., 252/728-2600, www.beaufort-inn.com, $200-250) is a large hotel on Gallants Channel, along one side of the colonial district. It's an easy walk to the main downtown attractions, and the hotel's outdoor hot tub and balconies with great views make it tempting to stay in as well. The **Pecan Tree Inn** (116 Queen St., 800/728-7871, www.pecantree.com, $135-175) is such a grand establishment that the town threw a parade in honor of the laying of its cornerstone in 1866. The house is still splendid, as are the 5,000-square-foot gardens. Catty-corner to the Old Burying Ground is the **Langdon House Bed and Breakfast** (135 Craven St., 252/728-5499, www.langdonhouse.com, $120-185). One of the oldest buildings in town, this gorgeous house was built in the 1730s on a foundation of English ballast stones.

# HARKERS ISLAND

The Core Sound region, which stretches to the east-northeast of Beaufort many miles up to the Pamlico Sound, is a region of birds and boats. Many Down Easterners also became expert decoy carvers. This art survives today, partly as art for art's sake, and also for its original purpose.

## Core Sound Waterfowl Museum

The **Core Sound Waterfowl Museum** (1785 Island Rd., Harkers Island, 252/728-1500, www.coresound.com, Mon.-Sat. 10am-5pm,

Sun. 2pm-5pm, free), which occupies a beautiful modern building on Shell Point, next to the Cape Lookout National Seashore headquarters, is a community labor of love. The museum is home to exhibits crafted by members of the communities represented, depicting Down East maritime life through decoys, nets, and other tools of the trades, everyday household objects, beautiful quilts and other utilitarian folk arts, and lots of other things held dear by local people.

## Food

**Captain's Choice Restaurant** (977 Island Rd., 252/728-7122, Fri.-Sun. 7am-9pm, Tues.-Thurs. 10am-9pm) is a great place to try traditional Down East chowder. Usually made of clams, but sometimes with other shellfish or fish, chowder in Carteret County is a point of pride. The point is the flavor of the seafood itself, which must be extremely fresh, and not hidden behind lots of milk and spices. Captain's Choice serves chowder in the old-time way—with dumplings.

# MOREHEAD CITY

Giovanni da Verrazano may have been the first European to set foot in present-day Morehead City when he sailed into Bogue Inlet. It wasn't until the mid-19th century that the town actually came into being, built as the terminus of the North Carolina Railroad to connect the state's overland commerce to the sea. Morehead is also an official state port, one of the best deepwater harbors on the Atlantic Coast. This admixture of tourism and gritty commerce gives Morehead City a likeable, real-life feel missing in many coastal towns today.

## Sights

Morehead City's history is on display at **The History Place** (1008 Arendell St., 252/247-7533, www.thehistoryplace.org, Tues.-Sat. 10am-4pm, free). The most striking exhibit is that of a carriage, clothes, and other items pertaining to Emeline Pigott, Morehead City's Confederate heroine. She was a busy girl all through the Civil War, working as a nurse, a spy, and a smuggler. The day she was captured, she was carrying 30 pounds of contraband hidden in her skirts, including Union troop movement plans, a collection of gloves, several dozen skeins of silk, needles, toothbrushes, a pair of boots, and five pounds of candy.

## Entertainment and Events

Seafood is a serious art in Morehead City. North Carolina's second-largest festival takes place in town every October—the enormous **North Carolina Seafood Festival** (252/726-6273, www.ncseafoodfestival.org). The city's streets shut down and over 150,000 visitors descend on the waterfront. Festivities kick off with a blessing of the fleet, followed with music, fireworks, competitions (including the flounder toss), and, of course, lots and lots of food.

If you're in the area on the right weekend in November, you'll not want to deprive yourself of the gluttonous splendor of the **Mill Creek Oyster Festival** (Mill Creek Volunteer Fire Department, 2370 Mill Creek Rd., Mill Creek, 252/247-4777). Food, and lots of it, is the focus of this event. It's a small-town fete, a benefit for the local volunteer fire department, and the meals are cooked by local experts.

## Sports and Recreation

Many of this region's most important historical and natural sites are underwater. From Morehead City's **Olympus Dive Center** (713 Shepard St., 252/726-9432, www.olympusdiving.com), divers of all levels of experience can take charter trips to dozens of natural and artificial reefs that teem with fish, including the ferocious-looking but not terribly dangerous eight-foot-long sand tiger shark. There are at least as many amazing shipwrecks to choose from, including an 18th-century schooner, a luxury liner, a German U-boat, and many Allied commercial and military ships that fell victim to the U-boats that infested this coast during World War II.

## Food

The **Sanitary Fish Market** (501 Evans St.,

252/247-3111, www.sanitaryfishmarket.com, daily 11:30am-9:30pm, $15-20) is probably Morehead City's best-known institution. The rather odd name reflects its 1930s origins as a seafood market that was bound by its lease and its fastidious landlord to be kept as clean as possible. Today it's a huge family seafood restaurant. Long lines in season and on weekends demonstrate its popularity. Be sure to buy a Sanitary T-shirt on the way out; it'll help you blend in everywhere else in the state.

The **Bistro-by-the-Sea** (4031 Arendell St., 252/247-2777, www.bistro-by-the-sea.com, Tues.-Thurs. 5pm-9:30pm, Fri.-Sat. 5pm-10pm, $10-25) participates in Carteret Catch, a program that brings together local fisherfolk with restaurants, fish markets, and wholesalers to ensure that fresh locally caught seafood graces the tables of Carteret County. In addition to seafood, specialties here are steak, tenderloin, and prime rib.

**Captain Bill's** (701 Evans St., 252/726-2166, www.captbills.com, daily 11:30am-9:30pm, $12-20) is Morehead City's oldest restaurant, founded in 1938. Try the conch stew, and be sure to visit the otters that live at the dock outside.

## BOGUE BANKS

The beaches of Bogue Banks are popular with visitors, but they have a typically North Carolinian, laid-back feel, a quieter atmosphere than the fun-fun-fun neon jungles of beaches in other states. The major attractions, Fort Macon State Park and the North Carolina Aquarium at Pine Knoll Shores, are a bit more cerebral than, say, amusement parks and bikini contests. In the surfing and boating, bars and restaurants, and the beach itself, there's also a bustle of activity to keep things hopping. Bogue, by the way, rhymes with "rogue."

### ★ North Carolina Aquarium

The **North Carolina Aquarium at Pine Knoll Shores** (1 Roosevelt Blvd., Pine Knoll Shores, 866/294-3477, www.ncaquariums.com, Aug.-June daily 9am-5pm, July Fri.-Wed. 9am-5pm, Thurs. 9am-9pm, $10.95 adults,

$8.95 children) is one of the state's three great coastal aquariums. Here at Pine Knoll Shores, exhibit highlights include a 300,000-gallon aquarium in which sharks and other aquatic beasts go about their business in and around a replica German U-Boat (plenty of originals lie right off the coast and form homes for reef creatures); a "jellyfish gallery" (they really can be beautiful); a pair of river otters; and many other wonderful animals and habitats.

### Fort Macon State Park

At the eastern tip of Atlantic Beach is **Fort Macon State Park** (2300 E. Fort Macon Rd., 252/726-3775, www.ncsparks.net/foma.html, park daily 9am-5:30pm, fort Oct.-Mar. daily 8am-6pm, Apr.-May and Sept. daily 8am-7pm, June-Aug. daily 8am-8pm, bathhouse area Nov.-Feb. daily 8am-5:30pm, Mar. and Oct. daily 8am-7pm, Apr.-May and Sept. daily 8am-8pm, June-Aug. daily 8am-9pm, bathhouse $4 adults, $3 children). The central feature of the park is Fort Macon itself, an 1820s federal fort that was a Confederate garrison for one year during the Civil War.

### Food

The **Channel Marker** (718 Atlantic Beach Causeway, Atlantic Beach, 252/247-2344, daily 11am-9:30pm, $15-25) is a more upscale alternative to some of the old-timey fried seafood joints on Bogue Banks (which are also great—read on). Try the crab cakes with mango chutney, or the Greek shrimp salad. The extensive wine list stars wines from the opposite side of North Carolina, from the Biltmore Estate in Asheville.

**White Swan Bar-B-Q and Chicken** (2500-A W. Fort Macon Rd., Atlantic Beach, 252/726-9607, Mon.-Sat. 7am-2pm, $8) has been serving the Carolina trinity of barbecue, coleslaw, and hush puppies since 1960. They also flip a mean egg for breakfast.

The ★ **Big Oak Drive-In and Bar-B-Q** (1167 Salter Path Rd., 252/247-2588, www.bigoakdrivein.com, Fri.-Sun. 11am-3pm) is a classic beach drive-in, a little red-white-and-blue-striped building with a walk-up counter and drive-up spaces. They're best known for their shrimp burgers (large $5), a fried affair slathered with Big Oak's signature red sauce, coleslaw, and tartar sauce. Then there are the scallop burgers, oyster burgers, clam burgers, hamburgers, and barbecue—all cheap, and made for snacking on the beach.

**Frost Seafood House** (1300 Salter Path Rd., Salter Path, 252/247-3202, Fri.-Sun. 7am-9pm, Mon.-Thurs. 4:30pm-9:30pm, $10) began in 1954 as a gas station and quickly became the restaurant that it is today. The Frost family catches its own shrimp and buys much of its other seafood locally. Be sure to request a taste of the "ching-a-ling sauce." Yet another community institution is the **Crab Shack** (140 Shore Dr., Salter Path, 252/247-3444, daily 11am-9pm, $9-25). You'll find it behind the Methodist church in Salter Path. The restaurant was wiped out in 2005 by Hurricane Ophelia, but they have since rebuilt, rolled up their sleeves, and plunged their hands back into the cornmeal.

## Accommodations

The **Atlantis Lodge** (123 Salter Path Rd., Atlantic Beach, 800/682-7057, www.atlantis-lodge.com, $70-220) is an old family-run motel. It has simple and reasonably priced efficiencies in a great beachfront location. Well-behaved pets are welcome for a per-pet, per-night fee. The **Clamdigger** (511 Salter Path Rd., Atlantic Beach, 800/338-1533, www.clamdiggerrama-dainn.com, $40-260) is another reliable choice, with all oceanfront guest rooms. Pets are not allowed. The **Windjammer** (103 Salter Path Rd., Atlantic Beach, 800/233-6466, www.wind-jammerinn.com, $50-200) is another simple, comfortable motel, with decent rates through the high season.

## Transportation

A 20-minute free **passenger ferry crosses the Neuse River** between Cherry Branch (near Cherry Point) and Minesott Beach in Pamlico County every 30 minutes (800/339-9156, pets allowed).

# Albemarle Sound

Referred to historically as the Albemarle, and sometimes today as the Inner Banks, the mainland portion of northeastern North Carolina is the hearth of the state's colonial history, the site of its first European towns and the earliest plantation and maritime economies.

The Great Dismal Swamp is here, a region thought of by early Carolinians and Virginians as a diseased and haunted wasteland, the sooner drained the better. They succeeded to some extent in beating back the swamp waters and vapors, but left enough for modern generations to recognize as one of the state's crown jewels.

## ★ THE GREAT DISMAL SWAMP

Viewed for centuries as an impediment to progress, the Great Dismal Swamp is now

recognized for the national treasure that it is, and tens of thousands of acres are protected. There are several points from which to gain access to the interior of the Dismal Swamp. A few miles south of the North Carolina-Virginia line, on U.S. 17, is the **Dismal Swamp Welcome Center** (2294 U.S. 17 N., visitors center 2356 U.S. 17 N., South Mills, 877/771-8333, www.dismalswamp.com, late May-Oct. daily 9am-5pm, Nov.-late May Tues.-Sat. 9am-5pm). Should you be arriving by water, you'll find the welcome center at mile 28 on the Intracoastal Waterway. You can tie up to the dock here and spend the night, if you wish, or wait for one of the four daily lock openings (8:30am, 11am, 1:30pm, and 3:30pm) to proceed. There are also picnic tables and grills here, and restrooms open day and night.

the Great Dismal Swamp

Another area of the swamp to explore is the **Great Dismal Swamp National Wildlife Refuge** (Suffolk, VA, 757/986-3705, www.albemarle-nc.com/gates/gdsnwr, daily dawn-dusk), which straddles the state line. Two main entrances are outside Suffolk, Virginia, off the White Marsh Road (Hwy. 642). These entrances, Washington Ditch and Jericho Lane, are open April-September daily 6:30am-8pm, October-March daily 6:30am-5pm. You may see all sorts of wildlife in the swamp—including poisonous cottonmouths, canebrake rattlers, copperheads, and possibly even black bears.

# WILLIAMSTON AND VICINITY

Williamston is at the junction of U.S. 17 and U.S. 64. If you're passing through town, Williamston is a great place to stop for barbecue or a fresh seafood meal.

## Sights

A little west of Williamston on U.S. 13/64 Alternate, you'll find the town of Robersonville and the **St. James Place Museum** (U.S. 64 Alt. and Outerbridge Rd., call Robersonville Public Library at 252/795-3591, by appointment, free). A Primitive Baptist church built in 1910 and restored by a local preservationist and folk art enthusiast, St. James Place is an unusual little museum that fans of Southern craft will not want to miss.

On the same highway is **East Carolina Motor Speedway** (4918 U.S. 64 Alt., 252/795-3968, www.ecmsracing.com, usually Apr.-Oct., pits open at 3pm, grandstands from 5pm), a 0.4-mile hard-surface track featuring several divisions, including late-model street stock, modified street stock, super-stock four-cylinder, and four-cylinder kids class.

## Food

Come to Williamston on an empty stomach. It has an assortment of old and very traditional eateries. The ★ **Sunny Side Oyster Bar** (1102 Washington St., 252/792-3416, www.sunnysideoysterbarnc.com, Sept.-Apr. Mon.-Thurs. 5:30pm-9pm, Fri.-Sat. from 5:30pm, Sun. 5pm-8pm, $12-20) is the best known, a seasonal oyster joint open in the months with the letter *r*—that is, oyster season. It's been in business since 1935, and is a historic as well as gastronomic landmark. The Sunny Side doesn't take reservations, and it fills to capacity in no time flat, so come early.

Down the road a piece, **Martin Supply** (118 Washington St., 252/792-2123), an old general store, is a good place to buy local produce and preserves, honey, molasses, and hoop cheese. **Griffin's Quick Lunch** (204 Washington St., 252/792-0002, Mon.-Fri. 6am-8:30pm, Sat. 6am-2pm, $8) is a popular old diner with good barbecue. Back on U.S. 64, **Shaw's Barbecue** (U.S. 64 Alt., 252/792-5339, Mon.-Sat. 6am-7pm, $7-10) serves eastern Carolina-style barbecue, as well as good greasy breakfasts.

East of Williamston at the intersection of U.S. 64 and Highway 171, the small Roanoke River town of Jamesville is home to a most unusual restaurant that draws attention from all over the country (it's even been featured in the *New York Times*). The ★ **Cypress Grill** (1520 Stewart St., off U.S. 64, 252/792-4175, mid-Jan.-Apr. Mon.-Sat. 11am-8pm, $7-10) is an unprepossessing wooden shack right-smack on the river, a survivor of the days when Jamesville made its living in the herring industry, dragging the fish out of the water with horse-drawn seine nets. Herring—breaded and seriously deep-fried, not pickled or sweet—is the main dish here, though they also dress the herring up in other outfits, and serve bass, flounder, perch, oyster, catfish, and other fish too. The Cypress Grill is open from the second Thursday in January through the end of April.

# EAST ON U.S. 64

The eastern stretch of U.S. 64 runs along the Albemarle Sound between Williamston and the Outer Banks. Here you'll encounter evidence of North Carolina's ancient past in the form of old-growth forests; of the recent past in a plantation with a long and complex history of slavery; and the present, in art galleries and abundant wildlife-watching and recreational opportunities.

## Somerset Place Historic Site
**Somerset Place Historic Site** (2572 Lake Shore Rd., Creswell, 252/797-4560, www.

ah.dcr.state.nc.us, Apr.-Oct. Mon.-Sat. 9am-5pm, Sun. 1pm-5pm, Nov.-Mar. Tues.-Sat. 10am-4pm, Sun. 1pm-4pm, free) was one of North Carolina's largest and most profitable plantations for the 80 years leading up to the Civil War. In the late 18th and early 19th centuries, 80 enslaved Africa-born men, women, and children were brought to Somerset to labor in the fields. The grief and spiritual disorientation they experienced, and the subsequent trials of the enslaved community that grew to include more than 300 people, are told by the historian Dorothy Spruill Redford in the amazing book *Somerset Homecoming*.

## Pettigrew State Park
On the banks of Lake Phelps, **Pettigrew State Park** (2252 Lakeshore Rd., Creswell, 252/797-4475, http://ncparks.gov, day-use hours June-Aug. 8am-9pm, Mar.-May and Sept.-Oct. 8am-8pm, Nov.-Feb. 8am-6pm, free) preserves a weird ancient waterscape that's unlike anywhere else in the state. Archaeological studies reveal that there was a human presence here a staggering 10,000 years ago. Visitors to Pettigrew State Park can camp at the family campground ($15), which has drive-in sites and access to restrooms and hot showers, or at primitive group campsites (from $9).

## Sports and Recreation
**Palmetto-Peartree Preserve** (Pot Licker Rd./Loop Rd./Hwy. 1220, east of Columbia, 252/796-0723 or 919/967-2223, www.palmettopeartree.org, daily dawn-dusk, free) is a 10,000-acre natural area, wrapped in 14 miles of shoreline along the Albemarle Sound and Little Alligator Creek. Originally established as a sanctuary for the red-cockaded woodpecker, this is a great location for bird-watching and spotting other wildlife, including alligators, wolves, bears, and bobcats; hiking, biking, and horseback riding along the old logging trails through the forest; and canoeing and kayaking.

Once the southern edge of the Great

Dismal Swamp, **Pocosin Lakes National Wildlife Refuge** (252/796-3004, www.fws.gov/pocosinlakes, daily dawn-dusk, free) is an important haven for many species of animals, including migratory waterfowl and reintroduced red wolves. The refuge headquarters is at Walter B. Jones Sr. Center for the Sounds (U.S. 64, 6 miles south of Columbia).

Also east of Columbia on U.S. 64 is the **Alligator River National Wildlife Refuge** (between Columbia and Roanoke Island, 252/473-1131, http://alligatorriver.fws.gov, daily dawn-dusk, free). This large swath of woods and pocosin represents one of the most important wildlife habitats in the state, home to over 200 species of birds.

# Pamlico Sound

## WASHINGTON, BATH, AND BELHAVEN

On the north side of the Pamlico River, as you head toward Mattamuskeet National Wildlife Refuge and the Outer Banks, the towns of Washington, Bath, and Belhaven offer short diversions into the nature and history of this region.

### North Carolina Estuarium

The **North Carolina Estuarium** (223 E. Water St., Washington, 252/948-0000, www.partnershipforthesounds.org, Tues.-Sat. 10am-4pm, $3 adults, $2 children) is a museum about both the natural and cultural history of the Tar-Pamlico River Basin. In addition to the exhibits, which include live native animals, historical artifacts, and much more, the Estuarium operates pontoon boat tours on the Pamlico River. River roving is free, but reservations are required.

### Moss House

Located in the Washington historic district, a block from the river, is the **Moss House** (129 Van Norden St., Washington, 252/975-3967, www.themosshouse.com, $110-235). This 1902 house is a cozy bed-and-breakfast with airy guest rooms and delicious breakfasts. An easy walk from the Moss House is **Bill's Hot Dogs** (109 Gladden St., Washington, 252/946-3343, daily 8:30am-5pm), a longtime local favorite for a quick snack.

### Goose Creek State Park

**Goose Creek State Park** (2190 Camp Leach Rd., 252/923-2191, http://ncparks.gov, daily 8am-dusk, free) is on the banks of the Pamlico, where Goose Creek empties into the river. It's an exotic environment of brackish marshes, freshwater swamps, and tall pine forests, home to a variety of wildlife, including bears, a multitude of bird species, and rather many snakes. Twelve primitive campsites ($13/day), with access to toilets and water, are available year-round, including one that is disabled-accessible.

### Historic Bath

North Carolina's oldest town, Bath, was chartered in 1705. For its first 70 or so years, Bath enjoyed the spotlight as one of the colony's most important centers of trade and politics—home of governors, refuge from conflicts with Native Americans, frequent host to and victim of Blackbeard. Today, almost all of Bath is designated as **Historic Bath** (252/923-3971, www.bath.nchistoricsites.org, visitors center and tours Apr.-Oct. Mon.-Sat. 9am-5pm, Sun. 1pm-5pm, Nov.-Mar. Tues.-Sat. 10am-4pm, Sun. 1pm-4pm, $2 admission for Palmer-Marsh and Bonner Houses). Important sites on the tour of the village are the 1734 St. Thomas Church, the 1751 Palmer-Marsh House, the 1790 Van Der Veer House, the 1830 Bonner House, and, from time immemorial, a set of indelible hoofprints said to have been made by the devil's own horse.

While in Bath, drop in at the **Old Town Country Kitchen** (436 Carteret St., 252/923-1840, Fri.-Sat. 7am-8:30pm, Sun.-Tues. 7am-2pm, Wed.-Thurs. 7am-8pm, $10) for some country cooking and seafood. If you decide to stay the night, try the **Inn on Bath Creek** (116 S. Main St., 252/923-9571, www.innonbathcreek.com, 2-night minimum Apr.-Nov. Fri.-Sat., $130-225). This bed-and-breakfast, built on the site of the former Buzzard Hotel, fits in nicely with the old architecture of the historic town, but because it was built in 1999, it has modern conveniences to make your stay especially comfortable.

## Belhaven

The name **Belhaven Memorial Museum** (210 E. Main St., Belhaven, 252/943-6817, www.beaufort-county.com, Thurs.-Tues. 1pm-5pm, free) gives no hint as to what a very strange little institution this is. The museum houses the collection of Miss Eva—Eva Blount Way, who died in 1962 at the age of 92—surely one of the most accomplished collectors of oddities ever. Miss Eva kept among her earthly treasures a collection of pickled tumors (one weighs 10 pounds), a pickled one-eyed pig, a pickled two-headed kitten, cataracts (pickled), and three pickled human babies.

Belhaven has an especially nice inn, the **Belhaven Water Street Bed and Breakfast** (567 E. Water St., 866/338-2825, www.belhavenwaterstreetbandb.com, $85-115). The guest rooms in this 100-year-old house face Pantego Creek and have their own fireplaces and private baths as well as wireless access.

## MATTAMUSKEET NATIONAL WILDLIFE REFUGE

Near the tiny town of Swan Quarter, the **Mattamuskeet National Wildlife Refuge** (Hwy. 94, between Swan Quarter and Englehard, 252/926-4021, www.fws.gov/mattamuskeet, daily dawn-dusk, free) preserves one of North Carolina's most remarkable natural features. Lake Mattamuskeet, 18 miles long by 6 miles wide, is the state's largest natural lake, and being an average of 1.5 feet deep—five feet at its deepest point—it is

Mattamuskeet National Wildlife Refuge

a most unusual environment. The hundreds of thousands of waterfowl who rest here on their seasonal rounds make this a world-famous location for bird-watching and wildlife photography.

Hiking and biking trails thread through the refuge, but camping is not permitted. Within the administration of the Mattamuskeet Refuge is the **Swan Quarter National Wildlife Refuge** (252/926-4021, www.fws.gov/swanquarter, daily dawn-dusk, free), located along the north shore of the Pamlico Sound, and mostly accessible only by water. This too is a gorgeous waterscape full of wildlife.

# New Bern

New Bern was settled in 1710 by a community of Swiss and German colonists. It also became North Carolina's capital in an era symbolized by the splendor of Tryon Palace, one of the most recognizable architectural landmarks in the state. Despite the considerable traffic it draws, New Bern is still a small and enormously pleasant city.

One all-important note: how to say it. It's your choice of "NYEW-bern" or "NOO-bern"—and in some folks' accents it sounds almost like "neighbor"—but never "new-BERN."

## SIGHTS
### ★ Tryon Palace

**Tryon Palace** (610 Pollock St., 252/514-4956 or 252/514-4900, www.tryonpalace. org, Mon.-Sat. 9am-5pm, Sun. 1pm-5pm, last tour 4pm, gardens summer Mon.-Sat. 9am-7pm, Sun. 1pm-7pm, shop Mon.-Sat. 9:30am-5:30pm, Sun. 1pm-5:30pm, $20 adults, $10 grades 1-12, gardens and stables only $8 adults, $3 grades 1-12) is a rather remarkable feat of historic re-creation, a from-the-ground-up reconstruction of the 1770 colonial capitol and governor's mansion.

the garden at Tryon Palace

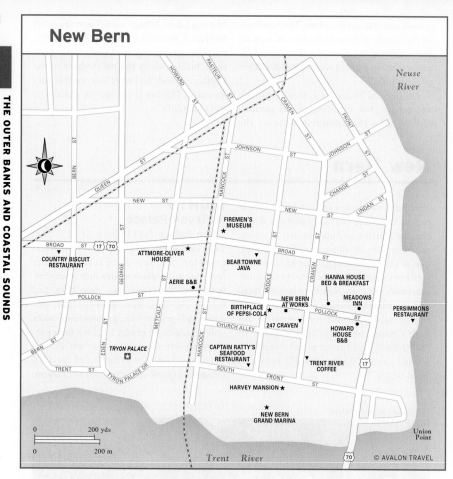

# New Bern

The original stood for a scant 25 years before burning down in 1798, and as the by-now state of North Carolina had relocated its governmental operations to Raleigh, there was no need to rebuild the New Bern estate.

The property continued, however, to live on in Carolinians' imaginations. In the early 20th century, a movement to rebuild Tryon Palace began. By the 1950s, both the funds and, incredibly, the original drawings and plans had been secured, and over a period of seven years the palace was rebuilt. When you visit, allow yourself plenty of time—a whole afternoon or even a full day.

In 2010, in honor of New Bern's 300th anniversary, Tryon Palace opened its **North Carolina History Center,** an enormous complex along the Trent River next to the Tryon Palace gardens, with galleries, a performance hall, outdoor interpretive areas, and more. You should begin your Tryon Palace adventure here.

## New Bern Firemen's Museum
The **New Bern Firemen's Museum** (408 Hancock St., 252/636-4087, www.newbernmuseums.com, Mon.-Sat. 10am-4pm, $5 adults, $2.50 children) is a fun little

museum—an idyll for the gearhead with an antiquarian bent. The museum houses a collection of 19th- and early 20th-century fire wagons and trucks, and chronicles the lively and contentious history of firefighting in New Bern.

## Attmore-Oliver House

The beautiful 1790 **Attmore-Oliver House** (510 Pollock St., 252/638-8558, www.new-bernhistorical.org, call for hours and tour schedule, $4 adults, free for students) is a nice historic house museum, with exhibits about New Bern's very significant Civil War history. It's also the headquarters of the New Bern Historical Society.

## Birthplace of Pepsi-Cola

We often think of Coca-Cola as the quintessential Southern drink, but it was here in New Bern that Caleb Bradham, a drugstore owner, put together what he called Brad's Drink—later Pepsi-Cola. Pepsi-Cola Bottling Company operates a soda fountain and gift shop at the location of Bradham's pharmacy, called the **Birthplace of Pepsi** (256 Middle St., 252/636-5898, www.pepsi-store.com).

## ENTERTAINMENT AND EVENTS

New Bern's historic Harvey Mansion has a cozy old-fashioned pub in its cellar, the **1797 Steamer Bar** (221 S. Front St., 252/635-3232). As one would gather from its name, the pub serves steamed seafood and other light fare. **Captain Ratty's Seafood Restaurant** (202-206 Middle St., 252/633-2088 or 800/633-5292, www.captainrattys.com) also has a bar that's a popular gathering spot for locals and visitors alike.

## SHOPPING

New Bern is a great place to shop for antiques. The majority of the shops are on the 220-240 blocks of Middle Street. There are also periodic antiques shows (and even a salvaged antique architectural hardware show) at the New Bern Convention Center. See www.visitnewbern.com for details.

Tryon Palace is a fun shopping spot for history buffs and home-and-garden fanciers.

the Birthplace of Pepsi-Cola

The historical site's **Museum Shop** (Jones House, Eden St. and Pollock St., 252/514-4932, Mon.-Sat. 9:30am-5:30pm, Sun. 1pm-5:30pm) has a nice variety of books about history and architecture as well as handicrafts and children's toy and games. The **Garden Shop** (610 Pollock St., 252/514-4932, Mon.-Sat. 10am-5pm, Sun. 1pm-5pm) sells special bulbs and plants, when in season, grown in Tryon Palace's own greenhouse.

## SPORTS AND RECREATION

At New Bern's Sheraton Marina, **Barnacle Bob's Boat and Jet Ski Rentals** (100 Middle St., Dock F, 252/634-4100, www.boatandjetskinewbern.com, daily 9am-7pm) rents one- and two-person Jet Skis ($65 per hour, half-hour $45) and 6- to 8-person pontoon boats ($65 per hour, 4 hours $220, 8 hours $420).

## FOOD

Down-home food choices include the **Country Biscuit Restaurant** (809 Broad St., 252/638-5151, Mon.-Tues. 5am-2pm, Wed.-Fri. 5am-2pm and 4pm-9pm, Sat. 5am-9pm, $7-12), which is open for breakfast, and is popular for, not surprisingly, its biscuits. **Moore's Olde Tyme Barbeque** (3711 U.S. 17 S./Martin Luther King Jr. Blvd., 252/638-3937, www.mooresbarbeque.com, Mon.-Sat. 10am-8pm, $6-9) is a family business, in operation (at a series of different locations) since 1945.

## ACCOMMODATIONS

The ★ **Aerie Bed and Breakfast** (509 Pollock St., 800/849-5553, www.aeriebedandbreakfast.com, $119-169) is the current incarnation of the 1880s Street-Ward residence. Its seven luxurious guest rooms are done up in Victorian furniture and earth-tone fabrics reflecting the house's earliest era. There is a lovely courtyard for guests to enjoy, and the inn is only one short block from Tryon Palace.

Also on Pollock Street, a few blocks away, are the **Harmony House Inn** (215 Pollock St., 800/636-3113, www.harmonyhouseinn.com, $99-175), the **Howard House Bed and Breakfast** (207 Pollock St., 252/514-6709, www.howardhousebnb.com, $89-149), and the **Meadows Inn** (212 Pollock St., 877/551-1776, www.meadowsinn-nc.com, $106-166). All three are appealing 19th-century houses decorated in the classic bed-and-breakfast style, and within easy walking distance to Tryon Palace and downtown.

# Wilmington and Cape Fear

Look for ★ to find recommended sights, activities, dining, and lodging.

# Highlights

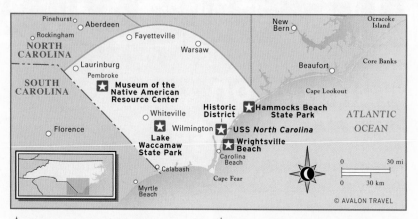

★ **Wilmington's Historic District:** North Carolina's largest historic district is a gorgeous collection of antebellum and late Victorian buildings (page 81).

★ **Wrightsville Beach:** Few other beaches in the state can compare with Wrightsville for its pretty strand, easy public access, clear waters, and overall beauty (page 82).

★ **USS North Carolina:** Take a tour of this enormous World War II battleship, permanently berthed on the Cape Fear River (page 83).

★ **Hammocks Beach State Park:** Accessible only by boat, one of the wildest and least disturbed Atlantic beaches is a popular stopover for migrating waterfowl and turtles (page 92).

★ **Museum of the Native American Resource Center:** This small but high-quality museum in Pembroke highlights the culture and artifacts of the local Lumbee people (page 100).

★ **Lake Waccamaw State Park:** The central feature of this scenic area is a Carolina bay, a unique geographical feature with a diverse surrounding ecosystem (page 100).

Cape Fear is part of the Caribbean culture that stretches up through the south Atlantic coast of North America—a world that reflects English, Spanish, and French adaptation to the tropics and, above all, the profound, trans-formative influence of African cultures brought to the New World by enslaved people. Wilmington is part of the sorority that includes Havana, Caracas, Port au Prince, Santo Domingo, New Orleans, Savannah, and Charleston. All exhibit the richness of Afro-Caribbean culture in their architecture, cuisine, folklore, and speech.

The area between Wilmington and Lumberton in the state's southeast corner is a strange, exotic waterscape (more so than a landscape) of seductively eerie swamps and backwaters. In this little band of coastal counties straddling the state line, within a 100-mile radius of Wilmington, is the native habitat—the only one in the world—of the Venus flytrap, a ferocious little plant of rather ghastly beauty. It somehow seems like an appropriate mascot for these weird backwaters.

The greatest draw to this region, even more than colonial cobblestones and carnivorous plants, are the beaches of Brunswick, New Hanover, Pender, and Onslow Counties. Some of them, like Wrightsville and Topsail, are well known, and others remain comparatively secluded barrier island strands. In some ways the "Brunswick Islands," as visitors bureaus designate them, can be thought of as the northern edge of the famous Grand Strand area around Myrtle Beach, South Carolina.

## HISTORY

The Cape Fear River, deep and wide, caught the attention of European explorers as early as 1524, when Giovanni de Verrazano drifted by, and two years later, when Lucas Vásquez de Ayllón and his men (including, possibly, the first enslaved Africans brought to the present-day United States) walked around before proceeding to their appointment for shipwreck near Winyah Bay in South Carolina. Almost 150 years later, William Hilton and explorers from the Massachusetts Bay Colony visited. They were either unimpressed with what

**Previous:** downtown Wilmington; the Wilmington waterfront. **Above:** fountain in Airlie Gardens.

# Wilmington and Cape Fear

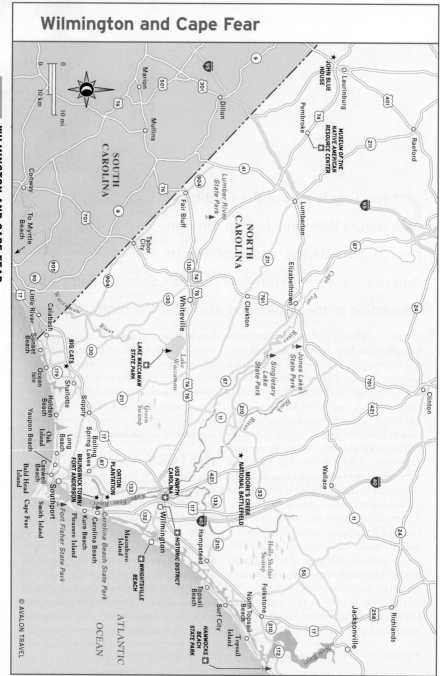

9

0 10 km

0 10 mi

95

501 301

Marion

76

Dillon

9

John Blue House

Laurinburg

401

211

Raeford

Museum of the Native American Resource Center

Pembroke

74

South Carolina

North Carolina

Mullins

Conway

701

9

905

90

17

Little River

Calabash

Sunset Beach

Big Cats

Ocean Isle

179

Shallotte

Holden Beach

Supply

Yaupon Beach

Oak Island

Long Beach

Caswell Beach

Bald Head Island

Southport

Cape Fear

Smith Island

Fort Fisher State Park

© AVALON TRAVEL

41

904

Fair Bluff

Lumber River State Park

Tabor City

130

74

76

Whiteville

130

211

Lake Waccamaw State Park

Lake Waccamaw

Waccamaw River

Green Swamp

74 76

Boiling Spring Lakes

17

87

Brunswick Town/ Fort Anderson

133

Orton Plantation

Cape Fear River

Pleasure Island

Kure Beach

Carolina Beach

Carolina Beach State Park

Kure Beach

Wrightsville Beach

Masonboro Island

Lumberton

95

Elizabethtown

701

Clarkton

87

Black River

Singletary Lake State Park

Jones Lake State Park

210

11

210

Moore's Creek National Battlefield

USS North Carolina

421

53

117

133

Wilmington

132

Historic District

210

Hampstead

50

Holly Shelter Swamp

Wallace

24

701

Clinton

421

40

11

North Topsail Beach

Folkstone

Topsail Beach

Surf City

Topsail Island

Hammocks Beach State Park

Jacksonville

258

Richlands

17

210

172

New River

Atlantic Ocean

To Myrtle Beach

they saw or knew they'd found a really good thing and wanted to discourage rival claims, because they left right away and posted a sign at the tip of the cape to the effect of, "Don't bother; the land's no good."

It wasn't until 1726 that European settlement took hold, when Maurice Moore claimed the banks of the river on behalf of a group of allied families holding a patent to the area. Moore platted Brunswick Town, and his brother Roger established his own personal domain at Orton. Brunswick was briefly an important port, but it was soon eclipsed by Wilmington, a new settlement up the river established by an upstart group. By the time of the Revolution, it was Wilmington that dominated trade along the river.

During the Civil War, Wilmington's port was a swarming hive of blockade-runners. Its fall to the Union at the late date of January 1865 was a severe blow to the sinking Confederacy. Commerce allowed the city to weather the Civil War and Reconstruction, and it continued to grow and flourish.

In the late 20th and early 21st centuries, southeastern North Carolina has gained prominence as a military center. Fort Bragg, in Fayetteville, is one of the country's largest army installations. Nearby Pope Air Force Base is the home of the 43rd Airlift Wing, and at Jacksonville, the U.S. Marine Corps' II Expeditionary Force, among other divisions, is stationed at Camp Lejeune.

## PLANNING YOUR TIME

Wilmington is an easy drive from pretty much anywhere in this region, giving ready access to the beaches to the north and south. It's so full of sights and activities that you'll probably want to stay here, and give yourself a day or more just to explore the city. If you're planning on visiting the beaches south of Wilmington, you might also want to consider staying in Myrtle Beach, South Carolina, about 20 minutes' drive (with no traffic—in

high season it's a very different story) on U.S. 17 from the state line. Farther inland, you'll find plenty of motels around Fayetteville and Lumberton, which are also a reasonable distance from Raleigh to make day trips.

## INFORMATION AND SERVICES

The several area hospitals include two in Wilmington, **Cape Fear Hospital** (5301 Wrightsville Ave., 910/452-8100, www.nhhn. org) and the **New Hanover Regional Medical Center** (2132 S. 17th St., 910/343-7000, www.nhhn.org); two in Brunswick County, **Brunswick Community Hospital** (1 Medical Center Dr., Supply, 910/755-8121, www.brunswickcommunityhospital.com) and **Dosher Memorial Hospital** (924 N. Howe St., Southport, 910/457-3800, www. dosher.org); two in Onslow County, **Onslow Memorial Hospital** (317 Western Blvd., Jacksonville, 910/577-2345, www.onslow-memorial.org) and the **Naval Hospital at Camp Lejeune** (100 Brewster Blvd., Camp Lejeune, 910/451-1113); and Fayetteville's **Cape Fear Valley Medical System** (1638 Owen Dr., Fayetteville, 910/609-4000, www. capefearvalley.com). Myrtle Beach's **Grand Strand Regional Medical Center** (809 82nd Pkwy., Myrtle Beach, SC, 843/692-1000, www.grandstrandmed.com) is not too far from the southernmost Brunswick communities. In an emergency, of course, calling 911 is the safest bet.

Extensive travel and visitor information is available from local convention and visitors bureaus: the **Wilmington/Cape Fear Coast CVB** (23 N. 3rd St., Wilmington, 877/406-2356, www.cape-fear.nc.us, Mon.-Fri. 8:30am-5pm, Sat. 9am-4pm, Sun. 1pm-4pm), and the **Brunswick County Chamber of Commerce** (4948 Main St., Shallotte, 800/426-6644, www.brunswickcountychamber.org, Mon.-Fri. 8:30am-5pm).

# Wilmington

In many cities, economic slumps have an unexpected benefit: historic preservation. With Wilmington's growth at a standstill for much of the 20th century, there was no need to replace the city's old buildings and neighborhoods. As a result, downtown Wilmington has remained a vast museum of beautiful architecture from its early days, and that historical appeal accounts for much of its popularity today as a destination.

Hollywood noticed the little city a couple of decades ago, and for a while Wilmington was one of the largest film and TV production sites east of Los Angeles. *Sleepy Hollow, Homeland,* and *Eastbound & Down* are just some of the recent series to have filmed here, and noteworthy movies filmed at least partly in Wilmington include *Forrest Gump, Iron Man 3, The Conjuring,* and many more (though not, ironically, either version of *Cape Fear*).

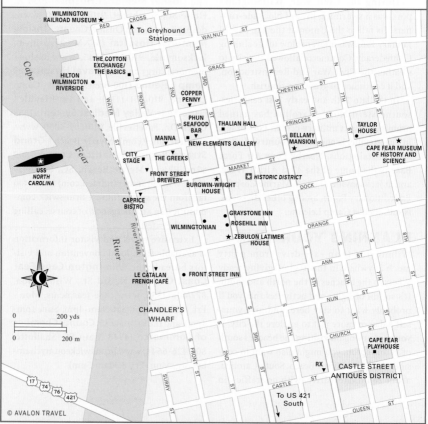

© AVALON TRAVEL

That said, North Carolina's state film industry tax incentives—once the most generous in the country—fell victim to politics and budget-slashing, with most of the work heading to Atlanta. There's no longer a film crew on every corner in Wilmington, but the evocative settings and sultry mood do remain. In addition to downtown's antebellum appeal, the long and well-done Riverwalk along the Cape Fear River is a nice place to stroll.

## SIGHTS
### ★ Historic District

Wilmington is to 19th-century architecture what Asheville is to that of the early 20th century. Having been the state's most populous city until around 1910, when Charlotte and its Piedmont neighbors left the old port city in their wake, Wilmington's downtown reflects its glory days of commerce and high society. This is North Carolina's largest 19th-century historic district, a gorgeous collection of antebellum and late Victorian town houses and commercial buildings, including many beautiful Southern iterations of the Italianate craze that preceded the Civil War.

The **Bellamy Mansion** (503 Market St., 910/251-3700, www.bellamymansion.org, tours hourly Tues.-Sat. 10am-5pm, Sun.

1pm-5pm, $12 adults, $6 under age 12) is a spectacular example of Wilmington's late-antebellum Italianate mansions. This enormous white porticoed house ranks among the loveliest Southern city houses of its era. Built by planter Dr. John Bellamy just before the outbreak of the Civil War, the house was commandeered by the Yankees after the fall of Fort Fisher, and a trip to Washington DC and a pardon granted personally by President Andrew Johnson, a fellow North Carolinian, were required before Bellamy could pry his home out of government hands. In addition to the mansion, another highly significant building stands on the property: the slave quarters. This confined but rather handsome two-story brick building is one of the few surviving examples in the country of urban slave dwellings. Extensive renovations are underway to restore the quarters to their early appearance.

The **Burgwin-Wright House** (224 Market St., 910/762-0570, www.burgwinwrighthouse.com, tours Tues.-Sat. 10am-4pm, $12 adults, $6 under age 12) has an oddly similar history to that of the Bellamy Mansion, despite being nearly a century older. John Burgwin (the emphasis is on the second syllable), a planter and the treasurer of the North Carolina colony, built the house in 1770 on top of the city's

the Bellamy Mansion

early jail. Soon thereafter, Wilmington became a theater of war, and the enemy, as was so often the case, took over the finest dwelling in town as its headquarters. In this case, the occupier, who had a particularly fine eye for rebel digs, was General Cornwallis, then on the last leg of his campaign before falling into George Washington's trap. The Burgwin-Wright House, like the Bellamy Mansion, is a vision of white-columned porticoes shaded by ancient magnolias, but the architectural style is a less ostentatious, though no less beautiful, 18th-century form, the mark of the wealthy merchant and planter class in the colonial South Atlantic and Caribbean world. Seven terraced sections of garden surround the house; they are filled with native plants and many original landscape features, making an intoxicating setting for an early spring stroll.

Yet another beautiful home in the historic district is the **Zebulon Latimer House** (126 S. 3rd St., 910/762-0492, www.latimer-house.org, Mon.-Sat. 10am-3pm, $12 adults, $6 children). The Latimer House is several years older than the Bellamy Mansion, but in its day was a little more fashion-forward, architecturally speaking. Latimer, a merchant from Connecticut, preferred a more urban expression of the Italianate style, a blocky, flat-roofed design with cast-iron cornices and other details that hint at the coming decades of Victorian aesthetics. Also located on the grounds is a very interesting two-story brick slave dwelling. The Latimer House is the headquarters of the Lower Cape Fear Historical Society, whose archive of regional history is important to genealogists and preservationists.

If you'd like to visit the Bellamy Mansion, Latimer House, and Burgwin-Wright House, be sure to buy a **three-house ticket** at the first house you visit. For $28, it will save you several bucks over what you'd pay were you to buy a ticket at each stop.

## ★ Wrightsville Beach

Wrightsville Beach, just outside of Wilmington, is easily one of the nicest beaches in the coastal Carolinas, which is a linear kingdom of beautiful strands. The beach is wide and easily accessible, visitor- and family-friendly, and simply beautiful. The water at Wrightsville often seems to be a brighter blue than one is accustomed to seeing this far north on the Atlantic coast, lending the feeling of a tropical beach. Wrightsville enjoys warm summertime water temperatures, a very wide strand, and lots of lodging and rental choices along the beach. Numerous public beach access points line Lumina Avenue, searchable at www.townofwrightsvillebeach.com; some are wheelchair accessible and some have showers or restrooms. The largest public parking lot, with 99 spaces, is at Beach Access No. 4 (2398 Lumina Ave.); No. 36 (650 Lumina Ave.) also has a large lot. They all fill up on busy days, but if you press on from one access point to the next, you'll eventually find a spot.

## Historic Sights Around Wilmington

### MOORE'S CREEK NATIONAL BATTLEFIELD

Not surprisingly, given their importance as a maritime center, the environs of Wilmington have seen much military action over the last 300 years. About 20 miles northwest of Wilmington, outside the town of Currie, near Burgaw, is **Moore's Creek National Battlefield** (40 Patriots Hall Dr., Currie, 910/283-5591, www.nps.gov/mocr, daily 9am-5pm except Thanksgiving Day, Dec. 25, and Jan. 1). The site commemorates the brief and bloody skirmish of February 1776 in which a Loyalist band of Scottish highlanders, kilted and piping, clashed with Patriot colonists. An important moment in the American Revolution, it was also noteworthy as the last major broadsword charge in Scottish history, led by the last Scottish clan army. The scenic "colonial garden" at Moore's Creek experienced significant damage in the flooding of 2016, but most of that has been mitigated and restored and the garden is back to normal.

## ★ USS *NORTH CAROLINA*

Docked in the Cape Fear River, across from the Wilmington waterfront at Eagles Island, is the startling gray colossus of the battleship **USS *North Carolina*** (Eagles Island, 910/251-5797, www.battleshipnc.com, Memorial Day-Labor Day daily 8am-8pm, Labor Day-Memorial Day daily 8am-5pm, $12 adults, $6 under age 13). This decommissioned World War II warship, which saw service at Guadalcanal, Iwo Jima, and many other important events in the Pacific theater, is a floating monument to the nearly 10,000 North Carolinians who died in World War II as well as a museum of what life was like in a floating metal city.

Tours are self-guided and include nine decks, the gun turrets and the bridge, crew quarters, the sick deck, and the Roll of Honor display of the names of North Carolina's war dead. Allow at least two hours to see it all. Visitors prone to claustrophobia might want to stay above deck; the passageways and quarters below are close, dark, and very deep. From the heart of the ship it can take quite a while to get back out, and on a busy day the crowds can make the space seem even more constricted. (Just imagine how it would have felt to be on this ship in the middle of the Pacific, with nearly 2,000 other sailors aboard.)

The battleship is also one of North Carolina's most famous haunted houses, as it were—allegedly home to several ghosts who have been seen and heard on many occasions. The ship has been featured on the Syfy Channel and on ghost-hunting television shows. Visit www.hauntednc.com to hear some chilling unexplained voices caught on tape.

### OAKDALE CEMETERY

In the mid-19th century, as Wilmington was bursting at the seams with new residents, the city's old cemeteries were becoming overcrowded with former residents. **Oakdale Cemetery** (520 N. 15th St., 910/762-5682, www.oakdalecemetery.org, daily 8am-5pm) was founded some distance from downtown to ease the subterranean traffic jam. It was designed in the parklike style of graveyards popular at the time, and soon filled up with splendid funerary art—weeping angels, obelisks, willows—to set off the natural beauty of the place. (Oakdale's website has a primer on Victorian grave art symbolism.) It's a fascinating place for a quiet stroll.

the USS *North Carolina*

## Anoles of Carolina

A little anole pauses on a downspout.

During your visit to the Wilmington area, you'll almost certainly see anoles. These are the tiny green lizards that skitter up and down trees and along railings—impossibly fast, beady-eyed little emerald beasts. Sometimes called "chameleons" by the locals, anoles can change color to camouflage themselves against their backgrounds. They also like to puff out their crescent-shaped dewlaps, the little scarlet pouches under their chins, when they're courting, fighting, or otherwise advertising their importance.

## Museums

### CAPE FEAR MUSEUM OF HISTORY AND SCIENCE

The **Cape Fear Museum of History and Science** (814 Market St., 910/798-4370, www.capefearmuseum.com, Tues.-Sat. 9am-5pm, Sun. 1pm-5pm, $8 adults, $7 students and seniors, $5 ages 3-17) has exhibits about the ecology of the Cape Fear region and its human history. Special treats are exhibits about giant indigenous life forms, including the prehistoric ground sloth and Michael Jordan.

### LOUISE WELLS CAMERON ART MUSEUM

The **Louise Wells Cameron Art Museum** (3201 S. 17th St., 910/395-5999, www.cameronartmuseum.com, Tues.-Wed. and Fri.-Sun. 10am-5pm, Thurs. 10am-8pm, $10 adults, $8 students), or "the CAM," is one of the major art museums in North Carolina, a very modern gallery with a good permanent collection of art in many media, with a special emphasis on North Carolina artists. Masters represented include Mary Cassatt and Utagawa Hiroshige. Special exhibits change throughout the year.

### WILMINGTON RAILROAD MUSEUM

The **Wilmington Railroad Museum** (505 Nutt St., 910/763-2634, www.wilmingtonrailroadmuseum.org, Apr.-Oct. Mon.-Sat. 10am-5pm, Sun. 1pm-5pm, Oct.-April. Mon.-Sat. 10am-4pm, $9.50 adults, $8.50 seniors and military, $5.50 ages 2-12) explores a crucial but now largely forgotten part of this city's history: its role as a railroad town. In 1840, Wilmington became the terminus for the world's longest continuous rail line, the Wilmington and Weldon Railroad. The

Atlantic Coast Line Railroad (into which the W&W merged around 1900) kept its headquarters at Wilmington until the 1960s, when it moved its offices, employees, and a devastatingly large portion of the city's economy to Florida. All manner of railroad artifacts are on display in this great little museum, from timetables to locomotives.

## Gardens and Parks
### AIRLIE GARDENS

**Airlie Gardens** (300 Airlie Rd., 910/798-7700, www.airliegardens.org, Mar. 20-Dec. daily 9am-5pm, longer hours Apr.-May, $9 adults, $3 ages 4-12, no pets) is most famous for its countless azaleas, but this 100-year-old formal garden park has many remarkable features, including an oak tree believed to be nearly 500 years old, and the Minnie Evans Sculpture Garden and Bottle Chapel. Evans, a visionary African American artist whose mystical work is among the most prized "outsider art," was the gatekeeper here for 25 of her 95 years. Golf cart tours are available with 48 hours' notice for visitors who are not mobile enough to walk the gardens.

### HALYBURTON PARK

A more natural landscape for hiking and biking is **Halyburton Park** (4099 S. 17th St., 910/341-7800, www.halyburtonpark.com, park daily dawn-dusk, nature center Tues.-Sat. 9am-5pm). The 58 acres of parkland, encircled by a 1.3-mile wheelchair-accessible trail and crisscrossed by interior trails, give a beautiful glimpse of the environment of sandhills, Carolina bays (elliptical, often boggy depressions), and longleaf pine and oak forest that used to make up so much of this area.

## ENTERTAINMENT AND EVENTS
### Performing Arts

**Thalian Hall** (310 Chestnut St., 800/523-2820, www.thalianhall.com) was built in the mid-1850s and today is the last standing theater designed by the prominent architect John Montague Trimble. It is still a major arts venue in the region, hosting performances of classical, jazz, bluegrass, and all sorts of other music. Its resident theater company is the **Thalian Association** (910/251-1788, www.thalian.org), which traces its roots back to 1788 and has been named the official community theater company of North Carolina. Wilmington City Hall is located contiguously within the building.

Often staging shows at Thalian Hall is **Big Dawg Productions** (http://bigdawgproductions.org). They put on a variety of plays and musicals of all genres throughout the year and host the **New Play Festival** of first-time productions by authors under age 18. Another Thalian company for nearly 25 years, the **Opera House Theatre Company** (910/762-4234, www.operahousetheatrecompany.net) has produced one varied season after another of big-name musicals and dramas, as well as the work of North Carolinian and Southern playwrights.

Also working in the Thalian is the critically acclaimed **Red Barn Studio Theatre** (1122 S. 3rd St., 910/762-0955, www.redbarnstudiotheatre.com). Actress Linda Lavin of *Alice* fame and her husband, Steve Bakunas, lived in Wilmington up until a few years ago and founded Red Barn while there.

## Festivals

Wilmington's best-known annual event is the **Azalea Festival** (910/794-4650, www.ncazaleafestival.org), which takes place in early April at venues throughout the city. It centers on the home and garden tours of Wilmington's most beautiful—and, at this time of year, azalea-festooned—historic sites. There is a dizzying slate of events, including a parade, a circus, gospel concerts, shag and step competitions, and even boxing matches. And like any self-respecting Southern town, it crowns royalty—in this case, the North Carolina Azalea Festival Queen as well as the Queen's Court. The Azalea Festival draws over 300,000 visitors, so book your accommodations well in advance. If you're traveling through the area in early April but aren't

# Greater Wilmington

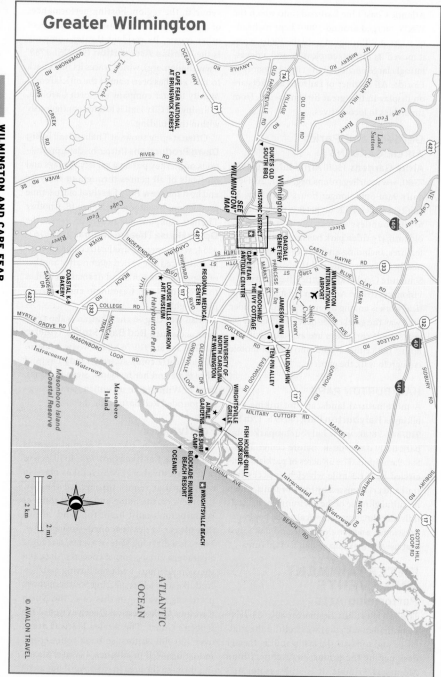

© AVALON TRAVEL

coming to the festival, be forewarned, this will be one crowded town.

Although Wilmington has become a magnet for Hollywood film production, there's also a passion here for independent films. Over the course of 20 years, November's **Cucalorus Film Festival** (910/343-5995, www.cucalorus.org) has become an important festival that draws viewers and filmmakers from around the world. Roughly 100 films are screened during each year's festival, which takes place at Thalian Hall and at the small Jengo's Playhouse (815 Princess St.), where the Cucalorus Foundation also holds regular screenings throughout the year.

## Nightlife

**Front Street Brewery** (9 N. Front St., 910/251-1935, http://frontstreetbrewery.com, Mon.-Wed. 11:30am-midnight, Thurs.-Sat. 11:30am-2am, Sun. 11:30am-10pm, late-night menu from 10:30pm) serves lunch and dinner, but what is most special is their menu of beers brewed on-site. They serve their own pilsner, IPA, and lager, Scottish and Belgian ales, and their specialty River City Raspberry Wheat ale. The space has an attractive dark-paneled saloon decor, and plenty of seating areas to choose from. Brewery tours are 3pm-5pm daily.

Billing itself as Wilmington's oldest bar, **Barbary Coast** (116 S. Front St., 910/762-8996, Mon.-Sat. 11am-2am) is a short walk from Front Street Brewery. It sports more of a classic dive bar atmosphere and is frequented by many locals. Enjoy craft beer on tap, a game of pool, and an old-fashioned jukebox.

## SHOPPING
### Shopping Centers

The buildings of **The Cotton Exchange** (Front St. and Grace St., 910/343-9896, www.shopcottonexchange.com) have housed all manner of businesses in over 150 years of continuous occupation: a flour and hominy mill, a Chinese laundry, a peanut cleaning operation (really), a "mariner's saloon" (we'll say no more about that), and, of course, a cotton

exchange. Today, they're home to dozens of boutiques, restaurants, and lovely little specialty shops selling kites, beads, and spices.

## Antiques and Consignment Stores

Along Castle Street, at the southern edge of the historic district, there is a growing district of antiques shops, all within two or three blocks of each other. **Castle Keep Antiques** (507 Castle St., 910/343-6046) occupies an old church building and has an absorbingly varied selection, with a more rural bent than the surrounding shops. Also be sure to stop in at **New Castle Antiques Center** (606 Castle St., 910/341-7228) and **Maggy's Antiques** (511 Castle St., 910/343-5200).

In the riverfront area, **Antiques of Old Wilmington** (25 S. Front St., 910/763-5188) and **Silk Road Antiques** (103 S. Front St., 910/343-1718) are within an easy walk of many restaurants and each other. On Market Street headed away from downtown is **Cape Fear Antique Center** (1606 Market St., 910/763-1837, www.capefearantiquecenter.com), which carries fancy vintage home furnishings, from bedroom and dining room furniture to desks and armoires in beautiful tones of wood, as well as a nice selection of antique jewelry.

## Books

Wilmington has quite a few nice bookstores, both retail and used. **McAllister & Solomon** (4402-1 Wrightsville Ave., 910/350-0189, www.mcallisterandsolomon.com) stocks over 20,000 used and rare books, a great treat for collectors to explore. **Two Sisters Bookery** (318 Nutt St., Cotton Exchange, 910/762-4444, Mon.-Sat. 10am-6pm, Sun. noon-6pm) is a nice little independent bookseller at the Cotton Exchange, with an inventory covering all genres and subject matters, and a calendar full of readings by favorite authors. Also excellent is **Pomegranate Books** (4418 Park Ave., 910/452-1107, www.pombooks.net, Mon.-Sat. 10am-6pm), which has a progressive bent and a wide selection of good reads.

## Art Galleries

Perhaps the most interesting arts experience in town is the "gallerium" **Expo 216** (216 Front St., 910/769-3899, www.expo216.com, Wed.-Sun. noon-6pm), a nonprofit museum/gallery in a 5,000-square-foot space downtown. Its theme-driven exhibits tend to focus on topical issues such as the environment, and it also features the work of regional artists for purchase.

**New Elements Gallery** (201 Princess St., 910/343-8997, www.newelementsgallery.com, Tues.-Sat. 11am-5:30pm) has been a leading institution in Wilmington's art scene since 1985. Featuring contemporary art in a wide variety of styles and media, New Elements has a special focus on artists from North Carolina and the wider Southeast.

## Music

**Finkelstein Music** (6 S. Front St., 910/762-5662, www.finkelsteins.com) is a family business that has been at this site, a great old commercial building on a busy downtown corner, for over 100 years. It began as a dry goods store but gradually evolved into today's music store, which carries a great selection of guitars, electric basses, and percussion.

## For Dogs

**Coastal K-9 Bakery** (5905 Carolina Beach Rd., Ste. 9, 866/794-4014, www.coastalk9bakery.com, Mon.-Sat. 10am-6pm, Sun. 1pm-5pm) sells fresh-baked gourmet dog treats, including various organic and hypoallergenic goodies, Carolina barbecue biscuits, liver brownies, and even vegetarian bacon bits.

# SPORTS AND RECREATION
## Masonboro Island

A 30-minute boat ride from Wrightsville Beach is Masonboro Island, an undeveloped barrier island that is a favorite spot for birding, shelling, and camping. **Wrightsville Beach Scenic Tours** (910/200-4002, www.wrightsvillebeachscenictours.com) operates the Wrightsville Water Taxi, which docks across the street from the Blockade Runner Hotel (275 Waynick Blvd.) and offers daily shuttle service ($20 round-trip) to the island in high season. The boat leaves the dock Monday-Saturday at 9am and returns at 3pm. Call ahead for reservations.

## Surfing

Wrightsville Beach is a very popular destination for East Coast surfers and is home to several surfing schools. **Surf Camp** (530 Causeway Dr., 866/844-7873, www.wb-surfcamp.com) is probably the area's largest surfing instruction provider. They teach a staggering number of multiday camps; one-day courses; kids-only, teenagers-only, women-only, and whole-family offerings; and classes in safety as well as technique. **Crystal South Surf Camp** (Public Access No. 39, on the beach, 910/395-4431, www.crystalsouthsurfcamp.com) is a family-run operation that gives group and individual five-day instruction for all ages.

## Spectator Sports

The **Wilmington Sharks** (910/343-5621, www.wilmingtonsharks.com, box seats $8, general admission $5), a Coastal Plains League baseball team, play at Legion Stadium (2149 Carolina Beach Rd.). This is college summer league ball, so they play with real wooden bats unlike in NCAA-administered play.

# FOOD
## Continental

★ **Caprice Bistro** (10 Market St., 910/815-0810, www.capricebistro.com, Sun.-Thurs. 5pm-10pm, Fri.-Sat. 5pm-midnight, bar until 2am, $13-22) is an absolutely wonderful little café and bar hosted by Thierry and Patricia Moity. The French cuisine here is delicious and the wine list is extensive. This is one of the best restaurants in town and well worth a visit.

**Le Catalan French Café** (224 S. Water St., 910/815-0200, www.lecatalan.com, fall-spring lunch and dinner Tues.-Sat. from 11:30am, summer Tues.-Sun. from 11:30am, $10-20) couldn't have a nicer location, on the

Riverwalk in the old downtown. They serve wonderful classic French food—quiches and *feuilletés,* beef bourguignon on winter Fridays, and a chocolate mousse for which they are famous. Their greatest draw, though, is the wine list (and the attached wine store). The proprietor, Pierre Penegre, is a Cordon Bleu-certified oenologist, and is frequently on hand to make recommendations.

## Seafood

Wrightsville Beach's **Bridge Tender** (1414 Airlie Rd., Wilmington, 910/256-4519, www. thebridgetender.com, lunch daily 11:30am-2pm, dinner daily from 5pm, $20-35) has been in business for over 30 years and is an icon of the local restaurant scene. The atmosphere is simple and elegant, with a dockside view. Entrées focus on seafood and Angus beef, with an extensive à la carte menu from which you can create delicious combinations of your favorite seafood and the Bridge Tender's special sauces. A sushi menu rounds out the appetizers, and a long wine list complements everything.

When you see a restaurant set in a really beautiful location, you dearly hope the food is as good as the view. Such is the case at Wrightsville's **Oceanic** (703 S. Lumina, Wrightsville Beach, 910/256-5551, www.oceanicrestaurant.com, Mon.-Sat. 11am-11pm, Sun. 10am-10pm, $10-27). The Wilmington *Star-News* has repeatedly voted it the Best Seafood Restaurant in Wilmington, and it receives similar word-of-mouth accolades right and left. It occupies a big old house right on the beach, with a wraparound porch and a pier. For an extra-special experience, ask for a table on the pier.

## Southern and Barbecue

Right downtown at the Cotton Exchange, facing Front Street, is **The Basics** (319 Front St., 910/343-1050, www.thebasicswilmington. com, breakfast Mon.-Fri. 8am-11am, lunch Mon.-Fri. 11am-4pm, dinner daily from 5pm, brunch Sat.-Sun. 11am-4pm, $10-18). In a streamlined, simple setting, The Basics serves comfort food classics, Southern-style. Be sure to try the Coca-Cola cake, a surprisingly delicious Southern delicacy. An ambitious renovation was particularly tasteful and well-done.

In business since 1984, ★ **Jackson's Big Oak Barbecue** (920 S. Kerr Ave., 910/799-1581, http://jacksonsbigoak.com, Mon.-Sat. 10:30am-8:45pm, under $8) is an old favorite. Their motto is, "We ain't fancy, but we sure

Le Catalan French Café

are good." Good old vinegary eastern North Carolina-style pork barbecue is the main item, though you can pick from Brunswick stew, fried chicken, and a mess of country vegetables. You'll get hush puppies and corn sticks at the table, but it will be worth your while not to fill up too fast—the cobblers and banana pudding are great.

### Eclectic American

**Flaming Amy's Burrito Barn** (4002 Oleander Dr., 910/799-2919, www.flamingamysburritobarn.com, daily 11am-10pm) is, in their own words, "Hot, fast, cheap, and easy." They have a long menu with 20 specialty burritos (Greek, Philly steak, Thai), eight fresh salsas, and bottled and on-tap beers. It's very inexpensive—you can eat well for under $10, drinks included. Frequent special promotions include Tattoo Tuesdays; if you show the cashier your tattoo (come on, we all know you've got one), you can take 10 percent off your meal.

**Boca Bay** (2025 Eastwood Rd., 910/256-1887, www.bocabayrestaurant.com, Mon.-Thurs. 5pm-10pm, Fri.-Sat. 5pm-11pm, brunch Sun. 9am-2pm, entrées $11-20) serves a tapas-style menu of sushi, stir-fries, and heartier entrées, all very tasty. Vegetarian options are fairly limited, but you can cobble together a meal of tapas, salad, and sides.

### Asian

**Indochine, A Far East Café** (7 Wayne Dr., at Market St., 910/251-9229, www.indochinewilmington.com, lunch Tues.-Thurs. 11am-2pm, Sat. 11am-3pm, dinner daily 5pm-10pm, $10-15) specializes in Thai and Vietnamese cuisine, has an extensive vegetarian menu, and has plenty of options for nonvegetarians as well. This restaurant is not downtown, but some distance out on Market Street; it's worth the drive. Try the vegetarian samosa egg rolls as an appetizer.

★ **Double Happiness** (4403 Wrightsville Ave., 910/313-1088, www.chinesedoublehappiness.com, daily lunch and dinner, $12-18) is a popular Chinese and Malaysian restaurant

known for serving traditional dishes that are a refreshing departure from the standard canon of American Chinese restaurants. The setting is original too, without, as one local food critic wrote, "a buffet or glamour food photos over a hospital-white take-out counter." You can choose between regular booths and traditional floor seating. If you're lucky, you might be present when the chef decides to send around rice balls, a sweet dessert snack, for everyone on the house.

### Coffee

**Port City Java** (21 N. Front St., 910/762-5282, Sun.-Thurs. 6:30am-10pm, Fri.-Sat. 6:30am-midnight) is my favorite coffeehouse in town. The java is great and the baristas very friendly, and the warm, wooden interior is conducive to relaxation.

## ACCOMMODATIONS
### Under $150

Affordable options are plentiful, especially on Market Street a couple of miles from downtown. Wilmington's **Holiday Inn** (5032 Market St., 866/553-0169, www.wilmingtonhi.com, $65-135) is clean and comfortable, and just a few minutes' drive from the historic district. Nearby is the **Jameson Inn** (5102 Dunlea Ct., 910/452-9828, www.jamesoninns.com, from $65), another fine choice. The Jameson Inn is a little hard to find, hidden behind other buildings. From Market Street, turn onto New Centre Drive and look for the sign across the street from Target.

### $150-300

Wilmington overflows with historic bed-and-breakfasts. ★ **Front Street Inn** (215 S. Front St., 800/336-8184, www.frontstreetinn.com, $139-239) is a tiny boutique hotel in the historic district, one block from the Cape Fear River and easy walking distance from the restaurants and shops at Market and Front Streets. The inn occupies the old Salvation Army of the Carolinas building, an attractive brick city building with arched windows and bright, airy guest rooms. For comfortable and classy lodging in the heart of the historic district, the Front Street Inn is a best bet.

The **Wilmingtonian** (101 S. 2nd St., 910/343-1800, www.thewilmingtonian.com, $87-325) is a complex of five buildings, four of which are renovated historic structures, from the 1841 De Rosset House to a 1950s convent. The De Rosset House is an utterly fabulous Italianate mansion, one of the most recognizable buildings in Wilmington. For $325 ($250 off-season), you can stay in the Cupola Suite, a spectacular aerie with a panoramic view of the port. The **Rosehill Inn** (114 S. 3rd St., 800/815-0250, www.rosehill.com, $90-200) occupies a pretty 1848 residence three blocks from the river. The flowery high-B&B-style decor suits the house well, making for elegant but comfy quarters. The **Taylor House** (14 N. 7th St., 800/382-9982, www.taylorhousebb.com, $125-140) is an absolutely lovely 1905 home—rather subdued in design when compared to some of the architectural manifestos nearby, but in a very attractive way. The pretty, sunny guest rooms promise relaxation. The famous ★ **Graystone Inn** (100 S. 3rd St., 888/763-4773, www.graystoneinn.com, $159-379) was built in the same year as the Taylor House, but its builder, the widow Elizabeth Bridgers, had a very different aesthetic. The splendor of the palace first known as the Bridgers House reflects the fortune of Mrs. Bridgers's late husband, a former Confederate congressman and one of the most influential figures in Wilmington's days as a railroad center.

These are by no means the only excellent bed-and-breakfast inns in Wilmington; the city is full of them. Check with the **Wilmington and Beaches Convention and Visitors Bureau** (www.wilmingtonandbeaches.com) for comprehensive listings.

A plush place to stay in the downtown area is the **Hilton Wilmington Riverside** (301 N. Water St., 888/324-8170, www.wilmington-hilton.com, $180-200). Located right on the river, many of the guest rooms have a great view. The shops, restaurants, and galleries of the riverfront are right outside the front door, making this a great place to stay if you're planning to enjoy Wilmington's downtown.

# NORTH OF WILMINGTON
## Topsail Island
In the manner of an old salt, Topsail is pronounced "Tops'l." The three towns on Topsail Island—Topsail Beach, North Topsail Beach, and Surf City—are popular beach communities. They're less commercial than some of

the Graystone Inn

their counterparts elsewhere along the coast, but still destinations for throngs of visitors in the summer months. A swing bridge gives access to the island at Surf City (the bridge opens around the beginning of each hour, so expect backups), and there is a high bridge between Sneads Ferry and North Topsail.

At Topsail Beach is the **Missiles and More Museum** (720 Channel Ave., 910/328-8663, www.missilesandmoremuseum.org, Memorial Day-Labor Day Mon.-Sat. 2pm-5pm, Labor Day-Memorial Day Mon.-Fri. 2pm-5pm, free). This little museum commemorates a rather peculiar chapter in the island's history: when it was used by the U.S. government for a project called Operation Bumblebee. During Operation Bumblebee, Topsail was a proving ground for missiles, and the work done here led to major advancements in missile technology and the development of a precursor of the ram jet engine used later in supersonic jet design. Exhibits include real warheads left over from the tests. Especially interesting to lovers of projectiles will be the 1940s color film of missile firings here at Topsail.

## ★ Hammocks Beach State Park

At the very appealing little fishing town of Swansboro, you'll find the mainland side of **Hammocks Beach State Park** (1572 Hammocks Beach Rd., 910/326-4881, http://ncparks.gov, Sept.-May daily 8am-6pm, June-Aug. daily 8am-7pm, free). Most of the park lies on the other side of a maze of marshes, on Bear and Huggins Islands. These wild, undeveloped islands are important havens for migratory waterfowl and nesting loggerhead sea turtles. Bear Island is 3.5 miles long and less than a mile wide, surrounded by the Atlantic Ocean, Intracoastal Waterway, Bogue and Bear Inlets, and wild salt marshes. A great place to swim, Bear Island has a bathhouse complex with a snack bar, restrooms, and outdoor showers. Huggins Island is the smaller of the two, and is covered in ecologically significant maritime forest and lowland marshes.

Two paddle trails, one just over 2.5 miles and the other 6 miles, weave through the marshes that surround the islands.

Camping is permitted on Bear Island, in reserved and first-come sites near the beach and inlet, with restrooms and showers available nearby.

A private boat or **passenger ferry** (910/326-4881, $5 adults, $3 seniors and children) are the only ways to reach the islands. The ferry's schedule varies by days of the week and season: in May and September Wednesday-Saturday and in April and October Friday-Saturday, the ferry departs from the mainland every half hour 9:30am-4:30pm, and departs from Bear Island every hour 10am-5pm. Memorial Day-Labor Day Monday-Tuesday, it departs from the mainland every hour 9:30am-5:30pm, and departs from the island every hour 10am-6pm; Wednesday-Sunday it departs from the mainland every half hour 9:30am-5:30pm, and departs from the island every half hour 10am-6pm.

## TRANSPORTATION

Wilmington is the eastern terminus of I-40, more than 300 miles east of Asheville, approximately 120 miles east of Raleigh. The Cape Fear region is also crossed by a major north-south route, U.S. 17, the old Kings Highway of colonial times. Wilmington is roughly equidistant along U.S. 17 between Jacksonville to the north and Myrtle Beach, South Carolina, to the south; both cities are about an hour away.

**Wilmington International Airport** (ILM, 1740 Airport Blvd., 910/341-4125, www.flyilm.com) serves the region with flights to East Coast cities. For a wider selection of routes, it may be worthwhile to fly into Myrtle Beach or Raleigh and rent a car. If driving to Wilmington from the Myrtle Beach airport, add another 30-60 minutes to get through Myrtle Beach traffic, particularly in summer, as the airport there is on the southern edge of town. If driving from Raleigh-Durham International

Airport, figure on the trip taking at least 2.5 hours. There is no passenger train service to Wilmington.

**Wave Transit** (910/343-0106, www. wavetransit.com), Wilmington's public transportation system, operates buses throughout the metropolitan area and trolleys in the historic district. They run a free downtown trolley that can take you to most areas of interest. Otherwise fares are $2 round-trip.

# The Southern Coast

From the beaches of Brunswick and New Hanover County to the swampy, subtropical fringes of land behind the dunes, this little corner of the state is one of the most beautiful parts of North Carolina.

There are a string of beaches here, starting with Carolina Beach and Kure, just south of Wilmington, and descending through the "Brunswick Islands," as designated in tourist literature. Most of these beaches are low-key, quiet family beaches, largely lined with residential and rental properties. They're crowded in the summertime, of course, but are still much more laid back than Myrtle Beach, over the state line to the south, and even Wrightsville and some of the "Crystal Coast" beaches.

You'll see some distinctive wildlife here. The first you'll notice, more likely than not, is the ubiquitous green anole (called "chameleons" by many locals). These tiny lizards, normally a bright lime green, but able to fade to brown when camouflage is called for, are everywhere—skittering up porch columns and along balcony railings, peering at you around corners, hiding between the fronds of palmetto trees. The males put on a big show by puffing out their strawberry-colored dewlaps.

This is also the part of the state where the greatest populations of alligators live. Alligators are nonchalant creatures that rarely appear better than comatose, but they are genuinely deadly if crossed. All along river and creek banks, bays, and swamps, you'll see their scaly hulks basking motionless in the sun. Keep small children and pets well clear of anywhere a gator might lurk.

In certain highly specialized environments—mainly in and around Carolina bays that offer both moistness and nutrient-poor soil—the Venus flytrap and other carnivorous plants thrive. To the average fly, these are more threatening than an alligator any day. The flytrap and some of its cousins are endangered, but in this region—and nowhere else in the world—you'll have plenty of opportunities to see them growing and gorging.

## KURE BEACH

Kure is a two-syllable name: pronounced "KYU-ree" (as in Marie Curie, not "curry"). This is a small beach community, not an extravaganza of neon lights and shark-doored towel shops. Most of the buildings on the island are houses, both rental houses for vacationers and the homes of Kure Beach's year-round residents. The beach itself, like all North Carolina ocean beaches, is public.

### Carolina Beach State Park

Just to the north of Kure is **Carolina Beach State Park** (1010 State Park Rd., off U.S. 421, Carolina Beach, 910/458-8206, http://ncparks. gov, Mar.-Apr. and Sept.-Oct. 8am-8pm, May-Aug. 8am-10pm, Nov.-Feb. 8am-6pm, free). Of all the state parks in the coastal region, this may be the one with the greatest ecological diversity. Within its boundaries are coastal pine and oak forests, pocosins between the dunes, saltwater marshes, a 50-foot sand dune, and lime-sink ponds; of the lime-sink ponds, one is a deep cypress swamp, one is a natural garden of water lilies, and one an ephemeral pond that dries into a swampy field every year, an ideal home for the many carnivorous plants that live here. You'll see Venus flytraps and their ferocious cousins, but resist the urge to dig or pick them, or to tempt them with your fingertips. Sort of like stinging insects that die after delivering their payload, the flytraps' traps can wither and fall off once they're sprung.

The park has 83 drive-to and walk-in campsites ($20), each with a grill and a picnic table. Two are wheelchair accessible. Restrooms and hot showers are nearby.

## Fort Fisher State Park

At the southern end of Kure Beach is **Fort Fisher State Park** (1000 Loggerhead Rd., off U.S. 421, 910/458-5798, http://ncparks. gov, June-Aug. daily 8am-9pm, Mar.-May and Sept.-Oct. daily 8am-8pm, Nov.-Feb. daily 8am-6pm, free). Fort Fisher has six miles of beautiful beach, a less crowded and commercial alternative to the other beaches of the area. A lifeguard is on duty Memorial Day-Labor Day daily 10am-5:45pm. The park also includes a 1.1-mile hiking trail that winds through marshes and along the sound, ending at an observation deck where visitors can watch wildlife.

This is also a significant historic site. Fort Fisher was a Civil War earthwork stronghold designed to withstand massive assault. Modeled in part on the Crimean War's Tower of Malakoff, Fort Fisher's construction was an epic saga in itself, as hundreds of Confederate soldiers, enslaved African Americans, and conscripted indigenous Lumbee people were brought in to build what became the Confederacy's largest fort. After the fall of Norfolk in 1862, Wilmington became the most important open port in the South, a vital harbor for blockade-runners and military vessels. Fisher held until nearly the end of the war. On December 24, 1864, U.S. general Benjamin "the Beast" Butler attacked the fort with 1,000 soldiers but was repulsed. A few weeks later, in January 1865, Fort Fisher was finally taken, but it required a Yankee force of 9,000 soldiers and 56 ships in what was to be the largest amphibious assault until World War II. Without its defenses at Fort Fisher, Wilmington soon fell, hastening the end of the war, which came only three months later. Thanks to the final assault by the Union forces and 150 subsequent years of winds, tides, and hurricanes, not a great deal of the massive earthworks survives. But the remains of this vitally important Civil War site are preserved in an oddly peaceful and pretty seaside park, which contains a restored gun emplacement and a visitors center with interpretive exhibits.

Also at Fort Fisher is a branch of the **North Carolina Aquarium** (910/458-8257, daily 9am-5pm, $10.95 adults, $9.95 seniors, $8.95 ages 3-12). Like its sisters at Roanoke and Pine Knoll Shores, this is a beautiful aquarium that specializes in the native marine life of the North Carolina waters. It's also a center for marine biology and conservation efforts, assisting in the rescue and rehabilitation of sea turtles, marine mammals, freshwater reptiles, and other creatures of the coast. While at the aquarium, be sure to visit the albino alligator.

## Accommodations

The beaches of the Carolinas used to be lined with boardinghouses, the old-time choice in lodging for generations of middle-class travelers. They were sort of a precursor to today's bed-and-breakfasts, cozy family homes where visitors dined together with the hosts and were treated not so much like customers as houseguests—which is just what they were. Hurricane Hazel razed countless guesthouses when it pummeled the coast in 1954, ushering in the next epoch, that of the family motel. The **Beacon House** (715 Carolina Beach Ave. N., 877/232-2666, www.beaconhouseinnb-b. com, from $150 high season, breakfast not included, some pets permitted in cottages with an extra fee) at Carolina Beach, just north of Kure, is a rare survivor from that era. The early-1950s boardinghouse has the typical upstairs and downstairs porches and dark wood paneling indoors. (Nearby cottages are also rented by the Beacon House.) The price is much higher than it was in those days, but you'll be treated to a lodging experience from a long-gone era.

# BALD HEAD ISLAND

Bald Head Island, an exclusive community where golf carts are the only traffic, is a two-mile, 20-minute ferry ride from Southport. More than 80 percent of the island is designated as a nature preserve, and at the southern tip stands "Old Baldy," the oldest lighthouse in North Carolina.

## Sights

The **Bald Head Island Lighthouse** (910/457-5003, www.oldbaldy.org, spring-fall Tues.-Sat. 10am-4pm, Sun. 11am-4pm, call for winter hours, $6 adults, $3 children) was built in 1818, replacing an even earlier tower that was completed in 1795. Despite being the new-comer at Bald Head, the 109-foot lighthouse is the oldest such structure surviving in North Carolina. A visit to the lighthouse includes a stop next door at the **Smith Island Museum**, housed in the lighthouse keeper's home. The

the Bald Head Island Lighthouse

development of Smith Island (of which Bald Head is the terminus) allowed almost 17,000 acres to be set aside as an ecological preserve. The Old Baldy Foundation leads **historical tours** (910/457-5003, Tues.-Sat. 10:30am, $57, includes round-trip ferry) of Bald Head, departing from Island Ferry Landing, a short walk from the lighthouse.

## Food

At Carolina Beach the **Shuckin' Shack** (6 N. Lake Park Blvd., 910/458-7380, www.theshuckinshack.com, Mon.-Sat. 11am-midnight, Sun. noon-midnight, $7-25) is a friendly little oyster bar that serves fresh local seafood, and oysters by the bucket. After a meal at the Shuckin' Shack, stop by **Britt's Donuts** (11 Boardwalk, 910/707-0755, Mon.-Thurs. and Sat.-Sun. 8:30am-10:30pm, Fri. 4pm-midnight, closed Oct.-Feb.). Britt's has been famous for its homemade doughnuts since opening its doors in 1939. Note they are very seasonal and close in the colder months.

# SOUTHPORT

One of North Carolina's prettiest towns, Southport is an 18th-century river hamlet whose port was overtaken in importance by Wilmington's—and hence it has remained small and quiet. It was the Brunswick County seat until the late 1970s, when that job was outsourced to Bolivia (Bolivia, North Carolina, that is). It's a wonderfully charming place, with block upon block of beautiful historic houses and public buildings. The old cemetery is a gorgeous spot, and in it you'll find many tombstones that bear witness to the town's seafaring history—epitaphs for sea captains who died while visiting Smithville (Southport's original name), and stones carved with pictures of ships on rolling waves.

## Sights

The **North Carolina Maritime Museum at Southport** (204 E. Moore St., 910/457-0003, www.ncmaritime.org, Tues.-Sat. 9am-5pm, $2 adults, $1 over age 62, free under age 16) is a small branch of the Maritime Museum at

Beaufort, where you can learn about the seafaring history of the Carolina coast. Among the many topics of interest here is the life of pirate Stede Bonnet, whose surname belies his infamous life of crime. Bonnet, who spent much time in the Southport area, was by turns the pillaging buddy and bitter rival of Blackbeard. Other cool displays in the museum include a section of a 2,000-year-old, 54-inch-long Indian canoe, and the eight-foot jawbone of a whale.

### Events

Southport hosts the state's best-known **Fourth of July Celebration** (910/457-6964, www.nc4thofjuly.com), attended each year by up to 50,000 people. (That's approximately 20 times the normal population of the town.) In addition to the requisite fireworks, food, and music, the festival features a special tribute to veterans, a flag retirement ceremony (that is, folks bring their old and worn-out flags), and a naturalization ceremony for new Americans.

### Food

The ★ **Yacht Basin Provision Company** (130 Yacht Basin St., 910/457-0654, www.provisioncompany.com, Sun.-Thurs. 11am-4pm, Fri.-Sat. 11am-9pm, $10-20) is a Southport seafood joint with a super-casual atmosphere. Customers place their orders at the counter and serve themselves drinks (on the honor system), then seat themselves dockside to await the arrival of their chow. Most popular here are the conch fritters and grouper salad sandwich, but anything you order will be good.

### Accommodations

**Lois Jane's Riverview Inn** (106 W. Bay St., 800/457-1152, www.loisjanes.com, $93-143, depending on season) is a Victorian waterfront home built by the innkeeper's grandfather. The guest rooms are comfortably furnished, bright and not froufrou, and a two-suite cottage behind the inn has its own kitchen and separate entrance. The front porch of the inn has a wonderful view of the harbor. Another affordable option is the **Inn at River Oaks** (512 N. Howe St., 910/457-1100, www.theinnatriveroaks.com, $65-135), a motel-style inn with very simple suites. The **Island Resort and Inn** (500 Ocean Dr., Oak Island, 910/278-5644, www.islandresortandinn.com, $75-190, depending on season) is a beachfront property with standard motel rooms and one- and two-bedroom apartment suites.

## OCEAN ISLE

Ocean Isle is the next-to-most-southerly beach in North Carolina, separated from South Carolina only by Bird Island and the town of Calabash. In October, Ocean Isle is the site of the **North Carolina Oyster Festival** (www.brunswickcountychamber.org), a huge event that's been happening for nearly 30 years. In addition to an oyster stew cook-off, surfing competition, and entertainment, this event features the North Carolina Oyster Shucking Competition. In the not-that-long-ago days when North Carolina's seafood industry was ascendant, workers—most often African American women—lined up on either side of long work tables in countless oyster houses along the coast and the creeks, and opened and cut out thousands of oysters a day. A complex occupational culture was at work in those rooms, one with its own vocabulary, stories, and songs. The speed at which these women worked was a source of collective and individual pride, and the fastest shuckers enjoyed quite a bit of prestige among their colleagues. The state shucking championship is the time when some of the best shuckers prove that although North Carolina may have changed around them, they haven't missed a beat.

## SOUTH ALONG U.S. 17

U.S. 17 is an old colonial road—in fact, its original name, still used in some stretches, is the Kings Highway. George Washington passed this way on his 1791 tour of the South, staying with the prominent planters of this area and leaving in his wake the legends about where he laid his head for an evening. Today, the Kings Highway, following roughly its original course, is still the main thoroughfare through Brunswick County into South Carolina.

## Brunswick Town and Fort Anderson

Near Orton is the **Brunswick Town/Fort Anderson State Historic Site** (8884 St. Philip's Rd. SE, Winnabow, 910/371-6613, www.ah.dcr.state.nc.us, Tues.-Sat. 9am-5pm, free), the site of what was a bustling little port town in the early and mid-1700s. In its brief life, Brunswick saw quite a bit of action. It was attacked in 1748 by a Spanish ship that, to residents' delight, blew up in the river. (One of that ship's cannons was dragged out of the river about 20 years ago and is on display here.) In 1765, the town's refusal to observe royal tax stamps was a successful precursor to the Boston Tea Party eight years later. But by the end of the Revolutionary War, Brunswick Town was completely gone, burned by the British and having been made obsolete anyway by the growth of Wilmington. Today, nothing remains of the colonial port except for the lovely ruins of the 1754 **St. Philip's Anglican Church** and some building foundations uncovered by archaeologists. During the Civil War, Fort Anderson, sand earthworks that were part of the crucial defenses of the Cape Fear, was built on this site, protecting the blockade-runners who came and went from Wilmington. A visitors center at the historic site tells the story of this surprisingly significant stretch of riverbank, and the grounds, with the town's foundations exposed and interpreted, are an intriguing vestige of a forgotten community.

## Nature Preserves

The Nature Conservancy's **Green Swamp Preserve** (Hwy. 211, 5.5 miles north of Supply, 910/395-5000, www.nature.org, daily dawn-dusk, free) contains nearly 16,000 acres of some of North Carolina's most precious coastal ecosystems, the longleaf pine savanna and evergreen shrub pocosin. Hiking is allowed in the preserve, but the paths are primitive. It's important to stay on the trails and not explore in the wilds because this is an intensely fragile ecosystem. In this preserve are communities of rare carnivorous plants, including the monstrous little pink-mawed Venus flytrap, four kinds of pitcher plant, and sticky-fingered sundew. It's also a habitat for the rare red-cockaded woodpecker, which is partial to diseased old-growth longleaf pines as a place to call home.

The Nature Conservancy maintains another nature preserve nearby, the **Boiling Spring Lakes Preserve** (off Hwy. 87, Boiling Spring Lakes, trail begins at community center, 910/395-5000, www.nature.org, daily dawn-dusk, free), with a trail that begins at the Boiling Spring Lakes Community Center. Brunswick County contains the state's greatest concentration of rare plant species, and the most diverse plant communities anywhere on the East Coast north of Florida. This preserve is owned by the Plant Conservation Program and includes over half the acreage of the town of Boiling Spring Lakes. The ecosystem comprises Carolina bays, pocosins, and longleaf pine forests. Like the Green Swamp Preserve, many of the species here are dependent on periodic fires to propagate and survive. The Nature Conservancy does controlled burning at both sites to maintain this rare habitat.

## Calabash and Vicinity

The once tiny fishing village of Calabash, just north of the South Carolina line, was founded in the early 18th century as Pea Landing, a shipping point for the bounteous local peanut crop. Calabashes, a kind of gourd, were used as dippers in the town supply of drinking water, and when the settlement was renamed in 1873, it was supposedly for that reason that it became Calabash.

In the early 1940s, a style of restaurant seafood was developed here that involves deep-frying lightly battered fish and shellfish. As the style caught on and more restaurants were built, the term "Calabash-style seafood" was born. Jimmy Durante was fond of dining in Calabash, and some people claim that it was in tribute to the food here that he signed off his shows by saying, "Good night, Mrs. Calabash, wherever you are." Though Calabash seafood is now advertised at restaurants all over the country, this little town has more than enough restaurants of its own to handle the yearly onslaught of visitors in search of an authentic Calabash meal. Local favorite spots for seafood are the **Calabash Seafood Hut** (1125 River Rd., 910/579-6723, daily 11am-9pm, $10-28) and, right on the docks, **Dockside Seafood House** (9955 Nance St. SW, 910/579-6775, daily 4pm-9pm, $9-17).

**Indigo Farms** (1542 Hickman Rd. NW, 910/287-6794, www.indigofarmsmarket.com, Mon.-Sat. 8:30am-5:30pm, longer hours in warm months), three miles north of the South Carolina line in Calabash, is a superb farm market, selling all manner of produce, preserves, and baked goods. It also has corn mazes and farm activities in the fall, and is a training site for porcine contestants in the prestigious local NASPIG races.

Sunset Beach, the southernmost of the Brunswick County beaches, is a wonderfully small-time place, a cozy town that until 2008 could only be reached via a one-lane pontoon bridge. One of the area's most popular restaurants is located just on the inland side of the bridge to Sunset Beach: **Twin Lakes**

**Seafood Restaurant** (102 Sunset Blvd., 910/579-6373, http://twinlakesseafood.com, daily 4:30pm-9:30pm, closed Nov.-Feb., $10-30) was built almost 40 years ago by Clarice and Ronnie Holden, both natives of the area. Clarice was born into a cooking family, the daughter of one of the founders of the Calabash restaurant tradition. Twin Lakes serves fresh locally caught seafood, a rarity in this time and place. In high season and on weekends, expect long lines.

## TRANSPORTATION

The Brunswick County beaches, including Holden, Ocean Isle, and Sunset, are an easy drive from Wilmington on U.S. 17. The beaches and islands along the cape, due south of Wilmington, are not as close to U.S. 17. They can be reached by taking U.S. 76 south from Wilmington, or by ferry from Southport. The **Southport-Fort Fisher Ferry** (800/293-3779 or 800/368-8969) is popular as a sightseeing jaunt as well as a means simply to get across the river. It's a 30-minute crossing; most departures are 45 minutes apart, from Southport in summer daily 5:30am-7:45pm, winter daily 5:30am-6:15pm, and leaving Fort Fisher in summer daily 6:15am-8:30pm, winter daily 6:15am-7pm. For most vehicles the fare is $5, but if you're driving a rig that's more than 20 feet long, boat trailers and the like included, the price can be as high as $15. It's $1 for pedestrians, $2 for bicyclists, and $3 for motorcyclists. Pets are permitted if leashed or in a vehicle, and there are restrooms on all ferries.

# Points Inland from Wilmington

Moving inland from the Wilmington area, you first pass through a lush world of wetlands distinguished by the peculiar Carolina bays. Not necessarily bodies of water, as the name would suggest, the bays are actually ovoid depressions in the earth, of unknown and much debated

origin. They are often water-filled, but by definition are fed by rainwater rather than creeks or groundwater. They create unique environments and are often surrounded by bay laurels (hence the name), and are guarded by a variety of carnivorous plants.

# The Legend of Henry Berry Lowry

In some places, the Civil War didn't end the day General Lee surrendered, but smoldered on in terrible local violence. One such place was the indigenous Lumbee community of Robeson County, in the days of the famous Lowry Band.

Then as now, Lowry (also spelled Lowrie) was a prominent surname among the Lumbee people. During the Civil War, Allen Lowry led a band of men who hid out in the swamps, eluding conscription into the backbreaking corps of semi-slave labor that was forced to build earthworks to defend Wilmington. When the war ended, violence against the Lumbees continued, and the Lowry Band retaliated, attacking the plantations of their wartime pursuers. Allen Lowry and his oldest son were captured in 1865 and executed. Henry Berry Lowry, the youngest son, inherited the mantle of leadership.

For the next several years, long after the end of the Civil War, the Lowry Band was pursued relentlessly. Arrested and imprisoned, Lowry and his men escaped from prison in Lumberton and Wilmington. Between 1868 and

Henry Berry Lowry

1872, the state and federal governments tried various ways to apprehend them—putting a bounty on Lowry's head, even sending in a federal artillery battalion. After an 11-month campaign of unsuccessful pursuit, the federal soldiers gave up. Soon afterward, the Lowry Band emerged from the swamps, raided Lumberton, and made off with a large amount of money. This was the end of the road for the Lowry Band, however, and one by one its members were killed in 1872—except, perhaps, Henry Berry. It's unknown whether he died, went back into hiding, or left the area altogether. As befits a legend, he seems simply to have disappeared.

Henry Berry Lowry is a source of fierce pride to modern Lumbee people, a symbol of the community's resistance and resilience. Every summer, members of the Lumbee community perform in the long-running outdoor drama *Strike at the Wind,* which tells the story of the Lowry Band. Another vivid retelling of the story is the 2001 novel *Nowhere Else on Earth* by Josephine Humphreys.

The next zone, bounded by the Waccamaw and Lumber Rivers, is largely farmland and small towns. This was for generations prime tobacco country, and that heritage is still very much evident in towns like Whiteville, where old tobacco warehouses line the railroad tracks. Culturally, this area—mostly in Columbus County, extending some distance into Robeson to the west and Brunswick to the east—is congruous with the three counties in South Carolina with which it shares a border—Horry, Marion, and Dillon.

The area around the Lumber River, especially in Robeson County, is the home of the indigenous Lumbee people, who have an amazing heritage of devotion to faith and family and steadfast resistance to oppression. If you turn on the radio while driving through this area, you'll likely find Lumbee gospel programming and get a sense of the cadences of Lumbee English.

At the edge of the region is Fayetteville. From its early days as the center of Cape Fear Scottish settlement to its current role as one of the most important military communities in the United States, Fayetteville has always been a significant North Carolina city.

# ALONG U.S. 74

A little way inland from Calabash, the countryside is threaded by the Waccamaw River, a gorgeous, dark channel full of cypress knees and dangerous reptiles. (The name is pronounced "WAW-cuh-MAW," with slightly more emphasis on the first syllable than the third.) It winds its way down from Lake Waccamaw through a swampy little portion of North Carolina, crossing Horry County, South Carolina (unofficial motto: "The *H* is silent"), before joining the Pee Dee and Lumber Rivers to flow into Winyah Bay at the colonial port of Georgetown. Through the little toenail of North Carolina that the Waccamaw crosses, it parallels the much longer Lumber River, surrounding the very rural Columbus County and part of Robeson County in an environment of deep subtropical wetlands.

## Sights

### ★ MUSEUM OF THE NATIVE AMERICAN RESOURCE CENTER

**Pembroke** is the town around which much of the indigenous Lumbee community revolves, and at the center of life here is the University of North Carolina at Pembroke (UNCP). Founded in 1887 as the Indian Normal School, UNCP's population is now only about one-quarter Native American, but it's still an important site in the history of North Carolina's indigenous people. The **Museum of the Native American Resource Center** (Old Main, UNCP, 910/521-6282, www.uncp.edu, Mon.-Sat. 8am-5pm, free) is on campus, occupying Old Main, a 1923 building that's a source of pride for the Pembroke community. The Resource Center has a small but very good collection of historical artifacts and contemporary art by Native Americans from across the country.

### JOHN BLUE HOUSE

Laurinburg's **John Blue House** (13040 X-way Rd., Laurinburg, 910/276-2495, www.johnbluecottonfestival.com, Tues.-Sat.

10am-noon and 1pm-4pm, free) is a spectacle of Victorian design, a polygonal house built entirely of heart pine harvested from the surrounding property and done up like a wedding cake with endless decorative devices. John Blue, the builder and original owner, was an inventor of machinery used in the processing of cotton. A pre-Civil War cotton gin stands on the property and is used for educational demonstrations throughout the year. This is the site of the **John Blue Cotton Festival,** an October event that showcases not only the ingenuity of the home's famous resident and the process of ginning cotton, but also lots of local and regional musicians and other artists.

## Sports and Recreation

Several beautiful state parks line the Waccamaw and Lumber Rivers.

**Yogi Bear's Jellystone Park** (626 Richard Wright Rd., 877/668-8586, www.taborcityjellystone.com, $30 tents, $120 cabins), formerly known as Daddy Joe's, is a popular campground with RV and tent spaces, rental cabins, and yurts. The facilities are clean and well maintained, and there are tons of children's activities on-site. Some of the camping is in wooded areas, but for the most part expect direct sun and plan accordingly.

In Fair Bluff is **River Bend Outfitters** (1206 Main St., 910/649-5998, www.whitevillenc.com/rbo), a canoe and kayak company that specializes in paddling and camping trips along the beautiful blackwater Lumber River.

### ★ LAKE WACCAMAW STATE PARK

**Lake Waccamaw State Park** (1866 State Park Dr., Lake Waccamaw, 910/646-4748, http://ncparks.gov, office daily 8am-5pm, park Nov.-Apr. daily 8am-6pm, Mar.-May and Sept.-Oct. daily 8am-8pm, June-Aug. daily 8am-9pm, free) encompasses the 9,000-acre Lake Waccamaw. The lake is technically a Carolina bay, a mysterious geological feature of this region. Carolina bays are large, oval depressions in the ground, many of which are boggy and filled with water, but which are actually named for the bay trees that typically grow in and around them. Lake Waccamaw has geological and hydrological characteristics that make it unique even within the odd category of Carolina bays. Because of its proximity to a large limestone deposit, the water is more neutral than its usually very acidic cousins and so supports a greater diversity of life. There are several aquatic creatures that live only here, with great names like the Waccamaw fatmucket and silverside (a mollusk and a fish, respectively). The park draws many boaters and paddlers, naturally, although the only available launches are outside the park. Primitive campsites are available in the park.

### JONES LAKE STATE PARK

North of Whiteville on U.S. 701 is Elizabethtown, location of **Jones Lake State Park** (4117 Hwy. 242, Elizabethtown, 910/588-4550, http://ncparks.gov, office Mon.-Fri. 8am-5pm, park Nov.-Feb. daily 8am-6pm, Mar.-May and Sept.-Oct. daily 8am-8pm, June-Aug. daily 8am-9pm). Visitors can go boating on Jones Lake, either in their own craft (no motors over 10 hp), or in canoes or paddleboats rented from the park ($5 per hour, $3 each additional hour). The lake is also great for swimming Memorial Day-Labor Day, with shallow, cool water and a sandy beach. There is a concession stand and a bathhouse at the beach. Camping is available in a wooded area, with drinking water and restrooms nearby. Visit the park's website for the rather complicated pricing system.

### SINGLETARY LAKE STATE PARK

**Singletary Lake State Park** (6707 Hwy. 53 E., Kelly, 910/669-2928, http://ncparks. gov, daily 8am-5pm, free), north of Lake Waccamaw in Kelly, centers on one of the largest of the Carolina bays, the 572-acre Singletary Lake, which lies within the Bladen Lakes State Forest. There is no individual

camping allowed, although there are facilities for large groups—including the entrancingly named Camp Ipecac—which date from the Civilian Conservation Corps (CCC) era. There is a nice one-mile hiking trail, the CCC-Carolina Bay Loop Trail, and a 500-foot pier extending over the bay. Some of the cypress trees here are estimated to have been saplings when the first English colonists set foot on Roanoke Island.

### LUMBER RIVER STATE PARK

**Lumber River State Park** (2819 Princess Ann Rd., Orrum, 910/628-4564, http://ncparks.gov, Nov.-Feb. 8am-6pm, Mar.-May and Sept.-Oct. 8am-8pm, June-Aug. 8am-9pm, free) has 115 miles of waterways, with numerous put-ins for canoes and kayaks. The river, referred to as the Lumber or Lumbee River, or, in areas farther upstream, Drowning Creek, traverses both the coastal plain region and the eastern edge of the sandhills. Camping is available at unimproved walk-in and canoe-in sites.

## Food

If you pass through Tabor City, don't neglect to have a meal at the ★ **Todd House** (102 Live Oak St., 910/653-3778, www.todd-house. com, Mon.-Fri. 11am-8pm, Sun. 11am-3pm, $12), which has been serving fine country cooking since 1923. The Todds are one of the oldest families in the area along the state line, and the first in the restaurant business was Mary Todd, who took to cooking meals for visiting tobacco buyers. Through her daughter's time, and a couple of subsequent owners, the Todd House has continued to serve famously good barbecue, fried chicken, and other down-home specialties. The wonderful pies are available for purchase, so pick one up for the road.

There's a take-out counter in Whiteville that chowhounds will drive an hour out of their way to reach because it's said to have the best burgers around. Next to the railroad tracks, **Ward's Grill** (706 S. Madison

St., 910/642-2004, Mon.-Tues. and Thurs. 7am-2pm, Wed. 7am-1pm, 1st two Sat. of the month 7am-noon, $8) has no seating, just a walk-up counter. Its burgers are famous, as are its chili dogs.

In Lumberton, try **Fuller's Old-Fashion BBQ** (3201 Roberts Ave., Lumberton, 910/738-8694, www.fullersbbq.com, Mon.-Sat. 11am-9pm, Sun. 11am-4pm, lunch buffet $7, dinner buffet $9.50). Fuller's has a great reputation for its barbecue, but it also makes all sorts of country specialties like chicken gizzards and chitterlings, and a special 12-layer cake.

## Transportation

This section of southeastern North Carolina is bisected by I-95, the largest highway on the East Coast. I-95 passes just outside both Fayetteville and Lumberton. Major east-west routes include U.S. 74, which crosses the Cape Fear at Wilmington and proceeds through Lake Waccamaw and Whiteville to pass just south of Lumberton and Pembroke, going to Laurinburg. Highway 87 goes through Elizabethtown, where you can choose to branch off onto Highway 211 to Lumberton, or bear north on Highway 87 to Fayetteville.

# FAYETTEVILLE

Fayetteville is North Carolina's sixth-largest city, and in its own quiet way has always been one of the state's most powerful engines of growth and change. In the early 1700s it became a hub for settlement by Scottish immigrants, who helped build it into a major commercial center. From the 1818 initiation of steamboat travel between Fayetteville and Wilmington along the Cape Fear—initially a voyage of six days!—to the building of the Plank Road, a huge boon to intrastate commerce, Fayetteville was well connected to commercial resources all through the Carolinas.

At a national level, Fayetteville serves as the location of the largest single U.S. Army base in existence. Fort Bragg is the home of the XVIII Airborne Corps, the 82nd Airborne, the Delta Force, and the John F. Kennedy Special Warfare Center and School. As such, it's also the home of many widows and children of soldiers who have died in Iraq and Afghanistan. Within Fort Bragg is Pope Field, formerly Pope Air Force Base, which provides air support for the Fort's varied missions.

## Sights

The **Museum of the Cape Fear Regional Complex** (801 Arsenal Ave., 910/486-1330, www.ncdcr.gov/ncmcf, Tues.-Sat. 10am-5pm, Sun. 1pm-5pm, free) has three components, each telling different stories of Fayetteville's history. The museum itself has exhibits on the history and prehistory of the region, including its vital role in developing transportation in the state, as well as its centrality as a military center. There is an 1897 house museum, the Poe House, which belonged to Edgar Allen Poe—not Edgar Allan, the writer, but Edgar Allen, a brickyard owner. The third section is the 4.5-acre Arsenal Park, site of a federal arms magazine built in 1836, claimed by the Confederacy in 1861, and destroyed by General Sherman in 1865.

The **Airborne and Special Operations Museum** (100 Bragg Blvd., 910/643-2766, www.asomf.org, Tues.-Sat. 10am-5pm, Sun. noon-5pm, free) is an impressive facility that presents the history of special operations paratroopers, from the first jump in 1940 to the divisions' present-day roles abroad in peacekeeping missions and war. In the museum's theater you can watch an amazing film of what it looks like when a paratrooper makes the jump, and the 24-seat Pitch, Roll, and Yaw Vista-Dome Motion Simulator makes the experience even more exciting.

The **JFK Special Warfare Museum** (Bldg. D-2502, Ardennes St. and Marion St., Fort Bragg, 910/432-4272, www.jfkwebstore. com, Tues.-Sun. 11am-4pm, ID required) tells the story of some interesting facets of the U.S. military, including Special Ops and Psychological Ops. The museum focuses on the Vietnam War era, but chronicles unconventional warfare from colonial times to the present.

Going back farther in time, the **Fayetteville Independent Light Infantry Armory and Museum** (210 Burgess St., 910/433-1612, by appointment, free) displays artifacts from the history of the Light Infantry. The Fayetteville Independent Light Infantry (FILI) is still active, dedicated as North Carolina's official historic military command, a ceremonial duty. But in its active-duty days, which began in 1793, FILI had some exciting times, particularly during the Civil War. In addition to the military artifacts, this museum also exhibits a carriage in which the Marquis de Lafayette was shown around Fayetteville—the only one of the towns bearing his name that he actually visited.

The 79-acre **Cape Fear Botanical Garden** (536 N. Eastern Blvd., 910/486-0221, www.capefearbg.org, Mar.-mid-Dec. Mon.-Sat. 10am-5pm, Sun. noon-5pm, mid-Dec.-Feb. Mon.-Sat. 10am-5pm, $10 adults, $5 children) is one of the loveliest horticultural sites in North Carolina. The camellia and azalea gardens are spectacular sights in the early spring, but the variety of plantings and environments represented makes the whole park a delight. Along the banks of the Paw Paw River and Cross Creek, visitors will find dozens of garden environments, including lily gardens, hosta gardens, woods, a bog, and an 1880s farmhouse garden. Without a doubt, this is the prettiest place in Fayetteville.

**Cross Creek Cemetery** (North Cool Spring St. and Grove St., 800/255-8217, daily dawn-dusk) is an attractively sad spot, the resting place of many Scottish men and women who crossed the ocean to settle the Cape Fear. Though all kinds of people were buried here over the years, it is the oldest section that is most poignant, where one stone after another commemorates Mr. or Mrs. Mac-So-and-So, Late of Glasgow or Perth, Merchant in This Town.

## Entertainment and Events

The **Cameo Theatre** (225 Hay St., 910/486-6633, www.cameoarthouse.com) is a cool early 20th-century movie house, originally known as the New Dixie. Today it is "Fayetteville's alternative cinematic experience," a place for independent and art-house movies.

The **Cape Fear Regional Theatre** (1209 Hay St., 910/323-4233, www.cfrt.org) began in 1962 as a tiny company with a bunch of borrowed equipment. Today it is a major regional theater with a wide reputation. Putting on several major productions each season, with a specialty in popular musicals, it draws actors and directors from around the country, but maintains its heart here in the Fayetteville arts community.

Fayetteville's late-April **Dogwood Festival** features rock, pop, and beach music bands; a dog show; a recycled art show; a "hogs and rags spring rally"; and the selection and coronation of Miss, Teen Miss, Young Miss, and Junior Miss Dogwood Festival.

## Food and Accommodations

Fayetteville's dining choices tend toward highway chains, though there are some exceptions. The ★ **Hilltop House** (1240 Fort Bragg Rd., 910/484-6699, www.hilltophousenc.com, lunch Mon.-Sat. 11am-2pm, dinner Mon.-Thurs. 5pm-9pm, Fri.-Sat. 5pm-10pm, brunch Sun. 10:30am-2:30pm, $15-25) serves hearty fare in an elegant setting, has complimentary wine-tasting Tuesday evening, and has been recognized with a Wine Spectator Award for Excellence—not surprising, given that the Hilltop House has a 74-page wine list. More casual is the **Mash House** (4150 Sycamore Dairy Rd., 910/867-9223, www.themashhouse.com, Mon.-Thurs. 5pm-10pm, Fri. 5pm-11pm, Sat. noon-11pm, Sun. noon-9pm, $8-16), which has a good variety of pizzas and sandwiches as well as heavier entrées and a selection of good homemade brews.

Likewise, the city's lodging options are

mostly chain motels, a multitude of which can be found at I-95's Fayetteville exits. You'll generally find a pretty reasonable deal at the old standards, but if you'd like to stay somewhere with more personality, Wilmington and Raleigh are both easily accessible.

## Information and Services

**Cape Fear Valley Health Services** (1638 Owen Dr., 910/615-4000, www.capefearvalley.com) is a large hospital complex with acute care services, a major cardiac care program, and everything else one would expect from a major regional hospital.

The website of the **Fayetteville Area Convention and Visitors Bureau** (www.visitfayettevillenc.com) is an excellent source of visitor information for this city. You'll find the basics as well as detailed driving tours, extensive historical information, and much more.

## Transportation

Fayetteville is a short hop off I-95. Fayetteville is also easily reached by Highway 24 via Jacksonville, Warsaw, and Clinton. **Fayetteville Regional Airport** (FAY, 400 Airport Rd., 910/433-1160, flyfay.ci.fayetteville.nc.us) has daily flights to Charlotte, Atlanta, and Washington DC on Delta and US Airways. The city is served by **Amtrak** (472 Hay St., 800/872-7245, www.amtrak.com, daily 10am-5:45pm and 10pm-5:45am) via the regional *Palmetto* and the New York-Miami *Silver Meteor* lines.

# Central North Carolina

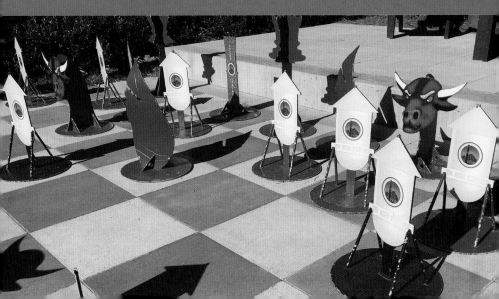

Look for ★ to find recommended
sights, activities, dining, and lodging.

# Highlights

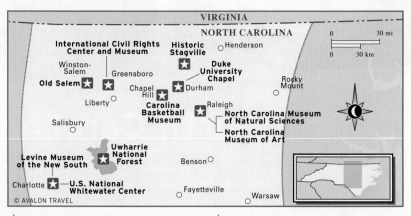

★ **North Carolina Museum of Natural Sciences:** Get close to massive whale and dinosaur skeletons and discover the many ecosystems of the region (page 109).

★ **North Carolina Museum of Art:** Amazingly varied collections encompass art from ancient Greece, Egypt, and the Americas as well as Judaica, pop art, and 18th- and 19th-century American and European masters (page 111).

★ **Duke University Chapel:** This beautiful and enormous Gothic edifice dominates the historic campus and hosts frequent concerts (page 118).

★ **Historic Stagville:** One of the South's largest enslaved populations lived and worked on this plantation. The story of their community is preserved here (page 118).

★ **Carolina Basketball Museum:** Learn more about the University of North Carolina's basketball program, one of the greatest collegiate athletic traditions in American sports (page 125).

★ **Old Salem:** Craftspeople and historical interpreters bring an 18th- and 19th-century religious community to life in this restored Moravian village (page 130).

★ **International Civil Rights Center and Museum:** Learn about the fight for integration and justice in North Carolina, a crucial front in the civil rights movement (page 134).

★ **Uwharrie National Forest:** Hiding under the canopy of forest are miles of hiking trails, wilderness campsites, and mysterious back roads (page 141).

★ **Levine Museum of the New South:** This innovative museum tells the complicated and sometimes painful story of the post-Civil War South, and Charlotte in particular (page 149).

★ **U.S. National Whitewater Center:** Home to the U.S. Olympic canoe and kayak teams, this facility is also designed for first-time paddlers and adventure sports enthusiasts (page 152).

# With a focus on the arts, civil rights, and educational institutions, Central North Carolina sets itself apart from the rest of the red state.

Long used to describe the Raleigh-Durham-Chapel Hill area, the Triangle originally referred to the three major universities here: the University of North Carolina (UNC) in Chapel Hill, Duke University in Durham, and North Carolina State University (NC State) in Raleigh. The concentration of colleges—there are over a dozen institutions of higher learning, including several prominent historically black universities—makes for a highly educated population with a deeply liberal bent. The Chapel Hill area is the epicenter of progressive politics in the area.

UNC's Creative Writing Program has a lot to do with the area's concentration of fine writers, having included such writers as Thomas Wolfe, Charles Kuralt, and David Sedaris. The music scene is just as rich, with great symphonies and chamber groups, a century-old blues tradition, and more old-time string band musicians than anywhere outside the mountains. If you like alternative country, you'll find a live music scene that rivals those of Austin and Nashville.

## PLANNING YOUR TIME

The ground covered in this chapter is best approached as three destinations for the purpose of setting out a practical itinerary. Raleigh calls for a full day, as it is large and flows in all directions. Durham and Chapel Hill are only nine miles apart, and can be used as a base for exploring the rest of the region.

If you choose one town in the Triangle to stay at night while exploring the whole area during the day, Durham is the most centrally located of the three and offers high-quality accommodations at reasonable prices. That said, I-40 and U.S. 70 link the whole Triangle area quite efficiently, and there are few points in the Triangle that are more than half an hour's drive from any other destination.

**Previous:** the University of North Carolina campus; the American Tobacco Campus. **Above:** the North Carolina State Capitol in Raleigh.

# Central North Carolina

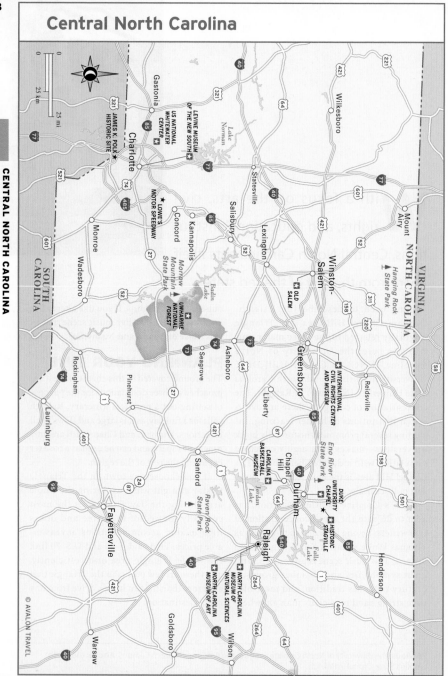

0

25 km

0

25 mi

Gastonia

JAMES K. POLK HISTORIC SITE ★

US NATIONAL WHITEWATER CENTER ✚

LEVINE MUSEUM OF THE NEW SOUTH ✚

Charlotte

Lake Norman

Statesville

Salisbury

Lexington

Winston-Salem

Mount Airy

Hanging Rock State Park ⚑

OLD SALEM ✚

VIRGINIA

NORTH CAROLINA

Wilkesboro

LOWE'S MOTOR SPEEDWAY ★

Concord

Kannapolis

Monroe

Wadesboro

SOUTH CAROLINA

Morrow Mountain State Park ⚑

Badin Lake

UWHARRIE NATIONAL FOREST

Seagrove

Asheboro

Rockingham

Pinehurst

Laurinburg

Fayetteville

Greensboro

INTERNATIONAL CIVIL RIGHTS CENTER AND MUSEUM ✚

Reidsville

Liberty

Sanford

Raven Rock State Park ⚑

CAROLINA BASKETBALL MUSEUM ✚

Chapel Hill

Eno River State Park ⚑

Durham

DUKE UNIVERSITY CHAPEL ⚑

HISTORIC STAGVILLE ✚ ★

Jordan Lake

Falls Lake

Raleigh

NORTH CAROLINA MUSEUM OF NATURAL SCIENCES ✚

NORTH CAROLINA MUSEUM OF ART ✚

Henderson

Wilson

Goldsboro

Warsaw

© AVALON TRAVEL

# Raleigh and Vicinity

Loyal watchers of *The Andy Griffith Show* know that when trouble came to Mayberry, it came from one of two places: Up North or Raleigh. But Raleigh is no hive of citified depravity. As the home of the state government and several universities, Raleigh is a spark that helps power the cultural engine of the rest of the state. North Carolina State University is here, as are two prominent historically black universities, Shaw and Saint Augustine's, and two small women's colleges, Peace and Meredith.

## SIGHTS
### ★ North Carolina Museum of Natural Sciences
The **North Carolina Museum of Natural Sciences** (Bicentennial Plaza, 11 W. Jones St., 877/462-8724, www.naturalsciences.org, Mon.-Sat. 9am-5pm, Sun. noon-5pm, 1st Fri. of the month 9am-9pm, free) hosts national traveling exhibitions and is home to excellent permanent exhibits. *Mountains to the Sea* is a re-creation of the regional environments of the state, populated with live and mounted animals and plants. *Stars of Prehistoric North Carolina* include the world's only publicly displayed skeleton of an *Acrocanthosaurus,* a 38-foot, 4.5-ton predatory dinosaur, and the remains of "Willo," a 66-million-year-old small vegetarian dinosaur, whose fossilized heart is a miraculous boon to paleontology. Visitors can also walk among hummingbirds and butterflies in the Living Conservatory,

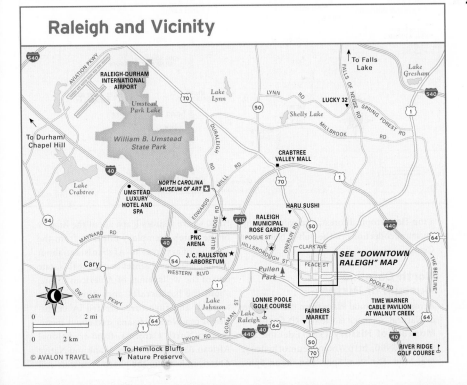
Raleigh and Vicinity

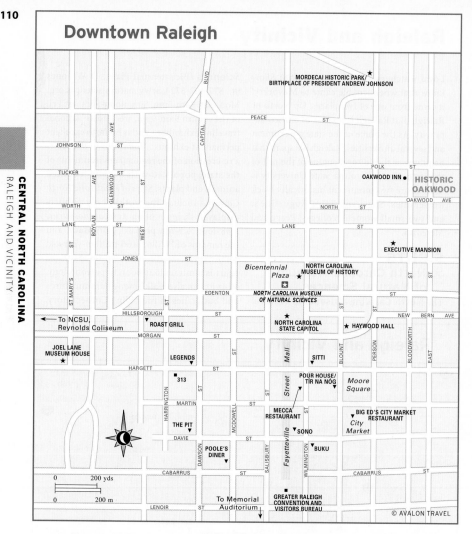

# Downtown Raleigh

MORDECAI HISTORIC PARK/
BIRTHPLACE OF PRESIDENT ANDREW JOHNSON

BLVD

PEACE ST

AVE

CAPITAL

JOHNSON ST

TUCKER ST

POLK ST

OAKWOOD INN ● **HISTORIC OAKWOOD**

GLENWOOD ST

OAKWOOD AVE

WORTH ST

NORTH ST

BOYLAN

WEST

LANE ST

LANE ST

ST

★ **EXECUTIVE MANSION**

JONES ST

*Bicentennial Plaza* ✚ **NORTH CAROLINA MUSEUM OF HISTORY**

ST MARY'S

EDENTON ST **NORTH CAROLINA MUSEUM OF NATURAL SCIENCES**

HILLSBOROUGH ST

NEW BERN AVE

← To NCSU, Reynolds Coliseum ▼ **ROAST GRILL**

**NORTH CAROLINA STATE CAPITOL**

★ **HAYWOOD HALL**

BLOODWORTH

MORGAN ST

**JOEL LANE MUSEUM HOUSE** ★

*Mall*

▼ **LEGENDS**

EAST

HARGETT ST

SITTI

BLOUNT

PERSON

■ 313

*Street*

**POUR HOUSE/ TIR NA NÓG**

*Moore Square*

HARRINGTON

MARTIN ST

**MECCA RESTAURANT**

**BIG ED'S CITY MARKET RESTAURANT**

▼ **THE PIT**

▼ SONO

*City Market*

DAVIE ST

*Fayetteville*

DAWSON

▼ **POOLE'S DINER**

SALISBURY

▼ **BUKU**

WILMINGTON

CABARRUS ST

CABARRUS ST

| 0 | 200 yds |
| 0 | 200 m |

LENOIR ST

To Memorial Auditorium ↓

■ **GREATER RALEIGH CONVENTION AND VISITORS BUREAU**

© AVALON TRAVEL

a top-floor tropical forest, and work among museum collections in the public Naturalist Center.

## North Carolina Museum of History

Across Bicentennial Plaza from the Museum of Natural Sciences is the **North Carolina Museum of History** (5 E. Edenton St., 919/807-7900, http://ncmuseumofhistory. org, Mon.-Sat. 9am-5pm, Sun. noon-5pm,

free), where visitors learn about the history of the state's exemplary military, from the Revolutionary War to Afghanistan; about the musicians and genres that make this state one of the wellsprings of American music; about the handicrafts, including pottery, textiles, and furniture, created by centuries of renowned artisans; and about medicine in North Carolina, from traditional African American root medicine and Native American herbs to the pharmaceuticals and technology that draw patients and researchers from around the world.

## ★ North Carolina Museum of Art

The **North Carolina Museum of Art** (2110 Blue Ridge Rd., 919/839-6262, http://ncartmuseum.org, Tues.-Thurs. and Sat.-Sun. 10am-5pm, Fri. 10am-9pm, free) is just outside the Beltline (I-440). Its collections are of the highest quality and include masterpieces of art from all eras and regions of the world, from ancient Egyptian, Greek, Roman, and pre-Columbian American art to the work of Botticelli, Giotto, and Raphael; Monet; Copley, Cole, Homer, Eakins, and Chase; Georgia O'Keeffe and Thomas Hart Benton; and many more. The gallery is also home to one of the nation's two Jewish ceremonial art collections, and to collections of 19th- and 20th-century African art.

## Historic Homes

The 1770s **Joel Lane Museum House** (St. Mary's St. and W. Hargett St., 919/833-3431, www.joellane.org, Wed.-Fri. 10am-2pm, tours 10am, 11am, noon, and 1pm, Sat. 1pm-4pm, tours 1pm, 2pm, and 3pm, $8 adults, $7 seniors, $4 children) is Wake County's oldest extant home. Costumed docents lead tours of the house and period gardens.

The 1799 **Haywood Hall** (211 New Bern Place, 919/832-8357, Thurs. 10:30am-1:30pm, free) is another of Raleigh's oldest extant buildings. Built for the state's first elected treasurer and his family, the house and gardens are open to the public and feature a historic doll collection. Tours are available for a fee.

**Mordecai Historic Park** (Mimosa St. and Wake Forest Rd., 919/857-4364, www.raleighnc.gov/mordecai, grounds daily dawn-dusk, hourly house tours Tues.-Sat. 9am-4pm, Sun. 1pm-4pm, $5 adults, $3 seniors, $3 ages 7-17) includes a late 18th-century and early 19th-century plantation house, restored dependencies, and other buildings, including the birthplace of President Andrew Johnson.

## Other Sights

The **North Carolina State Capitol** (1 E. Edenton St., 866/724-8687, www.ncstatecapitol.org, Mon.-Sat. 9am-5pm, free) and the **Executive Mansion** (200 N. Blount St., 919/807-7950), built in the 1830s and 1890s, respectively, are lovely examples of Victorian architecture. The Greek Revival capitol building has been restored to its antebellum

the North Carolina Museum of History

the North Carolina State Capitol

appearance. Free guided tours last approximately 45 minutes.

The **J. C. Raulston Arboretum** (4415 Beryl Rd., 919/515-3132, www.ncsu.edu/jcraulstonarboretum, Apr.-Oct. daily 8am-8pm, Nov.-Mar. daily 8am-5pm, free), across from Capitol City Lumber Company, is a free public garden focused on the development of ornamental plants suitable to the Southern climate. The **Raleigh Municipal Rose Garden** (301 Pogue St., near NC State, free) is home to over 1,000 roses of 60 varieties. Carolina roses are blessed with an extra-long growing season, and the Municipal Rose Garden also features bulbs and other ornamental plants, so a visit to the garden is special at any time of year.

## ENTERTAINMENT AND EVENTS
### Performing Arts

The **North Carolina Symphony** (919/733-2750, www.ncsymphony.org), a full-time 65-member orchestra under the direction of conductors Grant Llewellyn and William Henry Curry, tours throughout the state and beyond. Its home venue in Raleigh is the wonderful Meymandi Concert Hall at Progress Energy Center (2 E. South St., 919/831-6060).

The **North Carolina Opera** (919/792-3850, www.ncopera.org) has its home stage at Memorial Auditorium, also in the Progress Energy Center. The opera's rehearsals, held at a nearby church, are sometimes open to the public—see their website for details.

The **Time Warner Cable Music Pavilion at Walnut Creek** (3801 Rock Quarry Rd., 919/831-6400, www.livenation.com/raleigh) is a top local music venue, attracting pop and country chart-toppers. The **Lincoln Theatre** (126 E. Cabarrus St., 919/821-4111, www.lincolntheatre.com, all ages, $2 surcharge under age 18) is another important local performing arts institution where major rock, blues, jazz, and other bands fill the schedule.

### Nightlife

The best place to find out what's going on at Triangle-area clubs on any given night of the week is the *Independent Weekly* (www.indyweek.com), a free newspaper that's available at restaurants and shops throughout the region. By state law, establishments that serve liquor and make no more than 30 percent of their revenue from food must be private-membership clubs, but every club has ways of getting first-time visitors through the doors. Some clubs must be joined a few days in advance, while others accept applications with nominal dues at the door. Raleigh's popular nightspots are dance clubs, lots of live music venues, and gay clubs with great drag events.

The **Pour House Music Hall** (224 S. Blount St., 919/821-1120, www.the-pour-house.com) is a great venue with alternative country, rock and roll, bluegrass, and all sorts of other bands on the schedule. Visitors must print the membership form from the website, fill it out, and bring it to the door with $1. For Irish ambience, visit **Tír Na Nóg Irish Pub and Restaurant** (108 Hargett St., 919/833-7795), recently relocated from its longtime Blount Street location, and the **Hibernian Restaurant and Bar** (311 Glenwood Ave., 919/833-2258, www.hibernianpub.com).

**Legends** (330 W. Hargett St., 919/831-8888, www.legends-club.com, daily 9pm-close) is one of the most popular gay and lesbian clubs in the state, a fun bar that is also ground zero for the area's pageant circuit. Call for membership details.

### Fairs and Festivals

The 10-day **North Carolina State Fair** (1025 Blue Ridge Rd., 919/821-7400, www.ncstatefair.org), held each October, is the nation's largest agricultural fair, with an annual attendance of about 800,000. Plan on going back several times to take it all in. It has everything you might want in an agricultural fair: livestock and produce competitions, big-name bluegrass concerts, carnival rides, fighter jet flyovers, and lots of deep-fried food.

## SHOPPING

**Cameron Village** (Oberlin Rd. between Hillsborough St. and Wade Ave., www.shopcameronvillage.com) was one of the earliest shopping centers in the Southeast, a planned commercial neighborhood built on the grounds of the old Cameron plantation in the late 1940s. The complex opened with three stores, but today there are dozens. It tends toward independent boutiques and high-end chains and is a fun place to splurge. Some of the notable shops are **Uniquities** (450 Daniels St., 919/832-1234, www.uniquities.com, Mon.-Sat. 10am-7pm, Sun. 1pm-6pm), a great women's clothing boutique; and the **Junior League Bargain Box** (401 Woodburn Ave., 919/833-7587, Mon.-Sat. 10am-6pm), a nice thrift shop.

The 1914 **City Market** (214 E. Martin St., 919/821-8023, www.historiccitymarket.com) complex is another collection of nifty little shops and restaurants in a historic setting. **Crabtree Valley Mall** (Glenwood Ave./U.S. 70 at I-440) is the main conventional shopping mall in Raleigh.

## SPORTS AND RECREATION
### Spectator Sports

North Carolina State University is the southern terminus of Tobacco Road, the zone of legendary college sports traditions in the Atlantic Coast Conference (ACC). Though the UNC-Duke rivalry may score more media attention, NC State's **Wolfpack athletics** (www.gopack.com) is nothing to sniff at. Men's basketball games take place at the 20,000-seat **PNC Arena** (1400 Edwards Mill Rd., 919/861-2300, www.thepncarena.com) and football is next door at **Carter-Finley Stadium** (4600 Trinity Rd., 919/865-1510). Women's basketball and other Wolfpack sporting events take place at **Reynolds Coliseum** (2411 Dunn Ave., 919/515-2100) and **Doak Field** (1081 Varsity Dr., 919/515-2100).

During hockey season, PNC Arena is home to the **Carolina Hurricanes** (http://hurricanes.nhl.com). North Carolina may seem an unlikely place for an NHL franchise, but the Canes proved themselves in the 2005-2006 season, beating the Edmonton Oilers to win the Stanley Cup. Tickets can be purchased in person at the box office inside PNC Arena (919/861-2323, no phone sales) or through Ticketmaster (www.ticketmaster.com).

### Outdoor Recreation

**William B. Umstead State Park** (8801 Glenwood Ave., 919/571-4170, http://ncparks. gov, May-Aug. 8am-9pm, Mar.-Apr. and

# Scoring College Basketball Tickets

If you're visiting the Triangle during college basketball season and are hoping to catch a game in person, don't count on being able to buy a ticket at the box office. In fact, count on not being able to. The 20,000-seat Dean Dome, UNC's Dean E. Smith Center, routinely sells out for men's in-conference games, and PNC Arena, the NC State Wolfpack men's 20,000-seat home arena, often does as well. Duke plays at the comparatively quaint and tiny Cameron Indoor Stadium, and its 9,000 seats are the hardest of all to obtain.

The most prized and scarce treasure of all is a ticket to the Duke-UNC men's game. Unless a current student at one of the schools really, really likes you, or you're a major benefactor with a building named in your honor, your chances of paying face value for a ticket are slim to none. When the game is played at Duke, students follow an elaborately codified protocol of camping out next to Cameron in "Krzyzewskiville," a whimsical tent city named for the legendary Duke coach, for a chance at getting into the game. The university provides K-Ville with its own Wi-Fi; however, no heaters are allowed in the tents, and someone must always occupy a tent to keep its place in line or else the whole tent is disqualified. Some students spend the better part of a semester living at least part-time in K-Ville.

During basketball season, tickets appear on eBay, Craigslist, and ticket-scalping search engines. For a minor out-of-conference game, such as those played early in the season—the Wolfpack versus the Flying Menace of Snickelfritz County Community College, let's say—you should be able to get a reasonably good ticket for $10-20 above face value and without much difficulty. For a sold-out game between ACC teams, prices go up steeply. If you want to go to a UNC-Duke game, seats up in the rafters will be in the hundreds, and a good seat could easily set you back $1,000 or more.

Scalping is illegal in North Carolina; it's also pretty common. On game day, the scalpers are the people hanging around outside the arena, or on nearby street corners, holding signs that say "Need Tickets," code for "I've got tickets." If you ask one of them if he has a ticket, he'll ask cagily what you're looking for. Draw your line in the sand—you want a really good ticket for not a lot of money. If you ask for courtside seats for $20 each, you'll only get laughter and lose your bargaining chips, but if you start not too far from the bounds of reason, he'll talk business. Be firm, and be willing to turn down a best offer. There's another scalper just a few steps away. If you don't mind missing the first few minutes of the game, you'll find that prices start going down at tip-off.

Sept.-Oct. 8am-8pm, Nov.-Feb. 8am-6pm, free), between Raleigh and Durham, offers 20 miles of hiking trails, boat rentals in season, and mountain bike trails. The deep forests and creek banks feature flora normally found at higher elevations, including mountain laurel, and are frequented by a variety of wildlife. The Crabtree Creek entrance, where you'll find the visitors center, is 10 miles northwest of Raleigh off U.S. 70.

If your canoe or kayak is already strapped onto your car and all you need is a place to put in, try the **Neuse River Canoe Trail.** Over a stretch of 17 miles of the Neuse, you can choose from five different launches, beginning at the Falls Lake Dam. Visit www.raleighnc.gov for information on launch sites.

# FOOD
## Eclectic American

One of the most popular eateries in the Triangle since the 1970s, ★ **The Irregardless Café** (901 W. Morgan St., 919/833-8898, www.irregardless.com, lunch Tues.-Fri. 11:30am-2:30pm, dinner Tues.-Thurs. 5:30pm-10:30pm, Fri.-Sat. 5:30pm-10pm, brunch Sun. 10am-2pm, $15-25) began as a strictly vegetarian café, and has since expanded to include omnivorous fare—in fact, most of the entrées are now seafood and chicken dishes, but it still serves some good vegetarian and even vegan chow. From the long list of desserts, try the pear and almond caramelized tart and the vegan chocolate mocha raspberry cake.

**Lilly's Pizza** (1813 Glenwood Ave., 919/833-0226, www.lillyspizza.com, Sun.-Wed. 11am-10pm, Thurs. 11am-11pm, Fri.-Sat. 11am-midnight, under $10) is a locally owned, one-of-a-kind parlor that's been around for more than 15 years. They use lots of organic local ingredients, even in the homemade crusts. You can choose favorite ingredients for a custom pie, or have an equally tasty calzone, stromboli, or lasagna.

## Asian

A popular sushi spot is **Sono** (319 Fayetteville St., Ste. 101, 919/521-5328, www.sonoraleigh.com, lunch Mon.-Fri. 11am-2pm, dinner Sun.-Thurs. 5pm-10pm, Fri.-Sat. 5pm-11pm, $10-20), with many original sushi rolls as well as bento and noodle dishes.

## Middle Eastern

★ **Sitti** (137 S. Wilmington St., 919/239-4070, www.sitti-raleigh.com, Mon.-Thurs. 11am-10pm, Fri.-Sat. 11am-midnight, Sun. noon-10pm, $12-25) derives its name from the Lebanese nickname for grandmothers, and this restaurant draws from the owner-chef's Lebanese family traditions. Chef Ghassan Jarrouj prepares old family recipes, as well as specialties he has developed over his 30-year career, which has included jobs as chef for three U.S. ambassadors in Lebanon. The menu includes kebabs and hearty stews as well as special chef's creations such as pan-seared sea bass.

## Southern

Big Ed of **Big Ed's City Market Restaurant** (220 Wolfe St., 919/836-9909, Mon.-Fri. 7am-2pm, Sat. 7am-noon, lunch $10, cash only) has made some remarkable claims about his food over the years—asserting that a Big Ed's breakfast will make a tadpole slap a whale, and that the biscuits alone will empower a poodle to pull a freight train. The joint specializes in pork products—bacon, country ham, barbecue—and in-season regional vegetables.

Greek-American restaurateur families have had a strong influence on Southern cuisine for more than a century, often opening the first restaurants in small towns, and mastering the arts of frying chicken and boiling greens. Raleigh's **Mecca Restaurant** (13 E. Martin St., 919/832-5714, daily 7:30am-7pm) was opened in 1930 by the Dombalis family, and has become such a local institution—particularly a favorite of state government officials and workers—that when it marked its 75th anniversary, the whole city celebrated Mecca Restaurant Day.

Another such case is the Poniros family's **Roast Grill** (7 S. West St., 919/832-8292, www.roastgrill.com, Mon.-Sat. 11am-4pm, under $5), which has been serving hot dogs since 1940 but enjoyed a huge profile boost in 2009 by being featured on Adam Richman's *Man vs. Food*. You can get a hot dog blackened to your specifications, chili, a glass-bottle Coke or beer, pound cake, and baklava.

# ACCOMMODATIONS

Raleigh is still catching up to other North Carolina cities when it comes to small non-chain hotels. There are dozens of chain motels around the city, concentrated near the airport and downtown, and at various exits off I-40 and U.S. 70.

Some of Raleigh's notable bed-and-breakfasts have fallen victim to the Airbnb trend and gone out of business. One great stay in downtown Raleigh, however, is going strong. **The Hargett Bed and Breakfast** (1200 E. Hargett St., 919/588-3233, thehargett.com, from $99), while in a fairly undistinctive building, is notable for its three great rooms, very friendly service, excellent food, and a very central location.

If you don't need to stay inside the city limits and are craving some pampering, ★ **Umstead Luxury Hotel and Spa** (100 Woodland Pond, Cary, 866/877-4141, www.theumstead.com, from $299) in Cary shouldn't be missed. The Umstead's 14,000-square-foot spa has an incredible menu of services: 10 different specialized massages; many facial, manicure, and pedicure choices; milk, mineral, and aromatherapy baths; and a long list of body therapies and Asian body-care rituals. There's also a three-acre lake on the property, a 24-hour fitness center, and an outdoor heated pool. Guests have tee privileges at the Prestonwood Country Club, about 10 minutes away.

## INFORMATION AND SERVICES

The main hospital in Raleigh is **WakeMed** (3000 New Bern Ave., 919/350-8900), though Rex Healthcare and Duke Health also operate hospitals here. If you have an emergency, call 911 and let the EMTs decide which one is closest. There is at least one 24-hour pharmacy, **CVS** (3914 Capital Blvd., 919/876-5600).

Visitor information can be found at the **Greater Raleigh Convention and Visitors Bureau** (Bank of America Plaza, 421 Fayetteville St., 800/849-8499, www.visitraleigh.com), at the **Capital Area Visitor Information Desk** in the lobby of the Museum of History (5 E. Edenton St., 866/724-8687), the **Greater Raleigh Chamber of Commerce** (800 S. Salisbury St., 919/664-7000, www.raleighchamber.org), and the state **Department of Tourism** (301 N. Wilmington St., 1st Fl., 800/847-4862, www.visitnc.com).

For international travelers, Raleigh-Durham International Airport contains **Travelex** (919/840-0366, Terminal A daily 7am-8pm, Terminal C daily 2:30pm-6pm) outlets.

## GETTING THERE AND AROUND

I-40 and U.S. 70 are the main highways to and through town. The Raleigh Beltline, I-440, forms a loop around the city, with I-40, U.S. 70, and U.S. 64 radiating outward. I-40 is the quickest route to Chapel Hill, to the west, and east to I-95. I-40 and U.S. 70 are both good routes to Durham. U.S. 64 goes to Wilson, and on the other side of the city joins with U.S. 1 headed southeast toward Sanford and the Sandhills.

**Raleigh-Durham International Airport** (RDU, 2400 John Brantley Blvd, Morrisville, 919/840-2123, www.rdu.com) is one of the main airports in North Carolina, and the primary airport in the Triangle. It's located 15 minutes from Raleigh off I-40, and is a hub for major national airlines. There is a Raleigh **Amtrak Station** (320 W. Cabarrus St., 800/872-7245, www.amtrak.com) and a station in Cary (211 N. Academy St.).

Raleigh's **CAT System** (Capital Area Transit, 919/485-7433, www.gotriangle.org) runs buses all over the city, both inside and outside the Beltline, and links readily to other major transportation hubs. Many taxi and driver services are available, including **Yellow Cab** (919/875-1821), **Alliance Concierge** (919/815-6953), and **Blue Diamond Limousines and Sedans** (919/772-9595).

# Durham

Home of Duke University and North Carolina Central University (NCCU), Durham is an exciting place. Major arts festivals bring tens of thousands of visitors to Durham every year. Duke University's famous Blue Devils are one of the nation's dominant basketball teams, and NCCU's Eagles are a football powerhouse. There's a great deal of literary activity too, with one of the best selections of bookstores in the region.

## DUKE UNIVERSITY

Duke is often thought of as a sort of Southern Ivy League school, though much of its student body is actually from outside the region. The architecture of the Duke campus is done up in dark Gothic stonework, and it feels like a cross between Hogwarts and Oxford University in England.

Originally called Trinity College and located in Randolph County, it came to Durham and became Duke University under the

# Durham

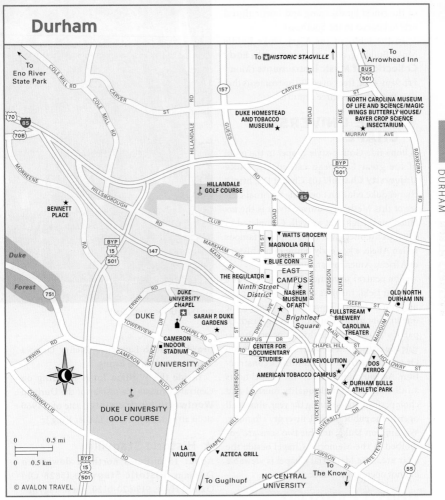

auspices of the Duke family, tobacco barons who were also responsible for the university's early policy of admitting women as students.

Duke's **Center for Documentary Studies** (1317 W. Pettigrew St., 919/660-3663, http://documentarystudies.duke.edu, gallery Mon.-Thurs. 9am-9pm, Fri. 9am-7pm, Sat. 9am-5pm) is an invaluable resource for artists, documentarians, and educators throughout the region as well as a fascinating place to visit.

**The Nasher Museum of Art** (2001 Campus Dr., 919/684-5135, www.nasher. duke.edu, Tues.-Wed. and Fri.-Sat. 10am-5pm, Thurs. 10am-9pm, Sun. noon-5pm, $5 adults, $4 seniors, $3 students, free under age 16) is home to extensive collections of ancient and medieval art, including one of the largest collections of pre-Columbian Latin American art in the United States. Adjoining the grounds of the Nasher are the **Sarah P. Duke Gardens** (919/684-3698, www.hr.duke.edu/dukegardens, daily 8am-dusk, free), 55 acres of some of the finest landscaping and horticultural arts to be seen in the Southeast.

In the lobby of the Mary Duke Biddle Music Building, on East Campus, is the **Eddy Collection of Music Instruments** (Mon.-Fri. 9am-4pm, free), over 500 instruments that date from the last three centuries.

# ★ DUKE UNIVERSITY CHAPEL

A bona fide Gothic-style chapel in the mold of the great European cathedrals, **Duke University Chapel** (401 Chapel Dr., http://chapel.duke.edu) isn't only the spiritual center of this Methodist university, it is the architectural highlight as well. Completed in 1932, its architect was Philadelphia's famous Julian Abele, a key early figure in the history of African American architects.

The central nave, nearly the length of a football field, inspires awe as you enter the building. The Bell Tower is modeled on the one in Canterbury Cathedral in England. Of particular note are the three pipe organs inside the chapel, one of which, the McClendon Organ, dates from the building's construction. As you might expect, the chapel hosts a full calendar of high-quality musical and choir performances during the year, almost all open to the public. Duke University's founder, Washington Duke, and his two sons are entombed in the Memorial Chapel beside the altar area; the Memorial Chapel is viewable but not open to the public.

# NORTH CAROLINA CENTRAL UNIVERSITY

NCCU was founded in 1910, the first public liberal arts college for African Americans in the United States. The **North Carolina Central University Art Museum** (NCCU campus, Lawson St. between Fine Arts Bldg. and Music Bldg., 919/530-6211, www.nccu.edu/artmuseum, Tues.-Fri. 9am-4:30pm, Sun. 2pm-5pm, free) specializes in the work of 19th- and 20th-century African American artists. The collections include work by such prominent and varied masters as Romare

the Duke University Chapel

Bearden, Jacob Lawrence, Henry Ossawa Tanner, and Minnie Evans.

Inside the William Jones Building on Central's campus is a display of the Durham **Woolworth lunch counter,** site of a 1960 sit-in attended by Martin Luther King Jr.

# ★ Historic Stagville

About 15 minutes north of downtown Durham, **Historic Stagville** (5828 Old Oxford Hwy., 919/620-0120, www.stagville.org, Tues.-Sat. 10am-5pm, tours 11am, 1pm, 3pm) preserves part of what was a staggeringly large plantation system. The Cameron-Bennehan family's holdings totaled nearly 30,000 acres in 1860, and the 900 enslaved African Americans who worked the land made up one of the South's largest enslaved communities. Historic Stagville includes 71 acres of the original plantations, with several notable vernacular structures that include two-story timber-frame slave quarters, a massive hipped-roof barn built in 1860, and the late 18th-century Bennehan plantation house.

## OTHER SIGHTS

A different side of 19th-century Durham life is presented at the **Duke Homestead and Tobacco Museum** (2828 Duke Homestead Rd., 919/477-5498, www.dukehomestead.nchistoricsites.org, Tues.-Sat. 9am-5pm, free), where the patriarch of Durham's tobacco industry, Washington Duke, began his career as a humble tobacco farmer. This was the start of North Carolina's rise to the top of the world tobacco market.

**Bennett Place** (4409 Bennett Memorial Rd., 919/383-4345, www.bennettplace.nchistoricsites.org, Tues.-Sat. 9am-5pm, free) is a historic site that commemorates the meeting of Confederate general Joseph Johnston and Union general William Tecumseh Sherman in April 1865. In the last days of the Civil War, when Confederate president Jefferson Davis was fleeing south to Georgia and Abraham Lincoln was dead, Johnston and Sherman had a series of negotiations here that led to the surrender of all the Confederate forces in the Carolinas, Georgia, and Florida.

The **North Carolina Museum of Life and Science** (433 Murray Ave., 919/220-5429, www.ncmls.org, Tues.-Sat. 10am-5pm, Sun. noon-5pm, $16 adults, $14 over age 64 and active military, $11 ages 3-12), home of the Magic Wings Butterfly House and Bayer Crop Science Insectarium, is the perfect place for children who enjoy meeting strange bugs, climbing inside tornadoes, and taking a trip on a locomotive to see red wolves.

## ENTERTAINMENT AND EVENTS

### American Tobacco Campus

**American Tobacco Campus** (318 Blackwell St., 919/433-1566, www.americantobaccocampus.com) is a wonderfully unique renovation and adaptive reuse of the sprawling old Lucky Strike plant in downtown Durham, once the largest cigarette factory in the world. Begun by Washington Duke—who later founded Duke University—American Tobacco was one of the 12 founding companies on the Dow Jones Industrial Average. Today it is the acknowledged entertainment district of Durham, in no small part due to the contiguous location of the ballpark where the Durham Bulls minor-league team plays. On the campus you'll find more than a dozen restaurants, bars, and shops, and even the headquarters of Burt's Bees, in addition to various startup firms.

### Full Frame Documentary Festival

April brings the **Full Frame Documentary Festival** (919/687-4100, www.fullframefest.org), which, before it had celebrated its 10th year, had already been identified by the *New York Times* as the premier documentary film festival in the United States. Venues throughout downtown host screenings, workshops, panels, and soirees, where documentary fans and aspiring filmmakers can mingle with the glitterati of the genre.

the American Tobacco Campus

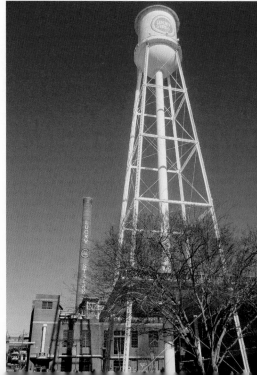

## Other Festivals

The **Grady Tate Jazz Festival** (www.nccu. edu) takes place in April at North Carolina Central University. North Carolina was home to such jazz legends as Thelonious Monk and John Coltrane, and Central has a widely respected jazz program, so it's only fitting that Durham should host this prestigious event.

For six weeks every summer, Durham is the site of the **American Dance Festival** (919/684-6402, www.americandancefestival. org), an internationally known event where the world's best choreographers often premiere new work. Durhamites and the visitors who come from around the world to ADF are one step ahead of the audiences in New York.

One of the region's most popular music festivals is the **Festival for the Eno** (www. enoriver.org), which takes place every Fourth of July weekend. The festival is held on the banks of the Eno River, so you can listen to the performances from the comfort of your inner tube while floating on the river.

August's **North Carolina Gay and Lesbian Film Festival** (ncglff.org) is the second-largest such event in the Southeast. Approximately 10,000 visitors attend the festival every year to watch new work by up-and-coming LGBT filmmakers at Durham's Carolina Theater.

## Nightlife

A unique and popular performance venue and party spot is **Motorco Music Hall** (723 Rigsbee Ave., www.motorcomusic.com), set in a repurposed car sales shop. They host a wide range of all-ages musical acts in "The Showroom" and have a great craft beer selection in their contiguous tavern area, the Garage Bar, and in their dining space, Parts & Labor (get it?).

Bingo parlors dot the landscape, but Durham is one of the few places where you can be part of the craze that is **Drag Bingo** (www.dragbingo.com, $15 in advance, $17 at the door). Once a month, tickets go on sale—and sell out fast—for a bingo event to benefit

area HIV/AIDS services. It's an incredibly fun scene—a mixture of gay and straight, folks in drag and in their usual attire, covetable prizes, a little bit of raunchy humor, and a lot of money going to a great cause.

# SPORTS AND RECREATION

## Hiking, Biking, and Water Sports

Durham is loaded with choices for hikers, joggers, and cyclists. The Eno River is surrounded by thousands of acres of parkland, much of which is marked for hiking. **Eno River State Park** (6101 Cole Mill. Rd., 919/383-1686, http://ncparks.gov, May-Aug. 8am-9pm, Mar.-Apr. and Sept.-Oct. 8am-8pm, Nov.-Feb. 8am-6pm, free), northwest of Durham, offers hiking, canoeing (Class I-III rapids), and camping ($13) in the beautiful and wild river valley. See the Eno River Association website (www.enoriver.org) for information on more places and ways to enjoy the river. **Frog Hollow Canoe and Kayak** (919/949-4315, www.froghollowoutdoors. com, Wed.-Fri. 10am-6pm, Sat.-Sun. 9am-6:30pm, by reservation only) rents boats and guides tours. During the warm months, you have the leisurely option of **Wafting the Eno** (919/471-3802, www.wafter.org, $12, reservations required). These guided float trips take off from West Point Park daily at 10am and 3:30pm, and at 9pm when there's a full moon.

## Spectator Sports

Thanks to the exploits of a demon and a smoke-snorting steer, Durham is probably even better known for its sports tradition than its history as a tobacco dynamo. The National Collegiate Athletic Association (NCAA) Division I **Duke Blue Devils** embody the gold standard in college basketball, and excel in many other sports. Their history is chronicled in the **Duke Sports Hall of Fame** (Towerview Rd., 919/613-7500), inside Cameron Indoor Stadium. Coach Mike Krzyzewski—that's pronounced "shuh-SHEV-skee," but you can call him Coach K—has shepherded the men's basketball team since 1980, leading them to a phenomenal number of championships.

Duke students are famous for living in tents for months on end outside Cameron Indoor Stadium, waiting first to buy tickets and then to snag good standing-room spots in the courtside student section of the arena. If you're on campus in season, take a look at their tent city, known as Krzyzewskiville.

The **Durham Bulls** (Durham Bulls Athletic Park, 409 Blackwell St., 919/956-2855, www.durhambulls.com)—yes, of *Bull Durham* fame—are one of the nation's most recognizable minor-league baseball teams. They are the Triple-A farm team for the Tampa Bay Rays, so you're likely to see big-league players rehabbing from injury and rookies on the brink of making it big. The spacious ballpark, designed by the architect who built Baltimore's Camden Yards, is comfortable and fun and ringed with food and beverage purveyors. A big wooden bull peers down from the end of the third-base line, and when a Bull hits a homer, the bull's eyes light up red, his tail flaps, and smoke billows from his nostrils.

# FOOD
## Eclectic American

★ **Watts Grocery** (1116 Broad St., 919/416-5040, www.wattsgrocery.com, $14-20), located in the Watts neighborhood of Durham, near the Duke campus, is the restaurant of Amy Tornquist, a master Southern chef. Tornquist makes use of locally grown produce in season, North Carolina seafood, and local artisanal cheeses. The menu features many gourmet variations on classic North Carolina dishes and is bound to please any fan of Southern food.

The ★ **Cosmic Cantina** (1920 Perry St., 919/286-1875, Mon. noon-4am, Tues.-Fri. 11am-3am, Sat. noon-4am, Sun. noon-midnight, under $10), a casual take-out-or-seat-yourself joint in the middle of the 9th Street neighborhood by the Duke campus, serves the best burritos you'll find just about anywhere.

The award-winning restaurant **Nana's** (2514 University Dr., 919/493-8545, www.nanasdurham.com, Mon.-Sat. 5:30pm-10pm, $18-30) is presided over by chef Scott Howell, a North Carolina native. The fare is hearty but elegant, and the wine list has won *Wine Spectator*'s Award of Excellence.

The Durham Bulls play downtown.

## Asian

The ★ **Thai Café** (2501 University Dr., 919/493-9794, www.thaicafenc.com, Mon.-Thurs. 11:30am-3pm and 5pm-10pm, Fri. 11:30am-3pm and 5pm-11pm, Sat. noon-11pm, Sun. noon-10pm, $10-20) is the sort of restaurant whose regulars might visit a dozen times before they'll try a second item on the menu, because whatever they tried on that first visit was so good they've been craving it ever since. The Thai Café serves all of the classic Thai restaurant dishes like pad thai, tom yum, and pad prik—all delicious—but the real masterpieces are the curries. You can choose between yellow, green, panang, and massaman with meat, seafood, tofu, or vegetables.

## Latin American

A star of Durham's food scene is **Dos Perros** (200 N. Mangum St., 919/956-2750, http://dosperrosrestaurant.com, breakfast Mon.-Fri. 7:30am-10:30am, lunch Mon.-Fri. 11:30am-2:30pm, dinner Mon.-Sat. 5pm-10:30pm, entrées $10-18), located in the heart of downtown. Try the pork roasted in banana leaves or the spice-rubbed grouper. There are also good vegetarian entrées. **Cuban Revolution** (318 Blackwell St., 919/687-4300, www.thecubanrevolution.com, Sun.-Thurs. 11am-midnight, Fri.-Sat. 11am-2am, entrées $10-16) is decorated with portraits of revolutionaries and trappings of circa-1959 Cuba. It serves classic Cuban dishes like *ropa vieja* and Cuban sandwiches as well as new inventions like the shrimp and maduro kebab. **Blue Corn** (716 9th St., 919/286-9600, www.bluecorncafedurham.com, Mon.-Thurs. 11:30am-9pm, Fri.-Sat. 11:30am-9:30pm, $12-15) is an award-winning pan-Latin restaurant. The menu includes Mexican favorites like fajitas and quesadillas, Cuban specialties like picadillo, and plenty of vegetarian choices.

Durham is bursting with wonderful Latin American restaurants and taco stands, more every year as the number of Latin American residents in the area swells. A local favorite is ★ **La Vaquita** (2700 Chapel Hill Rd.,

919/402-0209, http://lavaquitanc.com, daily 10am-9:30pm, $5-10), a little building with an outdoor walk-up counter and a huge fiberglass cow on the roof. It's very authentic Mexican cuisine, with many kinds of tacos, stews, tamales, ribs, *barbacoa,* and lots more.

## European

Best known as a bakery and patisserie, **Guglhupf** (2706 Durham-Chapel Hill Blvd., 919/401-2600, www.guglhupf.com, breakfast Tues.-Fri. 8am-11am, lunch Tues.-Fri. 11am-4:30pm, dinner Tues.-Thurs. 5:30pm-9:30pm, Fri.-Sat. 5:30pm-10pm, brunch Sat. 8am-4:30pm, Sun. 9am-3pm, dessert Sun. 3pm-5pm, $10-20) is also a wonderful café. Guglhupf's founder is from southern Germany, and the menu is based on that cuisine, with forays into other continental and American styles. Even if you don't have time for a full sit-down meal, do stop in here for

---

# Carolina Breads

The following catalog of Tar Heel taste in baked goods appeared in the 1955 *North Carolina Guide.*

> Outside of baker's bread, Tar Heels like (in an ascending scale from plain to fancy) cornbread, ashcakes, hoecakes, johnnycakes, cracklin' bread, potato bread, soda biscuits, buttermilk biscuits, rolls, muffins, popovers that pop, buckwheat cakes, eggbread or batterbread (called "spoonbread" in Virginia), bland Sally Lunn and flaky beaten biscuits; the last two are company bread.

The 1955 list should be updated for the 21st century's multiethnic and multinational culinary culture in North Carolina to include tortillas (there are dozens of *tortillerías* around the state), *papadum,* roti, chapati, naan, baguettes, madeleines, biscotti, pita, bagels, challah, matzo, and *banh mi.*

dessert, or to pick up a pastry or artisanal bread for the road.

## ACCOMMODATIONS

The most upscale place to stay in Durham is the **Washington Duke Inn and Golf Club** (3001 Cameron Blvd., 800/443-3853, www. washingtondukeinn.com, from $130). Located on the grounds of the Duke University Golf Course, on the Duke campus, the guest rooms and suites are sunny and plush, with the option of bunk beds for families traveling with kids. Babysitting services can be arranged by the concierge. Also convenient to the Duke campus, the **University Inn** (502 Elf St., 919/286-3817 or 800/313-3585, www.universityinnduke.com, from $70) is a basic motel, a good value in a good location.

Durham's most celebrated bed-and-breakfast is the ★ **Arrowhead Inn** (106 Mason Rd., 800/528-2207, http://arrowheadinn.com, from $135), a AAA Four Diamond awardee on a Revolution-era plantation about 15 minutes from downtown. All of the very luxurious guest rooms have their own fireplaces, and several have two-person whirlpools. On the inn's grounds are a garden cottage with a whirlpool and two-person steam shower, and a rather fabulous log cabin with a sleeping loft and spa-like bath appointments.

The **Old North Durham Inn** (922 N. Mangum St., 919/683-1885, www.bbonline. com, from $125) is a pretty house on one of the old primary roads in the city. It's been cited by the Durham Historic Preservation Society for its excellent renovation. Guests receive free tickets to Durham Bulls games, and can look out their bedroom windows across the street at the home where much of *Bull Durham* was filmed.

## INFORMATION AND SERVICES

**Duke University Medical Center** (2301 Erwin Rd., 919/416-3853) is the main hospital in Durham. **Durham Regional Hospital** (3643 N. Roxboro Rd., 919/470-4000) is also operated by Duke Health Systems. **Walgreens** (6405 Fayetteville St., 919/544-6430) has a 24-hour pharmacy.

Information for travelers is available from the **Durham Convention and Visitors Bureau** (101 E. Morgan St., 800/446-8604, www.durham-nc.com). The *Durham Herald-Sun* is the primary Durham-specific newspaper, though many people also read the Raleigh *News & Observer.* The *Independent* is a popular weekly cultural newspaper, available free throughout the region.

## GETTING THERE AND AROUND

Information about the Triangle's extensive network of **buses and shuttles** can be found at www.ridetta.org. **Raleigh-Durham International Airport** (RDU, 2400 John Brantley Blvd, Morrisville, 919/840-2123, www.rdu.com) is 10-20 minutes from Durham, reachable by an easy cab or shuttle ride. **Amtrak** (400 W. Chapel Hill St., 800/872-7245, www.amtrak.com, daily 7am-9pm) has direct service to Durham on the *Carolinian* line, pulling in to the station in the heart of downtown.

# Chapel Hill and Vicinity

The third corner of the Triangle is occupied by Chapel Hill. The University of North Carolina, the nation's oldest chartered state university, is the heart of the town and boasts many charming buildings on its historic campus. But the approximately 50,000 permanent residents, many of them former UNC students who grew so attached to Chapel Hill that they decided to stay, maintain a stimulating community in which the arts thrive.

The Chapel Hill area is the epicenter of progressive politics in North Carolina, most intensely concentrated in the emphatically left-wing little nearby town of Carrboro, which is so closely linked to Chapel Hill—it's difficult to tell exactly which block of Franklin Street and Main Street demarcates

their respective city limits—that they're often treated as if they were one town.

## SIGHTS
### University of North Carolina

The University of North Carolina campus, which dates to 1789, is made up of a couple of beautiful quads surrounded by many outlying complexes. Massive poplar trees on the quads make the campus an indulgently shady hideaway. Elegantly unpretentious Federal-style buildings were dorms and classrooms for 18th- and 19th-century scholars, and they're home to undergraduates today. Guided tours of the historic sites on campus depart from the **UNC Visitors Center** (250 E. Franklin St., 919/962-1630, www.unc.edu) Monday-Friday

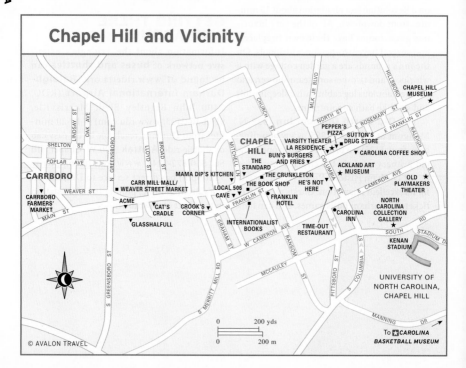

at 1:30pm. You can also pick up a brochure and walk through campus at your own pace.

The 1851 Old Playmakers Theater, at East Cameron Avenue in the middle of campus, was built by Alexander Jackson Davis, originally intended as a library and ballroom. In the 1920s the university converted the building to a theater.

At **Kenan Football Stadium** (Bell Tower Dr., off South Rd., 919/966-2575, www.tarheelblue.com), the **Charlie Justice Hall of Honors** chronicles the doughty deeds of UNC's football program. It's open Monday-Friday 8am-5pm and for three hours on home game days until half an hour before kickoff.

The **Ackland Art Museum** (919/966-5736, www.ackland.org, Wed.-Sat. 10am-5pm, Sun. 1pm-5pm, free), at the heart of the UNC campus near the intersection of Franklin and Columbia Streets, has a very special collection of European sculpture and painting spanning centuries, and an acclaimed collection of Asian art. The **North Carolina Collection Gallery** (919/962-1172, www.lib.unc.edu, Mon.-Fri. 9am-5pm, Sat. 9am-1pm, Sun. 1pm-5pm, free), on the ground floor of Wilson Library, is a cozy museum that will capture the fancy of any Southern history enthusiast.

## ★ Carolina Basketball Museum

While on campus, visit the **Carolina Basketball Museum** (Ernie Williamson Athletic Center, 450 Skipper Bowles Dr., www.tarheelblue.com, Mon.-Fri. 10am-4pm, closes 1 hour before weekday games, opens 3.5 hours before and closes 1 hour before weekend games, free). This multimillion-dollar 8,000-square-foot hagiological shrine holds mementos from a century of Carolina basketball. On a reproduction of the Heels' court, footprints and even players' actual shoes mark the spots from which some of the program's most memorable baskets were launched. There's a lot of video and interactive content, but the item most likely to please the Tar Heel faithful, and inspire hoots of derision, is a letter from Duke coach Mike Krzyzewski to a high school player from Wilmington, expressing his regret that the young man had chosen to attend UNC rather than Duke. The addressee was famed basketball player Michael Jordan.

## Other Museums

Across Franklin Street from the main quad is **Kidzu** (105 E. Franklin St., 919/933-1455,

on the UNC campus

www.kidzuchildrensmuseum.org, Tues.-Sat. 10am-5pm, Sun. 1pm-5pm, $5), a children's museum that features imaginative interactive exhibits for kids to explore, as well as a fun gift shop.

## Nostalgic College Spots

Every college town has a few emblematic hangouts—joints that would seem like no great shakes to the uninitiated, but that to generations of alumni are charged with nostalgia. At UNC, these icons are the **Carolina Coffee Shop** (138 E. Franklin St., 919/942-6875, Tues.-Thurs. 11am-9pm, Fri. 11am-10pm, Sat. 9am-10pm, Sun. 9am-2pm) and **Sutton's Drug Store** (159 E. Franklin St., 919/942-5161). The Carolina Coffee Shop, a dark, soporific retreat, has been the site of thousands of first dates over the last 90 years. It's a place to have an afternoon breakfast if you've been up studying all night, or to inhale a sandwich before heading across Franklin to a movie at the Varsity Theater. At night, the liquor license kicks in and it becomes a busy bar. Across the street is Sutton's Drug Store, a good place to catch a glimpse of members of the basketball team, who often stop here between classes.

## Weaver Street Market

**Weaver Street Market** (WSM, 101 E. Weaver St., 919/929-0010, www.weaverstreetmarket.coop, Mon.-Fri. 7:30am-9pm, Sat.-Sun. 8am-9pm) is the community hub of the politically liberal, artistically active, and often quite eccentric residents of Carrboro. WSM is an organic foods co-op with a small eating area—it's too plain to be called a café—inside and on the front lawn.

# ENTERTAINMENT AND EVENTS
## Movies

Like a good college town should, Chapel Hill has several movie theaters, including small theaters that show independent films. The **Varsity Theater** (123 E. Franklin St., 919/967-8665) is on the edge of campus, and the **Chelsea** (1129 Weaver Dairy Rd., 919/968-3005) and the **Movies at Timberlyne** (120 Banks Dr., 919/933-8600) are in the Timberlyne shopping center, up Highway 86 (Columbia Rd./Martin Luther King Jr. Dr.). The **Lumina Theater** (620 Market St., 919/932-9000, www.thelumina.com) is located in Southern Village, a development south of Chapel Hill on U.S. 15/501. The Lumina screens movies outdoors on summer evenings.

## Nightlife
### LIVE MUSIC

Chapel Hill-Carrboro is one of the best places in the Southeast to hear live music, and several small top-notch clubs here are legendary venues where major artists not only get their starts but return to again and again. The best known is probably the **Cat's Cradle** (300 E. Main St., Carrboro, 919/967-9053, www.catscradle.com). The artists who play the Cat's Cradle are leading lights in rock and roll, Americana, alt-country, and world music, and the audiences come to hear the music, not to play pool and shoot the breeze. Shows sell out quickly, so check the website. **Local 506** (506 W. Franklin St., Chapel Hill, 919/942-5506, www.local506.com) and the **Cave** (452½ W. Franklin St., Chapel Hill, 919/968-9308, http://caverntavern.com, no advance tickets) are also important local venues, tending more toward pop, rock, and punk. Note that to attend shows at Local 506, you must first join the club; membership is only $3, but it has to be arranged at least three days in advance.

### BEER AND WINE BARS

You have other options if you want to go out for a drink but haven't planned your barhopping three days in advance. The **West End Wine Bar** (450 W. Franklin St., Chapel Hill, 919/967-7599, www.westendwinebar.com, daily 5pm-2am) has a great rooftop patio, over 100 by-the-glass wines, and lots of "boutique beers." **He's Not Here** (112½ W. Franklin St., Chapel Hill, 919/942-7939, daily 1pm-2am) has been a hot spot since 1975. There's good live rock and roll with a low cover charge.

# SHOPPING
## Malls and Shopping Districts

**University Mall** (Estes Dr. between Franklin St. and Fordham Blvd./U.S. 15/501) is gradually evolving from a small 1970s-style mall to a collection of fancy boutiques and commercial art galleries. There are still a few fast-food counters and a discount shoe outlet or two, but these shops are being replaced by upscale jewelry and lingerie stores. Stop in at **Cameron's** (919/942-5554, www.camerons-gallery.com) for pretty one-of-a-kind jewelry and funky stationery, as well as sushi-shaped wind-up toys, librarian action figures, and other comical doodads. University Mall is anchored at its southern terminus by **A Southern Season** (800/253-3663, www.southernseason.com, Mon.-Fri. 10am-9pm, Sun. 11am-6pm), probably the region's most famous specialty foods retailer. With a strong emphasis on local and regional delicacies, Southern Season has a spectacular variety of gourmet foods and fine cookware.

## Books

Along Franklin Street, which becomes Carrboro's Main Street a few blocks west of campus, you'll find the usual college-town mix of textbook-exchanges, all-night convenience stores, and purveyors of sustainably crafted fair-trade bongs. There are also a handful of chichi women's clothing shops, trendy vintage-wear boutiques, and some great bookstores. Among the best in this last category is **The Book Shop** (400 W. Franklin St., 919/942-5178, www.bookshop-inc.com, Mon.-Fri. 11am-9pm, Sat. 11am-6pm, Sun. 1pm-5pm), a wonderful used and rare book dealer, where you can find a $5 paperback classic or a $1,000 rare first edition. **Internationalist Books** (405 W. Franklin St., 919/942-1740, www.internationalist-books.org, Mon.-Sat. 11am-8pm, Sun. 11am-6pm) is the area's best-known source for far-left-of-center political and philosophical literature and a hangout for progressive activists. **Nice Price Books** (100 Boyd St., Carrboro, 919/929-6222) sells good second-hand books and music, including a robust selection of used vinyl.

# SPORTS AND RECREATION
## Botanical Gardens

UNC's **North Carolina Botanical Garden** (Old Mason Farm Rd., off U.S. 15/501/Hwy. 54, 919/962-0522, www.ncbg.unc.edu, Mon.-Fri. 8am-5pm, Sat. 9am-5pm, Sun. 1pm-5pm, free) is the Southeast's largest botanical garden. The 800 acres contain beautiful hiking trails, an herb garden, an aquatic plant area, and a carnivorous plant garden. Back on campus, **Coker Arboretum** (E. Cameron St. and Raleigh St., daily dawn-dusk) is much smaller, but it's also a beautiful retreat. The five landscaped acres are most beautiful in springtime, when students will make detours on their way to class just to pass through the amazing 300-foot-long arbor of purple wisteria.

## Spectator Sports

**Tar Heel athletics** (www.tarheelblue.com) are well loved in Chapel Hill. The pinnacle of UNC sports is the men's basketball team—seven-time NCAA champions, coached for many years by the legendary Dean Smith and now by fellow Hall of Famer Roy Williams, and college home court to Michael Jordan, James Worthy, and a dizzying number of other all-time greats. The men play at the Dean E. Smith Center, a great glowing dome that seats more than 20,000. Carolina women's basketball is also of the highest caliber; the Tar Heel women play at historic Carmichael Auditorium in the heart of campus. (When the women play Duke at home, their biggest game of the year, they move over to the much larger Smith Center.) The football team's home field is the 1927 Kenan Stadium. The baseball team plays at Boshamer Stadium, which, like the Smith Center and Kenan Stadium, is off Manning Drive in the southern part of campus, in the area of the medical school. UNC excels in many other sports—soccer (Mia Hamm is an alumna), golf (Davis Love III), and track (Marion Jones), among others.

Acquiring tickets to UNC athletic events ranges from impossible to quite easy, with men's basketball tickets at the most precious end of the spectrum, followed by football and women's basketball. For all other tickets, try your luck with the main ticket office (800/722-4335, www.tarheelblue.com). Craigslist (www.craigslist.org) and eBay (www.ebay.com) are often reliable sources as well.

# FOOD

## Southern and Soul

★ **Crook's Corner** (610 W. Franklin St., 919/929-7643, www.crookscorner.com, dinner Tues.-Sun. 5:30pm, brunch Sun. 10:30am-2pm, $15-20) is one of the most influential restaurants in the South. It was the late Bill Eliot, its first chef, who put this restaurant on the culinary map with, among other brilliant creations, his now world-famous shrimp and grits recipe. Now led by chef Bill Smith, a native Tar Heel whose simple yet exquisite recipes include watermelon and tomato salad, honeysuckle sorbet, and some of the best fried green tomatoes you'll ever find, Crook's Corner continues to be a great innovator in Southern cuisine.

Just a few blocks from Crook's Corner is another legendary Carolina chef's restaurant, **Mama Dip's Kitchen** (408 W. Rosemary St., 919/942-5837, www.mamadips.com, Mon.-Sat. 8am-9:30pm, Sun. 8am-9pm, $10-12). Proprietress Mildred Council, "Mama Dip" herself, has been cooking since she was nine years old, and if you grew up in the South, you'll recognize at first bite the comfort-food recipes of a Southern matriarch. Dip's is known for its good fried chicken and for its vegetables.

## Eclectic American

**La Residence** (202 W. Rosemary St., 919/967-2506, www.laresidencedining.com, Tues.-Sun. 6pm-9:30pm, late menu and bar daily 9:30pm-2am, $20-25) has been a Chapel Hill favorite, though in different locations, for nearly 35 years. La Residence has an elegant continental-inspired menu created by chef Stephen Amos and delicious desserts by pastry chef Jill Lazarus.

Carrboro's **Glasshalfull** (106 S. Greensboro St., Carrboro, 919/967-9784, http://glasshalfullcarrboro.com, lunch Mon.-Fri. 11:30am-2:30pm, dinner Mon.-Sat. 5pm-10pm, late menu Fri.-Sat. after 10pm, $10-30) is equal parts restaurant and wine bar. The menu of contemporary American fare makes use of local ingredients and offers vegetarians plenty of good choices.

## Barbecue

If Chapel Hill's vegan/fusion vibe isn't what you want and smoked meat is what you crave, head to **Allen & Son BBQ** (6203 Millhouse Rd., 919/942-7576, Wed. 10am-4pm, Thurs.-Sat. 10am-8pm, around $15), whose handiwork is graced with the classic eastern North Carolina vinegar-based sauce and accompanied by some incredible hush puppies.

## Asian

**Lantern** (423 W. Franklin St., 919/969-8846, http://lanternrestaurant.com, Mon.-Sat. 5:30pm-10pm, bar Mon.-Sat. until 2am, $15-25) was named one of America's top 50 restaurants by *Gourmet Magazine*. The pan-Asian menu draws from fresh locally raised meats and North Carolina-caught seafood. The meals may be exotic, but the ingredients are down-home.

## Local Fare

The **Carrboro Farmers' Market** (301 W. Main St., http://carrborofarmersmarket.com, Sat. 7am-noon, Wed. 3:30pm-6:30pm) is a bustling, festive scene. The market features local organic produce in abundance as well as gorgeous cut flowers, artisanal cheeses, and charmingly cuckoo lawn art.

The Chapel Hill area is blessed with a local dairy, which supplies residents not only with old-fashioned bottled milk but with fantastic ice cream. To sample Mapleview Ice Cream, you have two choices beyond the freezer aisle of the grocery store. At the Carrboro **Mapleview Store** (100 E. Weaver St., 919/967-6842), you can pick up a cone or cup to eat while you listen to one of the free concerts on the lawn of Weaver Street Market, across the street. Alternatively, you might choose to make the scenic drive to the home store (3111 Dairyland Rd., 919/933-3600, www.mapleviewfarm.com, daily noon-10pm), out in the country toward Hillsborough.

## ACCOMMODATIONS
### Under $150

Chapel Hill's hotel infrastructure is well managed and affordable for the most part and there are plenty of options. My go-to choices are the adjacent properties of **Hampton Inn** (6121 Farrington Rd., 919/403-8700, www.hamptoninn.com) and **Holiday Inn Express** (6119 Farrington Rd., 919/489-7555, www.ihg.com), both very clean, well-run properties a short drive from downtown Chapel Hill.

### $150-300

One of the favorite inns in the state, the ★ **Carolina Inn** (211 Pittsboro St., 800/962-8519, www.carolinainn.com, from $180) has been a landmark on the UNC campus since it first opened in 1924. It's the place where visiting dignitaries are hosted, where the most important faculty functions take place, where lucky couples get married, and where old alumni couples celebrate their milestone anniversaries. The Carolina Inn is located at the center of the UNC campus and not far from the Dean Smith Center. Any special occasion related to the university will book the Carolina Inn far in advance—homecoming weekends, for example, and big basketball and football games. The inn's restaurant, **Carolina CrossRoads** (919/918-2735, $20-30), serves three elegant meals a day, created by chef Jimmy Reale, a believer in creative cuisine from local ingredients. Afternoon tea (Mon.-Sat. 3pm, $18-28) at the Carolina Inn is a popular treat in Chapel Hill; reservations are recommended.

The **Franklin Hotel** (311 W. Franklin St., 866/831-5999, www.franklinhotelnc.com, from $200) is a boutique hotel with a great location on Franklin Street near where Chapel Hill and Carrboro blend together. The furnishings are elegant and the beds extremely comfortable. Guest rooms have great modern touches like flat-screen TVs and iPod docks.

the historic Carolina Inn

The ★ **Inn at Bingham School** (Hwy. 54 and Mebane Oaks Rd., near Saxapahaw, 800/566-5583, www.chapel-hill-inn.com, rooms $150, cottage $195) is a 200-year-old home, originally the residence of the headmaster of the preparatory academy that operated here in the 18th and 19th centuries. The house sits in a region of sweeping countryside, near the little town of Saxapahaw, about 20 minutes outside Chapel Hill.

## GETTING THERE AND AROUND

Chapel Hill can be reached via the major highways, I-40 and I-85, as well as by U.S. 15/501, from Durham to the east and Pittsboro to the southwest.

# Winston-Salem

The village of Salem was established in the mid-18th century by the Unitas Fratrum, better known as the Moravians, a community of Protestants from Europe who migrated to the Americas and eventually into the hills of North Carolina.

The Winston part of Winston-Salem was founded as the seat of Forsyth County, and through the 19th and early 20th centuries it boomed as an industrial and trading hub, fed by what seemed for generations an endless stream of tobacco and textile money. Although the textile mills are nearly all gone in North Carolina, and the cigarette industry sputters along in fits and starts, Winston-Salem is still alive and well as a banking center and the home of Wake Forest University, Winston-Salem State University, and other important educational institutions.

## SIGHTS
### ★ Old Salem

Though nestled in the center of a modern city, **Old Salem** (900 Old Salem Rd., 888/653-7253, www.oldsalem.org, Tues.-Sat. 9:30am-4:30pm, Sun. 1pm-4:30pm, $23 adults, $11 children) was once a bustling independent village that was home to the industrious Moravians. That era is now re-created in the streets and homes of the old village, where costumed interpreters reconstruct the old Moravian ways and continue to make expertly crafted goods prized by fellow Carolinians.

Old Salem is also home to three museums, each a gem, and all housed in the Horton Museum Center. The **Museum of Early Southern Decorative Arts** (924 S. Main St., www.mesda.org, Tues.-Sat. 10am-4pm, Sun. 1pm-4pm, admission cost varies) re-creates 24 period rooms and six galleries to display the furniture, paintings, fabrics, and other distinctive decorative arts of the Old South, representing the years between 1670 and approximately 1850 in the Lowcountry, Chesapeake, and Backcountry regions.

## Museums

Winston-Salem's multitude of museums represents art of many places and centuries. **The Southeastern Center for Contemporary Art** (750 Marguerite Dr., 336/725-1904, www.secca.org, Tues.-Wed. and Fri.-Sat. 10am-5pm, Thurs. 10am-8pm, Sun. 1pm-5pm, free) hosts changing exhibits of stimulating modern work in a variety of media. The **Reynolda House Museum of American Art** (2250 Reynolda Rd., 888/663-1149, www.reynoldahouse.org, Tues.-Sat. 9:30am-4:30pm, Sun. 1:30pm-4:30pm, last entry 4pm, $14 adults, free students and under age 18) has a distinguished collection of American masterpieces from colonial times through the present day. The **Diggs Gallery** (601 S. Martin Luther King Dr., 336/750-2458, www.wssu.edu, Tues.-Sat. 11am-5pm, free) at Winston-Salem State University has excellent permanent and changing exhibitions of work by African

# Winston-Salem

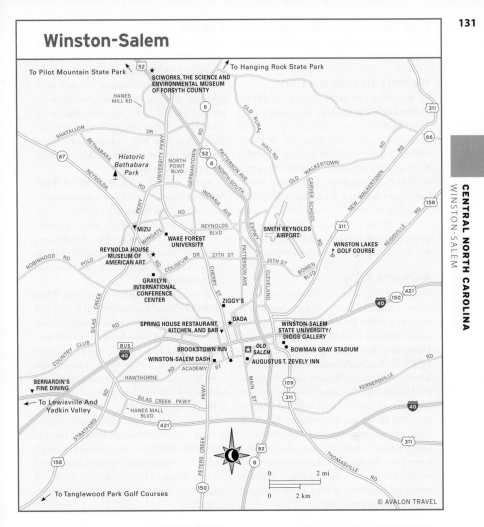

© AVALON TRAVEL

and African American artists, with a particular emphasis on North Carolina and the Southeast.

**SciWorks, the Science and Environmental Museum of Forsyth County** (400 W. Hanes Mill Rd., 336/767-6730, www.sciworks.org, Tues.-Fri. 10am-4pm, Sat. 10am-5pm, Sun. noon-5pm, $11 adults, $9 ages 3-19 and over age 62) was named one of the top 25 science museums by *Parents Magazine*. Here children can pet horseshoe crabs, play a floor piano with their feet, brush giant teeth, and learn about physics and biology.

A very different kind of gallery is the **Winston Cup Museum** (1355 N. Martin Luther King Dr., 336/724-4557, www.winstoncupmuseum.com, Tues.-Sat. 10am-5pm, $8 adults, $4 ages 5-12, free under age 5), which chronicles R. J. Reynolds's 33-year sponsorship of NASCAR. (There can be no more Carolinian combination than cigarettes and stock cars.) Here you'll see cars driven by Dale Senior and Dale Junior (as the

Earnhardts are known in these parts), drivers' helmets, winners' checks, and other great racing memorabilia.

## Historic Bethabara Park

In northern Winston-Salem, **Historic Bethabara Park** (2147 Bethabara Rd., 336/924-8191, www.bethabarapark.com, guided tours Apr.-Nov. Tues.-Fri. 10:30am-4:30pm, Sat.-Sun. 1:30pm-4:30pm, $4 adults, $1 children) explores an even earlier period of Moravian settlement than that of Salem. Bethabara was the first foothold of the Moravians in North Carolina. The 15 original settlers and the other Moravians who would soon join them constructed a sturdy, attractive little village in a very brief few years.

## Körner's Folly

Without a doubt, one of the most unforgettably strange places in North Carolina is **Körner's Folly** (413 S. Main St., 336/996-7922, www.kornersfolly.org, Thurs.-Sat. 10am-4pm, Sun. 1pm-4pm, $10 adults, $6 ages 5-16, free under age 5), located east of Winston-Salem in Kernersville. The seven-level house with 22 rooms of insanely ornate frippery and eccentric architectural contraptions fits all the requirements of the classic Victorian monstrosity. In its late-1870s infancy, Körner's Folly was intended not as a home but a display of designer Jule Körner's architectural innovations, a house of showrooms for his clients to tour. Little by little it also became Körner's home.

## ENTERTAINMENT AND EVENTS
### Performing Arts

The **Piedmont Opera** (336/725-7101, www.piedmontopera.org, $15-70) is a 30-year-old company that presents several operas each season, with a special emphasis on classic Italian opera. Now more than 60 years old, the **Winston-Salem Symphony** (336/725-1035, www.wssymphony.org, $15-60) has a performance schedule that includes a variety of music, from baroque to pop.

## Events

Starting at midnight and lasting into the early hours of Easter Sunday every year, **roving brass bands** play throughout the city, in a tradition that the Moravians of Salem practiced 200 years ago and that remains an important part of Easter worship. The bands' "rounds," as they're called, always begin with Bach's "Sleepers, Wake," a composition that was brand-new when the first Moravian band was organized in Saxony.

April brings the **RiverRun Film Festival** (336/724-1502, www.riverrunfilm.com), one of the largest film festivals in the Southeast. The festival is a great opportunity to see the work of both established and emerging filmmakers, and to attend workshops and panels about the art and business of moviemaking.

In June at the **North Carolina Wine Festival** (www.ncwinefestival.com), you can sample prize wines from dozens of vineyards across the state, from the sandy lowlands to steep mountainsides, and from the famously fertile Yadkin Valley, a short drive from Winston-Salem. The festival is held just outside the city in Clemmons, southwest of Winston-Salem on I-40.

The end of July and beginning of August is time for the **National Black Theater Festival** (336/723-2266, www.nbtf.org). The six-day gathering includes classic and modern dramas as well as poetry slams and many other events. It draws 60,000 visitors annually.

## SHOPPING

The Downtown Arts District, referred to as **DADA** (www.dadaws.org), is a neighborhood of galleries and boutiques located downtown between 5th, 6th, and Trade Streets. There are over a dozen commercial galleries, including the **Piedmont Craftsmen** (601 N. Trade St., 336/725-1516, www.piedmontcraftsmen.org, Tues.-Fri. 10:30am-5pm, Sat. 10am-5pm), which has a beautiful showroom where you'll find the work of hundreds of North Carolina's finest studio potters, fiber artists, jewelry designers, and craftspeople who work in many other media. Several restaurants, bars, and coffee shops are located in DADA.

The **Reynolda Village Shops** (2201 Reynolda Rd., 336/758-5584, www.reynoldavillage.com), near the historic Reynolda House and museum, is a cluster of specialty stores and boutiques full of unique jewelry, clothing, books, antiques, and more.

# SPORTS AND RECREATION
## Spectator Sports

Wake Forest University is the fourth school in the famous Tobacco Road athletic rivalry, and a worthy competitor to its nemeses in the Triangle: Duke, UNC, and NC State. The jewels in the crown of **Demon Deacon Athletics** (888/758-3322, www.wfu.edu) are Wake's ACC Division I football and basketball teams. As is the case at its Tobacco Road counterparts, obtaining a ticket to a Wake Forest football or basketball game can be quite difficult.

## NASCAR

NASCAR racing at **Bowman Gray Stadium** (1250 S. Martin Luther King Dr., 336/723-1819, www.bowmangrayracing.com, gates 6pm, races 8pm, $10 adults, $2 ages 6-11, free under age 6) is not only a classic Carolina experience—weekly races have been run here for 50 years—but is also a less daunting experience than race events at the massive stadiums elsewhere in the state. It's inexpensive too, making this an ideal place for your first NASCAR event. Weekly races include modified, street stock, sportsman, and stadium stock events.

# FOOD
## Eclectic American

**Bernardin's Fine Dining** (373 Jonestown Rd., 336/768-9365, www.bernardinsfinedining.com, lunch Mon.-Fri., dinner Mon.-Sat., $19-32) is one of the most lauded restaurants in Winston. In fact, the Greensboro *News & Record* labeled it "the Triad's only five-star restaurant." Seafood and hearty cuts of beef and veal dominate the menu. The wine list is extensive, and the desserts alone are worth a visit.

## Asian

**Downtown Thai and Sushi** (202 W. 4th St., 336/777-1422, www.downtownthai.com, lunch Mon.-Fri. 11am-2pm, dinner Mon.-Thurs. 5pm-10pm, Fri.-Sat. 5pm-11pm, Sun. 5pm-10pm, $20-25) is an elegant pan-Asian restaurant, specializing in sushi and Thai favorites such as pad thai and curries.

## Bakeries

Among the best-loved Moravian arts is that of baking, a tradition that is carried on by, among others, **Salem Baking Company** (224 S. Cherry St., 336/748-0230) and **Dewey's** (3121 Indiana Ave.; 2820 Reynolda Rd.; 262 Stratford Rd., 800/274-2994). At these Winston-Salem locations, and several shops elsewhere in the state, you'll find heavenly Moravian cookies, a thin, spiced wafer that is one of this state's most popular exports around Christmastime.

# ACCOMMODATIONS

A cotton mill built in the 1830s, the building that's home to the ★ **Brookstown Inn** (200 Brookstown Ave., 336/725-1120, www.brookstowninn.com, from $90) has been renovated and transformed into a luxurious hotel, with beautiful exposed brick walls and wooden floors. Guests enjoy wine and cheese in the evenings, and milk and cookies at night. The Brookstown Inn is within walking distance of Old Salem.

★ **Augustus T. Zevely Inn** (803 S. Main St., Old Salem, 800/928-9299, www.winston-salem-inn.com, from $95) is the only inn in Old Salem proper. The beautiful 1830s house is furnished in original and reproduction Moravian furniture, with special features peppered throughout, such as steam baths in some guest rooms, heated brick tile floors in others, and working cooking fireplaces.

## INFORMATION AND SERVICES

Winston-Salem's main emergency hospital is **Wake Forest University Baptist Medical Center** (Medical Center Blvd., 336/716-2255, www1.wfubmc.edu), located off Business I-40 between Cloverdale and Hawthorne. **Carolina Veterinary Specialists** (1600 Hanes Mall Blvd., 336/896-0902, www.carolinavet.com), a 24-hour emergency veterinary hospital, is located off I-40 just west of U.S. 421.

The **Winston-Salem Journal** (www.journalnow.com) is the city's main newspaper. The **Winston-Salem Visitors Center** (200 Brookstown Ave., 866/728-4200, www.visitwinstonsalem.com) has extensive travel information.

## GETTING THERE AND AROUND

Winston-Salem is on I-40, North Carolina's largest east-west highway. It is about 20 minutes from Greensboro, about 2 hours from Raleigh, and about 1.5 hours from Charlotte.

**Piedmont Triad International Airport** (GSO, 1000 A. Ted Johnson Pkwy., Greensboro, 336/665-5600, www.flyfrompti.com) is nearby on the northwest side of Greensboro. Winston-Salem's bus system, **WSTA** (336/727-2648, www.wstransit.com) is connected to that of Greensboro via Piedmont Area Regional Transit's **Express Bus** (336/662-0002, www.partnc.org).

# Greensboro and Vicinity

Greensboro might be more densely packed with colleges and universities than any other city in North Carolina. It's the home of the University of North Carolina at Greensboro, North Carolina A&T, the small Quaker college Guilford, and Bennett, a historically African American women's college known as the "Vassar of the South."

## SIGHTS
### Historic Parks

When one thinks of Revolutionary War battles, those that come first to mind are probably up north and in New England states. In truth, much of the Revolution was fought in the South, and some of the major turning points occurred here in North Carolina. **Guilford Courthouse National Military Park** (2332 New Garden Rd., 336/288-1776, www.nps.gov/guco, visitors center Tues.-Sat. 8:30am-5pm, free) commemorates the battle of Guilford Courthouse, at which 1,900 British troops led by General Cornwallis routed 4,500 Patriots under General Nathanael Greene, for whom the city of Greensboro was later named. It proved only a pyrrhic victory for the British,

however, as Cornwallis's army suffered very heavy casualties and was rendered unable to mount any more offensives for the remainder of the war. A 2.5-mile self-guided tour, which can be driven, hiked, or biked, stops at the essential spots on the battlefield.

### ★ International Civil Rights Center and Museum

Greensboro, the home of North Carolina A&T, a prominent historically black university, has played an important role in African American history. The **International Civil Rights Center and Museum** (134 S. Elm St., 800/748-7116, www.sitinmovement.org, Mon.-Sat. 9am-6pm, $12 adults, $10 students and seniors, $8 ages 6-12) is housed in Greensboro's old downtown Woolworth's building, the site of a famous 1960 lunch counter sit-in that lit a fire under North Carolina's civil rights movement. That whites-only counter is the touchstone for this museum's exploration of the civil rights movement. The four men who staged the sit-in—David Richmond, Franklin McCain, Jibreel Khazan, and Joseph McNeil—are honored on the A&T

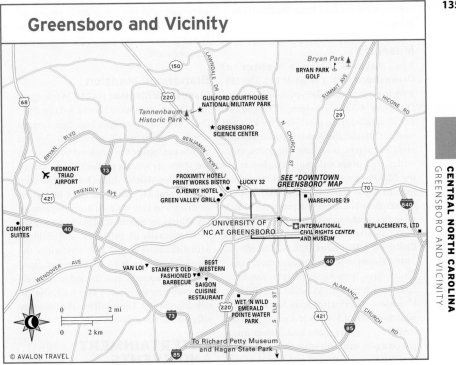

# Greensboro and Vicinity

Bryan Park
BRYAN PARK
GOLF

150

220

68

GUILFORD COURTHOUSE
NATIONAL MILITARY PARK

Tannenbaum
Historic Park

★ GREENSBORO
SCIENCE CENTER

29

SUMMIT AVE

HICONE RD

N. CHURCH ST

PIEDMONT
TRIAD
AIRPORT

73

PROXIMITY HOTEL/
PRINT WORKS BISTRO

LUCKY 32

*SEE "DOWNTOWN
GREENSBORO" MAP*

70

O.HENRY HOTEL

GREEN VALLEY GRILL

WAREHOUSE 29

840

421

FRIENDLY AVE

COMFORT
SUITES

40

UNIVERSITY OF
NC AT GREENSBORO

INTERNATIONAL
CIVIL RIGHTS CENTER
AND MUSEUM

REPLACEMENTS, LTD

WENDOVER AVE

VAN LOI

STAMEY'S OLD
FASHIONED
BARBECUE

BEST
WESTERN

SAIGON
CUISINE
RESTAURANT

40

ALAMANCE CHURCH RD

220

WET 'N WILD
EMERALD
POINTE WATER
PARK

S ELM ST

421

85

0   2 mi
0   2 km

73

To Richard Petty Museum
and Hagan State Park

85

© AVALON TRAVEL

a monument to General Nathanael Greene at Guilford Courthouse National Military Park

campus with the **A&T Four Statue** (1601 E. Market St.).

## Museums

The **Natural Science Center of Greensboro** (4301 Lawndale Dr., 336/288-3769, www.natsci.org, daily 9am-5pm, Animal Discovery daily 10am-4pm, $13.50 adults, $12.50 ages 3-13) is a great place for kids and adults. Outside, the Animal Discovery displays live tigers, meerkats, alligators, crocodiles, and other wild animals. Inside are the 22,000-square-foot Sciquarium, featuring sharks, stingrays, and otters, and the OmniSphere Theater, which projects 3-D digital shows on the domed planetarium ceiling.

For children under 10, the **Greensboro Children's Museum** (220 N. Church St., 336/574-2898, www.gcmuseum.com, Tues.-Thurs. 9am-5pm, Fri. 9am-8pm, Sat. 9am-5pm, Sun. 1pm-5pm, $8 adults and children, $7 seniors, $4 Fri. after 5pm) features a pretend town with a Main Street where kids can shop for groceries, bake and deliver pizza, put on a play with costumes and props, learn how houses are built, and scale a rock-climbing wall.

The **Green Hill Center for North Carolina Art** (200 N. Davie St., 336/333-7460, www.greenhillcenter.org, Tues.-Fri. noon-7pm, Sat. noon-5pm, Sun. 2pm-5pm, $5 donation) presents exhibits of work by artists who are from or have close ties to North Carolina. Much attention is given to North Carolina's folk art traditions, and deservedly so, but the state is also rich with practitioners of the formal studio arts. Some of the best of those artists are represented in this gallery.

The **Weatherspoon Art Museum** (Spring Garden St. and Tate St., 336/334-5770, http://weatherspoon.uncg.edu, Tues.-Wed. and Fri. 10am-5pm, Thurs. 10am-9pm, Sat.-Sun. 1pm-5pm, free), on the campus of UNC-Greensboro, has been dedicated to modern art since the early 1940s and has assembled a collection that includes works by Willem de Kooning, Andy Warhol, Cindy Sherman, and many other masters of 20th-century art. This is the best collection of modern art in North Carolina, and one of the very best in the Southeast.

## Blandwood Mansion

**Blandwood Mansion** (447 W. Washington St., 336/272-5003, www.blandwood.org, Feb.-Dec. Tues.-Sat. 11am-4pm, Sun. 2pm-5pm, $8 adults, $5 under age 12) was built in 1790 as a farmhouse, before the city itself was born. In the 1840s, its famous resident was Governor John Motley Morehead, the "Father of Modern North Carolina," one of the most important governors in this state's history because of his efforts to institute humane treatment of the mentally ill, prisoners, and children with disabilities as well as to modernize the state's schools. In 1844, Morehead engaged Alexander Jackson Davis, the architect largely responsible for the country's Gothic revival, to redo Blandwood. The result was the Italianate villa that stands today.

# ENTERTAINMENT AND EVENTS
## Nightlife

Greensboro is a college town several times over, so there's a lot of late-night mischief to enjoy. Popular pubs include **Natty Greene's Pub** (345 S. Elm St., 336/274-1373, www.nattygreenes.com, Mon.-Sat. 11am-2am, Sun. noon-midnight), bearing the moniker of the town's namesake, and the cigar-and-drinks bar **Churchill's on Elm** (213 S. Elm St., 336/275-6367, www.churchillscigarlounge.com).

## Performing Arts

The **Greensboro Symphony Orchestra** (multiple venues, 336/335-5456, ext. 223, www.greensborosymphony.org) was born in the 1920s as a student orchestra at Greensboro Women's College (now UNC Greensboro). It grew to become a beloved institution in the wider community of the city and a highly successful regional orchestra. Today's incarnation is conducted by Azerbaijani violinist

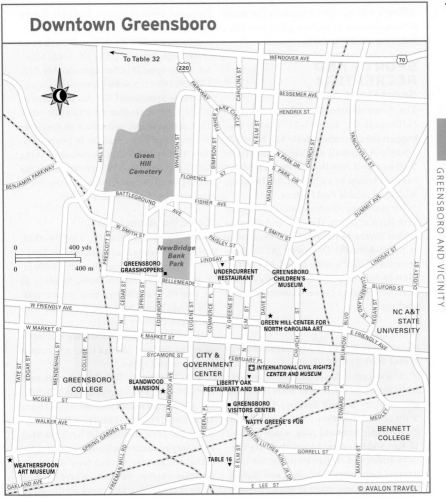

# Downtown Greensboro

Dmitry Sitkovetsky. The **Greensboro Opera** (multiple venues, 336/273-9472, www.greensboroopera.org) has been turning out wonderful performances of classical and modern opera for more than 25 years. The **Greensboro Ballet** (multiple venues, 336/333-7480, www.greensboroballet.org) presents several major productions each season, starring both longtime professional dancers and highly talented up-and-coming students.

## SHOPPING

Featured in a memorable early scene in the 2006 movie *Junebug,* **Replacements, Ltd.** (1089 Knox Rd., just off I-85 exit 132, between Greensboro and Burlington, 800/737-5223, www.replacements.com, daily 8am-10pm) is five football fields' worth of retail and behind-the-scenes space dedicated to what is surely the world's largest collection of tableware and flatware. What began in the 1970s as a small china collection in a North Carolina state auditor's attic has grown so much that today it comprises an 11-million-piece inventory featuring 250,000 patterns.

# SPORTS AND RECREATION
## Spectator Sports

The **Greensboro Grasshoppers** (408 Bellemeade St., 336/268-2255, www.gsohoppers.com, premium seats $11, lawn $7), a Single-A baseball affiliate of the Miami Marlins, play at First Horizon Park, a field that has been graced by all-star pitcher Dontrelle Willis and catcher Paul LoDuca.

For more than 50 years, central Carolinians have been enjoying the roar and burning rubber fumes of the racetrack experience at the **Piedmont Dragway** (6750 Holts Store Rd., Julian, 6 miles from I-85 exit 132, 336/449-7411, http://piedmontdragway.com, ticket prices vary), between Greensboro and Burlington.

## Recreation

Greensboro's **Wet 'N Wild Emerald Pointe Water Park** (3910 S. Holden Rd., 336/852-9721, www.emeraldpointe.com, May-Sept., hours vary, $36) offers more water rides than one could try in a full weekend. In addition to the central attraction, the two-million-gallon Thunder Bay wave pool, which features 48-foot-wide tsunami waves, there are five-story slides and riptide pools for the most intrepid swimmers, lazy rivers and shallow pools for those who prefer to relax, and many adventures in between.

# FOOD
## Southern

**Lucky 32** (1421 Westover Terrace, 336/370-0707, www.lucky32.com, Mon. 11:15am-9pm, Tues.-Thurs. 11:15am-10pm, Fri.-Sat. 11:15am-11pm, Sun. 10am-9pm, $11-27), just off Wendover Avenue, has been a Greensboro staple for 20 years. The menu features creative renditions of classic Southern fare. Standouts include chicken and dumplings,

cornmeal-crusted catfish, and pulled pork on johnnycakes.

**Stamey's Old Fashioned Barbecue** (2206 High Point Rd., 336/299-9888, Mon.-Sat. 10am-9pm; 2812 Battleground Ave./U.S. 220, 336/288-9275, www.stameys.com, Mon.-Sat. 11am-9pm, under $10) has been around in one form or another for almost 70 years. The Lexington-style barbecue is pit-fired over hickory wood for as much as 10 hours—old-time quality that's kept customers coming back for generations. The renovations at the Battleground Avenue location are new due to a serious fire that happened in 2016.

## Eclectic American

**Table 16** (600 S. Elm St., 336/279-8525, www.table16restaurant.com, lunch Tues.-Fri. 11:30am-2pm, dinner Tues.-Fri. 5:30pm-9:30pm, $22-34) is considered by many to be one of Greensboro's best restaurants. The menu blends New World cuisines with European culinary disciplines, resulting in such creations as honeyed salmon and kumquats, tilefish and country ham, and striped bass with fried apples.

The ★ **Liberty Oak Restaurant and Bar** (100-D W. Washington St., 336/273-7057, www.libertyoakrestaurant.com, Mon.-Thurs. 11am-10pm, Fri.-Sat. 11am-11pm, Sun. 10am-10pm, $10-27) is credited with having started a culinary revolution in Greensboro, a fad for casual restaurants serving New American gourmet cuisine. Specialties here include many seafood creations, duck confit, quail stuffed with andouille, and homemade red pepper and goat cheese ravioli.

## European

The award-winning **Print Works Bistro** (702 Green Valley Rd., 336/379-0699, www.printworksbistro.com, lunch Mon.-Fri. 11:15am-4pm, dinner Sun.-Thurs. 4pm-10:30pm, Fri.-Sat. 4pm-11pm, brunch Sat.-Sun. 7:30am-4pm, $11-31) is located at the Proximity Hotel and shares its clean, green aesthetic. The menu here comprises French bistro fare, from escargot to grilled pork tenderloin and duck confit.

Adjacent to the O.Henry Hotel and in the same restaurant family as Print Works is **Green Valley Grill** (622 Green Valley Rd., 336/854-2015, www.greenvalleygrill.com, Mon.-Thurs. 11:15am-10:30pm, Fri.-Sat. 11:15am-11pm, Sun. 9am-10pm, $18-31). The menu spans many European traditions, featuring dishes from paella to Jägerschnitzel. Green Valley Grill's wine list wins *Wine Spectator*'s Award of Excellence every year, with over 100 choices, including 50 by-the-glass selections.

## Asian

Greensboro has a long-established Vietnamese community and a wealth of Vietnamese restaurants. A favorite of local diners is **Saigon Cuisine Restaurant** (4205 High Point Rd., 336/294-9286, Mon.-Sat. 11am-2pm and 5pm-9pm), where some of the best dishes are the grilled pork over vermicelli and the flounder in basil sauce. **Van Loi** (3829-D High Point Rd., 336/855-5688, Wed.-Mon. 10am-10pm, $8) serves good *pho* and Vietnamese sandwiches.

## ACCOMMODATIONS

The **Proximity Hotel** (704 Green Valley Rd., 336/379-8200, www.proximityhotel.com, from $159) is a remarkable venture. Solar panels on the roof, huge windows in each guest room, recycled building materials, and many other green features mean that the Proximity reduces energy and water use by almost half over what would be expected of a comparable hotel.

The ★ **O.Henry Hotel** (624 Green Valley Rd., 336/854-2000, www.ohenryhotel.com, from $239), named for the Greensboro-born author of "Gift of the Magi," is a 1920s-style luxury hotel. The oversize guest rooms feature nine-foot ceilings, neighbor-silencing double walls, comfy beds, terrazzo showers and huge bathtubs, and, like the Proximity, windows that open. The O.Henry's own checkered cab will carry you to and from the airport free of charge.

## INFORMATION AND SERVICES

The **Greensboro Visitors Center** (317 S. Greene St., 800/344-2282, www.greensboronc.org, Mon.-Fri. 8:30am-5:30pm, Sat. 9am-4pm, Sun. 1pm-4pm), downtown across from the Carolina Theater, is open every day. Greensboro has several hospitals, the largest of which is **Moses H. Cone Memorial Hospital** (1200 N. Elm St., 336/832-7000, www.mosescone.com). Should your pet have an emergency, you can go to the **After Hours Veterinary Emergency Clinic** (5505 W. Friendly Ave., 336/851-1990, www.ahvec.com).

## GETTING THERE AND AROUND

Greensboro is connected to North Carolina's other cities by two of the state's major highways, I-40 and I-85. It is connected to the rest of the world by **Piedmont Triad International Airport** (GSO, 1000 A. Ted Johnson Pkwy., Greensboro, 336/665-5600, www.flyfrompti.com). The city is also a stop on the **Amtrak** (236 E. Washington St., 800/872-7245, station daily 24 hours) *Piedmont* and *Carolinian* lines. Greensboro's local bus system, the **Greensboro Transit Authority** (336/335-6499, www.greensboronc.gov), is connected to its counterpart in Winston-Salem by Piedmont Area Regional Transit's **Express Bus** (336/662-0002, www.partnc.org).

## LEXINGTON

The Piedmont town of Lexington is a veritable mecca for Southern chowhounds. Billing itself as the "Barbecue Capital of the World," Lexington is known as the epicenter of North Carolina's western barbecue tradition. Known locally as "honeymonk," Lexington barbecue comes from the pork shoulder, rather than whole-hog meat; also unlike in the east, the sauce usually has a dose of ketchup in it.

Foodies will argue endlessly about which barbecue purveyor in the Lexington area is the best, but an oft-cited favorite is **Lexington**

**Barbecue** (100 Smokehouse Ln., 704/249-9814, Mon.-Sat. 10am-9:30pm, $10). In this friendly eatery, the barbecue is slow-cooked over wood coals. The hush puppies, a category of food that can inspire nearly as much partisan debate as barbecue, are also quite special. Another top bet is **Speedy's** (1317 Winston Rd., 336/248-2410, http://speedysbbqinc.com, Mon.-Sat. 10:30am-9pm, $8). Not only is the food here good and plentiful, but the waitstaff will bring it right to the curb for you, old-time drive-in style.

October is officially Barbecue Month here in Davidson County, and late in the month every year, up to 100,000 people descend on Lexington for the **Barbecue Festival** (336/956-1880, www.barbecuefestival.com).

After a visit to one of Lexington's barbecue joints, make your way to **The Candy Factory** (15 N. Main St., 336/249-6770, www.thecandyfactory.net, Mon.-Thurs. 10am-5:30pm, Fri. 10am-7:30pm, Sat. 10am-4pm). A third-generation candy-making business, The Candy Factory is housed in a 1907 old-time hardware store, with beautiful creaky old floors. Barrels of candy line the shop.

# The Sandhills

Far from most of North Carolina's major highways, the region known as the Sandhills, an exceptionally beautiful part of the state, is often forgotten by travelers and travel writers.

## ASHEBORO AND VICINITY
### North Carolina Zoo
The **North Carolina Zoo** (Zoo Pkwy., 800/488-0444, www.nczoo.org, Apr.-Oct. daily 9am-5pm, Nov.-Mar. daily 9am-4pm, $12 adults, $10 college students and over age 62, $8 ages 2-12) sprawls over more than 500 acres of Purgatory Mountain, at the edge of the Uwharries. Animals that include elephants, zebras, polar bears, alligators, and many more live on large expanses of land planted and landscaped to approximate their native habitats. This acclaimed zoo is operated by the state of North Carolina.

### Other Sights and Activities
At the **North Carolina Aviation Museum** (2222-G Pilots View Rd., 336/625-0170, www.ncaviationmuseumhalloffame.com, Thurs.-Sun. 11am-5pm, $10 adults, $5 students), World War II through Vietnam War-era fighter aircraft gleam in restored splendor. After touring the two hangars where the airplanes and other military memorabilia are housed, check out the gift shop, which is a model plane lover's dream.

The **Asheboro Copperheads** (McCrary Stadium, Southway Rd., off McCrary St., 336/460-7018, www.teamcopperhead.com), part of the Coastal Plain League, are a summer wood-bat baseball team of college players from schools in North Carolina and throughout the South.

### Liberty Antiques Festival
Liberty, between Asheboro and I-85, hosts a twice-yearly antiques fair that draws crowds from all over the Southeast. At the **Liberty Antiques Festival** (2855 Pike Farm Rd., Staley, just outside Liberty, 800/626-2672, www.libertyantiquesfestival.com, $7), usually held over a three-day weekend in late April and again in late September, hundreds of vendors set up shop in a farm field, creating a huge outdoor antiques mall that offers many happy hours of browsing. There's huge variety among the dealers' wares, but overall the theme leans toward rustic Southern.

## SEAGROVE
The little crossroads town of Seagrove is built over beds of clay that perfectly suited the needs of 18th- and 19th-century potters. Several families of potters settled in this

region and, using the excellent red and gray clays so readily available, were soon supplying much of the rest of the region with jugs, crocks, plates, and other utilitarian wares.

## North Carolina Pottery Center

The **North Carolina Pottery Center** (233 East Ave., 336/873-8430, www.ncpotterycenter.org, Tues.-Sat. 10am-4pm, $2.50 adults, $1 high school students) is the ideal place to start your tour of Seagrove. Though the primary focus of the Pottery Center is to preserve and present the work of Seagrove-area potters, you'll also see representative work from the state's several other distinctive pottery traditions.

## Pottery Studios

**Ben Owen Pottery** (2199 Hwy. 705, 910/464-2261, www.benowenpottery.com), three miles south of the Pottery Center on Highway 705, "the Pottery Highway," is the studio and showroom of one of Seagrove's finest young potters. Ben Owen III learned the art from his grandfather, who was also a renowned area potter.

David and Mary Farrell of **Westmoore Pottery** (4622 Busbee Rd., Westmoore, 910/464-3700, www.westmoorepottery.com, Mon.-Sat. 9am-5pm) specialize in re-creating historical ceramics, primarily of North Carolina styles. Their work is so accurate that it appears in historic houses throughout the United States and has been featured in many movies, including *Amistad* and *Cold Mountain*.

**Luck's Ware** (1606 Adams Rd., Seagrove, 336/879-3261, Mon.-Fri. 9am-5pm) is the workshop of Sid Luck and his sons Matt and Jason, today's representatives of a generations-old family tradition. Sid fires (bakes) his pots in a groundhog kiln—an old-time Carolina form that has a long, arched brick tunnel, part of which is usually subterranean.

## Shopping

It's hard to imagine, but there is one shop in Seagrove with wares that rival the gleaming pottery in beauty. **Seagrove Orchids** (3451 Brower Mill Rd., 336/879-6677, www.seagroveorchids.com, Tues.-Sun. 10am-5pm and by appointment) is a wonderful place to visit even if your hobbies don't include exotic horticulture. There are over 220 kinds of orchids in the greenhouses here, from rare species to affordable plants good for beginners.

## Accommodations

The **Duck Smith House** (465 N. Broad St., 888/869-9018, www.ducksmithhouse.com, $125), a farmhouse built in 1914, is the classic Southern bed-and-breakfast, with a large wraparound porch and a hearty country breakfast. The location is perfect for a weekend of shopping for pottery.

# UWHARRIE MOUNTAINS

The Uwharrie Mountains are strange and beautiful, a range of hills covered in deep rocky woods and dotted with small quiet towns with names like Ether and Troy. Peaks of this range, one of the oldest in North America, once soared to 20,000 feet, but the millennia have worn them down until the highest mountain now stands at just over 1,000 feet.

## ★ Uwharrie National Forest

The trail system of the Uwharrie Forest has aptly been compared to a "mini-Appalachian Trail." Although the Uwharrie Mountains are significantly lower than the Blue Ridge Mountains and the Smokies, they do shelter delicate mountain ecosystems closely related to those of the Appalachians. Two major trails run through the park, the Uwharrie National Recreational Trail and the Dutchman's Creek Trail. Both begin 10 miles west of Troy, with parking at Highway 24/27. The 10-mile Dutchman's Creek Trail loops with the 20-mile Uwharrie Trail, which ends 2 miles east of Ophir at Highway 1306.

Two large campgrounds are located near Badin Lake, at the western edge of the park. **Arrowhead Campground** (Forest Rd. 597B, off Mullinix Rd./Forest Rd. 1154,

910/576-6391, reservations 877/833-6777, www.recreation.gov, $9 with electricity, $6 without electricity) has 48 sites with picnic tables and tent pads, 33 of which have electrical hookups. The Arrowhead Campground is 0.5 mile from Badin Lake. The **Badin Lake Campground** (Forest Rd. 576, off Hwy. 109, 910/576-6391, reservations 877/444-6777, www.recreation.gov, $8), which has 34 sites, is directly on the lake. Several smaller sites throughout the park are accessible for tent camping, and one, Canebrake Horse Camp near Badin Lake, is for folks traveling with their horses.

### Morrow Mountain State Park

Located catty-corner to Badin and Albemarle, **Morrow Mountain State Park** (49104 Morrow Mountain Rd., Albemarle, 704/982-4402, http://ncparks.gov, May-Aug. 8am-9pm, Mar.-Apr. and Sept.-Oct. 8am-8pm, Nov.-Feb. 8am-6pm, free) preserves one of the Uwharries' highest peaks, the 936-foot Morrow Mountain. Within the park, visitors can go boating on Lake Tillery or on the Pee Dee River, with rowboat and canoe rentals available in the spring and summer. Cabins are available for rent (summer $400 per week, off-season $80 per night, 2-night minimum). There are also over 100 campsites ($9-15) with water, restrooms, and showers nearby, but no electricity.

### INFORMATION AND SERVICES

Asheboro is the population center of Randolph County, where you'll find plenty of affordable chain motels and a fast-food jungle clustered along U.S. 64. This is also a center for area medical services. The **Asheboro/Randolph County Chamber of Commerce** (317 E. Dixie Dr., 336/626-2626, http://chamber.asheboro.com) can fix you up with all the logistical information you need as you venture into the Sandhills.

### GETTING THERE AND AROUND

U.S. 220, which runs from Greensboro almost to the South Carolina border, is the only major artery in this region, which is served by no major airports or rail lines. The Charlotte, Greensboro, and Raleigh-Durham airports are all within 1-2 hours' drive.

# Southern Pines and Pinehurst

Flip through the old postcards at any antiques shop in the Carolinas and you're likely to come across turn-of-the-20th-century images of the Southern Pines region of the North Carolina Sandhills. The area's development kicked into high gear in the 1890s, when Bostonian James Tufts constructed the Pinehurst Resort with money he made in the soda fountain industry. He commissioned Frederick Law Olmsted to design a village, which he named Pinehurst. The first hotel opened in 1895, followed by the Pinehurst golf course (now called Pinehurst No. 1) in 1898, and the Pinehurst No. 2 course in 1907.

Today, this whole section of Moore County, anchored by the picturesque towns of Pinehurst and Southern Pines, is a sea of golf courses and still a magnet for snowbirds and "halfbacks" (Northerners who retired to Florida, found it too hot, and came halfway back, to North Carolina). Primarily known for golf, the Pinehurst area has hosted the U.S. Open, the U.S. Women's Open, and the USGA National Championship. The spring months are exceptionally pretty, and the weather is usually warm but not dangerously hot (as it is in summer), so March-May, hotels and restaurants fill to the gills, and golf courses can book solid. The key to having a good golf vacation in the springtime is planning well in advance. Golf packages are key; by bundling lodging and greens fees, you can save cash and hassle.

# SPORTS AND RECREATION
## Golf

Given its background of Scottish settlement, it's no surprise that one of the most famous golf centers in the world is the Southern Pines, Pinehurst, and Aberdeen area, with more than 40 major courses. An epicenter of American golf for over 100 years, Pinehurst has been so influential in the development of the modern game that an entire format of play, the Pinehurst system—also called the Chapman system or American foursomes—was developed there.

The **Pinehurst Resort** (1 Carolina Vista Dr., Pinehurst, 800/487-4653, www.pinehurst.com) comprises eight major courses (called Pinehurst No. 1, No. 2, etc.), designed by some of the great golf course architects of the last century: Donald Ross, Ellis Maples, George and Tom Fazio, and Rees Jones. The circa-1907 Ross-designed Pinehurst No. 2 is considered the most important and has hosted numerous U.S. Open championships, including both the 2014 men's and women's championships. **Pine Needles** (Midland Rd., Southern Pines, 910/692-7111, www.pineneedles-midpines.com, greens fees $135-235) incorporates the Pine Needles (18 holes, par 71) and Mid-Pines (18 holes, par 72) courses, both Donald Ross creations. The **Talamore** (48 Talamore Dr., Southern Pines, 800/552-6292, www.talamoregolfresort.com, 18 holes, par 71, greens fees $60-130) was designed by Rees Jones. If you visit at the right time, you might be treated to the able caddying services of the Talamore llamas.

Other courses in the area were designed by Jack Nicklaus, Jack Nicklaus II, Dan Maples, Gary Player, and other leading lights of golf course architecture. Best of all, almost all of them are clustered within half an hour's drive or less from each other.

One of the most remarkable aspects of the Pinehurst golf scene, unlike some of the more vacation-oriented golfing centers of the country, is the prevalence of retired professionals, instructors, and skilled locals on the links. It makes for a more immersive and respectful golf experience, one with a certain addictive quality that keeps people coming back.

Your first stop online should be at the Pinehurst golf tourism website (www.homeofgolf.com). The Sandhills Golf Association website (www.sandhillsgolf.com) is another good source for golf-specific background and info. There are plenty of packages available and plenty of websites that offer them; among the best is www.villageofpinehurstgolf.com.

## Other Activities

This area pulsates to the rhythm of the links, but there are a few sights not related to golf. In the town of Southern Pines is **Campbell House** (482 E. Connecticut Ave., www.mooreart.org, Mon.-Fri. 9am-5pm, free), headquarters of the Moore County Arts Council and host to several galleries of local and regional artists. For those who want a touch of history, visit the **Tufts Archives** (150 Cherokee Rd., http://givettufts.org, Mon.-Fri. 9:30am-5pm, Sat. 9:30am-12:30pm, free) in Pinehurst.

## Hiking and Walking

**Weymouth Woods-Sandhills Nature Preserve** (1024 Fort Bragg Rd., Southern Pines, 910/692-2167, http://ncparks.gov, Nov.-Feb. daily 8am-6pm, Mar.-Oct. daily 8am-8pm, free) comprises nearly 900 acres and is home to red-cockaded woodpeckers, fox squirrels, and other natives of the longleaf pine barrens. Most of the preserve is a limited-use area, but several trails, most one mile long or shorter, let visitors explore the woods and swamps.

Another nice spot for walking is the **Horticultural Garden** (3395 Airport Rd., Pinehurst, 910/695-3882, http://sandhillshorticulturalgardens.com, daily dawn-dusk, free) at Sandhills Community College. A full acre of the property is dedicated to a formal English garden, while other areas show off plants of the woodlands and wetlands.

# FOOD

Some of the best places to dine in this area are at the Pinehurst Resort (800/487-4653). The **Carolina Dining Room** (Carolina Inn, 80 Carolina Vista Dr., Pinehurst, daily 6am-10am and 6:30pm-9pm, $36-37, dinner jacket required) is the resort's most formal dining room, serving fine chops and steaks presented with the chef's suggestions for wine accompaniment. At the **1895 Grille** (Holly Inn, 80 Carolina Vista Dr., Pinehurst, Wed.-Sat. 6pm-9pm, $24-35), specialties include savory grilled veal and steak, filet of grouper served over oyster risotto, and the signature cider-brined grilled pork chop with apple-pecan chutney. The **Tavern** (The Manor, 80 Carolina Vista Dr., Pinehurst, daily 11:30am-10pm, $16-27) serves lighter café fare, with entrée soups and sandwiches as well as an array of pasta dishes. Seven other restaurants, cafés, and tea shops are scattered throughout the Pinehurst Resort.

At the **Magnolia Inn** (Magnolia Rd. and Chinquapin Rd., Pinehurst, 800/526-5562, www.themagnoliainn.com, Tues.-Sat. 4:30pm-10pm, dining room $15-35, pub $6-12), the main dining room serves three-course meals with such specialties as lobster chimichanga, pork napoleon, fire-roasted pepper over grits, and the inn's special tomato bisque. At the pub, several of these specialties are served, along with sandwiches like the corned beef Reuben panini, barbecue pork sandwich, and pub burger with the works.

# ACCOMMODATIONS

A word to the wise: If you want to visit the Pinehurst area during a major tournament, you must book accommodations well in advance. When the U.S. Open is played in Pinehurst, as it often is, area hotel rooms are typically booked solid as the date approaches. Check the online calendar at www.vopnc.org to plan your dates.

## Resorts

A separate entity from the town of Pinehurst, the ★ **Pinehurst Resort** (80 Carolina Vista Dr., Pinehurst, 800/487-4653, www.pinehurst. com), opened in 1895, is the world's second-largest golf resort. The resort is built around eight golf courses, including the famed Pinehurst Nos. 1, 2, 3, and 4, designed by Donald Ross. There are three inns to choose from. The **Carolina** (from $250), built in 1901 and listed in the National Register of Historic Places, is a grand hotel in the Edwardian style, with long piazzas and lush lawns. The 1895 **Holly Inn** (from $230) was the first hotel built at the resort, and is a smaller and cozier club-like inn. The third inn, the **Manor** (from $150), is the smallest and most laid-back of the accommodations here.

For beginning golfers, as well as experienced players, the **Pinehurst Golf Academy** (from $1,329) gives weekend and weeklong classes, taught on Pinehurst Nos. 1, 3, and 5, with a stay at the Carolina included in the course fee. Also on the grounds is the four-star **Spa at Pinehurst,** with a long menu of skin and body care therapies. The **Pinehurst Tennis Club** is regarded as a top tennis resort nationally, with a high-quality pro shop and adult tennis camps. Golf, spa, and tennis packages can significantly reduce the overall cost of a stay at the Pinehurst, although surcharges for amenities might still apply.

## Inns

The **Pine Crest Inn** (Dogwood Rd., Pinehurst, 800/371-2545, www.pinecrestinnpinehurst. com, $70-120, plus 15 percent service charge) was owned for many years by Donald Ross, the golf course designer who helped make the Pinehurst Resort famous. Operated for the last 40 years by the Barrett family, the Pine Crest is a favorite for golfers and vacationers, and for local diners who come to the Pine Crest Inn Restaurant and Mr. B's Lounge.

The **Magnolia Inn** (Magnolia Rd. and Chinquapin Rd., Pinehurst, 800/526-5562, www.themagnoliainn.com, $75-190), built in 1896, sits in a great downtown location. Guests are just steps from local shopping and restaurants, and very close to the best area golfing. The ★ **Knollwood House** (1495 W. Connecticut Ave., Southern Pines,

910/692-9390, from $140) is one of the most popular inns in the area, a bed-and-breakfast located on the 15th green of the Mid-Pines golf course. The elegant house, built in 1927 as a Philadelphia family's vacation home, has a beautiful sunroom and front porch overlooking the azalea-spangled yard.

## GETTING THERE AND AROUND

Southern Pines and Pinehurst are most easily reached by U.S. 15/501 and U.S. 1, south from Chapel Hill and Raleigh, respectively, and can be reached easily from Fayetteville, just a short drive east. The region is also served by **Moore County Airport** (910/692-3212, www.moorecountyairport.com).

When you get here, it's a good idea to stop by the **Pinehurst-Aberdeen Convention and Visitors Bureau** (10677 U.S. 15/501, 800/346-5632, www.homeofgolf.com, Mon.-Fri. 9am-5pm) to stock up on timely information and brochures.

# Charlotte

There has only been one brief period, in Charlotte's earliest days, when it was not a boomtown. In the late 18th century it was a midsize county seat, but 1799 brought a taste of things to come when a child's creek-side discovery of a 17-pound lump of gold sparked a minor gold rush.

When the railroad came to the Carolina backcountry, Charlotte was first in line to get its ticket punched. Cotton farmers throughout the Carolina Piedmont carried their crops to Charlotte, and brokers funneled the raw cotton down the line to the port of Charleston. These early ties to South Carolina could arguably be the origin of the subtle but pervasive sense that Charlotte is only technically part of North Carolina.

Charlotte rebounded quickly after the Civil War, encouraging Northern and foreign investment—again drawing the disapprobation of other North Carolinians, but laying the groundwork for greater prosperity. Textile mill money enriched the city throughout the early 20th century. In more recent years,

view of Charlotte's Uptown

# Charlotte

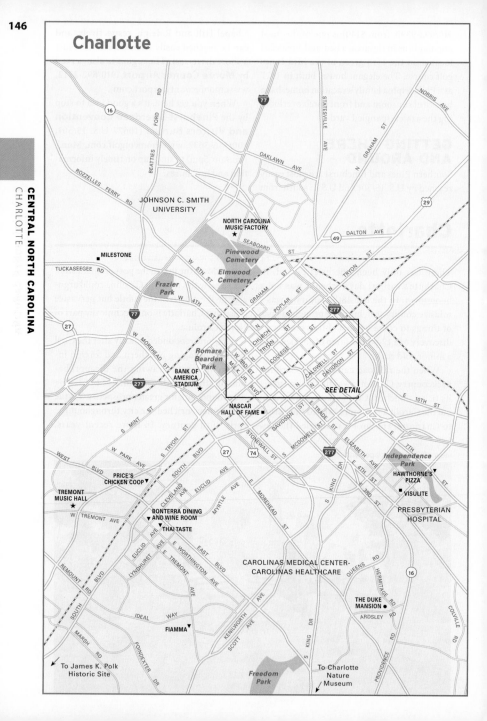

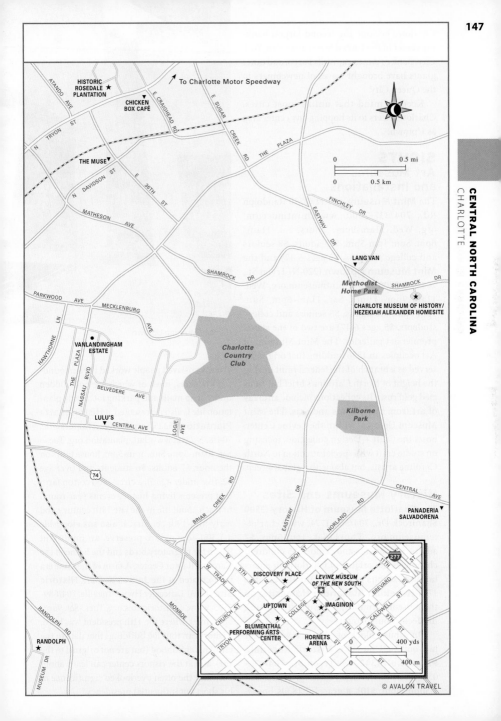

ATANDO AVE

HISTORIC ROSEDALE PLANTATION ★

To Charlotte Motor Speedway

CHICKEN BOX CAFÉ ▼

N TRYON ST

E CRAIGHEAD RD

E SUGAR CREEK RD

THE PLAZA

0      0.5 mi

0      0.5 km

THE MUSE ▼

N DAVIDSON ST

E 36TH ST

FINCHLEY DR

EASTWAY DR

MATHESON AVE

LANG VAN ▼

SHAMROCK DR

*Methodist Home Park*

SHAMROCK DR

CHARLOTTE MUSEUM OF HISTORY/ HEZEKIAH ALEXANDER HOMESITE

PARKWOOD AVE

HAWTHORNE LN

MECKLENBURG AVE

THE PLAZA

NASSAU BLVD

VANLANDINGHAM ESTATE ●

*Charlotte Country Club*

BELVEDERE AVE

*Kilborne Park*

LULU'S ▼

CENTRAL AVE

LOGIE AVE

74

CENTRAL AVE

BRIAR CREEK RD

EASTWAY DR

NORLAND RD

PANADERIA SALVADORENA ▼

RANDOLPH RD

MONROE

MUSEUM DR

RANDOLPH ★

CHURCH ST

277

W 5TH ST

W TRADE ST

DISCOVERY PLACE ★

LEVINE MUSEUM OF THE NEW SOUTH ✚

E 11TH ST

BREVARD ST

CALDWELL ST

S CHURCH ST

UPTOWN ★

N COLLEGE ST

6TH ST

IMAGINON ★

S TRYON ST

BLUMENTHAL PERFORMING ARTS CENTER

7TH ST

8TH ST

9TH ST

HORNETS ARENA ★

0      400 yds

0      400 m

© AVALON TRAVEL

Charlotte became the second-largest banking center of the United States after New York City. Bank of America, Wells Fargo, and other giants have brought waves of newcomers to the Queen City.

Keep in mind that unlike most cities, Charlotte refers to its hopping city center area as Uptown.

## SIGHTS
### Art Museums and Installations

The **Mint Museum of Art** (2730 Randolph Rd., 704/337-2000, www.mintmuseum.org, Wed. 11am-9pm, Thurs.-Sat. 11am-6pm, Sun. 1pm-5pm, $10 adults, $8 seniors and college students, $5 ages 6-17) and the **Mint Museum Uptown** (220 N. Tryon St., 704/337-2000, www.mintmuseum.org, Wed. 11am-9pm, Thurs.-Sat. 11am-6pm, Sun. 1pm-5pm, $10 adults, $8 seniors and college students, $5 ages 6-17) are two of the state's premier art galleries. The Mint Museum of Art occupies an 1836 building that originally served as a branch of the federal mint during the height of North Carolina's brief but frenzied gold rush. Its collections include an array of art from many lands and eras. The Mint Museum Uptown, within the Levine Center, hosts the Craft + Design collection, focusing on studio craft with special attention to North Carolina artists, but also with a global sweep.

### History Museums and Sites

The **Charlotte Museum of History** (3500 Shamrock Dr., 704/568-1774, www.charlottemuseum.org, Thurs.-Sat. 1pm-5pm, $7 adults, $5 students and seniors, $5 children) chronicles the origins of Charlotte in entertaining exhibits geared toward all ages; the 1774 **Hezekiah Alexander Homesite**, on the museum grounds, is the oldest structure in Mecklenburg County.

On a busy block of North Tryon Street just outside Uptown is **Historic Rosedale Plantation** (3427 N. Tryon St., 704/335-0325, www.historicrosedale.org, Thurs.-Sat. 1:30pm-3pm, $10), a graceful 1830s house.

the Mint Museum Uptown

Twenty enslaved people worked the surrounding 911 acres, most of which are now hidden under strip malls and parking lots. Early plantation life is also represented at **Historic Latta Plantation** (5225 Sample Rd., Huntersville, 704/875-2312, www.lattaplantation.org, Tues.-Sat. 10am-5pm, Sun. 1pm-5pm, house tours on the hour, $7 adults, $6 students and over age 62, free under age 5), a circa-1800 cotton farm that presents living-history events year-round to teach about life in the late 18th century and early-mid-19th century. It also sits alongside a 1,300-acre nature preserve, an important haven for migratory birds and the home of the Carolina Raptor Center. A farm of the same era is re-created at the **James K. Polk Historic Site** (12031 Lancaster Hwy., Pineville, 704/889-7145, www.nchistoricsites.org, Tues.-Sat. 9am-5pm, free), where the 11th president was born. Visitors can tour log buildings that date to the era of his childhood (but are not original to the site), and at the visitors center can learn about Polk and the often overlooked significance of his short but influential presidency.

the James K. Polk Historic Site, where the president was born

## ★ Levine Museum of the New South

The **Levine Museum of the New South** (200 E. 7th St., 704/333-1887, www.museumofthenewsouth.org, Mon.-Sat. 10am-5pm, Sun. noon-5pm, $8 adults, $6 seniors, $5 children) tells the story—in its permanent exhibit called *Cotton Fields to Skyscrapers*—of the South's emergence from the devastation of the Civil War and the rancor of Reconstruction, through the postwar reign of King Cotton, and the lives of the tobacco and textile industries that for so long were the staples of North Carolina's economy. Interwoven are stories of segregation and the civil rights movement, and the waves of globalization and immigration that are defining today's new New South. Changing exhibits address head-on, often in daring ways, community, race, nationality, stereotyping, religion, and other fascinating and extremely complex issues of Southern life.

the Levine Museum of the New South

## Museums and Activity Centers for Kids

**Discovery Place** (301 N. Tryon St., 704/372-6261, www.discoveryplace.org, Mon.-Fri. 9am-4pm, Sat. 10am-6pm, Sun. noon-5pm, museum $12, museum plus IMAX $17) is an interactive museum with an indoor rain forest, an IMAX theater, preserved human body parts, and much more. Discovery Place also operates the **Charlotte Nature Museum** (1658 Sterling Rd., 704/372-6261, www.charlottenaturemuseum.org, Tues.-Fri. 9am-5pm, Sat. 10am-5pm, Sun. noon-5pm, $6) next to Freedom Park, which is home to live animals and a walk-through butterfly pavilion. **ImaginOn** (300 E. 7th St., 704/416-4600, www.imaginon.org, Tues.-Thurs. 10am-7pm, Fri.-Sat. 10am-5pm, Sun. 1pm-5pm) is a major Uptown arts complex for children and teens. It has theaters, libraries, a story lab, and a teen center.

## ENTERTAINMENT AND EVENTS
### Performing Arts

Among the city's several excellent theater companies are **Theatre Charlotte** (501 Queens Rd., 704/376-3777, www.theatrecharlotte.org), which has been in business since the 1920s; the **Actor's Theatre of Charlotte** (650 E. Stonewall St., 704/342-2251, www.actorstheatrecharlotte.org), a company specializing in contemporary dramas; the **Carolina Actors Studio Theatre** (1118 Clement Ave., 704/455-8542, www.nccast.com) for experiential art; and the **Children's Theatre of Charlotte** (704/973-2800, www.ctcharlotte.org), which has its home at ImaginOn.

The **Blumenthal Performing Arts Center** (130 N. Tryon St., 704/372-1000, www.blumenthalcenter.org) in Uptown is the home theater of the **Charlotte Symphony** (www.charlottesymphony.org), which has been in existence for nearly 80 years. These days it puts together seasons of baroque, romantic, and modern classical music, as well as a series of pops-style concerts with guest artists. Almost 40 years old, the **North Carolina Dance Theater** (704/372-1000, www.ncdance.org) is another venerable institution in Charlotte's arts scene. They dance full-length classical ballets and modern works, and tour widely. **Opera Carolina** (704/372-1000, www.operacarolina.org), at 60 years old, is the leading opera company in the Carolinas. They produce four major operas each year, as well as an annual run of *Amahl and the Night Visitors* at Christmastime.

## Beyond Banktown

Charlotteans and outsiders alike often refer to the Queen City as Banktown, a name meant to conjure images of spotless sidewalks and shining office towers, a nine-to-five corporate culture with little room for the arts or nonconformity. But there's a lot more to Charlotte than the Bank of America tower (sometimes called the Taj McColl, for former CEO Hugh McColl).

I happen to think that Uptown, with its sparkly skyscrapers and stampeding suits, is kind of cool—a little bit of Washington's K Street in a more tropical clime. But we do a disservice to Charlotte and to ourselves as travelers if we overlook the beautiful variety of people who live here. In addition to the suggestions you'll find in this chapter, explore these websites and pick up these publications while you're in Banktown to find out what's happening outside the tower's shadow.

- *Creative Loafing* (http://clclt.com), a free weekly that you can find all over the city, does a bang-up job of covering the arts, food, politics, and everything else that makes Charlotte hum. The website is as good a resource as the print edition.

- **Weird Charlotte** (www.weirdcharlotte.com)—motto "Keep Charlotte weird? Make Charlotte weird!"—is an online compendium of "current weirdness," "historic weirdness," "random acts of weirdness," and "weirdos" in this fine city.

## Festivals

Each May, race fans take over several blocks of Uptown for **Speed Street** (704/455-5555, www.600festival.com). For three days, entertainers, race-car drivers, and thousands of enthusiasts celebrate the area's auto racing industry. Autograph sessions throughout the festival bring participants in close contact with racing royalty.

Charlotte is an incredible city for foodies, and one way to learn the culinary ropes here in a short time is to come to the early-June **Taste of Charlotte** (704/262-9847, www.tasteofcharlotte.com). Dozens of area restaurants make samples of their art available, from haute European masterpieces to soul food favorites, plus plenty of international flavors from this wonderfully diverse community.

Charlotte's rapidly expanding population of recent immigrants has filled the city's entertainment calendar with dozens of festivals and holidays from around the world. June's annual **Asian Festival** (704/540-6808) features dragon boat races on Ramsey Creek in Cornelius. Early September brings the **Yiasou Greek Festival** (704/334-4771, www.yiasoufestival.org), which celebrates one of the South's long-established Greek communities. October's **Latin American Festival** (704/531-3848, www.latinamericancoalition.org) celebrates the South's largest new immigrant group.

## Nightlife

The **North Carolina Music Factory** (1000 Seaboard St., 704/987-0612, http://ncmusicfactory.com) is a huge complex of clubs and theaters on the northeast side of Uptown. Its venues range from the 5,000-seat Uptown Amphitheater to Butter, a nightclub with top national DJs. Visit the website to find out about upcoming acts, and for a map of the factory; it helps to get your bearings before you go. **Tremont Music Hall** (400 W. Tremont Ave., 704/343-9494, www.tremontmusichall.com) has a capacity of more than 1,000 and hosts national acts in rock, punk, hardcore, ska, metal, and other styles. The smaller venue

on the site, the Casbah, holds 325 and often hosts regional and local acts. The **Visulite** (1625 Elizabeth Ave., 704/358-9200, www.visulite.com) is another major venue, hosting prominent rock and roll, reggae, world music, and other bands.

The **Milestone** (3400 Tuckasegee Rd., 704/398-0472, www.themilestoneclub.com) has been hosting underground and up-and-coming bands since 1969 and was a major landmark for punk music in the South in the 1980s. Artists who've made appearances in the club's history include R.E.M., Hasil Adkins, and Fugazi. Today's lineups are just as inspired. **Coyote Joe's** (4621 Wilkinson Blvd., 704/399-4946, www.coyote-joes.com) is a huge country dance hall and honky-tonk that hosts top Nashville artists. **Puckett's Farm Equipment** (2740 W. Sugar Creek Rd., 704/597-8230, www.puckettsfarm.com) is a smaller country juke joint with regular bluegrass and rockabilly shows.

The **Double Door Inn** (1218 Charlottetown Ave./Independence Blvd., 704/376-1446, http://doubledoorinn.com) calls itself "Charlotte's home of the blues." It has brought the glitterati of blues, roots, and roots-rock music to Charlotte for nearly four decades. The **Neighborhood Theatre** (511 E. 36th St., 704/358-9298, www.neighborhoodtheatre.com, all ages) in the NoDa (North Davidson) neighborhood is a place where artists already high on the charts, or new artists starting to make the climb to stardom, appear when they're in Charlotte. Visitors of all ages are admitted to most shows. NoDa also has a folk club, **The Muse** (3227 N. Davidson St., 704/376-3737, www.theeveningmuse.com, Wed.-Thurs. 6pm-midnight, Fri.-Sat. 6pm-late). This is an intimate listening room, and music fans of all ages are admitted.

# SPORTS AND RECREATION

## Spectator Sports

The Carolinas' only National Basketball Association franchise, the **Charlotte Hornets** (333 E. Trade St., 704/262-2287, www.nba.com/hornets), play in the massive Spectrum Center in Uptown. The Hornets attract a statewide following by recruiting talent from the ranks of UNC Tar Heel basketball alums. UNC alum and NBA legend Michael Jordon now owns the team.

Charlotte is also home to the Carolinas' only National Football League team, the **Carolina Panthers** (9800 S. Mint St., 704/358-7800, www.panthers.com), who play at the Bank of America Stadium at the edge of Uptown. Fans, twirling their growl-towels, cheered them on to National Football Conference titles in 2003 and 2015.

The Chicago White Sox Triple-A baseball affiliate is the **Charlotte Knights** (704/357-8071, www.charlotteknights.com), who play Uptown at BB&T Park (324 S. Mint St.). Single game tickets range $8-30.

Professional ECHL hockey team the **Charlotte Checkers** play at the Bojangles' Coliseum. Ticket and schedule information are available from 704/342-4423 and www.gocheckers.com.

## ★ U.S. National Whitewater Center

The **U.S. National Whitewater Center** (820 Hawfield Rd., 704/391-3900, www.usnwc.org, daily 10am-5pm, passes $20-54, canopy tours $89) features "the world's only multichannel recirculating white-water river"—that is, a complex of artificial rapids—designed for training athletes at the Olympic level (it is the home of the U.S. Olympic canoe and kayak team), as well as first-time thrill-seekers. The center's 300 acres also feature mountain biking trails, a climbing center, and more.

## FOOD

There are so many good new restaurants opening every week that it's hard to keep up, but for reviews of the newest restaurants (with lots of interesting cultural observation), check out *Creative Loafing* (free at many area businesses, http://clclt.com), and the food writing in the *Charlotte Observer* (www.charlotteobserver.com/restaurants).

## Southern and Soul

**Price's Chicken Coop** (1614 Camden Rd., 704/333-9866, www.priceschickencoop.com, Tues.-Sat. 10am-6pm, under $10) is one of Charlotte's favorite chicken places, a takeout counter where you can buy a box of deep-fried chicken, perch, shrimp, or liver and gizzards. Another venerable fried chicken laboratory is the **Chicken Box Café** (3726 N. Tryon St., 704/332-2636, daily 11am-9pm, under $10).

## Southeast Asian

Charlotte is a city of immigrants, with more arriving every year, and among the many benefits of this growing diversity is an amazingly rich culinary environment. Asian cuisines are prominent, especially Vietnamese, Thai, and Malaysian restaurants.

**Thai Taste** (324 East Blvd., 704/332-0001, www.thaitastecharlotte.com, lunch Mon.-Fri. 11:30am-2:30pm, dinner Sun.-Thurs. 5pm-9pm, Fri.-Sat. 5pm-10:30pm, $10-18) has been a favorite for more than 20 years. The menu includes a variety of curries, noodle dishes, and stir-fries, including many vegetarian options.

Charlotte has quite a few Vietnamese restaurants, which are great fun to sample. Perhaps the best known is ★ **Lang Van** (3019 Shamrock Dr., 704/531-9525, www.langvanrestaurant.com, Sun.-Thurs. 11am-9:45pm, Fri.-Sat. 11am-11pm, under $10). Lang Van has an incredibly long menu, with many *phos,* noodle soups, and vermicelli dishes. Like many Vietnamese restaurants, this is an ideal eatery for vegetarians. *Charlotte Observer* readers have voted Lang Van the area's top Asian restaurant multiple times.

## Pizza

Everyone seems to like **Brooklyn South Pizza** (19400 Jetton Rd., Cornelius, 704/896-2928, Mon.-Wed. 11am-9pm, Thurs.-Sat.

11am-10pm, Sun. noon-9pm, $10-15) in Cornelius, north of the city. **Tony's Pizza** (14027 Conlan Circle, 704/541-8225, http://tonysbigpizza.com, Mon.-Thurs. 11am-9pm, Fri.-Sat. 11am-10pm, Sun. noon-9pm, $5-25), founded by two Italian-born, Brooklyn-raised friends, is another favorite. Also loudly lauded is **Hawthorne's Pizza** (1701 E. 7th St., 704/358-9339; 5814 Prosperity Church Rd., 704/875-8502; 4100 Carmel Rd., Ste. A, 704/544-0299, http://hawthornespizza.com, Sun.-Thurs. 11am-midnight, Fri.-Sat. 11am-2am, $8-20).

## Latin American

Charlotte has a large Latino population, and its imprint on the culinary landscape of the city adds a welcome dimension to the diversity of restaurants here. Most immediately noticeable are the wealth of small home-style taquerias. Many can be found along Central Avenue. Try **Taquería Linares** (4918 Central Ave., 704/535-6716, daily 11am-9pm, $7), **Taquería las Delicias** (5111 Central Ave., 704/537-5156, daily 11am-9pm, $7), and **Taquería la Única** (2801 Central Ave., 704/347-5115, daily 11am-9pm, $8). **Lempira** (5906 South Blvd., 704/552-1515, Mon.-Thurs. 8am-11pm, Fri.-Sat. 8am-midnight, $12) is an especially good Central American restaurant on South Boulevard. Delicious Latin American bakeries also are popping up all over, like **Panadería Salvadoreña** (4800 Central Ave., 704/568-9161) and **Taste of Colombia** (212 N. Polk St., Pineville, 704/889-5328).

## European

**Fiamma** (2418 Park Rd., 704/333-4363, daily 11:30am-3:30pm and 5pm-11pm, under $30) is a special Italian restaurant in the Dilworth neighborhood. For its spectacular menu, Fiamma has fresh fish flown in every day from Italy, and they make their pasta and pizza crust dough twice daily from scratch. Such dedication to quality can be tasted at first bite.

## Indian

★ **Woodlands** (7128-A Albemarle Rd., 704/569-9193, Mon.-Fri. 11:30am-3pm and 5pm-9:30pm, Sat.-Sun. 11:30am-10pm, $7-15) serves absolutely wonderful vegetarian southern Indian cuisine, offering nearly 20 different curries, *utthapam* (rice and lentil pancakes), Chinese-influenced rice and noodle dishes, and dozens of other components with which to assemble one of the best Indian meals you'll find in North Carolina.

## Eclectic American

Among Charlotte's fanciest places to dine is **Bonterra Dining and Wine Room** (1829 Cleveland Ave. at E. Worthington Ave., 704/333-9463, http://bonterradining.com, $20-45). Bonterra, which has received both the Four Diamond Award from AAA and *Wine Spectator* magazine's Award of Excellence, makes its home in an old Methodist church. House specialties include New York strip steak, veal chops, and fried lobster tail. Really, though, it's as much about wine here as food. The wine list features many dozens of fine wines from California, France, Australia, and even North Carolina. There are also many choices of single-malt scotch, port, and cognac.

## ACCOMMODATIONS

When it comes to the languid elegance of the Old South, ★ **The Duke Mansion** (400 Hermitage Rd., 704/714-4400, www.dukemansion.com, from $179) is close kin to heaven. The circa-1915 mansion in Charlotte's lovely Myers Park neighborhood was home to North Carolina royalty, the Duke family, including the young Doris Duke. The downstairs foyer and gallery were clearly designed for entertaining high society, but the bedrooms—most restored to reflect the Duke family's tastes of around 1930—are simple and comfortable, and some of the en suite baths still have their original tubs and tiles.

The ★ **VanLandingham Estate** (2010

The Plaza, 704/334-8909 or 888/524-2020, www.vanlandinghamestate.com, from $140), built in 1913, provides a glimpse of the affluent infancy of the neighborhood known as Plaza-Midwood. A streetcar ran down the middle of The Plaza, and wealthy families established five- and six-acre estates in what was then a bucolic suburb. Plaza-Midwood now feels very close to the center of the city, and the lots have long since been subdivided, but it is still a charming enclave of early 20th-century craftsman-style bungalows. The VanLandingham is an architectural marriage of the best arts-and-crafts design elements and aesthetics individually tailored to the tastes of the builders, early textile magnates Ralph and Susie Harwood VanLandingham.

## INFORMATION AND SERVICES

Two Uptown locations serve as Charlotte **visitors centers:** one at 330 South Tryon Street (704/339-6040, www.crva.com, Mon.-Fri. 8:30am-5pm, Sat. 9am-3pm), and the other in the lobby of the Levine Museum of the New South (200 E. 7th St., 704/331-2753, www.museumofthenewsouth.org, Mon.-Sat. 10am-5pm, Sun. noon-5pm). The *Charlotte Observer* publishes an excellent annual guide to the region, geared toward new residents and visitors, called *Living Here.* You can pick it up at many major destinations, or read it at www.charlotteobserver.com. Another comprehensive resource is www.visitcharlotte.com.

**Carolinas Medical Center** (1000 Blythe Blvd., 704/355-2000, www.carolinasmedical-center.org) is one of the largest hospitals in the Carolinas. Emergency vet clinics include **Carolina Veterinary Specialists** (2225 Township Rd., 704/588-7015 or 704/504-9608, www.carolinavet.com) and **Emergency Veterinary Clinic** (2440 Plantation Center Dr., Matthews, 704/844-6440).

## GETTING THERE AND AROUND

**Charlotte Douglas International Airport** (CLT, 5501 Josh Birmingham Pkwy., 704/359-4013, www.charmeck,org) is the 10th-largest hub in the United States, with nonstop flights to and from over 120 destinations worldwide. Nearly 30 million passengers come through CLT each year. Charlotte's **Amtrak Station** (1914 N. Tryon St., 704/376-4416, www.amtrak.com) is a short cab ride from major Uptown hotels and attractions.

Charlotte's extensive and ever-expanding public transportation system provides affordable jaunts from place to place throughout the city. Some bus routes around the Center City and Uptown areas are free. The city has an ambitious light-rail system called **LYNX,** currently connecting Uptown to some southern neighborhoods and which will eventually provide rapid access to and from Charlotte's many far-flung neighborhoods and suburbs. Routes and fares are posted at www.charmeck.org, or call 704/336-7433.

# Vicinity of Charlotte

The number of NASCAR-related attractions and sites of interest to racing enthusiasts in general are too numerous to name, but you'll find a selection of the best listed here.

Several of the state's special food traditions intersect near Charlotte. The fumes of Lexington barbecue waft over the entire Piedmont, causing an irresistible urge to mix ketchup into one's barbecue sauce. Serious

aficionados of fried fish don't drive all the way to the coast to get their fix, but instead scout out inland fish camps on the back roads of Gaston and neighboring counties.

## MOORESVILLE AND LAKE NORMAN

Mooresville is home to some of the state's—and the nation's—most important car-racing facilities and attractions, as well as the home bases of more than 60 individual teams. There are several racing museums here, including the **North Carolina Auto Racing Hall of Fame** (Mooresville Visitor Center, 119 Knob Hill Rd., Mooresville, 704/663-5331, www. ncarhof.com, Mon.-Fri. 10am-5pm, Sat. 10am-3pm, $6 adults, $4 seniors and children). The **Memory Lane Motorsports Museum** (769 River Hwy., Mooresville, 704/662-3673, www. memorylaneautomuseum.com, daily 10am-5pm during race weeks, $10 adults, $6 ages 6-12, free under age 6) features the largest private collection of retired NASCAR automobiles and the world's largest collection of go-karts.

Major teams and racing companies are based here, and some operate facilities that are open to the public. **Dale Earnhardt Inc.** (1675 Coddle Creek Hwy./Hwy. 3, Mooresville, 704/334-9663, www.daleearnhardtinc.com, Mon.-Fri. 9am-5pm, Sat. 10am-4pm) has a showroom and a museum about the career of Dale Sr., a NASCAR legend. Teams' complexes are scattered throughout the area, including Dale Earnhardt Jr.'s **JR Motorsports** (349 Cayuga Dr., Mooresville, 704/799-4800, www.jrmotorsport.com), **Penske Racing** (200 Penske Way, Mooresville, 704/664-2300, www.penskeracing.com), and **Robert Yates Racing** (112 Byers Creek Rd., Mooresville, 704/662-9625, www.robertyatesracing.com).

Not to be missed either are the **NASCAR Technical Institute** (220 Byers Creek Rd., Mooresville, 877/201-2597, www.uti.edu), a formal training school for motorsports automotive technology, and **PIT Instruction and Training LLC** (156 Byers Creek Rd., Mooresville, 866/563-3566, www.5off5on. com), a pit-crew training school.

## Sports and Recreation

If it's too hot to be around all that asphalt, there's plenty to do on the water. **Lake Norman State Park** (159 Inland Sea Ln., Troutman, 704/528-6350, http://ncparks.gov, May-Aug. 8am-9pm, Mar.-Apr. and Sept.-Oct. 8am-8pm, Nov.-Feb. 8am-6pm, free) shelters the state's largest artificial lake, with boating, swimming, camping ($20), and more than six miles of biking and hiking trails.

# CONCORD AND KANNAPOLIS

Cabarrus County, which wraps around the northeastern corner of Charlotte, is one of the phonetic zones that give newcomers and longtime North Carolinians alike the fits. Banish from your mind all thoughts of three-headed dogs and celebrated jumping frogs: it's "cuh-BA-russ," and the *a* is pronounced as in "hat." Kannapolis rhymes with the capital of Maryland.

## Lowe's Motor Speedway

**Lowe's Motor Speedway** (5555 Concord Pkwy. S., Concord, 800/455-3267, www.lowesmotorspeedway.com, tours nonevent days Mon.-Sat. 9:30am, 10:30am, 11:30am, 1:30pm, 2:30pm, 3:30pm, Sun. 1:30pm, 3:30pm, $5), on U.S. 29 South, is Concord's best-known attraction. The 167,000-seat arena with a 1.5-mile track hosts the NASCAR Cup Series as well as other NASCAR, Xfinity, and Truck Series events. The speedway is also home to the **Richard Petty Driving Experience,** where you can ride—or even drive—a 600-hp stock car at speeds up to 165 mph, as well as the **Xtreme Measures Teen Driving School,** where teenage drivers can spend two days learning safe driving skills in an exhilarating environment. Oddly enough, the Speedway's Smith Tower, on the 2nd floor, hosts the **Carolinas Boxing Hall of Fame** (704/455-3200).

## Racing Sights

Not to be outdone by its neighbor Concord, Kannapolis honors racing and the life of its hometown star Dale Earnhardt Sr., with the **Dale Trail.** "Dale Senior" died at the age of 50 in an infamous last-lap crash at the 2001 Daytona 500, one of the tragedies in racing history that has most starkly illustrated the great danger to which drivers subject themselves. He is honored by a nine-foot bronze statue, a fan-financed granite monument, and huge murals, all at the **Dale Earnhardt Tribute** (Main St. and B St.) in the middle of Cannon Village, a historic shopping district in Kannapolis.

Opening Uptown in 2010, the **NASCAR Hall of Fame** (400 E. Martin Luther King Jr. Blvd., 888/902-6463, www.nascarhall. com, daily 10am-6pm, $19.95 adults, $12.95 ages 5-12) represents the state of the art of the South's second most popular sport (college football being the first, of course), suitably located in the spiritual heart of central North Carolina. The centerpiece is the Great Hall, where expansive rotating exhibits and displays reside, along with "Glory Road," an homage to great tracks and great cars from NASCAR history. The large "High Octane Theatre" shows a looping 12-minute film with exciting race highlights.

# Asheville and the Blue Ridge Parkway

# Highlights

© AVALON TRAVEL

★ **The Merry Go-Round Show:** Mount Airy is blessed with a rich musical tradition and a great small-town radio station, WPAQ. This weekly show is broadcast in front of a live audience (page 162).

★ **MerleFest:** For one long weekend in April, the best artists in American roots music are in North Wilkesboro, along with thousands of their fans (page 166).

★ **Grandfather Mountain:** Take a gander at the surrounding UN-designated International Biosphere Reserve from the famous Mile-High Swinging Bridge—if you dare (page 172).

★ **Mount Mitchell:** The tallest peak east of South Dakota was the subject of a scholarly feud in the mid-1800s. One of the antagonists, Mitchell himself, is buried at the summit (page 176).

★ **Chimney Rock:** A natural tower of stone growing out of a mountainside like a rhino's horn, Chimney Rock is the centerpiece of a large park with amazing hiking trails (page 181).

★ **Downtown Asheville Architecture:** In the early 20th century, wealthy summer vacationers left their mark in Asheville's downtown, a district packed with art deco and beaux arts masterpieces (page 182).

★ **Biltmore Estate:** This awe-inspiring palace of the Gilded Age hosts a collection of great little restaurants and shops, a winery, equestrian activities, and much more, all in a beautiful riverside setting (page 184).

★ **North Carolina Arboretum:** One of the most beautiful collections of horticulture in the country is framed by the surrounding Pisgah National Forest (page 186).

★ **Folk Art Center:** Learn about the master craftspeople of the Appalachians and purchase gorgeous handmade items, including unique jewelry, traditional weaving and woodcarving, and fine furniture (page 189).

★ **Pisgah Ranger District:** This 150,000-plus-acre section of the Pisgah National Forest encompasses the Cradle of Forestry Museum, Shining Rock Wilderness, Sliding Rock, Cold Mountain, and many other favorite outdoor destinations (page 199).

Oone of the first impressions re-corded by a visitor to North Carolina's Blue Ridge Mountains came in 1752, when Bishop Augustus Spangenberg came down from Pennsylvania in search of a prospective Southern home for the

Moravian Church. He eventually found a welcoming spot near present-day Winston-Salem, but it's a wonder he didn't turn back when he first saw the Blue Ridge, a sight that filled him with dread. This man, who had crossed the Atlantic and tramped all over the American frontier, wrote in his diary, "We have reached here after a hard journey over very high, terrible mountains and cliffs. . . . When we reached the top we saw mountains to the right, to the left, before and behind us, rising like great waves in a storm."

The Blue Ridge is still pretty daunting, and indeed nearly impenetrable in parts, but times have changed, and the region attracts visitors and adventurers from all over the world for its blend of rustic scenery and authentic folk culture.

Nestled in a valley along the colorfully named French Broad River, Asheville—western North Carolina's largest city—is something of a paradox. An outpost of left-leaning,

New Age-y thought in a generally very conservative area, Asheville boasts a large and influential creative community of artists, artisans, academics, and musicians of all types, from street buskers to classical performers (indeed, sometimes they're one and the same).

Begun in the 1930s as part of Franklin D. Roosevelt's Works Progress Administration, the Blue Ridge Parkway (BRP, www.blueridgeparkway.org) is 469 miles of road stretching from the North Carolina-Tennessee border into Virginia's Shenandoah Valley; the bulk of it is in the Tar Heel State. It's fun, accessible, tastefully done, and very scenic. The BRP took 50 years to complete—the final section was finished in 1987—and boasts 26 tunnels blasted out of the rock, 25 of them in North Carolina. Its complexion changes slightly as you wind your way farther north, but the twisty mountain driving at a maximum 45 mph is a constant.

Until the 20th century the farthest

**Previous:** the Blue Ridge Mountains above Asheville; a cabin near Stone Mountain. **Above:** a flat iron building in downtown Asheville.

# Asheville and the Blue Ridge Parkway

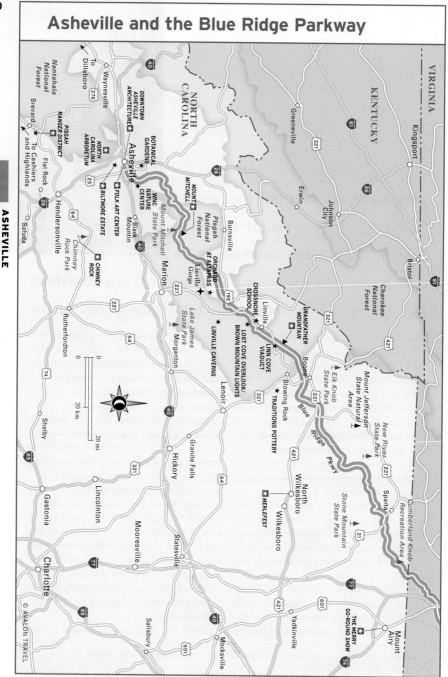

© AVALON TRAVEL

northwestern counties of North Carolina were so remote and so cut off from the rest of the state that they were known as the Lost Provinces. Gradually, improved roads and the BRP brought curious flatlanders up into the clouds, and the region evolved into a popular destination for vacationers. But stands of virgin forest are still hidden in remote coves, and places like the Linville Gorge dare the most accomplished outdoors enthusiasts.

On any given weekend in Mount Airy, and in many other mountain and foothills towns nearer to the heart of the Blue Ridge at the Virginia border, you can hear the old-time string band music that is as popular here today as it was in the days before the radio. Even if you've come to the mountains to ski or to eat at the gourmet restaurants in Boone and Blowing Rock, be sure to set aside a little time for the back roads.

## PLANNING YOUR TIME

Always keep the weather in mind when driving in the mountains here and all along the BRP, not only snow and ice from fall to spring but frequent dense fog throughout the year. Conditions can be completely different from one moment to the next and from one mountain to the next. Don't hesitate to pull over and wait out the fog. It often lifts and dissipates quickly.

Driving the BRP, while most satisfying, takes longer than it may look on a map due to the low speed limit and the winding nature of the road. The heavily traveled stretch from Asheville to Boone, for example, will take about four hours.

Asheville, to the south, boasts by far the greatest number of amenities, but there are fine restaurants and B&B-style lodging all through the towns of western North Carolina.

If you're planning on spending most of your time roaming the deep mountains around Mount Mitchell and Grandfather Mountain, the Linville area, and the Banner Elk and Beech Mountain areas, Boone is a convenient place to stay. Wilkesboro and Mount Airy are both at the edge of the mountains and easily accessible from the junction of I-77 and U.S. 421, a jumping-off point to almost any foothills location.

## INFORMATION AND SERVICES

The state Department of Transportation operates a real-time road conditions map (http://tims.ncdot.gov/tims). For current conditions along the Blue Ridge Parkway, you can check the recorded message at 828/298-0398.

Hospitals are located in most of the major towns in this region, but in case of an emergency, help might be delayed by weather, road conditions, or distance. In many areas—not just deep in the woods, but in populated areas as well—there may be no cell phone signal.

## GETTING THERE AND AROUND

The Blue Ridge Parkway is especially enjoyable in that there is no cross traffic. The BRP is bridged over interstate highways, and it has separate side roads for every intersection. Everything on the BRP is measured by milepost, with mile marker number 1 beginning in northwest Virginia, going all the way to number 469 at U.S. 441.

Along the BRP you'll be sharing the road with plenty of motorcyclists, drawn to the scenery and challenging roads. Always be aware of their presence, for their safety and for yours.

# Mount Airy and the Virginia Border

## MOUNT AIRY AND VICINITY
### Sights

In downtown Mount Airy you'll notice 1960s police squad cars, business names that may seem oddly familiar, and cardboard cutouts of Barney Fife peering out from shop windows. Mount Airy is the hometown of Andy Griffith and a mecca for fans of *The Andy Griffith Show*. TAGSRWC (www.mayberry.com) is an intentionally obtuse acronym for The Andy Griffith Show Rerun Watchers Club, the show's international fan club whose hundreds of chapters have in-reference names like "Her First Husband Got Runned over by a Team of Hogs" (Texas) and "Anxiety Magnifies Fearsome Objects" (Alabama). The Surry Arts Council hosts the citywide **Mayberry Days,** an annual fall festival entering its second decade, in which TAGSRWC members, other fans, cast members, and impersonators of Mayberry characters come to town and have a big time getting haircuts at Floyd's Barbershop, riding in squad cars, and arresting each other.

For a one-of-a-kind view of Mount Airy, hop into a Mayberry squad car to tour all the major sights in town. **Mayberry Squad Car Tours** (625 S. Main St., 336/789-6743, www.tourmayberry.com) leave from "Wally's Service Station," and cost "$35 for a carload."

Two roadside oddities in Mount Airy are not to be missed. At 594 North Andy Griffith Parkway/U.S. 52 stands the **Giant Milk Carton.** This 12-foot-tall metal milk carton now advertises Pet Milk, but since its creation in the 1940s it has also stood as an advertisement for Coble Dairy and Flavo-Rich Milk. At the intersection of U.S. 52 and Starlite Drive stands a **Great Big Man,** a very tall, friendly metal service station attendant. He is an old friend to out-of-towners who come to Mount Airy for the fiddlers' convention every year, who remember to turn off the highway to get to Veterans Park when they see "the Big Man."

### ★ *The Merry Go-Round* Show

In conjunction with WPAQ (AM 740), the Surry Arts Council hosts *The Merry Go-Round,* the country's third-longest-running live bluegrass and old-time music radio show. Come to the **Downtown Cinema Theater** (142 N. Main St., 800/286-6193, www.surryarts.org) for the show (Sat. 11am-1:30pm), or show up as early as 9am toting an instrument if you'd like to join in the preshow jam session. It's one of the state's great small-town treats.

### Other Entertainment and Events

When you visit Mount Airy or drive through the area, tune in to **WPAQ** (AM 740, also streaming online at www.wpaq740.com). For over 60 years, WPAQ has provided a venue for live local talent to perform old-time, bluegrass, and gospel music. Listen to the live Saturday-morning *The Merry Go-Round* show, or any other day of the week, when you'll hear local call-in shows, old-style country preaching, and more music. Another local institution that has a great deal to do with the vitality of Mount Airy's musical traditions is the **Bluegrass and Old-Time Fiddlers Convention** (631 W. Lebanon St., 800/286-6193, www.mtairyfiddlersconvention.com), held for almost 40 years during the first full weekend in June at Veterans Memorial Park. Thousands of people come to the festival from around the world to play old-time and bluegrass music with their friends and compete in what is a very prestigious competition in this genre of music.

The **Surry Arts Council** is one of the hubs of artistic activity in the Mount Airy-Surry County area. Located at the **Andy Griffith Theater** (218 Rockford St., 800/286-6193, www.surryarts.org), they sponsor and host

# Chang and Eng: Siamese Twins

Andy Griffith may be Mount Airy's most famous son, but in the middle of the 19th century, two of the most famous men in the world lived on a quiet farm in rural Surry County, just outside Mount Airy. Chang and Eng were born in Siam (now Thailand) in 1811, joined at the sternum by a cartilaginous band of flesh. Had they been born today, it probably would have been an easy operation to separate the brothers, but in 1811 they were lucky not to have been killed at birth. Beginning when they were teenagers, Chang and Eng toured the world, eventually becoming top draws at P. T. Barnum's shows.

During their travels through the United States, they took a shine to North Carolina, and when they burned out on show business, around age 30, they decided to settle in Wilkesboro. In North Carolina they adopted the last name of Bunker. Chang fell in love with a local girl named Addie Yates, and soon Eng took to courting her older sister Sally. The four married and moved in together, and raised a very large family—Eng and Sally had 11 children, and Chang and Addie had 10. Many of their descendants live in the area today.

In some ways Chang and Eng seemed like one person. When they first learned English, they referred to themselves as "I," and they were rarely observed to speak to each other, as if it was unnecessary. In one of countless medical experiments they underwent, the examining doctor tickled one brother, which caused the other brother to become angry. Yet in other ways they were very different, and inevitably this caused them great unhappiness. Chang was temperamental and vivid; Eng was reticent and contemplative. More dangerously, Chang liked to drink and Eng liked to gamble. Sometimes they had bitter arguments and, on a couple of occasions, fistfights. Perhaps it's best not to dwell too much on the Bunkers' conjugal relations, but their domestic arrangements required plenty of compromise. They divided their time between Chang and Addie's and Eng and Sally's houses, each brother being the other's houseguest half of the time.

In spite of the limitations that biology placed on them, the Bunkers became fairly conventional upper-middle-class farmers, owning slaves and sending two sons to fight in the Confederate Army. The war left them in dire financial straits, however, and in 1870 they sailed for Europe for another tour. On the voyage home, Chang had a severe stroke, from which he never fully recovered. He began to drink heavily, and his health declined. One January night in 1874, Eng awoke to find that Chang was dead. Within a few hours, Eng, who had been in excellent health, was also dead. An autopsy showed that Chang had died of a cerebral hemorrhage, but Eng's cause of death is still unknown. It's thought that he may have died of fright.

Chang and Eng Bunker, to whom we owe the existence of the phrase "Siamese twins," are buried at White Plains Baptist Church (506 Old Hwy. 601), south of Mount Airy.

many events throughout the year that showcase local talent in drama, visual arts, and especially music. On the third Saturday of the month, local and regional old-time and bluegrass bands perform in the **Voice of the Blue Ridge Series** ($10 adults, free under age 6).

## Sports and Recreation

Mount Airy and its neighbors are foothills towns, and you have to drive some distance farther west before you start to climb the Blue Ridge. This is why the geographical anomaly of Pilot Mountain is so startling. The 1,400-foot mountain, with a prominent rocky knob at the top, kind of looks like a giant dog's head, or the UHF knob of an old TV set that you could use to turn on *The Andy Griffith Show*. The surrounding **Pilot Mountain State Park** (792 Pilot Knob Park Rd., Pinnacle, 336/325-2355, http://ncparks.gov, mountain section May-Aug. 8am-9pm, Mar.-Apr. and Sept.-Oct. 8am-8pm, Nov.-Feb. 8am-6pm, river section May-Aug. 8:30am-8pm, Mar.-Apr. and Sept.-Oct. 8:30am-7pm, Nov.-Feb. 8:30am-5pm, free) is a beautiful place for hiking, swimming, rock climbing and rappelling (in designated areas), canoeing on the Yadkin River, and camping (Mar. 15-Nov. 30, $20, $15 over age 62) at 49 designated tent and trailer sites. Each site has a tent pad, a picnic table, and a grill as well as access to drinking water and hot showers.

A series of 400-foot rock faces, extending for two miles, are the most striking feature of **Hanging Rock State Park** (Hwy. 2015, 4 miles northwest of Danbury, 336/593-8480, http://ncparks.gov, Nov.-Feb. daily 8am-6pm, Mar. and Oct. daily 8am-7pm, Apr.-May and Sept. daily 8am-8pm, June-Aug. daily 8am-9pm, free). It's a great place for rock climbing and rappelling (which requires a permit and registration with park staff as well as a schedule that allows climbers to be finished and out of the park by closing time). You can also hike to waterfalls and beautiful overlooks, and swim in a nearby lake. Hanging Rock State Park has 73 tent and trailer campsites ($20), one of which is wheelchair accessible. There are also two-bedroom, four-bed vacation cabins available for rent during the summer by the week (about $450) and off-season nightly ($88) for a minimum of two nights. Registration is best arranged at least a month in advance; contact the park office for application details.

**Yadkin River Adventures** (104 Old Rockford Rd., Rockford, 336/374-5318, www.yadkinriveradventures.com) offers rentals of canoes, kayaks, and sit-on-tops, and shuttle service for full- and half-day paddling adventures. The Class I Yadkin River is great for paddlers of all ages and experience levels, and it has some beautiful views of Pilot Mountain.

Balloon pilots Tony and Claire Colburn lead tours of the Yadkin Valley by hot-air balloon, weather permitting, any time of year. **Yadkin Valley Hot Air Balloon Adventures** (336/922-7207, www.balloon-adventure.net) requires special arrangements—contact the Colburns for fees and availability—and it's an amazing way to see the Carolina foothills.

## Food

**The Snappy Lunch** (125 N. Main St., 336/786-4931, www.thesnappylunch.com,

Tues., Thurs., Sat. 5:45am-1:15pm, Mon., Wed., Fri. 5:45am-1:45pm, $4) is most famous for having been mentioned in *The Andy Griffith Show*. But having seated its first customer in 1923, The Snappy Lunch is much older than the show and predates even Andy himself. Pack your cholesterol drugs when you go to Mount Airy so that you can enjoy Snappy's signature pork chop sandwich.

There are at least two sources for good, strong coffee in Mount Airy. My favorites are the **Good Life Café** (Main-Oak Emporium, N. Main St. and E. Oak St., 336/789-2404, www.mainoakemporium.com, Mon.-Sat. 10am-6pm, Sun. 1pm-5pm), downtown, and **Moby's Coffee** (2123 Rockford St./U.S. 601, Ste. 200, 336/786-1222, Mon.-Thurs. 7am-10pm, Fri.-Sat. 7am-1pm).

## Accommodations

### UNDER $150

**The Rockford Bed and Breakfast** (4872 Rockford Rd., Dobson, 800/561-6652, www.rockfordbedandbreakfast.com, $120-140) is a beautiful mid-19th-century farmhouse south of Mount Airy in Dobson, convenient to many of the Yadkin Valley wineries.

In Mount Airy, try **Quality Inn** (2136 Rockford St., 336/789-2000, www.qualityinn.com, from $70), **Holiday Inn Express** (1320 Ems Dr., 336/719-1731, www.ichotels.group.com, from $80, pets allowed), and **Hampton Inn** (2029 Rockford St., 336/789-5999, www.hamptoninn.com, from $100).

### $150-300

**Pilot Knob Inn Bed and Breakfast** (361 New Pilot Knob Ln., Pinnacle, 336/325-2502, www.pilotknobinn.com, $129-249) is unusual in that guests can stay not only in suites in the main lodge but in one of several restored, century-old tobacco barns on the property. Each one-bedroom barn-turned-cabin is well equipped with modern conveniences, including two-person hot tubs and wood-burning stone fireplaces. Children are not allowed, nor are pets—other than your horse, that is, who can occupy a stall on the property for an additional $50 per night.

# STONE MOUNTAIN STATE PARK

In the town of Roaring Gap is **Stone Mountain State Park** (3042 Frank Pkwy., Roaring Gap, 336/957-8185, http://ncparks. gov, office daily 8am-5pm, park May-Aug. daily 8am-9pm, Mar.-Apr. and Sept.-Oct. daily 8am-8pm, Nov.-Feb. daily 8am-6pm, free). The centerpiece of the park, a National Natural Landmark, is the spectacular 600-foot smooth rock face of **Stone Mountain,** which, though similar in shape and texture, isn't to be confused with the much larger granite outcropping of the same name outside Atlanta.

This is, of course, a popular spot for rock climbing and rappelling, but adventurous hikers can make the strenuous trek to the summit on foot to enjoy the amazing view. Along one of the hiking trails are the multiple restored log-and-stone buildings of the historic Hutcheson homestead.

The park recommends that only experienced climbers attempt the faces in the park.

Be sure to register with the park office, and carefully read the park literature about climbing before setting out. Some very pleasant camping ($13-25) is available, both primitive backpack camping and family camping in sites near a washhouse with hot showers.

## Accommodations

The camping is great in Stone Mountain State Park, but those requiring more creature comforts might want to head to the nearby town of Elkin, near I-77. The best of the chain accommodations in the area is the **Fairfield Inn & Suites** (628 CC Camp Rd., 866/576-5693, www.marriott.com, $105).

# MOUNT JEFFERSON STATE NATURAL AREA

**Mount Jefferson State Natural Area** (SR 1152, Jefferson, 336/246-9653, http://ncparks. gov, May-Aug. 9am-8pm, Mar.-Apr. and Sept.-Oct. 9am-7pm, Nov.-Feb. 9am-5pm, free) preserves a peak that was known long ago as Panther Mountain as well as a couple of less savory names. Mount Jefferson has a forbidding countenance, with outcroppings of black volcanic rock and, on the north slope,

Stone Mountain State Park

a stunted forest of wind-whipped aspen and maple. Hiking trails, ranging from gentle to strenuous, wend along the crests and up to the peak, through laurel thickets and virgin red oak forests.

**New River State Park** (park office on Wagoner Access Rd./Hwy. 1590, east of Jefferson, 336/982-2587, http://ncparks.gov, May-Aug. 8am-9pm, Mar.-Apr. and Sept.-Oct. 8am-8pm, Nov.-Feb. 8am-6pm, free) threads along what is, despite the name, believed to be one of the oldest rivers in North America. The beautiful New is a very popular canoeing river, a gentle ride through some stunning countryside. Water is highest in May and June, lowest in August and September. Access points are all along the river. There are also many campsites, both canoe-in (no facilities, $13) and drive-to (with showers and restrooms, $25).

**New River Outfitters** (10725 U.S. 221 N., Jefferson, 800/982-9190, www.canoethenew.com) offers canoe runs, ranging from one hour to six days, and tubing trips along the New River. They operate from the old New River General Store, where you can buy mountain honey, hoop cheese, and local crafts. **Zaloo's Canoes** (3874 Hwy. 16 S., Jefferson, 800/535-4027, www.zaloos.com) is another long-established area outfitter that also offers canoe and raft trips.

## ELK KNOB STATE PARK

The small, scenic New River town of Todd is a slow, winding 12 miles north of Boone. **Elk Knob State Park** (5564 Meat Camp Rd., Todd, 828/297-7261, http://ncparks.gov, office daily 8am-5pm, park June-Aug. daily 8am-9pm, Mar.-May and Sept.-Oct. daily 8am-8pm, Nov.-Feb. daily 8am-6pm, free) currently offers three primitive campsites. The big draw is that it stays open during the winter, unlike many other state parks in the mountains, to enable visitors to enjoy cross-country skiing. Elk Knob, the second-highest peak in Watauga County at 5,520 feet, is a steep, strenuous hike along an old road leading to the summit. All facilities here are free of charge.

## WILKESBORO AND NORTH WILKESBORO

### ★ MerleFest

It began as a small folk festival more than 20 years ago, but **MerleFest** (www.merlefest.org, usually the last weekend in Apr.) has grown into one of the premier roots music events in the country. It was founded in honor of Merle Watson, the son of legendary guitarist Doc Watson. Merle, also a guitarist, passed away in 1985 in a tractor accident, cutting short an influential career. Doc Watson, who grew up in the nearby community of Deep Gap, continues to be the festival's ceremonial host, and nowadays he is joined by Merle's son Richard, who has also grown to be an expert guitarist. MerleFest draws thousands of visitors every year and many of the top-name performers in folk, country, and bluegrass music. Tickets cost $40-60 per day for general admission, $145-260 for multiday packages. Springtime in the mountains can be volatile; some years it's boiling hot and sunny at MerleFest, other times as damp and raw as winter, and sometimes it's both by turns. If you're traveling through the northern mountains during MerleFest, keep in mind that all the motels within an hour's drive of North Wilkesboro, and probably farther, will be booked solid, so be sure to put dibs on a room well in advance. Tenting and RV camping are available on the festival grounds.

### Food

North Wilkesboro's **Brushy Mountain Smokehouse and Creamery** (201 Wilkesboro Blvd., 336/667-9464, www.brushymtnsmokehouseandcreamery.com, Mon., Wed., and Thurs.-Sat. 11am-9pm, Sun. 11am-2pm) is famous for its pulled pork barbecue and country sides (biscuits, fried okra, baked apples), but it's also a great ice cream shop. The ice cream is made there, and they bake their own waffle cones, so it's as fresh as it can be. Fried apple pie, cobbler, and ice cream pie are all available by the slice as well as whole-hog.

# Deep Mountains

There's something exciting about the ascent into the High Country—glimpses of a shadowy mountain range on the horizon; cows grazing in steep, rocky fields; hairpin turns in the road around dynamited stone faces; the popping sound in your ears as you reach the first mountain. Most travelers experience this part of North Carolina by winding along the Blue Ridge Parkway (BRP), making side trips deeper into the mountains and peering down from the crest to the Piedmont below.

Boone is a fun and hip little city, the home of Appalachian State University, good antiques shops and organic markets, and a rambunctious green counterculture. Blowing Rock and Linville were tony summertime roosts for wealthy folks early in the 20th century, and much of that elegance remains, both in the stylish bungalows left behind and in the modern spas and resorts found here today.

Venturing off the Parkway and into the deep mountains leads to the little settlements of Penland and Crossnore, as well as Bakersville and other towns in the Toe River Valley. Here you'll find a thriving colony of artists. Many of them came to this area to be part of the folk school at Penland, which in its quiet way has exerted a great deal of influence on modern American craft movements.

## BOONE

Boone is the quintessential western North Carolina city, a blend of old and new, where proponents of homesteading and holistic living find a congenial habitat in the culture of rural Appalachia. It's also a college town, the home of Appalachian State University, and as such has an invigorating youthful verve.

### Shopping

Several antiques shops in Boone make the downtown a great place for browsing. **Appalachian Antiques** (631 W. King St., 828/268-9988, summer Mon.-Sat. 10am-6pm,

Sun. 11am-6pm, winter Mon.-Sat. 10am-5pm, Sun. noon-5pm) is one of the best and biggest.

**Footsloggers** (Depot St. and Howard St., 828/265-5111, www.footsloggers.com) has been selling gear for climbing, hiking, and camping for almost 40 years. At the Boone location (there's also a store in Blowing Rock) is a 40-foot climbing tower that simulates many conditions you might find climbing real rock faces.

There are several branches of the **Mast General Store** (Hwy. 194, Valle Crucis, 828/963-6511, www.mastgeneralstore.com, summer Mon.-Sat. 7am-6:30pm, Sun. noon-6pm, winter hours vary) in the Carolina High Country, but the original is in Valle Crucis, about 20 minutes west of Boone. Though it has been an attraction for more than 20 years now, the store's history as a community institution goes back generations, to the 1880s and before. When the Mast family owned it, the store had the reputation of carrying everything "from cradles to caskets," and today it still has an awfully varied inventory, with specialties in outdoor wear (Carhartt, Columbia, Teva), camping gear, and ever so much candy.

### Sports and Recreation
#### ROCK CLIMBING
**Rock Dimensions** (131 Depot St., 828/265-3544, www.rockdimensions.com) is a guide service that leads rock climbs and caving expeditions at gorgeous locations throughout western North Carolina and to parts of Tennessee and Virginia. Guides teach proper multi-pitch, top rope anchoring, and rappelling techniques.

#### SKIING
The Banner Elk area has some of the state's best ski slopes. **Sugar Mountain** (800/784-2768, www.skisugar.com) is North Carolina's largest winter resort, with 115 acres of ski slopes and 20 trails. In addition to skiing,

activities on the 5,300-foot-high mountain include snow tubing, skating, snowshoeing, and, in the summertime, the Showdown at Sugar National Mountain Bike Series. They offer lessons in skiing and snowboarding for adults and children. Nearby **Ski Beech Mountain Resort** (1007 Beech Mountain Pkwy., Beech Mountain, 800/438-2093, www.beechmountainresort.com) peaks at 300 feet higher than Sugar Mountain and has 15 slopes and 10 lifts, as well as skating and snowboarding areas. **Hawksnest** (2058 Skyland Dr., Seven Devils, 800/822-4295, www.hawksnest-resort.com) is on a 4,800-foot mountain in Seven Devils with 12 slopes, many geared toward beginner and intermediate skiers.

## HIKING, RAFTING, AND CAVE TRIPS

Down the road from the Mast General Store in Valle Crucis, **River and Earth Adventures** (3618 Broadstone Rd., 866/411-7238, www.raftcavehike.com) leads all sorts of exciting trips on the water, in the woods, and in the area's deep caves. Rafting expeditions ($65-85 adults, $55-65 children) ride the Lower Nolichucky (Class II-III), French Broad (Class III-IV), and Watauga (Class II-III) Rivers. Cave trips (year-round daily, $75 pp) meet at the Valle Crucis shop, from where you'll proceed to Elizabethton, Tennessee, about an hour away, for a day's spelunking in Worley's Cave. Guided hiking trips are also available, including all-day kids-only hikes (with adult guides, of course) to free up parents who'd like a day on their own.

**High Mountain Expeditions** (1380 Hwy. 105 S., Banner Elk, 800/262-9036, www.highmountainexpeditions.com), which also has a Boone location, leads rafting trips on the Watauga River (Class I-III) and the much more challenging Nolichucky River (Class III-IV). They also lead caving expeditions for adults and children, for which no experience is necessary.

## Food

The menu at **Our Daily Bread** (627 W. King St., 828/264-0173, www.ourdailybreadboone.com, Mon.-Thurs. 11am-8pm, Fri.-Sat. 11am-10pm, Sun. noon-6pm) includes no fewer than 30 specialty sandwiches, from their best-selling Jamaican turkey sub ($6.50) to the Elvis Prezz (bananas and peanut butter, the King's favorite, $5). Try the tempeh Reuben ($6.25), a daring mixture of flavors that features marinated tempeh, sauerkraut, Swiss cheese, and mustard on rye. Sounds outrageous, but it works. Our Daily Bread also makes a variety of fresh soups and chili (meat and veggie) every day.

★ **Melanie's Food Fantasy** (664 W. King St., 828/263-0300, www.melaniesfoodfantasy.com, Mon.-Sat. 8am-2:30pm, Sun. 8:30am-2:30pm) is worth a special trip to Boone. The breakfast menu is nothing short of spectacular, with its variety of whole-grain waffles, pancakes, and French toast ($4.25-8), all sorts of fancy omelets (try the spinach-garlic-provolone-Swiss, $6), and enough options to keep both carnivores and vegetarians full. Lunch at Melanie's is every bit as good.

The **Dan'l Boone Inn** (130 Hardin St., 828/264-8657, http://danlbooneinn.com, hours vary) serves old-time country food family-style. Despite the complicated pricing system (dinner $15 adults, $9 ages 9-11, $7 ages 6-8, $5 ages 4-5, free under age 4, breakfast $9 adults, $6 ages 9-11, $5 ages 6-8, $4 ages 4-5, free under age 4), the food is straightforward good. At breakfast you can feast on country ham and red-eye gravy, stewed apples, grits, and much more; at dinner there's fried chicken, country-style steak, ham biscuits, and lots of vegetable sides.

The **Gamekeeper Restaurant and Bar** (3005 Shull's Mill Rd., 828/963-7400, www.gamekeeper-nc.com, bar May-Oct. daily from 5pm, dinner May-Oct. Sun.-Fri. from 6pm, Sat. from 5:30pm, $20-50) is tucked away between Boone and Blowing Rock at the Yonahlossee Resort. This restaurant is making a stir as an innovator in high Southern fusion cuisine, with a menu that features appetizers like fried green tomatoes and fried okra, and entrées that include mountain trout, ostrich,

# Driving the Blue Ridge Parkway

Grandfather Mountain

The 250-mile length of the Blue Ridge Parkway in North Carolina is one of the most scenic and enjoyable drives in the country. Here are some highlights and suggested detours, north to south:

- **Milepost 238 to 244: Doughton Park** has hiking trails, a lodge, a restaurant, a picnic area, and a campground.
- **Milepost 272: E. B. Jeffress State Park** features a trail to a waterfall simply called the Cascades.
- **Milepost 292 to 295: Moses H. Cone Memorial Park** offers hiking, fishing, and equestrian trails and features the Parkway Craft Center.
- **Milepost 295 to 298: Julian Price Memorial Park** has trails, a campground, and a large lake, the only lake on the parkway where you can do some paddling.
- **Milepost 304:** The **Linn Cove Viaduct** runs alongside Grandfather Mountain. A visitors center leads to a trail under the viaduct.
- **Milepost 316: Linville Falls Recreation Area** has trails with overlooks of the namesake falls, along with a nice campground.
- **Milepost 331:** The little **Museum of North Carolina Minerals** explores the state's mining background.
- **Milepost 363 to 369: Craggy Gardens** is a great place to see blooming purple rhododendron in June.
- **Milepost 382:** The **Folk Art Center** sells and exhibits traditional Appalachian crafts.
- **Milepost 384:** The LEED-certified **Blue Ridge Parkway Visitors Center** includes a large theater showing a very good film about the region's history and culture.
- **Milepost 431: Richland Balsam** is the highest point on the parkway at 6,053 feet. A trail takes you through a small old-growth forest.
- **Detours: Mount Mitchell State Park** (via Hwy. 128); **Grandfather Mountain State Park** (via Blowing Rock Hwy./U.S. 221); **Linville Caverns** (via U.S. 221).

wapiti, and buffalo. Don't miss the bourbon pudding and white Russian cheesecake—or the seemingly endless wine list ($20-215 per bottle).

## Accommodations
### UNDER $150

The **Smoketree Lodge** (11914 Hwy. 105 S., 800/422-1880, www.smoketree-lodge.com, from $75 high season, from $55 off-season) is a large hotel with basic but comfortable guest rooms and efficiencies, a large rustic lobby, and a nice indoor pool and saunas.

The **Yonahlossee Resort** (Shulls Mill Rd., 800/962-1986, www.yonahlossee.com, from $109), between Boone and Blowing Rock, is a former girls' camp built in the 1920s. The resort has a big stone inn and studio cottages, a fitness center and a sauna, tennis courts with a pro shop, and a 75-foot indoor heated pool.

Among area motels, some good bets are **Fairfield Inn and Suites** (2060 Blowing Rock Rd., 828/268-0677, www.marriott.com, from $40), **Comfort Suites** (1184 Hwy. 105, 828/268-0099, www.choicehotels.com, from $100), **Holiday Inn Express** (1943 Blowing Rock Rd./U.S. 321 S., 828/264-2451, www.hi-express.com, from $90), and **Best Western Blue Ridge Plaza** (840 E. King St., 828/266-1100, www.bestwesternboone.com, from $65).

### $150-300

The **Lovill House Inn** (404 Old Bristol Rd., 800/849-9466, www.lovillhouseinn.com, $149-219) is close to the Appalachian State campus, and it was in the parlor of this 1875 farmhouse that the papers were drawn up that led to the founding of the university. The inn sits on 11 evergreen-shaded acres and is a lovely place to relax and read.

## BLOWING ROCK

The town of Blowing Rock, named for the nearby geological oddity, is an old rocking chair resort, graced by stately houses that were built long ago by early 20th-century captains of industry. Today, cafés and galleries make this a very pleasant place to stroll for a few

well-manicured touristy blocks, and the Blue Ridge Parkway gives easy access to the Moses Cone Manor and other notable local landmarks. The main street—called Main Street, of course—gets pretty crowded on summer weekends, the high season.

## Sights

**Blowing Rock** (U.S. 321 S., 828/295-7111, www.theblowingrock.com, hours vary, $6 adults, $1 children), just outside the cute town of Blowing Rock, is a strange rock outcropping purported (by *Ripley's Believe It or Not*) to be the only place in the world where snow falls upward. Indeed, light objects (think handkerchiefs, leaves, hats) thrown off Blowing Rock—not allowed, by the way, to prevent the valley from filling up with too-heavy litter—do tend to come floating back up. The view from the rock is quite lovely.

The **Moses Cone Manor** (BRP milepost 294, 828/295-7938, Mar. 15-Nov. daily 9am-5pm, free) is a huge white mountain palace, the 1901 country home of North Carolina textile baron Moses Cone. After making his fortune, Cone became a leading philanthropist, and as you drive around the state, particularly in the northern Piedmont, you'll notice that his name still graces quite a few institutions. Flat Top Manor, as the mansion on the Parkway was called, is a wonderfully crafted house, white and ornate like a wedding cake. Appropriately, it is home to one of the **Southern Highland Craft Guild** (828/298-7928, www.southernhighlandguild.org) stores, a place to buy beautiful textiles, pottery, jewelry, furniture, dolls, and much more, handmade by some of the best craftspeople of the Appalachian Mountains. There are also extensive hiking and riding trails on the estate.

## Food

**Storie Street Grille** (1167 Main St., 828/295-7075, www.storiestreetgrille.com, fall-spring Mon.-Sat. 11am-3pm and 5pm-9pm, later hours in summer, lunch $6-13, dinner $10-30) has a long lunch menu of sandwiches,

# Blowing Rock

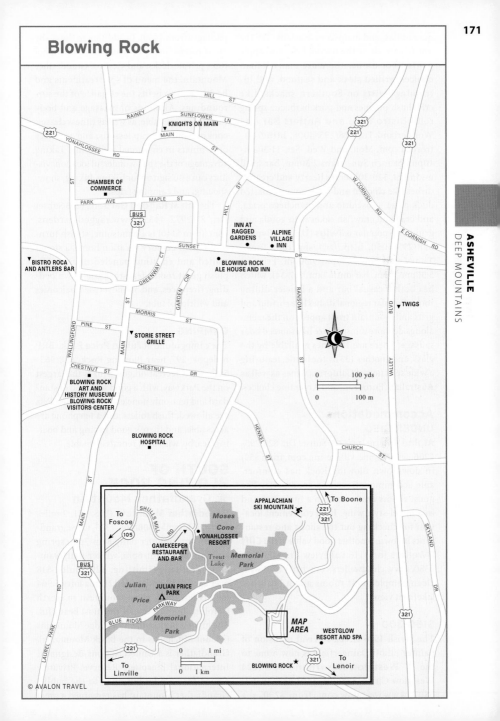

RAINEY ST

HILL ST

SUNFLOWER LN

221 YONAHLOSSEE RD

KNIGHTS ON MAIN

MAIN ST

221

321

321

W CORNISH RD

E CORNISH RD

CHAMBER OF COMMERCE

PARK AVE

MAPLE ST

HILL ST

BUS 321

INN AT RAGGED GARDENS

ALPINE VILLAGE INN

SUNSET ST

DR

RANSOM ST

VALLEY BLVD

BISTRO ROCA AND ANTLERS BAR

GREENWAY CT

GARDEN CIR

BLOWING ROCK ALE HOUSE AND INN

TWIGS

WALLINGFORD ST

PINE ST

MORRIS ST

ST

MAIN ST

STORIE STREET GRILLE

CHESTNUT ST

CHESTNUT DR

0        100 yds

0        100 m

BLOWING ROCK ART AND HISTORY MUSEUM/ BLOWING ROCK VISITORS CENTER

BLOWING ROCK HOSPITAL

HENKEL ST

CHURCH ST

To Foscoe

S MAIN ST

SHULLS MILL RD

APPALACHIAN SKI MOUNTAIN

To Boone

221

321

105

GAMEKEEPER RESTAURANT AND BAR

Moses Cone Memorial Park

YONAHLOSSEE RESORT

Trout Lake

SKYLAND DR

BUS 321

LAUREL PARK RD

Julian Price

JULIAN PRICE PARK

PARKWAY

BLUE RIDGE

Memorial Park

221

MAP AREA

WESTGLOW RESORT AND SPA

321

0        1 mi

0     1 km

To Linville

BLOWING ROCK

To Lenoir

quesadillas, and main-course salads. Try the pot-roast melt or the bacon, brie, and apple panini. For dinner there are many Italian choices, grilled steak and seafood, and intriguing twists on Southern snacks, like crab hush puppies and pork barbecue spring rolls. **Bistro Roca and Antlers Bar** (143 Wonderland Tr., 828/295-4008, http://bistroroca.com, Mon. and Wed.-Sat. 11:30am-10pm, brunch Sun. 11am-2:30pm, bar until midnight, $20-30) serves hearty and creative dishes like chicken and duck pot pie, roasted duck pizza, prosciutto and manchego pizza, and crab and crawfish cakes with gouda and grits. Also popular is **Twigs** (U.S. 321 Bypass, 828/295-5050, http://twigsbr.com, Tues.-Thurs. and Sun. 5:30pm-9:30pm, Fri.-Sat. 5:30pm-10pm, bar until 2am, $17-34), which has both a casual bar and a fancier dining room. Popular regional dishes like shrimp and grits and mountain trout appear on the menu alongside more unusual fare like sautéed boar sausage. There are 17 wines available by the glass, and another 133 by the bottle, featuring a wide selection of California wines as well as Australian, European, and Argentine choices.

## Accommodations
### UNDER $150
**Alpine Village Inn** (297 Sunset Dr., 828/295-7206, www.alpine-village-inn.com, from $50) in downtown Blowing Rock has comfortable accommodations at a good price. The guest rooms are located in a main inn and in a motel-style wing. It's a convenient location for checking out the shops and restaurants in town. Another good value is the **Cliff Dwellers Inn** (116 Lakeview Tr., 800/322-7380, www.cliffdwellers.com, from $70) with clean, simple guest rooms and a beautiful lakefront view.

### $150-300
The lavish 1916 Greek Revival mansion of painter Elliott Daingerfield is now home to the ★ **Westglow Resort and Spa** (224 Westglow Circle, 828/295-4463 or 800/562-0807, www.westglow.com, from $250, spa

packages from $450). In addition to the cushy guest rooms, many of which have whirlpool tubs, private decks, and views of Grandfather Mountain, the menu of spa treatments and health services befits the elegance of the surroundings. All kinds of massage and body therapy are available, as well as fitness classes, cooking and makeup lessons, and a variety of seminars in emotional well-being. Taking advantage of the spa's wonderful location, visitors can also sign up for hiking, biking, snowshoeing, and camping trips.

The **Inn at Ragged Gardens** (203 Sunset Dr., 877/972-4433, www.ragged-gardens.com, from $140) is a handsome, stylish turn-of-the-20th-century vacation home, a stone-walled and chestnut-paneled manor. The plush guest rooms feature goose-down bedding, fireplaces, and, in most cases, balconies and whirlpool tubs.

### CAMPING
The campground at **Julian Price Park** (BRP milepost 297, near Blowing Rock, 828/963-5911, www.recreation.gov, $16) is the largest on the Parkway, with a good selection of standard and tent-only nonelectric campsites. Pets are allowed, flush toilets and a telephone are accessible, and there's good hiking and boating nearby, with boat rentals available.

# SOUTH OF BLOWING ROCK
## ★ Grandfather Mountain
**Grandfather Mountain** (U.S. 221, 2 miles north of Linville, 800/468-7325, www.grandfather.com, summer daily 8am-7pm, spring and fall daily 8am-6pm, winter daily 8am-5pm, weather permitting, $20 adults, $18 over age 60, $9 under age 12), at a lofty 5,964 feet, is not the highest mountain in North Carolina, but it is one of the most beautiful. The highest peak in the Blue Ridge Mountains (Mount Mitchell is in the Black Mountains), Grandfather is a United Nations-designated International Biosphere Reserve. Privately owned for decades but open to the public, Grandfather Mountain has remained a great

expanse of deep forests and abundant wildlife, with many hiking trails. The main attraction is the summit, and the **Mile-High Swinging Bridge** (it's quite safe, but it is indeed a mile high and it swings in the breeze). The view from Grandfather Mountain is stunning, and the peak is easily accessible via the beautiful road that traces the skyward mile.

## Linn Cove Viaduct

Wrapping around Grandfather Mountain is a "bridge over land," the marvel of engineering known as the **Linn Cove Viaduct.** This last section of the Blue Ridge Parkway to be completed, in 1987, was intended to minimize environmental damage to the mountain. The National Park Service operates the **Linn Cove Visitor Center** (daily 10am-5pm) at the south end of the 0.25-mile viaduct, around BRP milepost 304. An adjacent hiking trail goes beside and beneath the viaduct.

## Linville Gorge

The deepest gorge in the United States, Linville Gorge is near Blue Ridge Parkway milepost 316 in a 12,000-acre federally designated wilderness area. Some of the hollers in this preserve are so remote that they still shelter virgin forests. **Linville Falls** (BRP milepost 316) is one of the most photographed places in North Carolina, a spectacular series of cataracts that fall crashing into the gorge. It can be seen from several short trails that depart from the **Linville Falls Visitors Center** (milepost 316, Apr. 25-Nov. 2 daily and weekends in Apr., 9am-5pm). The National Park Service operates the **Linville Falls Campground** (828/765-7818, www.recreation.gov, $19) near the falls at BRP milepost 316.3. Tent and RV sites are mixed together, and water and flush toilets are available May-October.

Linville Gorge has some great climbing spots. They range in difficulty from Table Rock, parts of which are popular with beginning climbers and other parts of which should only be attempted by experts, to the extremely strenuous Hawksbill cliff face and Sitting Bear

Mile-High Swinging Bridge at Grandfather Mountain

Linville Gorge

# South of Blowing Rock

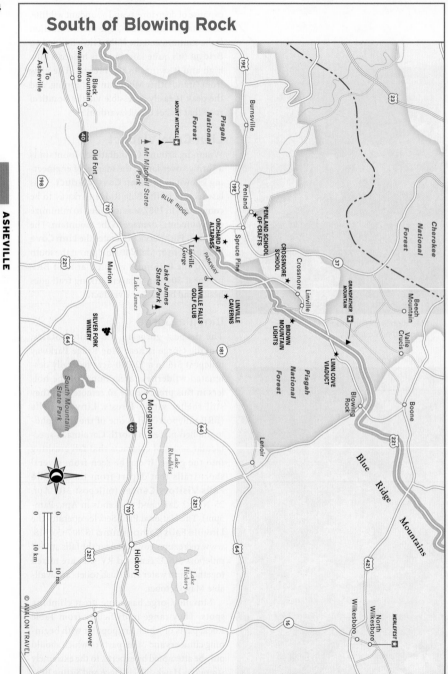

To Asheville

Black Mountain

Swannanoa

Old Fort

MOUNT MITCHELL

Pisgah National Forest

Mt Mitchell State Park

BLUE RIDGE

Burnsville

Penland

PENLAND SCHOOL OF CRAFTS

Spruce Pine

ORCHARD AT ALTAPASS

Linville Gorge

PARKWAY

CROSSNORE SCHOOL

Crossnore

Linville

LINVILLE FALLS GOLF CLUB

LINVILLE CAVERNS

Lake James State Park

Lake James

Marion

SILVER FORK WINERY

South Mountains State Park

Morganton

Lake Rhodhiss

BROWN MOUNTAIN LIGHTS

Pisgah National Forest

GRANDFATHER MOUNTAIN

Beech Mountain

Valle Crucis

LINN COVE VIADUCT

Blowing Rock

Boone

Cherokee National Forest

Lenoir

Blue Ridge Mountains

Hickory

Lake Hickory

Conover

Wilkesboro

North Wilkesboro

MERLEFEST

0

0

10 km

10 mi

© AVALON TRAVEL

rock pillar. Speak to the folks at the visitors center or at **Fox Mountain Guides** (3228 Asheville Hwy., Pisgah Forest, 888/284-8433, www.foxmountainguides), a Hendersonville-area service that leads climbs in the gorge, to determine which of Linville Gorge's many climbing faces would be best suited to your skill level.

## Linville Caverns

You can't visit the Blue Ridge Mountains without visiting caverns. **Linville Caverns** (U.S. 221, between Linville and Marion, south of BRP milepost 317, 800/419-0540, www.linvillecaverns.com, Mar. and Nov. daily 9am-4:30pm, Apr.-May and Sept.-Oct. daily 9am-5pm, June-Aug. daily 9am-6pm, Dec.-Feb. Sat.-Sun. 9am-4:30pm, $8 adults, $7 seniors, $6 children) is one of the venerable underground attractions of the Southern mountains. The natural limestone caverns feature all sorts of strange rock formations, underground trout streams, the occasional roosting bat, and, of course, a gift shop.

## Crossnore School

Since the early 1920s the master weavers of the **Crossnore Weaving Room** (Crossnore School, 100 D.A.R. Dr., Crossnore, 828/733-4305, www.crossnoreweavers.org) have produced beautiful textiles—afghans, rugs and runners, baby blankets, scarves, and more—which they've sold for the benefit of the Crossnore School. Founded in the 1910s for orphaned and disadvantaged children, the Crossnore School is today an actively operating children's home for western North Carolina kids who have no guardians—and for some local children who live with their families but whose educational needs are best served by the structure offered here. The fame of the weaving room is much more than a fund-raising program. The skills of the Crossnore Weavers are highly regarded among craftspeople throughout this region, and the sales gallery is an essential stop for the visitor interested in North Carolina's finest crafts.

## Orchard at Altapass

At milepost 328 on the Blue Ridge Parkway, the **Orchard at Altapass** (888/765-9531, www.altapassorchard.com, Mon. and Wed.-Sat. 10am-6pm, Sun. noon-6pm, free) is much more than an orchard, although it does produce apples in abundance. The land on which the orchard grows has been settled since the 1790s, when Charlie "Cove" McKinney and his large family lived here. McKinney had four wives—at the same time—who bore him 30 sons and a dozen daughters. Today, the Orchard at Altapass continues to turn out wonderful apples. It is also a favorite music venue in this region. On weekends, country, bluegrass, old-time, and gospel musicians, along with artists of a variety of other styles, perform at the Orchard.

## Penland School of Crafts

In the 1920s, Lucy Morgan, a teacher at a local Episcopal school, and her brother embarked on a mission to help the women of the mountains gain some hand in their own economic well-being. Several "folk schools" sprouted in the southern Appalachians in this era, most of them the projects of idealistic Northerners wanting to aid the benighted mountaineers. The Penland School, however, has the distinction of being one of the few such institutions that was truly homegrown, as Morgan was herself a child of the rural Carolina highlands. Today, the **Penland School of Crafts** (off Penland Rd., Penland, 828/765-2359, www.penland.org) is an arts instruction center of international fame. More than 1,000 people, from beginners to professionals, enroll in Penland's one-, two-, and eight-week courses every year to learn about craft in many different media. While the studios are not open to visitors, tours are given April-December on Tuesday and Thursday (advance reservations required).

## Museum of North Carolina Minerals

Right off the BRP at the junction with Highway 226, just in time for some science education as well as perhaps a restroom stop, is the delightful little **Museum of North Carolina Minerals** (milepost 331, 828/765-2761, daily 9am-5pm, free). This small but well-curated museum highlights the geology and topography of the Tar Heel State's portion of Appalachia, with a nod to the wealth of minerals and valuable gems extracted from the ground throughout its history.

## ★ Mount Mitchell

At 6,684 feet, **Mount Mitchell** (accessible from BRP milepost 355, near Burnsville) is the highest mountain east of South Dakota. It is the pinnacle of the Black Mountain range, a 15-mile-long, J-shaped ridge that was formerly considered to be one mountain. Now that the various peaks are designated as separate mountains, 6 of them are among the 10 highest in the eastern United States. Clingmans Dome, a mere 41 feet shorter, glares up at Mount Mitchell from the Tennessee border. **Mount Mitchell State Park** (BRP milepost 355, near Burnsville, 828/675-4611, http://ncparks.gov, May-Aug. 8am-9pm, Mar.-Apr. and Sept.-Oct. 8am-8pm, Nov.-Feb. 8am-6pm, free) is not only a place to catch an amazing panoramic view—up to 85 miles in clear weather—but it also has an education center, restaurant, gift shop, and nine campsites (late Apr.-late Oct. $20, $15 over age 60, Nov.-Apr. $12).

## Brown Mountain Lights

One of North Carolina's most enduring mysteries is that of the Brown Mountain Lights, glowing orbs that float in the air some evenings around Brown Mountain, at the Burke-Caldwell County line. According to the U.S. Geological Survey, the orbs may be reflections of car and train headlights in the valley below. This theory would seem to ignore the fact that the lights have been seen since at least 1833, long before the first headlights shone in this valley. The Brown Mountain Lights are widely believed to be of supernatural origin, and no scientific explanation has yet been proffered

that satisfactorily clears up the mystery. Ghost fanciers will be delighted to know that the Brown Mountain Lights can be observed by visitors from the Lost Cove overlook on the southeast side of the road, near milepost 310 on the Blue Ridge Parkway. Try a clear evening in the summer, right around dusk, and you might see them.

## Lake James State Park

**Lake James State Park** (Hwy. 126, 5 miles northeast of Marion, 828/652-5047, http://ncparks.gov, May-Aug. 8am-9pm, Mar.-Apr. and Sept.-Oct. 8am-8pm, Nov.-Feb. 8am-6pm, free) comprises a 6,500-acre lake and its 150 miles of shoreline. Lake James is artificial, created around 1920, but the graceful mountain setting among hemlocks and rhododendrons makes this a favorite natural area. The park rents canoes ($5 per hour), and campsites ($20) are open March 15-November 30; restrooms, showers, and drinking water are available nearby.

## Food

★ **Famous Louise's Rockhouse Restaurant** (23175 Rockhouse Ln., Linville Falls, near BRP milepost 321, 828/765-2702, daily 6am-8pm, $10), built in 1936 with stones taken from the Linville River, is not a large restaurant, but the dining room is spread out over three counties. The lines of Burke, McDowell, and Avery Counties meet on this exact spot, and customers, for reasons of loyalty or legality, often have preferences about where to take their repast. Famous Louise's is owned by a mother and daughter, and Louise, the mom, is a cook of some renown. The fare is traditional and homemade—the pimento cheese is mixed here, the corn bread and biscuits are whipped up from scratch, and the pot roast is stewed at a leisurely simmer.

## Accommodations

Linville's **Eseeola Lodge** (175 Linville Ave., 800/742-6717, www.eseeola.com, from $400) has been in the business of luxury mountain vacations for more than 100 years. The first lodge was built in the 1890s, along with a nine-hole golf course. The original lodge burned and was replaced by the present lodge, and in 1924 Donald Ross was engaged to build the championship golf course now known as the Linville Golf Club. Eseeola Lodge offers a complex but splendid array of lodging packages, with breakfast and dinner at the lodge's restaurant included and, depending on your predilections, tee times at the Linville Golf Club, spa services, and even croquet lessons. Greens fees for nonguests are $115 for the first round, $57.50 for same-day second rounds.

Scattered around a 92-acre private nature preserve in Marion, the six **Cottages at Spring House Farm** (219 Haynes Rd., Marion, 877/738-9798, www.springhouse-farm.com, from $245) are quiet hideaways with eco-conscious comforts. The proprietors, who live in a historic farmhouse on the property, stock the cabin kitchens with fresh bread and eggs and local honey. Each cottage has an outdoor hot tub and access to pond-side gazebos and hiking trails.

## GETTING THERE AND AROUND

There are no major airports in this region, but two are reasonably close: **Asheville Regional Airport** (AVL, 61 Terminal Dr., Fletcher, 828/684-2226, www.flyavl.com) and **Piedmont Triad International Airport** (GSO, 1000 A. Ted Johnson Pkwy., Greensboro, 336/665-5600, www.flyfrompti.com) in Greensboro. There is one major interstate highway, I-77, that runs north-south

along the edge of the mountains west of Mount Airy. Two other major highways run along or just beyond the boundaries of the northern mountains: I-40 to the east and south, running between Winston-Salem and Asheville, and I-26 to the south and west, between Asheville and Johnson City, Tennessee. U.S. 321 and U.S. 421 are the main roads here, and U.S. 19 winds through the southwest edge of the area covered in this chapter.

While it's probably the most fun and scenic route, the Blue Ridge Parkway is not the most efficient if you're trying to cover a lot of ground fast. The maximum speed is 45 mph, and because of weather, traffic, and twists and turns, you can count on driving slower than that most of the time.

Watauga County, which includes the towns of Blowing Rock, Boone, Deep Gap, and Zionville, is served by **AppalCart bus routes** (828/264-2278, www.appalcart.com). Riders must make reservations to ride, and the service is only available on weekdays, but the fares, which vary by route, are much cheaper than the gas it takes to get from place to place. AppalCart also runs routes to Charlotte, Winston-Salem, Hickory, Lenoir, and Wilkesboro, with fares ranging $10-50 round-trip. Another way to get to and from the area is via the **Mountaineer Express Bus** (336/662-0002 or 800/588-7787, www.partnc.org), which runs among Greensboro, Winston-Salem, Yadkinville, Wilkesboro, and Boone. The most expensive one-way trip (Greensboro-Boone) is only $10, and fares are half-price for students, wheelchair users, and passengers over age 60.

# East of the Blue Ridge Parkway

As you wind your way along the Blue Ridge Parkway, to the east you'll find several worthwhile detours, all within a half hour's drive of the Parkway.

## SOUTH ALONG U.S. 321
### Sights

**Traditions Pottery** (4443 Bolick Rd., 3 miles south of Blowing Rock, 828/295-5099, www.traditionspottery.com) is a hotbed of Piedmont and Appalachian folk traditions. The Owen-Bolick-Calhoun families trace their roots as potters back through six generations in the sandhills community of Seagrove and here in Caldwell County. They have also become renowned old-time musicians and storytellers. Traditions Pottery is not only a place to buy beautiful ceramics with an impeccable folk pedigree, but also the location of the Jack Tales Festival in August (Glenn Bolick learned his storytelling from the great Ray Hicks of Beech Mountain, a National Heritage Award winner), as well as numerous music jams and kiln openings throughout the year.

The **Antique Vending Company Museum** (30 S. Main St., Granite Falls, 828/962-9783, www.antiquevending.com, call for tour times) is a collection of more than 1,000 early soda machines (which North Carolinians are more likely to identify as "Coke machines," regardless of the brand of soft drink contained therein). The machines go back to the earliest days of automated cold drink dispensing, and include the only known remaining 1925 Icy-O Coca-Cola machine in the world.

The county seat of Caldwell County, Lenoir (pronounced "luh-NORE"), was named for General William Lenoir, a Revolutionary War hero and chronicler of the Battle of King's Mountain. **Fort Defiance** (1792 Fort Defiance Dr./Hwy. 268, Happy Valley, 828/758-1671, www.fortdefiancenc.org,

Apr.-Oct. Thurs.-Sat. 10am-5pm, Sun. 1pm-5pm, Nov.-Mar. Sat. 10am-5pm, Sun. 1pm-5pm and by appointment, $6 adults, $4 children), his 1792 plantation house in Happy Valley, is beautifully restored and open to the public. Among its unusual charms are a 200-year-old oriental chestnut tree, an English boxwood garden of the same vintage, and the largest beech tree in the state.

The **Hickory Museum of Art** (243 3rd Ave. NE, Hickory, 828/327-8576, www.hickorymuseumofart.org, Tues.-Sat. 10am-4pm, Sun. 1pm-4pm, free) was established in the early 1950s and was the first major museum of American art in the Southeast. Its early partnership with the National Academy of Design in New York City gained it the nickname of the "Southern Outpost of the National Academy." The museum has an impressive permanent collection, with special emphases on American painting, outsider and folk art, North Carolina folk pottery, and American studio pottery and glass.

### Festivals

Every Labor Day weekend, Caldwell County is home to the **Historic Happy Valley Old-Time Fiddlers' Convention** (828/726-0616, www.happyvalleyfiddlers.com), a laid-back event in a gorgeous location, the Jones Farm. The festival includes music competitions and concerts, drawing some great traditional artists from all over the hills. There is also a rubber duck race, demonstrations by instrument makers, tours of Fort Defiance, and visits to the grave of Laura Foster, the 1867 victim of North Carolina's most famous murderer, Tom "Dooley"—who happened to be a fiddler. Participants and visitors can camp along the Yadkin River on the Jones Farm during the festival for $10 per night. No alcohol is allowed; pets are permitted as long as they're leashed.

The Catawba Valley is one of the important pockets of North Carolina folk pottery,

# The Real Tom Dooley

What is probably North Carolina's most famous murder case, the 1867 murder of a young Wilkes County woman named Laura Foster by her lover, Tom Dula, is known around the world because of a 1950s recording by the Kingston Trio. "The Ballad of Tom Dooley," as it has come to be known, was sung in the North Carolina mountains long before its emergence as a folk revival standard. Most notably, the Watauga County banjo player and ballad singer Frank Profitt kept the story alive through song. Even today, almost 150 years later, the intricacies of the Dula case are debated in this area by descendants of the principal players, and by neighbors who have grown up with the legend.

The story is a sordid one. Tom Dula was 18 years old when he enlisted in the Confederate Army, and by that time he had already been involved for several years in a romantic relationship with a woman named Ann Melton. Following the Civil War, much of which he spent as a prisoner at the notoriously ghastly Point Lookout prison in Maryland, Dula came home to Wilkes County, older but apparently no wiser. He picked up where he left off with Ann Melton, by then married to another man, and at the same time commenced living with another local woman, Laura Foster. (In one version of the story, he was seeing yet a third woman, also a Melton.)

The subtleties of the motives and means that led to Laura Foster's death are still subjects of hot debate, but the facts are as follows. On May 25, 1866, Laura Foster set off from home riding her father's horse. The next day, the horse returned without her. After searchers had combed the woods and riverbanks for nearly a month, Laura Foster's body was finally discovered. She had been stabbed to death and buried in a shallow grave. When news got out that the body had been found, Dula disappeared.

Dula was caught a few weeks later in Tennessee. Back in Wilkes County, Tom Dula and Ann Melton were indicted for murder. Officials moved the trial down the mountain to nearby Iredell County, where a jury found Dula guilty (Ann Melton was acquitted). After a series of appeals and an eventual overturning of the verdict by the state supreme court, a new trial was convened, and Dula was again convicted. He was hanged on May 1, 1868, in Statesville. Historians write that even before the hanging was carried out, people in the area were singing a song with the verse, "Hang your head, Tom Dula / Hang your head and cry / You killed poor Laura Foster / And now you're bound to die."

with a tradition all its own dating back to the early 19th-century potter Daniel Seagle, and exemplified in modern times by the late Burlon Craig (one of the giants of Southern folk art) and contemporary master Kim Ellington. Hickory's annual **Catawba Valley Pottery and Antiques Festival** (Hickory Convention Center, late Mar., $6 adults, $2 children) brings together more than 100 potters and dealers in pottery and antiques. It's a great introduction to Southern folk pottery, and a danger zone if you're on a budget, because the wares sold here are most covetable.

## Sports and Recreation

Between Hickory and Morganton, outside the town of Connelly Springs, is **South Mountain State Park** (3001 South Mountain Park Ave., Connelly Springs, 828/433-4772, http://ncparks.gov, office Mon.-Fri. 8am-5pm, park May-Aug. daily 8am-9pm, Mar.-Apr. and Sept.-Oct. daily 8am-8pm, Nov.-Feb. daily 8am-6pm, free). One of the state's most rugged recreational areas, South Mountain State Park rises to elevations of 3,000 feet. One trail follows the Jacob Fork River to the top of 80-foot High Shoals Falls. Another trail, 0.75 mile long, runs along the lower reaches of Jacob Fork, and is wheelchair accessible. There are 17 miles of strenuous mountain biking trails. Primitive and equestrian campsites ($13) are located in various spots throughout the park, from 0.5 mile to 5.5 miles away from the Jacob Fork parking area. Pit toilets are located nearby campsites, but all supplies and water must be packed in. Watch out for bears!

The **Hickory Crawdads** (2500 Clement Blvd. NW, Hickory, 828/322-3000, www.hickorycrawdads.com) are a Single-A baseball affiliate of the Texas Rangers. The 2015 South Atlantic League Champions play at the modern Frans Stadium, where you may meet the mascot, Conrad—yes, Conrad—the Crawdad.

## Food

If you're traveling between Lenoir and Hickory on a weekend, take a detour to the little community of Dudley Shoals, where you'll find **Sims Country BBQ** (6160 Petra Mill Rd., Dudley Shoals, 828/396-5811, Fri.-Sat. 5pm-9pm, all-you-can-eat buffet $11). Sims is known not only for its all-you-can-eat Texas-style barbecue, which they pit-cook all day, but for live bluegrass music and clogging. It also hosts the annual Molasses Festival on the second Saturday in October, with bluegrass, dancing, and harvest-time activities. Check their Facebook page for details.

## BLACK MOUNTAIN
### Sights

Black Mountain is a beautiful little town only a short distance from Asheville. Step into the **Swannanoa Valley Museum** (223 W. State St., 828/669-9566, www.swannanoavalleymuseum.org, Tues.-Sat. 10am-5pm, Sun. 2pm-5pm, free) to learn about the history of this area, from its prehistory, Cherokee settlement, and early industrialization through the close of the all-important Beacon Blanket Factory to today. While you're here, stop in next door at the **Black Mountain Center for the Arts** (225 W. State St., 828/669-0930, www.blackmountainarts.org, Mon.-Fri. 10am-5pm, Sat. 1pm-4pm) to get a feel for what some of this region's many artists are up to.

East of Black Mountain, the **Mountain Gateway Museum** (102 Water St., Old Fort, 828/668-9259, http://ncmuseumofhistory.org, Mon.-Sat. 10am-5pm, Sun. noon-5pm, free) presents the cultural history of the North Carolina mountains from the time before the Revolution, when Old Fort was the wild frontier, through the present day. The museum hosts events throughout the year, showcasing all manner of traditional arts from this region.

## Entertainment and Events

Twice yearly, in the spring and fall, Black Mountain is the scene of the **Lake Eden Arts Festival** (828/686-8742, www.theleaf.com), better known as LEAF. Though based around the roots music of the world—and there are some amazing performers here every year—LEAF is also a festival of visual arts, poetry, food, and even the healing arts. LEAF is equal parts hippie festival and a delightful family-friendly event with an overlay of progressive thought and worldview. It takes place, appropriately, at Camp Rockmont, once the campus of Black Mountain College (377 Lake Eden Rd.).

### NIGHTLIFE

**Pisgah Brewing Company** (150 Eastside Dr., 828/669-0190, http://pisgahbrewing.com, Mon.-Wed. 4pm-9pm, Thurs.-Sat. usually 2pm-midnight, Sun. 2pm-9pm) is both a brewpub and music venue, featuring an eclectic mix of bands, from roots music to rock. Pisgah was the Southeast's first certified organic brewery. Several beers are on tap all year, including pale ale, porter, stout, and a long list of rotating seasonal brews. Tours are given Saturday at 2pm and 3pm.

## Shopping

**Black Mountain Books** (103 Cherry St., 828/669-8149, Mon.-Sat. 11am-5pm, Sun. 11am-3pm) specializes in rare and out-of-print titles, and is a great place to find unusual volumes on "North Carolina, Black Mountain College, the Southern Appalachians, nature, religion, and 18th- and 19th-century England and Scotland."

Down the road, stop in at **Chocolate Gems** (106 W. State St., 828/669-9105, www.chocgems.com) to see works of art of an entirely different flavor. This chocolatier makes all sorts of truffles and barks, and even chocolate sculptures, right on the premises.

## Food

A great local exponent of the farm-to-table movement is Black Mountain's **Blackbird Restaurant: A New American Tavern** (10 E. Market St., 828/669-5556, www.theblackbird-restaurant.com, Mon.-Sat. lunch 11am-2:30pm, bar 3pm-5:30pm, dinner 5:30pm-9:30pm, bar later, brunch Sun. 10am-2pm, $12-22). Blackbird brings fresh local ingredients to a Southern-inspired menu. It also has a long list of micro-brews and California wines.

Over on Church Street you'll find the **Black Mountain Bakery** (102 Church St., 828/669-1626, Tues.-Sat. 8am-4pm), a little café where you can order a quick soup and sandwich as well as a dessert or cookie for the road.

## Accommodations

The **Inn Around the Corner** (109 Church St., 800/393-6005, www.innaroundthecorner.com, no credit cards, $140-175) is a classic bed-and-breakfast in a lovely 1915 wooden house with a big front porch.

## CHIMNEY ROCK AND LAKE LURE
### ★ Chimney Rock

**Chimney Rock Park** (U.S. 64/74A, Chimney Rock, 800/277-9611, www.chimneyrockpark.com, hours vary, $15 adults, $7 ages 6-15) is home to some amazing rock formations. The star of the show, of course, is the Chimney Rock itself. Whether you climb the long series of steps to the top of this 315-foot tower of rock or take the elevator, you'll get there just the same, and the view is great. Also dazzling are the "Needle's Eye," the "Opera Box," and many more formations that visitors can explore.

The 400-foot **Hickory Nut Falls** can be reached by the Hickory Nut Falls Trail, a fairly leisurely 0.75-mile walk. An easy walk for children, the 0.6-mile Woodland Walk is dotted with animal sculptures and "journal entries" by Grady the Groundhog. The Skyline-Cliff Trail Loop is a good deal more strenuous, but this two-hour hike will carry you to some spectacular sights. (You may also recognize it from the 1992 film *The Last of the Mohicans*.) Chimney Rock's website (www.chimneyrockpark.com) has a nifty interactive trail map that will show you the lay of the land.

Needless to say, Chimney Rock Park is a mighty desirable location for rock climbing. By all means, give it a try—but remember that in this park, you must arrange your climb

Chimney Rock

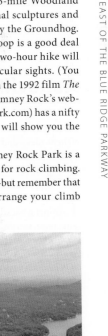

with **Fox Mountain Guides** (888/284-8433, www.foxmountainguides.com). They offer all sorts of instruction and guide services for climbers of all levels.

## Sports and Recreation

Lake Lure, a 720-acre highland lake, was created in the 1920s. Several local outfitters will guide you on or get you prepared for a day on the lake or on area rivers. Try **Lake Lure Adventure Company** (442 Memorial Hwy., 828/625-8066), or, for a relaxed sightseeing tour on the lake, **Lake Lure Tours** (next to Lake Lure Town Marina, 877/386-4255, www.lakelure.com, daily 9am-6pm, twilight cruises 6pm-9pm, dinner cruises 6pm and 7pm, $10-40 adults, $6-16 under age 12), which offers dinner and sunset cruises as well as daytime jaunts.

## Accommodations

The 1927 **Lake Lure Inn and Spa** (2771 Memorial Hwy., 888/434-4970, www.lakelure.com, from $109) is a grand old hotel that was one of the fashionable Southern resorts in its day. Franklin Roosevelt and Calvin Coolidge stayed here, and so did F. Scott Fitzgerald. The lobby is full of strange antiques that are the picture of obsolete opulence—such as a Baccarat chandelier much older than the hotel and a collection of upright disc music boxes (up to eight feet tall) that were all the rage before the invention of the phonograph. The Lake Lure Inn has been beautifully restored and is equipped with two restaurants, a bar, and a spa.

# Asheville

The steady year-round percolation of often offbeat ideas and art in the largest city in western North Carolina welcomes a sizable contingent of visitors each year, visiting the massive Biltmore Estate and enjoying the city's adventurous cuisine and nightlife. It's all against a backdrop of rock-ribbed mountain conservatism, reflected in the many and varied churches that dominate social life outside the bohemian, organically fed city center.

When the railroad finally came to town after the Civil War, Asheville became an important transportation hub, especially for the products of its burgeoning textile industry. Its dependence on the banking industry made it a casualty of the Great Depression, with the serendipitous side effect that much of its wonderful, often whimsical art deco architecture avoided the urban renewal that ruined so many cities in the post-World War II era.

Though Asheville's counterculture roots go back to the 1940s and nearby Black Mountain College, New Age and hippie culture first came to town in a big way in the 1960s, drawn by the climate, walkable downtown, and

relative isolation of the surrounding mountains. Its strains are everywhere, from the regular drum circles held in city parks to the offbeat shops to the political meetings advertised via leaflets stapled to power poles alongside the live band announcements.

## SIGHTS
### ★ Downtown Architecture

One of Asheville's chief charms is its striking architecture, which dates largely to the 1920s. Most famously, the creation of George Washington Vanderbilt's Biltmore Estate and its surrounding developments brought together the illustrious minds of landscape architect Frederick Law Olmsted and architect Richard Morris Hunt, who were, in their day, two of the leading lights in American design. The Montford neighborhood, contemporary to the Biltmore, is a striking mixture of ornate Queen Anne houses and craftsman-style bungalows. The Grove Park Inn was constructed in 1913, a huge, luxurious hotel fitted with rustic architectural devices to make vacationing New York nabobs feel like

# Asheville

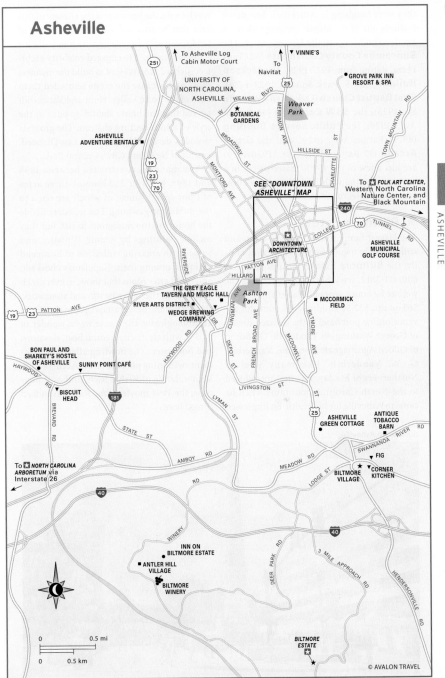

To Asheville Log Cabin Motor Court

▼ VINNIE'S

To Navitat

251

UNIVERSITY OF NORTH CAROLINA, ASHEVILLE

25

● GROVE PARK INN RESORT & SPA

WEAVER

W

BLVD

WEAVER AVE

MERRIMON AVE

Weaver Park

TOWN MOUNTAIN RD

★ BOTANICAL GARDENS

BROADWAY ST

MONTFORD AVE

HILLSIDE ST

CHARLOTTE ST

ASHEVILLE ADVENTURE RENTALS ■

19
23
70

SEE "DOWNTOWN ASHEVILLE" MAP

To ★ FOLK ART CENTER, Western North Carolina Nature Center, and Black Mountain

240

70

TUNNEL RD

RIVERSIDE DR

★ DOWNTOWN ARCHITECTURE

COLLEGE ST

ASHEVILLE MUNICIPAL GOLF COURSE

PATTON AVE

HILLARD AVE

19
23

PATTON AVE

THE GREY EAGLE TAVERN AND MUSIC HALL

RIVER ARTS DISTRICT ■

WEDGE BREWING COMPANY

Ashton Park

CLINGMAN AVE

FRENCH BROAD AVE

■ McCORMICK FIELD

HAYWOOD RD

DEPOT ST

BILTMORE AVE

McDOWELL ST

BON PAUL AND SHARKEY'S HOSTEL OF ASHEVILLE

SUNNY POINT CAFÉ

HAYWOOD RD

BREVARD RD

▼ BISCUIT HEAD

181

LIVINGSTON ST

LYMAN ST

25

ASHEVILLE GREEN COTTAGE

ANTIQUE TOBACCO BARN

RIVER RD

STATE ST

AMBOY RD

MEADOW RD

LODGE ST

SWANNANOA RIVER RD

▼ FIG

To ★ NORTH CAROLINA ARBORETUM via Interstate 26

40

★ CORNER KITCHEN

BILTMORE VILLAGE

WINERY RD

RD

40

DEER PARK RD

3 MILE APPROACH RD

HENDERSONVILLE RD

INN ON BILTMORE ESTATE

■ ANTLER HILL VILLAGE

BILTMORE WINERY

BILTMORE ESTATE ★

0      0.5 mi

0      0.5 km

© AVALON TRAVEL

they were roughing it. Asheville's downtown features one of the largest concentrations of art deco buildings in the United States. The **Buncombe County Courthouse** (60 Court Plaza, dating from 1927-1929), the **Jackson Building** (22 S. Pack Square, 1923-1924), **First Baptist Church** (Oak St. and Woodfin St., 1925), the **S&W Cafeteria** (56 Patton Ave., 1929), the **Public Service Building** (89-93 Patton Ave., 1929), and the **Grove Arcade** (37 Battery Park Ave., 1926-1929) are just a few of the 1920s masterpieces in a city overflowing with important early 20th-century architecture.

## ★ Biltmore Estate

The largest home in the United States, and still privately owned by the Vanderbilt family, the **Biltmore Estate** (1 Approach Rd., 800/411-3812, www.biltmore.com, check the website for hours, generally daily 9am-4:30pm, $65 adults, $32.50 children, discounts for advance online purchase) is the realized dream of George Washington Vanderbilt. Grandson of Gilded Age magnate Cornelius Vanderbilt, G. W. Vanderbilt, like many wealthy Northerners of his day, was first introduced to the North Carolina mountains when he came to Asheville for his health. So impressed

was he with the beauty and the climate of this area that he amassed a 125,000-acre tract of land south of Asheville on which to build his "country home." He engaged celebrity architect Richard Morris Hunt to build the mansion itself, and because the estate reminded them both of the Loire Valley, Hunt and Vanderbilt agreed that the house should be built in the style of a 16th-century château. The grounds would be designed by Frederick Law Olmsted, creator of New York City's Central Park.

The mansion, constructed between 1888 and 1895, has over 250 rooms—three acres of floor space!—most of which are open to the public for gawking. The wonders inside the house are too numerous to list, but they include paintings by Renoir, Whistler, and Sargent; an amazing collection of European antiques, among them Napoleon's chess set; and room after room that show, in every inch of paneling, tiles, woodwork, and stonework, the work of the best craftspeople of the 1890s. Technologically, the house was a wonder in its day, with electricity, central heat, elevators, and hot water. The bowling alley and basement swimming pool are reminiscent of Rich Manor, home of Richie Rich, and as it happens, the 1994 movie *Richie Rich* was indeed filmed here.

downtown Asheville

# Thomas Wolfe Looks Homeward

the Thomas Wolfe Memorial

A native son of Asheville, author Thomas Wolfe grew up in a boardinghouse that his mother ran, and which is operated today as the **Thomas Wolfe Memorial** (52 N. Market St., 828/253-8304, www.wolfememorial.com, Tues.-Sat. 9am-5pm, $5 adults, $2 students). He described the town of "Altamont" (Asheville) and its people so vividly in *Look Homeward, Angel* that the Asheville library refused to own it, and Wolfe himself avoided the town for almost eight years. In this passage, Wolfe describes the excitement of approaching Asheville as a traveler.

His destination was the little town of Altamont, twenty-four miles away beyond the rim of the great outer wall of the hills. As the horses strained slowly up the mountain road Oliver's spirit lifted a little. It was a gray-golden day in late October, bright and windy. There was a sharp bite and sparkle in the mountain air: the range soared above him, close, immense, clean, and barren. The trees rose gaunt and stark: they were almost leafless. The sky was full of windy white rags of cloud; a thick blade of mist washed slowly around the rampart of a mountain.

Below him a mountain stream foamed down its rocky bed, and he could see little dots of men laying the track that would coil across the hill toward Altamont. Then the sweating team lipped the gulch of the mountain, and, among soaring and lordly ranges that melted away in purple mist, they began the slow descent toward the high plateau on which the town of Altamont was built.

In the haunting eternity of these mountains, rimmed in their enormous cup, he found sprawled out on its hundred hills and hollows a town of four thousand people.

There were lands. His heart lifted.

There is more than enough to do and see here to occupy a full weekend. The **Biltmore Winery** operates in what was once the estate's dairy; daily tours and tastings allow visitors to sample the award-winning wines. **River Bend Farm** re-creates the working farm that supported the estate and its many workers. Blacksmiths, woodworkers, and other artisans work in the River Bend barn. The kitchen garden—backyard gardeners, just imagine this—is four acres.

The **Equestrian Center** gives lessons, and if you happen to travel with your own horse, the two of you can explore 80 miles of equestrian trails. Your horse can even have his or her own stall and board like a Vanderbilt steed. Visitors without the equestrian urge can also tour the estate by carriage, bike, raft, canoe, Segway, or, of course, on foot. Last but not least, you can zip around in a Land Rover after receiving expert training from Biltmore's own **Land Rover Experience Driving School.**

Admission to Biltmore varies by season; there is no charge for parking. Your ticket gets you in to the mansion itself, the gardens, the winery, and the farm. Some of the other features carry additional fees.

## ★ North Carolina Arboretum

The enormous **North Carolina Arboretum** (100 Frederick Law Olmsted Way, 828/665-2492, www.ncarboretum.org, Apr.-Oct. daily 8am-9pm, Nov.-Mar. daily 8am-7pm, greenhouse Mon.-Sat. 8am-2pm, parking $12) is considered by many to be one of the most beautiful such institutions in the country. The 434 natural and landscaped acres back onto the Pisgah National Forest, just off Blue Ridge Parkway milepost 393. Major collections include the National Native Azalea Repository, where you can see almost every species of azalea native to the United States, as well as several hybrids, and the very special Bonsai Collection, where staff horticulturists care for over 200 bonsais, many of their own creation. Bicycles and leashed dogs are permitted on many of the trails. Walking areas range from easy to fairly rugged.

The arboretum has a very nice café, the **Savory Thyme Café** (Mon.-Sat. 10am-4pm, Sun. noon-5pm) and gift shop, the **Garden Trellis** (Mon.-Sat. 10am-5pm, Sun. noon-5pm).

## aSHEville Museum

The unique and ambitious **aSHEville Museum** (35 Wall St., 828/222-0115, www.

The aSHEville Museum celebrates the history of women in Appalachia.

# Downtown Asheville

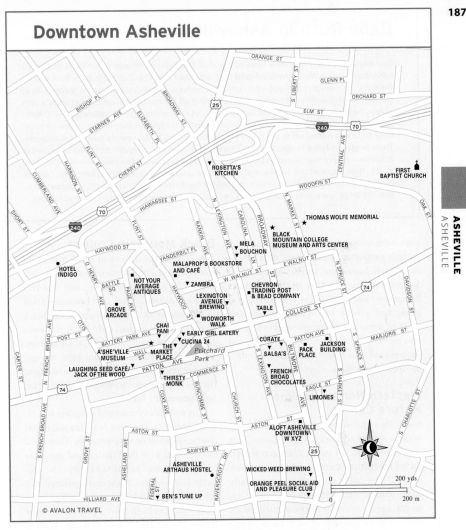

© AVALON TRAVEL

ashevillemuseum.com, Sun.-Thurs. 10am-9pm, Fri.-Sat. 10am-10pm, sliding scale donation $5-$15, under 10 free)—pronounced "a she ville"—is a small but growing and very earnest effort to highlight not only the regional history of women in this part of western North Carolina but women all over the world. With exhibits highlighting aspects from craftswomen to human trafficking, this is a must-see for the more progressively inclined visitor to Asheville.

## Botanical Gardens

The **Botanical Gardens** (151 W. T. Weaver Blvd., adjacent to the UNC-Asheville campus, 828/252-5190, www.ashevillebotanical-gardens.org, daily dawn-dusk, free) comprise a 10-acre preserve for the region's increasingly threatened native plants. Laid out in 1960 by landscape architect Doan Ogden, the gardens are an ecological haven. Spring blooms peak in mid-April, but the gardens are an absolutely lovely, visually rich place to visit any time of

## Babe Ruth in Asheville

One day in 1925, the New York Yankees baseball team was on its way to Asheville to play an exhibition game at **McCormick Field** (30 Buchanan Place, 828/258-0428). Babe Ruth was on the train, and he didn't feel well—a touch of flu, perhaps, or indigestion, but the bumpy rails of western North Carolina did him no good. Stepping off the train at Asheville, greeted by a rush of fans, he fainted and fell. Luckily, Ruth passed out next to the Yankees' catcher, Steve O'Neill, who did his job and caught his bulky teammate before the famous mug hit the station's marble floor. Ruth was rushed off to the Battery Park Hotel, where he apparently made a full recovery. The newspapers failed to note that fact, though, and it was briefly reported that Ruth had died in Asheville—a story that caused no small consternation. All was well a few years later when, on April 8, 1931, Ruth returned to Asheville, and both he and Lou Gehrig hit home runs here at McCormick Field. This august ground is now the home field of the **Asheville Tourists** (30 Buchanan Place, 828/258-0428, www.theashevilletourists.com), the Class A farm team of the Colorado Rockies.

year. Admission is free, but as the gardens are entirely supported by donations, your contribution will have a real impact. On the first Saturday in May, the **Day in the Gardens** brings food and music to this normally placid park, and garden and nature enthusiasts from all around come to tour and to buy native plants for their home gardens. The gift shop is open mid-March-December Monday-Saturday 10am-4pm.

### Western North Carolina Nature Center

Asheville—and western North Carolina generally—is very ecologically conscious. This concern is reflected in the **Western North Carolina Nature Center** (75 Gashes Creek Rd., 828/298-5600, www.wildwnc.org, daily 10am-5pm, $7 adults, $6 seniors, $3 ages 3-15, under age 16 must be accompanied by an adult). On the grounds of an old zoo—don't worry, it's not depressing—wild animals who are, for various reasons, unable to survive in the wild (they were injured, for example, or raised as pets and abandoned) live in wooded habitats where the public can view them. This is the place to see some of the mountains' rarest species, animals that most lifetime residents have never seen: cougars, wolves, coyotes, bobcats, and even the elusive hellbender. What's a hellbender, you ask? Come to the nature center and find out.

### Black Mountain College

Considering the history of Black Mountain College from a purely numerical standpoint, one might get the false impression that this little institution's brief, odd life was a flash in the pan. In its 23 years of operation, Black Mountain College had only 1,200 students, 55 of whom actually completed their degrees. But in fact, between 1933 and 1956, the unconventional school fired a shot heard round the world as an innovative model of education and community life.

The college's educational program was almost devoid of structure. Students had no set course schedule or requirements. They lived and farmed with the faculty, and no sense of hierarchy was permitted to separate students and teachers. Most distinguished as a school of arts, Black Mountain College hired Josef Albers as its first art director, when the Bauhaus icon fled Nazi Germany. Willem de Kooning taught here for a time, as did Buckminster Fuller, who began his design of the geodesic dome while he was in residence. Albert Einstein and William Carlos Williams were among the roster of guest lecturers.

Black Mountain College closed in 1956, due in part to the prevailing anti-leftist climate of that decade. The **Black Mountain College Museum and Arts Center** (56 Broadway, 828/350-8484, www.blackmountaincollege. org, Wed.-Sat. noon-4pm) is located not in the town of Black Mountain but in downtown Asheville. It's both an exhibition space and a resource center dedicated to the history and spirit of the college.

## ★ Folk Art Center

An essential sight near Asheville on the Blue Ridge Parkway is the **Folk Art Center** (BRP milepost 382, 828/298-7928, Jan.-Mar. daily 9am-5pm, Apr.-Dec. daily 9am-6pm). At this beautiful gallery, coupled with the oldest continuously operating craft shop in the United States, **Allanstand Craft Shop,** you'll find the work of members of the prestigious Southern Highland Craft Guild, a juried-membership organization that brings together many of the best artists in Appalachia. Though the folk arts are well represented here in the forms of beautiful pottery, baskets, weaving, and quilts, you'll also find the work of contemporary studio artists in an array of media, including gorgeous handcrafted furniture, clothing, jewelry, and toys. Bring your Christmas shopping list, even if it's April.

# ENTERTAINMENT AND EVENTS

Everywhere you turn in this city, you'll stumble on musicians—on street corners, in cafés, on front porches. There are also formal music venues where, on any given weekend and many weeknights, you can hear rock, bluegrass, Appalachian, "Afrolachian," blues, honky-tonk, country, and mountain swing.

## Bluegrass at The Fiddlin' Pig

The **Fiddlin' Pig** (28 Tunnel Rd., 828/251-1979, www.thefiddlinpig.com), a popular barbecue joint on U.S. 70, has live bluegrass music six nights a week. The host bands, the Whitewater Bluegrass Company and Balsam Range, are all-star locals whose fame spreads far beyond Asheville. The Pig has a good small dance floor, shared by clogging teams and dancing customers. There's also a full bar, but the restaurant remains a very child-friendly environment.

## Nightlife

The **Orange Peel Social Aid and Pleasure Club** (101 Biltmore Ave., 828/225-5851, www.theorangepeel.net) is another fabulous nightspot. Billed as "the nation's premier live music hall and concert venue," they can back up that claim by boasting of performances by Bob Dylan, Sonic Youth, Smashing Pumpkins, Blondie, and many other artists of that caliber—as well as some of the best up-and-coming acts from Asheville and the Southeast. There's a great dance floor and a cool bar. A leading host of roots music is the **Grey Eagle Tavern and Music Hall** (185 Clingman Ave., 828/232-5800, www.thegreyeagle.com). A listening room-style venue rather than a bar or club—that is, folks come here when they want to hear music, not bar-hop—the Grey Eagle does provide good Louisiana-style eats at its **Twin Cousins Kitchen,** and plenty of good beers and wines. Another favorite is **Jack of the Wood** (95 Patton Ave., 828/252-5445, www.jackofthewood.com). The shows here, which start on Friday and Saturday at 9:30,

the famous Orange Peel Social Aid and Pleasure Club

tend toward progressive approaches to traditional music, from bluegrass and old-time Appalachian to Irish and folk.

Asheville is home to some excellent microbreweries, and to visit them in the company of enthusiastic experts, try the **Asheville Brews Cruise** (828/545-5181, www.brewscruise.com, $37, $70 per couple). Mark and Trish Lyons take you all around town in the Brews Cruise van to sample some homegrown beers.

A hot spot downtown is **Wicked Weed Brewing Company** (91 Biltmore Dr., 828/575-9599, www.wickedweedbrewing. com), one of the youngest craft breweries in town, known for West Coast IPAs and sours. At this location you can enjoy their extensive brews on tap, some good gastropub-style food in a full sit-down restaurant, and a spacious patio/beer garden area.

At **Asheville Pizza and Brewing Company** (675 Merrimon Ave., 828/254-1281, www.ashevillepizza.com), you can start off the evening with one of this pizzeria, microbrewery, and movie house's tasty IPAs, and fortify yourself for the evening by filling up on good pizza.

The **French Broad Brewery** (101 Fairview Rd., 828/277-0222, www.french-broadbrewery.com) is another popular local nightspot that has grown up around a first-rate beer-making operation, and here you can choose from a varied menu that includes signature pilsners, lagers, ales, and more while listening to some good live music.

**Highland Brewing Company** (12 Old Charlotte Hwy., Ste. H, 828/299-3370, www. highlandbrewing.com) is Asheville's first microbrewery. They've been making beer and raking in awards for well over a decade, and on first sip you'll understand why they're one of the Southeast's favorite breweries.

Another good microbrewery is **Wedge Brewing Company** (125B Roberts St., 828/505-2792, www.wedgebrewing.com, daily noon-10pm), located in an old warehouse in the River Arts District. Wedge keeps about two dozen brews on tap, including pale ales, farmhouse ales, and a wheat beer flavored with cherries and raspberries.

## Festivals

Twice yearly, in late July and late October, the Southern Highland Craft Guild hosts the **Craft Fair of the Southern Highlands** (U.S. Cellular Center, 87 Haywood St., www. southernhighlandguild.org, Thurs.-Sun. 10am-6pm, $8). Since 1948 this event has brought much-deserved attention to the guild's more than 900 members, who live and work throughout the Appalachian Mountains. Hundreds of craftspeople participate in the fair, selling all sorts of handmade items.

Asheville's **Mountain Dance and Folk Festival** (828/258-6101, ext. 345, www. folkheritage.org, daily $20 adults, $10 under age 12, three days $54 adults, $24 under age 12) is the nation's longest-running folk festival, an event founded in the 1920s by musician and folklorist Bascom Lamar Lunsford to celebrate the heritage of his native Carolina mountains. Musicians and dancers from western North Carolina perform at the downtown Diana Wortham Theater at Pack Place for three nights each summer. On Saturday nights at Martin Luther King Jr. Park, also downtown, many of the same artists can be heard in the city's long-running and very popular **Shindig on the Green** concert series.

In October, a series of creepy and offbeat happenings take place in the monthlong festival called **Ashtoberfest** (www.ashtoberfest.com). Among the events are a horror film festival, a summit of horror writers, and—the pinnacle of Ashtoberfest—the Zombie Walk. Ashevillians (and a surprising number of out-of-towners) prepare for the Zombie Walk a month in advance by burying clothes in their yards. This way, when they dig them back up and don their zombie garb, they'll give off a properly fetid, sepulchral funk. Event dates and locations change each year, so take a look at Ashtoberfest's website.

# SHOPPING

## Antiques and Secondhand Goods

The best store in Asheville—of any kind—is the tiny curiosity shop **Not Your Average Antiques** (21 Page Ave., across from the Grove Arcade, 828/252-1333, www.notyouraverageantiques.com). This fine retailer trades almost exclusively in items that were coveted by 10-year-old boys between the years 1900 and 1960, approximately. Included in this bounty: tin robots and astronauts, ray guns, magician and circus posters, carousel animals, and cowboy accoutrements. Interspersed is some wonderful Southern folk art, birds made by area woodcarvers, and pottery from all over the state. You probably didn't realize until now that you needed a wind-up Buck Rogers toy from the 1930s—but you do.

It's an unusual sort of a town that has both the supply and demand necessary for a business like **Second Gear** (415-A Haywood Rd., 828/258-0757, www.secondgearwnc.com, daily 10am-6pm). This consignment shop deals exclusively in secondhand outdoor equipment and clothes. It's a great place to find canoes and kayaks, tents, climbing gear, men's and women's outdoor clothing and shoes, and many other items at very low prices.

## Galleries

One of Asheville's best places to shop is the 1929 **Grove Arcade** (1 Page Ave., 828/252-7799, www.grovearcade.com). The expansive Tudor Revival fortress, ornately filigreed inside and out in ivory-glazed terra-cotta, was originally meant to be the base of a 14-story building, a skyscraper for that time and place. As it is, the Grove Arcade is rather like an exposition hall at an early World's Fair. There are some great little galleries and boutiques here, including **Mountain Made** (828/350-0307, www.mtnmade.com, Mon.-Sat. 10am-6pm, Sun. noon-5pm) and the **Grove Arcade**

**ARTS & Heritage Gallery** (828/255-0775, www.grovearcade.com, Mon.-Sat. 10am-6pm, Sun. noon-5pm), both galleries of local artists' work; **Asheville Home Crafts** (828/350-7556, www.ashevillehomecrafts.com, Mon.-Sat. 10am-6pm, Sun. noon-6pm), which sells handmade quilts, dolls, afghans, and knit garments; several cafés; and a chocolatier.

## Books, Toys, and Crafts

One of the social hubs of this city is **Malaprop's Bookstore and Café** (55 Haywood St., 828/254-6734, www.malaprops.com, Mon.-Thurs. 8am-9pm, Fri.-Sat. 8am-10pm, Sun. 8am-7pm). The bookstore—progressive, with a deep selection in many subjects and a particular interest in regional literature—is joined to the requisite coffee bar. The variety of people who live here is striking, and among the young and artistic, there's a great deal of creativity invested in clothes, hairstyles, tattoos, and jewelry.

In the Grove Arcade you'll find the swanky yet very comfortable **Battery Park Book**

the Grove Arcade

Exchange and Champagne Bar (www. batteryparkbookexchange.com, Thurs.-Sat. 11am-11pm, Sun.-Wed. 11am-9pm). The clubby, dark wood interior is reminiscent of a Harry Potter movie, and it holds many spots to peruse the expansive stock. Enjoy bubbly or wine from a rather wide-ranging list.

**Dancing Bear Toys** (518 Kenilworth Rd., 800/659-8697, www.dancingbeartoys.com, Mon.-Sat. 10am-7pm, Sun. noon-5pm) has the ambience of a cozy village toy shop despite the more strip mall-looking exterior. Dancing Bear has toys for everyone, from babies to silly grown-ups—a fabulous selection of Playmobil figures and accessories, Lego, Brio, and other favorite lines of European toys; beautiful stuffed animals of all sizes; all sorts of educational kits and games; and comical doodads that would be a welcome find in an adult's or a child's stocking.

# FOOD
## Eclectic American

★ **Early Girl Eatery** (8 Wall St., 828/259-9292, www.earlygirleatery.com, Mon.-Wed. 7:30am-3pm, Thurs.-Fri. 7:30am-9pm, Sat.-Sun. 8am-9pm, $15) has caused a stir among area locavores. More than half of the vegetables, meat, and fish that go into Early Girl are raised or caught within 20 miles of the restaurant. The menu is very accommodating of Asheville's large vegetarian and vegan contingent, but nonveg diners can feast on pan-fried trout with green tomato-blackberry sauce, squash casserole, and hush puppies, or pan-seared duck with roasted shallots, sweet potato fritters, and sautéed greens—along with many other delicious New Southern creations. It's an especially popular spot for breakfast, served all day every day.

A few doors down, **Laughing Seed Café** (40 Wall St., 828/252-3445, www. laughingseed.com, Mon. and Wed.-Thurs. 11:30am-9pm, Fri.-Sat. 11:30am-10pm, Sun. 10am-9pm, under $20) achieves what vegetarian restaurants always aim for but are seldom able to achieve—its food is so good, and so widely praised, that a legion of nonvegetarians

have become loyal fans and customers. The restaurant describes its style as "international vegetarian cuisine," and it draws on Latin American, Thai, Indian, and other cuisines of the world to create hearty and addictively flavorful dishes.

Say you've been at the Grey Eagle or the Orange Peel, and the show has just let out. It's the middle of the night. You and your friends are not ready for the night to end, but you've got to refuel with some good food in order to keep going. The lights are on at **Rosetta's Kitchen** (111 Broadway Ave., 828/232-0738, www.rosettaskitchen.com, Mon.-Sat. 11am-11pm, $10-15), and the stove is hot. There's so much to recommend this place. First off, the food is good. It's all vegetarian, mostly vegan, and made with local produce in season. It's open late on weekends, 10pm-3am. They compost every scrap of organic material that makes its way back to the kitchen, and they make sure their used vegetable oil goes to power biodiesel cars. It's Asheville all over.

**Table** (48 College St., 828/254-8980, http:// tableasheville.com, lunch Mon. and Wed.-Sat. 11am-2:30pm, dinner Mon. and Wed.-Sat. 5:30pm-10pm, brunch Sun. 10:30am-2pm, $15-27) uses ingredients like locally caught bass and mountain-raised pork and lamb. Chef Jacob has created a menu that takes full advantage of the culinary riches of western North Carolina.

**The Market Place** (20 Wall St., 828/252-4162, www.marketplace-restaurant.com, Mon.-Fri. 5:30pm-10pm, Sat.-Sun. 10:30am-2:30pm and 5:30pm-10pm, $16-30) has graced downtown Asheville for 30 years. This local favorite constructs an elegant menu from ingredients raised or caught within 100 miles of the restaurant. Try the sweet potato ravioli, or the locally caught trout with roasted corn and black bean cakes.

West Asheville's **Sunny Point Café** (626 Haywood Rd., 828/252-0055, www.sunnypointcafe.com, Sun.-Mon. 8:30am-2:30pm, Tues.-Sat. 8:30am-9:30pm) serves three meals most days, but is so famous for its brunch that a line sometimes forms outside the door. The breakfast menu here is so popular that it is served at any time of day, even though the lunch and dinner menus are well worth a trip as well. This is a great bet for vegetarians—the meatless options are imaginative and beautifully created.

## BILTMORE VILLAGE

In one of the historic cottages of Biltmore Village is the ★ **Corner Kitchen** (3 Boston Way, 828/274-2439, www.thecornerkitchen. com, breakfast Mon.-Sat. 7:30am-11am, brunch Sun. 9am-3pm, lunch Mon.-Sat. 11:30am-3pm, dinner daily 5pm). Head chef Joe Scully counts among his illustrious former gigs the Waldorf Astoria and the United Nations. The elegant menu combines homestyle and haute most harmoniously. Try one of the heavenly appetizers (most around $9), like almond-fried brie served over a bed of greens with pear and apple conserve and a red-wine reduction, and then indulge in an entrée like the blackberry ketchup pork chop, which comes with sweet potatoes and fried green tomatoes ($21). For lunch you can choose from a nice selection of classic sandwiches, or order the Ploughman's Lunch ($9)—a cup of soup, a small salad, two cheeses, and either country-style terrine or roasted portabella mushroom. The cozy, cheerful dining room of this Victorian cottage opens into the kitchen, where guests can see every step of their meal's preparation while chatting with the staff.

## BILTMORE ESTATE

There are no fewer than nine places to eat on the Biltmore Estate (800/411-3812, www. biltmore.com, estate admission required to visit restaurants). The **Dining Room** (daily 5:30pm-9:30pm, reservations required) is an elegant restaurant, led by chef Richard Boyer, featuring estate-raised Angus beef, mountain trout, and Biltmore wines. Evening dress and reservations are suggested. At the **Biltmore Bistro** (daily 11am-9pm), chef Edwin French creates a fabulous gourmet menu from the Biltmore's own kitchen garden, locally raised heirloom crops, meat and seafood delicacies, and artisanal cheeses and breads. The dining room of the **Deerpark Restaurant** (Jan.-Mar. 14 Fri. 5pm-8pm, Sat.-Sun. 10am-3pm, Mar. 15-Dec. Mon.-Sat. 11am-3pm, Sun. 10am-3pm, buffet dinner Nov.-Dec. daily from 5pm) is a former barn designed by architect Richard Morris Hunt, now renovated to an airy splendor with walls of windows. Here, chef Angela Guiffreda creates hearty and homey meals based on Appalachian cuisine. Like the Deerpark, the **Stable Café** (lunch daily 11am-4pm, dinner daily from 5pm) is former livestock housing, and guests can sit in booths that were once horse stalls. This is a meat-eater's paradise, where you can order estate-raised Angus beef, pork barbecue with chef Don Spear's famous special sauce, and lots of other tasty dishes. The **Arbor Grill** (Mon.-Thurs. noon-7pm, Fri.-Sat. noon-8pm) is an alfresco café next to the winery, featuring live music on weekends. In the stable area near the mansion, both the **Bake Shop** and **Ice Cream Café** serve fresh treats. The **Creamery Grill** is the place for sandwiches and hand-dipped ice cream, and the **Conservatory Café** will keep the children happy with hot dogs and soft drinks.

## Indian

★ **Mela** (70 Lexington Ave., 828/225-8880, www.melaasheville.com, daily 11:30am-2:30pm and 5:30pm-9:30pm) is one of the best Indian restaurants in North Carolina. The elaborate menu offers dozens of choices, combining cuisines of both Northern and Southern India, with great meat, seafood, and vegetable dishes. The restaurant is dark and elegant, but the prices are surprisingly low. While the entrées are mostly in the $10-15 range, you can put together a great patchwork meal of appetizers (which start at $2), soup, and roti. Don't miss the samosas.

A local favorite is **Chai Pani** (22 Battery Park Ave., 828/254-4003, www.chaipaniasheville.com, Mon.-Thurs. 11:30am-3:30pm and 5pm-9:30pm, Fri.-Sat. 11:30am-3:30pm and 5:30pm-10pm, Sun. noon-3:30pm and 5pm-9:30pm, $10). "Chai pani" means "tea and water," a phrase that refers to a snack or a small gift. This restaurant is inspired by Indian street food vendors, and serves casual and affordable specialties from all over India.

## Latin American

Ask an Asheville resident for restaurant recommendations, and chances are ★ **Salsa's** (6 Patton Ave., 828/252-9805, www.salsas-asheville.com, Mon.-Thurs. 11:30am-2:30pm and 5:30pm-9pm, Fri. 11:30am-2:30pm and 5:30pm-10pm, Sat. noon-3pm and 5:30pm-10pm, Sun. noon-3pm and 5:30pm-9pm, $10-20) will be one of the first names intoned. It's definitely my favorite restaurant in town. Salsa's pan-Latin concoctions, from their famous fish burritos to exquisite cocktails, keep this tiny little café jam-packed with locals and with visitors who drive to Asheville just for a special meal. The flavors here are essentially earthy and hearty, but always topped with a refreshing touch of Caribbean lightness, courtesy largely of chef Hector Diaz's genius with various fruit-infused salsas, influenced by the cuisine of his Puerto Rico home.

Also delicious is **Limones** (13 Eagle St., 828/252-2327, http://limonesrestaurant.com, daily 10am-5pm, brunch Sun. 10:30am-2:30pm). Chef Hugo Ramirez, a native of Mexico City, combines his backgrounds in Mexican and French-inspired Californian cuisine to create a special menu.

## European

Chef Michael Baudouin grew up in France's Rhône Valley, the son of a winemaker and an excellent cook. He brings his culinary heritage to Asheville at his restaurant **Bouchon** (62 N. Lexington Ave., 828/350-1140, http://ashevillebouchon.com, daily from 5pm, small plates $5-13, large plates $10-20). Bouchon's "French comfort food" ranges from classics like rabbit in a Dijon mustard sauce and boeuf bourguignon to chicken thighs simmered in local apple cider. Delicious vegetarian options are available.

**Zambra** (85 Walnut St., 828/232-1060, www.zambratapas.com, dinner daily from 5pm, $10-20) combines cuisines of the western Mediterranean—Spanish, Gypsy, and North African—with fresh North Carolina ingredients. Specials change nightly and often feature North Carolina seafood. The long tapas menu has many choices for vegetarians.

**Vinnie's** (641 Merrimon Ave., 828/253-1077, www.vinniesitalian.com, Sun.-Thurs. 5pm-9:30pm, Fri.-Sat. 5pm-10:30pm, $10-20), on Merrimon Avenue downtown, is a good and reasonably priced Italian eatery. Pasta and pizza, heroes and calzone are offered in abundance, along with heartier veal and chicken dishes, lasagna, and eggplant parmigiana.

## Coffee and Sweets

Asheville has a unique coffee shop in **Double D's Coffee and Desserts** (41 Biltmore Ave., 828/505-2439, www.doubledscoffee.com, hours vary seasonally), which as the name implies is set within a permanently parked red double-decker bus, just like the ones in London. You step aboard and place your order downstairs (cash only), and you can walk up to the top level and relax and enjoy your drink in the cozily renovated interior. The coffee and treats are great, and there is also a nice picnic area if all the seats are full or you just want to enjoy the weather.

One of downtown's most popular breakfast-all-day spots is **Green Sage Café** (5 Broadway, 828/252-4450, www.greensage-cafe.com, Fri.-Sun. 7am-6pm, Mon.-Thurs. 7am-5pm), in a great corner location. Folks line up for morning coffee or tea (all sustainably grown and farmed) and fresh omelets and organic pancakes, along with lunch items like rice bowls and wraps.

**French Broad Chocolates** (10 S. Lexington Ave., 828/252-4181, http://frenchbroadchocolates.com, Sun.-Thurs. 11am-11pm, Fri.-Sat. 11am-midnight) is a mellow café serving a menu that celebrates chocolate, featuring French Broad Chocolates' own artisanal truffles, brownies, and pastries as well as sipping chocolates and floats. They're open early and late, perfect for an afternoon snack or a special dessert after a night on the town.

Enjoy a coffee on a real double-decker bus at Double D's Coffee and Desserts.

It's mentioned in the Shopping section, but many java aficionados insist the coffee at **Malaprop's Bookstore and Café** (55 Haywood St., 828/254-6734, www.malaprops. com, Mon.-Thurs. 8am-9pm, Fri.-Sat. 8am-10pm, Sun. 8am-7pm) is the best in town.

## ACCOMMODATIONS

With the recent tourism boom in Asheville has come dramatically higher hotel rates, as demand far outstrips supply. If you're not careful you can spend an enormous amount of money for a very subpar experience. I suggest sticking with these recommendations when possible, and otherwise go for newer properties. You'll likely already be paying a premium regardless, so you may as well go for the most modern hotels you can.

### Under $150

**Bon Paul and Sharky's Hostel of Asheville** (816 Haywood Rd., 828/350-9929, www.bonpaulandsharkys.com) is a pleasant old white house with a porch and porch swing, high-speed Internet access, and dorm-style bunks (in a shared room, women-only or coed, $27). You can camp in the yard for $20, or rent the private room ($70-100) with a TV and queen-size bed. Dogs are allowed in private rooms for an extra $12 per night. The

hostel offers pick-up service from the bus station or from the airport. Bon Paul and Sharky, by the way, were goldfish.

The **Asheville ArtHaus Hostel** (16 Ravenscroft Dr., 828/225-3278, http://aahostel.com) is a private room-only hostel. They offer two-person rooms (one with a queen bed and one with two twins) at about $60 per night, three-person rooms (one queen and one twin) at about $75, and family rooms (one queen and two twins) at about $90. The hostel's Tiny House is over $100. Pets are not permitted.

In the days before motels became the norm for budget lodging, the motor court or cottage court was a favorite overnight option for middle-class travelers. Several in the Asheville area are still in business and in good repair, providing today's travelers with charmingly retro accommodations. **Asheville Log Cabin Motor Court** (330 Weaverville Hwy., 828/645-6546, www.cabinlodging.com, $55-250, 2-night minimum, pets allowed for a fee) was constructed around 1930 and appears in the 1958 Robert Mitchum movie *Thunder Road*. The cabins have cable TV and wireless Internet access but no phones. Some are air-conditioned, but that's not usually a necessity at this elevation. Another great cabin court is the **Pines Cottages** (346 Weaverville Hwy.,

888/818-6477, http://ashevillepines.com, $45-175, depending on season, up to 2 pets allowed for $15 per pet). Billed as "A nice place for nice people," it's also a friendly place for pets.

My favorite is the quirky, kitschy **Mountaineer Inn** (155 Tunnel Rd., 828/254-5331, $70-100), run for decades by a Greek American family. The conveniently located Mountaineer sports one of the most awesome old-school neon signs you'll see anywhere. They offer a humble free breakfast in the tiny lobby, where the satellite TV is usually tuned to a Greek station.

## $150-300

Quality lodging at this price point is particularly underserved in Asheville, but one great candidate is **Hotel Indigo Asheville Downtown** (151 Haywood St., 877/859-5095, www.ihg.com, $275 and up), which does offer some very good rooms for under $300 in the heart of the very walkable downtown area.

## Over $300

The ★ **Omni Grove Park Inn Resort & Spa** (290 Macon Ave., 800/438-5800, www.groveparkinn.com, $400-600) is the sort of place to which Asheville residents will bring their out-of-town houseguests when giving them a grand tour of the city, simply to walk into the lobby and ooh and ah. The massive stone building—constructed by a crew of 400 workers who had only mule teams and a single steam shovel to aid them—was erected in 1912 and 1913, the project of St. Louis millionaire E. W. Grove. He was the Grove behind Grove's Tasteless Chill Tonic, a medicinal syrup that outsold Coca-Cola in the 1890s. You may have seen it in antiques shops; on the label was a picture of a wincing baby, who looks more like he's just been given a dose of the tonic than that he needs one.

The opening of the Grove Park Inn was cause for such fanfare that William Jennings Bryan addressed the celebratory dinner party. In the coming years, at least eight U.S.

presidents would be guests here, as would a glittering parade of early 20th-century big shots: Henry Ford, Thomas Edison, Eleanor Roosevelt, Harry Houdini, F. Scott Fitzgerald, Will Rogers, and George Gershwin. The lobby is quite amazing, like a cross between a Gilded Age hunting lodge and the great hall of a medieval castle. There are 14-foot fireplaces at each end, and the elevators are, believe it or not, inside the chimneys.

In addition to the spectacle of the lodge and its multiple restaurants, cafés, bars, and shops, guests have (for an additional charge) access to its world-famous spa. The pass gives access to the lounges, pools, waterfall, steam room, inhalation room, and outdoor whirlpool tub. For extra fees (ranging $75-500, with most around $200-300), guests can choose from a four-page menu of spa treatments: massage, facials, manicures, aromatherapy, body wraps, the works.

If you've spent the day touring the Biltmore Estate, viewing the incredible splendor in which a baron of the Gilded Age basked, it may be jarring to return to real life unless you're Richard Branson or the Queen of England. But you can soften the transition with a stay at the luxurious **Inn on Biltmore Estate** (800/411-3812, www.biltmore.com, $200-500). It's everything you'd wish for from a hotel in this location. The suites are beautifully furnished, the view is magnificent, and the lobby and dining room and library have the deluxe coziness of a turn-of-the-20th-century lodge.

If you do happen to be Richard Branson or the Queen of England, and simply need a mountain getaway, consider the inn's **Cottage on Biltmore Estate** (800/411-3812, www.biltmore.com, call for rates). This historic two-room cottage was designed by Richard Howland Hunt, the son of the mansion's designer, Richard Morris Hunt. Your own personal butler and chef come with the digs.

The **Doubletree Hotel Biltmore/**

Asheville (115 Hendersonville Rd., 855/605-0318, www.doubletree3.hilton.com, $300-400) is also a great place to stay for those centering their activities on the nearby Biltmore Estate, which is within walking distance and also served by a shuttle.

## INFORMATION AND SERVICES

The **Asheville Visitors Center** (36 Montford Ave., off I-240 exit 4C, 828/258-6129) can set you up with all the maps, brochures, and recommendations you could need. Other sources are www.exploreasheville.com and www.ashevillechamber.org.

**Mission Hospital** (509 Biltmore Ave. and 428 Biltmore Ave., 828/213-1948 or 828/213-4063, www.missionhospitals.org) in Asheville has two campuses and two emergency departments.

## GETTING THERE AND AROUND

Asheville lies spread-eagled at the crossroads of I-40, North Carolina's primary east-west highway, and I-26, a roughly north-south artery through the Southern highlands. Splitting the difference, U.S. 19 runs at a diagonal, deep into the Smokies in one direction and into the northern Blue Ridge in the other.

Asheville has an extensive public bus system, connecting most major points in the metropolitan area, including the airport, with downtown. Buses run Monday-Saturday 6am-11:30pm and cost $1 ($0.50 seniors). Visit www.ashevillenc.gov for routes and schedules.

**Asheville Regional Airport** (AVL, 61 Terminal Dr., Fletcher, 828/684-2226, www.flyavl.com) is a bit of a jog from the city, located to the south in Fletcher. It's an easy 20-minute drive on I-26.

# Southern Blue Ridge and Foothills

The mountains of Polk, Rutherford, and Henderson Counties, south of Asheville, have an air of enchantment to them. There are some quantifiable symptoms of this peculiarity. For one, Polk County has its own climate. Called the Thermal Belt, the meteorological pocket formed on this sheltered slope of the Blue Ridge has distinctly milder summers and winters than the surrounding areas. In the 19th century it became a favorite summering spot for the Charleston elite and other Southerners of the plantation class. Some lovely old houses and inns remain as vestiges of this genteel past.

## BREVARD

Brevard is the pleasant seat of the improbably named Transylvania County. As you might expect, Halloween is a big deal in this town. Brevard is also known for sheltering a population of rather startling white squirrels. The local legend about their origin goes that their ancestors escaped from an overturned circus truck in Florida in 1940 and made their way to Brevard as pets. More likely, say researchers, is that they came from an exotic pet breeder in Florida and were acquired by a Brevard-area family. In any case, the white squirrels escaped into the wilds of Transylvania County, and you'll probably see their descendants in the area when you visit.

### Entertainment and Events

The **Brevard Music Center** (349 Andante Ln., 828/862-2100, www.brevardmusic.org) has attracted the highest caliber of young musicians for more than 70 years for intensive summer-long classical music instruction. Throughout the summer, Brevard Music Center students as well as visiting soloists of international fame put on a world-class concert series, performing works by

# Southern Blue Ridge and Foothills

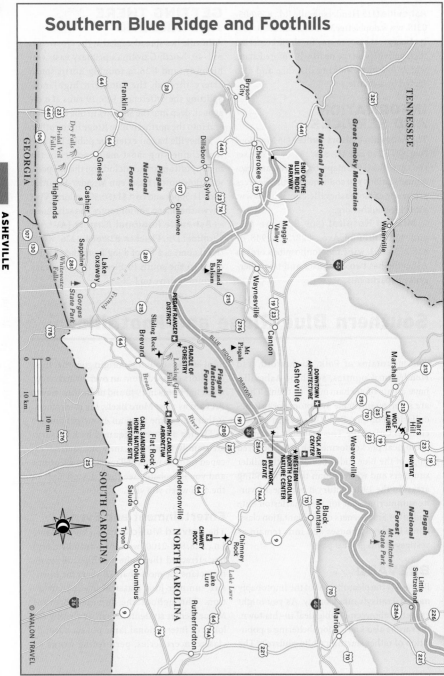

© AVALON TRAVEL

one of Brevard's white squirrels

the likes of Tchaikovsky and Gilbert and Sullivan.

## Shopping

A center for a very different sort of music is **Celestial Mountain Music** (16 W. Main St., 828/884-3575, www.celestialmtnmusic. com). This nice little shop carries, among the usual wares of a good music store, two lines of very special locally made instruments. Cedar Mountain Banjos, of the open-backed, old-time variety, are beautifully crafted and ring clear and pretty. The work of local fiddle builder Lyle Reedy is also sold at Celestial Mountain Music.

## Sports and Recreation

About 10 miles south of Brevard, **Dupont State Forest** (U.S. 276, 828/877-6527, www. dupontforest.com, daily dawn-dusk, free) has more than 90 miles of hiking trails covering 10,000 acres. Some of Transylvania County's beautiful waterfalls are located within the forest and accessible on foot (most trails in the forest are moderate or strenuous) or, with special permits and advance reservation for people with disabilities only, by vehicle. Visitors should use caution, wear brightly colored clothing, and leave their bearskin capes at home from September through the end of the year, when hikers share the woods with hunters.

## ★ PISGAH RANGER DISTRICT

Just to the north of Brevard in the town of Pisgah Forest is the main entrance to the **Pisgah Ranger District** (off U.S. 276, 828/877-3265, www.cs.unca.edu, park hours daily dawn-dusk, office hours Mon.-Fri. 8am-5pm, free) of the Pisgah National Forest. The forest covers half a million acres, a large swath of western North Carolina, but this 157,000-acre ranger district encompasses many of the forest's favorite attractions. A good topographical map of the ranger district is available from National Geographic (Map 780, $10, sold at the Cradle of Forestry store and at www.cradleofforestry.com). In the ranger district are more than 275 miles of hiking trails and several campgrounds, the most easily accessible of which is **Davidson River Campground,** 1.5 miles from the Brevard entrance (877/444-6777, www.recreation.gov, year-round, $10), with restrooms and showers.

The **Shining Rock Wilderness** and the **Middle Prong Wilderness** comprise rugged terrain that rises from 3,200 feet elevation at its lowest point along the West Pigeon River to a towering 6,400 feet at Richmond Balsam. **Cold Mountain,** made famous by the book and movie of the same name, is a real peak located within the Shining Rock Wilderness. These mountains are steep and the forests dense, and what trails there are have no signage. This is a popular area among experienced backwoods trekkers but is not recommended for casual visits, as it is exceedingly easy to get lost here. It's recommended that at a minimum, you should be adept at using both a compass and a topo map before venturing into these wilderness areas.

Sliding Rock in Pisgah Ranger District

Not to be confused with Shining Rock, **Sliding Rock** is an easily accessible waterfall and swimming spot with a parking lot, a bathhouse, and lifeguards (on duty Memorial Day-Labor Day daily 10am-6pm). You can actually ride down the 60-foot waterfall, a smooth rock face (not so smooth that you shouldn't wear sturdy britches) over which 11,000 gallons of water rush every minute into the chilly swimming hole below.

The **Cradle of Forestry** (U.S. 276, Pisgah Forest, 828/877-3130, www.cradleofforestry. com, mid-Apr.-early Nov. daily 9am-5pm, $5 adults, free under age 16) is a museum and activity complex commemorating the rise of the forestry profession in the United States, which originated here at a turn-of-the-20th-century training school in the forests once owned by George Washington Vanderbilt, master of the Biltmore Estate in Asheville. Plow days and living-history days throughout the year give an interesting glimpse into this region's old-time methods of farming and frontier living. Self-guided trails lead through the woods to many interesting locations on this former campus.

# HENDERSONVILLE

An easy drive from Asheville, Hendersonville is a comfortable small city with a walkable downtown filled with boutiques and cafés. It's also the heart of North Carolina's apple industry. Hundreds of orchards cover the hillsides of Henderson County, and all along the highway, long packinghouses bustle in the late summer as they process more than three million tons of apples. There are also many shops and produce stands run by members of old orchard-owning families, where you can buy apples singly or by the bushel, along with cider, preserves, and many other apple products.

## Sights

One of North Carolina's cool small transportation museums is located at the Hendersonville Airport. The **Western North Carolina Air Museum** (Hendersonville Airport, off U.S. 176/Spartanburg Hwy., 828/698-2482, www. wncairmuseum.com, Apr.-Oct. Sat. 10am-5pm, Wed. and Sun. noon-5pm, Nov.-Mar. Wed. and Sat.-Sun. noon-5pm, free) houses a collection of more than a dozen historic small aircraft, both originals and reproductions. Most are from the 1930s and 1940s, though some are even older, and they're all wonderfully fun contraptions to visit.

## Shopping

Hendersonville's downtown **Curb Market** (221 N. Church St. at 2nd Ave., 828/692-8012, www.curbmarket.com, Apr.-Dec. Tues., Thurs., and Sat. 8am-2pm, Jan.-Mar. Tues. and Sat. 8am-2pm) has been operating since 1924. Here you can buy fresh locally grown fruits, vegetables, and flowers; fresh-baked cakes, pies, and breads; jams, jellies, and pickles made in local home kitchens; and the work of local woodcarvers, weavers, and other craftspeople.

While in the Hendersonville area, keep an eye out for brightly colored, folk painting-adorned packages of **Immaculate Baking Company** (www.immaculatebaking.com) cookies. Besides making totally delicious cookies, this Hendersonville-based company helps support the work of visionary "outsider" artists throughout the South.

## FLAT ROCK
### Sights
Just south of Hendersonville is the historic village of Flat Rock. Founded in the early 19th century as a vacation spot for the Charleston plantation gentry, Flat Rock retains a delicate, cultured ambience. Many artists and writers have lived in this area, most famously Carl Sandburg, whose house, Connemara, is preserved as the **Carl Sandburg Home National Historic Site** (81 Carl Sandburg Ln., 828/693-4178, www.nps.gov/carl, daily 9am-5pm, house tour $5 adults, $3 over age 61, free under age 16). Here Sandburg and his family lived for more than 20 years, during which time he wrote, won the Pulitzer Prize for *Complete Poems,* and no doubt observed bemusedly as his wife and daughters raised champion dairy goats. (A herd of goats lives on the grounds today.) Thirty-minute tours take visitors through the house to see many of the Sandburgs' belongings. There is a bookstore in the house, and more than five miles of trails through the property.

### Entertainment and Events
Another literary landmark in the village is the **Flat Rock Playhouse** (2661 Greenville Hwy., 866/732-8008, www.flatrockplayhouse.org). Now the state theater of North Carolina, the

Flat Rock Playhouse's history dates to 1940, when a roving theater company called the Vagabonds wandered down from New York and converted an old gristmill here in the village into a stage. They now have a 10-month season, drawing more than 90,000 patrons yearly.

## SALUDA AND VICINITY
Just east and south of Hendersonville, bordering South Carolina, Polk County is home to several interesting little towns, most notably Tryon and Saluda, and a lot of beautiful mountain countryside. In Saluda you'll find a tiny downtown, laid out along the old Norfolk Southern Railway tracks. The tracks at Saluda are the top of the steepest standard-gauge mainline railroad grade in the United States.

### Entertainment and Events
For one weekend every July, Saluda busts at the seams with visitors to the **Coon Dog Day Festival** (800/440-7848, www.saluda.com). Hundreds of beautifully trained dogs from all over the region come to town to show off in a parade and trials, while the humans have a street fair and 5K race.

### Shopping
Six miles southeast of Columbus, Claude and Elaine Graves have been making distinctive pottery for 35 years at **Little Mountain Pottery** (6372 Peniel Rd., Tryon, www.crowsounds.com). The Graves's work draws on North Carolina's folk traditions in ceramics, but it's quite different from much of the pottery made in this area in that it also draws inspiration from the ceramics of North Africa, the Canary Islands, Spain, and Mexico. Don't miss Claude's wonderful portraits of influential North Carolina potters, arranged in an outdoor gallery along the walls of his barns and kiln.

### Sports and Recreation
The equestrian life plays a growing role in Polk and the surrounding counties of North Carolina's southern mountains. The

**Foothills Equestrian Nature Center** (3381 Hunting Country Rd., Tryon, 828/859-9021, www.fence.org), known as FENCE, occupies 380 beautiful acres along the border with South Carolina. The equestrian center has stables for 200 horses and two lighted show rings. FENCE hosts cross-country, three-day, A-rated hunter and jumper, dressage, and many other equestrian events throughout the year. The annual Block House Steeplechase has been held in Tryon for 60 years, and FENCE has hosted the event for 20 of those years. FENCE also offers regular hikes and bird-watching excursions on its beautiful property.

## Food

For such a tiny town, there are an awful lot of eating places in Saluda. Just stand in the middle of Main Street and look around; there are several choices, and you won't go wrong at any of them. The **Whistlestop Café** (173 Main St., 828/749-3310, Thurs.-Mon. 11am-5pm, $7) serves good hearty meals and strong coffee in its tiny dining room. The apple pound cake is perfect. **Wildflour Bakery** (173 E. Main, 828/749-9224, www.saluda.com, Wed.-Sat. 8am-3pm, Sun. 10am-2pm) stone-grinds wheat, with which it makes absolutely delicious breads, every single morning. Breakfast and lunch are served here, making this a great place to fill up before a day of kayaking or hiking.

# HIGHLANDS AND VICINITY
## Waterfalls

This country is blessed with beautiful waterfalls, some of which are easily visited. **Whitewater Falls** (Hwy. 281, on the state line, south of Highlands, daily dawn-dusk, $2 per vehicle), at over 400 feet, is reported to be the highest waterfall east of the Rockies. An upper-level viewing spot is at the end of a wheelchair-accessible paved trail, while a flight of more than 150 steps leads to the base of the falls. A much smaller but still very beautiful waterfall is **Silver Run Falls** (Hwy. 107,

4 miles south of Cashiers), reached by a short trail from a roadside pull-off. **Bridal Veil Falls** (U.S. 64, 2.5 miles west of Highlands) flows over a little track of road, right off U.S. 64. You'll see a sign from the main road where you can turn off and actually drive behind the waterfall, or park and walk behind it. Another falls that you can walk through is **Dry Falls** (U.S. 64, between Highlands and Franklin, daily dawn-dusk, $2 per vehicle), reached by a small trail off the highway, curving right into and behind the 75-foot waterfall.

## Sports and Recreation

One of North Carolina's newest state parks, **Gorges State Park** (Hwy. 281 S., Sapphire, 828/966-9099, http://ncparks.gov, May-Aug. 8am-9pm, Mar.-Apr. and Sept.-Oct. 8am-8pm, Nov.-Feb. 8am-6pm, free) is a lush mountain rain forest, receiving 80 inches of rain a year. The steep terrain rises 2,000 feet in four miles, creating a series of rocky waterfalls and challenging trails. Facilities are still under development, but primitive camping ($9) is permitted in designated areas.

## Food and Accommodations

The 3,500-foot-high town of Cashiers ("CASH-ers") is home to the **High Hampton Inn and Country Club** (1525 Hwy. 107 S., 800/334-2551, www.highhamptoninn.com, from $100, 3-night minimum), a popular resort for generations of North Carolinians. This was originally the home of Confederate general Wade Hampton, the dashing Charlestonian cavalryman. The lodge, a big old 1930s wooden chalet with huge, cozy fireplaces in the lobby, is surrounded by 1,400 acres of lakeside woodlands, with an 18-hole golf course, a good restaurant that serves buffet-style meals (dinner jacket requested in the evening), clay tennis courts, and a fitness center that features a climbing tower.

# INFORMATION AND SERVICES

In addition to Asheville's **Mission Hospital** (509 Biltmore Ave. and 428 Biltmore Ave.,

828/213-1948 or 828/213-4063, www.mis-sionhospitals.org), there are several re-gional hospitals with emergency or urgent care departments. **Park Ridge Hospital** (77 Airport Rd., Arden, 828/651-0098, www.parkridgehospital.org), located be-tween Asheville and Hendersonville, has urgent care (Mon.-Fri. 8am-7pm, Sat.-Sun. 11am-6pm). Hendersonville also has **Pardee Hospital** (800 N. Justice St., Hendersonville, 828/696-4270, www.pard-eehospital.org). In Brevard, the main hospi-tal is **Transylvania Community Hospital** (90 Hospital Dr., Brevard, 828/883-5243, www.tchospital.org), and in Rutherfordton it's **Rutherford Hospital** (288 S. Ridgecrest Ave., Rutherfordton, 828/286-5000, www.rutherfordhosp.org).

Maps and guides are available at the **Hendersonville and Flat Rock**

**Visitors Information Center** (201 S. Main St., Hendersonville, 800/828-4244, www.historichendersonville.com) and at the **Transylvania County Tourism Development Authority** (35 W. Main St., Brevard, 800/648-4523, www.visitwaterfalls.com).

## GETTING THERE AND AROUND

The Brevard-Hendersonville area is an easy drive from Asheville, with Hendersonville less than half an hour down I-26, and Brevard a short jog west from there on U.S. 64. To reach Tryon and Rutherfordton, follow U.S. 74 south and east from Hendersonville. **Asheville Regional Airport** (AVL, 61 Terminal Dr., Fletcher, 828/684-2226, www.flyavl.com), south of Asheville, is very convenient to this region.

# Waynesville and Vicinity

West of Asheville and near the Balsam Range, the town of Waynesville is an artistic com-munity where crafts galleries and studios line the downtown. In nearby Cullowhee, Western Carolina University is one of the mountain region's leading academic institutions, as well as the location of the wonderful Mountain Heritage Center museum and Mountain Heritage Day festival.

## WAYNESVILLE
Waynesville's downtown can keep a gallery-hopper or shopper happy for hours. Main Street is packed with studio artists' galler-ies, cafés and coffee shops, and a variety of boutiques.

### Shopping
**Blue Ridge Books & News** (152 S. Main St., 828/456-6000, www.brbooks-news.com, Mon.-Sat. 8am-8pm, Sun. 8am-5pm) is a very nice bookstore, with specialties in books of regional interest and cups of good coffee.

**Good Ol' Days Cigars** (46 N. Main St./145 Wall St., 828/456-2898, www.goodoldysci-gars.com, Mon.-Thurs. 10am-6pm, Fri.-Sat. 10am-7pm) offers a large selection of fine tobacco and smoking products—cigars, of course, as well as pipes, loose tobacco, rolling papers, and much more—and a TV lounge in which you can enjoy them.

One of the several locations of **Mast General Store** (63 N. Main St., 828/452-2101, www.mastgeneralstore.com, summer Mon.-Sat. 10am-6pm, Sun. noon-5pm, winter hours vary) is here in Waynesville. While the stores are perhaps best known among vacationers for making children clamor—they carry over 500 varieties of candy, many kept in big wooden barrels, old-time dry goods-store-style—they have an even larger selection of outdoor-fo-cused merchandise for adults.

### Galleries
Waynesville's galleries are many and varied, although the overarching aesthetic is one of

studio art with inspiration in the environmental and folk arts. **Twigs and Leaves** (98 N. Main St., 828/456-1940, www.twigsandleaves. com, Mon.-Sat. 10am-5:30pm, Sun. 1pm-4pm) carries splendid art furniture that is both fanciful and functional, pottery of many hand-thrown and hand-built varieties, jewelry, paintings, fabric hangings, mobiles, and many other beautiful and unusual items inspired by nature.

**Textures on Main** (142 N. Main St., 828/452-0058, www.texturesonmain.com, Mon.-Sat. 10am-6pm, Sun. noon-5pm) is a gallery showcasing the work of John and Suzanne Gernandt, furniture and fabric artists, respectively, and several other partners. Suzanne's fabric art is often abstract and features beautiful, deeply saturated colors. John's furniture and that of his fellow designers whose work is carried by Textures cover a stunning array of sensibilities—Jonathan Adler's hyper-mod pieces, Robin Bruce's gorgeous, understated upholstery, and Gernandt's own dazzling cabinetry, which has the grace of Shaker carpentry and the slightest hint of a Tim Burton-style offbeat aesthetic.

**Studio Thirty Three** (33 Pidgeon St., 828/456-3443, www.studio33jewelry.com) carries the work of a very small and select group of fine jewelers from western North Carolina. Their retail and custom inventory consists of spectacular handcrafted pieces in a variety of styles and an array of precious stones and metals. This is a must-see gallery if you are engaged or have another special occasion coming up.

## Food

A popular spot is **Bogart's** (303 S. Main St., 828/452-1313, Sun.-Thurs. 11am-9pm, Fri.-Sat. 11am-10pm, $10-20), which is locally famous for its filet mignon. If you're just passing through town and need a jolt of really strong, good coffee, visit **Panacea** (66 Commerce St., 828/452-6200, Mon.-Fri. 7am-5pm, Sat. 8am-5pm, under $5) in the funky Frog Level neighborhood downhill from downtown.

## Accommodations
### UNDER $150

Up on the Blue Ridge Parkway above Waynesville, and quite close to Asheville, is one of my favorite inns in all of North Carolina. The ★ **Pisgah Inn** (BRP milepost 410, 828/235-8228, www.pisgahinn. com, late Mar.-early Nov., from $100) is much like Skyland and Big Meadows on Virginia's Skyline Drive, with motel-style accommodations surrounding an old lodge with a large family-style dining room and a Parkway gift shop. The inn sits on a nearly 5,000-foot-high mountaintop, so the view is sensational. Trails surround the Pisgah like the spokes of a wheel, leading to short, pretty strolls and challenging daylong hikes. The restaurant, open for breakfast, lunch, and dinner (daily 7:30am-10:30am, 11:30am-4pm, and 5pm-9pm), has a mesmerizing view and an appetizing and varied menu ($5-25) of both country and fancy meals. The guest rooms are simple but comfortable, each with its own balcony and rocking chairs overlooking the valley, and TV but no telephones.

Waynesville also has quite a selection of luxury inns. The **Andon-Reid Inn** (92 Daisey Ave., 800/293-6190, www.andonreidinn.com, from $115, no pets, guests under 16 not encouraged) is a handsome turn-of-the-20th-century house close to downtown, with five tranquil rooms, each with its own fireplace, and a sumptuous four-course breakfast menu that might include sweet-potato pecan pancakes and pork tenderloin, homemade corn bread with honey butter, and many more treats.

### $150-300

Outside of Waynesville in the community of Balsam, the ★ **Balsam Mountain Inn** (68 Seven Springs Dr., Balsam, 800/224-9498, www.balsaminn.com, $139-219, dogs and cats permitted with prior approval) has stood watch for a century. It's a haunting, and haunted, location—an imposing old wooden hotel with huge double porches overlooking, in the foreground, a rather spooky little railroad platform, and, in the background, the beautiful ridges of Jackson and Haywood Counties. The interior has barely changed since the earliest days, paneled in white horizontal beadboard throughout, with 10-foot-wide hallways said to have been designed to accommodate steamer trunks. The one telephone is at the front desk, and there are no TVs, so plan to go hiking or to sit on the porch before dining in the downstairs restaurant, and then curl up and read in the library. (There is, paradoxically, fast Wi-Fi.) Among the inn's ghosts is a woman in a blue dress. She is said to originate in room 205, but comes and goes elsewhere on the 2nd floor.

The **Inn at Iris Meadows** (304 Love Ln., 888/466-4747, www.irismeadows.com, from $225, dogs permitted with advance notice, children discouraged) is another splendid house, on a hillside surrounded by lush trees and gardens. Shepherd-mix Scratch and gray tabby-cat Zephyrus help run the place, and are added attractions themselves.

## OVER $300

For tip-top luxury, try **The Swag** (2300 Swag Rd., 800/789-7672, www.theswag.com, $430-750). Superb guest rooms and cabins of rustic wood and stone each have a steam shower, and several have saunas, wet bars, and cathedral ceilings. The inn is at 5,000 feet elevation, at the very edge of Great Smoky Mountains National Park.

# CULLOWHEE

The unincorporated village of Cullowhee (pronounced "CULL-uh-wee"), located on Highway 107 between Sylva and Cashiers, is the home of Western Carolina University (WCU). The university's **Mountain Heritage Center** (lobby of the H. F. Robinson Administration Bldg., WCU campus, 1 University Way, 828/227-7129, www.wcu.edu, Nov.-May Mon.-Fri. 8am-5pm, June-Oct. Mon.-Fri. 8am-5pm, Sun. 2pm-5pm, free) is a small museum with a great collection that will fascinate anyone interested in Appalachian history. The permanent exhibit, *Migration of the Scotch-Irish People,* is full of artifacts like a 19th-century covered wagon, wonderful photographs, and homemade quilts, linens, musical instruments, and more. The Mountain Heritage Center also hosts two traveling exhibits at a time in addition to the permanent installation, and the annual **Mountain Heritage Day** festival (late Sept.), which brings together many of western North Carolina's best and most authentic traditional musicians and artisans in a free festival that draws up to 25,000 visitors.

# GETTING THERE AND AROUND

Waynesville is easily reached from Asheville by heading west on I-40, and then taking either U.S. 23 or U.S. 74. The Blue Ridge Parkway also passes a little to the south of the town near Balsam. Sylva is southwest of Waynesville on U.S. 23, and from there, Cullowhee is an easy drive down Highway 107.

# Great Smoky Mountains

**W**hen the Atlanta Olympic Park bomber, Eric Rudolph, was on the lam in the Smokies in 1996, there was a commonly held opinion among western North Carolinians that he would never be found. No doubt people

watching the news from living rooms around the country were mystified that a man couldn't be tracked down in this relatively small geographical area, a few sparsely populated counties largely made up of federal land. But after driving a little way into the high country south and west of Asheville, one can easily imagine that hundreds of people could hide in this wilderness and the outside world wouldn't notice so much as a rustling leaf.

In fact, exactly that occurred in the 1830s, although under very different circumstances, when President Martin Van Buren gave the final go-ahead to start the removal of the Cherokee people on the Trail of Tears. Several extended Cherokee families took to the deep mountains, and these resisters who refused to leave their homeland—choosing instead to brave months of living in fear, exposed to the elements—are the ancestors of many of today's Eastern Band of the Cherokee.

The ancient Cherokee culture has been rooted in the Smokies for thousands of years, from the early days described in their mythology, when the Ani-gituhwa-gi shared these mountains with witches and fairies, and birds and leeches as big as bears. The darkest hour came in the 19th century, when the Cherokee Nation was rent apart by forced exile to Oklahoma. But between those who stayed and hid out in the mountains, and those who walked home from Oklahoma to rebuild their lives in their ancestral home, the Cherokee people regained strength—and today the seat of the Eastern Band is here in far western North Carolina on the land known as the Qualla Boundary.

## PLANNING YOUR TIME

Many people plan their visits to the Smokies to coincide with what's blooming or blazing on the mountainsides. Spring wildflowers begin to bloom in late March, and peak in

---

**Previous:** turkeys in Cades Cove; autumn in Great Smoky Mountains National Park. **Above:** bear carving in downtown Cherokee.

Look for ★ to find recommended sights, activities, dining, and lodging.

# Highlights

★ **Museum of the Cherokee Indian:** The Cherokee people have lived in the Smoky Mountains for thousands of years. This excellent museum tells unforgettable tales of their history (page 212).

★ **Qualla Arts and Crafts Mutual:** Ancient craft traditions still thrive among Cherokee artists in western North Carolina. At the Qualla Mutual, visitors can learn about and purchase the work of today's masters (page 213).

★ **Cades Cove:** The most visited spot in Great Smoky Mountains National Park is a formerly bustling mountain village that is witness to the depth of history in the Southern highlands (page 218).

★ **Clingmans Dome:** From this third-highest peak in the eastern United States, set in a dramatic alpine environment, you'll have an astounding view of up to 100 miles on a clear day (page 219).

★ **Nantahala River Gorge:** So steep that in some places the water is only brushed by sunlight at high noon, this gorge is an unbeatable place for white-water rafting (page 225).

★ **John C. Campbell Folk School:** For nearly a century, the Folk School has been a leading light in promoting American craft heritage and nurturing new generations of artists (page 228).

# Great Smoky Mountains

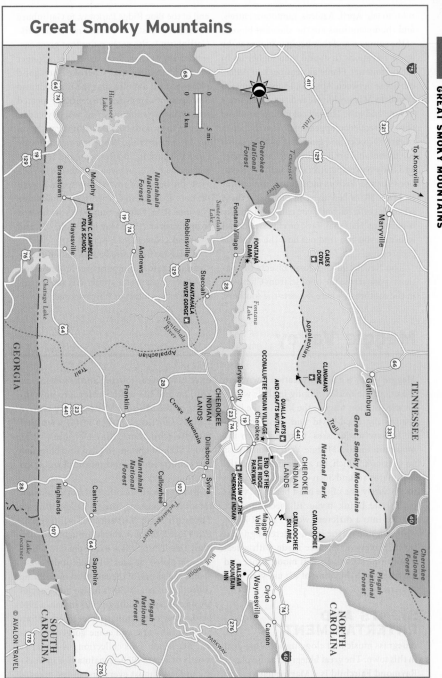

mid- to late April. Azaleas, mountain laurels, and rhododendrons are the showiest blooms of the summer, and they begin to bloom at the lower elevations first, and then higher up in the mountains. Flame azaleas peak in different areas between April and July, mountain laurels in May and June, and rhododendrons in June and July. The fall colors appear in the opposite sequence, appearing first at the peaks in early October, and gradually moving down the mountains until, in mid- to late October and early November, trees in the lower elevations change. Factors including summer heat and rainfall, or lack thereof, can throw these schedules off a bit, but if you call Great Smoky Mountains National Park or check regional websites, you can find out how the season is progressing.

The Newfound Gap Road bisects the national park across the middle, from Cherokee in the southeast, where it meets the southern end of the Blue Ridge Parkway, to Gatlinburg at the northwest. For a brief visit to the park, Gatlinburg is the entry point that gives easiest access to short loop roads. For a longer visit, Gatlinburg and Cherokee are good places to find a motel, and the Elkmont and Smokemont campsites are centrally located front-country camping areas where you can sleep in the woods but have your car with you for daytime driving. While you can certainly cross the park in an afternoon and see some sights, the more time you can devote to your visit, the better. Many visitors spend a week or more at a time in Great Smoky Mountains National Park. Campground stays are limited to one week at a time May 15-October 31, and two weeks November 1-May 14.

A massive forest fire in 2016 caused extensive damage to Gatlinburg over in Tennessee. However, most visitor attractions and amenities are either intact or fully restored.

# Maggie Valley

Maggie Valley is a family vacation town from the era of the nuclear family in their wood-paneled station wagon, the kids in the back seat eating Lik-M-Aid and wearing plastic Indian headdresses. Coming down the mountain toward Maggie Valley, you'll pass an overlook, which, on a morning when the mountains around Soco Gap are looped with fog, is surely one of the most beautiful vistas in the state. Drink in your fill, because you're headed into a different world. You'll know it when you pass the hand-lettered sign that says, "Have your picture made with a real moonshine still and a real moonshiner and his truck for a donation of $3; use your own camera."

## SIGHTS AND ENTERTAINMENT

Bluegrass music and clogging are a big deal in this town. The great bluegrass banjo player Raymond Fairchild is a Maggie native, and after his 50-year touring and recording career, he and his wife, Shirley, are now the hosts of the **Maggie Valley Opry House** (3605 Soco Rd., 828/648-7941, www.raymondfairchild.com, May-Oct. daily 8pm, about $12). In season, you can find bluegrass and country music concerts and clogging exhibitions every night.

In a state with countless attractions for automotive enthusiasts, Maggie Valley's **Wheels Through Time Museum** (62 Vintage Ln., 828/926-6266, www.wheelsthroughtime.com, Mar.-Dec. Thurs.-Mon. 9am-5pm, $12 adults, $10 over age 65, $6 ages 5-12, free under age 4) stands out as one of the most fun. A dazzling collection of nearly 300 vintage motorcycles are on display, including a 1908 Indian, a 1914 Harley Davidson, military motorcycles from both world wars, and some gorgeous post-war machines. This collection, which dates mostly to before 1950, is maintained in working order—almost every one of the bikes is revved up from time to time, and the museum's founder has been known to take a spin on one of the treasures.

## SPORTS AND RECREATION

Maggie Valley's **Cataloochee Ski Area** (1080 Ski Lodge Rd., off U.S. 19, 800/768-0285, slopes report 800/768-3588, www.cataloochee.com, lift tickets $20-60, equipment rentals $15-30) has slopes geared to every level of skier and snowboarder. Classes and private lessons are taught for all ages. At the nearby **Tube World** (U.S. 19, next to ski area, 800/768-0285, www.tubemaggievalley.com, $25 per session, must be over 42 inches tall, "Wee Bowl" area for smaller visitors $5 per session, call ahead for Wee Bowl, Thanksgiving-mid-Mar.), you can zip down the mountain on inner tubes.

## FOOD

**J. Arthurs Restaurant** (2843 Soco Rd., 828/926-1817, www.jarthurs.com, Wed.-Sat. 4:30pm-9pm, Sun. noon-8pm, $15-25) is a popular spot locally for steaks, which are the house specialty. The restaurant also has a variety of seafood and pasta dishes, but very little by way of vegetarian meals. Visit the website for a printable coupon.

## ACCOMMODATIONS

The main drag through Maggie Valley (Soco Rd./U.S. 19) is lined with motels, including some of the familiar national brands. Among the pleasant private motels are the **Valley Inn** (236 Soco Rd., 800/948-6880, www.thevalleyinn.com, from $39 off-season, rates vary in high season, call for specifics during your target dates) and **Jonathan Creek Inn and Villas** (4324 Soco Rd., 800/577-7812, www.jonathancreekinn.com, from about $90). The latter has creek-side guest rooms with screen porches.

## GETTING THERE AND AROUND

U.S. 19 is the main thoroughfare in these parts, leading from Asheville to Great Smoky Mountains National Park. Maggie is also a reasonably short jog off I-40 via exits 20, 24, and 27.

# Cherokee and the Qualla Boundary

The town of Cherokee is a mixture of seemingly contradictory forces: tradition and commerce, nature and development. Cherokee is the civic center of the Eastern Band of the Cherokee, a people who have lived in these mountains for many centuries and whose history, art, government, and language are very much alive. It is the seat of the Qualla (pronounced "KWA-lah," like the marsupial but with just two syllables) Boundary, which is not precisely a reservation, but a large tract of land owned and governed by the Cherokee people. Institutions like the Museum of the Cherokee Indian and the Qualla Arts and Crafts Mutual provide a rock-solid foundation for the Eastern Band of the Cherokee's cultural life. Take a look at the road signs as you drive around here. That beautiful, Asiatic-looking lettering below the English road names is the Cherokee language, in the written form famously created by Sequoyah in 1821. That language, once dying away with the Cherokee elders, is now taught to the community's youth; there are even plans for a Cherokee-language immersion school on the Qualla Boundary.

On the other hand, much of Cherokee's main drag is a classic old-timey tourist district. Here you'll find the "Indian" souvenirs—factory-made moccasins, plastic tomahawks, the works—so familiar to gift shop-goers across the country. In its own retro way, this side of Cherokee can actually be kind of charming, if you have a soft spot for the mid-20th-century family vacation aesthetic, the world of fudge counters and garish motel signs. (There are some incredible examples of the latter in Cherokee. Keep an eye out for the Princess, Warrior, and Chief Motels, each featuring a larger-than-life figure from the imaginary world of Hollywood and comic-book Indians.)

Enjoy this facet of Cherokee for what it's worth, but dig deeper—don't take this for the real Cherokee. The Cherokee are a people with thousands of years of history, much of which you can learn about here.

## SIGHTS

### ★ Museum of the Cherokee Indian

Make a visit to the **Museum of the Cherokee Indian** (589 Tsali Blvd., 828/497-3481, www.cherokeemuseum.org, daily 9am-5pm, $10 adults, $6 ages 6-13, free under age 6). Founded in 1948 and originally housed in a log cabin, this is now a widely acclaimed modern museum and community cultural locus. In the exhibits that trace the long history of the Cherokee people, you may notice the

disconcertingly realistic mannequins. Local members of the community volunteered to be models for these mannequins, allowing casts to be made of their faces and bodies so that the figures would not reflect an outsider's notion of what a Native American should look like, but rather the real people whose ancestors this museum honors. The Museum of the Cherokee Indian traces the tribe's history from the Paleo-Indian period, when the ancestral Cherokees were hunter-gatherers, through the ancient civilization into recorded history. A great deal of this exhibit area focuses on the 18th and 19th centuries, times when many tragedies befell the Cherokee as a result of the European invasion of their homeland. It was also a time of great cultural advancement, which included the development of Sequoyah's syllabary. The terrible Trail of Tears began near here, along the North Carolina-Georgia border. A small contingent of Cherokees remained in the Smokies at the time of the Trail of Tears, successfully eluding, and then negotiating with, the U.S. military, who were trying to send all of the Cherokee to Oklahoma. Those who lived out in the woods,

the town of Cherokee

the Museum of the Cherokee Indian

a great service to this community in providing a year-round market for the work of traditional Cherokee artists, whose stewardship of and innovation in traditional arts are so important.

## ENTERTAINMENT AND EVENTS

Of the several outdoor dramas for which North Carolina is known, among the longest running is Cherokee's *Unto These Hills* (Mountainside Theater, 688 Drama Rd., 866/554-4557, www.visitcherokeenc.com, summer Mon.-Sat. 8pm, $9.40-$29.40). For 60 summers, Cherokee actors have told the story of their nation's history, from ancient times through the Trail of Tears. Recently updated by Kiowa playwright Hanay Geiogomah, in consultation with the Cherokee people, the drama is now called *Unto These Hills: A Retelling.*

## ACCOMMODATIONS

The Eastern Band of the Cherokee operates **Harrah's Cherokee Casino and Hotel** (777 Casino Dr., 828/497-7777, www.harrahs.com, from $60). This full-bore Vegas-style casino with two towers of guest rooms has more than 3,000 games, mostly digital slots, with some digital table games run by croupiers. There's also a 1,500-seat theater that hosts major country artists throughout the year.

Cherokee has many motels, including **Holiday Inn** (37 Tsalagi Rd., 828/497-9181, www.holidayinn.com, from about $50) and **Econo Lodge** (20 River Rd./U.S. 19, 828/497-4575, www.econolodge.com, from about $80, pets allowed).

## GETTING THERE AND AROUND

Cherokee is located on a particularly pretty, winding section of U.S. 19, between Maggie Valley and Bryson City. Just north of Cherokee is the southern terminus of the Blue Ridge Parkway.

along with other Cherokees who were able to return home from Oklahoma, are the ancestors of today's Eastern Band, and their history is truly remarkable.

## ★ Qualla Arts and Crafts Mutual

Catty-corner to the museum is the **Qualla Arts and Crafts Mutual** (645 Tsali Blvd., 828/497-3103, www.visitcherokeenc.com, Mon.-Fri. 9am-5pm), a community arts co-op. Local artists sell their work here, and the gallery's high standards and the Cherokees' thousands of years of artistry make for a collection of very special pottery, baskets, masks, and other traditional art. As hard as it is to survive as an artist in Manhattan, artists in such rural areas as this have an exponentially more difficult go of it, trying to support themselves through the sale of their art, while at the same time maintaining the integrity of their vision and creativity. The Qualla co-op does

# Great Smoky Mountains National Park

An environment like no other, Great Smoky Mountains National Park (GSMNP) comprises over 800 square miles of high, cloud-ringed peaks and genuine rain forests. Tens of thousands of species of plants and animals live in the national park—80 different kinds of reptiles and amphibians alone (the park is sometimes called the Salamander Capital of the World), 200 species of birds, and more than 50 mammal species, from mice to mountain lions. The organization Discover Life in America (www.dlia.org) has for several years been conducting an All Taxa Biodiversity Inventory—that is, a census of all nonmicrobial life forms—in GSMNP, and have identified 17,000 of what they estimate to be a total of 100,000 separate species of plants and animals, including at least 900 hitherto unknown to science. The deep wilderness of the Great Smoky Mountains National Park is also a wonderful refuge for today's outdoors enthusiast, while the easy accessibility of ravishing scenery makes this the most visited national park in the United States.

## VISITING THE PARK
### Weather Considerations

To get a sense of the variability of the weather in GSMNP, keep in mind that elevation ranges from under 1,000 feet to over 6,600 feet. A low-lying area like that around Gatlinburg, Tennessee, is not a whole lot cooler than Raleigh in the summertime, with an average high of 88°F in July. For only three months of the year (Dec.-Feb.) does Gatlinburg have average lows under freezing, and then only by a few degrees. The opposite extreme is illustrated by Clingmans Dome, the highest elevation in the park. There the average high temperature is only 65°F in July—and only in June, July, and August can you be sure that it won't snow. If ever there were a place for layered clothing, this is it. No matter what

season the calendar tells you it is, be on the safe side and pack clothing for the other three as well. Keep these extremes in mind, too, in terms of safety; a snowstorm can bring two feet of snow to high elevations, and it's not at all unusual that the weather will be balmy at the foot of the mountain and icy at the top. At times, the temperature here has fallen to minus 20°F. Roads can be closed in the winter if the weather gets bad or restricted to vehicles with snow chains or four-wheel drive. Drive very slowly when it's icy. Leave plenty of room between you and the next car, and shift to a lower gear when going down slippery slopes. You can find out current conditions by calling the park (865/436-1200, ext. 630).

### Seasonal Considerations

The most crowded times in the park are mid-June-mid-August and all of October. Traffic is most likely to be heavy on the Cades Cove Loop Road and Newfound Gap Road. Several roads in the park are closed in the wintertime, though the dates vary. Among these are Balsam Mountain, Clingmans Dome, Little Greenbrier, Rich Mountain, and Round Bottom Roads and Roaring Fork Motor Nature Trail.

### Safety

Sometimes even the most experienced outdoorsy folks have emergencies. Whether going into the backcountry by yourself or with others, make sure that someone you trust knows where you're going, what your likely route is, and when to expect you back. The National Park Service recommends leaving this number with someone at home, to call if you're not back when expected: 865/436-1230.

Some of the basic safety rules may seem obvious, but it's good to review them. Climbing on rocks and waterfalls is always dangerous, and crossing a deep or flooded stream can be treacherous as well. If you have to cross a

# Great Smoky Mountains National Park

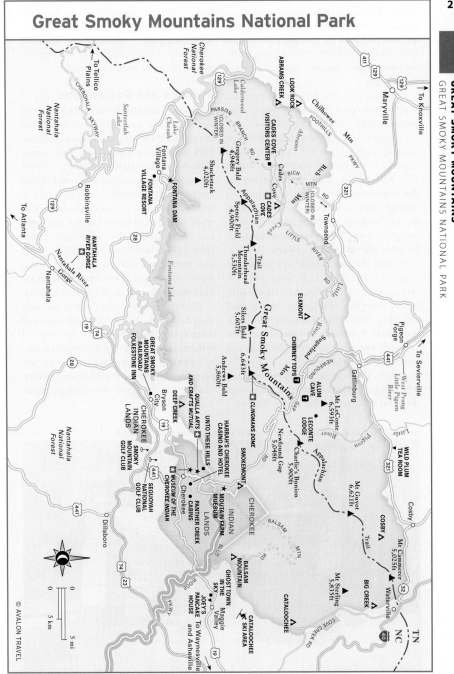

© AVALON TRAVEL

stream that's more than ankle-deep, it's recommended that you unbuckle the waist strap on your backpack (so you don't get pinned underwater if you fall), that you use a hiking stick to steady yourself, and that you wear nonslip shoes.

Cold is a concern, even in the summer. Wear layers, pack additional warm duds (warmer than you think you'll need), and try to stay dry. It may be shorts-and-T-shirt weather when you set out, but even in the summer it can be very cold here at night. Plan well, double-check before setting out that you have everything you could possibly need on your trek, and, says the National Park Service, "eat before you're hungry and rest before you're tired." Water from streams must be boiled or filtered before it's potable.

Wildlife can pose hazards here. Despite assurances to the contrary, there are still panthers (mountain lions) in these mountains. Ignore what the officials say in this (and only this) regard; locals see and hear them throughout Appalachia. But panthers are rare and reclusive, as are coyotes, wild hogs, and other resident tough guys.

Finally, if you're venturing out into the wild, it's good to remember that sometimes the greatest danger is other people. It's always better to hike or camp with at least one companion. A sturdy walking stick can be a lifesaver, and pepper spray, readily available and cheap in many different kinds of stores, should always be within easy reach.

## Permits and Regulations

Permits are required for camping in the national park and are quite easy to obtain. You can register at any of the more than a dozen visitors centers and ranger stations. This must be done in person, though, not online or over the phone. Fishing requires permits as well, which can be bought at outfitters and bait shops in nearby towns. Strict rules governing how, when, where, and what one can fish also apply, and can be read on the park website. Other rules apply to interaction with wildlife. Don't feed animals, and make sure to seal your foodstuffs to discourage night visitors. Firearms are forbidden in the park as, of course, is hunting.

Your dog is welcome in the park, but only in certain areas. To prevent transmission of diseases to or from the wildlife, and to avoid disrupting or frightening the resident fauna, as well as for their own safety, dogs are not permitted on hiking trails. They are, however, allowed to accompany you at campgrounds and picnic sites.

Historic mountain architecture abounds in Great Smoky Mountains National Park.

# WILDLIFE IN THE PARK

The largest animals in the park are also the most recently arrived. In the spring of 2001, the National Park Service experimentally reintroduced **elk** to the Great Smoky Mountains, a species that used to live here but was hunted to regional extinction in the 18th century. In the years since their reintroduction to the park, the herd has reproduced steadily, boding well for a successful future. If you hear a strange bellowing in the early autumn, it may be a male elk showing off for his beloved. One of the best places to see the elk is in the Cataloochee Valley, particularly in fields at dawn and dusk. Be sure to keep your distance; these animals can weigh up to 700 pounds, and the males have some formidable headgear.

An estimated 1,600 **black bears** live in GSMNP—two per square mile—so it's quite possible that you'll encounter one. Though they are a wonder to see, bears, which in this park weigh 100-400 pounds as adults, do pose a real risk to humans—and we to them—so it's important to be very aware of how we interact with them. It is illegal to come within 50 yards (150 feet) of a bear or elk, and those who knowingly get closer can be arrested. It sounds like a cliché, but the recommended procedure is this: If you see a bear, back away slowly. The National Park Service recommends that if the bear follows, you should stand your ground. If it keeps coming toward you persistently and looks menacing (and how could a bear persistently coming toward you not look menacing?), make yourself big and scary. Stand on a rock to look taller, or close to anyone else present, to show the bear that it's outnumbered. If it keeps coming closer, make a lot of noise and chuck things at it (rocks or sticks, that is; a bag of marshmallows or the fish you were just grilling would scarcely be deterrents). Should a bear actually attack you, the National Park Service recommends that you "fight back aggressively with any available object."

The best course of action is simply to avoid them and hope that any sightings you have will be from a safe distance. When camping, lock your food in the trunk of your car, if possible—or hoist it into a tree too high off the ground for a bear to reach it on its hind legs, and at a long enough length of rope from the nearest branch that one can't reach it by climbing the tree. Bears may approach in picnic areas. For goodness sake, don't feed them, no matter how winsome they look! "Habitual panhandler bears" (this is a real term) have

There's a good chance you'll see a black bear in the park.

been proven to die sooner than those that are afraid of humans, as they are more likely to be hit by cars, swallow indigestible food packaging, become easy targets for hunters, or even, if they are too problematic, be captured and euthanized.

Bears are hardly the only huge, ferocious animals in the park. Believe it or not, there are hundreds of snorting, tusky **wild hogs** here, descendants of a herd that escaped from a hunting preserve in Murphy in the 1910s. There are **coyotes, wolves,** and **bobcats,** and, though extremely rare, there are **mountain lions** (often called "panthers" or "painters" in this region) as well.

Of the many natural miracles in this park, one of the most astonishing is the light show put on for a couple of weeks each year by synchronous **fireflies.** Of the park's 14 species of firefly, only one, *Photinus carolinus,* flashes in this manner. While the average backyard's worth of fireflies twinkles like Christmas lights, synchronous fireflies, as their name implies, are capable of flashing in unison, by the hundreds or thousands. The sight is so amazing that, during the peak flashing period (usually in June), the park organizes nighttime expeditions to the best viewing spots.

If you go hiking in the backcountry, you might well see a **snake.** It's unlikely that you'll encounter a poisonous one, as there are only two kinds of vipers here—rattlesnakes and copperheads—that pose a danger to humans. There has never been a death from snakebite in the park, as far as anyone knows, but to be on the safe side, watch where you step or put your hands; it wouldn't do to be first on that list. But snakes are shy, so don't worry too much.

## SIGHTS
### Mountain Farm Museum

The area that is now Great Smoky Mountains National Park was once dotted with towns and farms, communities that were displaced for the establishment of the park. The **Mountain Farm Museum** (U.S. 441, 2 miles north of Cherokee, 828/497-1900),

next to the Oconaluftee Visitor Center, re-creates a mountain fastness of the late 19th and early 20th centuries. On the site of what was the Enloe family's farm, on the banks of the Oconaluftee River, a collection of historic buildings are preserved, some original to the site and others moved from elsewhere in the Smokies. The Davis House, a circa-1900 log house, is remarkable in that it is constructed from enormous chestnut timbers, a wood that has not been available in this region since the chestnut blight of the 1930s. A large cantilevered barn was constructed to allow wagons to be driven straight through, with stalls and haylofts to the sides. A variety of other dependencies—a meat house, a chicken house, an apple house, a corncrib, a gear shed, a blacksmith shop, and a springhouse—give a notion of the plethora of homesteading skills necessary for a mountain farm like this to prosper. Demonstrations are held here throughout the year, as well as two festivals, one a harvest festival and the other a commemoration of women's work in mountain farm life.

### ★ Cades Cove

On the Tennessee side of the park, an 11-mile one-way loop road traverses Cades Cove, a historic settlement dating to the late 18th century. Originally part of the Cherokee Nation, the land was ceded to the United States in 1819. The population grew through the 19th century until it was a busy town of several hundred people. The village is preserved today as it appeared around 1900, with homes, churches, barns, and a working gristmill, but minus the people—a mountain counterpart to Cape Lookout National Seashore's Portsmouth Village. Because of the cove's scenic beauty and abundance of wildlife, this is the most popular part of the nation's most visited national park. The loop road through Cades Cove takes about an hour to drive when visitors are sparse. On crowded days—in the peak summer and fall seasons, and most weekends—it can take several hours to cover the 11 miles.

The **Cades Cove Visitor Center**

(Dec.-Jan. daily 9am-4:30pm, Feb. and Nov. daily 9am-5pm, Mar. and Sept.-Oct. daily 9am-6pm, Apr.-Aug. daily 9am-7pm) is located at about the halfway point on the Cades Cove Loop. It has a bookstore, exhibits on Southern mountain culture, and seasonal ranger programs. At the southwestern side of the park, Cades Cove is most easily reached from the Laurel Creek Road inside the park, which links with Highway 73 near Townsend, Tennessee. Cades Cove Loop road begins and ends at Laurel Creek Road, but there are two outlets toward the western end—Forge Creek Road and Rich Mountain Road—that both lead out of the park, one-way, and are closed in wintertime.

## Cataloochee

Cataloochee in North Carolina was an even larger village than Cades Cove. Several important historic buildings from this extremely remote apple-growing town are standing and can be toured, including Palmer Chapel, the settlement's only church house, which was served by once-monthly visits by circuit-riding Methodist preachers. Cataloochee is also a prime spot for watching the park's elk, reintroduced in 2001 and prospering. Look for them in the open fields around sunrise and twilight. The Cataloochee area is at the far northeastern edge of the park, and it's a reasonably direct drive from I-40 via the Cove Creek Road. The National Park Service also recommends a more adventurous route for those with plenty of time and immunity to car sickness (it's a twisty road): Highway 32 from Cosby, Tennessee. Whichever way you go, part of the route will be on a gravel road. The park sells an auto tour booklet at the visitors centers, which will help guide you through Cataloochee. Several houses, a school, churches, and barns are open to the public.

## ★ Clingmans Dome

At 6,643 feet, Clingmans Dome is the third-highest mountain in the eastern United States, and the highest in the Great Smoky Mountains. A flying saucer-like observation tower at the end of a long, steep walkway gives 360-degree views of the surrounding mountains, and on a clear day, that view can be as far as 100 miles. More often, though, it's misty up here in the clouds, and Clingmans Dome receives so much precipitation that its woods are actually a coniferous rain forest. The road to the summit is closed December 1-March 31, but the observation tower remains open

the observation tower at Clingmans Dome

for those willing to make the hike. To get to Clingmans Dome, turn off Newfound Gap Road 0.1 mile south of Newfound Gap, and then take Clingmans Dome Road (closed in winter), which leads seven miles to the parking lot. The peak is right near the center of the park, due north as the crow flies (though not directly accessible) from Bryson City.

## Fontana Dam

At the southeastern edge of the park, Fontana Dam, 11,000 acres of water, is an artificial impoundment of the Little Tennessee River. This largest dam east of the Rockies was built in the 1940s, a stupendous wall of concrete the height of a 50-story skyscraper. It caused the river to flood back through little mountain towns, vestiges of which can be seen every five years when the water level is lowered for dam inspection. The **visitors center** (Hwy. 28, Fontana Dam, 828/498-2234 or 800/467-1388, May-Nov. daily 9am-7pm, free) is well worth a visit, and the Appalachian Trail goes right along the top of the dam.

## SPORTS AND RECREATION

Great Smoky Mountains National Park covers over half a million acres, and within that expanse are more than 800 miles of hiking trails, ranging from easy walks around major attractions to strenuous wilderness paths suited to the most experienced backpackers. A section of the Appalachian Trail goes through the park, crossing the Fontana Dam. There are dozens of books available about hiking in the Smokies, for sale at bookstores and outfitters throughout the region, as well as online. The park staffs a **Backcountry Information Office** (865/436-1297, daily 9am-noon), and the knowledgeable folks who work there are a good first resource when planning a hiking trip. The park website (www.nps.gov/grsm) has some downloadable maps to give you a general sense of the lay of the land. The Great Smoky Mountains Association website (www.

smokiesinformation.org) has a good online bookstore where you can find many books about hiking in the park.

## Hiking

Great Smoky Mountains National Park contains hundreds of miles of hiking trails, ranging from family-friendly loop trails to strenuous wilderness treks. Following are a sampling of hikes in the park. Before embarking on any of these trails, obtain a park map, and have a word with a park ranger to ascertain trail conditions and gauge whether it's well suited to your hiking skills.

A quick and easy foray into the woods is the **Spruce-Fir Trail,** off Clingmans Dome Road, a walk of just over 0.3 mile. Almost flat, and mostly following a wooden boardwalk, this is the ideal trail if you've been traveling in the car all day and simply want to stretch your legs and experience a bit of easily accessible forest atmosphere.

A longer but also fairly easy walk is the **Oconaluftee River Trail,** which begins behind the Oconaluftee Visitor Center. This path, which is gravel-covered, follows the river and goes through part of the Mountain Farm Museum grounds. Unlike nearly all other trails in the GSMNP, dogs and bicycles are allowed on this one.

The **Alum Cave Trail** has a trailhead off Newfound Gap Road. A 4.4-mile round-trip will carry you past some amazing views and interesting geological features, culminating at the Alum Cave, from which Epsom salts and saltpeter were mined beginning in the 1830s. The moderately strenuous couple of miles to Alum Cave represent the first leg of what becomes a much more difficult, treacherous hike, the 11 miles to the top of Mount LeConte.

The **Boogerman Trail** is a loop trail off the Cove Creek Road in the Cataloochee section of the park. This is a moderately strenuous, 7.5-mile round trip that takes 2-3 hours to complete. You'll pass old-growth trees, streams and cascades, and several old homesites, including that of "Boogerman" himself, an early resident named Robert Palmer.

As if the mountains and valleys, flora and fauna, and close-enough-to-touch clouds weren't wonder enough, GSMNP has literally hundreds of waterfalls. Several of the most popular and most beautiful are accessible from major trails.

Close to Bryson City, 25-foot **Indian Creek Falls** is a moderately difficult hike of less than two miles round-trip, and it's a two-for-one deal, as the path also goes by Tom Branch Falls. Crossing Deep Creek on bridges and logs and going by old homesites, this is an especially interesting hike. The Deep Creek-Indian Creek Trailhead is at the end of Deep Creek Road in Bryson City. It gets very crowded in nice weather, particularly because this is a popular area for tubing, and this makes parking quite difficult. Restrooms are available at the picnic area. Also accessible from the Indian Creek Trailhead is the path to 90-foot **Juney Whank Falls.** The hike to Juney Whank Falls is shorter but more difficult than that to Indian Creek Falls. Since it shares the same trailhead, you can expect to find the same crowds and parking difficulties as for the trail to Indian Creek Falls.

**Mingo Falls,** a beautiful 120-foot plume, is just outside the park, on the Qualla Boundary (Cherokee land). It can be seen from the Pigeon Creek Trail, which begins in the Mingo Falls Campground, off Big Cove Road south of Cherokee. The hike is very short, less than 0.5 mile round-trip, but is fairly strenuous.

Some longer hikes on the Tennessee side of the line lead to equally beautiful falls. **Rainbow Falls** is 80 feet high, and is as much a cloud of mist as it is a cataract—so much so that when the sun hits it just right, you can see a rainbow. In the winter, it sometimes freezes solid, an amazing sight. The Rainbow Falls Trail near Gatlinburg is difficult, and is almost 5.5 miles round-trip. It ascends about 1,500 vertical feet and is very rocky most of the way, but it provides some great views, both of the falls and of Gatlinburg. Parking is available on Cherokee Orchard Road in Gatlinburg, but it fills up pretty quickly; you may need to pay to park a little farther from the trailhead.

The tallest waterfall, 100-foot **Ramsey Cascades,** is also the most difficult to reach. Those able to make a strenuous eight-mile round-trip hike are richly rewarded with a journey through old-growth hardwood forests and along fast-moving rivers. The pool at the bottom of the falls is a great place to glimpse some of the creatures that make GSMNP the "Salamander Capital of the World."

It is never safe to climb on waterfalls, and quite a few people in the park have died doing that, so it's best to admire the cascading water from the trails. Ramsey Cascades is particularly dangerous. The parking area for the Ramsey Cascades Trail is off Greenbrier Road, a few miles southeast of Gatlinburg. The nearest portable toilets are at the picnic area on Greenbrier Road.

Maps and guides to the waterfalls are available at many locations in the park.

## Horseback Riding

Three commercial stables in the park offer "rental" horses on a by-the-hour basis (about $20 per hour). **Smokemont** (828/497-2373) is located in North Carolina near Cherokee. Two are in Tennessee: **Smoky Mountain** (865/436-5634, www.smokymountainridingstables.com) and **Cades Cove** (10018 Campground Dr., Townsend, TN, 865/448-6286, http://discovercadescove.com).

## Cycling

The **Cades Cove Store** (near Cades Cove Campground, 865/448-9034) rents bicycles in the summer and fall. From the second week in May to the second-to-last Saturday in September, the park closes off the loop road through Cades Cove on Wednesday and Saturday mornings, from sunrise until 10am, so that cyclists and hikers can enjoy the cove without having to worry about vehicular traffic.

### Field Schools

Two Tennessee-based organizations affiliated with GSMNP offer ways to get to know the park even better. The **Smoky Mountain Field School** (http://smfs.utk.edu) teaches workshops and leads excursions to educate participants in a wide array of fields related to the Smokies. One-day classes focus on the history and cultural heritage of the park, the lives of some of the park's most interesting animals, folk medicine and cooking of the southern Appalachians, and much more. Instructors also lead one-day and overnight hikes into the heart of the park.

The **Great Smoky Mountains Institute at Tremont** (9275 Tremont Rd., Townsend, TN, 865/448-6709, www.gsmit.org) teaches students of all ages about the ecology of the region, wilderness rescue and survival skills, and even nature photography. Many of the classes and guided trips are part of Road Scholar events, kids' camps, or teacher-training institutes; however, there are also rich opportunities for unaffiliated learners.

## FOOD

Unless you're staying at the LeConte Lodge or have packed a picnic or provisions, you'll have to leave the park for meals. The easiest way is simply to drive into Bryson City, Cherokee, or Gatlinburg, all right on the edge of the park. In Gatlinburg, try the **Smoky Mountain Brewery** (1004 Parkway, Ste. 501, 865/436-4200, www.smoky-mtn-brewery.com, daily 11:30am-1am, under $20), a popular brewpub and restaurant. The **Wild Plum Tea Room** (555 Buckhorn Rd., 865/436-3808, daily 11am-3pm, under $10) is a nice spot for soup and sandwiches, homemade desserts, and the signature wild plum muffins served with every entrée. The formal restaurant of the **Buckhorn Inn** (2140 Tudor Mountain Rd., 866/941-0460, www.buckhorninn.com, dinner seating daily at 7pm, breakfast daily 8am-9:30am, $30 prix fixe, reservations required)

has a different beautiful multicourse set menu every day of the week. Vegetarian meals can be prepared with advance notice.

## ACCOMMODATIONS

There is only one inn in the entire 500,000-acre park, and it's a highly unusual one. ★ **LeConte Lodge** (865/429-5704, www.lecontelodge.com, cabin beds $64 adults, $53 children, lodges $512-768, meals $33 adults, $23.50 children, cash or check only, no pets), built in the 1920s, is at an elevation of nearly 6,600 feet, and is accessible only on foot after a hike of several hours. The lodge is supplied by thrice-weekly llama train. There are flush toilets, but no showers. Nor is there electricity at the lodge, and though kerosene heaters will keep you toasty, remember that even in the summertime, temperatures can fall into the 30s at night. It's an amazing place, and enough people are willing to make the necessary trek to stay here that reservations are often required very far in advance.

Luckily for those who don't want to camp or to hike to a rustic lodge, there are countless motels just outside GSMNP. Reservations are always a good idea, especially in the summer and in leaf season, but you'll not want for choices in Cherokee, Maggie Valley, Bryson City, Pigeon Forge, Gatlinburg, Sevierville, and other neighboring communities. In addition to the many chain motels, affordable mom-and-pop motels also dot this landscape in abundance. A good choice is **Johnson's Inn** (242 Bishop Ln., Gatlinburg, 800/842-1930, www.johnsonsinn.com, $49-104, depending on season).

### Camping

GSMNP has many locations for camping, fees for which range $12-20. Campers can stay up to three nights at campsites, but only one night at a time in shelters. There are 10 front-country (car-accessible) campgrounds, each of which has cold running water and flush toilets in the restrooms, but no showers or power and water hookups. Most of these sites are first come, first served, but between May 15 and

October 15, sites at the Elkmont, Smokemont, Cades Cove, and Cosby Campgrounds can be reserved online (www.recreation.gov) or by calling 877/444-6777.

Within North Carolina, from northeast to southwest, the first campground is **Big Creek,** near I-40, at an elevation of 1,700 feet. This walk-in, tenting-only campsite features the beautifully soporific sound of rushing water from the nearby creek. It's open from spring to the beginning of November. The **Cataloochee Campground,** also reasonably close to I-40, is at 2,610 feet elevation and is also open from spring to the beginning of November.

The highest campground in the park, **Balsam Mountain Campground,** sits at a lofty 5,300 feet elevation and is a short drive from the terminus of the Blue Ridge Parkway. It's open only mid-May-late September and is less likely to be crowded than many of the other campgrounds. **Smokemont,** open year-round, is the closest to Cherokee, and sits at 2,198 feet elevation. **Deep Creek,** at 1,800 feet, is closest to Bryson City and is open spring-early November.

In Tennessee, again from northeast to southwest, **Cosby Campground,** at 2,459 feet elevation, open spring-early November, is closest to the town of Cosby and is not far from I-40. **Elkmont,** at 2,150 feet elevation on the Little River, open spring-early November, is the closest campsite to the Gatlinburg entrance to the park.

The **Cades Cove Campground,** located off the loop road at Cades Cove, at an elevation of 2,610 feet, is open year-round. Close to Cades Cove and to each other as the crow flies, though a considerable drive apart, are the southwestern-most Tennessee campsites, **Abrams Creek,** at 1,125 feet elevation, open spring-early November, and **Big Creek,** at 1,700 feet, open spring-early November.

**Backcountry camping** is abundant. It is only allowed at designated sites and shelters, and a permit is required, but the permits are free and can be obtained at any of 15 different visitors centers and campground offices throughout the park. There are also five drive-in horse camps ($20-25) and seven group campgrounds ($35-65). A map of the available campsites is downloadable at www.nps.gov/grsm/planyourvisit. Before camping at the GSMNP, be sure to familiarize yourself with the park's backcountry regulations and etiquette, available online and at locations in the park.

## INFORMATION AND SERVICES

The national park's official website is www.nps.gov/grsm. Much visitor information can be found to help you plan your trip at the websites of **Smoky Mountain Host** (www.visitsmokies.org) and the **Blue Ridge National Heritage Area** (www.blueridgeheritage.com). Detailed touring suggestions for sites associated with local history and heritage can be found at the **North Carolina Folklife Institute** (www.ncfolk.org) and in *Cherokee Heritage Trails,* an excellent guidebook that can be purchased online.

Area hospitals include those in Bryson City, Sylva, and Clyde, as well as a little farther afield in Asheville and in Knoxville and Maryville, Tennessee.

## GETTING THERE AND AROUND

The closest commercial airport to the Smokies is **Asheville Regional Airport** (AVL, 61 Terminal Dr., Fletcher, 828/684-2226, www.flyavl.com) in Fletcher; the **Gatlinburg-Pigeon Forge Airport** (GKT, 1255 Airport Rd., Sevierville, 865/453-6136), over the state line in Tennessee, is used by private planes but has no commercial passenger flights. Amtrak doesn't run anywhere in this area, but the closest stations, both hours away, are in Gastonia, near Charlotte, and in Spartanburg, South Carolina. Unless you're hiking through on the Appalachian Trail, the best way to get around the Smokies is by car. U.S. 19 and U.S. 23 stretch down from Asheville to the Georgia line, while U.S. 64, which stretches from Murphy to Manteo, snakes along the southern edge of the Smokies. Cresting the northern edge is I-40, running between Asheville and Knoxville.

# Bryson City and the Nantahala Forest

Mossy gorges, misty riverbanks, and cloud-ringed mountain peaks make the Nantahala region feel like a setting for fairy tales and conjuration. Cherokee mythology tells of a witch, Spearfinger, known to have frequented the Nantahala Gorge, which was also the abode of a monstrous snake and, of all things, an inchworm so large that it could span the top of the gorge and block out the light of the sun. Today, the Nantahala River, running through the narrow gorge, has become a favorite white-water rafting run.

Nearby Bryson City is an aqua-centric river town, one whose proximity to great white-water rapids makes it a favorite haunt for rafters and kayakers and their ilk. If you approach Bryson City from the north on U.S. 19, you're in for a strange sight: The banks of the Tuckasegee River are shored up with crushed cars. Look closely and you may recognize the fenders of trusty warhorses of your childhood.

## SIGHTS

The **Great Smoky Mountain Railroad** (Bryson City and Dillsboro depots, 800/872-4681, www.gsmr.com, from $30 adults, $16 children) is one of the best and most fun ways to see the Smokies. On historic trains, the GSMR carries sightseers on excursions, from two to several hours long, through some of the most beautiful scenery in the region. Trips between Dillsboro and Bryson City (with a layover at each end for shopping and dining) follow the banks of the Tuckasegee River, while round-trips from Bryson City follow the Little Tennessee and Nantahala Rivers deep into the Nantahala Gorge, and the Fontana Trestle Excursion crosses over the top of the Fontana Dam just at sunset. Many other excursions are offered, including gourmet dining and wine- and beer-tasting trips, *Thomas the Tank Engine* and *Little Engine That Could* themed trips for kids, and runs to and from river-rafting outfitters.

rafting on the Nantahala River Gorge

# SPORTS AND RECREATION

## ★ Nantahala River Gorge

The stunningly beautiful Nantahala River Gorge, just outside Bryson City in the Nantahala National Forest, supports scores of river guide companies, many clustered west along U.S. 19. "Nantahala" is said to mean "Land of the Noonday Sun," and there are indeed parts of this gorge where the sheer rock walls above the river are so steep that sunlight only hits the water at the noon hour. Eight miles of the Nantahala River flow through the gorge, over Class II and III rapids. The nearby Ocoee River is also a favorite of rafters, and the Cheoah River, on the occasions of controlled releases, has some of the South's most famous and difficult Class III and IV runs.

## Outfitters and Tours

**Endless River Adventures** (14157 U.S. 19 W., near Bryson City, 800/224-7238, www.endlessriveradventures.com) provides whitewater and flat-water kayaking instruction, rentals, and guided trips on the Nantahala, Ocoee, and Cheoah Rivers. They'll be able to suggest a run suited to your skill level. In addition to river guide services, **Wildwater Rafting** (10345 U.S. 19 W., 12 miles west of Bryson City, 800/451-9972, www.wildwaterrafting.com) leads **Wildwater Jeep Tours** ($40-90 adults, $25-70 children), half-day and full-day Jeep excursions on back roads and through wilderness to waterfalls and old mountain settlements.

Because some of these rapids can be quite dangerous, be sure to call ahead and speak to a guide if you have any doubts as to your readiness. If rafting with children, check the company's weight and age restrictions beforehand.

# ACCOMMODATIONS

The **★ Folkestone Inn** (101 Folkestone Rd., 888/812-3385, www.folkestoneinn.com, from $80) is one of the region's outstanding bed-and-breakfasts, a roomy 1920s farmhouse expanded and renovated into a charming and tranquil inn. Each guest room has a balcony or porch. Baked treats at breakfast include shortcake, kuchen, cobblers, and other delicacies.

An 85-year-old hotel in the National Register of Historic Places, the **Fryemont Inn** (245 Fryemont St., 800/845-4879, www.fryemontinn.com, spring-fall, from $125, including meals) has a cozy, rustic feel, with chestnut-paneled guest rooms and an inviting lobby with an enormous stone fireplace.

Some river outfitters offer lodging, which can be a very cheap way to pass the night if you don't mind roughing it. The **Rolling Thunder River Company** (10160 U.S. 19 W., near Bryson City, 800/408-7238, www.rollingthunderriverco.com, no alcohol permitted) operates a large bunkhouse, with beds ($8-12) available for its rafting customers. Carolina Outfitters offers a range of options at **Nantahala Cabins** (888/488-6345) www.carolinaoutfitters.com/vacation-rentals), including very simple guest rooms with private baths (from $40). Many of the outfitters also offer camping on their properties.

Way back in the forest by Fontana Lake, the **Fontana Village Resort** (Hwy. 28, Fontana Dam, 800/849-2258, www.fontanavillage.com, from $60) was originally built as housing for the workers constructing the dam, a massive World War II-era undertaking that created a whole town out here in the woods. Renovated into a comfortable resort, Fontana Village features a lodge, cabins, camping (from $25) and, for the more adventurous lodger, houseboats. Houseboats are a tradition on the lake, and the two that are rented by Fontana Village make for a most memorable vacation.

## Camping

For a look at the range of camping options available in the Nantahala National Forest, visit www.fs.usda.gov/nfsnc. Among the nicest is **Standing Indian Campground** (90 Sloan Rd., Franklin, 828/524-6441, Apr.-Nov., $16). Standing Indian has a nice diversity of campsites to choose from, from flat, grassy areas to cozy mountainside nooks. Drinking water, hot showers, flush toilets, and a phone are all available on-site, and leashed pets are permitted. At 3,400 feet elevation, the campground is close to the Appalachian Trail.

## GETTING THERE AND AROUND

Bryson City can be reached via U.S. 19, if you're coming south from Maggie Valley and Cherokee. U.S. 74 also passes very close by, an easy route from the east or west.

# Robbinsville and the Valley Towns

Another region at the heart of Cherokee life, both past and present, is found between Robbinsville and the Georgia state line. Near Robbinsville, the area known as Snowbird is one of the most traditional Cherokee communities, where the Cherokee language is still spoken as a first language, and the old crafts and folkways are alive as well. Here also is the grave of Junaluska, one of the Eastern Band's most prominent ancestors.

The town of Murphy is closely linked with the great tragedy of Cherokee history, the Trail of Tears. About 16,000 Cherokee people, including children, the elderly, and the infirm, were arrested and made to leave their homes and farms in North Carolina, Georgia, and Tennessee. They were brought here to Fort Butler, where they began their forced march to Oklahoma. The names of these people, many of whom died along the way, are inscribed in Cherokee on a memorial at the L&N Depot in Murphy.

In addition to the places of historical significance to Cherokee culture, this farthest southwest corner of North Carolina has other compelling sights. Brasstown, a tiny village on the Georgia line, is the home of the John C. Campbell Folk School, an artist colony nearly a century old, where visitors can stroll among studios and along trails, and stop in a gallery shop with some of the most beautiful crafts you'll find in the region. Back up toward Robbinsville, the relentlessly scenic Cherohala Skyway crosses 36 miles of the Cherokee and Nantahala National Forests. This road is a major destination for motorcyclists and sports-car drivers as well as day-trippers and vacationers.

## ROBBINSVILLE

The whole southwestern corner of North Carolina is rich with Cherokee history and culture, and the Robbinsville area has some of the deepest roots and sites of greatest significance to the modern and historical generations of the Cherokee people. In little towns and crossroads a few miles outside Robbinsville, several hundred people known as the Snowbird community keep alive some of the Cherokee's oldest ways. The Cherokee language is spoken here—it is still some residents' first language—and some of the Eastern Band's most admired basket makers, potters, and other artists continue to make and teach their traditional arts.

### Sights

Outside Robbinsville in the ancient Stecoah Valley, an imposing old rock schoolhouse built in 1930 and used as a school until the mid-1990s has been reborn as the **Stecoah Valley Center** (121 Schoolhouse Rd., Stecoah, 828/479-3364, www.stecoahvalley-center.com). This is the home of a weaver's guild, a native plants preservation group, a concert series, several festivals, and a great **gallery shop** (828/497-3098, May-Mar. Mon.-Fri. 10am-5pm, Apr. Mon.-Sat. 10am-5pm) of local artisans' work. Concerts in the Appalachian Evening summer series, featuring area musicians, are preceded by community suppers of traditional mountain cuisine.

On Robbinsville's Main Street is the **Junaluska Memorial** (Main St., about 0.5 mile north of the Graham County Courthouse, 828/479-4727, Mon.-Sat.

# Junaluska's Legacy to the Cherokee

Among the most important figures in the history of the Eastern Band of the Cherokee is Junaluska, who was born in 1776 near Dillard, Georgia. During the wars against the Creek people (1812-1814), the Cherokee fought alongside the U.S. military, and it's said that young Junaluska saved the life of Andrew Jackson at the battle of Horse Shoe Bend in Alabama.

Almost 20 years later, Andrew Jackson, now president, thanked the Cherokee by signing the Indian Removal Act, which ordered that they and four other major Southern nations be forced off their lands and marched to the new Indian Territory of Oklahoma. Junaluska traveled all the way to Washington to try to convince Jackson to change his mind, but his plea fell on deaf ears.

Junaluska was one of about 16,000 members of the Cherokee Nation who were made to walk the thousand miles to Oklahoma. In Tennessee, he led an attempted escape but was captured and forced to make the rest of the march in manacles and leg irons. In 1841 he was finally able to leave Oklahoma and made the 17-day trip by horseback all the way back to North Carolina. Supposedly Junaluska once said, "If I had known what Andrew Jackson would do to the Cherokees, I would have killed him myself that day at Horse Shoe Bend."

He spent his later years in Cherokee County, on land that was given to him by the state of North Carolina. He and his third wife, Nicie, are buried at Robbinsville, at what is now the Junaluska Memorial and Museum. A marker was commissioned in 1910 by the Daughters of the American Revolution, and during the dedication ceremony, a eulogy was delivered in the Cherokee language by the Reverend Armstrong Cornsilk, who said of Junaluska: "He was a good man. He was a good friend. […] He would ask the hungry man to eat. He would ask the cold one to warm by his fire. He would ask the tired one to rest, and he would give a good place to sleep. Juno's home was a good home for others."

9am-4pm). Here Junaluska and his third wife, Nicie, are buried. The marker was dedicated in 1910 by the Daughters of the American Revolution. The gravesite is maintained by the Friends of Junaluska, who also operate the **Heritage Center** (www.lakejunaluska.com) on the same site. At the museum you'll find ancient artifacts from life in Cheoah thousands of years ago. There are also contemporary Cherokee crafts on display, and outside you can walk a path that highlights the medicinal plants used for generations in this area.

Fourteen miles outside Robbinsville, down a winding country road, **Yellow Branch Pottery and Cheese** (136 Yellow Branch Circle, Robbinsville, 828/479-6710, www.yellowbranch.com, Tues.-Sat. noon-5pm, or by appointment) is a beautifully rustic spot for an afternoon's excursion. Bruce DeGroot, Karen Mickler, and their herd of Jersey cows produce prize-winning artisanal cheeses and graceful, functional pottery. (The cows don't actually help with the pottery.) Visitors are welcome at their farm and shop.

## Entertainment and Events

Every year in late May on the Saturday of Memorial Day weekend, the Snowbird Cherokee host the **Fading Voices Festival** (www.cherokeeheritagetrail.org) in Robbinsville. The festival features a mound-building ceremony, and all of the usual festival attractions—music, dancing, storytelling, crafts, and lots of food—but in the deeply traditional forms carried on by the Snowbird community.

## Sports and Recreation

The **Joyce Kilmer Memorial Forest** (Joyce Kilmer Rd., off Hwy. 143, west of Robbinsville, 828/479-6431, www.westernncattractions.com, daily dawn-dusk, free) is one of the largest remaining tracts of virgin forest in the eastern United States, where 450-year-old tulip poplar trees have grown to 100 feet tall and 20 feet around. The two-mile loop (or two one-mile loops) makes for an easy hike through a remarkable forest.

## Accommodations

The **Snowbird Mountain Lodge** (4633 Santeetlah Rd., 11 miles west of Robbinsville, 800/941-9290, www.snowbirdlodge.com, from $180) was built in the early 1940s, a rustic chestnut-and-stone inn atop a 3,000-foot mountain. The view is exquisite, and the lodge is perfectly situated between the Cherohala Skyway, Lake Santeetlah, and the Joyce Kilmer Forest. Guests enjoy a full breakfast, picnic lunch, and four-course supper created from seasonal local specialties. Another pleasant place to stay near Robbinsville is the **Tapoco Lodge Resort** (14981 Tapoco Rd., 15 miles north of Robbinsville, 800/822-5083, www.tapocolodge.com, Apr.-Nov., from $109 private bath, $75 shared bath). Built in 1930, the lodge is in the National Register of Historic Places and has the feel of an old-time hotel. Guest rooms in the main lodge and surrounding cabins are simple but comfortable, and the resort overlooks the Cheoah River, a legendary run for rafters several times each year when stored water is released to form crazy-fast rapids.

## HAYESVILLE AND BRASSTOWN

Between Hayesville and Brasstown, you can get a really good sense of the art that has come out of this region over the years. These two small towns are along the Georgia border on U.S. 64.

## ★ John C. Campbell Folk School

One of North Carolina's most remarkable cultural institutions, the **John C. Campbell Folk School** (1 Folk School Rd., Brasstown, 800/365-5724, www.folkschool.org) was born of the unusual honeymoon of unusual newlyweds from up north who traveled through Appalachia 100 years ago to educate themselves about Southern highland culture. John C. and Olive Dame Campbell, like other notable Northern liberals in their day, directed their humanitarian impulses toward the education and economic betterment of Southern

mountaineers. John Campbell died a decade later, but Olive, joining forces with her friend Marguerite Butler, set out to establish a "folk school" in the Southern mountains that she and John had visited. She was inspired by the model of the Danish *folkehøjskole*, workshops that preserved and taught traditional arts as a means of fostering economic self-determination and personal pride in rural communities. Brasstown, North Carolina, was chosen as the site for this grand experiment, and in 1925, the John C. Campbell Folk School opened its doors.

Today, thousands of artists travel every year to this uncommonly lovely remote valley, the site of an ancient Cherokee village. In weeklong and weekend-long classes, students of all ages and skill levels learn about traditional arts native to this region, such as pottery, weaving, dyeing, storytelling, and chair caning, as well as contemporary and exotic crafts, such as photography, kaleidoscope making, bookmaking, and paper marbling. By all means, visit the website or order a catalog, and see if any of the hundreds of courses offered every year strike your fancy. But even if you're passing through the area on a shorter visit, the Folk School welcomes you to explore the campus. Visitors are sincerely asked to help preserve the quiet atmosphere of learning and concentration when peering at artists' studios, but you can have an up-close look at some of their marvelous wares in the school's **Craft Shop** (bottom floor of Olive Dame Campbell Dining Hall, Mon.-Sat. 8am-5pm, Sun. 1pm-5pm), one of the nicest such shops in western North Carolina. Exhibits about the school's history, and historical examples of the work of local artists of past generations, are on display at the **History Center,** next to Keith House. There are several nature trails on campus that thread through this lovely valley. Be sure to visit the 0.25-mile **Rivercane Walk,** which features outdoor sculpture by some of the greatest living artists of the Eastern Band of the Cherokee. In the evenings you'll often find concerts by traditional musicians or community square, contra, and English country dances. A visit to the John C. Campbell Folk School, whether as a student or a traveler, is an exceptional opportunity to immerse yourself in a great creative tradition.

## Clay County Historical and Arts Council Museum

Hayesville's Old Clay County Jail, built in 1912, is now home to the **Clay County Historical and Arts Council Museum** (21 Davis Loop, Hayesville, 828/389-6814, June-Aug. daily 10am-4pm, call for hours off-season). This is a small and extremely interesting museum with varied collections, including the medical instruments of an early country doctor, an original jail cell (with a file hidden by a long-ago prisoner, discovered during renovations), an old moonshine still, a collection of beautiful Cherokee masks, and a remarkable crazy quilt embroidered with strange and charming illustrations.

### Food

Across from the courthouse in Hayesville, the **Café on the Square** (Mon.-Thurs. 6am-10pm, Fri.-Sat. 6am-11pm, under $10) is a spot to nip in for a good cup of coffee and a pastry as you set off on a mountain adventure.

## GETTING THERE AND AROUND

This is the southwesternmost corner of North Carolina, in some places as close to Atlanta as to Asheville. Robbinsville is located on U.S. 129, southwest of Bryson City. Hayesville and Brasstown are easily reached from U.S. 64, which closely parallels the Georgia border.

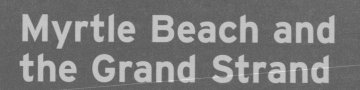

# Myrtle Beach and the Grand Strand

# The West has Las Vegas, Florida has Orlando, and South Carolina has Myrtle Beach.

There's no Bellagio Resort or Magic Kingdom here, but Myrtle Beach remains the number one travel destination in the state, with even more visitors than Charleston. Unlike Charleston, you'll find little history here. With several theme parks, 100 golf courses, 50 miniature golf courses, over 2,000 restaurants—not to mention miles of beautiful shoreline—Myrtle Beach is built for all-out vacation enjoyment. The hot, hazy height of the summer marks the busy season on the Strand, when its long main drag, Kings Highway (aka Business U.S. 17), is packed full of families eager for more swimming, more shopping, more eating, and just plain more.

While to many people the name Myrtle Beach conjures an image of tacky, downscale people doing tacky, downscale things, that's an outmoded stereotype. Tacky is certainly still in vogue here, but an influx of higher-quality development, both in accommodations and entertainment value, has lifted the bar significantly. Rather than slumming in a beat-up motel, quaffing PBR on the beach, and loading up on $2 T-shirts like in the "good old days," a typical Myrtle Beach vacation now involves a stay in a large condo apartment with flat-screen TVs, a full kitchen, and a sumptuous palmetto-lined pool; dining at the House of Blues; having drinks at the Hard Rock Café; stops at high-profile attractions like Ripley's Aquarium; and shopping at trendy retailers like Anthropologie and Abercrombie & Fitch.

The Grand Strand on which Myrtle Beach sits—a long, sandy peninsula stretching 60 miles from Winyah Bay to the North Carolina border—has been a vacation playground for generations of South Carolinians. Unlike Hilton Head, where New York and Midwestern accents are more common than Lowcountry drawls, Myrtle Beach and the Grand Strand remain largely homegrown passions, with many visitors living within a few hours' drive. Despite the steady increase of money and high-dollar development in the area, its strongly regional nature works to your advantage in that prices are generally lower than in Vegas or Orlando.

To the south of Myrtle proper lies the understated, affluent, and relaxing Pawleys Island, with nearby Murrells Inlet and its

**Previous:** family fun at Myrtle Beach; Ripley's Aquarium at Broadway at the Beach. **Above:** lounging chairs on Myrtle Beach.

Look for ★ to find recommended
sights, activities, dining, and lodging.

# Highlights

★ **Broadway at the Beach:** You'll find good cheesy fun along with tons of interesting shops, theme restaurants, and, of course, miniature golf (page 236).

★ **Barefoot Landing:** This commercial hub is North Myrtle Beach's answer to Broadway at the Beach, with the Alabama Theatre and the House of Blues nearby (page 238).

★ **Ocean Drive Beach:** The still-beating, still-shuffling heart of the Grand Strand is also the center of shag dancing culture (page 240).

★ **Carolina Opry:** This popular show offers corny but high quality family entertainment in an intimate, friendly setting (page 242).

★ **Brookgreen Gardens:** Enjoy the country's largest collection of outdoor sculptures, set amid a fine collection of formal gardens (page 262).

★ **Huntington Beach State Park:** The scenic beach combines with one-of-a-kind Atalaya Castle to make a unique getaway (page 262).

★ **Hampton Plantation:** This historic Georgian mansion on the scenic Wambaw Creek inspired a South Carolina poet laureate to give it to the state for posterity (page 268).

# Myrtle Beach and the Grand Strand

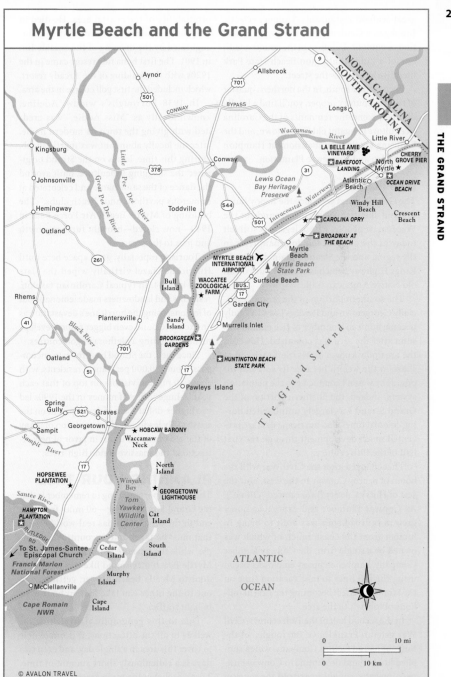

© AVALON TRAVEL

great seafood restaurants. Unique, eclectic Brookgreen Gardens hosts the largest collection of outdoor sculpture in the country, with one-of-a-kind Huntington Beach State Park literally right across the street.

Even farther south, in the northern quarter of the Lowcountry proper, you'll find a totally different scene: the remnants of the Carolina rice culture in quaint old Georgetown, and the haunting antebellum mansions at Hampton Plantation and Hopsewee Plantation.

## HISTORY

The Grand Strand was once the happy hunting and shellfish-gathering grounds of the Waccamaw people, whose legacy is still felt today in the name of the dominant river in the region and the Strand's main drag itself, Kings Highway, which is actually built on an old Native American trail.

The southern portion of the Strand, especially Georgetown and Pawleys Island, rapidly became home to a number of rice plantations soon after the area was colonized. However, the area now known as Myrtle Beach didn't share in the wealth because its soil and topography weren't conducive to the plantation system. Indeed, the northern portion of the Grand Strand was largely uninhabited during colonial times, and hurricane damage prevented much development through the first half of the 19th century.

That changed after the Civil War with the boom of nearby Conway to the west, now the seat of Horry County (pronounced "OR-ee"). As Conway's lumber and export economy grew, a railroad spur was built to bring in lumber from the coast, much of which was owned by a single firm, the Conway Lumber Company. Lumber company employees began using the rail lines to take vacation time on the Strand, in effect becoming the first of millions of tourists to the area.

In the second half of the 19th century, Civil War veteran Franklin G. Burroughs, of the Burroughs and Collins Company, which supplied lumber and turpentine to Conway business interests, sought to expand the tourism profitability of the coastal area. He died in 1897, but his heirs continued his dream, inaugurated by the opening of the Seaside Inn in 1901. The first bona fide resort came in the 1920s with the building of the Arcady resort, which included the first golf course in the area.

In 1938 Burroughs's widow, Adeline, known locally as "Miss Addie," was credited with giving the town its modern name, after the locally abundant wax myrtle shrub. During this time, locals on the Strand originated the shagging subculture, built around the dance of the same name and celebrated at numerous pavilions and "beach clubs." The building of Myrtle Beach Air Force Base in 1940—now closed—brought further growth and jobs to the area.

Tourism, especially, grew apace here until Hurricane Hazel virtually wiped the slate clean in 1954. In typical Carolinian fashion, residents and landowners made lemonade out of lemons, using the hurricane's devastation as an excuse to build even bigger resort developments, including a plethora of golf courses.

Since then, the Strand has grown to encompass about 250,000 permanent residents, with about 10 million visitors on top of that each year. A huge influx of money in the 1990s led to a higher-dollar form of development on the coast, sadly leading to the demolition of many of the old beach pavilions in favor of new attractions and massive condo high-rises.

## PLANNING YOUR TIME

The most important thing to remember is that the Grand Strand is *long*—60 miles from one end to the other. This has real-world effects that must be taken into account. For example, while the separate municipality of North Myrtle Beach may sound like it is right next door to Myrtle Beach proper, getting from one to the other can take half an hour even in light traffic.

Due to this geographical stretching, as well as to all the attractions, it is impossible to cover this area in a single day, and even two days is a ridiculously short amount of time. That's probably the main reason many folks indulge in a weekly rental. Not only does it give you enough time to see everything, but it enables you to relax, slow down, and enjoy the beaches and the general laid-back attitude.

In May, Memorial Day weekend and Bike Week have traditionally signaled the beginning of the tourism season in Myrtle Beach. The busy season exactly corresponds with the hottest months of the year, July and August. This is when crowds are at their peak, restaurants are most crowded, and the two spurs of U.S. 17 are at their most gridlocked.

Springtime in Myrtle Beach is quite nice, but keep in mind that water temperatures are still chilly through April. There is almost always one last cold snap in March that augurs the spring.

Personally, I recommend hitting Myrtle Beach just as the busy season wanes, right after Labor Day. Rooms are significantly cheaper, but most everything is still fully open and adequately staffed, with the added benefit of the biggest crush of visitors being absent. Similarly, for some really inexpensive room rates, try to hit town in late February.

Winter on the Grand Strand is very slow, as befitting this very seasonal locale. Many restaurants, especially down the Strand near Murrells Inlet, close entirely through February.

## ORIENTATION

This part of the Strand comprises several municipalities, from Surfside Beach to the south up to Little River near the North Carolina border, but for all intents and purposes it's one big place all its own. As a general rule, development (read: money) is moving more quickly to the North Myrtle Beach area rather than the older Myrtle Beach proper to the south.

**North Myrtle** is actually a recent aggregation of several historic beachfront communities: Windy Hill, Crescent Beach, Cherry Grove, and Ocean Drive. You'll see numerous signs announcing the entrance or exit into or out of these communities, but keep in mind you're still technically in North Myrtle Beach.

The **Grand Strand grid** is based on a system of east-west avenues beginning just north of Myrtle Beach State Park. Confusingly, these are separated into "North" and "South" avenues. Perhaps even more confusing, North Myrtle Beach also uses its own distinct north-and-south avenue system, also for roads running east-west. Got it?

It goes like this: Myrtle Beach starts with 29th Avenue South at the Myrtle Beach International Airport and goes up to 1st Avenue South just past Family Kingdom Amusement Park. From here, the avenues are labeled as "North" from 1st Avenue North up to 82nd Avenue North, which concludes Myrtle Beach proper. North Myrtle Beach begins at 48th Avenue South near Barefoot Landing and goes up to Main Street (the center of the shag culture). It continues with 1st Avenue North, goes up to 24th Avenue North (Cherry Grove Beach), and finally concludes at 61st Avenue North, near the North Carolina state line.

# Sights

TOP EXPERIENCE

## ★ BROADWAY AT THE BEACH

Love it or hate it, **Broadway at the Beach** (1325 Celebrity Circle, 800/386-4662, www.broadwayatthebeach.com, summer daily 10am-11pm, winter daily 10am-6pm), between 21st and 29th Avenues, is one of Myrtle's biggest and flashiest attractions—which is saying a lot. Opened in the late 1990s and expanded significantly since then, this collection of three hotels, over two dozen restaurants, about 50 shops, and a dozen kid-oriented activities sprawls over 350 acres with several other major attractions, restaurants, and clubs (such as the Hard Rock Café) on its periphery.

Just like the Magic Kingdom that many of Myrtle's attractions seek to emulate, Broadway at the Beach has at its center a large lagoon, around which everything else is situated. Needless to say, there's also a massive parking lot. Activity goes on all day and well into the wee hours, with the weekly Tuesday-night fireworks a big draw. While there's plenty to do, what with the great shops, tasty treats, and piped-in music following you everywhere, it's also fun just to walk around.

The biggest attraction at Broadway—and it's really big—is **Wonderworks** (1313 Celebrity Circle, 843/626-9962, www.wonderworksonline.com, Sun.-Thurs. 10am-8pm, Fri.-Sat. 10am-9pm, $23 adults, $15 children). You can't miss it—look for the thing that looks exactly like a massive, crumbling, upside-down creepy mansion. Inside you'll find a wide and quite varied assortment of interactive experiences designed to let you know what it's like to be upside down, or on a bed of nails, or in a hurricane, or freezing after the *Titanic* sank, and things of that nature. Think Ripley's Believe It or Not updated for a modern age, complete with laser tag.

Adjacent to the main Wonderworks building is the **Soar and Explore Zipline and Ropes Course** (daily noon-dusk, hours vary seasonally, zip line $19.95, ropes course $11.99, combo $26.99), where you can strap in and zip 1,000 feet overwater across the large lagoon around which Broadway at the Beach is constructed.

**Medieval Times** (2904 Fantasy Way, 843/236-4635, www.medievaltimes.com, $51 adults, $31 ages 3-12, free under age 3) is a combination dinner theater and medieval tournament reenactment. If the ticket prices sound high, keep in mind you're getting a three-course meal and a professional show done largely on horseback. Ask around for coupons to get a discount.

Now that almost all of the old-fashioned amusement parks at Myrtle Beach are gone, victims of "modernization," you can find a

Wonderworks is an upside-down mansion!

facsimile of sorts at **Pavilion Nostalgia Park** (843/913-9400, www.pavilionnostalgiapark. com, summer daily 11am-11pm, hours vary in other seasons, rides $3 each), which seeks to simulate the days of Myrtle gone by.

Of course, nowhere in Myrtle is really complete without miniature golf, and Broadway at the Beach's version is **Dragon's Lair Fantasy Golf** (1197 Celebrity Circle, 843/913-9301, $9), with two medieval-themed 18-hole courses boasting a fire-breathing dragon.

## Ripley's Aquarium

If you've been to Boston's New England Aquarium, don't expect something similar at **Ripley's Aquarium** (1110 Celebrity Circle, 800/734-8888, www.ripleysaquarium.com, Sun.-Thurs. 9am-9pm, Fri.-Sat. 9am-10pm, $22 adults, $11 ages 6-11, $4 ages 2-5, free under age 2) at Broadway at the Beach. This is a smaller but quite delightful aquarium built primarily for entertainment purposes rather than education. Calming music plays throughout, and a moving sidewalk takes you around and under a huge main tank filled with various marine creatures. There's even the requisite stingray-petting touch tank.

You might see the garish billboards for the aquarium up and down U.S. 17, featuring massive sharks baring rows of scary teeth. But don't expect an over-the-top shark exhibit—the truth is that most of the sharks in the aquarium are smaller and much more peaceful.

## Broadway Grand Prix

Just outside Broadway at the Beach you'll find the **Broadway Grand Prix** (1820 21st Ave. N., 843/839-4080, www.broadwaygrandprix. com, summer daily 10am-midnight, shorter hours in other seasons, from $20), where can you speed around in little go-karts on your choice of seven tracks, organized according to speed, age, and skill level. This being Myrtle Beach, there's other family-oriented entertainment offered here, including a rock-climbing wall and, of course, miniature golf.

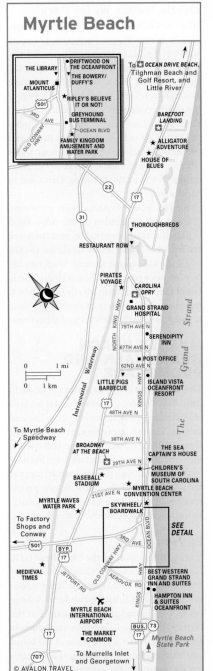

**THE GRAND STRAND**

SIGHTS

© AVALON TRAVEL

## Myrtle Waves Water Park

Billed as South Carolina's largest water park, **Myrtle Waves Water Park** (U.S. 17 Bypass and 10th Ave. N., 843/913-9260, www.myrtle-waves.com, May-Labor Day 10am-dusk, $25 ages 7 and over, $23 ages 3-6, free under age 3) is right across the street from Broadway at the Beach, covers 20 acres, and features all kinds of safe, fun "rides," such as the Ocean in Motion Wave Pool, the Layzee River, and the Saturation Station, where a huge water volcano absolutely soaks everybody in proximity every five minutes or so. That's just to name a few.

As you would expect, there are plenty of lifeguards on hand at all the rides. Food is plentiful if unremarkable, and there are shaded areas for the less adventurous to chill while the kids splash around. With one admission price covering all rides all day, this is one of the better deals in Myrtle Beach, which has more than its share of confusingly (and occasionally exorbitantly) priced attractions.

## MYRTLE BEACH BOARDWALK AND PROMENADE

The **Boardwalk** (www.visitmyrtlebeach.com, daily 24 hours, free) is the new pride of old Myrtle, greatly improving civic life and morale. The fun, meandering 1.2-mile jaunt from the 2nd Avenue Pier to the 14th Avenue Pier is built in three distinct sections, not only leading you through the commercial areas of the waterfront, but also allowing easy pedestrian beach access. One section provides a nice peaceful walking experience amid the dunes.

### Skywheel

You can't miss spotting the **Skywheel** (1110 N. Ocean Blvd., 843/839-9200, http://myrtle-beachskywheel.com, summer daily noon-midnight, $13 adults, $9 children), a huge Ferris wheel dominating the skyline at the Boardwalk. The cars are family-size and fully enclosed, and offer a great view of the ocean and surrounding area during the approximately 10-minute, three-rotation trip.

## ★ BAREFOOT LANDING

Before the arrival of Broadway at the Beach, the Strand's original high-concept retail and dining complex was **Barefoot Landing** (4898 U.S. 17 S., 843/272-8349, www.bflanding.com, hours vary). It's less flashy on the surface and certainly more tasteful, but just as commercial.

The centerpiece of the two-decade-old entertainment and shopping complex is **The Alabama Theatre** (4750 U.S. 17 S., 843/272-5758, www.alabama-theatre.com, ticket prices vary), a project of the famed country-and-western band of the same name, who despite their eponymous roots actually got their start gigging in juke joints in the Grand Strand. A stone's throw away is the **House of Blues** (4640 U.S. 17 S., 843/272-3000, www.hob.com, ticket prices vary), bringing in name acts on an almost nightly basis as well as diners to its excellent restaurant. On some nights you can pose for a picture with a real live tiger cub on your lap at **T.I.G.E.R.S. Preservation Station** (843/361-4552, www.tigerfriends.com, hours vary, free). Shopping is mostly the name of the game here, though.

### Alligator Adventure

One of the most popular attractions within Barefoot Landing is **Alligator Adventure** (843/361-0789, www.alligatoradventure.com, daily 9am-7pm, $21.99 adults, $16.99 ages 4-12, free under age 4). They have hundreds of alligators, yes, but also plenty of turtles, tortoises, snakes, and birds. The otters are a big hit as well. The highlight, though, comes during the daily alligator feedings, when you get a chance to see the real power and barely controlled aggression of these magnificent indigenous beasts. Keep in mind that due to the cold-blooded reptiles' dormant winter nature, the feedings are not held in the colder months.

## CHILDREN'S MUSEUM OF SOUTH CAROLINA

A less-expensive form of entertainment with an added educational component at Myrtle is the **Children's Museum of South Carolina**

(2501 N. Kings Hwy., 843/946-9469, www. cmsckids.org, summer Mon.-Sat. 9am-5pm, Sun. noon-5pm, $8). This facility tries hard to compete with the splashier attractions in town but still manages to keep a reasonably strong educational focus with programs like "Crime Lab Chemistry," "World of Art," and "Space Adventures."

## FAMILY KINGDOM AMUSEMENT AND WATER PARK

For a taste of old-time beachfront amusement park fun, try the **Family Kingdom** (300 4th Ave. S., 843/626-3471, www.family-kingdom. com, free admission, cost of rides varies) overlooking the Atlantic Ocean. It boasts several good old-school rides, such as the Sling Shot, the Yo-Yo, and everyone's favorite, the wooden Swamp Fox roller coaster with a crazy 110-foot free fall. The attached water park, though not a match to the one at Broadway at the Beach, is a lot of fun, with the requisite slides and a long "lazy river" floating ride.

There is no admission charge—you pay by the ride (although all-inclusive wristbands are available starting at $27). This means parents and grandparents without the stomach for the rides don't have to pay through the nose just to chauffeur the little ones who do.

## RIPLEY'S BELIEVE IT OR NOT!

Distinct in all but name from Ripley's Aquarium at Broadway at the Beach, this combo attraction down in the older area of Myrtle Beach—but very close to the brand-new Boardwalk—features several separate, though more or less adjacent, offerings from the venerable Ripley's franchise.

The **Ripley's Believe It or Not! Odditorium** (901 N. Ocean Blvd., 843/448-2331, www.ripleys.com, Sun.-Thurs. 10am-10pm, Fri.-Sat. 10am-11pm, $15 adults, $10 ages 6-11, free under age 6) is a repository of strange artifacts from around the world, updated with video and computer graphics for the new generation. It's fun and easy and takes no more than a half hour.

**Ripley's Haunted Adventure** (915 N. Ocean Blvd., 843/448-2331, www.ripleys.com, Sun.-Thurs. noon-10pm, Fri.-Sat. noon-11pm, $15 adults, $10 ages 6-11, free under age 6) is a sort of scaled-down version of Disney's famous Haunted House ride, with live actors scaring you through three floors.

Ripley's Believe It or Not!

**Ripley's Moving Theater** (917 N. Ocean Blvd., 843/448-2331, www.ripleys.com, Sun.-Thurs. 10am-10pm, Fri.-Sat. 10am-11pm, $15 adults, $10 ages 6-11, free under age 6) is a combined ride and movie theater featuring two motion-oriented films screened on a self-contained human conveyor belt, with a sort of kinetic IMAX effect.

## ★ OCEAN DRIVE BEACH

Less an actual place than a state of mind, the "OD" up in North Myrtle Beach is notable for its role in spawning one of America's great musical genres, beach music. Don't confuse beach music with the Beach Boys or Dick Dale—that's surf music. Beach music, simply put, is music to dance the shag to. Think the Drifters, the Platters, and the Swingin' Medallions.

To experience the OD, go to the intersection of Ocean Boulevard and Main Street and take in the vibe. There's still major shag action going on up here, specifically at several clubs specializing in the genre. If you don't want to shag, don't worry—this is still a charming, laid-back area that's a lot of fun simply to stroll around and enjoy a hot dog or ice cream cone.

## CHERRY GROVE PIER

One of the few grand old pavilions left on the Southeast coast, North Myrtle's **Cherry Grove Pier** (3500 N. Ocean Blvd., 843/249-1625, www.cherrygrovepier.com, Sun.-Thurs. 6am-midnight, Fri.-Sat. 6am-2am, free) was built in the 1950s. Despite renovations in the late 1990s, it still retains that nostalgic feel, with anglers casting into the waters and kids eating ice cream cones. There's a neat two-story observation deck, and on a clear day you can see North Carolina.

Unusually, this is a privately owned pier. It's particularly popular with anglers, who have their state licensing needs covered by the pier. Get bait or rent a fishing rod ($20 per day plus refundable $50 deposit) at the **Tackle and Gift Shop** (843/249-1625). They'll also sell you a crab net to cast off the pier ($6, licenses and permits included).

## TOURS

The number of tours offered in Myrtle Beach is nothing compared to Charleston, this being much more of a "doing" place than a "seeing" place. The most fun and comprehensive tour in the area is **Coastal Safari Jeep Tours** (843/497-5330, www.carolinasafari.com, $38 adults, $20 children), which takes you on a guided tour in a super-size Jeep (holding 12-14 people). You'll go well off the commercial path to see such sights on the Waccamaw Neck as old plantations, Civil War sites, and slave cabins, as well as hear lots of ghost stories. They'll pick you up at most area hotels.

# Entertainment and Events

## NIGHTLIFE

Any discussion of Myrtle Beach nightlife must begin with a nod to **The Bowery** (110 9th Ave. N., 843/626-3445, www.thebowerybar.com, daily 11am-2am), a country-and-western and Southern-rock spot right off the beach, which has survived several hurricanes since opening in 1944. Its roadhouse-style decor hasn't changed a whole lot since then, other than some cheesy marketing to play up its role in history as the place where the country band Alabama got its start playing for tips in 1973 under the name Wildcountry. They were still playing gigs here when their first big single, "Tennessee River," hit the charts in 1980.

Bands usually crank up here around 9pm, and there is a nominal cover charge. There's only one type of draft beer served at The Bowery, at $2.50 per mug, and there is no real dance floor to speak of. If the proud display of Confederate flags doesn't bother you, it's usually a lot of fun. Next door is The Bowery's

The Bowery

"sister bar," **Duffy's** (110 9th Ave. N., 843/626-3445, daily 11am-2am), owned by the same folks and with a similarly down-home vibe, except without the live music.

For a more upscale if definitely less personal and unique experience, Broadway at the Beach hosts the high-profile **Hard Rock Café** (1304 Celebrity Circle, 843/946-0007, www.hardrock.com, daily 11am-midnight). This is a new location as of 2016, the previous landmark pyramid having been demolished.

You don't have to be a Parrothead to enjoy **Jimmy Buffett's Margaritaville** (1114 Celebrity Circle, 843/448-5455, www.margaritavillemyrtlebeach.com, daily 11am-midnight) at Broadway at the Beach, actually a pretty enjoyable experience considering it's a national chain. The eponymous margaritas are, of course, the beverage highlight, but they also serve Jimmy's signature LandShark Lager on tap for beer lovers.

In addition to its attached live performance space, the **House of Blues** (4640 U.S. 17 S., 843/272-3000, www.hob.com) at Barefoot Landing features a hopping bar in its dining area, situated amid a plethora of folk art reminiscent of the Mississippi Delta. Most nights feature live entertainment starting at about 10pm, with one of the best-mixed sound systems you're likely to hear.

## SHAG DANCING

North Myrtle Beach is the nexus of that Carolina-based dance known as the shag. There are several clubs in town that have made a name for themselves as the unofficial "shag clubs" of South Carolina. The two main ones are **Duck's** (229 Main St., 843/249-3858, www.ducksatoceandrive.com) and **Fat Harold's** (210 Main St., 843/249-5779, www.fatharolds.com). There's also **The Pirate's Cove** (205 Main St., 843/249-8942).

Another fondly regarded spot is the **OD Pavilion** (91 S. Ocean Blvd., 843/280-0715), aka the Sunset Grill or "Pam's Palace," on the same site as the old Roberts Pavilion that was destroyed by 1954's Hurricane Hazel. Legend has it this was where the shag was born. Also in North Myrtle, the **Ocean Drive Beach Club** (98 N. Ocean Blvd., 843/249-6460), aka "the OD Lounge," inside the Ocean Drive Beach and Golf Resort, specializes in shag dancing most days after 4pm. The resort is a focal point of local shag conventions and is

# The Story of the Shag

Duck's is one of the oldest shag emporiums.

In South Carolina, the shag is neither a type of rug nor what Austin Powers does in his spare time. It's a dance—a smooth, laid-back, happy dance done to that equally smooth, laid-back, happy kind of rhythm and blues called beach music (not to be confused with surf music such as the Beach Boys). The boys twirl the girls while their feet kick and slide around with a minimum of upper-body movement—the better to stay cool in the Carolina heat.

Descended from the Charleston, another indigenous Palmetto State dance, the shag originated on the Strand sometime in the 1930s, when the popular Collegiate Shag was slowed down to

even home to the **Shaggers Hall of Fame.** Also inside the Ocean Drive Resort is another popular shag club, **The Spanish Galleon** (100 N. Ocean Blvd., 843/249-1047), aka "the Galleon."

Key local shag events, which are quite well attended, include the **National Shag Dance Championships** (www.shagnationals.com, Jan.-Mar.), the **Spring Safari** (www.shagdance.com, Apr.), and the **Fall Migration** (www.shagdance.com, mid-Sept.).

## SHOWS
### ★ Carolina Opry

Nothing can duplicate the experience of the Grand Ole Opry in Nashville, but don't snicker at Myrtle's **Carolina Opry** (8901-A Business U.S. 17, 800/843-6779, www.thecarolinaopry.com, showtimes and ticket prices vary). Since 1986 this well-respected stage show, begun by legendary promoter Calvin Gilmore, has packed 'em in at the Grand Strand. It is a hoot for country music fans and city slickers alike.

The main focus is the regular Opry show, done in the classic, freewheeling, fast-moving variety format known to generations of old-school country fans from the original Opry. Some of the humor is corny, and the brief but open displays of patriotic and faith-based music aren't necessarily for everyone. But there's no arguing the high energy and

the subgenre now called the Carolina Shag. While shag scholars differ as to the exact spawning ground, there's a consensus that North Myrtle Beach's Ocean Drive, or "OD" in local patois, became the home of the modern shag sometime in the mid-1940s.

Legend has it that the real shag was born when white teenagers, "jumping the Jim Crow rope" by watching dancers at black nightclubs in the segregated South, brought those moves back to the beach and added their own twists. Indeed, while the shag has always been primarily practiced by white people, many of the leading beach music bands were (and still are) African American.

By the mid-late 1950s, the shag, often called simply "the basic" or "the fas' dance," was all the rage with the Strand's young people, who gathered at beachfront pavilions and in local juke joints called beach clubs, courting each other to the sounds of early beach music greats like the Drifters, the Clovers, and Maurice Williams and the Zodiacs. This is the time period most fondly remembered by today's shaggers, a time of penny loafers (no socks!), poodle skirts, and 45-rpm records, when the sea breeze was the only air-conditioning.

The shag is practiced today by a graying but devoted cadre of older fans, with a vanguard of younger practitioners keeping the art form alive. A coterie of North Myrtle clubs specializes in the dance, while the area hosts several large-scale gatherings of shag aficionados each year.

To immerse yourself in shag culture, head on up to Ocean Drive Beach in North Myrtle at the intersection of Ocean Boulevard and Main Street and look down at the platters in the sidewalk marking the **Shaggers Walk of Fame.** Walk a couple of blocks up to the corner of Main Street and Hillside Drive and visit the mecca of beach music stores, **Judy's House of Oldies** (300 Main St., 843/249-8649, www.judyshouseofoldies.com, Mon.-Sat. 9am-6pm). They also sell instructional DVDs.

To get a taste of the dance itself, stop by the **OD Pavilion** (91 S. Ocean Blvd., 843/280-0715), **Duck's** (229 Main St., 843/249-3858, www.ducksatoceandrive.com), or **Fat Harold's** (210 Main St., 843/249-5779, www.fatharolds.com), or visit **The Spanish Galleon** (100 N. Ocean Blvd., 843/249-1047) inside the Ocean Drive Beach Resort. If you're interested, don't be shy; shaggers are notoriously gregarious and eager to show off their stock-in-trade. It's easy to learn, it's family-friendly, and there will be no shortage of pleasant young-at-heart shaggers around who will be happy to teach you the steps.

vocal and instrumental abilities of these very professional singers, instrumentalists, and dancers, who gamely take on hits through the generations ranging from bluegrass to Motown, pop, and modern country.

The Carolina Opry augments its regular music, comedy, and dance show with a seasonal Christmas special, which is extremely popular and sells out even faster than the regular shows, often six or more months in advance.

### Legends in Concert

Way down in Surfside Beach, where the big buildup on the Strand begins, you'll find **Legends in Concert** (301 Business U.S. 17, 843/238-7827, www.legendsinconcert.com,

ticket prices vary), a popular rotating show of celebrity impersonators from Elvis to Barbra Streisand. As cheesy as that sounds, the resemblances can be quite uncanny, and the shows are really entertaining.

### House of Blues

Besides being a great place for dinner, on the other side of the restaurant is the stage for the **House of Blues** (4640 U.S. 17 S., 843/272-3000, www.hob.com, ticket prices vary) at Barefoot Landing in North Myrtle Beach. They bring some pretty happening names in R&B, straight blues, and rock-and-roll to this fun venue dedicated to preserving old-school music and live performance, with a professional sound mix.

the Carolina Opry

## Medieval Times

Oh, come on—what's not to like about bountiful feasts, juggling jesters, skillful falconers, fetching maidens, and brave jousting knights? At **Medieval Times** (2904 Fantasy Way, 843/236-4635, www.medievaltimes.com, $51 adults, $31 under age 13) you'll get all that and more. The kitsch quotient is high at this Renaissance Faire on steroids, a live-action story line featuring plenty of stage combat, music, and a steady stream of culinary items for your enjoyment (and yes, there's a full bar for those of drinking age). The price may seem high at first glance, but keep in mind you're getting a hearty full dinner plus a two-hour stage and equestrian show.

## Pirate's Voyage

Sharing a parking lot with the Carolina Opry is **Pirate's Voyage** (8901-B N. Kings Hwy., 843/497-9700, www.piratesvoyage.com, from $44.99 adults, $26.99 ages 4-11, free under age 4), one of the newer entertainment attractions to hit Myrtle Beach. Affiliated with Dolly Parton's entertainment empire—her "Dixie Stampede" originally occupied this

the House of Blues

building—Pirate's Voyage takes you on a rollicking two-hour trip into the world of buccaneers, with fighting, lost treasure, dancing, acrobatics, mermaids, and assorted high-seas drama, all with photographers on hand to document your experience . . . for a price, me hearties. Like Medieval Times, this is essentially dinner theater, with three shows a day in the high season of late summer.

## The Alabama Theatre

The **Alabama Theatre** (4750 U.S. 17, 843/272-5758, www.alabama-theatre.com, ticket prices vary) at Barefoot Landing in North Myrtle Beach focuses on the long-running song-and-dance revue *One: The Show* as well as big-name acts who may be past their prime but are still able to fill seats, such as the Oak Ridge Boys, Kenny Rogers, and, of course, the eponymous troubadours Alabama, who got their big break while playing at Myrtle Beach. It's not all country, though—Motown and beach music acts like the Temptations and the Platters are often featured as well. As with the Carolina Opry, Barefoot Landing has its own Christmas special, and as with the Opry's offering, this one sells out well in advance.

## Palace Theatre

The **Palace Theatre** (1420 Celebrity Circle, 800/905-4228, www.palacetheatremyrtlebeach.com, ticket prices vary) at Broadway at the Beach offers a variety of toned-down Vegas-style entertainment. Recent shows included tributes to the Beatles and Queen.

## CINEMA

At Broadway at the Beach, there's a multiplex, Carmike's **Broadway Cinema 16** (843/445-1600, www.carmike.com). Other movie theaters include the **Cinemark** (2100 Coastal Grand Circle, 843/839-3221, www.cinemark.com) at the Coastal Grand Mall and the massive **Grand 14 at the Market Common** (4002 Deville St., 843/282-0550), part of a multiuse development on a repurposed Air Force base.

# FESTIVALS AND EVENTS

Interestingly, most events in Myrtle Beach don't happen during the three-month high season of June-August, mostly because it's so darn hot that all anyone wants to do is get in the water.

## Winter

The Grand Strand is the birthplace of the dance called the shag, and each winter for the last 25 years the **National Shag Dance Championships** (2000 N. Kings Hwy., 843/497-7369, www.shagnationals.com, from $15 per night) have been the pinnacle of the art form. Beginning with preliminaries in January, contestants in five age ranges compete for a variety of awards, culminating in the finals the first week in March. The level of professionalism might amaze you—for such a lazy-looking dance, these are serious competitors.

## Spring

You might not automatically associate our colder neighbor to the north with Myrtle Beach, but **Canadian American Days** (various venues, www.myrtlebeachinfo.com, free), or "Can Am," brings tens of thousands of visitors of both nationalities to sites all over the Strand each March to enjoy a variety of musical and cultural events. Always on top of marketing opportunities, the Myrtle Beach Chamber of Commerce makes sure this happens during Ontario's spring holidays to ensure maximum north-of-the-border attendance. While most of the events have little or nothing to do with Canada itself, this is basically a great excuse for Canucks to get some Carolina sunshine.

The **Spring Games and Kite Flying Contest** (843/448-7881, free) brings an exciting array of airborne craft to the Strand in front of Broadway at the Beach on an April weekend as the springtime winds peak.

Also in April is the area's second-largest shag event, the **Society of Stranders Spring Safari** (www.shagdance.com). Several clubs

# Motorcycle Madness

Growling engines? Spinning tires? Patriotic colors? Polished chrome? Bikini car washes? Erotic bull-riding contests? That is the spectacle known as **Myrtle Beach Bike Week,** one of the largest gatherings of Harley-Davidson enthusiasts on the East Coast and one of the oldest, at about 75 years.

The event has historically happened each May on the week and weekend before Memorial Day weekend, bringing over 250,000 motorcyclists and their entourages to town for 10 days of riding, bragging, and carousing. South Carolina's lack of a helmet law is a particular draw to these freedom-cherishing motorcyclists. A few days later, on Memorial Day weekend, there's another bike rally, this one simply called Black Bike Week. Nearly as large as the regular Bike Week, the focus is on African American riders and their machines.

Contrary to stereotype, there's not much of an increase in crime during either Bike Week. Regardless, they are widely known as a particularly bad time to bring families to the area, and therein lies the controversy. Joining other municipalities around the nation in discouraging motorcycle rallies, the city of Myrtle Beach has enacted tough measures to force the bike rallies to leave town and make the area more family-friendly during that time. Most controversial among recent measures was a municipal helmet law, enforceable only within Myrtle Beach city limits, that was later struck down by the South Carolina Supreme Court. Other still-standing measures include stringent noise ordinances designed to include the roaring, rattling tailpipes of pretty much every Harley ever made. The separate municipality of North Myrtle Beach, however, has made it clear that bikers are welcome there even if they're non grata a few miles to the south.

As of now, it seems that the rallies will remain on the Strand rather than gun their collective throttle and head elsewhere, as they occasionally threaten to do when relations with local municipalities and police departments get too tense. The upshot for the nonmotorcyclist visitor? Bikers are somewhat less of a factor than in years past, and certainly local police are taking them more seriously. But the time around Memorial Day is still as crowded as ever.

---

in North Myrtle Beach host shag dancers from all over for a week of, well, shagging.

The biggest single event in Myrtle Beach happens in May with the **Spring Bike Rally** (various venues, www.myrtlebeachbikeweek. com, free), always known simply as "Bike Week." In this 75-year-old event, over 250,000 Harley-Davidson riders and their entourages gather to cruise around the place, admire each other's custom rides, and generally party their patooties off. While the typical Harley dude these days is getting on in years and is probably a mild-mannered store manager in regular life, young or old they all do their best to let their hair down at this festive event. Dozens of related events go on throughout the week at venues all over the Strand, from tough-man contests to "foxy boxing" matches to wet T-shirt contests. You get the picture—it's not for the politically correct or for young children.

## Summer

Right after the Spring Bike Rally, on Memorial Day weekend, is the **Atlantic Beach Bikefest** (various venues), much more commonly referred to as "Black Bike Week." This event started in the 1980s and is spiritually based in Atlantic Beach, formerly the area's "black beach" during the days of segregation. It sees over 200,000 African American motorcycle enthusiasts gather in Myrtle Beach for a similar menu of partying, bikini contests, cruising, and the like. While the existence of separate events often reminds some people of the state's unfortunate history of segregation, supporters of both Bike Week and Black Bike Week insist it's not a big deal, and that bikers of either race are welcome at either event.

Kicking off with a festive parade, the 50-year-old **Sun Fun Festival** (various venues, www.grandstrandevents.com), generally held the weekend after Memorial Day weekend, signals the real beginning of the summer season with bikini contests, Jet Ski races, parades, air shows, and concerts galore.

The **City of Myrtle Beach Independence Day Celebration** (www.cityofmyrtlebeach.com, free) is held each July 4 weekend, when the largest number of visitors is in Myrtle Beach. It's fun, it's hot, there's fireworks aplenty, and boy, is it crowded.

## Fall

For a week in mid-September, North Myrtle Beach hosts one of the world's largest shag dancing celebrations, the **Society of Stranders Fall Migration** (www.shagdance.com, free). Head up to the intersection of Ocean Drive and Main Street to hear the sounds of this unique genre, and party with the shaggers at various local clubs. If you don't know the steps, don't worry—instructors are usually on hand.

There's another, smaller Harley riders' rally the first week in October, the **Fall Motorcycle Rally** (various venues, www.myrtlebeachbikeweek.com, free).

Thanksgiving weekend, when the beaches are much less crowded and the hotels much cheaper, is the **South Carolina Bluegrass Festival** (2101 N. Oak St., 706/864-7203, www.aandabluegrass.com, $30 adults, $20 ages 6-13, free under age 6), a delightful and well-attended event at the Myrtle Beach Convention Center, celebrating the Appalachian music tradition. It attracts some of the biggest names in the genre.

# Shopping

Shopping on the Grand Strand is strongly destination-oriented. You tend to find shops of similar price points and merchandise types clustered together in convenient locations: Upscale shops are in one place and discount and outlet stores in another. Here's a rundown of the main retail areas on the Strand with some of the standout shops.

## BROADWAY AT THE BEACH

The sprawling **Broadway at the Beach** (U.S. 17 Bypass and 21st Ave. N., www.broadwayatthebeach.com, hours vary) complex has scads of stores, some of which are quite interesting and rise well beyond tourist schlock. There are maps and directories of the site available at various kiosks around the area.

One of my favorite stores is **Retroactive** (843/916-1218, www.shopretroactive.com), a shop specializing in 1970s and 1980s styles and kitsch, with some of the best (and wittiest) pop-culture T-shirts I've seen. The owners are frank about their continuing obsession with '80s hair bands. Another awesome T-shirt and trinket shop that the kids and teens will particularly enjoy is **Stupid Factory** (843/448-1100). The kids—and those with a sweet tooth—will go crazy in the aptly named **It'SUGAR** (843/916-1300, www.itsugar.com), a store dedicated to just about any kind of candy and candy-themed merchandise you can think of, from modern brands to retro favorites. If the packaged or bulk varieties don't float your boat, you can design your own massive chocolate bar. And, of course, this being Myrtle Beach, there's a **Harley Davidson** (843/293-5555) gift store with Hog-oriented merch galore.

The bottom line on Broadway at the Beach, though, is that it's made for walking around and browsing. Just bring your walking shoes—the place is huge—and keep in mind that there's not a lot of shade.

## BAREFOOT LANDING

There are over 100 shops at **Barefoot Landing** (4898 U.S. 17 S., 843/272-8349, www.bflanding.com, hours vary) in North Myrtle Beach—as well as one cool old-fashioned carousel—but perhaps the most unique spot is **T.I.G.E.R.S. Preservation Station** (843/361-4552, www.tigerfriends.com, hours vary), where you get the opportunity to have your picture taken with a live tiger or lion cub. This is the fund-raising arm of a local organization for conservation of the big cats as well as gorillas and monkeys. Portraits begin at $100 to pose with a single critter and go up from there depending on the number of people you want to pose with in the shot. It's a lot of money, but this is truly a once-in-a-lifetime experience.

Relocated to the Strand from its grape yards in Chester, South Carolina, is **Carolina Vineyards Winery** (843/361-9181, www.carolinavineyards.com). Buy wine as a gift, or taste any seven of its labels for only $3.

There are magic shops, and then there are *magic shops.* **Trickmaster Magic Shop** (843/281-0705, http://trickmastermagicshop.com) is definitely the latter. Packed in this relatively small space is just about every legendary trick and trick deck known to the magician's art, along with a cool variety of magic books teaching you, in deadly serious fashion, the innermost secrets of the trade.

## THE MARKET COMMON

**The Market Common** (4017 Deville St., www.marketcommonmb.com, hours vary) is an ambitious residential-retail mixed-use development opened for business on the site of the decommissioned Myrtle Beach Air Force Base. While its location near the Myrtle Beach International Airport means it's not exactly amid the sun-and-fun action (possibly a good thing, depending on the season), the very pedestrian-friendly development style and tasteful shops might provide a refreshing change of pace.

There are three dozen (and counting) stores, including Anthropologie, Williams-Sonoma, Copper Penny, Chico's, Brooks Brothers, Fossil, Banana Republic, Barnes & Noble, and Jake and Company ("Life Is Good"). There are plenty of restaurants, including Ultimate California Pizza and P. F. Chang's, and a large multiplex movie theater.

For those interested in how the sprawling old base was closed in the 1990s and repurposed so completely, there's interpretive signage all around the pedestrian mall and along the roadways leading to it. At The Market Common's entrance is Warbird Park, a well-done veterans memorial featuring an Air Force A-10 attack aircraft, an F-100 Super Sabre, and a Corsair II.

## MALLS

The premier mall in the area is **Coastal Grand Mall** (2000 Coastal Grand Circle, 843/839-9100, www.coastalgrand.com, Mon.-Sat. 10am-9pm, Sun. noon-6pm) at the U.S. 17 Bypass and U.S. 501. It's anchored by Belk, J. C. Penney, Sears, Dillard's, and Dick's Sporting Goods.

Your basic meat-and-potatoes mall, **Myrtle Beach Mall** (10177 N. Kings Hwy., 843/272-4040, http://shopmyrtlebeachmall.com, Mon.-Sat. 10am-9pm, Sun. noon-6pm) is anchored by Belk, J. C. Penney, and Bass Pro Shops.

## DISCOUNT BEACHWEAR

Literally dozens of cavernous, tacky, deep-discount T-shirt-and-towel-type places are spread up and down Kings Highway like mushrooms after a rain. The vast majority of them belong to one of several well-established chains: **Eagles Beachwear** (www.eaglesbeachwear.net), **Whales** (www.whalesnauticalgifts.com), **Wing's Beachwear** (www.wingsbeachwear.com), and **Bargain Beachwear** (www.bargainbeachwear.com). These are the kinds of places to get assorted bric-a-brac and items for your beach visit. The quality isn't that bad, and the prices are uniformly low.

## OUTLET MALLS

There are two massive **Tanger Outlets** (www.tangeroutlet.com) at Myrtle Beach: **Tanger Outlet North** (10835 Kings Rd., 843/449-0491), off Kings Road/U.S. 17, and **Tanger Outlet South** (4635 Factory Stores

Blvd., 843/236-5100), off U.S. 501. Both offer over 100 factory outlet stores of almost every imaginable segment, from Fossil to Disney, OshKosh B'gosh to Timberland. Full food courts are available, and many folks easily spend an entire day here.

For years, busloads of hard-core shoppers from throughout the South have taken organized trips to the Grand Strand specifically to shop at **Waccamaw Factory Shoppes** (3071 Waccamaw Blvd., 843/236-8200). Their passion hasn't abated, as new generations of shopaholics get the fever to come here and browse the often deeply discounted offerings at row after row of outlet stores. There are actually two locations, the Factory Shoppes themselves and the nearby **Waccamaw Pottery** (3200 Pottery Dr., 843/236-6152). Bring your walking shoes (or buy some new ones at one of the many shoe stores), but don't worry about getting from one mall to the other—there's a free shuttle.

# Sports and Recreation

Myrtle Beach's middle name might as well be recreation. While some of the local variety tends toward overkill—I personally loathe Jet Skis, for example—there's no denying that if it involves outdoor activity, it's probably offered here. For general info, visit www.grandstrandevents.com. For municipal recreation info, visit www.cityofmyrtlebeach.com.

## ON THE WATER
### Beaches
The center of activity is the Strand itself, with its miles of user-friendly beaches. They're not the most beautiful in the world, but they're nice enough, and access is certainly no problem. In Myrtle Beach and North Myrtle Beach, you'll find clearly designated public access points off Ocean Boulevard, some with parking and some without. Both municipalities run well-marked public parking lots at various points, some of which are free during the off-season.

Dog owners will be pleased to know that May 15-September 15, dogs are allowed on the beach before 9am and after 5pm. September 15-May 15, dogs are allowed on the beach at any time of day.

Restrict your swimming to within 150 feet of shore. Surfside Beach to the south is a no-smoking beach with access points at 16th Avenue North, 6th Avenue North, 3rd Avenue North, Surfside Pier, 3rd Avenue South, 4th Avenue South, 13th Avenue South, and Melody Lane.

### Surfing
There's a steady, if low-key, surf scene in Myrtle Beach, despite the fact that the waves are not really that good and the sport is restricted to certain areas during the busy summer season. The rules are a little complicated.

In **Myrtle Beach proper,** surfing is only allowed April 15-September 15 daily 10am-5pm in the following zones:

• 29th Avenue South to the southern city limits
• 37th Avenue North to 47th Avenue North
• 62nd Avenue North to 68th Avenue North

82nd Avenue North to the northern city limits Up in **North Myrtle Beach,** surfers must stay in the following zones May 15-September 15 daily 9am-4pm:

• Cherry Grove Pier
• 6th Avenue North
• 13th Avenue South
• 28th Avenue South

38th Avenue South Down at **Surfside Beach,** surfing is restricted to the following zones, year-round daily 10am-5pm:

• 12th Avenue North to 14th Avenue North
• Melody Lane to 13th Avenue South

The oldest surf shop in the area, south of Myrtle Beach in Garden City Beach, is the

**Village Surf Shoppe** (500 Atlantic Ave., 843/651-6396, www.villagesurf.com), which has catered to the Strand's growing surf scene since 1969. Nearly as old is the **Surf City Surf Shop** (1758 U.S. 17 S., 843/272-1090; 3001 N. Kings Hwy., 843/626-5412, www.surfcitysurf-shop.com) franchise in Myrtle proper.

## Diving

Diving is popular on the Strand. As with fishing, many trips depart from Little River just above North Myrtle Beach. Offshore features include many historic wrecks, including the post-Civil War wreck of the **USS *Sherman*** offshore of Little River, and artificial reefs such as the famed **"Barracuda Alley,"** teeming with marine life, off Myrtle Beach.

**Coastal Scuba** (1901 U.S. 17 S., 843/361-3323, www.coastalscuba.com) in North Myrtle is a large operator, offering several different dive tours.

## Parasailing, Windsurfing, and Jet Skis

**Ocean Watersports** (405 S. Ocean Blvd., 843/445-7777, www.parasailmyrtlebeach. com) takes groups of up to six people on well-supervised, well-equipped parasailing adventures (about $50 pp), with tandem and triple flights available. Observers can go out on the boat for about $20. They also rent Jet Skis and offer "banana boat" rides ($15) in which a long—yes, banana-shaped—raft, straddled by several riders, is towed by a boat up and down the beach.

**Downwind Watersports** (2915 S. Ocean Blvd., 843/448-7245, www.downwindsails-myrtlebeach.com) has similar offerings, with the addition of good old-fashioned sailboat lessons and rentals ($16). Parasailing is about $65 per person for a single ride, banana boats are $16 for 20 minutes, and Jet Ski rentals are about $100 per hour.

Farther up the Strand in North Myrtle, between Cherry Grove Beach and Little River, you'll find **Thomas Outdoors Watersports** (2200 Little River Neck Rd., 843/280-2448, www.mbjetski.com), which rents kayaks in addition to Jet Skis and pontoon boats. They offer several Jet Ski tours ($75-125), including a dolphin-watching trip, as well as all-day kayak rental ($45 pp).

## Fishing

Most fishing on the Strand is saltwater, with charters, most based in Little River, taking anglers well into Atlantic waters. Tuna, wahoo, mackerel, and dolphin (not the mammal!) are big in the hot months, while snapper and grouper are caught year-round but are best in the colder months.

A good operator up in Little River is **Longway Fishing Charters** (843/249-7813, www.longwaycharters.com), which specializes in offshore fishing. Another in the same area is **Capt. Smiley's Inshore Fishing** (843/361-7445, www.captainsmiley-fishingcharters.com). **Fish Hook Charters** (2200 Little River Neck Rd., 843/283-7692, www.fishhookcharters.com) takes a 34-foot boat out from North Myrtle Beach.

For surf fishing on the beach, you do not need a license of any type. All other types of fishing require a valid South Carolina fishing license, available for a nominal fee online (http://dnr.sc.gov) or at any tackle shop and most grocery stores.

## Cruises

Except in the winter months, there are plenty of places to cruise in the Strand, from Little River down to Murrells Inlet, and from the Waccamaw River to the Intracoastal Waterway. The **Great American Riverboat Company** (8496 Enterprise Rd., 843/650-6600, www.mbriverboat.com) offers sightseeing and dinner cruises along the Intracoastal Waterway. **Island Song Charters** (4374 Landing Rd., 843/467-7088, www.sailingmyr-tlebeach.com) out of Little River takes you on sunset and dolphin cruises on the 32-foot sailboat *Island Song*.

Up in North Myrtle, **Getaway Adventures** (843/663-1100, www.myrtle-beachboatcruises.com) specializes in dolphin tours. Also in North Myrtle, **Thomas**

Outdoors Watersports (2200 Little River Neck Rd., 843/280-2448, www.mbjetski.com) runs dolphin cruises.

## ON LAND
### Golf

The Grand Strand in general, and Myrtle Beach in particular, is world golf central. There are over 120 courses in this comparatively small area, and if golfers can't find something they like here, they need to sell their clubs. While the number of truly great courses is few—the best courses are farther down the Strand near Pawleys Island—the quality overall is still quite high.

A great bonus is affordability. Partially because of dramatically increased competition due to the glut of courses, and partially because of savvy regional marketing, greens fees here are significantly lower than you might expect, in many cases under $100. For even more savings, finding a golf-lodging package deal in Myrtle Beach is like finding sand on the beach—almost too easy. Check with your hotel to see if they offer any golf packages. At any time of year, some good one-stop shops on the Internet are at www.mbn.com and www.myrtlebeachgolf.com.

Some highlights of area golf include the Davis Love III-designed course at **Barefoot Resort** (4980 Barefoot Resort Ridge Rd., 843/390-3200, www.barefootgolf.com, $105-185) in North Myrtle, maybe the best in the Strand outside Pawleys Island. Or would that be the Greg Norman course, or the Tom Fazio course, or the Pete Dye course, all also at Barefoot? You get the picture.

Also up near North Myrtle is a favorite with visitors and locals alike, the challenging **Glen Dornoch Golf Club** (4840 Glen Dornoch Way, 800/717-8784, www.glensgolfgroup.com, from $100), on 260 beautiful acres. Affiliated with Glen Dornoch are the 27 holes at Little River's **Heather Glen** (4650 Heather Glen Way, 800/868-4536, www.glensgolfgroup.com, $130), which are divided into Red, White, and Blue courses. They combine for what's consistently rated

one of the best public courses in the United States.

And no list of area golf is complete without a nod to **Myrtle Beach National** (4900 National Dr., 843/347-4298, www.mbn.com, from $80). With three distinct courses—King's North, West, and South Creek, with its South Carolina-shaped sand trap at hole 3—the National is one of the state's legendary courses, not to mention a heck of a deal.

### Miniature Golf

Don't scoff—miniature golf, or "putt-putt" to an older generation, is a big deal in Myrtle Beach. If you thought there were a lot of regular golf courses here, the 50 miniature golf courses will also blow your mind. Sadly, almost all of the classic old-school miniature golf courses are no more, victims of the demand for increased production values and modernized gimmick holes. But here are some of the standouts, including the best of the North Myrtle courses as well.

Down near the older section of Myrtle, the completely over-the-top **Mount Atlanticus Minotaur Goff** (707 N. Kings Hwy., 843/444-1008, $10 for 18 holes) is garish yet wonderful. And yes, that's how it's spelled—get it? Legend has it that this one course cost $3 million to build. Literally the stuff of dreams—or maybe hallucinations—this sprawling course mixes the mythological with the nautical to wonderful effect. You don't actually encounter the Minotaur until the bonus 19th hole, a fiendish water trap. If you get a hole in one, you get free golf here for life.

My favorite course is a bit farther north on the main drag. **Captain Hook's Miniature Golf** (2205 N. Kings Hwy., www.captainhooksminigolf.com, $10 for 18 holes) has two courses depicting the world of Peter Pan and Neverland, including a hole entirely on board the eponymous captain's pirate ship! I wouldn't call it particularly difficult, but it's a lot of fun.

**Hawaiian Rumble** (3210 U.S. 17, 843/458-2585, www.prominigolf.com) in North Myrtle is not only a heck of a fun, attractive course,

Mount Atlanticus Minotaur Goff

it's also the official training center for the U.S. Professional Miniature Golf Association (the folks who generally get a hole in one on every hole). The Rumble's sister course is **Hawaiian Village** (4205 U.S. 17, 843/361-9629, www.prominigolf.com) in North Myrtle, which is also the home of serious professional miniature golf competitions.

For a bit of retro action, try **Rainbow Falls** (9550 Kings Hwy., 843/497-2557). It's not as garish as some of the newer courses, but fans of old-school putt-putt will love it.

While at Broadway at the Beach, you might want to try the popular medieval-themed **Dragon's Lair** (1197 Celebrity Circle, 843/913-9301). Yep, it has a 30-foot fire-breathing dragon, Sir Alfred, that you have to make your way around. While the dinosaur craze has cooled somewhat, the golf at **Jurassic Golf** (445 29th Ave., 843/448-2116), festooned with dozens of velociraptors and the like, certainly has stayed hot. There is a similarly themed site in North Myrtle, the **Dinosaur Adventure** (700 7th Ave., 843/272-8041).

## Tennis

There are over 200 tennis courts in the Myrtle Beach area. The main municipal site is the **Myrtle Beach Tennis Center** (3302 Robert Grissom Pkwy., 843/918-2440, www.myrtlebeachtennis.com, $2 pp per hour), which has 10 courts, 8 of them lighted. The city also runs six lighted courts at **Midway Park** (U.S. 17 and 19th Ave. S.).

The privately owned **Kingston Plantation** (843/497-2444, www.kingstonplantation.com) specializes in tennis vacations, and you don't even have to be a guest. They have a pro on staff and offer lessons. Down in Pawleys Island, the **Litchfield Beach and Golf Resort** (14276 Ocean Hwy., 866/538-0187, www.litchfieldbeach.com) has two dozen nice courts.

## Cycling

In Myrtle Beach, when they say "biker," they mean a Harley dude. Bicycling—or safe bicycling, anyway—is largely limited to fat-tire riding along the beach and easy pedaling through the quiet residential neighborhoods near Little River. There is a bike lane on North Ocean Boulevard from about 29th Avenue North to about 82nd Avenue North. Riding on the sidewalk is strictly prohibited.

As for bike rentals, a good operator is **Beach Bike Shop** (711 Broadway St., 843/448-5335, www.beachbikeshop.com). In North Myrtle, try **Wheel Fun Rentals** (91 S. Ocean Blvd., 843/280-7900, www.wheelfunrentals.com).

## Horseback Riding

A horse ride along the surf is a nearly iconic image of South Carolina, combining two of the state's chief pursuits: equestrian sports and hanging out on the beach. A great way to enjoy a horseback ride along the Grand Strand without having to bring your own equine is to check out **Horseback Riding of Myrtle Beach** (843/294-1712, www.myrtlebeachhorserides. com). They offer a variety of group rides, each with a guide, going to nature-preserve or beach locales. While they'll take you out any day of the week, advance reservations are required. Ninety minutes on a nature preserve costs about $50 per person, while a 90-minute ride on the beach is about $75 per person.

You can go horseback riding on Myrtle Beach from the third Saturday in November until the end of February, with these conditions: You must access the beach from Myrtle Beach State Park, you cannot ride over sand dunes in any way, and you must clean up after your horse.

## SPECTATOR SPORTS

Playing April-early September in a large stadium near Broadway at the Beach are the **Myrtle Beach Pelicans** (1251 21st Ave. N., 843/918-6000, www.myrtlebeachpelicans. com, $8-11), a single-A affiliate of the Chicago Cubs.

NASCAR fans already know of the **Myrtle Beach Speedway** (455 Hospitality Ln., www.myrtlebeachspeedway.com, $12, free under age 10) off U.S. 501, one of the more vintage tracks in the country, dating back to 1958 (it was actually a dirt track well into the 1970s). Currently the main draws are the NASCAR Whelen All-American Series races (Apr.-Nov. Sat. 7:30pm).

Other spectator sports in the area tend to revolve around the Chanticleer teams of **Coastal Carolina University** (132 Chanticleer Dr. W., 843/347-8499, www. goccusports.com), just inland from Myrtle Beach in Conway. The baseball team won the school's first national title in 2016. By the way, *chanticleer* is an old name for a rooster, and in this case is a self-conscious derivative of the mascot of the University of South Carolina, the gamecock.

# Food

There are about 2,000 restaurants in the Myrtle Beach area, not counting hotel room service and buffets. You can find any dining option that floats your boat at almost any price level. Seafood, of course, is heartily recommended, but there are steak houses, rib joints, pizza places, and vegetarian restaurants galore as well. We can only explore a small fraction here, but following are some of the unique and tasty experiences on the bustling Grand Strand.

Food is never far away, with the biggest concentration of restaurants—including the gigantic seafood buffet places—on "Restaurant Row," a stretch of Kings Highway/U.S. 17

between Myrtle Beach and North Myrtle Beach, from about the merge of U.S. 17 Bypass and U.S. 17 Business in the south and the Tanger Outlets to the north.

## BREAKFAST

Pancakes are big on the Strand, with many flapjack places open daily 24 hours to accommodate partiers and night owls. A prime purveyor of pancakes is **Harry's Breakfast Pancakes** (2306 N. Kings Hwy., 843/448-8013, www.harryspancake.com, daily 5:30am-2pm, $4-10). They're not open all day, but there's enough time to enjoy their fluffy stacks and rich omelets.

## BARBECUE, BURGERS, AND STEAKS

The best barbecue in town—and a delightfully low-key experience in this often too-flashy area—is at ★ **Little Pigs Barbecue** (6102 Frontage Rd., 843/692-9774, Mon.-Sat. 11am-8pm, $8-12). This is a local-heavy place dealing in no-frills pulled pork, piled high at the counter and reasonably priced with a selection of sauces. The lack of atmosphere *is* the atmosphere, and they prefer to let the barbecue (and the hush puppies and onion rings) do the talking.

Since opening 30 years ago, ★ **Thoroughbreds** (9706 N. Kings Hwy., 843/497-2636, www.thoroughbredsrestaurant.com, Sun.-Thurs. 5pm-10pm, Fri.-Sat. 5pm-11pm, $20), on the old Restaurant Row, has been considered the premier fine-dining place in Myrtle Beach, dealing in the kind of wood-heavy, clubby, Old World-meets-New World ambience you'd expect to see in Palm Beach, Florida. That said, the prices are definitely more Myrtle Beach; you can easily have a romantic dinner for two for under $100. The menu is a carnivore's delight: Beef includes the signature prime rib, a great steak au poivre, and a nod to cowboy machismo, the 22-ounce bone-in rib eye.

The darling of the steak-loving set is **Rioz Brazilian Steakhouse** (2920 Hollywood Dr., 843/839-0777, www.rioz.com, daily 4pm-10pm, $20-40). It's not cheap—the recommended 15-item meat sampler is about $35 per person—but then again, an experience this awesome shouldn't be cheap (a big plus is that kids under age 7 eat for free). The meats are fresh and vibrant, slow-cooked over a wood fire in the simple but succulent style typical of the gaucho *churrascaria* tradition. The service is widely considered to be the best in the area. But the biggest surprise may turn out to be the salad and seafood bar, which even has sushi.

There is no dearth of places to nosh at Barefoot Landing, but meat lovers (not to mention golfers) will probably enjoy **Greg Norman's Australian Grille** (4930 Kings Hwy. S., 843/361-0000, www.gregnorman-saustraliangrille.com, lunch daily 11am-3pm, dinner daily 5pm-10pm, $20-30), which, despite the chain-sounding name, is the only restaurant of its kind. It's the place to enjoy a cocktail by the lake and a premium entrée like the lobster-crusted swordfish.

I normally shy away from mentioning national chain-type places, but I'll make an exception for Myrtle Beach, where you expect things to be a little cheesy. **Jimmy Buffett's Margaritaville** (1114 Celebrity Circle, 843/448-5455, www.margaritavillemyrtle-beach.com, Sun.-Thurs. 11am-10pm, Fri.-Sat. 11am-midnight, $13-22) at Broadway at the Beach is widely regarded as the best single location of the national chain. The signature Cheeseburger in Paradise is the obvious big hit. You get a lot of entertainment for your money as well, with balloon-twisting performers coming to your table and a bizarre whirling "hurricane" that acts up in the main dining area every now and then. As you'd expect, the margaritas are good, if expensive.

Many locals insist the better burger is at another Buffett-owned chain, the succinctly titled **Cheeseburger in Paradise** (7211 N. Kings Hwy., 843/497-3891, www.cheeseburgerinparadise.com, Sun.-Thurs. 11:30am-11pm, Fri.-Sat. 11:30am-midnight, $10-15), which offers a range of burgers on the menu with sweet potato chips on the side, all served up in a less flashy but still very boisterous atmosphere than the flagship restaurant.

## CLASSIC SOUTHERN

If you've got a hankering for some spicy Cajun-Creole food, go no farther than the **House of Blues** (4640 U.S. 17 S., 843/272-3000, www.hob.com, Mon.-Fri. 4pm-9pm, Sat. 8am-9pm, Sun. 9am-2pm and 3pm-9pm, $10-25) at Barefoot Landing in North Myrtle Beach. With 11 similarly themed locations around North America, this particular venue deals in the same kind of retro delta vibe, with specially commissioned folk art festooning the walls and live music cranking up at about 10pm. At your table, a gregarious server will walk you through the limited but intense menu, which includes such tasty bits as buffalo tenders (boneless chicken wings in a perfectly spicy sauce) and a couple of excellent jambalaya-type dishes. All portions are enormous and richly spiced. It's a loud, clanging room, so keep in mind that this is less a romantic experience than an exuberant, earthy one.

A special experience at House of Blues is the weekly **Gospel Brunch** (Sun. 9am-2pm, $20 adults, $10 ages 6-12, free under age 6), an opportunity not only to enjoy some tasty Southern-style brunch treats like cheese grits, jambalaya, and catfish tenders but to enjoy some outstanding gospel entertainment at the same time. The Gospel Brunch is served in seatings, and reservations are recommended.

## CONTINENTAL

In Myrtle Beach it can be difficult to find a good meal that's not fried or smothered or both. For a highbrow change of pace, try **The Library** (1212 N. Kings Hwy., 843/448-4527, www.thelibraryrestaurantsc.com, Mon.-Sat. 5pm-10pm, $20-50), which is hands-down the most romantic dining experience in Myrtle proper. It's not cheap, but then again, nothing about this place is pedestrian, from the very attentive European-style service to the savvy wine list and the signature dishes (many of them prepared tableside), like she-crab soup, Caesar salads, steak Diane, and the ultimate splurge, steak and lobster.

Like art? Like food? Try the **Collector's Café** (7726 N. Kings Hwy., 843/449-9370, www.collectorscafeandgallery.com, $10-20), which, as the name implies, is a combined gallery and dining space. Don't be daunted by the strip mall setting—inside is a totally different ball game with a trendy open kitchen and plush, eclectic furniture awaiting you amid the original artwork. As for the menu, you may as well go for what's widely regarded as the best single dish, the scallop cakes. Make sure you save room for dessert.

## ITALIAN

The best-regarded Italian place in Myrtle Beach—though it could just as easily go in the *Steaks* category, since that's its specialty—is **Angelo's** (2011 S. Kings Hwy., 843/626-2800, www.angelosteakandpasta.com, Sun.-Thurs. 4pm-8:30pm, Fri.-Sat. 4pm-9pm, $12-25). The signature dishes are intriguingly spiced cuts of steak (request beforehand if you don't want them seasoned), cooked medium and under for an exquisite tenderness. You can get spaghetti as a side with the steaks, or just go with the classic baked potato. Don't forget to check out the Italian buffet, including lasagna, Italian sausage, chicken cacciatore, ravioli, and, of course, pizza.

## MEXICAN

If you need a fix of absolutely authentic Mexican food, head straight to ★ **La Poblanita** (311 Hwy. 15, 843/448-3150, daily 11am-10pm, $7-10). Don't be put off by the humble exterior in a small strip mall; the food is simply amazing—and amazingly inexpensive. Eighty percent of the diners are Mexican American families, which attests to the authenticity of the cuisine. Everything on the menu is handmade, including the tortillas. The empanadas and burritos are quite simply the best I've eaten anywhere. Even the rice melts in your mouth. Don't forget the Mexican Coke!

## SEAFOOD

The grandest old Calabash seafood joint in town, **Original Benjamin's** (9593 N. Kings Hwy., 843/449-0821, daily 3:30pm-10pm, buffet $25 adults, $12 children), on the old Restaurant Row, is one of the more unique dining experiences in Myrtle Beach. With themed rooms overlooking the Intracoastal Waterway, including the concisely named Bus Room—yes, it has an old school bus in it—you'll find yourself in the mood to devour copious amounts of fresh seafood at its humongous 170-item buffet line.

Closer to Broadway at the Beach, try **George's** (1401 29th Ave. N., 843/916-2278, www.captaingeorges.com, Mon.-Sat. 3pm-10pm, Sun. noon-9pm, buffet $31, $16 ages 5-12, free under age 5). Despite the usual kitschy nautical decor, this is the kind of place even locals will admit going to for the enormous seafood buffet, widely considered a cut above the norm.

With old reliables like crab cakes and sea scallops as well as signature house dishes like pecan-encrusted grouper and stuffed flounder, you can't go wrong at **The Sea Captain's House** (3002 N. Ocean Blvd., 843/448-8082, daily 6am-10:30am, 11:30am-2:30pm, and 5pm-10pm, $10-20), one of Myrtle Beach's better seafood restaurants. This opinion is widely held, however, so prepare to wait—often up to two hours. Luckily, you can sip a cocktail and gaze out over the Atlantic Ocean as you do so. Old hands will tell you it's not as good as back in the day, but it's still a cut above.

When you're at Ocean Drive Beach up in North Myrtle, check out another venerable old name, the **Duffy Street Seafood Shack** (202 Main St., 843/281-9840, www.duffyst.com, daily noon-10pm, $10). This is a humble, unkempt roadside affair dealing in the kind of down-home treats Myrtle Beach seems to love ("pigskin" shrimp, fried pickles, and the like). Overall, it's a good place to get a tasty bite and soak in the flavor of this Cherry Grove neighborhood at the heart of the old shag culture.

# Accommodations

There is no dearth of lodging in the Myrtle Beach area, from the typical high-rise "resorts" (think condos on steroids) to chain hotels, vacation villas, house rentals, and camping. Because of the plethora of options, prices are generally reasonable, and competition to provide more and more on-site amenities—free breakfasts, "lazy river" pools, washers and dryers, hot tubs, poolside grills, and so on—has only increased. You are the beneficiary, so you might as well take advantage of it.

Note that the stated price range may be very broad because so many Myrtle Beach lodgings offer several room options, from one-bed guest rooms to full three-bedroom suites. Here are a few general tips to consider when booking a room:

- The larger suites are generally "condo apartments," meaning they're privately owned. While they're usually immaculately clean for your arrival, it means that housekeeping is minimal and you won't get lots of complimentary goodies whenever you call the front desk.

- The entire Myrtle Beach area is undergoing growth, and that includes the accommodations. This means that many properties have older sections and newer ones. Ask beforehand which section you're being booked in.

- Check www.myrtlebeachhotels.com for last-minute deals and specials at 11 well-run local resorts.

- By the end of September, prices drop dramatically.

- Almost all area lodgings, especially the high-rises, feature on-site pools galore; lounge chairs and tables are at a premium and go very quickly during high season when the sun's out.

- Always keep in mind that summer is the high season here, unlike the rest of South Carolina, and guest rooms, especially at beachfront places, get snapped up very early.

## UNDER $150

For 75 years, ★ **Driftwood on the Oceanfront** (1600 N. Ocean Blvd., 843/448-1544, www.driftwoodlodge.com, $100-120) has been a favorite place to stay. Upgraded over the years, but not *too* upgraded, this five-story, 90-room complex is family-owned and takes pride in delivering personalized service that is simply impossible to attain in the larger high-rises nearby. As you'd expect, the guest rooms and suites are a bit on the small side by modern Myrtle Beach standards—with none of the increasingly popular three-bedroom suites available—but most everyone is impressed by the value.

Probably the best-regarded bed-and-breakfast in Myrtle Beach (yes, there are a precious few) is the ★ **Serendipity Inn** (407 71st Ave. N., 843/449-5268, www.serendipityinn.com, $90-150). A short walk from the beach but sometimes seemingly light-years away from the typical Myrtle sprawl, this 15-room gem features a simple but elegant pool, an attractive courtyard, and sumptuous guest rooms. The full breakfast is simple but hearty. There's free Wi-Fi throughout the property.

If you're looking for a basic, inexpensive, one-bed hotel experience on the beach, ask for a room at the new oceanfront section of the **Best Western Grand Strand Inn and Suites** (1804 S. Ocean Blvd., 843/448-1461, $80-140), a smallish but clean and attentively run chain hotel. The property's other buildings are significantly older and are located across busy Ocean Boulevard, and the walk across the street to the beach can be difficult, especially if you have small kids. That said, this is a great value and a quality property.

If water park-style entertainment is your thing, try **Dunes Village Resort** (5200 N. Ocean Blvd., 877/828-2237, www.dunesvillage.com, $140-300), also one of the better values in Myrtle. Its huge indoor water park has copious waterslides, including several for adults, and various other aquatic diversions. The buildings themselves—the property comprises two high-rise towers—are modern and well equipped, although since this is a time-share-style property, housekeeping is minimal.

## $150-300

My favorite place to stay at Myrtle Beach is the ★ **Island Vista Oceanfront Resort** (6000 N. Ocean Blvd., 855/732-6250, www.island-vista.com). While not the flashiest or heaviest in amenities by any means, Island Vista's location in a quiet residential area overlooking a mile of the Strand's best and least-traveled beach makes it a standout alternative to the often crowded and logistically challenging environment you'll find in the more built-up high-rise blocks farther south on the beach. In the high season you'll pay about $300 for a one-bedroom suite, but the prices on the spacious and very well equipped two- and three-bedroom suites are competitive. They have the usual multiple-pool option, including an indoor heated pool area. A big plus is the fact that the in-house fine-dining restaurant, the **Cypress Room,** is a definite cut above most area hotel kitchens.

Consistently one of the best-regarded properties in Myrtle proper, the **Hampton Inn & Suites Oceanfront** (1803 S. Ocean Blvd., 843/946-6400, www.hamptoninnoceanfront.com, $169-259) has been made even better by a thorough upgrade. This is a classic beachfront high-rise (not to be confused with the Hampton Inn at Broadway at the Beach), clean inside and out, with elegant, tasteful guest rooms in various sizes. Guest rooms range from typical one-bed, one-bath hotel-style rooms to larger condo-style suites with a fridge.

Situated more toward North Myrtle, the **Sea Watch Resort** (161 Sea Watch Blvd., $171-395) is a good choice for those who want the full-on condo high-rise Myrtle Beach experience but not necessarily the crowds that usually go with it. Guest rooms are clean and well equipped.

One of the better-quality stays for the price in Myrtle is the **Roxanne Towers** (1604 N. Ocean Blvd., 843/839-1016, www.theroxanne.com, $150-250). Known for attentive service, this is a busy property in a busy area. Parking is historically something of a problem. Keep in mind that room size is capped at two bedrooms, so there are none of the sprawling three-bedroom suites that many other local places have.

For a quality stay in the heart of Myrtle's beach bustle, go for the **Sandy Beach Resort** (201 S. Ocean Blvd., 800/844-6534, www. sandybeachoceanfrontresort. com, $200-300). The guest rooms are top-notch, and the service is professional. As is the case with many local properties, there is a newer section, the Palmetto Tower, and an "old" section, the venerable Magnolia Tower. There are one-, two-, and three-bedroom units available, the latter a particularly good value.

Considered one of the major remaining centers of the shag subculture on the Strand, the **Ocean Drive Beach and Golf Resort** (98 N. Ocean Blvd., $200-350) up in North Myrtle Beach hosts many events surrounding the notable regional dance, including the Shaggers Hall of Fame. Its on-site lounge, **The Spanish Galleon,** specializes in beach music. It's also just a great place to stay, with amenities such as a "lazy river," a whirlpool, full galley-style kitchens, and, of course, proximity to the beach.

Also up in North Myrtle is the ★ **Tilghman Beach and Golf Resort** (1819 Ocean Blvd., 843/280-0913, www.tilghmanresort.com, $200-350), owned by the same company as the Ocean Drive Beach Resort. It's not directly on the beach, but since the buildings in front of it are pretty low, you can still get awesome ocean views. Even the views from the back of the building aren't bad, since they overlook a golf course. But you don't have to be a duffer to enjoy the Tilghman—the pool scene is great, the balconies are roomy, and the suites are huge and well enough equipped (a flat-screen TV in every room) to make you feel right at home.

## VACATION RENTALS

There are hundreds, probably thousands, of privately rented condo-style lodgings at Myrtle Beach, in all shapes and forms. Most, however, do a great job of catering to what vacationers here really seem to want: space, convenience, and a working kitchen. All rental agencies basically work with the same listings, so looking for and finding a rental is easier than you might think.

Some of the key brokers are **Myrtle Beach Vacation Rentals** (800/845-0833, www. mb-vacationrentals.com), **Beach Vacations** (866/453-4818, www.beachvacationsmb.com), **Barefoot Vacations** (800/845-0837, www. barefootvacations.info), **Elliott Realty and Beach Rentals** (www.elliottrealty.com), and **Atlantic Dunes Vacation Rentals** (866/544-2568, www.atlanticdunesvacations. com).

## BEACH CAMPING

Myrtle Beach is not where you go for a pristine, quiet camping experience. For that, I suggest Huntington State Park down near Murrells Inlet. However, there is plenty of camping, almost all of it heavily RV-oriented, if you want it. For more info, visit www.camp-myrtlebeach.com.

The closest thing to a real live campground is good old **Myrtle Beach State Park** (4401 S. Kings Hwy., 843/238-5325, www.southcarolinaparks.com, daily 6am-10pm, $4 adults, $1.50 ages 6-15, free under age 6), which despite being only a short drive from the rest of the beachfront sprawl is still a fairly relaxing place to stay, complete with its own scenic fishing pier (daily fishing fee $4.50). There's even a nature center with a little aquarium and exhibits.

The park's charming and educational atmosphere is largely due to the fact that this is one of the 17 Civilian Conservation Corps parks built during the Great Depression. There are four cabins ($54-125) available, all fully furnished and about 200 yards from the beach. The main campground is about 300 yards from the beach and comprises 300 sites with electricity and water ($23-25) and a 45-site tent and overflow campground ($17-19) that is only open during the summer high season.

The **Myrtle Beach KOA** (613 6th Ave. S., 800/562-7790, www.myrtlebeachkoa. com), though not at all cheap ($40-50 even for tenters), offers the usual safe, dependable amenities of that well-known chain, including rental "kabins" and activities for kids.

**Willow Tree RV Resort and Campground** (520 Southern Sights Dr., 843/756-4334, www.willowtreervr.com) is set inland on a well-wooded 300-acre tract with large sites well away from the sprawl, and it offers lakeside fishing and bike trails. In the summer high season, basic sites are $50-82, and the one- and two-bedroom cabins range $120-190.

# Information and Services

The main visitors center for Myrtle Beach is the **Myrtle Beach Area Chamber of Commerce and Visitor Center** (1200 N. Oak St., 843/626-7444, www.visitmybeach.com, Mon.-Fri. 8:30am-5pm, Sat. 10am-2pm). There's an **Airport Welcome Center** (1180 Jetport Rd., 843/626-7444) as well, and a visitors center in North Myrtle Beach, the **North Myrtle Beach Chamber of Commerce and Convention & Visitors Bureau** (270 U.S. 17 N., 843/281-2662, www.northmyrtlebeachchamber.com).

The main health care facility in the Myrtle Beach area is **Grand Strand Regional Medical Center** (809 82nd Pkwy., 843/692-1000, www.grandstrandmed.com). Myrtle Beach is served by the **Myrtle Beach Police Department** (1101 N. Oak St., 843/918-1382, www.cityofmyrtlebeach.com). The separate municipality of North Myrtle Beach is served by the **North Myrtle Beach Police Department** (843/280-5555, www.nmb.us).

# Transportation

## GETTING THERE

The Myrtle Beach area is served by the fast-growing **Myrtle Beach International Airport** (MYR, 1100 Jetport Rd., 843/448-1589, www.flymyrtlebeach.com), which hosts Allegiant (www.allegiantair.com), American (www.aa.com), Delta (www.delta.com), Porter Airlines (www.flyporter.com), Spirit (www.spiritair.com), United (www.ual.com), and WestJet (www.westjet.com).

Unusual for South Carolina, a state that is exceptionally well served by the interstate highway system, the main route into the area is the smaller U.S. 17, which runs north-south, with a parallel business spur, from Georgetown up to the North Carolina border. The approach from the west is by U.S. 501, called Black Skimmer Trail as it approaches Myrtle Beach.

The local **Greyhound Bus Terminal** (511 7th Ave. N., 843/231-2222, www.greyhound.com) is in "downtown" Myrtle Beach.

## GETTING AROUND

In practice, the Myrtle Beach municipalities blend and blur into each other in one long sprawl parallel to the main north-south route, U.S. 17. However, always keep this in mind: Just north of Murrells Inlet, U.S. 17 divides into two distinct portions. There's the U.S. 17 Bypass, which continues to the west of much of the coastal growth, and there's Business U.S. 17, also known as Kings Highway, the main drag along which most key attractions and places of interest are located.

The other key north-south route, Ocean Boulevard, runs along the beach. This is a two-lane road that can get pretty congested in the summer.

Thankfully, area planners have provided a

great safety valve for some of this often horrendous traffic. Highway 31, the Carolina Bays Parkway, begins inland from Myrtle Beach at about 16th Avenue. This wide and modern highway roughly parallels the Intracoastal Waterway and takes you on a straight shot, with a 65 mph speed limit, all the way to Highway 22 (the Conway Bypass) or all the way to Highway 9 at Cherry Grove Beach, the farthest extent of North Myrtle Beach. If time is of the essence, you should use Highway 31 whenever possible.

### Rental Car, Taxi, and Bus

You will need a vehicle to make the most of this area. Rental cars are available at the airport. Rental options outside the airport include **Enterprise** (1377 U.S. 501, 843/626-4277; 3401 U.S. 17 S., 843/361-4410, www.enterprise.com), **Hertz** (851 Jason Blvd., 843/839-9530, www.hertz.com), and the unique **Rent-a-Wreck** (901 3rd Ave. S., 843/626-9393).

Taxi service on the Strand is plentiful but fairly expensive. Look in the local Yellow Pages for full listings; a couple of good services are **Yellow Cab** (917 Oak St., 843/448-5555) and **Beach Checker Cab** (843/272-6212) in North Myrtle.

The area is served by the **Coastal Rapid Public Transit Authority** (1418 3rd Ave., 843/248-7277), which runs several bus routes up and down the Strand. Ask for information at a visitors center or call for a schedule.

### Bicycle

Bicyclists in Myrtle Beach can take advantage of some completed segments of the South Carolina portion of the **East Coast Greenway** (www.greenway.org), which, generally speaking, is Ocean Boulevard. You can actually ride Ocean Boulevard all the way from 82nd Avenue North down to the southern city limit.

In North Myrtle Beach, from Sea Mountain Highway in Cherry Grove, you can bike Ocean Boulevard clear down to 46th Avenue South, with a detour from 28th to 33rd Avenues. A right on 46th Avenue South takes you to Barefoot Landing. And, of course, for a scenic ride, you can pedal on the beach itself for miles. But remember: Bicycling on the sidewalk is strictly prohibited.

For bike rentals, try **Beach Bike Shop** (711 Broadway St., 843/448-5335, www.beach-bikeshop.com). In North Myrtle, try **Wheel Fun Rentals** (91 S. Ocean Blvd., 843/280-7900, www.wheelfunrentals.com).

# Points Inland

## CONWAY

A nice day trip west of Myrtle Beach—and a nice change from that area's intense development—is to the charming town of Conway, just northwest of Myrtle Beach on U.S. 501 and the Waccamaw River. Founded in 1733 with the name Kingston, it originally marked the frontier of the colony. It was later renamed Conwayborough, soon shortened to Conway, in honor of local leader Robert Conway, and now serves as the seat of Horry County.

Conway's heyday was during Reconstruction, when it became a major trade center for timber products and naval stores from the interior. The railroad came through town in 1887 (later being extended to Myrtle Beach), and most remaining buildings date from this period or later. The most notable Conway native is perhaps an unexpected name: William Gibson, originator of the cyberpunk genre of science fiction, was born here in 1948.

Conway is small and easily explored. Make your first stop the **Conway Visitors Center** (903 3rd Ave., 843/248-1700, www.cityofconway.com, Mon.-Fri. 9am-5pm), where you can pick up maps. It also offers guided tours ($2 pp) that depart from City Hall (3rd Ave. and Main St.); call for a schedule. You can also visit the **Conway Chamber of Commerce** (203 Main St.) for maps and information.

## Sights

Conway's chief attraction is the 850-foot **Riverwalk** (843/248-2273, www.conwayscchamber.com, daily dawn-dusk) along the blackwater Waccamaw River, a calming location with shops and restaurants nearby. Waterborne tours on the *Kingston Lady* leave from the Conway Marina at the end of the Riverwalk.

Another key stop is the **Horry County Museum** (428 Main St., 843/248-1542, www.horrycountymuseum.org, Tues.-Sat. 9am-4pm, free), which tells the story of this rather large South Carolina county from prehistory to the present. It holds an annual Quilt Gala in February, which features some great regional examples of the art.

Across from the campus of Coastal Carolina University is the circa-1972 Traveler's Chapel, aka **The Littlest Church in South Carolina** (U.S. 501 and Cox Ferry Rd.). At 12 by 24 feet, it seats no more than a dozen people. Weddings are held here throughout the year. Admission is free, but donations are accepted.

## Accommodations

The best stay in town is at the four-star **Cypress Inn** (16 Elm St., 843/248-8199, www.acypressinn.com, $145-235), a beautiful and well-appointed 12-room B&B right on the Waccamaw River.

## LEWIS OCEAN BAY HERITAGE PRESERVE

The humongous (over 9,000 acres) **Lewis Ocean Bay Heritage Preserve** (803/734-3886, www.dnr.sc.gov, daily dawn-dusk, free) is one of the more impressive phenomena in the Palmetto State, from a naturalist's viewpoint, made all the more special by its location a short drive from heavily developed Myrtle Beach. Managed by the state, it contains an amazing 23 Carolina bays, by far the largest concentration in South Carolina. These elliptical depressions, scattered throughout the Carolinas and all oriented in a northwest-southeast direction, are typified by a cypress-tupelo bog environment.

To get here from Myrtle Beach, take U.S. 501 north to Highway 90 and head east. After about seven miles, turn east onto the unpaved International Drive across from the Wild Horse subdivision. After about 1.5 miles on International Drive, veer left onto Old Kingston Road. The preserve is shortly ahead on both sides of the road; park along the shoulder.

# The Lower Grand Strand

Tiny **Pawleys Island** (year-round population about 200) likes to call itself "America's first resort" because of its early role, in the late 1700s, as a place for planters to go with their families to escape the mosquito-infested rice and cotton fields. It's still a vacation getaway and still has a certain elite understatement, an attitude the locals call "arrogantly shabby." While you can visit casually, most people who enjoy the famous Pawleys Island beaches do so from one of the many vacation rental properties.

Shabby arrogance does have its upside, however—there is a ban on further commercial development in the community, allowing Pawleys to remain slow and peaceful. For generations, Pawleys was famous for its cypress cottages, many on stilts. Sadly, 1989's Hurricane Hugo destroyed a great many of these iconic structures—27 out of 29 on the south end alone, most of which have been replaced by far less aesthetically pleasing homes. Hurricane Matthew in 2016, while nowhere near as catastrophic, caused extensive damage to the beach itself and surrounding dunes.

Directly adjacent to Pawleys, **Litchfield**

Beach offers similar low-key enjoyment along with a world-class golf resort. **Murrells Inlet** is chiefly known for a single block of seafood restaurants on its eponymous waterway.

## SIGHTS
### ★ Brookgreen Gardens

One of the unique—and most unlikely—sights in the developed Grand Strand area is bucolic **Brookgreen Gardens** (1931 Brookgreen Dr., 843/235-6000, www.brookgreen.org, May-Mar. daily 9:30am-5pm, Apr. daily 9:30am-8pm, $15 adults, $7 ages 6-12, free under age 6), directly across U.S. 17 from Huntington Beach State Park. Once one of several massive contiguous plantations in the Pawleys Island area, the modern Brookgreen is a result of the charity and passion of Archer Milton Huntington and his wife, Anna. Quite the sculptor in her own right, Anna Huntington saw to it that Brookgreen's 9,000 acres would host by far the largest single collection of outdoor sculpture in the United States. To learn more, visit the on-site **Carroll A. Campbell Jr. Center for American Sculpture,** which offers seminars and workshops throughout the year. A highlight of the year is the **Night of a Thousand Candles** in early December. It's actually closer to 6,000 candles, lit all across the grounds to gorgeous seasonal effect.

On the other end of the grounds opposite the gardens is the **E. Craig Wall Jr. Lowcountry Nature Center,** which includes a small enclosed cypress swamp with a boardwalk, herons and egrets, and a delightful river otter exhibit.

To add an extra layer of enjoyment to your visit, you can explore this massive preserve much more deeply by taking one of several tours offered on Brookgreen's pontoon boat ($7 adults, $4 children, on top of regular admission); check the website for a schedule.

### ★ Huntington Beach State Park

Right across the street from Brookgreen is **Huntington Beach State Park** (16148 Ocean Hwy., 843/237-4440, www.southcarolinaparks.com, daily 6am-10pm, $5 adults, $3 ages 6-15, free under age 6), probably the best of South Carolina's state parks not built by the Civilian Conservation Corps. Once a part of the same vast parcel of land owned by Archer Huntington and his wife, Anna, the state has leased it from the trustees of their estate since the 1960s.

You can tour the "castle" on the beach,

salt marsh at Huntington Beach State Park

**Atalaya,** former home of the Huntingtons and now the yearly site of the Atalaya Arts and Crafts Festival. This evocative Moorish-style National Historic Landmark is open to the public for free guided tours (Memorial Day-Sept. daily noon-1pm, Oct. Sun.-Mon. noon-1pm, Tues.-Sat. noon-2pm). You can stroll three miles of beach, view birds and wildlife from boardwalks into the marsh, hike several nature trails, and visit the well-done **Environmental Education Center** (843/235-8755, Tues.-Sun. 10am-5pm), which features a saltwater touch tank and a baby alligator.

While Hurricane Matthew in 2016 felled many trees at the park, thankfully it avoided major long-term damage.

## Pawleys Island Historic District

Although many of the island's homes were leveled by Hurricane Hugo, the **Pawleys Island Historic District** (843/237-1698, www.townofpawleysisland.com), in the central portion of the island, still has a dozen contributing structures, almost all on Myrtle Avenue. Among them are the **Weston House** (506 Myrtle Ave.), or Pelican Inn, and the **Ward House** (520 Myrtle Ave.), or Liberty Lodge. As you view the structures, many with their own historical markers, note the architecture. Because these were intended to be lived in May-November, they resemble open and airy Caribbean homes, with extensive porches and plenty of windows.

## EVENTS

The highlight of the lower Grand Strand calendar is the annual **Atalaya Arts and Crafts Festival** (www.atalayafestival.com, $6 adults, free under age 16), which takes place on the grounds of Huntington Beach State Park each September. There's music, food, and about 100 vendors who show their art and wares within the exotic Atalaya home. Admission to the park is free during the festival.

Also in September is the **Pawleys Island Festival of Music and Art** (www.

pawleysmusic.com, prices vary), which happens outdoors, across U.S. 17 under the stars in Brookgreen Gardens, with a few performances at nearby Litchfield Plantation.

A main event in Murrells Inlet is the annual **Fourth of July Boat Parade** (843/651-0900, free), which celebrates American independence with a patriotically themed procession of all kinds of streamer- and flag-bedecked watercraft down the inlet. It begins at about 6pm and ends, of course, with a big fireworks display.

Another big deal in Murrells Inlet is the annual **Blessing of the Inlet** (843/651-5099, www.belinumc.org), always held the first Saturday in May and sponsored by a local Methodist church. Enjoy food vendors, goods baked by local women, and a great family atmosphere.

## SHOPPING

The shopping scene revolves around the famous Pawleys Island hammock, a beautiful and practical bit of local handiwork sold primarily at the **Hammock Shops Village** (10880 Ocean Hwy., 843/237-8448, Mon.-Sat. 10am-6pm, Sun. 1pm-5pm). To purchase a Pawleys Island hammock, go to **The Original Hammock Shop** (843/237-9122, www.the-hammockshop.com), housed in a century-old cottage. Next door is the affiliated **Hammock Shop General Store,** which, as the name implies, sells a variety of other goods such as beachwear, books, and a notable style of local fudge. The actual hammocks are handcrafted in the shed next door, the way they have been since 1889.

## SPORTS AND RECREATION
### Beaches

Public access to the beach that remains after 2016's Hurricane Matthew is very limited. The best way to enjoy the beach is to rent one of the many private beach homes for a week or so. Beach access with parking at Pawleys Island includes a fairly large lot at the south end of the island and parking areas off Atlantic

Avenue at Hazard, 1st, Pearce, 2nd, and 3rd Streets, and Shell Road.

## Kayaking and Canoeing

The Waccamaw River and associated inlets and creeks are peaceful and scenic places to kayak, with plenty of bird-watching opportunities to boot. For a two-hour guided tour of the area salt marsh, reserve a spot on the kayak trips sponsored by the **Environmental Education Center** (Huntington Beach State Park, 843/235-8755, office Tues.-Sun. 10am-5pm, $30 pp). Call for tour days and times. Or you can put in yourself at Oyster Landing, about one mile from the entrance to the state park.

## Golf

Home to some of the best links in the Carolinas, the lower part of the Grand Strand recently organized its courses under the umbrella moniker **Waccamaw Golf Trail** (www.waccamawgolftrail.com), chiefly for marketing purposes. No matter, the courses are still as superb as ever, if generally pricier than their counterparts up the coast.

The best course in the area, and one of the best in the country, is the **Caledonia Golf and Fish Club** (369 Caledonia Dr., 843/237-3675, www.fishclub.com, $195). While the course itself is almost ridiculously young—it opened in 1995—this masterpiece is built, as so many area courses are, on the grounds of a former rice plantation. The clubhouse, in fact, dates from before the Civil War. Packages (800/449-4005, www.myrtlebeachcondo-rentals.com) are available. Affiliated with Caledonia is the fine **True Blue Golf Club** (900 Blue Stem Dr., 843/235-0900, www.fishclub.com, $100), considered perhaps the most challenging single course on the Strand.

Another excellent Pawleys course is the **Litchfield Country Club** (U.S. 17 and Magnolia Dr., 843/237-3411, www.litchcc.com, $60), one of the Grand Strand's oldest. The facilities are self-consciously dated—this is a country club, after all—setting it apart from the flashier, newer courses sprouting like mushrooms farther up the Strand. It's a deceptive course that's short on yards but heavy on doglegs.

The Jack Nicklaus-designed **Pawleys Plantation Golf and Country Club** (70 Tanglewood Dr., 843/237-6100, www.pawleysplantation.com, $150) has set a tough example for the last 20 years. The front nine is a traditional layout, while the back nine melts into the marsh.

# FOOD
## Breakfast and Brunch

The high-end strip mall setting isn't the most romantic, but by broad consensus the best breakfast on the entire Strand is at **Applewood House of Pancakes** (14361 Ocean Hwy., 843/979-1022, daily 6am-2pm, $5-10) in Pawleys. Eggs Benedict, specialty omelets, crepes, waffles, and pancakes abound in this roomy, unpretentious dining room. Do it; you won't regret it.

## Seafood

Murrells Inlet has several good places clustered together along the marsh on U.S. 17. The best is ★ **Lee's Inlet Kitchen** (4460 Business U.S. 17, 843/651-2881, www.leesinletkitchen.com, Mar.-Nov. Mon.-Sat. 4:30pm-10pm, $20-40), the only joint still in the original family—in this case the Lee family, who started the place in the mid-1940s. The seafood is simply but delectably prepared (your choice of fried or broiled). They close down December-February.

Everything from the fried green tomatoes to the crab cakes is fresh, hot, and tasty at **Flo's Place Restaurant** (3797 Business U.S. 17, 843/651-7222, www.flosplace.com, daily 11am-10pm, $15-25). Flo is sadly no longer with us, but her place still eschews schlock for a humble, down-home feel. In recent years the menu has added more New Orleans-style Creole seafood dishes.

On the other end of the spectrum stylewise is **Divine Fish House** (3993 Business U.S. 17, 843/651-5800, www.divinefishhouse.com, daily 5pm-10pm, $20-33), which offers more adventurous high-end cuisine like the fine San Antonio salmon (smothered with pepper-jack cheese and bacon) and the Asian-flavored banana leaf mangrove grouper.

## ACCOMMODATIONS
### Under $150

Similarly named but not to be confused with Litchfield Plantation is the nearby **Litchfield Beach and Golf Resort** (14276 Ocean Hwy., 866/538-0187, www.litchfieldbeach.com, $100-170). In typical Grand Strand fashion, this property delivers a lot of service for a surprisingly low price and offers a wide range of lodging choices, from a basic room at the Seaside Inn on the low end to four-bedroom villas ($230) on the other. A regular free shuttle takes you to the beach. There are also lots of water activities right on the premises, including a "lazy river" tube course.

### $150-300

The premier B&B-style lodging on the entire Grand Strand is ★ **Litchfield Plantation** (Kings River Rd., 843/237-9121, www.litchfieldplantation.com, $230-275) on Pawleys Island, built, as you've probably come to expect by now, on an old plantation. There is a host of lodging choices, all of them absolutely splendid. The Plantation House has four sumptuous suites, all impeccably decorated. The humbly named Guest House—actually an old mansion—has six bedrooms, and the entire 2nd floor is an executive suite. Lastly, the newer outparcel villas contain an assortment of two- and three-bedroom suites.

## Vacation Rentals

Many who enjoy the Pawleys area do so using a vacation rental as a home base rather than a traditional hotel or B&B. **Pawleys Island Realty** (88 N. Causeway Rd., 800/937-7352, www.pawleysislandrealty.com) can hook you up.

## Camping

At **Huntington Beach State Park** (16148 Ocean Hwy., 843/237-4440, www.southcarolinaparks.com, daily 6am-10pm, $5 adults, $3 ages 6-15, free under age 6), the beach is beautiful, there are trails and an education center, and the bird-watching is known as some of the best on the East Coast. While there are 131 RV-suitable sites ($23-28), tenters should go to one of the six walk-in tent sites ($17-19).

## INFORMATION AND SERVICES

On Pawleys Island is the **Georgetown County Visitors Bureau** (95-A Centermarsh Ln., 843/235-6595, www.visitgeorgetowncountysc.com). The **Myrtle Beach Area Chamber of Commerce** (1200 N. Oak St., 843/626-7444, www.visitmybeach.com) and the **Waccamaw Community Hospital** (4070 U.S. 17 Bypass, 843/652-1000, www.georgetownhospitalsystem.org) are in Murrells Inlet. Pawleys Island is served by the **Pawleys Island Police Department** (321 Myrtle Ave., 843/237-3008, www.townofpawleysisland.com).

# Georgetown and Vicinity

Think of Georgetown as Beaufort's lesser-known cousin. Like Beaufort, it's an hour away from Charleston, it boasts a tidy historic downtown, and it was once a major center of Lowcountry plantation culture. However, Georgetown gets significantly less attention and less traffic. The fact that the entrance to town is dominated by the sprawling, ominous-looking Georgetown Steel mill on one side of the road and the massive International Paper plant on the other has something to do with it. Making matters worse was a disastrous fire in September 2013, which destroyed seven historic waterfront buildings.

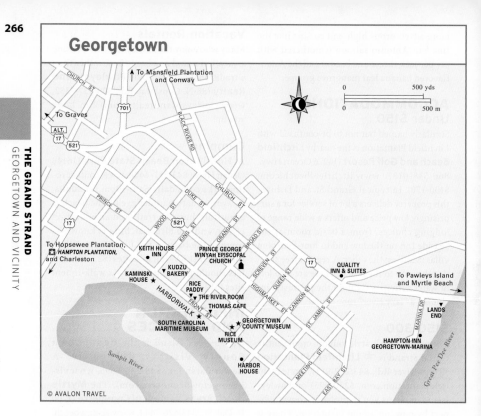

# Georgetown

To Mansfield Plantation and Conway
To Graves
ALT. 17
521
701
CHURCH ST
BLACK RIVER RD
PRINCE ST
DUKE ST
CHURCH ST
17
To Hopsewee Plantation,
HAMPTON PLANTATION,
and Charleston
KEITH HOUSE INN
KAMINSKI HOUSE
KUDZU BAKERY
WOOD ST
KING ST
521
ORANGE ST
PRINCE GEORGE WINYAH EPISCOPAL CHURCH
BROAD ST
SCREVEN ST
QUEEN ST
HIGHMARKET ST
CANNON ST
17
QUALITY INN & SUITES
To Pawleys Island and Myrtle Beach
HARBORWALK
RICE PADDY
FRONT ST
THE RIVER ROOM
THOMAS CAFE
SOUTH CAROLINA MARITIME MUSEUM
RICE MUSEUM
GEORGETOWN COUNTY MUSEUM
ST JAMES ST
MARINA DR
LANDS END
HAMPTON INN GEORGETOWN-MARINA
Sampit River
HARBOR HOUSE
MEETING ST
EAST BAY ST
Great Pee Dee River
0    500 yds
0    500 m
© AVALON TRAVEL

## HISTORY

The third-oldest city in South Carolina, after Charleston and Beaufort, Georgetown was founded in 1729 on a four- by eight-block grid, most of which still exists today, complete with original street names. The Revolutionary War hero Francis Marion, the "Swamp Fox," was born in nearby Berkeley County and conducted operations in and around the area throughout the war.

While Charleston-area plantations get most of the attention, the truth is that by 1840 about 150 rice plantations on the Sampit and Little Pee Dee Rivers were producing half of the entire national output of the staple crop. After the Civil War, the collapse of the slave-based economy (at its height, 90 percent of Georgetown's population were enslaved) meant the collapse of the rice economy as well.

In 1905, Bernard Baruch—native South

Carolinian, Wall Street mover and shaker, and adviser to presidents—came to town, purchasing Hobcaw Barony, a former plantation. It became his winter residence and hunting ground, and his legacy of conservation lives on there today in an education center on the site.

On the national level Georgetown is perhaps best known for being the hometown of comedian Chris Rock. Although he moved away long ago, many members of his family continue to live here.

## SIGHTS
### Kaminski House

The city of Georgetown owns and operates the historic **Kaminski House** (1003 Front St., 843/546-7706, www.kaminskimuseum.org, Mon.-Sat. 9am-5pm, $7 adults, $3 ages 6-12, free under age 6). Not to be confused with the

the Old Market building, part of the Rice Museum

1842 timepiece, hosts the bulk of the archival information on the impact of rice growing on the region's history and economy. The adjacent **Kaminski Hardware Building** includes a 17-minute video on the rice industry, a good Gullah-Geechee cultural exhibit, and a gift shop.

Most visitors to the Rice Museum take a one-hour **guided tour,** included in the price of admission. The highlight is the "Browns Ferry Vessel," the remains of a wrecked local colonial-era boat, circa 1730, which has its own listing in the National Register of Historic Places.

## South Carolina Maritime Museum

As the Palmetto State's second-largest port, Georgetown has more than its share of nautical history. Check it out at the burgeoning **South Carolina Maritime Museum** (729 Front St., 843/520-0111, www.scmaritime-museum.org, Mon.-Sat. 11am-5pm, free). The 2013 downtown fire caused a bit of damage to the building, but the museum is still humming. It sponsors the fun Wooden Boat Show each October on the waterfront.

## Georgetown County Museum

For a more complete look at various aspects of local history, check out the **Georgetown County Museum** (632 Prince St., 843/545-7020, Tues.-Fri. 10am-5pm, Sat. 10am-3pm, $4 adults, $2 ages 6-18, free under age 6). The highlight is a recently discovered letter written by Revolutionary War hero Francis Marion.

## Prince George Winyah Episcopal Church

It has seen better days—the British partially burned it during the Revolutionary War—but **Prince George Winyah Episcopal Church** (301 Broad St., 843/546-4358, www.pgwinyah.org, Mon.-Fri. 11:30am-4:30pm, services Sun. 8am, 9am, and 11am) is still a fine example of the Anglican tradition of the Lowcountry rice culture. Built in 1750 out

Kaminski Hardware Building down the block, this grand home was built in 1769 and was the executive residence of several city mayors. It is furnished with a particularly exquisite selection of 18th- and 19th-century antiques.

The grounds are beautiful as well, overlooking the Sampit River and lined with Spanish moss-covered oaks. Take the free 45-minute **guided tour** departing Monday-Saturday at 11am, 1pm, and 3pm; call ahead to confirm tour times.

## Rice Museum

The succinctly named **Rice Museum** (633 Front St., 843/546-7423, www.ricemuseum.org, Mon.-Sat. 10am-4:30pm, $7 adults, $3 ages 6-21, free under age 6) is a look back at the all-important staple crop and its massive effects on Georgetown, which at one point accounted for half of the country's rice production.

There are actually two parts of the museum. The **Old Market building,** often simply called "the Town Clock" because of its

# The Swamp Fox and the Coming of Guerrilla Warfare

Short, bowlegged, and moody, Francis Marion was as far away from the template of the war hero as his tactics were from the storybook exploits of military literature. The father of modern guerrilla warfare was born an unimpressively small and sickly baby, the youngest of seven, somewhere in Berkeley County, South Carolina, in 1732 to hardworking French Huguenot parents. Soon his family would move near Georgetown on the coast, and the teenage Marion became enamored with the sea. While his infatuation with maritime life lasted exactly one voyage—a whale rammed and sank his ship—a taste for adventure remained.

During the French and Indian War, Marion fought local Cherokee people, using irregular tactics that would resurface during the Revolutionary War. His first experience in the Revolutionary War was in more textbook engagements, such as the defenses of Fort Moultrie and Fort Sullivan and the siege of Savannah. But with the fall of Charleston in 1780, a vengeful Marion and his ragged band of volunteer fighters—who, unusual for the time, included African Americans—vanished into the bogs of the Pee Dee and took up a different way of warfare: ambush and retreat, harass and vanish. In a foreshadowing of the revolutionary movements of the 20th century, "Marion's Men" provisioned themselves with food and supplies from a sympathetic local populace, offering receipts for reimbursement after the war.

Astride small agile mounts called Marsh Tackies, descendants of horses originally left by the

of ballast stones (the parish itself dates from substantially earlier, 1721), the sanctuary features classic box pews, expert stained glass, and ornate woodwork on the inside. The bell tower dates from 1824.

## Hopsewee Plantation

Beautiful in an understated way, **Hopsewee Plantation** (494 Hopsewee Rd., 843/546-7891, www.hopsewee.com, Feb.-Nov. Tues.-Fri. 10am-4pm, Sat. 11am-4pm, Dec.-Jan. by appointment only, $17.50 adults, $10.50 ages 12-17, $7.50 ages 5-11, free under age 5), on the Santee River 12 miles south of Georgetown, was the birthplace of Thomas Lynch Jr., one of South Carolina's signers of the Declaration of Independence. Some key archaeological work is going on at the former slave village on this old indigo plantation; you can visit two of the original slave cabins on the tour. The 1740 main house is a masterpiece of colonial architecture, and all the more impressive because it's very nearly original, with the black cypress exterior largely intact. There's a fairly active calendar of events throughout the year, including sweetgrass basket-weaving classes.

## ★ Hampton Plantation

Tucked away three miles off U.S. 17 on the South Santee River is **Hampton Plantation State Historic Site** (1950 Rutledge Rd., 843/546-9361, www.southcarolinaparks.com, grounds daily 9am-5pm, free, house tours Sat.-Tues. 1pm, 2pm, and 3pm, $7.50 adults, $3.50 ages 6-15, free under age 6). This Georgian gem, one of the grandest of the antebellum Lowcountry homes, hosted George Washington in 1791. Supposedly the grand "Washington Oak" nearby provided shade for a picnic at which our first president dined. It was also the home of South Carolina poet laureate Archibald Rutledge, who sold it to the state in 1971. Because it's now a state-run project, admission fees are significantly lower than at most of the private plantation homes in the area. The imposing antebellum main house, built in 1735 and expanded in 1757, is magnificent both inside and out. If you want to skip the house tour, visiting the scenic grounds is free.

## St. James-Santee Episcopal Church

This redbrick church doesn't look that old,

Spanish, the Patriots rode where bigger British cavalry horses balked. Marion's nocturnal cunning and his superior intelligence network frustrated the British army and their Loyalist supporters to no end, leading to his nickname, "the Swamp Fox."

British colonel Banastre Tarleton, himself known as "the Butcher" for atrocities committed against civilians, was dispatched to neutralize Marion. The savage cat-and-mouse game between the two formed the basis for the storyline of Mel Gibson's *The Patriot* (Gibson's character was reportedly a composite of Marion and several other South Carolina irregulars). Filmed entirely in South Carolina—including at Middleton Plantation, Cypress Gardens, and Historic Brattonsville—*The Patriot* is far from an exact chronicle, but it does accurately portray the nature of the war in the Southern theater, in which quarter was rarely asked or given, and little distinction was made between combatant and civilian.

While certainly the most famous, the Swamp Fox was merely first among equals in a veritable menagerie of hit-and-run fighters. Thomas Sumter, a Virginian by birth, became known as "the Carolina Gamecock" for his ferocity on the battlefield; Andrew Pickens, "the Wizard Owl," and his militiamen played a key role in the Battle of Cowpens in the Upstate.

After the war, Marion served in elected office, married, and settled down at his Pine Bluff Plantation, now submerged under the lake that bears his name. He died in 1795 at the age of 63.

but the sanctuary of **St. James-Santee Episcopal Church** (Old Georgetown Rd., 843/887-4386), south of Georgetown near Hampton Plantation State Historic Site, dates from before the Revolutionary War. Known locally as "the Old Brick Church," this building dates from 1768, but the St. James-Santee parish it serves was actually the second in the colony after St. Michael's in Charleston. The parish was notable for incorporating large numbers of French Huguenots. The interior is nearly as Spartan as the exterior, featuring the rare sight of old-fashioned family box pews. While the brick was imported from Britain, the columns are made of cypress. Today, only one official service is held each year in the Old

Hampton Plantation

Brick Church, during Easter. You can have a look at the exterior and walk through the cemetery during daylight hours anytime, though. You get here by following the signs via a very long dirt road, not recommended in rainy weather unless you have a good four-wheel-drive vehicle.

## McClellanville

The almost unbearably cute little fishing village of McClellanville is nestled among the woods of Francis Marion National Forest and is known mostly for the annual **Lowcountry Shrimp Festival and Blessing of the Fleet** (http://lowcountryshrimpfestival.com), held on the waterfront in early May. This is the place to go for any kind of delectable fresh shrimp dish you might want, from fried shrimp to shrimp kebabs and shrimp tacos. The event culminates with the colorful and touching Blessing of the Fleet ceremony.

## Hobcaw Barony

Once a plantation, then a winter home for a Wall Street investor, **Hobcaw Barony** (22 Hobcaw Rd., 843/546-4623, www.hobcaw-barony.org, hours and prices vary) is now an environmental education center. Hobcaw entered its modern period when 11 former plantations were purchased en masse in 1905 by Wall Street investor Bernard Baruch, a South Carolina native who wanted a winter residence to escape the brutal Manhattan winters. Presidents and prime ministers came to hunt and relax on its nearly 18,000 acres. Fifty years later, Baruch died, and his progressive-minded daughter Belle took over, immediately wanting to open the grounds to universities for scientific research.

Still privately owned by the Belle W. Baruch Foundation, much of Hobcaw Barony is open only to researchers, but the **Hobcaw Barony Discovery Center** (843/546-4623, www.hob-cawbarony.org, Mon.-Fri. 9am-5pm, free) has various exhibits on local history and culture, including Native American artifacts and a modest but fun aquarium with a touch tank. To experience the rest of Hobcaw Barony, you

must take one of the various themed guided tours (call for days and times). The basic Hobcaw tour ($20) takes you on a three-hour van ride all around the grounds, including the main Hobcaw House, the historic stables, and the old slave quarters, with an emphasis on the natural as well as human history of the area. Other special tours include Birding on the Barony ($30), Christmas in the Quarters ($20), and a catch-and-release fly-fishing tour ($250) of local waters.

## Georgetown Lighthouse

While you can't access the state-owned **Georgetown Lighthouse,** you can indeed take a trip to the beach on North Island, where the lighthouse stands. The 1811 structure, repaired after heavy damage in the Civil War, is still an active beacon, now entirely automated.

North Island was part of lands bequeathed to the state by former Boston Red Sox owner Tom Yawkey; North Island is now part of a wildlife preserve bearing Yawkey's name. In 2001, the Georgetown Lighthouse, listed in the National Register of Historic Places, was added to the preserve.

## Tours and Cruises

One of the most sought-after tour tickets in the Georgetown area is for the annual **Plantation Home Tour** (843/545-8291). Sponsored by the Episcopal Church Women of Prince George Winyah Parish, this event, generally happening the first week in April, brings visitors onto many local private antebellum estates that are not open to the public at any other time. Each ticket is for either the Friday or Saturday tour, both of which feature a different set of homes. Tickets include tea at the Winyah Indigo Society Hall each afternoon.

For a standard downtown tour, get on one of the blue-and-white trams of **Swamp Fox Historic District Tours** (1001 Front St., 843/527-6469, $10 pp), which leave daily on the hour starting at 10am near the Harborwalk.

The best walking tour of Georgetown is

**Miss Nell's Tours** (843/546-3975, Tues. and Thurs. 10:30am and 2:30pm, other times by appointment, $7-24 depending on length of tour). Leaving from the Harborwalk Bookstore (723 Front St.), Miss Nell, who's been doing this for over 20 years, takes you on a delightful trek through Georgetown's charming downtown waterfront.

One of the more interesting local waterborne tours is on board the *Jolly Rover* and *Carolina Rover* (735 Front St., 843/546-8822, www.rovertours.com, Mon.-Sat., times and prices vary). The *Jolly Rover* is an honest-to-goodness tall ship that takes you on a two-hour tour of beautiful Winyah Bay and the Intracoastal Waterway, all with a crew in period dress. The *Carolina Rover* takes you on a three-hour ecotour to nearby North Island, site of the historic Georgetown Lighthouse. You can't tour the lighthouse itself, but you can get pretty darn close to it on this tour.

## ENTERTAINMENT AND EVENTS

The **Winyah Bay Heritage Festival** (632 Prince St., 843/833-9919, www.winyahbay.org, free) happens each January at various venues and benefits the local historical society. The focus is on wooden decoys and waterfowl paintings, similar to Charleston's well-known Southeast Wildlife Exposition.

Each October brings the delightful **Wooden Boat Show** (843/545-0015, www.woodenboatshow.com, free) to the waterfront, a celebration of, you guessed it, wooden boats. These aren't toys but the real thing—sleek, classic, and beautiful in the water. There are kids' activities, canoe-making demonstrations, a boat contest, and the highlight, a boatbuilding challenge involving two teams working to build a skiff in four hours.

## SPORTS AND RECREATION
### Kayaking and Canoeing

Kayakers and canoeists will find a lot to do in the Georgetown area, which includes the confluence of five rivers and the Atlantic Ocean.

A good trip for more advanced paddlers is to go out on **Winyah Bay** to undeveloped North Island. With advance permission from the state's Department of Natural Resources (803/734-3888), you can camp here. Any paddling in Winyah Bay is pleasant, whether you camp or not.

Another long trip is on the nine-mile blackwater **Wambaw Creek Wilderness Canoe Trail** in the Francis Marion National Forest, which takes you through some beautiful cypress and tupelo habitats. Launch sites are at the Wambaw Creek Boat Ramp and a bridge landing. Other good trips in the national forest are on the Santee River and Echaw Creek.

For rentals and guided tours, contact **Nature Adventures Outfitters** (800/673-0679), which runs daylong paddles (about $85 pp); and **Black River Outdoors Center and Expeditions** (21 Garden Ave., 843/546-4840, www.blackriveroutdoors.com), which runs a good half-day tour ($55 adults, $35 under age 13). For those who want to explore the intricate matrix of creeks and tidal canals that made up the Georgetown rice plantation empire, a guided tour is essential.

Occasional kayak ecotours leave from the **Hobcaw Barony Discovery Center** (22 Hobcaw Rd., 843/546-4623, www.hobcawbarony.org, Mon.-Fri. 9am-5pm, $50) under the auspices of the **North Inlet Winyah Bay National Estuarine Research Reserve** (843/546-6219, www.northinlet.sc.edu).

### Hiking

The **Francis Marion National Forest** (www.fs.fed.us) hosts a number of great hiking opportunities, chief among them the Swamp Fox passage of the **Palmetto Trail** (www.palmettoconservation.org). This 47-mile route winds through longleaf pine forests, cypress swamps, bottomland hardwood swamps, and various bogs, much of the way along an old logging railbed. The main entrance to the trail is near Steed Creek Road off U.S. 17; the entrance is clearly marked on the west side of the highway.

Another way to access the Swamp

Fox passage is at **Buck Hall Recreation Area** (843/887-3257) on the Intracoastal Waterway. This actually marks the trailhead of the Awendaw Connector of that part of the Palmetto Trail, a more maritime environment. Another trailhead from which to explore Francis Marion hiking trails is farther down U.S. 17 at the **Sewee Visitor Center** (5821 U.S. 17, 843/928-3368, www.fws.gov/seweecenter, Tues.-Sat. 9am-5pm).

## Golf

The closest really good links to Georgetown are the courses of the **Waccamaw Golf Trail** (www.waccamawgolftrail.com), a short drive north on U.S. 17. The best public course close to Georgetown is the **Wedgefield Plantation Golf Club** (129 Clubhouse Ln., 843/546-8587, www.wedgefield.com, $69), on the grounds of an old rice plantation on the Black River about four miles west of town.

# FOOD

Don't be fooled by Georgetown's small size—there's often a wait for tables at the better restaurants.

## Breakfast and Brunch

The *Southern Living*-recommended **Thomas Cafe** (703 Front St., 843/546-7776, www.thomascafe.net, Mon.-Fri. 7am-2pm, Sat. 7am-1pm, $5-9) offers awesome omelets and pancakes in addition to more Lowcountry-flavored lunch dishes like crab cake sandwiches and fried green tomatoes.

## Classic Southern

Georgetown's best-known fine-dining establishment is **The Rice Paddy** (732 Front St., 843/546-2021, www.ricepaddyrestaurant.com, lunch Mon.-Sat. 11:30am-2pm, dinner Mon.-Sat. 6pm-10pm, $20-30), with the name implying not an Asian menu but rather a nod to the town's Lowcountry culture. The seafood is strong, but they do a mean veal scaloppine and rack of lamb as well. Reservations are strongly recommended.

## Coffee, Tea, and Sweets

A perennial favorite is ★ **Kudzu Bakery** (120 King St., 843/546-1847, Mon.-Fri. 9am-5:30pm, Sat. 9am-2pm), renowned for its fresh-baked goodies such as delectable breakfast muffins, velvety chocolate cakes, and seasonal pies with fresh ingredients like strawberries, peaches, and pecans.

## Seafood

Find the best shrimp and grits in town at **The River Room** (801 Front St., 843/527-4110, www.riverroomgeorgetown.com, Mon.-Sat. 11:30am-2:30pm and 5pm-10pm, $15-25), which combines a gourmet attitude in the kitchen with a casual attitude on the floor. However, dishes like the herb-encrusted grouper or the signature crab cakes taste like fine dining all the way. Reservations are not accepted, and dress is casual. Literally right on the waterfront, the dining room in this former hardware store extends 50 feet over the Sampit River, adjacent to a public dock where many diners arrive by boat. There's even a large aquarium inside to complete the atmosphere.

# ACCOMMODATIONS
## Under $150

Close to the historic district is **Quality Inn & Suites** (210 Church St., 843/546-5656, www.qualityinn.com, $90-140), which has an outdoor pool and an included breakfast. On the north side of town on U.S. 17 you'll find the **Hampton Inn Georgetown-Marina** (420 Marina Dr., 843/545-5000, www.hamptoninn.com, $140-170), which also offers a pool and complimentary breakfast.

## $150-300

By far the most impressive lodging near Georgetown—and indeed among the most impressive in the Southeast—is ★ **Mansfield Plantation** (1776 Mansfield Rd., 843/546-6961, www.mansfieldplantation.com, $150-200), a bona fide antebellum estate dating from a 1718 king's grant. It is so evocative and so authentic that Mel Gibson shot part of his film *The Patriot* here, and renovation was recently completed on a historic slave chapel and cabin. You can stay in one of nine guest rooms situated in three guesthouses on the grounds, each within easy walking distance of the public areas in the main house, which include a 16-seat dining room.

With the closing of two longtime favorite B&Bs, the Dupre House and the Harbour House Inn, it's left to another B&B, the **Keith House Inn** (1012 Front St., 843/485-4324, www.thekeithhouseinn.com, $149-169), to carry on the tradition. Its four 2nd-floor suites, with balconies, each have a different theme. The public areas are wonderfully and whimsically furnished.

## INFORMATION AND SERVICES

In the historic waterfront area, you'll find the **Georgetown County Chamber of Commerce and Visitor Center** (531 Front St., 843/546-8436, www.georgetownchamber. com). **Georgetown Memorial Hospital** (606 Black River Rd., 843/527-7000, www. georgetownhospitalsystem.org) is the main medical center in the area. If you need non-emergency law-enforcement help, call the **Georgetown Police** (2222 Highmarket St., 843/545-4300, www.cityofgeorgetownsc. com).

## GETTING THERE AND AROUND

Georgetown is at the extreme southern tip of the Grand Strand, accessible by U.S. 17 from the east and south and U.S. 521 (called Highmarket St. in town) from the west. Very centrally located for a tour of the coast, it's about an hour north of Charleston and slightly less than an hour from Myrtle Beach.

Although there's no public transportation in Georgetown, its small size makes touring fairly simple. Metered parking is available downtown.

# Charleston

# Everyone who spends time in Charleston comes away with a story about the locals' courtesy and hospitality.

Mine came while walking through the French Quarter and admiring a handsome old single house on Church Street, one of the few that survived the fire of 1775. To my surprise, the woman chatting with a friend nearby turned out to be the homeowner. Noticing my interest, she invited me, a total stranger, inside to check out the progress of her renovation. This is a city that takes civic harmony seriously—it even boasts the country's only "Livability Court," a legally binding board that meets regularly to enforce local quality-of-life ordinances.

In 2015, however, Charleston gained national prominence when a white gunman murdered nine worshippers in the historically black Emanuel AME Church on Calhoun Street downtown. The nation was transfixed not only by the horror of the incident, but also by Charleston's community response, which was wholly in keeping with its character: hopeful, forgiving, resilient, and compassionate. Charleston's nickname, the "Holy City," derives from the skyline's abundance of church steeples rather than any excess of piety among its citizens, but its response to

the Mother Emanuel tragedy seemed to lend a new meaning.

While many visitors come to see the historical south of Charleston—finding it and then some, of course—they leave impressed by the diversity of Charlestonian life. It's a surprisingly cosmopolitan mix of students, professionals, and longtime inhabitants—who discuss the finer points of Civil War history as if it were last year, party on Saturday night like there's no tomorrow, and go to church on Sunday morning dressed in their finest.

This city, so known for its history, is also quietly booming as one of the nation's key centers of tech and digital development. Highly educated and motivated millennials from all over the country are flocking to Charleston for its blend of start-up friendliness, great nightlife, eco-friendly sensibilities, and vibrant arts and cultural scene.

## HISTORY

Unlike the many English colonies in America that were based on freedom from religious persecution, Carolina was strictly a commercial venture from the beginning. The tenure

---

**Previous:** the view down Broad Street from the Old Exchange; Charles Towne Landing. **Above:** the veranda at Husk.

Look for ★ to find recommended sights, activities, dining, and lodging.

# Highlights

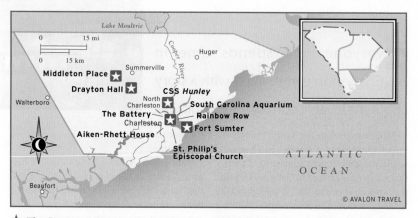

© AVALON TRAVEL

★ **The Battery:** Tranquil surroundings combine with beautiful views of Charleston Harbor, historical points key to the Civil War, and amazing mansions (page 281).

★ **Rainbow Row:** Painted in warm pastels, these old merchant homes near the cobblestoned waterfront take you on a journey to Charleston's antebellum heyday (page 283).

★ **South Carolina Aquarium:** Experience the state's surprising breadth of habitat (page 287).

★ **Fort Sumter:** Take the ferry to this historic place where the Civil War began, with gorgeous views along the way (page 287).

★ **St. Philip's Episcopal Church:** A sublimely beautiful sanctuary and two historic graveyards await you in the heart of the evocative French Quarter (page 289).

★ **Aiken-Rhett House:** There are certainly more ostentatious house museums in Charleston, but none that provide such a virtually intact glimpse into real antebellum life (page 296).

★ **Drayton Hall:** Don't miss Charleston's oldest surviving plantation home and one of the country's best examples of professional historic preservation (page 298).

★ **Middleton Place:** Wander around one of the world's most beautifully landscaped gardens—and the first in North America (page 299).

★ **CSS *Hunley*:** The first submarine to sink a ship in battle is a moving example of bravery and sacrifice (page 301).

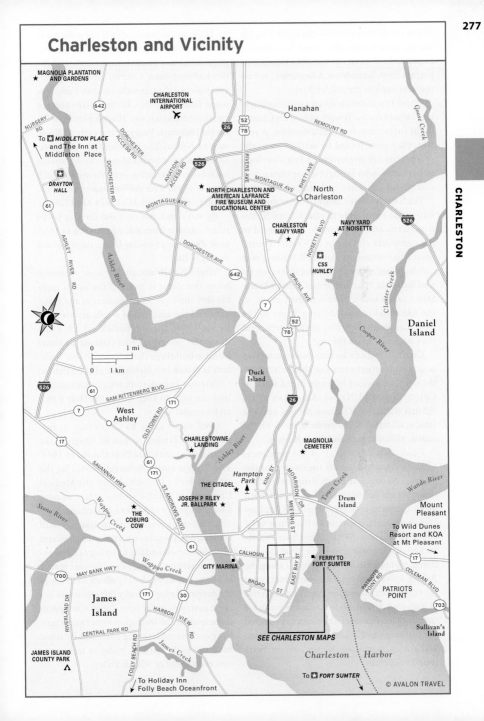

# Charleston and Vicinity

MAGNOLIA PLANTATION
AND GARDENS

CHARLESTON
INTERNATIONAL
AIRPORT

Hanahan

642

NURSERY
RD

To ⭐ MIDDLETON PLACE
and The Inn at
Middleton Place

DORCHESTER
ACCESS RD

AVIATION
ACCESS RD

DORCHESTER
RD

26

52
78

RIVERS AVE

REMOUNT RD

DRAYTON
HALL

61

MONTAGUE AVE

MONTAGUE AVE

RHETT AVE

526

NORTH CHARLESTON AND
AMERICAN LAFRANCE
FIRE MUSEUM AND
EDUCATIONAL CENTER

North
Charleston

526

Goose Creek

ASHLEY RIVER RD

Ashley River

DORCHESTER AVE

642

CHARLESTON
NAVY YARD

NAVY YARD
AT NOISETTE

NOISETTE BLVD

⭐ CSS
HUNLEY

SPRUILL AVE

Clouter Creek

Cooper River

Daniel
Island

7

52
78

0      1 mi

0    1 km

Duck
Island

26

526

61

SAM RITTENBERG BLVD

OLD TOWN RD

171

7

West
Ashley

171

CHARLES TOWNE
LANDING

MAGNOLIA
CEMETERY

Ashley River

Wando River

17

SAVANNAH HWY

61

171

ST ANDREWS BLVD

Hampton
Park

THE CITADEL

KING ST

MORRISON DR

Town Creek

Drum
Island

Mount
Pleasant

Stono River

Wappoo Creek

⭐ THE
COBURG
COW

JOSEPH P. RILEY
JR. BALLPARK ⭐

MEETING ST

To Wild Dunes
Resort and KOA
at Mt Pleasant

17

61

CALHOUN
ST

EAST BAY ST

FERRY TO
FORT SUMTER

PATRIOTS
POINT RD

COLEMAN BLVD

700

MAY BANK HWY

Wappoo Creek

CITY MARINA

BROAD
ST

PATRIOTS
POINT

703

James
Island

171

30

HARBOR VIEW RD

RIVERLAND DR

CENTRAL PARK RD

James Creek

SEE CHARLESTON MAPS

Sullivan's
Island

JAMES ISLAND
COUNTY PARK

FOLLY BEACH RD

To Holiday Inn
Folly Beach Oceanfront

Charleston   Harbor

To ⭐ FORT SUMTER

© AVALON TRAVEL

of the Lords Proprietors—the eight English aristocrats who literally owned the colony—began in 1670 when the *Carolina* finished its journey from Barbados at Albemarle Creek on the west bank of the Ashley River.

Those first colonists set up a small fortification called Charles Towne, named for Charles II, the first monarch of the Restoration. A year later they were joined by settlers from the prosperous but overcrowded British colony of Barbados, who brought a Caribbean sensibility that exists in Charleston to this day.

Finding the first Charles Towne not very fertile and vulnerable to attack from Native Americans and the Spanish, they moved to the peninsula and down to "Oyster Point," what Charlestonians now call White Point Gardens. Just above Oyster Point they set up a walled town, bounded by modern-day Water Street to the south (then a marshy creek, as the name indicates), Meeting Street to the west, Cumberland Street to the north, and the Cooper River on the east.

Charles Towne came into its own after two nearly concurrent events in the early 1700s: the decisive victory of a combined force of Carolinians and Native American allies against the fierce Yamasee people, and the final eradication of the pirate threat with the deaths of Blackbeard and Stede Bonnet.

Flush with a new spirit of independence, Charles Towne threw off the control of the anemic, disengaged Lords Proprietors, tore down the old defensive walls, and was reborn as an outward-looking, expansive, and increasingly cosmopolitan city that came to be called Charleston. With safety from hostile incursions came the time of the great rice and indigo plantations. Springing up all along the Ashley River soon after the introduction of the crops, they turned the labor and expertise of imported Africans into enormous profit for their owners. However, the planters preferred the pleasures and sea breezes of Charleston, and gradually summer homes became year-round residences.

As the storm clouds of civil war gathered in the early 1800s, the majority of Charleston's population was of African descent, and the city had long been America's main importation point for the transatlantic slave trade. The worst fears of white Charlestonians seemed confirmed during the alleged plot by slave leader Denmark Vesey in the early 1820s to start a rebellion. The Lowcountry's reliance on slave labor put it front and center in the coming national confrontation over abolition, which came to a head with the bombardment of Fort Sumter in Charleston Harbor in April 1861.

By war's end, not only did the city lay in ruins—mostly from a disastrous fire in 1861, as well as from a 545-day Union siege—so did its way of life.

World War II brought the same economic boom that came to much of the South, most notably through an expansion of the Navy Yard and the addition of a military air base. By the 1950s, the automobile suburb and a thirst for "progress" had claimed so many historic buildings that the inevitable backlash inspired the formation of the Historic Charleston Foundation, which continues to lead the fight to keep intact the Holy City's architectural legacy.

Civil rights came to Charleston in earnest with a landmark suit to integrate the Charleston Municipal Golf Course in 1960. The biggest battle, however, would be the 100-day strike in 1969 against the Medical University of South Carolina—then, as now, a large employer of African Americans.

Charleston's next great renaissance—still ongoing today—came with the redevelopment of its downtown and the fostering of the tourism industry under the nearly 40-year tenure of Mayor Joe Riley, during which so much of the current visitor-friendly infrastructure became part of daily life here. Today, Charleston is completing the transition away from a military and manufacturing base, and by some measures is the nation's leader in tech startups, even ahead of Silicon Valley.

# PLANNING YOUR TIME

Even if you're just going to confine yourself to the peninsula, plan on spending at least **two nights** in Charleston. You'll want half a day for shopping on King Street and a full day for seeing various attractions and museums. Keep in mind that one of Charleston's key sights, Fort Sumter, takes almost half a day to see once you factor in ticketing and boarding time for the ferry out to the fort and back; plan accordingly.

If you have a car, there are several great places to visit off the peninsula, especially the three plantations along the Ashley—Drayton Hall, Magnolia Plantation, and Middleton Place—and Charles Towne Landing. They are all no more than 30 minutes from downtown, and because they're roughly adjacent, you can visit all of them in a single day if you get an early start. The sites and excellent down-home restaurants on Johns Island are about 45 minutes out of downtown.

# ORIENTATION

Charleston occupies a peninsula bordered by the Ashley River to the west and the Cooper River to the east, which "come together to form the Atlantic Ocean," according to the haughty phrase once taught to generations of Charleston schoolchildren. Although the lower tip of the peninsula actually points closer to southeast, that direction is regarded locally as due south, and anything toward the top of the peninsula is considered due north.

The peninsula is ringed by islands, many of which have become heavily populated suburbs. Clockwise from the top of the peninsula, they are: Daniel Island, Mount Pleasant, Isle of Palms, Sullivan's Island, Morris Island, Folly Island, and James Island. The resort island of Kiawah and the less-developed Edisto Island are farther south down the coast.

Charleston is made up of many small neighborhoods, many of them quite old. The boundaries are confusing, so your best bet is to simply look at the street signs (signage in general is excellent in Charleston). If you're in a historic neighborhood, such as the French Quarter or Ansonborough, a smaller sign above the street name will indicate that.

Other key terms you'll hear are "the Crosstown," the portion of U.S. 17 that goes across the peninsula; "Savannah Highway," the portion of U.S. 17 that traverses "West Ashley," which is the suburb across the Ashley River; "East Cooper," the area across the Cooper River that includes Mount Pleasant, Isle of Palms, and Daniel and Sullivan's Islands; and "the Neck," up where the peninsula narrows. These are the terms that locals use, and hence what you'll see in this guide.

# Sights

TOP EXPERIENCE

## TOURS

Because of the city's small, fairly centralized layout, the best way to experience Charleston is on foot—either yours or via hooves of an equine nature. For more tour information in Charleston, visit the **Charleston Visitor Reception and Transportation Center** (375 Meeting St., 800/774-0006, www.charlestoncvb.com, Mon.-Fri. 8:30am-5pm), where they have entire walls of brochures for all the latest tours and an on-site staff of local tourism experts.

### Walking Tours

Since 1996, **Ed Grimball's Walking Tours** (Waterfront Park, Concord St., 843/813-4447, www.edgrimballtours.com, $22 adults, $8 children) has run twice-weekly historical tours that take you through the heart of Charleston, courtesy of the knowledgeable and sprightly Ed himself, a native Charlestonian. All of Ed's walks start from the big Pineapple Fountain in Waterfront Park, and reservations are a must.

**Original Charleston Walks** (Market St. and State St., 843/408-0010, www.charlestonwalks.com, times and prices vary) has received much national TV exposure. Its two-hour tours leave from the corner of Market and State Streets and cover a full slate, including a popular adults-only pub crawl.

**Charleston Strolls** (Mills House Hotel, 115 Meeting St., 843/722-8687, www.charlestonstrolls.com, daily 10am and 2pm, $25 adults, $10 children) is another popular tour good for a historical overview and tidbits. The two-hour tours leave twice daily from the Mills House Hotel.

Art lovers should check out the offerings from **Charleston Art Tours** (53 Broad St., 843/860-3327, www.charlestonarttours.com, $48-55). Sandra and Teri provide a selection of visual art-themed packages, including a French Quarter Tour and a Charleston Renaissance Tour.

Ghost tours are very popular in Charleston. **Bulldog Tours** (18 Anson St., 843/722-8687, www.bulldogtours.com, $22 adults, $10 children) has exclusive access to the Old City Jail, which features prominently in most of its tours. The most popular tour, the Haunted Jail Tour, leaves daily at 7pm, 8pm, 9pm, and 10pm; meet at the jail at 21 Magazine Street. The Ghosts and Dungeons Tour runs March-November Tuesday-Saturday at 7pm and 9pm and leaves from 18 Anson Street.

## Carriage Tours

There's not a lot of difference in service or price among the carriage companies, and that's chiefly by design. The city divides the tours into three routes, or "zones." Which zone your driver explores is determined by lottery at the embarkation point—you don't get to decide the zone and neither does your driver. Typically, rides take 1-1.5 hours and hover around $25 per adult, about half that per child.

Tours sometimes book up early, so call ahead. The oldest and in my opinion best service in town is **Palmetto Carriage Works** (40 N. Market St., 843/723-8145, www.palmettocarriage.com), which offers free parking at its "red barn" base near City Market. Another popular tour is **Old South Carriage Company** (14 Anson St., 843/723-9712, www.oldsouthcarriage.com) with its Confederate-clad drivers. **Carolina Polo & Carriage Company** (16 Hayne St., 843/577-6767, www.cpcc.com) leaves from several spots, including the Doubletree Hotel and the company's Hayne Street stables.

## Motorized Tours

**Adventure Sightseeing** (Charleston Visitor Reception and Transportation Center, 375 Meeting St., 843/762-0088, www.adventuresightseeing.com, daily various times, $20 adults, $11 children) offers several comfortable 1.5- to 2-hour rides, including the only motorized tour to the Citadel area, leaving the visitors center at various times throughout the day.

You can make a day of it with **Charleston's Finest Historic Tours** (Charleston Visitor Reception and Transportation Center, 375 Meeting St., 843/577-3311, www.historictoursofcharleston.com, daily 10:30am, $21 adults, $10.50 children), which has a basic two-hour city tour each day at 10:30am and offers some much longer tours to outlying plantations. The company offers free downtown pickup from most lodgings.

The old faithful **Gray Line of Charleston** (Charleston Visitor Reception and Transportation Center, 375 Meeting St., 843/722-4444, www.graylineofcharleston.com, Mar.-Nov. daily 9:30am-3pm, Dec.-Feb daily 9:30am-2pm, $21-34 adults, $12-19 children) offers a 90-minute Historic Charleston Tour. Tours depart from the visitors center every 30 minutes. Hotel pickup is available by reservation. The last tour leaves at 2pm during the off-season.

## African American History Tours

Al Miller's **Sites & Insights Tours**

(Charleston Visitor Reception and Transportation Center, 375 Meeting St., 843/552-9995, www.sitesandinsightstours.com, tour times vary, $13-18) has several packages, including a Black History and Porgy & Bess Tour as well as a good combo city and island tour, all departing from the visitors center.

Alphonso Brown's **Gullah Tours** (African American Art Gallery, 43 John St., 843/763-7551, www.gullahtours.com, Mon.-Fri. 11am and 1pm, Sat. 11am, 1pm, and 3pm, $18) features stories told in the Gullah dialect. Tours run Monday-Saturday and leave from the African American Art Gallery, near the visitors center.

# SOUTH OF BROAD

Wander among these narrow streets and marvel at the lovingly restored old homes, but keep in mind that almost everything down here is in private hands. Don't wander into a garden or take photos inside a window unless you're invited to do so.

The Battery

## ★ The Battery

For many, **The Battery** (S. Battery St. and Murray Blvd., 843/724-7321, daily 24 hours, free) is the single most iconic Charleston spot, drenched in history and boasting dramatic views. South is the Cooper River, with views of Fort Sumter, Castle Pinckney, and Sullivan's Island; north is the old carrier *Yorktown* moored at Mount Pleasant; and landward is the adjoining, peaceful **White Point Gardens,** the sumptuous mansions of the Battery.

Once the bustling (and sometimes seedy) heart of Charleston's maritime activity, the Battery was where "the gentleman pirate" Stede Bonnet and 21 of his men were hanged in 1718. The area got its name for hosting cannons during the War of 1812, with the current distinctive seawall structure built in the 1850s.

Contrary to popular belief, no guns fired from here on Fort Sumter, as they would have been out of range. However, many inoperable cannons, mortars, and piles of shot still reside here, much to the delight of kids. This is where Charlestonians gathered in a giddy, party-like atmosphere to watch the shelling of Fort Sumter in 1861, blissfully ignorant of the horrors to come.

### Edmondston-Alston House

The most noteworthy attraction on the Battery is the 1825 **Edmondston-Alston House** (21 E. Battery St., 843/722-7171, www.middletonplace.org, Sun.-Mon. 1pm-4:30pm, Tues.-Sat. 10am-4:30pm, $12 adults, $8 students), the only Battery home open to the public for tours. This is one of the most unique and well-preserved historic homes in the United States, thanks to the ongoing efforts of the Alston family, who acquired the house from shipping merchant Charles Edmondston after the Panic of 1837 and still lives on the 3rd floor (tours only visit the first two stories).

Over 90 percent of the home's furnishings are original items from the Alston era. Originally built in the Federal style, second owner Charles Alston added several Greek

# Charleston Sights

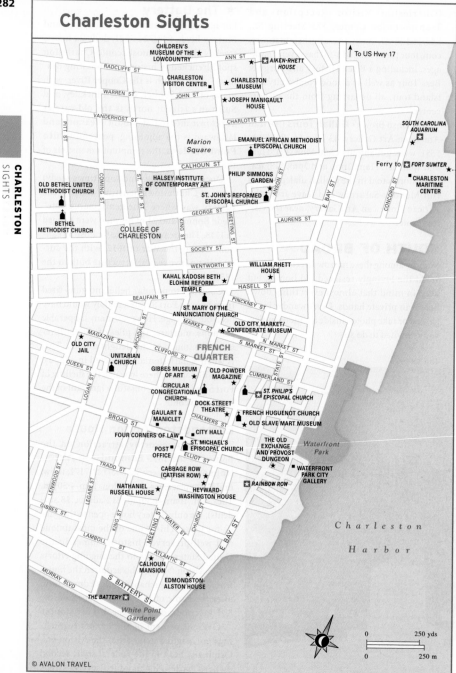

To US Hwy 17

RADCLIFFE ST

ANN ST

CHILDREN'S MUSEUM OF THE ★ LOWCOUNTRY

★ AIKEN-RHETT HOUSE

WARREN ST

JOHN ST

CHARLESTON VISITOR CENTER ■

★ CHARLESTON MUSEUM

VANDERHORST ST

★ JOSEPH MANIGAULT HOUSE

CHARLOTTE ST

*Marion Square*

SOUTH CAROLINA AQUARIUM ✚

EMANUEL AFRICAN METHODIST ✚ EPISCOPAL CHURCH

Ferry to ✚ FORT SUMTER ★

CALHOUN ST

■ CHARLESTON MARITIME CENTER

COMING ST

PITT ST

ST PHILIP ST

KING ST

MEETING ST

E BAY ST

CONCORD ST

OLD BETHEL UNITED METHODIST CHURCH ✚

HALSEY INSTITUTE ★ OF CONTEMPORARY ART

PHILIP SIMMONS ★ GARDEN

ANSON ST

✚ BETHEL METHODIST CHURCH

ST. JOHN'S REFORMED ✚ EPISCOPAL CHURCH

COLLEGE OF CHARLESTON

GEORGE ST

LAURENS ST

SOCIETY ST

WENTWORTH ST

WILLIAM RHETT ★ HOUSE

KAHAL KADOSH BETH ELOHIM REFORM ★ TEMPLE

HASELL ST

BEAUFAIN ST

PINCKNEY ST

ST. MARY OF THE ✚ ANNUNCIATION CHURCH

MARKET ST

MAGAZINE ST

ARCHDALE ST

OLD CITY MARKET/ ★ CONFEDERATE MUSEUM

★ OLD CITY JAIL

FRENCH QUARTER

S MARKET ST

N MARKET ST

STATE ST

UNITARIAN ✚ CHURCH

CLIFFORD ST

QUEEN ST

LOGAN ST

GIBBES MUSEUM OF ART ★

OLD POWDER ★ MAGAZINE

CUMBERLAND ST

CIRCULAR CONGREGATIONAL ✚ CHURCH

✚ ST. PHILIP'S EPISCOPAL CHURCH

DOCK STREET ★ THEATRE

GAULART & MANICLET ★

CHALMERS ST

FRENCH HUGUENOT CHURCH ✚

★ OLD SLAVE MART MUSEUM

BROAD ST

FOUR CORNERS OF LAW ■

★ CITY HALL

THE OLD EXCHANGE AND PROVOST DUNGEON ★

*Waterfront Park*

POST OFFICE ■

✚ ST. MICHAEL'S EPISCOPAL CHURCH

ELLIOT ST

TRADD ST

CABBAGE ROW (CATFISH ROW) ★

■ WATERFRONT PARK CITY GALLERY

LENWOOD ST

LEGARE ST

NATHANIEL RUSSELL HOUSE ★

HEYWARD- WASHINGTON HOUSE ★

✚ RAINBOW ROW

GIBBES ST

KING ST

MEETING ST

WATER ST

CHURCH ST

E BAY ST

LAMBOLL ST

ATLANTIC ST

*Charleston*

*Harbor*

MURRAY BLVD

CALHOUN MANSION ★

S BATTERY ST

EDMONDSTON- ALSTON HOUSE ★

THE BATTERY ✚

*White Point Gardens*

0      250 yds

0      250 m

© AVALON TRAVEL

Revival elements, notably the parapet, balcony, and piazza, from which General P. G. T. Beauregard watched the attack on Fort Sumter. Today, the house is owned and administered by the Middleton Place Foundation, best known for its stewardship of Middleton Place along the Ashley River.

## ★ Rainbow Row

At 79-107 East Bay Street, between Tradd and Elliot Streets, is one of the most photographed sights in the United States: colorful **Rainbow Row,** nine pastel-colored mansions facing the Cooper River. The bright, historically accurate colors are one of the vestiges of Charleston's Caribbean heritage, a legacy of the English settlers from the colony of Barbados who were among the city's first citizens.

The homes are unusually old for this fire-, hurricane-, and earthquake-ravaged city, with most dating from 1730 to 1750. These houses were originally right on the Cooper River, their lower stories serving as storefronts on the wharf. The street was created later on top of landfill, or "made land" as it's called locally.

Besides its grace and beauty, Rainbow Row is of vital importance to American historic preservation. These were the first Charleston homes to be renovated and brought back from early 20th-century seediness. The restoration projects on Rainbow Row directly inspired the creation of the Preservation Society of Charleston, the first such group in the United States.

## Nathaniel Russell House

Considered one of Charleston's grandest homes despite being built by an outsider from Rhode Island, the **Nathaniel Russell House** (51 Meeting St., 843/724-8481, www. historiccharleston.org, Mon.-Sat. 10am-5pm, Sun. 2pm-5pm, last tour begins 4:30pm, $12 adults, $5 children) is now a National Historic Landmark and one of the country's best examples of neoclassicism. Built in 1808 by Nathaniel Russell, aka "King of the Yankees," the home is furnished as accurately as possible to represent not only the lifestyle of the Russell family, but also the 18 African American servants who shared the premises.

When you visit, keep in mind that you're in the epicenter of not only Charleston's historic preservation movement but perhaps the nation's as well. In 1955 the Nathaniel Russell House was the first major project of the Historic Charleston Foundation, which raised $65,000 to purchase it. For an extra $6, you can gain admission to the Aiken-Rhett

Rainbow Row

# Know Your Charleston Houses

Charleston's homes boast not only a long pedigree, but an interesting and unique one as well. Here are the basics of local architecture.

- **Single House:** Thus named for its single-room width. With full-length piazzas, or long verandas, on the south side to take advantage of breezes, the single house is perhaps the nation's first sustainable house design. The house is lengthwise on the lot, with the entrance on the side. This means the "backyard" is actually the side yard. Church Street has great examples, including 90, 92, and 94 Church Street, and the oldest single house in town, the 1730 Robert Brewton House (71 Church St.).

- **Double House:** This layout is two rooms wide with a central hallway and a porched facade facing the street. Double houses often had separate carriage houses. The Aiken-Rhett and Heyward-Washington Houses are good examples.

- **Charleston Green:** This uniquely Charlestonian color—extremely dark green that looks pitch black in low light—has its roots in the aftermath of the Civil War. The government distributed surplus black paint to contribute to the reconstruction of the ravaged peninsula, but Charlestonians were too proud to use it as-is. So they added a tiny bit of yellow, producing Charleston green.

- **Earthquake Bolt:** Due to structural damage after the 1886 earthquake, many buildings were retrofitted with one or more wall-to-wall iron rods to keep them stable. The rod was capped at both ends by a "gib plate," often disguised with a decorative element such as a lion's head, an S or X shape, or some other design. Notable examples are at 235 Meeting Street, 198 East Bay Street, 407 King Street, and 51 East Battery (a rare star design); 190 East Bay Street is unusual for having both an X and an S plate on the same building.

- **Joggling Board:** This long (10-15 ft.) flexible plank of cypress, palm, or pine with a handle at each end served various recreational purposes. Babies were bounced to sleep, small children used it as a trampoline, and it was also a method of courtship. A couple would start out at opposite ends and bounce until they met in the middle.

- **Carolopolis Award:** The Preservation Society of Charleston hands out these badges, to be mounted near the doorway, to local homeowners who have renovated historic properties downtown. On the award is "Carolopolis," the Latinized name of the city; "Condita AD 1670," the Latin word for "founding" with the date of Charleston's inception; and the date the award was given.

- **Ironwork:** Wrought iron was a widely used ornament before the mid-1800s. Charleston's best-known blacksmith, Philip Simmons, worked in wrought iron. His masterpieces are visible most notably at the Philip Simmons Garden (91 Anson St.), a gate for the visitors center (375 Meeting St.), and the Philip Simmons Children's Garden at Josiah Smith Tennent House (Blake St. and E. Bay St.). Chevaux-de-frise are iron bars on top of a wall that project menacing spikes. They became popular after the Denmark Vesey slave revolt conspiracy of 1822. The best example is at the Miles Brewton House (27 King St.).

House farther uptown, also administered by the Historic Charleston Foundation.

## Calhoun Mansion

The single largest of Charleston's surviving grand homes, the 1876 **Calhoun Mansion** (16 Meeting St., 843/722-8205, www.calhounmansion.net, tours daily 11am-5pm, $16) boasts 35 opulent rooms (with 23 fireplaces!) in a striking Italianate design taking up a whopping 24,000 square feet. The grounds feature some charming garden spaces. A 90-minute "grand tour" is available for $75 per person; call for an appointment. Though the interiors at this privately run house are packed with antiques and furnishings, not all of them are accurate for the period.

## Heyward-Washington House

The **Heyward-Washington House** (87 Church St., 843/722-0354, www.charleston-museum.org, Mon.-Sat. 10am-5pm, Sun. noon-5pm, $12 adults, $5 children, combo tickets to Charleston Museum and Manigault House available) takes the regional practice of naming a historic home for the two most significant names in its pedigree to its logical extreme. Built in 1772 by the father of Declaration of Independence signer Thomas Heyward Jr., the house also hosted George Washington during the president's visit to Charleston in 1791. It's now owned and operated by the Charleston Museum. The main attraction at the Heyward-Washington House is its masterful woodwork, exemplified by the cabinetry of legendary Charleston carpenter Thomas Elfe.

## Cabbage Row

You'll recognize the addresses that make up **Cabbage Row** (89-91 Church St.) as "Catfish Row" from Gershwin's opera *Porgy and Bess* (based on the book *Porgy* by the Charleston author DuBose Heyward, who lived at 76 Church St.). Today this complex—which once housed 10 families—is certainly upgraded from years past, but the row still has the humble appeal of the tenement housing it once was, primarily for freed African American slaves after the Civil War. The house nearby at 94 Church Street was where John C. Calhoun and others drew up the infamous Nullification Acts that eventually led to the South's secession.

## St. Michael's Episcopal Church

The oldest church in South Carolina, **St. Michael's Episcopal Church** (71 Broad St., 843/723-0603, services Sun. 8am and 10:30am) is actually the second sanctuary built on this spot, the first being St. Philip's, which was rebuilt on Church Street. As a response to the overflowing congregation at the new St. Philip's, St. Michael's was built from 1752 to 1761, in the style of Christopher Wren. Other than a small addition on the southeast corner in 1883, the St. Michael's you see today is unchanged, including the massive pulpit, outsized in the style of the time.

Services here over the years hosted such luminaries as the Marquis de Lafayette, George Washington, and Robert E. Lee, the latter two of whom are known to have sat in the "governor's pew." Two signers of the U.S. Constitution, John Rutledge and Charles Cotesworth Pinckney, are buried in the sanctuary.

St. Michael's offers informal, free guided **tours** after Sunday services; contact the greeter for more information.

## Four Corners of Law

The famous intersection of Broad and Meeting Streets, named the **Four Corners of Law** for its confluence of federal law (the post office building), state law (the state courthouse), municipal law (city hall), and God's law (St. Michael's Episcopal Church), has been key to Charleston from the beginning. Meeting Street was laid out around 1672 and takes its name from the White Meeting House of early Dissenters, meaning non-Anglicans. Broad Street was also referred to as Cooper Street in the early days. Right in the middle of the street once stood the very first statue in the United States, a figure of William Pitt erected in 1766.

## WATERFRONT

### The Old Exchange and Provost Dungeon

The **Old Exchange and Provost Dungeon** (122 E. Bay St., 843/727-2165, www.oldexchange.com, daily 9am-5pm, $10 adults, $5 children and students) is brimming with history. The last building erected by the British before the American Revolution, it's also one of the three most historically significant colonial buildings in the United States, along with Philadelphia's Independence Hall and Boston's Faneuil Hall.

# The Great Charleston Earthquake

The Charleston peninsula is bordered by three faults: the Woodstock Fault above North Charleston, the Charleston Fault running along the east bank of the Cooper River, and the Ashley Fault to the west of the Ashley River. On August 31, 1886, one of them buckled, causing one of the most damaging earthquakes ever to hit the United States.

The earthquake of 1886 was signaled by foreshocks earlier that week, but Charlestonians remained unconcerned. Then, that Tuesday at 9:50pm, came the big one. With an epicenter somewhere near the Middleton Place Plantation, the Charleston earthquake is estimated to have measured about 7 on the Richter scale. Tremors were felt across half the country, with the ground shaking in Chicago and a church damaged in Indianapolis. A dam 120 miles away in Aiken gave way, washing a train off the tracks. Cracks opened up parallel to the Ashley River, with part of the riverbank falling into the water. Thousands of chimneys all over the state fell or were rendered useless. The quake brought a series of "sand blows," a phenomenon where craters open and spew sand and water into the air. In Charleston's case, some of the craters were 20 feet wide, shooting debris another 20 feet into the air. The whole event lasted less than a minute.

In crowded Charleston, the damage was horrific: over 2,000 buildings destroyed, a quarter of the city's value gone, 27 killed immediately and almost 100 more to die from injuries and disease. Because of the large numbers of newly homeless, tent cities sprang up in every available park and green space. The American Red Cross's first field mission soon brought some relief, but the scarcity of food and especially fresh water made life difficult.

Almost every surviving building had experienced structural damage, in some cases severe. This led to the widespread use of the "earthquake bolt" now seen throughout older Charleston homes. Essentially acting as a very long screw with a washer on each end, the idea of the earthquake bolt is simple: Poke a long iron rod through two walls that need stabilizing, and cap the ends. Charleston being Charleston, the caps were often decorated with a pattern or symbol.

The seismic activity of Charleston's earthquake was so intense that more than 300 aftershocks occurred in the 35 years after the event. Geologists think that most seismic events measured in the region today are probably also aftershocks.

This is actually the former Royal Exchange and Custom House, the cellar of which served as a British prison. The complex was built in 1771 over a portion of the original 1698 seawall, some of which you can see today during the short but fascinating tour of the "dungeon" (actually built as a warehouse). Three of Charleston's four signers of the Declaration of Independence did time downstairs for sedition against the crown. Later, happier times were experienced in the ballroom upstairs, as it was here that the state selected its delegates to the Continental Congress and ratified the U.S. Constitution; it's also where George Washington took a spin on the dance floor during his raucous "Farewell Tour" in 1791.

While the highlight for most is the basement dungeon, or provost, where the infamous "gentleman pirate" Stede Bonnet was imprisoned in 1718 before being hanged, visitors shouldn't miss the sunny upstairs ballroom and its selection of Washington-oriented history.

## Waterfront Park

Dubbing it "this generation's gift to the future," Mayor Joe Riley made this eight-acre project another part of his downtown renovation. Situated on Concord Street roughly between Exchange Street and Vendue Range, **Waterfront Park** (Concord St., 843/724-7327, daily dawn-dusk, free) was, like many waterfront locales in Charleston, built on what used to be marsh and water. This particularly massive chunk of "made land" juts about a football field's length farther out than the old waterline. Children will enjoy the large "Vendue" wading fountain at the park's entrance off Vendue Range, while a bit farther south is the large and quite artful Pineapple Fountain with its surrounding wading pool. Contemporary art lovers of all ages will appreciate the nearby **Waterfront Park City Gallery** (34 Prioleau St., www.citygalleryatwaterfrontpark.com, Tues.-Fri. 10am-6pm, Sat.-Sun. noon-5pm, free).

## ★ South Carolina Aquarium

The **South Carolina Aquarium** (100 Aquarium Wharf, 843/720-1990, www.scaquarium.org, Mar.-Aug. daily 9am-5pm, Sept.-Feb. daily 9am-4pm, $29.95 adults, $22.95 children, 4-D film extra, combo tickets with Fort Sumter tour available) is a great place for the whole family to have some fun while getting educated about the rich aquatic life off the coast and throughout this small but ecologically diverse state.

When you enter you're greeted with the 15,000-gallon Carolina Seas tank, with placid nurse sharks and vicious-looking moray eels. Other exhibits highlight the five key South Carolina ecosystems: beach, salt marsh, coastal plain, piedmont, and mountain forest. Another neat display is the Touch Tank, a hands-on collection of invertebrates found along the coast, such as sea urchins

and horseshoe crabs. The pièce de résistance, however, is the three-story Great Ocean Tank with its hundreds of deeper-water marine creatures, including sharks, puffer fish, and sea turtles.

A key part of the aquarium's research and outreach efforts is the Turtle Hospital, which, in partnership with the state of South Carolina, attempts to rehabilitate and save sick and injured specimens. The hospital has saved many sea turtles, the first one being a 270-pound female affectionately known as "Edisto Mama." Tour the hospital or visit the interactive Sea Turtle Recovery exhibit to learn more about these efforts.

## ★ Fort Sumter National Monument

This is the place that brought about the beginning of the Civil War, a Troy for modern times. Though many historians insist the war would have happened regardless of President Lincoln's decision to keep **Fort Sumter** (843/883-3123, www.nps.gov/fosu, hours seasonal, free) in federal hands, the stated casus belli was Major Robert Anderson's refusal to surrender the fort when requested to do so in the early-morning hours of April 12, 1861. A few hours later came the first shot of the

Fort Sumter National Monument

# Mayor Joe's Legacy

the entrance to Joseph P. Riley Jr. Park

Few cities anywhere have been as greatly influenced by one mayor as Charleston has by Joseph P. "Joe" Riley, who finally declined to run for reelection in 2015 after his 10th four-year term. "Mayor Joe," or just "Joe," as he's usually called, is not only responsible for the majority of redevelopment in the city; he also set the bar for its award-winning tourism industry.

Riley won his first mayoral race at the age of 32, the second Irish American mayor of the city. The lawyer, Citadel grad, and former member of the state legislature had a clear vision for his administration: to bring unprecedented numbers of women and minorities into city government, rejuvenate then-seedy King Street, and enlarge the city's tax base by annexing surrounding areas (during Riley's tenure the city grew from 16.7 square miles to over 100).

Here's only a partial list of the major projects and events Mayor Joe has made happen in Charleston:

- Charleston Maritime Center
- Charleston Place
- Children's Museum of the Lowcountry
- Hampton Park rehabilitation
- King Street-Market Street retail district
- Joseph P. Riley Jr. Park (named after the mayor at the insistence of city council)

- MOJA Arts Festival
- Piccolo Spoleto
- South Carolina Aquarium
- Spoleto USA
- Waterfront Park
- West Ashley Bikeway & Greenway

war, fired from Fort Johnson by Confederate captain George James. That 10-inch mortar shell, a signal for the general bombardment to begin, exploded above Fort Sumter. The first return shot from Fort Sumter was fired by none other than Captain Abner Doubleday, the man once credited as the father of baseball. Today the battered but still-standing Fort Sumter remains astride the entrance to Charleston Harbor on an artificial 70,000-ton sandbar, being part of the Third System of fortifications ordered after the War of 1812.

You can only visit by boats run by the approved concessionaire **Fort Sumter Tours** (843/881-7337, www.fortsumtertours.com, $18 adults, $11 ages 6-11, $16 seniors). Once at the fort, there's no charge for admission. Ferries leave from Liberty Square at Aquarium Wharf on the peninsula three times a day during the high season (Apr.-Oct.); call or check the website for times. Make sure to arrive about 30 minutes before the ferry departs. You can also get to Fort Sumter by ferry from Patriots Point at Mount Pleasant through the same concessionaire.

Budget at least 2.5 hours for the whole trip, including an hour at Fort Sumter. At Liberty Square on the peninsula is the **Fort Sumter Visitor Education Center** (340 Concord St., www.nps.gov/fosu, daily 8:30am-5pm, free), so you can learn more about where you're about to go. Once at the fort, you can be enlightened by the regular ranger talks on the fort's history and construction (generally at 11am and 2:30pm), take in the interpretive exhibits throughout the site, and enjoy the view of the spires of the Holy City from afar.

Some visitors are disappointed to find many of the fort's gun embrasures bricked over. This was done during the Spanish-American War, when the old fort was turned into an earthwork and the newer Battery Huger (huge-EE) was built on top of it.

# FRENCH QUARTER
## ★ St. Philip's Episcopal Church
With a pedigree dating back to the

colony's fledgling years, **St. Philip's Episcopal Church** (142 Church St., 843/722-7734, www.stphilipschurchsc.org, sanctuary Mon.-Fri. 10am-noon and 2pm-4pm, services Sun. 8:15am) is the oldest Anglican congregation south of Virginia. The first St. Philip's was built in 1680 at the corner of Meeting Street and Broad Street, the present site of St. Michael's Episcopal Church. It was badly damaged by a hurricane in 1710, so the city fathers approved the building of a new sanctuary dedicated to the saint on Church Street. Alas, the second St. Philip's burned to the ground in 1835. Construction immediately began on a replacement, and it's that building you see today. Heavily damaged by Hurricane Hugo in 1989, a $4.5 million renovation kept the church usable.

South Carolina's great statesman John C. Calhoun—who ironically despised Charlestonians for what he saw as their loose morals—was originally buried across Church Street in the former "stranger's churchyard," or West Cemetery, after his death in 1850. (Charles Pinckney and Edward Rutledge are two other notable South Carolinians buried here.) But near the end of the Civil War, Calhoun's body was moved to an unmarked grave closer to the sanctuary in an attempt to hide its location from Union troops.

## Circular Congregational Church
The historic **Circular Congregational Church** (150 Meeting St., 843/577-6400, www.circularchurch.org, services fall-spring Sun. 11am, summer Sun. 10:15am, tours Mon.-Fri. 10:30am) has one of the most interesting pedigrees of any house of worship in Charleston. Services were originally held on the site of the "White Meeting House," for which Meeting Street is named; they were moved here beginning in 1681 and catered to a polyglot mix of Congregationalists, Presbyterians, and Huguenots. For that reason it was often called the Church of Dissenters ("dissenter" being the common term at the time for anyone not an Anglican). As with many structures in

town, the 1886 earthquake necessitated a re-build, and the current edifice dates from 1891.

## French Huguenot Church

One of the oldest congregations in town, the **French Huguenot Church** (44 Queen St., 843/722-4385, www.frenchhuguenotchurch. org, liturgy Sun. 10:30am) also has the distinction of being the only remaining independent Huguenot church in the country. Founded around 1681 by French Calvinists, the church had about 450 congregants by 1700. The original sanctuary was built in 1687, but was deliberately destroyed as a firebreak during the great conflagration of 1796. The church was replaced in 1800, but that building was in turn demolished in favor of the picturesque, stucco-coated Gothic Revival sanctuary you see today, which was completed in 1845. Sunday services are conducted in English now, but a single annual service in French is still celebrated in April.

## Dock Street Theatre

Any thespian or lover of the stage must pay homage to the first theater built in North America, the **Dock Street Theatre** (135 Church St., 843/720-3968, www.charleston-stage.com, box office Mon.-Fri. 1pm-5pm, tickets $63-67). The original 1736 Dock Street Theatre burned down, but a second theater opened on the same site in 1754. That building was in turn demolished for a grander edifice in 1773, which, you guessed it, also burned down. The current building dates from 1809, when the Planter's Hotel was built near the site of the original Dock Street Theatre. To mark the theater's centennial, the hotel added a stage facility in 1835, and it's that building you see now. In addition to a very active and well-regarded annual season from the resident Charleston Stage Company, the 464-seat venue has hosted umpteen events of the Spoleto Festival over the past three decades and continues to do so.

## Old Powder Magazine

The **Old Powder Magazine** (79 Cumberland St., 843/722-9350, www.powdermag.org, Mon.-Sat. 10am-4pm, Sun. 1pm-4pm, $5 adults, $2 children) may be small, but the building is quite historically significant. The 1713 edifice is the oldest public building in South Carolina and the only one remaining from the days of the Lords Proprietors. As the name indicates, this was where the city's gunpowder was stored during the Revolution. The magazine is designed to implode rather than

the restored Dock Street Theatre

# French Huguenots

the French Huguenot Church

A visitor can't spend a few hours in Charleston without coming across many French-sounding names. Some are common surnames, such as Ravenel, Manigault (MAN-i-go), Gaillard, Laurens, or Huger (huge-EE). Some are street or place names, such as Mazyck or Legare (Le-GREE). The Gallic influence in Charleston was of the Calvinist Protestant variety. Known as Huguenots, these French immigrants—refugees from an increasingly intolerant Catholic regime in France—were numerous enough in the settlement by the 1690s that they were granted full citizenship and property rights if they swore allegiance to the British crown.

Unlike other colonies, Carolina never put much of a premium on religious conformity, a trait that exists to this day despite the area's overall conservatism. And unlike many who fled European monarchies to come to the New World, the French Huguenots were far from poverty-stricken. Most arrived already well educated and skilled in one or more useful trades. In Charleston's early days, they were mostly farmers or tar burners (makers of tar and pitch for maritime use). Their pragmatism and work ethic would lead them to higher positions in local society, such as lawyers, judges, and politicians. One of the wealthiest Charlestonians, the merchant Gabriel Manigault, was by some accounts the richest person in the American colonies during the early 1700s. South Carolina's most famous French Huguenot was Francis Marion, the "Swamp Fox" of Revolutionary War fame. Born on the Santee River, Marion grew up in Georgetown and is now interred near Moncks Corner.

The library of the **Huguenot Society of Carolina** (138 Logan St., 843/723-3235, www.huguenotsociety.org, Mon.-Fri. 9am-2pm) is a great research tool for anyone interested in French Protestant history and genealogy.

To this day, the spiritual home of Charleston's Huguenots is the same as always: the French Huguenot Church on Church Street, one of the earliest congregations in the city. The church still holds a liturgy in French every April.

explode in the event of a direct hit. This is another labor of love of the Historic Charleston Foundation, which has leased the building from The Colonial Dames since 1993. It was opened to the public as an attraction in 1997. Next door is the privately owned, circa-1709 **Trott's Cottage,** the first brick dwelling in Charleston.

## Old Slave Mart Museum

Slave auctions became big business in the South after 1808, when the United States banned the importation of slaves, thus increasing both price and demand. The auctions generally took place in public buildings where everyone could watch the wrenching spectacle. In the 1850s, public auctions in Charleston were put to a stop when city leaders discovered that visitors from European nations—all of which had banned slavery years before—were horrified at the practice. The slave trade was moved indoors to "marts" near the waterfront, where sales could be conducted out of the public eye. The last remaining such structure is the **Old Slave Mart Museum** (6 Chalmers St., 843/958-6467, www.charleston-sc.gov, Mon.-Sat. 9am-5pm, $7 adults, $5 children, free under age 6). Built in 1859, its last auction was held in November 1863. There are two main areas: the orientation area, where visitors learn about the transatlantic slave trade and the architectural history of the building itself, and the main exhibit area, where visitors can see documents, tools, and displays re-creating what happened inside during this sordid chapter in local history and celebrating the resilience of the area's African American population.

## NORTH OF BROAD
### Confederate Museum

Located on the 2nd floor of City Market's iconic main building, Market Hall on Meeting Street, the small **Confederate Museum** (188 Meeting St., 843/723-1541, Tues.-Sat. 11am-3:30pm, $5 adults, $3 children, cash only) hosts an interesting collection of Civil War memorabilia, with an emphasis on the military side, and is the local headquarters of the United Daughters of the Confederacy. Perhaps its best contribution, however, is its research library.

## Gibbes Museum of Art

The **Gibbes Museum of Art** (135 Meeting St., 843/722-2706, www.gibbesmuseum.org, Tues.-Sat. 10am-5pm, Sun. 1pm-5pm, $9 adults, $7 students, $5 ages 6-12) is one of those rare Southern museums that manages a good blend of the modern and the traditional, the local and the international. Their permanent collection spans a wide range of Southern art from the colonial era on, and they arguably have the most distinctive collection of portrait miniatures in the nation. Begun in 1905 as the Gibbes Art Gallery—the final wish of James Shoolbred Gibbes, who willed $100,000 for its construction—the complex has grown through the years in size and influence. The Gibbes Art School in the early 20th century formed a close association with the Woodstock School in New York, bringing important ties and prestige to the fledgling institution. Georgia O'Keeffe brought an exhibit here in 1955.

## Kahal Kadosh Beth Elohim Reform Temple

The birthplace of Reform Judaism in the United States and the oldest continuously active synagogue in the nation is **Kahal Kadosh Beth Elohim Reform Temple** (90 Hasell St., 843/723-1090, www.kkbe.org, services Sat. 11am, tours Mon.-Fri. 10am-noon, Sun. 10am-4pm). The congregation—*Kahal Kadosh* means "holy community" in Hebrew—was founded in 1749, with the current temple dating from 1840 and built in the Greek Revival style. The temple's Reform roots came about indirectly because of the great fire of 1838. In rebuilding, some congregants wanted to bring an organ into the temple, and the Orthodox contingent lost the debate. So the new building became the first home of Reform Judaism in the country, a fitting testament to Charleston's long-standing

# The New Charleston Green

Most people know "Charleston green" as a unique local color, the result of adding a few drops of yellow to post-Civil War surplus black paint. But these days the phrase also refers to environmentally friendly development in Charleston.

The most obvious example is the ambitious Navy Yard redevelopment, which seeks to repurpose the closed-down facility. From its inception in 1902 at the command of President Theodore Roosevelt through the end of the Cold War, the Charleston Navy Yard was one of the city's biggest employers. Though the yard was closed in 1995, a 340-acre section now hosts an intriguing mix of green-friendly design firms, small nonprofits, and commercial maritime companies. Clemson University—with the help of a massive federal grant, the largest in the school's history—will oversee one of the world's largest wind turbine research facilities, centered on Building 69.

Also in North Charleston, local retail chain Half Moon Outfitters has a green-friendly warehouse facility in an old grocery store. The first LEED (Leadership in Energy and Environmental Design) Platinum-certified building in South Carolina, the warehouse features solar panels, rainwater reservoirs, and locally harvested or salvaged interiors. There's also the LEED-certified North Charleston Elementary School as well as North Charleston's adoption of a "dark skies" ordinance to cut down on light pollution. On the peninsula, the historic meetinghouse of the Circular Congregational Church has a green addition with geothermal heating and cooling, rainwater cisterns, and Charleston's first vegetative roof.

For many Charlestonians, the green movement manifests in simpler things: the pedestrian and bike lanes on the Ravenel Bridge, the thriving city recycling program, and the Sustainable Seafood Initiative, a partnership of local restaurants, universities, and conservation groups that brings the freshest, most environmentally responsible dishes to your table when you dine out in Charleston.

This forward-thinking mode doesn't just mean enhanced quality of life for Charleston residents. It also pays off in attracting tech businesses and other cutting-edge employers, and the well-educated millennial knowledge workers who founded and staff them.

Charleston's tech economy is among the fastest growing in the nation, 26 percent faster than the national average, faster even than Austin, Texas, and Raleigh/Durham, North Carolina. Nearly 100 firms are part of the public/private Charleston Digital Corridor (www.charlestondigitalcorridor.com). The growth has garnered so much attention that some are using the nickname "Silicon Harbor" for the Charleston region.

ecumenical spirit of religious tolerance and inclusiveness.

## Old City Jail

If you were to make a movie called *Dracula Meets the Lord of the Rings,* the imposing **Old City Jail** (21 Magazine St., 843/577-5245) might make a great set. Its history is also the stuff from which movies are made. Built in 1802 on a lot set aside for public use since 1680, the edifice was the Charleston County lockup until 1939. Some of the last pirates were jailed here in 1822 while awaiting hanging, as was slave rebellion leader Denmark Vesey. During the Civil War, prisoners of both armies were held here at various times.

The Old City Jail currently houses the American College of the Building Arts. Unless you're a student there, the only way to tour the Old Jail is through **Bulldog Tours** (18 Anson St., 843/722-8687, www.bulldogtours. com). Their Haunted Jail Tour ($20 adults, $10 children) starts daily at 7pm, 8pm, 9pm, and 10pm; all tours are paid for at 40 North Market Street, within a short walk, with jail tours starting at the jail itself.

## Old City Market

Part kitschy tourist trap, part glimpse into the Old South, part community gathering place, **Old City Market** (Meeting St. and Market St., 843/973-7236, daily 6am-11:30pm) remains Charleston's most reliable attraction. It is certainly the practical center of the city's tourist trade, not least because so many tours originate nearby. No matter what anyone tries to tell you, Charleston's City Market never hosted a single slave auction. When the Pinckney family donated this land to the city for a "Publick Market," one stipulation was that no slaves were ever to be sold here—or else the property would immediately revert to the family's descendants. A recent multi-million-dollar renovation has prettified the bulk of City Market into more of a big-city air-conditioned pedestrian shopping mall. It's not as shabbily charming as it once was, but it certainly offers a more comfortable stroll during the warmer months.

## Philip Simmons Garden

Charleston's most beloved artisan is the late Philip Simmons. Born on nearby Daniel Island in 1912, Simmons became one of the most sought-after decorative ironworkers in the United States. In 1982 the National Endowment for the Arts awarded him its National Heritage Fellowship. His work is on display at the Smithsonian Institution and the Museum of International Folk Art in Santa Fe, New Mexico, among many other places. In 1989, the congregation at Simmons's **St. John's Reformed Episcopal Church** (91 Anson St., 843/722-4241, http://philipsimmons.us) voted to make the church garden a commemoration of the life and work of this legendary African American artisan, who died in 2009 at age 97. Completed in two phases, the Bell Garden and the Heart Garden, the project is a delightful blend of Simmons's signature graceful, sinuous style and fragrant flowers.

## Unitarian Church

In a town filled with cool old church cemeteries, the coolest belongs to the **Unitarian Church** (4 Archdale St., 843/723-4617, www.charlestonuu.org, services Sun. 11am, free tours Sat. 10am-1pm). As a nod to the beauty and power of nature, vegetation and shrubbery in the cemetery have been allowed to take their natural course (walkways excepted).

The church itself—the second-oldest such

the cemetery at Unitarian Church

edifice in Charleston and the oldest Unitarian sanctuary in the South—was built in 1776 because of overcrowding at the Circular Congregational Church, but the building saw rough usage by British troops during the Revolution. Repairs were made in 1787 and an extensive modernization took place in 1852. Sadly, the 1886 earthquake toppled the original tower, and the version you see today is a subsequent and less grand design.

To see the sanctuary at times other than weekend mornings, go by the office next door Monday-Friday 9am-2pm and they'll let you take a walk through the interior.

## William Rhett House

The oldest standing residence in Charleston is the circa-1713 **William Rhett House** (54 Hasell St.), which once belonged to the colonel who captured the pirate Stede Bonnet. It's now a private residence, but you can admire this excellent prototypical example of a Charleston single house easily from the street and read the nearby historical marker.

## Marion Square

While the Citadel moved lock, stock, and barrel almost a century ago, the college's old home, the South Carolina State Arsenal, still overlooks 6.5-acre **Marion Square** (between King St. and Meeting St. at Calhoun St., 843/965-4104, daily dawn-dusk), a reminder of the days when this was the institute's parade ground, the "Citadel Green" (the old Citadel is now a hotel). Marion Square is named for the "Swamp Fox" himself, Revolutionary War hero and father of modern guerrilla warfare Francis Marion. Marion Square hosts many events, including a farmers market every Saturday early April-late November.

## College of Charleston

The oldest college in South Carolina and the first municipal college in the country, the **College of Charleston** (66 George St., 843/805-5507, www.cofc.edu) represents a chunk of the city's history, but its 12,000-plus students bring a modern, youthful touch to many of the city's public activities. Though the college has its share of modernistic buildings, a stroll around the gorgeous campus will uncover some historic gems. The oldest building on campus, the Bishop Robert Smith House, dates from the year of the college's founding, 1770, and is now the president's house; find it on Glebe Street between Wentworth and George. Movies that have had scenes shot on campus include *Cold Mountain, The Patriot,* and *The Notebook.* If you have an iPhone or iPod Touch, you can download a neat self-guided tour, complete with video, from the iTunes App Store (www.apple.com, search "College of Charleston Tour," free).

## Emanuel African Methodist Episcopal Church

Known simply as "Mother Emanuel," **Emanuel African Methodist Episcopal Church** (110 Calhoun St., www.emanuelamechurch.org, services Sun. 9:30am) has a distinguished history as one of the South's oldest African American congregations. Prior to the Civil War, one of the church's founders, Denmark Vesey, was implicated in planning a slave uprising. The edifice was burned as retaliation for Vesey's involvement (and the founding of the Citadel as a military academy nearby was directly related to white unrest over the plot). In the wake of the Nat Turner revolt in 1834, open worship by African Americans was outlawed in Charleston and went underground until after the Civil War. The congregation adopted the "Emanuel" name with the building of a new church in 1872, a wooden structure that unfortunately didn't survive the great earthquake of 1886. The simple, elegant, and deceptively large church you see today dates from 1891, and has hosted luminaries such as Booker T. Washington, Dr. Martin Luther King Jr., and Coretta Scott King. In 2015, the historically black church was the site of the horrific murders of nine worshippers—including its pastor, Clementa Pinckney—by a white racist.

Emanuel African Methodist Episcopal Church

At Pinckney's memorial service, President Barack Obama spoke and led the congregation in singing *Amazing Grace.*

## Charleston Museum

During its long history, the **Charleston Museum** (360 Meeting St., 843/722-2996, www.charlestonmuseum.org, Mon.-Sat. 9am-5pm, Sun. noon-5pm, $12 adults, $5 children, combo tickets to Heyward-Washington and Manigault Houses available) has moved literally all over town. It's currently housed in a noticeably modern building, but make no mistake: This is the nation's oldest museum, founded in 1773. It strives to stay as fresh and relevant as any new museum, with a rotating schedule of special exhibits in addition to its very eclectic permanent collection. For a long time this was the only place to get a glimpse of the CSS *Hunley,* albeit just a fanciful replica in front of the main entrance. (Now you can see the real thing at its conservation site in North Charleston, and it's even smaller than the replica would indicate.) Much of the museum's collection focuses on aspects of everyday life of Charlestonians, from the aristocracy to slaves, including items such as utensils, clothing, and furniture. There are quirks as well, such as the Egyptian mummy and the fine lady's fan made out of turkey feathers. A particular and possibly surprising specialty includes work and research by noted regional naturalists like John James Audubon, André Michaux, and Mark Catesby.

## Joseph Manigault House

Owned and operated by the nearby Charleston Museum, the **Joseph Manigault House** (350 Meeting St., 843/723-2926, www.charlestonmuseum.org, Mon.-Sat. 10am-5pm, Sun. noon-5pm, last tour 4:30pm, $12 adults, $5 children, combo tickets to Charleston Museum and Heyward-Washington House available) is sometimes called the "Huguenot House." This grand circa-1803 National Historic Landmark was designed by wealthy merchant Gabriel Manigault for his brother, Joseph, a rice planter of local repute. The three-story brick town house is a great example of Adams, or Federal, architecture.

## ★ Aiken-Rhett House

An acquisition of the Historic Charleston Foundation, the **Aiken-Rhett House** (48 Elizabeth St., 843/723-1159, www.historic-charleston.org, Mon.-Sat. 10am-5pm, Sun. 2pm-5pm, last tour 4:15pm, $12 adults, $5 children) shows another side of the

the Aiken-Rhett House

# Family Fun in Charleston

Let's face it: A steady diet of house museums and long-ago history will bore anyone to tears, not just the young folks in your traveling party. Fortunately, Charleston has a range of options to please children of all ages. You just have to know where to look.

- **Children's Museum of the Lowcountry:** Conveniently located in the city's "Museum Row," this indoor playground offers a variety of hands-on activities for kids ages 3 months-12 years.

- **Old Exchange and Provost Dungeon:** For a real-life Pirates of the Caribbean experience, take a guided tour of this spooky spot from colonial times, complete with animatronic-style figures of pirates and scoundrels.

- **Sewee Visitor and Environmental Education Center:** Visit a pack of red wolves (indigenous to the coastal area) at this center devoted to preserving the species and educating people about these magnificent little animals.

- **South Carolina Aquarium:** The closest thing to a zoo, this easily managed and very informative installation features aspects of every habitat in the ecologically diverse Palmetto State—from Lowcountry marshland to Upstate mountain rivers—anchored by an enormous three-floor central observation tank filled with marine life.

- **Waterfront Park:** The park's outdoor fountain sculptures are sure to please any carefree spirit in your group.

organization's mission. Whereas the Historic Charleston-run Nathaniel Russell House seeks to re-create a specific point in time, work at the Aiken-Rhett House emphasizes conservation and research. Built in 1818 and expanded by South Carolina governor William Aiken Jr., after whom we know the house today, parts of this rambling, almost Dickensian house remained sealed from 1918 until 1975, when the family relinquished the property to the Charleston Museum. While the docents are friendly and helpful, the main way to enjoy the Aiken-Rhett House is by way of a self-guided MP3 player audio tour, which is unique in Charleston.

## Children's Museum of the Lowcountry

Another example of Charleston's savvy regarding the tourist industry is the **Children's Museum of the Lowcountry** (25 Ann St., 843/853-8962, www.explorecml.org, Tues.-Sat. 9am-5pm, Sun. noon-5pm, $12 non-SC residents). Recognizing that historic homes and Civil War memorabilia aren't enough to keep a family with young children in town for long, the city established this museum in 2005 specifically to give families with kids ages 3 months-12 years a reason to spend more time (and money) downtown.

## HAMPTON PARK
### The Citadel

**The Citadel** (171 Moultrie St., 843/953-3294, www.citadel.edu, grounds daily 8am-6pm) was originally sited at the Old State Arsenal at Marion Square, born out of panic over the threat of a slave rebellion organized in 1822 by Denmark Vesey. The school moved to its current 300-acre site farther up the peninsula along the Ashley River in 1922. The Citadel (technically named The Citadel, The Military College of South Carolina) has entered popular consciousness through the works of graduate Pat Conroy, especially his novel *Lords of Discipline,* starring a thinly disguised "Carolina Military Institute."

There's a lot for visitors to see, including **The Citadel Museum** (843/953-6779, daily noon-5pm, free), on your right just as you enter campus; the "Citadel Murals" in the Daniel Library; "Indian Hill," the highest point in Charleston and former site of an Indian trader's home; and the grave of U.S. general Mark Clark of World War II fame, who was Citadel president from 1954 to 1966. Ringing vast Summerall Field—the huge open space where you enter campus—are the many castle-like cadet barracks.

The most interesting single experience for visitors to the Citadel is the Friday afternoon dress parade on Summerall Field, in which cadets pass for review in full dress uniform (the fabled "long gray line") accompanied by a marching band and pipers. Often called "the best free show in Charleston," the parade happens almost every Friday at 3:45pm during the school year; you might want to consult the website before your visit to confirm. Arrive well in advance to avoid parking problems.

## WEST ASHLEY
### Charles Towne Landing

Any look at West Ashley must start where everything began, with the 600-acre state historic site **Charles Towne Landing** (1500 Old Town Plantation Rd., 843/852-4200, www.southcarolinaparks.com/ctl, daily 9am-5pm, $10 adults, $6 students, free under age 6). This

is where Charleston's original settlers first arrived and camped in 1670, remaining only a few years before eventually moving to the more defensible peninsula where the Holy City now resides. A beautiful and fully seaworthy replica of a settlers' ship is the main highlight, docked in the creek on the far side of the long and well-done exploration trail through the site.

## ★ Drayton Hall

A mecca for historic preservationists from all over the country, **Drayton Hall** (3380 Ashley River Rd., 843/769-2600, www.draytonhall. org, Mon.-Sat. 9am-5pm, Sun. 11am-5pm, tours on the half hour, $22 adults, $10 ages 12-18, $6 ages 6-11, grounds only $10) is remarkable not only for its pedigree, but also for the way in which it has been preserved. This stately redbrick Georgian-Palladian building, the oldest plantation home in the country open to the public, is literally historically preserved—as in no electricity, heat, or running water.

Since its construction in 1738 by John Drayton, son of Magnolia Plantation founder Thomas, Drayton Hall has survived almost completely intact through the ups and downs of Lowcountry history. In its heyday before

Drayton Hall

the American Revolution, Drayton Hall was widely considered the finest home in all the colonies, the very symbol of the extraordinary wealth of the South Carolina aristocracy. John Drayton died while fleeing the British in 1779; subsequently his house served as the headquarters of British generals Henry Clinton and Charles Cornwallis. During the Civil War, Drayton Hall escaped the depredations of the conquering Union army, one of only three area plantation homes to survive.

The guides hold degrees in the field, and a tour of the house, which starts on the half hour, takes every bit of 50 minutes. A separate 45-minute program called "Connections: From Africa to America" chronicles the diaspora of the slaves who originally worked this plantation, from their capture to their eventual freedom. "Connections" is presented at 11:15am, 1:15pm, and 3:15pm.

The site comprises not only the main house, but two self-guided walking trails as well, one along the peaceful Ashley River and another along the marsh. Also on-site is an African American cemetery with at least 33 known graves. It's kept deliberately untended and unlandscaped to honor the final wish of Richmond Bowens (1908-1998), the seventh-generation descendant of some of Drayton Hall's original slaves.

## Magnolia Plantation and Gardens

A different legacy of the Drayton family is **Magnolia Plantation and Gardens** (3550 Ashley River Rd., 843/571-1266, www.magnoliaplantation.com, daily 8:30am-4:30pm, $15 adults, $10 children, free under age 6). It claims not only the first garden in the United States, dating back to the 1680s, but also the first public garden, dating to 1872. Thomas Drayton Jr.—scion of Norman aristocracy, son of a wealthy Barbadian planter—came from the Caribbean to build his own fortune; he immediately married the daughter of Stephen Fox, who began this plantation in 1676. Magnolia has stayed in the possession

of an unbroken line of Drayton descendants to this day.

As a privately run attraction, Magnolia has little of the academic veneer of other plantation sites in the area, and there's a slightly kitschy feel here, the opposite of the quiet dignity of Drayton Hall. And unlike Middleton Place a few miles down the road, the gardens here are anything but manicured, with a wild, almost playful feel. That said, Magnolia can claim fame to being one of the earliest bona fide tourist attractions in the United States and the beginning of Charleston's now-booming tourist industry.

While spring remains the best—and the most crowded—time to come, a huge variety of camellias bloom in early winter, a time marked by a yearly Winter Camellia Festival. Children will enjoy finding their way through "the Maze" of manicured camellia and holly bushes, complete with a viewing stand to look within the giant puzzle. Plant lovers will enjoy the themed gardens such as the Biblical Garden, the Barbados Tropical Garden, and the Audubon Swamp Garden, complete with alligators and named after John James Audubon, who visited here in 1851. House tours, the 45-minute Nature Train tour, the 45-minute Nature Boat tour, and a visit to the Audubon Swamp Garden run about $8 per person extra for each offering.

## ★ Middleton Place

With the first landscaped garden in North America and still one of the most magnificent in the world, **Middleton Place** (4300 Ashley River Rd., 843/556-6020, www.middletonplace.org, daily 9am-5pm, $28 adults, $15 students, $10 children, guided house tour $15 extra) is a sublime, unforgettable combination of history and sheer natural beauty. Nestled along a quiet bend in the Ashley River, the grounds contain a historic restored home, working stables, 60 acres of breathtaking gardens, and the Inn at Middleton Place, a stunning piece of modern architecture.

First granted in 1675, Middleton Place is the culmination of the Lowcountry rice plantation aesthetic. In 1741 the plantation became the family seat of the Middletons, one of the most notable surnames in U.S. history. As the Civil War wound down, on February 22, 1865, the 56th New York Volunteers burned the main house and destroyed the gardens, leaving only the circa-1755 guest wing, which today is the excellently restored **Middleton Place House Museum** (4300 Ashley River Rd., 843/556-6020, www.middletonplace.org, guided tours Mon. 1:30pm-4:30pm, Tues.-Sun. 10am-4:30pm, $15). The 1886 earthquake added its mark, and it wasn't until 1916 that renovation of the property began. In 1971 Middleton Place was named a National Historic Landmark.

A short walk takes you to the **Plantation Stableyards,** where costumed craftspeople work using historically authentic tools and methods, all while surrounded by a happy family of domestic animals. The Stableyards is also home to a pair of magnificent male water buffalo. Henry Middleton originally imported a pair to work the rice fields—the first in North America—but these guys are just there to relax and add atmosphere. Meet them daily 9am-5pm.

The 53-room **Inn at Middleton Place** (www.theinnatmiddletonplace.com) has a bold Frank Lloyd Wright-influenced design, comprising four units joined by walkways. But both inside and outside it manages to blend quite well with the surrounding fields, trees, and riverbanks. The inn also offers kayak tours and instruction—a particularly nice way to enjoy the grounds from the waters of the Ashley—and features its own organic garden and labyrinth, intriguing modern counterpoints to the formal gardens of the plantation itself.

They still grow the exquisite Carolina Gold rice in a field at Middleton Place, harvested in the old style each September. You can sample some of it in many dishes at the **Middleton Place Restaurant** (843/556-6020, www.middletonplace.org, lunch daily 11am-3pm, dinner Tues.-Thurs. 6pm-8pm, Fri.-Sat. 6pm-9pm, Sun. 6pm-8pm, $15-25). You can tour the gardens for free if you arrive for a dinner reservation at 5:30pm or later.

## The Coburg Cow

The entire stretch of U.S. 17 (Savannah Hwy.) heading into Charleston from the west is redolent of a particularly Southern brand of retro Americana. The chief example is the famous **Coburg Cow,** a large, rotating dairy cow accompanied by a bottle of chocolate milk. The

Middleton Place

current installation dates from 1959, though a version of it was on this site as far back as the early 1930s, when this area was open countryside. During Hurricane Hugo the Coburg Cow was moved to a safe location. In 2001 the attached dairy closed down, and the city threatened to have the cow moved or demolished. But community outcry preserved the delightful landmark, which is visible today on the south side of U.S. 17 in the 900 block. You can't miss it—it's a big cow on the side of the road!

## Caw Caw Interpretive Center

About 10 minutes west of Charleston on U.S. 17 you'll find the unique **Caw Caw Interpretive Center** (5200 Savannah Hwy., Ravenel, 843/889-8898, www.ccprc.com, Tues.-Sun. 9am-5pm, $2), a treasure trove for history buffs and naturalists wanting to learn more about the old rice culture of the South. Most Wednesday and Saturday mornings, guided bird walks are held at 8:30am ($5 pp). You can put in your own canoe for $10 October-April on Saturdays and Sundays. Bikes and dogs aren't allowed on the grounds.

# NORTH CHARLESTON
## Magnolia Cemetery

Although not technically in North Charleston, historic **Magnolia Cemetery** (Cunnington Ave. at Huguenin Ave., 843/722-8638, Sept.-May daily 8am-5pm, June-Aug. daily 8am-6pm) is well north of the downtown tourist district in the area called "the Neck." This historic burial ground, while not quite the aesthetic equal of Savannah's famed Bonaventure Cemetery, is still a stirring site for its natural beauty and ornate memorials as well as for its historical aspects. Here are buried the crewmen who died aboard the CSS *Hunley,* reinterred after their retrieval from Charleston Harbor. In all, over 2,000 Civil War dead are buried here, including 5 Confederate generals and 84 rebels who fell at Gettysburg and were moved here.

## ★ CSS *Hunley*

In 1864, the Confederate submarine CSS *Hunley* mysteriously sank right after successfully destroying the USS *Housatonic* with the torpedo attached to its bow, marking the first time a sub ever sank a ship in battle. For the longest time, the only glimpse of the ill-fated Confederate submarine afforded to visitors was a not-quite-accurate replica outside the Charleston Museum. But in 1995, after a 15-year search, maritime novelist and adventurer Clive Cussler and his team finally found the submarine off Sullivan's Island. In 2000, a team comprising the nonprofit **Friends of the Hunley**, the federal government, and private partners successfully implemented a plan to safely raise the vessel.

Today you can view the sub, see the life-size model from the TNT movie *The Hunley,* and look at artifacts such as the "lucky" gold piece of the commander at the **Warren Lasch Conservation Center** (1250 Supply St., Bldg. 255, 866/866-9938, www.hunley.org, Sat. 10am-5pm, Sun. noon-5pm, $16 adults, $8 students, free under age 5). You can even see facial reconstructions of some of the eight sailors who died on board. The remains of the crew lie in Magnolia Cemetery, where they were buried in 2004 with full military honors.

The Lasch Center is only open to the public on weekends so that research and conservation can be performed during the week. Because of this limited window of opportunity and the popularity of the site, reserve tickets ahead of time.

To get to the Warren Lasch Conservation Center from Charleston, take I-26 north to exit 216B. Take a left onto Spruill Avenue and a right onto McMillan Avenue. Once in the Navy Yard, take a right on Hobson Avenue, and after about one mile take a left onto Supply Street. The Lasch Center is the low white building on the left.

## Fire Museum

The **North Charleston and American**

**LaFrance Fire Museum and Education Center** (4975 Centre Pointe Dr., North Charleston, 843/740-5550, www.legacyofheroes.org, Mon.-Sat. 10am-5pm, Sun. 1pm-5pm, last ticket 4pm, $6 adults, free under age 14), which shares a huge 25,000-square-foot space with the North Charleston Convention and Visitors Bureau, is primarily dedicated to maintaining and increasing its collection of antique American LaFrance firefighting vehicles and equipment. The 18 fire engines here date from 1857 to 1969. The museum's exhibits have taken on greater poignancy in the wake of the tragic loss of nine Charleston firefighters killed trying to extinguish a warehouse blaze on U.S. 17 in summer 2007—second only to the 9/11 attacks as the largest single loss of life for a U.S. firefighting department.

## SUMMERVILLE

Founded as Pineland Village in 1785, Summerville made its reputation as a place for plantation owners and their families to escape the insects and heat of the swampier areas of the Lowcountry. Summerville boasts a whopping 700 buildings in the National Register of Historic Places. For a walking tour of the historic district, download the map at www.visitsummerville.com or pick up a hard copy at the **Summerville Visitors Center** (402 N. Main St., 843/873-8535, Mon.-Fri. 9am-5pm, Sat. 10am-3pm, Sun. 1pm-4pm).

### Azalea Park

Much visitor activity in Summerville centers on **Azalea Park** (S. Main St. and W. 5th St. S., daily dawn-dusk, free), rather obviously named for its most scenic inhabitants. Several fun yearly events take place here, most notably the **Flowertown Festival** (www.flowertownfestival.com, free) each April, a three-day affair heralding the coming of spring and the blooming of the flowers. One of the biggest festivals in South Carolina, 250,000 people usually attend. Another event, **Sculpture in the South** (www.sculptureinthesouth.com) in May, takes advantage of the extensive public sculpture in the park.

## Colonial Dorchester State Historic Site

Just south of Summerville on the way back to Charleston is the interesting **Colonial Dorchester State Historic Site** (300 County Rd. S-18-373, 843/873-1740, www.southcarolinaparks.com, daily 9am-6pm, $2 adults, free under age 16), chronicling a virtually unknown segment of Carolina history. A contingent of Massachusetts Puritans ("Congregationalists" in the parlance of the time) were given special dispensation in 1697 to form a settlement of their own specifically to enhance commercial activity on the Ashley River. Today little is left of old Dorchester but the tabby walls of the 1757 fort overlooking the Ashley. Don't miss the unspectacular but still historically vital remains of the wooden wharf on the walking trail along the river, once the epicenter of a thriving port. The most-photographed thing on-site is the bell tower of the Anglican church of St. George—which actually wasn't where the original settlers worshipped and was in fact quite resented by them since they were forced to pay for its construction.

### Summerville-Dorchester Museum

To learn more about Summerville's interesting history, go just off Main Street to the **Summerville-Dorchester Museum** (100 E. Doty Ave., 843/875-9666, www.summervilledorchestermuseum.org, Mon.-Sat. 9am-2pm, donations accepted). Located in the former town police station, the museum has a wealth of good exhibits. The museum opened in 1992 thanks to a group of Summerville citizens who wanted to preserve the region's history.

## MOUNT PLEASANT AND EAST COOPER

The main destination in this area on the east bank of the Cooper River is the island of Mount Pleasant, primarily known as a peaceful, fairly affluent suburb of Charleston—a role it has played for about 300 years now.

# Greater Charleston

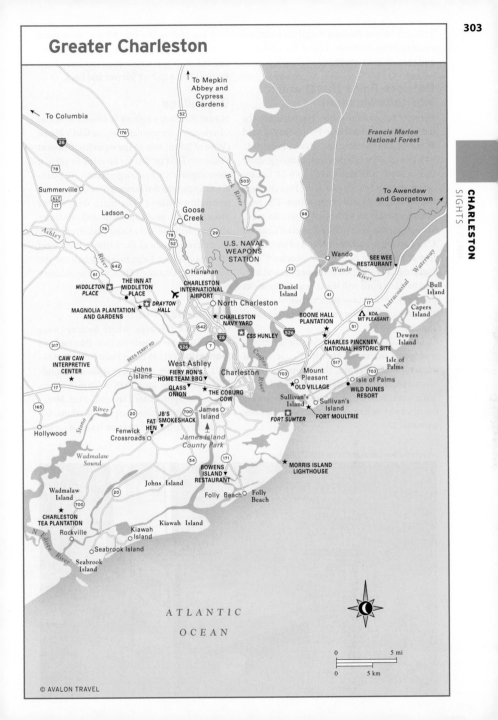

To Mepkin
Abbey and
Cypress
Gardens

To Columbia

52

176

26

78

Francis Marion
National Forest

503

Back River

Summerville

ALT 17

Ladson

98

To Awendaw
and Georgetown

Goose
Creek

Ashley River

76

78
52

29

U.S. NAVAL
WEAPONS
STATION

Wando

SEE WEE
RESTAURANT

Bull
Island

642

61

Hanahan

33

Wando River

MIDDLETON
PLACE

THE INN AT
MIDDLETON
PLACE

CHARLESTON
INTERNATIONAL
AIRPORT

DRAYTON
HALL

North Charleston

Daniel
Island

41

17

KOA
MT PLEASANT

Capers
Island

MAGNOLIA PLANTATION
AND GARDENS

BOONE HALL
PLANTATION

51

Dewees
Island

642

CHARLESTON
NAVY YARD

CSS HUNLEY

526

CHARLES PINCKNEY
NATIONAL HISTORIC SITE

317

BEES FERRY RD

526

7

26

Cooper River

517

Isle of
Palms

CAW CAW
INTERPRETIVE
CENTER

West Ashley

FIERY RON'S
HOME TEAM BBQ

Charleston

703

Mount
Pleasant

703

Johns
Island

GLASS
ONION

THE COBURG
COW

OLD VILLAGE

Isle of Palms

WILD DUNES
RESORT

17

165

Stono River

20

JB'S
SMOKESHACK

700

James
Island

Sullivan's
Island

Sullivan's
Island

FORT MOULTRIE

FAT
HEN

FORT SUMTER

Hollywood

Fenwick
Crossroads

James Island
County Park

Wadmalaw
Sound

54

171

BOWENS
ISLAND
RESTAURANT

MORRIS ISLAND
LIGHTHOUSE

Wadmalaw
Island

Johns Island

Folly Beach

Folly
Beach

700

20

CHARLESTON
TEA PLANTATION

Rockville

Kiawah
Island

Kiawah Island

Seabrook Island

N Edisto River

Seabrook
Island

ATLANTIC

OCEAN

0          5 mi

0          5 km

© AVALON TRAVEL

Through Mount Pleasant is also the only land route to access Sullivan's Island, Isle of Palms, and historic Fort Moultrie.

## Patriots Point Naval and Maritime Museum

Directly across Charleston Harbor from the old city lies the **Patriots Point Naval and Maritime Museum** (40 Patriots Point Rd., 843/884-2727, www.patriotspoint.org, daily 9am-6:30pm, $20 adults, $12 ages 6-11, free for active-duty military), one of the first chapters in Charleston's tourism renaissance. The project began in 1975 with what is still its main attraction, the World War II aircraft carrier USS *Yorktown*, named in honor of the carrier lost at the Battle of Midway. Much of "The Fighting Lady" is open to the public, and kids and nautical buffs will thrill to walk the decks and explore the many stations below deck on this massive 900-foot vessel, a veritable floating city.

Other ships moored beside the *Yorktown* and open for tours are the Coast Guard cutter USCG *Ingham,* the submarine USS *Clamagore,* and the destroyer USS *Laffey,* which survived being hit by three Japanese bombs and five kamikaze attacks—all within an hour.

A big plus is the free 90-minute guided tour. If you want to make a family history day out of it, you can hop on the ferry from Patriots Point to Fort Sumter and back.

## Old Village

Mount Pleasant's history is almost as old as Charleston's, encapsulated by the **Old Village** (West of Royall Ave. to the waterfront, Mount Pleasant). First settled for farming in 1680, it soon acquired cachet as a great place for planters to spend the hot summers away from the mosquitoes inland. The main drag is Pitt Street, where you can shop and meander among plenty of stores and restaurants (try an ice cream soda at the historic Pitt Street Pharmacy). The huge meeting hall on the waterfront, Alhambra Hall, was the old ferry terminal.

## Boone Hall Plantation

Unusual for this area, where fortunes were originally made mostly on rice, **Boone Hall Plantation**'s (1235 Long Point Rd., 843/884-4371, www.boonehallplantation.com, mid-Mar.-Labor Day Mon.-Sat. 8:30am-6:30pm, Sun. noon-5pm, Labor Day.-mid-Mar. Mon.-Sat. 9am-5pm, Sun. noon-5pm, $20 adults, $10 children) main claim to fame was as a cotton

restored slave cabin at Boone Hall Plantation

plantation as well as a noted brickmaking plant. Boone Hall takes the phrase "living history" to its extreme: It's not only an active agricultural facility, it also lets visitors go on "u-pick" walks through its fields, which boast succulent strawberries, peaches, tomatoes, and even pumpkins in October—as well as free hayrides. Keep in mind that the plantation's "big house" is not original; it's a 1935 reconstruction. The most poignant and educational structures by far are the nine humble brick slave cabins from the 1790s, expertly restored and most fitted with interpretive displays. Summers see some serious Civil War reenacting going on. In all, three different tours are available: a 30-minute house tour, a tour of Slave Street, and a garden tour.

## Charles Pinckney National Historic Site

The **Charles Pinckney National Historic Site** (1240 Long Point Rd., 843/881-5516, www.nps.gov/chpi, daily 9am-5pm, free) is one of my favorite sights in Charleston, for its uplifting, well-explored subject matter as well as its tastefully maintained house and grounds. Sometimes called "the forgotten founder," Charles Pinckney was not only a hero of the American Revolution and a notable early abolitionist, but also one of the main authors of the U.S. Constitution. His great-aunt Eliza Lucas Pinckney was the first woman agriculturalist in the United States, responsible for opening up the indigo trade. The current main house, doubling as the visitors center, dates from 1828, 11 years after Pinckney sold Snee Farm to pay off debts. That said, it's still a great example of Lowcountry architecture. It replaces Pinckney's original home, where President George Washington slept and had breakfast under a nearby oak tree in 1791 while touring the South.

## Isle of Palms

This primarily residential area of about 5,000 people received the state's first "Blue Wave" designation from the Clean Beaches Council for its well-managed and preserved beaches.

Like adjacent Sullivan's Island, there are pockets of great wealth here, but also a laid-back, windswept beach-town vibe. Aside from the whole scene, the main attraction here is the **Isle of Palms County Park** (14th Ave., 843/886-3863, www.ccprc.com, May-Labor Day daily 9am-7pm, Mar.-Apr. and Sept.-Oct. daily 10am-6pm, Nov.-Feb. daily 10am-5pm, $7 per vehicle, free for pedestrians and cyclists), with its oceanfront beach, complete with an umbrella rental front, volleyball court, playground, and lifeguards. The island's other claim to fame is the excellent (and surprisingly affordable) **Wild Dunes Resort** (5757 Palm Blvd., 888/778-1876, www.wilddunes.com), with its two Fazio golf courses and 17 clay tennis courts. Breach Inlet, between Isle of Palms and Sullivan's Island, is where the Confederate sub *Hunley* sortied to do battle with the USS *Housatonic*.

To get here from Mount Pleasant, take the Isle of Palms Connector (Hwy. 517) off U.S. 17 (Johnnie Dodds/Chuck Dawley Blvd.). To get to the county park, go through the light at Palm Boulevard and take the next left at the gate.

## Sullivan's Island

Part funky beach town, part ritzy getaway, Sullivan's Island has a certain timeless quality. While much of it was rebuilt after Hurricane Hugo's devastation, plenty of local character remains, as evidenced by some cool little bars in its tiny "business district" on the main drag of Middle Street. There's a ton of history on Sullivan's, but you can also just while the day away on the quiet, windswept beach on the Atlantic or ride a bike all over the island and back. Unless you have a boat, you can only get here from Mount Pleasant. From U.S. 17, follow the signs for Highway 703 and Sullivan's Island. Cross the Ben Sawyer Bridge, and then turn right onto Middle Street; continue for about 1.5 miles.

### FORT MOULTRIE

While Fort Sumter gets the bulk of the attention, the older **Fort Moultrie** (1214

Middle St., 843/883-3123, www.nps.gov/fosu, daily 9am-5pm, $3, free under age 16) on Sullivan's Island has a much more sweeping history. Furthering the irony, Major Robert Anderson's detachment at Fort Sumter at the opening of the Civil War was actually the Fort Moultrie garrison, reassigned to Sumter because Moultrie was thought too vulnerable from the landward side. Moultrie's first incarnation, a perimeter of felled palm trees, didn't even have a name when it was unsuccessfully attacked by the British in the summer of 1776, the first victory by the colonists in the Revolution. The redcoat cannonballs bounced off those flexible trunks, and thus was born South Carolina's nickname, "the Palmetto State."

In 1809 a brick fort was built here; it soon gained notoriety as the place where the great chief Osceola was detained after his capture. The chief died at the fort in 1838, and his modest grave site is still here, in front of the fort on the landward side. Other famous people to have trod on Sullivan's Island include Edgar Allan Poe, who was inspired by Sullivan's lonely, evocative environment to write *The Gold Bug* and other works. There's a Gold Bug Avenue and a Poe Avenue here today, and the local library is named after him as well. A young Lieutenant William Tecumseh Sherman was also stationed here during his Charleston stint in the 1830s, well before his encounter with history in the Civil War.

Moultrie's main Civil War role was as a target for Union shot during the long siege of Charleston. It was pounded so hard and for so long that its walls fell below a nearby sand hill and were finally unable to be hit anymore. A full military upgrade happened in the late 1800s, extending over most of Sullivan's Island (some private owners have even bought some of the old batteries and converted them into homes). It's the series of later forts that you'll visit on your trip to the Moultrie site, which is technically part of the Fort Sumter

National Monument and administered by the National Park Service.

Most of the outdoor tours are self-guided, but ranger programs typically happen Memorial Day-Labor Day daily at 11am and 2:30pm. There's a bookstore and visitors center across the street offering a 20-minute video on the hour and half hour 9am-4:30pm. Keep in mind there's no regular ferry to Fort Sumter from Fort Moultrie; the closest ferry to Sumter leaves from Patriots Point on Mount Pleasant.

### BENCH BY THE ROAD

Scholars say that about half of all African Americans alive today had an ancestor who once set foot on Sullivan's Island. As the first point of entry for at least half of all slaves imported to the United States, the island's "pest houses" acted as quarantine areas so slaves could be checked for communicable diseases before going to auction in Charleston proper. But few people seem to know this. In a 1989 magazine interview, African American author and Nobel laureate Toni Morrison said about historic sites concerning slavery, "There is no suitable memorial, or plaque, or wreath or wall, or park or skyscraper lobby. There's no 300-foot tower, there's no small bench by the road." In 2008, that last item became a reality, as the first of several planned "benches by the road" was installed on Sullivan's Island to mark the sacrifice of enslaved African Americans. It's a simple black steel bench with an attached marker and a nearby plaque. The Bench by the Road is at the Fort Moultrie visitors center (1214 Middle St.).

## Awendaw and Points North

This area just north of Charleston along U.S. 17—named for the Sewee Indian village originally located here and known to the world chiefly as the place where Hurricane Hugo made landfall in 1989—is seeing some new growth but still hews to its primarily rural, nature-loving roots.

## CAPE ROMAIN NATIONAL WILDLIFE REFUGE

One of the best natural experiences in the area is about a 30-minute drive north of Charleston at **Cape Romain National Wildlife Refuge** (5801 U.S. 17 N., 843/928-3264, www.fws.gov/caperomain, daily dawn-dusk, free). Essentially comprising four barrier islands, the 66,000-acre refuge—almost all of which is marsh—provides a lot of great paddling opportunities, chief among them **Bulls Island** (no overnight camping). A fairly lengthy trek from where you put in is famous Boneyard Beach, where hundreds of downed trees lie on the sand, bleached by sun and salt. Slightly to the south within the refuge, **Capers Island Heritage Preserve** (843/953-9300, www.dnr.sc.gov, daily dawn-dusk, free) is still a popular camping locale despite heavy damage from 1989's Hurricane Hugo. Get permits in advance by calling the South Carolina Department of Natural Resources. You can kayak to the refuge yourself or take the only approved ferry service from **Coastal Expeditions** (514-B Mill St., Mount Pleasant, 843/881-4582, www.coast-alexpeditions.com, $40 adults, $20 children, 30 minutes). **Barrier Island Eco Tours** (50 41st Ave., Isle of Palms, 843/886-5000, www.nature-tours.com, 3.5-hour boat excursions $38 adults, $28 children) on Isle of Palms also runs trips to the area.

## SEWEE VISITOR AND ENVIRONMENTAL EDUCATION CENTER

Twenty miles north of Charleston is the **Sewee Visitor and Environmental Education Center** (5821 U.S. 17, 843/928-3368, www.fws.gov/seweecenter, Wed.-Sat. 9am-5pm, free). Besides being a gateway of sorts for the almost entirely aquatic Cape Romain National Wildlife Refuge, Sewee is primarily known for housing several rare red wolves, which were part of a unique release program on nearby Bull Island begun in the late 1970s. They're kept at the center to maintain the genetic integrity of the species.

# FOLLY BEACH AND THE SOUTHWEST ISLANDS
## Folly Beach

A large percentage of the town of **Folly Beach** (south of Charleston via Hwy. 30 and Hwy. 171) was destroyed by Hurricane Hugo in 1989, and erosion since then has increased and hit the beach itself pretty hard. All that said, enough of Folly's funky charm is left to make it worth visiting. Called "the Edge of America" during its heyday as a swinging resort getaway from the 1930s through the 1950s, Folly Beach is now a slightly beaten but enjoyable little getaway on this barrier island. Folly's main claim to larger historical fame is playing host to George Gershwin, who stayed at a cottage on West Arctic Avenue to write the score for *Porgy and Bess,* set across the harbor in downtown Charleston. (Ironically, Gershwin's opera couldn't be performed in its original setting until 1970 because of segregationist Jim Crow laws.) Original *Porgy* author DuBose Heyward stayed around the corner at a summer cottage on West Ashley Avenue that he dubbed "Follywood."

Called Folly Road until it gets to the beach, Center Street is the main drag here, dividing the beach into east and west. In this area you'll find the **Folly Beach Fishing Pier** (101 E. Arctic Ave., 843/588-3474, Apr.-Oct. daily 6am-11pm, Nov. and Mar. daily 7am-7pm, Dec.-Feb. daily 8am-5pm, $5-7 parking, $8 fishing fee), which replaced the grand old wooden pier-and-pavilion structure that burned down in 1960.

To get to Folly Beach from Charleston, go west on Calhoun Street and take the James Island Connector. Take a left on Folly Road (Hwy. 171), which becomes Center Street once in Folly Beach.

At the far east end of Folly Island, about 300 yards offshore, you'll see the **Morris Island Lighthouse,** an 1876 beacon that was once surrounded by lush green landscape, but is now completely surrounded by water after the land eroded around it. Now privately owned, there's an extensive effort to save and preserve the lighthouse (www.savethelight.

org). There's also an effort to keep high-dollar condo development off beautiful bird-friendly Morris Island itself (www.morrisisland.org). To get there while there's still something left to enjoy, take East Ashley Street until it dead-ends. Park in the lot and take a 0.25-mile walk to the beach.

## Kiawah Island

The beautiful island of Kiawah—about 45 minutes from downtown Charleston—has as its main attraction the sumptuous **Kiawah Island Golf Resort** (12 Kiawah Beach Dr., 800/654-2924, www.kiawahgolf.com, $600-800), a key location for PGA tournaments. But even if you don't play golf, the resort is an amazing stay. The main component is **The Sanctuary,** an upscale hotel featuring an opulent lobby complete with grand stair-cases, a large pool area overlooking the beach, tasteful Spanish Colonial-style architecture, and 255 smallish but excellently appointed guest rooms. Several smaller private, family-friendly resorts also exist on Kiawah, with fully furnished homes and villas and every amenity you could ask for. Go to www.ex-plorekiawah.com for a full range of options or call 800/877-0837.

Through the efforts of the **Kiawah Island Conservancy** (23 Beachwalker Dr., 843/768-2029, www.kiawahconservancy.org), over 300 acres of the island have been kept as an unde-veloped nature preserve. The island's famous bobcat population has made quite a come-back; the bobcats are vital to the island eco-system, since as top predator they help cull what would otherwise become untenably large populations of deer and rabbit.

The beach at Kiawah is a particular delight, set as it is on such a comparatively undevel-oped island. No matter where you stay on Kiawah, a great thing about the island is the notable lack of light pollution—don't forget to look up at night and enjoy the stars!

## Seabrook Island

Like its neighbor Kiawah, **Seabrook Island** is a private resort-dominated island. In ad-dition to offering miles of beautiful beaches, on its 2,200 acres are a wide variety of golf-ing, tennis, equestrian, and swimming facil-ities as well as extensive dining and shopping options. There are a lot of kids' activities as well. For information on lodging options and packages, go to www.seabrook.com or call 866/249-9934. Seabrook Island is about 45 minutes from Charleston. From down-town, take Highway 30 West to Maybank Highway, then take a left onto Cherry Point Road.

## Johns Island

### ANGEL OAK PARK

The outlying community of Johns Island is where you'll find the inspiring **Angel Oak Park** (3688 Angel Oak Rd., Mon.-Sat. 9am-5pm, Sun. 1pm-5pm, free), home of a mas-sive live oak, 65 feet in circumference, that's over 1,000 years old and commonly consid-ered the oldest tree east of the Mississippi River. As is the case with all live oaks, don't expect impressive height—when oaks age they spread *out*, not up. The sprawling, pic-turesque tree and the park containing it are owned by the city of Charleston, and the scenic grounds are often used for weddings and special events. Angel Oak Park is about 30 minutes from Charleston. Take U.S. 17 over the Ashley River, then Highway 171 to Maybank Highway. Take a left onto Bohicket Road, and then look for signs on the right.

### LEGARE FARMS

**Legare Farms** (2620 Hanscombe Point Rd., 843/559-0763, www.legarefarms.com, hours vary) is open to the public for various activi-ties, including its annual pumpkin patch in October, its "sweet corn" festival in June, and bird walks (Sat. 8:30am, $6 adults, $3 chil-dren) in fall. To make the 20-minute drive from downtown Charleston, take Highway 30 West to Maybank Highway, then make a left onto River Road and a right onto Jenkins Farm Road.

the ancient Angel Oak

## Wadmalaw Island
### CHARLESTON TEA PLANTATION

Currently owned by the R. C. Bigelow Tea corporation, the **Charleston Tea Plantation** (6617 Maybank Hwy., 843/559-0383, www. charlestonteaplantation.com, Mon.-Sat. 10am-4pm, Sun. noon-4pm, free) is no cute living-history exhibit: It's a big working tea plantation—the only one in the United States—with acre after acre of *Camellia sinensis* being worked by modern farm machinery. Visitors get to see how the tea is brought "from the field to the cup." Factory tours are free, and a trolley tour of the "Back 40" is $10. And, of course, there's a gift shop where you can sample and buy all types of teas and tea-related products. Growing season is April-October. The tea bushes, direct descendants of plants brought over in the 1800s from India and China, "flush up" 2-3 inches every few weeks during growing season. Charleston Tea Plantation is about 30 minutes from Charleston. Take the Ashley River Bridge, stay left to Folly Road (Hwy. 171), turn right onto Maybank Highway and follow it 18 miles, and look for the sign on the left.

### DEEP WATER VINEYARDS

South Carolina has several good wineries, among them Wadmalaw's own **Deep Water Vineyards** (6775 Bears Bluff Rd., 843/559-6867, www.deepwatervineyard. com, Tues.-Sat. 10am-5pm), formerly Irvin House Vineyards, the Charleston area's only vineyard. They make several varieties of muscadine wine here, with $5 tastings and a gift shop. Every Saturday they host a "Wine-Down" party (noon-4pm). Also on the grounds you'll find **Firefly Distillery** (6775 Bears Bluff Rd., 843/559-6867, www.firefly-vodka.com, Tues.-Sat. 10am-5pm), home of their signature Firefly Sweet Tea Vodka. To get here from Charleston, go west on Maybank Highway about 10 miles to Bears Bluff Road, veering right on the latter. The vineyard entrance is on the left after about eight miles.

# Entertainment and Events

## NIGHTLIFE

Unlike the locals-versus-tourists divide you find so often in other destination cities, in Charleston it's nothing for a couple of visitors to find themselves at a table next to four or five college students enjoying themselves in true Charlestonian fashion: loudly and with lots of good food and strong drink nearby.

Bars close in Charleston at 2am, though there is a movement afoot to make the closing time earlier in some areas of town, mostly the Upper King neighborhood, the youngest and most vibrant nightlife area in Charleston. All hard-liquor sales stop at 7pm, with none at all on Sundays. You can buy beer and wine in grocery stores 24-7.

### Pubs and Bars

One of Charleston's favorite neighborhood spots is **Moe's Crosstown Tavern** (714 Rutledge Ave., 843/722-3287, daily 11am-2am) in the Hampton Square area.

In the French Quarter, the Guinness flows freely at touristy **Tommy Condon's Irish Pub** (160 Church St., 843/577-3818, www. tommycondons.com, Sun.-Thurs. 11am-2am, dinner until 10pm, Fri.-Sat. 11am-2am, dinner until 11pm), as do the patriotic Irish songs performed live most nights.

If it's a nice day, a good place to relax and enjoy happy hour outside is **Vickery's Bar and Grill** (15 Beaufain St., 843/577-5300, www.vickerysbarandgrill.com, Mon.-Sat. 11:30am-2am, Sun. 11am-1am, kitchen closes 1am), part of a small regional chain based in Atlanta. Start with the oyster bisque and maybe try the turkey and brie sandwich or crab cakes for your entrée.

The hottest hipster dive bar is the **Recovery Room** (685 King St., 843/727-0999, Mon.-Fri. 4pm-2am, Sat. 3pm-2am, Sun. noon-2am) in Upper King. The drinks are cheap and stiff, and the bar food is addictively tasty (two words: Tater Tots!).

Located not too far over the Ashley River on U.S. 17, Charleston institution **Gene's Haufbrau** (17 Savannah Hwy., 843/225-4363, www.geneshaufbrau.com, daily 11:30am-2am) is worth making a special trip into West Ashley. Boasting the largest beer selection in Charleston—from the Butte Creek Organic Ale from California to a can of PBR—Gene's also claims to be the oldest bar in town, established in 1952.

Though Sullivan's Island has a lot of high-dollar homes, it still has friendly watering holes like **Dunleavy's Pub** (2213-B Middle St., 843/883-9646, Sun.-Thurs. 11:30am-1am, Fri.-Sat. 11:30am-2am). Inside is a great bar festooned with memorabilia, or you can enjoy a patio table.

The other Sullivan's watering hole of note is **Poe's Tavern** (2210 Middle St., 843/883-0083, www.poestavern.com, daily 11am-2am, kitchen closes 10pm) across the street, a nod to Edgar Allan Poe and his service on the island as a clerk in the U.S. Army. It's a lively, mostly local scene, set within a fun but suitably dark interior (though you might opt for one of the outdoor tables on the raised patio). Simply put, no trip to Sullivan's is complete without a stop at one (or possibly both) of these two local landmarks, which are within a stone's throw of each other.

If you're in Folly Beach, enjoy the great views and cocktails at **Blu Restaurant and Bar** (1 Center St., 843/588-6658, www.blu-follybeach.com, daily 7am-10pm) inside the Tides Folly Beach hotel. There's nothing like a Spiked Lemonade on a hot Charleston day at the beach.

Another notable Folly Beach watering hole is the **Sand Dollar Social Club** (7 Center St., 843/588-9498, Sun.-Fri. noon-1am, Sat. noon-2am), the kind of cash-only, mostly local dive you often find in little beach towns. You have to pony up for a "membership" to this private club, but it's only a buck. There's a catch,

# Craft Breweries

The craft beer revolution has hit Charleston hard. Here are a few notable places to try:

- **Palmetto Brewing** (289 Huger St., 843/937-0903, www.palmettobrewery.com, tasting room Tues.-Wed. 3pm-7pm, Thurs. 3pm-9pm, Fri. 1pm-10pm, Sat. 1pm-7pm) has roots in Charleston going back before the Civil War and was the city's first post-Prohibition brewery. Known for their nitro beers and their Espresso Porter, among many others, they have an extensive outdoor seating area and often feature live music on weekends.

- **COAST Brewing** (1250 2nd St. N., 843/343-4727, www.coastbrewing.com, Thurs.-Fri. 4pm-7pm, Sat. 11am-4pm) in North Charleston focuses on sustainable and organic ingredients. Try the Blackbeerd Stout if it's available, and any Kölsch. This is more of a casual, all-outdoor tasting experience, so keep weather in mind.

- **Holy City Brewing** (4155C Dorchester Rd., www.holycitybrewing.com, Mon.-Thurs. 11am-8pm, Fri.-Sat. 11am-9pm, Sun. 11am-5pm), also in North Charleston, is known for its porters and stouts. This is also a great choice if you're hungry, as they have a full menu. Try the namesake Holy City Burger.

though: You can't get in until your 24-hour "waiting period" is over.

If you find yourself up in North Charleston, stop by **Madra Rua Irish Pub** (1034 E. Montague Ave., 843/554-2522, daily 11am-1am), an authentic watering hole with a better-than-average pub-food menu that's also a great place to watch a soccer game.

## Lounges

On the waterfront, the aptly named **Rooftop Bar and Restaurant** (23 Vendue Range, 843/723-0485, Tues.-Sat. 6pm-2am) at the Vendue is a very popular happy hour spot from which to enjoy the sunset over the Charleston skyline.

If artisan cocktails are your thing, head straight to another waterfront spot, **The Gin Joint** (182 E. Bay St., 843/577-6111, www.theginjoint.com, Thurs.-Fri. 5pm-2am, Sat. 3pm-2am, Sun.-Wed. 5pm-midnight), where you can get drinks with names like Thieve's Tonic (rum, turmeric, lime, coconut, ginger honey) and Studmuffin (Madeira, chicory liqueur, coffee liqueur, and bay leaf ice cubes). With most cocktails running about $11 each, they're actually bargains when you consider the curated ingredients going into each one. Got a big party? Order one of four signature punches to share, prepared tableside (about

$40). Fair warning: These aren't your typical office party punches and pack a commensurately large, well, punch. Thankfully, there is a good little menu of tapas to soak up all the alcohol.

Across the street from Gene's Haufbrau in West Ashley, the retro-chic **Voodoo Lounge** (15 Magnolia Rd., 843/769-0228, Mon.-Fri. 4pm-2am, Sat.-Sun. 5:30pm-2am, kitchen until 1am) is another very popular hangout. It has a wide selection of trendy cocktails and killer gourmet tacos.

## Live Music

Charleston's live music scene is hit or miss. With the long-ago passing of the heyday of Hootie & the Blowfish, there's no distinct "Charleston sound" to speak of (though Hootie frontman-turned-country-star Darius Rucker still plays frequently in the area), but the venues do a good job of bringing in well-regarded national and regional touring acts. The best place to find up-to-date music listings is the local free weekly *Charleston City Paper* (www.charlestoncitypaper.com).

The venerable **Music Farm** (32 Ann St., 843/722-8904, www.musicfarm.com) in Upper King isn't much to look at from the outside, but the cavernous space has played host to all sorts of bands over the past two

# Doin' the Charleston

It has been called the biggest song-and-dance craze of the 20th century. It first entered the American public consciousness via New York City in a 1923 Harlem musical called *Runnin' Wild*, but the roots of the dance soon to be known as the Charleston were indeed in the Holy City. No one is quite sure of the day and date, but local lore assures us that members of Charleston's legendary Jenkins Orphanage Band were the first to start dancing that crazy "Geechie step," a development that soon became part of the band's act.

The Jenkins Orphanage was started in 1891 by the African American Baptist minister Reverend D. J. Jenkins and was originally housed in the Old Marine Hospital at 20 Franklin Street (which you can see today, although it's not open to the public). To raise money, Reverend Jenkins acquired donated instruments and started a band comprising talented orphans from the house. The orphans traveled as far away as London, where they were a hit with the locals but not with the constabulary, who unceremoniously fined them for stopping traffic. A Charleston attorney who happened to be in London at the time, Augustine Smyth, paid their way back home, becoming a lifelong supporter of the orphanage in the process.

From then on, playing in donated old Citadel uniforms, the Jenkins Orphanage Band frequently took their act on the road. They played at the St. Louis and Buffalo expositions and even at President Taft's inauguration. They also frequently played in New York, and it was there that African American pianist and composer James P. Johnson heard the Charlestonians play and dance to their Gullah rhythms, considered exotic at the time. Johnson would incorporate what he heard into the tune "Charleston," one of many songs in the revue *Runnin' Wild*. The catchy song and its accompanying loose-limbed dance seemed tailor-made for the Roaring '20s and its liberated, hedonistic spirit. Before long the Charleston had swept the nation, becoming a staple of jazz clubs and speakeasies across the country and, indeed, the world.

decades. Recent concerts have included Fitz and the Tantrums, the Dropkick Murphys, and the Drive-By Truckers.

The hippest music spot in town is out on James Island at **The Pour House** (1977 Maybank Hwy., 843/571-4343, www.charlestonpourhouse.com, 9pm-2am on nights with music scheduled), where the local characters are sometimes just as entertaining as the acts onstage.

## Dance Clubs

The **Trio Club** (139 Calhoun St., 843/965-5333, Thurs.-Sat. 9pm-2am), right off Marion Square, is a favorite place to make the scene. There's a relaxing outdoor area with piped-in music, an intimate sofa-filled upstairs bar for dancing and chilling, and the dark candlelit downstairs with frequent live music leaning toward hip-hop sounds.

## Gay-Friendly

Most gay-oriented nightlife centers on the Upper King area. Charleston's hottest dance spot of any type, gay or straight, is **Cure** (28 Ann St., 843/577-2582, Fri.-Sun. 10pm-2am), on the lower level of the parking garage across from the visitors center (375 Meeting St.). This space was for years known as Club Pantheon but has changed ownership. Cover charges are typically not cheap, but it's worth it for the great DJs, the dancing, and the people watching, not to mention the frequent drag cabaret shows.

Just down the street from Cure—and owned by the same people—is a totally different kind of gay bar, **Dudley's** (42 Ann St., 843/577-6779, daily 4pm-2am). Mellower and more appropriate for conversation or a friendly game of pool, Dudley's is a nice contrast to the thumping club a few doors down.

North of Broad, **Vickery's Bar and Grill** (15 Beaufain St., 843/577-5300, www.vickerysbarandgrill.com, Mon.-Sat. 11:30am-2am, Sun. 11am-1am, kitchen closes 1am) does not market itself as a gay establishment, but it has nonetheless become quite popular with the gay community—not least because of the good reputation its parent tavern in Atlanta has with that city's large and influential gay community.

# PERFORMING ARTS
## Theater

Unlike the more (literally) puritanical colonies farther up the North American coast, Charleston was an arts-friendly settlement from the beginning. The first theatrical production on the continent happened in Charleston in January 1735, when a nomadic troupe rented a space at Church and Broad Streets to perform Thomas Otway's *The Orphan.* The play's success led to the building of the Dock Street Theatre on what is now Queen Street. Notable thespians performing in town included Edwin Booth, Junius Booth Jr. (brothers of Lincoln's assassin, John Wilkes), and Edgar Allan Poe's mother, Eliza.

Several high-quality troupes continue to keep Charleston's proud theater tradition alive, chief among them **Charleston Stage** (Dock Street Theatre, 135 Church St., 843/577-7183, www.charlestonstage.com), the resident company of the Dock Street Theatre. In addition to its well-received regular season of classics and modern staples, Charleston Stage has debuted more than 30 original scripts over the years, a recent example being *Gershwin at Folly,* recounting the composer's time at Folly Beach working on *Porgy and Bess.*

**The Footlight Players** (Footlight Players Theatre, 20 Queen St., 843/722-4487, www.footlightplayers.net) make up the oldest continuously active company in town, founded in 1931. This community-based amateur company performs a mix of crowd-pleasers (*Who's Afraid of Virginia Woolf?*) and creative adaptations (*Miracle in Bedford Falls,* a musical based on *It's a Wonderful Life*) at its space at 20 Queen Street.

The players of **PURE Theatre** (477 King St., 843/723-4444, www.puretheatre.org) perform in a black-box space in the heart of the Upper King entertainment/nightlife district.

Their shows emphasize compelling, mature drama, beautifully performed. This is where to catch less glitzy, grittier productions like *Rabbit Hole, American Buffalo,* and *Cold Tectonics,* a hit at Piccolo Spoleto.

The city's most unusual players are **The Have Nots!** (Theatre 99, 280 Meeting St., 843/853-6687, www.theatre99.com, Wed. 8pm, Fri.-Sat. 8pm and 10pm, $5-12.50), with a rotating ensemble of dozens of comedians who perform their brand of edgy, adults-only improv at Theatre 99. Friday is the most reliable improve night, while Wednesday and Saturday may feature more sketch comedy.

## Music

The **Charleston Symphony Orchestra** (Gaillard Center, 95 Calhoun St., 843/554-6060, www.charlestonsymphony.com) performed for the first time on December 28, 1936, at the Hibernian Hall on Meeting Street. During that first season the CSO accompanied *The Recruiting Officer,* the inaugural show at the renovated Dock Street Theatre. For seven decades, the CSO continued to provide world-class orchestral music, gaining "Metropolitan" status in the 1970s, when it accompanied the first-ever local performance of *Porgy and Bess,* which despite its Charleston setting couldn't be performed locally before then due to segregation laws. Now under the direction of conductor Ken Lam, the CSO performs at the renovated and reimagined Gaillard Center, modeled on European concert halls. Check the website for upcoming concerts.

The excellent music department at the College of Charleston sponsors the annual **Charleston Music Fest** (Simons Center for the Arts, 54 St. Philip St., $25), a series of chamber music concerts at various venues around the beautiful campus, featuring many faculty members of the college as well as visiting guest artists. Other college musical offerings include the **College of Charleston Concert Choir** (www.cofc.edu/music), which performs at various venues, usually churches, around town during the fall; the **College of**

Charleston Opera, which performs at least one full-length production during the school year and often takes the stage at Piccolo Spoleto; and the popular **Yuletide Madrigal Singers,** who sing in early December at a series of concerts in historic Randolph Hall.

**Chamber Music Charleston** (various locations, 843/763-4941, www.chambermusiccharleston.org), which relies on many core Charleston Symphony Orchestra musicians, continues to perform around town, including at Piccolo Spoleto. They play a wide variety of picturesque venues, including the **Sottile Theatre** (44 George St.) and Kiawah Island. They can also be found at private house concerts, which sell out quickly.

## CINEMA

The most interesting art-house and indie venue in town is **The Terrace** (1956D Maybank Hwy., 843/762-4247, www.terracetheater.com), and not only because it offers beer and wine that you can enjoy at your seat. Shows before 5pm are $7. It's west of Charleston on James Island; get there by taking U.S. 17 west from Charleston and going south on Highway 171, after which you take a right on Maybank Highway (Hwy. 700).

## FESTIVALS AND EVENTS

Charleston is a festival-mad city, especially in the spring and early fall. And new festivals are being added every year, further enhancing the hedonistic flavor of this city that has also mastered the art of hospitality.

### January

Held on a Sunday in late January at historic Boone Hall Plantation in Mount Pleasant, the **Lowcountry Oyster Festival** (www.charlestonlowcountry.com, Sun. 11am-5pm, $8, food additional) features literal truckloads of the sweet shellfish for your enjoyment. Gates open at 10:30am, and there's plenty of parking. Oysters are sold by the bucket and served with crackers and cocktail sauce. Bring your own shucking knife or glove, or buy them on-site.

### February

One of the unique events in town is the **Southeastern Wildlife Exposition** (various venues, 843/723-1748, www.sewe.com, $12.50 per day, $30 for three days, free under age 13). For the last quarter century, the Wildlife Expo has brought together hundreds of artists and exhibitors to showcase just about any kind of naturally themed art you can think of in over a dozen galleries and venues all over downtown. Kids will enjoy the live animals on hand as well.

North Charleston is home to **Brewvival** (adjacent to COAST Brewing, 1250 2nd St. N., www.brewvival.com, $75). This daylong craft brew-tasting festival features brewers from the rapidly growing South Carolina craft beer industry. There is live music, and food vendors are available as well.

### March

Generally straddling late February and the first days of March, the four-day **Charleston Food & Wine Festival** (www.charlestonfoodandwine.com, various venues and admission) is a glorious celebration of one of the Holy City's premier draws: its amazing culinary community. While the emphasis is on Lowcountry chefs, guest chefs from New York, New Orleans, and Los Angeles routinely come to show off their skills. Oenophiles, especially of domestic wines, will be in heaven as well. This event has boomed in recent years and downtown gets quite crowded. Tickets aren't cheap—an all-event pass is over $500 per person—but then again, this is one of the nation's great food cities.

Immediately before the Festival of Houses and Gardens is the **Charleston International Antiques Show** (40 E. Bay St., 843/722-3405, www.historiccharleston.org, admission varies), held at Historic Charleston's headquarters at the Missroon House on the High Battery. It features over 30 of the nation's best-regarded dealers and offers lectures and tours.

Mid-March-April, the perennial favorite **Festival of Houses and Gardens**

(843/722-3405, www.historiccharleston.org, admission varies) is sponsored by the Historic Charleston Foundation and held at the very peak of the spring blooming season for maximum effect. In all, the festival goes into a dozen historic neighborhoods to view about 150 homes. Each day sees a different three-hour tour of a different area, at about $50 per person. This is a fantastic opportunity to peek inside some amazing old privately owned properties that are inaccessible to visitors at all other times. A highlight is a big oyster roast and picnic at Drayton Hall.

Not to be confused with the above festival, the **Garden Club of Charleston House and Garden Tours** (843/530-5164, www. thegardenclubofcharleston.com, $35) are held over a weekend in late March. Highlights include the Heyward-Washington House and the private garden of the late great Charleston horticulturalist Emily Whaley.

One of Charleston's newest and most fun events, the five-night **Charleston Fashion Week** (www.charlestonfashionweek.com, admission varies) benefits local women's and children's charities. Mimicking New York's Fashion Week events under tenting in Bryant Park, Charleston's version features runway action under big tents in Marion Square—and, yes, past guests have included former contestants on *Project Runway*.

## April

The annual **Cooper River Bridge Run** (www.bridgerun.com) happens the first Saturday in April (unless that's Easter weekend, in which case it runs the week before) and features a six-mile jaunt across the massive Arthur Ravenel Bridge over the Cooper River, the longest cable span in the Western Hemisphere. It's not for those with a fear of heights, but it's still one of Charleston's best-attended events—there are well over 30,000 participants.

Previously known as the Family Circle Cup, the **Volvo Car Open** (161 Seven Farms Dr., Daniel Island, 843/856-7900, www.volvocaropen.com, admission varies) is held at Daniel Island's Family Circle Tennis Center, specifically built for the event. Almost 100,000 people attend the multiple-week event. Individual session tickets go on sale the preceding January.

Mount Pleasant is the home of Charleston's shrimping fleet, and each April sees all the boats parade by the Alhambra Hall and Park for the **Blessing of the Fleet** (843/884-8517, www.townofmountpleasant.com). Family events and lots and lots of seafood are also on tap.

## May

Free admission and free parking are not the only draws at the outdoor **North Charleston Arts Festival** (5000 Coliseum Dr., www.northcharleston.org), but let's face it, that's important. Held beside North Charleston's Performing Arts Center and Convention Center, the festival features music, dance, theater, multicultural performers, and storytellers. There are a lot of kids' events as well.

Held over three days at the Holy Trinity Greek Orthodox Church up toward the Neck, the **Charleston Greek Festival** (30 Race St., 843/577-2063, www.charlestongreekfestival.com, $5 admission, food extra) offers a plethora of live entertainment, dancing, Greek wares, and, of course, fantastic Greek cuisine cooked by the congregation. Parking is not a problem, and there's even a shuttle to the church from the lot.

Indisputably Charleston's single biggest and most important event, **Spoleto Festival USA** (843/579-3100, www.spoletousa.org, admission varies) has come a long way since it was a sparkle in the eye of the late Gian Carlo Menotti three decades ago. Though Spoleto long ago broke ties with its founder, his vision remains indelibly stamped on the event from start to finish. There's plenty of music, to be sure, in genres that include orchestral, opera, jazz, and avant-garde, but you'll find something in every other performing art, such as dance, drama, and spoken word, in traditions from Western to African to Southeast Asian. For 17 days from Memorial Day weekend through early June, Charleston hops and hums nearly 24 hours a day to the energy of this vibrant, cutting-edge (yet accessible) artistic celebration.

As if all the hubbub around Spoleto didn't give you enough to do, there's also **Piccolo Spoleto** (843/724-7305, www.piccolospoleto. com, various venues and admission), literally "little Spoleto," running concurrently. The intent of Piccolo Spoleto—begun just a couple of years after the larger festival came to town and run by the city's Office of Cultural Affairs—is to give local and regional performers a time to shine, sharing some of that larger spotlight on the national and international performers at the main event. Of particular interest to visiting families will be Piccolo's children's events, a good counter to some of the decidedly more adult fare at Spoleto USA.

## June

Technically part of Piccolo Spoleto but gathering its own following, the **Sweetgrass Cultural Arts Festival** (www.sweetgrass-festival.org) is held the first week in June in Mount Pleasant at the Laing Middle School (2213 U.S. 17 N.). The event celebrates the traditional sweetgrass basket-making skills of African Americans in the historic Christ Church Parish area of Mount Pleasant. If you want to buy some sweetgrass baskets made by the world's foremost experts in the field, this would be the time.

## July

Each year over 30,000 people come to see the **Patriots Point Fourth of July Blast** (866/831-1720), featuring a hefty barrage of fireworks shot off the deck of the USS *Yorktown* moored on the Cooper River in the Patriots Point complex. Food, live entertainment, and kids' activities are also featured.

## September

From late September into the first week of October, the city-sponsored **MOJA Arts Festival** (843/724-7305, www.mojafesti-val.com, various venues and admission) highlights the cultural contributions of African Americans and people from the Caribbean with dance, visual art, poetry, cuisine, crafts, and music in genres that include gospel, jazz, reggae, and classical. In existence since 1984, MOJA's name comes from the Swahili word for "one," and its diverse range of offerings in so many media have made it one of the Southeast's premier events. Some events are ticketed, while others, such as the kids' activities and many of the dance and film events, are free.

For five weeks from the last week of September into October, the Preservation Society of Charleston hosts the much-anticipated **Fall Tours of Homes & Gardens** (843/722-4630, www.preservationsociety. org, $45). The tour takes you into more than a dozen local residences and is the nearly 90-year-old organization's biggest fund-raiser. Tickets typically go on sale the previous June, and they tend to sell out very quickly.

Another great food event in this great food city, the **Taste of Charleston** (1235 Long Point Rd., 843/577-4030, www.charleston-restaurantassociation.com, 11am-5pm, $12) is held on a weekend in October at Boone Hall Plantation in Mount Pleasant and sponsored by the Greater Charleston Restaurant Association. Over 50 area chefs and restaurants come together so you can sample their wares, including a wine and food pairing, with proceeds going to charity.

## October

Local company **Half Moon Outfitters** (280 King St., 843/853-0990, 425 Coleman Blvd., 843/881-9472, www.halfmoonoutfitters.com, Mon.-Sat. 10am-7pm, Sun. noon-6pm) sponsors an annual six-mile Giant Kayak Race at Isle of Palms Marina in late October benefiting the Coastal Conservation League.

## November

**Plantation Days at Middleton Place** (4300 Ashley River Rd., 843/556-6020, www.middletonplace.org, daily 9am-5pm, last tour 4:30pm, guided tour $10) happen each Saturday in

# A Man, a Plan: Spoleto!

People gather in Marion Square to enjoy Piccolo Spoleto.

Sadly, Gian Carlo Menotti is no longer with us, having died in 2007 at the age of 95. But the overwhelming success of the composer's brainchild and labor of love, **Spoleto Festival USA,** lives on, enriching the cultural and social life of Charleston and serving as the city's chief calling card to the world at large.

Menotti began writing music at age seven in his native Italy. As a young man he moved to Philadelphia to study music, where he shared classes—and lifelong connections—with Leonard Bernstein and Samuel Barber. His first full-length opera, *The Consul,* would garner him the Pulitzer Prize, as would 1955's *The Saint of Bleecker Street.* But by far Menotti's best-known work is the beloved Christmas opera *Amahl and the Night Visitors,* composed especially for NBC television in 1951. At the height of his fame in 1958, the charismatic and mercurial genius—fluent and witty in five languages—founded the "Festival of Two Worlds" in Spoleto, Italy, specifically as a forum for young American artists in Europe. But it wasn't until nearly two decades later, in 1977, that Menotti was able to make his long-imagined dream of an American counterpart a reality.

Attracted to Charleston because of its long-standing support of the arts, its undeniable good taste, and its small size—ensuring that his festival would always be the number one activity in town while it was going on—Menotti worked closely with the man who was to become the other key part of the equation: Charleston mayor Joe Riley, then in his first term in office. Since then, the city has built on Spoleto's success by founding its own local version, **Piccolo Spoleto**—literally, "little Spoleto"—which focuses exclusively on local and regional talent.

Things haven't always gone smoothly. Menotti and the stateside festival parted ways in 1993, when he took over the Rome Opera. Making matters more uneasy, the Italian festival—run by Menotti's longtime partner (and later adopted son), Chip—also became estranged from what was intended to be its soul mate in South Carolina. (Chip was later replaced by the Italian Culture Ministry.) But perhaps this kind of creative tension is what Menotti intended all along. Indeed, each spring brings a Spoleto USA that seems to thrive on the inherent conflict between the festival's often cutting-edge offerings and the very traditional city that hosts it. Spoleto still challenges its audiences, just as Menotti intended it to. Depending on the critic and the audience member, that modern opera debut you see may be groundbreaking or gratuitous. The drama you check out may be exhilarating or tiresome.

Each year, a total of about 500,000 people attend both Spoleto and Piccolo Spoleto. Nearly one-third of the attendees are Charleston residents—the final proof that when it comes to supporting the arts, Charleston puts its money where its mouth is.

November, giving visitors a chance to wander the grounds and see artisans at work practicing authentic crafts, as they would have done in antebellum days, with a special emphasis on the contributions of African Americans. A special treat comes on Thanksgiving, when a full meal is offered on the grounds at the Middleton Place Restaurant (843/556-6020, www.middletonplace.org, reservations strongly recommended).

One of Charleston's newest annual events is the **Charleston International Film Festival** (843/817-1617, www.charlestoniff.com, various venues and prices). Despite being a relative latecomer to the film-festival circuit, the event is pulled off with Charleston's usual aplomb.

Though the **Battle of Secessionville** actually took place in June 1862 much farther south, November is the time the battle is reenacted at Boone Hall Plantation (1235 Long Point Rd., 843/884-4371, www.boonehallplantation.

com, $17.50 adults, $7.50 children) in Mount Pleasant. Call for specific dates and times.

## December

A yuletide in the Holy City is an experience you'll never forget, as the **Christmas in Charleston** (843/724-3705) events clustered around the first week of the month prove. For some reason—whether it's the old architecture, the friendly people, the churches, the carriages, or all of the above—Charleston feels right at home during Christmas. The festivities begin with the mayor lighting the city's 60-foot Tree of Lights in Marion Square, followed by a parade of brightly lit boats from Mount Pleasant all the way around Charleston up the Ashley River. The key event is the Sunday Christmas Parade through downtown, featuring bands, floats, and performers in the holiday spirit. The Saturday farmers market in the square continues through the middle of the month with a focus on holiday items.

# Shopping

Shopping in Charleston centers on King Street, unique not only for the fact that so many national-name stores are lined up so close to each other, but also because there are so many great restaurants of so many different types scattered in and among the retail outlets, ideally positioned for when you need to take a break to rest and refuel. **Lower King** is primarily top-of-the-line antiques stores (most are closed Sundays, so plan your trip accordingly); **Middle King** is where you'll find upscale name-brand outlets such as Banana Republic and American Apparel as well as some excellent shoe stores; and **Upper King,** north of Calhoun Street, is where you'll find funky housewares shops, generally locally owned.

## FRENCH QUARTER
### Antiques and Vintage

A cute little shop tucked away in an alley,

**Curiosity** (56 $^{1/2}$ Queen St., 843/647-7763, www.curiositycharleston.com) is a find even by the standards of antiques/vintage-crazy Charleston. A nice plus is the prices here are a bit lower than in the premier antiques shops on Lower King Street, which would never be accused of being bargain priced.

## Art Galleries

While not considered a visual arts mecca, the Holy City has been fertile ground for visual artists since native son Joseph Allen Smith began one of the country's first art collections in Charleston in the late 1700s. For most visitors, the center of gallery activity is in the French Quarter between South Market and Tradd Streets.

Incorporating works from the estate of Charleston legend Elizabeth O'Neill Verner is **Ann Long Fine Art** (54 Broad St., 843/577-0447, www.annlongfineart.com, Mon.-Sat.

# Art Walks

The best way to experience visual art galleries in Charleston is to go on one of the popular and free **Charleston Gallery Association ArtWalks** (843/724-3424, www.charlestongalleryassociation.com, first Friday of March, May, October, and December 5pm-8pm), which feature lots of wine, food, and, of course, art. Over 40 galleries throughout downtown, with a special focus on the French Quarter, are featured. You can download a map at the website and visit them all yourself, whether or not you're here for the ArtWalk.

11am-5pm), which seeks to combine the painterly aesthetic of the Old World with the edgy vision of the New.

One of the French Quarter's most beloved galleries, the **Corrigan Gallery** (62 Queen St., 843/722-9868, www.corrigangallery.com, daily 10am-5pm) deals in some of the best current local artists, along with a focus on the Charleston Renaissance and the Charleston printmaking tradition.

The **Pink House Gallery** (17 Chalmers St., 843/723-3608, http://pinkhousegallery.tripod.com, Mon.-Sat. 10am-5pm) is housed in the oldest tavern building in the South, built circa 1694. The exhibits here offer a glimpse into old Charleston, including exclusive antique prints.

**Robert Lange Studios** (2 Queen St., 843/805-8052, www.robertlangestudios.com, daily 11am-5pm) is oriented toward modern art. It hosts not only the work of its owners, Robert and Megan Lange, but also a slate of up-and-coming regional artists. This is a great place to be on the regular first Friday art walks and events.

## Books and Music
The great **Shops of Historic Charleston Foundation** (108 Meeting St., 843/724-8484, www.historiccharleston.org) is housed in a beautiful building and has plenty of tasteful Charleston-themed gift ideas, from books to kitchenware.

# NORTH OF BROAD
## Antiques
**Alexandra AD** (156 King St., 843/722-4897, Mon.-Sat. 10am-5pm) features great chandeliers, lamps, and fabrics.

Since 1929, **George C. Birlant & Co.** (191 King St., 843/722-3842, Mon.-Sat. 9am-5:30pm) has been importing 18th- and 19th-century furniture, silver, china, and crystal, and it deals in the famous "Charleston Battery Bench."

## Art Galleries
For a more modern take from local artists, check out the **Sylvan Gallery** (171 King St., 843/722-2172, www.thesylvangallery.com, Mon.-Fri. 9am-5pm, Sat. 10am-5pm, Sun. 11am-4pm), which specializes in 20th- and 21st-century art and sculpture.

Specializing in original Audubon prints and antique botanical prints is **The Audubon Gallery** (190 King St., 843/853-1100, www.audubonart.com, Mon.-Sat. 10am-5pm), the sister store of the Joel Oppenheimer Gallery in Chicago.

Within City Market is **Gallery Chuma** (188 Meeting St., 843/722-1702, www.gallerychuma.com, daily 9:30am-6pm), which specializes in the art of the Gullah people of the South Carolina coast. They put on lots of cultural and educational events about Gullah culture as well as display art on the subject.

**Art Mecca** (427 King St., 843/577-0603, www.artmeccaofcharleston.com, Mon.-Fri. 10am-6pm, Sat. 10am-7pm, Sun. 11am-5pm) is an inviting modernist space that specializes in local and regional contemporary artists. It's a great place to get a flavor of what Charleston's younger up-and-coming artists are doing.

## Books and Music
The charming **Pauline Books and Media** (243 King St., 843/577-0175, Mon.-Sat. 10am-6pm) is run by the Daughters of Saint Paul and

carries Christian books, Bibles, rosaries, and images from a Roman Catholic perspective.

It's easy to overlook at the far southern end of the retail development on King, but the excellent **Preservation Society of Charleston Book and Gift Shop** (147 King St., 843/722-4630, Mon.-Sat. 10am-5pm) is perhaps the best place in town to pick up books on Charleston lore and history as well as locally themed gift items.

## Clothes

A charmingly old-school and notable locally owned clothing store on King Street is the classy **Berlins Men's and Women's** (114-120 King St., 843/722-1665, Mon.-Sat. 9:30am-6pm), dating from 1883. Despite the name, Berlins focuses on men's clothing, offering designs from Canali, Coppley, Jack Victor, and more.

Big companies' losses are your gain at **Oops!** (326 King St., 843/722-7768, Mon.-Fri. 10am-6pm, Sat. 10am-7pm, Sun. noon-6pm), which buys factory mistakes and discontinued lines from major brands at a discount, passing along the savings to you. The range here tends toward colorful and preppy.

The incredible consignment store **The Trunk Show** (281 Meeting St., 843/722-0442, Mon.-Sat. 10am-6pm) offers one-of-a-kind vintage and designer wear and accessories. Some finds are bargains, some not so much, but there's no denying the quality and breadth of the offerings.

For a locally owned clothing shop, try the innovative **Worthwhile** (268 King St., 843/723-4418, www.shopworthwhile.com, Mon.-Sat. 10am-6pm, Sun. noon-5pm), which has lots of organic fashions.

## Jewelry

**Art Jewelry by Mikhail Smolkin** (312 King St., 843/722-3634, www.fineartjewelry.com, Mon.-Sat. 10am-5pm) features one-of-a-kind pieces by this St. Petersburg, Russia, native.

Since 1919, **Croghan's Jewel Box** (308 King St., 843/723-3594, www.

croghansjewelbox.com, Mon.-Fri. 9:30am-5:30pm, Sat. 10am-5pm) has offered amazing locally crafted diamonds, silver, and designer pieces to generations of Charlestonians. An expansion in the late 1990s tripled the size of the historic location.

**Joint Venture Estate Jewelers** (185 King St., 843/722-6730, www.jventure.com, Mon.-Sat. 10am-5:30pm) specializes in antique, vintage, and modern estate jewelry as well as pre-owned watches, including Rolex, Patek Philippe, and Cartier, with a fairly unique consignment emphasis.

## Shoes

A famous locally owned place for footwear is **Bob Ellis Shoe Store** (332 King St., 843/722-2515, www.bobellisshoes.com, Mon.-Sat. 10am-6pm), which has served Charleston's elite with high-end shoes since 1950.

**Copper Penny Shooz** (317 King St., 843/723-3838, Mon.-Sat. 10am-7pm, Sun. noon-6pm) combines hip and upscale footwear for women, "curated with a Southern eye," as this Charleston-based regional chain's motto goes.

Funky and fun **Phillips Shoes** (320 King St., 843/965-5270, Mon.-Sat. 10am-6pm) deals in Dansko for men, women, and kids (don't miss the awesome painting above the register of Elvis fitting a customer).

**Rangoni of Florence** (270 King St., 843/577-9554, Mon.-Sat. 9:30am-6pm, Sun. 12:30pm-5:30pm) imports the best women's shoes from Italy, with a few men's designs as well.

## Shopping Centers and Malls

**Belmond Charleston Place** (205 Meeting St., 843/722-4900, www.charlestonplace-shops.com, Mon.-Wed. 10am-6pm, Thurs.-Sat. 10am-8pm, Sun. noon-5pm), usually just called "Charleston Place," is a combined retail-hotel development with highlights such as Gucci, Talbots, Louis Vuitton, Yves Delorme, Everything But Water, and Godiva.

For years dominated by a flea market vibe,

City Market (Meeting St. and Market St., 843/973-7236, daily 9:30am-10:30pm) was recently upgraded and is now chockablock with boutique retail all along its lengthy interior. The humbler crafts tables are toward the back. If you must have one of the hand-crafted sweetgrass baskets, try out your haggling skills—the prices have wiggle room built in. In addition to the myriad tourist-oriented shops in the City Market itself, there are a few gems in the surrounding area that also appeal to locals.

## Sporting Goods

With retail locations in Charleston and throughout South Carolina and Georgia and a new cutting-edge, eco-friendly warehouse in North Charleston, **Half Moon Outfitters** (280 King St., 843/853-0990, www.halfmoonoutfitters.com, Mon.-Sat. 10am-7pm, Sun. noon-6pm) is something of a local legend. Here you can find not only top-of-the-line camping and outdoor gear and tips on local recreation, but also some really stylish outdoorsy apparel as well.

# UPPER KING
## Art Galleries

One of the most important single venues for art, the nonprofit **Redux Contemporary Art Center** (136 St. Philip St., 843/722-0697, www.reduxstudios.org, Tues.-Fri. 10am-6pm, Sat. noon-5pm) features modernistic work in a variety of media, including illustration, video installation, blueprints, performance art, and graffiti. Outreach is hugely important to this venture and includes lecture series, classes, workshops, and internships.

## Books and Music

Housed in an extremely long and narrow storefront, Jonathan Sanchez's funky and friendly **Blue Bicycle Books** (420 King St., 843/722-2666, www.bluebicyclebooks.com, Mon.-Sat. 10am-7:30pm, Sun. 1pm-6pm) deals primarily in used books and has a particularly nice stock of local and regional titles, art books, and fiction.

## Home Goods

Head to **Haute Design Studio** (489 King St., 843/577-9886, www.hautedesign.com, Mon.-Fri. 9am-5:30pm) for upper-end furnishings with an edgy feel.

# WATERFRONT
## Art Galleries

The **City Gallery at Waterfront** (34 Prioleau St., 843/958-6484, www.citygalleryatwaterfrontpark.com, Tues.-Fri. 10am-6pm, Sat.-Sun. noon-5pm) is funded by the city, with exhibits focusing on local and regional culture and folkways. It's mostly an exhibit space, though art is also sold here.

## Home Goods

Affiliated with the hip local restaurant chain Maverick Kitchens, **Charleston Cooks!** (194 E. Bay St., 843/722-1212, www.charlestoncooks.com, Mon.-Sat. 10am-9pm, Sun. 11am-6pm) has an almost overwhelming array of gourmet items and kitchenware, and even offers cooking classes.

**Indigo** (4 Vendue Range, 800/549-2513, Sun.-Thurs. 10am-6pm, Fri.-Sat. 10am-7pm), a favorite home accessories store, has plenty of one-of-a-kind pieces, many of them by regional artists and rustic in flavor, almost like outsider art.

# SOUTH OF BROAD
## Art Galleries

**Charleston Renaissance Gallery** (103 Church St., 843/723-0025, www.fineartsouth.com, Mon.-Sat. 10am-5pm) specializes in 19th- and 20th-century oils and sculpture and features artists from the American South, including some splendid pieces from the Charleston Renaissance.

**Helena Fox Fine Art** (106-A Church St., 843/723-0073, www.helenafoxfineart.com, Mon.-Sat. 10am-5pm) deals in 20th-century representational art.

# WEST ASHLEY
## Home Goods

Probably Charleston's best-regarded home

goods store is the nationally recognized **ESD, Elizabeth Stuart Design** (422 Savannah Hwy./U.S. 17, 843/225-6282, www.esdcharleston.com, Mon.-Sat. 10am-6pm), with a wide range of antique and new furnishings, art, lighting, jewelry, and more.

## Music

In an age when it's harder and harder to find brick-and-mortar music/movie stores, **Monster Music and Movies** (946 Orleans Rd., 843/571-4657, Mon.-Sat. 10am-9pm, Sun. noon-7pm) is a great discovery. They have new and used vinyl and CDs, and they feature great sales and in-store performances for the annual Record Store Day in April.

# NORTH CHARLESTON
## Music

**Fox Music House** (3005 W. Montague Ave., 843/740-7200, Mon.-Fri. 10am-6pm, Sat. 10am-5pm) is a neighborhood favorite, and has been locally owned since 1928. They specialize in pianos and keyboards.

## Shopping Centers

The **Tanger Outlet** (4840 Tanger Outlet Blvd., 843/529-3095, www.tangeroutlet.com, Mon.-Sat. 10am-9pm, Sun. 11am-6pm) has factory-priced bargains from stores such as Adidas, Banana Republic, Brooks Brothers, CorningWare, Old Navy, Timberland, and more.

# MOUNT PLEASANT AND EAST COOPER
## Antiques

Mount Pleasant boasts a fun antiques and auction spot, **Page's Thieves Market** (1460 Ben Sawyer Blvd., 843/884-9672, www.pagesthievesmarket.com, Mon.-Fri. 9am-5:30pm, Sat. 9am-5pm). Its rambling interior has hosted bargain and vintage shoppers for 50 years, and it's routinely voted Charleston's best antiques store.

## Shopping Centers

The most pleasant mall in the area is the retro-themed, pedestrian-friendly **Mount Pleasant Towne Center** (1600 Palmetto Grande Dr., 843/216-9900, www.mtpleasanttownecentre.com, Mon.-Sat. 10am-9pm, Sun. noon-6pm). In addition to national chains you'll find a few cool local stores in here, like Stella Nova spa and day salon and Copper Penny Shooz.

In a Harris Teeter grocery shopping center, **Gwynn's of Mount Pleasant** (916 Houston Northcutt Blvd., 843/884-9518, Mon.-Sat 10am-7pm) is an old-fashioned department store specializing in women's clothing and shoes, with a distinct local and Southern sensibility.

# Sports and Recreation

## ON THE WATER
### Beaches

In addition to the charming town of Folly Beach itself, there's the modest county-run **Folly Beach County Park** (1100 W. Ashley Ave., Folly Beach, 843/588-2426, www.ccprc.com, May-Labor Day 9am-8pm, Mar.-Apr. and Sept.-Oct. 10am-7pm, Nov.-Feb. 10am-6pm, $7 per vehicle, free for pedestrians and cyclists) at the far west end of Folly Island. It has a picnic area, restrooms, outdoor showers, and beach chair and umbrella rentals. Get there by taking Highway 171 (Folly Rd.) until it turns into Center Street, and then take a right on West Ashley Avenue.

On Isle of Palms you'll find **Isle of Palms County Park** (14th Ave., Isle of Palms, 843/886-3863, www.ccprc.com, fall-spring daily 10am-dark, summer daily 9am-dark, $5 per vehicle, free for pedestrians and cyclists), which has restrooms, showers, a picnic area, a beach volleyball area, and beach chair and umbrella rentals. Get there by taking the Isle of Palms Connector (Hwy. 517) to the island, go through the light at Palm Boulevard, and take the next left at the park gate. There's good public beach access near the Pavilion Shoppes on Ocean Boulevard, accessed via J. C. Long Boulevard.

On the west end of Kiawah Island to the south of Charleston is **Kiawah Island Beachwalker Park** (Kiawah Island, 843/768-2395, www.ccprc.com, Mar.-Apr. and Oct. Sat.-Sun. 10am-6pm, May-Aug. daily 9am-7pm, Sept. daily 10am-6pm, $7 per vehicle, free for pedestrians and cyclists), the only public facility on this mostly private resort island. It has restrooms, showers, a picnic area with grills, and beach chair and umbrella rentals. Get there from downtown Charleston by taking Lockwood Avenue onto the Highway 30 Connector bridge over the Ashley River. Turn right onto Folly Road, then take a left onto Maybank Highway. After about 20 minutes you'll take another left onto Bohicket Road, which leads you to Kiawah in 14 miles. Turn left from Bohicket Road onto the Kiawah Island Parkway. Just before the security gate, turn right on Beachwalker Drive and follow the signs to the park.

For a totally go-it-alone type of beach day, go to the three-mile-long beach on the Atlantic Ocean at **Sullivan's Island.** There are no facilities, no lifeguards, strong offshore currents, and no parking lots on this residential island (park on the side of the street). There's also a lot of dog walking on this beach, since no leash is required November-February. Get there from downtown by crossing the Ravenel Bridge over the Cooper River and bearing right onto Coleman Boulevard, which turns into Ben Sawyer Boulevard. Take the Ben Sawyer Bridge onto Sullivan's Island. Beach access is plentiful and marked.

## Diving

Offshore diving centers on a network of **artificial reefs** (see www.dnr.sc.gov for a list and locations), particularly the "Charleston 60" sunken barge and the popular "Train Wreck," comprising 50 deliberately sunk New York City subway cars. Probably Charleston's best-regarded outfitter and charter operator is **Charleston Scuba** (335 Savannah Hwy., 843/763-3483, www.charlestonscuba.com) in West Ashley. They offer training classes, charters, and offshore diving trips. In addition to Charleston Scuba, you also might want to check out **Cooper River Scuba** (843/572-0459, www.cooperriverdiving.com) and **Atlantic Coast Dive Center** (209 Scott St., 843/884-1500).

## Kayaking

Many kayakers put in at the Shem Creek Marina or the public Shem Creek Landing in Mount Pleasant. From here it's a safe, easy paddle—sometimes with appearances by dolphins or manatees—to the Intracoastal Waterway. Another good place to put in is at **Isle of Palms Marina** (50 41st Ave., 843/886-0209) behind the Wild Dunes Resort on Morgan Creek, which empties into the Intracoastal Waterway.

An excellent outfit for guided kayak tours is **Coastal Expeditions** (654 Serotina Ct., 843/881-4582, www.coastalexpeditions.com), which also runs the only approved ferry service to the Cape Romain National Wildlife Refuge. They'll rent you a kayak for roughly $50 per day. Coastal Expeditions also sells an outstanding kayaking, boating, and fishing map of the area (about $12).

The best tour operator close to downtown is **Nature Adventures Outfitters** (Shrimp Boat Ln., 843/568-3222, www.kayakcharlestonsc.com), which puts in on Shem Creek in Mount Pleasant for most of its 2-, 2.5-, 3-, and 3.5-hour and full-day guided trips, with prices from $40 to $85. They also offer blackwater tours out of landings at other locations; see the website for specific directions for those tours.

## Fishing and Boating

For casual fishing off a pier, try the well-equipped **Folly Beach Fishing Pier** (101 E. Arctic Ave., Folly Beach, 843/588-3474, daily dawn-dusk, $5-7 parking, $8 fishing fee, rod rentals available) on Folly Beach or the **North Charleston Riverfront Park** (843/745-1087, www.northcharleston.org, daily dawn-dusk) along the Cooper River on the grounds of the old Navy Yard. Get onto the Navy Yard grounds by taking I-26 north to exit 216B. Take a left onto Spruill Avenue and a right onto McMillan Avenue.

Key local marinas include **Shem Creek Marina** (526 Mill St., 843/884-3211, www.shemcreekmarina.com), **Charleston Harbor Marina** (24 Patriots Point Rd., 843/284-7062, www.charlestonharbormarina.com), **Charleston City Marina** (17 Lockwood Dr., 843/722-4968), **Charleston Maritime Center** (10 Wharfside St., 843/853-3625, www.cmcevents.com), and the **Cooper River Marina** (1010 Juneau Ave., 843/554-0790, www.ccprc.com).

Good fishing charter outfits include **Barrier Island Eco Tours** (50 41st Ave., 843/886-5000, www.nature-tours.com, about $80) out of Isle of Palms, **Bohicket Boat Adventure & Tour Co.** (2789 Cherry Point Rd., 843/559-3525, www.bohicketboat.com, $375 per half day for 1-2 passengers) out of the Edisto River, and **Reel Fish Finder Charters** (315 Yellow Jasmine Ct., Moncks Corner, 843/697-2081, www.reelfishfinder.com, $400 per half day for 1-3 passengers), which picks up clients at many different marinas in the area. For a list of all public landings in Charleston County, go to www.ccprc.com.

## Surfing and Kiteboarding

The surfing at the famous Washout area on the east side of Folly Beach isn't what it used to be due to storm activity and beach erosion. But diehards still gather at this area when the swell hits. Check out the conditions yourself from the three views of the **Folly Surfcam** (www.follysurfcam.com).

The best local surf shop is undoubtedly the historic **McKevlin's Surf Shop** (8 Center St., Folly Beach, 843/588-2247, www.mckevlins.com, spring-summer daily 10am-6pm, fall-winter daily 10am-5:30pm) on Folly Beach, one of the first surf shops on the East Coast, dating to 1965.

**Folly Beach Shaka Surf School** (107 E. Indian Ave., Folly Beach, 843/607-9911, www.shakasurfschool.com) offers private and group surf lessons, including youth surf camps throughout summer, women-only weekend outings, and yoga classes geared toward surfers. Surf camps are located on the east end of Folly Beach.

Mount Pleasant is home to **Sol Surfers Surf Camp** (1170 Lazy Ln., Mount Pleasant, 843/881-6700, www.solsurfers.net), which offers surf camps during the summer and private and group lessons throughout the year. The surf camp shuttle picks up students at the Parrot Surf Shop (811 Coleman Blvd.). Surf camps take place on the eastern end of Folly Beach.

## Water Parks

During the summer months, Charleston County operates three water parks: **Splash Island Waterpark** (444 Needlerush Pkwy., Mount Pleasant, 843/884-0832); **Whirlin' Waters Adventure Waterpark** (University Blvd., North Charleston, 843/572-7275); and **Splash Zone Waterpark at James Island County Park** (871 Riverland Dr., 843/795-7275), on James Island west of town. Admission runs about $10 per person. Go to www.ccprc.com for more information.

## Water Tours

The best all-around tour of Charleston Harbor is the 90-minute ride offered by **Spiritline Cruises** (Charleston Harbor, 800/789-3678, www.spiritlinecruises.com, $22 adults, $12 ages 4-11), which leaves from either Aquarium Wharf or Patriots Point. Allow about 30 minutes for ticketing and boarding. Spiritline also has a three-hour dinner cruise in the evening leaving from Patriots Point (about $50 pp) and a cruise to Fort Sumter.

**Sandlapper Water Tours** (Charleston Maritime Center, 10 Wharfside St., 843/849-8687, www.sandlappertours.com, Mar.-Aug., $20-27) offers many types of evening and dolphin cruises on a 45-foot catamaran. The company also offers Charleston's only waterborne ghost tour. Most of the tours leave from the Maritime Center near East Bay and Calhoun Streets.

**Barrier Island Eco Tours** (50 41st Ave., 843/886-5000, www.nature-tours.com, from $40) can take you on a passenger boat ride up to Cape Romain NWR out of Isle of Palms, with a focus on undeveloped Capers Island. Plan on seeing plenty of dolphins!

**Coastal Expeditions** (514-B Mill St., 843/884-7684, www.coastalexpeditions.com, prices vary) is based on Shem Creek in Mount Pleasant and offers several sea kayak adventures of varying lengths.

# ON LAND
## Golf
The country's first golf course was constructed in Charleston in 1786, so as you'd expect there's great golfing in the area, generally on the outlying islands. The folks at the nonprofit **Charleston Golf, Inc.** (423 King St., 843/958-3629, www.charlestongolfguide.com) are your best one-stop resource for tee times and packages.

The main public course is the 18-hole, renovated and upgraded **Charleston Municipal Golf Course** (2110 Maybank Hwy., 843/795-6517, www.charleston-sc.gov/golf, $22-24 for 18 holes), affectionately referred to as the Muni. To get there from the peninsula, take U.S. 17 south over the Ashley River, take Highway 171 (Folly Rd.) south, and then take a right onto Maybank Highway.

Probably the most renowned area facilities are at the acclaimed **Kiawah Island Golf Resort** (12 Kiawah Beach Dr., Kiawah Island, 800/654-2924, www.kiawahresort.com/golf, $150-350 for 18 holes, 25 percent discount for resort guests), about 20 miles from Charleston. The resort has five courses in all, the best known of which is the **Kiawah Island Ocean Course,** site of the famous "War by the Shore" 1991 Ryder Cup. This 2.5-mile course, which is walking-only until noon each day, hosted the Senior PGA Championship in 2007 and the PGA Championship in 2012. The resort offers a golf academy and private lessons galore. These are public courses, but be aware

that tee times are limited for golfers who aren't guests at the resort.

Two excellent resort-style public courses are at **Wild Dunes Resort** (5757 Palm Blvd., Isle of Palms, 888/845-8932, www.wilddunes.com, $165 for 18 holes) on Isle of Palms. The resort has been named one of the state's best by *Golf Digest*.

The 18-hole **Patriots Point Links** (1 Patriots Point Rd., Mount Pleasant, 843/881-0042, www.patriotspointlinks.com, $100 for 18 holes) on Charleston Harbor, right over the Ravenel Bridge, is one of the most convenient courses in the area, and it boasts some phenomenal views.

In Mount Pleasant you will find perhaps the best course in the area for the money, the award-winning **Rivertowne Golf Course** at the **Rivertowne Country Club** (1700 Rivertowne Country Club Dr., Mount Pleasant, 843/856-9808, www.rivertowne-countryclub.com, $150 for 18 holes). Opened in 2002, the course was designed by Arnold Palmer.

## Hiking and Biking
The **West Ashley Greenway** (South Windermere Shopping Center [80 Folly Rd.] to Johns Island, paralleling U.S. 17, dawn-dusk) is an urban walking and biking trail built on a former railbed. The 10-mile trail runs parallel to U.S. 17 and passes parks, schools, and the Clemson Experimental Farm, ending near Johns Island. To get to the trailhead from downtown, drive west on U.S. 17. About 0.5 mile after you cross the bridge, turn left onto Folly Road (Hwy. 171). At the second light, turn right into South Windermere Shopping Center; the trail is behind the center on the right.

The most ambitious trail in South Carolina is the **Palmetto Trail,** begun in 1997 and eventually covering 425 miles from the Atlantic to the Appalachians. The coastal terminus of the Palmetto Trail, the 7-mile **Awendaw Passage,** winds through the Francis Marion National Forest. It begins at the trailhead at the Buck Hall Recreational

Area (McClellanville, 843/887-3257, www.pal-mettoconservation.org, $5 vehicle fee), which has parking and restroom facilities. Get there by taking U.S. 17 north from Charleston about 20 miles and through the Francis Marion National Forest and then Awendaw. Take a right onto Buck Hall Landing Road.

Charleston-area beaches are perfect for a leisurely bike ride on the sand. Sullivan's Island is a particular favorite, and you might be surprised at how long you can ride in one direction on these beaches. Those desiring a more demanding use of their legs can walk or ride their bike in the dedicated pedestrian and bike lane on the massive **Arthur Ravenel Jr. Bridge** over the Cooper River, the longest cable-stayed bridge in the Western Hemisphere.

## Tennis

Tennis fans are in for a treat at the **Family Circle Tennis Center** (161 Seven Farms Dr., 800/677-2293, www.volvocaropen.com, Mon.-Thurs. 8am-8pm, Fri. 8am-7pm, Sat. 8am-5pm, Sun. 9am-5pm, $15/hour) on Daniel Island. This multimillion-dollar facility is owned by the city of Charleston and was built in 2001 specifically to host the annual Family Circle Cup women's competition, which is now known as the Volvo Car Open. But it's also open to the public year-round (except when the Volvo Car Open is on) with 17 courts.

The best resort tennis activity is at the **Kiawah Island Golf Resort** (12 Kiawah Beach Dr., Kiawah Island, 800/654-2924, www.kiawahresort.com, $44 per hour for nonguests). The resort's Roy Barth Tennis Center has nine clay and three hard courts, while the West Beach Tennis Club has 10 Har-Tru courts and 2 lighted hard courts.

There are four free, public, city-funded facilities on the peninsula: **Moultrie Playground** (Broad St. and Ashley Ave., 843/769-8258, www.charlestoncity.info, six lighted hard courts), **Jack Adams Tennis Center** (290 Congress St., six lighted hard courts), **Hazel Parker Playground** (70 E. Bay St., on the Cooper River, one hard court),

and **Corrine Jones Playground** (Marlowe St. and Peachtree St., two hard courts).

## Bird-Watching

Right in Charleston Harbor is the little **Crab Bank Seabird Sanctuary** (803/734-3886, www.dnr.sc.gov, Oct. 16-Mar. 14 daily dawn-dusk), where thousands of migratory birds can be seen, depending on the season. The sanctuary has been designated an Important Bird Area by Audubon. Mid-October-mid-March you can either kayak there yourself or take a charter with **Nature Adventures Outfitters** (1900 Iron Swamp Rd., Awendaw Island, 800/673-0679). During nesting season, mid-March-mid-October, the sanctuary is closed to the public.

On Johns Island southwest of Charleston is **Legare Farms** (2620 Hanscombe Point Rd., Johns Island, 843/559-0788, www.legare-farms.com, farm hours vary), which holds migratory bird walks ($6 adults, $3 children) in the fall each Saturday at 8:30am.

Once part of a rice plantation, the **I'on Swamp Trail** (15 miles northeast of Charleston via U.S. 17, 843/928-3368, www.fs.fed.us, daily dawn-dusk, free) is one of the premier bird-watching sites in South Carolina, particularly during spring and fall migrations. The rare Bachman's warbler, commonly considered one of the most elusive birds in North America, has been seen here. To get here, make the 10-minute drive to Mount Pleasant, then head north on U.S. 17 and take a left onto I'on Swamp Road (Forest Service Rd. 228). The parking area is 2.5 miles ahead on the left.

## Ice-Skating

Ice-skating in South Carolina? Yep, 100,000 square feet of it, year-round at the two NHL-size rinks of the **Carolina Ice Palace** (7665 Northwoods Blvd., North Charleston, 843/572-2717, www.carolinaicepalace.com, daily public sessions, $7 adults, $6 children). This is also the practice facility for the local hockey team, the Stingrays, as well as where the Citadel's hockey team plays.

## SPECTATOR SPORTS

A New York Yankees Class A affiliate in the South Atlantic League, the **Charleston River Dogs** play April-August at **Joseph P. Riley Jr. Park** (360 Fishburne St., 843/577-3647, www.riverdogs.com, $8-11 general admission), aka "the Joe." There are a lot of fun promotions to keep things interesting should the play on the field be less than stimulating. Expect to pay $5 for parking.

The professional USL Pro soccer team **Charleston Battery** plays April-July at **MUSC Health Stadium** (MUSC Health Stadium, 1990 Daniel Island Dr., 843/971-4625, www.charlestonbattery.com, about $10) on Daniel Island, north of Charleston.

An ECHL professional hockey team, the **South Carolina Stingrays** get a good crowd out to their rink at the **North Charleston Coliseum** (5001 Coliseum Dr., 843/744-2248, www.stingrayshockey.com, $15), playing October-April.

**The Citadel** (171 Moultrie St., 843/953-3294, www.citadelsports.com, ticket prices vary) plays Southern Conference football home games at **Johnson Hagood Stadium,** next to the campus on the Ashley River near Hampton Park. The basketball team plays home games at **McAlister Field House** on campus. The school's ice hockey team has its home games at the **Carolina Ice Palace** (7665 Northwoods Blvd., North Charleston).

# Food

Charleston's long history of good taste and livability combines with an affluent and sophisticated population to attract some of the brightest chefs and restaurateurs in the country. A long list of James Beard Award nominees each year confirms the city's role as perhaps the preeminent hub of culinary excellence in the American South.

Kitchens here eschew fickle trends, instead emphasizing quality, professionalism, and, most of all, freshness of ingredients. The farm-to-table movement is as strong here as anywhere in the country and drives the menus of most of the premier establishments.

If you come here in the first week or two of the New Year, keep in mind that is usually the time when Charleston's more popular restaurants might close briefly for renovations.

## WATERFRONT
### New Southern

Few restaurants in Charleston have inspired such impassioned advocates as legendary chef Sean Brock's flagship restaurant, ★ **McCrady's** (2 Unity Alley and 155 Bay St., www.mccradysrestaurant.com, Wed.-Thurs. and Sun. 7pm seating, Fri.-Sat. seatings at 6:30pm and 8:45pm, $125 pp, $85 pp wine pairing). In the restaurant's early days, Brock's then-groundbreaking sous vide (or vacuum cooking technique) was spoken of in reverent tones by his clientele. In an expansion and reimagining, Brock moved the original McCrady's to a spot right next door, where it continues to offer the sophisticated, almost frighteningly delicious tasting-menu experience for which it is renowned. Brock repurposed the former McCrady's space as **McCrady's Tavern,** a return to the original use of the building as a watering hole and community gathering spot back in the 1770s. In a nod to a more egalitarian dining experience, the tavern has a more casual New Southern menu. Either spot is a core stop of any Charleston foodie pilgrimage.

**Magnolias** (185 E. Bay St., 843/577-7771, www.magnoliascharleston.com, Mon.-Sat. 11:30am-10pm, Sun. 3:45pm-10pm, $25-35) began life as one of Charleston's first serious eating spots. While the interior has since been given a warm renovation, the menu remains as attractive as ever, with a delightful take on Southern classics like the lump crab cakes, the shellfish over grits, and the rainbow trout. The appetizers are particularly strong—start with the famous fried green tomatoes or maybe the boiled peanut hummus.

**Slightly North of Broad** (192 E. Bay St., 843/723-3424, www.snobcharleston.com, daily 11:30am-2:30pm and 5pm-10pm, $25-35), or "SNOB," is an ironic play on the often pejorative reference to the insular South of Broad neighborhood. This hot spot, routinely voted best restaurant in town in such contests, is anything but snobby. Hopping with happy foodies for lunch and dinner, the fun is enhanced by the long, open kitchen with its own counter area. The dynamic but comforting menu here is practically a bible of the new wave of Lowcountry cuisine, with dishes like beef tenderloin, jumbo lump crab cakes, grilled barbecue tuna—and, of course, the pan-seared flounder. An interesting twist at SNOB is the selection of "medium plates," dishes that are a little more generous than an appetizer but with the same adventurous spirit.

For many visitors to Charleston, there comes a point when they just get tired of stuffing themselves with seafood. If you find yourself in that situation, the perfect antidote is **High Cotton** (199 E. Bay St., 843/724-3815, www.mavericksouthernkitchens.com, Mon.-Thurs. 5:30pm-10pm, Fri. 5:30pm-11pm, Sat. 11:30am-2:30pm and 5:30pm-11pm, Sun. 10am-2pm and 5:30pm-10pm, $35-45), a meat lover's paradise offering some of the best steaks in town as well as a creative menu of assorted lamb and pork dishes. Chef Anthony Gray places heavy emphasis on using fresh local ingredients, both veggies and game, and the rotating menu always reflects that. None of this comes particularly cheap, but splurges rarely do. In the woody (and popular) bar area there's usually a solo live pianist or sax player after 6pm.

# NORTH OF BROAD
## Classic Southern

Executive chef Sean Brock of McCrady's fame already had a reputation as one of the country's leading purveyors of the farm-to-table fine-dining movement, but he cemented that reputation with **Husk** (76 Queen St., 843/577-2500, www.huskrestaurant.com, Mon.-Thurs. 11:30am-2pm and 5:30pm-10pm, Fri.-Sat. 11:30am-2pm and 5:30pm-11pm, Sun. 10am-2:30pm and 5:30pm-10pm, $25-35), voted "Best New Restaurant in the U.S." by *Bon Appétit* magazine soon after its 2011 opening. Brock says of his ingredients, "If it doesn't come from the South, it's not coming through the door." The spare, focused menu is constantly changing with the seasons. On a recent lunch visit my party enjoyed two types of catfish (a fried catfish BLT on Texas toast and a lightly cornmeal-dusted broiled catfish with local vegetables), Husk's signature cheeseburger, and—wait for it—lamb barbecue. Reservations are strongly recommended.

In business for over 40 years now, **Poogan's Porch** (72 Queen St., 843/577-2337, www.poogansporch.com, Mon.-Fri. 11:30am-2:30pm and 5pm-9:30pm, Sat.-Sun. 9am-3pm and 5pm-9:30pm, $25-30) is the prototype of a classic Charleston restaurant: lovingly restored old home, professional but unpretentious service, great fried green tomatoes, and rich, calorie-laden Lowcountry classics like crab cakes and shrimp and grits. Brunch is the big thing here, a bustling affair with ample portions, Bloody Marys, mimosas, and soft sunlight.

Walk through the gaslit courtyard of the Planter's Inn at Market and Meeting Streets into the intimate dining room of the ★ **Peninsula Grill** (112 N. Market St., 843/723-0700, www.peninsulagrill.com, daily from 5:30pm, $35-50) and begin an epicurean journey you'll not soon forget. Peninsula Grill might be Charleston's quintessential purveyor of high-style Lowcountry cuisine. You'll want to start with the sampler trio of soups and finish with the legendary coconut cake. Reservations are strongly recommended.

Follow Rachael Ray's lead and wait in the long lines outside **Jestine's Kitchen** (251 Meeting St., 843/722-7224, Tues.-Thurs. 11am-9:30pm, Fri.-Sat. 11am-10pm, $15-20) to enjoy a simple Southern take on such meat-and-three comfort food classics as meat loaf, pecan-fried fish, and fried green tomatoes. Most of the recipes are handed down from the restaurant's namesake, Jestine Matthews, the African American woman who raised owner Dana Berlin.

## New Southern

**Cru Café** (18 Pinckney St., 843/534-2434, www.crucafe.com, Tues.-Thurs. 11am-3pm and 5pm-10pm, Fri.-Sat. 11am-3pm and 5pm-11pm, $20-30) boasts an adventurous menu within a traditional-looking Charleston single house just around the corner from the main stable for the city's carriage tours, with a choice of interior or exterior seating. Sample entrées include poblano and mozzarella fried chicken and seared maple leaf duck breast.

The intimate bistro and stylish bar ★ **FIG** (232 Meeting St., 843/805-5900, www.eatat-fig.com, Mon.-Thurs. 6pm-11pm, Fri.-Sat. 6pm-midnight, $30-35) has a passion for fresh, simple ingredients. FIG—short for "Food Is Good"—attracts young professional scenesters as well as die-hard foodies. Chef Mike Lata won James Beard's Best Chef of the Southeast award in 2009. FIG is one of Charleston's great champions of the Sustainable Seafood Initiative, and the kitchen staff strives to work as closely as possible with local farmers and anglers in determining its seasonal menu.

Inside the plush Charleston Place Hotel you'll find **Charleston Grill** (224 King St., 843/577-4522, www.charlestongrill.com, dinner daily from 6pm, $30-60), one of the city's favorite (and priciest) fine-dining spots for locals and visitors alike. The menu specializes in French-influenced Lowcountry cuisine, with dishes like the niçoise vegetable tart. There are a lot of great fusion dishes as well, such as the tuna and *hamachi* sashimi topped with pomegranate molasses and lemongrass oil. Reservations are a must.

Focusing on purely seasonal offerings that never stay on the menu longer than three months, ★ **Circa 1886** (149 Wentworth St., 843/853-7828, www.circa1886.com,

Mon.-Sat. 5:30pm-9:30pm, $30-35) combines the best old-world tradition of Charleston with the vibrancy of its more adventurous kitchens. The restaurant—surprisingly little known despite its four-star Mobil rating—is located in the former carriage house of the grand Wentworth Mansion B&B just west of the main College of Charleston campus. The menu has featured such entrées as robust beef au poivre and shrimp-and-crab-stuffed flounder. Be sure to check the daily prix fixe offerings; they can be a great deal.

## Coffee, Tea, and Sweets

Considered the best coffeehouse in town, **Black Tap Coffee** (70 $^{1/2}$ Beaufain St., 843/793-4402, Mon.-Fri. 7am-7pm, Sat.-Sun. 8am-6pm) features an array of Counter Culture beans roasted and served to perfection by skilled baristas. Cold brew and pour-over cups are specialties of the house, as is their signature Lavender Latte. It's smallish and a bit off the beaten King Street path but still well within walking distance of that shopping thoroughfare.

If you find yourself needing a quick pick-me-up while shopping on King Street, avoid the lines at the two Starbucks locations on the avenue and instead turn east on Market Street and duck inside **City Lights Coffeehouse** (141 Market St., 843/853-7067, Mon.-Thurs. 7am-9pm, Fri.-Sat. 7am-10pm, Sun. 8am-6pm). The sweet goodies are delectable in this cozy little Euro-style place, and the Counter Culture organic coffee is to die for. If you're lucky, they'll have some of their Ethiopian Sidamo brewed.

Routinely voted as having the best desserts in the city, the cakes alone at **Kaminsky's** (78 N. Market St., 843/853-8270, daily noon-2am) are worth the trip to the City Market area. The fresh fruit torte, the red velvet, and the "Mountain of Chocolate" are the three best sellers.

## French

On the north side of Broad Street you'll find **Gaulart & Maliclet** (98 Broad St.,

843/577-9797, www.fastandfrenchcharles-ton.com, Mon. 8am-4pm, Tues.-Thurs. 8am-10pm, Fri.-Sat. 8am-10:30pm, $20-25), subtitled "Fast and French." This is a gourmet bistro with a strong takeout component. Prices are especially reasonable for this area of town, with great lunch specials under $10, Thursday night Fondue for Two specials at about $20, and breakfast all day.

**Queen Street Grocery** (133 Queen St., 843/723-4121, www.queenstreetgrocerycafe. com, kitchen Mon.-Sat. 10am-5pm, Sun. 11am-3pm, $10, store Mon.-Sat. 8am-8:30pm) is the kind of place frequented almost exclusively by locals. At this corner store you can load up on some of the tastiest made-to-order crepes this side of France—as well as light groceries, beer, wine, and cigarettes.

### Mediterranean

The cuisine of northern Italy comes alive in the bustling, dimly lit room of **Fulton Five** (5 Fulton St., 843/853-5555, www.fulton-five.com, Mon.-Sat. 5:30pm-close, $30-40), from the *insalata de funghi* to the sublime risotto. It's not cheap, and the portions aren't necessarily the largest, but with these tasty, non-tomato-based dishes and this romantic, gusto-filled atmosphere, you'll be satiated with life itself.

### Seafood

**Hyman's Seafood** (215 Meeting St., 843/723-6000, www.hymanseafood.com, Mon.-Thurs. 11am-9pm, Fri.-Sun. 11am-11pm, $20-40) is thought by many locals to border on a tourist trap, and it's mostly tourists who line up for hours to get in. To keep things manageable, Hyman's offers the same menu and prices for both lunch and dinner. After asking for some complimentary fresh boiled peanuts in lieu of bread, start with the Carolina Delight, a delicious appetizer (also available as an entrée) involving a lightly fried cake of grits topped with your choice of delectable seafood, or maybe a half-dozen oysters from the Half Shell oyster bar. Definitely

try the she-crab soup, one of the best you'll find anywhere. As for entrées, the ubiquitous Lowcountry crispy scored flounder is always a good bet.

## UPPER KING
### Classic Southern

One of a comparatively few great Charleston restaurants with an equally expert focus on breakfast as on the other meals, **Virginia's on King** (412 King St., 912/735-5800, www. holycityhospitality.com, Mon.-Fri. 7am-10pm, Sat. 8am-10pm, Sun. 10am-3pm, $15-25) is a great place to enjoy Southern classics like fried green tomatoes, tomato pie, and their signature she-crab soup. The salmon BLT lunch dish (or in their old Southern parlance, "dinner," with "supper" being the name of the last meal of the day) is one of the best seafood dishes I've had anywhere. As for breakfast, the omelets are solid and most of the lunch menu is also available.

Rapidly gaining a reputation as one of the best brunch scenes in town, **The Macintosh** (479 King St., 843/789-4299, www.themacin-toshcharleston.com, Mon.-Sat. 6:30am-7pm, Sun. 9am-6pm, $25-40) combines the best of Charleston's Classic/New South style with a gastropub sensibility, complete with an extensive craft beer menu. The chef is three-time James Beard semifinalist Jeremiah Bacon, which means you can't really go wrong. But for brunch I'd suggest the baked chorizo, and from the small but artfully curated dinner menu, any seafood dish is good. Happy hour (Mon.-Fri. 5pm-7pm) is also a big draw here, with its own special $5 small-plate bar food menu.

### American

Charleston's fave rave is ★ **Edmund's Oast** (1081 Morrison Dr., 843/727-1145, www.ed-mundsoast.com, Mon.-Thurs. 5:30pm-10pm, Fri.-Sat. 5:30pm-11pm, Sun. 10am-2:30pm and 5:30pm-10pm, $25-40), a boisterous beer garden/brewpub on the Upper Peninsula, boasting a 40-tap array, several brews made

# Lowcountry Locavores

Charleston has merged its own indigenous and abiding culinary tradition with the "new" idea that you should grow your food as naturally as possible and purchase it as close to home as you can. From bacon and snapper to sweet potatoes, the typical Charleston dish of today harkens back to its soulful Southern roots, before the days of factory food.

Spurred in part by an influx of trained chefs after the establishment of the Spoleto Festival in the 1970s, the locavore movement in Charleston came from the efforts of epicureans committed to sustainability and the principles of community-supported agriculture (CSA). Spearheaded by visionaries like the James Beard Award-winning Mike Lata of the bistro FIG and Sean Brock of Mc-Crady's, sustainable food initiatives have sprung up in Charleston and the Lowcountry, such as the South Carolina Aquarium's Sustainable Seafood Initiative (http://scaquarium.org), partnering with local restaurants to ensure a sustainable wild-caught harvest; Certified South Carolina (www.certifiedsc.com), guaranteeing that the food you eat was grown in the Palmetto State; and a local chapter of the Slow Food Movement (http://slowfoodcharleston.org).

The list of Holy City restaurants relying almost exclusively on local and sustainable sources is long, but here are a few notable examples:

- **Husk** (76 Queen St., 843/577-2500, www.huskrestaurant.com)
- **Charleston Grill** (224 King St., 843/577-4522, www.charlestongrill.com)
- **FIG** (232 Meeting St., 843/805-5900, www.eatatfig.com)
- **Al Di La** (25 Magnolia Rd., 843/571-2321, www.aldilarestaurant.com)
- **Queen Street Grocery** (133 Queen St., 843/723-4121, www.queenstreetgrocerycafe.com)
- **Middleton Place Restaurant** (4300 Ashley River Rd., 843/556-6020, www.middleton-place.org)
- **Circa 1886** (149 Wentworth St., 843/853-7828, www.circa1886.com)
- **COAST Bar and Grill** (39D John St., 843/722-8838, www.coastbarandgrill.com)
- **Cru Café** (18 Pinckney St., 843/534-2434, www.crucafe.com)
- **Hominy Grill** (207 Rutledge Ave., 912/937-0930, www.hominygrill.com)
- **Peninsula Grill** (112 N. Market St., 843/723-0700, www.peninsulagrill.com)

on-site, and, perhaps surprisingly, an excellent cocktail menu. The small plates, though, might be what stay with you. Expressive, excellent charcuterie and pitch-perfect sliders are the highlights. If you sit at the bar, the $4 per plate happy hour items (4:30pm-6:30pm) are a must-try; I suggest the smoked wings.

## Asian

There's usually a long wait to get a table at the great Thai place **Basil** (460 King St., 843/724-3490, www.basilthairestaurant.com, Mon.-Thurs. 11:30am-2:30pm and 5pm-10:30pm, Fri.-Sat. 5pm-11pm, Sun. 5pm-10pm, $15-20) on Upper King, since they don't take reservations. But Basil also has one of the hippest, most happening bar scenes in the area, so you won't necessarily mind. Revelers enjoy fresh, succulent takes on Thai classics like cashew chicken and pad thai. The signature dish is the basil duck.

## Barbecue

The Downtown/Upper Peninsula outpost of Charleston's favorite barbecue chain, **Fiery Ron's Home Team BBQ** (126 Williman St.,

843/225-7427, www.hometeambbq.com, daily 11am-10pm, $10-20), boasts a bit of an upscale feel from the original West Ashley location and the Sullivan's Island version. But don't be deceived by the excellent artisanal cocktail menu; the barbecue here is just as good.

## Coffee, Tea, and Sweets

One of the best java joints in Charleston is **Kudu Coffee** (4 Vanderhorst St., 843/853-7186, Mon.-Sat. 6:30am-7pm, Sun. 9am-6pm). A kudu is an African antelope, and the Africa theme extends to the beans, which all have an African pedigree. Poetry readings and occasional live music add to the mix. A lot of green-friendly, left-of-center community activism goes on here as well.

## French

The best mussels I've ever had were at ★ **39 Rue de Jean** (39 John St., 843/722-8881, www.holycityhospitality.com, Mon.-Thurs. 11:30am-11pm, Fri.-Sat. 11:30am-1am, Sun. 10am-11pm, $20-30). But anything off the bistro-style menu is unbelievably tasty, from the foie gras to the confit to the coq au vin to the steak frites. There are incredible Prohibition-style cocktails to go along with the extensive wine list.

## Italian

One of Upper King's "it" restaurants, **Indaco** (525 King St., 843/727-1218, www.indaco-charleston.com, Sun.-Thurs. 5pm-10pm, Fri.-Sat. 5pm-midnight, $15-25) features a small but well-curated menu of antipasti, custom wood-fired gourmet pizzas, and delicious Italian specialties like black pepper tagliatelle. Yes, there's brussels sprout pizza, and it's quite delicious! Indaco is set in a stylish, bustling restored warehouse.

## Mexican

The quesadillas at **Juanita Greenberg's Nacho Royale** (439 King St., 843/723-6224, www.juanitagreenbergs.com, daily 11am-11pm, $10-15) are perfectly packed with jack cheese, spicy sausage, and a delightful *pico de gallo*. This modest Mexican joint caters primarily to a college crowd, as you can tell from the reasonable prices, the large patio out back, the extensive tequila list, and the bar that stays open until 2am on weekends.

## Seafood

Near 39 Rue de Jean you'll find the affiliated **COAST Bar and Grill** (39D John St., 843/722-8838, www.coastbarandgrill.com, daily 5:30pm-close, $20-25), which makes the most of its loud, hip setting in a former warehouse. The raw bar is satisfying, with a particularly nice selection of ceviche. COAST is a strong local advocate of the Sustainable Seafood Initiative, whereby restaurants work directly with the local fishing industry.

# HAMPTON PARK
## Classic Southern

With a motto like "Grits are good for you," you know what you're in store for at **Hominy Grill** (207 Rutledge Ave., 912/937-0930, www.hominygrill.com, Mon.-Fri. 7:30am-8:30pm, Sat.-Sun. 9am-8:30pm, $15-20), set in a renovated barbershop at Rutledge Avenue and Cannon Street near the Medical University of South Carolina. Primarily revered for his Sunday brunch, chef Robert Stehling has fun—almost mischievously so—breathing new life into American and Southern classics. Because this is largely a locals' place, you can impress your friends back home by saying you had the rare pleasure of the Hominy's sautéed shad roe with bacon and mushrooms—when the shad are running, that is.

**Moe's Crosstown Tavern** (714 Rutledge Ave., 843/722-3287, Mon.-Sat. 11am-midnight, bar until 2am, $10-15) is not only one of the classic Southern dives, but also has one of the best kitchens on this side of town, known for hand-cut fries, great wings, and, most of all, excellent burgers. On Tuesdays, the burgers are half price at happy hour—one of Charleston's best deals.

## Italian

A rave of Charleston foodies is the

Tuscan-inspired fare of chef Ken Vedrinski at **Trattoria Lucca** (41 Bogard St., 843/973-3323, www.luccacharleston.com, Mon.-Sat. 6pm-10pm, $25-30). The menu is simple but perfectly focused, featuring handmade pasta and signature items like the pork chop or the fresh cheese plate. You'll be surprised at how much food your money gets you here. Monday evenings see a family-style prix fixe communal dinner.

# WEST ASHLEY
## Classic Southern
Tucked away on the grounds of the Middleton Place Plantation is the romantic **Middleton Place Restaurant** (4300 Ashley River Rd., 843/556-6020, www.middletonplace.org, Tues.-Thurs. and Sun. 11am-3pm and 6pm-8pm, Fri.-Sat. 11am-3pm and 6pm-9pm, $25-30). Theirs is a respectful take on traditional plantation fare like hoppin' John, gumbo, she-crab soup, and collards. The special annual Thanksgiving buffet is a real treat. Reservations are required for dinner. A nice plus is being able to wander the gorgeous landscaped gardens before dusk if you arrive at 5:30pm or later with a dinner reservation.

## New Southern
One of the more unassuming advocates of farm-to-table dining, ★ **The Glass Onion** (1219 Savannah Hwy., 843/225-1717, www.ilovetheglassonion.com, Mon.-Thurs. 11am-9pm, Fri. 11am-10pm, Sat. 10am-3pm and 4pm-10pm, $20-30) is in an equally unassuming location on U.S. 17 (Savannah Hwy.) on the western approach to town. That said, their food is right in the thick of the sustainable food movement and is incredibly tasty to boot (not to mention that there is more parking there than there is downtown). The interior says "diner," and indeed the emphasis here is on Southern soul and comfort-food classics. The Glass Onion also boasts a good variety of specialty craft brews to wash it all down. Another plus: In this town full of Sunday brunches, Glass Onion's specialty is a Saturday brunch!

## American
**Gene's Haufbrau** (17 Savannah Hwy., 843/225-4363, www.genes-haufbrau.com, daily 11:30am-2am, $10) is worth making a special trip into West Ashley. Claiming to be the oldest bar in continuous operation in town (1952), Gene's complements its fairly typical bar-food menu with some good wraps. Start with the "Drunken Trio" (beer-battered cheese sticks, mushrooms, and onion rings) and follow with a portobello wrap or a good old-fashioned crawfish po'boy. One of the best meals in town for the money is Gene's $8.50 blue plate special, a rotating comfort food entrée like country-fried steak or pot roast, offered Monday-Friday 11:30am-4pm. The late-night kitchen hours, until 1am, are a big plus.

If you're any kind of fan of fried chicken, whether good old-fashioned Southern fried or the type of sandwich you might get at Chick-fil-A, you will want to check out **Boxcar Betty's** (1922 Savannah Hwy., 843/225-7470, www.boxcarbetty.com, daily 11am-9pm, $10). Be warned, these juicy, incredibly tasty flour-breaded fried chicken sandwiches are addictive.

## Barbecue
My favorite barbecue joint, the rowdy and always hopping ★ **Fiery Ron's Home Team BBQ** (1205 Ashley River Rd., 843/225-7427, www.hometeambbq.com, Mon.-Sat. 11am-9pm, Sun. 11:30am-9pm, $10-20) has pulled pork and ribs that rank with the best I've had anywhere in the country. Even the sides are amazing here, including perfect collards and tasty mac and cheese. Pitmaster Madison Ruckel provides an array of tableside sauces, including hot sauce, indigenous South Carolina mustard sauce, and his own "Alabama white," a light and delicious mayonnaise-based sauce. As if that weren't enough, the owners' close ties to the regional jam-band community mean there's great live blues and indie rock after 10pm most nights (Thursday is bluegrass night) to spice up the bar action, which goes until 2am.

Fiery Ron's Home Team BBQ is one of the state's best.

## Mediterranean

Anything on this northern Italian-themed menu is good, but the risotto—a legacy of original chef John Marshall—is the specialty dish at **Al Di La** (25 Magnolia Rd., 843/571-2321, www.aldilarestaurant.com, Tues.-Sat. 6pm-10pm, $15-20), a very popular West Ashley fine-dining spot. Reservations are recommended.

# NORTH CHARLESTON
## Pizza

If you have a hankering for pizza in North Charleston, don't miss **EVO Pizzeria** (1075 E. Montague Ave., 843/225-1796, www.evo-pizza.com, Tues.-Fri. 11am-2:30pm and 5pm-10pm, Sat. 6pm-10pm, $15) in the Olde North Charleston area at Park Circle. They specialize in a small but rich menu of unusual gourmet pizza toppings, like pistachio pesto.

# SUMMERVILLE
## American

For a down-home-style pancakes-and-sandwich place that's popular with the locals at all hours of the day, try **Alex's Restaurant** (120 E. 5th N. St., 843/871-3202, daily 24 hours, $10).

A popular local landmark is **Guerin's Pharmacy** (140 S. Main St., 843/873-2531, Mon.-Fri. 9am-6pm, Sat. 9am-5pm, $5), which claims to be the state's oldest pharmacy. Complete with an old-fashioned soda fountain, they offer malted milk shakes and lemonade.

# MOUNT PLEASANT AND EAST COOPER

In Mount Pleasant, most of the restaurant action centers on the picturesque shrimping village of Shem Creek, which is dotted on both banks with bars and restaurants, most dealing in fresh local seafood. As with Murrells Inlet up the coast, some spots on Shem Creek border on tourist traps. Don't be afraid to go where the lines aren't.

## American

For a burger and an adult beverage or two, go straight to friendly **Poe's Tavern** (2210 Middle St., Sullivan's Island, 843/883-0083, www.poestavern.com, daily 11am-2am, kitchen until 10pm, $10-15), a nod to Edgar Allan Poe's stint at nearby Fort Moultrie.

## Seafood

At the **Red Drum Gastropub** (803 Coleman Blvd., 843/849-0313, www.reddrumrestaurant.com, daily 5:30pm-10pm, lunch/brunch

# To Market, to Market

A fun and favorite local fixture April-mid-December, the **Charleston Farmers Market** (843/724-7309, www.charlestoncity.info, Sat. 8am-2pm) rings beautiful Marion Square with stalls of local produce, street eats, local arts and crafts, and kids' activities.

Running April-October, East Cooper has its own version in the **Mount Pleasant Farmers Market** (843/884-8517, http://townofmountpleasant.com, Tues. 3pm-dark) at the Moultrie Middle School on Coleman Boulevard.

Sat.-Sun. 10:30am-2pm, $20-40), the food is just as important as the drink. While you're likely to need reservations for the dining room, where you can enjoy Lowcountry-Tex-Mex fusion-style cuisine with a typically Mount Pleasant-like emphasis on seafood, the bar scene is very hopping and fun, with live music every Wednesday-Thursday night.

A must-stop roadside diner in the Awendaw area is ★ **See Wee Restaurant** (4808 U.S. 17 N., 843/928-3609, Mon.-Thurs. 11am-8:30pm, Fri.-Sat. 11am-9:30pm, Sun. 11am-8pm, $15-25), about 20 minutes north of Charleston by car. Housed in a humble former general store on the west side of U.S. 17 (the restrooms are still outside), this diner draws folks from far and wide to enjoy signature menu items like the grouper and the unreal she-crab soup, considered by some epicures to be the best in the world. You can't miss with any of their seafood entrées. Occasionally the crowds can get thick, but rest assured it's worth any wait.

A popular spot, especially for the younger crowd, **Vickery's Shem Creek Bar and Grill** (1313 Shrimp Boat Ln., 843/884-4440, daily 11:30am-1am, $15-20) has a similar menu to its partner location on the peninsula, but this Vickery's has the pleasant added bonus of a beautiful view overlooking the creek. You'll get more of the Vickery's Cuban flair here, with a great black bean soup and an awesome Cuban sandwich.

A well-regarded spot on Shem Creek is **Water's Edge** (1407 Shrimp Boat Ln., 843/884-4074, daily 11am-11pm, $20-35), which consistently takes home a *Wine*

*Spectator* Award of Excellence for its great selection of vintages. Native Charlestonian Jimmy Purcell concentrates on fresh seafood with a slightly more upscale flair than many Shem Creek places.

## Vegetarian

For a real change of pace, try **The Sprout Cafe** (629 Johnnie Dodds Blvd., 843/849-8554, www.thehealthysprout.com, Mon.-Fri. 6am-8pm, Sat. 9am-3pm, Sun. 11am-3pm, $10) on U.S. 17. Dealing totally in raw foods, the restaurant emphasizes healthy and fresh ingredients. You might be surprised at the inventiveness of their breakfast-through-dinner seasonal menu, which might include a tasty crepe topped with a pear-and-nut puree and maple syrup, or a raw squash and zucchini "pasta" dish topped with walnut "meatballs."

## FOLLY BEACH AND THE SOUTHWEST ISLANDS
### American

Three words: duck fat fries. The **Tattooed Moose** (3328 Maybank Hwy., 843/277-2990, www.tattooedmoose.com, daily 11:30am-1am, $10-15) is a dive bar sensation on Johns Island, combining classic bar food with a typically Charlestonian touch of Old South culinary bravado. While the fries—served straight up with roasted garlic and blue cheese or with gravy—are the signature menu item, the sandwiches are simply fantastic. Try the duck confit sandwich or the pork belly sandwich. Brunch is becoming huge here, too, and live music is featured most nights.

## Barbecue

If barbecue is your thing, head straight to **JB's Smokeshack** (3406 Maybank Hwy., 843/557-0426, www.jbssmokeshack.com, Wed.-Sat. 11am-8:30pm, $8-18), considered one of the better 'cue joints in the Lowcountry. True connoisseurs will tell you it's the chicken that's really awesome, however. JB's offers a buffet for $8.88 per person ($5 under age 11), or you can opt for a barbecue plate, including hash, rice, and two sides. In a nice twist, the plates include a three-meat option: pork, chicken, ribs, or brisket.

## Breakfast and Brunch

The closest thing to a taste of old Folly is the **Lost Dog Café** (106 W. Huron Ave., 843/588-9669, daily 6:30am-3pm, $10-15), so named for its bulletin board stacked with alerts about lost pets, pets for adoption, and new pups and kittens for sale or giveaway. It opens early to offer a tasty, healthy breakfast to the surfing crowd. It's a great place to pick up a quick, inexpensive, and tasty meal while you're near the beach.

For a hearty and delicious breakfast, go to **Sunrise Bistro** (1797 Main Rd., 843/718-1858, www.sunrise-bistro.com, Tues.-Thurs. 7am-2:30pm, Fri.-Sat. 7am-2:30pm and 5pm-9pm, Sun. 9am-1pm, $10-15), one of those unassuming diners that always seems to have an eager crowd. Everything, from the omelets to the pancakes down to the simplest bagel with coffee, is spot-on, and a great value to boot. The best offerings here are during the day.

## French

★ **Fat Hen** (3140 Maybank Hwy., 843/559-9090, Tues.-Sat. 11:30am-3pm and 5:30pm-10pm, Sun. 10am-3pm, $20-40) is a self-styled "country French bistro" begun by a couple of old Charleston restaurant hands. The fried oysters are a particular specialty. There's also a bar menu (4pm-10pm).

## Mexican

**Taco Boy** (15 Center St., 843/588-9761, Sun.-Thurs. 11am-10pm, Fri.-Sat. 11am-11pm, $10) is a fun place to get a fish taco, have a margarita, and take a walk on the nearby beach afterward. Though no one is under any illusions that this is an authentic Mexican restaurant, the fresh guacamole is particularly rave-worthy, and there's a good selection of tequilas and beers *hecho en México,* with the bar staying open until 2am on weekends.

## Seafood

Set within the trendy Tides Folly Beach boutique hotel, **Blu** (1 Center St., 843/588-6658, www.blufollybeach.com, breakfast daily 7am-11am, lunch daily 11am-5pm, dinner Sun.-Thurs. 5pm-9pm, Fri.-Sat. 5pm-10pm, $15-30) offers an equally high standard of food and decor, along with some amazing views of the ocean. The menu isn't particularly pretentious, but it does offer high-quality Sustainable Seafood Initiative options, all of which are recommended.

Fans of the legendary **Bowens Island Restaurant** (1870 Bowens Island Rd., 843/795-2757, Tues.-Sat. 5pm-10pm, $15-20, cash only) on James Island went into mourning when it burned to the ground in 2006. But you can't keep a good oysterman down, and owner Robert Barber rebuilt. A universe removed from the Lexus-and-khaki scene downtown, Bowens Island isn't the place for the uptight. This is the spot to go when you want shovels of oysters literally thrown onto your table, freshly steamed and delicious and all-you-can-eat.

To get to Bowens Island from the peninsula, take Calhoun Street west onto the James Island Connector (Hwy. 30). Take exit 3 onto Highway 171 south and look for Bowens Island Road on the right. The restaurant will be on the left in a short while, after passing by several ritzy McMansions that in no way resemble the restaurant you're about to experience.

# Accommodations

Due to the city's long-standing tradition of hospitality and the high standards it has set for itself, hotels and bed-and-breakfasts are generally well maintained and have a high level of service.

The price differential is not that much between the peninsula and the outskirts. You'll pay more to stay in the tourist areas, but not *that* much more, with the bonus of being able to walk to most places you want to see. The farther south you go on the peninsula, the quieter and more affluent it tends to be. Folks looking for a more wild and woolly good time will be drawn to the Upper King area farther north.

## SOUTH OF BROAD
### $150-300

On the south side of Broad Street is a great old Charleston lodging, **Governor's House Inn** (117 Broad St., 843/720-2070, www.governorshouse.com, $200-350). This circa-1760 building, a National Historic Landmark, is associated with Edward Rutledge, signer of the Declaration of Independence. Though most of its 11 guest rooms—all with four-poster beds, period furnishings, and high ceilings—go for around $300, some of the smaller guest rooms can be had for closer to $200 in the off-season.

The nine guest rooms of ★ **Two Meeting Street Inn** (2 Meeting St., 843/723-7322, www.twomeetingstreet.com, $200-450) down by the Battery are individually appointed, with themes like "the Music Room" and the "the Spell Room." The decor in this 1892 Queen Anne bed-and-breakfast is very traditional, with lots of floral patterns and hunt club-style pieces and artwork. It's considered by many to be the most romantic lodging in town, and you won't soon forget the experience of sitting on the veranda enjoying the sights, sounds, and breezes. Three of the guest rooms—the Canton, Granite, and Roberts—can be had for not much over $200.

## WATERFRONT
### $150-300

The guest rooms and the thoroughly hospitable service are the focus at nearby ★ **The Vendue** (19 Vendue Range, 800/845-7900, www.thevendue.com, $250-450). All guest rooms are sumptuously appointed in boutique style, with lots of warm, rich fabrics, unique pieces, and high-end bath amenities. That said, the public spaces are cool as well, with a focus on featuring quality art that essentially turns the property into one huge exhibition space. The inn gets a lot of traffic in the evenings because of the popular and hopping Rooftop Bar, which has amazing views.

### Over $300

About as close to the Cooper River as a hotel gets, the **Harbourview Inn** (2 Vendue Range, 843/853-8439, www.harbourviewcharleston.com, $300-500) comprises a "historic wing" and a larger, newer, but still tastefully done main building. For the best of those eponymous harbor views, try to get a room on the 3rd floor or you might have some obstructions. It's the little touches that keep guests happy here, with wine, cheese, coffee, tea, and cookies galore and an emphasis on smiling, personalized service. The guest rooms are quite spacious, with big baths and 14-foot ceilings. You can take your complimentary breakfast—good but not great—in your room or eat it on the nice rooftop terrace.

## FRENCH QUARTER
### Over $300

A great place in this part of town is the **French Quarter Inn** (166 Church St., 843/722-1900, www.fqicharleston.com, $350-500). The decor in the 50 surprisingly spacious guest rooms is suitably high-period French, with low-style noncanopied beds and crisp fresh linens. Many guest rooms feature fireplaces, whirlpool baths, and private balconies.

# NORTH OF BROAD
## $150-300

It calls itself a boutique hotel, perhaps because each room is unique and sumptuously appointed. But the charming ★ **Andrew Pinckney Inn** (199 Church St., 843/937-8800, www.andrewpinckneyinn.com, $250-350) is very nearly in a class by itself in Charleston not only for its great rates but for its casual West Indies-style decor, charming courtyard, gorgeous three-story atrium, and rooftop terrace on which you can enjoy your complimentary (and delicious) breakfast. For the money and the amenities, it's possibly the single best lodging package in town.

If you plan on some serious shopping, you might want to stay right on the city's main shopping thoroughfare at the **Kings Courtyard Inn** (198 King St., 866/720-2949, www.kingscourtyardinn.com, $200-300). This 1853 Greek Revival building houses a lot more guest rooms—more than 40—than meets the eye, and it can get a little crowded at times. Still, its charming courtyard and awesome location on King Street are big bonuses, as is the convenient but cramped parking lot right next door (about $12 per day, a bargain for this part of town), with free in-and-out privileges.

Affiliated with the Kings Courtyard—and right next door, in fact—is the smaller, cozier **Fulton Lane Inn** (202 King St., 866/720-2940, www.fultonlaneinn.com, $240-350), with its lobby entrance on tiny Fulton Lane between the two inns. Small, simple guest rooms—some with fireplaces—have comfortable beds and spacious baths. This is the kind of place for active people who plan to spend most of their days out and about but want a cozy place to come back to at night. You mark down your continental breakfast order at night, leave it on your doorknob, and it shows up at the *exact* time you requested the next morning. Then when you're ready to shop and walk, just go down the stairs and take the exit right out onto busy King Street. Also nice is the $12-per-day parking with free in-and-out privileges.

Although it is a newer building by Charleston standards, the **Mills House Hotel** (115 Meeting St., 843/577-2400, www.millshouse.com, $250-400) boasts an important pedigree. Dating to 1853, the first incarnation was a grand edifice that hosted luminaries such as Robert E. Lee. Through the years, fire and restoration wrought their changes, and the modern version basically dates from an extensive renovation in the 1970s. The hotel

Andrew Pinckney Inn

has a very good restaurant and lounge inside, the Barbadoes Room (breakfast, lunch, dinner, and Sunday brunch), as well as a healthy banquet and event schedule. So this isn't the place to go for peace and quiet. Rather, this Wyndham-affiliated property is where you go to feel the bustle of downtown Charleston and to be conveniently close to its main sightseeing and shopping attractions. Some of the upper floors of this seven-story building offer spectacular views.

## Over $300

Considered Charleston's premier hotel, Charleston Place maintains a surprisingly high level of service and decor for its massive 440-room size. Currently owned by the London-based Orient-Express Hotels, ★ **Belmond Charleston Place** (205 Meeting St., 843/722-4900, www.charlestonplace.com, $300-500) is routinely rated as one of the best hotels in North America by *Condé Nast Traveler* and other publications. The guest rooms aren't especially large, but they are well appointed, featuring Italian marble baths, high-speed Internet, and voice messaging—and, of course, there's a pool available. A series of suite offerings—Junior, Junior Executive, Parlor, and the 800-square-foot Senior—feature enlarged living areas and multiple TVs and phones. The on-site **spa** (843/937-8522) offers all kinds of massages, including couples and "mommy to be" sessions. Diners and tipplers have three fine options to choose from: the famous **Charleston Grill** (843/577-4522, daily 6pm-close, $27-65) for fine dining; the breakfast, lunch, and brunch hot spot **Palmetto Cafe** (843/722-4900, daily 6:30am-3pm, $24-31); and the **Thoroughbred Club** (daily 11am-midnight) for cocktails and, for groups of 10 or more, afternoon tea.

On the north side of Broad Street, the magnificent ★ **John Rutledge House Inn** (116 Broad St., 843/723-7999, www.johnrutledgehouseinn.com, $300-400) is very close to the old South of Broad neighborhood not only in geography but in feel. Known as "America's most historic inn," the Rutledge House

boasts a fine old pedigree indeed: Built for Constitution signer John Rutledge in 1763, it's one of only 15 homes belonging to the original signers to survive. George Washington breakfasted here with Mrs. Rutledge in 1791. The interior is stunning: Italian marble fireplaces, original plaster moldings, and masterful ironwork abound in the public spaces. The inn's 19 guest rooms are divided among the original mansion and two carriage houses.

## UPPER KING
### $150-300

Stretching the bounds of the "Upper King" definition, the **Ashley Inn** (201 Ashley Ave., 843/723-1848, www.charleston-sc-inns.com, $200-300) is located well northwest of Marion Square, almost in the Citadel area. Although it's too far to walk from here to most any historical attraction in Charleston, the Ashley Inn does provide free bikes to its guests as well as free off-street parking, a particularly nice touch. It also deserves a special mention not only because of the romantic, well-appointed nature of its six guest rooms, suite, and carriage house but for its outstanding breakfasts. You get to pick a main dish, such as Carolina sausage pie, stuffed waffles, or cheese blintzes.

In a renovated 1924 building overlooking beautiful Marion Square, the **Francis Marion Hotel** (387 King St., 843/722-0600, www.francismarionhotel.com, $200-300) offers quality accommodations in the hippest, most bustling area of the peninsula—but be aware that it's quite a walk down to the Battery from here. The guest rooms are plush and big, though the baths can be cramped. The hotel's parking garage costs a reasonable $12 per day, with valet parking available until about 8pm. A Starbucks in the lobby pleases many guests on their way out or in. Most rooms hover around $300, but some are a real steal.

## HAMPTON PARK
### Under $150

Downtown Charleston's least-expensive lodging is also its most unique: the **Not So Hostel** (156 Spring St., 843/722-8383, www.

notsohostel.com, $30-70). The already-reasonable prices also include a make-your-own bagel breakfast, off-street parking, bikes, high-speed Internet access in the common room, and even an airport, train, and bus shuttle. The inn actually comprises three 1840s Charleston single houses, all with the obligatory piazzas. (However, unlike some hostels, there's air-conditioning in all the rooms.) Because the free bike usage makes up for its off-the-beaten-path location, a stay at the Not So Hostel is a fantastic way to enjoy the Holy City on a budget. They now have an annex at 33 Cannon Street with all-private rooms ($75-85).

## WEST ASHLEY
### $150-300
Looking like Frank Lloyd Wright parachuted into a 300-year-old plantation and got to work, ★ The Inn at Middleton Place (4290 Ashley River Rd., 843/556-0500, www.theinnatmiddletonplace.com, $200-300) is one of Charleston's unique lodgings—and not only because it's on the grounds of the historic and beautiful Middleton Place Plantation. The four connected buildings, comprising over 50 guest rooms, are modern yet deliberately blend in with the forested, neutral-colored surroundings. The spacious guest rooms have that same woodsy minimalism, with excellent fireplaces, spacious Euro-style baths, and huge floor-to-ceiling windows overlooking the grounds and the river. Guests also have full access to the rest of the gorgeous Middleton grounds. The only downside is that you're a lengthy drive from the peninsula and all its attractions, restaurants, and nightlife. But don't worry about food—the excellent Middleton Place Restaurant is open for lunch and dinner. There are nightly happy hours at the lodge, a great way to meet some of your fellow lodging mates and relax.

## SUMMERVILLE
### Over $300
The renowned Woodlands Resort & Inn (125 Parsons Rd., 843/875-2600, www.

woodlandsmansion.com, $500 and up) is one of a handful of inns in the United States with a five-star rating both for lodging and dining. Its 18 guest rooms within the 1906 great house are decorated in a mix of old-fashioned plantation high style and contemporary designer aesthetics, with modern, luxurious baths. There's also a freestanding guest cottage ($950) that seeks to replicate a hunting lodge vibe. There's a full day spa on the premises; the most basic offering, a one-hour massage, will run you about $120. Within Woodlands is its award-winning world-class restaurant, simply called The Dining Room (Mon.-Sat. 11am-2pm and 6pm-9pm, brunch Sun. 11:30am-2pm, $40-50). The 900-entry wine list and sommelier are collectively fantastic, as are the desserts. Jackets are required, and reservations are strongly advised.

## MOUNT PLEASANT AND EAST COOPER
### $150-300
One of the more accessible and enjoyable resort-type stays in the Charleston area is on the Isle of Palms at Wild Dunes Resort (5757 Palm Blvd., 888/778-1876, www.wilddunes.com, $275-350). This is the place to go for relaxing, beach-oriented vacation fun in your choice of a traditional hotel room, a house, or a villa. Bustling Mount Pleasant is only a couple of minutes away, and Charleston proper not much farther.

## FOLLY BEACH AND THE SOUTHWEST ISLANDS
### $150-300
The upbeat but still cozy Tides Folly Beach (1 Center St., 843/588-6464, www.tidesfollybeach.com, $200-300) boutique hotel has a combination of attentive staff, great oceanfront views, and an excellent on-site restaurant, Blu.

### Over $300
The beautiful island of Kiawah—about 45 minutes from downtown Charleston—has as its main attraction the sumptuous

★ **Kiawah Island Golf Resort** (1 Sanctuary Beach Dr., 800/654-2924, www.kiawahgolf.com, $500-1000), a frequent venue for PGA tournaments. But even if you don't play golf, the resort is an amazing stay. The main component is The Sanctuary, an upscale hotel featuring an opulent lobby complete with grand staircases, a large pool area overlooking the beach, tasteful Spanish Colonial-style architecture, and 255 smallish but excellently appointed guest rooms.

## CAMPING

Charleston County runs a family-friendly, fairly boisterous campground at **James**

**Island County Park** (871 Riverland Dr., 843/795-7275, www.ccprc.com, $31 tent site, $37 pull-through site). A neat feature here is the $5-per-person round-trip shuttle to the visitors center downtown, Folly Beach Pier, and Folly Beach County Park. The park also has 10 furnished cottages (843/795-4386, $138) for rent, sleeping up to eight people. Reservations are recommended. For more commercial camping in Mount Pleasant, try the **KOA of Mount Pleasant** (3157 U.S. 17 N., 843/849-5177, www.koa.com, from $30 tent sites, from $50 pull-through sites).

# Transportation and Services

## AIR

Way up in North Charleston is **Charleston International Airport** (CHS, 5500 International Blvd., 843/767-1100, www.chs-airport.com), served by American (www.aa.com), Delta (www.delta.com), JetBlue (www.jetblue.com), and Southwest (www.southwest.com).

It'll take about 20 minutes to make the 12-mile drive from the airport to downtown, and vice versa. The airport is conveniently located just off the I-526/Mark Clark Expressway perimeter highway off I-26. As in most cities, taxi service from the airport is regulated. This translates to about $30 for two people from the airport to Charleston Place downtown.

## CAR

There are two main routes into Charleston: I-26 from the west-northwest (which dead-ends downtown) and U.S. 17 from the west (called Savannah Highway when it gets close to Charleston proper), which continues east over the Ravenel Bridge into Mount Pleasant and beyond. There's a fairly new perimeter highway, I-526 (Mark Clark Expressway), which loops around the city from West Ashley to North Charleston to Daniel Island and into

Mount Pleasant. It's accessible both from I-26 and U.S. 17.

Keep in mind that I-95, while certainly a gateway to the region, is actually a good ways out of Charleston, about 30 miles west of the city. Charleston is almost exactly two hours from Savannah by car, and about an hour's drive from Beaufort and Hilton Head.

## Car Rentals

Charleston International Airport has rental kiosks for **Avis** (843/767-7031), **Budget** (843/767-7051), **Dollar** (843/767-1130), **Enterprise** (843/767-1109), **Hertz** (843/767-4550), **National** (843/767-3078), and **Thrifty** (843/647-4389). There are a couple of rental locations downtown: **Budget** (390 Meeting St., 843/577-5195) and **Enterprise** (398 Meeting St., 843/723-6215). **Hertz** has a location in West Ashley (3025 Ashley Town Center Dr., 843/573-2147), as does **Enterprise** (2004 Savannah Hwy., 843/556-7889).

## BUS

Public transportation by **Charleston Area Regional Transit Authority** (CARTA, 843/724-7420, www.ridecarta.com) is a convenient and inexpensive way to enjoy Charleston without the more structured nature of an organized tour. There's a wide variety of routes, but most visitors will limit their acquaintance to the tidy, trolley-like **DASH** (Downtown Area Shuttle, free) buses run by CARTA primarily for visitors. Keep in mind that DASH only stops at designated places.

## TAXI

The South is generally not big on taxis, and Charleston is no exception. The best bet is simply to call rather than try to flag one down. Charleston's most fun service is **Charleston Black Cabs** (843/216-2627, www.charleston-blackcabcompany.com), using Americanized versions of the classic British taxi. A one-way ride anywhere on the peninsula below the bridges is about $10 per person, and rates go up from there. They're very popular, so call as far ahead as you can or try to get one at their stand at Charleston Place. Two other good services are **Safety Cab** (843/722-4066) and **Yellow Cab** (843/577-6565).

You can also try a human-powered taxi service from **Charleston Rickshaw** (843/723-5685). A cheerful (and energetic) young cyclist will pull you and a friend to most points on the Lower Peninsula for about $10-15. Call 'em or find one by City Market. They work late on Friday and Saturday nights too.

## PARKING

As you'll quickly see, parking is at a premium in downtown Charleston. An exception seems to be the large number of free spaces all along the Battery, but unless you're an exceptionally strong walker, that's too far south to use as a reliable base from which to explore the whole peninsula.

Metered spaces are enforced 8am-6pm Monday-Saturday. Most metered parking downtown is on and around Calhoun Street, Meeting Street, King Street, Market Street, and East Bay Street.

The city has several conveniently located and comparatively inexpensive parking garages. I strongly suggest that you make use of them. They're located at the aquarium,

Camden and Exchange Streets, Charleston Place, Concord and Cumberland Streets, East Bay and Prioleau Streets, Marion Square, Gaillard Auditorium, Liberty and St. Philip Streets, Majestic Square, the Charleston Visitor Reception and Transportation Center, and Wentworth Street.

The city's website (www.charlestoncity.info) has a good interactive map of parking.

## TOURIST INFORMATION
### Visitors Centers

I highly recommend a stop at the **Charleston Visitor Reception and Transportation Center** (375 Meeting St., 800/774-0006, www.charlestoncvb.com, Mon.-Fri. 8:30am-5pm). I also recommend using the attached parking garage not only for your stop at the center but also anytime you want to see the many sights this part of town has to offer, such as the Charleston Museum, the Manigault and Aiken-Rhett Houses, and the Children's Museum. Go to the center to take advantage of the great deal offered by the **Charleston Heritage Passport** (www.heritagefederation.org), which gives you 40 percent off admission to all of Charleston's key historic homes, the Charleston Museum, and the two awesome plantation sites on the Ashley River: Drayton Hall and Middleton Place. You can get the Heritage Passport *only* at the Charleston Visitor Reception and Transportation Center on Meeting Street.

Other area visitors centers include the **Mount Pleasant-Isle of Palms Visitors Center** (99 Harry M. Hallman Jr. Blvd., 800/774-0006, daily 9am-5pm) and the **North Charleston Visitors Center** (4975B Centre Pointe Dr., 843/853-8000, Mon.-Sat. 10am-5pm).

### Hospitals

If there's a silver lining in getting sick or injured in Charleston, it's that there are plenty of high-quality medical facilities available. The premier institution is the **Medical University of South Carolina** (171 Ashley Ave., 843/792-2300, www.muschealth.com)

in the northwest part of the peninsula. Two notable facilities are near each other downtown: **Roper Hospital** (316 Calhoun St., 843/402-2273, www.roperhospital.com) and **Charleston Memorial Hospital** (326 Calhoun St., 843/792-2300). In Mount Pleasant there's **East Cooper Regional Medical Center** (1200 Johnnie Dodds Blvd., www.eastcoopermedctr.com). In West Ashley there's **Bon Secours St. Francis Hospital** (2095 Henry Tecklenburg Ave., 843/402-2273, www.ropersaintfrancis.com).

## Police

For nonemergencies in Charleston, West Ashley, and James Island, contact the **Charleston Police Department** (843/577-7434, www.charlestoncity.info). You can also contact the police department in Mount Pleasant (843/884-4176). North Charleston is a separate municipality with its own police department (843/308-4718, www.northcharleston.org). Of course, for emergencies always call **911.**

## Media

The daily newspaper of record is the *Post and Courier* (www.charleston.net). Its entertainment insert, *Preview,* comes out on Thursdays. The free alternative weekly is the *Charleston City Paper* (www.charlestoncitypaper.com), which comes out on Wednesdays and is the best place to find local music and arts listings. A particularly well-done and lively metro glossy is *Charleston* magazine (www.charlestonmag.com), which comes out once a month.

The National Public Radio affiliate is the South Carolina ETV radio station WSCI at 89.3 FM. South Carolina ETV is on television at WITV. The local NBC affiliate is WCBD, the CBS affiliate is WCSC, the ABC affiliate is WCIV, and the Fox affiliate is WTAT.

## Libraries

The main branch of the **Charleston County Public Library** (68 Calhoun St.,

843/805-6801, www.ccpl.org, Mon.-Thurs. 9am-9pm, Fri.-Sat. 9am-6pm, Sun. 2pm-5pm) has been at its current site since 1998. Named for Sullivan's Island's most famous visitor, the **Edgar Allan Poe Library** (1921 I'on Ave., 843/883-3914, www.ccpl.org, Mon. and Fri. 2pm-6pm, Tues., Thurs., and Sat. 10am-2pm) has been housed in Battery Gadsden, a former Spanish-American War gun emplacement, since 1977.

The College of Charleston's main library is the **Marlene and Nathan Addlestone Library** (205 Calhoun St., 843/953-5530, www.cofc.edu), home to special collections, the Center for Student Learning, the main computer lab, the media collection, and even a café. The college's **Avery Research Center for African American History and Culture** (125 Bull St., 843/953-7609, www.cofc.edu/avery, Mon.-Fri. 10am-5pm, Sat. noon-5pm) houses documents relating to the history and culture of African Americans in the Lowcountry.

For other historical research on the area, check out the collections of the **South Carolina Historical Society** (100 Meeting St., 843/723-3225, www.southcarolinahistoricalsociety.org, Mon.-Fri. 9am-4pm, Sat. 9am-2pm). There's a $5 research fee for nonmembers.

## LGBTQ Resources

Contrary to many media portrayals of the region, Charleston is quite open to the LGBTQ community, which plays a major role in arts, culture, and business. As with any other place in the South, however, it's generally expected that people—straights as well—will keep personal matters and politics to themselves in public settings. A key local advocacy group is the **Alliance for Full Acceptance** (29 Leinbach Dr., Ste. D-3, 843/883-0343, www.affa-sc.org). The **Lowcountry Gay and Lesbian Alliance** (843/720-8088) holds a potluck the last Sunday of each month. For the most up-to-date happenings, try the *Charleston City Paper.*

# Hilton Head and the Lowcountry

# For many people around the world, the Lowcountry is the first image that comes to mind when they think of the American South.

History hangs in the humid air where first the Spanish and French came to interrupt the native tribes' ancient reverie, followed by the English. Although time, erosion, and development have erased most traces of these various occupants, you can almost hear their ghosts in the rustle of the branches in a sudden sea breeze or in the piercing call of a heron over the marsh.

The defining characteristic of the Lowcountry is its liquid nature—not only literally, in the creeks and waterways that dominate every vista and the seafood cooked in all manner of ways, but figuratively too, in the slow but deep quality of life here. Not so very long ago, before the influx of resort development, retirement subdivisions, and tourism, much of the Lowcountry was like a flatter, more humid Appalachia—poverty-stricken and desperately underserved. While the archetypal South has been marketed in any number of ways to the rest of the world, here you get a sense that this is the real thing—timeless, endlessly alluring, but somehow very familiar.

South of Beaufort is the historically significant Port Royal area and the East Coast Marine Corps Recruit Depot of Parris Island. East of Beaufort is the center of Gullah culture, St. Helena Island, and the scenic gem of Hunting Island. To the south is the scenic but entirely developed golf and tennis mecca, Hilton Head Island, and Hilton Head's close neighbor but diametrical opposite in every other way, Daufuskie Island, another important Gullah center. Nestled between is the close-knit and gossipy little village of Bluffton on the gossamer May River.

## PLANNING YOUR TIME

A commonsense game plan is to use centrally located Beaufort as a home base and spend **three days** exploring the region. Take at least half a day of leisure to walk all over Beaufort, a delightfully walkable place. If you're in the mood for a road trip, dedicate a full day to tour the area to the north and northeast, with

---

**Previous:** yoga on the beach; the Harbour Town Lighthouse. **Above:** Old Town Bluffton.

Look for ★ to find recommended
sights, activities, dining, and lodging.

# Highlights

★ **Henry C. Chambers Waterfront Park:** While away the time on a porch swing at this clean and inviting gathering place on the serene Beaufort River (page 349).

★ **St. Helena's Episcopal Church:** To walk through this Beaufort sanctuary and its walled graveyard is to walk through history (page 351).

★ **Penn Center:** Visit the center of modern Gullah culture and education—and a key site in the history of the civil rights movement (page 360).

★ **Hunting Island State Park:** One of the most peaceful natural getaways on the East Coast is only minutes away from the civilized temptations of Beaufort (page 363).

★ **ACE Basin:** You can take a lifetime to learn your way around this massive, marshy estuary—or just a few hours to soak in its lush beauty (page 363).

★ **Edisto Beach State Park:** Relax at this quiet, friendly, and relatively undeveloped park on Sea Island, a mecca for shell collectors (page 367).

★ **Pinckney Island National Wildlife Refuge:** This well-maintained sanctuary is a major birding location and a great getaway from nearby Hilton Head (page 370).

★ **Coastal Discovery Museum at Honey Horn:** This beautifully repurposed plantation house with spacious grounds is a great place to learn about Hilton Head history, both human and natural (page 371).

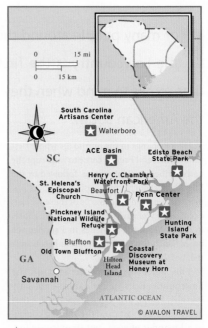

© AVALON TRAVEL

★ **Old Town Bluffton:** By turns gossipy and gorgeous, the charming "Old Town" on the May River centers on a thriving artist colony (page 382).

★ **South Carolina Artisans Center:** Visual artists and fine craftspeople from all over the state contribute work to this high-quality collective in Walterboro (page 387).

# Hilton Head and the Lowcountry

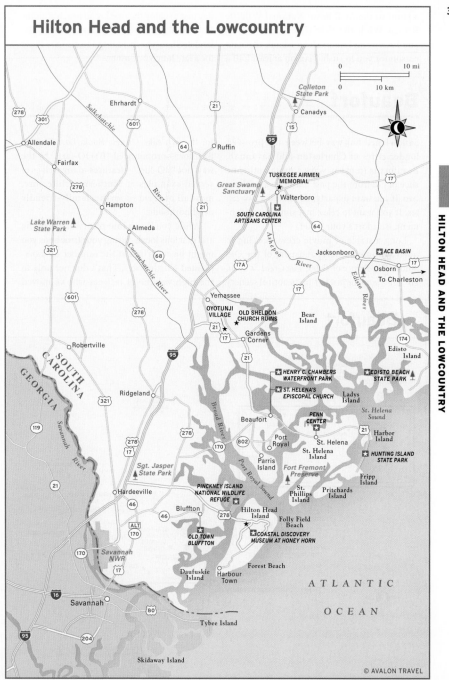

© AVALON TRAVEL

a jaunt to the ACE Basin National Wildlife Refuge. While the New York accents fly fast and furious on Hilton Head Island, that's no reason for you to rush. Plan on at least half a day just to enjoy the fine broad beaches alone. I recommend another half day to tour the island itself, maybe including a stop in Sea Pines for a late lunch or dinner.

# Beaufort

Sandwiched halfway between the prouder, louder cities of Charleston and Savannah, Beaufort is in many ways a more authentic slice of life from the past than either of those two. If you want to party, stay in those two cities. If you want to relax in a similar environment, Beaufort's your ticket.

Long a staple of movie crews seeking to portray some archetypal aspect of the Old South (*The Prince of Tides, The Great Santini, Forrest Gump*) or just to film beautiful scenery for its own sake (*Jungle Book, Last Dance*), Beaufort—pronounced "BYOO-fert," by the way, not "BO-fort"—features many well-preserved examples of Southern architecture, most all of them in idyllic, family-friendly neighborhoods.

While you'll run into plenty of charming and gracious locals during your time here, you might be surprised at the number of transplanted Northerners. That's due not only to the high volume of retirees who've moved

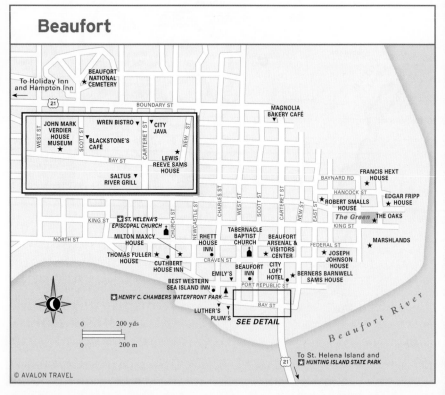

to the area, but also to the active presence of three major U.S. Navy facilities: the Marine Corps Air Station Beaufort, the Marine Corps Recruit Depot on nearby Parris Island, and the Beaufort Naval Hospital.

The two main avenues to remember are Bay Street, along the Beaufort River and the real center of downtown; and Boundary Street, which becomes Carteret Street as you arrive into downtown proper.

## HISTORY

This was the site of the second landing by the Spanish on the North American continent, the expedition of Captain Pedro de Salazar in 1514 (Ponce de León's more famous landing at St. Augustine was but a year earlier). A Spanish slaver made a brief stop in 1521, long enough to name the area Santa Elena. Port Royal Sound didn't get its modern name until the first serious attempt at a permanent settlement, Jean Ribault's exploration in 1562. Though ultimately disastrous, Ribault's base of Charlesfort was the first French settlement in America.

In 1776, Beaufort planter Thomas Heyward Jr. was a signer of the Declaration of Independence. After independence, Lowcountry planters turned to cotton as the main cash crop, since England had been their prime customer for indigo. The gambit paid off, and Beaufort soon became one of the wealthiest towns in the new nation. In 1861, only seven months after secessionists fired on Fort Sumter in nearby Charleston, a Union fleet sailed into Port Royal and occupied the Lowcountry for the duration of the war.

Gradually developing their own distinct dialect and culture, much of it linked to their West African roots, isolated Lowcountry African Americans became known as the Gullah. Evolving from an effort by abolitionist missionaries early in the Civil War, in 1864 the Penn School was formed on St. Helena Island specifically to teach the children of the Gullah communities. Now known as the Penn Center, the facility has been a beacon for the study of this aspect of African American culture ever since.

## SIGHTS
### ★ Henry C. Chambers Waterfront Park

A tastefully designed, well-maintained, and user-friendly mix of walkways, bandstands, and patios, **Henry C. Chambers Waterfront Park** (843/525-7054, www. cityofbeaufort.org, daily 24 hours) is a favorite gathering place for locals and visitors

the Henry C. Chambers Waterfront Park

# Pat Conroy's Lowcountry

No person was as closely associated with the South Carolina Lowcountry as beloved author Pat Conroy, who passed away in 2016. After moving around as a child in a military family, he began high school in Beaufort. His painful teen years there formed the basis of his first novel, a brutal portrait of his domineering Marine pilot father, Colonel Donald Conroy, aka Colonel Bull Meecham of *The Great Santini* (1976). Many scenes from the 1979 film adaptation were filmed at the famous Tidalholm, the Edgar Fripp House (1 Laurens St.) in Beaufort. (The house was also front and center in *The Big Chill*.)

Conroy's pattern of thinly veiled autobiography actually began with his first book, the self-published *The Boo*, a tribute to a teacher at the Citadel in Charleston while Conroy was still a student there. His second work, *The Water is Wide* (1972), is a chronicle of his experiences teaching in a one-room African American school on Daufuskie Island. Though ostensibly a straightforward first-person journalistic effort, Conroy changed the location to the fictional Yamacraw Island, supposedly to protect Daufuskie's fragile culture from curious outsiders. The 1974 film adaptation starring Jon Voight was titled *Conrack* after the way his students mispronounced his name. You can visit that same one-room school today on Daufuskie. Known as the Mary Field School, the building is now a local community center.

Conroy would go on to publish in 1980 *The Lords of Discipline*, a reading of his real-life experience with the often-savage environment faced by cadets at the Citadel—though Conroy would change the name, calling it the Carolina Military Institute. Still, when it came time to make a film adaptation in 1983, the Citadel refused to allow it to be shot there, so the "Carolina Military Institute" was filmed in England instead. Conroy also wrote the foreword to the cookbook *Gullah Home Cooking the Daufuskie Way: Smokin' Joe Butter Beans, Ol' 'Fuskie Fried Crab Rice, Sticky-Bush Blackberry Dumpling, and Other Sea Island Favorites* by Daufuskie native and current Savannah resident Sallie Ann Robinson.

For many of his fans, Conroy's *The Prince of Tides* is his ultimate homage to the Lowcountry. Surely, the 1991 film version starring Barbra Streisand and Nick Nolte—shot on location and awash in gorgeous shots of the Beaufort River marsh—did much to implant an idyllic image of the area with audiences around the world. According to local legend, Streisand originally didn't intend to make the film in Beaufort, but a behind-the-scenes lobbying effort allegedly coordinated by Conroy himself, and including a stay at the Rhett House Inn, convinced her.

The Bay Street Inn (601 Bay St.) in Beaufort was seen in the film, as was the football field at the old Beaufort High School. The beach scenes were shot on nearby Fripp Island. Interestingly, some scenes set in a Manhattan apartment were actually shot within the old Beaufort Arsenal (713 Craven St.), now a visitors center. Similarly, the Beaufort Naval Hospital doubled as New York's Bellevue.

Despite the many personal tribulations he faced in the area, to the end Conroy never gave up on the Lowcountry. He is interred in the old Gullah Cemetery on St. Helena Island, near the historic Penn Center, beside civil rights heroine Agnes Sherman. As for the "Great Santini" himself, you can visit the final resting place of Colonel Conroy in the Beaufort National Cemetery—Section 62, Grave 182.

alike, beckoning one and all with its open green space and wonderful marsh-front views.

## John Mark Verdier House Museum

A smallish but stately Federalist building on the busiest downtown corner, the **John Mark Verdier House Museum** (801 Bay St., 843/379-6335, www.historicbeaufort.org, tours on the half hour Mon.-Sat. 10:30am-3:30pm, $5) is the only historic Beaufort planter's home open to regular tours. Built in 1805 for John Mark Verdier, its main claims to fame are acting as the Union headquarters during the long occupation of Beaufort during the Civil War and hosting Revolutionary War

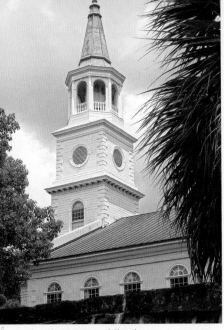

St. Helena's Episcopal Church

**Helena's Episcopal Church** (505 Church St., 843/522-1712, Tues.-Fri. 10am-4pm, Sat. 10am-1pm) has witnessed some of Beaufort's most compelling tales. Built in 1724, this was the parish church of Thomas Heyward, one of South Carolina's signers of the Declaration of Independence. John "Tuscarora Jack" Barnwell, one of Beaufort's founders, is buried on the grounds.

While the cemetery and sanctuary interior are likely to be your focus, take a close look at the church exterior—many of the bricks are actually ships' ballast stones. Also be aware that you're not looking at the church's original footprint; the building has been expanded several times since its construction (a hurricane in 1896 destroyed the entire east end). A nearly $3 million restoration, mostly for structural repairs, was completed in 2000.

## Reconstruction Era National Monument

One of Barack Obama's last acts as president was the creation of the **Reconstruction Era National Monument** (www.nps.gov/reer, hours vary, free). Encompassing several sites in the Beaufort area, this isn't a single park you visit but rather a collection of locations that were important in the years immediately following the Civil War.

The easiest site to visit is the Beaufort Firehouse (706 Craven St.) downtown across from the Beaufort Arsenal/Museum. Once home to private businesses and now deeded to the National Park Service, the firehouse marks the site of community gatherings in the post-Civil War occupation era. As the national monument takes shape, it is likely to be a visitors center of some sort.

Two key sites on St. Helena Island are Darrah Hall on the Penn Center campus (for which there's a separate listing in this chapter) and the Brick Baptist Church, just across the street from the Penn Center. Darrah Hall is the epicenter of one of the nation's first schools for emancipated slaves. The Brick Baptist Church was built by slaves in 1855 and is the oldest church on St. Helena Island.

hero the Marquis de Lafayette, who stayed at the Verdier House on his 1825 U.S. tour. In 2011 the Verdier House was extensively and professionally restored, with exterior paint reflecting the home's authentic 1863 look.

## Beaufort Arsenal Visitors Center and History Museum

The imposing yellow-gray tabby facade of the 1852 **Beaufort Arsenal** (713 Craven St.) houses the **Beaufort Visitors Center** (843/986-5400, www.beaufortsc.org, Mon.-Sat. 9am-5pm, Sun. noon-5pm) and **Beaufort History Museum** (www.beauforthistorymuseum.com, Mon.-Sat. 10am-4pm, $5). The visitors center is a great place to purchase various tour tickets, and the adjacent museum is a small but informative stop to learn more about the area's long and important history. There are also public restrooms.

## ★ St. Helena's Episcopal Church

Nestled within a low brick wall surrounding this historic church and cemetery, **St.**

The Camp Saxton/Emancipation Oak site is on the grounds of the Beaufort Naval Hospital. While currently not open to the public, that will likely change at some point in the future.

## Tabernacle Baptist Church

Built in 1845, the handsome **Tabernacle Baptist Church** (911 Craven St., 843/524-0376) had a congregation of over 3,000 before the Civil War. Slaves made up most of the congregation, and during the war freed slaves purchased the church. A congregant was the war hero Robert Smalls, who seized the Confederate steamer he was forced to serve on and delivered it to Union forces. He is buried in the church cemetery and has a nice memorial dedicated to him facing the street.

## Beaufort National Cemetery

Begun by order of Abraham Lincoln in 1863, **Beaufort National Cemetery** (1601 Boundary St., daily 8am-sunset) is one of the few cemeteries containing the graves of both Union and Confederate troops. This national cemetery is where 19 soldiers of the all-black 54th and 55th Massachusetts Infantries were reinterred after being found on Folly Island near Charleston. Also buried here is "the Great Santini" himself, novelist Pat Conroy's father, Donald.

## Santa Elena History Center

The actual historic site is on nearby Parris Island, but in downtown Beaufort you'll find the **Santa Elena History Center** (1501 Bay St., 843/379-1550, www.santa-elena.org, Tues.-Sat. 10am-4pm, Sun. 1pm-4pm, free), detailing the Spanish occupation of the area beginning 450 years ago, long before English-speaking settlers arrived. This is a new and growing venture, and exhibits and resources will be added as funds become available.

## A Walking Tour of Beaufort Homes

Here's a walking tour of some of Beaufort's fine historic homes in private hands. You won't be taking any tours of the interiors, but these homes are part of the legacy of the area and are locally valued as such. Be sure to respect the privacy of the inhabitants by keeping the noise level down and not trespassing on private property to take photos.

- **Thomas Fuller House:** Begin at the corner of Harrington and Bay Streets and view the 1796 Thomas Fuller House (1211 Bay St.), one of the oldest in Beaufort and unique in that much of the building material is tabby (hence the home's other name, the Tabby Manse).

- **Milton Maxcy House:** Walk east on Bay Street one block and take a left on Church Street; walk up to the corner of Church and Craven Streets. Otherwise known as the Secession House (113 Craven St.), this 1813 home was built on a tabby foundation dating from 1743. In 1860, when it was the residence of attorney Edmund Rhett, the first Ordinance of Secession was signed here, and the rest, as they say, is history.

- **Lewis Reeve Sams House:** Resume the walking tour on the other side of the historic district at the foot of the bridge in the old neighborhood simply called "the Point." The beautiful Lewis Reeve Sams House (601 Bay St.) at the corner of Bay and New Streets, with its double-decker veranda, dates from 1852 and like many Beaufort mansions served as a Union hospital during the Civil War.

- **Berners Barnwell Sams House:** Continue up New Street, where shortly ahead on the left you'll find the 1818 Berners Barnwell Sams House (310 New St.), which served as the African American hospital during the Union occupation. Harriet Tubman of Underground Railroad fame worked here for a time as a nurse.

- **Joseph Johnson House:** Continue up New Street and take a right on Craven Street. Cross East Street to find the 1850 Joseph Johnson House (411 Craven St.), with the massive live oak in the front yard.

Legend has it that when the Yankees occupied Hilton Head, Mr. Johnson buried his valuables under an outhouse. After the war he returned to find his home for sale due to unpaid back taxes. He dug up his valuables, paid the taxes, and resumed living in the home. You might recognize the home from the film *Forces of Nature*.

- **Marshlands:** Backtrack to East Street, walk north to Federal Street, and go to its end. Built by James R. Verdier, Marshlands (501 Pinckney St.) was used as a hospital during the Civil War, as many Beaufort homes were, and is now a National Historic Landmark. It was the setting of Francis Griswold's 1931 novel *A Sea Island Lady*.

- **The Oaks:** Walk up to King Street and take a right. Soon after you pass a large open park on the left, King Street dead-ends at Short Street. The Oaks (100 Laurens St.) at this corner was owned by the Hamilton family, who lost a son who served with General Wade Hampton's cavalry in the Civil War. After the conflict, the family couldn't afford the back taxes; neighbors paid the debts and returned the deed to the Hamiltons.

- **Edgar Fripp House:** Continue east on Laurens Street toward the water to find this handsome Lowcountry mansion, sometimes called Tidalholm (1 Laurens St.). Built in 1856 by the wealthy planter for whom nearby Fripp Island is named, this house was a key setting in *The Big Chill* and *The Great Santini*.

- **Francis Hext House:** Go back to Short Street, walk north to Hancock Street, and take a left. A short way ahead on the right, the handsome red-roofed estate known as Riverview (207 Hancock St.) is one of the oldest structures in Beaufort; it was built in 1720.

- **Robert Smalls House:** Continue west on Hancock Street, take a short left on East Street, and then a quick right on Prince Street. The 1834 Robert Smalls House (511 Prince St.) was the birthplace of Robert

Smalls, a former slave and Beaufort native who stole the Confederate ship *Planter* from Charleston Harbor while serving as helmsman and delivered it to Union troops in Hilton Head. Smalls and a few compatriots commandeered the ship while the officers were at a party at Fort Sumter. Smalls used the bounty he earned for the act of bravery to buy his boyhood home. After the war, Smalls was a longtime U.S. congressman.

# ENTERTAINMENT AND NIGHTLIFE
## Performing Arts

Beaufort's fine arts scene is small but professional in outlook. Most performances are based in the nice Performing Arts Center on the oak-lined campus of the **University of South Carolina Beaufort** (USCB, 801 Carteret St., 843/521-4100, www.uscb.edu). A prime mover of the local performing arts scene is **Beaufort Performing Arts Inc.,** formed by a mayoral task force in 2003 specifically to encourage arts and cultural development within the area. Ticket prices typically range $12-40.

Perhaps surprising for such a small place, Beaufort boasts its own full orchestra, the **Beaufort Orchestra** (1106 Carteret St., 843/986-5400, www.beaufortorchestra.org), which plays in the Performing Arts Center.

## Cinema

One of only two functional drive-ins in the state, the **Highway 21 Drive In** (55 Parker Dr., 843/846-4500, www.hwy21drivein.com) has two screens, great sound, movies Friday-Sunday, and awesome concessions that include Angus beef hamburgers. All you need to provide is the car and the company.

## Festivals and Events

Surprising for a town so prominent in so many films, Beaufort didn't have its own film festival until 2007. The **Beaufort Film Festival** (843/986-5400, www.beaufortfilmfestival.com) is held in February. It's small in scale but growing steadily each year and boasts a diverse range of high-quality, cutting-edge entries, including shorts and animation. Most events are held at the University of South Carolina Beaufort campus.

Now over 20 years old, the **Gullah Festival of South Carolina** (www.theoriginalgullahfestival.org) celebrates Gullah history and culture on Memorial Day weekend at various locations throughout town, mostly focusing on Waterfront Park.

By far the biggest single event on the local festival calendar is the over 50-year-old **Beaufort Water Festival** (www.bftwaterfestival.com), held over two weeks in June or July each year, centering on the Waterfront Park area.

Fall in the Lowcountry means shrimping season, and early October brings the **Beaufort Shrimp Festival** (www.beaufortsc.org). Various cooking competitions are held, obviously centering on the versatile crustaceans that are the raison d'être of the shrimp fleet.

St. Helena Island hosts the three-day **Penn Center Heritage Days** (www.penncenter.com) each November, without a doubt the Beaufort area's second-biggest celebration after the Water Festival. Focusing on Gullah culture, history, and delicious food, Heritage Days does a great job of combining fun with education.

## SHOPS

The recently renovated Old Bay Marketplace, with a facade so bright red you can't miss it, hosts a few cute shops, most notably the stylish **Lulu Burgess** (917 Bay St., 843/524-5858, Mon.-Sat. 10am-6pm, Sun. noon-5pm), an eclectic store that brings a rich, quirky sense of humor to its otherwise tasteful assortment of gift items for the whole family.

A great women's clothing store nearby is **Go Fish** (719 Bay St., 843/379-8448, www.shopgofish.com, Mon.-Thurs. 10am-6pm, Fri.-Sat. 10am-8pm), a regional chain with particularly high-quality but affordable garments, jewelry, and shoes.

At the far end of Bay Street is **Bay Street Treasures** (1001 Bay St., 843/379-4488, Mon.-Sat. 10am-5pm), an eclectic home goods/furnishings store, strong with regional and Lowcountry appeal.

My favorite shop in Beaufort is **Nevermore Books** (201 Carteret St., 843/812-9460, www.nevermorebooks.com, Tues.-Fri. 10am-5pm, Sat. 11am-4pm), a very short walk off Bay Street around the corner on Carteret. While Edgar Allan Poe is the ostensible theme of this locally owned shop—check out the awesome window display!—they specialize in fiction of all types and have a range of regional books as well.

## Art Galleries

A complete art experience blending the traditional with the cutting edge is at the **I. Pinckney Simons Art Gallery** (711 Bay St., 843/379-4774, www.ipinckneysimonsgallery.com, Tues.-Fri. 11am-5pm, Sat. 11am-3pm), which is pronounced "Simmons" despite the spelling.

For a taste of Gullah-themed art, head to **LyBenson's Gallery & Studio** (211 Charles St., 843/525-9006, www.lybensons.com). Not just a place to enjoy and purchase art, they have some small exhibits on local history and culture, including a room dedicated to local African American hero Robert Smalls.

Right on the water is a fun local favorite, the **Longo Gallery** (103 Charles St., 843/522-8933, Mon.-Sat. 11am-5pm). Owners Suzanne and Eric Longo provide a whimsical assortment of less traditional art than you might find in the more touristy waterfront area. Take Charles Street as it works its way toward the waterfront, and the gallery is right behind a storefront on the corner of Charles and Bay Streets.

You'll find perhaps the area's best-known gallery over the bridge on St. Helena Island. Known regionally as one of the best places to find Gullah folk art, **Red Piano Too** (870 Sea Island Pkwy., 843/838-2241, www.redpianotoo.com, Mon.-Sat. 10am-5pm) is on the corner before you turn onto the road to the historic Penn Center. Over 150 artists from a diverse range of traditions and styles are represented in this charming little 1940 building with a red tin awning.

# SPORTS AND ACTIVITIES

Beaufort County comprises over 60 islands, so it's no surprise that nearly all recreation in the area revolves around the water, which dominates so many aspects of life in the Lowcountry. The closer to the ocean you get, the more it's a salt marsh environment. But as you explore more inland, including the sprawling ACE Basin, you'll encounter primarily blackwater.

## Kayaking

The Lowcountry is tailor-made for kayaking. Most kayakers put in at the public landings in nearby **Port Royal** (1 Port Royal Landing Dr., 843/525-6664) or **Lady's Island** (73 Sea Island Pkwy., 843/522-0430), across the river from downtown Beaufort. If you don't feel comfortable with your navigation skills, it's a good idea to contact Kim and David at **Beaufort Kayak Tours** (843/525-0810, www.beaufortkayaktours.com), who rent kayaks and can guide you on a number of excellent tours. They charge about $40 for adults and $30 for children for a two-hour trip. A tour with Beaufort Kayak Tours is also the best (and nearly the only) way to access the historically significant ruins of the early British tabby Fort Frederick, now located on the grounds of the Beaufort Naval Hospital and inaccessible by car.

## Fishing and Boating

Key marinas in the area are the **Downtown Marina** (1006 Bay St., 843/524-4422) in Beaufort, the **Lady's Island Marina** (73 Sea Island Pkwy., 843/522-0430), and the **Port Royal Landing Marina** (1 Port Royal Landing Dr., 843/525-6664). Hunting Island has a popular 1,000-foot fishing pier at its south end. A good local fishing charter service is Captain Josh Utsey's **Lowcountry Guide Service** (843/812-4919, www.

beaufortscfishing.com). Captain Ed Hardee (843/441-6880) offers good inshore charters.

## Biking

Despite the Lowcountry's, well, lowness, biking opportunities abound. It might not get your heart rate up like a ride in the Rockies, but the area lends itself to laid-back two-wheeled enjoyment. Many local B&Bs provide bikes free for guests, and you can rent your own just across the river from Beaufort in Lady's Island at **Lowcountry Bikes** (102 Sea Island Pkwy., 843/524-9585, Mon.-Tues. and Thurs.-Fri. 10am-6pm, Wed. 10am-1pm, Sat. 10am-3pm, about $5 per hour). They can also hook you up with some good routes around the area.

## Tours

Colorful character Jon Sharp has retired from his popular walking tours, but filling his shoes is Janet Matlock, who took over the venture and now runs the equally popular **Janet's Walking History Tour** (843/226-4412, www.janetswalkinghistory.com, $25). This highly recommended two-hour jaunt begins and ends at the Downtown Marina (1006 Bay St.) and takes you all through the downtown area. Tours leave at 12:30pm Monday and 11am Tuesday-Saturday; during the hot months of June-September they leave at 10am Monday-Saturday.

**The Spirit of Old Beaufort** (103 West St. Extension, 843/525-0459, www.thespiritofoldbeaufort.com, Mon.-Sat. 10:30am, 2pm, and 7pm, $18) runs a good year-round series of themed walking tours, roughly two hours long, with guides usually in period dress. If you don't want to walk, you can hire one of their guides to join you in your own vehicle (from $50).

As you might expect, few things could be more Lowcountry than an easygoing carriage ride through the historic neighborhoods. **Southurn Rose Buggy Tours** (843/524-2900, www.southurnrose.com, daily 10am-5pm, $18 adults, $7 children)—yes, that's how they spell it—offers 50-minute narrated

# Lowcountry Boil or Frogmore Stew?

Near Beaufort it's called Frogmore stew after the township (now named St. Helena) just over the river. Closer to Savannah it's simply called Lowcountry boil. Supposedly the first pot of this delectable, hearty concoction was made by Richard Gay of the Gay Fish Company. As with any vernacular dish, dozens of local and family variants abound. The key ingredient that makes Lowcountry boil/Frogmore stew what it is—a well-blended mélange with a character all its own rather than just a bunch of stuff thrown together in a pot of boiling water—is some type of crab-boil seasoning. You'll find Zatarain's seasoning suggested on a lot of websites, but Old Bay is far more common in the eponymous Lowcountry where the dish originated.

In any case, here's a simple six-serving recipe to get you started. The only downside is that it's pretty much impossible to make it for just a few people. The dish is intended for large gatherings, whether a football tailgate party on a Saturday or a family afternoon after church on Sunday. Note the typical ratio of one ear of corn and 0.5 pound each of meat and shrimp per person.

- 6 ears fresh corn on the cob, cut into 3-inch sections
- 3 pounds smoked pork sausage, cut into 3-inch sections
- 3 pounds fresh shrimp, shells on
- 5 pounds new potatoes, halved or quartered
- 3 ounces Old Bay Seasoning

Put the sausage and potato pieces, along with the Old Bay, in two gallons of boiling water. When the potatoes are about halfway done, about 15 minutes in, add the corn and boil for about half that time, 7 minutes. Add the shrimp and boil for another 3 minutes, until they just turn pink. Do not overcook the shrimp. Take the pot off the heat and drain; serve immediately. If you cook the shrimp just right, the oil from the sausage will cause those shells to slip right off.

This is but one of dozens of recipes. Some cooks add some lemon juice and beer in the water as it's coming to a boil; others add onion, garlic, or green peppers.

---

carriage rides of the Point, including movie locations, embarking and disembarking near the Downtown Marina about every 40 minutes.

An important specialty bus tour in the area is **Gullah-N-Geechie Man Tours** (843/838-7516, www.gullahngeechietours.net, $20 adults, $18 children), focusing on the rich Gullah history and culture of the St. Helena Island area, including the historic Penn Center. Call for pickup information.

## FOOD

Because of Beaufort's small size and insular nature, many of its restaurants double as nightlife hot spots, with hopping bar scenes—or as hopping as it gets here, anyway—at dinner hours and beyond, often with a crowd of regulars. That said, those looking for a rowdy late-night time will be happier seeking it in the notorious party towns of Charleston and Savannah.

### New Southern

The stylishly appointed **Wren Bistro, Bar and Market** (210 Carteret St., 843/524-9463, www.wrenbistroandbar.com, Mon.-Sat. 11am-11pm, $15-25) is known for any of its chicken dishes. While the food is great, the interior is particularly well done, simultaneously warm and classy. As seems to be typical of Beaufort, the lunches are as good as the dinners, and the bar scene is quite active.

### Breakfast and Brunch

One of the best breakfasts I've had anywhere was a humble two-egg plate for five bucks at Beaufort's most popular morning

Common Ground Coffeehouse and Market Cafe

well-kept little modernist space next to the similarly modernist City Loft Hotel. Their espresso is big-city quality, their periodicals are timely, and their pastries and sandwiches are good for tiding you over when you need some quick energy for more walking around town.

A few blocks across downtown is a great coffee place, **Common Ground Coffeehouse and Market Cafe** (102 West St., 843/524-2326, daily 7:30am-10pm). Located in a historic building facing the river, this is not just a serenely pleasant and convenient place to enjoy your coffee, but the cakes, cookies, light sandwiches, and fresh Italian gelatos are all delightfully delicious. Get here by strolling down Bay Street; it's at the end of an alley between two blocks, and is right on the Waterfront Park. There's an open mike every Friday night.

## Seafood

The hottest dinner table in town is at the ★ **Saltus River Grill** (802 Bay St., 843/379-3474, Sun.-Thurs. 5pm-9pm, Fri.-Sat. 5pm-10pm, $10-39), famous throughout the state for its raw bar. Other specialties include she-crab bisque, lump crab cakes, and the ubiquitous shrimp and grits. The Saltus River Grill is more upscale in feel and in price than most Lowcountry places, with a very see-and-be-seen attitude and a hopping bar. Reservations are recommended.

The short and focused menu at **Plum's** (904½ Bay St., 843/525-1946, lunch daily 11am-4pm, dinner daily 5pm-10pm, $15-25) keys in on entrées highlighting local ingredients, such as the shrimp penne *all'amatriciana* and fresh black mussel pasta. An outstanding microbrew selection makes Plum's a big nightlife hangout as well.

## Steaks

★ **Luther's Rare & Well Done** (910 Bay St., 843/521-1888, daily 10am-midnight, from $8) on the waterfront is the kind of meat-lover's place where even the French onion soup has a morsel of rib eye in it. While the patented

hangout, ★ **Blackstone's Café** (205 Scott St., 843/524-4330, Mon.-Sat. 7:30am-2:30pm, Sun. 7:30am-2pm, under $10). The dish is complete with tasty hash browns, a comparative rarity in this part of the country, where grits rule as the breakfast starch of choice.

## Burgers and Sandwiches

A lunch favorite is **Magnolia Bakery Café** (703 Congress St., 843/524-1961, Mon.-Sat. 9am-5pm, under $10). Lump crab cakes are a specialty item, but you can't go wrong with any of the sandwiches. Vegetarian diners are particularly well taken care of with a large selection of black bean burger plates. As the name indicates, the range of desserts here is tantalizing, with the added bonus of a serious espresso bar.

## Coffee, Tea, and Sweets

The closest thing to a hipster coffeehouse in Beaufort is **City Java and News** (301 Carteret St., 843/379-5282, Mon.-Sat. 6am-6:30pm, Sun. 7am-6:30pm), a sunny and

succulent rubbed steaks are a no-brainer here, the handcrafted specialty pizzas are also quite popular. Housed in a historic pharmacy building, Luther's is also a great place for late eats after many other places in this quiet town have rolled up the sidewalk. A limited menu of appetizers and bar food to nosh on at the inviting and popular bar is available after 10pm.

### Tapas

**Emily's** (906 Port Republic St., 843/522-1866, www.emilysrestaurantandtapasbar.com, dinner Mon.-Sat. 4pm-10pm, bar until 2am, $10-20) is a very popular fine-dining spot that specializes in a more traditional brand of rich, tasty tapas and is known for its active bar scene.

## ACCOMMODATIONS

Beaufort's historic district is blessed with an abundance of high-quality accommodations that blend well with their surroundings.

### Under $150

The **Best Western Sea Island Inn** (1015 Bay St., 843/522-2090, www.bestwestern. com, $135-170) is a good value for those for whom the B&B experience is not paramount. Anchoring the southern end of the historic district in a tasteful low brick building, the Best Western offers decent service, basic amenities, and surprisingly attractive rates for the location on Beaufort's busiest street.

### $150-300

Any list of upscale Beaufort lodging must highlight the ★ **Beaufort Inn** (809 Port Republic St., 843/379-4667, www.beaufortinn. com, $152-425), consistently voted one of the best B&Bs in the nation. It's sort of a hybrid in that it comprises not only the 1897 historic central home, but also a cluster of freestanding historic cottages, each with a charming little porch and rocking chairs.

The 18-room circa-1820 **Rhett House Inn** (1009 Craven St., 843/524-9030, www. rhetthouseinn.com, $175-320) is the local vacation getaway for the stars. Such arts and entertainment luminaries as Robert Redford, Julia Roberts, Ben Affleck, Barbra Streisand, Dennis Quaid, and Demi Moore have all stayed here at one time or another.

the Beaufort Inn

There's nothing like enjoying the view of the Beaufort River from the expansive porches of the ★ **Cuthbert House Inn** (1203 Bay St., 843/521-1315, www.cuthberthouseinn.com, $205-250). This grand old circa-1790 Federal mansion was once the home of the wealthy Cuthbert family of rice and indigo planters. Some of the king rooms have fireplaces and claw-foot tubs. Of course you get a full Southern breakfast in addition to sunset hors d'oeuvres on the veranda.

While a stay at a B&B is the classic way to enjoy Beaufort, many travelers swear by the **City Loft Hotel** (301 Carteret St., 843/379-5638, www.citylofthotel.com, $200). Housed in a former motel, City Loft represents a total modernist makeover, gleaming from stem to stern with chrome and various art deco touches.

# TRANSPORTATION AND SERVICES

The **Beaufort Visitors Information Center** (713 Craven St., 843/986-5400, www.beaufortsc.org, Mon.-Sat. 9am-5pm, Sun. noon-5pm), the headquarters of the Beaufort Chamber of Commerce and Convention and Visitors Bureau, has relocated from its old Carteret Street location and can now be found within the Beaufort Arsenal.

## Air

While the Marines can fly their F-18s directly into Beaufort Naval Air Station, you won't have that luxury. The closest major airport to Beaufort is the **Savannah/ Hilton Head International Airport** (SAV, 400 Airways Ave., 912/964-0514, www.savannahairport.com) off I-95 outside Savannah. From there it's about an hour to Beaufort. If you're not going into Savannah for any reason, the easiest route to the Beaufort area from the airport is to take I-95's exit 8, and from there take U.S. 278 east to Highway 170.

Alternatively, you could fly into **Charleston International Airport** (CHS, 5500 International Blvd., www.chs-airport.com), but because that facility is on the far north side of Charleston, it will take a bit longer (about an hour and 20 minutes) to get to Beaufort. From the Charleston Airport the best route south to Beaufort is U.S. 17 south, exiting onto U.S. 21 at Gardens Corner and then into Beaufort.

## Car

If you're coming into the region by car, I-95 will be your likely primary route, with your main point of entry being exit 8 off I-95 connecting to U.S. 278 east to Highway 170. Beaufort is a little over an hour from Charleston.

Don't be discouraged by the big-box sprawl that assaults you on the approaches to Beaufort on Boundary Street, lined with the usual discount megastores, fast-food outlets, and budget motels. After you make the big 90-degree bend where Boundary turns into Carteret Street—known locally as the "Bellamy Curve"—it's like entering a whole new world of slow-paced, Spanish moss-lined avenues, friendly people, gentle breezes, and inviting storefronts.

# Outside Beaufort

The areas outside tourist-traveled Beaufort can take you even further back into sepia-toned Americana, into a time of sharecropper homesteads, sturdy oystermen, and an altogether variable and subjective sense of time.

About 15 minutes east of Beaufort is the center of Gullah culture, St. Helena Island, and the scenic gem of Hunting Island. Just a few minutes south of Beaufort is the East Coast Marine Corps Recruit Depot of Parris Island. About 10 minutes away is the little community of Port Royal.

## SIGHTS
### ★ Penn Center

By going across the Richard V. Woods Memorial Bridge over the Beaufort River on the Sea Island Parkway (which turns into U.S. 21), you'll pass through Lady's Island and reach St. Helena Island. Known to old-timers as Frogmore, the area took back its old Spanish-derived place name in the 1980s. Today St. Helena Island is most famous for the **Penn Center** (16 Martin Luther King Jr. Dr., 843/838-2474, www.penncenter.com, Mon.-Sat. 11am-4pm, $4 adults, $2 seniors and children), the spiritual home of Gullah culture and history. When you visit here among the live oaks and humble but well-preserved buildings, you'll instantly see why Martin Luther King Jr. chose this as one of his major retreat and planning sites during the civil rights era. The Penn Center continues to serve an important civil rights role by providing legal counsel to African American homeowners in St. Helena. Because clear title is difficult to acquire in the area due to the fact that so much of the land has stayed in the families of former slaves, developers are constantly making shady offers so that ancestral land can be opened up to upscale development.

The 50-acre campus is part of the Penn School Historic District, a National Historic Landmark comprising 19 buildings, most of historical significance. The Retreat House was intended for Dr. King to continue his strategy meetings, but he was assassinated before being able to stay there. The museum and bookshop

Penn Center played an important role during the civil rights movement.

are housed in the Cope Building, now called the York W. Bailey Museum, situated right along MLK Jr. Drive.

To get to the Penn Center from Beaufort (about 10 miles), proceed over the bridge until you get to St. Helena Island. Take a right onto MLK Jr. Drive when you see the Red Piano Too Art Gallery. The Penn Center is a few hundred yards down on your right. If you drive past the Penn Center and continue a few hundred yards down MLK Jr. Drive, look for the ancient tabby ruins on the left side of the road. This is the **Chapel of Ease,** the remnant of a 1740 church destroyed by forest fire in the late 1800s.

### Fort Fremont Preserve

Military historians and sightseers of a particularly adventurous type will want to drive several miles past the Penn Center on St. Helena Island to visit **Fort Fremont Preserve** (Lands End Rd., www.fortfremont. org, daily 9am-dusk, free). Two artillery batteries remain of this Spanish-American War-era coastal defense fort (an adjacent private residence is actually the old army hospital). The fort was active until 1921, but now the big guns are long gone. Their heavy concrete emplacements, however—along with many dark tunnels and small rooms—are still here and make for a very interesting visit. Guided docent tours happen the fourth Saturday of the month starting at 10:30am at the St. Helena Branch of the Beaufort County Library (6355 Jonathan Francis Senior Rd.). The two-hour tours are free, and reservations aren't required.

### Old Sheldon Church

About 20 minutes north of Beaufort are the poignantly desolate ruins of the once-magnificent **Old Sheldon Church** (Old Sheldon Church Rd., off U.S. 17 just past Gardens Corner, daily dawn-dusk, free). One of the first Greek Revival structures in the United States, the house of worship held its first service in 1757. The sanctuary was first burned by the British in 1779. After being rebuilt in 1826, the sanctuary survived until General Sherman's arrival in 1865, whereupon Union troops razed it once more. Nothing remains now but these towering walls and columns made of red brick instead of the tabby often seen in similar ruins on the coast. It's now owned by the nearby St. Helena's Episcopal Church in Beaufort, which holds outdoor services here the second Sunday after Easter.

the ruins of Old Sheldon Church

## Port Royal

This sleepy hamlet between Beaufort and Parris Island touts itself as a leader in "small-town New Urbanism," with an emphasis on livability, retro-themed shopping areas, and relaxing walking trails. However, **Port Royal** is still pretty sleepy—but not without very real charms, not the least of which is the fact that everything is within easy walking distance of everything else. The highlight of the year is the annual Softshell Crab Festival, held each April to mark the short-lived harvesting season for that favorite crustacean.

While much of the tiny historic district has a scrubbed, tidy feel, the main historic structure is the charming little **Union Church** (11th St., 843/524-4333, Mon.-Fri. 10am-4pm, donation), one of the oldest buildings in town, with guided docent tours.

Don't miss the boardwalk and observation tower at **The Sands** municipal beach and boat ramp. The 50-foot-tall structure provides a commanding view of Battery Creek. The little beach is artificial (made from dredged material) but still somewhat unusual in this area. To get to The Sands, head east onto 7th Street off the main drag of Parris Avenue. Seventh Street turns into Sands Beach Road for a brief stretch and then merges with 6th Street, taking you directly to The Sands.

A must-stop for families is the **Port Royal Maritime Center** (310 Okatie Hwy., 843/645-7774, www.portroyalsoundfoundation.org, Tues.-Sat. 10am-5pm, free), a new venture that is a great resource for learning about the area's ecological history. Another environmentally oriented point of pride is the **Lowcountry Estuarium** (1402 Parris Ave., 843/524-6600, www.lowcountryestuarium.org, Wed.-Sat. 10am-5pm, feedings at 11:30am and 3pm, $5 adults, $3 children).

If you get hungry in Port Royal, try the waterfront seafood haven **11th Street Dockside** (1699 11th St., 843/524-7433, daily 4:30pm-10pm, $17-27). The Dockside Dinner is a great sampler plate with lobster tail, scallops, crab legs, and shrimp. The views of the waterfront and the adjoining shrimp-boat docks are relaxing and beautiful.

## Parris Island

Though more commonly known as the home of the legendary **Marine Corps Recruit Depot Parris Island** (283 Blvd. de France, 843/228-3650, www.mcrdpi.marines.mil, free), the island is also of historical significance as the site of some of the earliest European presence in the New World. Today it's where all female U.S. Marine recruits and most male recruits east of the Mississippi River go through the Corps' grueling 13-week boot camp. Almost every Friday during the year marks the graduation of a company of newly minted Marines. That's why you might notice an influx of visitors to the area each Thursday, aka "Family Day," with the requisite amount of celebration on Fridays after that morning's ceremony.

Unlike many military facilities in the post-9/11 era, Parris Island still hosts plenty of visitors. Just check in with the sentry at the gate and show your valid driver's license, registration, and proof of insurance. Rental car drivers must show a copy of the rental agreement. On your way to the depot proper, there are a couple of beautiful picnic areas. Once inside, stop first at the **Douglas Visitor Center** (Bldg. 283, Blvd. de France, 843/228-3650, Mon. 7:30am-noon, Tues.-Wed. 7:30am-4:30pm, Thurs. 6:30am-7pm, Fri. 7:30am-3pm), a great place to find maps and information. As you go by the big parade ground, or "deck," be sure to check out the beautiful sculpture re-creating the famous photo of Marines raising the flag on Iwo Jima. A short way ahead is the **Parris Island Museum** (Bldg. 111, 111 Panama St., 843/228-2951, www.mcrdpimuseum.com, daily 10am-4:30pm, free), detailing the proud history of the Corps with a particular focus on this Recruit Depot.

The Spanish built Santa Elena nearby the original French settlement, Charlesfort. They then built two other settlements, San Felipe and San Marcos. The Santa Elena site, now on the circa-1950s Parris Island Depot golf course, is a National Historic Landmark. So far, archaeologists have found a residence of a wealthy family in the town and have identified two of Santa Elena's five forts. Many artifacts are viewable at the nearby **clubhouse-interpretive center** (daily 7am-5pm, free). You can take a self-guided tour; to get to the site from the museum, continue on Panama Street and take a right on Cuba Street. Follow the signs to the golf course and continue through the main parking lot of the course.

## ★ Hunting Island State Park

Rumored to be a hideaway for Blackbeard himself, the aptly named Hunting Island was indeed for many years a notable hunting preserve, and its abundance of wildlife remains to this day. The island is one of the East Coast's best birding spots and also hosts dolphins, loggerheads, alligators, and deer. A true family-friendly outdoor adventure spot, **Hunting Island State Park** (2555 Sea Island Pkwy., 866/345-7275, www.huntingisland.com, winter daily 6am-6pm, during daylight saving time daily 6am-9pm, $5 adults, $3 children) has something for everyone—kids, parents, and newlyweds. Yet it still retains a certain sense of lush wildness—so much so that it doubled as Vietnam in the movie *Forrest Gump.*

At the north end past the campground is the island's main landmark, the historic **Hunting Island Light,** which dates from 1875. Although the lighthouse ceased operations in 1933, a rotating light—not strong enough to serve as an actual navigational aid—is turned on at night. While the 167-step trek to the top (donation $2 pp) is strenuous, the view is stunning.

## ★ ACE Basin

Occupying pretty much the entire area between Beaufort and Charleston, the **ACE Basin**—the acronym signifies its role as the collective estuary of the Ashepoo, Combahee, and Edisto Rivers—is one of the most enriching natural experiences the country has to offer. The ACE Basin's three core rivers, the Edisto being the largest, are the framework for a matrix of waterways crisscrossing its approximately 350,000 acres of salt marsh. While the ACE Basin can in no way be called "pristine," it's a testament to the power of nature that after 6,000 years of human presence and often intense cultivation, the basin manages to retain much of its untamed feel.

About 12,000 acres of the ACE Basin Project comprise the **Ernest F. Hollings ACE Basin National Wildlife Refuge** (8675

the view from the Hunting Island Light

# The Lost Art of Tabby

Tabby is a unique construction technique combining oyster shells, lime, water, and sand found along the South Carolina and Georgia coasts.

Contrary to popular belief, it did not originate with Native Americans. The confusion is due to the fact that the native population left behind many middens, or trash heaps, of oyster shells. While these middens indeed provided the bulk of the shells for tabby buildings to come, Native Americans had little else to do with it. Also contrary to lore, although the Spanish were responsible for the first use of tabby in the Americas, almost all remaining tabby in the area dates from later English settlement. The British first fell in love with tabby after the siege of Spanish-held St. Augustine, Florida, and quickly began building with it in their colonies to the north.

Scholars are divided as to whether tabby was invented by West Africans or its use spread to Africa from Spain and Portugal, circuitously coming to the United States through the knowledge of imported slaves. The origin of the word itself is also unclear, as similar words exist in Spanish, Portuguese, Gullah, and Arabic to describe various types of wall.

We do know for sure how tabby is made: The primary technique was to burn alternating layers of oyster shells and logs in a deep hole in the ground, thus creating lime. The lime was then mixed with oyster shells, sand, and freshwater and poured into wooden molds, or "forms," to dry and then be used as building blocks, much like large bricks. Tabby walls were usually plastered with stucco. Tabby is remarkably strong and resilient, able to survive the hurricanes that often batter the area. It also stays cool in the summer and is insect-resistant, two enormous advantages down here.

Following are some great examples of true tabby you can see today on the South Carolina and Georgia coasts, from north to south:

- **Dorchester State Historic Site** in Summerville, north of Charleston, contains a well-preserved tabby fort.

- Several younger tabby buildings still exist in downtown Beaufort: the **Barnwell-Gough House** (705 Washington St.); the Thomas Fuller House, or **"Tabby Manse"** (1211 Bay St.); and the **Saltus House** (800 block of Bay St.), perhaps the tallest surviving tabby structure.

- The **Chapel of Ease** on St. Helena Island dates from the 1740s. If someone tells you Sherman burned it down, don't believe it; the culprit was a forest fire.

Willtown Rd., 843/889-3084, www.fws.gov/acebasin, grounds year-round daily dawn-dusk, office Mon.-Fri. 7:30am-4pm, free), run by the U.S. Fish and Wildlife Service. The historic 1828 **Grove Plantation House** is in this portion of the basin and houses the refuge's headquarters. Sometimes featured on local tours of homes, it's one of only three antebellum homes left in the ACE Basin. Surrounded by lush, ancient oak trees, it's really a sight in and of itself.

This section of the refuge, the **Edisto Unit,** is about an hour's drive from Beaufort. To get to the Edisto Unit of the Hollings/ACE Basin National Wildlife Refuge, take U.S. 17 to Highway 174 (going all the way down this route takes you to Edisto Island) and turn right onto Willtown Road. The unpaved entrance road is about two miles ahead on the left. There are restrooms and a few picnic tables.

You can also visit the two parts of the **Combahee Unit** of the refuge, which offers a similar scene of trails among impounded wetlands along the Combahee River, with parking; it's farther west near Yemassee. The Combahee Unit is about 30 minutes from Beaufort. Get here by taking a left off U.S. 17 onto Highway 33. The larger portion of the Combahee Unit is soon after the turnoff, and the smaller, more northerly portion is about five miles up the road.

the Chapel of Ease on St. Helena Island

- The **Stoney-Baynard Ruins** in Sea Pines Plantation on Hilton Head are all that's left of the home of the old Braddock's Point Plantation. Foundations of a slave quarters are nearby.

- **Wormsloe Plantation** near Savannah has the remains of Noble Jones's fortification on the Skidaway Narrows.

- **St. Cyprian's Episcopal Church** in Darien is one of the largest tabby structures still in use.

- **Fort Frederica** on St. Simons Island has not only the remains of a tabby fort but many foundations of tabby houses in the surrounding settlement.

- The remarkably intact walls of the **Horton-DuBignon House** on Jekyll Island, Georgia, date from 1738, and the house was occupied into the 1850s.

## Recreation
### KAYAKING

A good service for rentals and knowledgeable guided tours of the ACE Basin is **Outpost Moe's** (843/844-2514, www.geocities.ws/outpostmoe), where the basic 2.5-hour tour costs $40 per person, and an all-day extravaganza through the basin is $80. Moe's provides lunch for most of its tours. Another premier local outfitter for ACE Basin tours is **Carolina Heritage Outfitters** (U.S. 15 in Canadys, 843/563-5051, www.canoesc.com), which focuses on the Edisto River trail. In addition to guided tours ($30) and rentals, you can camp overnight in their cute tree houses ($125) along the kayak routes. They load you

up with your gear and drive you 22 miles upriver, then you paddle downriver to the tree house for the evening. The next day, you paddle yourself the rest of the way downriver back to home base.

To have a drier experience of the ACE Basin from the deck of a larger vessel, try **ACE Basin Tours** (1 Coosaw River Dr., Beaufort, 843/521-3099, www.acebasintours.com, Mar.-Nov. Wed. and Sat. 10am, $35 adults, $15 children), which will take you on a three-hour tour in the 40-passenger *Dixie Lady*. To get to their dock from Beaufort, take Carteret Street over the bridge to St. Helena Island, and then take a left on Highway 802 east (Sam's Point Rd.). Continue until you cross Lucy Point Creek;

the ACE Basin Tours marina is on your immediate left after you cross the bridge.

The state of South Carolina has conveniently gathered some of the best self-guided kayak trips at www.acebasin.net/canoe.html.

## GOLF

Golf is much bigger in Hilton Head than in the Beaufort area, but there are some local highlights. The best-regarded public course in the area, and indeed one of the best military courses in the world, is **Legends at Parris Island** (Bldg. 299, Parris Island, 843/228-2240, www.mccssc.com, $30). Call in advance for a tee time.

Another popular public course is **South Carolina National Golf Club** (8 Waveland Ave., Cat Island, 843/524-0300, www.sc-national.com, $70). Get to secluded Cat Island by taking the Sea Island Parkway onto Lady's Island and continuing south as it turns into Lady's Island Drive. Turn onto Island Causeway and continue for about three miles.

## CAMPING

**Hunting Island State Park** (2555 Sea Island Pkwy., 866/345-7275, www.huntingisland.com, winter daily 6am-6pm, during daylight saving time daily 6am-9pm, $5 adults, $3 children, $25 RV sites, $19 tent sites, $87-172 cabin) has 200 campsites with individual water and electric hookups on the north end of the island. There used to be plenty of cabins for rent, but beach erosion has sadly made the ones near the water uninhabitable. One cabin near the lighthouse is still available for rent, and it is in such high demand that the park encourages you to camp instead.

Another neat place to camp is **Tuck in the Wood** (22 Tuc In De Wood Ln., St. Helena, 843/838-2267, $25), a very well-maintained 74-site private campground just past the Penn Center on St. Helena Island.

# Edisto Island

One of the last truly unspoiled places in the Lowcountry, Edisto Island has been highly regarded as a getaway spot since the Edisto people first started coming here for shellfish. In fact, locals here swear that the island was settled by English-speaking colonists even before Charleston was settled in 1670.

There are rental homes galore on Edisto Island. Because of the lack of hotels, this is the most popular option for most vacationers here—indeed, it's just about the only option. Contact **Edisto Sales and Rentals Realty** (1405 Palmetto Blvd., 800/868-5398, www.edistorealty.com).

## SIGHTS

The **Edisto Museum** (8123 Chisolm Plantation Rd., 843/869-1954, www.edistomuseum.org, Tues.-Sat. noon-5pm, $4 adults, $2 children, free under age 10), a project of the Edisto Island Historic Preservation Society, has recently expanded and incorporated a nearby slave cabin. Its well-done exhibits of local lore and history are complemented by a gift shop. The Edisto Museum is before you get to the main part of the island, off Highway 174.

Opened in 1999 by local snake hunters the Clamp brothers, the **Edisto Island Serpentarium** (1374 Hwy. 174, 843/869-1171, www.edistoserpentarium.com, hours vary, $14.95 adults, $10.95 ages 4-12, free age 3 and younger) is educational and fun, taking you up close and personal with a variety of reptilian creatures native to the area. They usually close Labor Day-April 30.

The **Botany Bay Wildlife Management Area** (www.preserveedisto.org, Wed.-Mon. dawn-dusk, free) is a great way to enjoy the unspoiled nature of Edisto Island. On the grounds of two former rice and indigo plantations comprising 4,000 acres, Botany Bay features several remains of the old plantations and a small, wonderful beach. There are no facilities to speak of, so pack and plan accordingly. Botany Bay is closed on hunt days, which vary depending on the hunting season but are fairly rare.

## SPORTS AND ACTIVITIES

As the largest river of the ACE (Ashepoo, Combahee, Edisto) Basin complex, the Edisto River figures large in the lifestyle of residents and visitors. A good public landing is at Steamboat Creek off Highway 174 on the way down to the island. Take Steamboat Landing Road (Hwy. 968) from Highway 174 near the James Edwards School. Live Oak Landing is farther up Big Bay Creek near the interpretive center at the state park. The **Edisto Marina** (3702 Docksite Rd., 843/869-3504) is on the far west side of the island.

Captain Ron Elliott of **Edisto Island Tours** (843/869-1937) offers various ecotours and fishing trips as well as canoe and kayak rentals for about $25 per day. A typical kayak tour runs about $35 per person for a 1.5-2-hour trip, and he offers a "beachcombing" trip for $15 per person. Riding a bike on Edisto

Beach and all around the island is a great and relaxing way to get some exercise and enjoy its scenic, laid-back beauty. The best place to rent a bike—or a kayak or canoe, for that matter—is **Island Bikes and Outfitters** (140 Jungle Rd., 843/869-4444, Mon.-Sat. 9am-4pm). Bike rentals run about $16 per day; single kayaks are about $60 per day.

### ★ Edisto Beach State Park

**Edisto Beach State Park** (8377 State Cabin Rd., 843/869-2156, www.southcarolinaparks.com, Nov.-mid-Mar. daily 8am-6pm, mid-Mar.-Oct. daily 6am-10pm, $5 adults, $3 children, free under age 6) is one of the world's foremost destinations for shell collectors. Largely because of fresh loads of silt from the adjacent ACE Basin, there are always new specimens, many of them fossils, washing ashore. The park stretches almost three miles and features the state's longest system of fully accessible hiking and biking trails, including one leading to a 4,000-year-old shell midden, now much eroded from past millennia. The particularly well-done **interpretive center** (Tues.-Sat. 9am-4pm) has plenty of interesting exhibits about the nature and history of the park as well as the surrounding ACE Basin.

Edisto Island

## CAMPING

A great thing about Edisto Island is the total absence of ugly chain lodging or beachfront condo development. My recommended option is staying at **Edisto Beach State Park** (843/869-2156, www.southcarolinaparks.com, $25 tent sites, $75-100 cabins) itself, either at a campsite on the Atlantic side or in a marsh-front cabin on the northern edge. During high season (Apr.-Nov.), there's a minimum week-long stay in the cabins; during the off-season, the minimum stay is two days. You can book cabins up to 11 months in advance.

## FOOD

One of the all-time great barbecue places in South Carolina is on Edisto: ★ **Po Pigs Bo-B-Q** (2410 Hwy. 174, 843/869-9003, Wed.-Sat. 11:30am-9pm, $4-10), on the way into town. This is the real thing, the full pig cooked in all its many ways: white meat, dark meat, crack-lin's, and hash, served in the local style of "all you care to eat." Unlike many barbecue spots, they do serve beer and wine.

Another popular joint on the island is **Whaley's** (2801 Myrtle St., 843/869-2161, Tues.-Sat. 11:30am-2pm and 5pm-9pm, bar daily 5pm-2am, $5-15), a down-home place in an old gas station a few blocks off the beach. This is a good place for casual seafood like boiled shrimp, washed down with a lot of beer. The bar is open seven days a week.

The legendary ★ **Old Post Office** (1442 Hwy. 174, 843/869-2339, www.theoldpost-officerestaurant.com, Tues.-Sun. 5:30pm-10pm, $20), a Lowcountry-style fine-dining spot, served a devoted clientele for 20 years. It recently reopened with a bang and thankfully kept its old-school mystique intact. Specialties include fine crab cakes drizzled with mousseline sauce, the pecan-encrusted Veal Edistonian, and a Carolina rib eye topped with a pimiento cheese sauce.

## TRANSPORTATION

Edisto Island is basically halfway between Beaufort and Charleston. There's one main land route here, south on Highway 174 off U.S. 17. It's a long way down from U.S. 17 to Edisto, but the 20- to 30-minute drive is scenic and enjoyable. Most activity on the island centers on the township of Edisto Beach, which voted to align itself with Colleton County for its lower taxes (the rest of Edisto Island is part of Charleston County).

### Tours

Edisto has many beautiful plantation homes, relics of the island's longtime role as host to cotton plantations. While all are in private hands and therefore off-limits to the public, an exception is offered through **Edisto Island Tours & T'ings** (843/869-9092, $20 adults, $10 under age 13). You'll take a van tour around Edisto's beautiful churches and old plantations.

# Hilton Head Island

Literally the prototype of the modern planned resort community, Hilton Head Island is also a case study in how a landscape can change when money is introduced. From Reconstruction until the post-World War II era, the island consisted almost entirely of African Americans with deep roots in the area. In the mid-1950s Hilton Head began its transformation into an almost all-white, upscale golf, tennis, and shopping mecca populated largely by Northern transplants and retirees. As you can imagine, the flavor here is now quite different from surrounding areas of the Lowcountry, to say the least, with an emphasis on material excellence, top prices, get-it-done-yesterday punctuality, and the attendant aggressive traffic.

These days, Hilton Head gets the most national media attention for the RBC Heritage golf tournament each April, when the entire

# Hilton Head Island

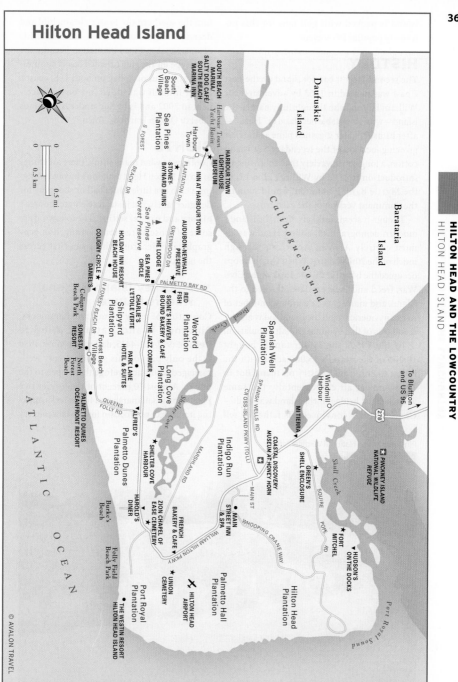

SOUTH BEACH MARINA
SALTY DOG CAFÉ/
SOUTH BEACH
MARINA INN

South
Beach
Village

Daufuskie
Island

Sea Pines
Plantation

Harbour Town

Hilton Town Yacht Basin

Barataria
Island

HARBOUR TOWN
LIGHTHOUSE
MUSEUM

INN AT HARBOUR TOWN

STONEY-
BAYNARD RUINS

Calibogue Sound

AUDUBON-NEWHALL
PRESERVE

Sea Pines
Forest Preserve

THE LODGE

GREENWOOD DR

PLANTATION DR

SEA PINES
CIRCLE

COLIGNY CIRCLE

HOLIDAY INN RESORT
BEACH HOUSE

DANIEL'S

Coligny
Beach Park

SONESTA
RESORT

PALMETTO DUNES
OCEANFRONT RESORT

PALMETTO BAY RD

CHARLIE'S

L'ETOILE VERTE

Shipyard
Plantation

PARK LANE
HOTEL & SUITES

N FOREST BEACH DR

Forest Beach
Village

N FOREST BEACH DR

Forest
Beach

North
Forest
Beach

QUEENS
FOLLY RD

RED
FISH

SIGNE'S HEAVEN
BOUND BAKERY & CAFÉ

THE JAZZ CORNER

ALFRED'S

Wexford
Plantation

Long Cove
Plantation

Spanish Wells
Plantation

Broad Creek

Shelter Cove

SHELTER COVE
HARBOUR

Palmetto Dunes
Plantation

HAROLD'S
DINER

ZION CHAPEL OF
EASE CEMETERY

FRENCH
BAKERY & CAFÉ

CROSS-ISLAND PKWY (TOLL)

SPANISH WELLS RD

Indigo Run
Plantation

COASTAL DISCOVERY
MUSEUM AT HONEY HORN

GREEN'S
SHELL ENCLOSURE

MI TIERRA

Windmill
Harbour

MAIN ST

MAIN
STREET INN
& SPA

WILLIAM HILTON PKWY

MARSHLAND RD

Skull Creek

HILTON HEAD
AIRPORT

UNION
CEMETERY

Port Royal
Plantation

THE WESTIN RESORT
HILTON HEAD ISLAND

Palmetto Hall
Plantation

Hilton Head
Plantation

WHOOPING CRANE WAY

SQUIRE
POPE RD

FORT
MITCHEL

HUDSON'S
ON THE DOCKS

Skull Creek

PINCKNEY ISLAND
NATIONAL WILDLIFE
REFUGE

To Bluffton
and US 95

278

Port Royal Sound

ATLANTIC OCEAN

Burke's
Beach

Folly Field
Beach Park

0     0.5 mi

0     0.5 km

island is packed with golf fans for this extremely popular PGA event.

## HISTORY

The second-largest barrier island on the East Coast was named in 1663 by adventurer Sir William Hilton, who thoughtfully named the island—with its notable headland or "Head"—after himself. Later it gained fame as the first growing location of the legendary Sea Island cotton, a long-grain variety that, following its introduction in 1790 by William Elliott II of the Myrtle Bank Plantation, would soon be the dominant version of the cash crop.

Though it seems unlikely given the island's modern demographics, Hilton Head was almost entirely African American through much of the 20th century. When Union troops occupied the island at the outbreak of the Civil War, freed and escaped slaves flocked to the island, and many of the dwindling number of African Americans on the island today are descendants of this original Gullah population.

In the 1950s the Fraser family bought 19,000 of the island's 25,000 acres with the intent to continue forestry on them. But in 1956—not at all coincidentally the same year the first bridge to the island was built—Charles Fraser convinced his father to sell him the southern tip. Fraser's brainchild and decades-long labor of love—some said his obsession—Sea Pines Plantation became the prototype for the golf-oriented resort communities so common today on both U.S. coasts. Fraser himself was killed in a boating accident in 2002 and is buried under the famous Liberty Oak in Harbour Town.

## SIGHTS

Contrary to what many think, there are things to do on Hilton Head that don't involve swinging a club at a little white ball or shopping for designer labels, but instead celebrate the area's history and natural setting. The following are some of those attractions, arranged in geographical order from where you first access the island.

### ★ Pinckney Island National Wildlife Refuge

Consisting of many islands and hammocks, **Pinckney Island National Wildlife Refuge** (912/652-4415, daily dawn-dusk, free) is the only part of this small but very well-managed 4,000-acre refuge that's open to the public. Almost 70 percent of the former rice plantation is salt marsh and tidal creeks, making it a perfect microcosm for the Lowcountry

Pinckney Island National Wildlife Refuge

as a whole, as well as a great place to kayak or canoe. Some of the state's richest birding opportunities abound here.

## Green's Shell Enclosure

Less known than the larger Native American shell ring farther south at Sea Pines, **Green's Shell Enclosure** (803/734-3886, daily dawn-dusk) is certainly easier to find, and you don't have to pay $5 to enter the area, as with Sea Pines. This three-acre heritage preserve dates back to at least the 1300s. The heart of the site comprises a low embankment, part of the original fortified village. To get here, take a left at the intersection of U.S. 278 and Squire Pope Road. Turn left into Green's Park, pass the office on the left, and park. The entrance to the shell enclosure is on the left behind a fence.

## ★ Coastal Discovery Museum at Honey Horn

With the acquisition of Honey Horn's 70-acre spread of historic plantation land, Hilton Head finally has a full-fledged museum worthy of the name, and the magnificent **Coastal Discovery Museum** (70 Honey Horn Dr., 843/689-6767, www.coastaldiscovery.org, Mon.-Sat. 9am-4:30pm, Sun. 11am-3pm, free)

is a must-see, even for those who came to the island mostly to golf and soak up sun.

The facility centers on the expertly restored Discovery House, the only antebellum house still existing on Hilton Head, with exhibits and displays devoted to the history of the island. The museum is also a great one-stop place to sign up for a variety of specialty on-site and off-site guided tours, such as birding and Gullah history tours. The cost for most on-site tours is a reasonable $10 adults and $5 children.

But the real draw is the 0.5-mile trail through the Honey Horn grounds, including several boardwalk viewpoints over the marsh, a neat little butterfly habitat, a few gardens, and a stable and pasture that host Honey Horn May and Tadpole, the museum's two Marsh Tackies—short, tough little ponies descended from Spanish horses and used to great effect by Francis "Swamp Fox" Marion and his freedom fighters in the American Revolution.

While a glance at a map and area signage might convince you that you must pay the $1.25 toll on the Cross Island Parkway to get to Honey Horn, that isn't so. The exit to Honey Horn on the parkway is actually before you get to the toll plaza; therefore access is free.

one of the Coastal Discovery Museum's Marsh Tackies

## Union Cemetery

A modest but key aspect of African American history on Hilton Head is at **Union Cemetery** (Union Cemetery Rd.), a small burial ground featuring several graves of black Union Army troops (you can tell by the designation "USCI" on the tombstone, for "United States Colored Infantry"). Also of interest are the charming hand-carved cement tombstones of nonveterans. To get here, turn north off William Hilton Parkway onto Union Cemetery Road. The cemetery is a short way ahead on the left. There is no signage or site interpretation.

## Zion Chapel of Ease Cemetery

More like one of the gloriously desolate scenes common to the rest of the Lowcountry, this little cemetery in full view of the William Hilton Parkway at Folly Field Road is all that remains of one of the "Chapels of Ease," a string of chapels set up in the 1700s. The **Zion Chapel of Ease Cemetery** (daily dawn-dusk, free) is said to be haunted by the ghost of William Baynard, whose final resting place is in a mausoleum on the site (the remains of his ancestral home are farther south at Sea Pines Plantation).

## Audubon-Newhall Preserve

Plant lovers shouldn't miss this small but very well-maintained 50-acre wooded tract in the south-central part of the island on Palmetto Bay Road between the Cross Island Parkway and the Sea Pines Circle. Almost all plant life, even that in the water, is helpfully marked and identified. The **Audubon-Newhall Preserve** (year-round dawn-dusk, free) is open to the public, but you can't camp here. For more information, call the **Hilton Head Audubon Society** (843/842-9246).

## Sea Pines Plantation

This private residential resort development at the extreme west end of the island—the first on Hilton Head and the prototype for every other such development in the country—hosts several attractions that collectively are well worth the $5 per vehicle "road use" fee, which you pay at the main entrance gate.

### HARBOUR TOWN

It's not particularly historic and not all that natural, but **Harbour Town** is still pretty cool. The dominant element is the squat, colorful **Harbour Town Lighthouse Museum** (149 Lighthouse Rd., 843/671-2810, www.harbourtownlighthouse.com, daily 10am-dusk, $4.25, free age 5 and under), which has never really helped a ship navigate its way near the island. The 90-foot structure was built in 1970 purely to give visitors a little atmosphere, and that it does, as kids especially love climbing the stairs to the top and looking out over the island's expanse.

### STONEY-BAYNARD RUINS

The **Stoney-Baynard ruins** (Plantation Dr., dawn-dusk, free), tabby ruins in a residential neighborhood, are what remains of the circa-1790 central building of the old Braddock's Point Plantation, first owned by patriot and raconteur Captain "Saucy Jack" Stoney and later by the Baynard family. Active during the island's heyday as a cotton center, the plantation was destroyed after the Civil War.

### SEA PINES FOREST PRESERVE

The **Sea Pines Forest Preserve** (175 Greenwood Dr., 843/363-4530, free) is set amid the Sea Pines Plantation golf resort development, but you don't need a bag of clubs to enjoy this 600-acre preserve, which is built on the site of an old rice plantation (dikes and logging trails are still visible). Here you can ride a horse, fish, or just take a walk on the eight miles of trails (dawn-dusk) and enjoy the natural beauty around you. No bike riding is allowed on the trails, however.

In addition to the Native American shell ring farther north off Squire Pope Road, the Sea Pines Forest Preserve also boasts a shell ring set within a canopy of tall pines.

## Tours and Cruises

Most guided tours on Hilton Head focus on

the water. **Harbour Town Cruises** (843/363-9023, www.vagabondcruise.com, $30-60) offers several sightseeing tours as well as excursions to Daufuskie and Savannah. They also offer a tour on a former America's Cup racing yacht.

"Dolphin tours" are extremely popular on Hilton Head, and there is no shortage of operators. **Dolphin Watch Nature Cruises** (843/785-4558, $25 adults, $10 children) departs from Shelter Cove, as does **Lowcountry Nature Tours** (843/683-0187, www.lowcountrynaturetours.com, $40 adults, $35 children, free under age 3). **Outside Hilton Head** (843/686-6996, www.outsidehiltonhead.com) runs a variety of water ecotours and dolphin tours as well as a guided day-trip excursion to Daufuskie, complete with golf cart rental.

There is a notable land-based tour by **Gullah Heritage Trail Tours** (leaves from Coastal Discovery Museum at Honey Horn, 843/681-7066, www.gullahheritage.com, $32 adults, $15 children) delving into the island's rich, if poorly preserved, African American history from slavery through the time of the freedmen.

## ENTERTAINMENT AND NIGHTLIFE
### Nightlife

The highest-quality live entertainment on the island is at **The Jazz Corner** (1000 William Hilton Pkwy., 843/842-8620, www.thejazzcorner.com, dinner daily 6pm-9pm, late-night menu after 9pm, dinner $15-20, cover varies), which brings in big names in the genre to perform in this space in the unlikely setting of a boutique mall, the Village at Wexford. The dinners are actually quite good, but the attraction is definitely the music. Reservations are recommended. Live music starts around 7pm.

For years islanders jokingly referred to the "Barmuda Triangle," an area named for the preponderance of bars within vague walking distance of Sea Pines Circle. While some of the names have changed over the years, the longtime anchor of the Barmuda Triangle is the **Tiki Hut** (1 S. Forest Beach Dr., 843/785-5126,

Sun.-Thurs. 11am-8pm, Fri.-Sat. 11am-10pm, bar until 2am), actually part of The Beach House hotel at the entrance to Sea Pines. This popular watering hole is the only beachfront bar on the island, which technically makes it the only place you can legally drink alcohol on a Hilton Head beach. Another Triangle fave is **The Lodge** (7 Greenwood Dr., 843/842-8966, www.hiltonheadlodge.com, daily 11:30am-midnight). After the martini-and-cigar craze waned, this popular spot successfully remade itself into a beer-centric place with 36 rotating taps.

Despite its location in the upscale strip mall of the Village at Wexford, the **British Open Pub** (1000 William Hilton Pkwy./Hwy. 278, 843/686-6736, daily 11am-10pm) offers a fairly convincing English vibe with, as the name suggests, a heavy golf theme. The fish-and-chips and shepherd's pie are both magnificent.

Inside Sea Pines is the **Quarterdeck Lounge and Patio** (843/842-1999, www.seapines.com, Sun.-Thurs. 5:30pm-10pm, Fri.-Sat. 5:30pm-midnight) at the base of the Harbour Town Lighthouse. This is where the party's at after a long day on the fairways during the Heritage golf tournament. Within Sea Pines at the South Beach Marina is also where you'll find **The Salty Dog Cafe** (232 S. Sea Pines Dr., 843/671-2233, www.saltydog.com, lunch daily 11am-3pm, dinner daily 5pm-10pm, bar daily until 2am), one of the area's most popular institutions (some might even call it a tourist trap) and something akin to an island empire, with popular T-shirts, a gift shop, books, and an ice cream shop, all overlooking the marina. My suggestion, however, is to make the short walk to the affiliated **Wreck of the Salty Dog** (843/671-7327, daily until 2am), where the marsh views are better and the atmosphere not quite so tacky.

A gay-friendly bar on Hilton Head is **Cool Cats Lounge** (32 Palmetto Bay Rd., Mon.-Fri. 8pm-3am, Sat. 8pm-2am), with a welcoming dive-bar atmosphere and a small but lively dance floor.

## Performing Arts

Because so many residents migrated here from art-savvy metropolitan areas in the Northeast, Hilton Head maintains a very high standard of top-quality entertainment. Much of the activity centers on the multimillion-dollar **Arts Center of Coastal Carolina** (14 Shelter Cove Ln., 843/842-2787, www.artshhi.com), which hosts touring shows, resident companies, musical concerts, dance performances, and visual arts exhibits.

Under the direction of maestro John Morris Russell, the **Hilton Head Symphony Orchestra** (843/842-2055, www.hhso.org) performs a year-round season of masterworks and pops programs at various venues, primarily the First Presbyterian Church (540 William Hilton Pkwy./Hwy. 278). They also take their show on the road with several concerts in Bluffton and even perform several "Symphony Under the Stars" programs at Shelter Cove. **Chamber Music Hilton Head** (www.cmhh. org) performs throughout the year with selections ranging from Brahms to Smetana at All Saints Episcopal Church (3001 Meeting St.).

## Cinema

There's an art house on Hilton Head, the charming **Coligny Theatre** (843/686-3500, www.colignytheatre.com) in the Coligny Plaza shopping center before you get to Sea Pines. For years this was the only movie theater for miles around, but it has reincarnated as a primarily indie film venue. Look for the entertaining murals by local artist Ralph Sutton. Showtimes are Monday 11:30am and 4pm, Tuesday and Friday 11:30am, 4pm, and 7pm, Wednesday-Thursday and Saturday-Sunday 4pm and 7pm.

## Festivals and Events

Late February-early March brings the **Hilton Head Wine and Food Festival** (www.hiltonheadhospitality.org), culminating in what they call "the East Coast's Largest Outdoor Public Tasting and Auction," which is generally held at the Coastal Discovery Museum at Honey Horn. Some events charge admission.

Without question, Hilton Head's premier event is the **RBC Heritage Golf Tournament** (843/671-2248, http://theheritagegolfsc.com), held each April (usually the week after the Masters) at the Harbour Town Golf Links on Sea Pines Plantation. Formerly known as the Verizon Heritage Classic, the event is South Carolina's only PGA Tour event and brings thousands of visitors to town. The entire island gets *quite* crowded during this time, so be aware.

A fun and fondly anticipated yearly event is the **Kiwanis Club Chili Cookoff** (www. hiltonheadkiwanis.org), held each October at Honey Horn on the south end. A low admission price gets you all the chili you can eat plus free antacids. All funds go to charity, and all excess chili goes to a local food bank.

Every November brings Hilton Head's second-largest event, the **Hilton Head Concours d'Elegance & Motoring Festival** (www.hhiconcours.com), a multiday affair bringing together vintage car clubs from throughout the nation and culminating in a prestigious "Best of Show" competition. It started as a fund-raiser for the Hilton Head Symphony, but now people come from all over the country to see these fine vintage cars in a beautiful setting.

# SHOPS

As you'd expect, Hilton Head is a shopper's delight, with an emphasis on upscale stores and prices to match. Keep in mind that hours may be shortened in the off-season (Nov.-Mar.). Here's a rundown of the main island shopping areas in the order you'll encounter them as you enter the island.

## Shelter Cove

**Shelter Cove Towne Centre** (40 Shelter Cove Ln., www.sheltercovetownecentre), a repurposed former mall space, centers on a Belk anchor store and a Kroger. New retail locations are steadily opening there. The nearby **Plaza at Shelter Cove** (50 Shelter Cove Ln., www.theplazaatsheltercove.com) features a Whole Foods and the flagship location of **Outside Hilton Head** (843/686-6996, www.outsidehiltonhead.com, Mon.-Sat. 10am-5:30pm, Sun. 11am-5:30pm), a complete outdoor outfitter with a knowledgeable staff.

## Village at Wexford

Easily my favorite place to shop on Hilton Head, this well-shaded shopping center on William Hilton Parkway (Hwy. 278) hosts plenty of well-tended shops, including the foodie equipment store **Le Cookery** (843/785-7171, Mon.-Sat. 10am-6pm), the Lily Pulitzer signature women's store **S. M. Bradford Co.** (843/686-6161, Mon.-Sat. 10am-6pm), and the aromatic **Scents of Hilton Head** (843/842-7866, Mon.-Fri. 10am-6pm, Sat. 10am-5pm).

My favorite shop on all Hilton Head is at Wexford, **The Oilerie** (843/681-2722, www.oilerie.com, Mon.-Sat. 10am-7pm, Sun. noon-5pm). This franchise provides free samples of all its high-quality Italian olive oils and vinegars. After you taste around awhile, you pick what you want and the friendly staff bottles it for you in souvenir-quality glassware. They also have a selection of spices, soaps, and other goodies.

## Coligny Circle

This is the closest Hilton Head comes to funkier beach towns like Tybee Island or Folly Beach, although it doesn't really come that close. You'll find dozens of delightful and somewhat quirky stores here, many keeping long hours in the summer, like the self-explanatory **Coligny Kite & Flag Co.** (843/785-5483, Mon.-Sat. 10am-9pm, Sun. 11am-6pm), the comprehensive and stylish **Quiet Storm Surf Shop** (843/671-2551, daily 10am-9pm), and **Fresh Produce** (843/842-3410, www.freshproduceclothes.com, Mon.-Sat. 10am-10pm, Sun. 10am-9pm), actually a very cute women's clothing store. Kids will love both **The Shell Shop** (843/785-4900, Mon.-Sat. 10am-9pm, Sun. noon-9pm) and **Black Market Minerals** (843/785-7090, Mon.-Sat. 10am-10pm, Sun. 11am-8pm).

## Harbour Town

The **Shoppes at Harbour Town** (www.seapines.com) are a collection of about 20 mostly boutique stores along Lighthouse Road in Sea Pines Plantation. At **Planet Hilton Head** (843/363-5177, www.planethiltonhead.com, daily 10am-9pm) you'll find some cute, eclectic gifts and home goods. Other clothing highlights include **Knickers Men's Store** (843/671-2291, daily 10am-9pm) and **Radiance** (843/363-5176, Mon.-Tues. 10am-5pm, Wed.-Sat. 10am-9pm, Sun. 11am-9pm), a very cute and fashion-forward women's store.

The **Top of the Lighthouse Shoppe** (843/671-2810, www.harbourtownlighthouse.com, daily 10am-9pm) is where many a climbing visitor has been coaxed to part with some of their disposable income. And, of course, as you'd expect being near the legendary Harbour Town links, there's the **Harbour Town Pro Shop** (843/671-4485, daily 7am-5pm), routinely voted one of the best pro shops in the nation.

## South Beach Marina

On South Sea Pines Drive at the marina you'll find several worthwhile shops, including a good marine store and all-around grocery dealer **South Beach General Store** (843/671-6784, daily 8am-10pm). I like to stop in **Blue Water Bait and Tackle** (843/671-3060, daily 7am-8pm) and check out the cool nautical stuff. They can also hook you up with a variety of kayak trips and fishing charters. And, of course, right on the water there's the ever-popular **Salty Dog Cafe** (843/671-2233, www.saltydog.com, lunch daily 11am-3pm, dinner daily 5pm-10pm), whose ubiquitous T-shirts seem to adorn every other person on the island.

## Art Galleries

Despite the abundant wealth apparent in some quarters here, there's no freestanding art museum in the area, that role being filled by independent galleries. A good representative example is **Morris & Whiteside Galleries** (220 Cordillo Pkwy., 843/842-4433, www.morris-whiteside.com, Mon.-Fri. 9am-5pm,

Sat. 10am-4pm), located in the historic Red Piano Too Art Gallery building, which features a variety of paintings and sculpture, heavy on landscapes but also showing some fine figurative work. The nonprofit **Art League of Hilton Head** (14 Shelter Cove Ln., 843/681-5060, Mon.-Sat. 10am-6pm) is located in the Walter Greer Art Gallery within the Arts Center of Coastal Carolina and displays work by member artists in all media. The **Nash Gallery** (13 Harbourside Ln., 843/785-6424, Mon.-Fri. 10am-9pm, Sat. 10am-8pm, Sun. 11am-5pm) in Shelter Cove Harbour deals more in North American craft styles. Hilton Head art isn't exactly known for its avant-garde nature, but you can find some whimsical stuff at **Picture This** (78D Arrow Rd., 843/842-5299, Mon.-Fri. 9:30am-5:30pm, Sat. 9:30am-12:30pm), including a selection of Gullah craft items.

# SPORTS AND ACTIVITIES
## Beaches

First, the good news: Hilton Head Island has 12 miles of some of the most beautiful, safe beaches you'll find anywhere. The bad news is that there are only a few ways to gain access, generally at locations referred to as "beach parks." Don't just drive into a residential neighborhood and think you'll be able to park and find your way to the beach.

Driessen Beach Park has 207 long-term parking spaces, costing $0.25 for 30 minutes. There's free parking but fewer spaces at the Coligny Beach Park entrance and at Fish Haul Creek Park. Also, there are 22 metered spaces at Alder Lane Beach Access, 51 at Folly Field Beach Park, and 13 at Burkes Beach Road. Most other beach parks have permit parking only. Clean, well-maintained public restrooms are available at all the beach parks. You can find **beach information** at 843/342-4580 and www.hiltonheadislandsc.gov. Beach park hours vary: Coligny Beach Park is open daily 24 hours; all other beach parks are open March-September daily 6am-8pm and October-February daily 6am-5pm.

Alcohol is strictly prohibited on Hilton Head's beaches.

## Kayaking

Kayakers will enjoy Hilton Head Island, which offers several gorgeous routes, including Calibogue Sound to the south and west and Port Royal Sound to the north. For particularly good views of life on the salt marsh, try Broad Creek, which nearly bisects Hilton Head Island, and Skull Creek, which separates Hilton Head from the natural beauty of Pinckney Island. Broad Creek Marina is a good place to put in.

If you want a guided tour, there are plenty of great kayak tour outfits to choose from in the area. Chief among them is **Outside Hilton Head** (32 Shelter Cove Ln., 800/686-6996, www.outsidehiltonhead.com).

## Biking

Although the very flat terrain is not challenging, Hilton Head provides some scenic and relaxing cycling opportunities. Thanks to wise planning and foresight, the island has an extensive and award-winning 50-mile network of biking trails that does a great job of keeping cyclists out of traffic. A big plus is the long bike path paralleling the William Hilton Parkway, enabling cyclists to use that key artery without braving its traffic. There is even an underground bike path beneath the parkway to facilitate crossing that busy road. In addition, there are also routes along Pope Avenue as well as North and South Forest Beach Drive. Go to www.hiltonheadisland.org/biking to download a map of the island's entire bike path network.

**Palmetto Dunes Oceanfront Resort** (4 Queens Folly Rd., 800/827-3006, www.palmettodunes.com) has a particularly nice 25-mile network of bike paths that all link up to the island's larger framework. Within the resort is **Palmetto Dunes Outfitters** (843/785-2449, www.pdoutfitters.com, daily 9am-5pm), which will rent you any type of bike you might need. Sea Pines Plantation also has an extensive 17-mile network of bike

# Golf Galore

With great weather, beautiful land, and an abundance of retirees, the Carolinas and Georgia offer some of the best golf courses in the world. While a handful of courses are more exclusive, many of the best are public and even have reasonable prices.

Here are some fantastic places to tee-off:

- **Pinehurst Resort** (page 143), north of Charlotte, N.C., is a world center of golf and golf history, with eight premier links to choose from. Pinehurst Number Two, in particular, is among the sport's most beloved courses. There are dozens of other courses in the area as well.

- On Hilton Head, the best public course—and one of the most highly-regarded in the world—is **Harbour Town Golf Links** (page 378), also home of the RBC Heritage tournament. **Palmetto Dunes Resort** (page 378) also offers some excellent playing.

- While the Myrtle Beach area has a reputation as being somewhat downscale, there are some great courses here—over 50 in fact. Chief among them are **Myrtle Beach National** (page 251) and the **Barefoot Resort** (page 251).

- Down the road from Myrtle Beach and near Pawleys Island is the **Waccamaw Golf Trail** (page 264), which features some of the best courses in the Carolinas, including that of the famous Litchfield Resort.

- The Pete Dye Ocean Course at **Kiaweh Island Golf Resort** (page 308) near Charleston is famous for its difficulty.

- The **Westin Savannah Harbor Golf Resort** (page 630) is a great course along the Savannah River.

- Most golf in the Atlanta area centers on private clubs like Augusta National, but one notable public course is **Stone Mountain Golf Club** (page 503), a short drive east of downtown.

trails; you can pick up a map at most information kiosks within the plantation.

There's a plethora of bike rental facilities on Hilton Head with competitive rates. Be sure to ask if they offer free pickup and delivery. Try **Hilton Head Bicycle Company** (112 Arrow Rd., 843/686-6888, daily 9am-5pm, $16 per day).

## Horseback Riding

Within the Sea Pines Forest Preserve is **Lawton Stables** (190 Greenwood Dr., 843/671-2586, www.lawtonstableshhi.com), which features pony rides, a small-animal farm, and guided horseback rides through the preserve. You don't need any riding experience, but you do need reservations.

## Bird-Watching

The premier birding locale in the area is the **Pinckney Island National Wildlife Refuge** (U.S. 278 east, just before Hilton Head, 912/652-4415, www.fws.gov, free). You can see bald eagles, ibis, wood storks, painted buntings, and many more species. Birding is best in spring and fall. The refuge has several freshwater ponds that serve as wading bird rookeries. During migration season, so many beautiful birds make such a ruckus that you'll think you've wandered onto an Animal Planet shoot.

## Golf

Hilton Head is one of the world's great golf centers, with no fewer than 23 courses. Perhaps contrary to what you might expect, most courses on the island are public, and some are downright affordable. All courses are 18 holes unless otherwise described; greens fees are averages and vary with season and tee time.

The best-regarded course, with prices to match, is **Harbour Town Golf Links** (Sea Pines Plantation, 843/363-4485, www.seapines.com, $239). It's on the island's south end at Sea Pines and is the home of the annual RBC Heritage Classic, far and away the island's number one tourist draw.

There are two Arthur Hills-designed courses on the island, **Arthur Hills at Palmetto Dunes Resort** (843/785-1140, www.palmettodunes.com, $125) and **Arthur Hills at Palmetto Hall** (Palmetto Hall Plantation, 843/689-4100, www.palmettohallgolf.com, $130), both of which now offer the use of Segway vehicles on the fairways. The reasonably priced **Barony Course** at Port Royal Plantation (843/686-8801, www.portroyalgolfclub.com, $98) also boasts some of the toughest greens on the island. Another challenging and affordable course is the **George Fazio at Palmetto Dunes** Resort (843/785-1130, www.palmettodunes.com, $105).

It's wise to book tee times through the **Golf Island Call Center** (888/465-3475, www.golfisland.com), which can also hook you up with good packages.

## Tennis

One of the top tennis destinations in the country, Hilton Head has over 20 tennis clubs, some of which offer court time to the public (walk-on rates vary; call for information). They are: **Palmetto Dunes Tennis Center** (Palmetto Dunes Resort, 843/785-1152, www.palmettodunes.com, $30 per hour), **Port Royal Racquet Club** (Port Royal Plantation, 843/686-8803, www.portroyalgolfclub.com, $25 per hour), **Sea Pines Racquet Club** (Sea Pines Plantation, 843/363-4495, www.seapines.com, $25 per hour), **South Beach Racquet Club** (Sea Pines Plantation, 843/671-2215, www.seapines.com, $25 per hour), and **Shipyard Racquet Club** (Shipyard Plantation, 843/686-8804, $25 per hour).

Free, first-come, first-served play is available at the following public courts, maintained by the Island Recreation Association (www.islandreccenter.org): **Chaplin Community Park** (Singleton Beach Rd., four courts, lighted), **Cordillo Courts** (Cordillo Pkwy., four courts, lighted), **Fairfield Square** (Adrianna Ln., two courts), **Hilton Head High School** (School Rd., six courts), and **Hilton Head Middle School** (Wilborn Rd., four courts).

## Zip Line

Billing itself as the only zip line experience within 250 miles, the **Zip Line Hilton Head** (33 Broad Creek Marina Way, 843/682-6000, www.ziplinehiltonhead.com) offers an extensive canopy tour making great use of the area's natural scenery and features. You generally "fly" in groups of about eight. Reservations are strongly encouraged. The latest offering is "Aerial Adventure," a challenging two-hour trip ($50) with about 50 obstacles.

# FOOD

Because of the cosmopolitan nature of the population, with so many transplants from the northeastern United States and Europe, there is uniformly high quality in Hilton Head restaurants. Hilton Head has shed its reputation as a somewhat stodgy food town and does offer some fun, cutting-edge, big-city-style spots to enjoy.

## Bistro

Combining rib-sticking comfort food with hearty European-style cuisine is ★ **Lucky Rooster** (841 William Hilton Pkwy., 843/681-3474, www.luckyroosterhhi.com, daily 5pm-10pm, $15). This really is one of the most vibrant and satisfying menus on the island, from the fried green tomatoes to the pan-fried sweetbread starters, to the short rib and shrimp and grits and mushroom lasagna entrées. A lively full bar complements the bistro-style scene.

An upgrade of a longtime island favorite called simply Daniel's, **Crave by Daniel's** (2 N. Forest Beach Dr., 843/341-9379, http://danielshhi.com, daily 4pm-2am, $25) is now an upscale steak house with a twist. In addition to offering gorgeous cuts of meat like a center-cut filet mignon, they specialize in what they call "big small plates." Try a sizzling cinnamon steak kebab or a gyro pizzetta.

## Breakfast and Brunch

There are a couple of great diner-style places on the island. Though known more for its hamburgers and Philly cheesesteaks, **Harold's Diner** (641 William Hilton Pkwy., 843/842-9292, Mon.-Sat. 7am-3pm, $4-6) has great pancakes as well as its trademark brand of sarcastic service. The place is small, popular, and does not take reservations.

If you need a bite in the Coligny Plaza area, go to **Skillets** (1 N. Forest Beach Dr., 843/785-3131, www.skilletscafe.com, breakfast daily 7am-5pm, dinner daily 5pm-9pm, $5-23) in Coligny Plaza. Their eponymous stock-in-trade is a layered breakfast dish of sautéed ingredients served in a porcelain skillet, like the "Kitchen Sink" (pancakes ringed with potatoes, sausage, and bacon, topped with two poached eggs).

A great all-day breakfast place with a twist is ★ **Signe's Heaven Bound Bakery & Café** (93 Arrow Rd., 843/785-9118, www.signesbakery.com, Mon.-Fri. 8am-4pm, Sat. 9am-2pm, $5-10). Breakfast is tasty dishes like frittatas and breakfast polenta, while the twist is the extensive artisanal bakery, with delicious specialties like the signature key lime pound cake. Expect a wait during peak periods.

## German

I'm pretty sure you didn't come all the way to South Carolina to eat traditional German food, but while you're here, check out ★ **Alfred's** (807 William Hilton Pkwy./Hwy. 278, 843/341-3117, wwww.alfredshiltonhead.com, Mon.-Sat. 5pm-11pm, $20-30), one of the more unique spots on Hilton Head and a big favorite with the locals. Expect a wait. Bratwurst, veal cordon bleu, and of course Wiener schnitzel are all standouts. I recommend the German Mix Platter ($25), which features a brat, some sauerbraten, and a schnitzel.

## Seafood and Southern

Honest-to-goodness Southern cookin' isn't always that easy to come by on this island full of transplants from outside the South. But a great place to find it is **A Lowcountry Backyard** (32 Palmetto Bay Rd., #4A, www.hhbackyard.com, Mon.-Sat. 11am-3pm and 4:30pm-9pm, Sat. brunch 9am-noon, Sun. brunch 9am-3pm, $15). As the name implies, this is regional cuisine served in a relaxed and casual atmosphere fitting for island life. As with many Hilton Head establishments, it's located within a strip mall setting, the Village Exchange.

Not to be confused with Charley's Crab House next door to Hudson's, seafood lovers will enjoy the experience down near Sea Pines at ★ **Charlie's L'Etoile Verte** (8 New Orleans Rd., 843/785-9277, http://charliesgreenstar.com, lunch Tues.-Sat. 11:30am-2pm, dinner Mon.-Sat. 5:30pm-10pm, $25-40), which is considered by many connoisseurs to be Hilton Head's single best restaurant. The emphasis here is on "French country kitchen" cuisine—think Provence, not Paris. In keeping with that theme, each day's menu is concocted from scratch and handwritten. Reservations are essential.

A longtime Hilton Head favorite is **Red Fish** (8 Archer Rd., 843/686-3388, www.redfishofhiltonhead.com, lunch Mon.-Sat. 11:30am-2pm, dinner daily beginning with early-bird specials at 5pm, $20-37). Strongly Caribbean in decor as well as menu, with romanticism and panache to match, this is a great place for couples. Reservations are essential.

Fresh seafood lovers will enjoy one of Hilton Head's staples, the huge **Hudson's on the Docks** (1 Hudson Rd., 843/681-2772, www.hudsonsonthedocks.com, lunch daily 11am-4pm, dinner daily from 5pm, $14-23) on Skull Creek just off Squire Pope Road on the less-developed north side. Much of the catch—though not all of it, by any means—comes directly off the boats you'll see dockside. Try the stuffed shrimp filled with crabmeat. Leave room for one of the homemade desserts crafted by Ms. Bessie, a 30-year veteran employee of Hudson's.

## ACCOMMODATIONS

Generally speaking, accommodations on Hilton Head are often surprisingly affordable given their overall high quality and the breadth of their amenities.

### Under $150

You can't beat the price at **Park Lane Hotel and Suites** (12 Park Ln., 843/686-5700, www.hiltonheadparklanehotel.com, $130). This is your basic suite-type hotel (formerly a Residence Inn) with kitchens, laundry, a pool, and a tennis court. The allure here is the price, hard to find anywhere these days at a resort location. For a nonrefundable fee, you can bring your pet. The one drawback is that the beach is a good distance away. The hotel does offer a free shuttle, however, so it would be wise to take advantage of that and avoid the usual beach-parking hassles. As you'd expect given the price, rooms here tend to go quickly; reserve early.

### $150-300

A great place for the price is the **South Beach Inn** (232 S. Sea Pines Dr., 843/671-6498, www.sbinn.com, $186) in Sea Pines. Located near the famous Salty Dog Cafe and outfitted in a similar nautical theme, the inn not only has some pretty large guest rooms for the price, it offers a lovely view of the marina and has a very friendly feel. As with all Sea Pines accommodations, staying on the plantation means you don't have to wait in line with other visitors to pay the $5-per-day "road fee." Sea Pines also offers a free trolley to get around the plantation.

One of Hilton Head's favorite hotels for beach lovers is **The Beach House** (1 S. Forest Beach Dr., 855/474-2882, www.beachhousehhi.com, $200), formerly the Holiday Inn Oceanfront and home of the famed Tiki Hut bar on the beach. Staff turnover is less frequent here than at other local accommodations, and while it's no Ritz-Carlton and

occasionally shows signs of wear, it's a good value in a bustling area of the island.

One of the better resort-type places for those who prefer the putter and the racquet to the Frisbee and the surfboard is the **Inn and Club at Harbour Town** (7 Lighthouse Ln., 843/363-8100, www.seapines.com, $199) in Sea Pines. The big draw here is the impeccable service, delivered by a staff of "butlers" in kilts, mostly Europeans who take the venerable trade quite seriously. While it's not on the beach, you can take advantage of the free Sea Pines Trolley every 20 minutes.

Recently rated the number one family resort in the United States by *Travel + Leisure*, the well-run ★ **Palmetto Dunes Oceanfront Resort** (4 Queens Folly Rd., 800/827-3006, www.palmettodunes.com, $150-300) offers something for everybody in terms of lodging. There are small, cozy condos by the beach or larger villas overlooking the golf course, and pretty much everything in between. The prices are perhaps disarmingly affordable considering the relative luxury and copious recreational amenities, which include 25 miles of very well-done bike trails, 11 miles of kayak and canoe trails, and, of course, three signature links. As with most developments of this type on Hilton Head, the majority of the condos are privately owned, and therefore each has its own particular set of guidelines and cleaning schedules.

A little farther down the island you'll find the **Sonesta Resort** (130 Shipyard Dr., 843/842-2400, www.sonesta.com/hiltonhead-island, $160-200), which styles itself as Hilton Head's only green-certified accommodations. The guest rooms are indeed state-of-the-art, and the expansive, shaded grounds near the beach are great for relaxation. No on-site golf here, but immediately adjacent is a well-regarded tennis facility with 20 courts.

Another good resort-style experience heavy on the golf is on the grounds of the Port Royal Plantation on the island's north side, **The Westin Resort Hilton Head Island** (2 Grasslawn Ave., 843/681-4000, www.westin.com/hiltonhead, from $200), which hosts three PGA-caliber links. The beach is also but a short walk away. This AAA four diamond-winning Westin offers a mix of suites and larger villas.

## Vacation Rentals

Many visitors to Hilton Head choose to rent a home or villa for an extended stay, and there is no scarcity of availability. Try **Resort Rentals of Hilton Head** (www.hhivacations.com) or **Destination Vacation** (www.destinationvacationhhi.com).

# TRANSPORTATION AND SERVICES

The best place to get information on Hilton Head, book a room, or secure a tee time is just as you come onto the island at the **Hilton Head Island Chamber of Commerce Welcome Center** (100 William Hilton Pkwy., 843/785-3673, www.hiltonheadisland.org, daily 9am-6pm).

## Air

A few years back, the **Savannah/Hilton Head International Airport** (SAV, 400 Airways Ave., Savannah, 912/964-0514, www.savannahairport.com) added Hilton Head to its name specifically to identify itself with that lucrative market. Keep in mind that when your plane touches down in Savannah, you're still about a 45-minute drive to Hilton Head proper. From the airport, go north on I-95 into South Carolina, and take exit 8 onto U.S. 278 east.

There is a local regional airport as well, the **Hilton Head Island Airport** (HXD, 120 Beach City Rd., 843/689-5400, www.bcgov.net). While attractive and convenient, keep in mind that it only hosts propeller-driven commuter planes because of the runway length and concerns about noise.

## Getting Around

Hilton Head Islanders have long referred to their island as the "shoe" and speak of driving to the toe or going to the heel. If you take a look at a map, you'll see why: Hilton Head bears an uncanny resemblance to a running shoe pointed toward the southwest, with the aptly named Broad Creek forming a near facsimile of the Nike "swoosh" symbol.

Running the length and circumference of the shoe is the main drag, U.S. 278 Business (William Hilton Parkway), which crosses onto Hilton Head right at the "tongue" of the shoe, a relatively undeveloped area. The Cross Island Parkway toll route (U.S. 278), beginning up toward the ankle as you first get on the island, is a quicker route straight to the toe near Sea Pines.

While making your way around the island, always keep in mind that the bulk of it consists of private developments, and local law enforcement frowns on people who aimlessly wander among the condos and villas.

Other than taxi services, there is no public transportation to speak of in Hilton Head, unless you want to count the free shuttle around Sea Pines Plantation. Taxi services include **Yellow Cab** (843/686-6666), **Island Taxi** (843/683-6363), and **Ferguson Transportation** (843/842-8088).

# Bluffton and Daufuskie Island

Just outside Hilton Head are two of the Lowcountry's true gems, Bluffton and Daufuskie Island. While Bluffton's outskirts have been taken over by the same gated community and upscale strip mall sprawl spreading throughout the coast, at its core it is a delightfully charming little community on the quiet May River, now called Old Bluffton, where you'd swear you just entered a time warp.

Daufuskie Island still maintains much of its age-old isolated, timeless personality, and the island—still accessible only by boat—is one of the spiritual centers of the Gullah culture and lifestyle.

## ★ OLD TOWN BLUFFTON

Similar to Beaufort, but even quieter and smaller, historic Bluffton is an idyllic village on the banks of the serene May River. Bluffton was the original hotbed of secession, with Charleston diarist Mary Chesnut famously referring to the town as "the center spot of the fire eaters." During their Civil War occupation, Union troops repaid the favor of those original Bluffton secessionists, which is why only nine homes in Bluffton are of antebellum vintage; the rest were torched in a search for Confederate guerrillas.

The center of tourist activity is "Old Town," the **Old Bluffton Historic District,** several blocks of 1800s-vintage buildings clustered between the parallel Boundary and Calhoun Streets (old-timers sometimes call this "the original square mile"). Many of the buildings are private residences, but most have been converted into art studios and antiques stores.

### Heyward House
### Historic Center

The **Heyward House Historic Center** (70 Boundary St., 843/757-6293, www.heywardhouse.org, Mon.-Fri. 10am-5pm, Sat. 10am-4pm, tours $5 adults, $2 students) is not only open to tours but also serves as Bluffton's

visitors center. Built in 1840 as a summer home for the owner of Moreland Plantation, John Cole, the house was later owned by George Cuthbert Heyward, grandson of Declaration of Independence signer Thomas Heyward. (Remarkably, it stayed in the family until the 1990s.) The Heyward House also sponsors walking tours of the historic district (843/757-6293, $15, by appointment only). Download your own walking tour map at www.heywardhouse.org.

### Church of the Cross

Don't fail to go all the way to the end of Calhoun Street, as it dead-ends on a high bluff on the May River at the Bluffton Public Dock. Overlooking this peaceful marsh-front vista is the photogenic **Church of the Cross** (110 Calhoun St., 843/757-2661, www.thechurchofthecross.net, free tours Mon.-Sat. 10am-2pm). The current sanctuary was built in 1854 and is one of only two local churches not burned in the Civil War. The parish itself began in 1767, with the first services on this spot held in the late 1830s. While the church looks as if it were made of cypress, it's actually constructed of heart pine.

### Bluffton Oyster Company

You might want to get a gander at the state's last remaining working oyster house, the **Bluffton Oyster Company** (63 Wharf St., 843/757-4010, www.blufftonoyster.com, Mon.-Sat. 9am-5:30pm), and possibly purchase some of their maritime bounty. Larry and Tina Toomer continue to oversee the oyster-harvesting-and-shucking family enterprise, which has its roots in the early 1900s.

## SHOPS

Bluffton's eccentric little art studios, most clustered in a two-block stretch on Calhoun Street, are by far its main shopping draw. Named for the Lowcountry phenomenon you find in the marsh at low tide among the fiddler crabs, Bluffton's **Pluff Mudd Art** (27 Calhoun St., 843/757-5551, Mon.-Sat. 10am-5:30pm) is a cooperative of 16 talented young painters and photographers from throughout the area. The **Guild of Bluffton Artists** (20 Calhoun St., 843/757-5590, Mon.-Sat. 10am-4:30pm) features works from many local artists, as does the outstanding **Society of Bluffton Artists** (48 Boundary St., 843/757-6586, Mon.-Sat. 10am-5pm, Sun. 11:30am-3pm). For cool, custom handcrafted pottery, try **Preston Pottery and Gallery** (10 Church St., 843/757-3084, Tues.-Sat. 10am-5pm). Another great Bluffton place is the hard-to-define **Eggs'n'tricities** (71 Calhoun St., 843/757-3446, Mon.-Sat. 10am-5pm). The name pretty much says it all for this fun and eclectic vintage, junk, jewelry, and folk art store.

If you want to score some fresh local seafood for your own culinary adventure, the no-brainer choice is the **Bluffton Oyster Company** (63 Wharf St., 843/757-4010, Mon.-Sat. 9am-5:30pm), the state's only active oyster facility. They also have shrimp, crab, clams, and fish, nearly all of it from the nearly pristine May River on whose banks the facility sits.

For a much more commercially intense experience, head just outside of town on U.S. 278 on the way to Hilton Head to find the dual **Tanger Outlet Centers** (1414 Fording Island Rd., 843/837-4339, Mon.-Sat. 10am-9pm, Sun. 11am-6pm), an outlet-shopper's paradise with virtually every major brand represented.

# FOOD
## American

Probably the single most popular place in Bluffton is the friendly **Old Town Dispensary** (15 Captains Cove, 843/837-1893, daily 11am-2am, $15-25), just off the Calhoun Street center of activity. This is an outstanding place to go for some cut-above pub/bar food or casual drinks, with plenty of outdoor seating and usually some live music going on.

Another very popular casual spot in Old Town, and frequented by many locals, is **Captain Woody's Bar & Grill** (17 State of Mind St., 843/757-6222, $10-15). Unpretentious and friendly, this is a good place to enjoy a

Bluffton Oyster Company on the May River

burger and a beer in a relaxed, patio-style environment with plenty going on around you.

## Breakfast and Brunch

No discussion of Bluffton cuisine is complete without the famous **Squat 'n' Gobble** (1231 May River Rd., 843/757-4242, daily 24 hours). Long a site of gossiping and politicking as well as, um, squatting and gobbling, this humble diner on May River Road is an indelible part of the local consciousness.

## Coffee

If you're looking for a coffeehouse in Old Town, go no farther than ★ **Corner Perk** (1297 May River Rd., Fording Island Rd., 843/816-5674, Tues.-Thurs. 7am-4pm., Fri.-Sat. 7am-11pm, Sun. brunch 7am-4pm, $10-20) in The Promenade, just off the main drag. Their coffee is truly wonderful, and the sandwich-heavy lunch menu compares with anything else in town. Upstairs is The Roasting Room, a more upscale, full-service bourbon bar.

## French

Most dining in Bluffton is pretty casual, but you'll get the white-tablecloth treatment at **Claude & Uli's Signature Bistro** (1533 Fording Island Rd., 843/837-3336, lunch Mon.-Fri. 11:30am-2:30pm, dinner Mon.-Sat. from 5pm, $18-25) just outside of town in Moss Village. Chef Claude does a great veal cordon bleu as well as a number of fine seafood entrées, such as an almond-crusted tilapia and an excellent seafood pasta.

## Mexican

My favorite restaurant in Bluffton is ★ **Mi Tierra** (101 Mellichamp Center, 843/757-7200, lunch daily 11am-4pm, dinner Mon.-Fri. 4pm-9pm, Sat.-Sun. 4pm-10pm, $3-15). They serve very high-quality but unpretentious Tex-Mex-style food in a fun atmosphere at affordable prices.

## ACCOMMODATIONS
### Under $150

A quality bargain stay right between Bluffton

and Hilton Head is the **Holiday Inn Express Bluffton** (35 Bluffton Rd., 843/757-2002, www.ichotelsgroup.com, $120), on U.S. 278 as you make the run onto Hilton Head proper. It's not close to the beach or to Old Town Bluffton, so you'll definitely be using your car, but its central location will appeal to those who want to keep their options open.

### Over $300

For an ultra-upscale spa and golf resort environment near Bluffton, the clear pick is the **Inn at Palmetto Bluff** (19 Village Park Square, 843/706-6500, www.palmettobluffresort.com, $650-900) just across the May River. This property was picked recently as the number two U.S. resort by *Condé Nast Traveler* magazine. There are three top-flight dining options on the grounds: the fine-dining **River House Restaurant** (843/706-6542, breakfast daily 7am-11am, lunch or "porch" menu daily 11am-10pm, dinner daily 6pm-10pm, $30-40); the **May River Grill** (Tues.-Sat. 11am-4pm, $9-13) at the golf clubhouse; and the casual **Buffalo's** (843/706-6630, Sun.-Tues. 11:30am-5pm, Wed.-Sat. 11:30am-9pm, $10-15).

## DAUFUSKIE ISLAND

Sitting between Savannah and Hilton Head Island and accessible only by water, Daufuskie Island—pronounced "da-FUSK-ee"—has about 500 full-time residents, most of whom ride around on golf carts or bikes (there's only one paved road, Haig Point Road). Once the home of rice and indigo plantations and rich oyster beds—the latter destroyed by pollution and overharvesting—the two upscale residential resort communities on the island, begun in the 1980s, give a clue as to where the future might lie, although the recent global economic downturn, perhaps thankfully, slowed development to a standstill.

The area of prime interest to visitors is the unincorporated western portion, or **Historic District,** the old stomping grounds of Pat Conroy during his stint as a teacher of resident African American children. His old

# Who Are the Gullah?

A language, a culture, and a people with a shared history, Gullah is more than that—it's also a state of mind. Simply put, the Gullah are African Americans of the Sea Islands of South Carolina and Georgia. (In Georgia, the term *Geechee,* from the nearby Ogeechee River, is more or less interchangeable.) Protected from outside influence by the isolation of this coastal region after the Civil War, Gullah culture is the closest living cousin to the West African traditions of those brought to this country as slaves.

While you might hear that *Gullah* is a corruption of "Angola," some linguists think it simply means "people" in a West African language. In any case, the Gullah speak what is known as a creole language, meaning one derived from several sources. Gullah combines elements of Elizabethan English, Jamaican patois, and several West African dialects; for example, "goober" (peanut) comes from the Congo *n'guba.* Another creole element is a word with multiple uses; for example, Gullah's *shum* could mean "see them," "see him," "see her," or "see it" in either past or present tense, depending on context. Several white writers in the 1900s published collections of Gullah folk tales, but it wasn't until later linguistic research was done that the Gullah tongue was recognized as something more than just broken English. Lorenzo Dow Turner's groundbreaking *Africanisms in the Gullah Dialect,* published in 1949, traced elements of the language to Sierra Leone in West Africa and more than 300 Gullah words directly to Africa.

Gullah is typically spoken very rapidly, which of course only adds to its impenetrability to the outsider. Gullah also relies on colorful turns of phrase. *"E tru mout"* ("He true mouth") means the speaker is referring to someone who doesn't lie. *"Le een crack muh teet"* ("I didn't even crack my teeth") means "I kept quiet." A forgetful Gullah speaker might say, *"Mah head leab me"* ("My head left me").

Gullah music, as practiced by the world-famous Hallelujah Singers of St. Helena Island, also uses many distinctly African techniques, such as call-and-response (the folk hymn "Michael Row the Boat Ashore" is a good example). The most famous Americans with Gullah roots are late boxer Joe Frazier (Beaufort), hip-hop star Jazzy Jay (Beaufort), NFL great Jim Brown (St. Simons Island, Georgia), and Supreme Court justice Clarence Thomas (Pin Point, Georgia, near Savannah).

Upscale development continues to claim more and more traditional Gullah areas, generally by pricing the Gullah out through rapidly increasing property values. Today, the major pockets of living Gullah culture in South Carolina are in Beaufort, St. Helena Island, Daufuskie Island, Edisto Island, and a northern section of Hilton Head Island.

The old ways are not as prevalent as they were, but several key institutions are keeping alive the spirit of Gullah: the **Penn Center** (16 Martin Luther King Dr., St. Helena, 843/838-2474, www. penncenter.com, Mon.-Sat. 11am-4pm, $4 adults, $2 seniors and children) on St. Helena Island near Beaufort; the **Avery Research Center** (66 George St., Charleston, 843/953-7609, www. cofc.edu/avery, Mon.-Fri. 10am-5pm, Sat. noon-5pm) at the College of Charleston; and **Geechee Kunda** (622 Ways Temple Rd., Riceboro, Georgia, 912/884-4440, www.geecheekunda.com) near Midway off U.S. 17.

one-room schoolhouse of *The Water is Wide* fame, the **Mary Field School,** is still here, as is the adjacent 140-year-old **Union Baptist Church,** but Daufuskie students now have a surprisingly modern new facility (middle school students are still ferried to mainland schools every day). Farther north on Haig Point Road is the new **Billie Burn Museum,** housed in the old Mount Carmel Church and named after the island's resident historian.

On the southern end you'll find the **Bloody Point Lighthouse,** named for the vicious battle fought nearby during the Yamasee War of 1815 (the light was actually moved inland in the early 1900s). Other areas of interest throughout the island include Native American sites, tabby ruins, the old Baptist church, and a couple of cemeteries.

Download a very well-done, free self-guided tour of Daufuskie's historic sites at www.hiltonheadisland.org; look for the "Robert Kennedy Historic Trail Guide" (not a nod to the former attorney general and U.S. senator, but a longtime island resident and historian).

For overnight stays, you can rent a humble but cozy cabin at **Freeport Marina** (843/785-8242, $100-150, golf cart $60 extra per day), near the ferry dock and overlooking the water. There are vacation rental options island-wide as well; go to www.daufuskieislandrentals.com for info on a wide variety of offerings. Sorry, no camping available!

There are no grocery stores as commonly understood on Daufuskie, only a couple of general store-type places. So if you've booked a vacation rental, most grocery items will need to be brought in with you.

For the freshest island seafood, check out the **Old Daufuskie Crab Company** (Freeport Marina, 843/785-6652, daily 11:30am-9pm, $8-22). The deviled crab is the house specialty. The other place to dine out on the island is **Marshside Mama's** (15 Haig Point Rd., 843/785-4755, www.marshsidemamas.com, hours change frequently, $10-15), a laid-back spot to enjoy grouper, gumbo, and Lowcountry boil, and frequent live music. Reservations are strongly encouraged.

For hand-crafted island art, go to **Iron Fish Gallery** (168 Benjies Point Rd., 843/842-9448, call ahead for hours), featuring the work of Chase Allen. His "coastal sculptures" include fanciful depictions of fish, stingrays, and even mermaids.

## Transportation and Services

The main public ferry between Daufuskie and Hilton Head is operated by **Calibogue Cruises** (18 Simmons Rd., 843/342-8687, www.daufuskiefreeport.com). Taking off from Broad Creek Marina on Hilton Head, the pleasant short ride—30 minutes each way—brings you in on the landward side of the island. Cost is $33 per person round-trip, or $64 per person round-trip including a meal at the Old Daufuskie Crab Company and a golf cart rental. Ferries run three times a day Monday, Wednesday, and Friday, and twice a day Tuesday, Thursday, Saturday, and Sunday. Ferry reservations are essential!

While the ferry trip and many vacation rentals include the rental of a golf cart, for *a la carte* service—get it?—rent one near Freeport Marina by calling 843/342-8687 (rates vary but hover around $30 per person per day). As the amount of golf carts is limited, I strongly recommend reserving yours in advance. All standard rules of the road apply, including needing a valid driver's license.

# Points Inland

It's likely that at some point you'll find yourself traveling inland from Beaufort, given that region's proximity to I-95. While this area is generally more known for offering interstate drivers a bite to eat and a place to rest their heads, there are several spots worth checking out in their own right, especially Walterboro and the Savannah National Wildlife Refuge.

## WALTERBORO

Walterboro is chiefly known to the world at large for being one of the best antiquing locales on the East Coast. Indeed, many of the high-dollar antiques shops on Charleston's King Street actually do their picking right here in the local stores, selling their finds at a significant markup in Charleston! (Another advantage Walterboro antiques shopping has over Charleston: plenty of free parking.)

Convenient and walkable, the two-block **Arts and Antiques District** on Washington Street centers on more than a dozen antiques and collectible stores, interspersed with a few gift shops and eateries. The best shop, though by no means the only one you should check out, is **Bachelor Hill Antiques** (255

E. Washington St., 843/549-1300, Mon.-Sat. 9am-6pm, Sun. 9am-4pm), which has several rooms packed with interesting and unique items, from collectibles to furniture to most everything in between.

## Sights
### ★ SOUTH CAROLINA ARTISANS CENTER

Don't miss the **South Carolina Artisans Center** (334 Wichman St., 843/549-0011, www.scartisanscenter.com, Mon.-Sat. 9am-5pm, Sun. 1pm-5pm, free), an expansive and vibrant collection of the best work of local and regional painters, sculptors, jewelers, and other craftspeople, for sale and for enjoyment. The Artisans Center hosts numerous receptions, and every third Saturday of the month they hold live artist demonstrations 11am-3pm.

### MUSEUMS

Walterboro boasts three small museums. The relocated and upgraded **Colleton Museum** (506 E. Washington St., 843/549-2303, www.colletonmuseum.org, Tues. noon-6pm, Wed.-Fri. 10am-5pm, Sat. 10am-2pm, free) is one of the best examples of a small-town museum you're likely to find. Adjacent is the farmers market, open Tuesday 2pm-6pm and Saturday 10am-2pm May-end of October.

The **Bedon-Lucas House Museum** (205 Church St., 843/549-9633, Thurs.-Sat. 1pm-4pm, $3 adults, free under age 8) was built by a local planter in 1820. An example of the local style of "high house," built off the ground to escape mosquitoes and catch the breeze, the house today is a nice mix of period furnishings and unadorned simplicity.

The **Slave Relic Museum** (208 Carn St., 843/549-9130, www.slaverelics.org, by appointment, $6 adults, $5 children) houses the Center for Research and Preservation of the African American Culture. It features artifacts, photos, and documents detailing the Atlantic passage, slave life, and the Underground Railroad.

### TUSKEGEE AIRMEN MEMORIAL

Yes, the Tuskegee Airmen of World War II fame were from Alabama, not South Carolina. But a contingent trained in Walterboro, at the site of the present-day **Lowcountry Regional Airport** (537 Aviation Way, 843/549-2549), a little north of downtown on U.S. 17. A publicly accessible, low-security area of the airport hosts the **Tuskegee Airmen Memorial,** an outdoor monument

the South Carolina Artisans Center

# Tuskegee Airmen in Walterboro

In a state where all too often African American history is studied in the context of slavery, a refreshing change is the tale of the Tuskegee Airmen, one of the most lauded American military units of World War II. Though named for their origins at Alabama's Tuskegee Institute, the pilots of the famed 332nd Fighter Group actually completed their final training in South Carolina at Walterboro Army Airfield, where the regional airport now sits.

The U.S. military was segregated during World War II, with African Americans mostly relegated to support roles. An interesting exception was the case of the 332nd, formed in 1941 as the 99th Pursuit Squadron by an act of Congress and the only all-black flying unit in the American military at the time. Mostly flying P-47 Thunderbolts and P-51 Mustangs, the pilots of the 332nd had one of the toughest missions of the war: escorting bombers over the skies of Germany and protecting them from Luftwaffe fighters. Though initially viewed with skepticism, the Tuskegee Airmen wasted no time in proving their mettle.

In fact, it wasn't long before U.S. bomber crews—who were, needless to say, all white—specifically requested that they be escorted by the airmen, who were given the nickname "Red-tail Angels" because of the distinctive markings of their aircraft. While legend has it that the 332nd never lost a bomber, this claim has been debunked. But as Tuskegee Airman Bill Holloman said, "The Tuskegee story is about pilots who rose above adversity and discrimination and opened a door once closed to black America, not about whether their record is perfect." The 332nd's reputation for aggressiveness in air combat was so widely known that the Germans also had a nickname for them—*Schwartze Vogelmenschen*, or "Black Birdmen."

Today Walterboro honors the airmen with a monument on the grounds of the Lowcountry Regional Airport, on U.S. 17 just northeast of town. In an easily accessible part of the airport grounds, the monument features a bronze statue and several interpretive exhibits. Another place to catch up on Tuskegee Airmen history is at the **Colleton Museum** (506 E. Washington St., 843/549-2303, www.colletonmuseum.org, Tues. noon-6pm, Wed.-Fri. 10am-5pm, Sat. 10am-2pm, free), which has a permanent exhibit on the pilots and their history in the Walterboro area.

Walterboro Army Airfield's contribution to the war effort was not limited to the Tuskegee Airmen. Seven of the famed Doolittle Raiders were trained here, there was a compound for holding German prisoners of war, and it was also the site of the U.S. military's largest camouflage school.

---

to these brave flyers. There's a bronze statue and several interpretive exhibits.

### GREAT SWAMP SANCTUARY

Just south of town is the **Great Swamp Sanctuary** (www.thegreatswamp.org, daily dawn-dusk, free), a still-developing ecotourism project focusing on the Lowcountry environment. Located in one of the region's few braided-creek habitats accessible to the public, the 842-acre sanctuary has three miles of walking and biking trails, some along the path of the old Charleston-Savannah stagecoach route. Kayakers and canoeists can paddle more than two miles of winding creeks. There are three entry points to the Great Swamp Sanctuary, all off Jefferies Boulevard. In west-to-east order from I-95: north onto

Beach Road, north onto Detreville Street (this is considered the main entrance), and west onto Washington Street.

## Festivals and Events

In keeping with South Carolina's tradition of towns hosting annual events to celebrate signature crops and products, Walterboro's **Colleton County Rice Festival** (http://the-ricefestival.org, free) happens every April. There's a parade, live music, a 5K run, and the crowning of the year's "Rice Queen."

## Food

The story of food in Walterboro revolves around ★ **Duke's Barbecue** (949 Robertson Blvd., 843/549-1446, $7), one of the best-regarded barbecue spots in the Lowcountry and one of the top two joints named "Duke's" in the state (the other, by common consensus, is in Orangeburg). The pulled pork is delectable, cooked with the indigenous South Carolina mustard-based sauce.

## Accommodations

If you're looking for big-box lodging, the section of Walterboro close to I-95 is chockablock with it. The quality is surprisingly good, perhaps because they tend to cater to Northerners on their way to and from Florida. A good choice is **Holiday Inn Express & Suites** (1834 Sniders Hwy., 843/538-2700, www.hiexpress.com, $85), or try the **Comfort Inn & Suites** (97 Downs Ln., 843/538-5911, www.choicehotels.com, $95).

If you'd like something with a bit more character, there are two B&Bs on Hampton Street downtown. **Old Academy Bed & Breakfast** (904 Hampton St., 843/549-3232, www.oldacademybandb.com, $80-115) has four guest rooms housed in Walterboro's first school building. They offer a full continental breakfast. Note that credit cards are not accepted. Although built recently (by local standards), the 1912 **Hampton House Bed and Breakfast** (500 Hampton St., 843/542-9498, www.hamptonhousebandb.com, $125-145) has three well-appointed guest rooms and offers a full country breakfast. By appointment only, you can see its Forde Doll and Dollhouse Collection, with over 50 dollhouses and oodles of antique dolls.

## SAVANNAH NATIONAL WILDLIFE REFUGE

Roughly equally divided between Georgia and South Carolina, the sprawling, 30,000-acre **Savannah National Wildlife Refuge** (912/652-4415, www.fws.gov/savannah, daily dawn-dusk, free) is one of the premier bird-watching and nature-observing locales in the Southeast. The system of dikes and paddy fields once used to grow rice now helps make this an attractive stopover for migrating birds. Bird-watching is best October-April. While you can kayak on your own on miles of creeks, you can also call **Swamp Girls Kayak Tours** (843/784-2249, www.swampgirls.com), who work out of nearby Hardeeville, for a guided tour. The wildlife refuge is about 20 minutes from Savannah, two hours from Charleston, and an hour from Beaufort. To get here, take exit 5 off I-95 onto U.S. 17. Go south to U.S. 170 and look for Laurel Hill Wildlife Drive. Be sure to stop by the **visitors center** (off U.S. 170 at Laurel Hill Wildlife Dr., Mon.-Sat. 9am-4:30pm).

# Columbia and the Midlands

The "real" South Carolina, this large area stretching across the wide waist of the Palmetto State, is often neglected in discussions of tourism.

Between the living movie set that is the Lowcountry and the more dramatic landscape of the Upstate, the Midlands—flat and crisscrossed with interstate highways—sometimes seem plain by comparison. But the Midlands have long been something of an honest broker between the Lowcountry and the Upcountry, from Columbia's original role as compromise state capital to the region's default mode as a cultural buffer zone between the insouciant coast and the staunch mountains.

In addition to great fishing, throughout the region there's an abundance of outdoor activity, including some of the best white-water rafting in the South near Columbia and the unique Congaree National Park, home to some of the most ancient old-growth forest on the planet.

## PLANNING YOUR TIME

Columbia is an easy city to get around in. Reserve half a day for the Riverbanks Zoo and a minimum of another half day for the other major sights. Two days will allow you to see more of the city, including a night out in the Vista and an evening in Five Points.

Because of the physical breadth of the Midlands, one day is not nearly enough to enjoy the rest of the region outside Columbia. Reserve half a day alone for Congaree National Park. If you only have a day or a day and a half, choose between two areas: the Pee Dee or Santee Cooper.

**Previous:** Riverbanks Zoo and Garden; South Carolina State House. **Above:** Maurice's Piggie Park BBQ.

Look for ★ to find recommended
sights, activities, dining, and lodging.

# Highlights

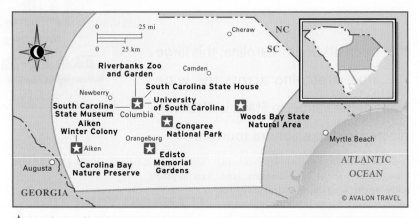

★ **South Carolina State House:** The resilient and grand state capitol features gorgeous grounds and interesting monuments (page 396).

★ **South Carolina State Museum:** Learn all about the Palmetto State in an excellently restored warehouse in the Congaree Vista (page 398).

★ **University of South Carolina:** The elegant Horseshoe area is the oldest, most beautiful part of one of the South's oldest universities (page 398).

★ **Riverbanks Zoo and Garden:** One of the country's best zoos has a dynamic educational and conservation component as well as a beautiful botanical garden (page 399).

★ **Congaree National Park:** This park features an ancient cypress swamp with what may be the tallest old-growth canopy remaining on earth (page 404).

★ **Woods Bay State Natural Area:** This well-preserved Carolina bay features a canoe trail and scenic boardwalk (page 407).

★ **Edisto Memorial Gardens:** The pride of Orangeburg showcases thousands of varieties of roses (page 409).

★ **Aiken Winter Colony:** See the cozy, historic cottages of the wealthy Northerners who put Aiken on the map (page 412).

★ **Carolina Bay Nature Preserve:** This scenic and accessible Carolina bay features a good walking trail around its circumference (page 414).

# Columbia and the Midlands

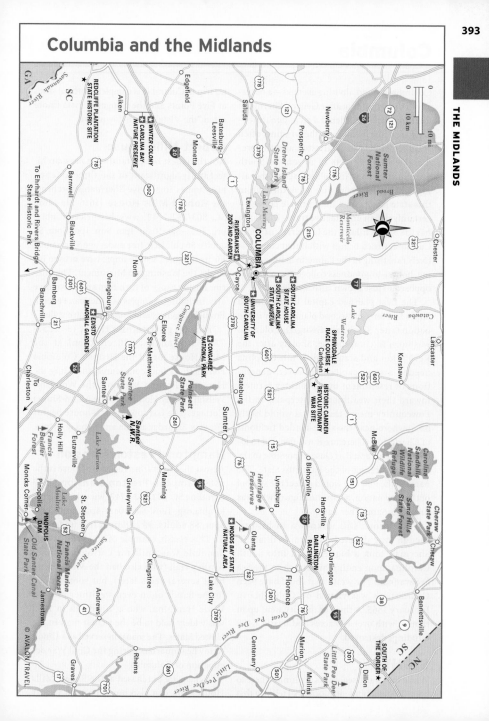

© AVALON TRAVEL

# Columbia

Columbia's broad, inviting avenues—a necessity of the rebuilding after General Sherman's torching, now considered a civic signature—are a welcome break from the winding, often cramped streets of Charleston and the predictable Main Streets of dozens of South Carolina hamlets. And while it seems that almost every little burg you drive through in this state has its own little private college—certainly not an unattractive trait—Columbia has the big enchilada, the University of South Carolina, which brings with it that comparatively rare thing in the Palmetto State: a genuine, honest-to-goodness college-town vibe, as opposed to just a town with a college.

The first planned capital in the United States and only the second planned city in the nation (after Savannah, Georgia), Columbia was born in compromise. Shortly after the Revolution and statehood, South Carolina needed a state capital. However, generations of resentment by Upcountry farmers toward their wealthier counterparts in the Lowcountry meant the capital would likely be nowhere near the slave-tended fiefdoms of Charleston. Therefore it was decided to locate the new capital as close as possible to the geographic center of the Palmetto State. The name of the new city would reflect the symbol of the new nation, a feminine figure who was the Uncle Sam of her day.

For reasons still unknown to history, though long debated, General William T. Sherman took a big left turn into South Carolina upon ending his March to the Sea at Savannah. The wrath that could have been Charleston's was visited on Columbia in February 1865. A third of the city went up in flames, with over 300 acres and nearly 1,400 buildings destroyed.

## SIGHTS

While the "must-see" picks are limited here to specific attractions, any local will tell you that

no trip to Columbia is complete without stops at Five Points and the Congaree Vista (more often "the Vista"), both downtown.

## Robert Mills House

Not the oldest but certainly the most architecturally significant of the three antebellum homes to survive Sherman's torching, the **Robert Mills House** (1616 Blanding St., 803/252-7742, www.historiccolumbia.org, Tues.-Sat. 10am-4pm, Sun. 1pm-5pm, $8 adults, $6 children, free under age 5) is named for its designer, whose impressive oeuvre includes the Washington Monument. The interior hosts a range of furniture and decorative arts, including examples of American Federal, English Regency, and French Empire styles.

You can get a **combo ticket** (803/252-7742, $28 adults, $20 children) at the Mills House for all the Historic Columbia Foundation's house museums, including the Hampton-Preston Mansion, the Woodrow Wilson Family Home, and the Mann-Simon Cottage. The last tour at each house begins Tuesday-Saturday at 3pm and Sunday at 4pm.

## Hampton-Preston Mansion

Across the street from the Mills House is the 1818 **Hampton-Preston Mansion** (1615 Blanding St., 803/252-7742, www.historiccolumbia.org, Tues.-Sat. 10am-4pm, Sun. 1pm-5pm, $8 adults, $6 children, free under age 6). This classic example of an elite planter's domicile was built for cotton merchant Ainsley Hall (who also had the Mills House built several years later), but soon landed in the hands of an even wealthier planter, Wade Hampton, who at his death in 1835 was widely held to be the richest man in the United States. The mansion served as a Union Army headquarters during the Civil War occupation of Columbia.

Tickets are purchased at the Robert Mills House. You can also buy a **combo ticket**

# Columbia

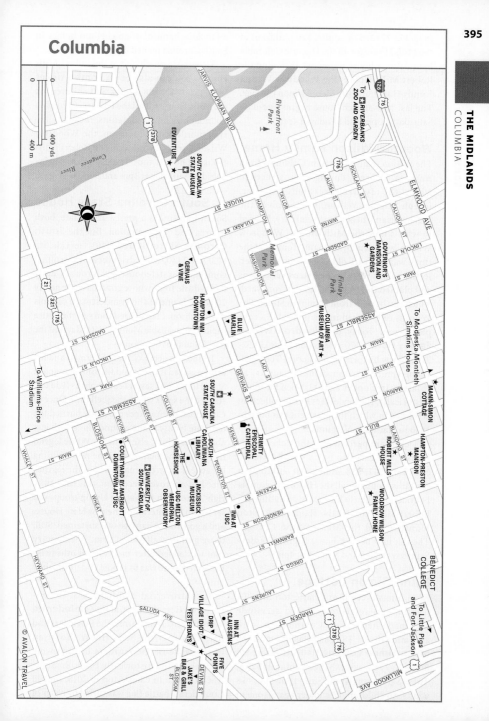

To Riverbanks Zoo and Garden

126
76

Riverfront Park

1 378
EDVENTURE ★

Congaree River

SOUTH CAROLINA STATE MUSEUM ★

JARVIS KLARMAN BLVD

HUGER ST
PULASKI ST
HAMPTON ST
TAYLOR ST
LAUREL ST
RICHLAND ST
176
WAYNE ST
CALHOUN ST
ELMWOOD AVE
LINCOLN ST
PARK ST

GOVERNOR'S MANSION AND GARDENS ★

Memorial Park

WASHINGTON ST

GADSDEN ST

Finlay Park

COLUMBIA MUSEUM OF ART ★

21
321
176

GADSDEN ST
LINCOLN ST
PARK ST
ASSEMBLY ST
GERVAIS & VINE ▲

HAMPTON INN DOWNTOWN ▲

BLUE MARLIN ●

GERVAIS ST
LADY ST
MAIN ST
SUMTER ST
MARION ST
BULL ST
ASSEMBLY ST

To Modjeska Monteith Simkins House

MANN-SIMON COTTAGE ★

COLLEGE ST
GREENE ST
DEVINE ST
BLOSSOM ST

SOUTH CAROLINA STATE HOUSE ★

SOUTH CAROLINIANA LIBRARY ■

THE HORSESHOE

TRINITY EPISCOPAL CATHEDRAL ✝

SENATE ST
PENDLETON ST
PICKENS ST
HENDERSON ST
BARNWELL ST

HAMPTON-PRESTON MANSION ★
BLANDING ST
ROBERT MILLS HOUSE ★

WOODROW WILSON FAMILY HOME ★

To Williams-Brice Stadium

WHALEY ST
MAIN ST
HEYWARD ST

UNIVERSITY OF SOUTH CAROLINA ✚

MCKISSICK MUSEUM ■

USC MELTON MEMORIAL OBSERVATORY ■

INN AT USC ●

COURTYARD BY MARRIOTT DOWNTOWN AT USC ●

GREGG ST
LAURENS ST
HARDEN ST

BENEDICT COLLEGE

To Little Pigs and Fort Jackson

SALUDA AVE
VILLAGE IDIOT ▲
YESTERDAY'S ▲
DRIP ●
INN AT CLAUSSENS ●

FIVE POINTS

JAKE'S BAR & GRILL ▲

11 378
76
1

DEVINE ST
BLOSSOM ST
MILLWOOD AVE

WHEAT ST

© AVALON TRAVEL

0      400 yds
0      400 m

(803/252-7742, $28 adults, $20 children) at the Mills House for all the Historic Columbia Foundation's house museums, including the Robert Mills House, the Woodrow Wilson Family Home, and the Mann-Simon Cottage. The last tour at each house begins Tuesday-Saturday at 3pm and Sunday at 4pm.

## Woodrow Wilson Family Home

The Wilson family arrived in Columbia from Augusta, Georgia, during Reconstruction, when the future president's father, Joseph Ruggles Wilson, took a job at the Presbyterian Theological Seminary, housed in what's now the Mills House. Woodrow Wilson, who went by the name Tommy at the time, was 14 years old. Woodrow's mother, Jessie, held sway over the extensive gardens and planted the magnolias in the front yard, which can be seen from Hampton Street. The Wilsons only stayed in the house for a couple of years. Today, the **Woodrow Wilson Family Home** (1705 Hampton St., 803/252-7742, www.historiccolumbia.org, Tues.-Sat. 10am-4pm, Sun. 1pm-5pm, $8 adults, $6 children, free under age 6) is open for tours. Historically, the key object in the collection is the bed in which the president was born in 1856 in Staunton, Virginia.

Tickets are purchased at the Robert Mills House. You can also buy a **combo ticket** (803/252-7742, $28 adults, $20 children) at the Mills House for all the Historic Columbia Foundation's house museums, including the Robert Mills House, the Hampton-Preston Mansion, and the Mann-Simon Cottage. The last tour at each house begins Tuesday-Saturday at 3pm and Sunday at 4pm.

## Mann-Simon Cottage

Born into slavery near Charleston in 1799, Celia Mann somehow escaped servitude and made her way to Columbia to work as a midwife. By 1844 she was living in the **Mann-Simon Cottage** (1403 Richland St., 803/252-7742, www.historiccolumbia.org, Tues.-Sat. 10am-4pm, Sun. 1pm-5pm, $8 adults, $6 children, free under age 6), one of

a precious handful of antebellum homes in South Carolina owned by free blacks.

Tickets are purchased at the Robert Mills House. You can also buy a **combo ticket** (803/252-7742, $28 adults, $20 children) at the Mills House for all the Historic Columbia Foundation's house museums, including the Hampton-Preston Mansion, the Woodrow Wilson Family Home, and the Robert Mills House. The last tour at each house begins Tuesday-Saturday at 3pm and Sunday at 4pm.

## ★ South Carolina State House

South Carolina is a pretty small state, both in area and in population. But the **South Carolina State House** (1101 Gervais St., 803/734-2430, www.discoversouthcarolina. com, www.scstatehouse.gov, grounds daily dawn-dusk, free), whose grounds cover nearly 20 acres, is one of the grandest state capitols in the nation. Free guided tours of the entire capitol are available Monday-Saturday and the first Sunday of the month.

In 1865 General William Sherman and his army assailed the city, and the still incomplete State House took several cannonballs (you can still see the spots where the shells hit). Once in Columbia, the Yankees promptly burned the old State House to the ground along with just about everything else in town. While legend has it that Sherman spared the new building because it wasn't actually where the legislature had approved secession, this isn't quite right. The truth is that the Union troops did set fire to the interior of the new State House, and a good bit of damage was sustained. Still, those granite walls stood firm. A temporary roof was added after the war, but otherwise the State House was to sit idle and unfinished until 1907.

A controversial highlight is at the entrance on Gervais Street, at the **Confederate Monument.** At one time, the rebel Stars and Bars flew over the State House. However, in the wake of the murders of nine worshippers at the historically black Emanuel AME Church in Charleston in 2015, the old Confederate battle flag was furled by order of

the South Carolina State House

the governor and the state legislature. It is no longer present on the State House grounds.

The **African American History Monument** is a comparatively late addition to the property and the first of its kind on any American capitol grounds. The dozen vignettes on the monument depict various chapters in the struggle for civil rights from slavery through today. At the base of the monument are four rubbing stones, each representing a different region of Africa from which slaves were imported.

The imposing and impressive **George Washington Statue** at the capitol's front steps is sculpted of bronze on a granite base and is supposedly Washington's exact height: six feet, two inches tall. If you're here after hours, you may notice joggers running up and down the front steps, *Rocky*-style.

## Trinity Episcopal Cathedral

The beautiful buffed-brick **Trinity Episcopal Cathedral** (1100 Sumter St., 803/771-7300, www.trinitysc.org), near the State House, is a fine example of Gothic Revival church architecture, and a recent renovation has made it even more attractive. Its congregation has roots back to the very first backcountry Episcopalian church in the state, around 1812.

The current sanctuary hosts deceased luminaries in the attached cemetery, including five governors of South Carolina and three Confederate generals (and one who was both: Wade Hampton III). Good construction and

Trinity Episcopal Cathedral

benevolent wind patterns (and divine intervention?) saved the church from Yankee fires in 1865.

## ★ South Carolina State Museum

The mother lode of all history of the Palmetto State, the **South Carolina State Museum** (301 Gervais St., 803/898-4921, www.scmuseum.org, Mon. and Wed.-Fri. 10am-5pm, Tues. 10am-8pm, Sat. 10am-6pm, Sun. noon-5pm, $13.95 adults, $11.95 children, free under age 3) occupies the 1893 Columbia Mill textile building. Open since 1988, there are over 70,000 artifacts in its growing collection. There's a constant menu of rotating exhibits as well as a standing collection of art, archaeology, and natural history. Kids love the giant shark display, a 43-foot-long replica of a prehistoric shark skeleton typical of the species that once roamed this area back when water levels were significantly higher than today. But the real highlights are the detailed and vibrant exhibits on particular segments of the human history of South Carolina.

Housed within the State Museum complex is the small but well-tended **South Carolina Relic Room & Military Museum** (301 Gervais St., 803/737-8095, www.crr.sc.gov, Tues.-Sat. 10am-5pm, 1st Sun. of the month 1pm-5pm, $6 adults, $3 youth, free under age 12, $1 1st Sun. of the month), which maintains an interesting collection of artifacts and memorabilia highlighting the state's significant contributions to American military history, with a strong focus on the Civil War era. A combo ticket ($9) provides admission to both the State Museum and the Relic Room.

## EdVenture

The new-fangled children's museum **EdVenture** (211 Gervais St., 803/779-3100, www.edventure.org, Tues.-Sat. 9am-5pm, Sun. noon-5pm, $11.50), within the State Museum complex but in a separate building, was built specifically for those ages 12 and under. In it are over 350 hands-on exhibits, mostly concentrating on science and nature. A highlight is "Eddie," a 40-foot-tall schoolboy within whose simulated innards kids can climb and slide.

## Columbia Museum of Art

The small but well-done **Columbia Museum of Art** (Main St. and Hampton St., 803/799-2810, www.columbiamuseum.org, Tues.-Fri. 11am-5pm, Sat. 10am-5pm, Sun. noon-5pm, $12 adults, $5 children, free under age 5) is in a suitably modern-looking building, erected in 1998. The highlight of its permanent collection is the Samuel H. Kress Collection on the upper floor, including some wonderful Renaissance and baroque pieces. The most notable single works here are Botticelli's matchless *Nativity* and Claude Monet's *The Seine at Giverny*. Occasionally hours and admission cost are different during special exhibits; check the website for details.

## ★ University of South Carolina

Columbia isn't just the state capital; it's a college town as well. The **University of South Carolina** (USC, 803/777-0169, www.sc.edu) hosts nearly 30,000 students at its main campus in Columbia, although apparently only a few attend during summer, which is dead compared to the busy fall and spring.

On Sumter Street at College Street you'll find the wrought-iron gates opening onto **The Horseshoe,** the oldest and most beautiful part of campus. The grand **McKissick Museum** (816 Bull St., 803/777-7251, www.artsandsciences.sc.edu, Mon.-Fri. 8:30am-5pm, Sat. 11am-3pm, free), a New Deal-era public works project, houses USC's many collections and has diverse exhibits on public life and history in the state. There are two galleries on the 2nd floor, a natural history component on the 3rd floor, and a visitors center on the 1st floor.

The key building to note during your walking tour of The Horseshoe is one near the Sumter Street entrance, the **South Caroliniana Library** (910 Sumter St., 803/777-3131, www.sc.edu, Mon.-Fri.

# Walter Edgar's Journal

He's originally from Alabama, but you could call University of South Carolina professor Walter Edgar the modern voice of the Palmetto State. From the rich diversity of barbecue to the inner workings of the poultry business and the charms of beach music, Edgar covers the gamut of South Carolina culture and experience on his popular weekly radio show *Walter Edgar's Journal*, airing on South Carolina public radio stations throughout the state.

Currently director of the USC Institute of Southern Studies, the Vietnam vet and certified barbecue contest judge explains the show like this: "On the *Journal* we look at current events in a broader perspective, trying to provide context that is often missing in the mainstream media." More specifically, Edgar devotes each one-hour show to a single guest, usually a South Carolinian—by birth or by choice—with a unique perspective on some aspect of state culture, business, arts, or folkways. By the time the interview ends, you not only have a much deeper understanding of the topic of the show but of the interviewee as well. And because of Edgar's unique way of tying strands of his own vast knowledge and experience into every interview, he'll also leave you with a deeper understanding of South Carolina itself.

In these days of media saturation, a public radio show might sound like a rather insignificant perch from which to influence an entire state. But remember that South Carolina is a small, close-knit place, a state of Main Street towns rather than impersonal metro areas. During any given show, many listeners in Edgar's audience will know his guests on a personal basis. And by the end of the show, the rest of the listeners will feel as if they did.

Listen to *Walter Edgar's Journal* Friday at noon on South Carolina public radio, with a repeat Sunday at 8pm. Hear podcasts of previous editions at www.scetv.org.

8:30am-5pm, Sat. 9am-1pm, free). Designed by renowned American architect Robert Mills, who also designed Columbia's premier house museum, the Caroliniana is the first freestanding college library in the country (two fireproof wings were added in 1927). The library has one of the most significant collections on Southern history anywhere, with a particularly distinguished reading room full of stately busts and Harry Potter-esque alcoves. It's open to the public; all you need is a photo ID. Keep in mind that it's open only when classes are in session.

## Governor's Mansion and Gardens

The executive branch of the Palmetto State is headquartered at the **Governor's Mansion and Gardens** (800 Richland St., 803/737-1710, www.scgovernorsmansion.org, gardens Mon.-Fri. 9am-5pm, free). Built in 1855 as the Arsenal Military Academy, the building, which now houses the governor and family, survived the burning of the city in 1865

and hosted its first chief executive in 1869. The six rooms of the mansion open to the public contain an impressive collection of furnishings and artwork from various eras. Call or visit the website to make an appointment for a free tour.

## ★ Riverbanks Zoo and Garden

One of the nation's best, if underrated, zoos and South Carolina's most popular single attraction, **Riverbanks Zoo and Garden** (500 Wildlife Pkwy., 803/779-8717, www.riverbanks.org, fall-winter daily 9am-5pm, spring-summer Mon.-Fri. 9am-5pm, Sat.-Sun. 9am-6pm, $15.95 adults, $13.50 children, free under age 2) is a unique combo site. Not only do you get a crackerjack zoo, with nearly 400 species represented and an extensive environmental and educational component, but there's a beautiful botanical garden as well. A $36 million expansion includes a new seal/sea lion exhibit, an upgraded grizzly bear environment, and more kids' activities.

Some tips on enjoying Riverbanks: It gets

hot in Columbia. Go early or late in the day to see the animals at their best. Regardless of the heat, Riverbanks begins attracting heavy crowds just before lunchtime. If crowds bother you, get there right as it opens. When you enter, take stock of the rotating schedule of exhibits, programs, showtimes, and feeding times *before* you set off on your trek through the zoo.

Riverbanks couldn't be easier to get to. It's just off I-26 at the Greystone Boulevard exit.

## ENTERTAINMENT

Columbia is a fun town with plenty of nightlife, especially when USC is in session. In addition to the campus's cultural offerings, there are two main areas to remember for entertainment, dining, and shopping: Five Points, the intersection of Harden and Greene Streets and Saluda Avenue; and the Vista (sometimes called the Congaree Vista), a more recently restored area closer to downtown amid former mill buildings.

Riverbanks Zoo and Garden

### Festivals and Events

The main public event on the calendar for downtown Columbia is March's annual **St. Patrick's Day Festival** (www.stpats5points.com, $15) in Five Points. The conglomeration of bars and the cozy streets make for a vivacious Celtic celebration. There are five stages of live music, various kids' activities, and, of course, a big parade.

Each October, Five Points hosts the **Columbia Blues Festival** (803/733-8452, www.wordofmouthproductions.org), a celebration of that indigenous American art form, mostly relying on regional talent. Also in October comes the biggest single local event, the **South Carolina State Fair** (1200 Rosewood Dr., 803/799-3387, www.scstatefair.org, $8 adults, $2 children) at the sprawling state fairgrounds near Williams-Brice Stadium.

### Nightlife

As you'd expect, nightlife here is plentiful, boisterous, and centers on the college scene, especially in Five Points. The Vista appeals to visitors as well as trendy and well-heeled locals. There's no smoking in all bars, restaurants, and public places in Columbia.

Any discussion of nightlife in Columbia, and specifically in Five Points, should begin with **Jake's Bar & Grill** (2112 Devine St., 803/708-4788, Tues.-Fri. 4pm-4am, Sat. 2pm-2am, Sun. 5pm-2am). Formerly called Rockafella's, it often hosted Hootie and the Blowfish when they were getting their start, and it remains the quintessential Five Points neighborhood joint.

In the Vista, for great live bar bands go to the spacious and bustling **Tin Roof** (1022 Senate St., 803/771-1558, www.tinroofbars.com). This is a South Carolina outpost of a Nashville chain of revival juke joints and "shotgun shacks" catering to college crowds. The closest thing to a Five Points-style dive in the Vista is **The Whig** (1200 Main St., 803/931-8852, daily 4pm-2am, kitchen until 10pm), a bohemian-slacker joint with what's generally considered the best jukebox in town.

## Performing Arts

The nearly half-century-old **South Carolina Philharmonic** (721 Lady St., 803/771-7937, www.scphilharmonic.com) plays most of its classical music concerts at the **Koger Center for the Arts** (1051 Greene St., 803/777-7500, www.koger.sc.edu) under the baton of Morihiko Nakahara.

**Columbia City Ballet** (www.columbiacityballet.com), a professional troupe, generally dances at the Koger Center for the Arts. They offer one of the more eclectic seasons you'll find outside New York City, with a ballet about Dracula every Halloween, and even a ballet chronicling the history of Hootie and the Blowfish. Of course, there's an annual holiday *Nutcracker* as well.

## SHOPPING

Other than malls, the main shopping area in Columbia is at Five Points. The Vista also has a growing range of good stores.

As with much of South Carolina, the capital has some good antiques action, mostly in the West Columbia area. **Old Mill Antique Mall** (310 State St., 803/796-4229, www.oldantiquemill.com, Mon.-Sat. 10am-5:30pm, Sun. 1:30pm-5:30pm), represents vendors on a consignment basis. **763 Antique Mall** (763 Meeting St., 803/796-1516, www.763antiquemall.com, Mon.-Sat. 10am-6pm, Sun. 1:30pm-6pm) is in an 11,000 square foot space and has a wide range of collectibles.

The acclaimed **Blue Sky Gallery** (733 Saluda Ave., 803/779-4242, www.blueskyart.com, by appointment) in Five Points is where you'll find original work from none other than Blue Sky himself, aka Warren Edward Johnson, a nationally renowned local artist who specializes in murals and folk art. Call for an appointment.

**Sid Nancy** (733 Saluda Ave., 803/779-6454, www.shopsidnancy.com, Mon.-Fri. noon-8pm, Sat. 11am-7pm, Sun. 1pm-3pm) in Five Points, as the name might indicate, is an awesome vintage and thrift store with a definite cutting-edge post-punk appeal. Adjacent is the excellent consignment shop **Revente** (737 Saluda Ave., 803/256-3076, www.shoprevente.com, Mon.-Sat. 10am-6pm, Sun. noon-6pm), which tends to cater to the upper end of the scale, though with some great bargains if your timing is right.

Serious vinyl junkies should head straight to Five Points to check out **Papa Jazz** (2014 Greene St., 803/256-0096, www.papajazz.com, Mon.-Sat. 10am-7pm, Sun. 1pm-6pm). Besides the eponymous genre, they deal in used vinyl of all types, including rare funk records and the occasional punk gem. It's a tiny store packed to the gills with music, but it has been a Columbia tradition for over 25 years.

## RECREATION

Because of its position at the confluence of the Saluda, Broad, and Congaree Rivers and the presence of Lake Murray nearby, Columbia is a haven for water-based pastimes. Generally speaking, most put-in spots are in West Columbia, using the large Gervais Street Bridge from downtown as a major landmark. The **Three Rivers Greenway** (803/765-2200, www.riveralliance.org, daily dawn-dusk, free) joins several different hiking and biking paths and provides numerous river access points.

A great place to put in on the Saluda River is **Saluda Shoals Park** (5605 Bush River Rd., 803/731-5208, www.icrc.net, daily dawn-dusk, $4 per vehicle), a 350-acre park on the Saluda River outside of town with a good launch ramp. The park offers periodic guided kayak trips; call for details.

There are several good outfitters in town for rental, purchase, or guided tours. **Adventure Carolina** (1107 State St., 803/796-4505, www.adventurecarolina.com) runs several trips on all area rivers, including a quick and easy selection of three-hour, three-mile paddles (about $50 pp). They also rent anything you might need. **River Runner Outdoor Center** (905 Gervais St., 803/771-0353, www.riverrunner.us, Mon.-Sat. 10am-6pm) is the designated outfitter for Saluda Shoals Park but will rent for any trip at about $40 per day.

On the other side of the rivers in West

Columbia and the suburb of Cayce are the **West Columbia Riverwalk** (from town, cross over the Gervais St. Bridge, take a left on Alexander Rd., and you'll see the amphitheater and parking lot on the left) and the **Cayce Riverwalk** (take Blossom St. over the river, then a left onto Axtell Dr./Jessamine St., and the entrance is on the left).

## Spectator Sports

As part of the Southeastern Conference, the **University of South Carolina's Gamecocks** (www.gamecocksonline.cstv. com) play football in front of a passionate fan base at **Williams-Brice Stadium** (1127 George Rogers Blvd., 803/254-2950). They play basketball downtown at the **Colonial Center** (801 Lincoln St., 803/576-9200).

The brand-new **Columbia Fireflies** (www.columbiafireflies.com) play baseball in the also brand-new **Spirit Communications Park** (1640 Freed St., 803/726-4487, single game tickets $10), built especially for them. The Single-A level farm team of the New York Mets made a big impact their inaugural year in 2017 by signing former University of Florida and NFL player Tim Tebow to play for them.

## FOOD

Columbia may not be challenging Charleston on the food front anytime soon, but a growing number of very tasty establishments have sprung up in the Five Points and Vista districts to go along with other longtime favorites in town. And if you're a barbecue fan, you're definitely in luck.

### American

Columbians swear by the pimento cheeseburgers and the pimento cheese fries at **Rockaway's** (2719 Rosewood Dr., 803/256-1075, daily 11am-11pm, $8), an under-the-radar, locals-only type place in a nondescript building on the south side of the USC campus. For a brewpub, **Hunter Gatherer Brewery** (900 Main St., 803/748-0540, Tues.-Sat. 4pm-midnight, $10) has an excellent kitchen, and

many locals insist the best burger in town is actually here.

### Barbecue and Ribs

**Maurice's Piggie Park BBQ** (1600 Charleston Hwy., 803/796-0220, www.mauricesbbq.com, Sun.-Thurs. 10am-10pm, Fri.-Sat. 10am-11pm, $7-12) in West Columbia is the real thing: mustard-based Carolina pulled pork, and lots of it. This barbecue is the traditional Midlands variety, in a yellow mustard sauce.

Many locals insist however that ★ **Little Pigs** (4927 Alpine Rd., 803/788-8238, www. littlepigs.biz, Wed. 11am-2pm, Thurs.-Sat. 11am-9pm, $8) outside downtown near Fort Jackson has much better 'cue, despite not cooking with wood (a sticky issue with connoisseurs). This is all-you-can-eat buffet-style dining in a simple setting, with the focus purely on the pig itself—literally, since you can see it all right there in the buffet line.

### Classic Southern

Not Columbia's best restaurant, but certainly its best-known, ★ **Yesterday's** (2030 Devine St., 803/799-0196, www.yesterdayssc. com, Sun.-Thurs. 11:30am-midnight, Fri.-Sat. 11:30am-1am, $6-12), in the heart of Five Points, is as close to a Southern institution as the city offers. This simple, always-crowded diner has a menu perfect for a Southern gameday meal for the whole family: "Confederate fried" steak, special-recipe fried chicken, fried catfish, and, of course, the signature meat loaf. Yes, meat loaf. They also have all kinds of sandwiches, including wraps, burgers, clubs, and southwestern chicken.

### Coffee, Tea, and Sweets

Probably the best cuppa joe in Columbia is at **Drip** (729 Saluda Ave., 803/661-9545, www. dripcolumbia.com, Mon.-Sat. 7am-6pm, Sun. 8am-6pm) in the heart of Five Points, which, as the name implies, specializes in the hot trend of pour-over drip coffee. There is also wine and beer.

A favorite, if quirky, spot in the Vista is

**Nonnah's** (930 Gervais St., 803/779-9599, Mon.-Fri. 11:30am-2pm and 5pm-10pm, Sat. 6pm-midnight), an eatery better known for its bar scene and for its great desserts.

## Mediterranean and Middle Eastern

Generally considered one of the best restaurants in Columbia and certainly the most romantic, ★ **Gervais & Vine** (620A Gervais St., 803/799-8463, www.gervine.com, Mon.-Sat. 4:30pm-close, $8-10) specializes in Spanish-style tapas. An extensive vibrant menu of both hot and cold tapas awaits, including seared pork tenderloin with cucumber-melon salsa and lavender honey, and marinated manchego cheese with thyme and garlic.

## New Southern

A longtime favorite with locals, visitors, and the college crowd alike, the **Blue Marlin** (1200 Lincoln St., 803/799-3838, www.bluemarlincolumbia.com, lunch Mon.-Fri. 11:30am-2:30pm, dinner Mon.-Thurs. 5pm-10pm, Fri. 5pm-11pm, Sat. 4pm-11pm, Sun. 11:30am-9pm, $16-25) in the Vista is known for its mix of Lowcountry and New Orleans-style entrées, like the oyster and shrimp Bienville, seafood gumbo, and shrimp and grits. Each table gets a community-style bowl of collard greens.

## Vegetarian

The premier vegan and vegetarian spot in Columbia is **Blue Cactus Café** (2002 Greene St., 803/929-0782, Tues.-Fri. 11am-3pm and 5pm-9pm, Sat. noon-9pm, $7-10). While the veggie burrito is to die for, carnivores will be pleased at the various spicy meat dishes offered, especially in southwestern and Korean cuisine.

# ACCOMMODATIONS

Columbia has plenty of lodging but is somewhat underserved in terms of quality accommodations for travelers and businesspeople. This is slowly changing, however. These are the best picks close to major attractions.

## Under $150

Perhaps the most beloved stay in Columbia is the ★ **Inn at USC** (1619 Pendleton St., 866/455-4753, www.innatusc.com, $145), a real hidden gem right on campus. A particular emphasis is placed on a certain clubby collegiality. A plus is the complimentary cooked-to-order breakfast in the Palmetto Room.

The **Courtyard by Marriott Downtown at USC** (630 Assembly St., 803/799-7800, www.marriott.com, $120-125) puts you a short walk from several performing arts facilities, the State House, and the Vista. There's a small and somewhat windy rooftop pool.

There aren't many bed-and-breakfasts in Columbia—thanks to General Sherman, the stock of nostalgic old homes is small—but one well-regarded B&B is the **1425 Inn** (1425 Richland St., 803/252-7225, $130-150). Formerly the Richland Inn, this property has had a slight but tasteful makeover since a management change.

## $150-300

It's hard to beat the ★ **Hampton Inn Downtown** (822 Gervais St., 803/231-2000, www.hamptoninncolumbia.com, $159) for its combination of location and service. Right in the Vista and close by the State House, this property has the usual high standards associated with the Hampton brand, along with the usual price premium. The only problematic thing about this property is its continuing tight parking issue.

Housed in a former bakery building, the **Inn at Claussen's** (2003 Greene St., 803/765-0440, www.theinnatclaussens.com, $150-200) is the premier lodging in Five Points proper.

# INFORMATION AND SERVICES
## Visitors Centers

The main visitors center in the area is the **Columbia Regional Visitors Center** (1101 Lincoln St., 803/545-0000, Mon.-Fri. 8am-6pm, Sat. 10am-4pm, Sun. 1pm-5pm, www.columbiacvb.com), on the upper floor of the Columbia Metropolitan Convention Center in the Vista. The Lake Murray area has its own, the **Capital City/Lake Murray Country Visitors Center** (2184 North Lake Dr., Irmo, 800/725-3935, www.scjewel.com, Mon.-Fri. 9am-5pm, Sat. 10am-4pm, Sun. 1pm-5pm), northwest of town near the lake. The university runs an excellent visitors center as well, the **University of South Carolina Visitors Center** (816 Bull St., 803/777-0169, www.sc.edu/visitorcenter, Mon.-Fri. 8:30am-5pm, Sat. 11am-3pm) in the McKissick Museum. Visitor parking is available at the corner of Pendleton and Bull Streets.

## TRANSPORTATION
### Getting There
Columbia is served by **Columbia Metropolitan Airport** (CAE, 3000 Aviation Way, 803/822-5000, www.columbiaairport.com), southwest of town, which hosts American, Delta, and United.

If you're driving, three interstate highways—I-20, I-26, and I-77—intersect near the city. Signage is plentiful and accurate from all three.

**Amtrak** (850 Pulaski St., 803/252-8246 or 800/872-7245, www.amtrak.com) has a station downtown with daily New York-Miami *Silver Star* trains. There's a **Greyhound bus station** (2015 Gervais St., 803/256-6465, www.greyhound.com, daily 24 hours) downtown as well.

### Getting Around
The airport has numerous **car rental** kiosks, including Alamo, Avis, Budget, Hertz, and Thrifty. In town you'll find an abundance of Enterprise (www.enterprise.com) locations; several Hertz locations, including one downtown (508 Gervais St., 803/252-2561, www.hertz.com); and a Budget location downtown (408 Blossom St., 803/779-3707, www.budget.com).

The **Central Midlands Regional Transit Authority** (803/255-7100, www.gocmrta.com) is the city's public transportation system. Buses run throughout the area, including a full schedule of downtown routes. Single trips are $1.50, or you can purchase a 10-ride pass for $10.

# Outside Columbia

## ★ CONGAREE NATIONAL PARK
There's literally nothing like it on the planet. Set on a pristine tract of land close to Columbia's sprawl but seemingly a galaxy away, **Congaree National Park** (100 National Park Rd., 803/776-4396, www.nps.gov/cong, daily dawn-dusk, free) contains the most ancient stands of old-growth cypress left in the world. It is, quite simply, one of my favorite places. And like many truly great experiences, it's free.

Adjacent to the **Harry Hampton Visitor Center** (daily 8:30am-5pm), which has a great gift shop in addition to good educational exhibits, you'll embark on a system of elevated boardwalks and trails, 20 miles in total, that takes you into and through a good portion

of Congaree's 22,000 acres. A well-done self-guided tour brochure explains the fascinating aspects of this unique environment, almost unknown today.

You'll see cypresses towering over 130 feet into the air (Congaree is said to have the tallest forest canopy on earth, taller than the boreal forests of Canada and the Himalayas). At ground level you'll see hundreds of cypress "knees," parts of the trees' root systems that jut aboveground. You'll see unbelievably massive loblolly pines—a larger, immeasurably grander species than the sad slash pine tree farms that took over much of the South's available acreage with the arrival of the big paper plants in the 1930s.

You'll have the rare experience of seeing what an old-growth forest actually looks like

Congaree National Park

by Native Americans. The town's main drag, Broad Street, is actually on the route of the old Catawba trading path. Archaeologists now think the great and influential Creek town of Cofitachequi, which gained fame for its contact with Spanish explorer Hernando De Soto, was headquartered nearby. Most notably, it was the home of Mary Boykin Chesnut, famed Civil War diarist. Camden's resurgence came in the late 1800s, when it became home to a series of affluent Northerners who brought their wealth and their love of horses to town. To this day Camden is a major equestrian center, nicknamed the "Steeplechase Capital of the World."

and why it's so peaceful: Because the canopy shuts off so much light, there is almost no understory. You can walk among the great trees as if you were in a scene from *Lord of the Rings*. You'll view gorgeous Weston Lake, actually an oxbow lake that was once part of the Congaree River, isolated as the river changed course over time. You'll see—and much more often, hear—a wide range of wildlife, including owls, waterfowl, and several species of woodpecker, including the rare red-cockaded woodpecker.

You can kayak Cedar Creek, or take one of the free guided canoe tours every Saturday and Sunday, with canoes provided. And serious hikers will enjoy the expansive series of trails that go even deeper into the wilderness than the standard boardwalk loop (sorry pedal-pushers—no bikes are allowed on the trails or boardwalks).

## CAMDEN

Camden's attractive and practical geographic location on the Wateree River was recognized

### Historic Camden Revolutionary War Site

Unlike most historic battlefields in the state, the **Historic Camden Revolutionary War Site** (803/432-9841, www.historic-camden.net, Tues.-Sat. 10am-5pm, Sun. 2pm-5pm, free) commemorates a British victory. In this "Empire Strikes Back" scenario, American general Horatio Gates, hero of the Battle of Saratoga, and his combined force of Continental troops and untrained militia were defeated by a large British force from Charleston under the command of Lord Cornwallis, better known to history for surrendering to George Washington at Yorktown several years later. The 107-acre "outdoor museum" includes the townsite of Camden, the oldest inland city in South Carolina. One caveat: This is not the actual battle site, which is several miles away and largely uninterpreted. To get to the actual battlefield, go north from Historic Camden about seven miles on U.S. 521, then take a left onto Flat Rock Road. The marker commemorating the battle is about two miles on the right.

### Springdale Race Course

Northwest of town is the nearly 100-year-old **Springdale Race Course** (200 Knights Hill Rd., 803/432-6513), which also hosts the town's two biggest steeplechase events. At the entrance to the track, you'll find the **National Steeplechase Museum** (803/432-6513, www.nationalsteeplechase-museum.org, Sept.-May Wed.-Sat. 10am-4pm, other times by appointment, free), containing a well-managed and exhaustive collection of vintage photos, artifacts, trophies, racing colors, and archival records. Get to Springdale Race Course by taking U.S. 521 (Broad St.) north through Camden, and then turn left onto Knights Hill Road. The track is a little way up on the right.

### Food and Accommodations

The best-regarded eating spot in the Camden area is actually a short drive outside Camden in Boykin, a historic little hamlet just south of town on U.S. 521, past I-20. **The Mill Pond Steakhouse** (84 Boykin Mill Rd., 803/424-0261, www.themillpondsteakhouse.com, Tues.-Sat. 5pm-10pm, $20-40) serves awesome high-end, connoisseur-style steaks and Southern classics like crab cakes and shrimp and grits.

There are several great B&Bs in town, chief among them the outstanding **Bloomsbury Inn** (1707 Lyttleton St., 803/432-5858, www.bloomsburyinn.com, $150-180), widely rated one of the best in the United States. The 1849 property itself is of great historical importance as the onetime home of James and Mary Chesnut, he a Confederate general and she a famous wartime diarist.

# The Pee Dee

Named for the Pee Dee River running through it, this region in the extreme northeast of the state—always called "the Pee Dee," not just "Pee Dee"—is largely off the tourism radar. That's a shame, because it offers a particularly relaxing, rolling landscape and a plethora of charming small towns. Though Florence is by far the major city in the region—largely due to its location straddling the region's interstate highways—it has very little to offer. Where possible, stay off the beaten path to explore the region further.

### Cheraw Historic District

The beguiling little town of Cheraw on the Pee Dee River is my favorite place in the Pee Dee and one of the Palmetto State's great, but underrated, gems. How gemlike? To tour some of its historic buildings, you simply sign out the keys at the little visitors center. Only in South Carolina, folks. Primarily known today as the birthplace of jazz great Dizzy Gillespie, Cheraw—pronounced "chuh-RAW"—was actually one of the first settlements in the state, dating from the 1730s.

The **Cheraw Visitors Bureau** (221 Market St., 843/537-8425, www.cheraw.com,

Mon.-Fri. 9am-5pm) inside the chamber of commerce building puts out an excellent walking-tour map; call or stop by to get one. You can even make appointments to tour sites on the weekend, but make sure to call ahead.

A natural first stop is the place where Cheraw's favorite son grew up, the **Dizzy Gillespie Home Site Park** (300 block of Huger St., daily dawn-dusk, free). Get here by taking Huger Street a couple of blocks north of Market Street as you come into town. A particularly cool aspect of the park is the chrome fence along Huger Street, illustrating several bars from Gillespie's biggest hit, "Salt Peanuts." (No statue of Dizzy? No worries. There's a nice one a few blocks farther into town.) The premier event in Cheraw, as you'd expect, given its favorite son, is the **South Carolina Jazz Festival** (various venues, 843/537-8420, www.scjazzfestival.com, $20 per day), held each autumn.

### Carolina Sandhills National Wildlife Refuge

Established in 1939, **Carolina Sandhills NWR** (23734 U.S. 1, 843/335-8401, www.fws.gov/carolinasandhills, daily dawn-dusk, free)

is one of the last, best places to find the once-ubiquitous longleaf pine and wiregrass habitat, home of the endangered red-cockaded woodpecker. Several well-maintained hiking trails allow you to fully explore and observe this rare ecosystem, and a handful of lakes are available for fishing; a state fishing license (www.dnr.sc.gov) is required.

## Darlington Raceway

**Darlington Raceway** (1301 Harry Byrd Hwy./U.S. 52, 843/395-8499, www.darlingtonraceway.com, dates vary, $35-150) is the granddad of all NASCAR tracks, the first ever to host a major race. While it's not as plush as the ritzier raceways built to accommodate the sport's push to gentrify its ranks, this is still an impressive sight right on U.S. 52. Racing fans can celebrate the return of the NASCAR Cup Series Southern 500 to its customary slot on Labor Day weekend. If you're not in town that weekend, you can call ahead for tours (Mon.-Fri., $5 pp). Sharing a parking area is the **Darlington Raceway Stock Car Museum** (1301 Harry Byrd Hwy./U.S. 52, 843/395-8862, www.darlingtonraceway.com, Mon.-Fri. 10am-5pm, Sat. 10am-4pm, Sun. 11am-4pm, $5 adults, free under age 13).

## ★ Woods Bay State Natural Area

The best site associated with Florence is actually south of town in the country, near tiny Olanta but still conveniently close to I-95. **Woods Bay State Natural Area** (11020 Woods Bay Rd., 843/659-4445, www.south-carolinaparks.com, daily 9am-6pm, free) is one of the largest remaining Carolina bays, a unique and somewhat mysterious geological phenomenon. These elliptical depressions, scattered throughout the Carolinas and all oriented in a northwest-southeast direction, are typified by a cypress-tupelo bog environment. There's also a rich variety of flora and fauna, including the Cooper's hawk and southern twayblade orchid.

Although the signage is good, it can still be a little tricky getting here. The quickest route is I-95 exit 146, but if you're coming from Florence, take U.S. 52 (Irby St.) through the city and turn right onto U.S. 301 south of town. When you get to Olanta, start looking for the brown signs for Woods Bay. To get back on I-95, take a left onto Woods Bay Road and continue on to little Shiloh. I-95 is a short distance away.

Cheraw is the birthplace of the great jazz artist Dizzy Gillespie.

# SOUTH OF THE BORDER

As you're traveling along I-95, you'll inevitably notice billboards with a stereotyped Mexican named Pedro with a penchant for puns exhorting people to visit **South of the Border** (I-95 and U.S. 301/501, 843/774-2411, www.thesouthoftheborder.com, daily 24 hours, free). Begun in 1950 by Al Schafer as a beer stand servicing a dry North Carolina county just across the state line—"south of the border"—the entertainment empire near Dillon gradually grew to encompass motels, restaurants (Mexican and otherwise), gas stations, RV campgrounds, fireworks stands, sprawling gift shops, and even an adult entertainment store, the Dirty Old Man's Shop. At one point, South of the Border, which covers nearly 150 acres, had its own police and fire departments.

In 1997, the racist content of the billboards was watered down, and employees stopped wearing "Pedro" name tags. Today, a more evolved world and vastly increased entertainment options mean that South of the Border is a ghost town. The main landmark is the 75-foot sombrero-clad Pedro himself, between whose massive legs you can drive your car.

# TRANSPORTATION

## Air

The airport serving the Pee Dee is **Florence Regional Airport** (FLO, 2100 Terminal Dr., 843/669-5001, www.florencescairport.com), which hosts American Airlines. However, most travelers drive to the Pee Dee or arrive at larger airports in the region such as Greenville, Charleston, or Charlotte.

## Car

Interstate highways I-95 and I-20 intersect in the Pee Dee, and they are by far the dominant arteries. Other major highways include U.S. 1 from Camden to Cheraw; U.S. 301, which largely parallels I-95 to the east; and U.S. 52 from Cheraw through Darlington to Florence.

Florence Regional Airport has several **car rental** kiosks, including Hertz, Budget, and Avis. There's an Enterprise location (213 S. Coit St., 843/317-6857) downtown. Hartsville has a couple of locations, including Hertz (1 N. 2nd St., 843/662-7930) and Enterprise (826 N. 5th St., 843/857-9088).

## Train

Two cities in the Pee Dee have **Amtrak** (www.amtrak.com) passenger train stations with daily New York City-Miami *Silver Meteor* trains: Florence (807 E. Day St.) and Dillon (100 N. Railroad Ave.), near the North Carolina border.

## Bus

**Greyhound** (www.greyhound.com) has bus stations in Florence (611 S. Irby St., 843/662-8407) and in Sumter (129 S. Harvin St., 803/775-3849).

# The Santee Cooper Region

As primordial as Lakes Marion and Moultrie seem to be, they're actually artificial. Both are by-products of a New Deal-era hydroelectric project under the auspices of the Santee Cooper Authority, named after the two rivers impounded to form the lakes. One of the largest public works projects in history, the Santee Cooper project was so expansive that eventually the entire region would be known by the same name; the area's chief utility company also goes by that moniker. World War II interrupted the clearing of Lake Marion—hence all those gnarled cypress trees still poking above the waves to this day. Somewhere under its waters, in fact, is Pond Bluff, the old homestead of "the Swamp Fox," Francis Marion himself.

## ★ Edisto Memorial Gardens

By far the main attraction in Orangeburg is **Edisto Memorial Gardens** (200 Riverside Dr., 800/545-6153, www.orangeburg.sc.us/gardens, daily dawn-dusk, free). The "memorial" aspect is because they're dedicated to the memory of local veterans who died in both world wars. But other than the nice sculpture at the entrance, there is little else remotely military about this wonderful free venue right next to Orangeburg's downtown.

As a nod to the city's popular annual Festival of Roses, the keynotes are the vast fields of heirloom roses in a dazzling variety of colors, which you'll be able to see approximately April-November, with May being the best month. You can't pick the roses, but you can just about get lost wandering among the rows. A scenic duck pond provides a relaxing backdrop. The site takes on added brilliance—literally—in November and December, as Christmas-themed light displays occupy seemingly every corner of the gardens.

The biggest event of the year is the **Festival of Roses** (803/534-6821, www.festivalofroses.com, free), held, fittingly, the weekend before

Mother's Day. About 30,000 people attend this weekend-long event, which culminates in a Parade of Roses downtown, with a special float carrying the Queen of Roses.

Food in Orangeburg largely begins and ends with ★ **Duke's Barbecue,** the legacy of the legendary Earl Duke. There are two locations, one uptown (789 Chestnut St., 803/534-9418, call for hours, $8) and one downtown (1298 Whitman St., 803/534-2916, call for hours, $8). Connoisseurs of 'cue clearly prefer the original, more Spartan spot on Whitman Street downtown, commonly referred to around town as "the one by the Pepsi plant." In both cases, you get freshly cooked pulled pork served all-you-can-eat buffet-style with a local version of the indigenous mustard-based sauce, plenty of sweet tea, and loaves of Sunbeam white bread on the tables. Both locations serve what could be the finest examples of the traditional South Carolina side called hash, a pork-based stew. Duke's hours vary; call ahead to make sure they're open.

## LAKES MARION AND MOULTRIE

Wild-looking Lake Marion on the Santee River, known for its plethora of striped bass, is the larger of the two lakes, covering over 100,000 acres. To the south, more manicured Lake Moultrie on the Cooper River covers about 60,000 acres and is known for its massive catfish; blue cats over 40 pounds are not uncommon, and some over 50 pounds have been caught. There are numerous marinas, public landings, and fish camps around the circumference of both lakes.

### Santee National Wildlife Refuge

Located an easy jaunt off I-95, **Santee NWR** (2125 Fort Watson Rd., 803/478-2217, www.fws.gov/santee, daily dawn-dusk, free)

Lake Marion in the Santee National Wildlife Refuge

actually comprises several federally run locations on the eastern shore of Lake Marion. The well-done **visitors center** (Tues.-Fri. 8am-4pm, 1st, 2nd, and 3rd Sat. of the month 8am-4pm) is at the main Bluff Unit of the refuge, with a nice overlook of the lake and an easy walk down to the sandy shore. A very short drive away is the site of Fort Watson, built by the British on a 3,000-year-old Indian mound. Francis Marion caused the British surrender of Fort Watson in 1781. Each October sees a Revolutionary War encampment at the site in honor of the victory.

Bird-watchers will enjoy the rich variety of migratory ducks, geese, and swans that make their way to Santee NWR November-February.

## Pinopolis Dam

The tallest single-step lock in North America and the second tallest in the world, the Pinopolis Dam at the south end of Lake Moultrie separates the impounded lake from the Cooper River. If you're in a boat or kayak, it's a whopping 75-foot, half-hour drop from the lake to the 1940s-era Tailrace Canal, a short trip on which takes you to the river. For a guided kayak tour that includes a jaunt through the lock, contact **Blackwater Adventures** (843/761-1850, www.blackwateradventure.com, about $50).

## Francis Beidler Forest

The **Francis Beidler Forest** (336 Sanctuary Rd., Harleyville, 843/462-2150, www. sc.audubon.org, Tues.-Sun. 9am-5pm, $8 adults, $4 ages 6-18, free under age 6) is jointly owned by The Nature Conservancy and the Audubon Society. It conserves a rare and special 15,000-acre habitat in the blackwater Four Holes Swamp. An 1,800-acre section of the forest contains some of the largest and most ancient old-growth stands of bald cypress and tupelo trees in the world.

To get here from Charleston, take I-26 west out of town to exit 187. Make a left onto Highway 27 south to U.S. 78, where you turn right. Veer right on U.S. 178, and then take a right on Francis Beidler Forest Road. To get to the visitors center, veer right onto Mims Road after a few miles.

## Recreation

A good way for the casual traveler to enjoy the lakes is at **Santee State Park** (251 State Park Rd., 803/854-2408, www.southcarolinaparks.com, daily 6am-10pm, $2 adults, free under age 16) on Lake Marion near the town of Santee. A nature-based boat tour of the lake (Wed. and Fri.-Sun., call for times) run by **Fish Eagle Tours** (803/854-4005) departs from the Tackle Shop. The park also has two boat ramps.

All fishing on the lakes for those over age 16 requires a valid South Carolina fishing license, available at any tackle shop, online (www.dnr.sc.gov), or by phone (888/434-7472). A seven-day nonresident license is $11. A total of 40 game fish can be kept any one day, with no more than 10 black bass, 5 striped bass, and only 1 catfish over 36 inches long.

There are three golf courses of note on Lake Marion around the town of Santee: **Santee Cooper Country Club** (630 Santee Dr., 803/854-2467, www.santeecoopergolf.com, $30-60), the area's first; **Lake Marion Golf Course** (9069 Old Hwy. 6, 803/854-2554, www.santeecoopergolf.com, $27-51), built in 1979; and **Santee National Golf Club** (8638 Old Hwy. 6, 803/854-3531, www.santeenational.com, $40-60). **Wyboo Golf Club** (1 Warrens Way, 803/478-7899, www.wyboogolfclub.com, $40-50), a Tom Jackson design near Manning (take I-95 exit 119), is consistently rated one of the top 10 public courses in South Carolina. There are tons of golf packages available in the area; call the Santee Cooper Country Commission (800/227-8510) for more info.

### Food

Any discussion of great food in South Carolina must include ★ **Sweatman's Bar-b-que** (1313 Gemini Dr., 803/492-7543, Fri.-Sat. 11:30am-9:30pm, $8-15), outside the town of Holly Hill on the western side of the lakes. People drive two or three hours, literally from the other side of the state, just to eat here on a weekend. While a certain amount of this popularity is driven by the media's trendy fondness for "authentic" Americana—Sweatman's proudly displays signed items by TV gourmand Anthony Bourdain—there's no doubt that this is a special kind of place, if a humble one.

They cook their pork the old-fashioned way: the proverbial whole hog, slow-cooked over wood in a blockhouse out back. The result is served buffet-style, in two types: the dry white portion, the "inside meat," and the glazed outer portion, "the outside meat." Don't miss the "cracklin's," crunchy fried pigskin.

Sweatman's closes for most of August. To get here, take I-95 exit 90 and then head east on U.S. 176, which becomes Main Street in Holly Hill. Turn left onto Highway 453 and head north for a few miles, and Sweatman's is on the right. When in Holly Hill looking for the turn, keep in mind that Highway 453 is not contiguous through town. You're looking for the spur of Highway 453 that begins on the west side of the railroad tracks.

Sweatman's has only one serious competitor in the area, and that's ★ **McCabe's Bar-B-Que** (480 N. Brooks St., 803/435-2833, Thurs.-Sat. 5:30pm-9pm, $10) on the eastern side of Lake Marion in the town of Manning. The pork is finely pulled, and the sauce is the tangy, kicky Pee Dee-style pepper-and-vinegar variety. Served with that distinctive hash side dish and sliced tomatoes, this plate is often considered the equal of Sweatman's.

## MONCKS CORNER

The town of Moncks Corner, seat of Berkeley County, is at the southern tip of Lake Moultrie at the headwaters of the Cooper River; it is a gateway of sorts to the greater Charleston area.

### Mepkin Abbey

The burg of Moncks Corner is actually named for a person, not a vocation, but nonetheless that's where you'll find a fully active, practicing Trappist monastery, **Mepkin Abbey** (1098 Mepkin Abbey Rd., 843/761-8509, www.mepkinabbey.org, Tues.-Fri. 9am-4:30pm, Sat. 9am-4pm, Sun. 1pm-4pm, free), notable for the fact that it's not only open to visitors but welcomes them.

The beautiful abbey and grounds on the Cooper River are on what was once the plantation of great Carolina statesman Henry Laurens, whose ashes are buried here, and later the home of the famous publisher Henry Luce and his wife, Clare Boothe Luce. The focal point of natural beauty is the Luce-commissioned **Mepkin Abbey Botanical Garden** (Tues.-Sun.), a 3,200-acre tract with a camellia garden designed by noted landscape architect Loutrel Briggs, a native New Yorker who made Charleston his adopted home.

When they're not in prayer, the monks generally observe silence. In accordance with the emphasis the order puts on the spiritual value of manual labor, farming is the main physical occupation, with the monks' efforts producing eggs, honey, preserves, soap, and even compost from the gardens, all of which you can purchase in the abbey gift shop in the reception center, which will always be your first stop. Tours of the abbey itself are usually given Tuesday-Sunday 11:30am and 3pm.

## INFORMATION AND SERVICES

The centrally located visitors center for Santee Cooper is the **Santee Cooper Country Visitor Information Center** (9302 Old Hwy. 6, Santee, 803/854-2131, www.santeecoopercountry.org) in the town of Santee, right off I-95.

## TRANSPORTATION

I-95 goes directly through Santee Cooper, making it one of the more accessible parts of South Carolina. U.S. 301 is another key route, cutting through the region and serving Orangeburg before briefly joining I-95 and crossing Lake Marion to Manning. U.S. 17 is the main road to Moncks Corner.

A car is a must in Santee Cooper, unless you're planning on simply boating to the lakes from the Intracoastal Waterway, which is theoretically possible. Rental cars are available in Orangeburg from **Enterprise** (1624 Saint Matthews Rd., 803/534-0143, www.enterprise.com) and **Hertz** (907 Chestnut St., 803/534-0447, www.hertz.com).

# Aiken

There are towns with horses, and then there are horse towns. Aiken is the latter. How can you tell the difference? Let's put it this way: Horses have the right of way over cars within Aiken city limits. Indeed, roads in Aiken's Horse District are intentionally kept unpaved so as not to cause stress to tender equine hooves. Several Kentucky Derby winners have Aiken roots, including Pleasant Colony (1981), Swale (1984), and Sea Hero (1993). Visitors can enjoy the clean retro-tinged downtown area, with its wide attractive streets and its very good selection of cafés, restaurants, and stores, a clear cut above most South Carolina towns its size.

## SIGHTS

Aiken manages a good mix of horse-related attractions and those having nothing to do with our fast four-legged friends. The majority of attractions in town, whether horsey or not, make the most of Aiken's easygoing natural beauty and optimistic all-American atmosphere.

## ★ Winter Colony

The old homes of the wealthy Northerners who really put Aiken on the map are almost all privately owned. But a drive or a walk through the **Winter Colony Historic Districts** (www.nationalregister.sc.gov), which are three nationally recognized areas, will give you a good idea not only of their wealth but of their taste as well. Major sectors include the area just west of the intersection of Richland Avenue and Laurens Street; Highland Park Drive near the railroad tracks; the Hitchcock Woods-Hopelands-Rye Patch area off Whiskey Road, south of downtown; and the matchless oak-lined canopy along Boundary Street. Key estates—all private—in the Winter Colony include **Let's Pretend,**

# Aiken

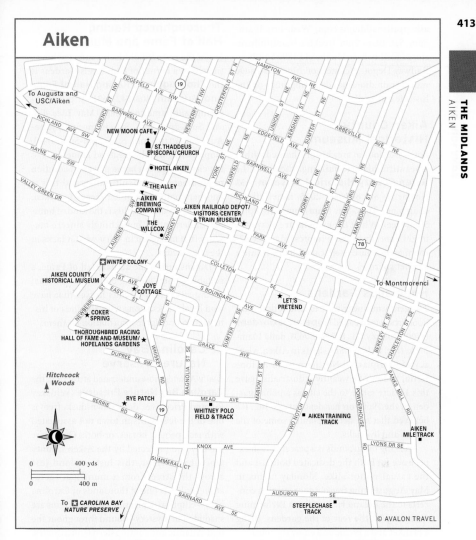

© AVALON TRAVEL

**Joye Cottage,** and **Sandhurst.** The best way to tour the historic areas of Aiken, including the Winter Colony, is to join the city's tour (803/642-7631, www.cityofaikensc.gov, Sat. 10am, $15) leaving from the Visitors Center and Train Museum (406 Park Ave.) downtown.

You'll often hear the phrase **Horse District** in Aiken. This is actually an informal name for the residential area within the Winter Colony near two vintage racetracks,

the Aiken Mile Track (Banks Mill Rd.) and the Aiken Training Track (538 Two Notch Rd.). Keep in mind that during the warmer months there are precious few horses to see—most will be racing or training up north (this is, after all, a *winter* colony).

## Aiken Railroad Depot

The Aiken Railroad Depot, also called the **Visitors Center and Train Museum** (406 Park Ave., 803/293-7846, www.

aikenrailroaddepot.com, Wed.-Fri. 10am-5pm, Sat. 10am-2pm, free) is a beautifully restored facility based in the old 1899 Southern Railway Depot. It centers on nine HO-gauge model train dioramas depicting stops on the historic railroad.

## Aiken County Historical Museum

For a good look at area history, housed within a beautiful historic building, check out the **Aiken County Historical Museum** (433 Newberry St., 803/642-2015, http://aiken-county.net, Tues.-Sat. 10am-5pm, Sun. 2pm-5pm, free). While the exhibits are okay, you might honestly be more impressed by the 32-room great house itself, called Banksia (after a variety of rose).

## Hopelands Gardens

The gently meandering, exquisitely done outdoor arboretum called **Hopelands Gardens** (1700 Whiskey Rd., 803/642-7631, daily 10am-dusk, free) is, like many sights in Aiken, a legacy of transplanted Northern wealth. Hope Iselin, widow of a wealthy industrialist, gave this 14-acre estate to the city as a public garden in the 1960s on her death at age 102. It's believed that she herself planted some of the cedars and live oaks.

Walking the grounds is a peaceful, lush experience for both the dedicated botanist and the casual visitor alike. Monday nights in May-August bring free outdoor evening concerts to the Roland H. Windham Performing Arts Stage at the rear of the gardens. Bring a blanket and a picnic and enjoy the music.

Also on the grounds is the Dollhouse, once a playhouse and erstwhile schoolroom of the Iselin kids. Actually an old Sears Roebuck catalog house, today the Dollhouse hosts the Aiken Garden Club Council. It's open to the public every Sunday 2pm-5pm, and during the Christmas season it is decorated in fine holiday fashion.

To get here from downtown, just head south on Chesterfield Street, which shortly turns into Whiskey Road.

## Thoroughbred Racing Hall of Fame and Museum

Set in the restored old Iselin carriage house (natch) in a corner of Hopelands Gardens is the **Thoroughbred Racing Hall of Fame and Museum** (803/642-7631, http://aiken-racinghalloffame.com, Sept.-May Tues.-Fri. and Sun. 2pm-5pm, Sat. 10am-5pm, June-Aug. Sat. 10am-5pm, Sun. 2pm-5pm, free). Hope Iselin, who bequeathed Hopelands to the city, was quite a horse maven in addition to an amateur horticulturalist, and this is another component of her legacy to Aiken. Staffed by volunteers, this is the kind of humble, underfunded, but achingly sincere museum that makes up in spirit what it lacks in the wow factor.

Downstairs is the actual Hall of Fame, a suitably clubby-looking collection of actual racing silks from famous horses that have trod local tracks, along with all kinds of historical and pedigree information on them.

## ★ Carolina Bay Nature Preserve

Easily Aiken's most underrated attraction, the **Carolina Bay Nature Preserve** (Whiskey Rd. and Price Ave., daily dawn-dusk, free) is one of the few sights in town not associated with rich people, horses, or both. Owned by the city and protected by the Aiken County Open Land Trust, this lush wetland just across the street from a municipal recreation facility is one of thousands of Carolina bays—elliptical depressions whose origins are shrouded in mystery—found throughout the mid-Atlantic and southeastern United States.

Like most Carolina bays, Aiken's is far from pristine, having been farmed for many years. But this particular specimen is a great example of a restored Carolina bay, with some indigenous flora reintroduced, including a wildflower meadow. A discreet system of pumps keeps it full of water and conversely keeps it from overflowing and flooding the surrounding development. More and more birds are visiting the bay as the years go by. A trail takes you around the circumference of

Carolina Bay Nature Preserve

the bay, and the scenery is beautiful at each point; you can even fish.

To get here, take Whiskey Road well south of Hopelands Gardens until you get to Price Avenue, where you turn east; the preserve parking area is shortly ahead on the left.

## Hitchcock Woods

Once the fox-hunting grounds of Thomas Hitchcock, New Yorker and avid sportsman, **Hitchcock Woods** (South Boundary Rd. and Whiskey Rd., 803/642-0528, www.hitchcockwoods.org, daily dawn-dusk, free) is now considered the largest urban forest preserve in the country at a whopping 2,000 acres. It's a great place to hike and stroll, though oddly—given that any number of horse-related activities is allowed—no bicycling is allowed. There are seven main entrances, each with a kiosk that has maps to the woods; or go to the website for a printable, delightfully *Lord of the Rings*-like map. The closest entrance to downtown is on South Boundary Road west of Laurens

Street. Another is on Coker Spring Road just west of the spring.

## Tours

The key tour in Aiken is provided by the city (803/642-7631, www.visitaikensc.com, Sat. 10am, $15), leaving from the Visitors Center and Train Museum (406 Park Ave.) downtown. Lasting about two hours, it takes you by trolley to all significant areas of town, including through the Winter Colony, with a stop for a walk through Hopelands Gardens. Call for reservations or information.

## SHOPPING

There are at least half a dozen antiques shops downtown, many with Sunday hours—a nice change from a lot of sleepy South Carolina towns. The most notable examples are **Aiken Antique Mall** (112 Laurens St., 803/648-6700, Mon.-Sat. 10am-6pm, Sun. 1:30pm-6pm), **Aiken Antiques and Auction** (1060A Park Ave., 803/642-0107, Mon.-Sat. 9am-6pm, Sun. 1:30pm-6pm), and **Swan Antique Mall**

# High Cotton and Hot Steam

The big cotton boom of the early 1800s in South Carolina created a demand for a quick way to get the cash crop to market in Charleston, then hotly competing with Savannah, Georgia, for the title of nation's leading cotton export center. That's how South Carolina became home to the first steam rail system in the world, an incredibly little-known fact today.

In 1827, the South Carolina Canal and Rail Road Company was chartered to build a line that would expedite trade from the Upcountry. The resulting 137-mile Charleston-Hamburg line, begun in 1833, was at the time the longest railroad in the world. By 1858 the line was joined with tracks going all the way to Memphis, Tennessee.

However, competing railroads—such as subsequent tracks to Greenville and Augusta—kept profit margins on the Charleston-Hamburg line so low that further expansion was not feasible. With the rise of Augusta and then Atlanta as major rail centers, the line gradually became a backwater run. While the original line stayed in some form of service until the 1980s, its glory days were far in the past.

Today, U.S. 78 roughly follows the old railbed through towns like Aiken, Blackville, Williston, and, of course, tiny Branchville, which became the world's first rail junction when a spur to Columbia was built off the Charleston-Hamburg line.

(321 Richland Ave., 803/643-9922, Mon.-Sat. 10am-5:30pm, Sun. 1pm-5pm). **The Iron Pony** (210 York St., 803/642-5004, Wed.-Sat. 11am-5pm) is set in an antebellum home.

If you like paintings of horses, boy, are you in luck. **Equine Divine** (135 Laurens St., 803/642-9772, www.equinedivineonline. com, Mon.-Sat. 10am-5pm) deals in plenty of equestrian-related artwork and doodads, and it even stays open an hour later during polo season. **Jackson Gallery** (300 Park Ave., 803/648-7397, by appointment) features high-end horse sculpture.

## FOOD

Good dining options are scattered throughout the central downtown area, with several in "The Alley," a short lane off Laurens Street.

### American

The **Aiken Brewing Company** (140 Laurens St., 803/502-0707, www.aikenbrewingcompany.com, Mon.-Sat. 11am-2am, $10) is a popular restaurant and microbrewery at the entrance to The Alley. While it is best known for its surprisingly wide selection of hand-crafted brews, it also offers above-average bar food, such as quesadillas and beer-battered (of course) chicken tenders and wings.

### Coffee and Treats

For a cup of joe, some hipster attitude, and a light wrap, sandwich, or sweet treat, go to ★ **New Moon Cafe** (116 Laurens St., 803/643-7088, http://newmoondowntown. com, Mon.-Fri. 8am-5pm, Sat.-Sun. 9am-2pm, $5), certainly the closest thing to an alternative place in this preppy town, although note the weird hours.

## ACCOMMODATIONS

The most important thing to remember about staying in Aiken is that all lodging is at a premium during the week of the Masters golf tournament, held each year in early April in nearby Augusta, Georgia.

### Under $150

For an interesting and remarkably inexpensive stay right downtown, try the **Hotel Aiken** (235 Richland Ave., 803/648-4265, www.hotelaiken.com, $65-100), a historic property built in 1898 at the height of the Winter Colony's glory. Renovated in 2001, it still retains a certain well-worn patina. However, this isn't where to go for peace and quiet: The hotel's two attached bars, the clubby **Polo Tavern** and the ritzy **One Hundred Laurens,** are centers of downtown nightlife. In fact, things

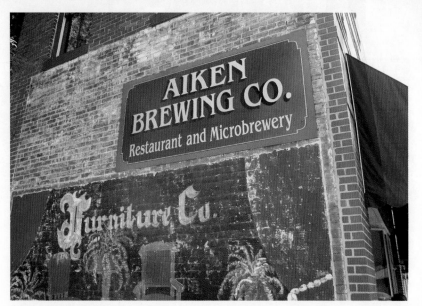

the Aiken Brewing Company

get so noisy that the guest rooms directly over the bar area are discounted.

## $150-300

For a truly grand historic hotel experience downtown, try ★ **The Willcox** (100 Colleton Ave., 877/648-2200, www.thewillcox.com, $185-425), which once hosted Franklin D. Roosevelt as well as a throng of well-heeled visitors during Aiken's Winter Colony glory days.

## INFORMATION AND SERVICES

The main **Aiken Visitors Center** (113 Laurens St., 803/642-7557, www.aikenis.com) is inside the historic Holley Building. The **Visitors Center and Train Museum** (406 Park Ave., 803/293-7846, www.aikenrailroaddepot.com) also features good visitor info.

## TRANSPORTATION

Aiken is very accessible either from I-20 just to the north or directly from Augusta, Georgia, via U.S. 78, which is called Jefferson Davis Highway in Augusta and becomes Richland Avenue in downtown Aiken.

The closest airport to Aiken is the small **Augusta Regional Airport** (AGS, 1501 Aviation Way, 706/798-3236, www.flyags. com) in Georgia, hosting carriers Delta Connection and American Eagle. Indeed, when in Aiken it's important to remember that much larger Augusta is a short drive away and is for all intents and purposes considered a part of the local economy.

In Aiken, there's a **Greyhound bus station** (153 Pendleton St., 803/648-6894, www.greyhound.com).

# Greenville and the Upstate

C onservative in culture and world-view, the Upstate—you'll also hear it called the Upcountry—is the fastest-growing region of South Carolina.

As such, it's becoming much more diverse each passing year, but the area's hospitality and small-town values remain largely intact. You don't read about it much in the history books, but the Upstate was the most pivotal theater of the American Revolution, in which groups of Upcountry militia and Loyalist Tories savagely battled back and forth while the uniformed regular armies in New England were at a stalemate.

By far the region's main metro area, Greenville is rapidly outpacing its reputation for conservatism. It does so through a devotion to smart urban redevelopment and a forward-looking business sense that has allowed it to move beyond the old mill-based economy that long ago moved offshore.

In the northernmost part of the state, along the fringes of the Blue Ridge Mountains, you'll find stunning natural beauty and plenty of outdoor recreation, all at prices much lower than in the heavily visited havens across the border in trendier North Carolina.

## PLANNING YOUR TIME

You can spend as much or as little time in the Upstate as you want. For the full flavor, you'll need at least three days and two nights. Remember to budget time to explore Greenville's Main Street. For a more focused stay—say, one devoted to hiking or fishing along the Cherokee Foothills Scenic Highway (Hwy. 11)—a couple of nights, or perhaps even one, will do.

**Previous:** riding horses in the Upstate; Falls Park on the Reedy. **Above:** Trinity Church in downtown Greenville.

Look for ★ to find recommended
sights, activities, dining, and lodging.

# Highlights

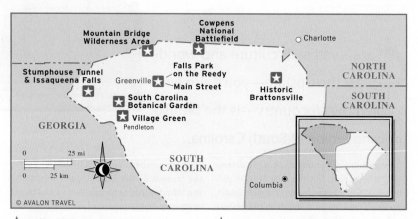

★ **Falls Park on the Reedy:** This rolling green oasis is in excellently restored downtown Greenville (page 421).

★ **Greenville's Main Street:** A nationally renowned example of walkable urban redesign (page 421).

★ **Cowpens National Battlefield:** This interpretive site commemorates a key Patriot victory in the American Revolution (page 432).

★ **Stumphouse Tunnel and Issaqueena Falls:** This fun twofer features a tunnel with a unique history and a scenic waterfall (page 436).

★ **Mountain Bridge Wilderness Area:** The wildest area of the Upstate combines Jones Gap State Park with Caesars Head State Park (page 438).

★ **South Carolina Botanical Garden:** The state's official gardens are on the scenic campus of Clemson University (page 440).

★ **Pendleton Village Green:** This historic hamlet has a delightful central square (page 442).

★ **Historic Brattonsville:** Living history and educational fun for the whole family can be found at this restored Upcountry village (page 444).

# Greenville

Greenville, South Carolina, might be the coolest city you've never heard of. It's a source of frustration to Greenville residents that so few of their fellow Americans—heck, even their fellow South Carolinians—are aware of the city's modern renaissance. Greenville has its fair share of well-scrubbed block-long megachurches, but the only crusade most residents of Greenville seem to be on is spreading the word that their city—inevitably pronounced in the local foothills twang as "GRUHN-vul"—is actually a rapidly growing and increasingly wealthy city nestled in the scenic foothills of the Appalachians.

Like much of the Upstate, modern-day Greenville is located on what used to be the heart of the Cherokee Nation. The first white settler of note was Richard Pearis, who began a plantation around 1770 in what's now downtown Greenville at East Court and South Main Streets.

By the turn of the 20th century, Greenville began promoting itself as the "Textile Center of the South." After World War II, that slogan was expanded to "Textile Center of the World." In the 1960s, however, as farsighted community and business leaders foresaw the coming decline of the U.S. textile industry, Greenville began pursuing a more diversified economy, concentrating on increasing foreign investment.

## SIGHTS
### ★ Falls Park on the Reedy

In a fun quirk of fate, Greenville's most historic spot, the place it began, is also its coolest visitor attraction. **Falls Park on the Reedy** (864/232-2273, www.greatergreenville.com, daily dawn-dusk, free), a rambling, manicured, eclectic outdoor experience along the Reedy River, is where Richard Pearis, the area's first nonnative settler, set up his trading post and gristmill in 1768 on what was then Cherokee land. The scenic **Reedy River Falls**

powered Pearis's mill and helped spawn the city you see today. While the Pearis mill is long gone, you can still see some ruins of the later Vardry and McBee mills from the early 1800s on the riverbank.

You can keep up with the historical events that happened here through a series of markers, but Falls Park is more of an all-around pedestrian experience. Walk the 355-foot **Liberty Bridge**—the only curved pedestrian suspension bridge in the country—over the Reedy River Falls, and see the nearby **Falls Cottage,** built by George Dryer in 1840.

### ★ Greenville's Main Street

To get the true feel of Greenville's revitalization, take a leisurely walk down historic **Main Street,** which in a nice reversal of the usual situation was actually narrowed from four lanes to the current cozy two. The renovated area—one of the most well-done I've seen in the country—runs roughly from the Hyatt Regency Hotel slightly downhill to the newest restored area, the West End. In between are quality stores, cafés, and restaurants of all descriptions, all under a particularly well-crafted and shady tree canopy.

### Shoeless Joe Jackson Museum

With memorabilia from the life and career of Greenville's favorite native son, the **Shoeless Joe Jackson Museum** (356 Field St., 864/235-6280, www.shoelessjoejackson. org, Sat. 10am-4pm and Greenville Drive home game nights, free) suitably sits adjacent to the Fluor Field minor-league ballpark in the historic West End. The house, formerly the home of Joe and his family, was moved to this site from 119 East Wilborn Street, and it houses a variety of photos and artifacts, all in a cozy, loving setting. Parking next to the museum is free except on Greenville Drive game days.

# Greenville and the Upstate

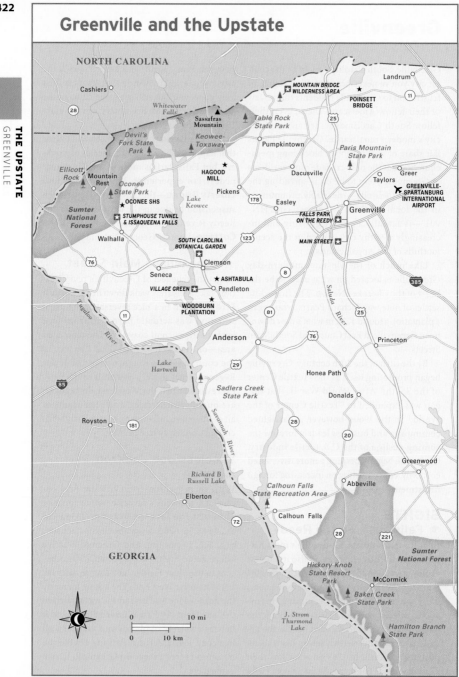

NORTH CAROLINA

Cashiers

28

Whitewater Falls

Devil's Fork State Park

Ellicott Rock

Mountain Rest

Oconee State Park

OCONEE SHS

STUMPHOUSE TUNNEL & ISSAQUEENA FALLS

Sumter National Forest

Walhalla

76

Seneca

VILLAGE GREEN

11

Tugaloo River

85

Royston

181

Lake Hartwell

GEORGIA

Richard B Russell Lake

Elberton

72

Sassafras Mountain

Keowee-Toxaway

HAGOOD MILL

Lake Keowee

Pickens

178

SOUTH CAROLINA BOTANICAL GARDEN

Clemson

ASHTABULA

Pendleton

WOODBURN PLANTATION

81

Anderson

29

Sadlers Creek State Park

28

Savannah River

Calhoun Falls State Recreation Area

Calhoun Falls

MOUNTAIN BRIDGE WILDERNESS AREA

Table Rock State Park

Pumpkintown

Dacusville

Easley

123

8

76

Honea Path

Donalds

20

Landrum

11

POINSETT BRIDGE

25

Paris Mountain State Park

Taylors

Greer

GREENVILLE-SPARTANBURG INTERNATIONAL AIRPORT

FALLS PARK ON THE REEDY

Greenville

MAIN STREET

385

25

Princeton

Greenwood

Abbeville

221

Sumter National Forest

McCormick

Hickory Knob State Resort Park

Baker Creek State Park

J. Strom Thurmond Lake

Hamilton Branch State Park

Saluda River

0     10 mi

0     10 km

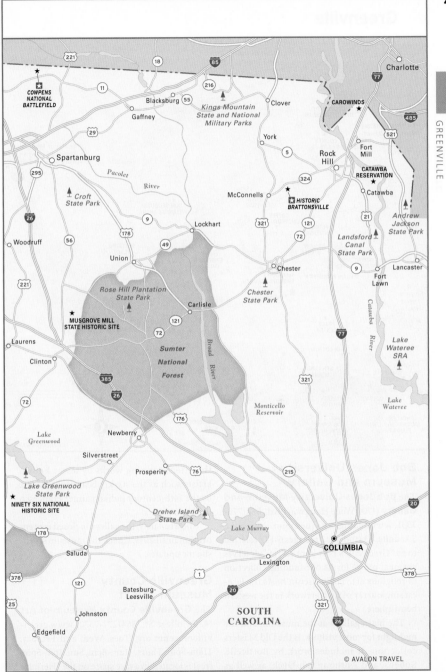

© AVALON TRAVEL

# Greenville

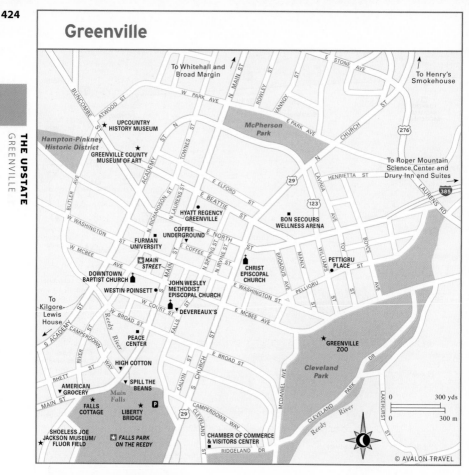

© AVALON TRAVEL

## Bob Jones University Museum and Gallery

The **Bob Jones University Museum and Gallery** (1700 Wade Hampton Blvd., 864/770-1331, www.bjumg.org, Tues.-Sun. 2pm-5pm, $5 adults, $3 students, free ages 6-12), referred to as "Greenville's best-kept secret," deserves national praise for its outstanding collection of religious art. The museum hosts the largest single array of such artwork in the western hemisphere.

The main gallery at the museum, and the highlight for most visitors, is the Old Masters collection. It includes work by Botticelli, Rubens, and Anthony van Dyck, as well as the often stunning works by lesser-known artists such as the starkly beautiful *Crucifix* by the 14th-century Italian painter Francesco di Vannuccio.

Unfortunately, the gallery is closed for renovation until 2019. Check the museum's website for updates.

## Greenville County Museum of Art

The **Greenville County Museum of Art** (420 College St., 864/271-7570, www.greenvillemuseum.org, Tues.-Wed. and Fri.-Sat. 11am-5pm, Thurs. 11am-8pm, Sun. 1pm-5pm, free) is located in a nice space on the "Heritage

downtown Greenville

# Paris Mountain State Park

My favorite park in the Greenville area, and one of South Carolina's coolest state parks (and that's saying a lot), is **Paris Mountain State Park** (2401 State Park Rd., 864/244-5565, www.southcarolinaparks.com, daily 8am-sunset, $2 adults, free under age 16). This is yet another of the state parks built by the Civilian Conservation Corps in the mid-1930s, with many of the sturdily built, evocative structures typical of that effort. To get to Paris Mountain State Park, take the North Pleasantburg Drive/Highway 291 exit from I-385. Go north on Piney Mountain Road, take a right onto State Park Road, and continue to the park entrance.

# TOURS

Carriage rides downtown are available from **Whispering Winds Carriage Co.** (864/220-3650, www.downtowncarriage.com, Fri.-Sat. 6pm-11pm, adults $15, under five $5). They last about half an hour and depart from the Westin Poinsett and Courtyard Marriott.

For more detailed guided tours, check out **Greenville History Tours** (864/567-3940, www.greenvillehistorytours.com, $12, culinary tour $39), which offers several options.

# ENTERTAINMENT AND EVENTS

Since the closure of longtime local favorite The Handlebar, the local live music scene has been hurting. Trying to pick up the slack is **The Radio Room** (2845 N. Pleasantburg Dr., 864/263-7868, www.wpbrradioroom.com), an excellent hipster dive bar a bit north of downtown that books the best indie touring bands.

In the restored West End across from Falls Park is **Chicora Alley** (608 S. Main St., 864/232-4100, www.chicoraalley.com, Tues.-Sat. 5pm-2am, Sun.-Mon. 5pm-midnight), a great place to grab a bite, have a brew, and listen to reggae or jazz.

One might not rank the **Greenville Symphony Orchestra** (GSO, 200 S. Main St., 864/232-0344, www.greenvillesymphony. org) among the world's greatest ensembles,

Green" downtown at the corner of Academy and College Streets. The feather in its cap is the resident collection, always on display, of 32 of what Andrew Wyeth himself called his best watercolors. The museum also has an eclectic collection of American contemporary artists such as Josef Albers, Jasper Johns, Andy Warhol, Edward Hopper, and Romare Bearden.

# Upcountry History Museum

Also at Heritage Green is the **Upcountry History Museum** (540 Buncombe St., 864/467-3100, www.upcountryhistory.org, Tues.-Sat. 10am-5pm, Sun. 1pm-5pm, $6 adults, $4 ages 4-12, free under age 4).

# Greenville Zoo

The smallish **Greenville Zoo** (150 Cleveland Park Dr., 864/467-4300, www.greenvillezoo. com, daily 10am-4:30pm, $8.75 adults, $5.50 children, free under age 4) is good for an hour or so of fun if you're in the downtown area. It comprises 10 acres tucked into verdant Cleveland Park.

# The Story of Shoeless Joe

With the possible exception of another controversial man with the same surname—civil rights leader Jesse Jackson—Greenville's most famous native son is Joseph Jefferson "Shoeless Joe" Jackson, one of a handful of baseball players whose name is mentioned in the same breath as Babe Ruth (who eagerly took hitting tips from the South Carolinian, in fact). Baseball purists remember him for his powerful natural swing and his claim on the third-highest career batting average at .356. But to much of the general public, he's best known for his role in the Black Sox gambling scandal, which he seems to have actually had little to do with.

Born in next-door Pickens County in 1888 (or 1889, some scholars believe), Jackson began working in a textile mill while still a young child, and had no formal education. In those days each mill fielded its own team, and "textile ball" was a popular local pastime for mill workers and area spectators alike. Jackson soon became a standout on the Brandon Mill nine, gaining his nickname when, during a game in nearby Anderson, he took the batter's box in his socks because his new cleats were aggravating a bad blister. After he then swatted a triple, a frustrated fan of the opposing team called Jackson a "shoeless son of a gun," and the name stuck—along with an unfortunate image of a clueless Southern bumpkin.

In 1908 Jackson went on to play minor-league ball for the Greenville Spinners. He was then signed for a short stint with the Philadelphia Athletics, an unproductive relationship that soon had him moonlighting around the South Atlantic League with the Savannah minor-league team. Settling into life in the big leagues, he went on to a five-year run with the Cleveland Indians, chalking up a .408 batting average his rookie season. The gangly left fielder signed with the Chicago White Sox in 1915, and he still holds the career triples and batting average records for that team.

Jackson's aw-shucks persona would come back to haunt him during the 1919 Black Sox scandal, when the White Sox were accused of throwing that year's World Series. Although he had by far the best performance of both teams during the series, his output dipped notably in the games the White Sox lost. The Chicago papers had a field day savaging the Southerner when under oath he admitted he'd participated. Modern scholarship has shown, however, that an unscrupulous lawyer manipulated him into making the admission. Years later, his teammates admitted he was at none of the meetings where the fix was discussed.

While the jury acquitted Jackson, baseball commissioner Kennesaw Mountain Landis banned him from the sport anyway. A hangdog Jackson returned to the familiar South, opening up a successful dry-cleaning business back in Savannah. He also quietly managed and played on several Georgia semipro and "outlaw" teams. He moved back to Greenville with his wife in 1933, continuing to play and manage. For the rest of his life Jackson proclaimed his innocence, though he fatalistically accepted his tarnished place in history. While working at a Greenville liquor store he owned late in life, none other than the great Ty Cobb and sportswriter Grantland Rice came in. According to Rice, after Cobb paid for his bottle, he asked Jackson, "Don't you know me, Joe?" Jackson said, "Sure, I know you, Ty, but I wasn't sure you wanted to speak to me. A lot of them don't."

Jackson died of a heart attack in 1951 and is buried in Woodlawn Memorial Park in Greenville, section 5, plot 333. You can find a striking bronze statue of Shoeless Joe in downtown Greenville in the West End on Main Street. The **Shoeless Joe Jackson Museum** (356 Field St., 864-235-6280, www.shoelessjoejackson.org, Sat. 10am-4pm and Greenville Drive home game nights, free) is adjacent to the ballpark in the West End. Once the Jackson family home, the structure was moved from 119 East Wilborn Street to this location. Another effort to honor him is the dedication of **Shoeless Joe Jackson Memorial Park** (406 West Ave., 864-288-6470, daily dawn-dusk, free), farther out on the West End on the site of an old ball field where the man himself once played.

Today, Jackson's legacy is in a bit of a renaissance, and you can find out more about the advocacy effort to get him into the Baseball Hall of Fame at www.blackbetsy.com, a website bearing the nickname of his favorite bat.

but it is an impressive group nonetheless and is the city's performing arts crown jewel. The GSO now plays most of its concerts at the Peace Center Concert Hall on the banks of the Reedy River.

My favorite Greenville event—and perhaps the most surprising one to outsiders who assume the city is populated by clueless hayseeds—is the summer-long **Upstate Shakespeare Festival** (Falls Park, S. Main St., 864/787-4016, performances May-Aug. Thurs.-Sun. 7pm, free). The festival brings two complete productions by the Bard downtown, separated by a period classic by another well-known playwright. The setting is the rolling Falls Park, where the audience lolls around on the grass, enjoys a bottle of wine and a picnic dinner, and takes in the show in the gradually cooling air of a fine Upstate evening.

## SHOPPING

Shopping in Greenville comes in two forms: on Main Street and off. Don't neglect Main Street's restored West End.

The most unique shopping experience on Main Street is at the **Mast General Store** (111 N. Main St., 864/235-1883, Mon.-Thurs. 10am-6pm, Fri.-Sat. 10am-9pm, Sun. noon-5pm), a branch of a North Carolina-based regional chain. This hard-to-define and sprawling store, restored to a 1920s vibe, has camping gear, outdoor clothing, preppy clothes, local books, maps, gifts, and an entire candy section in the back.

Paying homage to one of the area's largest employers is **Michelin on Main** (550 S. Main St., 864/241-4450), which contains every kind of Michelin-branded thing you can imagine. The funky **Christopher Park Gallery** (608-A S. Main St., 864/232-6744, www.chickenmanart.com) in the West End has a variety of outsider paintings and sculptures and locally crafted jewelry. On the other end of Main is the **Mary Praytor Gallery** (26 S. Main St., 864/235-1800, www.themarypraytorgallery.com, Tues.-Sat. 10am-5pm), which features eclectic folk art and contemporary paintings from regional artists.

Despite its bland name, the **Clothing Warehouse** (123 N. Main St., 864/467-1238, www.theclothingwarehouse.com, Mon.-Wed. 11am-8pm, Thurs.-Sat. 11am-9pm, Sun. 11am-7pm), a branch of a popular Southern chain, is the hippest vintage clothing and shoe store in town, with a great selection from various eras.

Into beading? Try **The Beaded Frog** (233 N. Main St., 864/235-2323, www.beadedfrog.com, Tues.-Wed. and Fri.-Sat. 11am-5:30pm, Thurs. 11am-8pm, Sun. 1pm-5pm), a locally owned store with every type of bead you could imagine. Take the kids to **O. P. Taylor's** (117 N. Main St., 864/467-1984, www.optaylors.com, Mon.-Sat. 10am-6pm, Sun. 1pm-5pm), a fine toy store with a variety of European toys, Thomas the Tank Engine gear, and games. As military surplus stores go, **Greenville Army Store** (660 S. Main St., 864/232-3168, www.greenvillearmystore.com, Mon.-Sat. 9:30am-5:30pm) is outstanding—which makes sense when one considers it's been in business for half a century and has served many generations of martial Upstaters.

There aren't many indie record stores left in the United States, but a great one is still thriving at **Horizon Records** (2-A W. Stone Ave., 864/235-7922, http://blog.horizonrecords.net), catering to true music enthusiasts since 1975 with a variety of new and used product on CD, DVD, and vinyl. Owner Gene Berger and his helpful staff often host some fairly high-profile musicians for workshops and in-house concerts; check the website for details.

## SPECTATOR SPORTS

If you ask the typical Greenville resident what is the most important sports event in the area, they'll say Clemson football. But technically speaking, a more pertinent spectator pastime in Greenville comes courtesy of the **Greenville Drive** (945 S. Main St., 864/240-4528, www.greenvilledrive.com, box seats $8), an affiliate of the Boston Red Sox playing in the South Atlantic League. They play in the retro-style Fluor Field in the historic West

End, built in 2005 as a nearly exact facsimile of Boston's Fenway Park.

# FOOD
## Barbecue

Don't be put off by the nondescript exterior and small dining room at ★ **Henry's Smokehouse** (240 Wade Hampton Blvd., 864/232-7774, www.henryssmokehouse. com, call for hours, $4-10). This is one of the best, if not *the* best, Upstate barbecue joints and a true Greenville tradition, even though they have taken on some trappings of Midlands 'cue cooking, offering a mustard-based sauce. If the mustard sauce is too much of an acquired taste for you, they also offer the indigenous Upcountry tomato-based sauce. There are two other locations, one on Woodruff Road and the other in nearby suburban Simpsonville.

## Classic Southern

Like its older sister location in Charleston, ★ **High Cotton** (550 S. Main St., 864/335-4200, www.mavericksouthernkitchens.com, daily 5:30pm-10pm, Sun. jazz brunch 10am-2pm, $20-40) deals in robust, no-nonsense takes on Southern and American classics. Meats and game are a particular specialty. Reservations are recommended.

The word *quaint* seems to be applied quite often to dining at **Mary's Restaurant at Falls Cottage** (615 S. Main St., 864/298-0005, www.fallscottage.com, Tues.-Sat. 11am-2pm, Sun. 10am-2pm, $10-15), and rightly so for an experience in this daintily restored little cottage scenically overlooking Falls Park. Breakfast buffet, lunches, and brunches are popular. Reservations are strongly recommended.

## Coffee, Tea, and Sweets

The java trend has hit Greenville big time, and while there is indeed a Starbucks on Main Street, there are some excellent indie coffeehouses in the restored downtown area as well. If you're walking near Falls Park on the Reedy, take a coffee and snack break at **Spill the Beans** (531 S. Main St., 864/242-6355, http://stbdowntown.com, Mon.-Sat. 6:30am-11pm, Sun. 1:30pm-9:30pm), right at the entrance to the park. Besides a great selection of coffees, they have the best fresh, hot (and huge!) waffles in town and good yogurt and smoothie offerings.

For truth in advertising, you can't beat **Coffee Underground** (1 E. Coffee St., 864/298-0494, www.coffeeunderground.info, Mon.-Thurs. 7am-11pm, Fri. 7am-midnight, Sat. 8am-midnight, Sun. 8am-10pm), literally located underground and on Coffee Street. Walk down the stairs below ground level at the intersection of Main and Coffee Streets to enter this spacious bistro with an art gallery atmosphere, which also hosts frequent theatre performances. There is a nice brunch menu in addition to breakfast and snack goodies.

## New Southern

Trendy **American Grocery Restaurant** (732 S. Main St., 864/232-7665, www.americangr. com, Tues.-Sat. 6pm-10pm, $15-25) is not a grocery store at all but an upscale advocate for *very* locally sourced organic and all-natural meats and produce.

# ACCOMMODATIONS

Visitors to Greenville will be pleasantly surprised at the low rates for lodging compared to other American metropolitan areas, a surprise made even more pleasant by the generally high standards.

## Under $150

The best accommodations value in Greenville, the **Drury Inn and Suites** (10 Carolina Point Pkwy., 800/378-7946, www.druryhotels.com, $96-175) has excellent facilities, classy decor, prompt, attentive service, and most rooms under $150.

The best and most popular B&B in town is ★ **Pettigru Place** (302 Pettigru St., 864/242-4529, www.pettigruplace.com, $115-195), and not only because of its proximity to scenic Cleveland Park and being a 20-minute walk from Main Street's activity. Pettigru's five guest rooms are decorated tastefully along particular themes.

## $150-300

The only four-diamond hotel in Greenville and easily its most pedigreed, the ★ **Westin Poinsett** (120 S. Main St., 864/421-9700, www.westinpoinsettgreenville.com, $185-245) isn't for those who insist on a brand-new building. This is a historic inn built in 1925, and the elegantly simple guest rooms and decor reflect this. The staff is professional and friendly, and you can't beat the location—right on top of the old town center on bustling Main Street.

Anchoring the east end of Main Street's revitalization is the **Hyatt Regency Greenville** (220 N. Main St., 864/235-1234, www.greenville.hyatt.com, $159-259), which is somewhat dated in its monolithic style, typical of the chain. When people downtown talk about going "up near the Hyatt," this is what they're referencing.

## INFORMATION AND SERVICES

The main visitors center in Greenville is the **Greenville Downtown Visitor Center** (206 S. Main St., 864/233-0461, www.greenvillecvb.com, Mon.-Fri. 8:30am-5pm). Another one close by is the **Greenville Convention and Visitors Bureau** (631 S. Main St., 864/421-0000, www.greenvillecvb.com, Mon.-Fri. 8:30am-5pm), which has brochures and maps only.

## TRANSPORTATION

### Air

This rapidly growing metro area is served by the **Greenville-Spartanburg International Airport** (GSP, 864/877-7426, www.gspairport.com), the busiest in the state, at I-85 exit 57. Airlines here include Allegiant (www.allegiant-air.com), American Airlines (www.aa.com), Delta (www.delta.com), Southwest (www.southwest.com), and United (www.ual.com).

### Train

Trains stop at the **Greenville Amtrak Station** (1120 W. Washington St., 864/255-4221, www.amtrak.com), with daily service in each direction on the New Orleans-New York City *Crescent.*

### Car

The main routes into Greenville are I-85 and I-185, which enters the city from the west side and becomes Mills Avenue, then shortly becomes Church Street. From there, most attractions of interest are to the west (on your left) as you drive into town. Signage is generally excellent in Greenville.

A spur off I-85 called I-385 enters Greenville from the east and runs by the airport. Keep in mind, however, that this is a toll road. There really is no need to use it unless you are coming in and out of the airport. Laurens Road (U.S. 276) on the other side of the airport leads into town in virtually the same place.

### Bus

**Greenlink** (864/467-5000, www.ridegreenlink.com) is an all-biodiesel fleet with various routes throughout Greenville County. Each ride is $1.25, and transfers are $0.50. Children under age six ride free.

# Spartanburg

Not as enveloped in new construction as Greenville or as thick with newer residents, Spartanburg retains its small-town attitude while hosting a growing contingent of progressive thinkers. The late legendary gospel great Ira Tucker was from here, as is the Southern rock group the Marshall Tucker Band (no relation to Ira, and no, there's not actually anyone in the band named Marshall Tucker).

One of the Revolutionary War's key engagements took place at nearby Cowpens, where a combined force of colonial militia and Continental Army soldiers soundly defeated a British contingent of redcoats and Loyalists. Spartanburg resident Kate Barry entered legend as South Carolina's own version of Paul Revere, warning local commanders of the approach of the British in time for them to prepare for the battle.

The town got its modern name in 1785, when it was named for the local Spartan Rifles militia regiment. In the nineteenth century, Spartanburg, along with Greenville, grew in importance as major textile centers. It was during this time that Spartanburg got its nickname, "Hub City."

## SIGHTS
### Morgan Square

The best place to start your explorations in Spartanburg is downtown at **Morgan Square** (daily 24 hours), the center of the city's efforts to transform into a model of pedestrian-friendly downtown redevelopment. Nearby is a throwback to Spartanburg's rail heyday, the restored **Magnolia Street Train Depot** (Magnolia St. and Morgan Ave.), which now hosts the local Amtrak station, the visitors bureau, and the **Hub City Farmer's Market** (Sat. 8am-noon).

### Seay House

Vernacular architecture buffs will enjoy viewing the oldest extant building in Spartanburg, the **Seay House** (106 Darby Rd., 864/596-3501, Apr.-Oct. Sat. 11am-5pm, $5), built by farmer Kinsman Seay around 1800. Take Crescent Drive off John B. White Boulevard, and then a left onto Darby Road.

Morgan Square in downtown Spartanburg

Hatcher Garden and Woodland Preserve

## Hatcher Garden and Woodland Preserve

The delightful **Hatcher Garden and Woodland Preserve** (832 John B. White Sr. Blvd., 864/574-7724, www.hatchergarden.org, daily dawn-dusk, free) was the labor of love of Harold and Josephine Hatcher, who in 1969 began planting over 10,000 trees and flowering bushes to realize their vision of a community garden. Now an expertly and lovingly tended 10-acre public garden, the site boasts gorgeous flower displays, little ponds, and tastefully arranged viewing platforms.

## Walnut Grove Plantation

The most notable historic structure in the Spartanburg area is the **Walnut Grove Plantation** (1200 Otts Shoals Rd., Roebuck, 864/576-6546, Apr.-Oct. Tues.-Sat. 11am-5pm, Sun. 2pm-5pm, Nov.-Mar. Sat. 11am-5pm, $6 adults, $3 children, free under age 6), outside of town in little Roebuck. It was built in 1765 on land granted by King George III to the family of planter Charles Moore.

## BMW Zentrum

Although it's technically located in Greer, right next door, Spartanburg tends to claim the **BMW Zentrum** (1400 Hwy. 101 S., Greer, 888/868-7269, www.bmwusfactory.com/zentrum) as its own. Currently the only place outside Germany where BMWs are manufactured, the Zentrum is an interesting hybrid exhibit combining a factory and a museum. You can't miss the Zentrum—it's between Greenville and Spartanburg right on I-85. Take exit 60 and follow the signs.

While tours of the factory itself have been suspended until 2018 so that a billion-dollar renovation can take place, you can visit on-site static displays for free, featuring numerous vintage and noteworthy BMWs.

## Spartanburg Museum of Art

The aggressively local **Spartanburg Museum of Art** (200 E. St. John St., 864/948-5364, www.spartanburgartmuseum.org, Tues.-Sat. 10am-5pm, Sun. 1pm-5pm, $5 adults, $3 students and ages 4-17, free under age 4, first Thurs. of the month free) began with the acquisition of *The Girl with Red Hair* by Robert Henri in 1907. Since then, the museum has acquired over 400 pieces of art and sculpture for its permanent collection, which focuses on regional artists. It's housed in the big Chapman Cultural Center downtown.

## Spartanburg Regional Museum of History

In the same building as the Museum of Art is the **Spartanburg Regional Museum of History** (200 E. St. John St., 864/596-3501, Tues.-Wed. and Fri.-Sat. 10am-5pm, Thurs. 10am-8pm, Sun. 1pm-5pm, $5 adults, $3 students and ages 4-17, free under age 4, first Thurs. of the month free), run by the Spartanburg County Historical Association. Perhaps the single most historically important item in the collection is the Pardo Stone, a boulder supposedly bearing graffiti from the first Spanish explorer to come through the Upstate, Juan Pardo.

## ★ Cowpens National Battlefield

The most significant historic site in the Spartanburg area is **Cowpens National Battlefield** (4001 Chesnee Hwy., 864/461-2828, www.nps.gov/cowp, daily 9am-5pm, free), which commemorates one of the key victories over the British in the Revolutionary War. Fought literally in an old cattle pasture, hence the name, the dreaded British cavalry colonel Banastre Tarleton was driven from the field by a combined force of General Daniel Morgan's continentals and local militia (Morgan is memorialized with a park bearing his name in nearby downtown Spartanburg). The British would remain on the defensive for the rest of the war.

In addition to seeing the battlefield and learning about the history of the period in the interpretive center, the other big attraction at Cowpens is the trails, some of which have historical significance. The 1.3-mile **Battlefield Trail** includes exhibits, the 1856 Washington Light Infantry Monument, and the Green River Road, along which the battle was fought. If you want to stay in your car, take the 3.8-mile **Auto Loop Road,** which includes exhibits and parking areas with short trails to the Green River Road, an 1818 log cabin, and a picnic area.

April-October you can take advantage of free one-hour guided walks of the battlefield (Sat. 9:30am, Sun. 1:30pm). Each year on the weekend closest to January 17, the anniversary of the battle, the park celebrates with various demonstrations of period weaponry and a cool living-history encampment.

## Poinsett Bridge

The oldest bridge in the state is the beautiful little 14-foot **Poinsett Bridge** (Callahan Mountain Rd., Lyman), built around 1820 by Joel T. Poinsett, city father of Greenville and the man for whom the poinsettia is named. Get there by taking U.S. 25 north past its intersection with Highway 11 and turn right onto Old Highway 25. Take a right onto Callahan Road.

# ENTERTAINMENT AND EVENTS

## Nightlife

On Morgan Square you can't miss the popular, cavernous **Delaney's Irish Pub** (117 W. Main St., 864/583-3100, Mon.-Sat. 11am-2am, Sun. 3pm-2am). They have a great selection of beer on tap and in the bottle as well as a very good menu of pub food. Dating from 1938, the **Nu-Way Restaurant and Lounge** (373 E. Kennedy St., 864/582-9685) is Spartanburg's version of every town's lovable old dive. This is the place to go for that ironically hip night out on the town, not to mention some truly satisfying burgers.

## Performing Arts

Some vibrant stuff goes on downtown at the **Hub-Bub** (149 S. Daniel Morgan Ave., Ste. 2, 864/582-0056, www.hub-bub.com, admission varies). Housed in a former Nash Rambler dealership, Hub-Bub hosts over 100 evenings a year of concerts, film, art exhibits, plays, and workshops, almost all of it with a countercultural edge for this conservative area.

The very definition of a "multiuse" venue, the beautiful **Chapman Cultural Center** (200 E. St. John St., 864/542-2787, www. chapmanculturalcenter.org, admission varies) next to Barnet Park has a 500-seat theater that hosts performances by several local theater groups as well as Ballet Spartanburg. It also houses the city's two main museums, the Spartanburg Museum of Art and the Spartanburg Regional Museum of History.

# SHOPPING

My favorite shop in Spartanburg is the nonprofit **Hub City Bookshop** (186 W. Main St., 864/577-9349, www.hubcity.org, Mon.-Thurs. 10am-7pm, Fri.-Sat. 10am-9pm), which has a great selection of new and used tomes and also serves as the central meeting point for the Hub City Writers Project and houses the Hub City Press. There's also an attached coffee shop.

# How South Carolina Saved America

Cowpens National Battlefield

To read most history books, you'd think the Revolutionary War took place almost entirely in Boston. But South Carolina was the location of the conflict's fiercest fighting, suffering the most men killed of all 13 colonies. Savage and personal, the fighting here usually involved not uniformed regulars but Patriot and Tory militia.

In a span of 90 days, Upstate South Carolina hosted two of the most important Patriot victories of the war, Kings Mountain and Cowpens. Sent to pacify the backcountry's independent-minded Scots-Irish colonists, British major Patrick Ferguson led 1,000 Tory militiamen to a stronghold at the base of Kings Mountain on the border of the Carolinas. On October 7, 1780, an equal number of Appalachian militiamen assaulted the position using tactics they'd learned fighting Native Americans. Rather than marching as a unit and shooting en masse as a European army would, each militiaman fired at will as he attacked, hiding behind rocks to reload.

The battle seesawed for an hour. The end came when Ferguson, attempting to rally his men, was riddled with eight bullets. As the Tory line collapsed, colonists initially sounded the cry "Tarleton's Quarter!," an ironic reference to the brutal British colonel Banastre Tarleton, infamous for murdering prisoners. But cooler heads prevailed, and 700 Loyalists were taken prisoner.

By January 1781 many Kings Mountain veterans had joined General Daniel Morgan, who chose a large cattle-grazing area—literally, the "cow pens"—outside modern-day Spartanburg to make a stand. Learning from the debacle at Camden, Morgan picked a wide-open battlefield with no place for potentially panicking militiamen to run and hide. To further bolster the colonists, he posted regular Continental Army troops behind them.

Thinking the retreating militiamen were panicking, Tarleton's men advanced into a firestorm of bullets. Sending militiamen out on both wings, Morgan surrounded the British in a classic double envelopment, studied by military leaders to this day.

In a very real way, Cowpens led directly to American victory in the war. With the exception of his stronghold at Charleston, General Cornwallis wrote off South Carolina and moved his troops into North Carolina instead. A series of engagements led to his retreat up the Virginia coast to Yorktown, where, bottled up by Washington's army and the French fleet, he was forced to surrender.

You can visit both battle sites today, at **Kings Mountain National Military Park** (2625 Park Rd., 803/222-3209, www.nps.gov/kimo, Labor Day-Memorial Day daily 9am-5pm, Memorial Day-Labor Day daily 9am-6pm, free) near Blacksburg and **Cowpens National Battlefield** (4001 Chesnee Hwy., 864/461-2828, www.nps.gov/cowp, daily 9am-5pm, free) near Gaffney.

# SPORTS AND RECREATION
## Hiking and Biking

Spartanburg is becoming a mecca of sorts for bicyclists. The city is the launching point for the **Assault on Mt. Mitchell** (www.freewheelers.info) each May, an amateur race over 100 miles long taking participants from Spartanburg to Mount Mitchell, North Carolina, the highest point east of the Mississippi River.

The main recreation area close to Spartanburg is **Croft State Natural Area** (450 Croft State Park Rd., 864/585-1283, www.southcarolinaparks.com, daily 7am-9pm, $2 adults, free under age 16), which offers 12 miles of biking and hiking trails within its massive acreage, once a U.S. Army training ground. As the Palmetto Trail nears completion, a section is expected to join Croft with the rest of the trail.

# FOOD
## Asian

A great Thai place, right downtown on Morgan Square, is **Lime Leaf** (101 E. Main St., 864/542-2171, Mon.-Fri. 11:30am-3pm and 5pm-10pm, Sat. 5pm-11pm, $9-15). For a sushi fix, check out **Wasabi** (1529 John B. White Sr. Blvd., 864/576-8998, www.wasabispartanburg.com, Tues.-Sat. 11:30am-2:30pm and 5pm-10pm, $5-10).

## Classic Southern

No visit to Spartanburg is complete without a visit to the **Beacon Drive-In** (255 John B. White Blvd., 864/585-9387, www.beacondrivein.com, Mon.-Sat. 6:30am-10pm, $5-7). As is the case with many surviving greasy spoon-type places with retro allure, the media hype now surrounding the Beacon doesn't quite match the food, which is really very simple when you get down to it. The signature offering is the Chili Cheese A-Plenty, which sounds like a chili dog but is actually a burger topped with chili and cheese ("A-Plenty" means you get a huge mound of fries and onion rings tossed on top).

Once considered the best barbecue place in Spartanburg, **Wade's Restaurant** (1000 N. Pine St., 864/582-3800, www.eatatwades.com, Mon.-Sat. 10:45am-8:30pm, Sun. 10:45am-3pm, $6-9) has branched out and now deals out all kinds of Southern comfort food, meat-and-two style, including collard greens, fried chicken, and dinner rolls. Wednesday nights are big here, so if you don't like waiting in line, be forewarned.

## Coffee, Tea, and Sweets

The most happening coffee and sweet-treat shop in town is ★ **The Coffee Bar** (188-A W. Main St., 864/582-1227, www.littlerivercoffeebar.com, Mon.-Thurs. 7am-7pm, Fri.-Sat. 7am-9pm), located in the historic Masonic Temple downtown and adjacent to the Hub City Bookshop and the nonprofit goings-on there.

## Pizza

There's a continuing rivalry over who has the best pizza in Spartanburg: **Venus Pie Pizza** (400 E. Main St., 864/582-4200, Mon.-Tues. 11:30am-9pm, Wed. 11:30am-9:30pm, Thurs.-Fri. 11:30am-10:30pm, Sat. 11:30am-10pm, $6-12) or **The Mellow Mushroom** (464 E. Main St., 864/582-5495, Mon.-Thurs. 11am-10pm, Fri.-Sat. 11am-midnight, Sun. noon-9pm, $7-14) down the block. The former is a totally local venture, while the latter is a regional chain.

# ACCOMMODATIONS
## Under $150

The first and still best-regarded B&B in Spartanburg is the award-winning ★ **Inn on Main** (319 E. Main St., 864/585-5001, www.innonmainofspartanburg.com, $95-155). Located in a historic 1904 building right on the main drag, Inn on Main offers six distinctive, exquisitely furnished suites that wouldn't be out of place in one of the classic B&Bs in Charleston or Beaufort (and at about half the price). The beds alone, some of which are genuine antiques, will wow you. Of course, you get the requisite full Southern breakfast served in a clubby setting typical of the inn's common areas. Keep in mind they discourage kids under age 12.

The spacious **Spartanburg Marriott at Renaissance Park** (299 N. Church St., 864/596-1211, $109-179) has 240 smoke-free rooms within walking distance of the downtown area.

## TRANSPORTATION

While Spartanburg does have its own small municipal airport, **Spartanburg Downtown Memorial Airport** (SPA, 500 Ammons Rd., 864/574-8552, www.cityof-spartanburg.org), it has no commercial flights, and most visitors fly into the area at the much larger **Greenville-Spartanburg International Airport** (GSP, 2000 GSP Dr., 864/877-7426, www.gspairport.com), a short distance west of town along I-85. Another option is **Charlotte-Douglas International Airport** (CLT, 5501 Josh Birmingham Pkwy., 704/359-4000, www.clt.com), 70 miles east of Spartanburg in North Carolina.

**Amtrak** (290 Magnolia St., 800/872-7245, www.amtrak.com) has a station downtown, with daily service in each direction on the New Orleans-New York City *Crescent*. There's also a **Greyhound bus station** (100 N. Liberty St., www.greyhound.com).

Public transportation by bus in Spartanburg is offered by **Spartanburg Area Regional Transit Agency (SPARTA)** (100 N. Liberty St., 864/562-4287, www.spartabus. com). Fares run $1.25 per trip, and eight interlocking routes take you all over town, including the mall area.

# Along the Blue Ridge

While the landscape is not as stark as north of the border, the Blue Ridge in South Carolina has the dual advantages of being both more easily accessible and much less expensive than the increasingly upscale area of the North Carolina mountains.

## ELLICOTT ROCK WILDERNESS AREA

One of the oldest trails in the Southeast can be found in the **Ellicott Rock Wilderness Area** (803/561-4000, www.fs.fed.us, year-round daily, free), which has acreage in three states. It takes you through the Chattooga River gorge in the Sumter National Forest, with about half the trail in North Carolina and a small portion in Georgia. Ellicott Rock itself, once inaccurately considered the meeting point of the three states, is actually in North Carolina. You can reach it on one of the trails in the wilderness area.

Get here by taking Forest Road 708 (Burrells Ford Rd.) west of Highway 107.

There's a parking area near the Burrells Ford Campground, and it's a short hike to the Chattooga River. Since the Chattooga River became designated a Wild and Scenic River, you can no longer drive your car all the way into **Burrells Ford Campground** in the Sumter National Forest. But if you don't mind hiking a short distance, you'll be happy to be away from the RV crowd. As you'd expect, this is a no-frills campground, with a hand-pumped well and minimal toilet facilities.

## OCONEE STATE PARK

One of the gems of the Civilian Conservation Corps era in South Carolina, **Oconee State Park** (624 State Park Rd., Mountain Rest, 864/638-5353, www.southcarolinaparks.com, during daylight saving time daily 7am-9pm, other seasons Sun.-Thurs. 7am-7pm, Fri.-Sat. 7am-9pm, $2 adults, free under age 16), a few miles north of Walhalla, is also one of the Upstate's most popular campgrounds. Its two lakes are picturesque, with paddleboat

camping at Oconee State Park

and johnboat rentals available ($10 per day). There's a good network of trails on-site, including the beginning of the Foothills Trail.

## ★ STUMPHOUSE TUNNEL AND ISSAQUEENA FALLS

This combo free attraction, a neat place to bring the family, is overseen by the nearby town of Walhalla as part of a conservation agreement among the town, local landowners, and a few nonprofit groups. You'll find it clearly marked on the east side of Highway 28 several miles north of Walhalla. If you're up this way checking out the Chattooga River, there's no reason not to stop by.

The **Stumphouse Tunnel** (864/638-4343, daily 8am-5pm, free) is a cool (literally) and possibly slightly frightening experience that kids will either really enjoy or be really petrified of. You won't know until you get them here. In the early 1800s somebody hatched a plan to run a railroad from Charleston to the Midwest, to be known as the Blue Ridge Rail Line. The line was built from Charleston to nearby Pendleton, but one big problem remained: Stumphouse Mountain was in the

way. Residing in a hastily formed rough-and-rowdy burg called, suitably enough, Tunneltown, 1,500 workers managed to dig about 1,600 feet of the planned mile-long tunnel through the mountain before funds ran out. Then the Civil War started, and thus ended the Blue Ridge Line.

The 25-foot-high tunnel stayed empty until the 1940s, when Clemson University professor Paul Miller discovered that the tunnel's interior stayed a consistent 56°F with 85 percent humidity year-round, making it a perfect natural cooler to store and age the signature Clemson blue cheese.

Today, a walk in the tunnel—about 500 feet of it is still open—is like a scary, albeit very low-budget, thrill ride. Take your flashlight if you go inside because once you're a few feet in, there is no light at all. If you're brave enough, you'll eventually come to a brick doorway, behind which is another couple of hundred feet of even darker tunnel before it's finally closed off.

A short walking distance from Stumphouse Tunnel is another charming attraction, **Issaqueena Falls** (864/638-4343, daily 8am-5pm, free). It's a popular place to visit and

# The Legend of Issaqueena Falls

Oconee County lore says that sometime in the late 1700s, Cherokee maiden Issaqueena fell in love with an English trader named Allan Francis. When the local Cherokee planned an attack on an English outpost, Issaqueena got on her pony and took a 96-mile ride to warn the settlers, which fittingly ended at the English fort at Ninety Six. She began a family with Francis back at Stumphouse Mountain where she had grown up.

But one day a group of Cherokee attempted to kidnap Issaqueena. She ran from them, but they eventually caught up to her at the 200-foot waterfall at the base of the mountain. Legend has it that Issaqueena pretended to fling herself to her death over the falls but actually hid under a ledge until her pursuers left. Another version has it that she hid under the falls because the Cherokee supposedly thought evil spirits dwelled in waterfalls.

So is the story true? In the frontier memoirs of Ann Matthews, we read about an Indian woman who "disliked very much to think that the white women who had been so good to her in giving her clothes and bread and butter in trading parties would be killed, [so] she became determined to let them know their danger [...] and walked 96 miles in twenty-four hours spreading news as she went." Other accounts confirm this story. Some recent scholars, however, doubt her existence at all, citing an abundance of elaborately embellished tales from the Victorian era about comely Indian maidens falling in love with white settlers.

If she did exist, however, perhaps the best clue to Issaqueena's psychology has as much to do with lineage as with love. Legend says that Issaqueena was actually one of the Choctaw people kidnapped by the Cherokee, and her given name at birth was Cateechee.

admire the water's forceful path down over the rocks, many of which you can climb out on if you're feeling adventurous.

## OCONEE STATION STATE HISTORIC SITE

Not to be confused with nearby Oconee State Park, **Oconee Station State Historic Site** (500 Oconee Station Rd., 864/638-0079, www. southcarolinaparks.com, daily 9am-6pm, free) is a much smaller park with no camping facilities, geared toward the enjoyment of two historic sites within it as well as a popular and easily accessible waterfall.

The main structure is **Oconee Station** (Sat.-Sun. 1pm-5pm, free), a reconstructed late-1700s blockhouse (fort), used to defend what was then the frontier against Cherokee and other Native American attacks. The other structure is the **William Richards House** (Sat.-Sun. 1pm-5pm, free), built in 1805 by the Irish settler of that name and used as a trading post.

Get here by taking Highway 11 (Cherokee Foothills Scenic Byway) north of West Union

and Walhalla a few miles and following the signs.

## DEVIL'S FORK STATE PARK

Don't be put off by the name—**Devil's Fork State Park** (161 Holcombe Circle, 864/944-2639, www.southcarolinaparks. com, spring-summer daily 7am-9pm, fall-winter Sat.-Thurs. 7am-6pm, Fri. 7am-8pm, $2 adults, free under age 16) is one of the easier and more picturesque modern, non-Civilian Conservation Corps South Carolina state parks. Its claim to fame is being the only public access to Lake Jocassee, which despite its artificial nature is pretty picturesque. As you might expect, this park, with four boat ramps, is popular with boaters and anglers (Jocassee is the only lake in South Carolina offering both trophy trout and smallmouth bass).

## KEOWEE-TOXAWAY STATE NATURAL AREA

At the halfway point between the two ends of the Cherokee Foothills Scenic Byway (Hwy.

11) lies **Keowee-Toxaway State Natural Area** (108 Residence Dr., Sunset, 864/868-2605, www.southcarolinaparks.com, during daylight saving time daily 7am-9pm, other seasons Sat.-Thurs. 9am-6pm, Fri. 9am-8pm, free). This is one of the state's newer and smaller campgrounds, built in the 1970s on 1,000 acres of land donated by Duke Power, which is also responsible for the existence of Lake Keowee, on which the site resides and under which are the remains of an ancient Cherokee town.

While you're here, or even if you're just driving by, don't miss the **Cherokee Heritage Interpretive Center** (daily 11am-noon and 4pm-5pm, free) on-site. There's a modest museum explaining the natural and human history of the area, including the inundation of the ancient village of Keowee.

## TABLE ROCK STATE PARK

A very popular state park with the casual RV crowd as well as with serious hikers is **Table Rock State Park** (158 E. Ellison Ln., 864/878-9813, www.southcarolinaparks.com, during daylight saving time Sun.-Thurs. 7am-9pm, Fri.-Sat. 7am-10pm, other seasons Sun.-Thurs. 7am-7pm, Fri.-Sat. 7am-9pm, $2 adults, free under age 16), just off Highway 11, the Cherokee Foothills Scenic Byway. With two lakes, well-appointed cabins, tent and RV sites, and some exceptional examples of Civilian Conservation Corps handiwork, there is plenty to do and see. But perhaps the key element is Table Rock itself, dominating the northern sky-scape and compelling hikers like a large magnet. Serving as the eastern trailhead for the 76-mile-long Foothills Trail, the park provides access to several strenuous but ultimately rewarding journeys.

Just off the Cherokee Foothills Scenic Highway is **The Inn at Table Rock** (117 Hiawatha Tr., 864/878-0078, www.theinnattablerock.com, $129-179). This six-room historic Victorian offers a bucolic, sumptuous setting on four acres, with views of Table Rock and the Blue Ridge. They discourage guests under age 18.

## ★ MOUNTAIN BRIDGE WILDERNESS AREA

By far the most wild and woolly nature experience in the Upstate is at **Mountain Bridge Wilderness Area** (8155 Geer Hwy./U.S. 276, Cleveland, 864/836-6115, www.southcarolinaparks.com, spring-summer daily 9am-9pm, fall-winter daily 9am-6pm, $2 adults, free under age 16), just shy of the border with North Carolina. Technically speaking, this site actually comprises two well-known parks, **Caesars Head State Park** and **Jones Gap State Park,** but these are very atypical South Carolina state parks, so don't be fooled by the designation.

The focal point of the area is the hike to Caesars Head, a fancifully shaped 3,622-foot-tall rock outcropping along the Blue Ridge Escarpment. The other major landmark is the 420-foot **Raven Cliff Falls,** one of the most stunning cataracts in the state. It waits at the end of a moderately strenuous 2.2-mile hike, with a suspension bridge available for your scenic vertigo-inducing pleasure.

Campers will find 24 primitive trail-side sites ($8-20), 18 of which have fire rings and 6 of which allow no fires. You must have a permit in advance to camp in the Mountain Bridge Wilderness; call 866/345-7275 or go to the website.

## GETTING AROUND

Getting around is quite easy. The main route is Highway 11, the Cherokee Foothills Scenic Byway, running roughly east-west along the base of the Blue Ridge. Other key routes are U.S. 76 in the northwest corner, which takes you from Westminster up to the Chattooga River and into Georgia; Highway 28, which links Highway 11 and U.S. 76 through the cute town of Walhalla; and U.S. 276, a spur from Highway 11 to the Caesars Head area.

# Waterfalls of the Upstate

Because of South Carolina's location on the Blue Ridge Escarpment—the so-called "Blue Wall" marking the sudden end of the Appalachians—it contains dozens of waterfalls, from grand to humble. While there are plenty of brochures and websites out there guiding you to the locations of South Carolina's waterfalls, keep in mind that some falls are significantly more difficult to get to than others, especially if there has been a recent rain to turn the old logging roads into muck. Also remember that some of the more remote falls require strenuous, if enjoyable, hikes.

Here is a sampling of some of the more accessible falls in the Upstate. For more info, go to www.alleneasler.com/waterfalls.html or www.sctrails.net.

Issaqueena Falls

· At 420 feet, **Raven Cliff Falls** are the highest in South Carolina, and by some measures, the highest in the eastern United States. Get here by way of a moderately strenuous 4.4-mile round-trip hike out of Caesars Head State Park in the Mountain Bridge Wilderness Area. There's a parking area off U.S. 276.

· Table Rock State Park has several smaller falls on its network of trails, with most on the two-mile **Carrick Creek** loop.

· **Issaqueena Falls** just north of Walhalla on Highway 28 comes with its own legend of a love-struck Cherokee princess. The parking area is near the head of the falls, and there's a nice trail down the falls with a scenic overlook.

· **Spoon Auger Falls** up near the Chattooga River in the northwest corner of the state has a 40-foot drop. It's a short hike out of the Burrells Ford Campground parking area. To get here from Walhalla, take Highway 107 north 17 miles to Forest Road 708 (Burrells Ford Rd.). The parking lot is three miles ahead.

· The comically misnamed **Hidden Falls** are easily found within Oconee State Park. Get to this 40-foot cascade by taking the two-mile yellow-blazed Hidden Falls Trail.

· Just up the road on Highway 11 are the 60-foot **Station Cove Falls,** easily found on a short trail within the Oconee Station State Historic Site.

· The picturesque 30-foot **Reedy Branch Falls** are very easy to get to. From Westminster, take U.S. 76 about 15 miles north and look for a pull-off on the left after you pass Chattooga Ridge Road on the right. The falls are about a 300-yard walk from the road.

· Perhaps the easiest cascade to find—and one of the more enjoyable—is 30-foot **Chau-Ram Falls** in Oconee County's Chau-Ram County Park. (The name derives from the Chauga River and Ramsey Creek.) Drive west of Westminster on U.S. 76 for about three miles; the park entrance is on the left. Unlike most local waterfalls, this one has a nice campground nearby.

# Clemson and Vicinity

Like any great American college town, the home of the Clemson University Tigers is vocally proud of its local sports teams. This is especially true in the wake of their dramatic NCAA Football National Championship win in 2017, Clemson University's second. If you're the type to scoff at the Southern passion for college football—or if you're a fan of the Tigers' archrival, the University of South Carolina—OR if you don't like the color orange—you might not enjoy Clemson very much.

## Sights

The following attractions are all on the Clemson University campus, which welcomes visitors. Catch a campus tour at the **Clemson University Visitors Center** (109 Daniel Dr., 864/656-4789, www.clemson.edu) most days at 9:45am and 1:45pm.

### JOHN C. CALHOUN HOME

The ancestral home of the great South Carolina statesman and subsequently that of his daughter and Thomas Clemson, the **John C. Calhoun Home** (101 Fort Hill St., 864/656-2475, www.clemson.edu, Mon.-Sat. 10am-noon and 1pm-4:30pm, Sun. 2pm-4:30pm, $5 adults, $2 ages 6-12, free under age 6) is the spiritual center of Clemson. Also known as Fort Hill, the Greek Revival mansion, a National Historic Landmark, is essentially all that remains of the original plantation.

### ★ SOUTH CAROLINA BOTANICAL GARDEN

The official botanical garden of the Palmetto State since 1992, the **South Carolina Botanical Garden** (150 Discovery Ln., 864/656-3405, www.clemson.edu, daily dawn-dusk, free) takes up the entire southeastern tip of the Clemson campus and is a delightful place to stroll, relax, and take in the aromas of the tens of thousands of types of plants, flowers, and herbs planted on the site's 300 acres. There are 70 acres of display gardens, including the impressive camellia garden, a dwarf conifer garden, a hosta garden, and a butterfly garden. A 40-acre arboretum and nearly 100 acres of woodlands with walking trails complete the outdoor package. The best times to visit are spring and fall; in the summer there are significantly fewer flowering plants, and the heat can be stifling.

Within the grounds of the South Carolina Botanical Garden is the **Bob Campbell Geology Museum** (140 Discovery Ln., 864/656-4600, www.clemson.edu/public/geomuseum, Wed.-Sat. 10am-5pm, Sun. 1pm-5pm, closed home football Sat., free), which has its roots in a small rock collection in the Clemson geology department.

the South Carolina Botanical Garden

## Entertainment and Events

Like everything else in Clemson, local entertainment here moves with the ebb and flow of student life—especially during football season.

### NIGHTLIFE

The most famous college bar in Clemson is **The Esso Club** (129 Old Greenville Hwy., 864/654-5120, www.theessoclub.com), on the edge of campus. As the name indicates, it's in an old gas station, built in 1933 on what was then the main road to Atlanta. You could actually fill up your car until the mid-1980s, when it became a full-time bar and tavern.

The other key watering hole in town is the **Tiger Town Tavern** (368 College Ave., 864/654-5901, www.tigertowntavern.com), aka Triple T's. Upstairs is Top of Tiger Town Tavern, a "private club"—meaning that for a few bucks a year its members can drink there on Sundays. You can too if you come as a current member's guest and pony up.

## Sports and Recreation
### SPECTATOR SPORTS

Clemson University plays about seven Saturday home football games during the regular season, August-November. During this time, everything in town focuses on the game, to the exclusion of all else except basic bodily functions. Many attractions in town are closed on home football Saturdays. The games are played in **Clemson Memorial Stadium** (Centennial Blvd., 864/656-2118, www.clemsontigers.com), aka "Death Valley," at the western edge of campus. You can buy advance tickets to a Clemson University home game at the school's official ticket site (www.clemsontigers.com) or by calling the school directly at 800/253-6766.

## Food

Whatever you do in Clemson, don't miss a stop by the Hendrix Student Center on campus, where you'll find ★ **'55 Exchange** (864/656-2155, www.clemson.edu/icecream, Aug.-May Mon.-Fri. 11:30am-6pm, Sat.-Sun. 1pm-6pm, June-July Mon.-Thurs. 11:30am-8pm, Fri. 11:30am-6pm, Sat.-Sun. 1pm-6pm, $4-10). They have what I believe to be the best ice cream and milk shakes on the planet, courtesy of the Clemson University Dairy Sciences Department. Open to the public, this little corner shop—named for the Clemson graduating class that funded its opening—features rich, robust ice cream in the old style, served in a multitude of equally fresh and tasty cones and edible cups.

Considered the finest of fine dining in Clemson, **Pixie & Bill's** (1058 Tiger Blvd., 864/654-1210, www.tigergourmet.com, lunch Mon.-Fri. 11:30am-1:30pm, dinner Mon.-Sat. 5:30pm-9:30pm, $18-26) is a favorite of students and visiting alumni alike.

## Accommodations

There are several nice places to stay in Clemson, but don't stay near Tiger Boulevard unless you enjoy the sound of trains—there are busy railroad tracks that cut through town in that area. Also keep in mind that rates here skyrocket on home-game weekends.

Not near the train tracks and right next to the campus's Walker Golf Course—and like that facility, completely open to the public—is the **James F. Martin Inn** (100 Madren Center Dr., 864/654-9020, www.clemson.edu, $100). Many of its 89 guest rooms overlook Lake Hartwell. There's an outdoor pool, tennis courts, Wi-Fi, and included continental breakfast.

The circa-1837 **Sleepy Hollow Bed and Breakfast** (220 Issaqueena Tr., 864/207-1540, www.sleepyhollow.ws, $100-175) is reportedly the site of the introduction of Percheron horses and Jersey cows to South Carolina, in addition to what's purported to be the state's largest white oak tree out back. A full breakfast is offered on weekends and a continental breakfast is served during the week.

# PENDLETON

Right next door to Clemson and basically contiguous with it, the significantly older Pendleton is one of the most impossibly

# Carolina Kitsch

the Jockey Lot and Farmers Market

Need a T-shirt that says "Jesus was nailed for my sins"? How about a NASCAR handbag? Some used gospel CDs? Karate movies on VHS? Fresh grapefruit by the basket? Over-the-counter medicines for a buck? You'll find it all and then some in the dollar-store-run-wild atmosphere of the sprawling **Jockey Lot and Farmers Market** (4530 U.S. 29, Belton, 864/224-2027, www.jockeylot.com, Sat. 7am-5pm, Sun. 8am-5pm, free), which claims to be South Carolina's single most-visited attraction and the South's biggest flea market. *Attraction* really isn't the word, however, because this is hardly intended for tourists; it's mostly for the benefit of budget shoppers from around the Upstate, who jam the sheds and roam the display tables of this huge complex, just over twenty miles southwest of Greenville and Anderson on U.S. 29. Table after table of merchandise, ranging from personal junk to odd lots of cheap Chinese-made stuff, spread before you like a vast discount smorgasbord. Honestly, the sheer bulk of the offerings can be overwhelming.

Walk slowly through the place, soaking in the rustic vibe. Smile and talk with people as you pass. If you're really meant to buy something here, it will jump out at you. Most of this stuff… you can live without.

cute small towns you'll ever see. Founded in 1790, Pendleton's origin came over a century after Charleston's founding, but you'll find this Upstate town oddly familiar if you've been to that great Lowcountry city: Most of the finer buildings in Pendleton were built by Lowcountry planters who kept summer homes here.

## Sights
### ★ VILLAGE GREEN

Pendleton's main claim to fame is its central **Village Green** (125 E. Queen St., 864/646-3782, www.pendleton-district.org). Now surrounded by cute shops and cafés, it's the center of the area of Pendleton that's in the National Register of Historic Places—over 50 buildings in town date from before 1850. The focal point is the circa-1828 **Farmers Society Hall** (255 Old Depot Rd., 864/646-8161) in the center of the green.

### ASHTABULA

Stately **Ashtabula** (444 Hwy. 88, 864/646-7249, www.pendletonhistoricfoundation.org, Thurs.-Sun. 1pm-4pm, $6 adults, $2 children), pronounced "ash-ta-BYEW-la," was built in the 1820s by Charleston's well-connected Lewis Ladson Gibbes. He was a descendant of the first English settler in South Carolina, Dr. Henry Woodward, and married Maria Henrietta Drayton, daughter of Dr. Charles Drayton of Drayton Hall fame and Esther Middleton, of the magnificent Middleton Place and sister of Arthur Middleton, who signed the Declaration of Independence.

## WOODBURN PLANTATION

Another magnificent home with historical roots is **Woodburn Plantation** (328 U.S. 76, 864/646-7249, www.pendletonhistoric-foundation.org, Fri. 2:30pm-5pm, $6 adults, $2 children). Like Ashtabula, it is a very short drive from Pendleton, although on the other side of town. And like Ashtabula, this four-story house with high ceilings, spacious verandas, and great cross-ventilation was owned as a summer home by a Lowcountry planter and statesman, in this case Charles Cotesworth Pinckney.

## HISTORIC TOURS

Try **Historic Pendleton District Tours** (125 E. Queen St., 864/646-3782), inside the historic Hunter's Store building, which also houses the **Pendleton District Historical, Recreational, and Tourism Commission** (864/646-3782, Mon.-Fri. 9am-4:30pm, Sat. 10am-3pm); they can hook you up with materials to take your own self-guided tour.

## Shopping

Antiques buffs will find themselves in heaven in Pendleton, with several good stores ringing the Village Green. Keep in mind that store hours are not always religiously observed. The best is **Past Times** (165 S. Mechanic St., 864/654-5985, Tues.-Sat. 11am-5pm), which boasts the largest collection of vintage Edgefield pottery in the nation. Colonial and Shaker furniture is the specialty of **The Renaissance Man** (130 S. Mechanic St., 864/646-8862).

# Old English District

In the early days of the Revolution, this area was considered safe ground for British soldiers and settlers due to the Loyalist sentiments of the local population. All that changed due to the heavy-handed occupation by the redcoats. With Loyalists in shorter supply than promised, the British soon found themselves on the run, especially after key defeats at Cowpens and Kings Mountain.

## KINGS MOUNTAIN NATIONAL MILITARY PARK

Nestled against the North Carolina border (the actual town of Kings Mountain is in the Tar Heel State) is **Kings Mountain National Military Park** (2625 Park Rd., 803/222-3209, www.nps.gov/kimo, Labor Day-Memorial Day daily 9am-5pm, Memorial Day-Labor

Day daily 9am-6pm, free). The site marks the battle of October 7, 1780, when American militia defeated a band of Loyalists under British major Patrick Ferguson. While the Patriots clearly carried the day, only later did it become clear that the Battle of Kings Mountain was the turning point in the Revolutionary War, after which the British never again gained the offensive.

Kings Mountain is the end point of the **Overmountain Victory National Historic Trail** (864/936-3477, www.nps.gov/ovvi), marking the route of the victorious militia forces through the Carolinas. It's important to note that this is a federal site, therefore no battle reenactments are allowed.

Not to be confused with the nearby Kings Mountain State Park, campers can spend the night within the National Military Park only

Historic Brattonsville

at the Garner Creek campsite, intended for a single large party. No reservations are taken, but you must get a permit (free) at the park's visitors center. Oh, and another catch: It's a three-mile hike to the campsite.

## KINGS MOUNTAIN STATE PARK

Not to be confused with the adjacent National Military Park of the same name, **Kings Mountain State Park** (1277 Park Rd., Blacksburg, 803/222-3209, www.southcarolinaparks.com, during daylight saving time daily 7am-8pm, other seasons daily 8am-6pm, $2 adults, free under age 16) offers plenty to do amid the picturesque setting of one of the classic South Carolina state parks built in the 1930s by the Civilian Conservation Corps. There are miles of good trails, two fishing lakes with boat rentals ($20 per day), and a living-history farm replicating the look, feel, and livestock of a typical piedmont farm in the early 1800s.

For the horse lover, there are 20 miles of equestrian trails that connect to the National Military Park. The state park has 15 equestrian campsites ($12)—but bring your own horse. For regular campers, the park has a whopping 115 RV and gravel tent sites with electricity and water ($16-18) and 10 primitive campsites with no water or electricity ($12-13).

## ★ HISTORIC BRATTONSVILLE

Near the town of McConnells, **Historic Brattonsville** (1444 Brattonsville Rd., 803/684-2327, www.chmuseums.org, Tues.-Sat. 10am-5pm, Sun. 1pm-5pm, $6 adults, $3 ages 4-17, free under age 4) includes the site of the Revolutionary War battle of Huck's Defeat, a pivotal victory of Patriot militia over the Tories. But the chief allure of this 775-acre site is the impressive grouping of more than 30 well-restored historic structures (although not all are open to the public), including the circa-1840 visitors center, a reconstruction of a backwoods log cabin, and a mid-1800s milk barn and hog pen. The crown jewel is the 1766 **William Bratton House,** probably the oldest building in this part of the state and where some scenes in Mel Gibson's *The Patriot* were filmed.

# Atlanta

Look for ★ to find recommended
sights, activities, dining, and lodging.

# Highlights

★ **Georgia Aquarium:** The largest single aquarium tank in the world is the centerpiece of this major tourist attraction (page 452).

★ **Martin Luther King Jr. National Historic Site:** This stirring and expansive tribute to the civil rights leader contains many historically significant buildings, such as his birth home (page 454).

★ **Zoo Atlanta:** A world-class gorilla habitat and two charming pandas are among the highlights (page 458).

★ **High Museum of Art:** The multistory modern building contains a plethora of American arts and crafts, from folk art to high art, with some Old Masters mixed in as well (page 459).

★ **Fox Theatre:** This ornate, Moorish-themed venue remains in constant use. It's Midtown's most cherished locale (page 462).

★ **Michael C. Carlos Museum:** This small but significant museum hosts intriguing Egyptian and Greek artifacts in an intimate setting (page 464).

★ **Atlanta History Center and Swan House:** View the excellent Civil War exhibit and tour the magnificent, one-of-a-kind Swan House (page 465).

★ **Decatur:** This small city adjacent to Atlanta has one of the nation's most happening foodie and café scenes, all within a couple of blocks (page 499).

© AVALON TRAVEL

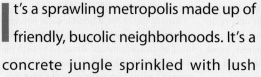

**I**t's a sprawling metropolis made up of friendly, bucolic neighborhoods. It's a concrete jungle sprinkled with lush green space. It's a center of dyed-in-the-wool Southern arts and culture filled to the brim with transplants from elsewhere.

It's in the middle of the Bible Belt but is legendary, even notorious, for its nightlife. All these things are true in their own ways, and there's no use trying to sort them out. Indeed, the only constant in Atlanta life is change.

To the rest of Georgia, Atlanta is often an object of derision, both for its role as state capital as well as for its traffic and rampant growth. Atlanta is far and away the most commercially important city in the Southeast. Love it or hate it, everyone knows the city is a vast and vigorous economic engine that has almost single-handedly catapulted Georgia into the top nine most populous states.

Befitting a city that literally rose from the ashes of the Civil War, you can be anything you want here without worrying too much about who or what came before. Unlike some of the more rigidly stratified cities in the South, with historic social and economic divides, "the city too busy to hate" just wants to know what you're doing right now. This

isn't always good—as Atlantans themselves will frankly admit, they've done a horrible job of preserving their history—but sometimes it can be almost as refreshing as an ice-cold "Coke-Cola" on a summer day.

## HISTORY

The words "Atlanta" and "history" rarely seem to occupy the same sentence, but the truth is that Atlanta's history is more interesting than it's generally given credit for. While Georgia's first city, Savannah, was founded over a century before Atlanta, in typical spirit once Atlanta got going, it moved fast.

In 1837, after the cruel mass removal of Creek and Cherokee people and the subsequent influx of white settlers, the Western & Atlantic Railroad chose a spot just east of the Chattahoochee River as the southern end of a track into Tennessee. The little town that emerged around the zero milepost was simply called Terminus. In 1843 its

---

**Previous:** Atlanta's skyline; Jimmy Carter Library and Museum. **Above:** the Fox Theatre.

name was changed to Marthasville, in honor of the daughter of former Governor Wilson Lumpkin, a major railroad booster. A scant two years later the name was changed again to its modern version. There are conflicting stories: One theory says Atlanta is a feminine version of "Atlantic" and a nod to its first railroad line. Another much more romantic version says it was renamed in honor of Martha Lumpkin's middle name, Atalanta, itself an homage to a Greek goddess.

Despite its modern association with the Confederacy, largely due to *Gone with the Wind,* business-oriented Atlanta was far less enamored with the idea of secession than most of the South. The Civil War initially provided an enormous economic boost to Atlanta, which rapidly became one of the Confederacy's largest industrial centers.

After a lengthy bombardment and General William T. Sherman's outmaneuvering of Confederate general John Bell Hood, Atlanta fell to Union troops on September 2, 1864. The 4,000 citizens who hadn't already fled the siege were ordered to evacuate. On November 15, a massive fire swept the city: It originated in the planned destruction of industrial and manufacturing areas, but through the carelessness of Union troops quickly spread to residential areas. Most of the city was burned to the ground and all its rail lines were destroyed. The fall of Atlanta crippled the Confederate war effort, secured the reelection of Abraham Lincoln, and kicked off Sherman's "March to the Sea," which would conclude in Savannah that Christmas.

The railroad again came to Atlanta's rescue. Only a few months after the war's end, all five of its main lines were up and running. The new spirit of rebirth was so contagious, in fact, that in 1868 Georgia politicos decided to move the state capital from Milledgeville—so symbolic of the old South—to Atlanta, its new commercial powerhouse.

Though segregation was very much in effect, Atlanta quickly became not only the birthplace of a large black middle class but the home of four institutions of higher learning for African Americans: Morris Brown College, Clark College, Morehouse College, and Spelman College, all of which joined existing white institutions such as Georgia Tech, Oglethorpe University, Agnes Scott College, and Emory University.

Auburn Avenue became the city's center of African American culture and commerce, with "Daddy King," Martin Luther King Sr., in the pulpit at Ebenezer Baptist Church. The "roar" in the Roaring Twenties in Atlanta came from its burgeoning airfield, soon to be named for its chief advocate, city councilman and mayor William Hartsfield.

Also in the 1920s, a humble local newspaper reporter named Margaret Mitchell, sidelined by an ankle injury, wrote *Gone with the Wind,* another of Atlanta's great exports. The premiere of the film came in 1939 with a star-studded gala; in a precursor to Atlanta's reputation as a racially enlightened Southern city, costar Hattie McDaniel became the first-ever African American Oscar winner.

The 1960s, in particular, gave proof of Atlanta's new nickname, "the city too busy to hate," actually coined by Hartsfield as mayor. His successor, Ivan Allen Jr., himself the son of an Atlanta mayor, formed a close partnership with local black civil rights leaders, chief among them Martin Luther King Jr., in order to promote fair housing and equal opportunity in the workplace as well as send a signal to the private sector at large that Atlanta was a great place to do business. In 1969, with the election of the city's first African American mayor, Maynard Jackson, Atlanta proper had become a majority-black city. Three years later, Atlantan Andrew Young was elected Georgia's first black congressman since Reconstruction.

In 1971 the airport was renamed Hartsfield Atlanta International Airport and within a decade was the world's busiest (Maynard Jackson's name was added in 2003). By the middle of the decade, Atlanta was America's third-busiest convention center. Those trends continued through the go-go 1980s and well into the 1990s.

Little Five Points is home to Atlanta's counterculture.

them. That said, for the most part traveling around Atlanta is a pleasure and not unusually time-consuming.

Afternoons in July and August are uncomfortably hot, so plan accordingly, especially if visiting an outdoor site like Stone Mountain. Zoo Atlanta is well worth a visit, but if the weather's hot, go right when it opens before the animals seek refuge from the heat.

## NEIGHBORHOODS

Despite its ever-growing size, Atlanta remains a city of neighborhoods, and neighborhoods within neighborhoods, each with a separate character and feel. The specific geography is an inexact and debatable science, but here's an overview:

**Downtown:** This is the beating commercial and political heart of Atlanta as well as its most socioeconomically challenged area. Neighborhoods within Downtown include **Sweet Auburn, Fairlie-Poplar,** up-and-coming **Old Fourth Ward,** and **So-No** (South of North Ave.).

**Five Points:** Not to be confused with Little Five Points, this downtown area adjacent to Underground Atlanta is literally the city center. During the first days of settlement, the intersection of Peachtree, Decatur, and Marietta Streets with Edgewood Avenue was chosen as the central point around which all development would radiate.

**Grant Park:** This verdant Victorian area southeast of Downtown hosts Zoo Atlanta and Oakland Cemetery. Up-and-coming **Cabbagetown** is adjacent.

**Midtown:** The culture-rich area between Downtown and Buckhead includes the Georgia Tech campus as well as the Margaret Mitchell House and the Fox Theatre.

**Inman Park:** This rejuvenated, gentrified Queen Anne garden suburb was Atlanta's first planned neighborhood.

**Little Five Points:** The gateway to East Atlanta at the intersection of Moreland and Euclid Streets is also the center of Atlanta's bohemian culture.

**Atlantic Station:** This planned New

Though unfortunately remembered most for the terrorist bombing that took place, the 1996 Summer Olympics in Atlanta was actually a successful staging overall and resulted in several important infrastructure improvements, chiefly Turner Field, athlete dorms that became housing for Georgia Tech and Georgia State University, and, of course, Centennial Olympic Park, site of the bombing and currently the hub of several major attractions.

## PLANNING YOUR TIME

Atlanta is fun for a day or for several days, and there's always something to do any day of the week. Shoppers, be sure to carve out time to enjoy the city's many shopping opportunities, whether they be in the Lenox and Phipps malls in Buckhead or the little shops in Virginia-Highland and Decatur.

If you're driving a car, at some point you will be faced with Atlanta's heavy traffic. Weekday morning and afternoon rush hours are ridiculous; plan to be as near your destination as possible before getting caught up in

# Atlanta

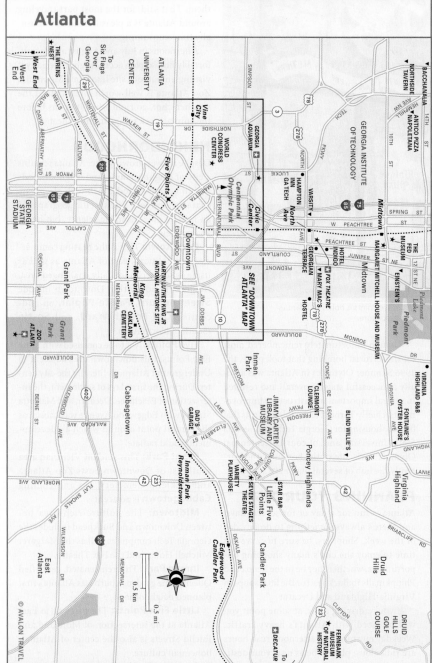

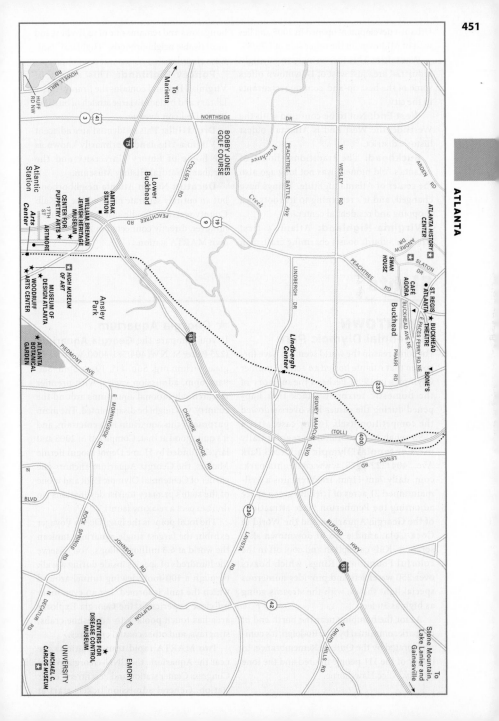

Urbanist development opened in 2005 and lies west of Midtown on the other side of I-75/85.

**Westside:** This increasingly trendy light industrial area just west of Downtown offers some of the best up-and-coming restaurants in the city.

**West End:** Not to be confused with the Westside, the West End is Atlanta's oldest historic district.

**Buckhead:** The traditional home of Atlanta's "old money" was not long ago also the center of Atlanta nightlife. Things have changed, and it's returning to its roots as a shopping and residential center.

**Virginia-Highland:** Atlanta's first streetcar suburb boasts charming craftsman bungalows and remains one of its liveliest and most livable neighborhoods. "Highland" is always singular.

**Poncey-Highland:** This subset of Virginia-Highland contains the Jimmy Carter Library and includes a large stretch of bustling Ponce De Leon Avenue.

**Druid Hills:** This residential area adjacent to Virginia-Highland is primarily known as the home of Emory University and the Fernbank Natural History Museum.

**Decatur:** Not an Atlanta neighborhood but an entirely separate city and the DeKalb County seat, fun, foodie-oriented Decatur is, however, directly connected to Atlanta by its own MARTA station.

# Sights

## DOWNTOWN
### Centennial Olympic Park

For some reason the world seems to have forgotten that Atlanta hosted an actual Summer Olympics in 1996. Perhaps the memory of the domestic terrorist attack that happened during the games has overshadowed the competition itself. In any case, after a 1998 rehab to accommodate regular daily use, **Centennial Olympic Park** (265 Park Ave., 404/222-7275, www.centennialpark. com, daily 7am-11pm, free) remains a well-maintained 21 acres of friendly green space adjoining the Pemberton Place attractions of the Georgia Aquarium and the World of Coca-Cola, amid a sea of downtown skyscrapers. Kids can splash and cool off in the colorful Fountain of Rings, which boasts over 250 water jets and provides numerous special light shows, with the streams going as high as 30 feet.

As for the bombing near the north end of the park committed by Eric Rudolph, it's commemorated by the Quilt of Remembrance, in honor of the 111 people injured and the lone fatality, Alice Hawthorne.

### ★ Georgia Aquarium

If you compare the **Georgia Aquarium** (225 Baker St. NW, 404/581-4000, www.georgiaaquarium.org, Sun.-Fri. 10am-5pm, Sat. 9am-6pm, admission varies) with premier research-educational aquariums around the country, you might be disappointed. The main purpose of this aquarium is to entertain, and it's quite good at that. Completed in 2005 and largely funded by Home Depot mogul Bernie Marcus, the Georgia Aquarium anchors one corner of Centennial Olympic Park and is one of the state's primary tourist destinations (so don't expect a relaxing jaunt).

The focal point is the huge Ocean Voyager exhibit, the largest single aquarium tank in the world at 6.3 million gallons. You observe the hundreds of species inside during a walk through a 100-foot viewing tunnel around which the tank is formed. For an even more up-close experience, the Georgia Explorer area has touch pools with horseshoe crabs, stingrays, and other coastal creatures.

Two MARTA rapid transit stations are near the Aquarium: the CNN-Georgia World Congress Center station and Peachtree Center station. General admission tickets start at

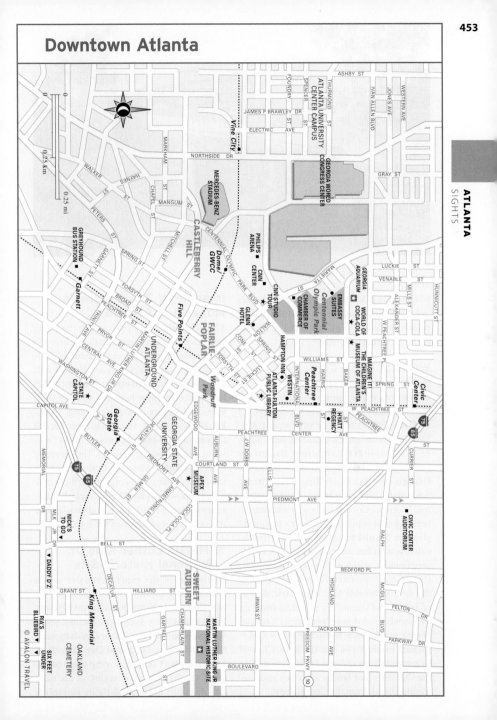

the Georgia Aquarium

$39.95 adults, $33.95 children. But various online advance and early admission tickets receive small discounts, so check the website for the full range of prices.

## World of Coca-Cola

If you want to immerse yourself in Atlanta's number one export, or if you really just love the taste, don't miss the over-the-top **World of Coca-Cola** (121 Baker St. NW, 404/676-5151, www.worldofcoca-cola.com, daily, hours vary, $16 adults, $12 children). Essentially one long, cheerful commercial for the iconic Georgia creation (including a mandatory six-minute video prior to entering the exhibits), World of Coca-Cola is a quick, fun experience that is perhaps Atlanta's top guilty pleasure. Think Disney with syrup. After the video, you get free rein to examine Coca-Cola memorabilia, watch endless loops of historic Coca-Cola commercials, and take part in the unquestionable highlight: taste dozens of samples of Coca-Cola products from six continents to your heart's content. Of course, there's a gift shop featuring every Coke-themed product you can imagine. Cheesy? Commercial? Yes and yes. But also good clean fun that the whole family will enjoy and a refreshing break from the Georgia heat.

## Imagine It! The Children's Museum of Atlanta

The now-prime territory across the street from Centennial Olympic Park is where the city chose to build its entry into the burgeoning kids museum category. **Imagine It! The Children's Museum of Atlanta** (275 Centennial Olympic Park Dr., 404/659-5437, www.childrensmuseumatlanta.org, Mon.-Fri. 10am-4pm, Sat.-Sun. 10am-5pm, $12.75) opened in 2003 and is a pioneer in the "museum without walls" concept. Unlike many other children's museums, which seem to have one eye on what parents expect, the focus here is on the power of play. There's a splash space, a farm space, a crawl space, and even a place where kids just get to paint the walls.

## ★ Martin Luther King Jr. National Historic Site

Easily one of the most expansive urban National Park Service-administered sites, the **Martin Luther King Jr. National Historic Site** (450 Auburn Ave., 404/331-5190, www.nps.gov, Memorial Day-Labor Day daily 9am-6pm, Labor Day-Memorial Day daily 9am-5pm, free) isn't only a moving elegy to the great Atlantan but an overview of the most crucial epoch of the civil rights movement

# A "Coke-Cola" and a Smile

the World of Coca-Cola

In the years after the Civil War, Atlanta was a boomtown, with its forward-looking business community using the city's destruction as a reason to rebuild bigger and better. By 1868, Atlanta was the new capital of Georgia, and a year later a former Confederate officer and druggist from Columbus, Georgia, moved here seeking opportunity.

John Pemberton was interested in the growing market for health tonics and hit upon a recipe using kola nut and coca leaf extracts. The first version was "French Wine Cola," but one of Pemberton's partners came up with "Coca-Cola," and the world's premier brand name was born. (While the company is called Coca-Cola, Atlantans often ask to drink a "Coke-Cola.")

Twenty years later Asa Griggs Candler bought Pemberton's company and had two great ideas. First was the idea of selling the product—the ingredients of which were secret, as they are to this day—in syrup form, to be carbonated right at the soda fountain. The second was franchising bottling rights nationwide, which catapulted Coca-Cola to prominence and created a number of family fortunes.

When the Woodruff family acquired Coca-Cola in 1919, president Robert Woodruff set his sights on global expansion. During World War II, in a brilliant blend of patriotism and business savvy, he promised a five-cent bottle to every U.S. serviceman no matter where they were stationed. It was not only a step toward expanding into 200 countries; by gaining the label of "wartime production" Coca-Cola could circumvent the rationing of sugar, its syrup's main ingredient!

There've been missteps along the way, chiefly the "New Coke" debacle, humorously chronicled at the **World of Coca-Cola** (121 Baker St. NW, 404/676-5151, www.worldofcoca-cola.com, daily, hours vary, $16 adults, $12 children), where you can sample a room full of Coke products. The company got in trouble when it was revealed that its Dasani bottled water was just purified City of Atlanta tap water. While the company maintains its flagship product never contained actual cocaine (the drug wasn't made illegal until 1906), many analysts say it likely contained very minimal traces through the 1920s.

Coca-Cola's philanthropic legacy is felt in Atlanta today at the Robert Woodruff Memorial Arts Center, Emory University, and the Centers for Disease Control and Prevention, among many others. Individually, the late Robert Woodruff's acts of philanthropy changed the face of the state, but exactly how much we may never know; most of his gifts are reckoned to be anonymous.

the tomb of Dr. King and his wife Coretta Scott King at the King Center for Nonviolent Social Change

itself. The facility, itself part of an even larger National Preservation District, comprises several wide-ranging features, all within a single block of historic (and historically African American) Auburn Avenue: the **visitors center** (450 Auburn Ave.); the restored original sanctuary of **Historic Ebenezer Baptist Church** (corner of Auburn Ave. and Jackson St.); the **King Center for Nonviolent Social Change** (449 Auburn Ave.), directly across the street, and where King and his wife are buried; the heavily visited **King Birth Home** (501 Auburn Ave.); and the nearby **Fire Station Number 6,** which played a key role in the desegregation of Atlanta's fire department.

Most visitors save time to pay their respects at the tomb of Dr. King and his wife, Coretta Scott King, at the King Center, situated at the end of a beautiful reflective pool and marked by an eternal flame (Dr. King was originally interred at Southview Cemetery).

A good bit more emotional in content than the typical education-heavy federally preserved site, the visitors center focuses on the sacrifice of King and his family, with an entire room devoted to a display of the humble wagon that served as his hearse following his assassination in 1968.

Even more moving than King's tomb is the experience within the church where he preached, Ebenezer Baptist, now called the Heritage Sanctuary to differentiate itself from the Horizon Sanctuary across the street (the church that the Ebenezer congregation built and moved into in 1999). The Heritage Sanctuary was restored and opened to the public in 2001.

A visit to the King Birth Home is also quite touching in that you really get a taste of life on Auburn Avenue in the 1930s, which, while segregated, at that time lacked the more modern type of urban blight that unfortunately is endemic along most of the street today. Within, the family rooms are preserved in a slice-of-life manner, with games and clothes strewn around the children's rooms, for example, instead of the more typical bare-bones aspect of many house museums. While most pieces are period and not actually King family items, the dishes in the kitchen are indeed relics of their time here. (Photography in the house is prohibited by request of the King family.)

The free tour of the Birth Home is quite popular, but there are no advance reservations. To secure a spot, you need to show up early the same day of the tour and book your space, preferably right at 9am when they open. If you arrive later in the day, you'll almost certainly be out of luck. However, as park rangers are quick to point out, there's a well-done video in the visitors center that gives you an extensive virtual tour.

## CNN Studio Tour

Cable news may not be the groundbreaking novelty it once was, but the **CNN Studio Tour** (1 CNN Center, 404/827-2300, www.cnn.com, daily 9am-5pm, $15 adults, $12 children) offers an opportunity to see how the world's first 24-hour cable news channel operates, as well as to get a glimpse further inside two other landmark Ted Turner enterprises, Turner Network Television (TNT) and Turner Broadcasting Systems (TBS). If you'd like, you can take a crack at anchoring your own "show" with the option to buy the demo tape! The walking tours, departing every 10 minutes, are 55 minutes long and sell out very quickly, so book ahead. There are daily elevator-assisted tours at 10:30am, 1:30pm, and 3:30pm. The CNN Tour is one of the featured attractions in the Atlanta CityPASS (www.citypass.com, five attractions for $69).

## Center for Human and Civil Rights

Atlanta's newest major attraction is the **Center for Human and Civil Rights** (100 Ivan Allen Jr. Blvd., www.civilandhumanrights.org, Mon.-Sat. 10am-5pm, Sun. noon-5pm, $18.25) at Centennial Olympic Park. This multilevel building has three main focuses: The main floor chronicling the civil rights movement in the U.S.; the top floor dealing with global struggles such as the fights against human trafficking and torture/detention; and the ground floor containing priceless manuscripts on display by Martin Luther King Jr. Because of the ongoing nature of the museum's mission, it hosts frequent rotating exhibits and timely speakers on current events.

## State Capitol

Known colloquially as "the Gold Dome" for its shiny gilded top (among other less charitable, more descriptive names), the circa-1889 **Georgia State Capitol** (206 Washington St. SW, 404/330-6150, Mon.-Fri. 8am-5pm) is where the Peach State's making of laws happens. The state legislature, officially called the General Assembly, only meets for about

the Horizon Sanctuary, where the Ebenezer congregation now worships

the Georgia State Capitol

40 days each winter. But despite that brief annual meeting (or because of it?), Georgia has gained a reputation as one of the most corrupt states in the union. Until very recently, rural legislators routinely ate so many roasted peanuts during extended sessions that the floors would be covered with shells.

To learn more about the history of the General Assembly and see various historical and political artifacts, you can get a brochure and take a self-guided tour of the **Capitol Museum** (www.libs.uga.edu, Mon.-Fri. 8am-5pm, free). A free iPhone app is also available at the website. The grounds, while not the equal of the gorgeous State House grounds one state over in Columbia, South Carolina, are attractively maintained and feature various statuary, including a tribute to a group of African American legislators who were briefly kicked out of the capitol during Reconstruction.

### APEX Museum

Another place to learn about Georgia black history is at the **APEX Museum** (135 Auburn Ave., 404/523-2739, www.apexmuseum.org, Tues.-Sat. 10am-5pm, $6 adults, $5 children), short for African American Panoramic Experience. APEX centers on

three permanent exhibits: "Africa: The Untold Story," which chronicles humanity's rise in the African continent on to the trans-Atlantic slave trade; "Sweet Auburn: Street of Pride"; and "The Georgia Negro," based on W. E. B. Du Bois's historic exhibit from the 1900 Paris Expo documenting black middle-class life in Georgia.

## GRANT PARK
### ★ Zoo Atlanta

There are larger zoos and there are more significant zoos. But few combine size with educational enjoyment as well as **Zoo Atlanta** (800 Cherokee Ave. SE, 404/624-9453, www.zooatlanta.org, daily 9:30am-5:30pm, $21 adults, $16 ages 3-11), the pride of Grant Park. Primates are the prime specialty of Zoo Atlanta, and their expansive open gorilla habitat isn't only very enjoyable, it's a center of global gorilla research (Dian Fossey was a key collaborator). Venerable old Willie B., a silverback gorilla, lived at the zoo from 1961 until his death in 2000, but his garrulous image remains a symbol of Zoo Atlanta, especially since the zoo's significant upgrade and renovation in the late 1980s.

While there's a strong emphasis on crowd favorites from the African plains, like gorillas,

Zoo Atlanta

elephants, giraffes, zebras, and a lion who sleeps 23 hours a day, the other key attraction at Zoo Atlanta is its family of delightful giant pandas, Lun Lun and Yang Yang, and their offspring Ya Lun and Xi Lun. Despite the sumptuous, specially built pagoda in which they cavort for your enjoyment, the pandas are actually the property of China, on indefinite loan.

As with any zoo in the South, you'll want to get here as early in the day as possible to catch the animals before the heat drives them into shade and sleep (not to mention avoiding the crush of deluxe double-wide baby strollers when the crowd starts hitting at about 11am). Getting to Grant Park early will also help you get a parking space in the smallish zoo lot.

## Oakland Cemetery

Atlanta's **Oakland Cemetery** (248 Oakland Ave., www.oaklandcemetery.com, daily 8am-8pm, free) is a visually compelling and strangely relaxing location filled with history. The three most famous perpetual denizens are legendary golfer Bobby Jones; Atlanta's first African American mayor, Maynard Jackson; and, of course, iconic writer Margaret Mitchell. (There are lots of Mitchells buried in Oakland Cemetery, but technically the

author of *Gone with the Wind* is not buried as a Mitchell; she was married to John Marsh when she died and her tombstone here bears that surname.)

The visitors center on-site offers tour information, and, perhaps oddly, cemetery-themed souvenirs. Cemetery-sponsored guided tours are available Saturday and Sunday at 10am, 2pm, and 4pm, no reservations required and all leaving from the visitors center.

## MIDTOWN
### ★ High Museum of Art

It bills itself as the most important art museum in the Southeast, and while that may be somewhat arguable, there's no doubt that the **High Museum of Art** (1280 Peachtree St. NE, 404/733-4400, www.high.org, $19.50 adults, $12 ages 6-17) is a crucial element of Atlanta cultural life and represents a significant collection of American art in its own right. The building itself, a gleaming white modernist structure not dissimilar in look and feel to New York's Guggenheim (here you also take a winding staircase up through the exhibits), seems strangely at home in posh Midtown, despite its architecture having absolutely nothing to do with any other building in the area. A major reason for the High's physical harmony with its neighborhood has to do with being set back within a well-maintained urban green space.

Once inside the cavernous interior, you'd be excused for briefly thinking that no amount of art could ever fill the space adequately. Indeed, you should take a few minutes to study the somewhat confusing layout of the three separate buildings (all linked by a sky bridge) that make up the High. The bulk of the museum's noteworthy permanent collection occupies three floors in the Stent wing, expertly arranged in viewing areas that split the huge square footage into manageable chunks. Don't miss the folk art collection upstairs, with a significant representation of work by noted Georgia outsider artist Howard Finster.

## Margaret Mitchell House and Museum

Perhaps more accurately called Margaret Mitchell's apartment, this charmingly restored "Dump," as the great author and her husband John Marsh affectionately referred to it, takes you back in time to that 10-year span in the 1920s and 1930s when Mitchell wrote *Gone with the Wind* while recovering from a nasty ankle injury.

The furnishings at the **Margaret Mitchell House and Museum** (990 Peachtree St., 404/249-7015, www.margaretmitchellhouse.com, Mon.-Sat. 10am-5:30pm, Sun. noon-5:30pm, $13 adults, $8.50 children) aren't even close to original, since the three-story 1899 building, converted to an apartment in 1919, was severely blighted in the late 1970s, vandalized and essentially open to the elements. Indeed, it was slated for demolition until a cadre of local residents and donors teamed up to save the house in the late 1980s. However, the Dump's tribulations still weren't over: After renovations had begun, two separate fires struck, one in 1994 and another in 1996.

Using Mitchell's own journal notes, restorationists furnished the tiny one-bedroom second-story apartment as closely as they could to what they thought was authentic when the building housed the Crescent Apartments, with the Marshes in apartment number 1. Your experience is by guided tour, leaving every half hour and meeting in the cute and well-stocked gift shop. While the house opens at 10am, the first tour of the day doesn't begin until 10:30am. A charming tour guide will walk you through a small set of displays about Mitchell's young life and burgeoning journalism career before escorting you into the actual apartment.

The High Museum of Art is the Southeast's premier art museum.

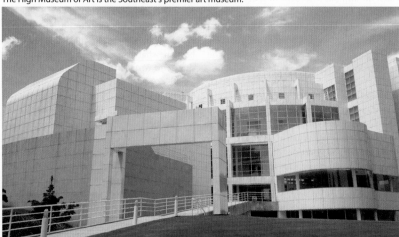

# Margaret Mitchell's Legacy

Margaret Mitchell changed the world. Her novel *Gone with the Wind* would become one of the planet's most printed books and inspire one of cinema's most popular films.

Mitchell was a reporter for the *Atlanta Journal-Constitution* when she had to quit due to a nagging ankle injury. Her husband, John, anxious to give her something to do while confined to the ramshackle apartment on Peachtree Street they called "the Dump," urged her to write a book. It took nearly 10 years to write, but once published in 1936, *Gone with the Wind* took the world by storm. A scant three years later the blockbuster film premiered at Atlanta's now-demolished Loew's Grand Theatre, with a crowd of one million gathered to see the greatest stars of the day. Generally shy, Mitchell spoke briefly at the premiere.

Coming from a long line of Atlantans, she was well equipped to write the ultimate tale of the Old South. Her grandfather told her stories about serving in the Confederate army. Like her heroine Scarlett O'Hara, Mitchell was rebellious: During the Roaring Twenties, "Peggy," as she styled herself, adopted the flapper look and lifestyle, at one point calling herself an "unscrupulous flirt." At age 22, she married an abusive alcoholic. The best man at her wedding, John Marsh, would become her second husband. They were together when she was killed at age 48, hit by a speeding car just a few blocks from her house.

The best place to experience Mitchell's legacy is at "the Dump" itself, the **Margaret Mitchell House and Museum** (990 Peachtree St., 404/249-7015, www.margaretmitchellhouse.com, Mon.-Sat. 10am-5:30pm, Sun. noon-5:30pm, $13 adults, $8.50 children). The typewriter she used to write *Gone with the Wind*, however, is at a special Mitchell exhibit on the 5th floor of the **Atlanta-Fulton Public Library** (1 Margaret Mitchell Square, 404/730-1700, www.afplweb.com, Mon.-Thurs. 9am-8pm, Fri.-Sat. 9am-6pm, Sun. 2pm-6pm, free). Down Peachtree Street, you can visit the Georgian Terrace Hotel, where Clark Gable and Vivien Leigh stayed during the premiere. Up in Marietta you can visit the *Gone with the Wind* Museum: Scarlett on the Square.

The author is buried in **Oakland Cemetery** (248 Oakland Ave., www.oaklandcemetery.com, daily 8am-8pm, free) in the Grant Park area near Zoo Atlanta. But don't look for the name "Mitchell"; she lies next to her husband, John Marsh, and bears his name.

---

Be sure to check out the small but interesting exhibit on the filming of *Gone with the Wind* in the restored building across the courtyard. A combo ticket ($22 adults, $12 children) with admission to the Mitchell House and the Atlanta History Center is available at either location or online.

## The Fed Museum

Directly across the street from the Margaret Mitchell House, though utterly different in look and purpose, is the Atlanta Monetary Museum, more commonly called **The Fed Museum** (1000 Peachtree St., www.frbatlanta.org, Mon.-Fri. 9am-4pm, free). Within the hulking Federal Reserve Bank of Atlanta building, the Fed Museum offers not only some surprisingly interesting exhibits on the history of money, from barter to modern times, but some amazing behind-the-scenes looks at enormous amounts of cash being counted, sorted, and bundled in various ways. It doesn't take long to visit, but this is one of the best free, fun, and informative hours you'll spend in Atlanta.

## Atlanta Botanical Garden

If you love orchids, you'll go nuts for the **Atlanta Botanical Garden** (1345 Piedmont Ave., 404/876-5859, www.atlantabotanical-garden.org, Nov.-Mar. Tues.-Sun. 9am-5pm, Apr.-Oct. Tues.-Wed. and Fri.-Sun. 9am-7pm, Thurs. 9am-10pm, $19 adults, $13 children, parking $2 per hour). The centerpiece of this gorgeous 30-acre gem right beside Piedmont Park is the **Dorothy Chapman Fuqua Conservatory,** which specializes in rain forest habitat. Within the conservatory you'll find the pièce de résistance, the **Fuqua Orchid Center,** which bills itself as the largest collection of orchid species in the United States. It features a special section devoted purely to mountain-habitat orchids as well as a massive display of tropical rain forest species.

The sprawling grounds are a collection of themed gardens, including a Japanese garden, a rose garden, a working organic herb garden, and a children's garden with sculptures and exhibits. A good way to enjoy it, albeit in the dark, is during the Concert in the Garden series. Past performers have included Merle Haggard, Aaron Neville, and Neko Case.

## ★ Fox Theatre

Truly one of the all-time classic vintage venues, the **Fox Theatre** (660 Peachtree St. NE, 404/881-2100, www.foxtheatre.org) is without question Atlanta's most beloved landmark and a priceless piece of Americana. Its rococo Moorish-Egyptian theme, complete with a faux minaret and stylized hieroglyphics, is a nod to its original incarnation, never realized, of being a Shriners temple. When completed in 1929 it was as a movie theater in a popular chain developed by William Fox. The 4,600-seat "Arabian courtyard" auditorium, including nearly 100 crystal stars, did

not actually host the world premiere of *Gone with the Wind* in 1939, but the Fox Theatre was the only theater in Atlanta at the time that allowed both white and black patrons. The "Colored" box-office window is still here, at the back entrance.

Over 300 performances a year are held at "the Fabulous Fox," from traveling Broadway shows to musical performances to, yes, movies—today usually shown on a state-of-the-art digital projector. However, the audience singalongs that occasionally precede the features are shown on the original 1929 projector.

The grand Egyptian Ballroom, designed after a temple for Pharaoh Ramses II (the mezzanine ladies' lounge has a replica of King Tut's throne), continues to host large gala events and dances. The Fox also features its original pipe organ, nicknamed "Mighty Mo," occasionally played during special performances such as Atlanta Ballet's annual *Nutcracker.*

## Jimmy Carter Library and Museum

First, to clear up any confusion: The **Jimmy Carter Library and Museum** (441 Freedom Pkwy., 404/865-7100, www.jimmycarterlibrary.gov, museum Mon.-Sat. 9am-4:45pm,

the Fox Theatre

Sun. noon-4:45pm, library Mon.-Fri. 8:30am-4:30pm, $8 adults, free under age 17) is on the grounds of the globally renowned **Carter Center,** but they're not the same entity.

The nonprofit Carter Center pursues the former president's goals of international cooperation, free and fair elections, and human rights, and isn't usually open to the public. Since 1986 the public component has belonged to the Jimmy Carter Library and Museum, which houses not only about 27 million of the president's papers and records but exhibits of his life and work both in the White House and after. (If you're looking for political memorabilia from Carter's campaigns, you might be disappointed; most of that is in various buildings in the Jimmy Carter National Historic District in his hometown of Plains, Georgia, a couple of hours south.)

The spacious boulevard called Freedom Parkway links the Carter Center to the Martin Luther King Jr. National Historic Site, and indeed the two sites are only about five minutes apart by car. The president and his wife, Rosalynn, both maintain offices at the Carter Center and can occasionally be seen coming and going. The grounds are particularly nice and are free and open to the public whether or not you enter the museum building.

## William Breman Jewish Heritage Museum

The **William Breman Jewish Heritage Museum** (1440 Spring St., 678/222-3700, www.thebreman.org, Mon.-Thurs. 10am-5pm, Fri. 10am-3pm, Sun. 1pm-5pm, $12 adults, $6 children), often just called the Breman, aspires to chronicle and honor the whole of the Jewish experience in Atlanta since antebellum times, but with a nod to greater events such as the Holocaust and aspects of social justice.

## Museum of Design Atlanta

It bills itself as the only museum in the South devoted purely to design. In any event, **Museum of Design Atlanta** (MODA, 1315 Peachtree St. NE, 404/979-6455, www.museumofdesign.org, Tues.-Sat. 10am-5pm, Sun. noon-5pm, $10 adults, $5 students and children) is 5,000 square feet of display space devoted to a constantly shifting array of exhibits, focusing on some aspect of modern design; there are no permanent displays. It's a fun visit in a hip environment. On the last Thursday of the month the museum stays open until 8pm and admission includes a cocktail. MODA is near the Woodruff Arts Center, and the nearby Arts Center MARTA transit station is very convenient. However, MODA has no parking lot; you're urged to pay to park at the LAZ lot (1337 Peachtree St.).

# DRUID HILLS
## Fernbank Museum of Natural History

Since opening in the early 1990s, the **Fernbank Museum of Natural History** (767 Clifton Rd. NE, 404/929-6300, www.fernbankmuseum.org, Mon.-Sat. 10am-5pm, Sun. noon-5pm, $17.50 adults, $15.50 children) in Druid Hills has become a staple of the Atlanta cultural scene as well as a regular stop for local schoolchildren. While now a separate entity, the museum is an offshoot of the nearby Fernbank Science Center, a project of the DeKalb County Public Schools.

The main permanent exhibit at Fernbank and by far the most attention-demanding is the "Giants of the Mesozoic" display of massive, life-size dinosaur sculptures, including a 120-foot *Argentinosaurus,* the largest dinosaur known to science. Another permanent exhibit is "A Walk through Time in Georgia," which tells the story of the Peach State in geological and biological terms. For many visitors, though, the highlight is the 300-seat IMAX theater, which hosts a steady schedule of beautifully shot nature films. Every Friday evening sees another edition of "Martinis and IMAX," featuring a movie, finger food, and access to a cash bar for one low admission cost.

The **Fernbank Science Center** (156 Heaton Park Dr., 678/874-7102, http://fsc.fernbank.edu, Mon.-Wed. 9am-5pm, Thurs.-Fri. 9am-9pm, Sat. 10am-5pm, free), though a

the Fernbank Museum of Natural History

separate facility, has a cool observatory with frequent planetarium shows (Thurs.-Fri. 9am-10:30pm).

## ★ Michael C. Carlos Museum

One of the most enriching small museums I've found anywhere, the **Michael C. Carlos Museum** (571 S. Kilgo Circle NE, 404/727-4282, www.carlos.emory.edu, Tues.-Fri. 10am-4pm, Sat. 10am-5pm, Sun. noon-5pm, $8 adults, $6 children) on the Emory University quadrangle is one of Atlanta's hidden gems. The comparatively young age of the museum building itself, built in 1985 and majorly upgraded in 1993, is matched by its dynamic, intimate approach to its subject matter, primarily Greco-Roman, pre-Columbian, and Egyptian antiquities.

The collections, some of which date from an early collegiate collection in the Victorian era, are small, but their presentation is extremely well curated and annotated, as befitting a university-affiliated institution. You can get up close and personal with just about everything, including the priceless sculptures.

These days the centerpiece of the Carlos is its extremely well-preserved collection of Egyptian funerary artifacts (interestingly, many were acquired from a curiosity museum

in upstate New York). You enter the Egyptian section on a dramatically lighted, gradual ramp bearing a huge stylized map of the Nile River. Inside the hall are several mummies, most bearing incredibly vivid, unrestored,

the Michael C. Carlos Museum

and unretouched paint from thousands of years ago. If mummies aren't your thing, the top floor has an impressive collection of African folk masks and crafts, and the museum has a vibrant collection of pre-Columbian Native American antiquities.

The museum is near the main entrance to the Emory campus off the traffic circle at Oxford and Decatur Roads. Parking is available in a nearby parking garage.

## Centers for Disease Control Museum

Possibly Atlanta's most offbeat museum and perhaps its most interesting is the **David J. Sencer Centers for Disease Control Museum** (1600 Clifton Rd. NE, 404/639-0830, www.cdc.gov, Mon.-Fri. 9am-5pm, free), located on the world-famous campus of the crucial public health research institution. Until recently called "Global Odyssey of Health," the CDC Museum is a bit less clinical in nature than you might expect, the emphasis being on vibrant multimedia. Ongoing exhibits include a "Global Symphony," a 100-foot-long chronicle of the fight against diseases like polio and HIV/AIDS; "The Story of CDC," a history of the CDC and the evolution of its role; and the massive sculpture *Messengers*. Indeed, at the museum's rotating exhibits, you're just as likely to see cutting-edge art dealing with sociopolitical topics as you are anything of an overtly medical nature.

## BUCKHEAD
### ★ Atlanta History Center and Swan House

The **Atlanta History Center** (130 W. Paces Ferry Rd., 404/814-4000, www.atlantahistorycenter.com, Mon.-Sat. 10am-5:30pm, Sun. 1pm-4pm, $16.50 adults, $11 children) is a well-run city museum with a huge added bonus: the historic and beautifully restored **Swan House** (tours Mon.-Sat. 11am-4pm, Sun. 1pm-4pm), one of the finest house museums in the South. The History Center itself offers a multitude of well-curated exhibits, including the obligatory city history section (try to catch one of the free guided docent tours for much more information than the exhibits show).

The History Center purchased the Swan House directly from Mrs. Inman, heir to the Inman fortune (and whose son is the namesake for nearby Inman Park), exactly as she left it. What this means to visitors is that they have an opportunity to tour this magnificent, 14,000-square-foot, elegantly and charmingly appointed mansion stocked almost completely with original furnishings. This is almost unheard of in the house museum world, which generally depends on approximating furnishings by period and almost never has the luxury of featuring original items.

Designed by Philip Trammell Shutze, the multistory Swan House dates from "only" 1928, but looks and feels significantly older thanks to the tastes of the owners, Edward and Emily Inman. Edward made his fortune as a cotton middleman. You'll get a distinct *Downton Abbey* vibe as you take your guided tour from room to room and note how marvelously clubby and cozy the house feels despite its swank opulence.

The most exciting news for the History Center is the planned opening in 2017 of the new Lloyd and Mary Ann Whitaker Cyclorama Building, which will house the famous 128-year-old circular painting of the Battle of Atlanta, formerly housed in a museum in Grant Park near Zoo Atlanta. The plan is not only to restore the Victorian-era painting but to restore the original way it was intended to be displayed.

The Atlanta History Center also operates the Margaret Mitchell House, and you can purchase a combo ticket ($22 adults, $12 children) from either place. The center is also one of several attractions featured in the Atlanta CityPASS package ticket (www.citypass.com, $69).

### Governor's Mansion

The official residence of the chief executive of the Peach State, the **Governor's Mansion** (391 W. Paces Ferry Rd. NW, http://

the historic Swan House at the Atlanta History Center

mansion.georgia.gov, tours Tues.-Thurs. 10am-11:30am, free) is not to be confused with the much larger and more ornate State Capitol or "Gold Dome" downtown. This handsomely appointed, 30-room Greek Revival home in Buckhead is open for free tours for a short window each week. Keep in mind it's not exactly historic, given that it was only built in 1967.

## WEST END
### The Wren's Nest

Generations of Americans have enjoyed the folktales of Uncle Remus and Brer Rabbit, the brainchildren of the great Joel Chandler Harris. The memory of the author and his creations is preserved at Harris's West End home, **The Wren's Nest** (1050 Ralph David Abernathy Blvd., 404/753-7735, www.wrensnestonline.com, Tues.-Sat. 10:30am-2:30pm, $8 adults, $5 children), including many original furnishings. Atlanta's oldest house museum, the Wren's Nest's preservation was encouraged in the early 20th century by Andrew Carnegie and President Theodore Roosevelt.

Harris, also known as a vigorous and progressive editor at the *Atlanta Journal-Constitution,* lived in this Queen Anne house from 1881 to 1908, during which time he wrote many of his most famous tales gathered in the global best-seller *Uncle Remus: His Songs and His Sayings.* A particular highlight is storytelling time each Saturday at 1pm, courtesy of the "Wren's Nest Ramblers," the resident group of African American storytellers who bring Harris's tales to life. (Those who want to further their Brer Rabbit experience can drive a couple of hours south to Eatonton, Georgia, and visit Harris's birthplace at the Uncle Remus Museum.)

### Six Flags over Georgia

A favorite day-trip destination of generations of Georgians, **Six Flags over Georgia** (275 Riverside Pkwy. SW, 770/739-3400, www.six-flags.com, $57, $40 children under 48 inches tall, free under age 2, parking $20) is known to thrill seekers the world over for its vast assortment of roller coasters. Many are authentically wooden and structured for maximum speed in the old-school way, while the newer variety emphasize the modern focus on heavy G-force and twists and turns. The 100-acre park features no less than 37 "thrill rides" ranging from the mild kiddie ride Tweetie's Tree House (Six Flags has an extensive licensing agreement with Warner Bros. movie and cartoon characters; Batman and Superman feature prominently here) to the world-class "hypercoaster" Goliath. Of course, you can still ride that vintage classic, the Great American Scream Machine.

It's not cheap, and it can get pretty crowded. Your best bet for a slightly thinner crowd is to come on weekdays during summer as well as April-May and September-October.

# UNIVERSITIES AND COLLEGES
## Georgia Tech

Anchoring a large portion of downtown and midtown Atlanta, the **Georgia Institute of Technology** (North Ave., 404/894-2000, www.gatech.edu), always simply called "Georgia Tech" or even just "Tech," is one of the nation's oldest, largest, and best engineering schools. Founded in 1885 specifically as an effort to reboot the South's industrial efforts in the wake of the Civil War, it is one of the few premier engineering-research schools in the United States that is a fully public institution.

By far the most interesting portion of campus for visitors is the nine-acre "Old Campus" or Hill District, the original Tech campus and site of a dozen of its oldest and most picturesque buildings. A highlight is Tech Tower, named for its large, lighted "Tech" signage on each of its four sides.

The Georgia Tech Yellow Jackets play football at Bobby Dodd Stadium at Historic Grant Field. While improved since its early days, Grant Field is the oldest major university gridiron in the United States, built in 1905. As skyscrapers have sprung up around it, the view from a typical Jacket home game is quite different from the bucolic setting of the typical college football stadium.

Don't be surprised to hear an old-fashioned steam whistle while walking around the Tech campus. An old school tradition, the whistle blows five minutes before the top of each hour during regular class times.

## Emory University

A private university occupying 630 acres in the verdant, quiet Druid Hills residential area in northeast Atlanta, **Emory University** (1615 Pierce Dr. NE, 404/727-6123, www.emory.edu) hasn't been in town the entire time; it was founded in 1836 in Oxford, Georgia. However, in 1915 a land grant by Asa Griggs Candler, then-president of Coca-Cola, enabled the school to move to the state capital, beginning a long association with the locally based soft-drink giant. In 1979, another Coca-Cola president, Robert W. Woodruff, donated over $100 million in Coke stock to Emory, the largest-ever gift to a university up to that time. In 1994 the Emory business school was renamed for Roberto Goizueta, yet another Coca-Cola president and college benefactor.

However, you'll find very few commercial nods to Coca-Cola on Emory's understated, wooded campus. Despite Emory's old-fashioned roots as a Methodist institution, it is on the leading edge of design, with over two million square feet of building space LEED-certified to meet state-of-the-art sustainability and conservation standards. By far the main attraction for visitors is the **Michael C. Carlos Museum** (571 S. Kilgo Circle, 404/727-4282, www.carlos.emory.edu, Tues.-Fri. 10am-4pm, Sat. 10am-5pm, Sun. noon-5pm, $8 adults, $6 children), an excellently designed and curated museum devoted to Egyptian, Greco-Roman, and ancient Native American artifacts.

## Historically Black Colleges and Universities

Perhaps nowhere else is Atlanta's importance to African American history as clear as in the presence of several of the country's oldest and most influential historically black colleges and universities (HBCUs), all nearby to each other in southwest Atlanta and since 1929 gathered in a consortium called the Atlanta University Center.

All member institutions share the **Robert W. Woodruff Library** (111 James P. Brawley Dr. SW, 404/978-2067, www.auctr.edu), whose main claim to fame these days is as the home of an expansive collection of papers from Martin Luther King Jr., purchased from the King estate in 2006 and deeded to King's alma mater, Morehouse College. The papers are available for public research use.

The first higher education institution in the United States established especially for African Americans to attain graduate degrees was Atlanta College, founded in conjunction with the Freedmen's Bureau in the months immediately following the Civil War. A few years later, Clark College was founded to grant undergraduate degrees. In 1929 they merged to form **Clark Atlanta University** (223 James P. Brawley Dr., 404/880-8000, www.cau.edu), which today has about 4,000 students and maintains its Methodist affiliation. It's one of only four HBCUs with full research institution status. Famed author and civil rights activist W. E. B. Du Bois was a longtime sociology professor here.

Easily the best known of Atlanta's HBCUs, however, are **Morehouse College** (830 Westview Dr., 404/681-2800, www.morehouse.edu) and **Spelman College** (350 Spelman Ln., 404/681-3643, www.spelman.edu). While technically unaffiliated, they're often mentioned in the same breath not only because of their academic excellence but because of their unique nature; Morehouse is an all-men's school, while Spelman is all women. Between them they account for an amazing variety of high-profile alumni, including Martin Luther King Jr. and his daughters,

filmmaker Spike Lee, actor Samuel L. Jackson, authors Alice Walker and Tina McElroy Ansa, and Atlanta's first black mayor, Maynard Jackson. The **Spelman College Museum of Fine Art** (350 Spelman Ln., 404/681-3643, www.spelman.edu, Tues.-Fri. 10am-4pm, Sat. noon-4pm, $3 donation) is in the Cosby Academic Center and is devoted purely to artwork by female artists covering the African diaspora.

**Morris Brown College** (643 MLK Jr. Dr., 404/739-1010, www.morrisbrown.edu) has the distinction of being the first African American college self-funded entirely by African Americans, almost all of them formerly enslaved. However, Morris Brown lost accreditation in 2002 after a financial scandal. No longer technically a member of the Atlanta University Center organization, Morris Brown currently has fewer than 40 students and faces a very uncertain future.

## Georgia State University

Despite its heavily urban setting downtown, **Georgia State University** (30 Courtland St., 404/413-2000, www.gsu.edu) is actually not as young as you'd think, with roots dating back to 1913. It's not as small as you'd think either; its enrollment is now the largest in the state. Of prime interest to visitors is the school-run **Rialto Center for the Arts** (80 Forsyth St., 404/413-9849, www.rialtocenter.org) in the Fairlie-Poplar district, hosting most performances of Georgia State's esteemed music department.

# Entertainment and Events

## NIGHTLIFE
### Live Music

The main rock-and-roll bar in happening Little Five Points is **The Star Community Bar** (437 Moreland Ave., 404/500-4942, www.starbaratlanta.com, Thurs.-Sun. 4pm-3am), more colloquially just called "Star Bar" and known far and wide as a Southern hipster

mecca and live-music joint. It also boasts one of the coolest Elvis shrines outside of Memphis, upstairs in a special "vault."

The premier bigger-name live-music venue in Little Five Points is **Variety Playhouse** (1099 Euclid Ave. NE, 404/524-7354, www.variety-playhouse.com), a former movie theater converted into a concert space, with a mix of assigned seating and a dance floor up front near the stage. They do have beer and wine, but the best way to enjoy a night out at Variety Playhouse is to sample food and drink elsewhere in this lively entertainment district before (and after!) the show. Unlike most nightspots in Atlanta, no smoking is allowed here.

The best blues joint in Atlanta proper and easily one of the more authentic dive bars in town as well, **Northside Tavern** (1058 Howell Mill Rd., 404/874-8745, www.northsidetavern.com, daily noon-3am) features live blues and jazz seven nights a week and has a beat-up interior to match that crushing schedule.

One of Atlanta's most iconic live-music hubs, **Blind Willie's** (828 N. Highland Ave., 404/873-2583, www.blindwilliesblues.com) brings the blues (and some jazz) six nights a week in the hip Virginia-Highland neighborhood.

Renowned as a late-night party place and metal club for the last 20 years, **The Highlander** (931 Monroe Circle, 404/872-0060, www.thehighlanderatlanta.com, Mon.-Sat. 11am-3am, Sun. 12:30pm-midnight) in Midtown has experienced a renewed popularity in the wake of an episode of *Diners, Drive-ins, and Dives* on the Food Channel. The focus food-wise is on the delectable burgers, which some call the best in Atlanta.

One of Atlanta's premier live-music clubs, East Atlanta's **The Earl** (488 Flat Shoals Ave., 404/522-3950, www.badearl.com) also boasts some of its best burgers (the guacamole burger is a fave rave, and don't forget the sweet-potato fries). The acts tend toward the indie or heavy side, and are generally bands on their way up to better things; in short, a great place to catch great bands in an intimate venue while you still can.

Like great, loud music? Love unicorns? Then **The Drunken Unicorn** (736 Ponce de Leon Ave., no phone, www.thedrunkenunicorn.net) in Poncey-Highland is for you. In classic rock-bar style, it's basically a dark dungeon with a smallish stage and a really good sound system. The focus is on the bands—metal, punk, indie, basically anything not mainstream—and cheap and flowing beer. It's directly underneath **Friends on Ponce** (736 Ponce de Leon Ave., 404/817-3820, www.friendsonponce-atl.com), a neighborhood gay bar.

No ATL pub crawl is complete without a visit to **Smith's Olde Bar** (1578 Piedmont Ave., 404/875-1522, www.smithsoldebar.com, Mon.-Sat. noon-3am, Sun. noon-midnight)—or "SOB," get it?—in the Piedmont Park-Morningside area just northeast of Midtown. Combine an Irish pub with a blues-rock club with a pool hall with a sports bar, but with a more open-minded attitude in this gay-friendly area of town, and you have a fairly complete nightlife experience.

## Dive Bars

In a city that already has its share of quirky one-of-a-kind bars and clubs, the **Clermont Lounge** (789 Ponce de Leon Ave., 404/874-4783, www.clermontlounge.net, Mon.-Sat. 1pm-3am) in Virginia-Highland is perhaps the quirkiest. Originally a 1960s hotel bar in a hotel that has since shut down, the Clermont is a combination strip club-hipster dive with kitsch cachet to burn. The vibe isn't so much classic gentlemen's club as it is sheer spectacle, with the generally over-the-hill but spirited topless dancers being an assortment of ages and body types. The booze is plentiful and cheap, the ubiquitous PBR running a buck apiece most nights, the company interesting and varied, and the burlesque entertainment . . . well, it is what it is.

No look at Atlanta nightlife is complete without a look at **Sister Louisa's Church of the Living Room & Ping Pong Emporium** (466 Edgewood Ave., 404/522-8275, www.sisterlouisaschurch.com, Mon.-Sat. 5pm-3am, Sun. 5pm-midnight), which, amazingly, is exactly what the name implies—except "Sister Louisa" is actually a guy, specifically Grant Henry, a former priest who now serves libations and has painted some interesting quasi-religious-themed artwork for the walls. As for the Ping-Pong, yes, there's one table upstairs. The main show at "Church," as everyone calls it, is the clientele itself, a mix of über-hipsters, freaks, those of vague gender, and, of course, lookie-loos in search of the wild side of Atlanta life.

You'll find **El Bar** (939 Ponce de Leon Ave., 404/881-6040, Wed.-Sat. 10pm-3am) right behind and sort of underneath El Azteca restaurant in Virginia-Highland, and if you like crazy nights, a combination of hip-hop and club music, and excellent and creative drink specials (the house specialty is a shot of tequila with a Miller High Life), you will have lots of *amor* for El Bar. It's cozy and crowded late on weekend nights.

## Taverns and Pubs

The personification of the neighborhood bar and grill, **Manuel's Tavern** (602 N. Highland Ave., 404/525-3447, www.manuelstavern.com, Tues.-Sat. 11am-2am, Sun.-Mon. 11am-midnight) is nearly as well known for its food as its spirits and convivial atmosphere. Older generations knew "Mannie's" as where Atlanta's old-school power structure let their hair down and exchanged scuttlebutt. Fresh off a loving restoration, Manuel's remains a Poncey-Highland must-visit for the beer connoisseur and comfort-food maven alike.

Virginia-Highland's favorite bar is **The Righteous Room** (1051 Ponce de Leon Ave., 404/874-0939, Mon.-Thurs. 11:30am-2am, Fri. 11:30am-3am, Sat. noon-3am, Sun. noon-2am), which also gets most everyone's vote for best bar food in Atlanta. The burgers in particular deserve the raves they get, but the menu is surprisingly extensive, with good veggie selections and even a salmon quesadilla.

Yes, the name's a joke: **Euclid Avenue Yacht Club** (1136 Euclid Ave. NE, 404/688-2582, www.theeayc.com, Mon.-Thurs. 3pm-2am, Fri.-Sat. noon-3am, Sun. noon-midnight) has nothing to do with boats of any kind. But this staple of the Little Five Points (L5P) bar scene does have something of a clubby atmosphere in the sense that it's really more of an old-school neighborhood blue-collar bar than some of the more hipster-oriented dives that have sprung up in L5P over the past few years.

## Nightclubs and Dancing

For a cover in the $5-10 range, you can go underground, literally, and dance all night to the DJs spinning old-school hip-hop and dance-pop at the epicenter of the ATL club scene, **MJQ** (736 Ponce de Leon Ave., 404/870-0575, Mon.-Wed. 10pm-4am, Thurs.-Fri. 11pm-4am, Sat. 11pm-3am), situated in the same complex as the also-popular Drunken Unicorn.

Probably Atlanta's premier gay dance club, **The Jungle Club** (215 Faulkner Rd. NE, 404/844-8800, www.jungleclubatlanta.com, daily 5pm-3am) is also one of the more serious purveyors of straight-up house music and its subvariants, often bringing in world-class DJs for a long night of partying until dawn.

Atlanta's go-to spot for authentic Latin and salsa dancing—actually, the DJs spin everything from reggaeton to merengue—**La Rumba II** (4300 Buford Hwy., 678/789-2888, www.larumba2.com, Thurs.-Sun. 10pm-4am) is the latest incarnation of a local Latino favorite.

If you're looking for the classic multilevel high-dollar hip-hop club, dance, and Red Bull-and-vodka scene, with all that that implies, go straight to **Compound** (1008 Brady Ave., 404/898-1702, www.compoundatl.com, Thurs.-Sat. 9pm-3am) and hope you look good enough to make it in.

## Craft Breweries

While Georgia itself is a bit behind the curve of the national craft brew trend, Atlanta has a number of excellent, established breweries open for tour. Chief among these is the nationally known **Sweetwater Brewery** (195 Ottley Dr., 404/691-2537, www.sweetwaterbrew.com), where $12 gets you a tasting and tour. These can get pretty crowded on the weekends, so get there early for the best shot at the taps.

Calling itself the oldest brewery in Georgia,

Red Brick Brewing (2323 Defoors Hill Rd, 404/355-5558, www.redbrickbrewing.com) in West Atlanta features very well-attended tastings and tours most evenings, with afternoon sessions on the weekend.

Not to be confused with Red Brick, up in Marietta the **Red Hare Brewing Company** (1998 Delk Industrial Blvd., 678/401-0600, www.redharebrewing.com) offers tastings and tours a roughly half-hour drive from the center of Atlanta.

The first-rate beers of the smaller-batch **Three Taverns Brewing** (121 New St., 404/600-3355, www.threetavernsbrewery.com) in Decatur have an excellent reputation around the state. They offer tastings and tours in their "Parlour" Thursday and Friday evenings and Saturday afternoons for $14 per person.

Another brilliant small-batch brewery, strong on saisons and sours, is **Orpheus Brewing** (1440 Dutch Valley Place, www.orpheusbrewing.com), in the middle of the Midtown party mix. Because of the trendier location, their tasting and touring experience ($12) is a bit more upscale than some others around town.

One of the newest breweries in the city is **Scofflaw Brewing Company** (1738 MacArthur Blvd., www.scofflawbeer.com) in West Atlanta, specializing in sublime IPAs that are often also available at local taps. Tours are offered Thursday-Sunday.

## PERFORMING ARTS

Because of its size, wealth, and population of affluent transplants, Atlanta offers a huge variety of fine arts performance and takes its place among the country's leading cultural centers.

### Venues

Atlanta's leading overall cultural venue is the **Robert W. Woodruff Memorial Arts Center** (1280 Peachtree St. NE, 404/733-4200, www.woodruffcenter.org). You'd be forgiven for thinking the *memorial* in the name refers to legendary philanthropist Woodruff, who provided much of the funding for its

construction. The memorializing in question, however, refers to the tragic 1962 airplane crash in Paris that claimed the lives of eight Atlanta art community movers and shakers, leading to the establishment of the arts center in 1968. This attractive 12-acre campus, around which Midtown has built a reputation as a leading arts center, includes 1,800-seat Symphony Hall, home of the Atlanta Symphony Orchestra, and the High Museum of Art, which comprises several buildings.

One of the country's great historic venues, the 4,600-seat **Fox Theatre** (660 Peachtree St. NE, 404/881-2100, box office 855/285-8499, www.foxtheatre.org) continues to host a full slate of productions, generally touring road shows and benefit performances. Its charmingly over-the-top design makes it worth seeing even if you're not attending a show here.

For many years it was known to Atlanta music fans as the Roxy, anchor of the Buckhead nightlife scene and host to some of the greatest names in rock and roll. Today, the fully restored and renamed, circa-1930 **Buckhead Theatre** (3110 Roswell Rd., 404/843-2825, www.thebuckheadtheatre.com) hosts some of the biggest names in indie music as well as the occasional theatrical production.

The **Verizon Wireless Amphitheatre** (2200 Encore Pkwy., 404/733-5010, www.vzwamp.com), one of many bearing that name throughout the United States, is in the northern suburb of Alpharetta and hosts some of the biggest names in music in its 12,000-seat setting with lots of amenities.

Verdant **Piedmont Park** (1320 Monroe Dr., 404/875-7275, www.piedmontpark.org) in Midtown hosts some of Atlanta's most popular live shows, often free ones, such as Music Midtown and the Pride Fest. Nearby **Atlanta Botanical Garden** (1345 Piedmont Ave. NE, 404/876-5859, www.atlantabotanicalgarden.org) also hosts a well-received concert series during the summer. Buckhead's answer to Piedmont Park, the amphitheater at **Chastain Park** (4469 Stella Dr., 404/233-2227, http://chastainseries.com) is also a popular place to see a live show during the summer.

# Atlanta's New South

the Ponce City Market's rooftop

Atlanta is one of America's most diverse cities, both in population and in culture. In 2016, *Vogue* even proposed that Atlanta was becoming the South's new cultural capital. And it was a good year for the city: The Atlanta Falcons beat the Green Bay Packers to head to the Super Bowl, Donald Glover's *Atlanta* won Best Television Series at the Golden Globes, and trap artists from Atlanta were No. 1 on the Billboard charts.

Atlanta has long been an economic and social center for the Southeast, from playing a key role in the civil rights movement to being the country's epicenter of hip hop. Today, the city continues to prove that it's on the cutting-edge.

## ART

- The **High Museum of Art** (page 459) is the largest art museum between New York and Houston, offering great rotating exhibits in addition to a vast permanent collection on display.

- The **Museum of Design Atlanta** (page 463) bills itself as the only museum in the South devoted purely to design. On the last Thursday of the month the museum stays open until 8pm and admission includes a cocktail.

For years, the Omni was a premier local sports and entertainment venue. In 1999 that decaying cavern was demolished, and on that site now sits the 18,000-seat **Philips Arena** (1 Philips Dr., 404/878-3000, www.philipsarena. com), adjoining the CNN Center. (Local resident Elton John played its inaugural show.) "The Phil" is home of the Atlanta Hawks basketball team and is considered the third-busiest concert facility in the United States.

**Infinite Energy Center** (6400 Sugarloaf Pkwy., 770/813-7600, www.infiniteenergy-center.com), just off the Perimeter northwest of Atlanta in the exurb of Duluth, hosts frequent large-scale touring acts. Another of Atlanta's large-scale venues, **Cobb Energy**

## MUSIC

### Festivals

- One of Atlanta's most highly regarded music events, **Music Midtown** (page 478) offers a stunning variety of top-name artists.

- **Shaky Knees Music Festival** (page 477) is rapidly becoming one of the South's major rock/indie/pop festivals.

- The **Atlanta Jazz Festival** (page 477) is one of the largest free jazz fests in the country.

### Venues

- The classic **Fox Theatre** (page 471) is one of the nation's great restored vintage concert halls.

- See a big stadium show at **Philips Arena** (page 472) or at the modern **Infinite Energy Center** and **Cobb Energy Centre** (page 472), both right on the Perimeter (I-285).

- Go underground, literally, and dance all night to the DJs spinning old-school hip-hop and dance-pop at the epicenter of the ATL club scene, **MJQ** (page 470).

## SOCIAL AWARENESS

- The **Center for Civil and Human Rights** (page 457) is Atlanta's newest museum, a compelling and up-to-the-minute look at the history of the ongoing struggle for equality and justice the world over.

- The **National Black Arts Festival** (page 478) focuses on the African American cultural experience, including music, theater, literature, and film.

- The South's largest such event and one of the oldest Pride festivals in the United States, the over-40-year-old **Atlanta Pride** (page 478) attracts huge crowds.

## RECREATION

- At **Ponce City Market** (page 486), housed in the repurposed circa-1920's Sears building, you can shop and eat inside, and on the roof you can drink, play miniature golf, and take in the view.

- The **Atlanta BeltLine** (page 483) seeks to connect nearly 50 neighborhoods throughout the entire metro area to a nearly 40-mile network of multiuse trails loosely based on old rail lines, with at least five MARTA public transit stops along the way.

---

**Performing Arts Centre** (2800 Cobb Galleria Pkwy., 770/916-2800, www.cobbenergycentre.com), is situated right at the intersection of I-75 and the I-285 Perimeter just northwest of town.

## Music and Dance

Long considered the leading orchestra of the Southeast and one of the best in the country, the nearly 70-year-old **Atlanta Symphony Orchestra** (1280 Peachtree St. NE, 404/733-5000, www.atlantasymphony. org) performs under the baton of conductor and music director Robert Spano, whose vision includes championing new works by up-and-coming conductors. The affiliated

**Atlanta Symphony Chorus** is an award-winning entity in its own right and is one of the world's leading groups of its kind. The Atlanta Symphony Orchestra (ASO) performs at least 200 concerts a year, most at the Atlanta Symphony Center in the Woodruff Memorial Arts Center on Peachtree Street. But they can frequently be seen at huge outdoor shows as well, at places like Verizon Wireless Amphitheatre and Chastain Park.

Since its inception in the 1970s, the **Atlanta Chamber Players** (www.atlantachamberplayers.com) has relied on a core group from the ASO to perform intimate small-scale concerts from the chamber repertoire. They play a wide variety of venues, including the High Museum of Art, college campuses, and local churches.

The first dedicated baroque ensemble in the Southeast, the **Atlanta Baroque Orchestra** (770/557-7582, www.atlantabaroque.org) is under the direction of Julie Andrijeski and makes its home base well outside the Perimeter in the northern suburb of Roswell, playing mostly at the Roswell Presbyterian Church.

Once the Marietta Symphony, then the Cobb Symphony, and now the **Georgia Symphony Orchestra** (770/429-7016, www.georgiasymphony.org), this all-professional group performs at various venues just north of Atlanta, with its main base at the Bailey Center at Kennesaw State University.

The **Georgia State University Symphony Orchestra** (404/413-5900, www.music.gsu.edu) is affiliated with Georgia State University, which has a sprawling campus downtown. Its music department is excellent, and audiences at their performances are the beneficiaries. They typically play at the Rialto Center for the Arts in Fairlie-Poplar.

The highly regarded **Atlanta Opera** (404/881-8801, www.atlantaopera.org) has had to move locations a lot over the years to accommodate growing crowds, from the Woodruff Center to the Fox Theatre to the Civic Center, and now to the huge, plush Cobb Energy Performing Arts Centre (2800 Cobb Galleria Pkwy.) in northwest Atlanta at I-75 and I-285.

The smaller **Capitol City Opera** (678/301-8013, www.ccityopera.org) concentrates more on light opera, such as *Cosi Fan Tutte,* and operates in close affiliation with Oglethorpe University. Capitol City generally performs at the university's Conant Performing Arts Center.

Closing in on the century mark, the **Atlanta Ballet** (404/873-5811, www.atlantaballet.com) has a long and storied history, but it's not hidebound by any means. These days it's as known for its innovation as for its tradition, regularly performing work by new choreographers. The Atlanta Ballet juggles three main performance venues: the massive Cobb Energy Performing Arts Centre (2800 Cobb Galleria Pkwy.), the Fox Theatre (660 Peachtree St. NE), and the Gwinnett Performing Arts Center (6500 Sugarloaf Pkwy.), east of town.

Billing itself as the nation's only fully integrated dance company, **Full Radius Dance** (404/724-9663, www.fullradiusdance.org) incorporates dancers with disabilities into its calendar of original choreography, with wheelchairs and dancers moving together in rhythm. Most of their shows are at 7 Stages (1105 Euclid Ave. NE) in Little Five Points.

## Theater

The "establishment" company in Atlanta is **Alliance Theatre** (404/733-4650, www.alliancetheatre.org), performing primarily at the Woodruff Memorial Arts Center (1280 Peachtree St. NE) in Midtown. Since its founding in 1968, Alliance has served not only as the city's premier theater company but also as a developing ground for theatrical acting and directing talent from all over the Southeast.

The 30-year-old **Horizon Theatre** (1083 Austin Ave., 404/584-7450, www.horizontheatre.com) performs in an intimate space in Little Five Points, but don't let the small size of the room fool you: This is a fully professional theater presenting important work through the course of its five-show main season, and it's probably Atlanta's favorite theater company.

Since 1988, **Actor's Express** (887 W. Marietta St., 404/607-7469, www.actors-express.com) has provided Atlanta audiences with an enriching alternative to the usual chestnut offerings, with just enough familiarity to keep a high profile. They currently perform in the historic restored space of the King Plow Art Center just west of Downtown proper.

Atlanta's most politically vibrant theater, **7 Stages** (1105 Euclid Ave. NE, 404/523-7647, www.7stages.org) operates in its own space in the heart of Little Five Points, and appropriate to its bohemian location, provides a steady season of compelling, often controversial performances.

The professional **Theatrical Outfit** (84 Luckie St., 678/528-1500, www.theatricaloutfit.org), Atlanta's third-oldest theater group, operates out of the first LEED-certified theater building in the United States, the Balzer Theatre at Herren's in Midtown. It's on the site of the old Herren's, the first restaurant in Atlanta to voluntarily desegregate. Theatrical Outfit focuses heavily on developing Atlanta-area writers, directors, and actors.

The **Center for Puppetry Arts** (1404 Spring St. NW, 404/873-3089, www.puppet.org) is the largest U.S. group dedicated to the art form. It not only hosts a regular season of performances at its space in Midtown, but there is a puppetry museum on-site, which includes a Jim Henson Wing, memorializing the Muppets founder (and ribbon-cutter of the center itself, back in 1978).

The improv gurus at **Dad's Garage** (280 Elizabeth St. NE, 404/523-3141, www.dadsgarage.com) near Inman Park specialize in staging bawdy original scripts and also feature a heavy weekly schedule of improv, some of it themed and quite long-running. The audience gets to drink beer and wine throughout the shows; this is not for kids.

In both look and feel, the **New American**

**Shakespeare Tavern** (499 Peachtree St. NE, 404/874-5299, www.shakespearetavern.com) is intended to closely replicate the Elizabethan play-going experience, right down to the Globe Theatre-inspired facade of the building itself in the SoNo district on Peachtree Street. This beloved project of the Atlanta Shakespeare Company seeks to break down the barriers that sometimes make the enjoyment of the Bard's work a rather stuffy experience.

The company **Georgia Shakespeare** (4484 Peachtree Rd. NE, 404/504-1473, www.gashakespeare.org) puts on a full season of the Bard within the confines of host institution Oglethorpe University. While the shows are within a theater venue, many people opt for a preshow picnic on the scenic grounds just outside.

## CINEMA

In addition to a plethora of the usual generic multiplexes, Atlanta offers several unique moviegoing experiences. The oldest operating movie theater in Atlanta is the **Plaza Theatre** (1049 Ponce de Leon Ave., 404/873-1939, www.plazaatlanta.com) in Midtown. It delivers a steady diet of kitschy classics and pulp fiction-style movies, with frequent midnight screenings of *The Rocky Horror Picture Show*.

For a flavor of high-quality Los Angeles-style cinema, head to Landmark Theatres' **Midtown Art Cinema** (931 Monroe Dr., 404/879-0160, www.landmarktheatres.com), generally considered the best new-release theater in the city, and with the best atmosphere.

There are two IMAX theaters in Atlanta: the Fernbank Museum of Natural History's **Rankin M. Smith IMAX Theater** (767 Clifton Rd., 404/929-6400, www.fernbankmuseum.org), which shows science and nature-related films; and **Regal Atlantic Station Stadium 16 & IMAX** (261 19th St., 404/347-9894, www.imax.com), which offers various IMAX-formatted films in addition to a wide variety of non-IMAX new releases.

# What Happened to Buckhead?

Back in the 1980s and 1990s, Buckhead was a nationally renowned party central, specifically in the several-block entertainment area known as Buckhead Village. It was jammed with bars and live-music venues that stayed hopping every night until 4am and attracted everybody from college students to yuppies to visiting CEOs. Here's how it happened, and how it all went away:

A gradual downturn through the 1970s convinced city officials to lift minimum parking requirements for nightclubs in order to encourage development. That it did, and soon the village was chockablock with popular watering holes and hordes of partiers pub-crawling between them, an atmosphere that was likened to "Mardi Gras every night." The 1980s were the glory days, with the Roxy Theatre (now the restored Buckhead Theatre) hosting some of the hottest bands on a weekly basis. By the mid-1990s, however, the village had over 100 liquor licenses, gangsta rap was more popular than rock and roll, and the crowds and cruising became unrulier.

Everything came to a head one Sunday in January 2000 when the Super Bowl was being played in Atlanta. Two people were shot and killed at a club called Cobalt in a high-profile case involving National Football League player Ray Lewis, who was implicated in the killings. Though Lewis was later acquitted, the PR damage was done. Another multiple shooting a couple of years later involving the rapper P. Diddy's entourage sealed Buckhead Village's fate. Residents persuaded the city to make last call at 2:30am and to tighten up on liquor licenses.

Partying gradually followed the path of least resistance to other areas of town. Developer Ben Carter began buying up the village's nine acres to make way for his massive and ambitious Buckhead Atlanta multiuse planned development. In 2007, acknowledging the imminent demise of the village's old character, a Bye Bye Buckhead party was held that attracted thousands. Soon nearly all the clubs were bulldozed, just in time for the 2008 economic collapse. The last of the old bars to close was Fado's Irish Pub.

In 2011 the OliverMcMillan company took over the stalled development, and in 2014 opened The Shops Buckhead Atlanta, a six-block commercial center with upscale shops, restaurants, apartments, and offices. More commercial development is currently in the works.

# FESTIVALS AND EVENTS

## January

Understandably, a huge focus in his hometown is the **Martin Luther King Jr. Birthday Celebration** (404/526-8900, www.thekingcenter.org). The civil rights leader's birthday is a national holiday marked with a variety of events, most centering on the MLK Jr. National Historic Site (www.nps.gov) in Downtown. The keynote event is the annual march down Auburn Avenue from Peachtree Street to Jackson Street. Ebenezer Baptist Church typically hosts an annual memorial service, and the MLK Jr. Birth Home often holds an open house. While the Atlanta Symphony Orchestra has generally played a memorial concert at King's alma mater, Morehouse College, in recent years they've been playing the concert at Atlanta Symphony Hall on Peachtree Street.

## March

Since 1976 the **Atlanta Film Festival** (678/929-8103, www.atlantafilmfestival.com) has brought Academy Award-qualifying indie and first-run films to town. Its main venue these days is the Landmark Midtown Art Cinema (931 Monroe Dr. NE, 404/879-0408, www.landmarktheatres.com).

## April

For 75 years Atlantans have gathered in Piedmont Park for the annual **Dogwood Festival** (Piedmont Park, 404/817-6642, www.dogwood.org). While the focus is obviously on the blooming dogwoods, the festival itself is largely an open-air arts-and-crafts market featuring vendors from all over the Southeast, plus, of course, lots of food and music.

It's not often that a neighborhood festival

Shaky Knees Music festival is nationally renowned.

event. The typical host venue is the Loews Atlanta Hotel (11th St. and Peachtree St.), with booths including the popular Tasting Tents radiating out a couple of blocks. Tiered ticketing provides various levels of access, from the basic one-event ticket at $65 to an all-inclusive weekend pass for $500.

Rapidly becoming one of the South's major rock/indie/pop festivals, **Shaky Knees Music Festival** (www.shakykneesfestival. com) happens over a weekend and is one of the better-run and more organized such events you'll attend. Lineups are announced in February, and one-day tickets are available. The most recent edition was held in Centennial Olympic Park downtown, but the event occasionally changes venue.

The **Atlanta Jazz Festival** (404/546-6820, www.atlantafestivals.com) is one of the largest free jazz fests in the country. The location and timing of the festival have bounced around over the years, but the current incarnation in Piedmont Park over the Memorial Day Weekend seems to be a real crowd-pleaser.

is recommended for out-of-town visitors, but that's the case with the always fun and festive **Inman Park Festival** (www.inmanparkfestival.org), which happens the last weekend in April. Set in Atlanta's first planned neighborhood and now one of its most vibrant and up-and-coming, the festival features music, an eccentric and fun Saturday parade, and a popular tour of homes on Friday. Of course, the area's many awesome new restaurants are open, often with extended hours. It's a festival of a neighborhood artfully reclaimed from blight, and the overall sense of optimism pervades.

## May

The city's premier foodie event is the **Atlanta Food & Wine Festival** (404/474-7330, www.atlfoodandwinefestival.com). Perhaps strangely, given Atlanta's long association with high-profile chefs, it's a comparatively young event, having started in 2006. Eateries and eaters, both highfalutin and lowbrow, come together for this popular Midtown

## June

If you're in Atlanta in June, it seems a shame to miss the **Virginia-Highland Summer Fest** (http://vahi.org), which offers the chance to enjoy the full measure of fun in one of the city's most popular and vibrant neighborhoods.

## July

**Stone Mountain Fourth of July** (1000 Robert E. Lee Blvd., Stone Mountain, 770/498-5690, www.stonemountainpark.com, parking $10) celebrations are always hugely well attended and feature a variety of events, culminating, of course, in a big fireworks display launched from areas at the top and bottom of Stone Mountain itself. Immediately before the fireworks, which are actually done on two consecutive nights, is a special laser show. I strongly advise getting here early as parking places and good spots on the lawn from which to observe the fireworks fill up fast.

A large section of Midtown shuts down for the annual **Peachtree Road Race** (404/231-9064, www.peachtreeroadrace.org), happening each Fourth of July, rain or shine. Even MARTA adjusts its schedule, starting trains at 5am that day to accommodate the lack of automobile traffic and the rush of runners and observers. The six-mile course starts in Buckhead and winds down Peachtree to take 10th Street to the finish in Piedmont Park, where an assortment of food, drink, and fun awaits. The foot race starts at 7:30am, with a wheelchair race beginning at 6:45am.

The **Chattahoochee River Summer Splash** (678/538-1200, www.nps.gov) in late July offers a festive opportunity for a six-mile float down the Chattahoochee River National Recreation Area.

The **National Black Arts Festival** (404/730-7315, http://nbaf.org) focuses on the African American cultural experience, including music, theater, literature, and film. The main weekend event centers on activities in Centennial Olympic Park, but satellite events happen at venues all around, including a gallery crawl and multiple jazz concerts.

## September

Definitely not to be confused with Underground Atlanta, the **Atlanta Underground Film Festival** (1200 Foster St., www.auff.org) hosts edgy short films curated from national submissions. The venue, the Goat Farm Arts Center, is a restored warehouse and multiuse performing arts hub for Atlanta's more cutting-edge arts community.

One of Atlanta's most highly regarded music events, **Music Midtown** (www.musicmidtown.com) in Piedmont Park still offers a stunning variety of top-name artists despite the economic downturn having taken a toll on its attendance in recent years. What used to be a three-day event is now down to

two, but past years have featured The Killers, Beck, Deadmau5, Pearl Jam, and local hero Ludacris. Not too shabby.

## October

The South's largest such event and one of the oldest Pride festivals in the United States, the over-40-year-old **Atlanta Pride** (404/382-7588, www.atlantapride.org) attracts huge crowds to Piedmont Park and satellite venues over the course of an October weekend, timed to mark National Coming Out Day. Entertainment is top-notch, with past performers including Nicki Minaj and the Indigo Girls. And, of course, the main event is the Pride Parade down Peachtree Street to Piedmont Park on Saturday and its spinoff parades, the Dyke March and the Trans March.

Technically separate from Atlanta Pride but happening concurrently, **Out on Film** (404/296-3807, www.outonfilm.org) has been screening gay- and lesbian-oriented fare for a quarter century. Based at the Landmark Midtown Art Cinema (931 Monroe Dr. NE, 404/879-0408, www.landmarktheatres.com), the festival also offers extensive Q&As with filmmakers and a host of special events.

The **Little Five Points Halloween** (404/230-2884, www.l5phalloween.com) celebration is everything you'd expect from this hipster-bohemian area. Let's just say it's probably not for small children.

Atlanta has a large and influential Greek American community, and the annual **Atlanta Greek Festival** (404/633-5870, www.atlantagreekfestival.org) packs in the crowds for a taste of souvlaki, baklava, and other goodies. There is, of course, music and dancing as well. It happens at the grounds of the Greek Orthodox Cathedral of the Annunciation (2500 Clairmont Rd. NE) in North Druid Hills.

# Shopping

Atlanta is the Southeastern mecca of shopping. Every possible chain and boutique brand is represented, along with a vibrant independent retail community. Mall shoppers won't be disappointed either; Atlanta has some of the nation's oldest, all substantially renovated since their early days.

Atlanta's key shopping districts are the Buckhead-Perimeter area north of Downtown; Midtown (including Virginia-Highland, Little Five Points, and Atlantic Station); and Downtown.

## ANTIQUES

Easily Atlanta's most beloved antiques-vintage store, **Paris on Ponce** (716 Ponce de Leon Ave., 404/249-9965, www.parisonponce. com, Mon.-Sat. 11am-6pm, Sun. noon-6pm), in Virginia-Highland, is, as the name implies, redolent of old Europe and full of unique furniture and assorted decorative items, all with a certain whimsical and quirky allure that treads the line between classic and kitsch.

The **Miami Circle Design District** (www. miamicircleshops.com) in Buckhead is commonly considered the headquarters of the hard-core Atlanta antiquing community, and indeed of the entire Southeast. Located in a large cul-de-sac, it comprises about 80 antiques shops, home goods stores, and art galleries; the enormity of its offerings is beyond our scope here, but a few highlights are the ornate home goods of **Burroughs Wellington** (631 Miami Circle, 404/264-1616, www.burroughswellington.com, Mon.-Sat. 10am-5pm); the fabrics and furniture of **Curran Designers** (737 Miami Circle, 404/237-4246, www.curran-aat.com, Mon.-Sat. 10am-5:30pm); the classic Euro stylings at **Foxglove Antiques** (699 Miami Circle, 404/233-0222, www.foxgloveantiques. com, Mon.-Sat. 10am-5pm); and the unique Chinese offerings at **Mandarin Antiques** (700 Miami Circle, 404/467-1727, www.

mandarinantiquesinc.com, Mon.-Fri. 10am-5:30pm, Sat. 10am-5pm).

Another antiques center in Buckhead is the **West Village** (www.westvillagega.com), a loose collection of quaint and quirky antiques and home goods merchants within the triangle formed by East Andrews Drive, Roswell Road, and West Paces Ferry Road.

Up near the Perimeter, in the town of Chamblee, is the perennially popular **Chamblee Antique Row** (3519 Broad St., 770/458-6316, www.antiquerow.com), a retail district comprising nearly two dozen clothing and antiques stores, plus a few restaurants. Charming and pedestrian-friendly, it's a quick three blocks from the Chamblee MARTA station.

## ART GALLERIES

While you're taking in the more traditional exhibits at the High Museum, you might want to extend your Midtown art crawl to **Atlanta Contemporary Art Center** (535 Means St., 404/688-1970, www.thecontemporary.org, Tues.-Sat. 11am-5pm, Sun. noon-5pm), a nonprofit cooperative established in 1973 and in its current space since 1989, dedicated to the work of new Atlanta artists.

A massive converted warehouse hosting about 300 individual studios and performing arts spaces, **Goat Farm Arts Center** (1200 Foster St.), on the west edge of Midtown, is one of Atlanta's most unique cultural spaces. It has two indoor performance spaces and three outdoor stages, all hosting experimental or indie-style work. The Goat Farm is performance- and exhibition-based, and doesn't really have regular hours. You can visit anytime, and the on-site coffee shop is open daily 10:30am-7pm.

An important part of the burgeoning art scene in the Atlantic Station area, **Sandler Hudson Gallery** (1009 Marietta St., 404/817-3300, www.sandlerhudson.com, Tues.-Fri.

10am-5pm, Sat. noon-5pm) focuses on contemporary Southern artists. In addition to its display space, there's a sculpture area on the roof.

A key arts anchor in the up-and-coming Castleberry Hill area, **Besharat Gallery** (175 Peters St., 404/524-4781, www.besharatgallery.com, Fri.-Sat. 11am-6pm) and its companion space **Besharat Contemporary** (163 Peters St., 404/577-3660, www.besharatcontemporary.com, Tues.-Sat. 10am-5pm) together are one of the most balanced visual arts experiences in the city, blending a respect for craft and tradition with a real commitment to showcasing more modern sensibilities. Nearby is **Zucot Gallery** (100 Centennial Olympic Park Dr., 404/380-1040, www.zucotgallery.com, Tues.-Fri. 3pm-9pm, Sat. noon-10pm), which keeps things fresh in its compellingly minimalist space by completely changing out the entire exhibit every two months or so.

Since 1997, **Young Blood Gallery and Boutique** (636 N. Highland Ave., 404/254-4127, www.youngbloodgallery.com, Tues.-Sat. noon-8pm, Sun. noon-6pm) has been a key part of the renaissance of the Virginia-Highland area as well as a leading exponent of the Atlanta underground arts and music scene. Their offerings tend toward the bold, modern, and vibrant, with a strong nod toward sequential art.

## BOOKS

Since 1989, Inman Park has been home to **A Cappella Books** (208 Haralson Ave., 404/681-5128, www.acapellabooks.com, Mon.-Sat. 11am-7pm, Sun. noon-6pm), which deals in new, used, and rare volumes and features a remarkably well-informed, engaged staff.

**Bound to Be Read Books** (481 Flat Shoals Ave., 404/522-0877, www.boundtobereadbooks.com, Tues.-Thurs. 11am-9pm, Fri.-Sat. 11am-10pm, Sun. 1pm-6pm), an East Atlanta staple, has a very wide assortment, from fiction to technical books to gay and lesbian studies and literature.

**The Green Room Actors Lounge** (25 Bennett St., 404/351-4736, www.thegreenroomatl.com, Wed. noon-9pm, Thurs. noon-6pm, Fri. noon-11pm, Sat. 1pm-midnight) combines racks of books on acting, directing, and other aspects of show business with a stocked bar in a tony atmosphere. This is a favorite hangout of Atlanta's sizable theater community.

## CLOTHES AND FASHION

The funky **Little Five Points** (L5P) neighborhood is a major thrift-vintage-counterculture shopping destination. The closest thing to an anchor store is **Junkman's Daughter** (464 Moreland Ave., 404/577-3188, www.thejunkmansdaughter.com, Mon.-Fri. 11am-7pm, Sat. 11am-8pm, Sun. noon-7pm), a combination vintage-novelty-tchotchke store and quasi tourist trap. My favorite vintage shop in L5P is **Stefan's Vintage** (1160 Euclid Ave., 404/688-4929, www.stefansvintageclothing.com, Mon.-Sat. 11am-7pm, Sun. noon-6pm), the oldest store of its kind in Atlanta and where you can score some remarkable wearable finds.

In the **Peachtree Battle** (2341 Peachtree Rd., www.branchprop.com) shopping center in Buckhead, a sort of deluxe strip mall setting, you'll find fun locally owned stores such as the **Frolic Boutique** (2385 Peachtree Rd., 404/846-8002, www.frolicboutique.com, Mon.-Sat. 11am-6pm) and **Mint Julep** (2353 Peachtree Rd., 404/814-9155, www.mintjulepga.com, Mon.-Sat. 10am-6pm, Sun. 1pm-5pm), Atlanta's Lilly Pulitzer outlet.

The vibrant and friendly Virginia-Highland neighborhood offers a charming array of largely independent locally owned stores, often with a twist, such as the vintage store **Mooncake** (1019 Virginia Ave., 404/892-8043, Mon.-Sat. 11am-7pm), which hosts frequent trunk shows, and the original location of **Bill Hallman** (792 N. Highland Ave., 404/876-6055, www.billhallman.com, Mon.-Sat. 11am-8pm, Sun. noon-7pm), which features a sleek take on both men's and women's up-to-the-moment fashions.

# HOME GOODS

Virginia-Highland is the main neighborhood for fun home goods shopping. Don't miss the quirky attraction of **Richards Variety** (931 Monroe Dr., 404/879-9877, www.richards-varietystore.com, Mon.-Sat. 10am-8pm, Sun. noon-6pm), a half-century-old staple featuring unusual novelties, toys, costumes, and other assorted party supplies.

Into recycling and sustainable living? Hit the **Re-Inspiration Store** (591 N. Highland Ave., 404/352-1971, www.reinspirationstore.com, Mon.-Thurs. 11am-6pm, Fri.-Sat. 10am-6pm, Sun. noon-5pm), right across from the iconic Manuel's Tavern. You'll find funky items and gifts made from repurposed things like spark plugs, pop-tops, and shell casings.

Also in Virginia-Highland you'll find the charming and unique **Indie-pendent** (1052 St. Charles Ave., 404/313-0004, www.theindie-pendent.com, Thurs.-Sat. 11am-5pm, Sun. 1pm-5pm), a hip and happening collection of DIY-style regionally handcrafted kitchen, home, and garden goods along with jewelry and art.

# MALLS

Atlanta's premier mall and one of the nation's oldest, having opened in 1959, is **Lenox Square** (3393 Peachtree Rd. NE, 404/233-6767, www.simon.com, Mon.-Sat. 10am-9pm, Sun. noon-6pm) in Buckhead, with about 250 stores on four levels. Of course, the current incarnation bears no resemblance whatsoever to the Eisenhower administration version. Anchor stores are Macy's, Bloomingdale's, and Neiman Marcus, and there's a massive Forever 21 as well as an Apple retail location. This being Buckhead, there are also many high-dollar boutique outlets of note: Façonnable, Nicole Miller, Bulgari, Fendi, Cartier, Burberry, and Prada, to name but a few. There's a convenient MARTA stop.

Close to Lenox Square and owned by the same investment group is **Phipps Plaza** (3500 Peachtree Rd. NE, 404/262-0992, www.simon.com, Mon.-Sat. 10am-9pm, Sun. noon-5:30pm), an even more upscale Buckhead mall. Its anchors are Saks Fifth Avenue, Nordstrom, and Belk, with an impressive list of boutiques that include Armani, Valentino, Jimmy Choo, Versace, and Tiffany.

The simply and aptly named **Perimeter Mall** (4400 Ashford Dunwoody Rd., 770/394-4270, www.perimetermall.com, Mon.-Sat. 10am-9pm, Sun. noon-7pm) was the first such project along the I-285 corridor north of Atlanta proper in the satellite city of Dunwoody (it's served by the Dunwoody MARTA station). Current anchors are Von Maur, Dillard's, Macy's, and Nordstrom, and there's an Apple retail store.

Way outside the Perimeter in Buford, Georgia, about 30 miles from Downtown Atlanta, is the massive **Mall of Georgia** (3333 Buford Dr., Buford, 678/482-8788, www.mallofgeorgia.com, Mon.-Sat. 10am-9pm, Sun. noon-6pm). It has over 200 stores on three levels, including anchors Belk, Dillard's, JCPenney, Macy's, Nordstrom, Dick's Sporting Goods, and Havertys, plus an Apple retail store. Food opportunities are plentiful, and the Mall of Georgia is very attractively landscaped.

A reclaimed light industrial area turned mixed-use, **Atlantic Station** (1380 Atlantic Dr., 404/733-1221, www.atlanticstation.com, Mon.-Sat. 10am-9pm, Sun. noon-7pm) offers an outdoor pedestrian-style mall featuring H&M, Z Gallerie, and more familiar chain stores such as Banana Republic, American Eagle, and Nine West. Atlantic Station occasionally hosts traveling exhibits, such as a recent stop by a show of artifacts from the *Titanic*.

About halfway between Atlanta and Macon off I-75 you'll find the sprawling **Tanger Outlet Center** (1000 Tanger Dr., Locust Grove, 770/957-5310, www.tangeroutlet.com, Mon.-Sat. 9am-9pm, Sun. 11am-7pm), which has bargain outlets ranging from J.Crew to Lucky Brand to Skechers.

As the name implies, **Underground Atlanta** (50 Upper Alabama St., 404/523-2311, www.underground-atlanta.com, Mon.-Thurs. 10am-8pm, Fri.-Sat. 10am-9pm, Sun.

noon-6pm) is an underground mall, the legacy of an urban layer built up in the 1920s over previously existing rail lines. It has gone through several incarnations over the last half century, as the city tries to keep it afloat as a viable entertainment and shopping destination (a recent effort involved extending bar closing times to 4am). Sketchy and long removed from its heyday in the 1980s, Underground Atlanta today is an idea that sounds cooler than it really is; even the shops are mostly downscale here in an area of town that, frankly, is not Atlanta's safest or most welcoming. There will be many signs and ads urging you to visit, but I advise against it.

## MUSIC AND RECORDS

In Little Five Points you'll find a couple of neat indie record stores. **Criminal Records** (1154 Euclid Ave., 404/215-9511, www.criminalatl. com, Mon.-Sat. 11am-9pm, Sun. noon-7pm) not only has an outstanding selection of happening music, they often host record release parties with live entertainment by the hottest regional bands.

**Wax 'n' Facts** (432 Moreland Ave., 404/525-2275, www.waxnfacts.com, Mon.-Sat. 11am-8pm, Sun. noon-6pm), in business since 1976, has an awesome vinyl collection and also hosts performances.

## OUTDOOR OUTFITTERS

Huge outdoor retailer **REI** (www.rei.com) has two locations in the metro area: one near Druid Hills (1800 Northeast Expressway, 404/633-6508, Mon.-Sat. 10am-9pm, Sun. 11am-6pm) and the other on the Perimeter (1165 Perimeter Center, 770/901-9200, Mon.-Sat. 10am-9pm, Sun. 11am-6pm).

Regional chain **Half Moon Outfitters** (1034 Highland Ave., 404/249-7921, www. halfmoonoutfitters.com, Mon-Fri. 10am-7pm, Sat. 10am-8pm, Sun. 11am-6pm) has a friendly location in Virginia-Highland, selling clothing in addition to gear. In Buckhead, go to **High Country Outfitters** (3906 Roswell Rd., 404/814-0999, www.highcountryoutfitters.com, Mon.-Fri. 10am-8pm, Sat. 10am-6pm, Sun. noon-6pm), serving Atlanta since 1975. For those wanting trendy adventurous outerwear, head to the retail store of **North Face** (35A W. Paces Ferry Rd., 404/467-0119, www.thenorthface.com, Mon.-Sat. 10am-8pm, Sun. 11am-6pm) in Buckhead.

# Sports and Recreation

Atlanta's generally moderate weather and fairly mild winters mean residents spend a lot of time outdoors, a nice break from the city's legendary congestion. Generally considered an awful spectator sports town, Atlanta is better oriented to those of the more active persuasion, and it has plenty of parks and facilities to accommodate them.

## PARKS

For a city known for its well-used superhighways, Atlanta has a surprisingly large amount of green space, and it is heavily used and admired by residents.

First landscaped in 1904, **Piedmont Park** (1320 Monroe Dr., 404/875-7275, www. piedmontpark.org, daily 6am-11pm, free) in Midtown is the most popular public park, not to mention the most conveniently located. Two major expansions, one in 2008 and one in 2011, brought its area to 190 acres and added a bathhouse-pool area. In addition to miles of jogging and biking paths, there's a boccie court and an off-leash dog park. A legacy of Atlanta's Victorian-era expansion, Piedmont Park includes some areas of the old Civil War battlefield. It has hosted much sports history as well, being the home of the Atlanta Crackers pro baseball team and, during the leather helmet era, the home of the great University of Georgia and Georgia Tech football rivalry.

Chastain Park (Lake Forest Dr. and Powers Ferry Rd., www.chastainpark.org, daily dawn-dusk, free) in Buckhead is actually Atlanta's largest park at nearly 300 acres. It includes a popular amphitheater, a pool, a golf course, a new tennis center, and lots of jogging and biking opportunities.

Atlanta's oldest park is **Grant Park** (bounded by Boulevard SE, Atlanta Ave., Cherokee Ave., Sydney St., Park Ave., and Berne St.), where you'll find Zoo Atlanta. It fell into neglect until the 1990s and is sort of playing catch-up with the other city parks. It is currently under the stewardship of the Grant Park Conservancy (404/521-0938, www.gp-conservancy.org), which offers walking tours exploring the rich Victorian history of the park and surrounding neighborhood of the same name.

Downtown has the 200-acre, six-mile-long **Freedom Park** (North Ave. and Moreland Ave., www.freedompark.org, daily dawn-dusk) linear green space between the Martin Luther King Jr. National Historic Site and the Jimmy Carter Library. It is best known in local lore as the former civic battleground of the "Freeway Revolt," a successful grassroots effort in the 1970s to stop the massive proposed Stone Mountain Freeway from paving over the entire area.

# RUNNING, WALKING, AND BIKING

**Piedmont Park** (1320 Monroe Dr., 404/875-7275, www.piedmontpark.org, daily 6am-11pm, free) has three basic footpaths (no bicycles allowed): the Active Oval, the Lake Loop, and the Park Loop; they interlock for a customized experience. Cycling is only allowed on the main roadway through the park and the meadow paths at 10th Street. **Chastain Park** (www.chastainpark.org) has two freshly renovated 5K loops and a 3K loop. Park at Powers Ferry Road near the amphitheater.

An ambitious, evolving, ongoing project, the **Atlanta BeltLine** (http://beltline.org) seeks to connect nearly 50 neighborhoods throughout the entire metro area to a nearly 40-mile network of multiuse trails loosely based on old rail lines, with at least five MARTA public transit stops along the way. The first phase of the BeltLine to open is the Eastside Trail, which connects Piedmont Park, Inman Park, and the Old Fourth Ward; it is probably the most germane to visitors. Art displays and businesses spring up all along its length. The BeltLine is so heavily used and so popular that it is literally driving economic and residential development along its path, especially in the Midtown area. And the phenomenon is really only just beginning.

Atlanta has a robust running community, with a roster of marathons, triathlons, 5Ks, and 10Ks. Though it's a fairly short race, the city's marquee runner's event is the **Peachtree Road Race** (404/231-9064, www.peachtreeroadrace.org), a very popular six-mile course down the city's main street each Fourth of July morning, ending in Piedmont Park. Other key events on the running calendar include the **ATL 20K Relay and 10K** on Labor Day weekend, the **Allstate Half-Marathon** in October, and the **Atlanta-Chattanooga-Atlanta Relay** in October. Go to http://rungeorgia.com for more info.

The moderately hilly terrain of the Georgia Piedmont makes it good bicycling territory. There's a bike path from Piedmont Avenue downtown all the way to Stone Mountain. Within **Stone Mountain Park** (1000 Robert E. Lee Blvd., 770/498-5690, www.stonemountainpark.com, daily 10am-10pm, $10 admission) are a lot of opportunities as well. The **Atlanta BeltLine** (http://beltline.org) offers multiuse trails all around metro Atlanta, with a completed course connecting Piedmont Park, Inman Park, and the Old Fourth Ward. See www.atlantabike.org for more info.

There's an actual velodrome in the Atlanta area, **Dick Lane Velodrome** (1889 Lexington Ave., 404/769-0012, www.dicklanevelodrome.com) in East Point, one of only a few dozen such facilities in the United States. Races are every Saturday night.

## RAFTING AND BOATING

White-water rafting in the ATL? Most definitely. **"Shootin' the Hootch,"** or rafting down the Chattahoochee, has been a rite of passage for environmentalists and partying college students alike for decades. A 50-mile stretch of the river is managed by the National Park Service as the **Chattahoochee River National Recreation Area** (www.nps. gov). Several private companies are authorized to offer tube and raft rental; the two recommended options are **Chattahoochee Outfitters** (203 Azalea Dr., 770/650-1008, Apr.-Nov. daily, Dec.-Mar. Fri.-Sun.), which leaves from the northern suburb of Roswell, and **High Country Outfitters** (3906B Roswell Rd., 404/814-0999, www.highcountryoutfitters.com, Mon.-Fri. 10am-8pm, Sat. 10am-6pm, Sun. noon-6pm), which puts in at two locations (Johnson Ferry and Powers Island). Keep in mind that generally speaking, children under age five aren't allowed to "shoot the Hootch" at all for safety reasons. Of course, you can put your own vessel into the Hootch.

## SWIMMING

Piedmont Park sports an **Aquatic Center** (404/875-7275, www.piedmontpark.org, summer Mon.-Fri. 10am-5pm, Sat.-Sun. noon-5pm, $4 adults, $2 children). **The Grant Park Pool** (625 Park Ave. SE, 404/622-3041, $4 adults, $2 children) has weekend hours during the summer. The **Candler Park Pool** (1500 McLendon Ave. NE, 404/373-4349, $4 adults, $2 children) is operated by the City of Atlanta.

## GOLF

Two public courses of note are in Buckhead. The 18-hole public **Bobby Jones Golf Course** (384 Woodward Way, 404/355-1009, www.bobbyjonesgc.com, $30-45) has been around since 1932 and sits atop part of the old Battle of Peachtree Creek site. The suitably named Peachtree Battle Creek winds amid five holes. **North Fulton Municipal Golf Course** (216 W. Wieuca Rd. NW, 404/255-0723, www.americangolf.com, $40) is in Chastain Park and gets very crowded.

## TENNIS

The **Sharon J. Lester Tennis Center** (400 Park Dr., 404/853-3461, www.utatennis. com, Mon.-Thurs. 9am-10pm, Fri. 9am-9pm, Sat.-Sun. 9am-6pm) at Piedmont Park offers 12 lighted hard courts. The **Chastain Park Tennis Center** (110 W. Wieuca Rd. NW, 404/255-3210, www.utatennis.com, Mon.-Thurs. 9am-9pm, Fri. 9am-1pm and 3pm-7pm, Sat. 9am-7pm, Sun. 11am-7pm) is a brand-new EarthCraft building with nine lighted hard courts.

## SPECTATOR SPORTS

The Major League Baseball **Atlanta Braves** (www.atlanta.braves.mlb.com) no longer play in Atlanta proper. In the 2017 season they moved to the northern suburb of Cobb County and the new Suntrust Park (http://homeofthebraves.com). The ballpark is designed to have a slightly smaller capacity than the Braves' former digs, Turner Field, to give fans a more intimate, old-school experience—albeit with extensive food courts and craft beer and signature cocktail vendors.

The National Football League **Atlanta Falcons** (www.atlantafalcons.com), two-time NFC champions, play in the brand-new Mercedes-Benz Stadium, right next to their former home, the Georgia Dome. There is a nearby MARTA stop, but the Vine City Station is about as close. The Falcons have an interactive site at http://vsv.falcons.com, which is designed to help with seating and parking issues.

The National Basketball Association **Atlanta Hawks** (www.nba.com, www.philipsarena.com) play in the Philips Arena, next to the CNN Center Downtown. While the team is much better these days than in some eras past, the games almost never sell out, and single-game tickets are quite affordable considering the upscale experience in "the Phil" (even the restrooms are nice). There's a Philips Arena MARTA station right here, so transportation and parking are no excuses not to go.

The **Atlanta Silverbacks** (3200 Silverbacks Way, 404/969-4900, www.

atlantasilverbacks.com) play professional soccer at the second-tier level in the North American Soccer League. Their home pitch is the soccer-specific Silverbacks Park in Chamblee, just outside town.

Atlanta had two professional ice hockey teams in the past, the Atlanta Flames (which departed for Calgary in 1980) and the Atlanta Thrashers (which moved to Winnipeg in 2011). Currently the only pro action on the ice is from the **Gwinnett Gladiators** (Arena at Gwinnett Center, 6400 Sugarloaf Pkwy., 770/497-5100, www.gwinnettgladiators.com), who play in Duluth's Infinite Energy Center.

Autumn in the South means college football. Like most Georgians, Atlanta mostly roots for the Georgia Bulldogs in Athens, but in town, the hottest ticket is for **Georgia Tech** (www.ramblinwreck.com) home football games. The Yellow Jackets play Downtown at Bobby Dodd Stadium at Historic Grant Field (North Ave. and Techwood Dr.) on the corner of campus (the Yellow Jackets' chief rivals, the Georgia Bulldogs, jokingly refer to Tech as the "North Avenue Trade School").

For years Georgia State University was primarily known as an urban commuter school, but the addition of a high-level football program in 2010 immediately made the **Georgia State Panthers** (www.georgiastatesports.com) a high-profile enterprise. They now play in Turner Field, the former home of the Atlanta Braves, which the university purchased in 2016.

# Food

Atlanta isn't known as one of the nation's great food towns, but it's getting there. A remarkable resurgence of foodie culture with a typically Atlantan overlay of Southern charm is happening across town, particularly in Midtown, on the Westside, in Virginia-Highland, and in the Cabbagetown-Grant Park area.

## DOWNTOWN
### American
No other restaurant qualifies for the title of "Atlanta institution" more than **The Varsity** (61 North Ave. NW, 404/881-1706, www.the-varsity.com, Sun.-Thurs. 10am-11:30pm, Fri.-Sat. 10am-12:30am, $5), which since 1928 has fed generations of budget-conscious Georgia Tech students and is one of the last surviving quirky Southern fast-food diners. The cavernous space—the largest drive-in restaurant in the world, they say—is daunting enough, but the counter experience is really what amps up your adrenaline. In decidedly non-Southern fashion, the grimly determined counter staff, like something out of a *Seinfeld* episode, demand to know, "What'll you have?" You'll quickly stammer something off the greasy-spoon-style menu, probably a chili-cheese dog and onion rings washed down with their signature orange drink. (And don't forget Coca-Cola. The downtown Varsity is allegedly the world's largest single sales point of the iconic Georgia drink.) There are several satellite Varsities throughout Georgia now, as far afield as Athens and Dawsonville, but this original location on North Avenue astride I-75 is the one and only, in this author's opinion.

If you're as hooked on bison burgers as I am, you'll take comfort in the presence of **Ted's Montana Grill** (133 Luckie St., 404/521-9796, www.tedsmontanagrill.com, Sun.-Thurs. 11am-10pm, Fri.-Sat. 11am-11pm, $15) in Fairlie-Poplar. Atlanta icon Ted Turner opened the now-national chain in 2002 with restaurateur George McKerrow Jr. This is the original flagship location, and it still serves as a reminder of Turner's pioneering, hugely important work in bringing back the bison population of the West. The payoff, of course, is delicious bison meat served up in a variety of dishes at the restaurant. If buffalo is a little too adventurous for you, there's also a good

# Ponce City Market

While Atlanta isn't known for historic preservation, it is increasingly known for creative repurposing of its older buildings that are still left. There's no better example than **Ponce City Market** (675 Ponce de Leon Ave., www.poncecitymarket.com, food mall open Mon.-Sat. 11am-9pm, Sun. noon-6pm), an incredibly ambitious makeover of the enormous old circa-1920s Sears Building, which later served as Atlanta's "City Hall East."

Today the edifice is home to apartments and an expansive two-level boutique shopping mall and food court, featuring a mix of upscale grab 'n' go items and a few sit-down eateries. The real treat is on the roof, however, where $10 per person gets you onto the old service elevator and up to the top of the building. There, you can enjoy an expansive view of the entire city—including a glimpse of Stone Mountain—as well as a complete mini-golf course, various old-school carnival games, and a full bar. Food, drink, and games are all additional purchases. While pay parking is available on-site, the rapid success of Ponce City Market is in part due to its location right on the most popular section of the Beltline. You can walk or bike from many locations in the city.

selection of classic seafood, beef, and poultry dishes. Ted's work doesn't stop with ranching, however; his place is 99 percent plastic-free. Even the straws are recyclable paper. There are now several other locations in the metro area, including a Midtown edition (1874 Peachtree St., 404/355-3897).

If you're staying in one of the large swank hotels in or near Peachtree Center close to Centennial Olympic Park and you don't particularly feel like eating in the hotel but also don't want to go too far, take a stroll to **Max Lager's** (320 Peachtree St., 404/525-4400, www.maxlagers.com, Mon.-Sat. 11:30am-11pm, Sun. 4pm-11pm, $15). At the oldest brewpub in the city, you can enjoy a pint of one of their very good handcrafted beers and a tasty dinner cooked on their signature wood-fired grill (my favorite is the bison burger, but any of the salmon dishes are also recommended).

## GRANT PARK
### Brunch

Though it comes across as a venerable institution, **Ria's Bluebird** (421 Memorial Dr., 404/521-3737, daily 8am-3pm, $15), near Grant Park, is actually a fairly new place. Hipsters and preppies alike pack the place for its large, delicious breakfasts and brunches, served by a cadre of inked servers who are

nicer than they might appear. All of the omelets are great, and Ria's is very good about offering a range of veggie options (two words: tempeh reuben). There's almost always a line to get in.

### Coffee and Sweets

Known all over town for their dark arts with a French press, making espresso, and raising latte foam-pulling to a fine art, the folks at **Octane Coffee** (437 Memorial Dr., 404/815-9886, http://octanecoffee.com, Mon. 7am-6pm, Tues.-Fri. 7am-midnight, Sat. 8am-midnight, Sun. 8am-10pm) take coffee seriously. They take painting seriously too, and the main Grant Park location (there's another on the Westside) features works by local artists all over the walls on steady rotation. The vibe is crisp and ultramodern rather than cozy and quirky, with hipsters and mover-shaker types alike enjoying the range of java, chai, and yes, craft brews.

### Greek

If you gotta get your gyro on, go no farther than ★ **Nick's To-Go** (240 Martin Luther King Jr. Blvd., 404/521-2220, www.nicksfood. com, Mon.-Fri. 11am-7:30pm, Sat. noon-7pm, $7), a local food icon and one of the best little Greek joints I've found stateside. It's not much to look at: a nearly windowless

# To Market, To Market

Each Saturday April-mid-December in Midtown you'll find the **Peachtree Road Farmers Market** (2744 Peachtree Rd., www.peachtreeroadfarmersmarket.com, Apr.-mid-Dec. Sat. 9am-noon), on the grounds of the Cathedral of St. Philip. It is one of the largest in the metro area.

The most diverse farmers market is up in Doraville at the **Buford Highway Farmers Market** (5600 Buford Hwy., 770/455-0770, www.aofwc.com, daily 8am-10pm), which takes full advantage of the many cultural groups present in the area to provide a stunning array of produce and goods you're unlikely to find elsewhere.

The **Grant Park Farmers Market** (600 Cherokee Ave., www.grantparkmarket.org, Apr.-Dec. Sun. 9:30am-1:30pm) is open April-December.

Downtown near the Martin Luther King Jr. Historic Site you'll find the indoor **Sweet Auburn Curb Market** (Edgewood Ave. and Jessie Hill Pkwy., 404/659-1665, www.sweetauburncurbmarket.com, Mon.-Sat. 8am-6pm), whose roots go back to the 1920s when it was called the Municipal Market and was a center of the local black community.

cinderblock building with faded blue paint in a less-than-upscale part of town. Sometimes you'll order from Nick himself, who's well known to many local politicos who come here from the nearby state capitol for a quick lunch. But the food—authentic, perfectly spiced, and made to order with fresh ingredients—is more than worth the eyesore. This is one of the few places left where you can get an honest-to-Athena lamb gyro (other meats are available). As the name implies, the food is all technically to-go (you pick up at a window facing the parking lot), but there are a couple of picnic tables on-site.

## Seafood

Yep, it's called **Six Feet Under Pub and Fish House** (437 Memorial Dr., 404/525-6664, www.sixfeetunderatlanta.com, Mon.-Thurs. 11am-1am, Fri.-Sat. 11am-2am, Sun. 11am-midnight, $15) because it's right across the street from historic Oakland Cemetery. In fact, from a perch on the 3rd-floor deck, you can count the headstones. The menu at this multilevel wood-paneled gastropub leans heavily to the seafood side, with some great raw bar stuff and fried oysters and shrimp and the like. It's not a microbrewery, but craft beers are a big part of the experience, with frequent brew-related events and contests. There's a second location on the Westside (the

first restaurant in town to use wind power), but the cemetery location is the original.

Look for the full parking lot at the corner of Memorial Drive and Martin Luther King Jr. Drive and you've found **Daddy D'z BBQ Joynt** (264 Memorial Dr., 404/222-0206, www.daddydz.com, Sun.-Thurs. 11am-10:30pm, Fri.-Sat. 11am-midnight, Sun. noon-9:30pm, $12), generally considered one of the city's best barbecue restaurants. Atlanta isn't known as a 'cue capital—too many Northern transplants, you see—but Daddy's is certainly the real thing, especially when it comes to their signature ribs ($25 for a full slab). Portions are enormous and generally come with Texas toast.

# MIDTOWN
## Classic Southern

The closest thing Atlanta has to Paula Deen's Lady & Sons in Savannah, in both menu and media hype if not in the sheer volume of butter, is **Mary Mac's Tea Room** (224 Ponce de Leon Ave., 404/876-1800, www.marymacs.com, daily 11am-9pm, $20). On Ponce just down from the Georgian Terrace Hotel, Mary Mac's has packed in visitors and locals alike for 60 years with its range of Deep South specialties, some served family-style, like baked chicken, meat loaf, and grilled liver and onions. They have seafood as well, mostly of the tried-and-true fried variety. And yes, there's a fried green tomato appetizer.

At the other end of the price scale and with status as the best inexpensive joint in Atlanta, **Eats** (600 Ponce de Leon Ave., 404/888-9149, www.eatsonponce.com, daily 11am-10pm, $5) lives up (or down?) to its name in gloriously humble fashion. The specialty is the excellent jerk chicken, served in heaping portions (not on Friday, though, when you get jerk tilapia). Barbecue and lemon pepper flavors are available for the spice-averse. How inexpensive? The meat-and-three-veggie combo plate, and we're talking very large servings here, runs a paltry $4.75. Because of the inclusive hours, you see a large slice of Atlanta life come in and out of these doors on one of the city's most interesting thoroughfares.

## New Southern

If you're looking for a cool place for drinks or a meal near Piedmont, perhaps before a concert, look no further than **Einstein's** (1077 Juniper St., 404/876-7925, www.metrocafes. com, Mon.-Thurs. 11am-11pm, Fri. 11am-midnight, Sat. 9am-midnight, Sun. 9am-11pm, $15). With plenty of indoor and outdoor seating, a large and very friendly staff, great signature drinks, excellent burgers, and a solid small-plates menu, they've pretty much got all your social needs covered. The location, a block off Peachtree Street and another block or so to the park, cannot be topped and is one of Atlanta's favorite see-and-be-seen locales, especially at Sunday brunch.

What's that you say? You want a great taqueria with Korean flair and flavor? That would be **Takorea** (818 Juniper St., 404/532-1944, www.mytakorea.com, Mon.-Thurs. 11:30am-10pm, Fri.-Sat. 11:30am-11pm, Sun. noon-10pm, $10), a concept restaurant that has actually managed to make the concept work. Chef Tomas Lee combined both of his culinary loves into this unique Midtown spot, which has a surprisingly sleek and sexy interior for a self-described "street food" joint. They also have a very interesting cocktail list, including a specialty martini made with a distinctive Korean liquor called *soju*.

Chef Ryan Smith has worked in some of Atlanta's finest restaurants, and now he's running his own kitchen at ★ **Empire State South** (999 Peachtree St. NE, 404/541-1105, www.empirestatesouth.com, Mon.-Thurs. 7am-10pm, Fri. 7am-11pm, Sat.-Sun. 10:30am-11pm, $25-35) in Midtown right on Peachtree Street, across the street from Margaret Mitchell's house. Empire State is somewhat unusual among the city's better restaurants in two ways: (1) the menu is extremely pared down; and (2) it offers breakfast on weekdays in addition to lunch and dinner. Did I mention the boccie ball courtyard? The morning meal is a simple yet versatile menu of Southern biscuits and New York bagels (get it? Empire State?), while the lunch menu focuses on high-quality sandwiches and one or two more savory dishes, such as a great pork belly. Dinner is a more heavy-hitting affair, with a full range of delicious, quirky appetizers like farm egg and octopus sausage (!) and entrées like Georgia trout and rib eye for two.

# INMAN PARK AND LITTLE FIVE POINTS
## Breakfast and Brunch

A beloved metro chain with nine Atlanta franchises, **Flying Biscuit Cafe** (1655 McLendon Ave., 404/687-8888, www.flyingbiscuit.com, daily 7am-10pm, $10) began in Candler Park near Little Five Points as an organic-friendly culinary project funded by Indigo Girls member and native Atlantan Emily Saliers. While not every location offers a dinner menu, all are best known for their delicious and cost-effective brunches served all day, which emphasize various specialty omelets such as the Piedmont with tasty chicken sausage. Even their namesake biscuits and gravy features an egg on top. That said, Flying Biscuit is also a big hit with the vegan crowd, offering a range of items. Cozy and often crowded, expect a wait at peak periods at all locations.

## Coffee and Sweets

Atlanta has its share of good-to-great coffee-houses, but my favorite is **Inman Perk** (240 N. Highland Ave., 678/705-4545, www.in-manperkcoffee.com, Mon.-Thurs. 6am-11pm, Fri. 6am-10pm, Sat. 7am-10pm, Sun. 8am-11pm) in, yes, Inman Park. In keeping with some of the New Urbanist vibe you often see throughout Atlanta's up-and-coming neighborhoods, Inman Perk's exterior is resolutely modernist, even Bauhaus. Inside it's a little more like a typical coffeehouse, with a large amount of seating and good Wi-Fi. Not only is the coffee several cuts above a Starbucks or even the usual locally owned java joint, they boast a wide selection of teas as well. And if you prefer alcohol to caffeine, there's a good menu of craft beers and interesting wines.

## Italian

Upscale Italian is the name of the game at Inman Park, with the one-two combination of **Sotto Sotto** (313 N. Highland Ave., 404/523-6678, www.urestaurants.net, Mon.-Thurs. 5:30pm-11pm, Fri.-Sat. 5:30pm-midnight, Sun. 5:30pm-10pm, $18-40) and its adjacent sibling **Fritti** (309 N. Highland Ave., 404/880-9559, www.urestaurants.net, Mon.-Thurs. 11:30am-11pm, Fri.-Sat. 11:30am-midnight, Sun. 12:30pm-10pm, $10-20). Sotto Sotto specializes in Tuscan cuisine, which is quite a bit different from the tomato-dominated stereotype of Italian food (though they do have a killer lasagna). Fritti is where you go for wood-fired pizza in the trendy thin-crust genre from farther south in Italy's boot. Typical offerings are the gorgonzola, pineapple, and balsamic vinegar pizza and the Funghi di Bosco with white truffle oil and portobello mushrooms.

## Steaks and Burgers

Small plates, big plates, cold plates, "second mortgage plates," **Rathbun's** (112 Krog St., 404/524-8280, www.rathbunsrestaurant.com, Mon.-Thurs. 5:30pm-10pm, Fri.-Sat. 5:30pm-11pm, $18-40) has it all. A new toast of the ATL foodie scene—exec chefs Kevin and Kent Rathbun beat Bobby Flay in an episode of *Iron Chef America*—this aspirational enterprise in Inman Park injects innovation and flavor across a wide-ranging menu. Where else can you find a hot smoked-salmon tostada, a 22-ounce bone-in rib eye, char-grilled octopus, roasted bone marrow, elk, duck breast with Thai risotto, and eggplant steak fries all in one place?

As much tourist attraction as burger spot, **Vortex** (438 Moreland Ave., 404/688-1828, www.thevortexbarandgrill.com, Sun.-Thurs. 11am-midnight, Fri.-Sat. 11am-2am, $10) dominates one approach to Little Five Points with its iconic zombie monster entrance. After walking through the demonic skull's mouth, you sit down in a rather boisterous atmosphere and enjoy some of the larger, better burgers in town, with attitude to spare. The catch: Because this is specifically a "smoking allowed inside" restaurant, by law no one under 18 is permitted inside. There's a second version in Midtown.

## Pub Fare

L5P's most highly rated spot is ★ **The Porter Beer Bar** (1156 Euclid Ave, 404/223-0393, www.theporterbeerbar.com, $12-20), which despite its name is a full-service restaurant serving lunch, dinner, and Sunday "Hair of the Dog" brunch. The small but well-curated menus are in constant rotation, but highlights include the Cuban and the "Porn Dog" (use your imagination). There is always a good selection of vegetarian fare as well. Wash it all down from a massive selection of over 400 beers, on tap and in the bottle.

## Food Mall

One of the more pleasant new mixed-use developments in Atlanta is **Krog Street Market** (99 Krog St., www.krogstreetmarket.com, Mon.-Thurs. 7am-9pm, Fri. 7am-10pm, Sat. 8am-10pm, Sun. 8am-9pm), in a renovated 1920s warehouse in the Inman Park area. Its central food court features many counter-style locations for grab 'n' go food, coffee, and smoothies. Shops include the vintage/home goods store **The Collective** and the craft beer/growler store **Hop City.** The sit-down Tex-Mex spot **Superica** has a streetside patio. Inside, you might want to try **Richard's Southern Fried,** dealing in the new trend for "hot" fried chicken.

# BUCKHEAD
## Classic Southern

A "diner" pretty much in name only—it's not cheap, and it offers valet parking—**Buckhead Diner** (3075 Piedmont Rd. NE, 404/262-3336, www.buckheadrestaurants.com, Mon.-Sat. 11am-midnight, Sun. 10am-10pm, $15-25) is primarily known as a place where celebrities can get a bite to eat in an atmosphere that is neither problematic for them nor exclusive from the rest of us. What this means in practice is you will get a mighty fine yet simply envisioned comfort-food meal, perhaps the signature roast beef sandwich with an opener of pimento cheese fritters, and maybe spot someone like Jane Fonda a few tables over.

## Mediterranean

The crispiest, tastiest, fluffiest, most melt-in-your-mouth falafel I've had anywhere is at **Cafe Agora** (262 E. Paces Ferry Rd., 404/949-0900, www.cafeagora.com, Mon.-Thurs. 11am-10pm, Fri.-Sat. 11am-4am, Sun. 11am-9pm, $7-12), a Buckhead staple that specializes in freshly cooked, authentic Greek-Turkish cuisine made by the owners themselves using old-world recipes. They also deal a mean gyro and have a full range of homemade hummus, tabbouleh, dolmades, and baba ghanoush. You can't go wrong with anything on the menu. And on weekends it's all served till 4am! There's another location in Midtown (92 Peachtree Place NE, 404/253-2997, Mon.-Sat. 10am-10pm), just around the corner from the Margaret Mitchell House.

## Steaks

Widely considered one of the best steak houses in the United States, ★ **Bone's** (3130 Piedmont Rd. NE, 404/237-2663, www.bonesrestaurant.com, Mon.-Fri. 11:30am-2:30pm and 5:30pm-10pm, Sat.-Sun. 5:30pm-10pm, $30-50) is a throwback to the time when corporate movers and shakers gathered for three-martini lunches and enormous slabs of expertly seared beef. Some of that still goes on, of course, but in a changing world, Bone's has gained slightly more universal appeal while still retaining that flavor of clubby nostalgia. There are some great seafood dishes on the menu, but obviously the steaks are the draw here. All are amazing, but I call your attention to the two dry-aged items on the beef menu: a bone-in rib eye and a porterhouse for two. Needless to say, this isn't a particularly vegetarian-friendly restaurant.

## Vietnamese

Good Vietnamese food in Buckhead is at **Chateau de Saigon** (4300 Buford Hwy. NE, 404/929-0034, www.chateaudesaigon.com, Sun.-Mon. and Wed.-Thurs. 11am-10pm, Fri.-Sat. 11am-11pm, $10-25). The menu is quite extensive, and you'll find all the usual fare, including *pho, bun,* fried rice entrées, and spring rolls. But don't stop there. There are some real gems here, including "shaken beef" filet mignon; "hot pots," where raw ingredients are cooked tableside; "sizzling fish," also cooked while you watch; and an entire page of clay pot offerings. There's even an entire submenu of tofu dishes.

# VIRGINIA-HIGHLAND
## Breakfast and Brunch

A Virginia-Highland brunch staple, **Murphy's** (997 Virginia Ave., 404/872-0904, www.murphys-atlanta-restaurant.com, Mon.-Thurs. 11am-10pm, Fri. 11am-11pm, Sat. 8am-11pm, Sun. 8am-10pm, $20) nearly always has a wait on Sunday, but most will say it's worth it. Crab cake Benedict and shrimp and grits are particular faves, and the smoked salmon is highly recommended for fans of that delicacy. Every table gets a basket of delicious muffins and biscuits with jam.

While it did indeed start out chiefly as a purveyor of sweet treats, **Highland Bakery** (655 Highland Ave. NE, 404/586-0772, www.highlandbakery.com, Mon.-Fri. 7am-4pm,

Sat.-Sun. 8am-4pm, $4-12) in nearby Old Fourth Ward has expanded its menu far beyond muffins and the like. Nowadays it's better known for its delectable breakfast and brunch offerings, from ricotta pancakes to fried chicken Benedict. The combination of down-home comfort food and the assortment of hipster servers has attracted a devoted following that has spread out to Highland Bakery's two subsequent locations, one in Midtown and one in Buckhead.

## Italian

The Virginia-Highland neighborhood is picture-perfect for a relaxing lunch or dinner, and a great place to get just that is at one of the area's most beloved restaurants, ★ **La Tavola** (992 Virginia Ave., 404/873-5430, www.latavolatrattoria.com, Mon.-Thurs. 5:30pm-10pm, Fri.-Sat. 5:30pm-11pm, Sun. 11am-3pm and 5:30pm-10pm, $15-25). As the name implies, this is essentially an old-school trattoria with just enough bistro-style, open-kitchen atmosphere to keep a trendy edge. Northern Italian specialties such as risotto and mussels are the order of the day here, along with delights such as delicious prosciutto and perfect crusty bread. There's a full antipasti menu and a delightful assortment of Italian desserts such as tiramisu, panna cotta, and crostata. It's an excellent choice for a low-key romantic experience.

## Seafood

A raw bar may not be the first thing that comes to mind when you think of Atlanta, but ★ **Fontaine's Oyster House** (1026 N. Highland Ave., 404/872-0869, www.nnnwcorp.com, Mon. 11:30am-1am, Tues. 4pm-2:30am, Wed.-Sat. 11:30am-2:30am, Sun. noon-midnight) is easily the best shellfish joint in town, as well as just a fun place to hang out into the wee hours, with the bar staying open past the usual kitchen closing time of midnight on weekends (11pm during the week). You can sit at a booth or at the bar to enjoy the range of fresh seafood. Gulf oysters, raw or steamed, will run you about

$10 per dozen, and "specialty" oysters about twice that. In keeping with the vaguely New Orleans-Cajun approach to the menu, their po'boys are amazing: You get your choice of oyster, shrimp, scallops, catfish, or crawfish.

# DRUID HILLS
## Ethiopian

Yes, Atlanta has Ethiopian cuisine, along with a fairly large Ethiopian population, and the best place for it is **Desta Ethiopian Kitchen** (3086 Briarcliff Rd. NE, 404/929-0011, www.destaethiopiankitchen.com, Mon.-Thurs. 9am-midnight, Fri.-Sun. 9am-1am, $10-15). You eat Ethiopian food with thin, tasty bread rather than utensils, and your friendly server will provide plenty of it. The cuisine ranges from delectable stews to split-pea soup and expertly prepared tilapia.

# PERIMETER
## Chinese

North of Buckhead, just outside the Perimeter, is Atlanta's closest thing to a classic Chinatown spot, **Canton Cooks** (5984 Roswell Rd. NE, 404/250-0515, Thurs.-Tues. 11am-2:30am, $10-15), offering delicacies such as fried fish maw, Peking spare ribs, fried squid, and, of course, General Tso's chicken. Possibly the best Chinese restaurant in the city, this humble spot is in a strip mall near a Whole Foods in the northern Atlanta suburb of Sandy Springs and is a favorite of that area's burgeoning Chinese population.

# WESTSIDE
## Italian

One of Atlanta's more full-immersion dining experiences is at ★ **Antico Pizza Napoletana** (1093 Hemphill Ave. NW, 404/724-2333, www.anticoatl.com, Mon.-Sat. 11:30am-"until they run out of dough," about 11pm or midnight, pizza $20), where you'll find authentic Naples-via-Brooklyn pizza in a hot, loud environment seemingly tailor-made for enjoying a big tasty pie. It's not all a bed of roses: The wait is usually quite long, they're closed on Sunday, and you can only add one topping to the pie of your choice. That's right: only one ingredient, no exceptions. But all the major ingredients (prosciutto, pecorino, soppressata, etc.) come directly from Italy, and the pies are exactly as you would find them in Naples. Each pizza feeds a lot of people.

You'll never set foot in an Olive Garden again after a visit to **Osteria del Figo** (1210 Howell Mill Rd., 404/351-3700, www.figo-pasta.com, Mon.-Thurs. 11:30am-9:30pm, Fri. 11:30am-10pm, Sat. noon-10pm, Sun. noon-9:30pm, $12), a unique pasta restaurant that matches flavor with value. Though overshadowed in the local culinary scene by the five-star Bacchanalia across the parking lot, Figo, part of a citywide chain of similar pasta places, is no slouch, offering a wide-ranging menu of pastas, regional Italian sauces (tomato-based and cream-based), and specialty melt-in-your-mouth meatballs. You place your order and pay for it first, then sit in the well-appointed dining room, where you're served by the waitstaff.

## New Southern

The most sought-after table in Atlanta is at ★ **Bacchanalia** (1198 Howell Mill Rd., 404/365-0410, www.starprovisions.com, Mon.-Sat. from 6pm, $25-35, five-course prix fixe $85), a Southeastern mecca of so-called New American cuisine that continues to top most of the foodie lists for the city. Through their Star Provisions cooperative-conglomerate (you actually enter the restaurant through the retail arm), chef-owners Anne Quatrano and Clifford Harrison concentrate on sourcing all foods organically, locally, and regionally, many from their own Summerland Farm and associated abattoir. The menu centers on a five-course prix fixe that includes a cold appetizer, fish, entrée, cheese course, and dessert (*amuse-bouche* generally comes around as well). Typical dishes include a delectable slow-roasted porchetta, a perfect red snapper, the signature crab fritter, and yes, foie gras. You can order à la carte from the bar area. Don't expect to walk in and get a table; reservations fill up months in advance. Directly next door, chef David Carson runs the kitchen at **Quinones at Bacchanalia** (1198 Howell Mill Rd., 404/365-0410, www.starprovisions.com, Mon.-Sat. from 6pm), a smaller, more Southern-tinged dining room that also relies on the tried-and-true five-course prix fixe.

# Accommodations

As a major commercial center, convention location, and home to the world's busiest airport, Atlanta understandably offers a truly mind-boggling number of hotel rooms. As you might expect, there is a huge range in quality, from world-class to miserable. One local plus, however, is that because of the massive volume of lodging, prices are often surprisingly reasonable; that said, always be sure to inquire beforehand about common and typically poorly publicized surcharges, such as for parking and Internet access.

Hartsfield-Jackson International Airport is virtually a city of its own, with an extensive lodging infrastructure to match—there are at least 60 hotels in the immediate area. Prices are a bit lower than in more desirable areas of town, but the service is typically poorer as well, not to mention the high stress level of most guests, who are either rushing to catch a plane or dead tired from flying all day.

Because of Atlanta's size and the fact that there's not a huge price variation throughout the city, these accommodations are organized by area first and then by price.

## DOWNTOWN
### $150-300

Fresh off a $65 million renovation, one of downtown's oldest flagship properties is now one of the plushest. Built in the late 1960s and a harbinger of Atlanta's boom period, the ★ **Hyatt Regency** (265 Peachtree St. NE, 404/577-1234, www.atlantaregency. hyatt.com, $190-230) offers all the crisp professionalism of that chain with a modernist minimalism. The renovated rooms are geared to tourists as well as business travelers and conventioneers, with all the in-room amenities everyone demands these days. Designed by noted Atlanta architect John Portman (a nearby street is named after him), the Hyatt's atrium is something of an architectural legend in its own right: The ultrafast glass elevators were the first of their kind in Atlanta and still offer a thrill for guests of all ages. When first built, the 24-story Hyatt was considered very tall and featured a revolving restaurant at the top, which subsequently closed as much taller skyscrapers rose all around it. The Hyatt now offers two good dining options on the ground floor. The attractions of Centennial Olympic Park, such as the Georgia Aquarium and the World of Coca-Cola, are a short walk away.

It's no longer the tallest hotel in the world, as it briefly was when first built in 1976, but the 73-story **Westin Peachtree Plaza** (210 Peachtree St. NE, 404/659-1400, www.starwood.com, from $250) still offers stunning views, not the least of which can be found at its famous revolving rooftop restaurant, the Sun Dial (daily lunch and dinner, $20). Each of the nearly 1,100 guest rooms in this John Portman-designed edifice (he also designed the Hyatt Regency and the nearby Marriott Marquis) feature floor-to-ceiling windows. While taller than Portman's Hyatt, the Westin looks very similar and is often mistaken for it. The rooms aren't large, but they are well equipped and tastefully furnished.

One of the better Downtown stays and probably the best stay for any Georgia Tech-oriented visit is the **Hampton Inn Atlanta-Georgia Tech** (244 North Ave. NW, 404/881-0881, www.hamptoninn.com, $160). Situated literally on the edge of Tech's sprawling urban campus, the Hampton Inn is also quite convenient to the Centennial Olympic Park attractions like the Georgia Aquarium and the World of Coca-Cola. Be aware, however, that as with many Downtown hotels, parking is valet-only and not cheap.

If it's access to the Centennial Olympic Park area you're looking for, look no further than the **Embassy Suites Hotel** (267 Marietta St., 404/223-2300, www.embassy-suites.com, $180-300), adjacent to the park and within a stone's throw of the Georgia Aquarium (ask about package deals). The pool area overlooks the well-maintained park, which is a nice touch.

## Over $300

Now run by the Marriott chain, Atlanta's first entry into the boutique hotel market was **Glenn Hotel** (110 Marietta St., 404/521-2250, www.glennhotel.com, from $300). The main attraction of this property in the renovated Fairlie-Poplar district is the use of "personal hosts," that is, butlers, who are on call for you daily 24 hours. There's a popular rooftop bar, the SkyLounge, which is worth a visit for the scintillating views as well as the signature cocktails. The in-house restaurant, Glenn's Kitchen, is a cut above most hotel offerings and specializes in New Southern cuisine.

# MIDTOWN
## $150-300

Perhaps surprisingly, Atlanta is actually behind the curve in the boutique hotel trend. One of the newest and most charming is the ★ **Artmore** (1302 W. Peachtree St., 404/876-6100, www.artmorehotel.com, around $150), an independently owned delight in Midtown. This restored 1925 Spanish Mediterranean, with an art deco look inside and out, offers a little taste of Beverly Hills in this older area of Atlanta, but without the exorbitant rates. Unlike most boutique hotels, the guest rooms are quite roomy. While the breakfast is called continental, it's likely one of the most extensive and well-prepared continental breakfasts you'll find.

While occasionally overlooked because of its location across the street from the Fox Theatre and right next to the equally historic (and huge) Georgian Terrace Hotel, **Hotel**

**Indigo** (683 Peachtree St., 404/874-9200, www.hotelindigo.com, $175) offers one of Atlanta's few real boutique-hotel experiences. Like most boutique hotels, the emphasis is on quality rather than size, and the Indigo's guest rooms and baths are pretty small. Pet friendly and personable, the Indigo is a nice break from the occasionally impersonal level of service at Atlanta's bigger chain hotels.

Atlanta doesn't have much history left, but the **Georgian Terrace Hotel** (659 Peachtree St. NE, 866/845-7551, www.thegeorgianterrace.com, $175-350) is still here. This grand 1911 beaux arts masterpiece hosted Clark Gable, Vivien Leigh, and other *Gone with the Wind* cast members for the film's premiere, and the Georgian Terrace still retains that old Hollywood appeal. Contrary to popular opinion, the film's premiere didn't take place across the street at the Fox Theatre; nonetheless, it's thrilling to have that ornate historic venue to gaze on, and of course to visit for a show. Other famous guests at the Georgian Terrace have included F. Scott Fitzgerald, Walt Disney, President Calvin Coolidge, and Arthur Murray, who began his dance instruction career in the hotel's ballroom. While the guest rooms have undergone regular renovations since then, keep in mind this is a historic property with the usual eccentricities, including slow elevators and guest rooms that vary widely in size and orientation. And, two words: rooftop pool!

## BUCKHEAD
### Over $300
Atlanta's premier luxury-spa hotel, the ★ **Mandarin Oriental** (3376 Peachtree St. NE, 404/995-7500, www.mandarinoriental.com) is an oasis of calm in busy Buckhead, but with every bit of the swank expected in that tony area. The emphasis at the Mandarin is on pampering guests to the nth degree, from the plush and spacious guest rooms to the luxurious baths to the state-of-the-art high-def plasma TVs artfully arranged throughout. There are several tiers of rooms, from the "budget" two-person king ($325) up to the incredible Mandarin Suite ($7,000). The level of relaxed attentiveness and confident professionalism of the staff is something of a local legend.

Buckhead's other premier luxury-spa lodging, the Starwood property ★ **St. Regis Atlanta** (88 W. Paces Ferry Rd., 404/563-7900, www.stregis.com, $450-700), is particularly recommended for those for whom a swank old-school hotel pool experience is a must (it's open daily 24 hours!). The guest rooms are world-class as well, with a level of taste and furnishing that seems almost too good to be true. The extremely high level of customer service is vectored through butlers, who seemingly exist to serve your every whim at any hour of the day, providing everything from ice (no loud vending machines) to wakeup calls. As at the Mandarin, there's an ultra-exclusive penthouse suite, the Empire.

## PERIMETER
### Under $150
For a stay up near "the Perimeter," aka I-285 north of Buckhead, you'll do no better than ★ **Holiday Inn Perimeter/Dunwoody** (4386 Chamblee-Dunwoody Rd., 770/457-6363, www.holidayinn.com, under $150), one of the more well-appointed and professionally staffed examples of that hotel chain, at incredibly low prices for Atlanta. They have state-of-the-art guest room renovations (including the trendy Keurig one-cup coffeemakers) and a hotel bar that's a step above the usual.

### $150-300
Another good stay in the clean and safe (if overly commercial) Perimeter area is the **Sheraton Atlanta Perimeter** (800 Hammond Dr., 404/564-3000, www.sheraton-perimeter.com, under $200). While it's clearly designed with the business traveler in mind, the hotel boasts an attentive staff and guest rooms that are well appointed and cleanly maintained.

## BED-AND-BREAKFASTS AND HOSTELS
### Under $150

For a quiet experience more typical of Southern B&Bs, try **Sugar Magnolia Bed and Breakfast** (804 Edgewood Ave., 404/222-0226, www.sugarmagnoliabb.com, under $150) in peaceful Inman Park, which still manages to be plenty close to a lot of key attractions. There are four guest rooms, all at quite reasonable rates, in this historic property, including the extravagant Royal Suite, which features a king bed in a curtained alcove and a whirlpool tub.

Atlanta doesn't offer much in the way of hostels. In fact, as of this writing there's only one, the 85-bed Atlanta **International Hostel** (223 Ponce de Leon Ave., 404/875-9449, www.atlantahostel.com, under $30), offering stable, safe accommodations in a restored Victorian. There's free continental breakfast every day, free parking, a pool table, and an assortment of cute pets; Wi-Fi, however, is an added daily cost. The Midtown location on bustling, fun Ponce de Leon Avenue near the Fox Theatre and locally renowned Mary Mac's Tea Room is not the world's safest locale, but is primed for access to dining and nightlife as well as for public transportation (only four blocks from the North Avenue MARTA station).

### $150-300

Atlanta has precious few true B&Bs, but a good one is **Virginia Highland Bed & Breakfast** (630 Orme Circle, 404/892-2735, www.virginiahighlandbb.com, $119-219), which capitalizes on the charms of its namesake neighborhood with sumptuous beds and a much more private, intimate setting than you'll get at one of the many hundreds of hotels in the rest of the city. There are four guest rooms; the largest is the garden apartment, which sleeps four with two bedrooms and two baths.

The five-suite eco-friendly **Stonehurst Place** (923 Piedmont Ave., 404/881-0722, www.stonehurstplace.com, $160-400) offers a top-of-the-line B&B experience in Midtown. The guest rooms, including the art on the walls, are impeccably furnished with a good mix of old-school traditional taste and cutting-edge amenities like iPod-iPhone docking stations. It's even pet friendly. The breakfasts are to die for, with unique but still comfort-oriented dishes such as a green chili egg puff and goat cheese phyllo bites.

# Information and Services

## HOSPITALS

The main trauma center in Atlanta and in the entire Southeast is **Grady Memorial Hospital** (80 Jesse Hill Jr. Dr., 404/616-1000, www.gradyhealth.org). If you're in a serious accident while near Atlanta this is definitely the place to go.

Other important facilities include **Piedmont Atlanta Hospital** (1968 Peachtree Rd., 404/605-5000, www.piedmonthospital.org), north of Downtown, part of a metro-wide hospital chain; and **St. Joseph's Hospital** (5665 Peachtree Dunwoody Rd., 678/843-7001, www.stjosephsatlanta.org), even farther north at the Perimeter.

## MEDIA
### Newspapers

The newspaper of record in Atlanta is the venerable *Atlanta Journal-Constitution* (www.ajc.com). Famous alumni include Margaret Mitchell and Henry Grady. For complete arts and entertainment listings, in addition to a good amount of counterculture politics, you'll want to check out *Creative Loafing* (www.clatl.com), the city's longtime alt-weekly,

# ATL Lingo

- **AJC:** nickname for the city's daily newspaper of record, the *Atlanta Journal-Constitution*.

- **The ATL:** hip-hop slang for Atlanta.

- **Brookwood Split:** the spot south of Buckhead where I-75 and I-85 separate north of the Connector.

- **The Connector:** that portion of I-75 and I-85 that passes directly through the center of Downtown.

- **Dirty South:** subgenre of hip-hop produced in the ATL.

- **Grady:** shorthand for the hulking Downtown presence of Grady Memorial Hospital, the South's premier trauma center. The Connector goes around it at the "Grady Curve."

- **The Hootch:** the Chattahoochee River. One "shoots the Hootch," that is, rides a white-water raft or inner tube downstream. The Chattahoochee is also a key source of drinking water for Atlanta.

- **Hotlanta:** Using this nickname for Atlanta will mark you as a tourist or a generally lame person. Avoid it at all costs.

- **L5P:** acronym for Little Five Points.

- **Peachtree:** generally refers to Peachtree Street, the historic north-south main avenue through the heart of Atlanta. Do not confuse it with the 70 other roads in Atlanta bearing some variant of "Peachtree." Movers and shakers all wanted a prestigious address on Peachtree Street. If they couldn't have that, nearby streets were named to feature the word, for example, Peachtree Circle, Peachtree Lane, and so on. Adding to the confusion is the fact that Peachtree Street becomes Peachtree Road in Buckhead. While Georgia is the Peach State, local folklore says Peachtree is probably a corruption of "pitch tree," a pine tree used for sap.

- **The Perimeter:** the vast swath of I-285 encircling the city and the demarcation between Atlanta proper and its fast-growing suburbs. Rush-hour traffic jams are the stuff of nightmares, with the northern portion, or "Top End," the most congested.

- **Ponce:** what locals call Ponce de Leon Avenue. The most upscale area during Atlanta's Victorian heyday, this sinuous street is a center of dining and nightlife. If you insist on the full name, avoid Spanish inflection and say "LEE-on."

- **Spaghetti Junction:** the sprawling 14-bridge cloverleaf that includes the intersection of "The Perimeter" (I-285) and I-85 and handles over 250,000 vehicles a day.

- **The Ted:** nickname for Turner Field, the home of the Atlanta Braves major league baseball team until 2017, when they moved to SunTrust Park in the northern suburb of Cobb County. Following the Braves' move, the Georgia State University Panthers will play college football in the reconfigured venue.

which by some reckonings actually has the higher circulation of the two.

Atlanta's sizable LGBTQ community is served by *Project Q Atlanta* (www.projectqatlanta.com) and by *Edge* (www.edgeatlanta.com).

## Radio

Traffic reports are very important in Atlanta, and many locals tune to **WSB** (750 AM and 95.5 FM). **SiriusXM** also has Atlanta traffic at channel 134.

The Atlanta radio dial is full of options,

but one of the more unique is the Georgia Tech student-run station, **WREK** (91.1 FM). The local Georgia Public Broadcasting public radio station is **WABE** (90.1 FM).

## LIBRARIES

The main branch of the **Atlanta-Fulton Public Library System** (1 Margaret Mitchell Square, 404/730-1700, www.afplweb.com, Mon.-Thurs. 9am-8pm, Fri.-Sat. 9am-6pm, Sun. 2pm-6pm) frequently hosts exhibits,

and its most notable standing exhibit is the Margaret Mitchell room on the 5th floor.

The major universities also have worthy libraries: the vast **Georgia Tech Library** (704 Cherry St., 404/894-4500, www.library. gatech.edu, Mon.-Thurs. 7:30am-10pm, Fri. 7:30am-6pm, Sat. 9am-6pm, Sun. noon-10pm) and the **Georgia State University Library** (100 Decatur St., 404/413-2820, www.library. gsu.edu, Mon.-Fri. 8:30am-5:15pm), which are open to nonstudents.

# Transportation

## CAR

Often to the chagrin of residents, Atlanta is a major nexus of interstate highways, and that's how most drivers enter and leave. Major thoroughfares are north-south arteries **I-75** and **I-85,** which actually combine into a single road through Downtown, separating a little south of Buckhead (from there I-75 heads into Chattanooga, Tennessee, and I-85 into Greenville, South Carolina). Northeast on I-85 is the infamous **"Spaghetti Junction,"** a vast collection of interchanges and one portion of highway with an incredible 18 lanes.

**I-285,** called **"The Perimeter"** by locals, and in portions labeled the "Atlanta Bypass," forms a vast circle around the metro area and serves primarily as a commuter avenue. It carries 250,000 vehicles a day at speeds ranging from blindingly fast to a barely perceptible crawl. Traffic is much worse at the **"Top End"** of the Perimeter, north of Atlanta near the city's most populous suburbs. New variable speed limit signs have been installed in portions of the Top End to adjust the speed limit from a max of 65 mph to lower limits to account for congestion and delays. Nonetheless, try to avoid it during rush hour if at all possible.

**I-20** runs east-west along the bottom of the Atlanta metro area, its eastern end passing through Augusta and its western end

going into Alabama. It's called Ralph David Abernathy Parkway near Downtown.

A key non-interstate route is **Highway 78,** called Stone Mountain Parkway east of the city and Ponce de Leon Avenue in town.

With Atlanta's heavy traffic and frequent accident and road construction delays, monitoring traffic conditions is a full-time job that's never dull. Local radio station **WSB** (95.5 FM and 750 AM) generally has the most frequent and up-to-date reports. **SiriusXM** also has a good satellite station covering DC-Baltimore-Atlanta traffic at channel 134.

On-street metered parking is available in increments of a half hour and 1-4 hours. Parking enforcement in Atlanta is extremely aggressive. While meter enforcement times vary depending on the zone, most in the visitor-frequented areas are enforced Monday-Saturday 7am-10pm. As of this writing there's talk of 24-hour meter enforcement. There are many dozens of parking garages and public and private parking lots at various costs; an excellent resource with interactive mapping is www.atlantadowntown.com.

## AIR

**Hartsfield-Jackson Atlanta International Airport** (ATL, 6000 North Terminal Pkwy., 404/530-6600, www.atlanta-airport.com) is the world's busiest, serving nearly 100 million passengers a year. Situated seven miles south of Atlanta proper astride Fulton and Clayton Counties, Hartsfield-Jackson is Georgia's largest employer and is in many ways a city unto itself. In one spot, I-75/85 actually goes under one of the runways.

Its flagship airline is Delta, whose hub here is the largest in the world, making up 60 percent of the airport's traffic. In all, about two dozen airlines fly in and out; domestic highlights include Southwest, American, and United, with international highlights including Air France, British Airways, KLM, Korean Air, and Lufthansa.

The massive **Hartsfield-Jackson Rental Car Center** houses 10 airport rental agencies, with room for more. Though freestanding, it is fully integrated with the airport by a people-moving transportation system, the ATL Skytrain, as well as its own access highway. The airport's transit system is the Plane Train, which provides full transport from terminal to terminal, including the Maynard Jackson International Terminal.

Parking at the domestic terminal is in two tiers. The four-level Daily Parking area ($3 per hour, $16 per day) is closest to the terminal and provides a large number of covered spots. The open-air Economy lots ($3 per hour, $12 per day) are the cheapest, and have a free shuttle that runs daily 8am-midnight.

There is an international shuttle connector (daily 24 hours, free) to link international passengers with both the rental car center and the domestic terminal, where the MARTA station is located. The airport MARTA rapid transit station is on the north side of the airport near the baggage claim area. Unlike some metro transit systems that use a rotating fare system, all rides on MARTA, regardless of distance, are $2.50 one-way, including to and from Hartsfield-Jackson.

Various taxi services operate out of Hartsfield-Jackson, and the fare from the airport to Downtown will run you about $40.

# MARTA PUBLIC TRANSIT

Atlanta's main public transit entity is **MARTA** (Metropolitan Atlanta Rapid Transit Authority, www.itsmarta.com, $2.50 one-way). While often the butt of jokes locally and certainly not on par with more expansive transit systems such as New York City's or San Francisco's, MARTA is a very handy and extremely cost-effective way to avoid the snarling traffic jams prevalent throughout Atlanta. There are two main components: the rapid transit trains and the extended bus system.

The train system layout is very simple: The two north-south lines, Gold and Red, go from Hartsfield-Jackson International Airport in the south and split in Buckhead, the Red Line going to Sandy Springs and the Gold Line to Doraville. The main east-west route is the Blue Line, spanning the diameter of the I-285 Perimeter, with a shorter Green Line serving Downtown. There's only one transfer station: Five Points in Downtown.

There are nearly 40 MARTA train stops, with one convenient to just about every notable destination. Generally speaking, trains run about every 15-20 minutes Monday-Friday 5am-1am, Saturday-Sunday and most holidays 6am-1am. There is full access for riders with disabilities, and bicycles are accommodated on trains and buses anytime. One-way fares are $2.50 regardless of the length of the trip, which makes MARTA a remarkable bargain compared to other big-city transit systems. The best option is to purchase a reloadable BreezeCard at any MARTA station; you then just tap it to a card reader to board.

Bus routes are fully integrated into MARTA. You can transfer to a bus line for free for one-way trips finished within three hours. The free transfer is automatically activated when used at the airport. Tap the card on the fare box on the bus.

The MARTA website features a handy downloadable *Rookie's Guide*, which is worth a quick look.

## BUS AND TRAIN

The Atlanta **Amtrak** (1688 Peachtree St., 404/881-3060, www.amtrak.com) train station is smack-dab Downtown.

Atlanta has two **Greyhound** bus stations: one in Downtown (232 Forsyth St., 404/584-1728, www.greyhound.com) and another at Hartsfield-Jackson International Airport (404/765-9598, www.greyhound.com).

## TAXI SERVICE

While not a taxi-centric town, there are plenty of cab companies. Try **Atlanta Checker Cab** (404/351-1111, www.atlantacheckercab.com) or **Atlanta Lenox Taxi Company** (404/872-2600, www.atlantalenoxtaxi.com).

# Greater Atlanta

The idea of Greater Atlanta might seem funny, or at least redundant, to those who live in Atlanta, considering the city's notorious sprawl. But there are indeed several separate municipalities worth visiting, which, though largely subsumed within the metro area, still have managed to retain their individual identity. One of Georgia's most popular attractions, Stone Mountain, is just east of town, as is the happening little city of Decatur. North of Atlanta are Marietta and Gainesville, the latter a gateway to North Georgia. And southeast of Atlanta is the unique and well-preserved natural getaway of Arabia Mountain.

## ★ DECATUR

Decatur is that rarest of birds: a place with a true small-town vibe directly adjacent to a massive metro area. Despite its proximity to the city, when you're here, you feel like you're away from Atlanta's sometimes oppressive sprawl.

Decatur has had that feel from the beginning. Technically older than Atlanta, Decatur dates back to 1822. Citizens didn't want the rampant growth that would come with a major rail terminal, so they refused one; the settlement that would later be Atlanta was founded a bit west in 1837.

Today, Decatur (www.visitdecaturgeorgia.com) is known for the success of its downtown revitalization, which has resulted in one of the most vibrant café, restaurant, and shopping scenes in the South. It's also one of the most assertively progressive little cities in the region, a trait that showed itself with the recent grassroots effort against a new Wal-Mart.

### Waffle House Museum

The national chain boasts over 1,600 locations today, but the very first Waffle House was in little old Decatur, founded in 1955 when neighbors Joe Roger and Tom Forkner went into business together. The **Waffle House Museum** (2719 E. College Ave., 770/326-7086, www.wafflehouse.com, by appointment, free) contains memorabilia from back in the day. Aside from a few annual open houses, it's only open by appointment, so call ahead and check the website.

### Nightlife and Food

The draw in Decatur, other than its beautiful, modernist town square, is its compelling food and nightlife, and the two pursuits are deeply intertwined here. Many of the city's hottest nightspots offer great food in addition to world-class craft beer selections, and many other venues offer frequent live music.

It's fittingly Decatur-ish that its most famous nightspot, **Eddie's Attic** (515 N. McDonough St., 404/377-4976, www.eddiesattic.com, daily from 5pm) is located literally right next door to city hall. One of the most influential folk-acoustic venues in the South, Eddie's upstairs performance space is where the Indigo Girls got their start. The main listening room isn't the place to get

# Greater Atlanta

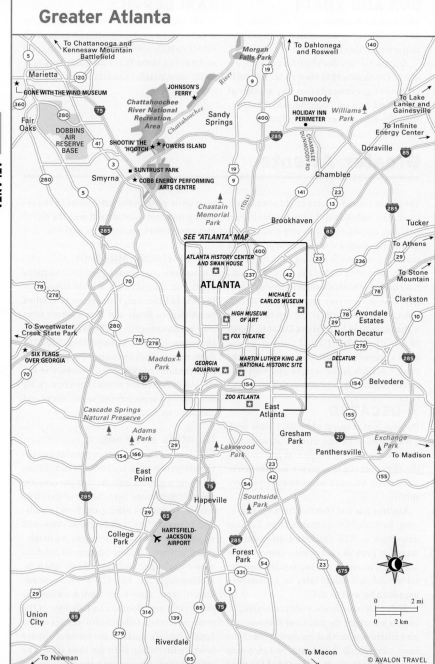

To Chattanooga and Kennesaw Mountain Battlefield

Marietta

GONE WITH THE WIND MUSEUM

Fair Oaks

DOBBINS AIR RESERVE BASE

Smyrna

SHOOTIN' THE 'HOOTCH ★ ★ POWERS ISLAND

SUNTRUST PARK

★ COBB ENERGY PERFORMING ARTS CENTRE

Chattahoochee River National Recreation Area

JOHNSON'S FERRY

Sandy Springs

Morgan Falls Park

Chattahoochee River

To Dahlonega and Roswell

Dunwoody

HOLIDAY INN PERIMETER

Williams Park

To Lake Lanier and Gainesville

To Infinite Energy Center

Doraville

Chamblee

CHAMBLEE DUNWOODY RD

Chastain Memorial Park

Brookhaven

Tucker

To Athens

SEE "ATLANTA" MAP

ATLANTA HISTORY CENTER AND SWAN HOUSE

ATLANTA

MICHAEL C CARLOS MUSEUM

HIGH MUSEUM OF ART

FOX THEATRE

GEORGIA AQUARIUM

MARTIN LUTHER KING JR NATIONAL HISTORIC SITE

ZOO ATLANTA

East Atlanta

To Stone Mountain

Clarkston

Avondale Estates

North Decatur

DECATUR

Belvedere

To Sweetwater Creek State Park

SIX FLAGS OVER GEORGIA

Maddox Park

Cascade Springs Natural Preserve

Adams Park

Lakewood Park

Gresham Park

Panthersville

Exchange Park

To Madison

East Point

College Park

HARTSFIELD-JACKSON AIRPORT

Hapeville

Southside Park

Forest Park

Union City

Riverdale

To Newnan

To Macon

0    2 mi
0    2 km

© AVALON TRAVEL

rowdy, or even to spend quality time with your smartphone; you're expected to pay attention to the performers. Mondays are standard open-mike nights, and the quality is top-notch. For a louder good time, there is rooftop patio seating.

The first-rate beers of the smaller-batch **Three Taverns Brewing** (121 New St., 404/600-3355, www.threetavernsbrewery. com) have an excellent reputation around the state. They offer tastings and tours in their "Parlour" Thursday and Friday evenings and Saturday afternoons for $14 per person.

With a name taken from Shakespeare, **Cakes & Ale** (155 Sycamore St., 404/377-7994, www.cakesandalerestaurant.com, Tues.-Thurs. 6pm-11pm, kitchen closes 10pm, Fri.-Sat. 5:30pm-midnight, kitchen closes 10:30pm) recently moved into a larger space closer to the city center, the better to accommodate the crowds that come to enjoy the adventurous farm-to-table cuisine of Napa-trained lead chef Billy Allin, formerly of another great (and sadly now defunct) local spot, Watershed.

For an Irish pub atmosphere with that thing that most Irish pubs lack—really good food—try **The Marlay House** (426 W. Ponce de Leon Ave., 404/270-9950, www.themarlayhouse.com, Mon.-Thurs. 11:30am-10:30pm, bar until midnight, Fri. 11:30am-11:30pm, bar until 2am, Sat. 10:30am-11:30pm, bar until 2am, Sun. 10:30am-10:30pm, bar until midnight, $15). They are known for their righteous roast and Yorkshire pudding. Of course, they have a great tap selection and pride themselves on pouring a pint of Guinness just as you would get it in Dublin. Most nights there is live traditional Irish music.

An intriguing and beguiling mix of neighborhood bar, signature cocktail joint, craft brew headquarters, and farm-to-table restaurant, **Leon's Full Service** (131 E. Ponce de Leon Ave., 404/687-0500, www.leonsfullservice.com, Mon. 5pm-1am, Tues.-Thurs. 11:30am-1am, Fri.-Sat. 11:30am-2am, Sun. 11:30am-1am, kitchen closes 1 hour earlier, $15-20) lives up to its name. The range

of old-school specialty cocktails, hovering around $10, is inspiring; check out the seasonal offerings. The main-plate menu is small but finely honed; try the grilled flatiron steak or the veggie loaf. In any case, don't miss out on the "pub frites," with your choice of two sauces, such as goat cheese fondue or horseradish mayo.

The first spot to really put Decatur's downtown renaissance on the map, **Brick Store Pub** (125 E. Court Square, 404/687-0990, www.brickstorepub.com, Mon. 11am-1am, Tues.-Sat. 11am-2am, Sun. noon-1am, $10) continues to offer a unique selection of amped-up yet affordable comfort food and pub fare, such as "Shepherd's Daughter's Pie," a great Cornish game hen, and an Italian-themed pierogi. The beer list includes a raft of great Belgians served in a dedicated space upstairs.

An outrageously popular tapas place, **Iberian Pig** (121 Sycamore St., 404/371-8800, www.iberianpigatl.com, Mon.-Thurs. 5pm-10pm, Fri.-Sat. 3pm-11pm, Sun. 5pm-9pm, tapas $5-15) offers great small plates and, as the name suggests, a remarkable variety of authentic Spanish pork dishes in a boisterous atmosphere. The best deal is the charcuterie sampler; don't miss the rare and incredible *jamón ibérico*.

For a real Italian wood-oven pizza experience, head to **No. 246** (129 E. Ponce de Leon Ave., 678/399-8246, www.no246.com, Mon.-Thurs. 11am-3pm and 5pm-10pm, Fri.-Sat. 11am-3pm and 5pm-11pm, Sun. 11am-3pm and 5pm-9pm, $12-24). They also offer a pasta and gnocchi menu and a special chicken scaloppine for two.

There are several coffeehouses in Decatur, but my favorite is **Java Monkey** (425 Church St., 404/378-5002, www.javamonkeydecatur.com, Mon.-Fri. 6:30am-midnight). They have tasty goodies in addition to great coffee, and every Tuesday night they host a surprisingly dynamic open-mike night for musicians.

Decatur has two great farmers markets. **Your Dekalb Farmers Market** (3000 E. Ponce de Leon Ave., www.

dekalbfarmersmarket.com, daily 9am-9pm) is an enormous collection of goods and produce not only from regional sources but literally from around the world. **The Decatur Farmers Market** (163 Clairemont Ave., Wed. 4pm-7pm; 498 N. McDonough St., Sat. 9am-1pm, www.decaturfarmersmarket.com) is a more modest and typical collection of locally sourced organic produce.

## Shopping

Decatur hosts numerous boutique-style retail establishments, including über-trendy **Squash Blossom** (113 E. Court Square, 404/373-1864, www.squashblossomboutique.com, Mon. 11am-7pm, Tues.-Thurs. 11am-8pm, Fri. 11am-9pm, Sat. 10am-9pm, Sun. 11am-6pm), a great place for hip women's apparel and accessories from companies like Free People, Michael Stars, and Echo. There's fun and fresh **World of Collage** (114 E. Ponce de Leon Ave., 404/377-1280, www.worldofcollage.com, Mon.-Sat. 11am-9pm, Sun. noon-6pm), which actually has little to do with collage and is a boutique with hard-to-find designers like Desigual and Johnny Was. For a slightly more mature take but still a lot of color, browse **Boutique Karma** (145 Sycamore St., 404/373-7533, www.boutique-karma.com, Mon.-Sat. 10:30am-7:30pm, Sun. 12:30pm-6pm).

Their branch in Athens, Georgia, is much more famous, but only two years after that one opened in 1976, another branch of **Wuxtry Records** (2096 N. Decatur Rd., 404/329-0020, www.wuxtry-records.com, Mon.-Sat. 11am-8pm, Sun. noon-6pm) opened in Decatur. Like its sister store, it's a gathering place for local musicians and hipsters alike.

The local arts and crafts scene is well represented at two cooperative galleries: **Wild Oats and Billy Goats** (112 E. Ponce de Leon Ave., 404/378-4088, www.wildoatsandbillygoats.com, Wed.-Fri. 11am-6pm, Sat. 11am-7pm, Sun. 1pm-5pm) and **HomeGrown Decatur** (412 Church St., 404/373-1147, www.home-growndecatur.com, Mon.-Sat. 10am-9pm, Sun. noon-8pm).

One of the most unique shops in town is **Houndstooth Road** (316 Church St., 404/220-8957, www.h2rd.com, Wed.-Sat. noon-7pm, Sun. noon-5pm, Tues. by appointment), a high-end Euro-style bicycle retailer, which also offers a range of clothing and accessories for the upwardly mobile cyclist.

### Getting There and Around

Getting to Decatur from Atlanta proper couldn't be easier. The dedicated Decatur MARTA station is literally yards away from the town center, something that was quite controversial at first. Conversely, you can just drive east on Ponce de Leon Avenue from the heart of Atlanta's midtown on Peachtree Street, and end up directly in downtown Decatur. Once in Decatur, a car isn't necessary. It's very walkable, with almost every place you might want to visit within a couple of blocks.

## STONE MOUNTAIN

Stone Mountain is both an iconic feature of the Atlanta landscape and a fairly cheesy tourist destination. In any case, it's certainly unique. The massive outcropping itself, a nearly 1,700-foot dome of quartz and granite five miles around at the base, is incredible and geologically fascinating. The bas-relief sculpture on the north side of Stone Mountain, of Confederate general Robert E. Lee flanked by General Stonewall Jackson and Confederate president Jefferson Davis, all on horseback, is also an impressive work, regardless of what you may think of the implied message. The nightly narrated 45-minute laser shows, included with basic admission, have been a staple of the scene for generations at **Stone Mountain Park** (1000 Robert E. Lee Blvd., 770/498-5690, www.stonemountainpark.com, daily 10am-10pm, $10 admission, other attractions extra).

What is distinctly less unique about Stone Mountain is the theme park that has been built up around it since a major "upgrade" in the 1990s. A cynic might say that the Confederates in the rock have themselves become an afterthought, playing second, third, and fourth fiddles to the associated rides and seasonal attractions (extra ticket required) that have blossomed literally in the mountain's shadow, including an actual locomotive train that takes you, Magic Kingdom-style, around the park's periphery.

The Confederates on the rock look down on Memorial Hall, where you enter for the laser shows. Adjacent to Memorial Hall is where you hop on the Skyride tram to and from the top of the mountain (extra ticket required), which, I must say, is worth the price. Closer to the mountain are individual interpretive memorials to each state of the Confederacy, detailing their involvement and sacrifice in the Civil War. At the horses' feet lies a large reflective pool complete with fountains.

While summer brings a steady crowd, Christmastime is a really big deal at Stone Mountain Park, with a cordoned-off area with a festival-of-lights-style show (extra charge) and even a fake "snow mountain" between Memorial Hall and the mountain. Perhaps understandably, the associated Confederate history museum has been shunted off to one side of the park, where you can park and take a hiking trail to the top of the mountain if you're so inclined.

Your $10 basic entrance fee also entitles you to the use of various picnic areas and walking-biking trails within the park's vast expanse. There are over 400 tent and RV camping sites ($45-60) available within the park, as well as the attached Stone Mountain Inn ($170-200) and Evergreen Marriott Conference Resort ($190-230).

Also in the park is the **Stone Mountain Golf Club** (1145 Stonewall Jackson Dr., 770/465-3278, www.stonemountaingolf.com, $39-73), widely regarded as one of the state's best public golfing opportunities. It's an accessible and pleasant experience on two 18-hole courses. The Stonemont course, designed by Robert Trent Jones Sr., is a staple on the state amateur championship circuit. Both courses offer great views of Stone Mountain itself as well as Stone Mountain Lake.

## Getting There and Around

When most folks talk about Stone Mountain, they're talking about the outcropping and theme park, not the separate small municipality. In any case, the best way to get to either is to take one of three routes east of Atlanta: Stone Mountain Parkway/U.S. 78, Ponce de Leon Avenue, or Memorial Drive. There is no MARTA train service to Stone Mountain,

Stone Mountain

# Stone Mountain Stories

"Let freedom ring from Stone Mountain of Georgia . . ."

When Dr. Martin Luther King Jr. included those famous words in his 1963 "I Have a Dream" speech, it wasn't a nod to the huge carving of three Confederate figures on the face of the granite outcropping, the largest bas-relief sculpture in the world. Commissioned in 1916, the carving wasn't actually completed until 1972, several years after King's assassination.

King was almost certainly referring to the fact—not generally mentioned in the Atlanta area today—that the modern incarnation of the Ku Klux Klan was founded in November 1915 on the summit of Stone Mountain. Those "Knights of Mary Phagan," as the hooded group called itself, burned a cross and took an oath administered by the grandson of the first KKK Grand Wizard, Confederate general Nathan Bedford Forrest. Also present that night was Sam Venable, owner of Stone Mountain, who would oversee efforts by various sculptors to finish the carving, one of which was Gutzon Borglum of Mount Rushmore fame, all the while allowing the KKK to hold meetings here. Frustrated by a 30-year hiatus in the carving, the state of Georgia finally purchased Stone Mountain from Venable in 1958 for $1 million.

Today, the carving of Confederate generals Robert E. Lee and Stonewall Jackson and Confederate president Jefferson Davis forms the central attraction of **Stone Mountain Park** (1000 Robert E. Lee Blvd., 770/498-5690, www.stonemountainpark.com, daily 10am-10pm, $10 admission, other attractions extra), one of Georgia's biggest tourist draws and a place where the KKK most certainly is not welcome anymore.

Truthfully, the most interesting history on Stone Mountain's summit happened long before the Civil War, when Creek and later Cherokee people held ceremonies up here. In the early 1800s, when it was called Rock Mountain, the summit was a frequent destination for daylong horseback trips. Contrary to what you might think, Stone Mountain was actually heavily quarried for granite throughout the history of nonnative settlement of the area. Stone Mountain rock is in the U.S. Capitol in Washington DC and was offered for use in the Martin Luther King Jr. Memorial, but it was turned down in favor of granite from China.

but you can take a MARTA bus from the Kensington Station.

## MARIETTA

One of the largest municipalities in the Atlanta metro area, Marietta (www.mariettasquare.com) is the Cobb County seat, with well over 50,000 residents within its city limits alone. Sadly it has even less remaining antebellum history than Atlanta, given that General Sherman's troops left only four buildings intact during their torching of Marietta in 1864. A major battle was fought at nearby Kennesaw Mountain, now a National Park Service-administered site. During World War II, the city and Cobb County got a boost with the construction of the enormous Bell airplane factory (later Lockheed Martin), which produced B-29 bombers by the thousands for the strategic bombing campaign on Japan. Cultural life in Marietta today revolves around the city's charming town square.

### Gone with the Wind Museum: Scarlett on the Square

Marietta doesn't play a role in Margaret Mitchell's novel, but the city does host one of the few *Gone with the Wind* museums outside Atlanta proper. The **Gone with the Wind Museum** (18 Whitlock Ave., 770/794-5576, www.gwtwmarietta.com, Mon.-Sat. 10am-5pm, $7 adults, $6 children), also called "Scarlett on the Square" and set within a restored 1875 cotton warehouse, offers a modest collection of memorabilia, mostly from the movie, most notably the honeymoon gown worn by Vivien Leigh in the film.

### Marietta Museum of History

The **Marietta Museum of History** (1 Depot

St., 770/794-5710, www.mariettahistory.org, Mon.-Sat. 10am-4pm, $5 adults, $3 children) is on the 2nd floor of the 1845 Kennesaw House, one of a handful of antebellum structures left in town. There are displays on Native Americans, the region's gold rush, and of course the localized aspects of the Civil War. A separate **Aviation Wing** (S. Cobb Dr. and Atlanta Rd. SE, 770/794-5710, www.mariettahistory.org, Thurs.-Sat. 10am-3pm) is on 15 acres of land and has vintage airplane displays focusing on Marietta's considerable contribution to the World War II production effort.

## Marietta/Cobb Museum of Art

Dedicated purely to American art, mostly from the 19th and 20th centuries, the **Marietta/Cobb Museum of Art** (30 Atlanta St., 770/528-1444, www.mariettacobbartmuseum.org, Tues.-Fri. 11am-5pm, Sat. 11am-4pm, Sun. 1pm-4pm, $8 adults, $5 children) is housed in Marietta's first post office. It hosts frequent community-oriented art instruction workshops, such as plein air and figure drawing.

## Kennesaw Mountain National Battlefield Park

In June 1864, General Sherman's advance on Atlanta was temporarily stopped by Confederate troops and artillery dug in along the top of Kennesaw Mountain outside of Marietta. The 3,000-acre **Kennesaw Mountain National Battlefield Park** (900 Kennesaw Mountain Dr., 770/427-4686, www.nps.gov, daily 8:30am-5pm, free) preserves and interprets the vast battleground. There are four self-guided driving-tour stops and an incredible 18 miles of hiking trails (no bikes) throughout the battlefield area, all interpreted. Visit the website for info on a cell phone audio tour.

## Marietta Confederate Cemetery

Over 3,000 Confederate veterans, including many killed in the Battle of Kennesaw Mountain, are laid to rest in **Marietta**

**Confederate Cemetery** (395 Powder Springs St., 770/794-5606, www.mariettaga. gov, daily 8:30am-dusk, free), the largest Confederate cemetery south of Richmond, Virginia, the Confederate capital. The graveyard was founded in 1863 when a local woman donated land on her plantation to bury 20 soldiers who had died in a train wreck.

## The Big Chicken

For generations of Atlantans, the main attraction in "May-retta" has been what is universally called **The Big Chicken** (U.S. 41 and Hwy. 120). It's actually a vintage Kentucky Fried Chicken franchise started in 1956. The seven-story, 56-foot-tall chicken was designed by a Georgia Tech architecture student and erected in 1963. Severe storm damage in 1993 nearly caused it to be demolished, but it was saved by a public outcry, which included Air Force pilots who use the Big Chicken as a navigation point while landing at a nearby base.

## Food, Nightlife, and Accommodations

Marietta's most beloved spot is the ★ **Marietta Diner** (306 Cobb Pkwy. S., 770/423-9390, www.mariettadiner.com, daily 24 hours, $15), a 24-hour meet-and-eat place known to generations of locals. It's getting a good amount of national buzz these days for its well-crafted menu of Southern comfort food (with a few twists, like kebabs and Romanian steak), all served in massive portions. Yes, they serve breakfast all day.

There's no shortage of good eats around Marietta's downtown square (www.eatonthesquare.com), but your best bets include the unusual but delicious Tex-Mex-Asian fusion of **Taqueria Tsunami** (70 S. Park Square, 678/324-7491, www.taqueriatsunami.com, Mon.-Thurs. 11am-9pm, Fri.-Sat. 11am-10pm, Sun. 10:30am-9pm, $12-20); the Thai-Japanese blend at **Thaicoon & Sushi** (34 Mill St., 678/766-0641, www.thaicoonmarietta.com, Mon.-Thurs. 11:30am-2:30pm and 5pm-10pm, Fri. 11:30am-2:30pm and 5pm-11pm, Sat. 5pm-11pm, Sun. 5pm-10pm,

$12-18); and the hearty pizzeria **Marietta Pizza Company** (3 Whitlock Ave., 770/419-0900, www.mariettapizza.com, Mon.-Thurs. 11am-10pm, Fri.-Sat. 11am-11pm, Sun. 12:30pm-10pm, $15), which offers a focused and well-conceived menu, including great subs and a gluten-free crust.

A favorite location to fuel up before or after a Kennesaw Mountain hike is **Mountain Biscuits** (1718 Old Hwy. 41, 770/419-3311, Mon.-Fri. 6am-2pm, Sat. 7am-2pm, $10), where all the namesake baked items are enormous, made from scratch, and served with delicious gravy and tasty country ham and eggs.

The **Red Hare Brewing Company** (1998 Delk Industrial Blvd., 678/401-0600, www. redharebrewing.com) offers tastings and tours.

There are plenty of chain hotels in Cobb County, but for a more unique stay try the **Stanley House Bed & Breakfast** (236 Church St., 770/426-1881, www.thestanleyhouse.com, $125), housed in a beautiful Victorian a short walk from the main town square.

### Getting There and Around

Unfortunately MARTA doesn't go directly to Marietta, but you can take a MARTA rapid transit train to the Holmes Station and then take a Cobb Community Transit bus (http://dot.cobbcountyga.gov) to where you need to go. MARTA and Cobb Community Transit are both $2.50. By car from Atlanta, take I-75 north to exit 265; take a left on the North Marietta Parkway (Hwy. 120).

## LAKE LANIER

As the prime reservoir on the Chattahoochee River, Lake Lanier is the main drinking water source for Atlanta. It's also one of the most popular recreation spots in the metro area, a fact driven not only by its proximity to the big city but by its sheer size: nearly 700 miles of shoreline. The U.S. Army Corps of Engineers operates Lake Lanier and also runs more than 70 recreation and boat access areas, over 40 of which are operated directly by the corps with the rest leased out to various other government entities. In addition to the ubiquitous boat ramps, there are eight marinas.

Periodic drought in the region has also led to frequently low water levels. While there are over 100 boat ramp lanes in theory, in practice a percentage are often closed due to low water levels. The lowest level recorded since the lake's construction in the 1950s was during the severe drought of 2007.

By far the most upscale and comprehensive lodging on the lake is ★ **Lake Lanier Islands Resort** (7000 Lanier Islands Pkwy., 770/945-8787, www.lakelanierislands.com, $200-600). In addition to a variety of guest rooms, suites, lake houses, and villas, it has its own **golf course** (greens fees start at $50), **Canopy Zip-Line Tours** ($200 full day, $30 "express"), a boat landing, an **Equestrian Center** (rides from $35), and even its own water park, **LanierWorld** ($35 adults, $20 children, lower after dark). Other amenities and activities include miniature golf, tennis, and volleyball. The main Legacy Lodge building features frequent live entertainment. Business travelers have use of the attached conference center. For those who want a more laid-back or luxurious vibe, there is a campground and hiking trails, and of course a full-service spa. While the intent is to provide anything and everything for the whole family with full lake access, interestingly there are no pet-friendly facilities at the resort. You don't have to be a registered guest to enjoy many of the à la carte amenities; the $10 gate fee (which guests also have to pay) entitles you to entrance and parking.

The Corps of Engineers operates several reservable **campgrounds** (www.recreation.gov, $30) on Lake Lanier with nearly 500 campsites: Bald Ridge Creek, Bolding Mill, Duckett Mill, Old Federal, Sawnee, and Van Pugh South Campground. Keep in mind they are seasonal, mostly due to lower water levels in the winter; check the website in advance. While there are many islands strewn throughout the lake and accessible by boat, you're not supposed to camp on them.

# GAINESVILLE

Gainesville is chiefly known for two things: Its supposed status as "Poultry Capital of the World," a nod to the many chicken processing plants in the area; and as the home of Confederate general James Longstreet, Robert E. Lee's second-in-command. Despite his Confederate bona fides, Longstreet was quick to embrace northern Reconstruction policies after the Civil War, even becoming an active Republican during a time when that was considered borderline traitorous for a white Southerner. Get to Gainesville from Atlanta via I-85 north; take I-985/Lanier Parkway into town.

## Piedmont Hotel

Opened by General James Longstreet in 1876, over the years the **Piedmont Hotel** (827 Maple St., 770/539-9005, www.longstreet-society.org, Tues.-Sat. 10am-4pm, free) has been reduced to only the ground floor of its former three-story opulence. It's a museum of sorts now and home to the Longstreet Society (www.longstreetsociety.org), dedicated to preserving the memory of the general. Longtime *Atlanta Journal-Constitution* editor Henry Grady was a frequent guest, as was Joel Chandler Harris of "Uncle Remus" fame. Local lore has it that what we now know as Southern fried chicken was first cooked in the Piedmont's kitchen.

## Alta Vista Cemetery

General James Longstreet was laid to rest in **Alta Vista Cemetery** (1080 Jesse Jewell Pkwy.). Well-wishers often leave cigars at his gravesite, an homage to the general's favorite vice. You'll also find the graves of many other Confederate veterans, a space shuttle astronaut, and Daniel Boone, though not *that* Daniel Boone. The cemetery's name means "high view" in Spanish, and the scenic hilltop location certainly provides that. Download a walking tour at www.gainesville.org.

# Northeast Georgia History Center

The little **Northeast Georgia History Center** (322 Academy St., 770/297-5900, Tues.-Sat. 10am-4pm, $5 adults, $3 children) has some modest exhibits from the Gainesville area's history, including the Northeast Georgia Sports Hall of Fame and the restored circa-1780 log cabin of Chief White Path of the Cherokee people. There's also a little Freedom Garden dedicated to veterans.

# ARABIA MOUNTAIN NATIONAL HERITAGE AREA

Two wonderful areas of pristine nature right outside the concrete jungle of Atlanta are **Panola Mountain State Park** (2600 Hwy. 155, 770/389-7801, www.gastate-parks.org, daily 7am-dusk, parking $5), near the suburban town of Stockbridge, and **Davidson-Arabia Nature Preserve** (3787 Klondike Rd., 770/492-5231, www.arabi-aalliance.org, daily dawn-dusk, free) near Lithonia. Both areas are part of the Arabia Mountain National Heritage Area, administered by a cooperative partnership of local groups, and both are centered on enormous granite outcroppings similar to the larger Stone Mountain but without the attendant development.

Panola Mountain is known for its rich and rare botanical treasure, such as yellow daisies and Diamorpha. Because of its fragile ecosystem, hiking is allowed only through guided tours (depart from the park's nature center, generally Wed. and Fri.-Sun. 8am, $7 pp). Hikers have full use of Davidson-Arabia, with trails accessible from Klondike Road or by trailheads on the paved, 20-mile Rockdale River-Panola Mountain PATH Trail, which is open to bicycles and leashed dogs.

Panola Mountain and Arabia Mountain are both easily accessible from Atlanta by taking I-20 east. For Panola Mountain, get off at exit 68 and take Highway 155. For Arabia Mountain get off at Klondike Road, exit 74.

# SENOIA

At the very edge of metro Atlanta—about 25 miles south—is Senoia (pronounced "seh-NOY"), better known to fans of the cable TV series *The Walking Dead* as Woodbury. In fact, shooting of the incredibly popular show has been so integral to the economy of this 3,000-person burg that several buildings on Main Street, purpose-built for the show, still bear the name of the fictional town, such as Woodbury Town Hall.

The unofficial hub of town activity is **Senoia Coffee & Café** (1 Main St., 770/599-8000, http://senoiacoffeeandcafe.com, Mon.-Thurs. 6:30am-3pm, Fri. 6:30am-9pm, Sat. 7:30am-9pm), also known as the Woodbury Coffee House from the show. Have a cup of Zombie Dark java and maybe overhear chatter from "Walker Stalkers"—admittedly obsessive fans—while the crew is in town filming.

For pub-style eats and entertainment, go to **Southern Ground Social Club** (18 Main St., 770/727-9014, www.southerngroundsocialclub.com, Tues.-Sat. 11am-2am, $15), owned by native son and country star Zac Brown. The limited menu is tasty; try the fried green tomato BLT. As you'd expect, most nights feature live music.

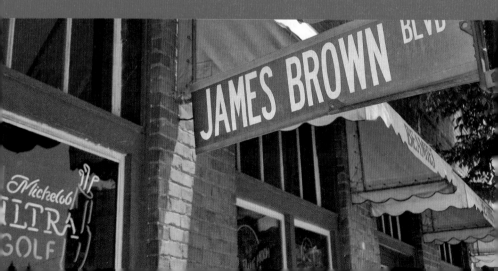

# North Georgia

## Highlights

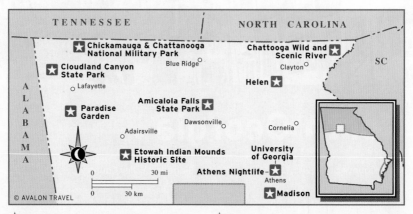

★ **Chattooga Wild and Scenic River:**
Take a raft ride on the Carolina border down
through *Deliverance* country (page 513).

★ **Helen:** A little cheesy and a lot of fun, this
"Alpine village" re-creates *The Sound of Music*
experience, but with beer (page 516).

★ **Amicalola Falls State Park:** View the
tallest waterfall east of the Mississippi River, near
where the Appalachian Trail begins (page 519).

★ **Etowah Indian Mounds Historic
Site:** Climb to the top of an ancient Native
American temple mound at this excellently pre-
served site and museum (page 525).

★ **Chickamauga & Chattanooga
National Military Park:** Take in the huge
battlefield where the Confederacy won its last
major victory (page 526).

★ **Paradise Garden:** Immerse yourself in
the eccentric, prolific vision of iconic folk artist
Howard Finster (page 528).

★ **Cloudland Canyon State Park:** Dotted
with caves, this fascinating geological feature
offers jaw-dropping views and great hiking and
spelunking (page 529).

★ **University of Georgia:** The nation's oldest chartered university is on a beautiful shaded
campus full of historic buildings (page 530).

★ **Athens Nightlife:** The legacy of the B-52s
and R.E.M. live on in this college town's robust
live music scene (page 533).

★ **Madison:** One of the most charming and
well-preserved old Southern towns is chock-full
of eclectic and interesting architecture (page
537).

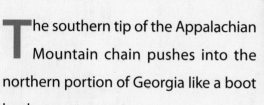

The southern tip of the Appalachian Mountain chain pushes into the northern portion of Georgia like a boot heel.

Though crisscrossed by gorges, rivers, creeks, and hollows, North Georgia is a distinctly accessible mountainous area, more logistically forgiving than many areas farther into the Blue Ridge, but with a similar culture of self-sufficiency.

The northeastern portion of Georgia between the great coastal plain to the south and the mountainous regions of the far north has been a hotbed of activity from the earliest days of the colony. Today, exurban Atlanta has encroached on its western edge.

## PLANNING YOUR TIME

It's theoretically possible to barnstorm through North Georgia in a day or two by car, just seeing the highlights. The northeast section has more sights and more and better roads; that said, in the summer those two-lane roads, especially in the Helen area, can get pretty crowded with vacationers.

The Piedmont hosts the state's flagship (and oldest) university, in Athens. It can easily be experienced by car with a minimum of travel time. Using Athens as a base, you can take a fun day-trip circle route to Madison, Greensboro, Washington, and back.

---

**Previous:** the alpine village of Helen; James Brown Boulevard street sign in Augusta. **Above:** Tallulah Gorge.

# North Georgia

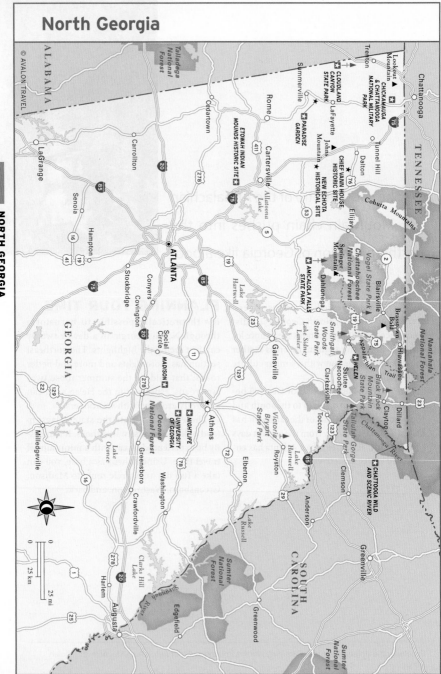

ALABAMA

Talladega
National
Forest

TENNESSEE

Trenton

Lookout
Mountain ▲

Chattanooga

75

Summerville

CLOUDLAND
CANYON
STATE PARK ✚

CHICKAMAUGA
& CHATTANOOGA
NATIONAL MILITARY
PARK ✚

LaFayette

Cohutta Mountains

Rome

PARADISE
GARDEN ✚

Johns
Mountain

Tunnel Hill

Dalton

76

CHIEF VANN HOUSE
HISTORIC SITE ★

Cedartown

411

ETOWAH INDIAN
MOUNDS HISTORIC SITE ✚

Cartersville

Allatoona
Lake

NEW ECHOTA
HISTORICAL SITE ★

53

Ellijay

Nantahala
National Forest

20

278

LaGrange

Carrollton

85

Senoia

Hampton

16

41

19

ATLANTA

75

85

Stockbridge

Covington

Conyers

Social
Circle

20

Lake
Allatoona

5

19

Lake
Hartwell

23

Springer
Mountain

AMICALOLA FALLS
STATE PARK ✚

Dahlonega

Chattahoochee
National Forest

Vogel
State Park

2

Blairsville

Brasstown
Bald ▲

Black Rock
Mountain
State Park

75

HELEN ✚

Sautee
Nacoochee

Clarkesville

Appalachian
Trail

Hiawassee

19

Smithgall
Woods
State Park

Clayton

23

Dillard

GEORGIA

MADISON ✚

22

129

Milledgeville

278

11

Gainesville

Lake Sidney
Lanier

129

Athens

UNIVERSITY
OF GEORGIA ✚

NIGHTLIFE ✚

78

Oconee
National Forest

Greensboro

Crawfordville

Lake
Oconee

Washington

Clarks Hill
Lake

72

Victoria
Bryant
State Park

Elberton

Royston

Lake
Hartwell

Toccoa

123

Tallulah Gorge
State Park

Clarkesville

Chattooga River

CHATTOOGA WILD
AND SCENIC RIVER ✚

Clemson

Anderson

85

29

Greenville

SOUTH
CAROLINA

Lake
Russell

Sumter
National
Forest

Greenwood

Sumter
National
Forest

278

20

Harlem

1

23

Augusta

Savannah River

Edgefield

0

0

25 km

25 mi

N

# Rabun County

In the northeast corner of the state on the border of the Carolinas, the Rabun County area (www.gamountains.com) is one of the most visited portions of North Georgia. It's where you'll find some of the state's most scenic vistas.

Rabun hit the global map in the 1890s, when the high Tallulah Falls Railway was constructed along the Tallulah Gorge, the deepest east of the Mississippi River. The railway brought vacationers to various Victorian-style mountain resorts, and the area served as the scenic location for several movies, including *The Great Locomotive Chase* and the Burt Reynolds film *Deliverance*.

## CLAYTON

The Rabun County seat is Clayton (www. downtownclaytonga.org), a diverse little mountain town with rustic charm to spare but still a full slate of offerings for the more sophisticated traveler to this very conservative part of the country.

The **Rabun County Welcome Center** (232 U.S. 441, 706/782-4812, www.gamountains.com) is a good first stop. For a quick look at local history, go to the museum and research library at the **Rabun County Historical Society** (81 N. Church St., Mon. 10am-2pm, Wed. 12:30pm-4:30pm, Fri. 10am-2pm) near the county courthouse.

My favorite restaurant in this part of North Georgia is ★ **Zeppelin's** (88 Main St., 706/212-0101, www.zeppelinspastahouse. com, Mon.-Thurs. 11:30am-9pm, Fri.-Sat. 11am-10pm, Sun. 11am-9pm, $12). A menu of perfectly crispy flatbread pizzas (about $15 and big enough for two) are their main claim to fame, but their burgers are incredible as well, including a bison option.

## Foxfire Museum & Heritage Center

For nearly 50 years, the *Foxfire* book and

magazine series has chronicled and preserved the dwindling folkways of the southern Appalachians in North Georgia. The Foxfire organization funds and runs the **Foxfire Museum & Heritage Center** (Black Mountain Pkwy., 706/746-5828, www.foxfire. org, Mon.-Sat. 8:30am-4:30pm, $6 over age 10, $3 ages 7-10, free 6 and under) in Mountain City, a few minutes north of Clayton. This collection of vernacular log buildings just off U.S. 441 contains a wealth of authentic displays and equipment portraying the daily life of mountain people in this area. Each October in downtown Clayton is the **Foxfire Mountaineer Festival** (www.foxfire.org).

## ★ CHATTOOGA WILD AND SCENIC RIVER

If you've seen the 1972 film *Deliverance*, you've seen the Chattooga River (www.rivers.gov), the South's best white-water rafting locale (in the movie it bore the fictional name "Cahulawassee"). The Chattooga River forms part of the Georgia-South Carolina border. If you're white-water rafting, you'll likely be putting in farther upstream, but the easiest way to get to the Chattooga is to take U.S. 76 until you just cross the Chattooga River Bridge into South Carolina. On the Carolina side is a sizable parking area, unfortunately with subpar restroom facilities. You can park in Georgia if you'd like, but there's a $2 parking fee and fewer spaces.

**Bull Sluice Falls** is a popular thrill-seeking point for rafters and kayakers at the end of Section III of the river, with a 14-foot drop when the river is at full level (Bull Sluice also had a starring role in *Deliverance*). Bull Sluice is also a popular free place for area families to enjoy a dip in the cool water amid the roaring sounds of the sluice.

For recreational purposes the Chattooga is divided into four sections. Section I is primarily for anglers. Section II begins at Highway 28 and ends at Earl's Ford, where there's a 0.25-mile hike to reach the parking area. This is a great little seven-mile run for families, tubers, and novice rafters. The real action begins at Section III, a 14-mile run from Earl's Ford to the U.S. 76 bridge, with a 0.25-mile walk to put in. Beginning with Warwoman Rapid, you'll get a lot of Class II, III, and IV rapids, including the final Class IV-V rapid at Bull Sluice, which concludes Section III. In all, Section III will take 6-8 hours from beginning to end. The most challenging ride is Section IV, from the U.S. 76 bridge to the river's end at Lake Tugaloo.

For serious rafting, the starting points are upriver on the South Carolina side. The main professional rafting tour company on the river is **Nantahala Outdoor Center** (888/905-7238, www.noc.com, prices vary). Expect to pay at least $85 per person, more during the high season in the summer. While walk-ins are welcome, I recommend reserving your trip in advance. Another popular Chattooga rafting guide is **Wildwater Rafting** (800/451-9972, www.wildwaterrafting.com, prices vary).

The prime independent outfitter is **Chattooga Whitewater Outfitters** (14239 U.S. 76, Long Creek, 864/647-9083, www.

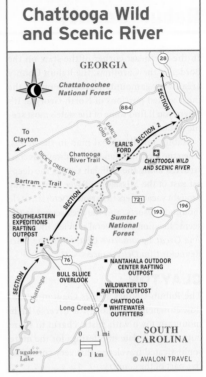

rafting on the Chattooga River

chattoogawhitewatershop.com). If you find yourself craving some carbs after a day of white-water rafting on the Chattooga, check out the pizza joint **Humble Pie** (14239 U.S. 76, Long Creek, 864/647-9083, www.chattoogawhitewatershop.com, Tues.-Sun. 3pm-10pm, $10), within and owned by Chattooga Whitewater Outfitters.

## BLACK ROCK MOUNTAIN STATE PARK

The highest state park in Georgia and one of the most enjoyable, **Black Rock Mountain State Park** (3085 Black Rock Mountain Pkwy., 706/746-2141, www.gastateparks.org, Mar.-Nov. daily 7am-10pm, parking $5, campsites $25-28, walk-in campsites $15, cottages $125-145) attracts particularly large crowds during leaf-turning season in the fall. The visitors center at the summit of the mountain is a popular place for its relaxing views. Campers will find 44 tent and RV sites, 10 cottages, and a dozen walk-in campsites.

## MOCCASIN CREEK STATE PARK

**Moccasin Creek State Park** (3655 Hwy. 197, 706/947-3194, www.gastateparks.org,

Mar.-Nov. daily 7am-10pm, parking $5, campsites $25), nestled up against quiet, pretty Lake Burton, is focused on boating and fishing. Camping is a little snug here, with tent and RV gravel sites fairly close together. But it's a fine place for water recreation, with docks, a boat ramp, and a fishing pier open only to disabled people, seniors, and children.

## Wildcat Creek

Just around the corner from Lake Burton is the access road to the hidden gem of **Wildcat Creek** (Forest Rd. 26, www.fs.usda.gov, campsites $10, first come, first served, no water) in Chattahoochee-Oconee National Forest. You'll find outstanding fishing in the creek stocked with rainbow trout. Lining Wildcat Creek are two primitive campgrounds run by the U.S. Forest Service. Hikers can access the Appalachian Trail from this route as well. A sturdy 4WD vehicle is strongly recommended.

## TALLULAH GORGE STATE PARK

**Tallulah Gorge State Park** (338 Jane Hurt Yarn Dr., 706/754-7981, www.gastateparks. org, daily 8am-dusk, parking $5) has been one of the state's most visited parks since its

Moccasin Creek State Park

inception in the 1990s. It contains the eponymous and iconic Tallulah Falls as well as a vast area on either side of the deepest gorge (1,000 feet) in the eastern United States.

Your first stop is the **Jane Hurt Yarn Interpretive Center** (daily 8am-5pm), a combined visitors center and museum. This is where you get your free permit to hike to the floor of the gorge (only permit holders can go all the way to the bottom, and only 100 permits are given out each day; get here as early as you can).

For the less adventurous or those with less time, a simple walk along the north rim includes several viewing points. You may choose to go down the 531-step staircase and across a suspension walking bridge to the bottom of the gorge (you'll need a permit to actually walk onto the rocky bottom). Along the way you'll see the old iron towers used to stage Karl Wallenda's famous tightrope walk across the gorge in 1970. The most adventurous hikers can take the long trek from there to **Bridal Veil Falls,** where the only swimming in the park is allowed. At 600 feet, the second-tallest waterfall in the state is **Caledonia Cascade,** sometimes called Cascade Falls, near the beginning of Tallulah Gorge. You can see it from the hiking trail around the rim.

The trail system within the park is extensive. Lodging within the park includes 50 tent and RV sites and three backcountry shelters ($15).

# Helen and Vicinity

The area around Helen is picturesque, easily accessible, and offers plenty of visitor amenities. No wonder, then, that it's an extremely popular summer and fall vacation spot, especially for day-trippers from metro Atlanta.

## ★ HELEN

For generations of Georgians, the word "Helen" has either meant a fun place to get away in the mountains, a hilariously cheesy living theme park, or a combination of both. Situated in a neat little valley at the headwaters of the Chattahoochee River, this once-decrepit former logging town was literally rebuilt from scratch in the late 1960s specifically to mimic a stereotypical German-Swiss mountain village. Local regulations require that every structure conform to a classic Alpine motif that will feel familiar to anyone who has seen *The Sound of Music.*

The highlight of the year is the annual **Oktoberfest** (706/878-1908, www.helen-chamber.com, $8 Mon.-Fri., $9 Sat., free Sun.) centering on the town's Festhalle (1074 Edelweiss Strasse). Unlike many towns that hold similar events, Oktoberfest in Helen is no mere long weekend: It lasts from mid-September through the end of October. In true German style, the Festhalle is filled with rows of long tables for you to enjoy your beer and brats and listen to oompah music.

## Sights

**Charlemagne's Kingdom** (8808 N. Main St., 706/878-2200, www.georgiamodelrailroad.com, Thurs.-Tues. 10am-5pm, $5) is the labor of love of a German couple who, over the course of the last two decades, have built an entirely self-contained little part of Germany traversed by an extensive model railroad, featuring over 400 feet of indoor track.

Directly adjacent to Helen is the more tasteful little community of Sautee Nacoochee. The **Folk Pottery Museum of Northeast Georgia** (283 Hwy. 255, 706/878-3300, www.folkpotterymuseum.com, Mon.-Sat. 10am-5pm, Sun. 1pm-5pm, $5 adults, $2 children) is within the Sautee Nacoochee Cultural Center.

## Food and Accommodations

The oldest German restaurant in Helen, the iconic **Old Heidelberg** (8660 N. Main St., 706/878-3273, spring-fall daily 11:30am-9pm, $20) calls itself the "most photographed

windmill in Helen

building in Georgia." The menu has an entire page of schnitzel (about $20) and another for sausage dishes ($15). Conveniently across the street from the town's Festhalle, ★ **Bodensee** (64 Munich Strasse, 706/878-1026, www.bodenseerestaurant.com, spring-fall daily 11:30am-8pm, $15) serves a mean jaeger schnitzel along with all the other staples.

Quality chain lodging in Helen is scarce, but you can try the entirely Alpine-themed **Hampton Inn** (147 Unicoi St., 706/878-3310, www.hamptoninn.com, $100) or the **Country Inn & Suites** (877 Edelweiss Strasse, 706/878-9000, www.countryinns.com, $110-150) for a cut above the typical chain experience. For a romantic, and yes, German-themed getaway, head to **Black Forest Bed & Breakfast** (8902 N. Main St., 706/878-3995, www.black-forestvacationrentals.com, $135-250).

## RAVEN CLIFF FALLS

Situated within the massive **Raven Cliffs Wilderness Area** (www.fs.usda.gov), itself a major trout-fishing and hiking mecca, Raven Cliff Falls on Dodd Creek is one of North Georgia's most popular cascades despite being a relatively strenuous five-mile round-trip hike. The falls, with a total drop of 400 feet, are present in several sections along the hike. There is walk-in camping, but it's not particularly recommended due to the crowds. To get here, take Highway 75 north from Helen about 1.5 miles and turn left onto Highway 356. From there go about 2.5 miles to the Richard B. Russell Scenic Highway, then turn right and go 3 miles to the well-marked trailhead and parking area.

## SMITHGALL WOODS STATE PARK

With a focus on education, **Smithgall Woods State Park** (61 Tsalaki Tr., 706/878-3087, www.gastateparks.org, visitors center daily 8am-5pm, parking $5) is a delightful gem a bit north of Helen. The rustically attractive main visitors center contains displays on flora and fauna, with the highlight being the nearby raptor aviary, where rescued birds of prey live under care. There is no camping at Smithgall Woods per se, but there are five reservable and perhaps surprisingly upscale cottages ($150-500).

## UNICOI STATE PARK

**Unicoi State Park and Lodge** (1788 Hwy. 356, 706/878-2201, www.gastateparks.org, parking $5, tents and RVs $29-35, walk-in campsites $25, cottages $80-100) offers something for everyone on a sprawling 1,000 acres within a few miles of Helen. There are nearly 100 camping spaces for tents and RVs and a couple dozen walk-in tent sites, a vast array of charming cottages in various multilevel clusters, and the associated 100-room lodge (800/573-9659, $75-100).

### Anna Ruby Falls

Although it is within Unicoi State Park, **Anna Ruby Falls** (www.fs.usda.gov, daily 9am-6pm, entry gate closes 5pm, $3) is run by the U.S. Forest Service and requires a

Anna Ruby Falls

separate admission. However, it's worth the nominal fee, not only for the perfectly situated twin falls themselves—uniting to form Smith Creek at the bottom, which itself empties into Unicoi Lake and, much later, the Gulf of Mexico—but for the relaxing, scenic walk from the parking area and visitors center to the falls.

## CLARKESVILLE

The seat of Habersham County, Clarkesville is primarily known for its tidy downtown shopping area and one of the premier B&B's in the state: ★ **Glen-Ella Springs Inn** (1789 Bear Gap Rd., 706/754-7295, www.glenella.com, $150-275). Set in a restored yet still rustic-feeling 1800s building on a scenic 12 acres, Glen-Ella's 16 guest rooms all boast covered porches with rocking chairs. The attached restaurant (daily 6pm-10pm, $25) is considered one of Georgia's best, and it's open to nonguests.

A few miles north of Clarkesville on Highway 197 is the venerable and charming pottery makers' collective **Mark of the Potter** (9982 Hwy. 197 N., 706/947-3440, www.markofthepotter.com, daily 10am-6pm), set within the restored Watts gristmill.

# The Appalachian Trail

Following the lead of the country's first conservationist president, Theodore Roosevelt, the first stirrings of the concept of a national "super-trail" began making the rounds in the early 1920s. Work soon began on what was then called "America's Footpath."

By 1937 the entire Appalachian Trail was finished on both ends, from Georgia to Maine. However, almost immediately a hurricane did heavy damage to the path, and Skyline Drive was extended to the Blue Ridge Parkway in the 1940s, which destroyed a 120-mile-long section of the trail.

Renewed interest in the trail came in the postwar years. The designation of the Appalachian Trail, or "AT" as it's often known, as a National Scenic Trail in 1968 cemented its status as a national treasure under federal protection.

Amicalola Falls State Park

# ★ AMICALOLA FALLS STATE PARK

Home of the tallest cascade east of the Mississippi River, **Amicalola Falls State Park** (418 Amicalola Falls State Park Rd., 706/265-8888, www.gastateparks.org, daily 7am-10pm, visitors center daily 8:30am-5pm, parking $5) also happens to be a main gateway to the Appalachian Trail. It's an extremely popular park, especially during leaf-viewing season in the fall. The magnificent 730-foot falls are one of the "Seven Natural Wonders of Georgia" and are worth the crowds.

Lodging at Amicalola (www.galodges.com) includes the **Amicalola Falls Lodge** (from $150) near the top of the falls. You can also stay in one of 14 rustic cottages. However, the most distinctive lodging at Amicalola is the ★ **Len Foote Hike Inn** (www.hike-inn.com,

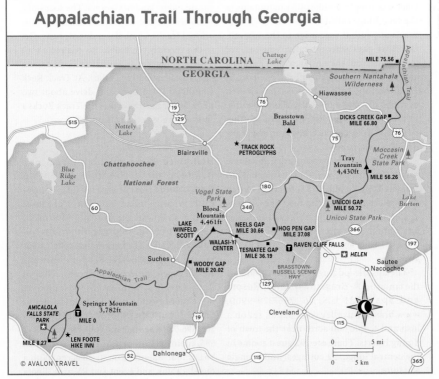

# Appalachian Trail Through Georgia

NORTH CAROLINA
GEORGIA
Chatuge Lake
Appalachian Trail
MILE 75.56

Southern Nantahala Wilderness
Hiawassee

19
129
76
Nottely Lake
Brasstown Bald
DICKS CREEK GAP
MILE 66.80
515
76

★ TRACK ROCK PETROGLYPHS
Blairsville
75
Moccasin Creek State Park

Blue Ridge Lake
Chattahoochee
Tray Mountain 4,430ft
MILE 56.26

National Forest
Vogel State Park
180
Lake Burton

60
Blood Mountain 4,461ft
348
UNICOI GAP MILE 50.72
Unicoi State Park

LAKE WINFELD SCOTT
NEELS GAP MILE 30.66
HOG PEN GAP MILE 37.08
366
197

WALASI-YI CENTER
TESNATEE GAP MILE 36.19
RAVEN CLIFF FALLS
★ HELEN

Suches
WOODY GAP MILE 20.02
BRASSTOWN-RUSSELL SCENIC HWY
Sautee Nacoochee

Appalachian Trail
129

AMICALOLA FALLS STATE PARK
Springer Mountain 3,782ft
MILE 0
Cleveland
115

MILE 8.27
19

LEN FOOTE HIKE INN

52
Dahlonega
115
365

© AVALON TRAVEL

0        5 mi
0    5 km

$100-140), an eco-friendly hiker's lodge that's a five-mile trek from the main park area. Run by a nonprofit, the inn has a staff that lives on-site. The 20 guest rooms are really only intended for sleeping, but the communal areas are charmingly appointed. From the Hike Inn, it is another mile to reach the AT.

There is a total of 12 miles of trails in the park, with the most popular and famous being the 8.5-mile **Southern Terminus Approach Trail** from the falls to Springer Mountain, the bottom tip of the AT.

Georgia's section of the AT (www.appalachiantrail.org) is 76 miles long, from Springer Mountain to Bly Gap and on into North Carolina. At its highest point in Georgia, Blood Mountain, the AT is 4,460 feet above sea level; its low spot is Dicks Creek Gap at 2,675 feet. White rectangular blazes mark the trail, and turns are marked with double blazes.

# Brasstown Bald

At 4,784 feet, Georgia's highest point is the summit of **Brasstown Bald** (770/297-3000, www.fs.usda.gov, visitors center daily 10am-4pm, $3 pp). Deep in the Chattahoochee-Oconee National Forest and historic Cherokee country, the mountain is called Enotah by the Cherokee people. Unlike other mountains in the Blue Ridge called balds, Brasstown Bald is actually full of vegetation to the summit. On clear days, theoretically, you can see four states from the nostalgically charming and well-built observation deck: Georgia, Tennessee, and both Carolinas. You can even occasionally make out the Atlanta skyline. (The very top of the tower is for fire-spotting by the U.S. Forest Service, however, and is off-limits to visitors.)

Hike up from the parking area, about one mile round-trip, or wait for the frequent but seasonal shuttle buses ($3) to chug you up the winding path to the top. The visitors center underneath the observation tower has a number of interesting exhibits. Pack a lunch—the views from the picnic area are awesome.

The upscale lodging of note in the area is the fantastic ★ **Brasstown Valley Resort and Spa** (6321 U.S. 76, 706/379-9900, www.brasstownvalley.com, $200), set on a lush and scenic 500 acres near the town of Young Harris. There are 102 guest rooms in the central lodge, 32 cottages, and a single spa suite.

## TRACK ROCK PETROGLYPHS

**Track Rock Gap** (Track Rock Gap Rd., 706/745-6928, www.fs.usda.gov, daily dawn-dusk, free), with its ancient Native American rock carvings, or petroglyphs, is the only such site on public land in Georgia. The soapstone rocks feature over 100 depictions of wildlife, animal tracks, symbols, and footprints. Get to this recently renovated site, complete with a historic marker, from Blairsville by taking U.S. 76 east about five miles. At Track Rock Gap Road, turn right and drive about two miles to the gap. Drive past the Track Rocks a short distance to the parking lot.

## HIAWASSEE

Hiawassee (www.mountaintopga.com) is known for its **Georgia Mountain Fairgrounds** (1311 Music Hall Rd., 706/896-4191, www.georgiamountainfairgrounds.com), which hosts the **Georgia Mountain Fair** (July) and the **Georgia Mountain Fall Festival** (Oct.). The fairgrounds offer camping as well (706/896-4191, $21-34) with nearly 100 sites open year-round and nearly 200 open April-October, both paved and unpaved. For a more rustic brush with nature stay at **Enota Mountain Retreat** (1000 Hwy. 180, 706/896-7504, www.enota.com, tents $25, RVs $35, cabins $110-165) near Hiawassee, which boasts four waterfalls on its 60 acres. With a motel, cabins, and a tent and RV area, Enota combines a truly beautiful setting with no-frills, communal, pet-friendly living complete with attached 10-acre organic farm.

## VOGEL STATE PARK

**Vogel State Park** (405 State Rt. 129, 706/745-2628, www.gastateparks.org, daily 7am-10pm, parking $5) is one of Georgia's oldest and most beloved. There's plenty of hiking with lots to see, including a peaceful 22-acre lake (no motorized watercraft allowed), complete with a little beachfront area, and the small but wonderful **Trahlyta Falls.** There's a 13-mile backcountry trail, and you can access the Appalachian Trail from the park as well. Perhaps the most unique aspect is the museum dedicated to the Civilian Conservation Corps (CCC), which constructed Vogel (along with many other Southern state parks) in the 1930s. This is also one of the better Georgia parks for camping, with roomy, woodsy sites.

# Dahlonega

Epicenter of one of the first gold rushes in the United States, Dahlonega (www.dahlonega.org) still retains a fitting frontier vibe. Most everything in town revolves around either the town's literally golden history or the student life of North Georgia College and State University, the distinctive gold-leaf steeple of its administration building dominating the skyline. However, "purple gold" is making a big impact on the area these days in the form of a burgeoning wine region. The highlight of the Dahlonega calendar is the **Gold Rush Days** (www.dahlonegajaycees.com) festival every October, which features food, fun, and music in the square.

## SIGHTS
### Dahlonega Gold Museum State Historic Site

The **Dahlonega Gold Museum State**

Dahlonega's Gold Rush Days, held in October

**Historic Site** (1 Public Square, 706/864-2257, www.gastateparks.org, Mon.-Sat. 9am-5pm, Sun. 10am-5pm, $6 adults, $3.50 children) is in the old 1836 courthouse building, itself of great significance as the oldest surviving courthouse in Georgia. The museum commemorates and explains the phenomenon of the Georgia gold rush. Don't miss the excellent short film upstairs documenting the gold rush with oral history from Georgians who worked the mines, many still open well into the 20th century. The seats in the theater are the courthouse's original courtroom benches.

### Crisson Gold Mine

The only remaining working gold mine in Georgia is the **Crisson Gold Mine** (2736 Morrison Moore Pkwy., 706/864-6363, www.crissongoldmine.com, daily 10am-6pm, cost varies). You can pan for gold or just shop for jewelry made from gold that is still mined on-site for the souvenir market. You can also opt to buy their ore by the bucket and take it home with you to see if you get lucky. Those who purchase six buckets of ore can use the mine's own tools for a really authentic experience. Tours are given of the old stamp mill on the grounds.

### Consolidated Gold Mines

It's not a working mine anymore, but **Consolidated Gold Mines** (185 Consolidated Gold Mine Rd., 706/864-8473, daily 10am-5pm, $15 adults, $9 children) is the actual site of what was once one of the largest gold processing plants in the world, only open for about 10 years at the turn of the 20th century. Some of the old mine shafts, including the legendary "Glory Hole," have been excavated and restored for public tours, 200 feet underground, by knowledgeable guides.

## WINERIES

The Dahlonega area has made quite a name for itself over the past 10-15 years or so as a

a rock-crusher at Consolidated Gold Mines

regional wine center. The wine business is seasonal, however, so the wineries often take an extended hiatus from public visitation during the winter.

**Wolf Mountain Vineyards** (180 Wolf Mountain Tr., 706/867-9862, www.wolf-mountainvineyards.com, tastings Thurs.-Sat. noon-5pm, Sun. 12:30pm-5pm, from $10) has rapidly established itself as Georgia's leading winemaker. **Frogtown Cellars** (700 Ridge Point Dr., 706/865-0687, www.frogtownwine.com, Mon.-Fri. noon-5pm, Sat. noon-6pm, Sun. 12:30pm-5pm, tastings from $15) has 42 acres on the outskirts of Dahlonega and a satellite tasting room in Helen (7601 S. Main St., daily). **Montaluce Estates** (946 Via Montaluce, 706/867-4060, www.montaluce.com, Tues.-Sat. 11am-5pm, Sun. noon-5pm, tastings from $16) boasts a state-of-the-art upscale facility. The first Dahlonega winery of the modern era is **Three Sisters Vineyards** (439 Vineyard Way, 706/865-9463, www.threesistersvineyards.com, Thurs.-Sat. 11am-5pm, Sun. 1pm-5pm, tastings $5-30). **Kaya Vineyards** (5400 Town Creek Rd., 706/219-3514, www.kayavineyards.com, Wed.-Sat. 11am-5pm, Sun. 12:30pm-5pm) offers several varietals, with tastings ranging $14-25.

## FOOD AND ACCOMMODATIONS

The signature shepherd's pie at ★ **Shenanigan's Irish Pub** (87 N. Chestatee St., 706/482-0114, www.theshenaniganspub.com, Mon.-Thurs. 11am-10pm, Fri.-Sat. 11am-midnight, Sun. noon-7pm, $10) is just what the doctor ordered to warm you up from the inside on a brisk day in the foothills.

**Mountain Laurel Creek Inn & Spa** (202 Talmer Grizzle Rd., 706/867-8134, www.mountainlaurelcreek.com, rooms $150-200, cottage $220) offers six guest rooms and the freestanding Dancing Bear Cottage, all in a well-maintained scenic foothills setting. Children are not allowed.

# Gold in Them Thar Hills

An accident of geology put one of the world's largest, most accessible, and purest veins of gold in North Georgia, a diagonal swath running northeast to southwest with its epicenter in Lumpkin County. Millions of years after being formed it would spur one of the first gold rushes in the United States.

Georgia gold is legendary for its extraordinary purity, in some places as high as 98 percent (most miners are happy with 80 percent). While the quality was certainly part of its allure, most of the draw was its easy abundance. Indeed, local legend has it that a hunter began the rush in 1828 by literally tripping over a huge nugget.

The earliest method was placer mining (pronounced "plasser"), which involves sorting through alluvial deposits by an open-pit technique or by the old familiar "panning for gold." However, within a few years the most easily accessible gold in North Georgia had been discovered. Mining techniques became much more invasive, including hydraulic mining—essentially erasing entire mountainsides with very powerful hoses—or the classic dynamite-in-the-shaft method. Above and below ground, the mines were everywhere, and the environmental devastation they caused can be seen to this day. The human devastation included the brutal removal of Native Americans and the Trail of Tears.

The sheer volume of gold extracted from these Appalachian foothills was so impressive that the U.S. Mint decided it would be more efficient to build a new branch in Dahlonega in 1838; it stayed open until the Civil War. You can see examples of the remarkably brilliant coins made at the Dahlonega Mint at the **Dahlonega Gold Museum State Historic Site** (1 Public Square, 706/864-2257, www.gastateparks.org, Mon.-Sat. 9am-5pm, Sun. 10am-5pm, $6 adults, $3.50 children) in the main square. Technically, Dahlonega wasn't the country's first gold rush town; that distinction belongs to nearby Auraria, which soon went extinct, with hardly a trace of the town remaining today.

As for the guy who first said, "There's gold in them thar hills," he was U.S. Mint chief assayer M. F. Stephenson, and what he really said was "There's millions in it." Ironically, he wasn't trying to kick off the Georgia gold rush; he was trying to convince prospectors to stay in Dahlonega instead of going to California, where another, and eventually much more famous, gold rush had just begun in 1849.

# Cohutta Mountains

The central portion of North Georgia is dominated by the Cohutta Mountain range, which though technically not part of the Blue Ridge is for most purposes contiguous with it. The area is less populated than the Blue Ridge portion just to the east and almost completely dominated by the enormous Cohutta Wilderness Area.

## ELLIJAY

For most of the year not much goes on in tiny, cute Ellijay, but it boasts one of Georgia's most popular annual festivals: the **Georgia Apple Festival** (www.georgiaapplefestival.org). Happening over two weekends each October, the Apple Festival celebrates the harvest of this area's chief crop—over 600,000 bushels a year. For a scenic look at the farms where the apples are grown, take a drive down "Apple Alley," Highway 52. Many farms are open in the autumn harvest season for tours, hayrides, and pick-your-own apples.

About 20 miles north of Ellijay is the popular and versatile **Fort Mountain State Park** (181 Fort Mountain Park Rd., 706/422-1932, www.gastateparks.org, parking $5, campsites $25-28, cottages $125-145), within the Chattahoochee National Forest and adjacent to the Cohutta Wilderness. The specialty here is 27 miles of mountain biking trails.

## COHUTTA WILDERNESS AREA

The most heavily used in the region, the **Cohutta Wilderness Area** (706/695-6736, www.georgiawildlife.com, free) includes 36,000 acres in Georgia and another 1,000 acres in Tennessee. It has about 100 miles of hiking trails for various skill levels, running through some very beautiful and extremely interesting country. Anglers come from all over to fly-fish on the numerous rivers cutting through.

While camping without a permit is allowed anywhere in Cohutta except directly on trails, usage regulations severely limit campfires; consult the website or call ahead.

# Cartersville to the Tennessee Border

Conveniently located roughly along I-75 from northwestern metro Atlanta up to the Tennessee border at Chattanooga are several areas of historical and educational significance. Here they are listed in geographical order northward from Atlanta.

## CARTERSVILLE

Benefiting from its proximity to the Atlanta metro area, Cartersville is a fairly bustling old railroad town with an active town square and several notable attractions.

### Booth Western Art Museum

North Georgia isn't where you'd expect to find a huge shiny museum dedicated to cowboy and Native American art, but you'll find that and more at the 120,000-square-foot limestone **Booth Western Art Museum** (501 Museum Dr., 770/387-1300, www.boothmuseum.org, Tues.-Wed. and Fri.-Sat. 10am-5pm, Thurs. 10am-8pm, Sun. 1pm-5pm, $10 adults, $8 students, free under age 12), which claims to be Georgia's biggest museum after the High in Atlanta. While the highlight for many is the permanent and succinctly named Cowboy Gallery, the entire multistory edifice does a good job of inclusivity, with artwork by and about Native Americans, African Americans, and women.

## Tellus Science Museum

The **Tellus Science Museum** (100 Tellus Dr., 770/606-5700, www.tellusmuseum.org, daily 10am-5pm, $14 adults, $10 children, planetarium shows $3.50) focuses on astronomy and geology, with mineral and fossil exhibits galore. The building is constructed around a central observatory, open during monthly special events (check the website). The all-digital planetarium provides frequent shows at additional cost.

## Rose Lawn House Museum

A short walk from the town square is **Rose Lawn House Museum** (224 W. Cherokee Ave., 770/387-5162, www.roselawnmuseum.com, Tues.-Fri. 10am-noon and 1pm-5pm, $5 adults, $2 children), former home of influential 19th-century evangelist Samuel Porter Jones. The museum features period furnishings and serves as a home for memorabilia of another famous Bartow County native, Rebecca Latimer Felton, the first woman to serve in the U.S. Senate.

## Food

Tasty dining options downtown include **Appalachian Grill** (14 E. Church St., 770/607-5357, Mon.-Thurs. 11am-9pm, Fri.

11am-10pm, Sat. noon-10pm, $15), with its signature trout dishes and combo platters, and **Jefferson's** (28 W. Main St., 770/334-2069, www.jeffersonsrestaurant.com, Mon.-Wed. 11am-10pm, Thurs.-Sat. 11am-11pm, Sun. 11:30am-10pm, $10), known for its wings and oysters.

## ★ ETOWAH INDIAN MOUNDS HISTORIC SITE

The **Etowah Indian Mounds Historic Site** (813 Indian Mounds Rd., 770/387-3747, www.gastateparks.org, Wed.-Sat. 9am-5pm, $5), outside Cartersville, is the most intact mound-builder site in the Southeast. On this 54 acres was one of the most influential communities of the Mississippian culture from about AD 1000 to 1500. Its six masterfully constructed earthen mounds are in surprisingly good shape today, with full access to the top, providing a beautiful panorama of the surrounding area and the other mounds.

The small but well-curated visitors center has a nice museum with some stunning artifacts retrieved from the site. Bring a picnic lunch and enjoy the tranquil serenity of the shaded picnic area on the banks of the Etowah River directly beside the mound site.

the Etowah Indian Mounds Historic Site

## NEW ECHOTA HISTORIC SITE

The beneficiary of a recent upgrade and renovation, **New Echota Historic Site** (1211 Chatsworth Hwy., 706/624-1321, www.gastateparks.org, Thurs.-Sat. 9am-5pm, $7 adults, $5.50 children) outside Calhoun has an especially bittersweet nature, serving both as capital of the Cherokee Nation from 1825 to 1838 and as the place where the Trail of Tears began. Today there are a dozen original and reconstructed period buildings. The visitors center plays a 17-minute film about the history of the site and hosts the Cherokee Research Library.

## CHIEF VANN HOUSE HISTORIC SITE

A short drive east of Dalton is the **Chief Vann House Historic Site** (82 Hwy. 225 N., 706/695-2598, www.gastateparks.org, Thurs.-Sat. 9am-5pm, $6 adults, $3.50 children), the best-preserved extant house of the Cherokee Nation.

## TUNNEL HILL

The chief attraction in this little mountain town is the **Historic Western & Atlantic Railroad Tunnel** (215 Clisby Austin Dr., 706/876-1571, www.tunnelhillheritagecenter.com, Mon.-Sat. 9am-5pm, $7 adults, $5 children), part of the first railroad through the Appalachians. For a few minutes in 1862 it hosted part of the Great Locomotive Chase. The tunnel can be toured at the top of each hour.

## ★ CHICKAMAUGA & CHATTANOOGA NATIONAL MILITARY PARK

Directly south of Fort Oglethorpe on Highway 1 (or off I-75's exit 350) is the **Chickamauga & Chattanooga National Military Park** (3370 LaFayette Rd., www.nps.gov, visitors center daily 8:30am-5pm, grounds daily dawn-dusk, free), preserving and interpreting the site of one of the last major Confederate victories of the Civil War. The focus is primarily on the savage fighting around Chickamauga in September 1863.

There's a small and well-done visitors center and museum with a 20-minute video explaining the rather complicated action of the battle. The main draw is the seven-mile walking tour over the battlefield, culminating in a trip up an observation tower to view the entire area. There are interpretive maps, or you can dial a number on your cell phone to listen to an audio tour (get the number from the rangers at the visitors center).

the Chickamauga & Chattanooga National Military Park

# Ridge and Valley Country

The northwestern portion of Georgia is geologically and culturally somewhat different from the rest of North Georgia. It's often called the Ridge and Valley Country, an area to the west of the Cartersville-Great Smoky Fault and a clear differentiation from the Blue Ridge Mountains to the east. Rome is by far its biggest city.

## ROME

Like the great Italian capital that is its namesake, Rome, Georgia, was built on seven hills. In front of **City Hall** (601 Broad St.) is a statue of Romulus and Remus nursing from a wolf, a nod to the creation story of the European city. A gift to the city from Italian dictator Benito Mussolini in 1929, the statue was taken down to prevent vandalism during World War II and returned in the 1950s. Today, Rome is a center of regional higher education, health care, and manufacturing. You might first want to check out the **Rome-Floyd County Visitors Center** (402 Civic Center Dr., 800/444-1834, www.romegeorgia.org).

### Berry College

Rome's chief claim to fame is big and beautiful **Berry College** (2277 Martha Berry Hwy., 706/232-374, www.berry.edu), a liberal arts school on an expansive campus, the largest contiguous college campus in the world. Founder Martha Berry was the daughter of a wealthy area planter and was struck by the profound lack of educational opportunities for most young people in these hardscrabble foothills. She began an impromptu Sunday school at her home, which eventually expanded to a family log cabin, still on campus today. Much of the campus land is administered by the state as hunting and conservation areas; other parts are open to the public for walking and biking.

The highlight is **Oak Hill & The Martha Berry Museum** (24 Veterans Memorial Hwy., 706/368-6789, www.berry.edu, Mon.-Sat. 10am-5pm, tours every 30 minutes 10am-3:30pm, $5 adults, $3 children), Berry's Greek Revival home where you can learn much more about the school's history.

### Clocktower Museum

Downtown Rome's most famous sight is the 1872 **Clocktower** (E. 2nd St., Mon.-Fri. 9am-3pm, free), a massive clock atop the 100-foot-tall former city water tower. There's a small museum inside, and visitors can climb to the top.

### Chieftains Museum and Major Ridge Home

One of the key remaining sites along the Trail of Tears, the **Chieftains Museum** (501 Riverside Pkwy., 706/291-9494, www.chieftainsmuseum.org, Fri.-Sat. 1pm-5pm, $5 adults, $3 children) is within the home of Major Ridge, who gathered a band of Cherokee people to fight alongside colonists during the American Revolution. Out of gratitude, Andrew Jackson gave him the rank of major, which Ridge would adopt as his first name. However, by the 1830s, pressure on the Cherokee to give up their lands was so intense he felt compelled to sign the controversial Treaty of New Echota, which resulted in the Trail of Tears.

### Food and Accommodations

A couple of good places to get a bite right downtown are **Harvest Moon Cafe** (234 Broad St., 706/292-0099, www.myharvestmooncafe.com, Mon. 11am-2:30pm, Tues.-Thurs. 11am-9pm, Fri.-Sat. 11am-10pm, $15), with good steaks, salmon, and catfish, and **Jefferson's** (340 Broad St., 706/378-0222, www.jeffersonsrestaurant.com, Mon.-Wed. 11am-10pm, Thurs.-Sat. 11am-11pm, Sun. 11:30am-10pm, $10), a regional chain famous for its wings and oysters.

The premier lodging in Rome is the ★ **Claremont House** (906 E. 2nd Ave.,

706/291-0900, www.theclaremonthouse.net, $150-170), set in an absolutely stunning high Victorian masterpiece of a building. There are four charming guest rooms with 14-foot ceilings and canopy beds.

## NEAR ROME
### ★ Paradise Garden

You'd be forgiven for thinking that the late, great Georgia folk artist Howard Finster lived in Athens, Georgia, on the other side of the state. His collaborations on album-cover art for the iconic Athens band R.E.M. and later with the Talking Heads put Finster on the global map. He became known not only as one of the South's greatest and certainly hippest outsider artists but as a classic Southern showman-raconteur.

Finster's memory lives on in Athens, but the best place to view his fertile, almost feverish imagination in action is at **Paradise Garden** (200 N. Lewis St., 706/808-0800, www.paradisegardenfoundation.org, Wed.-Sat. 10am-4pm, Sun. 1pm-4pm, donation), his Summerville studio on a swampy four acres of land off a side street. Like the world's most eccentric theme park, Finster's drawing,

painting, and craftwork cover just about every foot of available space on every structure. Here, you fully understand the provenance of the phrase, "one man's junk is another man's treasure." Each May the town park at Summerville hosts **Finster Fest,** an expansive celebration not only of Finster's work but that of regional folk artists from all around.

To get to the Garden, head north through Summerville on U.S. 27. Take a right on Rena Street, looking for the signs, and then make another right onto North Lewis Street. You can't miss it!

If you need a bite to eat while you're in Summerville, head straight for the delectable fried catfish at ★ **Jim's Family Restaurant** (6 Lyerly St., 706/857-2123, daily 8am-8pm, $10). Camp for the night at little **James H. "Sloppy" Floyd State Park** (2800 Sloppy Floyd Lake Rd., 706/857-0826, www.gastateparks.org, parking $5, campsites $25-28, cottages $135-145), one of Georgia's smaller yet still picturesque parks.

## TAG CORNER

The extreme northwestern tip of Georgia, sometimes called "TAG corner," an acronym

Howard Finster's Paradise Garden

referring to its position astride the borders of Tennessee, Alabama, and Georgia, is yet another geological substratum. Part of the Cumberland Plateau, it's a flat-topped highland area, one of whose dominant features is limestone. Long story short, this means lots of caves.

## Lookout Mountain

By far the main geological feature of the area is Lookout Mountain, part of the Cumberland Plateau. Most of the 84-mile-long mountain is in Tennessee, including the remnants of a key Civil War battlefield and the popular Raccoon Mountain and Ruby Falls caves.

The East Coast's premier hang gliding location is **Lookout Mountain Flight Park and Training Center** (7201 Scenic Hwy., 800/688-5637, www.hanglide.com, Thurs.-Tues. 9am-6pm). Under the tutelage of certified staff, hang gliding enthusiasts launch from 1,340-foot McCarty's Bluff into the wild blue yonder off Lookout Mountain.

## ★ Cloudland Canyon State Park

Lookout Mountain's most dramatic feature is the 1,000-foot canyon at Sitton's Gulch,

renamed Cloudland Canyon in the 1930s during the park's construction by the Civilian Conservation Corps. **Cloudland Canyon State Park** (122 Cloudland Canyon Park Rd., 706/657-4050, www.gastateparks.org, daily 7am-10pm, parking $5, backcountry trails $3 pp, campsites $25-28) is quite simply one of the most striking of all Southern state parks. Its steep sandstone walls are the remnants of a 200-million-year-old shoreline. From the various lookout points along the West Rim Loop Trail skirting the edge of the main picnic area and parking lot along the canyon's edge, you can also see the entrances to some of the canyon's many limestone caves.

The rim trail is about five miles in length and gives you overlook opportunities into three canyon gorges. There is another five-mile network of backcountry trails, along which primitive camping is permitted, a particularly recommended option for those so inclined. You can hike to the bottom of the canyon via some steep but well-maintained and staircase-augmented trails. There are another 72 tent and RV sites divided between the east and west rims, and 16 cottages along the west rim, two of which are dog friendly.

Cloudland Canyon State Park

# Athens

Home to the University of Georgia, Athens is a heady and often quirky mix of culture, partying, football, and progressive thought in an otherwise conservative area. What really makes Athens stand out, and clearly puts it head and shoulders above most college towns, is the fabled "Athens scene," a musical ethos that for the past 30 years has virtually defined, and in some cases directly authored, the sound of American indie rock and roll.

A forward-thinking state legislature in 1785 made a bold step to endow a "college or seminary of learning," essentially giving birth to the idea of state-supported higher education in the United States. The surrounding town, created in 1806, was to be called Athens to channel the spirit of the great artistic, literary, and scientific accomplishments of the ancient Greeks. Athens's most famous resident in the antebellum era was Henry W. Grady, who would go on to be a seminal editor of the *Atlanta Journal-Constitution* and founder of the University of Georgia school of journalism, which bears his name.

## SIGHTS
### Church-Waddel-Brumby House

The main Athens visitors center is within the restored **Church-Waddel-Brumby House** (280 E. Dougherty St., 706/353-1820, www. athenswelcomecenter.com, Mon.-Sat. 10am-5pm, Sun. noon-5pm, free), a circa-1820 house museum alleged to be the oldest residence in the city.

### ★ University of Georgia

As befitting its deep roots in the Deep South, the **University of Georgia** (www.uga.edu), "Georgia" or UGA in common parlance, boasts not only a devotion to tradition, but a large (over 600 acres) and scenic campus that is worth exploring whether you're affiliated with the university or not. You can take free student-guided tours leaving from the visitors

center on South Campus or download a walking tour map (http://visit.uga.edu). Here's a quick look at the highlights:

Every visit to UGA should begin with the famous **Arch** at the old North Campus entrance on Broad Street. Old Bulldog etiquette demands that underclass students only walk around the Arch, not under it. As you walk through the Arch you'll see the Greek Revival **Hunter Holmes Academic Building,** actually two antebellum buildings combined in the early 20th century. In 2001 it was renamed to honor the first two African American students admitted to UGA: Hamilton Holmes and Charlayne Hunter-Gault (later a

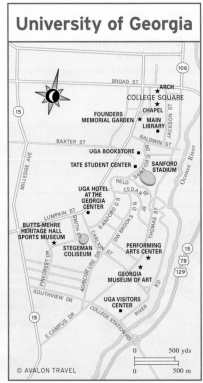

## University of Georgia

# Athens

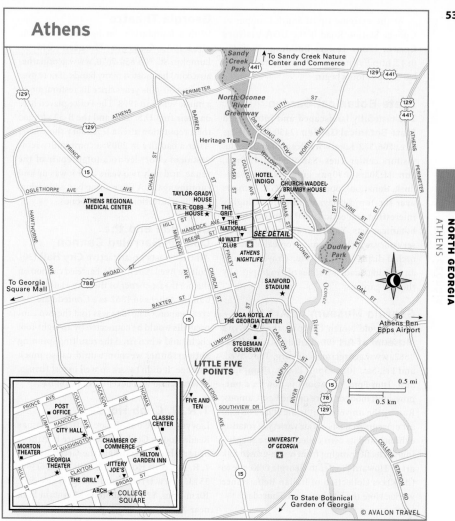

To Sandy Creek Nature Center and Commerce

Sandy Creek Park

North Oconee River Greenway

Heritage Trail

HOTEL INDIGO

CHURCH-WADDEL-BRUMBY HOUSE

TAYLOR-GRADY HOUSE

ATHENS REGIONAL MEDICAL CENTER

T.R.R. COBB HOUSE ★

THE GRIT ▼

THE NATIONAL ▼

40 WATT CLUB ▼

ATHENS NIGHTLIFE

SEE DETAIL

Dudley Park

To Georgia Square Mall ←

SANFORD STADIUM ★

To Athens Ben Epps Airport →

UGA HOTEL AT THE GEORGIA CENTER

STEGEMAN COLISEUM

LITTLE FIVE POINTS

FIVE AND TEN ▼

UNIVERSITY OF GEORGIA

0       0.5 mi
0       0.5 km

To State Botanical Garden of Georgia

© AVALON TRAVEL

POST OFFICE ■
CITY HALL ★
MORTON THEATER
GEORGIA THEATER ★
THE GRILL ▼
ARCH ★
COLLEGE SQUARE
CLASSIC CENTER
CHAMBER OF COMMERCE ■
HILTON GARDEN INN ■
JITTERY JOE'S ▼

renowned broadcast journalist), who began classes in 1961.

Nearby is the 1832 **Chapel,** where students once attended services three days a week. These days, students take turns ringing the old chapel bell, now in a small tower nearby, until midnight after every Georgia football victory.

South of the Chapel and off to the right you'll run across verdant little **Herty Field,** where the Bulldogs played their first football game in 1892 (beating Mercer University

50-0) under the direction of coach Charles Herty, also a chemist of national repute. A parking lot actually occupied this rectangle from the 1940s to 1999, when the hallowed athletic ground was reclaimed as relaxing green space for casual enjoyment.

Continue down Sanford Drive to the impossible-to-miss, enormous **Sanford Stadium,** where the Bulldogs play home games "between the hedges" growing all along the sidelines.

At the extreme tip of South Campus at College Station Road is the **UGA Visitors Center** (Four Towers Building, 706/542-0842, http://visit.uga.edu), where the student-led campus tours begin.

## State Botanical Garden

The tastefully landscaped and interpreted **State Botanical Garden** (2450 S. Milledge Ave., 706/542-1244, www.botgarden.uga.edu, visitors center Tues.-Sat. 9:30am-4:30pm, Sun. 11:30am-4:30pm, grounds daily 8am-dusk, donation), operated by UGA, eschews over-the-top displays of flora for a highly interesting and educational approach to the botanical arts. You enter through the conservatory, which has a nice tropical plant and orchid display. Just outside, arrayed around an inviting quad, is a series of geographically themed gardens.

## Georgia Museum of Art

Once on old North Campus, the **Georgia Museum of Art** (90 Carlton St., 706/542-4662, www.georgiamuseum.org, Tues.-Wed. and Fri.-Sat. 10am-5pm, Thurs. 10am-9pm, Sun. 1pm-5pm, donation) is now in a purpose-built modern space on the East Campus. Run by the university, it is the state's official art museum. It hosts a wide variety of rotating exhibits, and its own collections are surprisingly eclectic, ranging from home-grown folk art by Howard Finster to Georgia O'Keeffe to the Kress Collection of Italian Renaissance works. Note the late hours on Thursday.

## Butts-Mehre Heritage Hall Sports Museum

For fans of "the Dawgs," the **Butts-Mehre Heritage Hall Sports Museum** (1 Selig Circle, www.georgiadogs.com, Mon.-Fri. 8am-5pm, free) is a must-see. Football takes center stage, including the two Heisman Trophies won by UGA players Frank Sinkwich and Herschel Walker, and the national championship trophy won by the Dawgs in 1980 during Walker's tenure.

## Georgia Theatre

With a foundation dating from 1889, the circa-1935 **Georgia Theatre** (215 N. Lumpkin St., 706/850-7670, www.georgiatheatre.com) has hosted many bands of note over the past 30-plus years since its restoration as a music venue in 1978. The Police played here on their first U.S. tour, and the B-52's forged their reputation after a legendary show here. After a bad fire in 2009, a community reinvestment effort led to a total repair of the venue, and only two years later it was up and running again. A fun rooftop bar, added during the renovation, is a great bonus.

## City Hall and the Double-Barreled Cannon

Athens boasts an attractive **City Hall** (301 College Ave.). The double-barreled cannon on the northeast corner of the City Hall lot was built in Athens in 1862 as a Confederate "secret weapon." The idea was that the two cannonballs would be connected by an eight-foot chain, and when fired the resulting spinning antipersonnel weapon would cause much damage. It didn't work so well in test firings, however, and was never used in combat.

## T. R. R. Cobb House

Lawyer and Confederate officer Thomas Reade Rootes Cobb is a key figure in Athens history, but interestingly the Greek Revival **T. R. R. Cobb House** (175 Hill St., 706/369-3513, www.trrcobbhouse.org, Tues.-Sat. 10am-4pm, $2) was at Stone Mountain Park near Atlanta for 20 years. It has since been returned to this site, about a block from the original location where it was first built in 1834. The ground floor is expertly restored to antebellum furnishings. The 2nd floor is more of a museum format.

## Taylor-Grady House

Named for its two most notable owners, Confederate officer and Irish native Robert Taylor and *Atlanta Journal-Constitution* editor and UGA journalism school founder

Henry W. Grady, the **Taylor-Grady House** (634 Prince Ave., 706/549-8688, www.taylor-gradyhouse.com, Mon., Wed., and Fri. 9am-3pm, Tues. and Thurs. 9am-1pm, $3) was built in 1844 as a summer home for Taylor and his family. It's now a house museum.

# ENTERTAINMENT AND EVENTS
## ★ Athens Nightlife

In a matter of great local pride, the University of Georgia is usually at or near the top of the annual lists of best party schools in the country. Indeed, urban legend maintains that Athens has the highest number of bars per capita in the United States.

First among equals, the legendary **40 Watt Club** (285 W. Washington St., 706/549-7871, www.40watt.com, open show nights only) has been at the forefront of the Athens music scene since 1978, when it was cofounded by Curtis Crowe, drummer with local legends Pylon (it's now owned by the ex-wife of R.E.M. guitarist Peter Buck). It's the CBGB of the South, but unlike that NYC club, it's still open for business, albeit in its fifth location.

Despite its swank name, **Manhattan Cafe** (337 N. Hull St., 706/369-9767, Mon.-Sat. 4pm-2am) is one of Athens's most humbly charming bars, a cross between a dive, a hipster bar, and a Prohibition-era speakeasy. The house cocktail is a refreshing blend of Maker's Mark and spicy Blenheim Ginger Ale. **Little Kings** (223 W. Hancock St., 706/369-3144, Mon.-Sat. 7pm-2am) is a go-to for high-profile indie acts; local legends Pylon chose it to kick off a reunion tour. If you're into concerts where even the band wears earplugs, **Caledonia Lounge** (256 W. Clayton St., 706/549-5577, www.caledonialounge.com, Mon.-Sat. 5pm-2am) is the place for you. Small and sweaty, **Go Bar** (195 Prince Ave., 706/546-5609, Mon.-Sat. 9pm-2am), next to the popular restaurant The Grit in a block restored and owned by R.E.M.'s Michael Stipe, is a popular spot to dance and enjoy live music.

Another great way to enjoy the local music scene is at **AthFest** (www.athfest.com). Happening every June in a blocked-off portion of downtown, this music festival features plenty of free live outdoor concerts,

the famous double-barreled cannon at City Hall

# Rock-and-Roll Legacy

Athens is renowned for its contributions to rock and roll, spawning names such as R.E.M., the B-52's, Widespread Panic, and Pylon, among many others. An entertaining 1987 documentary chronicling the scene, *Athens, GA: Inside/Out*, is available on DVD. Here's a brief tour of venues that played a role in forming Athens's rock-and-roll legacy. Go to www.visitathensga.com for a full version courtesy of alt-weekly the *Flagpole*.

the trestle from R.E.M.'s *Murmur* album

- **40 Watt Club:** Named because its first incarnation was lit by a single lightbulb, Athens's most legendary club has hosted every major name in local rock history. It's had several locations, in this order: 2nd floor of 171 College Avenue (above The Grill); 2nd floor of 100 College Avenue (above Starbucks); 256 W. Clayton St.; 382 East Broad Street (now university offices), and 285 West Washington Street, where it is now.

- **Georgia Theatre:** 215 North Lumpkin Avenue. The century-old venue reopened after a 2009 fire; The Police played here on their first U.S. tour.

- *Murmur* **Railroad Trestle:** 270 South Poplar Street. The railroad trestle on the back cover of R.E.M.'s *Murmur* album was recently restored through a community effort. Park at the lot near Dudley Park around the corner.

- **140 East Washington Street:** This was once the Uptown Lounge, which in the 1980s hosted The Pixies, Jane's Addiction, R.E.M., and Black Flag. Now it's home to Copper Creek Brewing Co.

- **St. Mary's Steeple:** An Episcopal church was here until it was demolished in 1990, leaving only this steeple. R.E.M. rehearsed and played their first concert here, a birthday party for a friend in April 1980. It's now surrounded by condos but easily accessible from the street.

- **312 East Broad Street:** The "Frigidaire" building was built in the 1880s as the Athens Opera House. For 10 years beginning in 1997, Tasty World operated here and hosted acts such as The Shins and Kings of Leon.

- **260 North Jackson Street:** Now Jackson Street Books, it was record store Wax Jr. Facts in the early 1980s, managed by Pylon bassist Michael Lachowski, who now owns a local design firm.

- **Wuxtry Records:** 197 East Clayton Street. R.E.M.'s Peter Buck once worked here, among many other local musicians. It's been in business since 1975.

film screenings, arts and crafts displays, and product and food booths. The core experience, however, involves the ticketed bracelets ($17-20), which allow you to club-crawl.

## SHOPPING

Before he became a rock star, R.E.M.'s Peter Buck once managed **Wuxtry Records** (197 E. Clayton St., 706/369-9428, www.wuxtry-records.com, Mon.-Fri. 10am-7pm, Sat. 11am-7pm, Sun. noon-6pm), and it remains one of the Southeast's best (and quirkiest) sources for vintage vinyl and hard-to-get recordings. Go upstairs to their even more eccentric cousin store **Bizarro Wuxtry Comics, Toys & Records** (197 E. Clayton St., 706/353-7938,

Mon.-Fri. 10am-7pm, Sat. 11am-7pm, Sun. noon-6pm), which has an extensive collection of alternative zines as well as shirts and offbeat items.

The best bookstore in town for the past 25 years has been **Jackson Street Books** (260 N. Jackson St., 706/546-0245, Mon.-Sat. 11am-6pm, Sun. noon-4pm), which deals in plenty of good-condition used and rare volumes.

## SPORTS AND RECREATION

The premier overall outdoor activity in Athens is the **North Oconee River Greenway** (70 Sunset Dr., www.athensclarkecounty.com, daily dawn-dusk), a well-done project that has reclaimed much of the north bank of the Oconee, once the home of a thriving mill industry. Four miles of multi-level walking, jogging, and biking trails, including one along the river, meander through the peaceful wooded bank. Interpretive signage explains the rich heritage of the river's industry.

Needless to say, the premier spectator sport in Athens involves the **Georgia Bulldogs football team** (tickets from $55). They play in enormous Sanford Stadium on UGA's South Campus. The Dawgs are a huge deal around here, and for most big games, tickets are hard to come by, though there are often tickets for sale by enterprising individuals on game day. For less competitive games, check online. The home court of the Dawgs men's and women's **basketball teams** is venerable Stegeman Coliseum (100 Smith St.). The baseball-playing **Diamond Dawgs** play at Foley Field. The UGA **women's soccer team** consistently plays at the highest level of NCAA competition, and you can watch their games for free at their specially built soccer stadium. Ten-time national champs, the women's gymnastics team the **Gym Dogs** competes at Stegeman Coliseum (100 Smith St.). Go to georgiadogs.com to find out more information about any of these teams.

## FOOD
### Burgers and Barbecue

One of Athens's great food traditions, ★ **The Grill** (171 College Ave., 706/543-4770, www.thegrillathensga.com, daily 24 hours, breakfast daily midnight-noon, $7) is open 24-7 right on the town's most traveled block, so there's no excuse not to check it out. They serve traditional diner food amid 1950s retro decor. Upstairs is where the first incarnation of local music venue 40 Watt Club opened in the late 1970s.

### Coffeehouses

An expanding local chain, ★ **Jittery Joe's** (www.jitteryjoes.com) has several locations around town, and all of them offer a delicious variety of expertly roasted beans. The flagship "tasting room" location (780 E. Broad St., 706/227-2161, Mon.-Fri. 7am-6pm, Sat.-Sun. 8am-6pm), just east of the main downtown area, is a nice getaway inside a rustic former warehouse. There's a smaller location farther into downtown (297 E. Broad St., 706/613-7449, Mon.-Fri. 6:30am-midnight, Sat.-Sun. 7:30am-midnight) and one south of downtown in the Five Points neighborhood (1230 S. Milledge Ave., 706/208-1979, Mon.-Fri. 6:30am-midnight, Sat.-Sun. 7:30am-midnight), along with several others around town.

**Walker's Pub & Coffee** (128 College Ave., 706/543-1433, www.walkerscoffee.com, Mon.-Sat. 7am-2am, Sun. 7am-9pm), ironically a couple of doors down from a Starbucks, is, as the name indicates, a hybrid spot: During the day, it's a lounge-worthy coffeehouse, with roomy wooden booths, and after about 10pm, it turns into a full-service bar.

### Organic and Vegetarian

The kind of vegetarian and vegan place that even a carnivore could love, ★ **The Grit** (199 Prince Ave., 706/543-6592, www.thegrit.com, Mon.-Fri. 11am-10pm, Sat.-Sun. 10am-3pm and 5pm-10pm, $10) offers fresh, lovingly prepared, and extremely affordable meatless delicacies. Most are locally sourced, such as the grilled seitan steak, scintillating noodle bowls, and the signature must-try black bean chili.

A combination of natural food mecca and fine-dining date spot, ★ **The National** (232 W. Hancock St., 706/549-3450, www.the-nationalrestaurant.com, Mon.-Thurs. 11am-3pm and 5pm-10pm, Fri.-Sat. 11am-3pm and 5pm-11pm, Sun. 5pm-10pm, $15-25) has perhaps the most tightly focused rotating menu in the city, all changing with the seasons. A recent visit featured pan-roasted North Carolina trout and a grilled hanger steak with marinated roasted peppers. There are always great veggie and vegan options. Or you could just content yourself with two or three starters, the "pizzettes" being particularly good choices. On Sunday-Tuesday nights they offer a dinner-and-a-movie deal with the Cine BarCafe theater next door.

### Pizza

As the often-long line at both locations indicates, the most popular pizza place in town is **Transmetropolitan,** almost always just called "Transmet" (145 E. Clayton St., 706/613-8773, daily 11am-11pm, pizza $10). The vibe is combination college pizza joint, hipster bar, and sports bar. Any of the signature pizzas are great and affordable, with some adventurous options including, yes, the Hungry Sasquatch.

## ACCOMMODATIONS

If you're coming to Athens on a graduation weekend or on one of the autumn Saturdays the Bulldogs play here, book your room well in advance or you'll be out of luck. Prices listed are for non-football nights; they double (or triple!) for football weekends.

### Under $150

My favorite place to stay in Athens is the ★ **UGA Hotel at the Georgia Center** (1197 S. Lumpkin St., 800/884-1381, www.georgia-center.uga.edu, $90-200). While constructed to serve as a lodging center for university-based conventions and for alumni, anyone can book a room. The location on campus is

unbeatable and the 200 guest rooms and various public spaces are top-notch. Forget about staying here on a football weekend unless you've booked well in advance.

Athens has one B&B of note: **The Colonels** (3890 Barnett Shoals Rd., 706/559-9595, www.thecolonels.net, $115-200), a classic renovated seven-room antebellum farmhouse on historic Angel Oak Farm run by, yes, "Colonels" Marc and Beth. The breakfasts are magnificent. The location is about a 10-minute drive from downtown, but very convenient to the State Botanical Garden.

### $150-300

The city's newest lodging, and Athens's first entry in the boutique category, is ★ **Hotel Indigo** (500 College Ave., 706/546-0430, www.hotelindigoathens.com, $145-235). Its swank decor, frequent generous receptions, LEED-certified green attitude, and downtown location make it a no-brainer.

## INFORMATION AND SERVICES
### Hospitals

The main hospital in town is **Athens Regional Medical Center** (1199 Prince Ave., 706/475-7000, www.athenshealth.org), with a Level II emergency room. Their **Regional FirstCare Clinic** (485 Hwy. 29 N.) offers walk-in service for nonemergencies.

### Media

The newspaper of record in Athens is the *Athens Banner-Herald* (www.onlineathens.com). However, a more popular media outlet and certainly the one to consult for music and entertainment is the *Flagpole* (www.flagpole.com), the independent alt-weekly. Now weekly, *The Red and Black* (www.redandblack.com) is run by University of Georgia students, most of them in the journalism school. It is independent from the school administration, however.

The most unique radio station in town is the student-staffed and university-run **WUOG** (90.5 FM), which airs the usual eclectic and quirky blend of indie college rock, Americana, blues, and jazz.

## GETTING THERE AND AROUND
### Car

The main route to Athens from Atlanta is U.S. 78, the old "Atlanta Highway." It turns into Broad Street when you reach town. The main route into Athens from the south is U.S. 441, which runs into the Athens Perimeter (Hwy. 10), often called "the Loop" or the "Ten Loop," before you hit town.

### Public Transit

The Athens city and county government runs a good bus system called simply **The Bus** (www.athenstransit.com, $1.60 per ride, free for UGA students). The Bus runs a UGA football shuttle ($5 round-trip, purchase ticket at airport) on home game Saturdays from Ben Epps Airport to the Arch on North Campus.

# Madison and Vicinity

About 30 minutes south of Athens, this charming and well-kept little burg, named for founding father James Madison, routinely tops travel magazines' lists of best small town in the country and provides location sets for movies seeking Old South authenticity. Visitor traffic in Madison (www.madisonga. org) is steady, driven not only by the nostalgically picturesque town itself but also by an upscale real estate boom on nearby Lake Oconee.

Madison likes to market itself as "the town Sherman refused to burn." While technically true—Madison was the home of Unionist senator Joshua Hill, a friend of Sherman's brother—there are plenty of Georgia towns that Union troops spared from the torch. In any case, Madison is well worth a visit, not only to see its eclectic historic district but to enjoy its trim, pleasant vibe.

## ★ MADISON

The best way to enjoy Madison's sizable historic district is to pick up the official walking tour brochure at the **Madison Visitors**

Madison boasts beautiful antebellum architecture.

Center (115 E. Jefferson St., 706/342-4454, www.madisonga.org, Mon.-Fri. 9:30am-4pm, Sat. 10am-5pm, Sun. 1pm-4pm), itself inside the 1887 firehouse and original city hall.

Highlights include the magnificent 1811 Greek Revival **Heritage Hall** (277 S. Main St., 706/342-9627, www.friendsofheritage-hall.org, Mon.-Sat. 11am-4pm, Sun. 1:30pm-4:30pm, $7 adults, $3 children), now home of the Morgan County Historical Society and open for tours daily. Other homes of aesthetic and historical significance, now private residences, are the Queen Anne gingerbread-style **Hunter House** (580 S. Main St.) and the **Joshua Hill Home** (485 Old Post Rd.), home of the senator credited with saving Madison from General Sherman's fires. The **Rogers House and Rose Cottage** (179 E. Jefferson St., 706/343-1090, Mon.-Sat. 10am-4:30pm, Sun. 1:30pm-4:30pm, $5 adults, $3 children) are Madison's two house museums, side by side and adorably hard to resist from the outside. The former is a rarely seen Piedmont Plain cottage from the early 1800s, charmingly restored, and the latter is the restored home of Adeline Rose, who built the home after being emancipated from slavery.

The **Madison Museum of Art** (300 Hancock St., 706/485-4530, mmofa.org, call for hours, donation) has a small but intriguing collection of work by European and regional artists. The **Morgan County African American Museum** (154 Academy St., 706/342-9191, www.mcaam.org, Tues.-Sat. 10am-4pm, $5) is actually more of an arts and crafts co-op focusing on African American artists and culture. It features several small but well-curated collections in an adorable 1895 cottage.

## Shopping

There are several good antiques stores near each other in the town center, making for a fine afternoon of browsing. Some highlights are three stores owned by the same folks and within shouting distance of each other:

sprawling, fascinating **J&K Fleas An'Tiques** (184 S. Main St., 706/342-3009, www.j-and-k-enterprises.com, Mon.-Fri. 10:30am-5:30pm, Sat. 10:30am-6pm, Sun. 1pm-5:30pm), **J&K Antiques Etc.** (159 S. Main St., 706/752-0009, www.j-and-k-enterprises.com, Mon.-Sat. 10:30am-5:30pm), and the consignment shop **Just Out of the Kloset** (179 S. Main St., 706/752-1960, www.j-and-k-enterprises.com, Tues.-Sat. 10:30am-5:30pm).

## Food and Accommodations

Madison's fine-dining spot is ★ **Town 220** (220 W. Washington St., 706/752-1445, www.town220.com, Tues.-Thurs. 11am-2:30pm and 5pm-9pm, Fri.-Sat. 11am-2:30pm and 5pm-10pm, $15-30), just behind the James Madison Inn, featuring chef Fransisco De La Torre's hip take on fusion-style cuisine. Your best bet for casual dining is **Madison Chop House Grille** (202 S. Main St., 706/342-9009, daily 7am-10am and 11:30am-9:30pm, $10-15), on the main drag, for killer burgers and fresh salads.

The small and plush boutique hotel **James Madison Inn** (260 W. Washington St., 706/342-7040, www.jamesmadisoninn.com, $190-220) is right off the big town park and offers full concierge service. The guest rooms are remarkably well appointed, both in terms of decor and technological compatibility. Book early; these rooms are in high demand. The ★ **Farmhouse Inn** (1051 Meadow Ln., 706/342-7933, www.thefarmhouseinn.com, rooms $100-170, farmhouse $400-500) offers a delightful getaway-style experience in a charmingly rustic (but not *too* rustic) farm setting on 100 green and glorious acres outside of town.

## Information and Services

The **Madison Visitors Center** (115 E. Jefferson St., 706/342-4454, www.madisonga.org, Mon.-Fri. 9:30am-4pm, Sat. 10am-5pm, Sun. 1pm-4pm) is the place to go for brochures and information.

## EAST ALONG I-20

### Lake Oconee

The second-largest body of water in the state, Lake Oconee benefits from a gated-community boom and robust recreational tourism, including an internationally ranked Ritz-Carlton resort. Most residents live "behind the gates," as locals refer to the plethora of exclusive upscale communities. A good first stop for general visitor information is the **Lake Oconee Welcome Center** (5820 Lake Oconee Pkwy., Mon.-Fri. noon-8pm, Sat. 10am-5pm).

By far the premier property on Lake Oconee is the ★ **Ritz-Carlton Lodge, Reynolds Plantation** (1 Lake Oconee Tr., 706/467-0600, www.ritzcarlton.com, $260-450), one of the nation's top resorts. While more casual in approach than other properties in the brand, the level of attentiveness is everything you'd expect, with a nice retro feel to the buildings themselves. While technically closed to everyone but guests, you can generally get on the grounds if you are dining at one of the facilities. You can book an upscale golf package (starting around $300 per night) at **Reynolds Plantation** (800/800-5250, www.reynoldsplantation.com), which offers 99 holes of golf on five world-class public courses, including the Plantation Course and the Jack Nicklaus-designed Great Waters.

**NORTH GEORGIA**
MADISON AND VICINITY

## "I Will Make Georgia Howl"

Scorched-earth campaigns have been a part of war for centuries. But the first formal targeting of civilian infrastructure in modern times was **General William T. Sherman**'s infamous **"March to the Sea"** from Atlanta to Savannah during the Civil War. It took little more than a month, but by the time Sherman "gave" Savannah to President Abraham Lincoln as a Christmas present in December 1864, the March would enter Southern mythology as one of the war's most bitter memories, with Sherman himself regarded as satanic.

To keep the Confederates guessing, Sherman originally split his forces, 60,000 strong, into two wings deep in enemy territory with no supply lines—a daring, some said foolhardy, move that defied conventional military theory. The right wing headed toward Macon, while the left wing, farther north, headed to Augusta. Ironically, Sherman himself rode with a bodyguard unit made up entirely of Southerners, the Unionist 1st Alabama Cavalry Regiment.

Sherman's goal wasn't to starve Georgians into submission, but to break their will to resist and destroy confidence in the Confederate Army, to "make Georgia howl," as he told his boss, General Ulysses S. Grant. Sherman wanted his soldiers to feed on the move with local supplies. Foraging Union troops were called "bummers," and their behavior ranged from professional to atrocious. The destruction Sherman intended was for anything Confederates might use for military purposes: mills, manufacturing, bridges, and especially railroads, the tracks heated intensely and twisted into "Sherman's neckties."

So how much destruction did Sherman actually cause? If you travel today in the footsteps of his army, from Madison to Milledgeville, from Forsyth to Swainsboro, you'll see plenty of antebellum structures still standing, used as bed-and-breakfasts, law offices, and private homes. Contrary to reputation, the March's swath of destruction was actually quite narrow. (South Carolina, however, as the cradle of secession, would feel Northern vengeance intensely.)

Also contrary to opinion, Sherman never saw emancipating slaves as a chief goal. As crowds of freed slaves began following his army, Sherman just saw more mouths to feed: In his own orders, "Negroes who are able-bodied and can be of service to the several columns may be taken along, but each army commander will bear in mind that the question of supplies is a very important one and that his first duty is to see to them who bear arms."

## Greensboro

Named for Revolutionary War hero Nathanael Greene, little Greensboro (www.visitlakeoconee.com) isn't as energetically marketed as Madison but offers much of the same friendly confidence. The highlight, as far as I'm concerned, is the historic 1807 **Old Gaol** (E. Greene St., 706/453-7592), the oldest jail still standing in Georgia. This sturdy, two-story little fortress has actual dungeons inside and includes an ominous hanging area with a trapdoor, complete with hangman's noose. You have to get the key from the nice folks around the corner at the **Greensboro Chamber of Commerce** (111 N. Main St., 706/453-7592, www.greeneccoc.org, Mon.-Sat. 10am-5pm) on the main drag.

# Augusta

Yes, this is the home of the affluently aloof Augusta National Golf Club, which has refused to admit U.S. presidents on more than one occasion. But this is also where you'll find Tobacco Road, as in the actual Tobacco Road of Erskine Caldwell's eponymous novel about hardscrabble life in the Old South during the Great Depression. There it is, right there, on the outskirts of town when you come in on U.S. 25.

## SIGHTS

### Augusta Riverwalk

There are few better places to enjoy the natural vistas of the Savannah River than the **Augusta Riverwalk** (daily dawn-dusk, free), which stretches for about five city blocks, from 6th to 10th Streets.

In order to better negotiate the steepness of the bluff, the Riverwalk actually comprises two bricked walkways. Access the upper level by ramps at the ends of 10th Street, 8th Street Plaza, and 6th Street; get to the lower level via RiverWalk Marina (5th St.), 8th Street Plaza, the Jessye Norman Amphitheatre, and 10th Street Plaza (in front of the Marriott and where the Morris Museum of Art is located).

### Morris Museum of Art

The **Morris Museum of Art** (1 10th St., 706/724-7501, http://themorris.org, Tues.-Sat. 10am-5pm, Sun. noon-5pm, $5 adults, $3 children) has quickly become one of the most important second-tier art museums in the South.

The core of its all-Southern collections is the life's gatherings of Robert P. Coggins, whose collection was acquired by the nascent Morris board in the late 1980s.

### Augusta Museum of History

Standouts among the well-curated exhibits at the **Augusta Museum of History** (560 Reynolds St., 706/722-8454, www.augustamuseum.org, Tues.-Sat. 10am-5pm, Sun. 1pm-5pm, $4 adults, $3 children) include the Civil War section, the exhibit of Savannah River Edgefield pottery, including works by the renowned Dave "The Slave" Drake, and an homage to Augusta's golf heritage.

### James Brown Statue

It took a while, but a bronze commemoration of the Godfather of Soul in his hometown was erected in 2005 in the median of Broad Street between 8th and 9th Streets, within sight of the Imperial Theatre where Brown rehearsed and performed, and a block from the portion of 9th Street renamed James Brown Boulevard, where he shined shoes as a child.

The **James Brown Cam,** installed by the Augusta Arts Council, enables you to dial a number on your cell phone and have a picture taken for download later.

### Laney-Walker Historic District

The city's old African American business district is commemorated today in the Laney-Walker Historic District north of

# Augusta

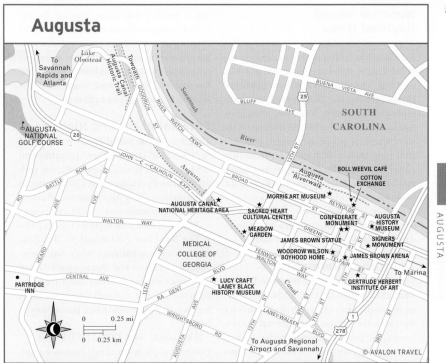

Laney-Walker Boulevard (formerly Gwinnett St.), bounded on the west by Phillips and Harrison Streets and on the east by 7th and Twiggs Streets (Twiggs St. was the boyhood neighborhood of James Brown).

The key attraction in Laney-Walker is the **Lucy Craft Laney Museum of Black History** (1116 Phillips St., 706/724-3546, www.lucycraftlaneymuseum.com, Tues.-Fri. 9am-5pm, Sat. 10am-4pm, $5 adults, $2 children). Ms. Laney herself, whose former home hosts the museum named for her, was one of the first black educators in the South.

## Augusta Canal National Heritage Area

Fairly unique among American canals in that it wasn't built for commercial transportation but for hydromechanical power, the Augusta Canal is the South's only industrial canal in continuous use. The **Augusta Canal Interpretive Center** (1450 Greene St.,

706/823-0440, www.augustacanal.com, Apr.-Nov. Mon.-Sat. 9:30am-5:30pm, Sun. 1pm-5:30pm, Dec.-Mar. Tues.-Sat. 9am-5:30pm, $6 adults, $4 children, free with $12.50-25 boat tour) at the well-restored Enterprise Mill building is the place to see related exhibits and artifacts and take boat tours on it.

The headgate area is best explored at **Savannah Rapids Park** (3300 Evans to Locks Rd., Martinez, 706/868-3349, www.co-lumbiacountyga.gov, daily dawn-dusk, free) in the next county over. You can launch your own canoe or kayak from a low point along the bank at the launch dock at Petersburg Boat Dock at the headgate.

You can rent a canoe or kayak at **Broadway Tackle & Canoe Rentals** (1730 Broad St., 706/738-8848, www.broadway-tackle.com). The old towpath runs alongside this entire section and can be walked or biked. Get a free self-guided tour map at the Augusta Canal Interpretive Center.

## Woodrow Wilson Boyhood Home

A native of Virginia, the future president led a peripatetic life before occupying the White House, never staying in one place for very long. The **Woodrow Wilson Boyhood Home** (419 7th St., 706/722-9828, www.wilsonboyhoodhome.org, Tues.-Sat. 10am-5pm, tours on the hour, $5 adults, $3 students) is the place where he stayed the longest, a 10-year stint from 1860 to 1870 while his father was pastor of the local First Presbyterian Church and before the family's move to Columbia, South Carolina (which boasts a Wilson home of its own). The 14 rooms are furnished with period pieces, including about a dozen originals that the Wilsons owned and used.

## Tours and Information

The main city tour is the **Historic Trolley Tour** (560 Reynolds St., 706/724-4067, $12) on board the Lady Liberty trolley. You'll see the canal, the Wilson home, several historic homes, and more. It leaves from the Augusta Museum of History each Saturday at 1:30pm

and is roughly two hours; they ask for 24-hour advance reservations. Admission to the Augusta Museum of History is included with the price of the tour. In the atrium of the museum is the **Augusta Visitors Center** (560 Reynolds St., 706/724-4067, Mon.-Sat. 10am-5pm, Sun. 1pm-5pm) and gift shop.

## Entertainment and Nightlife

The circa-1918 **Imperial Theatre** (749 Broad St., 706/722-8341, www.imperialtheatre.com) is where James Brown often rehearsed with his notoriously micromanaged bands prior to going on tour. These days it hosts a full calendar of various musicals and film screenings.

The most hallowed nightspot in Augusta is **The Soul Bar** (984 Broad St., 706/724-8880, www.soulbar.com, Mon.-Sat. 4pm-3am), a cavernous and charming old-school rock-punk-hipster dive just down from the Imperial Theatre and well known for hosting local musicians, including James Brown's band.

The larger **Sky City** (1157 Broad St., 706/945-1270, www.skycityaugusta.com,

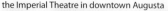

the Imperial Theatre in downtown Augusta

Mon.-Sat. 6pm-3am), down the road, is where to go for bigger-name touring acts such as Drive-By Truckers and Justin Townes Earle.

If only an Irish pub will do, head straight for **Tipsey McStumble's** (214 7th St., 706/955-8507, Mon.-Sat. 11:30am-3am), reportedly on the site of Augusta's first strip club. The current staff respects that spirit in that the women wear naughty Catholic schoolgirl outfits.

## Festivals

Augusta's premier event is **The Masters** (www.themasters.com) golf tournament, which takes place each year on the first full weekend in April. While tickets to the actual weekend competition are notoriously difficult to come by, tickets to the qualifying rounds during the week are actually not so hard to score. Lucky members of the general public can score tickets to the Masters through a lottery system (apply at the website) nearly a full year ahead. Augusta's other event of note is the **Westobou Festival** (www.westoboufestival.com, ticket prices vary), which takes place the first week in October at various downtown venues and features a ton of regional and national performing and artistic talent.

## SHOPPING

Head straight to **Artists Row** (www.artistsrowaugusta.com), a delightful consortium of galleries within restored Victorian storefronts, many complete with lofts and wrought-iron balconies, clustered in and around the 1000 block of Broad Street. One of Broad Street's most classically Augustan establishments is the kitschy antiques and bric-a-brac nostalgia market called **Merry's Trash & Treasures** (1236 Broad St., 706/722-3244, www.merrystrashandtreasures.com, Mon.-Fri. 9am-5:30pm, Sat. 9am-5pm). Forty years of history and 25,000 square feet of display space mean you can get a lot here among the various furniture and home goods offerings.

# SPORTS AND RECREATION

## Spectator Sports

The minor-league **Augusta GreenJackets** (www.milb.com), a single-A farm team of the San Francisco Giants, play at Lake Olmstead Stadium (78 Milledge Rd.). The great and infamous Ty Cobb, who was born near town, once played ball in Augusta.

## Golf

If you're a member of **Augusta National Golf Club** (www.masters.com) or an invitee of a member, and hence eligible to play here, you already know who you are. Even to members, it's open for play only a few weeks out of the year. Area public courses include the renovated links-style **Augusta Municipal** (2023 Highland Ave., 706/731-9344, www.thepatchaugusta.com, greens fees $20), aka "the Patch," and a very good state park course over the Savannah River in South Carolina, **Hickory Knob State Resort Park** (1591 Resort Dr., McCormick, SC, 864/391-1764, www.hickoryknobresort.com, greens fees $30-35).

# FOOD AND ACCOMMODATIONS

Most Augustans will tell you the best barbecue in town is at **Sconyer's** (2250 Sconyers Way, 706/790-5411, www.sconyersbar-b-que.com, Thurs.-Sat. 10am-10pm, $10). The hickory-smoked 'cue is delicious, with a tangy sauce a cut above the usual too-sweet variety you'll find in other parts of Georgia. You can get a beer here, not a given with most authentic barbecue joints in the Bible Belt. ★ **Boll Weevil Cafe & Sweetery** (10 9th St., 706/722-7772, http://thebollweevil.com, daily 11am-9pm, $20) is Augusta's nod to traditional, classic Southern cuisine. The best hushpuppies—those addictive fried cornmeal fritters renowned throughout the South—I've ever had were at **T's Restaurant** (3416 Mike Padgett Hwy., 706/798-4145, www.tsrestaurant.com,

Tues.-Thurs. 11am-9pm, Fri. 11am-10pm, Sat. 4:30pm-10pm, $10).

With few exceptions, the Augusta hotel scene is dominated by national chains. Keep in mind that during Masters week in early April, accommodations in Augusta and the surrounding area are not only extremely difficult to obtain at the last minute, they are extraordinarily expensive. Augusta's premier accommodations option is the ★ **Partridge Inn** (2110 Walton Way, 706/737-8888, www.partridgeinn.com, $130-150). This hotel and attached spa in a century-old building features 144 guest rooms. For maximum ease of access to the Riverwalk and downtown sights, go straight to the **Augusta Marriott at the Convention Center** (2 10th St., 706/722-8900, www.marriott.com, $150).

## GETTING THERE AND AROUND

Augusta is very conveniently located near east-west I-20. A loop highway, I-520, circles the city. Keep in mind that just north of the Savannah River is North Augusta, South Carolina, part of the greater Augusta metro area.

The city is served by **Augusta Regional Airport** (AGS, 1501 Aviation Way, 706/798-3236, www.flyags.com), which hosts flights by Delta and American.

**Greyhound** (1128 Greene St., 706/722-6411, www.greyhound.com) offers bus service into and out of town. As for public transit, the city runs **Augusta Public Transit** (www.augustaga.gov, $1.25 per ride), with frequent bus routes around town.

## OUTSIDE AUGUSTA
### Harlem

Named after the famous neighborhood in New York City, Harlem was the birthplace in 1892 of Oliver Hardy, of the famed Laurel and Hardy comedy team. He wasn't here long, but Harlem really plays it up.

The main stop is the **Laurel & Hardy Museum** (250 N. Louisville St., 706/556-0401, www.harlemga.org, Tues.-Sat. 10am-4pm, free) on the main road, where the man's youth and life and times are celebrated in an exhibit and video. Old-timey cars and costumes abound the first weekend of each October as the entire town celebrates their native son's legacy at the **Oliver Hardy Festival** (http://harlemga.org), which brings as many as 30,000 people to this town that is normally home to fewer than 2,000 residents.

# Washington

Founded in 1780, the first city in America named after George Washington (the nation's capital didn't bear his name until nearly 20 years later), stately Washington is also possibly the resting place of the legendary missing Confederate gold! In addition to the mythical lost treasure, the city figures large in Southern symbolism as onetime home of Alexander H. Stephens, vice president of the Confederacy, and as the place where Jefferson Davis convened the last meeting of his cabinet on May 5, 1865.

## SIGHTS
### Robert Toombs House

A hugely influential figure in U.S. and Georgia politics, Robert Toombs was a staunch Unionist for most of his political career (though also a slave-owning planter) who morphed into the state's most vocal advocate of secession. The **Robert Toombs House** (216 E. Robert Toombs Ave., 706/678-2226, www.gastateparks.org, Tues.-Sat. 9am-5pm, tours 10am-4pm, $5 adults, $3 children) brings his life, well, to life with guided tours of this antebellum Greek Revival mansion.

## Washington Historical Museum

Run by the Washington-Wilkes Historical Foundation, the **Washington Historical Museum** (308 E. Robert Toombs Ave., 706/678-5001, www.historyofwilkes.org, Tues.-Sat. 10am-5pm, $3) is particularly interesting to Civil War buffs, chiefly because Wilkes County was so well connected at that time.

## Tours

The delightful **"Miss Fanny"** (706/318-3128, http://missfanny.com, $20), whose real name is Elaine, gives very entertaining and informative tours that cover dozens of key homes and usually include a few invitations to come inside. And yes, you'll no doubt hear about the lost Confederate gold.

## PRACTICALITIES

The well-restored 17-room **Fitzpatrick Hotel** (16 W. Square, 706/678-5900, www.thefitzpatrickhotel.com, $120-225) is oriented to weekend guests, so if you'd like to stay on a weekday, give them a call well ahead of time. The premier B&B in town is the circa-1828 **Washington Plantation Bed & Breakfast** (15 Lexington Ave., 877/405-9956, www.washingtonplantation.com, $160-230), known for its gourmet breakfasts and beautiful seven-acre grounds.

You don't have to look too hard for the best place to eat in town. The ★ **Washington Jockey Club** (5 E. Square, 706/678-1672, www.washingtonjockeyclub.com, Wed.-Thurs. 5pm-9:30pm, Fri.-Sat. 11am-2pm and 5pm-9:30pm, $10-30) is right on the courthouse square. Signature entrées are the pecan chicken and the shrimp and grits. There's also a full-service bar, pretty much the only watering hole in this sleepy town.

The **Washington-Wilkes Chamber of Commerce** (22 W. Square, 706/678-5111, www.washingtonwilkes.org, Mon.-Fri. 10am-4pm), right on the main courthouse square, is where to get brochures and other information.

# Savannah River Lakes

The mighty Savannah River forms the border of Georgia and South Carolina, and since the 1950s the U.S. Army Corps of Engineers has controlled its flow. Dams make lakes, and millions come to frolic on three of them on the Savannah River each year; from north to south, they are Lake Hartwell, Lake Russell, and Clark's Hill-Lake Thurmond.

For a general overview, go to www.sas.usace.army.mil. Lakes Hartwell and Thurmond have **campgrounds** (877/444-6777, www.ReserveUSA.com) operated by the Corps. The general websites for reservations and info on Georgia and South Carolina state parks are www.gastateparks.org and www.discoversouthcarolina.com. Many recreation areas and campgrounds close in the off-season, after Labor Day, though most boat ramps stay open all year. Drought conditions can also affect water levels on Lakes Hartwell and Thurmond (Lake Russell is kept near full at all times). Check the Corps website for up-to-date info.

## LAKE HARTWELL

Of the three lakes, northernmost Lake Hartwell (www.sas.usace.army.mil), named after Revolutionary War heroine Nancy Hart, has the most upscale feel and is focused more on private docks and private vacation rentals. For full information, stop by the **Hartwell Dam & Lake Office & Visitor Center** (5625 Anderson Hwy., Hartwell, 706/856-0300, year-round Mon.-Fri. 8am-4:30pm, summer

Sat.-Sun. 9am-5:30pm, fall-spring Sat.-Sun. 8am-4:30pm).

Optimized for serious anglers, **Tugaloo State Park** (1763 Tugaloo State Park Rd., 706/356-4362, www.gastateparks.org, office daily 8am-5pm, RV and tent sites $23-30, primitive campsites $15, cottages $135) has one of the biggest boat ramps in the area. There are over 100 RV and tent sites, 5 primitive campsites, and 20 cottages.

**Hart Outdoor Recreation Area** (330 Hart Park Rd., 706/213-2045, www.gastateparks.org, campsites $19-26, walk-in campsites $19) is a good base of operations for fishing, and also offers self-registration seasonal camping with nice views of the lake (62 sites), as well as 16 walk-in campsites. The boat ramp is open year-round.

## Royston

Nestled near the South Carolina line, Royston's main contribution to history is as the hometown of baseball legend Ty Cobb, the "Georgia Peach," whose impressive and often controversial career is memorialized at the **Ty Cobb Museum** (461 Cook St., 706/245-1825, www.tycobbmuseum.org, Mon.-Fri. 9am-5pm, Sat. 10am-4pm, $5 adults, $3 children). The museum is actually inside the Ty Cobb Healthcare Center, a philanthropic legacy of Cobb himself, an astute investor who amassed a large personal fortune.

If you're in the area on a weekend, head straight to ★ **Vanna's Country Barbecue** (Hwy. 17 S., 706/246-0952, Fri.-Sat. 11am-9pm, Sun. 11am-3pm, $5) to get a bite in "beautiful downtown Vanna," a bit south of Royston. While the pulled pork is delectably soft and the Brunswick stew most excellent, I'd head straight for their legendary ribs.

## Victoria Bryant State Park

Considered one of the best lesser-known state parks in Georgia, **Victoria Bryant State Park** (1105 Bryant Park Rd., 706/245-6270, www.gastateparks.org, parking $5, campsites $25-28) has a nice creek that runs through the camping area, with 27 tent and RV sites. The highlight is the selection of eight raised-platform tenting sites. The adjacent **Highland Walk Golf Course** (706/245-6770, http://georgiagolf.com, daily from 8am) offers 18 holes.

## LAKE RUSSELL

Named after long-serving Georgia senator Richard B. Russell Jr., Lake Russell (www.sas.usace.army.mil) is the youngest of the three lakes. Because it was built after the Water Projects Act of 1974, private development on its shores is prohibited. For more information, stop by the **Russell Dam & Lake Office & Visitors Center** (4144 Russell Dam Dr., 706/213-3400, Mon.-Fri. 8am-4:30pm, Sat.-Sun. 8am-4pm).

Along Lake Russell is one of the gems in the Georgia state park system, **Richard B. Russell State Park** (2650 Russell State Park Rd., 706/213-2045, www.gastateparks.org, parking $5, tent and RV sites $25-28, cottages $130-140). It is home to the 18-hole **Arrowhead Pointe Golf Course** ($45-50) as well as a well-regarded disc golf course. There are only 28 RV and tent sites and no primitive sites, but there are 20 very nice lakefront cottages, two of which are dog-friendly ($40 per dog, maximum two).

## CLARK'S HILL LAKE

Clark's Hill Lake is technically called Lake Strom Thurmond (www.sas.usace.army.mil); in 1988 Congress renamed it in honor of the controversial long-serving South Carolina politician. Georgia politicians refused to honor the change, and on Georgia maps it's still called Clark's Hill. It is the oldest of the three Army Corps of Engineers lakes on the Savannah River, and its 70,000 acres make it the largest such project east of the Mississippi. For more info, go across the border into South Carolina and visit the **Thurmond Lake Office & Visitors Center** (510 Clarks Hill

Hwy., Clarks Hill, SC, 864/333-1147, daily 8am-4:30pm).

A great way to enjoy the lake with the family is **Elijah Clark State Park** (2959 McCormick Hwy., 706/359-3458, www.gastateparks.org, parking $5, tent and RV sites $25, walk-in campsites $15, Pioneer campground $35, cottages $120). There are 165 RV and tent sites, 10 walk-in tent sites, the Pioneer campground, and 20 lakefront cottages, two of which are dog friendly ($40 per dog, maximum two).

Bass anglers should head straight to **Mistletoe State Park** (3725 Mistletoe Rd., 706/541-0321, www.gastateparks.org, parking $5, tent and RV sites $25, walk-in campsites $15, backcountry sites $10, cottages $140).

## Elberton

The town of Elberton prides itself on being the "Granite Capital of the World." Fittingly, its chief attraction is made of granite as well, specifically the **Georgia Guidestones** (Guidestones Rd.) off Highway 77 north of town, known as "America's Stonehenge" because of the vague resemblance of the 19-foot-tall stones to the Druid monument. The Guidestones, erected in 1980, feature an assortment of New-Agey exhortations in 12 languages, including four ancient tongues.

# Middle and South Georgia

M iddle Georgia is full of surprises. Besides being the home of the Allman Brothers and Otis Redding, Macon also has one of the most beautifully ornate cathedrals you'll see outside Europe. Columbus is where the inventor of

Coca-Cola was born. President Franklin Roosevelt was inspired by the healing properties of Warm Springs to found the March of Dimes. The nation's first state park was at Indian Springs. And polite Milledgeville once housed the largest insane asylum on the planet.

South Georgia is the least populous part of the state and unquestionably the hottest during the summer. One might be tempted to ask, "Why go to South Georgia?" Where else can you find an entire town devoted almost entirely to celebrating the life and times of a president born there, as is the case with Plains and native son Jimmy Carter? Where else can you find a swamp the size of Delaware, filled with blackwater that is as clean as what comes out of your tap at home, as is the case with the Okefenokee? Where else can you walk in the footsteps of Civil War POWs and visit a stirring national museum devoted to the memory of American POWs from all wars, as you can at Andersonville?

## PLANNING YOUR TIME

Basically, there are three routes of particular interest in South Georgia. The area occasionally called "Presidential Pathways" includes sites related to Jimmy Carter as well as the Andersonville POW camp and museum and the Kolomoki Mounds and Providence Canyon sights. Then there's the southern band along the Florida border, with Thomasville as the main stop; and finally, the huge Okefenokee Swamp, taking up virtually the entire southeastern corner of Georgia. The Okefenokee is something of a special case, as you can easily spend several days exploring it or simply confine it to a day trip.

**Previous:** an alligator in Okefenokee Swamp; the National Civil War Naval Museum in Columbus.
**Above:** FDR's Llittle White House.

# Middle and South Georgia

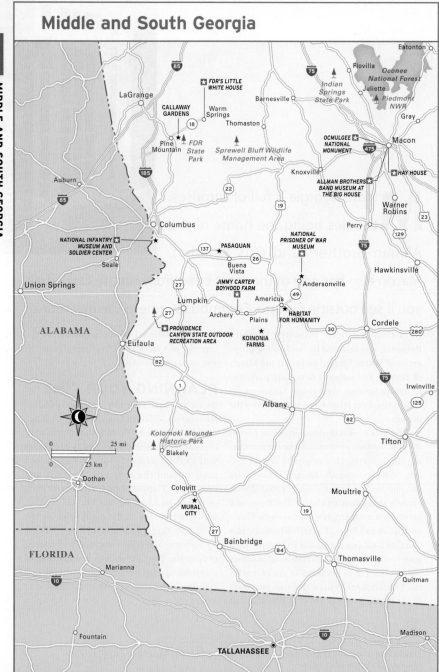

Eatonton

Flovilla

Oconee National Forest

Indian Springs State Park

Juliette

Piedmont NWR

Gray

LaGrange

FDR'S LITTLE WHITE HOUSE

Barnesville

CALLAWAY GARDENS

Warm Springs

Thomaston

OCMULGEE NATIONAL MONUMENT

Macon

HAY HOUSE

Pine Mountain

FDR State Park

Sprewell Bluff Wildlife Management Area

Knoxville

ALLMAN BROTHERS BAND MUSEUM AT THE BIG HOUSE

Auburn

Warner Robins

Columbus

Perry

NATIONAL INFANTRY MUSEUM AND SOLDIER CENTER

PASAQUAN

NATIONAL PRISONER OF WAR MUSEUM

Seale

Buena Vista

Hawkinsville

Union Springs

JIMMY CARTER BOYHOOD FARM

Andersonville

Lumpkin

Americus

ALABAMA

Archery

Plains

HABITAT FOR HUMANITY

Cordele

PROVIDENCE CANYON STATE OUTDOOR RECREATION AREA

KOINONIA FARMS

Eufaula

0    25 mi

0    25 km

Kolomoki Mounds Historic Park

Albany

Irwinville

Blakely

Tifton

Dothan

Colquitt

Moultrie

MURAL CITY

FLORIDA

Bainbridge

Thomasville

Marianna

Quitman

Fountain

Madison

TALLAHASSEE

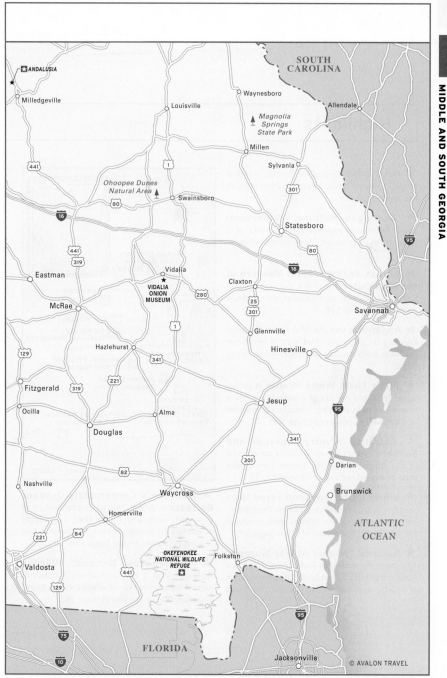

© AVALON TRAVEL

Look for ★ to find recommended
sights, activities, dining, and lodging.

# Highlights

★ **Hay House:** One of the South's grandest house museums is also fascinatingly individualistic (page 553).

★ **Ocmulgee National Monument:** These enormous mounds are remnants of a once-glorious Native American civilization (page 555).

★ **Allman Brothers Band Museum at the Big House:** One of the country's favorite bands has a lovingly curated collection of unique memorabilia (page 557).

★ **Andalusia:** Visit the farm where the great Flannery O'Connor authored most of her classic Southern Gothic novels and short stories (page 562).

★ **FDR's Little White House:** A bittersweet look into the life of a pioneering figure is enriched with amazing memorabilia from his transformative presidency (page 566).

★ **National Infantry Museum and Soldier Center:** A stirring look at the exploits of the American fighting soldier comes with state-of-the-art technology (page 570).

★ **Jimmy Carter Boyhood Farm:** Take a nostalgic and insightful look into the Depression-era experiences of the Georgia-born president just outside his hometown of Plains (page 576).

★ **National Prisoner of War Museum:** The site of the notorious Andersonville Civil War POW camp hosts a deeply affecting exploration of cruelty and bravery during wartime (page 577).

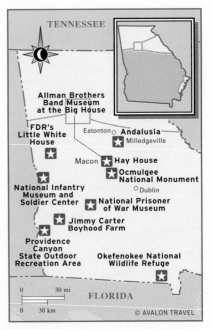

★ **Providence Canyon State Outdoor Recreation Area:** This geological feature of high white walls and a deep floor, surprisingly developed by human impact, has been called "Georgia's Grand Canyon" (page 578).

★ **Okefenokee National Wildlife Refuge:** Visit a vast and wholly fascinating natural feature the likes of which can't be found anywhere else on the planet (page 582).

# Macon

It's fitting that Macon is pretty much dead center in the middle of Georgia, since in many ways it's the archetypal Georgia town: laid-back, churchified, heavy on fried food, built by the railroad, surrounded by seemingly endless farmland, and a center of cross-pollinating musical traditions.

## SIGHTS

### ★ Hay House

Easily one of the most splendid and splendidly restored antebellum mansions in the South, the Hay House (934 Georgia Ave., 478/742-8155, www.georgiatrust.org, Sept.-Dec. and Mar.-June Tues.-Sat. 10am-4pm, Sun. 1pm-4pm, Jan.-Feb. and July-Aug. Tues.-Sat. 10am-4pm, last tour 3pm, $9 adults, $5 students) in the stately Intown neighborhood is worthy of a tour. Built in the Italian Renaissance Revival style and completed a scant five years before the outbreak of the Civil War, the Hay House was built by William Butler Johnston. It passed into the hands of insurance magnate Parks Lee Hay during the 1920s. The magnificent abode stayed in the Hay family until

1977, when it was given to the Georgia Trust for Historic Preservation.

## St. Joseph Catholic Church

Oddly for this rigidly Baptist region, one of the most beautiful and ornate Roman Catholic churches pretty much anywhere is right in Macon's historic Intown neighborhood. St. Joseph Catholic Church (830 Poplar St., 478/745-1631, www.stjosephmacon.com, office Mon.-Fri. 9:30am-4:30pm) was completed at the turn of the 20th century, though it harks back to a much older tradition of grand European cathedrals. At the top of the church's left tower, as you face the sanctuary from Poplar Street, you'll see three huge bronze bells, named Jesus, Mary, and Joseph. You can hear them rung daily at 6am, noon, and 6pm.

## Sidney Lanier Cottage

Just around the corner from St. Joseph, the Sidney Lanier Cottage (935 High St., 478/743-3851, Mon.-Sat. 10am-4pm, last tour 3:30pm, $5 adults, $3 children) is where that

the Hay House in downtown Macon

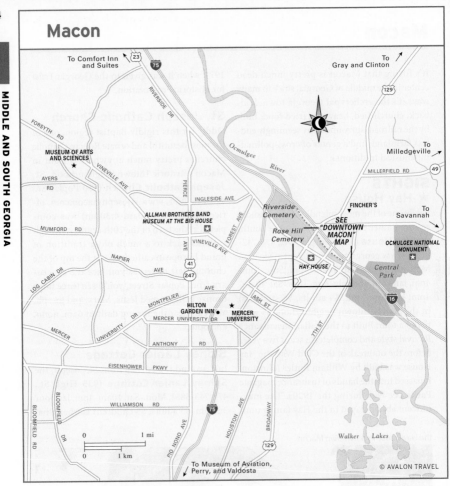

# Macon

To Comfort Inn and Suites

To Gray and Clinton

To Milledgeville

To Savannah

Ocmulgee River

RIVERSIDE DR

FORSYTH RD

MUSEUM OF ARTS AND SCIENCES

VINEVILLE AVE

AYERS RD

PIERCE

INGLESIDE AVE

MILLERFIELD RD

Riverside Cemetery

FINCHER'S

ALLMAN BROTHERS BAND MUSEUM AT THE BIG HOUSE

FOREST AVE

Rose Hill Cemetery

SEE "DOWNTOWN MACON" MAP

OCMULGEE NATIONAL MONUMENT

MUMFORD RD

VINEVILLE AVE

AVE

HAY HOUSE

Central Park

NAPIER

AVE

ASH ST

LOG CABIN DR

MONTPELIER

HILTON GARDEN INN

MERCER UNIVERSITY

MERCER

UNIVERSITY DR

MERCER UNIVERSITY DR

7TH ST

ANTHONY RD

EISENHOWER PKWY

BLOOMFIELD RD

WILLIAMSON RD

BLOOMFIELD DR

PIO NONO AVE

HOUSTON AVE

BROADWAY

Walker Lakes

0    1 mi

0    1 km

To Museum of Aviation, Perry, and Valdosta

© AVALON TRAVEL

---

great man of letters was born in 1842; this was actually his grandparents' home at the time. While he didn't live in this house most of his life, he did spend much of his time in the Macon area.

## Cannonball House

While General Sherman and his troops left Macon alone, an exchange of artillery fire led to some random shells hitting and embedding themselves into the antebellum **Cannonball House** (856 Mulberry St., 478/745-5982,

www.cannonballhouse.org, Jan.-Feb. Mon.-Fri. 11am-last tour at 4:15pm, Sat. 10am-last tour at 4:15pm, Mar.-Dec. Mon.-Sat. 10am-last tour at 4:15pm, $8 adults, $6 students, free under age 4). Tours last 45 minutes and include the main house, with its furnishings and Civil War memorabilia, and the historically notable two-story brick kitchen building with servants quarters.

## Grand Opera House

The 1,000-seat **Grand Opera House** (651

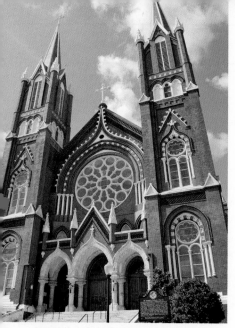

St. Joseph Catholic Church

Mulberry St., 478/301-5470, www.thegrand-macon.com, Mon.-Fri. 10am-5pm, showtimes vary), built in 1883, represents the height of Macon's opulent Victorian heyday. While Reconstruction and its aftermath were difficult throughout the South, Macon fared noticeably better than most Southern cities, and "the Grand" is proof.

## Museum District

While not all offerings have worked out—the Georgia Music Hall of Fame was forced to close in 2011—Macon does boast its own fledgling museum district in a walkable, renovated section of downtown.

### MUSEUM OF ARTS AND SCIENCES

Billing itself as Georgia's largest general-purpose museum, the **Museum of Arts and Sciences** (4182 Forsyth Rd., 478/477-3232, www.masmacon.org, Tues.-Sat. 10am-5pm, Sun. 1pm-5pm, $10 adults, $7 students, $5 ages 2-17) features a wide range of natural history

exhibits and regionally oriented historical artifacts.

### GEORGIA CHILDREN'S MUSEUM

Four floors of enriching, educational children's activities, some still under development, are the attraction in this handsome building in the heart of downtown, which also includes a decent café for the refreshment of the adults. Highlights of the **Georgia Children's Museum** (382 Cherry St., 478/755-9539, www.georgiachildrens-museum.com, Tues.-Sat. 10am-5pm, $4) include a hands-on TV studio and an exhibit on the indigenous Creek people.

### TUBMAN AFRICAN AMERICAN MUSEUM

Actually more of an art and art-history destination than strictly a historical museum, the **Tubman African American Museum** (340 Walnut St., 478/743-8544, www.tubmanmuseum.com, Tues.-Sat. 9am-5pm, $10 adults, $6 children) explores the African American experience and culture.

## ★ Ocmulgee National Monument

There are a couple of sites elsewhere with somewhat better-preserved Native American mounds, but none quite so extensive as the sprawling and entirely fascinating **Ocmulgee National Monument** (1207 Emery Hwy., 478/752-8257, www.nps.gov, daily 9am-5pm, free). To early white settlers of the region they were simply called the "Old Fields," but to the Mississippian people that lived here from about 900 to 1650, it was a bustling center of activity, from the enormous temple mound (from the top you can see most of downtown Macon) to the intimate and striking Earth Lodge, which, though completely restored, boasts the only original and unchanged lodge floor in North America.

Begin and end your visit at the charming art deco visitors center. Inside you'll find an extensive series of displays illustrating not

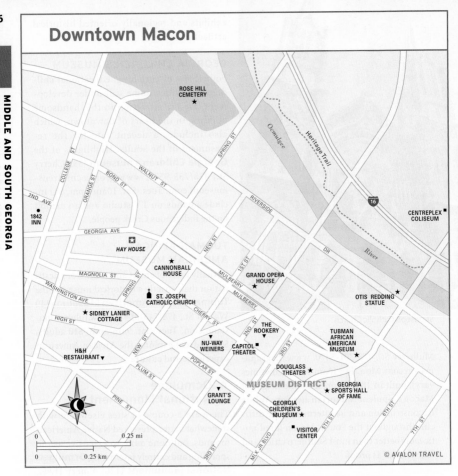

# Downtown Macon

ROSE HILL CEMETERY ★

Ocmulgee

Heritage Trail

16

CENTREPLEX COLISEUM ■

SPRING ST
COLLEGE ST
ORANGE ST
BOND ST
WALNUT ST
2ND AVE
RIVERSIDE
DR
River

1842 INN ●

GEORGIA AVE

HAY HOUSE ✦

MAGNOLIA ST

CANNONBALL HOUSE ★

GRAND OPERA HOUSE ★

OTIS REDDING STATUE ★

WASHINGTON AVE

SPRING ST

MULBERRY ST

MULBERRY ST

ST. JOSEPH CATHOLIC CHURCH ⌖

SIDNEY LANIER COTTAGE ★

HIGH ST

CHERRY ST

NEW ST

1ST ST

2ND ST

THE ROOKERY ★

TUBMAN AFRICAN AMERICAN MUSEUM ★

NU-WAY WEINERS ▼

CAPITOL THEATER ■

H&H RESTAURANT ▼

3RD ST

DOUGLASS THEATER ★

PLUM ST

POPLAR ST

PINE ST

GRANT'S LOUNGE ▼

MUSEUM DISTRICT

GEORGIA SPORTS HALL OF FAME ★

GEORGIA CHILDREN'S MUSEUM ★

VISITOR CENTER ■

MLK JR BLVD

3RD ST

5TH ST

6TH ST

7TH ST

0        0.25 mi

0        0.25 km

© AVALON TRAVEL

only artifacts from the area, but the scope of Native American life in the region covering at least 17,000 years. From the visitors center you take the trails through the actual mounds, which may not look like much more than grassy knolls until you fully digest the significance of this site, which some scholars say at its peak was more populous than modern-day Macon.

A major planned expansion of the grounds was announced in 2016; check the website for updates.

## Otis Redding Statue

Just as you cross the bridge over the Ocmulgee

River from downtown into east Macon, on your left you'll see Gateway Park and the beginning of the Ocmulgee Heritage Trail. The key landmark here, however, is the small but well-done memorial plaza to the late great Otis Redding, Macon native and beloved R&B-soul musician who influenced an entire generation before dying in a plane crash at the age of 26. A nice touch is the buried, vandalism-proof speakers surrounding the statue, which play a steady 24-hour diet of Redding songs.

## Rose Hill Cemetery

One of two adjacent historic cemeteries along

Ocmulgee National Monument

Riverside Drive, **Rose Hill Cemetery** (1071 Riverside Dr., 478/751-9119, www.historicrosehillcemetery.org, daily dawn-dusk, free) is generally of more interest to visitors. This is where Duane Allman and Berry Oakley are buried side by side; they died in separate motorcycle accidents about a year and three blocks apart. A few feet away, in a separate plot across a walkway, is where Duane's brother Greg Allman was laid to rest after his death in 2017. Allman Brothers fans can also see the poignant graves of "Little Martha" Ellis and Elizabeth Reed, both of whom inspired band tunes.

## Riverside Cemetery

While adjacent Rose Hill Cemetery tends to get more attention, **Riverside Cemetery** (1301 Riverside Dr., 478/742-5328, www.riversidecemetery.com, daily dawn-dusk, free) is much more walkable. Notable sites include the poignant Babyland (a late 19th-century plot where small children are buried) and the grave of Charles Reb Messenburg, who, at his request, was buried standing up.

## ★ Allman Brothers Band Museum at the Big House

If you're any kind of a fan of the Allman Brothers Band, or if the idea of vintage tube amps, beautiful guitars, well-used drums, handwritten set lists, and flamboyant 1970s outfits gets you excited, head straight to the wonderfully done **Allman Brothers Band Museum at the Big House** (2321 Vineville Ave., 478/741-5551, www.thebighousemuseum.com, Thurs.-Sun. 11am-6pm, $8 adults, $4 children). The rambling Tudor mansion, or "Big House," is a very short drive northwest of downtown. It's where the band lived as an extended community from 1970 to 1973, and where many of their iconic hits were written, and it has been beautifully and tastefully restored. In some cases the intent is to replicate rooms where the Allmans and friends hung out; others create light-filled and joyously celebratory display areas for the enormous volume of Allman-related memorabilia and vintage instruments.

## Tours and Information

Easily the most distinctive tour in town is **Lights on Macon** (www.lightsonmacon.com), a free, self-guided, illuminated nighttime walking tour available every night of the year. A neighborhood of historic Intown Macon leaves its lights on every night so tourgoers can view at their leisure. Download the

# Allman Brothers Tour

Though their family roots are actually in north Florida, perhaps no other musical name is so associated with Macon and middle Georgia as the Allman Brothers Band. Far ahead of their time musically in their sinuous and rhythmic blend of rock, blues, soul, and even country, they were also one of the first true multiracial bands.

Duane and Gregg Allman grew up as competing siblings, with Duane's fiery personality and virtuosic slide guitar work driving their early success. Touring with what would become a close-knit bunch of friends in various incarnations through the mid- to late 1960s, the whole bunch ended up in Macon as the Allman Brothers Band. With the 1969 release of their eponymous debut album, nothing in the rock world—or in Macon, for that matter—was ever the same.

The city is chock-full of Allman sites that have inspired pilgrimages for decades. The band had various residences, including **309 College Street** and **315 College Street,** which was on the cover of the band's first album. The most famous was the "Big House," a large Tudor rented by bassist Berry Oakley and his wife, Linda, and memorialized today in the **Allman Brothers Band Museum at the Big House** (2321 Vineville Ave., 478/741-5551, www.thebighouse-museum.com, Thurs.-Sun. 11am-6pm, $8 adults, $4 children).

Alas, the Allmans' heyday was short-lived. In October 1971 Duane perished in a motorcycle crash at **Hillcrest Avenue and Bartlett Street.** Barely a year later, Oakley died in another motorcycle crash at **Napier and Inverness Avenues.** Both were only 24. They are buried side by side at **Rose Hill Cemetery.** Greg Allman, who passed away in 2017, is laid to rest in a nearby plot a few feet away. At Rose Hill you can also see two gravesites that inspired Allman songs, "Little Martha" Ellis and Elizabeth Napier Reed. The Bond tomb at Rose Hill was on the back cover of the band's debut record.

Not all is gloom and doom, however. Down the road from the Big House you can have the best fried chicken and collard greens for miles around at **H & H Restaurant** (807 Forsyth St., 478/742-9810, www.mamalouise.com, Mon.-Sat. 6:30am-4pm, $12), where the band frequently ate and which features much Allmans memorabilia.

While in Macon, the band's label was **Capricorn Records** (535 D.T. Walton Sr. Way/Cotton Ave.), which, though now in other hands, still retains the old signage and exterior. The actual Capricorn studios were at **536 Martin Luther King Jr. Boulevard;** that exterior can be seen on the *Allman Brothers Band at Fillmore East* album.

the Allman Brothers Band Museum at the Big House

# On the Chitlin Circuit

In the days of racial segregation, there was even a color line for music. Thus began the legendary "chitlin circuit" of African American entertainers playing to black audiences, with Macon as a key stop.

While an actual chitlin is an ingredient in Southern food, specifically fried pig intestine, or "chitterling," the chitlin circuit is best exemplified by four enormously influential Georgia artists: **Ray Charles, James Brown,** and two who grew up blocks apart in Macon's Pleasant Hill neighborhood, **Little Richard** and **Otis Redding.**

Richard "Little Richard" Penniman is considered in some circles the real father of rock and roll, emulated by white artists such as Elvis Presley and Jerry Lee Lewis. Little Richard wrote "Long Tall Sally" while working as a dishwasher at **Ann's Tic-Toc Room** (408 Broadway, now Martin Luther King Jr. Blvd.) about a waitress there. It's now a swank bar, but it's still the Tic-Toc Room, and a plaque outside explains the history of the building. A stone's throw away is the restored circa-1921 **Douglass Theatre** (355 Martin Luther King Jr. Blvd.), a major chitlin circuit venue that continues to host a full calendar of shows. Contrary to what many assume, the venue isn't named after early abolitionist Frederick Douglass but rather local black entrepreneur Charles Henry Douglass.

Otis Redding, though born in nearby Dawson, came of age in Macon. It's said that he won so many teen talent shows at the Douglass that he was eventually barred from competing. He sang at the Baptist church (850 Armory Dr.), where his father was pastor.

Redding nearly single-handedly brought chitlin circuit R&B to a white counterculture audience with his short but electrifying headlining appearance at the Monterey Pop Festival in 1967. Redding died in a plane crash only six months later, but his memory lives on at Macon's **Gateway Park,** where he is memorialized with a statue and plaza.

tour guide from the website or get the brochure at the **Downtown Macon Visitor Information Center** (450 Martin Luther King Jr. Blvd., 478/743-3401, www.maconga. org, Mon.-Fri. 9am-5pm, Sat. 10am-4pm). Begin your tour at one of two iconic Macon locations, the Hay House (934 Georgia Ave.) or 1842 Inn (353 College St.). Download a handy free daytime walking tour of downtown Macon at www.maconwalkingtours. com.

## ENTERTAINMENT AND EVENTS
### Nightlife

The premier rock club in town and a key part of Georgia's music history is **Grant's Lounge** (576 Poplar St., 478/746-9191, www.grantslounge.com, Mon.-Sat. noon-2am), the "original home of Southern rock," which still hosts regular live music after over four decades of nourishing the budding careers of Southern names like Lynyrd Skynyrd, Tom Petty, and the Marshall Tucker Band.

For another neat bit of Southern music history, have a cocktail at the **Tic-Toc Room** (408 Broadway, 478/744-0123, Mon.-Sat. 5pm-2am). It's more of a martini bar and swank café these days, but in the days before integration it was a key venue on the "chitlin circuit" of African American entertainment; James Brown, Little Richard, and Otis Redding all performed here. (Little Richard also worked here, and it's said he wrote "Long Tall Sally" about a coworker.)

### Festivals

Without question Macon's premier event is the "pinkest party on earth," the **Cherry Blossom Festival** (www.cherryblossom. com, Mar.), which takes place in mid- to late March to take advantage of the annual blossoming of the city's estimated 300,000-plus Yoshino cherry trees, which are not indigenous but were imported from Japan. Events are varied, from a Bed Race to nightly concerts to, of course, the Cherry Blossom Parade, and take place at various venues, including Cherry

Street downtown, Central City Park (Willie Smokie Glover Dr.), Mercer University, and Wesleyan College. A free trolley takes festivalgoers from spot to spot. While some events and concerts are ticketed, the majority are free and open to the public.

Easily the most unique event in the area is the **Ocmulgee Indian Celebration** (www.nps.gov, Sept.), which takes place on the grounds of the National Park Service-operated Ocmulgee National Monument and celebrates the heritage and culture of the descendants of the Creek people, who built the enormous mound complex here.

## FOOD

Because of Macon's central location near several interstate highways, pretty much every type of fast-food and chain restaurant you can think of has an outpost in town. Instead, here are some of the unique and recommended local and regional offerings.

### American

With an active bar scene to go along with its well-received menu, ★ **The Rookery Restaurant & Bar** (543 Cherry St., 478/746-8658, www.rookerymacon.com, Mon. 11am-3pm, Tues.-Thurs. 11am-9:30pm, Fri.-Sat. 11am-10pm, Sun. 11:30am-9pm, $8-15) is a great all-purpose stop in the most happening area of Macon's restored downtown, with history back to 1976. Specialties include Betsy's Grilled Pimento Cheese, a Southern delicacy, and a range of great burgers, all half a pound and all named after famous Georgians, from the Allman Brothers (Swiss cheese and mushrooms) to Jerry Reed (pepper jack cheese and jalapeños) to Jimmy Carter (peanut butter and bacon).

Perhaps the most unique restaurant in Macon is **Nu-Way Weiners** (430 Cotton Ave., 478/743-1368, www.nu-wayweiners. com, Mon.-Fri. 6am-7pm, Sat. 7am-6pm, $2-4), which has grown to nine locations in its nearly 100-year history. At all of them you'll find the same inexpensive menu of hot dogs built around Nu-Way's "secret" chili topping.

### Soul Food

Allman Brothers fans will know ★ **H & H Restaurant** (807 Forsyth St., 478/742-9810, www.mamalouise.com, Mon.-Sat. 6:30am-4pm, $12) as the band's favorite hangout in Macon, but "Mama Louise" Hudson's place is also one of the best soul food diners anywhere. It's very informal: When you're ready to leave, you come back behind the counter and pay the cook, who also runs the register. The menu is as simple as it has been for the last 50 years; you pick a meat (go with the fried chicken) and three veggies, such as perfect collard greens and their signature squash. The walls are covered with memorabilia of Southern rock, particularly the Allman Brothers, who were taken under Mama Louise's wing during their early days as starving artists.

## ACCOMMODATIONS
### Under $150

Due to its very central location at the confluence of three interstate highways (I-75, I-475, and I-16), Macon offers a vast range of budget chain accommodations that tend to group in large clusters.

The I-75 cluster is just north of downtown, about a five-minute drive. I'd recommend the **Comfort Inn & Suites** (3935 Arkwright Rd., 478/757-8688, www.comfortinn.com, $75-100) or the pet-friendly **Candlewood Suites** (3957 River Place Dr., 478/254-3531, www.ichotelsgroup.com, $75-100). The densest cluster is off I-475 on the western edge of Macon, with downtown about 10 minutes away. Try **Comfort Inn West** (4951 Eisenhower Pkwy., 478/788-5500, www.comfortinn.com, $75-100), with renovated guest rooms, or the pet-friendly **Sleep Inn West** (140 Plantation Inn Dr., 478/476-8111, www.sleepinn.com, $75-100).

A good budget choice a bit closer to downtown is the **Hilton Garden Inn** (1220

Stadium Dr., 478/741-5527, www.hilton. com, $130) adjacent to the tranquil Mercer University campus.

## $150-300

The premier lodging in Macon is the ★ **1842 Inn** (353 College St., 478/741-1842, www.1842inn.com, $140-255), and I urge you to make every effort to secure a room if you're planning to visit the city. It's in a particularly striking Greek Revival building that was once the home of a mayor, with "opulent" a fair description of its interior. Ten of the inn's 19 guest rooms are in the main building, which boasts a classic wraparound veranda with 17 columns. There's a separate Victorian Cottage, which was actually moved onto this parcel of land in the 1980s and has nine guest rooms.

## SOUTH OF MACON
### Museum of Aviation

There's one very worthwhile reason to visit the town of Warner Robins, 14 miles south of Macon, and that's the excellent **Museum of Aviation** (Russell Pkwy., 478/926-6870, www.museumofaviation.org, daily 9am-5pm, free) on the massive Robins Air Force Base. Comprising several very large buildings with roughly outlined chronological themes, the core collection of the museum is its impressive array of many, many dozens of military aircraft from all eras of American aviation. Airplane buffs of all ages will go nuts seeing these beauties up close, from World War II classics like the P-51 Mustang to the host of Cold War and Vietnam War-era jets to the starkly elegant U-2 and SR-71 spy planes. A nice plus with the museum is that, despite being on a military installation, it's in an area where you don't have to go through the usual checkpoints for your driver's license and proof of car insurance.

## INFORMATION AND SERVICES

The centrally located **Downtown Macon Visitor Information Center** (450 Martin Luther King Jr. Blvd., 478/743-3401, www. maconga.org, Mon.-Sat. 9am-5pm, Sat. 10am-4pm) is in the offices of the local convention and visitors bureau and is a must-stop. For those who prefer a visitors center off the interstate highway, go to the I-75 **Southbound Rest Area** (478/994-8181, info kiosk Mon.-Fri. 9am-5pm), a mile south of exit 181.

## GETTING THERE AND AROUND

Macon is extraordinarily well served by the interstate highway system. I-75 passes through town north-south, and the western terminus of I-16 is here.

The small **Middle Georgia Regional Airport** (MCN, 1000 Terminal Dr., 478/788-3760, www.cityofmacon.net) hosts flights by Silver Airways to Atlanta and Orlando.

Macon is served by **Greyhound** (65 Spring St., 478/743-5411, www.greyhound.com). In town, the **Macon Transit Authority** (www. mta-mac.com, $1.25) runs buses and trolleys on various routes.

# Milledgeville

Milledgeville may not get as much attention as some other cities in Georgia, but it's worth a visit and is actually vital to the state's history. It served as state capital during the antebellum era—Atlanta didn't get that title until after the Civil War—and so boasts more than its share of intriguing political shenanigans. Milledgeville's eccentric combination of lively social gatherings and Southern Gothic darkness meant that it was the perfect breeding ground for writer Flannery O'Connor's brand of darkly humorous symbolic fiction.

## SIGHTS
### Old Governor's Mansion

One of the preeminent examples of Greek Revival architecture in the country, the **Old Governor's Mansion** (120 S. Clark St., 478/445-4545, www.gcsu.edu, Tues.-Sat. 10am-4pm, Sun. 2pm-4pm, $10 adults, $2 children) was built in Georgia's antebellum heyday in the late 1830s. It hosted 10 Georgia governors and their families, until Atlanta became the state capital in 1868. It also briefly hosted General Sherman, who made it his headquarters during a portion of his March to the Sea. Tours begin at the top of each hour, and self-guided tours are not possible. There's a cute gift shop in a well-restored outbuilding to the mansion's rear.

## Stetson-Sanford House

A great example of the local "Milledgeville federal" architectural style, the **Stetson-Sanford House** (601 W. Hancock St., 478/453-1803, www.oldcapitalmuseum.org, Thurs.-Sat., visit via Milledgeville Trolley Tours) was originally on North Wilkinson Street and hosted visiting dignitaries during Milledgeville's tenure as state capital. You can visit by taking a trolley tour; go to the Milledgeville Visitors Center (200 W. Hancock St.) to catch the trolley (Mon.-Fri. 10am, Sat. 2pm, $12 adults, $5 children).

## ★ Andalusia

On a 550-acre plot of wooded land north of the city center, **Andalusia** (U.S. 441, 4 miles northwest of Milledgeville, 478/454-4029, www.andalusiafarm.org, Mon.-Tues. and

Flannery O'Connor wrote her famous works at Andalusia.

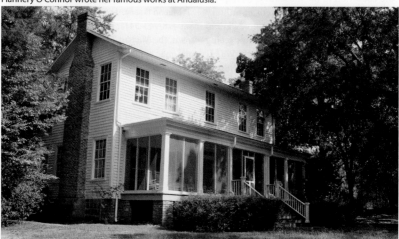

# Finding Flannery

Though born and raised in Savannah, Flannery O'Connor attended college in Milledgeville and did the bulk of her writing here. Her family had deep roots in the area and their imprint is felt all over town. Here are some related sites:

Her first home here is the **Cline-O'Connor-Florencourt House** (311 W. Greene St.), now a private residence, where she lived until her beloved father's early death from lupus (a hereditary disease that would later claim her life as well). As an aside, this handsome building briefly served as the governor's residence in the 1830s; indeed, it's a stone's throw from the grand Old Governor's Mansion.

Flannery and family faithfully attended **Sacred Heart Catholic Church** (110 N. Jefferson St.), which was actually built on land donated to the church by her great-grandmother. After her father died, Flannery became quite close with her mother, Regina Cline O'Connor, and the two often lunched at the tearoom and enjoyed peppermint chiffon pie in the **Stetson-Sanford House** (601 W. Hancock St., 478/453-1803, www.oldcapitalmuseum.org), now a house museum.

During World War II, Flannery attended Georgia State College for Women, now Georgia College & State University. Visit the **Flannery O'Connor Room** of the college museum to see vintage photos and personal items, including the manual typewriter on which those amazing novels and short stories were written.

The major stop is at **Andalusia** (U.S. 441, 4 miles northwest of Milledgeville, 478/454-4029, www.andalusiafarm.org, Mon.-Tues. and Thurs.-Sat. 10am-4pm, $5 donation), the ancestral Cline-O'Connor family dairy farm. After studying at the prestigious University of Iowa Writer's Workshop writing program and a brief stay at the Yaddo writer's retreat in New York, O'Connor was diagnosed, as she feared, with lupus. She returned to Milledgeville under the burden of the pessimistic prognosis to live out her days with her mother and write in the downstairs parlor, converted into a bedroom.

However, Flannery defied expectations and lived another 14 years at Andalusia before passing away at the age of 39. Visit her simple gravesite at **Memory Hill Cemetery** (Liberty St. and Franklin St., www.friendsofcems.org, daily 8am-5pm). Well-wishers often leave a single peacock feather at her tomb in memory of Flannery's well-known fondness for "the king of the birds."

Thurs.-Sat. 10am-4pm, $5 donation) is the name given to the dairy farm of the O'Connor family, where iconic Southern writer Flannery O'Connor lived most of her adult life. She wrote all her major works in a bedroom on the ground floor of the main house, actually a parlor converted so that the ailing Flannery, suffering from lupus, wouldn't have to climb the stairs (her crutches are right there by the bed).

Five rooms are open for viewing: Flannery's bedroom, the kitchen area, the dining room, a porch area with displays and a video, and an upstairs bedroom, plus there's a small reception area with a small but delightful selection of unique O'Connor-related items, some of them created by family members still in the area. Most of the furnishings are original, even the refrigerator.

The entrance to Andalusia isn't particularly obvious; heading north out of Milledgeville, pass the Wal-Mart on your left, then look for a Babcock furniture store on the right. The driveway entrance is directly across U.S. 441 on the left.

## Central State Hospital

Fans of poignant abandoned sites will find themselves drawn to the evocative decay of the sprawling 1,700-acre Central State Hospital, one of the oldest in the United States and at one time the biggest. However, while you can drive around the buildings, you may not trespass within. You'll have to content yourself with a visit to the **Central State Hospital Museum** (620 Broad St., 478/445-4878, www.centralstatehospital.org, by appointment, free) in the old 1891 depot on the hospital campus, which chronicles the history of this darkly fascinating institution.

In 1837 the state legislature authorized a "State Lunatic, Idiot, and Epileptic Asylum," which admitted its first patient in 1842. By the time it was renamed again in 1967 as Central State Hospital, it was the largest mental hospital in the country. Shock therapy was common, as was outright neglect and abuse.

Today, the bulk of the 150 years' worth of buildings, some of them oddly ornate, are vacant and unused, except for the tortured ghosts that many swear walk the halls and stairwells each night.

## Georgia College & State University Museums

Georgia's dedicated public liberal arts university, which has a variety of buildings all over downtown, offers a trio of small but solid museums, all free of charge. **Georgia College Museum** (221 N. Clark St., 478/445-4391, www.gcsu.edu, Mon.-Sat. 10am-4pm, free) is primarily known for its Flannery O'Connor Room, a repository of personal items specific to the Milledgeville-based author, including mementos from her time at the college. The highlight is the manual typewriter on which she typed most of her works. The **Natural History Museum and Planetarium** (Herty Hall, W. Montgomery St. and N. Wilkinson St., 478/445-2395, www.gscu.edu, Mon.-Fri. 8am-4pm, first Sat. of month 10am-4pm, free) features a region-leading collection of fossils and other paleontology-related artifacts as well as a state-of-the-art digital planetarium. The **Museum of Fine Arts** (102 S. Columbia St., 478/445-4572, www.gcsu.edu, by appointment, free) is housed in the beautiful restored 1935 Napier-Underwood House.

## FOOD AND ACCOMMODATIONS

The "satellite location"—if that phrase can be used for such an old-school institution—of the original location in Gray, ★ **Old Clinton BBQ** (2645 N. Columbia St., 478/454-0084, www.oldclintonbbq.com, Mon.-Thurs. 10am-8pm, Fri.-Sat. 10am-9pm, Sun. 10am-4pm, $5) is considered one of Georgia's top-tier barbecue spots. Their sauce, atypical for Georgia, is of the tangier North Carolina variety. A full platter with the works is under $7, and a no-frills pulled-pork sandwich less than $3.

The premier accommodations in Milledgeville are at the ★ **Antebellum Inn** (200 N. Columbia St., 478/453-3993, www.antebelluminn.com, rooms $110-150, cottage $170), which has five guest rooms in the Greek Revival main house plus an adorable pool cottage with a full-size pool, quite a rarity for B&Bs in these parts. Standard hotels in the area aren't very impressive, but you might try the **Holiday Inn Express** (1839 N. Columbia St., 877/859-5095, www.hiexpress.com, $80-110).

# NORTH OF MILLEDGEVILLE
## Eatonton

A short drive from Milledgeville in Putnam County is the small, neat town of Eatonton (http://eatonton.com), whose main claim to fame is as the birthplace of writers Joel Chandler Harris and Alice Walker. Don't be deceived by the moribund main drag of U.S. 441 through town; Eatonton has some magnificent antebellum architecture one block west, on Madison Avenue.

The **Uncle Remus Museum** (214 Oak St., 706/485-6856, www.uncleremusmuseum.org, Mon.-Sat. 10am-5pm, Sun. 2pm-5pm, free) is right on the main drag on the site of the original homestead of Joseph Sidney Turner, the "Little Boy" in the classic folk tales told by Uncle Remus and chronicled by Joel Chandler Harris. The small but charming museum is within a log cabin, which actually comprises three slave cabins moved from a nearby location and intended to simulate Remus's cabin.

There isn't a museum about Alice Walker, but Eatonton markets the **Alice Walker Driving Trail** that includes her girlhood church, Wards Chapel AME Church. Get

the Uncle Remus Museum in Eatonton

the tour brochure at the **Eatonton-Putnam Chamber of Commerce** (305 N. Madison Ave., 706/485-7701, Mon.-Fri. 9am-5pm).

## INFORMATION AND SERVICES

Pick up your brochures and tour info at the friendly **Milledgeville Visitors Center** (200 W. Hancock St., 478/452-4687, Mon.-Fri. 9am-5pm, Sat. 10am-4pm). While you're there, make sure you get the Milledgeville Historic Walking Tour brochure, a particularly well-done, user-friendly, and attractive little document. This is also where you can catch the **Guided Trolley Tour** (Mon.-Fri. 10am, Sat. 2pm, $12 adults, $5 children), including visits to the Old State Capitol and Lockerly Hall.

# FDR Country

As you'll quickly notice from all the things named after him here, this entire area reflects the enormous impact of President Franklin D. Roosevelt (FDR). As governor of New York, FDR began visiting the town now called Warm Springs, eventually building his picturesque Little White House here, today a state historic site and museum. The expansive FDR State Park near Pine Mountain isn't only a mecca for area hikers, it also commemorates the president's legacy of community building and conservation, with some particularly well-preserved Depression-era Civilian Conservation Corps-built structures enjoyed by visitors to this day.

## WARM SPRINGS

While Warm Springs owes its fame to FDR, the healing properties of its natural spring were well known to the indigenous Creek people. In the 18th and 19th centuries, the town, originally called Bullochville, was a familiar name to Southerners seeking relief from various ailments.

Franklin D. Roosevelt, at the time the governor of New York, began visiting the therapeutic springs in 1924, purchasing the historic Meriwether Inn and the 1,700 acres that the now-demolished building stood on. The 88°F water from sources deep within the surrounding hills (milder than the near-scalding water that some natural spas are known for) gave the town its more descriptive modern name. The gently warming, mineral-infused springs aided the management of Roosevelt's debilitation from polio.

## ★ FDR's Little White House

While Franklin D. Roosevelt began visiting Warm Springs in 1924, it wasn't until 1932—the year he was first elected president—that he had the charming six-room **Little White House** (401 Little White House Rd., 706/655-5870, www.gastateparks.org, daily 9am-4:45pm, $12 adults, $7 children) built from Georgia pine in a wooded area down the road from the town center. (The first building you'll see when walking toward the Little White House from the entrance building and museum is actually a servants quarters.)

While the president enjoyed all the amenities you'd expect, including a cook, a live-in secretary, servants, and constant U.S. Marine and Secret Service protection, the estate has a cozy and rustic feeling. Fascinating memorabilia are on hand, all arranged as they might have been during FDR's 16 visits here during his presidency.

While the Little White House itself is well worth seeing, the state of Georgia oversees the

extensive **FDR Memorial Museum** on-site, contiguous with the entrance building and gift shop. Here you'll learn not only about FDR's political career but about his life and times in Warm Springs and how that community shaped some of his domestic policies.

## Roosevelt Warm Springs Institute for Rehabilitation

Right around the corner from the Little White House on U.S. 27 is the **Roosevelt Warm Springs Institute for Rehabilitation** (6135 Roosevelt Hwy., 706/655-5670, www.roosevelttrehab.org, daily 9am-5pm, free), on the site of FDR's first land purchase in the Warm Springs area. It's a working hospital, not an attraction, but you can take a free self-guided tour of the grounds. Note the Roosevelt Warm Springs Institute is not the same as the FDR Historic Pools site. Both are on U.S. 27 and both have entrances on the same side of the road, which confuses a lot of visitors, but they are separate entities.

## FDR Historic Pools and Springs

Just down the road from the Roosevelt Warm Springs Institute are the **FDR Historic Pools and Springs** (U.S. 27, 706/655-5870, www.

FDR's Little White House

gastateparks.org, daily 9am-4:45pm, $10, includes admission to the Little White House). At this simple, lovingly curated site, you can walk around the famous pools (usually empty) in which the president enjoyed the healing spring waters from beneath the nearby hills.

The pools are used occasionally, specifically on Labor Day each year, when they are open to the public. You have to sign up in advance, though, and swim time is limited to 90 minutes per person.

If you visit the Little White House, admission to the historic pools is included. Note the historic pools are not on the campus of the Roosevelt Warm Springs Institute, which is just down the road. Though both sites use the same spring water, they are unaffiliated and have completely separate entrances.

### Food and Accommodations

The classic Warm Springs experience is a stay at the ★ **Warm Springs Hotel** (47 Broad St., 706/655-2114, www.hotelwarmspringsbb.org, $65-160) on the little main block. During the Roosevelt era, this circa-1907 inn hosted luminaries from all over the world who came to visit the president at the Little White House, including the king and queen of Spain. The guest rooms are cute and come in all sizes, hence the wide range of rates. The associated Tuscawilla Soda Shop downstairs is a great place for a cool drink or some tasty ice cream and fudge, in addition to being historic in its own right: FDR often snacked here.

For other dining, I strongly recommend heading north a few minutes to Pine Mountain, which offers a much better and wider variety of food options. However, if you simply must eat in Warm Springs, try **Mac's Barbecue** (5711 Spring St., 706/655-2472, daily 11am-8pm, $5), about one minute's walk from the Warm Springs Hotel.

# PINE MOUNTAIN

The thoroughly charming little burg of Pine Mountain, while owing much of its current success to the nearby Callaway Gardens attraction, is worthy of a visit in and of itself.

The main town area consists of a couple of well-restored blocks of shops and cafés, two very good barbecue spots, and the friendly little **visitors center** (101 Broad St., 706/663-4000, www.pinemountain.org, Mon.-Sat. 10am-5pm).

## Callaway Gardens

It's a bit hard to describe **Callaway Gardens** (17800 U.S. 27, 800/225-5292, www.callawaygardens.com, daily 9am-5pm, $20 adults, $10 children) to those who don't know anything about it. Part nature preserve, part kids' theme park, part retiree playground, and part recreational dream, its 13,000 acres encompass all those pursuits as gracefully as could reasonably be expected.

Most visits start with a walk through the $12 million **Virginia Hand Callaway Discovery Center,** which features info kiosks and an orientation video in the big theater. A particular highlight at Callaway is the **Cecil B. Day Butterfly Center,** one of the largest butterfly observatories in North America. This LEED-certified building hosts at least 1,000 butterflies at any given time. The **John A. Sibley Horticultural Center** is a five-acre designed landscape featuring a hybrid garden-greenhouse-indoor waterfall area. Other offerings include a regular birds-of-prey show, a zip line, a beach, stocked fishing lakes, a nearly 10-mile bike trail, and miles of themed nature and garden walking trails. The annual Christmas lights show is always a huge hit.

Callaway Gardens' famous **Mountain View Golf Course** has hosted PGA events in the past and is a consistently high-rated course at the national level. The older course, **Lake View,** is less challenging but more scenic and quietly enjoyable.

Callaway Gardens' well-stocked lakes are known far and wide among anglers. **Mountain Creek Lake** is particularly known for its bass fishing; you can rent a boat or even go on a guided fishing trip. **Robin Lake** at Callaway Gardens bills itself as the world's largest artificial white-sand beach, stretching for a mile around the huge lake.

## FDR State Park

It's fitting that **Franklin D. Roosevelt State Park** (2970 Hwy. 190, 706/663-4858, www.gastateparks.org, daily 7am-10pm, parking $5) would bear the president's name, since the circa-1935 park was one of the first built under the auspices of his now-legendary Civilian Conservation Corps (CCC). Of course, it had a head start; Roosevelt owned most of the land that the park now sits on.

Georgia's largest state park, the centerpiece is the 23-mile **Pine Mountain Trail.** The historic main building and ranger station offers numerous trail maps; you'll need one if you plan on doing any serious hiking. Pay a visit to **Dowdell's Knob,** the highest point in the park, where the president enjoyed picnics. Several of the cottages in the park are original CCC-era constructions. Take a dip in the historic **Liberty Bell Swimming Pool,** also a CCC project and a very enjoyable pool fed by natural springs.

## Food

I recommend dining in town rather than at the Callaway Gardens facilities if you can. If barbecue's your thing, head straight to ★ **The Whistlin' Pig Cafe** (572 S. Main Ave., 706/663-4647, Mon.-Sat. 10:30am-3pm, $7), a real local favorite that's also known far and wide for its pulled pork, absolutely out-of-this-world ribs, and excellent Brunswick stew. Don't confuse it with **Three Lil Pigs** (146 S. Main Ave., 706/307-7109, daily 11am-7pm, $7, cash only), which is not far away on the same side of the road and also has a local following. Stick with the pig that whistles.

If you must eat at Callaway Gardens, the best bet is the **Country Kitchen** (17800 U.S. 27, 800/225-5292, www.callawaygardens.com, Sun.-Thurs. 8am-8pm, Fri.-Sat. 8am-9pm, $12), inside the Country Store, with offerings a cut above the usual meat-and-three Southern fare at diners like this all over Georgia.

## Accommodations
### UNDER $150

A surprisingly good stay for a low rate can be found at the **Days Inn & Suites** (368 S. Main Ave., 706/663-2121, www.daysinn.com, under $100) in Pine Mountain near Callaway Gardens. A nice B&B experience is in the heart of Pine Mountain proper at the charming **Chipley Murrah House** (207 W. Harris St., 706/663-9801, www.chipleymurrah.com, $95-150), with four guest rooms in the main house and three cottages.

Franklin D. Roosevelt State Park is one of Georgia's oldest.

## $150-300

**Callaway Gardens** (17800 U.S. 27, 800/225-5292, www.callawaygardens.com) offers a variety of lodging, mostly geared for family getaways and often offering packages that include park admission. For larger families and groups, cottage and villa stays are available from about $300 per night. The 150-room ★ **Lodge at Callaway Gardens** (4500 Southern Pine Dr., 706/489-3300, www.callawaygardens.com, from $220), actually a Marriott property, is the choice for swank upscale lodging, complete with a large beautiful pool area and the on-site Spa Prunifolia. Packages that include park admission are available.

### CAMPING

If camping or cabin life is your thing, choose among the 22 cottages and 140 tent and RV campsites offered at historic **FDR State Park** (2970 Hwy. 190, 706/663-4858, www.gastateparks.org, parking $5, primitive campsites $9 pp, tent and RV sites $25, cottages $100-135,

5-night minimum). Many of the tent and RV sites are on scenic Lake Delanor, which also has canoe rental. There are 16 primitive campsites as well along the Pine Mountain Trail.

## INFORMATION AND SERVICES

The **Pine Mountain Visitors Center** (101 Broad St., 706/663-4000, www.pinemountain.org) provides a range of information for the entire area. The tiny **Warm Springs Welcome Center** (1 Broad St., 706/655-3322, hours vary) is in a restored train depot.

**Oconee Regional Medical Center** (821 N. Cobb St., Milledgeville, 478/454-3505, www.oconeeregional.com) provides a full range of emergency care.

## GETTING THERE AND AROUND

U.S. 27 is the main route into and out of Warm Springs. The Pine Mountain area and all other FDR-related sites are along Highway 190.

# Columbus

Unlike some of the more visually monotonous rural areas of Georgia, the state's western edge is scenically inviting and has a gently rolling landscape. Billing itself as the last city founded in the original 13 colonies and site of the last engagement of the Civil War, Columbus has retained a robust presence into the 21st century, due in no small part to its very close association with the massive U.S. Army installation at Fort Benning.

In recent years, downtown revitalization and the long, scenic Riverwalk on the Chattahoochee River have sparked visitor interest. To the world at large, however, Columbus is best known as the hometown of several key figures in Southern arts and commerce: author Carson McCullers *(The Heart Is a Lonely Hunter),* "Mother of the Blues" Ma Rainey, Coca-Cola inventor John Pemberton, and longtime Coca-Cola

president and philanthropist extraordinaire Robert Woodruff.

## SIGHTS
### National Civil War Naval Museum

It surprises many people to hear that the **National Civil War Naval Museum** (1002 Victory Dr., 706/327-9798, www.portcolumbus.org, Sun.-Mon. 12:30pm-4:30pm, Tues.-Sat. 10am-4:30pm, $7.50 adults, $6 children) is located far away from the nearest ocean, but any Civil War buff will tell you that naval warfare during that conflict was mostly of a riverine nature, not out on the deep blue sea. That said, all maritime phases of the war are well represented here, from coastal to blue water.

Both the Civil War Naval Museum and the National Infantry Museum at Fort Benning are located off Victory Parkway, a short drive

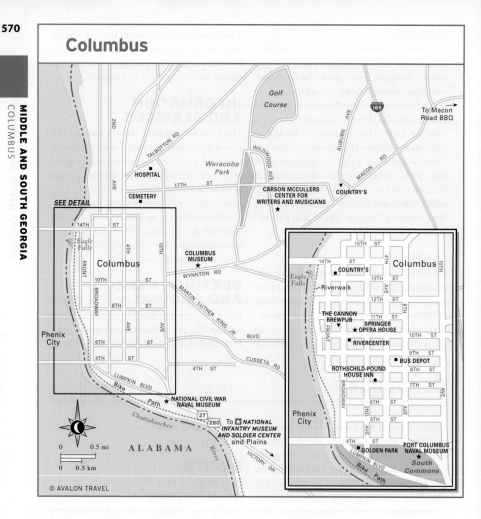

# Columbus

© AVALON TRAVEL

from each other, so one can easily make an afternoon of visiting the pair.

## ★ National Infantry Museum and Soldier Center

The **National Infantry Museum and Soldier Center** (1775 Legacy Way, 706/685-5800, www.nationalinfantrymuseum.org, Tues.-Sat. 9am-5pm, Sun. 11am-5pm, $5 donation) is a well-funded and well-designed extended love letter to the soldiers, paratroopers, and Rangers of the U.S. Army Infantry, a large portion of whom received their training at Fort Benning, where the museum resides.

The grand entrance, featuring a giant statue of a World War II-era squad leader exhorting his men to attack, sets the tone. From there you enter a series of stimulating multimedia vignettes highlighting notable small-unit infantry actions from the Revolutionary War through the Vietnam War. From there, the bulk of the museum comprises separate galleries, each dealing with a specific period of U.S. Army history. The galleries are well assembled and informative, featuring a range of uniforms, armaments, memorabilia, and instructional multimedia about individual campaigns and engagements through the present day. The Ranger Hall of Honor memorializes 200 individual U.S. Army Rangers of note.

An affiliated IMAX theater shows thematic movies in the IMAX format, in addition to special seasonal films. Check the website for showtimes and ticket prices.

## Uptown Columbus

Most cities would call this "downtown," but in Columbus it's Uptown (www.uptown-columbusga.com). It's a National Historic District and the center of Columbus social and nightlife. The bulk of the activity centers on Broadway, which has a grassy median with a fountain.

Just a couple of blocks off Broadway is the renowned **Springer Opera House** (103 10th St., 706/324-5714, www.springeroperahouse.org), a handsome, cast iron, balcony-bedecked late 19th-century venue of 700 seats that has hosted luminaries such as Oscar Wilde, Will Rogers, Tom Thumb, Franklin D. Roosevelt, and Garrison Keilor (see the "Walk of Stars" on the sidewalk in front of the building). Built in 1871, the Springer was declared the official state theater of Georgia in the 1970s by then-governor Jimmy Carter. It continues to host a regular schedule of performances by its in-house theater company.

## Columbus Museum

The **Columbus Museum** (1251 Wynnton Rd., 706/748-2562, www.columbusmuseum.com, Tues.-Wed. and Fri.-Sat. 10am-5pm, Thurs. 10am-8pm, Sun. 1pm-5pm, free) is among the best-curated museums I've seen in a medium-small city, with the not-trivial added benefit of having free admission every day. The space itself is bright, inviting, clean, and contemporary in feel, but without the sense of lonely emptiness that many such modern museums tend to evoke. The permanent collection boasts an excellent variety of stimulating American impressionists, and the 3rd floor hosts rotating exhibits of national and international value and interest. There's a standing exhibit on Columbus history as well, with a particular focus on the Native American presence.

## RECREATION

Most recreation in Columbus centers on the **Chattahoochee River.** The most obvious choice is a walk or ride along the **Chattahoochee River Trail,** which extends

the Springer Opera House

# Rebels at Sea

Though the Union blockaded the Southern coast almost immediately with war's outbreak, that didn't stop the Confederacy from embarking on a crash course to build its own navy. At its peak, the Confederate Navy counted only about 5,000 personnel—outnumbered literally 10 to 1 by the U.S. Navy in both vessels and sailors. However, what the rebels lacked in numbers they made up for in innovation and bravery.

Confederate subs made the first submarine attacks in history. The rebel raider CSS *Alabama* sank U.S. ships as far away as the coast of France. A particularly feared Southern innovation—as represented by the CSS *Virginia* or "Merrimac" in its epic fight with the USS *Monitor*—was the ironclad, a regular wooden warship stripped to its berth deck and topped with an impenetrable iron superstructure. By war's end a menagerie of bizarre-looking contraptions was the norm in both fleets. As awkward as some vessels were—many were simply too underpowered to drag around that extra metal—they were the forerunners of the sophisticated warships to come.

The best place to find out more is at the **National Civil War Naval Museum** (1002 Victory Dr., 706/327-9798, www.portcolumbus.org, Sun.-Mon. 12:30pm-4:30pm, Tues.-Sat. 10am-4:30pm, $7.50 adults, $6 children) in Columbus. You'll leave not only with a certain admiration for the ragtag but plucky Confederate Navy, but also with an appreciation of the profound paradigm shift in naval technology, which echoes in the present day.

roughly 15 miles from Uptown Columbus all the way to Fort Benning, concluding at Oxbow Meadows. The trail includes the Riverwalk section adjacent to the popular Uptown area of restaurants and nightlife.

By far the biggest news in Columbus outdoors life is **Whitewater Express** (1000 Bay Ave., 706/321-4720, www.columbusgawhitewater.com, daily 9am-6pm, raft trips $33-49), more popularly known as "River City Rush." Two antiquated earthen dams near the falls on the river have been demolished to reveal a magnificent 2.5-mile white-water run that goes from Class I all the way to Class IV. The city, which bills the white-water project as the longest urban white-water course in the world, hopes it will spur ecotourism development.

# FOOD

Every imaginable chain restaurant is available in the Columbus area. Otherwise, your best bet is to stick with pub food, which seems to set the standard here.

## American

Known for its lively bar scene, ★ **The Cannon Brewpub** (1041 Broadway, 706/653-2337, www.thecannonbrewpub.com,

Mon.-Thurs. 11am-10pm, Fri.-Sun. 11am-11pm, $15) is a linchpin of Uptown nightlife. All of the burgers are excellent, and you can get them with the Cannon's signature sweet potato "sunspots." Of course, you have your selection of handcrafted beers brewed on-site. Try the sampler flight of beers if you can't quite decide.

## Barbecue

There are two major purveyors of Columbus 'cue, and each has its fan base. The best-known and the one with the longest tradition is ★ **Country's** (3137 Mercury Dr., 706/563-7604, www.countrysbarbecue.com, Sun.-Thurs. 11am-10pm, Fri.-Sat. 11am-11pm, $8-12), which has a well-rounded menu featuring equally good pulled pork, grilled chicken, ribs, and brisket. Seasonal favorites are always welcomed by regular patrons. Tuesday night is all-you-can-eat barbecue chicken, and Friday and Saturday nights bring live bluegrass to the original location. There is also an Uptown location (1329 Broadway), a little closer to the action.

Some aficionados will tell you that the humble **Pepper's** (4620 Warm Springs Rd., 706/569-0051, Mon.-Tues. and Sat.

10:30am-2:30pm, Wed.-Fri. 10:30am-8pm, $7) is at least as good, with a leaner cut of meat, and offers a particularly tasty take on that Georgia side dish known as Brunswick stew.

## ACCOMMODATIONS

The vast military presence in Columbus means there is plenty of inexpensive lodging. While quality can vary, generally speaking you can book a brand-name hotel for well under what you'd pay in other markets.

### Under $150

The pet-friendly ★ **Staybridge Suites Columbus** (1678 Whittlesley Rd., 706/507-7700, www.sbscolumbus.com, $100) is close to I-185 and has a nice kitchen in each suite, and there is a hot breakfast each morning included in the rates. The **Hampton Inn Columbus** (7390 Bear Ln., 706/256-2222, www.hamptoninn.com, $100) is also off I-185 and is one of the least expensive Hampton Inns you'll find, with the guarantee of quality typical of the chain. There are no hidden charges here, and the Wi-Fi and parking really are included in the rates.

### $150-300

The ★ **Rothschild-Pound House Inn** (201 7th St., 706/322-4075, www.thepoundhouseinn.com, $185-365) is the premier B&B in Columbus, set in an ornately appointed Second Empire-style home. There are four sumptuous suites in the main house, with another six spread out in three cottages that are part of the whole enterprise.

## INFORMATION AND SERVICES

The spacious and well-done **Columbus Visitors Center** (900 Front Ave., 706/322-1613, www.visitcolumbusga.com, Mon.-Fri. 8:30am-5:30pm, Sat. 10am-2pm) is conveniently located. For emergencies go to **The Medical Center** of the Columbus Regional Healthcare System (710 Center St., 706/571-1000, www.columbusregional.com). The newspaper of record is the **Ledger-Enquirer** (www.ledger-enquirer.com).

## GETTING THERE AND AROUND

### Car

Columbus is on the Georgia-Alabama border, and several highways lead directly to and from both states over the Chattahoochee River. A major interstate highway doesn't pass through, but a spur of I-75 called I-185 takes you directly to Columbus. When driving in Columbus, keep in mind that Fort Benning in effect surrounds the city on the Georgia side. While highways going through that military facility are open to the public, traffic laws tend to be more strictly enforced.

### Air

**Columbus Metropolitan Airport** (CSG, 3250 W. Britt David Rd., 706/324-2449, www.flycolumbusga.com) has flights to Atlanta on Delta.

### Bus

Columbus is served by **Greyhound** (818 Veterans Pkwy., 706/322-7391, www.greyhound.com). There's a good public transportation service, **METRA** (www.columbusga.org, $1.30), with extensive routes throughout the city. It runs a charming trolley service through the Uptown-downtown-historic areas.

## OUTSIDE COLUMBUS

### Pasaquan

On the outskirts of Buena Vista about 20 miles outside Columbus is a unique place, the folk-art compound of **Pasaquan** (238 Eddie Martin Rd., 229/649-9444, www.pasaquan.blogspot.com, Apr.-Nov. first Sat. of the month 10am-4pm, $5). The sprawling collection of almost psychedelic pagoda-like temples, statues, and masonry walls, all of them brightly painted, is the product of the late visionary artist Eddie Owens Martin, known as "Saint EOM." Sadly, Martin committed suicide in 1986.

Note the very limited hours, although for a $100 donation you can make an appointment for a private visit. To get here from the Buena Vista town square, drive north 1.5 miles on Highway 41, then veer left onto Highway 137. Go about 4.5 miles and take a right on Eddie Martin Road. Pasaquan is 0.5 mile north.

# Jimmy Carter Country

With the notable exception of Providence Canyon, the deeply rural farm country around Americus isn't very scenically stimulating, but it contains some of the nation's most important and interesting history.

Many come just to see tiny Plains, population under 700, birthplace of the 39th U.S. president, Jimmy Carter. The former president and his wife, Rosalynn, still live on the main road in the only house they've ever owned, and Carter himself still teaches Sunday school (open to the public) many times a year at his church on the outskirts of town.

Every American should visit the National Prisoner of War Museum, at the site of the notorious Andersonville POW camp. The Civil War site is grimly fascinating, and the adjacent museum is deeply moving in its portrayal of the plight and ingenuity of U.S. prisoners of war throughout history.

## AMERICUS

Americus is the best base of operations from which to explore Carter Country, and this cute town perched on a little hill offers a few things of its own worth seeing as well. Because it's home to Georgia Southwestern University and is the international headquarters of Habitat for Humanity, Americus is a little more resistant to the ups and downs of the economy than many comparatively hard-hit rural towns.

### Habitat for Humanity Global Village and Discovery Center

Its administrative offices are in Atlanta, but the global operations center for Habitat for Humanity and the associated **Global Village and Discovery Center** (721 W. Church St., 229/410-7937, www.habitat.org, Mon.-Fri. 9am-5pm, Sat. 10am-2pm, $4 adults, $3 children) is in its hometown of Americus. The centerpiece of the experience is seeing replicas of typical third world housing, along with tours of 15 of the special low-cost sustainable buildings that Habitat for Humanity seeks to build in those areas, each design customized for the particular area's climate and terrain.

### Koinonia Farms

Before founding Habitat for Humanity, Millard and Linda Fuller met at **Koinonia Farms** (1324 Hwy. 49, 877/738-1741, www.koinoniapartners.org, Mon.-Sat. 9am-5pm, Sun. 1pm-5pm, free). This 70-year-old agricultural and ministerial institution was established by two couples, Clarence and Florence Jordan and Martin and Mabel England, specifically to embody what they saw as the ideals of early Christianity. By growing and providing food and spreading fellowship, they aimed to overcome the then-ingrained racism and economic disparity endemic to the South Georgia region and to be an example to other "intentional communities."

Today, visitors are always welcome at this working farm, especially at the weekday noon community lunches. The emphasis is on *working,* however, and Koinonia is mainly a place where people come to volunteer their labor on the farm or their trade skills, or even their musicianship, in exchange for a stay at the attached RV and lodging area, where people can stay for up to two weeks (longer during harvest time). Koinonia goods can be purchased on-site or at shops around the Americus and Plains area.

## Georgia Rural Telephone Museum

About 20 minutes south of Americus in a restored cotton warehouse in tiny Leslie is one of the quirkiest and most fun little museums around, the **Georgia Rural Telephone Museum** (135 N. Bailey Ave., 229/874-4786, www.grtm.org, Mon.-Fri. 9am-3:30pm, nominal fee). We're not just talking rotary phones here; we're talking the old-timey phone exchanges with live operators who manually connected your call.

## Food and Accommodations

Your best bet for lodging in Americus is the historic ★ **Windsor Hotel** (125 Lamar St., 229/924-1555, www.windsor-americus.com, $200), itself a landmark worth visiting. Now a Best Western property, it's a stirring image of Victoriana with its imposing turrets and broad balcony. Book in advance, as the Windsor often hosts dignitaries in the area to visit Carter and Habitat for Humanity.

Another recommended lodging option is the well-run, clean, and recently upgraded **Jameson Inn** (1605 E. Lamar St., 229/924-2726, www.jamesoninns.com, $100), several blocks away, which offers a free full breakfast.

The Windsor also happens to be your best bet for food and adult beverages in this corner of the Bible Belt. The Windsor has two excellent dining options: the sit-down, farm-to-table **Rosemary & Thyme** (125 Lamar St., 229/924-1555, www.windsor-americus.com, Mon.-Fri. 6:30am-9:30am and 5pm-9pm, Sat. 6:30am-10am and 5pm-9pm, Sun. 6:30am-10am, $20) and the upstairs ★ **Floyd's Pub** (125 Lamar St., 229/924-1555, www.windsor-americus.com, Mon.-Sat. from 5pm, $15), named after a longtime bellman. My favorite meal in Americus consists of sitting down at the bar at Floyd's and ordering the sublime gyro wrap; any of their sandwiches are excellent.

## PLAINS

Plains (www.plainsgeorgia.com) itself is little more than a single block of businesses and a few houses and churches. For most intents and purposes, the entire town is the Jimmy Carter National Historic Site and can be enjoyed within a single day. It's surrounded by intensively cultivated farmland, which includes the exceptionally well-interpreted Jimmy Carter Boyhood Farm. All the Carter-oriented sites are free of charge.

As you'd expect from the place where a peanut farmer became president, the big

Main Street, Plains

annual event is the **Plains Peanut Festival** (www.plainsgeorgia.com), happening each September, which almost always features appearances by the Jimmy and Rosalynn Carter.

## Jimmy Carter National Historic Site

Start your visit at the Victorian-era **Plains Depot Museum and Presidential Campaign Headquarters** (Main St., 229/824-4104, www.nps.gov, daily 9am-4:30pm, free) on Main Street next to the block of shops comprising Plains's "downtown." Not just the train depot and oldest building in the area, it was where Jimmy Carter symbolically based his presidential campaign and is a must-stop for any political junkie. The interior of the depot (warning: no air-conditioning) features much memorabilia about Carter's insurgent run in the post-Watergate years, shocking not only the Democratic Party establishment but the entire globe, which marveled at a peanut farmer becoming leader of the free world.

Technically, the **Plains High School Visitors Center and Museum** (300 N. Bond St., 229/824-4104, www.nps.gov, daily 9am-5pm, free), housed in the old Plains High School, is the premier Carter-oriented site in Plains, but for those expecting an in-depth interpretation of his legacy and influential post-presidential activity, it might be underwhelming (for that, go to the Carter Center in Atlanta). But certainly, it's neat to walk around in the same school where both the future president and his future wife, Rosalynn, attended classes, and the museum does a good job in explaining the social and political circumstances of the times in which Carter grew up and his motivations for running for office after a successful career in the U.S. Navy submarine service.

**Maranatha Baptist Church** (148 Hwy. 45 N., 229/824-7896, www.mbcplains.com) isn't nearly the largest church in Plains (that distinction goes to Plains Baptist, which Jimmy and Rosalynn left decades ago in protest of its now-repudiated policy of refusing

African American congregants). But it's where the Carters still attend church each Sunday. Dozens of times a year Carter himself gives an hour-long Sunday school lesson right before the regular 11am service. You can stay for the service or just attend the lesson; all you have to do is show up about 8am or 9am, get checked out quickly by the Secret Service, take a seat at a pew, listen to an orientation, and enjoy.

You won't be able to tour the **Carter Family Compound** on the town's main road, but you'll spot it instantly by the tall fence and the Secret Service checkpoint at the entrance. The simple 1961 ranch home is on 4.5 acres of land and is the only home Carter and his wife have ever owned. There's a video tour at the museum in the old Plains High School.

## ★ Jimmy Carter Boyhood Farm

It's not in Plains proper—it's actually in even smaller Archery—but the impeccably maintained **Jimmy Carter Boyhood Farm** (Old Plains Hwy., 229/824-4104, www.nps.gov, daily 10am-5pm, free) a few miles out of town, is a must-see, not only to get a better perspective on Carter's boyhood but for a charming and educational slice-of-life of rural and agricultural Americana gone by.

While the centerpiece is the well-restored one-story farmhouse where Earl and Lillian Carter raised the future president and his siblings during the Depression era, there's plenty more to see, including lovingly tended native-plant gardens, the old Carter general store, domestic animals, and the restored home of the Clarks, an African American family who were often employed by the Carters and who provided a window on the real need for social justice in the Jim Crow-era South.

The farm itself is expertly maintained by the National Park Service, but keep in mind that there's no air-conditioning on-site, just as when the Carters lived here. There are restrooms and a water fountain at the entrance by the parking lot, and a park ranger is always around if you have any questions. Stay

the restored home of the Carters at the Jimmy Carter Boyhood Farm

hydrated and use sunscreen. Walking tours of the farm are led on Saturday and Sunday at 11:30am and 3:30pm.

Get there by taking U.S. 280 west out of Plains for 0.5 mile, then bearing left on Old Plains Highway for 1.5 miles. The farm is on the right side of the road. The family burial ground in Lebanon Cemetery is along the same road; Carter's parents and brother and sister are interred here.

## SAM Shortline

The railroads are still very active in this part of Georgia, and the tracks through Plains host the tourist-oriented passenger shuttle **SAM Shortline** (877/427-2457, www.samshortline. com). These 1949 vintage cars are a fun way to get around from the Boyhood Farm with stops in Plains, Americus, and Leslie (site of the Georgia Rural Telephone Museum). Check the website for schedules and fares.

## ★ NATIONAL PRISONER OF WAR MUSEUM

First off, don't be confused: The **National Prisoner of War Museum** (760 POW Rd., 229/924-0343, www.nps.gov, museum daily 9am-5pm, grounds and cemetery daily

8am-5pm, free), about 12 miles north of Americus, is also where you'll find Camp Sumter, the infamous Civil War prison camp, now called Andersonville Prison, as well as Andersonville National Cemetery. The multiple nature of the site is deliberate and entirely appropriate.

The museum not only describes the history, atmosphere, and ensuing controversy of the Andersonville POW camp (called Camp Sumter at the time) through exhibits and an excellent short film, it also delves into the poignant human chronicle of American prisoners of war from all conflicts, from the Revolution to the world wars, the Korean War, the Vietnam War, and the Iraq War. Young children might find some of the exhibits disturbing, but I consider the museum a must-visit for any American high schooler or older.

Behind the air-conditioned and fully appointed museum is the entrance to the **Andersonville Prison,** formerly known as **Camp Sumter,** demarcated by a memorial wall and sculpture. You're greeted by an expanse of open space, split by a still-existing creek. At one point nearly 40,000 Union POWs were confined here, completely exposed to the elements, using the creek as both

the National Prisoner of War Museum

a toilet and for drinking water. The site was picked clean of artifacts decades ago, but the National Park Service has done a great job of maintaining replicas of the 18-foot stockade wall and associated "deadline," as well as facsimiles of the "she-bangs," or makeshift tents, of the otherwise sun-blasted prisoners. There are a series of ornate monuments erected by various Northern states to memorialize their citizens' sacrifices while in captivity.

You can drive a small loop road around the entire Andersonville camp, but unless the afternoon sun is just too intense, I recommend walking the site to get the full impact of what actually went on here 150 years ago. Adjacent to Camp Sumter is **Andersonville National Cemetery,** which contains graves of POWs and Civil War veterans and was established specifically to keep the lessons of Andersonville in public memory.

## Food

Really good food is hard to find in this area, but one notable exception is ★ **Yoder's Deitsch Haus** (5252 Hwy. 26, 478/472-2024, Tues. and Thurs.-Sat. 11:30am-2pm and 5pm-8:30pm, Wed. 11:30am-2pm, $8) near the otherwise bereft town of Montezuma a few miles from Andersonville. Yoder's menu— cooked and served by local Mennonites, part of a sizable contingent in the surrounding area—draws people from miles around. The delectable, hearty Southern-meets-German cuisine is served in a clean, open, community-style buffet atmosphere. Save room for the amazing pies and other desserts, which are signature items. The only drinks are iced tea, coffee, and water. Dress conservatively.

## POINTS WEST
### ★ Providence Canyon State Outdoor Recreation Area

While at first glance it looks like a cluster of little canyons parachuted in from out west, the truth about **Providence Canyon State Outdoor Recreation Area** (8930 Canyon Rd., 229/838-6870, www.gastateparks.org, mid-Sept.-mid-Apr. daily 7am-6pm, mid-Apr.-mid-Sept. daily 7am-9pm, $5, backcountry campsites $9), aka "Georgia's Grand Canyon," is a bit more complicated. Though it doesn't look that way when you wander among these steep white walls dotted with trees and patrolled overhead by circling hawks, the canyons are actually products of human activity. Poor farming practices in the early 1800s in

# Ambiguity and Andersonville

The very word *Andersonville* is synonymous with harsh cruelty to captives, one reason the National Prisoner of War Museum was established a stone's throw from the notorious Confederate camp. From February 1864 to May 1865, 45,000 Union prisoners lived on this bare 26-acre plot, with no roof or shelter of any kind to shield them from the blistering South Georgia sun, nor from the winter cold. Nearly 13,000 died.

Within Andersonville's 20-foot stockade walls was a grotesque city all its own, with its own rules and rulers. Food was thrown into the compound to be fought over, sold, and resold by prisoners. The only drinking water was a fetid creek running through the middle of the camp, with the downstream portion the camp's only latrine. The world's first war crimes trial came out of the Andersonville experience, as camp commandant Colonel Henry Wirz was hanged for his role after the war in a court-martial presided over by Union general Lew Wallace, who would later write *Ben-Hur*.

As horrible as Andersonville was, however, the only reason the camp existed at all was because of a decision by Union general Ulysses S. Grant to stop the practice of POW exchanges, previously the norm throughout the war. The concept was simple: Regular agreements were made to trade roughly equal numbers of prisoners, thus relieving the burden on both sides of feeding and caring for them. But the sudden halt in exchanges and the deterioration of Southern military and civilian standards meant that Confederates suddenly found themselves responsible for thousands of prisoners, but with dwindling supplies and people to devote to them. Colonel Wirz sent a petition north asking that POW exchanges be reinstated; it was denied. By late 1864 the Confederacy even offered to release all prisoners if the Union would provide transportation; it refused.

So, as awful as it was, Andersonville represented a deeply flawed and imperfect response to a nearly impossible situation, a situation mirrored by similarly horrific POW camps in the North such as Camp Elmira, New York. Southerners were far from immune to the degrading effect of the prisoners' plight. Many Andersonville prison guards themselves broke down under the strain and guilt.

this soft-soil area led to topsoil erosion followed by dramatic washouts, carving the deep gulches that now form a picturesque attraction.

There are plenty of opportunities to drive or walk around the rim and look down into the fingers of Providence Canyon, but the best way to enjoy the 16 separate canyons that form the park is to take the short, pleasant hike onto the canyon floor. (It's strictly forbidden to climb the fragile walls once you're down here.) You might consider joining the **Canyon Climbers Club** (www.gastateparks.org, $10), which coordinates activity in Providence Canyon and two other Georgia parks with similar topography, Tallulah Gorge and Cloudland Canyon. Backpackers can camp on the seven-mile backcountry trail.

There is a **visitors center** (Sept. 1-Nov. 30 and Mar. 1-May 31 Sat.-Sun. 8am-5pm) where you can find restrooms and park-related information.

## INFORMATION AND SERVICES

The **Plains Welcome Center** (1763 U.S. 280 W., 229/824-7477) is a short way outside the tiny town, and as of this writing was facing budget issues. The best bet for information in Plains is at the **Plains High School Visitors Center and Museum** (300 N. Bond St., 229/824-4104, www.nps.gov, daily 9am-5pm, free), also the main portal for exploring all Jimmy Carter-related sights.

If you pass through Americus, check out the **Americus Welcome Center** (123 W. Lamar St., 229/928-6059, www.visitamericusga.com) on the 1st floor of the town's municipal building.

## GETTING THERE AND AROUND

This part of South Georgia is very well served by roads and is fairly easy to get around by car. Americus, the best base of operations, is easily accessible from I-75 south of Atlanta. U.S. 280/27 heads due west out of Americus and takes you right through Plains, and on to Westville and Providence Canyon. To get to Andersonville, head north out of Americus on Highway 49.

A unique way to get around Carter County is by the **SAM Shortline** (877/427-2457, www.samshortline.com), a light passenger rail running a route from Plains to Cordele and points between. Check the website for frequently changing schedules and fares.

# Southwest Georgia

Agriculture is the name of the game down here in this sparsely populated area, with peanuts, pecans, and cotton, including the state's dedicated agricultural college. Though largely free of fighting during the Civil War, this is where the Confederacy ended for good with the capture of Confederate president Jefferson Davis. The city of Albany played a key role in national civil rights, chiefly with the groundbreaking Albany Movement, orchestrated in part by Martin Luther King Jr. The main natural attraction is the scenic and intriguing Flint River.

## ALBANY

South Georgia's largest city, Albany (www.visitalbanyga.com) owes its history to the scenic Flint River, one of the South's great waterways. The Flint's bounty sparked the city's founding as a trade center, named after the capital of New York State, in case anyone didn't get the hint. Although the former Food Network icon moved her operations to Savannah long ago, Paula Deen is actually an Albany native—and by the way, locals like Paula pronounce it "all-BEN-ee," not "ALL-buh-ny." It ain't in New York, y'all!

Learn about the area's human and natural history at the **Thronateeska Heritage Center** (100 W. Roosevelt Ave., 229/432-6955, www.heritagecenter.org, Thurs.-Sat. 10am-4pm, free), named for the ancient Native American word for the area. There's a Museum of History, a Science Discovery Center, and a good model train layout within its cavernous interior—the main building is the repurposed 1913 rail depot—but for many the highlight is the **Wetherbee**

## How Do You Say Pecan?

PEA-can or pe-CON? The debate continues in South Georgia, where the meadows are dotted with picturesque pecan orchards and roadside stands sell bushels of the freshly harvested nut each autumn. What's the right way to pronounce *pecan*? Old-timers insist it ain't French, and the emphasis should be on the first syllable: PEA-can. More recent arrivals—perhaps enamored of the nut's newly acquired foodie cachet as a key part of reinvented Southern cuisine—say it's the more refined pe-CON. The Georgia Department of Agriculture has actually come up with a Solomonic answer to the debate. The official pronunciation of *pecan* for state agricultural purposes is with the emphasis on the first syllable: PEA-can. However, the Agriculture Department also says the original pronunciation of the word, derived from an ancient Native American tongue, was almost certainly pe-CON. So you're not nuts. You can say it any way you like.

Planetarium (showtimes vary, $3) in the adjacent building, which holds various themed shows on the night sky.

Albany's chief claim to fame to the world at large is as the boyhood home of the great Ray Charles, one of the first performers to move traditional gospel into the realm of popular R&B. He is commemorated in the neat **Ray Charles Plaza** (Front St.) on the Flint Riverwalk. The elaborate memorial features Charles at a rotating baby grand piano. He "plays" music through a discreet sound system, and each evening there is a light and fountain show. The audience sits in the round on huge piano keys.

The centerpiece of a recent public-private effort to revitalize downtown Albany is the **Flint RiverQuarium** (117 Pine Ave., 229/639-2650, www.flintriverquarium.com, Tues.-Sat. 10am-5pm, Sun. 1pm-5pm, $9 adults, $6.50 children), a 175,000-gallon, 22-foot-deep aquarium on the river—one of the few such open-air facilities you'll find—exploring the area's interesting riverine ecosystem.

Albany's key role in the national struggle for civil rights is documented at the **Albany Civil Rights Institute** (326 Whitney Ave., 229/432-1698, www.albanycivilrightsinstitute.org, Tues.-Sat. 10am-4pm, $6 adults, $5 students), a new facility next to the historic 1906 Mt. Zion Baptist Church, where Martin Luther King Jr. made speeches during the push to integrate Albany public facilities in the early 1960s. The entire history of the Albany Movement is chronicled in fascinating detail. The second Saturday of the month you can hear a performance by the Freedom Singers, a group with roots going back to 1962.

The **Albany Museum of Art** (311 Meadowlark Dr., 229/439-8300, www.albanymuseum.com, Tues.-Sat. 10am-5pm, $4 adults, $2 children) has a solid collection of European and American art, but it's chiefly known for the Davis collection of sub-Saharan African art, one of the largest in the country. The museum hosts a performance series by the Albany Symphony Orchestra.

# WEST OF ALBANY
## Kolomoki Mounds Historic Park

One of the best-preserved pre-Columbian mound-builder sites in the United States, **Kolomoki Mounds Historic Park** (205 Indian Mounds Rd., 229/724-2150, www.gastateparks.org, daily 7am-10pm, parking $5, campsites $25-27) is also Georgia's oldest, its sprawling complex inhabited from AD 350 to 750, nearly 1,000 years older than the Etowah Mounds up in Cartersville.

You'll see the mounds on the drive in, but you'll first want to go to the end of the road to the visitors center, which incorporates a theater and boardwalk within a partially excavated mound, opened in the less enlightened era of the 1930s. The film explores the history of the site and the culture of the Woodland people who built it, part of a thriving network of similar compounds across the Southeast.

The real highlight is a trip up the stairs to the top of the enormous great temple mound, the tallest in Georgia at 57 feet. It feels much higher than that because of its dominant view overlooking a broad plain featuring two smaller burial mounds and several even smaller ceremonial mounds. Because this is a relatively isolated area, there are times you can have the entire top of the mound to yourself—quite a powerful experience.

Kolomoki offers 27 tent and RV sites. There are a couple of small lakes to boat and fish on, a boat ramp, and a swimming beach. Hikers will find a lake trail and a forest trail with a total of five miles of paths.

## Colquitt, "Mural City"

With not even 2,000 residents and tucked away deep into some of Georgia's most productive farmland, Colquitt (www.colquitt-georgia.com) wouldn't seem to merit much attention from visitors. But over the last decade the tiny town has been rejuvenated through cultural tourism.

The most obvious aspect is the nearly 20 large-scale murals throughout the downtown area, seemingly on every flat surface. Initiated with the Millennium Mural Project and representing various aspects of regional life and history, the murals are of extremely high artistic quality and are a photographer's dream.

The other component of Colquitt's vibrant cultural scene for its small size is *Swamp Gravy* (229/758-5450, www.swampgravy.com, $27), Georgia's "official folk-life play" performed at the historic **Cotton Hall** (158 E. Main St.), a renovated cotton warehouse turned into a 300-seat venue, which also hosts other productions throughout the year. *Swamp Gravy* is a humorous musical performed by a huge volunteer cast. A new edition premieres each October, portraying segments of local life, history, and culture, and is reprised each March.

# The Okefenokee Swamp

Scientists often refer to Okefenokee as an "analogue," an accurate representation of a totally different epoch in the earth's history. In this case it's the Carboniferous Period, about 350 million years ago, when the living plants were lush and green and the dead plants simmered in a slow-decaying peat that would one day end up as the oil that powers our civilization.

But for the casual visitor, Okefenokee might also be simply a wonderful place to get almost completely away from human influence and witness firsthand some of the country's most interesting wildlife in its natural habitat. Despite the enormous wildfires of the spring of 2007 and the summer of 2011—some of the largest the Southeast has seen in half a century, so large they were visible from space—the swamp has bounced back, for the most part, and is once again hosting visitors who wish to experience its timeless beauty.

## ★ OKEFENOKEE NATIONAL WILDLIFE REFUGE

It's nearly the size of Rhode Island and just a short drive off I-95, but the massive and endlessly fascinating **Okefenokee National Wildlife Refuge** (912/496-7836, www.fws.gov/okefenokee, Mar.-Oct. daily dawn-7:30pm, Nov.-Feb. daily dawn-5:30pm, $5 per vehicle) is one of the lesser-visited national public lands. Is it that very name "swamp" that keeps people away, with its connotations of fetid misery and lurking danger? Or simply its location, out of sight and out of mind in South Georgia?

In any case, while it long ago entered the collective subconscious as a metaphor for the most untamed, darkly dangerous aspects of the American South—as well as the place where Pogo the Possum lived—the Okefenokee remains one of the most intriguing natural areas on the planet.

The Okefenokee Swamp was created by an accident of geology. About 250,000 years ago, the Atlantic Ocean washed ashore about 70 miles farther inland from where it does today. Over time, a massive barrier island formed off this primeval Georgia coastline, running from what is now Jesup, Georgia, south to Starke, Florida. When the ocean level dropped during the Pleistocene Era, this sandy island became a topographical feature known today as the Trail Ridge, its height effectively creating a basin to its west. Approximately 90 percent of the Okefenokee's water comes from rainfall into that basin, which drains slowly via the Suwannee and St. Marys Rivers.

Native Americans used the swamp as a hunting ground and gave us its current name, which means "Land of the Trembling Earth," a reference to the floating peat islands, called "houses," that dominate the landscape.

It's a common mistake to call the Okefenokee "pristine," because like much of the heavily timbered and farmed southeastern coast, it is anything but. The swamp's ancient cypress stands and primordial longleaf

# The Okefenokee Swamp

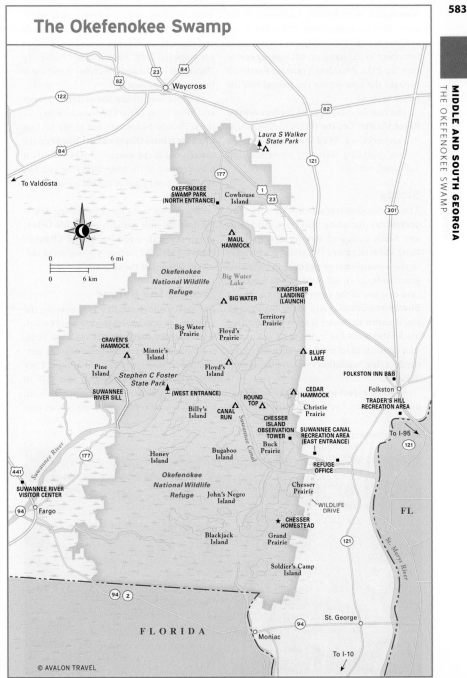

To Valdosta

0      6 mi

0      6 km

Waycross

Laura S Walker State Park

OKEFENOKEE SWAMP PARK (NORTH ENTRANCE)

Cowhouse Island

MAUL HAMMOCK

*Okefenokee National Wildlife Refuge*

Big Water Lake

BIG WATER

KINGFISHER LANDING (LAUNCH)

Territory Prairie

Big Water Prairie

Floyd's Prairie

CRAVEN'S HAMMOCK

Minnie's Island

Floyd's Island

BLUFF LAKE

Pine Island

Stephen C Foster State Park

FOLKSTON INN B&B

Folkston

SUWANNEE RIVER SILL

(WEST ENTRANCE)

CEDAR HAMMOCK

TRADER'S HILL RECREATION AREA

ROUND TOP

Christie Prairie

To I-95

Billy's Island

CANAL RUN

CHESSER ISLAND OBSERVATION TOWER

SUWANNEE CANAL RECREATION AREA (EAST ENTRANCE)

Honey Island

Bugaboo Island

Buck Prairie

REFUGE OFFICE

*Okefenokee National Wildlife Refuge*

John's Negro Island

Chesser Prairie

WILDLIFE DRIVE

FL

SUWANNEE RIVER VISITOR CENTER

CHESSER HOMESTEAD

Fargo

Blackjack Island

Grand Prairie

Soldier's Camp Island

*Suwannee River*

*St. Marys River*

**FLORIDA**

Moniac

St. George

To I-10

© AVALON TRAVEL

pine forests were heavily harvested in the early 20th century. About 200 miles of old railbed through the swamp remain as a silent testament to the scope of that logging operation. In 1937, President Franklin Roosevelt brought the area within the federal wildlife refuge system.

The state has also opened the **Suwannee River Visitor Center** (912/637-5274, www.gastateparks.org, Wed.-Sun. 9am-5pm), a "green" building featuring an orientation video and exhibits.

## Sights

The Okefenokee features a wide variety of ecosystems, including peat bogs, sand hills, and black gum and bay forests. Perhaps most surprising are the wide-open vistas of the swamp's many prairies or extended grasslands, 22 in all. And as you kayak or canoe on one of the water trails or on the old **Suwannee Canal** (a relic of the logging era), you'll notice the water is all very dark. This blackwater is not due to dirt or silt but to natural tannic acid released into the water from the decaying vegetation that gave the swamp its name.

As you'd expect in a national wildlife refuge, the Okefenokee hosts a huge variety of animal life—more than 400 species of vertebrates, including over 200 varieties of birds and more than 60 types of reptiles. Birders get a special treat in late November-early December when sandhill cranes come south to winter in the swamp.

A great way to see the sandhill cranes and other birds of the Okefenokee is to hike the 0.75-mile boardwalk out to the 50-foot **Chesser Island Observation Tower** on the eastern end of the swamp. This boardwalk is a by-product of the huge 2011 fire; you can see the charred piers of the old boardwalk as you stroll.

You can get to the tower by driving or biking the eight-mile round-trip **Wildlife Drive,** which also takes you by the old **Chesser Homestead,** the remnants of one of the oldest settlements in the swamp.

## Touring the Refuge

For most visitors, the best way to enjoy the Okefenokee is to book a guided tour through **Okefenokee Adventures** (866/843-7926, www.okefenokeeadventures.com), the designated concessionaire of the refuge. They offer a 90-minute guided boat tour ($18.50 adults, $11.25 children) that leaves each hour, and a 2.5-hour reservation-only sunset tour

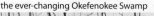

the ever-changing Okefenokee Swamp

($25 adults, $17 children) that takes you to see the gorgeous sunset over Chesser Prairie. Extended or custom tours, including multiday wilderness excursions, are also available. They also rent bikes, canoes, and camping gear, and even run a decent little café where you can either sit down and have a meal or take it to go out on the trail.

Privately owned canoes and boats with motors under 10 hp may put in with no launch fee, but you must sign in and out. No ATVs are allowed on the refuge, and bicycles are allowed only on designated bike trails. Keep in mind that some hunting goes on in the refuge at designated times. Pets must be leashed at all times.

## Camping

If fire and water levels permit, it's possible to stay the night in the swamp, canoeing to one of the primitive camping "islands" in the middle of the refuge. You need to make reservations up to two months in advance, however, by calling **U.S. Fish and Wildlife** (912/496-3331, Mon.-Fri. 7am-10am). A nonrefundable fee of $10 per person (which also covers your entrance fee) must be received 16 days before you arrive (mailing address: Okefenokee National Wildlife Refuge, Route 2, Box 3330, Folkston, GA 31537). Campfires are allowed only at Canal Run and Floyds Island. A camp stove is required for cooking at all other shelters. (Keep in mind that in times of extreme drought or fire threat, boat trips may not be allowed. Always check the website for the latest announcements.)

At **Stephen Foster State Park** (17515 Hwy. 177, 912/637-5274, fall-winter daily 7am-7pm, spring-summer daily 6:30am-8:30pm), aka the **West Entrance,** near Fargo, Georgia, there are 66 tent sites ($24) and nine cottages ($100). This part of the Okefenokee is widely considered the best way to get that "true swamp" experience.

## Transportation and Services

For anyone using this guide as a travel resource, the best way to access the Okefenokee—and the one I recommend—is the **East Entrance** (912/496-7836, www.fws.gov/okefenokee, Mar.-Oct. daily dawn-7:30pm, Nov.-Feb. daily dawn-5:30pm, $5 per vehicle), otherwise known as the **Suwannee Canal Recreation Area.** This is the main U.S. Fish and Wildlife Service entrance and the most convenient way to hike, rent boating and camping gear, and observe nature. The **Richard S. Bolt Visitor Center** (912/496-7836) has some cool nature exhibits and a surround-sound orientation video. Get to the East Entrance by taking I-95 exit 3 for Kingsland onto Highway 40 west. Go through Kingsland and into Folkston until Highway 40 dead-ends. Take a right, and then an immediate left onto Main Street. At the third light, make a left onto Okefenokee Drive (Hwy. 121) south.

Families with kids may want to hit the **North Entrance** at the privately run **Okefenokee Swamp Park** (U.S. 1, 912/283-0583, www.okeswamp.com, daily 9am-5:30pm, $12 adults, $11 ages 3-11) near Waycross, Georgia. (Fans of the old *Pogo* will recall Waycross from the comic strip, and yes, there's a real "Fort Mudge" nearby.) Here you will find a more touristy vibe, with a reconstructed pioneer village, a serpentarium, and animals in captivity. From here you can take various guided tours for an additional fee.

There's camping at the nearby but unaffiliated **Laura S. Walker State Park** (5653 Laura Walker Rd., 800/864-7275, www.gastateparks.org). Be aware the state park is not in the swamp and isn't very swampy, but it does have a nice man-made lake where you can rent canoes. Get to the North Entrance by taking I-95 exit 29 and going west on U.S. 82 about 45 miles to Highway 177 (Laura Walker Rd.). Go south through Laura S. Walker State Park; the Swamp Park is several miles farther.

If you really want that cypress-festooned, classic swamp look, take the long way around the Okefenokee to **Stephen Foster State Park** (17515 Hwy. 177, 912/637-5274, fall-winter daily 7am-7pm, spring-summer daily 6:30am-8:30pm), aka the **West Entrance,** near Fargo, Georgia. Guided tours are available. Get to Stephen Foster State Park by taking I-95 exit 3 and following the signs to Folkston. Get on Highway 121 south to St. George, and then go west on Highway 94.

# FOLKSTON

The chief attraction in Folkston and its main claim to fame is the viewing depot for the **Folkston Funnel** (912/496-2536, www.folkston.com), a veritable train-watcher's paradise. This is the spot where the big CSX double-track rail line—following the top of the ancient Trail Ridge—hosts 60 or more trains a day. They say 90 percent of all freight trains to and from Florida use this track.

Railroad buffs from all over the South congregate here, anticipating the next train by listening to their scanners. The first Saturday each April brings buffs together for the all-day Folkston RailWatch.

The old Atlantic Coast Line depot across the track from the viewing platform has been converted into the very interesting **Folkston Railroad Transportation Museum** (3795 Main St., 912/496-2536, www.charltoncountyga.us, Mon.-Fri. 9am-5pm, Sat. 10am-3pm,

free), with lots of history, maps, and technical stuff for the hard-core rail buff and novice alike.

## Food

To fuel up in Folkston for your trek in the swamp, go no further than the friendly ★ **Okefenokee Restaurant** (1507 Third St., 912/496-3263, daily 11am-8pm, $10-20), across from the handsome county courthouse. Their huge buffet is a steal at under $10; come on Friday nights for a massive seafood buffet (mostly fried) for under $20 per person. In any case don't miss the fried catfish, featured at both buffets. It's some of the best I've had anywhere in the South.

## Accommodations

For a bit of luxury in town, right outside the refuge's East Entrance is the excellent ★ **Inn at Folkston Bed and Breakfast** (509 W. Main St., 888/509-6246, www.innatfolkston.com, $120-170). There is nothing like coming back to its cozy Victorian charms after a long day out in the swamp. The four-room inn boasts an absolutely outstanding breakfast, an extensive reading library, and a whirlpool tub.

# Savannah

Look for ★ to find recommended sights, activities, dining, and lodging.

# Highlights

★ **River Street:** Despite River Street's tourist tackiness, there's nothing like strolling the cobblestones amid the old cotton warehouses, enjoying the cool breeze off the river, and watching the huge ships on their way to the bustling port (page 595).

★ **First African Baptist Church:** The oldest black congregation in the United States still meets in this historic sanctuary, a key stop on the Underground Railroad (page 597).

★ **Telfair Museums:** Old school meets new school in this museum complex that comprises the traditional **Telfair Academy of Arts and Sciences** (page 602) and the ultramodern **Jepson Center for the Arts** (page 602).

★ **Owens-Thomas House:** Savannah's single greatest historic home is one of the country's best examples of Regency architecture and a fine example of state-of-the-art historical preservation (page 603).

★ **Cathedral of St. John the Baptist:** This soaring Gothic Revival edifice is complemented by its ornate interior and its matchless location on verdant Lafayette Square, stomping

ground of the young Flannery O'Connor (page 606).

★ **Monterey Square:** Savannah's quintessential square has some of the best examples of local architecture and world-class ironwork all around its periphery (page 608).

★ **Forsyth Park:** This verdant expanse ringed by old live oaks is the true center of downtown life; it's Savannah's backyard (page 612).

★ **Bonaventure Cemetery:** This historic burial ground is the final resting place for some of Savannah's favorite citizens, including the great Johnny Mercer (page 615).

★ **Fort Pulaski National Monument:** This well-run site, built with the help of a young Robert E. Lee, is not only historically significant, its beautiful setting makes it a great place for the entire family (page 617).

★ **National Museum of the Mighty Eighth Air Force:** This museum tells the story of the U.S. Eighth Air Force, who executed American bombing missions over Nazi Germany, and includes restored WWII and Cold War-era aircraft (page 620).

**I**n an increasingly homogenized society, Savannah is one of the last places where eccentricity is celebrated and even encouraged. This outspoken, often stubborn determination to make one's own way in the world is personified by the

old Georgia joke about Savannah being the capital of "the state of Chatham," a reference to the county in which it resides. In typical contrarian fashion, Savannahians take this nickname as a compliment.

Savannah was built as a series of rectangular "wards," each constructed around a central square. As the city grew, each square took on its own characteristics, depending on who lived on the square and how they made their livelihood. Sounds simple—and it is. That's why its effectiveness has lasted so long.

It is this individuality that is so well documented in John Berendt's *Midnight in the Garden of Good and Evil*. The squares of Savannah's downtown—since 1965 a National Landmark Historic District—are also responsible for the city's walkability, another defining characteristic. Just as cars entering a square must yield to traffic already within,

pedestrians are obliged to slow down and interact with the surrounding environment, both constructed and natural. You become participant and audience simultaneously, a feat made easier by the local penchant for easy conversation.

This spirit of independence extends to Savannah's growing hipster culture, helped along by the steady expansion of the Savannah College of Art and Design (SCAD), which boasts much of downtown Savannah as its campus.

Savannah is also known for being able to show you a rowdy good time, and not only during its massive, world-famous St. Patrick's Day celebration. Savannahians will use any excuse for a party, exemplified by the city's very liberal open-container law—adults can walk with alcoholic beverages around downtown—which adds to the generally merry atmosphere.

---

**Previous:** the Cathedral of St. John the Baptist; Bonaventure Cemetery. **Above:** a cannon at Fort Pulaski National Monument.

# HISTORY

To understand the inferiority complex that Savannah occasionally feels with regards to Charleston, you have to remember that from day one Savannah was intended to play second fiddle to its older, richer neighbor to the north. By the early 1700s, the land south of Charleston had become a staging area for attacks on the settlement by the Spanish and Native Americans. So in 1732, King George II granted a charter to the Trustees of Georgia, a proprietary venture that was the brainchild of a 36-year-old general and member of parliament, General James Edward Oglethorpe. Though the mission was to found a colony to buffer Charleston from the Spanish, Oglethorpe had a far more sweeping vision in mind.

On February 12, 1733, the *Anne* landed with 114 passengers along the high bluff on the south bank of the Savannah River. Oglethorpe laid out his settlement in a deceptively simple plan that is still studied the world over as a model of nearly perfect urban design. He bonded with Tomochichi, the local Creek Indian chief, and the colony prospered. Ever the idealist, Oglethorpe had a plan for the new "classless society" in Savannah that prohibited slavery, rum, and—wait for it—lawyers! But as the settlers enviously eyed the dominance of Charleston's slave-based rice economy, the Trustees bowed to public pressure and relaxed restrictions on slavery and rum.

By 1753, the crown reclaimed the charter, making Georgia England's 13th American colony. Though part of the new United States in 1776, Savannah was captured by British forces in 1778, who held the city against a combined assault a year later. After the Revolution, Savannah became the first capital of Georgia, a role it had until 1786.

Despite hurricanes and yellow fever epidemics, Savannah's heyday was the antebellum period from 1800 to 1860, when for a time it outstripped Charleston as a center of commerce. Savannah's population boomed after an influx of European immigrants, chief among them Irish workers coming to lay track on the new Central of Georgia line.

Blockaded for most of the Civil War, Savannah didn't see much action other than the fall of Fort Pulaski in April 1862, when a Union force successfully laid siege using rifled artillery, a revolutionary technology that instantly rendered the world's masonry forts obsolete. War came to Savannah's doorstep when General William T. Sherman's March to the Sea concluded with his capture of the town in December 1864. On December 22, Sherman sent a now-legendary telegram to President Lincoln bearing these words: "I beg to present you as a Christmas gift, the City of Savannah with 150 heavy guns and plenty of ammunition and also about 25,000 bales of cotton."

After a lengthy Reconstruction period, Savannah began reaching out to the outside world. From 1908 to 1911 it was a national center of road racing. In the Roaring '20s, native son Johnny Mercer rose to prominence, and the great Flannery O'Connor was born in downtown Savannah. World War II provided an economic lift, but the city was still known as the "pretty woman with a dirty face," as Britain's Lady Astor famously described it in 1946.

Almost in answer to Astor's quip, city leaders in the 1950s began a misguided program to retrofit the city's infrastructure for the automobile era. Savannah's preservation movement had its seed in the fight by seven Savannah women to save the Davenport House and other buildings from demolition.

Savannah played a pioneering, though largely unsung, role in the civil rights movement. Ralph Mark Gilbert, pastor of the historic First African Baptist Church, launched one of the first black voter registration drives in the South. Gilbert's efforts were kept alive in the 1950s and 1960s by the beloved W. W. Law, a letter carrier who was head of the local chapter of the NAACP for many years.

The opening of the Savannah College of Art and Design in 1979 ushered another important chapter in Savannah's renaissance, which is ongoing to this day.

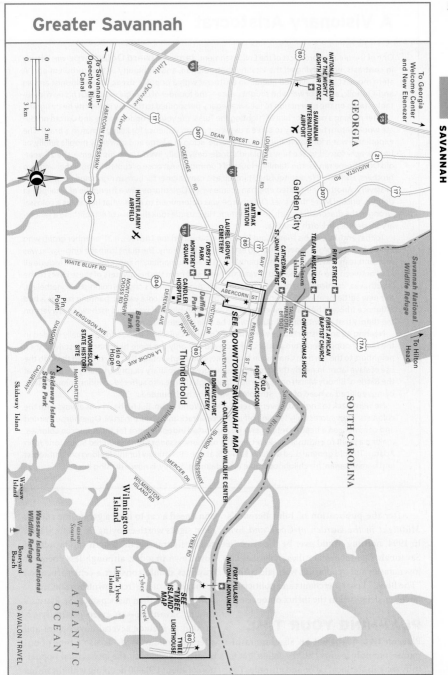

# Greater Savannah

To Georgia
Ogeechee Canal

To Savannah–
Ogeechee River
and New Ebenezer

NATIONAL MUSEUM
OF THE MIGHTY
EIGHTH AIR FORCE

GEORGIA

SAVANNAH
INTERNATIONAL
AIRPORT

DEAN FOREST RD

LOUISVILLE RD

AUGUSTA RD

Garden City

AMTRAK
STATION

HUNTER ARMY
AIRFIELD

LAUREL GROVE
CEMETERY

FORSYTH
PARK

MONTEREY
SQUARE

CANDLER
HOSPITAL

Daffin
Park

WHITE BLUFF RD

MONTGOMERY
CROSS RD

VICTORY DR

TRUMAN PKWY

BONAVENTURE RD

ST. JOHN THE BAPTIST

CATHEDRAL OF

BAY ST

ABERCORN ST

TELFAIR MUSEUMS

Hutchinson
Island

RIVER STREET

Savannah National
Wildlife Refuge

SOUTH CAROLINA

FIRST AFRICAN
BAPTIST CHURCH

OWENS-THOMAS HOUSE

TALMADGE
MEMORIAL
BRIDGE

To Hilton
Head

OLD
FORT JACKSON

SEE "DOWNTOWN SAVANNAH" MAP

Pin
Point

FERGUSON AVE

Bacon
Park

Isle of
Hope

WORMSLOE
STATE HISTORIC
SITE

Skidaway Island
State Park

Skidaway
Island

MCWHORTER

LA ROCHE AVE

Thunderbolt

BONAVENTURE
CEMETERY

OATLAND ISLAND WILDLIFE CENTER

Savannah River

MERCER DR

WILMINGTON
ISLAND RD

Wilmington
Island

Wassaw
Island

Wassaw
Sound

Wassaw Island National
Wildlife Refuge

Boneyard
Beach

ATLANTIC OCEAN

Little Tybee
Island

TYBEE RD

Tybee
Creek

FORT PULASKI
NATIONAL MONUMENT

SEE "TYBEE
ISLAND" MAP

TYBEE
LIGHTHOUSE

© AVALON TRAVEL

0
3 km

0
3 mi

ABERCORN EXPRESSWAY

Little Ogeechee River

Ogeechee River

Ogeechee RD

DERENNE AVE

DIAMOND CAUSEWAY

WILMINGTON ISLAND

PRESIDENT ST. EXT.

ISLANDS EXPRESSWAY

# A Visionary Aristocrat

One of the greatest products of the Enlightenment, **James Edward Oglethorpe** was a study in contrasts, embodying all the vitality, contradiction, and ambiguity of that turbulent age. A stern moralist yet an avowed liberal, an aristocrat with a populist streak, an abolitionist and an anti-Catholic, a man of war who sought peace—the founder of Georgia would put his own inimitable stamp on the new nation to follow, a legacy personified to this day in the city he designed.

After making a name for himself fighting the Turks, the young London native and Oxford graduate would return home only to serve a two-year prison sentence for killing a man in a brawl. The experience was a formative one for Oglethorpe, scion of a large and upwardly mobile family, as he was now forced to see how England's underbelly really lived. Upon his release, the 25-year-old Oglethorpe ran for the "family" House of Commons seat once occupied by his father and two brothers, and won. He distinguished himself as a campaigner for human rights and an opponent of slavery. Another jail-related epiphany came when Oglethorpe saw a friend die of smallpox in debtors prison. More than ever, Oglethorpe was determined to right what he saw as a colossal wrong in the draconian English justice system. His crusade took the form of establishing a sanctuary for debtors in North America.

To that end, he and his friend Lord Perceval established the Trustees, a 21-member group who lobbied King George for permission to establish such a colony. The grant from the king—who was more interested in containing the Spanish than in any humanitarian concerns—would include all land between the Altamaha and Savannah Rivers and from the headwaters of these rivers to the "south seas." Ironically, there were no debtors among Savannah's original colonists. Nonetheless, the new settlement was indeed a reflection of its founder's core values, banning rum as a bad influence (though beer and wine were allowed), prohibiting slavery, and eschewing lawyers on the theory that a gentleman should always be able to defend himself.

Nearing 40 and distracted by war with the Spanish, Oglethorpe's agenda gradually eroded in the face of opposition from settlers, who craved not only the more hedonistic lifestyle of their neighbors to the north in Charleston but the economic advantage that city enjoyed through the use of slave labor. In nearly the same hour as his greatest military victory, crushing the Spanish at the Battle of Bloody Marsh on St. Simons Island, Oglethorpe also suffered an ignominious defeat: being replaced as head of the 13th colony, which he had founded.

He went back to England, never to see the New World again. But his heart was always with the colonists. After successfully fending off a political attack and a court-martial, Oglethorpe married and commenced a healthy retirement. He supported independence for the American colonies, making a point to enthusiastically receive the new ambassador from the United States, one John Adams. The old general died on June 30, 1785, at age 88. Fittingly for this lifelong philanthropist and humanitarian, his childhood home in Godalming, Surrey, is now a nursing home.

After the publication of John Berendt's *Midnight in the Garden of Good and Evil* in 1994, nothing would ever be the same in Savannah. Old-money families cringed as idiosyncrasies and hypocrisies were laid bare in "The Book." Local merchants and politicians, however, delighted in the influx of tourists.

## PLANNING YOUR TIME

Plan on **two nights** at an absolute minimum—not only to enjoy all the sights, but to fully soak in the local color and attitude. You don't need a car to have a great time and see most sights worth enjoying. A strong walker can easily traverse the length and breadth of downtown in a day, although less energetic travelers should consider a central location or make use of the free downtown shuttle.

Much more than just a parade, St. Patrick's Day in Savannah—an event generally expanded to include several days before and after the holiday itself—is also a time of immense crowds, with the city's usual population of about 150,000 doubling with the influx of partying visitors. Be aware that lodging on and around March 17 fills up well in advance.

## ORIENTATION

The downtown area is bounded on the east by East Broad Street and on the west by Martin Luther King Jr. Boulevard (formerly West Broad St.). Technically, Gwinnett Street is the southern boundary of the National Historic Landmark District, though in practice locals extend the boundary several blocks southward.

# Sights

It's best to introduce yourself to the sights of Savannah by traveling from the river southward. It's no small task to navigate the nation's largest contiguous historic district, but when in doubt it's best to follow James Oglethorpe's original plan of using the five "monumental" squares on Bull Street (Johnson, Wright, Chippewa, Madison, and Monterey) as focal points.

TOP EXPERIENCE

## TOURS

Fair warning: Although local tour guides technically must pass a competency test demonstrating their knowledge of Savannah history, facts sometimes get thrown out the window in favor of whatever sounds good at the time. Keep in mind that not everything you hear from a tour guide may be true.

### Trolley Tours

The vehicles of choice for the bulk of the masses visiting Savannah, trolleys allow you to sit back and enjoy the views in reasonable comfort. As in other cities, the guides provide commentary while attempting, with various degrees of success, to navigate the cramped downtown traffic environment. The main trolley companies in town are **Old Savannah Tours** (912/234-8128, www.oldsavannah-tours.com, basic on-off tour $27 adults, $12 children), **Old Town Trolley Tours** (800/213-2474, www.trolleytours.com, basic on-off tour $27.99 adults, $10 children), and **Oglethorpe Trolley Tours** (912/233-8380, www.oglethorpetours.com, basic on-off tour $22.50 adults,

$10 children). All embark from the Savannah Visitors Center on Martin Luther King Jr. Boulevard about every 20-30 minutes on the same schedule, daily 9am-4:30pm.

Frankly there's not much difference between them, as they all offer a very similar range of services for similar prices, with most offering pickup at your downtown hotel. While the common "on-off privileges" allow trolley riders to disembark for a while and pick up another of the same company's trolleys at marked stops, be aware there's no guarantee the next trolley—or the one after that—will have enough room to take you on board.

### Horse and Carriage Tours

Ah, yes—what could be more romantic and more traditional than enjoying downtown Savannah the way it was originally intended to be traveled, by horse-drawn carriage? This is one of the most fun ways to see the city, for couples as well as for those with horse-enamored children. There are three main purveyors of equine tourism in town: **Carriage Tours of Savannah** (912/236-6756, www.carriagetoursofsavannah.com), **Historic Savannah Carriage Tours** (888/837-1011, www.savannahcarriage.com), and **Plantation Carriage Company** (912/201-0001, http://plantationcarriagecompany.com). The length of the basic tour and the price are about the same for all—45-60 minutes, about $25 adults and $15 children. All offer specialty tours as well, from ghost tours to evening romantic rides with champagne. Embarkation points vary;

check company websites for pickup points. Some will pick you up at your hotel.

## Specialty Tours

The premium tour option is **Old City Walks** (E. Jones Ln., 912/358-0700, www.oldcitywalks.com, $48), explorations of well-known and of little-known Savannah attractions, guided by longtime local expert Phil Sellers. These aren't budget tours, but they are the state of the art locally. There are several tours and many times; Sellers also offers privately scheduled tours.

Consistently one of the highest-quality tours in town, **Savannah Taste Experience** (meets on River Street outside the Bohemian Hotel, 912/221-4439, www.savannahtasteexperience.com, $49 adults, $37 children) takes you on several foodie stops to taste, sip, and learn about Savannah's culinary scene. The basic tour is "First Squares," which focuses on spots within easy walking distance of the waterfront.

Longtime tour guide and raconteur Greg Proffit and his staff offer fun walking "pub crawls" through **Savannah Tours by Foot** (527 E. Gordon St., 912/238-3843, www.savannahtours.com, $10-18 adults), wherein the point is to meet your guide at some local tavern, ramble around, learn a little bit, and imbibe a lot, though not necessarily in that order. The adult tour is the "Creepy Crawl" ($25), whereas the tour suitable for kids and Girl Scouts is the "Creepy Stroll" ($16 adults, $10 children). You may not want to believe everything you hear, but you're sure to have a lot of fun. The tours book up early, so make arrangements in advance.

Storyteller and author Ted Eldridge leads **A Walk Through Savannah Tours** (meeting point at various locations in the historic district, 912/921-4455, www.awalkthroughsavannah.bravehost.com, $15 adults, $5 ages 6-12, free under age 6) and offers all kinds of specialty walking tours, such as a garden tour, a ghost tour, a historic churches tour, and, of course, a *Midnight in the Garden of Good and Evil* tour.

To learn about Savannah's history of film-making and to enjoy the best of local cuisine, try a **Savannah Movie Tour** (meets at Savannah Visitors Center, 301 MLK Jr. Blvd., 912/234-3440, www.savannahmovietours.com, $25 adults, $15 children), which takes you to various film locations in town. The company also offers the Foody Tour ($48) featuring local eateries.

## Ghost Tours

The copious ghost tours can be fun for the casual visitor who wants entertainment rather than actual history. Students of the paranormal are likely to be disappointed by the cartoonish, Halloween aspect of some of the tours.

A standout in the ghost field is **Hearse Ghost Tours** (various pickup locations, 912/695-1578, www.hearseghosttours.com, $15), a unique company that also operates tours in New Orleans and St. Augustine, Florida. Up to eight guests at a time ride around in the open top of a converted hearse—painted all-black, of course—and get a 90-minute, suitably over-the-top narration from the driver-guide. It's still pretty cheesy, but a hip kind of cheesy.

For those who take their paranormal activity *very* seriously, there's Shannon Scott's **Sixth Sense Savannah Ghost Tour** (meets at Clary's Cafe, 404 Abercorn St., 866/666-3323, www.sixthsensesavannah.com, $20, midnight tour $38.50), an uncensored, straightforward look at Savannah's poltergeist population.

## Biking Tours

To see downtown Savannah by bicycle—quite a refreshing experience—try **Savannah Bike Tours** (41 Habersham St., 912/704-4043, www.savannahbiketours.com, $15 adults, $10 under age 12) for a two-hour trip through 19 squares and Forsyth Park with your "rolling concierge." Pedaling around the squares and stopping to explore certain sights is a unique pleasure. Tours leave daily at 9:30am,

12:30pm, and 4pm. Rent bikes from them or ride your own.

For a unique tour experience, take a seat on the **Savannah Slow Ride** (various meeting points, 912/414-5634, www.savannahslow-ride.com, $25), a sort of combination bar, bicycle, and carriage ride. You get on with a group and everyone helps pedal around the squares on about a two-hour ride at five miles per hour or less. You can even bring your to-go cup with you. Pickup points depend on the tour; call for details.

# WATERFRONT
## ★ River Street

It's much tamer than it was 30 years ago—when muscle cars cruised its cobblestones and a volatile mix of local teenagers, sailors on shore leave, and soldiers on liberty made things less than family-friendly after dark—but River Street still has more than enough edginess to keep things interesting. Families are safe and welcome here, but energetic pub crawling remains a favorite pastime for locals and visitors alike.

If you have a car, park it somewhere else and walk. The cobblestones—actually old ballast stones from some of the innumerable ships that docked here over the years—are tough on the suspension, and much of River Street is dedicated to pedestrian traffic anyway.

### THE WAVING GIRL

At the east end of River Street is the statue of Florence Martus, aka *The Waving Girl,* set in the emerald-green expanse of little Morrell Park. Beginning in 1887 at the age of 19, Martus—who actually lived several miles downriver on Elba Island—took to greeting every passing ship with a wave of a handkerchief by day and a lantern at night, without fail for the next 40 years. Ship captains returned the greeting with a salute of their own on the ship's whistle, and word spread all over the world of the beguiling woman who waited on the balcony of that lonely house. Martus became such an enduring symbol of the personality and spirit of Savannah that a U.S. Liberty ship was named for her in 1943.

### WORLD WAR II MEMORIAL

Near the foot of the Bohemian Hotel Savannah Riverfront on River Street is a 21st-century addition to Savannah's public monuments. Installed in 2010, the **World War II Memorial**—fairly modernist by local standards—features a copper-and-bronze globe torn in half to represent the European and Pacific theaters of the war. The more than 500 local people who gave their lives in that conflict are memorialized by name.

## Bay Street

Because so few downtown streets can accommodate 18-wheelers, Bay Street unfortunately has become the default route for industrial traffic in the area on its way to and from the industrial west side of town. In front of the Hyatt Regency Savannah is a concrete bench marking the spot on which Oglethorpe pitched his first tent.

Dominating Bay Street is **City Hall** (2 E. Bay St.), with its gold-leaf dome. The 1907 building was designed by acclaimed architect Hyman Witcover and erected on the site of Savannah's first town hall. Directly adjacent to City Hall on the east is a small canopy sheltering two cannons, which together compose the oldest monument in Savannah. These are the **Chatham Artillery Guns,** presented to the local militia group of the same name by President George Washington during his one and only visit to town in 1791.

Behind the Chatham Artillery Guns is the ornate **Savannah Cotton Exchange** (100 E. Bay St.), built in 1886 to facilitate the city's huge cotton export business. The fanciful lion figure in front—sometimes mistakenly referred to as a griffin—represents Mark the Evangelist. However, it isn't original—the first lion was destroyed in 2009 in a bizarre traffic accident.

# Downtown Savannah

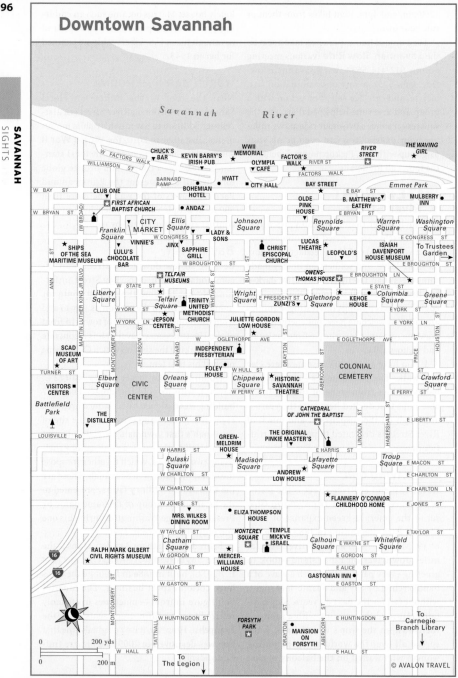

Savannah River

W. FACTORS WALK
WILLIAMSON ST
CHUCK'S BAR
KEVIN BARRY'S IRISH PUB
WWII MEMORIAL
FACTOR'S WALK
RIVER ST
RIVER STREET
THE WAVING GIRL
BARNARD RAMP
OLYMPIA CAFÉ
HYATT
E. FACTORS WALK

W BAY ST
CLUB ONE
BOHEMIAN HOTEL
CITY HALL
BAY STREET
E BAY ST
Emmet Park

FIRST AFRICAN BAPTIST CHURCH
ANDAZ
OLDE PINK HOUSE
B. MATTHEW'S EATERY
MULBERRY INN

W BRYAN ST
CITY MARKET
Ellis Square
E BRYAN ST

Franklin Square
VINNIE'S
W CONGRESS ST
LADY & SONS
Johnson Square
Reynolds Square
Warren Square
Washington Square

SHIPS OF THE SEA MARITIME MUSEUM
LULU'S CHOCOLATE BAR
JINX
SAPPHIRE GRILL
CHRIST EPISCOPAL CHURCH
LUCAS THEATRE
LEOPOLD'S
ISAIAH DAVENPORT HOUSE MUSEUM
To Trustees Garden

W BROUGHTON ST
E BROUGHTON ST

TELFAIR MUSEUMS
OWENS-THOMAS HOUSE
E BROUGHTON LN

W STATE ST
Wright Square
E STATE ST
Greene Square

Liberty Square
Telfair Square
TRINITY UNITED METHODIST CHURCH
E PRESIDENT ST
Oglethorpe Square
ZUNZI'S
KEHOE HOUSE
Columbia Square

W YORK ST
JEPSON CENTER
E YORK ST
E YORK LN

ANN ST
MARTIN LUTHER KING JR BLVD
JEFFERSON ST
BARNARD ST
WHITAKER ST
BULL ST
DRAYTON ST
ABERCORN ST
LINCOLN ST
HABERSHAM ST
PRICE ST
HOUSTON ST

W YORK LN

JULIETTE GORDON LOW HOUSE

W OGLETHORPE AVE
E OGLETHORPE AVE

SCAD MUSEUM OF ART
INDEPENDENT PRESBYTERIAN

TURNER ST
FOLEY HOUSE
W HULL ST
COLONIAL CEMETERY
E HULL ST

VISITORS CENTER
Elbert Square
Orleans Square
Chippewa Square
HISTORIC SAVANNAH THEATRE
Crawford Square

Battlefield Park
CIVIC CENTER
W PERRY ST
E PERRY ST

LOUISVILLE RD
THE DISTILLERY
W LIBERTY ST
CATHEDRAL OF JOHN THE BAPTIST
E LIBERTY ST

GREEN-MELDRIM HOUSE
THE ORIGINAL PINKIE MASTER'S

W HARRIS ST
E HARRIS ST

Pulaski Square
Madison Square
Lafayette Square
Troup Square
E MACON ST

W CHARLTON ST
ANDREW LOW HOUSE
E CHARLTON ST

W CHARLTON LN
E CHARLTON LN

W JONES ST
FLANNERY O'CONNOR CHILDHOOD HOME
E JONES ST

MRS. WILKES DINING ROOM
ELIZA THOMPSON HOUSE
E TAYLOR ST

W TAYLOR ST
MONTEREY SQUARE
TEMPLE MICKVE ISRAEL

Chatham Square
W GORDON ST
Calhoun Square
E WAYNE ST
Whitefield Square

RALPH MARK GILBERT CIVIL RIGHTS MUSEUM
MERCER-WILLIAMS HOUSE
E GORDON ST

W ALICE ST
E ALICE ST
GASTONIAN INN

W GASTON ST
E GASTON ST

TATTNALL ST
MONTGOMERY ST
DRAYTON ST
ABERCORN ST

W HUNTINGDON ST
E HUNTINGDON ST
To Carnegie Branch Library

FORSYTH PARK
MANSION ON FORSYTH

W HALL ST
E HALL ST

0    200 yds
0    200 m

To The Legion

© AVALON TRAVEL

the First African Baptist Church

Oscar-winning lyricist Johnny Mercer on the square's western edge.

## Franklin Square

Until recently, Franklin Square was, like Ellis Square, a victim of "progress," this time in the form of a highway going right through the middle of it. But as part of the city's effort to reclaim its history, Franklin Square was returned to its original state in the mid-1980s. The **Haitian Monument** in the center of the square commemorates the sacrifice and service of "Les Chasseurs Volontaires de Saint-Domingue," the 750 Haitian volunteers who fought for American independence and lost many of their number during the unsuccessful attempt to wrest Savannah back from the British in 1779.

## ★ FIRST AFRICAN BAPTIST CHURCH

The premier historical attraction on Franklin Square is the **First African Baptist Church** (23 Montgomery St., 912/233-2244, http://firstafricanbc.com, tours Tues.-Sat. 11am and 2pm, Sun. 1pm, $7 adults, $6 students/seniors), the oldest black congregation in North America, dating from 1777. The church also hosted the first African American Sunday school, begun in 1826. The church's founding pastor, George Liele, was the first black Baptist in Georgia and perhaps the first black missionary in the country. The present building dates from 1859 and was built almost entirely by members of the congregation themselves, some of whom redirected savings intended to purchase their freedom toward the building of the church. A key staging area for the Underground Railroad, First African Baptist still bears the scars of that turbulent time. In the floor of the fellowship hall—where many civil rights meetings were held, because it was safer for white citizens to go there instead of black activists going outside the church—you'll see breathing holes, drilled for use by escaped slaves hiding in a cramped crawlspace.

# CITY MARKET
## Ellis Square

Ellis Square's history as Savannah's main open-air marketplace goes back to 1755, when there was a single City Market building in the square itself. The fourth City Market was built in 1872, an ornate Romanesque affair with a 50-foot roofline. In 1954, the city decided to build a parking garage in the square. So the magnificent City Market building—and Ellis Square—simply ceased to exist.

Several large warehouses surrounding City Market survived. Now a hub of tourism, City Market encompasses working art studios, hip bars, cute cafés, live music in the east end of the courtyard, cutting-edge art galleries, gift shops, and restaurants.

The eyesore that was the Ellis Square parking garage is gone, and the square has been rebuilt as a pedestrian hangout, complete with a fountain, all atop a huge underground parking garage. Be sure to check out the smallish bronze of native Savannahian and

# In the Footsteps of Bartram

The West has its stirring tale of Lewis and Clark, but the Southeast has its own fascinating—if somewhat less dramatic—tale of discovery, in the odyssey of William Bartram. In March 1773, the 33-year-old Bartram—son of royal botanist John Bartram and definitely a chip off the old block—arrived in Savannah to begin what would become a four-year journey through eight colonies. As Lewis and Clark would do in the following century, Bartram not only exhaustively documented his encounters with nature and with Native Americans, he also made discoveries whose impact has stayed with us to this day.

William Bartram

Young "Willie," born near Philadelphia in 1739, had a talent for drawing and for plants. A failure at business, Bartram was happy to settle on a traveling lifestyle that mixed both his loves. After accompanying his father on several early trips, Bartram set out on his own at the request of an old friend of his father's in England, Dr. John Fothergill, who paid Bartram 50 pounds per year plus expenses to send back specimens and drawings.

Though Bartram's quest would eventually move farther inland and encompass much of the modern American South, most of its first year was spent in coastal Georgia. After arriving in Savannah he moved southward, roughly paralleling modern U.S. 17, to the now-dead town of Sunbury, through Midway, and on to Darien, where he stayed at the plantation of Lachlan McIntosh on the great Altamaha River, which inspired Bartram to pen some of his most beautiful writing. Bartram also journeyed to Sapelo Island, Brunswick, St. Marys, and even into the great Okefenokee Swamp. Using Savannah and Charleston as bases, Bartram mostly traveled alone, either by horse, by boat, or on foot. Word of his trip preceded him, and he was usually greeted warmly by local traders and Indian chiefs (except for one encounter with a hostile Native American near the St. Marys River). In many places, he was the first European seen since De Soto and the Spanish. His epic journey ended in late 1776, when Bartram gazed on his beloved Altamaha for the last time. Heading north and crossing the Savannah River south of Ebenezer, he proceeded to Charleston and from there to his hometown of Philadelphia—where he would remain for the rest of his days.

At its publication, his 1791 chronicle, *Travels Through North and South Carolina, Georgia, East and West Florida,* was hailed as "the most astounding verbal artifact of the early republic." In that unassuming yet timeless work, Bartram cemented his reputation as the country's first native-born naturalist and practically invented the modern travelogue. Thanks to the establishment of the William Bartram Trail in 1976, you can walk in his footsteps—or close to them, anyway, since historians are not sure of his route. The trail uses a rather liberal interpretation, including memorials, trails, and gardens, but many specific "heritage sites" in coastal Georgia have their own markers, as follows:

· River and Barnard Streets in Savannah to mark the beginning of Bartram's trek

· LeConte-Woodmanston Plantation in Liberty County (Barrington Ferry Rd. south of Sandy Run Rd. near Riceboro)

· 1.5 miles south of the South Newport River off U.S. 17

· St. Simon's Island on Frederica Road near the Fort Frederica entrance

· Off Highway 275 at Old Ebenezer Cemetery in Effingham County

Among the indigenous species Bartram was the first to record are the Fraser magnolia, gopher tortoise, Florida sandhill crane, flame azalea, and oakleaf hydrangea.

# HISTORIC DISTRICT NORTH

## Johnson Square

Due east of City Market, Johnson Square, Oglethorpe's very first square, is named for Robert Johnson, governor of South Carolina at the time of Georgia's founding. The roomy, shaded square, ringed with major bank branches and insurance firms, is dominated by the **Nathanael Greene Monument** in honor of George Washington's second-in-command, who was granted nearby Mulberry Grove plantation for his efforts. In typically maddening Savannah fashion, there is a separate square named for Greene, which has no monument to him at all.

## Reynolds Square

Walk directly east of Johnson Square to find yourself at Reynolds Square, named for John Reynolds, the first (and exceedingly unpopular) royal governor of Georgia. First called "Lower New Square," Reynolds Square originally served as site of the filature, or cocoon storage warehouse, during the fledgling colony's ill-fated flirtation with the silk industry (a federal building now occupies the site). As with Johnson Square, the monument in Reynolds Square has nothing to do with its namesake, but is instead a likeness of John Wesley dedicated in 1969 near the spot believed to have been his home.

### OLDE PINK HOUSE

A Reynolds Square landmark, the **Olde Pink House** (23 Abercorn St.) is not only one of Savannah's most romantic restaurants but quite a historic site as well. It's the oldest Savannah mansion from the 18th century still standing as well as the first place in Savannah where the Declaration of Independence was read aloud. The Georgian mansion was built in 1771 for rice planter James Habersham Jr., one of America's richest men at the time and a member of the notorious "Liberty Boys" who plotted revolution. The building's pink exterior was a matter of serendipity, resulting from its core

redbrick seeping through the formerly white stucco outer covering.

### LUCAS THEATRE FOR THE ARTS

Built in 1921 as part of Arthur Lucas's regional chain of movie houses, the **Lucas Theatre for the Arts** (32 Abercorn St., 912/525-5040, www.lucastheatre.com) also featured a stage for road shows. In 1976, the Lucas closed after a screening of *The Exorcist*. When the building faced demolition in 1986, a group of citizens created a nonprofit to save it. Despite numerous starts and stops, the 14-year campaign finally paid off in a grand reopening in 2000, an event helped immeasurably by timely donations from *Midnight* star Kevin Spacey and the cast and crew of the locally shot *Forrest Gump*. The theater's schedule stays pretty busy, so it should be easy to check out a show while you're in town.

### Columbia Square

Named for the mythical patroness of America, Columbia Square features at its center not an expected portrait of that female warrior figure but the original fountain from Noble Jones's Wormsloe Plantation, placed there in 1970.

### ISAIAH DAVENPORT HOUSE MUSEUM

Columbia Square is primarily known as the home of the **Isaiah Davenport House Museum** (324 E. State St., 912/236-8097, www.davenporthousemuseum.org, Mon.-Sat. 10am-4pm, Sun. 1pm-4pm, $9 adults, $5 children). The house museum is a delightful stop in and of itself because of its elegant simplicity, sweeping double staircase, and near-perfect representation of the Federalist style. But the Davenport House occupies an exalted place in Savannah history as well, because the fight to save it began the preservation movement in the city. In 1955 the Davenport House, then a tenement, was to be demolished for a parking lot. But Emma Adler and six other Savannah women, angered by the recent destruction of Ellis Square, refused to let it go down quietly. Together they formed the Historic Savannah Foundation in order to raise the $22,500 needed to purchase the Davenport House.

## Warren and Washington Squares

Warren Square and its neighbor Washington Square formed the first extension of Oglethorpe's original four squares, and they boast some of the oldest houses in the historic district. Both squares are lovely little garden spots, ideal for a picnic in the shade. Two houses near Washington Square were restored by the late Jim Williams of *Midnight* fame: the **Hampton Lillibridge House** (507 E. St. Julian St.), which once hosted an Episcopal exorcism, and the **Charles Oddingsells House** (510 E. St. Julian St.).

## Greene Square

Named for Revolutionary War hero Nathanael Greene, but bearing no monument to him whatsoever, Greene Square is of particular importance to local African American history. At the corner of Houston (pronounced "HOUSE-ton") and East State Streets is the 1810 **Cunningham House,** built for Henry Cunningham, former slave and founding pastor of the **Second African Baptist Church** (124 Houston St., 912/233-6163, www.secondafrican.org), on the west side of the square, in which General Sherman made his famous promise of "40 acres and a mule." In 1818, the residence at 542 East State Street was constructed for free blacks Charlotte and William Wall. The property at 513 East York Street was built for Catherine DeVeaux, part of a prominent African American family.

## Old Fort

One of the lesser-known aspects of Savannah history is this well-trod neighborhood at the east end of Bay Street, once the site of groundbreaking experiments and piratical intrigue, and then a diverse melting pot of Savannah citizenry.

## EMMET PARK

Just north of Reynolds Square on the north side of Bay Street you'll come to **Emmet Park** (E. Bay St. west of E. Broad St.), first a Native American burial ground and then known as "the Strand" or "Irish Green" because of its proximity to the Irish slums of the Old Fort. In 1902 the park was named for Robert Emmet, an Irish patriot of the early 1800s, who was executed by the British for treason. Within it is the eight-foot **Celtic Cross,** erected in 1983 and carved of Irish limestone. The Celtic Cross is at the center of a key ceremony for local Irish Catholics during the week prior to St. Patrick's Day.

## TRUSTEES' GARDEN

At the east end of Bay Street where it meets East Broad Street rises a bluff behind a masonry wall—at 40 feet off the river, still the highest point in Chatham County. This is **Trustees' Garden** (10 E. Broad St., 912/443-3277, http://trusteesgarden.com), the nation's first experimental garden. Trustees' Garden became the site of Fort Wayne, named after General "Mad Anthony" Wayne of Revolutionary War fame, who retired to a plantation near Savannah. The Fort Wayne area—still called the "Old Fort" neighborhood by old-timers—fell from grace and became associated with the "lowest elements" of Savannah society, which in the 19th and early 20th centuries were Irish and African Americans. It also became known for its illegal activity and as the haunt of sea salts such as the ones who frequented what is now the delightfully schlocky **Pirates' House** restaurant. That building began life in 1753 as a seamen's inn and was later chronicled by Robert Louis Stevenson in *Treasure Island* as a rogue's gallery of pirates and nautical ne'er-do-wells.

Find the **Herb House** on East Broad Street, the older-looking clapboard structure next to the Pirates' House entrance. You're looking at what is considered the single oldest building in Georgia and one of the oldest in the United States. Constructed in 1734, it was originally the home of Trustees' Garden's chief gardener.

# A Southern St. Paddy's Day

Savannah hosts the second-largest St. Patrick's Day celebration in the world, second only to New York City's. With its fine spring weather and walkability—not to mention its liberal rules allowing you to carry an adult beverage on the street—Savannah is tailor-made for a boisterous outdoor celebration.

Ironically, given St. Patrick's Day's current close association with the Catholic faith, the first parade in Savannah was organized by Irish Protestants. Thirteen members of the local Hibernian Society—the country's oldest Irish society—took part in a private procession to Independent Presbyterian Church in 1813. The first public procession was in 1824, when the Hibernians invited all local Irishmen to parade through the streets. The first recognizably modern parade, with bands and a "grand marshal," happened in 1870.

Organized by a "committee" of about 700 local Irish residents, today's three-hour procession includes marchers from all the local Irish organizations, in addition to marching bands and floats representing many local groups. The assembled clans wear kelly-green blazers, brandishing their walking canes and to-go cups, some pushing future committee members in strollers.

## Broughton Street

Downtown's main shopping district for most of the 20th century was Broughton Street. Postwar suburbs and white flight brought neglect to the area by the 1960s, and many thought Broughton was gone for good. But with the downtown renaissance brought about largely by the Savannah College of Art and Design (SCAD), Broughton was able not only to get back on its feet, but also to thrive as a commercial center once again.

### JEN LIBRARY

The Savannah College of Art and Design's **Jen Library** (201 E. Broughton St.) is a state-of-the-art facility set in the circa-1890 Levy and Maas Brothers department stores.

### TRUSTEES THEATER

Around the corner from the Lucas Theatre on Reynolds Square is the art moderne **Trustees Theater** (216 E. Broughton St., 912/525-5051, www.trusteestheater.com), a Savannah College of Art and Design (SCAD) operation that seats 1,200 and hosts concerts, film screenings, and the school's much-anticipated spring fashion show. It began life in the postwar boom of 1946 as the Weis Theatre, another one of those ornate Southern movie

houses that took full commercial advantage of being the only buildings at the time to have air-conditioning. But by the end of the 1970s it had followed the fate of Broughton Street, lying dormant and neglected until its purchase and renovation by SCAD in 1989.

## Wright Square

The big monument in Wright Square, Oglethorpe's second square, has nothing to do with James Wright, royal governor of Georgia before the Revolution, for whom it's named. Instead the monument honors William Gordon, former mayor and founder of the Central of Georgia Railway. But more importantly, Wright Square is the final resting place for the great Yamacraw chief Tomochichi, buried in 1737 in an elaborate state funeral at James Oglethorpe's insistence. A huge boulder of North Georgia granite honoring the chief was placed in a corner of the square in 1899. However, Tomochichi is not buried under the boulder but rather somewhere underneath the Gordon monument.

## Telfair Square

Telfair Square was named for Mary Telfair, last heir of a family that was one of the most important in Savannah history. Mary bequeathed the family mansion to the Georgia Historical Society upon her death in 1875 to serve as a museum. Originally called St. James Square after a similar square in London, Telfair was the last of Oglethorpe's original four squares.

Telfair Square hosts two of the three buildings operated by **Telfair Museums,** an umbrella organization that relies on a combination of private and public funding and has driven much of the arts agenda in Savannah for the last 125 years. The third building operated by Telfair Museums is the Owens-Thomas House on Oglethorpe Square.

Get a triple-site pass to the Jepson Center, the Telfair Academy, and the Owens-Thomas House for $20 per person.

## ★ JEPSON CENTER FOR THE ARTS

The proudest addition to the Telfair Museums group is the striking, 64,000-square-foot **Jepson Center for the Arts** (207 W. York Ln., 912/790-8800, www.telfair.org, Sun.-Mon. noon-5pm, Tues.-Sat. 10am-5pm, $12 adults, $5 students), whose ultramodern exterior sits catty-corner from the Telfair Academy of Arts and Sciences. Promoting a massive, daringly designed new facility

devoted to nothing but modern art was a hard sell in this traditional town, especially when renowned architect Moshe Safdie insisted on building a glassed-in flyover across a lane between two buildings. After a few delays in construction, the Jepson opened its doors in 2006 and has since wowed locals and visitors alike with its cutting-edge traveling exhibits and rotating assortment of late 20th-century and 21st-century modern art. If you get hungry, you can enjoy lunch in the expansive atrium café, and, of course, there's a nice gift shop.

Each late January-early February the Jepson Center hosts most events of the unique Pulse Art + Technology Festival, a celebration of the intersection of cutting-edge technology and performing and visual arts.

## ★ TELFAIR ACADEMY OF ARTS AND SCIENCES

The oldest public art museum in the South, the **Telfair Academy of Arts and Sciences** (121 Barnard St., 912/790-8800, www.telfair. org, Sun.-Mon. noon-5pm, Tues.-Sat. 10am-5pm, $12 adults, $5 students) was built in 1821 by the great William Jay for Alexander Telfair, scion of that famous Georgia family. The five statues in front are of Phidias, Raphael,

the Jepson Center for the Arts

Rubens, Michelangelo, and Rembrandt. As well as displaying Sylvia Judson Shaw's now-famous *Bird Girl* sculpture, which originally stood in Bonaventure Cemetery (actually the third of four casts by the sculptor), the Telfair Academy features an outstanding collection of primarily 18th- and 20th-century works, most notably the largest public collection of visual art by Khalil Gibran. Major paintings include works by Childe Hassam, Frederick Frieseke, Gari Melchers, and the massive *Black Prince of Crécy* by Julian Story.

## TRINITY UNITED METHODIST CHURCH

Directly between the Telfair and the Jepson stands **Trinity United Methodist Church** (225 W. President St., 912/233-4766, www.trinitychurch1848.org, sanctuary daily 9am-5pm, services Sun. 8:45am and 11am), Savannah's first Methodist church. Built in 1848 on the site of the Telfair family garden, its masonry walls are of famous "Savannah Gray" bricks—a lighter, more porous, and elegant variety—under stucco. Virgin longleaf pine was used for most of the interior, fully restored in 1969. Call ahead for a tour.

## Oglethorpe Square

Don't look for a monument to Georgia's founder in the square named for him. His monument is in Chippewa Square. Originally called "Upper New Square," Oglethorpe Square was created in 1742.

### JULIETTE GORDON LOW BIRTHPLACE

Around the corner from Wright Square at Oglethorpe and Bull is the **Juliette Gordon Low Birthplace** (10 E. Oglethorpe Ave., 912/233-4501, www.juliettegordonlowbirthplace.org, Mar.-Oct. Mon.-Sat. 10am-4pm, $15 adults, $12 children, $10 Girl Scouts), declared the city's very first National Historic Landmark in 1965, and fresh off a significant restoration effort. The founder of the Girl Scouts of the USA lived here from her birth in 1860 until her marriage. The house was

completed in 1821 for Mayor James Moore Wayne, future Supreme Court justice, but the current furnishings, many original, are intended to reflect the home during the 1880s.

Also called the Girl Scout National Center, the Low birthplace is probably Savannah's most festive historic site because of the heavy traffic of Girl Scout troops from across the United States. They flock here year-round to take part in programs and learn more about their organization's founder, whose family sold the house to the Girl Scouts in 1953. You don't have to be affiliated with the Girl Scouts to tour the home. Tours are given every 15 minutes, and tickets are available at the Oglethorpe Avenue entrance.

### ★ OWENS-THOMAS HOUSE

The square's main claim to fame, the **Owens-Thomas House** (124 Abercorn St., 912/233-9743, www.telfair.org, Sun.-Mon. noon-5pm, Tues.-Sat. 10am-5pm, last tour 4:30pm, $20 adults, $15 students, ticket includes Jepson Center and Telfair Academy), lies on the northeast corner. Widely known as the finest example of Regency architecture in the United States, the Owens-Thomas House was designed by brilliant young English architect William Jay. One of the first professionally trained architects in the United States, Jay was only 24 when he designed the home for cotton merchant or "factor" Richard Richardson, who lost the house in the depression of 1820 (all that remains of Richardson's tenure are three marble-top tables). The house's current name is derived from Savannah mayor George Owens, who bought the house in 1830.

Perhaps most interestingly, a complex plumbing system features rain-fed cisterns, flushing toilets, sinks, bathtubs, and a shower. When built, the Owens-Thomas House in fact had the first indoor plumbing in Savannah. On the south facade is a beautiful cast-iron veranda from which Revolutionary War hero Marquis de Lafayette addressed a crowd of starstruck Savannahians during his visit in 1825. The associated slave quarters are in a surprisingly intact state, including the original

# Scout's Honor

Known as "Daisy" to family and friends, **Juliette Magill Kinzie Gordon** was born to be a pioneer. Her father's family took part in the original settlement of Georgia, and her mother's kin were among the founders of Chicago. Mostly known as the founder of the **Girl Scouts of the USA,** Daisy was also an artist, adventurer, and healer. Born and raised in the house on Oglethorpe Avenue in Savannah known to Girl Scouts across the nation as simply "the Birthplace," she was an animal lover with an early penchant for theater, drawing, and poetry.

In 1911 while in England, Daisy met Robert Baden-Powell, founder of the Boy Scouts and Girl Guides in Britain. Struck by the simplicity and usefulness of his project, she carried the seeds of a similar idea back with her to the United States. "I've got something for the girls of Savannah, and all of America, and all the world, and we're going to start it tonight," were her famous words in a phone call to a cousin after meeting Baden-Powell. So on March 12, 1912, Daisy gathered 18 girls to register the first troop of American Girl Guides, later the Girl Scouts of the USA.

Juliette "Daisy" Gordon Low died of breast cancer in her bed in the Andrew Low House on January 17, 1927. She was buried in Laurel Grove Cemetery. Girl Scout troops from all over the United States visit her birthplace, the Andrew Low House, and her gravesite to this day, often leaving flowers and small personal objects near her tombstone as tokens of respect and gratitude.

"haint blue" paint. The carriage house, where all tours begin, is now the home's gift shop.

The Owens-Thomas House is owned and operated by the Telfair Museums. Get a combination pass to all Telfair sites—the Jepson Center for the Arts, the Telfair Academy of Arts and Sciences, and the Owens-Thomas House—for $20 per person.

## Martin Luther King Jr. Boulevard
### SHIPS OF THE SEA MARITIME MUSEUM

One of Savannah's more unique museums is the quirky **Ships of the Sea Maritime Museum** (41 MLK Jr. Blvd., 912/232-1511, http://shipsofthesea.org, Tues.-Sun. 10am-5pm, $9 adults, $7 students). The stunning Greek Revival building in which it resides is known as the Scarbrough House because it was initially built in 1819 by the great William Jay for local shipping merchant William Scarbrough, co-owner of the SS *Savannah*, the first steamship to cross the Atlantic. After the Scarbroughs sold the property, it became the West Broad School for African Americans from Reconstruction through integration.

Inside, children, maritime buffs, and crafts connoisseurs can find intricate and detailed scale models of various historic vessels, such as Oglethorpe's *Anne*, the SS *Savannah*, and the NS *Savannah*, the world's first nuclear-powered surface vessel. There's even a model of the *Titanic*.

# HISTORIC DISTRICT SOUTH
## Chippewa Square

Named for a battle in the War of 1812, Chippewa Square has a large monument not to the battle, natch, but to James Oglethorpe, clad in full soldier's regalia. Notice the general is still facing south, toward the Spanish.

Yes, the bench on the square's north side is in the same location as the one Tom Hanks occupied in *Forrest Gump*, but it's not the same bench that hosted the two-time Oscar winner's backside—that one was donated by Paramount Pictures to be displayed in the Savannah History Museum on MLK Jr. Boulevard.

### COLONIAL CEMETERY

Just north of Chippewa Square is Oglethorpe Avenue, originally called South Broad and the southern boundary of the original colony. At Oglethorpe and Abercorn Streets is **Colonial Cemetery** (Oglethorpe St. and Abercorn

St., www.savannahga.gov, daily 8am-dusk, free), first active in 1750. You'd be forgiven for assuming it's the "DAR" cemetery; the Daughters of the American Revolution contributed the ornate iron entranceway in 1913, thoughtfully dedicating it to themselves instead of the cemetery itself.

This is the final resting ground of many of Savannah's yellow fever victims. Famous people buried here include Button Gwinnett, one of Georgia's three signers of the Declaration of Independence. The man who reluctantly killed Gwinnett in a duel, General Lachlan McIntosh, is also buried here. The original burial vault of Nathanael Greene is in the cemetery, although the Revolutionary War hero's remains were moved to Johnson Square over a century ago.

### HISTORIC SAVANNAH THEATRE

At the square's northeast corner is the **Historic Savannah Theatre** (222 Bull St., 912/233-7764, www.savannahtheatre.com), which claims to be the oldest continuously operating theater in the United States. Designed by William Jay, it opened in 1818 with a production of *The Soldier's Daughter*. In the glory days of gaslight theater in the 1800s, some of the nation's best actors, including Edwin Booth, brother to Lincoln's assassin, regularly trod the boards of its stage. Due to a fire in 1948, little remains of Jay's original design except a small section of exterior wall. The building is currently home to a semiprofessional revue company specializing in oldies shows.

### INDEPENDENT PRESBYTERIAN CHURCH

Built in 1818, possibly by William Jay—scholars are unsure of the scope of his involvement—**Independent Presbyterian Church** (207 Bull St., 912/236-3346, www.ipcsav.org, services Sun. 11am, Wed. noon) is called the "mother of Georgia Presbyterianism." A fire destroyed most of Independent Presbyterian's original structure in 1889, but the subsequent rebuilding was a very faithful rendering of the original design, based on London's St. Martin-in-the-Fields. The church's steeple made a cameo appearance in *Forrest Gump* as a white feather floated by. In 1885 Woodrow Wilson married local parishioner Ellen Louise Axson in the manse to the rear of the church. Call ahead for a tour.

## Madison Square

Named for the nation's fourth president, Madison Square memorializes a local hero who gave his life for his city during the American Revolution. Irish immigrant Sergeant William Jasper, hero of the Battle of Fort Moultrie in Charleston three years earlier, was killed leading the American charge during the 1779 Siege of Savannah, when an allied army failed to retake the city from the British. The monument in the square honors Jasper, but he isn't buried here.

### GREEN-MELDRIM HOUSE

Given the house's beauty and history, visitors will be forgiven for not immediately realizing that the **Green-Meldrim House** (1 W. Macon St., 912/232-1251, www.stjohnssav.org, tours every 30 minutes Tues. and Thurs.-Fri. 10am-4pm, Sat. 10am-1pm, $8 adults, $5 students and children) is also the rectory of the adjacent St. John's Episcopal Church, which acquired it in 1892. This is the place where Sherman formulated his ill-fated "40 acres and a mule" Field Order No. 15, giving most of the Sea Islands of Georgia and South Carolina to freed blacks. A tasteful example of Gothic Revival architecture, this 1850 design by John Norris features a beautiful external gallery of filigree ironwork.

## Lafayette Square

One of Savannah's favorite squares, especially on St. Patrick's Day, verdant Lafayette Square boasts a number of important sights and attractions.

### ANDREW LOW HOUSE MUSEUM

A major landmark on Lafayette Square is the **Andrew Low House Museum** (329

Abercorn St., 912/233-6854, www.andrew-lowhouse.com, Mon.-Sat. 10am-4pm, Sun. noon-4pm, $10 adults, $8 children), once the home of Juliette "Daisy" Gordon Low, the founder of the Girl Scouts of the USA, who was married to cotton heir William "Billow" Low, Andrew Low's son. Despite their happy-go-lucky nicknames, the union of Daisy and Billow was a notably unhappy one. Still, divorce was out of the question, so the couple lived separate lives until William's death in 1905. The one good thing that came out of the marriage was the germ for the idea for the Girl Scouts, which Juliette got from England's "Girl Guides" while living there with her husband, Savannah being the couple's winter residence. Designed by the great New York architect John Norris, the Low House is a magnificent example of the Italianate style. Author William Makepeace Thackeray ate in the dining room, now sporting full French porcelain service, and slept in an upstairs room; he also wrote at the desk by the bed. Also on the 2nd floor you'll see the room where Robert E. Lee stayed during his visit and the bed where Juliette Gordon Low died.

## ★ CATHEDRAL OF ST. JOHN THE BAPTIST

Spiritual home to Savannah's Irish community and the oldest Catholic church in Georgia, the **Cathedral of St. John the Baptist** (222. E. Harris St., 912/233-4709, www.savannahcathedral.org, daily 9am-noon and 12:30pm-5pm, mass Sun. 8am, 10am, 11:30am, Mon.-Sat. noon, Latin mass Sun. 1pm) was initially known as Our Lady of Perpetual Help. It's the place to be for mass the morning of March 17 at 8am, as the clans gather in their green jackets and white dresses to take a sip of communion wine before moving on to harder stuff in honor of St. Patrick.

Despite its overt Celtic character today, the parish was originally founded by French émigrés from Haiti who arrived after the successful overthrow of the colonial government by a slave uprising on the island in the late 1700s. The first sanctuary on the site was built in 1873. In a distressingly common event back then in Savannah, fire swept through the edifice in 1898, leaving only two spires and the external walls. The cathedral was completely rebuilt within a year and a half. In the years since, many renovations have been

the Cathedral of St. John the Baptist

## The Story of "Jingle Bells"

Boston and Savannah vie over bragging rights as to where the classic Christmas song "Jingle Bells" was written. The song's composer, James L. Pierpont, led a life at times as carefree as the song itself. Born in Boston, Pierpont ventured from his wife and young children in 1849 to follow the gold rush to San Francisco. When his brother John was named minister of the new Unitarian congregation in Savannah in 1853, Pierpont followed him, becoming music director and organist, again leaving behind his wife and children in Boston. During this time Pierpont became a prolific composer of secular tunes, including polkas, ballads, and minstrel songs.

In August 1857, a Boston-based publisher, Oliver Ditson and Co., published Pierpont's song "One Horse Open Sleigh." Two years later it was rereleased with the current title, "Jingle Bells." At neither time, however, was the song a popular hit. It took action by his son Juriah in 1880 to renew the copyright to what would become one of the most famous songs of all time.

In Massachusetts, they swear Pierpont wrote the song while at the home of one Mrs. Otis Waterman. In Georgia, scholars assure us a homesick Pierpont wrote the tune during a winter at a house at Oglethorpe and Whitaker Streets, long since demolished. The Savannah contingent's ace in the hole is the fact that "Jingle Bells" was first performed in public at a Thanksgiving program at the local Unitarian Universalist Church in 1857. And despite persistent claims in Massachusetts that he wrote the song there in 1850, Southern scholars point out that Pierpont was actually in California in 1850.

undertaken. The most recent, from 1998 to 2000, involved the intricate removal, cleaning, and re-leading of more than 50 of the cathedral's stained-glass windows, a roof replacement, and an interior makeover.

### FLANNERY O'CONNOR CHILDHOOD HOME

On a corner of Lafayette Square stands the rather Spartan facade of the **Flannery O'Connor Childhood Home** (207 E. Charlton St., 912/233-6014, www.flanneryoconnorhome.org, Fri.-Wed. 1pm-4pm, $6 adults, $5 students, free under age 15). The Savannah-born novelist lived in this three-story townhome from her birth in 1925 until 1938 and attended church at the cathedral across the square. Once a fairly nondescript attraction for so favorite a native daughter, a recent round of renovations has returned the two main floors to the state Flannery would have known, including an extensive library.

### HAMILTON-TURNER INN

Across from the O'Connor house is the **Hamilton-Turner Inn** (330 Abercorn St., 912/233-1833, www.hamilton-turnerinn.

com). Now a privately owned bed-and-breakfast, this 1873 Second Empire mansion is best known for the showmanship of its over-the-top Victorian appointments and its role in *Midnight in the Garden of Good and Evil* as the home of Joe Odom's girlfriend, "Mandy Nichols" (real name Nancy Hillis). In 1883 it was reportedly the first house in Savannah to have electricity.

## Troup Square

Low-key Troup Square boasts the most modern-looking monument downtown, the **Armillary Sphere.** Essentially an elaborate sundial, the sphere is a series of astrologically themed rings with an arrow that marks the time by shadow. It is supported by six tortoises.

### BEACH INSTITUTE

Just east of Troup Square, near the intersection of Harris and Price Streets, is the **Beach Institute** (502 E. Harris St., 912/234-8000, Tues.-Sun. noon-5pm, $4). Built as a school by the Freedmen's Bureau soon after the Civil War, it was named after its prime benefactor, Alfred Beach, editor of *Scientific American*.

It served as an African American school through 1919. Restored by SCAD and given back to the city to serve as a museum, the Beach Institute houses the permanent Ulysses Davis collection and a rotating calendar of art events with a connection to black history.

## JONES STREET

There aren't a lot of individual attractions on Jones Street, the east-west avenue between Taylor and Charlton Streets just north of Monterey Square. Rather, it's the small-scale, throwback feel of the place and its tasteful, dignified homes, including the former home of **Joe Odom** (16 E. Jones St.), that are the attraction. The **Eliza Thompson House** (5 W. Jones St.), now a bed-and-breakfast, was the first home on Jones Street.

## UNITARIAN UNIVERSALIST CHURCH OF SAVANNAH

Troup Square is the home of the historic **Unitarian Universalist Church of Savannah** (313 E. Harris St., 912/234-0980, www.jinglebellschurch.org, service Sun. 11am). This original home of Savannah's Unitarians, who sold the church when the Civil War came, was recently reacquired by the congregation. It is where James L. Pierpont first performed his immortal tune "Jingle Bells." When he did so, however, the church was actually on Oglethorpe Square. The entire building was moved to Troup Square in the mid-1800s.

## ★ Monterey Square

Originally named "Monterrey Square" to commemorate the local Irish Jasper Greens' participation in a victorious Mexican-American War battle in 1846, the spelling morphed into its current version somewhere along the way. But Monterey Square remains one of the most visually beautiful and serene spots in all of Savannah. At the center of the square is a monument not to the victory for which it is named but to Count Casimir Pulaski, killed while attempting to retake the city from the British, and whose remains

Amazing ironwork surrounds Monterey Square.

supposedly lie under the 55-foot monument. Fans of ironwork will enjoy the ornate masterpieces in wrought iron featured at many houses on the periphery of the square.

## MERCER-WILLIAMS HOUSE MUSEUM

Many visitors come to see the **Mercer-Williams House Museum** (429 Bull St., 912/236-6352, www.mercerhouse.com, Mon.-Sat. 10:30am-4pm, Sun. noon-4pm, $12.50 adults, $8 students). While locals never begrudge the business Savannah has enjoyed since the publishing of "The Book," *Midnight in the Garden of Good and Evil,* it's a shame that this grand John Norris building is now primarily known as a crime scene involving late antiques dealer Jim Williams and his lover. Therefore it might come as no surprise that if you take a tour of the home, you might hear less about "The Book" than you may have expected. Now proudly owned by Jim Williams's sister Dorothy Kingery, an established academic in her own right, the Mercer-Williams House deliberately concentrates on the early

the Mercer-Williams House Museum

history of the home and Jim Williams's prodigious talent as a collector and conservator of fine art and antiques. That said, Dr. Kingery's mama didn't raise no fool, as we say down here. The house was known to generations of Savannahians as simply the Mercer House until *Midnight in the Garden of Good and Evil* took off, at which time the eponymous nod to the late Mr. Williams was added.

The house was built for General Hugh W. Mercer, Johnny Mercer's great-grandfather, in 1860. Just so you know, and despite what any tour guide might tell you, the great Johnny Mercer himself never lived in the house. Tours of the home's four main rooms begin in the carriage house to the rear of the mansion. They're worth it for art aficionados even though the upstairs, Dr. Kingery's residence, is off-limits. Be forewarned that if you're coming just to see things about the book or movie, you might be disappointed.

### TEMPLE MICKVE ISRAEL

Directly across Monterey Square from the Mercer House is Temple Mickve Israel (20 E. Gordon St., 912/233-1547, www.mickveisrael.org, Mon.-Fri. 10am-1pm and 2pm-4pm, closed Jewish holidays, $4 suggested donation), a notable structure for many reasons: It's Georgia's first synagogue; it's the only Gothic

synagogue in the country; and it's the third-oldest Jewish congregation in North America (following those in New York and Newport, Rhode Island). Notable congregants have included Dr. Samuel Nunes Ribeiro, who helped stop an epidemic in 1733, and his descendant

Temple Mickve Israel

Raphael Moses, considered the father of the peach industry in the Peach State.

Mickve Israel offers 30- to 45-minute tours of the sanctuary and museum. No reservations are necessary for tours.

## Calhoun Square

The last of the 24 squares in Savannah's original grid, Calhoun Square is also the only square with all its original buildings intact.

### MASSIE HERITAGE CENTER

Dominating the south side of Calhoun Square is Savannah's first public elementary school and the spiritual home of Savannah educators, the **Massie Heritage Center** (207 E. Gordon St., 912/201-5070, www.massieschool. com, Mon.-Sat. 10am-4pm, Sun. noon-4pm, $8 adults, $5 youth). In 1841, Peter Massie, a Scots planter with a populist streak, endowed the school to give poor children as good an education as the children of rich families (like Massie's own) received. After the Civil War, the "Massie School," as it's known locally, was designated as the area's African American public school. Classes ceased in 1974, and it now operates as a living-history museum, centering on the period-appointed one-room "heritage classroom" but with several other exhibit spaces of note.

A million-dollar renovation in 2012 added an interactive model of Oglethorpe's urban design and several interesting exhibits on aspects of Savannah architecture and history. In all, Massie provides possibly the best one-stop tour for an all-encompassing look at Savannah history and culture. You can either do a self-guided tour or take the very informative guided tour at 11am or 2pm for the same admission price.

### WESLEY MONUMENTAL
### UNITED METHODIST CHURCH

The **Wesley Monumental United Methodist Church** (429 Abercorn St., 912/232-0191, www.wesleymonumental. org, sanctuary daily 9am-5pm, services Sun. 8:45am and 11am), named not only for

movement founder John Wesley but also for his musical younger brother Charles, is home to Savannah's first Methodist parish. Built in 1875 on the model of Queen's Kirk in Amsterdam and the fourth incarnation of the parish home, this is another great example of Savannah's Gothic churches.

## Martin Luther King Jr. Boulevard
### BATTLEFIELD PARK

Right off MLK Jr. Boulevard is **Battlefield Park** (corner of MLK Jr. Blvd. and Louisville Rd., dawn-dusk, free), aka the Spring Hill Redoubt, a reconstruction of the British fortifications at the Siege of Savannah with an interpretive site. Note that the redoubt is not at the actual location of the original fort; that lies underneath the nearby Sons of the Revolution marker. Eight hundred granite markers signify the battle's casualties, most of whom were buried in mass graves soon afterward. Sadly, most of the remains of these brave men were simply bulldozed up and discarded without ceremony during later construction projects.

### GEORGIA STATE
### RAILROAD MUSEUM

The **Georgia State Railroad Museum** (601 W. Harris St., 912/651-6823, www. chsgeorgia.org, daily 9am-5pm, $10 adults, $6 students), aka "The Roundhouse," is an ongoing homage to the deep and strangely underreported influence of the railroad industry on Savannah. Constructed in 1830 for the brand-new Central of Georgia line, the Roundhouse's design was cutting-edge for the time, the first building to put all the railroad's key facilities in one place. Spared by Sherman, the site saw its heyday after the Civil War. The highlight of the Roundhouse is the thing in the middle that gave the structure its name, a huge central turntable for positioning rolling stock for repair and maintenance. Frequent demonstrations occur with an actual steam locomotive firing up and taking a spin on the turntable.

# Family Fun in Savannah

Savannah is more than historic mansions and to-go-cup pub crawls. There's plenty for tykes to see and do. Here are a few spots:

- **Ellis Square:** This square's modernist renovation includes a large wading fountain—a great spot to cool off when it gets hot.

- **Georgia State Railroad Museum:** Climb aboard these big machines, which feature frequent train rides along a short length of track complete with old-fashioned steam whistle. As a bonus, located within the Railroad Museum complex is the small but growing **Savannah Children's Museum.**

- **Jepson Center for the Arts:** In addition to being that rarity—a shiny new modernist building in this very historic old city—there is a neat children's section inside this arts center, the **Artzeum.**

- **Massie School Heritage Center:** This restored historic schoolhouse was the first school for emancipated African Americans in Savannah, and indeed was a public school in the 1970s. Not only is this a charming slice of nostalgia, but a recent upgrade and renovation also possibly makes it the single best stop for an all-around Savannah history lesson.

- **Oatland Island Educational Center:** To view wildlife up close and personal, head a few minutes east of town to this facility, which houses cougars and an entire wolf pack, in addition to many other animals along its winding marsh-side nature trail.

- **Fort Pulaski National Monument:** Kids can climb on the parapets, earthworks, and cannons, and burn off calories on the great nature trail nearby. Along the way they'll no doubt learn a few things as well.

## SAVANNAH CHILDREN'S MUSEUM

Next to the Railroad Museum is the **Savannah Children's Museum** (655 Louisville Rd., 912/651-6823, www.savannahchildrensmuseum.org, Tues.-Sat. 10am-4pm, Sun. 11am-4pm, $7.50), open since 2012. The children's museum is a work in progress that currently has an outdoor "Exploration Station" and a pending larger facility.

## RALPH MARK GILBERT CIVIL RIGHTS MUSEUM

One of the former black-owned bank buildings on MLK Jr. Boulevard is now home to the **Ralph Mark Gilbert Civil Rights Museum** (460 MLK Jr. Blvd., 912/231-8900, Tues.-Sat. 10am-4pm, $10). Named for a pastor of the First African Baptist Church and a key early civil rights organizer, the building was also the local NAACP headquarters for a time. Three floors of exhibits here include photos and interactive displays, the highlight for

historians being a fiber-optic map of nearly 100 significant civil rights sites.

## SAVANNAH HISTORY MUSEUM

The **Savannah History Museum** (303 MLK Jr. Blvd., 912/651-6825, www.chsgeorgia.org, daily 9am-5:30pm, $7 adults, $4 children) is the first stop for many a visitor to town because it's in the same restored Central of Georgia passenger shed as the visitors center. It contains many interesting exhibits on local history, concentrating mostly on colonial times. Toward the rear of the museum is a room for rotating exhibits, as well as one of Johnny Mercer's four Oscars, and, of course, the historic "Forrest Gump bench" that Tom Hanks sat on during his scenes in Chippewa Square.

## SCAD MUSEUM OF ART

In 2011, the **Savannah College of Art and Design Museum of Art** (601 Turner Blvd.,

912/525-5220, www.scadmoa.org, Tues.-Wed. and Fri.-Sat. 10am-5pm, Thurs. 10am-8pm, Sun. noon-5pm, $10 adults, $5 students) expanded this handsome building into an old railroad facility immediately behind it, more than doubling its exhibition space and adding the impressive Walter O. Evans Collection of African American Art. The SCAD Museum of Art now hosts a rotating series of exhibits, from standard painting to video installations, many of them commissioned by the school itself.

## VICTORIAN DISTRICT
### CARNEGIE BRANCH LIBRARY
The **Carnegie Branch Library** (537 E. Henry St., 912/652-3600, www.liveoakpl.org, Mon. 10am-8pm, Tues.-Thurs. 10am-6pm, Fri. 2pm-6pm, Sat. 10am-6pm) is the only example of prairie architecture in town, designed by Savannah architect Julian de Bruyn Kops and built, as the name implies, with funding from tycoon-philanthropist Andrew Carnegie in 1914. But more importantly, the Carnegie Library was for decades the only public library for African Americans in Savannah. One of its patrons was a young Clarence Thomas, who would of course grow up to be a U.S. Supreme Court justice.

★ **FORSYTH PARK**
A favorite with locals and visitors alike, the vast, lush expanse of **Forsyth Park** (bordered by Drayton St., Gaston St., Whitaker St., and Park Ave., 912/351-3850, daily 8am-dusk) is a center of local life, abuzz with activity and events year-round. The park owes its existence to William B. Hodgson, who donated its core 10 acres to the city for use as a park. Deeply influenced by the then-trendy design of green-space areas in France, Forsyth Park's landscape design by William Bischoff dates to 1851.

## SOFO DISTRICT
### LAUREL GROVE CEMETERY
Its natural vista isn't as alluring as Bonaventure Cemetery's, but **Laurel Grove Cemetery** (802 W. Anderson St. and 2101 Kollock St., daily 8am-5pm, free) boasts its own exquisitely carved memorials and a distinctly Victorian type of surreal beauty that not even Bonaventure can match. In keeping with the racial apartheid of Savannah's early days, there are actually two cemeteries: **Laurel Grove North** (802 W. Anderson St.) for whites, and **Laurel Grove South** (2101 Kollock St.) for blacks. Both are well worth visiting.

By far the most high-profile plot in the

Laurel Grove Cemetery

# A Walking Tour of Forsyth Park

As you approach the park, don't miss the ornate ironwork on the west side of Bull Street marking the **Armstrong House,** designed by Henrik Wallin. Featured in the 1962 film *Cape Fear* as well as 1997's *Midnight in the Garden of Good and Evil,* this Italianate mansion was once home to Armstrong Junior College before its move to the city's south side. Directly across Bull Street is another site of *Midnight* fame, the **Oglethorpe Club,** one of the many brick and terra-cotta designs by local architect Alfred Eichberg.

Forsyth Fountain

It's easy to miss, but as you enter the park's north side, you encounter the **Marine Memorial,** erected in 1947 to honor the 24 Chatham County Marines killed in World War II. Subsequently, the names of Marines killed in Korea and Vietnam were added. Look west at the corner of Whitaker and Gaston Streets; that's **Hodgson Hall,** home of the Georgia Historical Society. This 1876 building was commissioned by Margaret Telfair to honor her late husband, William Hodgson.

Looking east at the corner of Drayton and Gaston Streets, you'll see the old **Poor House and Hospital,** in use until 1854, when it was converted to serve as the headquarters for the Medical College of Georgia. During the Civil War, General Sherman used the hospital to treat Federal soldiers. From 1930 to 1980 the building was the site of Candler Hospital. Behind the old hospital's cast-iron fence is Savannah's most famous tree, the 300-year-old **Candler Oak.** During Sherman's occupation, wounded Confederate prisoners were treated within a barricade around the oak. The tree is in the National Register of Historic Trees and was the maiden preservation project of the Savannah Tree Foundation, which secured the country's first-ever conservation easement on a single tree.

Walking south into the park proper, you can't miss the world-famous **Forsyth Fountain,** an iconic Savannah sight. Cast in iron on a French model, the fountain was dedicated in 1858. Two other versions of this fountain exist—one in Poughkeepsie, New York, and the other in, of all places, the central plaza in Cusco, Peru.

Continuing south, you'll encounter two low buildings in the center of the park. The one on the east side is the so-called "Dummy Fort," circa 1909, formerly a training ground for local militia. Now it's the **Forsyth Park Café** (daily 7am-dusk). To the west is the charming **Fragrant Garden for the Blind.** One of those precious little Savannah gems that is too often overlooked, the Fragrant Garden was initially sponsored by the local Garden Club and based on others of its type throughout the United States.

The tall monument dominating Forsyth Park's central mall is the **Confederate Memorial.** Dedicated in 1875, it wasn't finished until several years later. A New York sculptor carved the Confederate soldier atop the monument.

My favorite Forsyth Park landmark is at the extreme southern end. It's the Memorial to Georgia Veterans of the Spanish-American War, more commonly known as *The Hiker* because of the subject's casual demeanor and confident stride. Savannah was a major staging area for the 1898 conflict, and many troops were bivouacked in the park. Sculpted in 1902 by Alice Ruggles Kitson, more than 50 replicas of *The Hiker* were made and put up all over the United States.

North Cemetery is that of Juliette Gordon Low, founder of the Girl Scouts of the USA. Other historically significant sites there include the graves of 8th Air Force founder Frank O. Hunter, Central of Georgia Railway founder William Gordon, and "Jingle Bells" composer James Pierpont.

Laurel Grove South features the graves of Savannah's early black Baptist ministers, such as Andrew Bryan and Andrew Cox Marshall. Some of the most evocative gravesites are those of African Americans who obtained their freedom and built prosperous lives for themselves and their families.

## SOUTHSIDE

### WORMSLOE STATE HISTORIC SITE

The one-of-a-kind **Wormsloe State Historic Site** (7601 Skidaway Rd., 912/353-3023, www.gastateparks.org/info/wormsloe, Tues.-Sun. 9am-5pm, $10 adults, $4.50 children) was first settled by Noble Jones, who landed with Oglethorpe on the *Anne* and fought beside him in the War of Jenkins' Ear. One of the great renaissance men of history, this soldier was also an accomplished carpenter, surveyor,

forester, botanist, and physician. The house, dating from 1828, and 65.5 acres of land are still owned by his family, and no, you can't visit them.

The stunning entrance canopy of 400 live oaks, Spanish moss dripping down the entire length, is one of those iconic images of Savannah that will stay with you forever. A small interpretive museum, a one-mile nature walk, and occasional living-history demonstrations make this a great site for the entire family. Walk all the way to the Jones Narrows to see the ruins of the site's original 1739 fortification, one of the oldest and finest examples of tabby construction in the United States.

### Pin Point

Off Whitefield Avenue (Diamond Causeway) on the route to Skidaway Island is tiny Pin Point, a predominantly African American township better known as the boyhood home of Supreme Court justice Clarence Thomas. Pin Point traces its roots to a community of former slaves on Ossabaw Island. Displaced by a hurricane, they settled at this idyllic site overlooking the Moon River, itself a former plantation.

## Pin Point on the Moon River

On Ossabaw Island, former slaves had settled into freedom as subsistence farmers after the Civil War. But when a massive hurricane devastated the island in 1893, many moved to the mainland, south of Savannah along what would later be known as Moon River, to a place called Pin Point. While many continued farming, plenty gained employment at local factories, where crabs and oysters were packed and sold. The largest and longest-lived of those factories was A. S. Varn & Son, which employed nearly 100 Pin Point residents—about half of the adult population.

Because so many local people worked at the same place, Pin Point developed a strong community bond, one that was instrumental in forging the life and career of future Supreme Court justice Clarence Thomas, who was born at Pin Point in 1948. Until he was seven, Thomas lived in a tiny house there with his parents, one without plumbing and insulated with newspapers. After a house fire, Thomas moved to Savannah with his grandparents.

While times have certainly changed here—paved roads finally came in the 1970s, and most of the old shotgun shacks have been replaced with mobile homes—Pin Point remains a small, close-knit community of about 300 people, with most property still owned by descendants of the freedmen who bought it after Reconstruction. The Varn factory remained the economic heart of Pin Point until it shut down in 1985. Today, the old factory forms the heart of an ambitious new project, the **Pin Point Heritage Museum** (www.pinpointheritagemuseum.com), which conveys the spirit and history of that community, including its most famous native son, through a series of exhibits and demonstrations.

## PIN POINT HERITAGE MUSEUM

Many Pin Point residents made their living by shucking oysters at the Varn Oyster Company, the central shed of which still remains and forms the basis of the **Pin Point Heritage Museum** (9924 Pin Point Ave., http://chsgeorgia.org/PHM, Thurs.-Sat. 9am-5pm, $8 adults, $4 children), opened in 2012. The museum tells the story of the Pin Point community through exhibits, a film, and demonstrations of some of the maritime activities at the Varn Oyster Company through the decades, such as crabbing, canning, shucking, and shrimp-net making.

## Skidaway Island

Skidaway Island is notable for two beautiful and educational nature-oriented sites.

### SKIDAWAY ISLAND STATE PARK

A site of interest to visitors is **Skidaway Island State Park** (52 Diamond Causeway, 912/598-2300, www.gastateparks.org/info/skidaway, daily 7am-10pm, parking $5). You can camp here ($25-28), but the awesome nature trails leading out to the marsh—featuring an ancient Native American shell midden and an old whiskey still—are worth a trip just on their own, especially when combined with the Marine Educational Center and Aquarium. To get here, take Victory Drive (U.S. 80) until you get to Waters Avenue and continue south as it turns into Whitefield Avenue and then the Diamond Causeway. The park is on your left after the drawbridge. An alternative route from downtown is to take the Truman Parkway all the way to its dead end at Whitefield Avenue; then take a left on Whitefield and continue as it turns into Diamond Causeway where it enters Skidaway.

### UNIVERSITY OF GEORGIA MARINE EDUCATIONAL CENTER AND AQUARIUM

The **University of Georgia Marine Educational Center and Aquarium** (30 Ocean Science Circle, 912/598-3474, www.marex.uga.edu, Mon.-Fri. 9am-4pm, Sat. 10am-5pm, $6 adults, $3 children, cash only) shares a picturesque 700-acre campus on the scenic Skidaway River with the research-oriented **Skidaway Institute of Oceanography,** also University of Georgia (UGA) affiliated. It hosts scientists and grad students from around the nation, often for trips on its research vessel, the RV *Sea Dawg.* The main attraction of the Marine Center is the small but well-done and recently upgraded aquarium featuring 14 tanks with 200 live animals.

## EASTSIDE

### ★ BONAVENTURE CEMETERY

On the banks of the Wilmington River just east of town lies one of Savannah's most distinctive sights, **Bonaventure Cemetery** (330 Bonaventure Rd., 912/651-6843, daily 8am-5pm, free). While its pedigree as Savannah's premier public cemetery goes back 100 years, it was used as a burial ground as early as 1794. In the years since, this achingly poignant vista of live oaks and azaleas has been the final resting place of such local and national luminaries as Johnny Mercer, Conrad Aiken, and, of course, the Trosdal plot, former home of the famous *Bird Girl* statue (the original is now in the Telfair Academy of Arts and Sciences). Fittingly, the late, great Jack Leigh, who took the *Bird Girl* photo for the cover of *Midnight in the Garden of Good and Evil,* is interred here as well.

If you're doing a self-guided tour, go by the small visitors center at the entrance and pick up one of the free guides to the cemetery, assembled by the Bonaventure Historical Society. By all means, do the tourist thing and pay your respects at Johnny Mercer's final resting place, and go visit beautiful little "Gracie" in Section E, Lot 99.

### OATLAND ISLAND WILDLIFE CENTER

The closest thing to a zoo in Savannah is the vast, multipurpose **Oatland Island Wildlife Center** (711 Sandtown Rd., 912/898-3980,

# Johnny Mercer's Black Magic

The great Johnny Mercer is not only without a doubt Savannah's most noteworthy progeny, he is also one of the greatest lyricists music has ever known. Born in 1909, he grew up in southside Savannah on a small river then called the Back River but since renamed Moon River in honor of his best-known song.

Armed with an innate talent for rhythm and a curious ear for dialogue—both qualities honed by his frequent boyhood contact with Savannah African American culture and musicians during the Jazz Age—Mercer wrote what is arguably his greatest song, "Moon River," in 1961. The song, debuted by Audrey Hepburn in the film *Breakfast at Tiffany's*, won an Academy Award for Best Original Song. In addition to "Moon River," Mercer won three other Oscars, for "On the Atchison, Topeka and the Santa Fe" (1946), "In the Cool, Cool, Cool of the Evening" (1951), and "Days of Wine and Roses" (1962).

Today you can pay your respects to Mercer in three places: his boyhood home (509 E. Gwinnett St., look for the historical marker in front of this private residence); the bronze sculpture of Mercer in the revitalized Ellis Square near City Market; and at his gravesite in beautiful Bonaventure Cemetery. And regardless of what anyone tells you, neither Johnny Mercer nor any member of his family ever lived in the Mercer-Williams House on Monterey Square, of *Midnight in the Garden of Good and Evil* fame. Although it was built for his great-grandfather, the home was sold to someone else before it was completed.

www.oatlandisland.org, daily 10am-5pm, $5 adults, $3 children). Set on a former Centers for Disease Control site, it has undergone an extensive environmental cleanup and is now owned by the local school system, although supported purely by donations. Families by the hundreds come here for a number of special Saturdays throughout the year, including an old-fashioned cane grinding in November and a day of sheep shearing in April.

The main attractions here are the critters, located at various points along a meandering two-mile nature trail through the woods and along the marsh. All animals at Oatland are there because they're somehow unable to return to the wild. Highlights include a tight-knit pack of eastern wolves, a pair of bison, cougars (once indigenous to the region), some really cute foxes, and an extensive raptor aviary. Kids will love the petting zoo of farm animals, some of which are free to roam the grounds at will.

## OLD FORT JACKSON
The oldest standing brick fort in Georgia, **Old Fort Jackson** (Fort Jackson Rd., 912/232-3945, http://chsgeorgia.org, daily 9am-5pm, $7 adults, $4 children), named for Georgia

governor James Jackson (1798-1801), is also one of eight remaining examples of the so-called Second System of American forts built prior to the War of 1812. Operated by the non-profit Coastal Heritage Society, Fort Jackson is in an excellent state of preservation and provides loads of information for history buffs as well as for kids. Most visitors especially love the daily cannon firings during the summer. If you're really lucky, you'll be around when Fort Jackson fires a salute to passing military vessels on the river—the only historic fort in the United States that does so.

To get to Fort Jackson, take the President Street Extension (Islands Expressway) east out of downtown. The entrance is several miles down on the left.

## TYBEE ISLAND
Its name means "salt" in the old Euchee tongue, indicative of the island's chief export in those days. Eighteen miles and about a half-hour drive from Savannah, in truth Tybee is part and parcel of the city's social and cultural fabric. Many of the island's 3,000 full-time residents, known for their boozy bonhomie and quirky personal style, commute to work in the city.

# Tybee Island

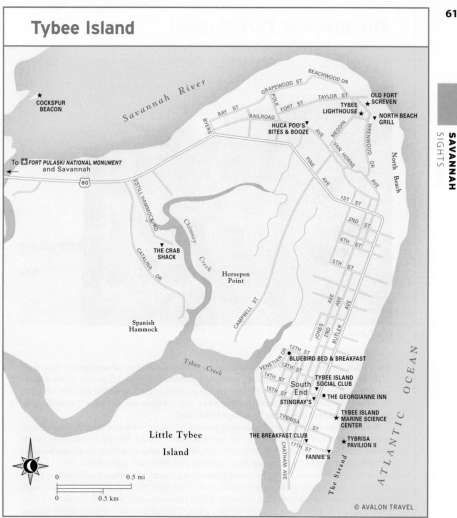

© AVALON TRAVEL

The entire island has become a focal point of Georgia's booming film industry. The 2017 reboot of *Baywatch* with Dwayne "the Rock" Johnson was filmed on Tybee's beach, as was the Miley Cyrus film *The Last Song*.

## ★ FORT PULASKI NATIONAL MONUMENT

There's one must-see before you get to Tybee Island proper. On Cockspur Island you'll find **Fort Pulaski National Monument** (U.S. 80 E., 912/786-5787, www.nps.gov/fopu, daily 9am-5pm, $7, free under age 16), a delight for any history buff. The pleasure starts when you cross the drawbridge over the moat and see a cannon pointed at you from a narrow gun port. Enter the inside of the fort and take in just how big it is—Union occupiers regularly played baseball on the huge, grassy parade ground. Take a walk around the perimeter, underneath the ramparts. This is where the soldiers lived and worked, and you'll

# The Siege of Fort Pulaski

Fort Pulaski

Fort Pulaski's construction was part of a broader initiative by President James Madison in the wake of the War of 1812, which dramatically revealed the shortcomings of U.S. coastal defense. Based on state-of-the-art European design forged in the cauldron of the Napoleonic Wars, Fort Pulaski's thick masonry construction used 25 million bricks, many of them of the famous "Savannah Gray" variety handmade at the nearby Hermitage Plantation.

When Georgia seceded from the Union in January 1861, a small force of Confederates immediately took control of Fort Pulaski and Fort Jackson. In early 1862 a Union sea-land force came to covertly lay the groundwork for a siege of Fort Pulaski. The siege would rely on several batteries secretly set up across the Savannah River. Some of the Union guns utilized new rifled-chamber technology, which dramatically increased the accuracy, muzzle velocity, and penetrating power of their shells. The Union barrage began at 8:15am on April 10, 1862, and Fort Pulaski's walls crumbled under the withering fire. At least one shell struck a powder magazine, igniting an enormous explosion. After 30 hours, Confederate general Charles Olmstead surrendered the fortress.

It was not only Fort Pulaski that was rendered obsolete—it was the whole concept of masonry fortification. From that point forward, military forts would rely on earthwork rather than brick. The section of earthwork you see as you enter Fort Pulaski, the "demilune," was added after the Civil War.

see re-creations of officers' quarters, meeting areas, sick rooms, and prisoners' bunks among the cannons, where Confederate prisoners of war were held after the fort's surrender. Cannon firings happen most Saturdays.

## TYBEE ISLAND
## MARINE SCIENCE CENTER

At the foot of the Tybrisa Pavilion is the little **Tybee Island Marine Science Center** (1510 Strand Ave., 912/786-5917, www.tybeemarinescience.org, daily 10am-5pm, $4 adults, $3 children), with nine aquariums and a touch tank featuring native species. Here is the nerve center for the Tybee Island Sea Turtle Project, an ongoing effort to document and preserve the local comings and goings of the island's most beloved inhabitant and unofficial mascot, the endangered sea turtle.

## TYBEE ISLAND
## LIGHT STATION AND MUSEUM

At North Campbell Avenue is the entrance to the less-populated, more historically significant north end of Tybee Island, once almost entirely taken up by Fort Screven, a coastal defense fortification of the early 1900s. Rebuilt several times in its history, the **Tybee Island Light Station** (30 Meddin Ave., 912/786-5801, www.tybeelighthouse.org, Wed.-Mon. 9am-5:30pm, last ticket sold 4:30pm, $9 adults, $7 children) traces its construction to the first year of the colony, based on a design by the multitalented Noble Jones. At its completion in 1736, it was the tallest structure in the United States. One of a handful of working 18th-century lighthouses today, the facility has been restored to its 1916-1964 incarnation, featuring a nine-foot-tall first-order Fresnel lens installed in 1867.

All the outbuildings on the lighthouse grounds are original, including the residence of the lighthouse keeper, also the oldest building on the island. If you've got the legs and the lungs, definitely take all 178 steps up to the top of the lighthouse for a stunning view of Tybee, the Atlantic, and Hilton Head Island.

Tybee Island Light Station

# The Tybee Bomb

On a dark night in 1958 at the height of the Cold War, a USAF B-47 Stratojet bomber made a simulated nuclear bombing run over southeast Georgia. A Charleston-based F-86 fighter on a mock intercept came too close, clipping the bomber's wing. Before bringing down the wounded B-47 at Savannah's Hunter Airfield, Commander Howard Richardson decided to jettison his lethal cargo: a 7,000-pound Mark 15 hydrogen bomb, serial number 47782. Richardson, who won the Distinguished Flying Cross for his efforts that night, jettisoned the bomb over water. What no one knows is exactly where. And thus began the legend of "the Tybee Bomb." Speculation ran wild, with some locals fearing a nuclear explosion, radioactive contamination, or even that a team of scuba-diving terrorists would secretly retrieve the weapon.

Commander Richardson, now retired, says the bomb wasn't armed when he jettisoned it. Environmentalists say that doesn't matter, because the enriched uranium the Air Force admits was in the bomb is toxic whether or not there's the risk of a nuclear detonation. People who work in the fishing industry on Tybee say the fact that the bomb also had 400 pounds of high explosive "nuclear trigger" is reason enough to get it out of the waterways.

The Air Force has made several attempts to locate the weapon. In 2000 it sent a team to Savannah to find the bomb, concluding it was buried somewhere off the coast in 5-15 feet of mud. In 2005, in another attempt to find the weapon, it sent another team of experts down to look one last time. Their verdict: The bomb's still lost.

All around the area of the north end around the lighthouse complex you'll see low-lying concrete bunkers. These are remains of Fort Screven's coastal defense batteries, and many are in private hands. Battery Garland is open to tours, and also houses the **Tybee Island Museum,** a charming, almost whimsical little collection of exhibits from various eras of local history.

One entrance fee gives you admission to the lighthouse, the lighthouse museum, and the Tybee Island Museum.

### TYBEE POST THEATER

The new pride of the north end is the **Tybee Post Theater** (10 Van Horne Ave., 912/472-4790, www.tybeeposttheater.org, prices vary), a fully restored performing arts venue that was once, as the name implies, the theater for the Fort Screven military facility. The small but cozy 200-seat space now offers a range of programming from live music to live theatre to film screenings, the latter its original purpose when built in 1930. Indeed, the theater was one of the first in Georgia to host the new "talkie" films.

## Pooler
### ★ NATIONAL MUSEUM OF THE MIGHTY EIGHTH AIR FORCE

Military and aviation buffs should not miss the **National Museum of the Mighty Eighth Air Force** (175 Bourne Ave., Pooler, 912/748-8888, www.mightyeighth.org, daily 9am-5pm, $10 adults, $6 children and active-duty military) in Pooler, Georgia, right off I-95. The 8th Air Force was born at Hunter Field in Savannah as the 8th Bomber Command in 1942, becoming the 8th Air Force in 1944; it is now based in Louisiana.

A moving testament to the men and machines that conducted those strategic bombing campaigns over Europe in World War II, the museum also features later 8th Air Force history such as the Korean War, the Linebacker II bombing campaigns over North Vietnam, and the Persian Gulf. Inside you'll find airplanes like the P-51 Mustang and the German ME-109. The centerpiece, however, is the restored B-17 bomber *City of Savannah*, the newest jewel of the collection, acquired from the National Air and Space Museum in Washington DC.

# Entertainment and Events

## NIGHTLIFE

Savannah is a hard-drinking town, and not just on St. Patrick's Day. The ability to legally walk downtown streets with beer, wine, or a cocktail in hand definitely contributes to the overall joie de vivre. Bars close in Savannah at 3am, a full hour later than in Charleston. A citywide indoor smoking ban is in effect and you may not smoke cigarettes in any bar in Savannah.

## Bars and Pubs

One of Savannah's favorite and most raucous historic taverns is possibly the River Street bar most visited by actual locals. The **Bayou Café** (4 N. Abercorn Ramp, 912/233-6411, daily 11am-3am), overlooking River Street but situated on one of the cobblestone "ramps" going down from Bay Street to the waterfront, offers a convivial dive-bar-type atmosphere and a solid Cajun-style pub food menu. The main floor is the traditional tavern, where the best local blues musicians play frequent gigs. The 2nd floor is more of a game room and general younger folks' party area.

For over 65 years, perhaps Savannah's most beloved dive bar/watering hole has been **The Original Pinkie Master's** (318 Drayton St., 912/999-7106, www.theoriginalsavannah.com, Mon.-Thurs. 3pm-3am, Fri.-Sat. noon-3am). For decades this has been a gathering place for local politicos; according to local lore, this is where then-governor Jimmy Carter announced his run for presidency (even though he's a teetotaler). A recent change of ownership has managed that rarest of accomplishments: They've lovingly retained the kitschy dive bar motif, complete with historic memorabilia, while expanding the drink menu and making things a bit more palatable for the general public.

The main landmark on the west end of River Street is the famous (or infamous, depending on which side of "the Troubles"

you're on) **Kevin Barry's Irish Pub** (117 W. River St., 912/233-9626, www.kevinbarrys.com, daily 11am-3am), one of Savannah's most beloved establishments. KB's is open seven days a week, with evenings seeing performances by a number of Irish troubadours, all veterans of the East Coast trad circuit.

Without question, the place in Savannah that comes closest to replicating an actual, authentic Irish pub environment is tiny, cozy **O'Connell's** (42 Drayton St., 912/231-2298, daily 3pm-3am), where they know how to pour a Guinness, feature Magners cider on tap, and the house specialty is the "pickleback"—a shot of Jameson's followed by a shot of, yes, pickle brine. In classic Emerald Isle tradition, most seating is bench-style, to encourage conversation.

Uncharacteristically, Savannah now sports several good hotel bars, and one of the best is **Rocks on the Roof** (102 W. Bay St., 912/721-3800, Fri.-Sat. 11am-1am, Sun.-Thurs. 11am-midnight), atop the Bohemian Hotel Savannah Riverfront on the waterfront. In good weather the exterior walls are opened up to reveal a large wraparound seating area with stunning views of downtown on one side and of the Savannah River on the other.

No, Lincoln Street in Savannah isn't named for Abraham Lincoln. But dark, fun little **Abe's on Lincoln Street** (17 Lincoln St., 912/349-0525, http://abesonlincoln.com, Mon.-Sat. 4pm-3am) is the oldest bar in town, with a very eclectic clientele.

On Whitaker Street is a hip hangout with an excellent menu, **Circa 1875** (48 Whitaker St., 912/443-1875, www.circa1875.com, Mon.-Thurs. 6pm-10pm, Fri.-Sat. 6pm-11pm), where the burgers are as good as the martinis. The vintage vibe takes you back to the days of the Parisian salons.

Yes, **The Distillery** (416 W. Liberty St., 912/236-1772, www.distillerysavannah.com, Mon.-Sat. 11am-close, Sun. noon-close) is located in a former distillery. As such, the atmosphere isn't exactly dark and romantic—it's sort of one big open room—but the excellent location at the corner of MLK Jr. Boulevard and Liberty Street, the long vintage bar, and the great selection of beers on tap combine to make this a happening spot. The fish-and-chips are also great.

Gamers and geeks alike will enjoy video and board game action—as well as the food and drink—at **The Chromatic Dragon** (514 MLK Jr. Blvd., 912/289-0350, www.chromaticdragon.com, Thurs.-Sat. 11am-2am, Sun.-Wed. 11am-11pm). While you can get a meal and a brew here, the focus is on the gaming, so much so that you are asked "analog or digital?" as you walk in; in other words, board games or video consoles, the latter mainly Xbox360 and PS3. They offer a vast array of both, or you can bring your own.

**Moon River Brewing Company** (21 W. Bay St., 912/447-0943, www.moonriverbrewing.com, Mon.-Thurs. 11am-11pm, Fri.-Sat. 11am-midnight, Sun. 11am-10pm) is directly across from the Hyatt Regency Savannah and offers half a dozen handcrafted beers in a rambling old space that housed Savannah's premier hotel in antebellum days. The particular highlight these days, however, is the dog-friendly enclosed beer garden on the busy corner of Bay and Whitaker.

In the City Market area, your best bet is **The Rail Pub** (405 W. Congress St., 912/238-1311, www.therailpub.com, Mon.-Sat. 3pm-3am), one of Savannah's oldest and most beloved taverns. This two-story spot is a great place to get a pint or a shot or do karaoke in a boisterous but still cozy and friendly environment.

## Craft Breweries

Savannah is finally catching up to the craft brewery trend, and **Southbound Brewing Company**'s (107 E. Lathrop Ave., 912/335-7716, http://southboundbrewingco.com, tours 5:30pm Wed.-Fri., 2pm Sat., $15) tasting events are getting rave reviews. Tours include 36 ounces of beer served on-site and your choice of a 22-ounce bomber, a 32-ounce growler fill, a six-pack, or a pint glass. The tastings attract a large crowd, so don't dillydally. Southbound's offerings include a rotating series of special-event beers and the occasional rock concert. As is the case with many up-and-coming breweries, the large, restored warehouse space isn't in the most scenic neighborhood.

Savannah's other key craft brewery is **Service Brewing** (574 Indian St., http://servicebrewing.com, tours 5:30pm-7:30pm Thurs.-Fri., 2pm-4pm Sat., $12 pp), so named because its founders are former military; they donate a portion of all profits to veterans service organizations. Basic tastings include either a 36-ounce flight of 6 ounces per pour or three 12-ounce pours. Service is a wee bit

## The To-Go Cup Tradition

Arguably the single most civilized trait of Savannah, and certainly one of the things that most sets it apart, is the glorious old tradition of the "to-go cup." True to its history of hard partying and general open-mindedness, Savannah, like New Orleans, legally allows you to walk the streets downtown with an open container of your favorite adult beverage. Of course, you have to be 21 or over, and the cup must be Styrofoam or plastic, never glass or metal, and no more than 16 ounces. While there are boundaries to where to-go cups are legal, in practice this includes almost all areas of the historic district frequented by visitors. The quick and easy rule of thumb is to keep your to-go cups north of Jones Street.

Every downtown watering hole has stacks of cups at the bar for patrons to use. You can either ask the bartender for a to-go cup—aka a "go cup"—or just reach out and grab one yourself. Don't be shy; it's the Savannah way.

closer to downtown than is Southbound, and within walking distance of the River Street/ City Market area.

## Live Music and Karaoke

Savannah's undisputed karaoke champion is **McDonough's** (21 E. McDonough St., 912/233-6136, www.mcdonoughsofsavannah. com, Mon.-Sat. 8pm-3am, Sun. 8pm-2am), an advantage compounded by the fact that a lot more goes on here than karaoke. The kitchen at McDonough's is quite capable, and many locals swear you can get the best burger in town here. Despite the sports bar atmosphere, the emphasis is on the karaoke, which ramps up every night at 9:30pm.

Despite its high-volume offerings, **The Jinx** (127 W. Congress St., 912/236-2281, www.thejinx.net, Mon.-Sat. 4pm-3am) is a friendly watering hole and the closest thing Savannah has to a full-on music club, with a very active calendar of rock and metal shows. Shows start late here, never before 11pm and often later than that. If you're here for the music and have sensitive ears, bring earplugs. The beer offerings are good, but this is the kind of place where many regular patrons opt for tallboy PBRs.

## LGBTQ-Friendly

Any examination of LGBTQ nightlife in Savannah must, of course, begin with **Club One Jefferson** (1 Jefferson St., 912/232-0200, www.clubone-online.com, Mon.-Sat. 5pm-3am, Sun. 5pm-2am) of *Midnight in the Garden of Good and Evil* fame, with its famous drag shows, including the notorious Lady Chablis, upstairs in the cabaret, and its rockin' 1,000-square-foot dance floor downstairs. Cabaret showtimes are Thursday-Saturday 10:30pm and 12:30am, Sunday 10:30pm, and Monday 11:30pm. Call for Lady Chablis's showtimes.

A friendly, kitschy little tavern at the far west end of River Street near the Jefferson Street ramp, **Chuck's Bar** (301 W. River St., 912/232-1005, Mon.-Wed. 8pm-3am, Thurs.-Sat. 7pm-3am) is a great place to relax and see

some interesting local characters. Karaoke at Chuck's is especially a hoot, and they keep the Christmas lights up all year.

# PERFORMING ARTS
## Theater

The semipro troupe at the **Historic Savannah Theatre** (222 Bull St., 912/233-7764, www.savannahtheatre.com) performs a busy rotating schedule of oldies revues (a typical title: *Return to the '50s*), but they make up for their lack of originality with the tightness and energy of their talented young cast of regulars.

## Music

The **Savannah Philharmonic** (box office 216 E. Broughton St., 912/525-5050, www. savannahphilharmonic.org, Mon.-Fri 10am-5pm) is a professional symphony orchestra that performs concertos and sonatas at various venues around town and is always worth checking out.

## Cinema

The ornate, beautifully restored **Lucas Theatre for the Arts** (32 Abercorn St., 912/525-5040, www.lucastheatre.com, most screenings under $10) downtown is a classic Southern movie house. The Savannah Film Society and Savannah College of Art and Design host screenings there throughout the year. Check the website for schedules.

# FESTIVALS AND EVENTS

Savannah's calendar fairly bursts with festivals, many outdoors. Dates shift from year to year, so it's best to consult the listed websites for details.

## January

Floats and bands take part in the **Martin Luther King Jr. Day Parade** downtown to commemorate the civil rights leader and Georgia native. The bulk of the route is on historic MLK Jr. Boulevard, formerly West Broad Street.

Straddling January and February is the weeklong **PULSE Art + Technology Festival** (www.telfair.org), an adventurous event that brings video artists and offbeat electronic performance art into the modern Jepson Center for the Arts.

## February

Definitely not to be confused with St. Patrick's Day, the **Savannah Irish Festival** (912/232-3448, www.savannahirish.org) focuses on Celtic music.

Hosted by the historically black Savannah State University at various venues around town, the monthlong **Black Heritage Festival** (912/691-6847) is tied into Black History Month and boasts name entertainers like the Alvin Ailey Dance Theatre (performing free!). This event also usually features plenty of historical lectures devoted to the very interesting and rich history of African Americans in Savannah.

Also in February is the quickly growing **Savannah Book Festival** (www.savannahbookfestival.org), modeled after a similar event in Washington DC and featuring many national and regional authors at various venues downtown.

## March

One of Savannah's unique festivals is the multiday indie rock festival **Savannah Stopover** (www.savannahstopover.com) in early or mid-March. The idea is simple: Book bands that are already driving down to Austin, Texas, for the following week's South By Southwest so they can "stop over" and play at various venues in downtown Savannah. Get it?

More than just a day, the citywide **St. Patrick's Day** (www.savannahsaintpatricksday.com) celebration generally lasts at least half a week and temporarily triples the population. The nearly three-hour parade—second biggest in the United States—always begins at 10am on St. Patrick's Day (unless that falls on a Sunday, in which case it's generally on the previous Saturday) and includes an interesting mix of marching bands, wacky floats, and sauntering local Irishmen in kelly-green jackets. The appeal comes not only from the festive atmosphere and generally beautiful spring weather, but also from Savannah's unique law allowing partiers to walk the streets with a cup filled with the adult beverage of their choice.

The three-week **Savannah Music Festival** (912/234-3378, www.savannahmusic

Savannah's St. Patrick's Day Parade is the nation's second-largest.

festival.org) is held at various historic venues around town and begins right after St. Patrick's Day. Past festivals have featured Wynton Marsalis, Dianne Reeves, and the Avett Brothers.

## April

Short for "North of Gaston Street," the **NOGS Tour of Hidden Gardens** (912/961-4805, www.gcofsavnogstour.org, $30) is available two days in April and focuses on a selection of Savannah's amazing private gardens chosen for excellence of design, historical interest, and beauty.

Everyone loves the annual free **Sidewalk Arts Festival** (912/525-5865, www.scad.edu) presented by the Savannah College of Art and Design in Forsyth Park. Contestants claim a rectangular section of sidewalk on which to display their chalk art talent. There's a non-contest section with chalk provided.

## May

The SCAD-sponsored **Sand Arts Festival** (www.scad.edu) on Tybee Island's North Beach centers on a competition of sand castle design, sand sculpture, sand relief, and wind sculpture. You might be amazed at the level of artistry lavished on the sometimes-wondrous creations, only for them to wash away with the tide.

If you don't want to get wet, don't show up at the **Tybee Beach Bum Parade,** an uproarious event held the weekend prior to Memorial Day weekend. With a distinctly boozy overtone, this unique 20-year-old event features homemade floats filled with partiers who squirt the assembled crowds with various water pistols. The crowds, of course, pack their own heat and squirt back.

## September

The second-largest LGBTQ event in Georgia (only Atlanta's version is larger), the **Savannah Pride Festival** (www.savannahpride.org, various venues, free) happens every September. Crowds get pretty big for this festive, fun event, which usually features lots of dance acts and political booths.

Over Labor Day weekend you can check out the **Savannah Craft Brew Festival** (International Trade & Convention Center, 1 International Dr., www.savannahcraftbrewfest.com, $50). This daylong tasting event features a healthy range of breweries from around the nation, not only from Georgia's own burgeoning craft brew industry.

## October

The Savannah Philharmonic Orchestra plays a free **Picnic In The Park** concert in Forsyth Park that draws thousands of noshers. Arrive early to check out the ostentatious, whimsical picnic displays, which compete for prizes. Then set out your blanket, pop open a bottle of wine, and enjoy the sweet sounds.

The combined aroma of beer, sauerkraut, and sausage that you smell coming from the waterfront is the annual **Oktoberfest on the River** (www.riverstreetsavannah.com), which has evolved to be Savannah's second-largest celebration (behind only St. Patrick's Day). Live entertainment of varying quality is featured, though the attraction, of course, is the aforementioned beer and German food. A highlight is Saturday morning's "Weiner Dog Races" involving, you guessed it, competing dachshunds.

It's a fairly new festival, but the **Tybee Island Pirate Festival** (http://tybeepiratefest.com) is a fun and typically rollicking Tybee event in October featuring, well, everybody dressing up like pirates, saying "Arr" a lot, eating, drinking, and listening to cover bands. It may not sound like much, and it's really not, but it's typically very well attended.

Sponsored by St. Paul's Greek Orthodox Church, the popular **Savannah Greek Festival** (www.stpaulsgreekorthodox.org) features food, music, and Greek souvenirs. The weekend event is held across the street from the church at the parish center—in the gym, to be exact, right on the basketball court. Despite the pedestrian location, the food is authentic and delicious, and the atmosphere convivial and friendly.

Hosted by the Savannah College of Art and Design, the weeklong **Savannah Film Festival** (www.scad.edu) beginning in late October is rapidly growing not only in size but in prestige as well. Lots of older, more established Hollywood names appear as honored guests for the evening events, while buzzworthy up-and-coming actors, directors, producers, writers, and animators give excellent workshops during the day.

One of Savannah's most unique events is late October's **"Shalom Y'all" Jewish Food Festival** (912/233-1547, www.mickveisrael.org), held in Forsyth Park and sponsored by the historic Temple Mickve Israel. Latkes, matzo, and other nibbles are all featured along with entertainment.

# Shopping

Downtown Savannah's main shopping district is **Broughton Street.** There are many vibrant local shops as well as national chain stores on the avenue.

A bit south of downtown proper, but still a short drive away, is the **Starland District**. This up-and-coming mixed-use area is home to a growing variety of more hipster-oriented shops.

Focusing on upscale art and home goods, the small but chic and friendly **Downtown Design District** runs three blocks on Whitaker Street, a short walk from Forsyth Park.

## WATERFRONT
### Antiques
One of the coolest antiques shops in town is **Jere's Antiques** (9 N. Jefferson St., 912/236-2815, www.jeresantiques.com, Mon.-Sat. 9:30am-5pm). It's in a huge historic warehouse on Factor's Walk and has a concentration on fine European pieces.

### Gourmet Treats
Cater to your sweet tooth—and buy some goodies to bring back with you—at **River Street Sweets** (13 E. River St., 912/234-4608, www.riverstreetsweets.com, daily 9am-11pm), where you can witness Southern delicacies like pralines being made as you shop. And of course, there are free samples.

## HISTORIC DISTRICT NORTH
### Art Supply
A great art town needs a great art supply store, and in Savannah that would be **Blick Art Materials** (318 E. Broughton St., 912/234-0456, www.dickblick.com, Mon.-Fri. 8am-8pm, Sat. 10am-7pm, Sun. 11am-6pm), which has all the equipment and tools for the serious artist—priced to be affordable for students. But casual shoppers will enjoy it as well for its collection of offbeat gift items.

### Clothes and Fashion
Perhaps Broughton Street's most beloved old shop is **Globe Shoe Co.** (17 E. Broughton St., 912/232-8161, Mon.-Sat. 10am-6pm), a Savannah institution and a real throwback to a time of personalized retail service. They have no website and no Facebook page—they're all about simple one-to-one service, like in the old days.

Inhabiting a well-restored upstairs space, **Civvie's New and Recycled Clothing** (14 E. Broughton St., 912/236-1551, Mon.-Sat. 11am-7pm, Sun. 11am-5pm) is perhaps Savannah's most well-regarded vintage store, with a variety of retro clothes and shoes and a strong local following. They also have a nifty section of campy, kitschy gift items.

Now at what's considered Savannah's prime downtown corner, at Bull and Broughton, is

# A City of Art

There are more art galleries per capita in Savannah than in New York City—one gallery for every 2,191 residents, to be exact. Savannah College of Art and Design (SCAD) galleries are in abundance all over town, displaying the handiwork of students, faculty, alumni, and important regional and national artists. Savannah's arts scene also shines a spotlight on theatre, classical music, and cool movie houses.

For art lovers, the no-brainer package experience for the visitor is the combo of the **Telfair Academy of Arts and Sciences** (121 Barnard St., 912/790-8800, www.telfair.org) and the **Jepson Center for the Arts** (207 W. York St., 912/790-8800, www.telfair.org). These two arms of the Telfair Museums run the gamut of art, from old-school portraiture to cutting-edge contemporary art.

**SCAD galleries** (912/525-5225, www.scad.edu) are abundant. Outposts with consistently impressive exhibits are the **Gutstein Gallery** (201 E. Broughton St.) and **Pinnacle Gallery** (320 E. Liberty St.). The college also runs its own museum, the **SCAD Museum of Art** (227 MLK Jr. Blvd., 912/525-7191, www.scad.edu), which recently doubled in size to accommodate a new wing devoted to the Walter O. Evans Collection of African American Art.

The small and avant-garde **ArtRise Savannah** (2427 DeSoto Ave., 912/335-8204, www.artrisesavannah.org) helps coordinate "Art March" gallery crawls in the SoFo (South of Forsyth) district the first Friday of the month. **Non-Fiction Gallery** (1522 Bull St., 912/662-5152), also in SoFo, exhibits work by many of Savannah's up-and-coming talents. Nearby is **Sulfur Studios** (2301 Bull St., sulfurstudios.org), which not only hosts rotating exhibits, but also coordinates many community forums and events of a cutting-edge nature.

Overlooking Ellis Square downtown is well-regarded **Kobo Gallery** (33 Barnard St., 912/201-0304, www.kobogallery.com), a local artist co-op featuring some of Savannah's best contemporary artists who frequently put on group shows. One of the featured artists is always on duty, so stopping in can be a very informative experience.

There are several good galleries in the beach town of Tybee Island as well, chief among them **Dragonfly Studio** (1204 Hwy 80, 912/786-4431, www.dragonflystudioarts.com), which hosts work by the very best coastal artists in a cute little roadside shack.

century-old family-owned **Levy Jewelers** (2 E. Broughton St., 912/233-1163, Mon.-Sat. 10am-9pm, Sun. noon-6pm). They have a complete showcase of necklaces, watches, and rings from two dozen internationally recognized designers.

## Gourmet Treats

One of the more unique Savannah retail shops is the **Savannah Bee Company** (104 W. Broughton St., 912/233-7873, www.savannahbee.com, Mon.-Sat. 10am-7pm, Sun. 11am-5pm), which carries an extensive line of honey and honey-based merchandise, from foot lotion to lip balm. All the honey comes from area hives owned by company founder and owner Ted Dennard. The flagship Broughton location provides plenty of

sampling opportunities at the little café area and even boasts a small theater space for instructional films. There is also a location on **River Street** (1 W. River St., 912/234-7088, Mon.-Sat. 10am-7pm, Sun. 11am-8pm) on the ground floor of the Hyatt Regency hotel.

Chocolate lovers need to head straight to **Chocolat by Adam Turoni** (323 W. Broughton St., 912/335-2914, www.chocolat-tat.com, daily 11am-6pm), a tiny space with a big taste. Adam's handcrafted, high-quality chocolates are miniature works of art—and delicious ones at that. Be prepared to be overwhelmed.

## Home Goods

While Savannah is an Anglophile's dream, Francophiles will enjoy **The Paris Market**

& Brocante (36 W. Broughton St., 912/232-1500, www.theparismarket.com, Mon.-Sat. 10am-6pm, Sun. 11am-4pm), set on a beautifully restored corner of Broughton Street. Home and garden goods, bed and bath accoutrements, and a great selection of antique and vintage items combine for a rather opulent shopping experience. Plus there's an old-school Euro café inside, where you can enjoy a coffee, tea, or hot chocolate.

Those looking for home decorating ideas with inspiration from both global and Southern aesthetics, traditional as well as sleekly modern, should check out **24e Furnishings at Broughton** (24 E. Broughton St., 912/233-2274, www.twenty-foure.com, Mon.-Thurs. 10am-6pm, Fri.-Sat. 10am-7pm, Sun. noon-5pm), located in an excellently restored 1921 storefront. Be sure to check out the expansive 2nd-floor showroom.

## HISTORIC DISTRICT SOUTH
### Antiques

Possibly the most beloved antiques store in town is **Alex Raskin Antiques** (441 Bull St., 912/232-8205, www.alexraskinantiques.com, Mon.-Sat. 10am-5pm) in Monterey Square, catty-corner from the Mercer-Williams House Museum, set in the historic Hardee Mansion. A visit is worth it just to explore the home. But the goods Alex lovingly curates are among the best and most tasteful in the region.

**Small Pleasures** (412 Whitaker St., 912/234-0277, Mon.-Sat. 10:30am-5pm) is one of Savannah's hidden gems. They deal in a tasteful range of vintage and estate jewelry, in a suitably small but delightfully appointed space in the Downtown Design District.

### Books and Music

Specializing in "gently used" books in good condition, **The Book Lady** (6 E. Liberty St., 912/233-3628, Mon.-Sat. 10am-5:30pm) on Liberty Street features many rare first editions. Enjoy a gourmet coffee while you browse the stacks.

The fact that **E. Shaver Bookseller** (326 Bull St., 912/234-7257, Mon.-Sat. 9am-6pm) is one of the few locally owned independent bookstores left in town should not diminish the fact that it is also one of the best bookstores in town. The friendly, well-read staff can help you around the rambling old interior of their ground-level store and its generous stock of regionally themed books.

The beautiful Monterey Square location and a mention in *Midnight in the Garden of Good and Evil* combine to make **V&J Duncan** (12 E. Taylor St., 912/232-0338, www.vjduncan.com, Mon.-Sat. 10:30am-4:30pm) a Savannah "must-shop." Owner John Duncan and his wife, Virginia ("Ginger" to friends), have collected an impressive array of prints, books, and maps over the past quarter century, and are themselves a treasure trove of information.

### Clothes

**Custard Boutique** (414 Whitaker St., 912/232-4733, Mon.-Sat. 10:30am-6pm, Sun. noon-5pm) in the Downtown Design District has a cute, cutting-edge selection of women's clothes in a range of styles and is easily the match of any other women's clothing store in town.

### Gifts and Souvenirs

Set in a stunningly restored multilevel Victorian within a block of Forsyth Park, the globally conscious **Folklorico** (440 Bull St., 912/232-9300, Mon.-Sat. 10am-5pm, Sun. 1pm-5pm) brings in a fascinating and diverse collection of sustainably made jewelry, gifts, and home goods from around the world, focusing on Central and South America and Asia.

In this town so enamored of all things Irish, a great little locally owned shop is **Saints and Shamrocks** (309 Bull St., 912/233-8858, www.saintsandshamrocks.org, Mon.-Sat. 9:30am-5:30pm, Sun. 11am-4pm), across the intersection from the Book Lady. Pick up your St. Patrick's-themed gear and gifts to celebrate Savannah's highest holiday along with high-quality Irish imports.

Not only a valuable outlet for SCAD students and faculty to sell their artistic wares, **shopSCAD** (340 Bull St., 912/525-5180, www.shopscadonline.com, Mon.-Wed. 9am-5:30pm, Thurs.-Fri. 9am-8pm, Sat. 10am-8pm, Sun. noon-5pm) is also one of Savannah's most unique boutiques. You never really know what you'll find, but whatever it is, it will be one-of-a-kind. The jewelry in particular is always cutting edge and showcases good craftsmanship. The designer T-shirts are a hoot too.

# Sports and Recreation

Savannah offers copious outdoor options that take full advantage of the city's temperate climate and the natural beauty of its marshy environment next to the Atlantic Ocean.

## WATER TOURS

The heavy industrial buildup on the Savannah River means that the main river tours, all departing from the docks in front of the Hyatt Regency Savannah, tend to be disappointing in their unrelenting views of cranes, docks, storage tanks, and smokestacks. Still, for those into that kind of thing, narrated trips up and down the river on the *Georgia Queen* and the *Savannah River Queen* are offered by **Savannah Riverboat Cruises** (9 E. River St., 800/786-6404, www.savannahriverboat. com, starts at $22.95 adults, $13.95 ages 4-12). You can opt for just sightseeing, or add a dinner cruise.

If you've just *got* to get out on the river for a short time, by far the best bargain is to take one of the four little water ferries of **Savannah Belles** (River St. at City Hall and Waving Girl Landing, www.catchacat. org, daily 7:30am-10:30pm, free), named after famous women in Savannah history, which shuttle passengers from River Street to Hutchinson Island and back every 15-20 minutes. Pick one up on River Street in front of City Hall or at the Waving Girl Landing a few blocks east.

one of the Savannah Belles ferries

# KAYAKING AND CANOEING

Maybe the single best kayak or canoe adventure in Savannah is the run across the Back River from Tybee to **Little Tybee Island,** an undeveloped state heritage site that is actually twice as big as Tybee, albeit mostly marsh. To get here, take Butler Avenue all the way to 18th Street and take a right, then another quick right onto Chatham Avenue. The parking lot for the landing is a short way up Chatham Avenue on your left. Warning: Do not attempt to swim to Little Tybee, no matter how strong a swimmer you think you are.

**Lazaretto Creek,** on the western edge of Tybee Island, is a great place to explore Tybee and environs. From here you can meander several miles through the marsh, or go the other way and head into a channel of the Savannah River. Put in at the Lazaretto Creek landing, at the foot of the Lazaretto Creek bridge on the south side of U.S. 80 on the way to Tybee Island. You can also put in at the nearby **Tybee Marina** (4 Old Tybee Rd., 912/786-5554, www.tybeeislandmarina.com), also on Lazaretto Creek.

One of the great overall natural experiences in the area is the massive **Savannah National Wildlife Refuge** (694 Beech Hill Ln., Hardeeville, SC, 843/784-2468, www.fws.gov/refuge/savannah, daily dawn-dusk, free). This 30,000-acre reserve—half in Georgia, half in South Carolina—is on the Atlantic flyway, so you'll be able to see birdlife in abundance, in addition to alligators and manatees. Earthen dikes crisscrossing the refuge are vestigial remnants of paddy fields from plantation days.

You can kayak on your own, but many opt to take guided tours offered by **Wilderness Southeast** (912/897-5108, www.wildernesssoutheast.org, two-hour trips from $37.50 for two people), **Sea Kayak Georgia** (888/529-2542, www.seakayakgeorgia.com, $55 pp), and **Swamp Girls Kayak Tours** (843/784-2249, www.swampgirls.com, $45). To get to the refuge, take U.S. 17 north over the big Talmadge Bridge, over the Savannah River into South Carolina. Turn left on Highway 170 south and look for the entrance to Laurel Hill Wildlife Drive on the left.

# HIKING

A relic of the pre-railroad days, the **Savannah-Ogeechee River Canal** (681 Ft. Argyle Rd., 912/748-8068, www.savannahogeecheecanal.com, daily 9am-5pm, $2 adults, $1 students) is a 17-mile barge route joining the two rivers. Finished in 1830, it saw three decades of prosperous trade in cotton, rice, bricks, guano, naval stores, and food crops before the coming of the railroads finished it off. You can walk some of its length today near the Ogeechee River terminus, admiring the impressive engineering of its multiple locks used to stabilize the water level.

To get here, get on I-95 south, take exit 94, and go west on Fort Argyle Road (Hwy. 204). The canal is a little over two miles from the exit.

# BIKING

Many locals like to load up their bikes and go to **Fort Pulaski National Monument** (912/786-5787, www.nps.gov, daily 9am-5pm, $7 pp, free under age 16). From the grounds you can ride all over scenic and historic Cockspur Island.

Outside of town, much biking activity centers on Tybee Island, with the six-mile **McQueen's Island Trail** (U.S. 80 near Fort Pulaski National Monument) being a popular and simple ride. The trail started as a rail route for the Central of Georgia Railway and was converted to a multiuse trail in the 1990s.

# GOLF

The **Club at Savannah Harbor** (2 Resort Dr., 912/201-2007, www.theclubatsavannahharbor.com, greens fees $135, $70 for twilight) is across the Savannah River on Hutchinson Island, adjacent to the Westin Savannah Harbor Resort. Home to the Liberty Mutual Legends of Golf Tournament each spring, the club's tee times are 7:30am-3pm.

# FISHING

A highly regarded local fishing charter is Tybee-based **Amick's Deep Sea Fishing** (1 Old Hwy. 80, Tybee Island, 912/897-6759, www.amicksdeepseafishing.com, from $120 pp). Captain Steve Amick and crew run offshore charters daily. Go east on U.S. 80 and turn right just past the Lazaretto Creek Bridge.

# BIRD-WATCHING

An excellent birding spot on the **Colonial Coast Birding Trail** (http://georgiawildlife.dnr.state.ga.us) is Tybee Island's **North Beach area** (Savannah River to 1st St., Tybee Island, parking $5 per day, meters available). You'll see a wide variety of shorebirds and gulls, as well as piping plovers, northern gannets, and purple sandpipers (winter).

# SPECTATOR SPORTS

For sports action that's hard-hitting and comes with a certain hipster kitsch quotient, check out the bruising bouts of the women of the **Savannah Derby Devils** (Savannah Civic Center, 301 W. Oglethorpe Ave., 912/651-6556, www.savannahderby.com), who bring the roller derby thunder against other regional teams. They skate downtown at the Savannah Civic Center.

The newest hit on the Savannah sports scene is the college summer league team **The Savannah Bananas** (1401 E. Victory Dr., 912/712-2482, thesavannahbananas.com). This very popular local summer pasttime happens at historic Grayson Stadium, where greats such as Babe Ruth and Jackie Robinson played back in the day. This isn't NCAA ball—these young players use real wooden bats and play for the love of the game while they're out of class for the summer. Single game tickets start at $9. Most games sell out, so get your tickets early.

# Food

Savannah is a fun food town, with a selection of cuisine concocted by a cast of executive chefs who despite their many personal idiosyncrasies tend to go with what works rather than experiment for the sake of experimentation.

For the freshest seafood, consider a trip to Tybee Island or Thunderbolt (which is on the way to Tybee).

## WATERFRONT
### Classic Southern

The bustling, friendly interior of **Treylor Park** (115 E. Bay St., 912/495-5557, www.treylorpark.com, Mon.-Fri. noon-1am, Sat. 10am-2am, Sun. 10am-1am, $10-15) plays up the shabby-chic undertone of Savannah life, with tasty gourmet takes on downmarket Southern classics like the chicken biscuit, pot pie, and sloppy joe. Don't miss their signature starter dish, the PB&J Wings. A particularly tasteful cocktail menu and a well-curated craft beer list round out the experience.

Very few restaurants on River Street rise above tourist schlock, but a standout is **Vic's on the River** (16 E. River St., 912/721-1000, www.vicsontheriver.com, Sun.-Thurs. 11am-10pm, Fri.-Sat. 11am-11pm, $25-35). With dishes like wild Georgia shrimp, stone-ground grits, and blue crab cakes with a three-pepper relish, Vic's combines a romantic old Savannah atmosphere with an adventurous take on Lowcountry cuisine. Note the entrance to the dining room is not on River Street but on the Bay Street level on Upper Factor's Walk.

### Breakfast

★ **B. Matthew's Eatery** (325 E. Bay St., 912/233-1319, www.bmatthewseatery.com, Mon.-Thurs. 8am-9pm, Fri.-Sat. 8am-10pm, Sun. 9am-3pm, $10-15) serves what is widely considered the best breakfast in the entire Savannah historic district. The omelets—most under $10—are uniformly wonderful, and the sausage and bacon are excellent and not greasy. There are healthier selections as well, and you can actually get a decent bowl of oatmeal—but I suggest something more decadent. Sunday brunch is incredible.

## CITY MARKET
### Classic Southern

Every year, thousands of visitors come to Savannah to wait for hours for a chance to sample some of local celebrity Paula Deen's "home" cooking at **The Lady & Sons** (102 W. Congress St., 912/233-2600, www.ladyandsons.com, Mon.-Sat. 11am-3pm and 5pm-close, Sun. 11am-5pm, $15-20). There's actually a fairly typical Southern buffet with some decent fried chicken, collard greens, and mac and cheese. For the privilege, you must begin waiting in line as early as 9:30am for lunch and as early as 3:30pm for dinner in order to be assigned a dining time.

### Coffee, Tea, and Sweets

Combine a hip bar with outrageously tasty dessert items and you get ★ **Lulu's Chocolate Bar** (42 MLK Jr. Blvd., 912/238-2012, www.luluschocolatebar.net, Sun.-Thurs. noon-midnight, Fri.-Sat. 2pm-2am,). While the whole family is welcome before 10pm to enjoy chocolate-chip cheesecake and the like, after that it's 21-and-over. The late crowd is younger and trendier and comes mostly for the unique specialty martinis like the pineapple upside-down martini. The prices are quite reasonable at this fun place.

### Italian

One would never call Savannah a great pizza town, but the best pizza here is **Vinnie VanGoGo's** (317 W. Bryan St., 912/233-6394, www.vinnievangogos.com, Mon.-Thurs. 4pm-11:30pm, Fri. 4pm-1am, Sat. noon-1am, Sun. noon-11:30pm, $10-15, cash only), at the west end of City Market on Franklin Square. Their pizza is a thin-crust Neapolitan

style—although the menu claims it to be New York style—with a delightful tangy sauce and fresh cheese. Individual slices are huge, so don't feel obliged to order a whole pie. The waiting list for a table can get pretty long.

## HISTORIC DISTRICT NORTH
### Classic Southern

Savannah's most dramatic restaurant success story is ★ **The Grey** (109 MLK Jr. Blvd., 912/662-5999, www.thegreyrestaurant.com, Sun. and Tues.-Thurs. 5:30pm-10pm, Fri.-Sat. 5:30pm-11pm, supper every third Sunday of the month, $25-35), located in a stunningly restored former bus depot. It has taken the national foodie world by storm with its take on beloved regional vernacular and soul food cuisine classics like seafood boudin, veal sweetbreads, roasted yardbird, fisherman's stew, and more, depending on seasonal whim and sourcing availabilities. A James Beard Award finalist in 2015, the Grey features the talents of standout executive chef Mashama Bailey, who grew up in Savannah and has a close eye for what makes the South tick food-wise. At the entrance is the "Diner Bar," a smaller offset bar area offering a punchy bar food menu strong on sandwiches.

The best lunch on Broughton Street is at **Kayak Kafe** (1 E. Broughton St., 912/233-6044, www.eatkayak.com, Mon.-Thurs. 11am-10pm, Fri.-Sat. 11am-11pm, Sun. 11am-5pm, $10-15), where you can get a killer fresh salad or a fish taco to refresh your energy level during a busy day of shopping or sightseeing. Vegetarians, vegans, and those on a gluten-free diet will be especially pleased by the available options. As one of the very few Broughton Street places with outdoor sidewalk tables, this is also a great people-watching spot.

**Olde Pink House** (23 Abercorn St., 912/232-4286, Sun.-Thurs. 5:30pm-10:30pm, Fri.-Sat. 5:30pm-11pm, $20-30) is known for its savvy (and often sassy) service and the uniquely regional flair it adds to traditional dishes, with liberal doses of pecans, Vidalia onions, shrimp, and crab. The she-crab soup

# To Market, To Market

Savannah's first and still premier health-food market, **Brighter Day Natural Foods** (1102 Bull St., 912-236-4703, www.brighterdayfoods.com, Mon.-Sat. 9am-7pm, Sun. noon-5:30pm) has been the labor of love of Janie and Peter Brodhead for 30 years, all of them in the same location at the southern tip of Forsyth Park. Boasting organic groceries, regional produce, a sandwich and smoothie bar with a takeout window, and an extensive vitamin, supplement, and herb section, Brighter Day is an oasis in Savannah's sea of chain supermarkets.

Opened in 2013, **Whole Foods Market** (1815 E. Victory Dr., www.wholefoodsmarket.com, daily 8am-9pm) offers the chain's usual assortment of organic produce, with a very good fresh meat and seafood selection.

Fairly new but already thriving, the **Forsyth Park Farmers Market** (www.forsythfarmersmarket.org, Sat. 9am-1pm) happens in the south end of scenic and wooded Forsyth Park. You'll find very fresh fruit and produce from a variety of fun and friendly regional farmers. If you have access to a real kitchen while you're in town, you might be glad to know there's usually a very good selection of organic, sustainably grown meat and poultry products as well—not always a given at farmers markets.

If you need some good-quality groceries downtown—especially after hours—try **Parker's Market** (222 E. Drayton St., 912/231-1001, daily 24 hours). In addition to a pretty wide array of gourmet-style grab 'n' go victuals inside, there are gas pumps outside to fuel your vehicle.

There's one 24-hour full-service supermarket in downtown Savannah: **Kroger** (311 E. Gwinnett St., 912/231-2260, daily 24 hours).

and lamb chops in particular are crowd-pleasers, and the scored crispy flounder stacks up to similar versions of this dish at several other spots in town. Reservations are recommended.

## Coffee, Tea, and Sweets

The best coffee on Broughton is at **The Coffee Fox** (102 W. Broughton St., 912/401-0399, www.thecoffeefox.com, Mon.-Sat. 7am-11pm, Sun. 8am-4pm), a locally owned joint that expertly treads the fine line between hipster hangout and accessible hot spot. The freshly baked goodies are nearly as good as the freshly brewed java, which includes cold-brew and pour-over offerings.

He helped produce *Mission Impossible III* and other movies, but Savannah native Stratton Leopold's other claim to fame is running the 100-year-old family business at ★ **Leopold's Ice Cream** (212 E. Broughton St., 912/234-4442, www.leopoldsicecream.com, Sun.-Thurs. 11am-10pm, Fri.-Sat. 11am-11pm). Leopold's also offers soup and sandwiches to go with its delicious family ice

cream recipe and sweet treats. Memorabilia from Stratton's various movies is all around the shop, which stays open after every evening performance at the Lucas Theatre around the corner. You can occasionally find Stratton himself behind the counter doling out scoops.

## Mexican

The best Mexican spot downtown is **Tequila's Town** (109 Whitaker St., 912/236-3222, www.tequilastown.com, Mon.-Thurs. 11am-10pm, Fri.-Sat. 11am-11pm, Sun. noon-10pm, $15-25), a relatively new place that fills an oft-noted void in the Savannah foodie scene. The menu is comprehensive and authentic, a clear step above the usual gringo-oriented fat-fest. Highlights include the chilies rellenos and the seafood, not to mention the guacamole prepared tableside.

## South African

Look for the long lunchtime line outside the tiny storefront that is **Zunzi's** (108 E. York St., 912/443-9555, http://zunzis.com, Mon.-Sat. 11am-6pm, $10). This takeout joint is one of

Savannah's favorite lunch spots, the labor of love of South African expatriates Gabby and Johnny DeBeer, who've gotten a lot of national attention for their robust, rich dishes like the exquisite South African-style sausage.

# HISTORIC DISTRICT SOUTH
## Classic Southern

A very popular spot with locals and tourists alike, the **Crystal Beer Parlor** (301 W. Jones St., 912/349-1000, www.crystalbeerparlor. com, daily 11am-10pm, $15-20) offers one of the best burgers downtown. With a history going back to the 1930s, this has been a friendly family tradition for generations of Savannahians. The lively bar area has a very wide range of craft brews, and there are plenty of snug booths to sit in and enjoy the solid American menu.

The rise of Paula Deen and her Lady & Sons restaurant has only made local epicures even more exuberant in their praise for ★ **Mrs. Wilkes' Dining Room** (107 W. Jones St., 912/232-5997, www.mrswilkes.com, Mon.-Fri. 11am-2pm, $25), Savannah's original comfort-food mecca. The delightful Sema Wilkes herself has passed on, but nothing has changed—not the communal dining room, the cheerful service, the care taken with takeout customers, nor, most of all, the food, which is a succulent mélange of the South's greatest hits, including the best fried chicken in town, snap beans, black-eyed peas, and collard greens. Be prepared for a long wait, however; lines begin forming early in the morning.

# SOFO DISTRICT
## New Southern

Before there was Paula Deen, there was Elizabeth Terry, Savannah's first high-profile chef and founder of ★ **Elizabeth on 37th** (105 E. 37th St., 912/236-5547, daily 6pm-10pm, $30-40), Savannah's most elegant restaurant. Executive chef Kelly Yambor uses eclectic, seasonally shifting ingredients that blend the South with the south of France. Reservations are recommended.

## Burgers

The cozy **Green Truck Neighborhood Pub** (2430 Habersham St., 912/234-5885, http:// greentruckpub.com, Tues.-Sat. 11am-11pm, $15) earns rave reviews with its delicious regionally sourced meat and produce offered at reasonable prices. (The large selection of craft beers on tap is a big draw too.) The marquee item is the signature five-ounce grass-fed burger. It's a small room that often has a big line, and they don't take reservations, so be prepared.

## Coffee, Tea, and Sweets

Primarily known for its sublime sweet treats, James Beard Award-nominated **Back in the Day Bakery** (2403 Bull St., 912/495-9292, www.backinthedaybakery.com, Tues.-Fri. 9am-5pm, Sat. 8am-3pm) also offers a small but delightfully tasty (and tasteful) range of lunch soups, salads, and sandwiches (11am-2pm). Lunch highlights include the baguette with camembert, roasted red peppers, and lettuce, as well as the caprese, the classic tomato, mozzarella, and basil trifecta on a perfect ciabatta. But whatever you do, save room for dessert, which runs the full sugar spectrum: red velvet cupcakes, lemon bars, macaroons, carrot cake, and many others.

**Foxy Loxy** (1919 Bull St., 912/401-0543, www.foxyloxycafe.com, Mon.-Sat. 7am-11pm) is a classic coffeehouse set within a cozy multistory Victorian on Bull Street. Pluses include the authentic Tex-Mex menu, wine and beer offerings, and freshly baked sweet treats.

The coffee at **The Sentient Bean** (13 E. Park Ave., 912/232-4447, www.sentientbean. com, daily 7:30am-10pm) is all fair trade and organic, and the all-vegetarian fare is a major upgrade above the usual coffeehouse offerings. But "the Bean" is more than a coffeehouse—it's a community. Probably the best indie film venue in town, the Bean regularly hosts screenings of cutting-edge left-of-center documentary and kitsch films, as well as rotating art exhibits.

# EASTSIDE
## Classic Southern
Located just across the Wilmington River from the fishing village of Thunderbolt, **Desposito's** (187 Old Tybee Rd., 912/897-9963, www.despositosseafood.com, Tues.-Fri. 5pm-10pm, Sat. noon-10pm, $20) is a big hit with locals and visitors alike, although it's not in all the guidebooks. The focus here is on crab, shrimp, and oysters, and lots of them, all caught wild in local waters and served humbly on tables covered with newspapers.

## Barbecue
If you're out this way visiting Wormsloe or Skidaway Island State Park, or if you're just crazy about good barbecue, make a point to hit little ★ **Sandfly BBQ** (8413 Ferguson Ave. 912/356-5463, www.sandflybbq.com, Mon.-Sat. 11am-8pm, $10), unique in the area for its dedication to real Memphis-style barbecue. Anything is great—this is the best brisket in the area—but for the best overall experience try the Hog Wild platter.

# TYBEE ISLAND
## Breakfast and Brunch
Considered the best breakfast in the Savannah area for 30 years and counting, **The Breakfast Club** (1500 Butler Ave., 912/786-5984, http://tybeeisland.com/breakfast-club, daily 6:30am-1pm, $15), with its brisk diner atmosphere and hearty Polish sausage-filled omelets, is like a little bit of Chicago in the South. Lines start early for a chance to enjoy such house specialties as Helen's Solidarity, the Athena Omelet, and the Chicago Bear Burger.

## Casual Dining
Set in a large former fishing camp overlooking Chimney Creek, **The Crab Shack** (40 Estill Hammock Rd., 912/786-9857, www.thecrabshack.com, Mon.-Thurs. 11:30am-10pm, Fri.-Sun. 11:30am-11pm, $20) is a favorite local seafood place and something of an attraction in itself. Don't expect gourmet fare or quiet seaside dining; the emphasis is on mounds of fresh, tasty seafood, heavy on the raw-bar action. Getting there is a little tricky: Take U.S. 80 to Tybee, cross the bridge over Lazaretto Creek, and begin looking for Estill Hammock Road to Chimney Creek on the right. Take Estill Hammock Road and veer right. After that, it's hard to miss.

One of Tybee's more cherished restaurants is on the north end in the shadow of the Tybee Light Station. Like a little slice of Jamaica near the dunes, the laid-back **North Beach Grill** (33 Meddin Ave., 912/786-4442, daily 11:30am-10pm, $15) deals in tasty Caribbean fare, such as its signature jerk chicken, fish sandwiches, and, of course, delicious fried plantains, all overseen by chef-owner "Big George" Spriggs. Frequent live music adds to the island vibe.

For a leisurely and tasty dinner, try **Tybee Island Social Club** (1311 Butler Ave., 912/472-4044, http://tybeeislandsocialclub.com, Tues. 5pm-9:30pm, Wed.-Fri. noon-9:30pm, Sat.-Sun. 11:30am-10pm, $20). Their menu is somewhat unusual for this seafood-heavy island: It's primarily an assortment of gourmet-ish tacos, including fish, duck, and lime- and tequila-marinated steak, all under $10 each. The beer and wine list is accomplished, and the live entertainment is usually very good—which is fortunate, since the service here is on the slow side.

# Accommodations

The good news for visitors is that there are now many comparatively new hotels of note directly in the downtown area within walking distance of most sites. Some of them are the more widely recognized chains, and others represent more boutique companies and provide a commensurately higher level of service. The less-good news, especially for locals, is that the ominously rising skyline the newer, bigger hotels represent is a change from the friendly small-scale historical footprint Savannah is known for in the first place.

## WATERFRONT
### $150-300

The ★ **Bohemian Hotel Savannah Riverfront** (102 W. Bay St., 912/721-3800, www.bohemianhotelsavannah.com, $225-350) is gaining a reputation as one of Savannah's premier hotels, both for the casual visitor as well as visiting celebrities. Located between busy River Street and bustling City Market, this isn't the place for peace and quiet, but its combination of boutique-style retro-hip decor and happening rooftop bar scene makes it a great place to go for a fun stay that's as much Manhattan as Savannah. Valet parking is available, which you will come to appreciate.

It's not exactly brand-new—it occupies the space formerly occupied by the well-regarded Mulberry Inn—but ★ **The Brice** (601 E. Bay St., 912/238-1200, www.thebricehotel.com, $175-225) features a complete boutique-style upgrade to this historic building, which formerly housed Savannah's first Coca-Cola bottling plant, on the eastern edge of the historic district. With great service and 145 rooms, most complete with a modernized four-poster bed, the Brice also features **Pacci Italian Kitchen + Bar** (breakfast daily 7am-10:30am, brunch Sat.-Sun. 8am-3pm, dinner Sun.-Thurs. 5pm-10pm, Fri.-Sat. 5pm-10:30pm, $15-25), one of the better hotel restaurant/bar combos in town.

For years critics have called it an insult to architecture and to history. The modernist **Hyatt Regency Savannah** (2 E. Bay St., 912/238-1234, www.savannah.hyatt.com, $200-250) is more than three decades old, but a competent renovation means that the Hyatt—a sort of exercise in cubism straddling an entire block of River Street—has avoided the neglect of many older chain properties downtown. Three sides of the hotel offer views of the bustling Savannah waterfront, with its massive ships coming in from all over the world.

If you require a swank pool, look no further than the **Westin Savannah Harbor Golf Resort and Spa** (1 Resort Dr., 912/201-2000, www.westinsavannah.com, $250-500), which has a beautiful resort-style pool across the Savannah River from downtown and overlooking the old city. Accessing the hotel—located on a cross-channel island—is a bit of a process, but one made easier by charming river ferries that run regularly and free of charge. The attached golf course is a good one, and packages are available.

## CITY MARKET
### $150-300

Providing a suitably modernist decor to go with its somewhat atypical architecture for Savannah, the ★ **Andaz Savannah** (14 Barnard St., 912/233-2116, www.savannah.andaz.hyatt.com, $250-350) overlooks restored Ellis Square and abuts City Market with its shopping, restaurants, and nightlife. A boutique offering from Hyatt, the Andaz's guest rooms and suites feature top-of-the-line linens, extra-large and well-equipped baths, in-room snack bars, and technological features such as MP3 docking stations, free Wi-Fi, and, of course, the ubiquitous flat-screen TV. Customer service is a particular strong suit. Just off the lobby is a very hip lounge-wine bar that attracts locals as well as hotel guests. Keep in mind things can get a little noisy in this area at night on weekends.

# HISTORIC DISTRICT NORTH
## Under $150

Famous for its host of resident ghosts—which many employees do swear aren't just tourist tales—**17hundred90 Inn** (307 E. President St., 912/236-7122, www.17hundred90.com, $140) offers 14 cozy rooms within a historic building that dates from, yep, 1790. The addition of several nearby guesthouses, booked through the inn, has expanded the footprint of this great old Savannah name. The great plus here—other than the ghost stories, of course—is the excellent on-site restaurant and bar, popular with both locals and tourists alike.

## $150-300

Once a bordello, the 1838 mansion that is home to the 16-room **Ballastone Inn** (14 E. Oglethorpe Ave., 912/236-1484, www.ballastone.com, $250-400) is one of Savannah's favorite inns. Highlights include an afternoon tea service and one of the better full breakfasts in town. Note that some guest rooms are at what Savannah calls the "garden level," meaning sunken basement-level rooms with what amounts to a worm's-eye view.

One of Savannah's favorite bed-and-breakfasts, **The Kehoe House** (123 Habersham St., 912/232-1020, www.kehoehouse.com, $225-300) is a great choice for its charm and attention to guests. Its historic location, on quiet little Columbia Square catty-corner to the Isaiah Davenport House, is within walking distance to all the downtown action, but far enough from the bustle to get some peace out on one of the rocking chairs on the veranda.

# HISTORIC DISTRICT SOUTH
## $150-300

One of Savannah's original historic B&Bs, the **Eliza Thompson House** (5 W. Jones St., 912/236-3620, www.elizathompsonhouse.

com, $200-250) is a bit out of the bustle on serene, beautiful Jones Street, but still close enough for you to get involved whenever you feel the urge. You can enjoy the various culinary offerings—breakfast, wine and cheese, nighttime munchies—either in the parlor or on the patio overlooking the house's classic Savannah garden.

The circa-1896 ★ **Foley House Inn** (14 W. Hull St., 912/232-6622, www.foleyinn.com, $220-350) is a four-diamond B&B with some rooms available at a three-diamond price. Its 19 individualized Victorian-decor guest rooms, in two town houses, range from the smaller Newport overlooking the "grotto courtyard" to the four-poster, bay-windowed Essex room, complete with a fireplace and a whirlpool bath. The location on Chippewa Square is pretty much perfect: well off the busy east-west thoroughfares but in the heart of Savannah's active theater district and within walking distance of anywhere.

# VICTORIAN DISTRICT
## $150-300

★ **The Gastonian** (220 E. Gaston St., 912/232-2869, www.gastonian.com, $225-350), circa 1868, is a favorite choice for travelers to Savannah, mostly for its 17 sumptuously decorated guest rooms and suites, all with working fireplaces, and the always outstanding full breakfast. They pile on the epicurean delights with teatime, evening nightcaps, and complimentary wine. This is one of the six properties owned by the local firm HLC, which seems to have consistently higher standards than most out-of-town chains.

How ironic that a hotel built in a former mortuary would be one of the few Savannah hotels not to have a resident ghost story. But that's the case with **Mansion on Forsyth Park** (700 Drayton St., 912/238-5158, www.mansiononforsythpark.com, $200-350), which dominates an entire block alongside Forsyth Park, including partially within the high-Victorian former Fox & Weeks Mortuary building. Its sumptuous guest rooms, equipped with big beds, big baths, and big-screen TVs, scream "boutique hotel," as does the swank little bar and the alfresco patio area.

## TYBEE ISLAND

Most of the hotels on Tybee Island are what we describe in the South as "rode hard and put away wet," meaning that they see a lot of wear and tear from eager vacationers. I encourage a B&B stay. Also be aware that places on Butler Avenue, even the substandard ones, charge a premium during the high season (Mar.-Oct.).

### $150-300

For those looking for the offbeat, try the **Atlantis Inn** (20 Silver Ave., 912/786-8558, www.atlantisinntybee.com, $150-200). Its reasonably priced, whimsically themed rooms are a hoot, and you're a short walk from the ocean and a very easy jaunt around the corner from busy Tybrisa Street. The downside, however, is no dedicated parking.

The best B&B-style experience on Tybee can be found at **The Georgianne Inn** (1312 Butler Ave., 912/786-8710, www.georgianne-inn.com, $175-250), a short walk off the beach and close to most of the island's action, yet not so close that you can't get away when you want to. The complimentary bikes to use while you're there are a nice plus.

## CAMPING

The best campground in town is at the well-managed and rarely crowded **Skidaway Island State Park** (52 Diamond Causeway, 912/598-2300, www.gastateparks.org, parking $5 per vehicle per day, tent and RV sites $26-40). There are 88 sites with 30-amp electric hookups. A two-night minimum stay is required on weekends, and there's a three-night minimum for Memorial Day, Labor Day, Independence Day, and Thanksgiving.

There's one campground on Tybee Island, the **River's End Campground and RV Park** (915 Polk St., 912/786-5518, www.cityoftybee.org, water-and-electric sites $34, 50-amp full-hookup sites $45, cabins $150) on the north side. River's End offers 100 full-service sites plus some primitive tent sites. The highlights, however, are the incredibly cute little cabins; book well in advance. During Tybee's sometimes-chilly off-season (Nov.-Mar.), you can relax and get warm inside the common River Room. River's End also offers a swimming pool and laundry facilities.

# Transportation and Services

## AIR

Savannah is served by the fairly efficient **Savannah/Hilton Head International Airport** (SAV, 400 Airways Ave., 912/964-0514, www.savannahairport.com), directly off I-95 at exit 104. The airport is about 20 minutes from downtown Savannah and 45 minutes from Hilton Head Island. Airlines with routes to SAV include American Airlines (www.aa.com), Allegiant (www.allegiant.com), Delta (www.delta.com), JetBlue (www.jetblue.com), Sun Country (www.suncountry.com), and United (www.ual.com).

Taxis and Uber provide transportation into Savannah. The maximum cab fare for destinations in the historic district is $28.

## CAR

Savannah is the eastern terminus of I-16, and that interstate is the most common entrance to the city. However, most travelers get to I-16 via I-95, taking the exit for downtown Savannah (Historic District).

Paralleling I-95 is the old coastal highway, now U.S. 17, which goes through Savannah. U.S. 80 is Victory Drive for most of its length through town; after you pass through Thunderbolt on your way to the islands area, however, it reverts to U.S. 80, the only route to and from Tybee Island.

When you're driving downtown and come to a square, the law says traffic within the square *always* has the right of way. In other words, if you haven't yet entered the square, you must yield to any vehicles already in the square.

## Car Rentals

The majority of rental car facilities are at the Savannah/Hilton Head International Airport, including **Avis** (800/831-2847), **Budget** (800/527-0700), **Dollar** (912/964-9001), **Enterprise** (800/736-8222), **Hertz** (800/654-3131), **National** (800/227-7368), and **Thrifty** (800/367-2277). Rental locations away from the airport are **Avis** (7810 Abercorn St., 912/354-4718), **Budget** (7070 Abercorn St., 912/355-0805), and **Enterprise** (3028 Skidaway Rd., 912/352-1424; 9505 Abercorn St., 912/925-0060; 11506-A Abercorn Expressway, 912/920-1093; 7510 White Bluff Rd., 912/355-6622).

## TRAIN

Savannah is on the New York-Miami *Silver Service* of **Amtrak** (2611 Seaboard Coastline Dr., 912/234-2611, www.amtrak.com). To get to the station on the west side of town, take I-16 west and then I-516 north. Immediately take the Gwinnett Street-Railroad Station exit and follow the Amtrak signs.

## BUS

**Chatham Area Transit** (www.catchacat. org, Mon.-Sat. 5:30am-11:30pm, Sun. 7am-9pm, $1.25, includes one transfer, free for children under 41 inches tall, exact change only), Savannah's publicly supported bus system, is quite thorough and efficient considering Savannah's relatively small size. Plenty of routes crisscross the entire area.

Of primary interest to visitors is the free **Dot Express Shuttle** (daily 7am-9pm), which travels a continuous circuit route through the historic district with 11 stops at hotels, historic sites, and the Savannah Visitors Center. The shuttle is wheelchair accessible.

## TAXI

Taxi services in Georgia tend to be less regulated than in other states, but service is plentiful in Savannah and is generally reasonable. The chief local provider is **Yellow Cab** (866/319-9646, www.savannahyellowcab.com). For wheelchair accessibility, request cab number 14. Other providers include **Adam Cab** (912/927-7466), **Magikal Taxi Service** (912/897-8294), and **Sunshine Cab** (912/272-0971).

If you're not in a big hurry, it's always fun to take a **Savannah Pedicab** (912/232-7900, www.savannahpedicab.com) for quick trips around downtown, or with the competing company **Royal Bike Taxi** (912/341-3944, www.royalbiketaxi.com). In both cases your friendly driver will pedal one or two passengers anywhere within the historic district, and you essentially pay what you think is fair (I recommend $5 per person minimum).

## PARKING

Parking is at a premium in downtown Savannah. Traditional coin-operated meter parking is available throughout the city, but more and more the city is going to self-pay kiosks, which accept debit/credit cards. Bottom line: Be sure to pay for all parking weekdays 8:30am-5pm.

As of this writing, one big plus is there is *no* enforcement of parking meters at all on weekends or any day after 5pm. However, there is a very unpopular political move afoot to expand paid parking to Saturdays and evenings, so check the meters on arrival.

The city operates several parking garages at various rates and hours: the **Bryan Street Garage** (100 E. Bryan St.), the **Robinson Garage** (132 Montgomery St.), the **State Street Garage** (100 E. State St.), the **Liberty Street Garage** (401 W. Liberty St.), and the new **Whitaker Street Garage** underneath revitalized Ellis Square.

Tybee Island has paid parking year-round daily 8am-8pm.

# TOURIST INFORMATION
## Visitors Centers

The main clearinghouse for visitor information is the downtown **Savannah Visitors Center** (301 MLK Jr. Blvd., 912/944-0455, Mon.-Fri. 8:30am-5pm, Sat.-Sun. and holidays 9am-5pm). The newly revitalized Ellis Square features a small visitors kiosk (Mon.-Fri. 8am-6pm) at the northwest corner of the square, with public restrooms and elevators to the underground parking garage beneath the square.

Other visitors centers in the area include the **River Street Hospitality Center** (1 River St., 912/651-6662, daily 10am-10pm), the **Tybee Island Visitor Center** (S. Campbell Ave. and U.S. 80, 912/786-5444, daily 9am-5:30pm), and the **Savannah Airport Visitor Center** (464 Airways Ave., 912/964-1109, daily 10am-6pm).

**Visit Savannah** (101 E. Bay St., 877/728-2662, www.savannahvisit.com), the local convention and visitors bureau, maintains a list of lodgings on its website.

## Hospitals

Savannah has two very good hospital systems. Centrally located near midtown, **Memorial Health University Hospital** (4700 Waters Ave., 912/350-8000, www.memorialhealth.com) is the region's only Level 1 Trauma Center and is one of the best in the nation. The St. Joseph's-Candler Hospital System (www.sjchs.org) has two units, **St. Joseph's Hospital** (11705 Mercy Blvd., 912/819-4100) on the extreme south side and **Candler Hospital** (5401 Paulsen St., 912/819-6000), closer to midtown.

## Police

The Savannah-Chatham County Metropolitan Police Department has jurisdiction throughout the city of Savannah and unincorporated Chatham County. For non-emergencies, call 912/651-6675; for emergencies, call 911.

## Media

The daily newspaper of record is the *Savannah Morning News* (912/525-0796, www.savannahnow.com). It puts out an entertainment insert, called "Do," on Thursdays. The free weekly newspaper in town is *Connect Savannah* (912/721-4350, www.connectsavannah.com), hitting stands each Wednesday. Look to it for culture and music coverage as well as an alternative take on local politics and issues.

Two glossy magazines compete: the hipper *The South* magazine (912/236-5501, www.thesouthmag.com) and the more establishment *Savannah* magazine (912/652-0293, www.savannahmagazine.com).

# The Golden Isles

Look for ★ to find recommended sights, activities, dining, and lodging.

# Highlights

★ **Jekyll Island Historic District:** Relax and soak in the salty breeze at this onetime playground of the country's richest people (page 651).

★ **The Village:** The center of social life on St. Simons Island has shops, restaurants, a pier, and a beachside playground (page 656).

★ **Fort Frederica National Monument:** An excellently preserved tabby fortress dates from the first days of English settlement in Georgia (page 657).

★ **Harris Neck National Wildlife Refuge:** This former wartime airfield is now one of the East Coast's best birding locations (page 663).

★ **Cumberland Island National Seashore:** This undeveloped island paradise has wild horses, evocative abandoned ruins, and over 16 miles of gorgeous beach (page 668).

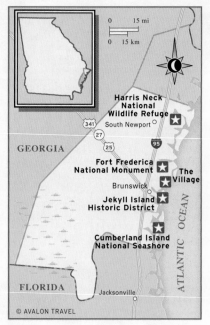

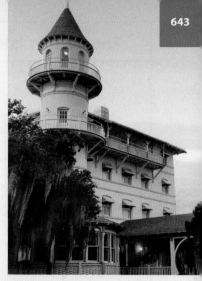

# The Georgia coast retains a timeless mystique evocative of an era before the coming of Europeans, even before humankind itself.

Often called the Golden Isles because of the play of the afternoon sun on the vistas of marsh grass, its other nickname, "the Debatable Land," is a nod to its centuries-long role as a constantly shifting battleground of European powers.

On the map it looks relatively short, but Georgia's coastline is the longest contiguous salt marsh environment in the world—a third of the country's remaining salt marsh. Abundant with wildlife, vibrant with exotic, earthy aromas, constantly refreshed by a steady, salty sea breeze, it's a place with no real match anywhere else.

Ancient Native Americans held the area in special regard. Avaricious for gold as they were, the Spanish also admired the almost monastic enchantment of Georgia's coast, choosing it as the site of their first colony in North America. They built a subsequent chain of Roman Catholic missions, now long gone.

While the American tycoons who used these barrier islands as personal playgrounds had avarice of their own, we must give credit where it's due: Their self-interest kept these places largely untouched by the kind of development that has plagued many of South Carolina's barrier islands to the north.

## PLANNING YOUR TIME

Many travelers take I-95 south from Savannah to the Golden Isles, but **U.S. 17** roughly parallels the interstate—in some cases so closely that drivers on the two roads can see each other—and is a far more scenic and enriching drive for those with a little extra time to spend. Indeed, U.S. 17 is an intrinsic part of the life and lore of the region, and you are likely to spend a fair amount of time on it regardless.

Geographically, Brunswick is similar to Charleston in that it lies on a peninsula laid out roughly north-south. And like Charleston, it's separated from the Atlantic by barrier islands, in Brunswick's case St. Simons Island and Jekyll Island. Once you get within city limits, however, Brunswick has more in common with Savannah due

---

**Previous:** Fort Frederica National Monument; a wild horse at Cumberland Island National Seashore.
**Above:** the legendary Jekyll Island Club.

# The Golden Isles

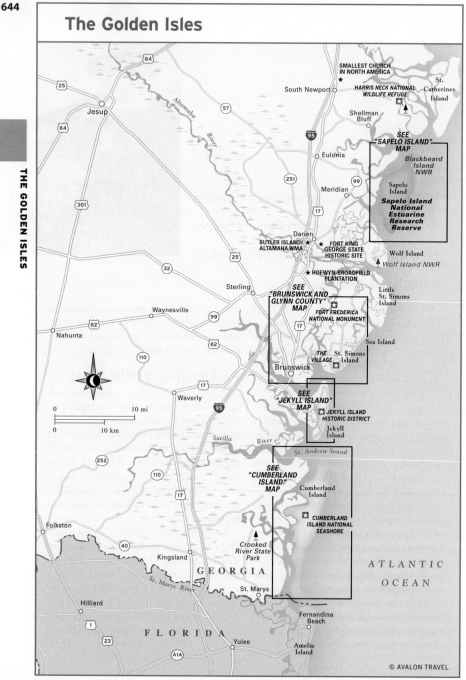

SMALLEST CHURCH
IN NORTH AMERICA ★

South Newport

HARRIS NECK NATIONAL
WILDLIFE REFUGE

St.
Catherines
Island

Jesup

Shellman
Bluff

SEE
"SAPELO ISLAND"
MAP

Blackbeard
Island
NWR

Eulonia

Sapelo
Island

Meridian

Sapelo Island
National
Estuarine
Research
Reserve

Altamaha River

Darien

BUTLER ISLAND/
ALTAMAHA WMA ★

★ FORT KING
GEORGE STATE
HISTORIC SITE

Wolf Island

↟ Wolf Island NWR

★ HOFWYN-BROADFIELD
PLANTATION

Sterling

SEE
"BRUNSWICK AND
GLYNN COUNTY"
MAP

Little
St. Simons
Island

Waynesville

FORT FREDERICA
NATIONAL MONUMENT

Nahunta

Sea Island

St. Simons
Island

THE
VILLAGE

Brunswick

SEE
"JEKYLL ISLAND"
MAP

Waverly

★ JEKYLL ISLAND
HISTORIC DISTRICT

Jekyll
Island

0        10 mi

0        10 km

Satilla    River

St. Andrew Sound

SEE
"CUMBERLAND
ISLAND"
MAP

Cumberland
Island

252

CUMBERLAND
ISLAND NATIONAL
SEASHORE

Folkston

Crooked
River State
Park

Kingsland

GEORGIA

ATLANTIC

OCEAN

Hilliard

St. Marys River

St. Marys

FLORIDA

Fernandina
Beach

Yulee

Amelia
Island

© AVALON TRAVEL

to its Oglethorpe-designed grid layout. Brunswick itself can easily be fully experienced in a **single afternoon.** But really—as its nickname "Gateway to the Golden Isles" indicates—Brunswick is an economic and governmental center for Glynn County, to which Jekyll Island and St. Simons Island, the real attractions in this area, belong.

Both Jekyll Island and St. Simons Island are well worth visiting, and have their own separate pleasures—Jekyll more contemplative, St. Simons more upscale. Give an **entire day to Jekyll** so you can take full advantage of its relaxing, open feel. A **half day** can suffice for **St. Simons** because most of its attractions are clustered in the Village area near the pier, and there's little beach recreation to speak of.

Getting to the undeveloped barrier islands, Sapelo and Cumberland, takes planning because there is no bridge to either. Both require a ferry booking and hence a more substantial commitment of time. There are no real stores and few facilities on these islands, so pack along whatever you think you'll need, including food, water, medicine, suntan lotion, insect repellent, and so on. **Sapelo Island** is limited to **day use** unless you have prior reservations, with the town of Darien in McIntosh County as the gateway. The same is true for Cumberland Island National Seashore, with the town of St. Marys in Camden County as the gateway.

# Brunswick and Glynn County

Consider Brunswick sort of a junior Savannah, sharing with that larger city to the north a heavily English flavor, great manners, a city plan with squares courtesy of General James Oglethorpe, a thriving but environmentally intrusive seaport, and a busy shrimping fleet. Despite an admirable effort at downtown revitalization, most visitors to the area seem content to employ Brunswick, as its nickname implies, as a "Gateway to the Golden Isles" rather than as a destination in itself.

## SIGHTS
### Brunswick Historic District

Most of the visitor-friendly activity centers on **Newcastle Street,** where you'll find the bulk of the galleries, shops, and restored buildings. Adjacent in the historic areas are some nice residential homes.

The new pride of downtown is **Old City Hall** (1212 Newcastle St., 912/265-4032, www.brunswickgeorgia.net/och2.html), an amazing circa-1889 Richardsonian Romanesque edifice designed by noted regional architect Alfred Eichberg, who also planned many similarly imposing buildings in Savannah. Today it doubles as a rental event facility as well as a part-time courthouse; call ahead to take a gander inside.

Another active restored building is the charming **Ritz Theatre** (1530 Newcastle St., 912/262-6934, www.goldenislearts.org), built in 1898 to house the Grand Opera House and the offices of the Brunswick and Birmingham Railroad. This ornate three-story Victorian transitioned with the times, becoming a vaudeville venue, then a movie house.

### Mary Ross Waterfront Park

**Mary Ross Waterfront Park,** a downtown gathering place at Bay and Gloucester Streets, also has economic importance as a center of local industry—it's here where Brunswick's shrimp fleet is moored and the town's large port facilities begin. In 1989 the park was dedicated to Mary Ross, member of a longtime Brunswick shrimping family and author of the popular Georgia history book *The Debatable Land.*

### Lover's Oak

At the intersection of Prince and Albany Streets is the **Lover's Oak,** a nearly 1,000-year-old tree. Local lore tells us that it has been a secret

# Brunswick and Glynn County

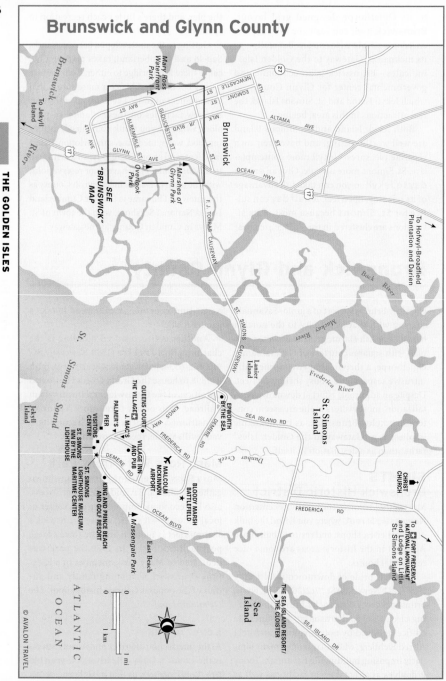

© AVALON TRAVEL

# Brunswick

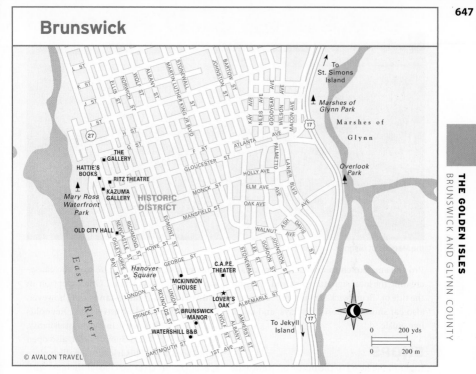

meeting place for young lovers for centuries (though one does wonder how much of a secret it actually could have been). It's about 13 feet in diameter and has 10 sprawling limbs.

Amid the light industrial sprawl of this area of the Golden Isles Parkway is the interesting little **Overlook Park,** just south of the visitors center on U.S. 17—a good, if loud, place for a picnic. From the park's picnic grounds or overlook you can see the fabled **Marshes of Glynn,** which inspired Georgia poet Sidney Lanier to write his famous poem of the same title under the **Lanier Oak,** located a little farther up the road in the median.

## Hofwyl-Broadfield Plantation

South Carolina doesn't own the patent on well-preserved old rice plantations, as the **Hofwyl-Broadfield Plantation** (5556 U.S. 17, 912/264-7333, www.gastateparks.org, Wed.-Sun. 9am-5pm, last main house tour 4pm, $8 adults, $5 children), a short

drive north of Brunswick, proves. With its old paddy fields along the gorgeous and relatively undeveloped Altamaha River estuary, the plantation's main home is an antebellum wonder, with an expansive porch and a nice house museum that includes silver, a model of a rice plantation, and a slide show. There's also a pleasant nature trail.

## FESTIVALS AND EVENTS

Each Mother's Day at noon, parishioners of the local St. Francis Xavier Church hold the **Our Lady of Fatima Processional and Blessing of the Fleet** (www.brunswick.net), begun in 1938 by the local Portuguese fishing community. After the procession, at about 3pm at Mary Ross Waterfront Park, comes the actual blessing of the shrimping fleet.

Foodies will enjoy the **Brunswick Stewbilee** ($9 adults, $4 children), held on the second Saturday in October 11:30am-3pm.

the Marshes of Glynn at Overlook Park

Pro and amateur chefs showcase their skills in creating the local signature dish and vying for the title of "Brunswick Stewmaster." There are also car shows, contests, displays, and much live music.

## SHOPS

Right in the heart of the bustle on Newcastle is a good indie bookstore, **Hattie's Books** (1531 Newcastle St., 912/554-8677, www.hattiesbooks.com, Mon.-Fri. 10am-5:30pm, Sat. 10am-4pm). Not only do they have a good selection of local and regional authors, you can also get a good cup of coffee.

Like Beaufort, South Carolina, Brunswick has made the art gallery a central component of its downtown revitalization, with nearly all of them on Newcastle Street. Near Hattie's you'll find the **Ritz Theatre** (1530 Newcastle St., 912/262-6934, Tues.-Fri. 9am-5pm, Sat. 10am-2pm), which has its own art gallery inside. Farther down is **The Gallery on Newcastle Street** (1626 Newcastle St., 912/554-0056, www.thegalleryonnewcastle.com, Thurs.-Sat. 11am-5pm), showcasing the original oils of owner Janet Powers.

## FOOD

Brunswick isn't known for its breadth of cuisine options, and, frankly, most discriminating diners make the short drive over the causeway to St. Simons Island. One exception in Brunswick that really stands out, however, is **Indigo Coastal Shanty** (1402 Reynolds St., 912/265-2007, www.indigocoastalshanty.com, Tues.-Fri. 11am-3pm, Fri.-Sat. also open 5pm-10pm, $12). This friendly, smallish place specializes in creative coastal themes, with dishes like the Charleston Sauté (shrimp and ham with peppers), Fisherman's Bowl (shrimp and fish in a nice broth), and even that old Southern favorite, a pimento cheeseburger.

## ACCOMMODATIONS

In addition to the usual variety of chain hotels—most of which you should stay far away from—there are some nice places to stay in Brunswick at very reasonable prices if you want to make the city a base of operations. In the heart of Old Town in a gorgeous Victorian is the ★ **McKinnon House** (1001 Egmont St., 912/261-9100, www.mckinnonhousebandb.com, $125), which had a cameo role in the 1974 film *Conrack*. Today, this bed-and-breakfast is Jo Miller's labor of love, a three-suite affair with some plush interiors and an exterior that is one of Brunswick's most photographed spots. Surprisingly affordable for its elegance, the **WatersHill Bed & Breakfast** (728 Union St., 912/264-4262,

# Brunswick Stew

Virginians insist that the distinctive Southern dish known as Brunswick stew was named for Brunswick County, Virginia, in 1828, where a political rally featured stew made from squirrel meat. But all real Southern foodies know the dish is named for Brunswick, Georgia. Hey, there's a plaque to prove it in downtown Brunswick—although it says the first pot was cooked on July 2, 1898, on St. Simons Island, not in Brunswick at all. However, I think we can all agree that "Brunswick stew" rolls off the tongue much more easily than "St. Simons stew." You can find the famous pot in which the first batch was cooked on F Street near Mary Ross Waterfront Park.

The first Brunswick Stew was cooked in this pot.

It seems likely that what we now know as Brunswick stew is based on an old colonial recipe, adapted from Native Americans, that relied on the meat of small game—originally squirrel or rabbit but nowadays mostly chicken or pork—along with vegetables like corn, onions, and okra simmered over an open fire. Today, this tangy, thick, tomato-based delight is a typical accompaniment to barbecue throughout the Lowcountry and the Georgia coast, as well as a freestanding entrée on its own. Here's a typical recipe from Glynn County, home of the famous Brunswick Stewbilee festival held the second Saturday of October:

## SAUCE

Melt ¼ cup butter over low heat, then add:
1¾ cups ketchup
¼ cup yellow mustard
¼ cup white vinegar

Blend until smooth, then add:
½ tablespoon chopped garlic
1 teaspoon ground black pepper
½ teaspoon crushed red pepper
½ ounce Liquid Smoke
1 ounce Worcestershire sauce
1 ounce hot sauce
½ tablespoon fresh lemon juice

Blend until smooth, then add:
¼ cup dark brown sugar
Stir constantly and simmer for 10 minutes, being careful not to boil. Set aside.

## STEW

Melt ¼ pound butter in a two-gallon pot, then add:
3 cups diced small potatoes
1 cup diced small onion
2 14½-ounce cans chicken broth
1 pound baked chicken
8-10 ounces smoked pork

Bring to a boil, stirring until potatoes are nearly done, then add:
1 8½-ounce can early peas
2 14½-ounce cans stewed tomatoes
1 16-ounce can baby lima beans
¼ cup Liquid Smoke
1 14½-ounce can creamed corn

Stir in sauce. Simmer slowly for two hours. Makes one gallon of Brunswick stew.

www.watershill.com, $100) serves a full break-fast and offers a choice of five themed suites, such as the French country Elliot Wynell Room or the large Mariana Mahlaney Room way up in the restored attic. Another good B&B is the **Brunswick Manor** (825 Egmont St., 912/265-6889, www.brunswickmanor. com, $130), offering four suites in a classic Victorian and a tasty meal each day.

The most unique lodging in the area is the ★ **Hostel in the Forest** (Hwy. 82, 912/264-9738, www.foresthostel.com, $25, cash only). Formed more than 30 years ago as an International Youth Hostel, the place initially gives off a hippie vibe, with an evening communal meal (included in the rates) and a near-total ban on cell phones. But don't expect a wild time: No pets are allowed, the hostel discourages young children, and quiet time is strictly enforced beginning at 11pm. To reach the hostel, take I-95 exit 29 and go west for two miles. Make a U-turn at the intersection at mile marker 11. Continue east on Highway 82 for 0.5 mile. Look for a dirt road on the right with a gate and signage. This is now a "membership" organization so you'll need to join before booking.

## TRANSPORTATION AND SERVICES

Brunswick is directly off I-95. Take exit 38 to the Golden Isles Parkway, and take a right on U.S. 17. The quickest way to the historic district is to make a right onto Gloucester Street. Plans and funding for a citywide public transit system are pending, but currently Brunswick has no public transportation.

A downtown **information station** is in the Ritz Theatre (1530 Newcastle St., 912/262-6934, Tues.-Fri. 9am-5pm, Sat. 10am-2pm).

The newspaper of record in town is the **Brunswick News** (www.thebrunswicknews. com). The main **post office** (805 Gloucester St., 912/280-1250) is downtown.

# Jekyll Island

Few places in the United States have as paradoxical a story as Jekyll Island (www.jekyllisland.com). Once the playground of the world's richest people—whose indulgence allowed the island to escape the overdevelopment that plagues nearby St. Simons—Jekyll then became a dedicated vacation area for Georgians of modest means, by order of the state legislature. Today, it's somewhere in the middle—a great place for a relaxing nature-oriented vacation that retains some of the perks of luxury of its Gilded Age pedigree.

After securing safe access to the island from the Creeks in 1733, Georgia's founder, General James Oglethorpe, gave the island its modern name, after his friend Sir Joseph Jekyll. In 1858, Jekyll Island was the final port of entry for the infamous voyage of *The Wanderer,* the last American slave ship. After intercepting the ship and its contraband manifest of 409 African slaves—the importation of slaves having been banned in 1808—its owners and crew were put on trial and acquitted in Savannah.

As a home away from home for the country's richest industrialists—including J. P. Morgan, William Rockefeller, and William Vanderbilt—in the late 1800s and early 1900s, Jekyll Island was the unlikely seat of some of the most crucial events in modern American history. It was at the Jekyll Island Club in 1910 that the Federal Reserve banking system was set up, the result of a secret convocation of investors and tycoons. Five years later on the grounds of the club, AT&T president Theodore Vail would listen in on the first transcontinental phone call.

## ORIENTATION

You'll have to stop at the entrance gate and pay a $6 "parking fee" to gain daily access to this state-owned island; a weeklong pass is $28. (Bicyclists and pedestrians don't need to pay.)

# Jekyll Island

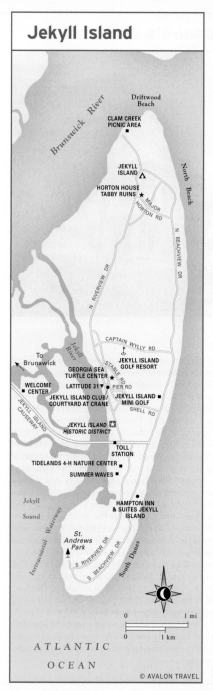

ATLANTIC
OCEAN

© AVALON TRAVEL

A friendly attendant will give you a map and a newsletter, and from there you're free to enjoy the whole island at your leisure.

## SIGHTS
### ★ Jekyll Island Historic District

A living link to one of the most glamorous eras of American history, the **Jekyll Island Historic District** is also one of the largest on-going restoration projects in the southeastern United States. A visit to this 240-acre riverfront area is like stepping back in time to the Gilded Age, with croquet grounds, manicured gardens, and even ferry boats with names like the *Rockefeller* and the *J. P. Morgan*. The historic district essentially comprises the buildings and grounds of the old **Jekyll Island Club,** not only a full-service resort complex—consisting of the main building and several amazing "cottages" that are mansions themselves—but a sort of living-history exhibit chronicling that time when Jekyll was a gathering place for the world's richest and most influential people.

The Queen Anne-style main clubhouse, with its iconic turret, dates from 1886. Within a couple of years the club had already outgrown it, and the millionaires began building the ornate cottages on the grounds surrounding it. In 2000 renovations were done on the most magnificent outbuilding, the 24-bedroom Crane Cottage, a Mediterranean villa that also hosts a fine restaurant.

The **Jekyll Island Museum** (100 Stable Rd., 912/635-4036, www.jekyllisland.com, daily 9am-5pm, free), in the historic district at the old club stables, houses some good history exhibits.

## Georgia Sea Turtle Center

Within the historic district in a whimsically renovated 1903 building is the **Georgia Sea Turtle Center** (214 Stable Rd., 912/635-4444, www.georgiaseaturtlecenter.org, daily 9am-5pm, $7 adults, $5 children), which features interactive exhibits on these important marine creatures, for whom Jekyll Island is a major nesting ground. Don't miss the attached rehabilitation building, where you can see the center's turtles

# Jekyll Island's Millionaire's Club

the Jekyll Island Club

After the Civil War, as the Industrial Revolution gathered momentum seemingly everywhere but Georgia's Golden Isles, a couple of men decided to do something to break the foggy miasma of Reconstruction that had settled into the area and make some money in the process. In the late 1870s, John Eugene DuBignon and his brother-in-law Newton Finney came up with a plan to combine DuBignon's long family ties to Jekyll with Finney's extensive Wall Street connections in order to turn Jekyll into an exclusive winter hunting club. Their targeted clientele was a no-brainer: the newly minted American mega-tycoons of the Industrial Age. Finney found 53 such elite millionaires willing to pony up to become charter members of the venture, dubbed the Jekyll Island Club. Among them were William Vanderbilt, J. P. Morgan, and Joseph Pulitzer. As part of the original business model, in 1886 Finney purchased the island from DuBignon for $125,000.

With the formal opening two years later began Jekyll Island's half century as a premier playground for the country's richest citizens, centered on the Victorian winter homes, called "cottages," built by each member and preserved today in the historic district.

In 1910, secret meetings of the so-called "First Name Club" led to the development of the Aldrich Plan, which laid the groundwork for the modern Federal Reserve System. A few years later, AT&T president Theodore Vail, nursing a broken leg at his Mound Cottage on Jekyll, participated in the first transcontinental telephone call on January 25, 1915, among New York City, San Francisco, and the special line strung down the coast from New York and across Jekyll Sound to the club grounds. Also on the line were the telephone's inventor, Alexander Graham Bell, his assistant Thomas Watson, the mayors of New York and San Francisco, and President Woodrow Wilson.

The millionaires continued to frolic on Jekyll through the Great Depression, but worsening international economic conditions reduced the club's numbers, even though the cost of membership was lowered in 1933. The outbreak of World War II and the resulting drain of labor into the armed forces put a further cramp in the club's workings, and it finally closed for good in 1942. The state would acquire the island after the war in 1947, turning the once-exclusive playground of millionaires into a playground for all the people.

in various states of treatment and rehabilitation before they are released into the wild. Children and adults alike will enjoy this unique opportunity to see these creatures up close and learn about the latest efforts to protect them.

In an effort to raise awareness about the need to protect the nesting areas of the big loggerheads that lay eggs on Jekyll each summer, the Sea Turtle Center also guides **nighttime tours** (early June-Aug. daily 8:30pm and 9:30pm) on the beach in order to explain about the animals and their habitat and hopefully to see some loggerheads in action. These tours fill up fast, so make reservations in advance.

### Driftwood Beach

Barrier islands like Jekyll are in a constant state of southward flux as currents erode the north end and push sand down the beach to the south end. This phenomenon has created **Driftwood Beach,** as the soil has eroded from under the large trees, causing them to fall and settle into the sand. In addition to being a naturalist's wonderland, it's also a starkly beautiful and strangely romantic spot. Drive north on Beachview Drive until you see a pullover on your right immediately after the Villas by the Sea (there's no signage). Park and take the short trail through the maritime forest, and you'll find yourself right there among the fallen trees and sand.

### Horton House Tabby Ruins

Round the curve and go south on Riverview Drive, and you'll see the large frame of a two-story house on the left (east) side of the road. That is the ruins of the old **Horton House,** built by Jekyll's original English-speaking settler, William Horton. The house has survived two wars, a couple of hurricanes, and a clumsy restoration in 1898. Its current state of preservation is thanks to the Jekyll Island Authority and various federal, state, and local partners.

Frenchman Christophe Poulain du Bignon would live in the Horton House for a while after purchasing the island in the 1790s. Across the street from the house is the poignant little **Du Bignon Cemetery,** around which winds a nicely done pedestrian and bike path overlooking one of the most beautiful areas of marsh you'll see in all the Golden Isles.

## ENTERTAINMENT AND NIGHTLIFE

There's no real nightlife to speak of on Jekyll, it being intended for quiet, affordable daytime relaxation. The focus instead is on several annual events held at the **Jekyll Island Convention Center** (1 N. Beachview Dr., 912/635-3400), which has undergone a massive restoration to bring it in line with modern convention standards.

At the beginning of the New Year comes one of the area's most beloved and well-attended events, the **Jekyll Island Bluegrass Festival** (www.adamsbluegrass.com). Many of the genre's biggest traditional names come to play at this casual multiday gathering. The focus here is on the music, not the trappings, so come prepared to enjoy wall-to-wall bluegrass played by the best in the business.

In September as the harvest comes in off the boats, the **Wild Georgia Shrimp and Grits Festival** (www.jekyllisland.com, free admission) promotes the value of the Georgia shrimping industry by focusing on how good the little critters taste in various regional recipes.

## SPORTS AND ACTIVITIES
### Hiking and Biking

Quite simply, Jekyll Island is a paradise for bicyclists and walkers, with a well-developed and very safe system of paths totaling about 20 miles and running the circumference of the island. The paths go by all major sights, including the Jekyll Island Club in the historic district. In addition, walkers and bicyclists can enjoy much of the seven miles of beachfront at low tide.

Rent your bikes at **Jekyll Island Miniature Golf** (100 James Rd., 912/635-2648, daily 9am-8pm, $5.25 per hour, $11.50 per day). Take a left when you dead-end after the entrance gate, then another left.

### Golf and Tennis

True to Jekyll Island's intended role as a playground for Georgians of low to medium income, its golf and tennis facilities—all centrally located at the middle of the island—are quite reasonably priced. The **Jekyll Island Golf Resort** (322 Captain Wylly Rd., 912/635-2368, www.jekyllisland.com, greens fees $40-60) comprises the largest public golf resort in Georgia. A total of 63 holes on four courses—Pine Lakes, Indian Mound, Oleander, and Ocean Dunes (nine holes)—await. Check the resort's website for "golf passport" packages that include local lodging.

The adjacent **Jekyll Island Tennis Center** (400 Captain Wylly Rd., 912/635-3154, www.gate.net/~jitc, $25 per hour) boasts 13 courts, 7 of them lighted, as well as a pro shop (daily 9am-6pm).

### Water Parks

**Summer Waves** (210 S. Riverview Dr., 912/635-2074, www.jekyllisland.com, Memorial Day-Labor Day, $20 adults, $16 children under 48 inches tall) is just what the doctor ordered for kids with a surplus of energy. The 11-acre facility has a separate section for toddlers to splash around in, with the requisite more daring rides for hard-charging preteens. Hours vary, so call ahead.

### Horseback Riding and Tours

**Victoria's Carriages and Trail** (100 Stable Rd., 912/635-9500, Mon.-Sat. 11am-4pm) offers numerous options, both on horseback as well as in a horse-drawn carriage, including carriage tours of the island (Mon.-Sat. every hour 11am-4pm, $15 adults, $7 children). There's a 6pm-8pm night ride ($38 per couple). Horseback rides include a one-hour beach ride ($55) that leaves at 11am, 1pm, and 3pm and a sunset ride (6:30pm, $65) that lasts a little over an hour. Victoria's is at the entrance to the Clam Creek Picnic Area on the north end of the island, directly across the street from the Jekyll Island Campground.

The **Tidelands 4-H Center** (912/635-5032) gives 1.5-2-hour Marsh Walks (Mon. 9am, $5 adults, $3 children) leaving from Clam Creek Picnic Area, and Beach Walks ($5 adults, $3 children) leaving Wednesdays at 9am from the St. Andrews Picnic Area and Fridays at 9am from South Dunes Picnic Area.

## FOOD

Cuisine offerings are few and far between on Jekyll. I'd suggest you patronize one of the three dining facilities at the **Jekyll Island Club** (371 Riverview Dr.), which are all open to nonguests. They're not only delicious but pretty reasonable as well, considering the swank setting. My favorite is the ★ **Courtyard at Crane** (912/635-2400, lunch Sun.-Fri. 11am-4pm, Sat. 11am-2pm, dinner Sun.-Thurs. 5:30pm-9pm, $27-38). Located in the circa-1917 Crane Cottage, one of the beautifully restored tycoon villas, the Courtyard offers romantic evening dining (call for reservations) as well as tasty and stylish lunch dining in the alfresco courtyard area or inside.

For a real and figurative taste of history, make a reservation at the **Grand Dining Room** (912/635-2400, breakfast Mon.-Sat. 7am-11am, Sun. 7am-10am, lunch Mon.-Sat. 11:30am-2pm, brunch Sun. 10:45am-2pm, dinner daily 6pm-10pm, dinner $26-35), the club's full-service restaurant. Focusing on continental cuisine—ordered either à la carte or as a prix fixe "sunset dinner"—the Dining Room features a pianist each evening and for Sunday brunch. Jackets or collared shirts are required for men.

For a tasty breakfast, lunch, or dinner on the go or at odd hours, check out **Café Solterra** (912/635-2600, daily 7am-10pm), great for deli-type food and equipped with Starbucks coffee. There are two places for seaside dining and cocktails at the historic Jekyll Island Club Wharf: **Latitude 31** (1 Pier Rd., 912/635-3800, www.crossoverjekyll.com, Tues.-Sun. 5:30pm-10pm, $15-25, no reservations) is an upscale seafood-oriented fine-dining place, while the attached **Rah Bar** (Tues.-Sat. 11am-close, Sun. 1pm-close, depending on weather) serves up oysters and shellfish in a very casual setting; try the Lowcountry boil or the crab legs.

the Courtyard at Crane

## ACCOMMODATIONS
### Under $150

While most bargain lodging on Jekyll is sadly subpar, the old **Days Inn** (60 S. Beachview Dr., 912/635-9800, www.daysinnjekyll.com, $100) has undergone remodeling lately and is the best choice if budget is a concern (and you don't want to camp, that is). It has a good location on the south side of the island with nice ocean views.

### $150-300

Any discussion of lodging on Jekyll Island begins with the legendary ★ **Jekyll Island Club** (371 Riverview Dr., 800/535-9547, www.jekyllclub.com, $199-490), which is reasonably priced considering its history, postcard-perfect setting, and delightful guest rooms. Some of its 157 guest rooms in the club and annex areas are available for under $200. There are 60 guest rooms in the main club building, and several outlying cottages, chief among them the Crane, Cherokee, and Sans Souci Cottages, are also available. All rates include use of the big outdoor pool overlooking the river, and a neat amenity is a choice of meal plans for an extra daily fee.

The first hotel built on the island in 35 years, the ★ **Hampton Inn & Suites Jekyll Island** (200 S. Beachview Dr., 912/635-3733, www.hamptoninn.com, $180-210) was constructed according to an exacting set of conservation guidelines, conserving much of the original tree canopy and employing various low-impact design and building techniques. It's one of the best eco-friendly hotel designs I've experienced.

### Camping

One of the niftiest campgrounds in the area is the **Jekyll Island Campground** (197 Riverview Dr., 912/635-3021, tent sites $25, RV sites $32). It's a friendly place with an excellent location at the north end of the island. There are more than 200 sites, from tent to full-service pull-through RV sites. There's a two-night minimum on weekends and a three-night minimum on holiday and special-event weekends; reservations are recommended.

## TRANSPORTATION AND SERVICES

Jekyll Island is immediately south of Brunswick. You'll have to pay a $6 per vehicle fee to get onto the island. Once on the island, most sites are on the north end (a left as you reach the dead-end at Beachview Dr.).

The main circuit route around the island is Beachview Drive, which suitably enough changes into Riverview Drive as it rounds the bend to landward at the north end.

Many visitors choose to bicycle around the island once they're here, which is certainly the best way to experience both the sights and the beach itself at low tide.

The **Jekyll Island Visitor Center** (901 Downing Musgrove Causeway, 912/635-3636, daily 9am-5pm) is on the long causeway along the marsh before you get to the island. Set in a charming little cottage it shares with the Georgia State Patrol, the center has a nice gift shop and loads of brochures on the entire Golden Isles region.

# St. Simons Island

Despite a reputation for aloof affluence, the truth is that St. Simons Island is also very visitor friendly, and there's more to do here than meets the eye.

Fort Frederica, now a National Monument, was a key base of operations for the British struggle to evict the Spanish from Georgia—which culminated in 1742 in the decisive Battle of Bloody Marsh. In the years after American independence, St. Simons woke up from its slumber as acre after acre of virgin live oak was felled to make the massive timbers of new warships for the U.S. Navy, including the USS *Constitution*. In their place was planted a new crop—cotton. The island's antebellum plantations boomed to world-class heights of profit and prestige when the superior strain of the crop known as Sea Island cotton came in the 1820s.

The next landmark development for St. Simons didn't come until the building of the first causeway in 1924, which led directly to the island's resort development by the mega-rich industrialist Howard Coffin of Hudson Motors fame, who also owned nearby Sapelo Island to the north.

## ORIENTATION

Because it's only a short drive from downtown Brunswick on the Torras Causeway, St. Simons has much less of a remote feel than most other Georgia barrier islands, and it's much more densely populated than any other Georgia island except for Tybee. Most visitor-oriented activity on this 12-mile-long, heavily residential island is clustered at the south end, where St. Simons Sound meets the Atlantic.

## SIGHTS
### ★ The Village

Think of **"The Village"** at the extreme south end of St. Simons as a mix of Tybee's downscale accessibility and Hilton Head's upscale exclusivity. This compact, bustling area only a few blocks long offers not only boutique shops and stylish cafés, but also vintage stores and busking musicians.

### St. Simons Lighthouse Museum

Unlike many East Coast lighthouses, which tend to be in hard-to-reach places, anyone can walk right up to the **St. Simons Lighthouse Museum** (101 12th St., 912/638-4666, www.saintsimonslighthouse.org, Mon.-Sat. 10am-5pm, Sun. 1:30pm-5pm, $12 adults, $5 children). Once inside, you can enjoy the museum's exhibit and take the 129 steps up to the top of the 104-foot beacon—which is, unusually, still active—for a gorgeous view of the island and the ocean beyond.

### Maritime Center

A short walk from the lighthouse and also administered by the Coastal Georgia Historical Society, the **Maritime Center** (4201 1st St., 912/638-4666, www.saintsimonslighthouse.org, Mon.-Sat. 10am-5pm, Sun. 1:30pm-5pm, $12 adults, $5 children) is at the historic East Beach Coast Guard Station. Authorized by

# Golden Isles on the Page

And now from the Vast of the Lord will the waters of sleep
Roll in on the souls of men,
But who will reveal to our waking ken
The forms that swim and the shapes that creep
Under the waters of sleep?
And I would I could know what swimmeth below when the tide comes in
On the length and the breadth of the marvelous marshes of Glynn.

Sidney Lanier

Many authors have been inspired by their time in the Golden Isles, whether to pen flights of poetic fancy, page-turning novels, or politically oriented chronicles. Here are a few of the most notable names:

- **Sidney Lanier:** Born in Macon, Georgia, Lanier was a renowned linguist, mathematician, and legal scholar. Fighting for the Confederacy during the Civil War, he was captured while commanding a blockade runner and taken to a POW camp in Maryland, where he came down with tuberculosis. After the war, he stayed at his brother-in-law's house in Brunswick to recuperate, and it was during that time that he took up poetry, writing the famous "Marshes of Glynn," quoted above.

- **Eugenia Price:** Although not originally from St. Simons, Price remains the best-known local cultural figure, setting her *St. Simons Trilogy* here. After relocating to the island in 1965, she stayed here until her death in 1996. She's buried in the Christ Church cemetery on Frederica Road.

- **Tina McElroy Ansa:** Probably the most notable literary figure currently living on St. Simons Island is award-winning African American author Tina McElroy Ansa. Few of her books are set in the Golden Isles region, but they all deal with life in the South, and Ansa is an ardent devotee of St. Simons and its relaxed, friendly ways.

- **Fanny Kemble:** In 1834, this renowned English actress married Georgia plantation heir Pierce Butler, who would become one of the largest slave owners in the United States. Horrified by the treatment of Butler's slaves at Butler Island, just south of Darien, Georgia, Kemble penned one of the earliest antislavery chronicles, *Journal of a Residence on a Georgian Plantation in 1838-1839*. Kemble's disagreement with her husband over slavery hastened their divorce in 1849.

President Franklin Roosevelt in 1933 and completed in 1937 by the Works Progress Administration, the East Beach Station took part in military action in World War II, an episode chronicled in exhibits at the Maritime Center.

## ★ Fort Frederica National Monument

The expansive and well-researched **Fort Frederica National Monument** (Frederica Rd., 912/638-3639, www.nps.gov/fofr, daily 9am-5pm, free) lies on the landward side of the island. Established by General James Oglethorpe in 1736 to protect Georgia's southern flank from the Spanish, the fort (as well as the village that sprang up around it, in which the Wesley brothers preached for a short time) was named for Frederick Louis, the Prince of Wales. The feminine suffix -*a* was added to distinguish it from the older Fort Frederick in South Carolina.

You don't just get to see a military fort here (actually the remains of the old powder magazine; most of the fort itself eroded into the river long ago); this is an entire colonial townsite a mile in circumference, originally modeled after a typical English village. A self-guided walking tour through the beautiful grounds shows foundations of building sites that have been uncovered, including taverns, shops, and the private homes of influential citizens. Closer to the river is the large tabby structure of the garrison barracks.

## Bloody Marsh Battlefield

There's not a lot to see at the site of the **Battle of Bloody Marsh** (Frederica Rd., 912/638-3639, www.nps.gov/fofr, daily 8am-4pm, free). Essentially just a few interpretive signs overlooking a beautiful piece of salt marsh, the site is believed to be near the place where British soldiers from nearby Fort Frederica ambushed a force of Spanish regulars on their way to besiege the fort. The battle wasn't actually that bloody—some accounts say the Spanish lost only seven men—but the stout British presence convinced the Spanish to leave St. Simons a few days later, never again to project their once-potent military power that far north in the New World.

While the Battle of Bloody Marsh site is part of the National Park Service's Fort Frederica unit, it's not at the same location. Get to the battlefield from the fort by taking Frederica Road south, and then a left (east)

on Demere Road. The site is on your left as Demere Road veers right, in the 1800 block.

## Christ Church

Just down the road from Fort Frederica is historic **Christ Church** (6329 Frederica Rd., 912/638-8683, www.christchurchfrederica. org, daily 2pm-5pm). The first sanctuary dates from 1820, but the original congregation at the now-defunct town of Frederica held services under the oaks at the site as early as 1736. The founder of Methodism, John Wesley, and his brother Charles both ministered to island residents during 1736-1737.

Christ Church's claim to fame in modern culture is as the setting of local novelist Eugenia Price's *The Beloved Invader,* the first work in her Georgia trilogy. The late Price, who died in 1996, is buried in the church cemetery.

## Tours

**St. Simons Island Trolley Tours** (912/638-8954, www.stsimonstours.com, daily 11am, $22 adults, $10 ages 4-12, free under age 4) offers just that, a ride around the island in comparative comfort, leaving from the pier.

Fort Frederica National Monument

# ENTERTAINMENT AND NIGHTLIFE

## Nightlife

Unlike some areas this far south on the Georgia coast, there's usually a sizable contingent of young people on St. Simons out looking for a good time. The island's premier club, **Rafters Blues and Raw Bar** (315½ Mallory St., 912/634-9755, www.raftersblues. com, Mon.-Sat. 4:30pm-2am), known simply as "Rafters," brings in live music most every Thursday-Saturday night, focusing on the best acts on the regional rock circuit.

My favorite spot on St. Simons for a drink or an espresso—or a panini, for that matter—is **Palm Coast Coffee, Cafe, and Pub** (316 Mallory St., 912/634-7517, www.palmcoastssi. com, daily 8am-10pm). This handy little spot, combining a hip, relaxing coffeehouse with a hearty menu of brunchy items, is in the heart of the Village. The kicker, though, is the cute little bar the size of a large walk-in closet right off the side of the main room—a little bit of Key West on St. Simons.

Inside the Village Inn is the popular nightspot the **Village Pub** (500 Mallory St., 912/634-6056, www.villageinnandpub. com, Mon.-Sat. 5pm-midnight, Sun. 5pm-10pm). Slightly more upscale than most watering holes on the island, this is the best place for a quality martini or other premium cocktail.

# SHOPS

Most shopping on St. Simons is concentrated in the Village and is a typical beach town mix of hardware and tackle, casual clothing, and souvenir stores. A funky highlight is **Beachview Books** (215 Mallory St., 912/638-7282, Mon.-Sat. 10:30am-5:30pm, Sun. 11:30am-3pm), a rambling used bookstore with lots of regional and local goodies, including books by the late great local author Eugenia Price. Probably the best antiques shop in this part of town is **Village Mews** (504 Beachview Dr., 912/634-1235, Mon.-Sat. 10am-5pm).

# SPORTS AND ACTIVITIES

## Beaches

Keep going from the pier past the lighthouse to find **Massengale Park** (daily dawn-dusk), with a playground, picnic tables, and restrooms right off the beach on the Atlantic side. The beach itself on St. Simons is underwhelming compared to some in these parts, but it's easily accessible from the pier area and good for a romantic stroll if it's not high tide. There's a great playground, Neptune Park, right next to the pier overlooking the waterfront.

## Kayaking and Boating

With its relatively sheltered landward side nestled in the marsh and an abundance of wildlife, St. Simons Island is an outstanding kayaking site, attracting connoisseurs from all over. A good spot to put in on the Frederica River is the **Golden Isles Marina** (206 Marina Dr., 912/634-1128, www.gima-rina.com), which is actually on little Lanier Island on the Torras Causeway right before you enter St. Simons proper. For a real adventure, put in at the ramp at the end of South Harrington Street off Frederica Road, which will take you out Village Creek on the seaward side of the island.

Undoubtedly the best kayaking outfitter and tour operator in this part of the Golden Isles is **SouthEast Adventure Outfitters** (313 Mallory St., 912/638-6732, www.south-eastadventure.com, daily 10am-6pm), which also has a location in nearby Brunswick.

## Biking

The best place to rent bikes is **Monkey Wrench Bicycles** (1700 Frederica Rd., 912/634-5551). You can rent another kind of pedal-power at **Wheel Fun Rentals** (532 Ocean Blvd., 912/634-0606), which deals in four-seat pedaled carts with steering wheels.

## Golf and Tennis

A popular place for both sports is the **Sea Palms Golf and Tennis Resort** (5445

Frederica Rd., 800/841-6268, www.seapalms. com, greens fees $70-80) in the middle of the island, with three 9-hole public courses and three clay courts. The **Sea Island Golf Club** (100 Retreat Rd., 800/732-4752, www.seaisland.com, greens fees $185-260) on the old Retreat Plantation as you first come onto the island has two award-winning 18-hole courses, the Seaside and the Plantation. Another public course is the 18-hole **Hampton Club** (100 Tabbystone Rd., 912/634-0255, www.hamptonclub.com, greens fees $95) on the north side of the island, part of the King and Prince Beach and Golf Resort.

## FOOD

While the ambience at St. Simons has an upscale feel, don't feel like you have to dress up to get a bite to eat—the emphasis is on relaxation and having a good time.

### Breakfast and Brunch

★ **Palmer's Village Cafe** (223 Mallory St., 912/634-5515, www.palmersvillagecafe.com, Tues.-Sun. 7:30am-2pm, $10-15), formerly called Dressner's, is right in the middle of the Village's bustle. It's one of the island's most popular places but still has enough seats that you usually don't have to wait. Sandwiches and burgers are great, but breakfast all day is the real attraction and includes lovingly crafted omelets, hearty pancakes, and a "build your own biscuit" menu.

### Seafood

A popular seafood place right in the action in the Village is **Barbara Jean's** (214 Mallory St., 912/634-6500, www.barbarajeans.com, Sun.-Thurs. 11am-9pm, Fri.-Sat. 11am-10pm, $7-20), which also has a variety of imaginative veggie dishes to go along with its formidable seafood menu, including some excellent she-crab soup and crab cakes. They also have plenty of good landlubber treats.

### Fine Dining

★ **Nancy** (26 Market St., 912/634-0885,

www.nancyssi.com, lunch Tues.-Sat. 11:30am-2pm, dinner Thurs.-Sat. 6pm-10pm, $30) is an interesting concept: An upscale fine-dining spot with an affiliated boutique women's clothing shop. Nancy Herdlinger and chef Abney Harper run this enterprise in a newer area a short drive outside the Village. It's one of the premier fine-dining spots on the Georgia coast south of Savannah. Any seafood dish is great, but I suggest the short ribs if they're on the tightly curated menu.

Inside the King and Prince Resort, you'll find the old-school glory of the **Blue Dolphin** (201 Arnold Rd., 800/342-0212, lunch daily 11am-4pm, dinner daily 5pm-10pm, $15-30), redolent of the *Great Gatsby* era. The Blue Dolphin claims to be the only oceanfront dining on the island, and the views are certainly magnificent.

## ACCOMMODATIONS
### Under $150

A charming and reasonable place a stone's throw from the Village is ★ **Queens Court** (437 Kings Way, 912/638-8459, $85-135), a traditional roadside motel from the late 1940s, with modern upgrades that include a nice outdoor pool in the central courtyard area. Despite its convenient location, you'll feel fairly secluded.

You couldn't ask for a better location than that of the **St. Simons' Inn by the Lighthouse** (609 Beachview Dr., 912/638-1101, www.saintsimonsinn.com, $120-300), which is indeed in the shadow of the historic lighthouse and right next to the hopping Village area. A so-called "condo-hotel," each of the standard and deluxe suites at the inn are individually owned by off-site owners—however, each guest gets full maid service and a complimentary breakfast.

### $150-300

The best-known lodging on St. Simons Island is the ★ **King and Prince Beach and Golf Resort** (201 Arnold Rd., 800/342-0212, $249-320). Originally opened as a dance club in

1935, the King and Prince brings a swank old-school glamour similar to the Jekyll Island Club (though less imposing). And like the Jekyll Island Club, the King and Prince is also designated as one of the Historic Hotels of America. Its nearly 200 guest rooms are spread over a complex that includes several buildings, including the historic main building, beach villas, and freestanding guesthouses. Some standard rooms can go for under $200 even in the spring high season. Winter rates for all guest rooms are appreciably lower and represent a great bargain. For a dining spot overlooking the sea, try the **Blue Dolphin** (lunch daily 11am-4pm, dinner daily 5pm-10pm, $15-30). The resort's Hampton Club provides golf for guests and the public.

An interesting B&B on the island that's also within walking distance of most of the action on the south end is the 28-room **Village Inn & Pub** (500 Mallory St., 912/634-6056, www.villageinnandpub.com, $160-245), nestled among shady palm trees and live oaks. The pub, a popular local hangout in a renovated 1930 cottage, is a nice plus.

### Over $300

Affiliated with the Sea Island Resort, the **Lodge at Sea Island** (100 Retreat Ave., 912/638-3611, $650-2,500) is actually on the south end of St. Simons Island on the old Retreat Plantation. Its 40 grand guest rooms and suites all have great views of the Atlantic Ocean, the associated Plantation Course links, or both. Full butler service makes this an especially pampered and aristocratic stay.

## TRANSPORTATION AND SERVICES

Get to St. Simons through the gateway city of Brunswick. Take I-95 exit 38 for Golden Isles, which will take you to the Golden Isles Parkway. Take a right onto U.S. 17 and look for the intersection with the Torras Causeway, a toll-free road that takes you the short distance onto St. Simons.

The **St. Simons Visitors Center** (530-B Beachview Dr., 912/638-9014, www.bgivb.com, daily 9am-5pm) is in the St. Simons Casino Building near Neptune Park and the Village. The main newspaper in St. Simons is the **Brunswick News** (www.thebrunswicknews.com). The **U.S. Postal Service** (800/275-8777) has an office at 620 Beachview Drive.

## LITTLE ST. SIMONS ISLAND

This 10,000-acre privately owned island, accessible only by water, is almost totally undeveloped—thanks to its salt-stressed trees, which discouraged timbering—and boasts seven miles of beautiful beaches. All activity centers on the circa-1917 ★ **Lodge on Little St. Simons Island** (1000 Hampton Point Dr., 888/733-5774, www.littlestsimonsisland.com, from $625), named one of the top five U.S. resorts by *Condé Nast Traveler* in 2016. Within it lies the famed Hunting Lodge, where meals and cocktails are served. With 15 ultra-plush guest rooms and suites in an assortment of historic buildings, all set amid gorgeous natural beauty—there are five full-time naturalists on staff—the Lodge is a reminder of what St. Simons proper used to look like. The guest count is limited to 30 people.

### Transportation

Unless you enlist the aid of a local kayaking charter company, you have to be a guest of the Lodge to have access to Little St. Simons. The ferry, a 15-minute ride, leaves from a landing at the northern end of St. Simons at the end of Lawrence Road. Guests have full use of bicycles once on the island and can also request shuttle transportation just about anywhere.

## SEA ISLAND

The only way to enjoy Sea Island—basically a tiny appendage of St. Simons facing the Atlantic Ocean—is to be a guest at ★ **The Sea Island Resort** (888/732-4752, www.seaisland.com, from $700). The legendary facility, which underwent extensive renovations in 2008, is routinely ranked as one of the best resorts in the United States. The rooms at the resort's premier lodging institution, **The Cloister,** nearly defy description—enveloped in old-world luxury, they also boast 21st-century technology.

## Transportation

Get to Sea Island by taking Torras Causeway onto the island and then making a left onto Sea Island Causeway, which takes you all the way to the gate marking the only land entrance to the island.

# Darien and McIntosh County

The small fishing and shrimping village of Darien in McIntosh County has an interesting and historic pedigree of its own. It is centrally located near some of the best treasures the Georgia coast has to offer, including the Harris Neck National Wildlife Refuge, the beautiful Altamaha River, and the sea island of Sapelo, and it also boasts what many believe to be the best traditional seafood restaurants in the state.

Unlike Anglophilic Savannah to the north, the Darien area has had a distinctly Scottish flavor from the beginning. In 1736, Scottish Highlanders established a settlement at the mouth of the Altamaha River at the bequest of General James Oglethorpe, who wanted the tough Scots protecting his southern border from the Spanish.

Darien's heyday was in that antebellum period, when for a brief time the town was the world's largest exporter of cotton, floated down the Altamaha on barges and shipped out through the town's port. The Bank of Darien was the largest bank south of Philadelphia in the early 1800s. Almost nothing from this period remains, however, because on June 11, 1863, a force of mostly African American Union troops burned Darien to the ground, with all its homes and warehouses going up in smoke (the incident was portrayed in the movie *Glory*).

In the pre-interstate highway days, U.S. 17 was the main route south to booming Florida. McIntosh County got a bad reputation for "clip joints," which would fleece gullible travelers with a variety of illegal schemes. This

the Darien shrimping fleet

period is recounted in the best seller *Praying for Sheetrock* by Melissa Fay Greene.

## SIGHTS
### Smallest Church in North America

While several other churches claim that title, fans of the devout and of roadside kitsch alike will enjoy the tiny and charming little **Memory Park Christ Chapel** (U.S. 17, daily 24 hours). The original 12-seat chapel was built in 1949 by local grocer Agnes Harper, when the church was intended as a round-the-clock travelers' sanctuary on what was then the main coastal road, U.S. 17. Upon her death, Harper simply willed the church to Jesus Christ. Sadly, in late 2015 an arsonist burned Mrs. Harper's church to the ground. A community effort, however, rebuilt it as closely as possible. Get there by taking I-95 exit 67 and going south a short way on U.S. 17; the church is on the east side of the road.

### ★ Harris Neck National Wildlife Refuge

Literally a stone's throw away from the "Smallest Church" is the turnoff onto the seven-mile Harris Neck Road leading east to the **Harris Neck National Wildlife Refuge**

(912/832-4608, www.fws.gov/harrisneck, daily dawn-dusk, free). In addition to being one of the single best sites in the South from which to view wading birds and waterfowl in their natural habitat, Harris Neck also has something of a poignant backstory. For generations after the Civil War, an African American community descended from the area's original slaves quietly struggled to eke out a living here by fishing and farming.

The settlers' land was taken by the federal government during World War II to build a U.S. Army Air Force base. Now a nearly 3,000-acre nationally protected refuge, Harris Neck gets about 50,000 visitors a year to experience its mix of marsh, woods, and grassland ecosystems and for its nearly matchless bird-watching. Most visitors use the four-mile "wildlife drive" to travel through the refuge, stopping occasionally for hiking or bird-watching.

Kayaks and canoes can put in at the public boat ramp on the Barbour River. Near the landing is the **Gould Cemetery,** an old African American cemetery that is publicly accessible. Charming handmade tombstones evoke the post-Civil War era of Harris Neck before the displacement of local citizens to build the airfield.

old cemetery at Harris Neck National Wildlife Refuge

To get here, take I-95 exit 67 and go south on U.S. 17 about one mile, then east on Harris Neck Road (Hwy. 131) for seven miles to the entrance gate on the left.

## Shellman Bluff

Just northeast of Darien is the old oystering community of **Shellman Bluff.** It's notable not only for the stunning views from the high bluff, but also for fresh seafood. Go to **Shellman's Fish Camp** (1058 River Rd., 912/832-4331, call ahead) to put in for a kayak or canoe ride. Save room for a meal; there are some great seafood places here.

## Fort King George State Historic Site

The oldest English settlement in what would become Georgia, **Fort King George State Historic Site** (1600 Wayne St., 912/437-4770, www.gastateparks.org/fortkinggeorge, Tues.-Sun. 9am-5pm, $7.50 adults, $4.50 children) for a short time protected the Carolinas from attack, from its establishment in 1721 to its abandonment in 1727. Walking onto the site, with its restored 40-foot-tall cypress blockhouse fort, instantly reveals why this place was so important: It guards a key bend in the wide Altamaha River, vital to any attempt to establish transportation and trade in the area.

### Tours

**Altamaha Coastal Tours** (229 Ft. King George Rd., 912/437-6010, www.altamaha. com) is your best bet for taking a guided kayak tour (from $50) or renting a kayak (from $20 per day) to explore the beautiful Altamaha River.

## FOOD

McIntosh County is a powerhouse in the food department, and as you might expect, fresh and delicious seafood in a casual atmosphere is the order of the day here.

**The Old School Diner** (1080 Jesse Grant Rd. NE, Townsend, 912/832-2136, http://old-schooldiner.com, Wed.-Fri. 5:30pm-9:30pm, Sat.-Sun. noon-9:30pm, $15-30, cash only) is located in a whimsical semirural compound seven miles off U.S. 17, just off Harris Neck Road on the way to the wildlife refuge. The draw here is succulent fresh seafood in the coastal Georgia tradition. Old School's prices aren't so old school, but keep in mind that the portions are huge, rich, and filling.

Even farther off the main roads than the Old School Diner, the community of Shellman Bluff is well worth the drive. Find ★ **Hunters Café** (Shellman Bluff, 912/832-5771, lunch Mon.-Fri. 11am-2pm, dinner Mon.-Fri. 5pm-10pm, Sat.-Sun. 7am-10pm, $10-20) and get anything that floats your boat—it's all fresh and local. Wild Georgia shrimp are a particular specialty, as is the hearty cream-based crab stew. Take a right off Shellman Bluff Road onto Sutherland Bluff Drive, then a left onto New Shellman Road. Take a right onto the unpaved River Road and you can't miss it.

Another Shellman Bluff favorite is ★ **Speed's Kitchen** (Shellman Bluff, 912/832-4763, Thurs.-Sat. 5pm-close, Sun. noon-close, $10-20), where people move anything but fast, and the fried fish and crab-stuffed flounder are out of this world. Take a right off Shellman Bluff Road onto Sutherland Bluff Drive. Take a right onto Speed's Kitchen Road.

## ACCOMMODATIONS

If you want to stay in McIntosh County, I strongly recommend booking one of the five charming guest rooms at ★ **Open Gates Bed and Breakfast** (301 Franklin St., Darien, 912/437-6985, www.opengatesbnb. com, $125-140). This lovingly restored and reasonably priced inn is on historic and relaxing Vernon Square in downtown Darien.

## SAPELO ISLAND

One of those amazing, undeveloped Georgia barrier islands that can only be reached by boat, Sapelo also shares with some of those islands a link to the Gilded Age.

# Sapelo Island

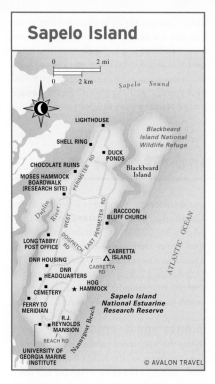

© AVALON TRAVEL

island to the state, again with the exception of the 430 acres of Hog Hammock, which at the time had slightly more than 100 residents. Today most of the island is administered for marine research purposes under the designation of **Sapelo Island National Estuarine Research Reserve** (www.sapelonerr.org).

## Sights

Once on the island, you can take guided tours under the auspices of the Georgia Department of Natural Resources. Wednesday 8:30am-12:30pm is a tour of the island that includes the **R. J. Reynolds Mansion** (www.reynoldsonsapelo.com) on the south end as well as Hog Hammock and the Long Tabby ruins. Saturday 9am-1pm is a tour of the historic **Sapelo Lighthouse** on the north end along with the rest of the island. June-Labor Day there's an extra lighthouse and island tour Friday 8:30am-12:30pm. March-October on the last Tuesday of the month they do an extra-long day trip, 8:30am-3pm. Tours cost $10 adults, $6 children, free under age 6. Call 912/437-3224 for reservations. You can also arrange private tours.

Another key sight on Sapelo is a 4,500-year-old **Native American shell ring** on the north end, one of the oldest and best preserved anywhere. Beach lovers will especially enjoy the unspoiled strands on Sapelo, including the famous **Nannygoat Beach.**

## Accommodations

While it's theoretically possible to stay overnight at the **R. J. Reynolds Mansion** (www.reynoldsonsapelo.com), it is limited to groups of at least 16 people. Realistically, to stay overnight on Sapelo you need a reservation with one of the locally owned guesthouses. One recommendation is Cornelia Bailey's six-room **The Wallow** (912/485-2206, call for rates) in historic Hog Hammock. The Baileys also run a small campground, **Comyam's Campground** (912/485-2206, $10 pp). Another option is **The Weekender** (912/485-2277, call for rates).

## History

The Spanish established a Franciscan mission on the north end of the island in the 1500s. Sapelo didn't become fully integrated into the Lowcountry plantation culture until its purchase by Thomas Spalding in the early 1800s. After the Civil War, many of the nearly 500 former slaves on the island remained, with a partnership of freedmen buying land as early as 1871.

Hudson Motors mogul Howard Coffin bought all of Sapelo, except for the African American communities, in 1912, building a palatial home and introducing a modern infrastructure. Coffin hit hard times in the Great Depression and in 1934 sold Sapelo to tobacco heir R. J. Reynolds, who consolidated the island's African Americans into the single Hog Hammock community. By the mid-1970s the Reynolds family had sold the

## Transportation and Services

Visitors to Sapelo must embark on the ferry at the **Sapelo Island Visitors Center** (912/437-3224, www.sapelonerr.org, Tues.-Fri. 7:30am-5:30pm, Sat. 8am-5:30pm, Sun. 1:30pm-5pm, $10 adults, $6 ages 6-18) in little Meridian, Georgia, on Highway 99 north of Darien. The visitors center actually has a nice nature hike of its own as well as an auditorium where you can see an informative video. From here it's a half-hour trip to Sapelo over the Doboy Sound. Keep in mind you must call in advance for reservations before showing up at the visitors center. April-October it's recommended to call at least a week in advance.

# Cumberland Island and St. Marys

Actually two islands—Great Cumberland and Little Cumberland—Cumberland Island National Seashore is the largest and one of the oldest of Georgia's barrier islands, and also one of its most remote and least developed. Currently administered by the National Park Service, it's accessible only by ferry or private boat. Most visitors to Cumberland get here from the gateway town of St. Marys, Georgia, a nifty little fishing village.

## ST. MARYS

Much like Brunswick to the north, the fishing town of St. Marys plays mostly a gateway role, in this case to the Cumberland Island National Seashore. During the colonial period, St. Marys was the southernmost U.S. city. In 1812 a British force took over Cumberland Island and St. Marys, with a contingent embarking up the St. Marys River to track down the customs collector.

Unlike towns such as Darien, which was put to the torch by Union troops, St. Marys was saved from destruction in the Civil War. A hotel was built in 1916 (and hosted Marjorie Kinnan Rawlings, author of *The Yearling*), but tourists didn't discover the area until the 1970s. It was also then that the U.S. Navy built the huge nuclear submarine base at Kings Bay, currently the area's largest employer with almost 10,000 workers.

## Orientation

Most activity in downtown St. Marys happens up and down Osborne Street, which perhaps not coincidentally is also how you get to the **Cumberland Island Visitor Center** (113 St. Marys St., 912/882-4335, daily 8am-4:30pm) and from there board the *Cumberland Queen* for the trip to the island. (Note: The Cumberland Island Visitor Center and the Cumberland Island Museum are in two different places, about a block apart.)

## Sights and Events

Tying the past to the present, it's only fitting that the home of the Kings Bay Submarine Base (which is not open to the public) has a museum dedicated to the "Silent Service." The **St. Marys Submarine Museum** (102 St. Marys St., 912/882-2782, www.stmaryswelcome.com, Tues.-Sat. 10am-4pm, Sun. 1pm-5pm, $5 adults, $3 children) on the riverfront has a variety of exhibits honoring the contribution of American submariners, including a bunch of cool models. There's a neat interactive exhibit where you can look through the genuine sub periscope that sticks out of the roof of the museum.

A block down Osborne Street from the waterfront—and *not* at the actual Cumberland Island Visitor Center or the actual ferry dock—is the handsome little **Cumberland Island National Seashore Museum** (129 Osborne St., 912/882-4336, www.stmaryswelcome.com, Wed.-Sun. 1pm-4pm, free). It has several very informative exhibits on the natural and human history of Cumberland, as well as a room devoted to the short but fascinating role the island played in the War of 1812.

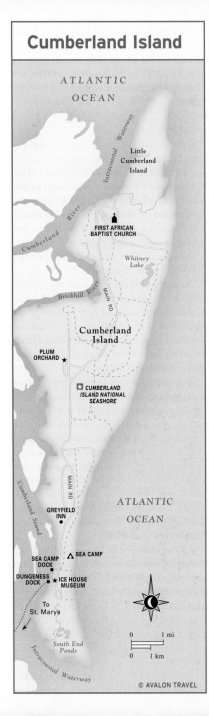

# Cumberland Island

ATLANTIC OCEAN

Little Cumberland Island

*Intracoastal Waterway*

*Cumberland River*

FIRST AFRICAN BAPTIST CHURCH

Whitney Lake

*Brickhill River*

MAIN RD

Cumberland Island

PLUM ORCHARD

CUMBERLAND ISLAND NATIONAL SEASHORE

MAIN RD

ATLANTIC OCEAN

*Cumberland Sound*

GREYFIELD INN

SEA CAMP DOCK  △ SEA CAMP

DUNGENESS DOCK  ★ ICE HOUSE MUSEUM

To St. Marys

South End Ponds

0    1 mi

0    1 km

*Intracoastal Waterway*

© AVALON TRAVEL

The most notable historic home in St. Marys is the **Orange Hall House Museum** (311 Osborne St., 912/576-3644, www.orange-hall.org, Tues.-Sat. 9am-4pm, Sun. 1pm-4pm, $3 adults, $1 children). This beautiful Greek Revival home, circa 1830, survived the Civil War and was the center of town social life during the Roaring '20s.

## Food

St. Marys cannot compete in culinary sophistication with Charleston or Savannah, but it does have some of the freshest seafood around. One of the best places to eat seafood on the waterfront in St. Marys is at **Lang's Marina Restaurant** (307 W. St. Marys St., 912/882-4432, lunch Tues.-Fri. 11am-2pm, dinner Wed.-Sat. 5pm-9pm, $15-20). Another pair of good waterfront spots, right next to each other, are **The Shark Bite** (104 W. St. Marys St., 912/576-6993, Tues.-Sat. 11am-9pm, $12-20), which has great burgers and live music, and **Riverside Café** (106 W. St. Marys St., 912/882-3466, Tues.-Sat. 11am-9pm, $15-20), which specializes in Greek favorites.

## Accommodations

The most notable lodging for historical as well as economic value is the 18-room **Riverview Hotel** (105 Osborne St., 912/882-3242, www.riverviewhotelstmarys.com, under $100). It was built in the 1920s and has hosted such notables as author Marjorie Rawlings, John Rockefeller, poet Sidney Lanier, and Andrew Carnegie. ★ **Emma's Bed and Breakfast** (300 W. Conyers St., 912/882-4199, www.emmasbedandbreakfast.com, under $200) is situated on four beautiful acres in downtown St. Marys in a grand Southern-style mansion with all the trappings and hospitality you'd expect.

More outdoorsy visitors can stay at cottage, tent, or RV sites at **Crooked River State Park** (6222 Charlie Smith Sr. Hwy., 912/882-5256, www.gastateparks.org). There are 62 tent and RV sites (about $22) and 11 cottages ($85-110) as well as primitive camping ($25).

## Transportation and Services

Take I-95 exit 3 for Kingsland-St. Marys Road (Hwy. 40). This becomes Osborne Road, the main drag of St. Marys, as it gets closer to town. The road by the waterfront is St. Marys Street.

The **St. Marys Convention and Visitors Bureau** (406 Osborne St., 912/882-4000, www.stmaryswelcome.com) is a good source of information not only for the town but for Cumberland Island, but keep in mind that this is not actually where you catch the ferry to the island.

## ★ CUMBERLAND ISLAND NATIONAL SEASHORE

Not only one of the richest estuarine and maritime forest environments in the world, **Cumberland Island National Seashore** (912/882-4335, reservations 877/860-6787, www.nps.gov/cuis) is one of the most beautiful places on the planet, as everyone learned when the "it" couple of their day, John F. Kennedy Jr. and Carolyn Bessette, were wed on the island in 1996. With more than 16 miles of gorgeous beach and an area of over 17,000 acres, there's no shortage of scenery.

Cumberland is far from pristine: It has been used for timbering and cotton, is dotted with evocative abandoned ruins, and hosts a band of beautiful but voracious wild horses. But it is still a remarkable island paradise in a world where those kinds of locations are getting harder and harder to find.

There are two ways to enjoy Cumberland: day trip or overnight stay. An early arrival and departure on the late ferry, combined with bike rental and a tour, still leaves plenty of time for day-trippers to relax. Camping overnight on Cumberland is quite enjoyable, but it's a bit rustic and probably isn't for novices.

Important note: Distances on the map can be deceiving. Cumberland is very narrow but also very long—about 18 miles tip to tip. You can walk the width of the island in minutes, but you will not be able to hike its length even in a day.

You can have a perfectly enjoyable time on Cumberland just hanging out on the more populated south end, but those who want to explore the island fully should consider renting a bike or booking seats on the new National Park Service van tour around the island.

## History

The Timucuan Indians revered this site, visiting it often for shellfish and for sassafras, a medicinal herb common on the island. Cumberland's size and great natural harbor made it a perfect base for Spanish friars, who established the first mission on the island, San Pedro Mocama, in 1587. In fact, the first Christian martyr in Georgia was created on Cumberland, when Father Pedro Martinez was killed by the Indians.

As part of his effort to push the Spanish back into Florida for good, General James Oglethorpe established Fort William at the south end of Cumberland—the remains of which are now underwater—as well as a hunting lodge named Dungeness, an island placename that persists today.

But inevitably, the Lowcountry planters' culture made its way down to Cumberland, which was soon the site of 15 thriving plantations and small farms. After the Civil War, Cumberland was set aside as a home for freed African Americans—part of the famous and ill-fated "40 acres and a mule" proposal—but politics intervened: Most of Cumberland's slaves were rounded up and taken to Amelia Island, Florida, although some remained and settled at Cumberland's north end (the "Settlement" area today).

As elsewhere on the Georgia coast, the Industrial Revolution came to Cumberland in the form of a vacation getaway for a mega-tycoon, in this case Thomas Carnegie, industrialist and brother of the better-known Andrew Carnegie of Carnegie Library fame. Carnegie built a new, even grander Dungeness, which suffered the same fate as its predecessor in a 1959 fire.

Cumberland Island narrowly avoided becoming the next Hilton Head—literally—in

# Wild Horses of Cumberland

the wild horses of Cumberland Island

Contrary to popular opinion, Cumberland Island's famous wild horses are not direct descendants of the first horses brought to the island by Spanish and English settlers, although feral horses have certainly ranged the island for most of recorded history. The current population of about 140 or so is actually descended from horses brought to the island by the Carnegie family in the 1920s. Responding to overwhelming public opinion, the National Park Service leaves the herd virtually untended and unsupervised. The horses eat, live, fight, grow up, give birth, and pass away largely without human influence, other than euthanizing animals who are clearly suffering and have no hope of recovery.

You're not guaranteed to see wild horses on Cumberland, but the odds are heavily in your favor. They often congregate to graze around the Dungeness ruins, and indeed any open space. Over the years they've made trails through the forest and sand dunes, and can often be seen cavorting on the windy beach in the late afternoon and early evening.

Each stallion usually acquires a "harem" of dependent mares, and occasionally you might even witness spirited competition between stallions for mares and/or territory.

Gorgeous and evocative though these magnificent animals are, they have a big appetite for vegetation and frankly are not the best thing for this sensitive barrier island ecosystem. But their beauty and visceral impact on the visitor is undeniable, which means the horses are likely to stay as long as nature will have them.

And yes, these really are *wild* horses, meaning you should never try to feed or pet them, and you certainly won't be riding them.

1969 when Hilton Head developer Charles Fraser bought the northern tip of the island and began bulldozing a runway. The dwindling but still influential Carnegies joined with the Georgia Conservancy to broker an agreement that resulted in dubbing Cumberland a National Seashore in 1972, saving it from further development. A $7.5 million gift from the Mellon Foundation enabled the purchase of Fraser's tract and the eventual incorporation of the island within the National Park Service.

To learn more about Cumberland's fascinating history, visit the **Cumberland Island National Seashore Museum** (129 Osborne St., 912/882-4336, www.stmaryswelcome.com,

Plum Orchard can be toured on the second and fourth Sunday of the month.

Wed.-Sun. 1pm-4pm, free) while you're in St. Marys, a block away from the actual ferry docks.

## Sights

The ferry typically stops at two docks a short distance from each other, the Sea Camp dock and the Dungeness dock. At 4pm, rangers offer a "dockside" interpretive program at the Sea Camp. A short way farther north at the Dungeness Dock, rangers lead a highly recommended "Dungeness Footsteps Tour" at 10am and 12:45pm, concentrating on the historic sites at the southern end of the island. Also at the Dungeness dock is the little **Ice House Museum** (912/882-4336, daily 9am-5pm, free), containing a range of exhibits on the island's history from Native American times to the present day.

Down near the docks are also where you'll find the stirring, almost spooky **Dungeness Ruins** and the nearby grave marker of Light-Horse Harry Lee. (You're very likely to see some wild horses around this area too.) The cause of the 1866 fire that destroyed the old Dungeness home is still unknown. Another even grander home was built on the same site during the Victorian era, but also fell victim to fire in the 1950s. It's these Victorian ruins you see today.

A very nice addition to the National Park Service offerings is a daily "Lands and Legacies" van tour (reservations 877/860-6787, $15 adults, $12 seniors and children) that takes you all around the island, eliminating the need for lengthy hikes. It's ideal for day-trippers—if a bit long at six hours—but anyone can take the ride. It leaves from the Sea Camp Ranger Station soon after the first morning ferry arrives. Reservations are strongly recommended.

Moving north on the Main Road (Grand Ave.)—a dirt path and the only route for motor vehicles—you come to the **Greyfield Inn** (904/261-6408, www.greyfieldinn.com). Because it is a privately owned hotel, don't trespass through the grounds. A good way farther north, just off the main road, you'll find the restored, rambling 20-room mansion **Plum Orchard,** another Carnegie legacy. Guided tours of Plum Orchard are available on the second and fourth Sunday of the month ($6 plus ferry fare); reserve a space at 912/882-4335.

At the very north end of the island, accessible only by foot or by bicycle, is the former freedmen's community simply known as **The Settlement,** featuring a small cemetery and the now-famous **First African Baptist Church** (daily dawn-dusk)—a 1937 version of the 1893 original—a humble and rustic one-room church made of whitewashed logs and in which the 1996 Kennedy-Bessette wedding took place.

## Sports and Activities

There are more than 50 miles of hiking trails all over Cumberland, about 15 miles of nearly isolated beach to comb, and acres of maritime forest to explore—the latter an artifact of Cumberland's unusually old age for a barrier island. Upon arrival, you might want to rent a bicycle at the **Sea Camp dock** (no reservations, arrange rentals on the ferry, adult bikes $16 per day, youth bikes $10, $20 overnight). The only catch with the bikes is that you shouldn't plan on taking them to the up-country campsites.

Shell-and-sharks-teeth collectors might want to explore south of Dungeness Beach as well as between the docks. Unlike some parks, you are allowed to take shells and fossils off the island.

Wildlife enthusiasts will be in heaven. More than 300 species of birds have been recorded on the island, which is also a favorite nesting ground for female loggerhead turtles in the late summer. Of course, the most iconic image of Cumberland Island is its famous **wild horses,** a free-roaming band of feral equines who traverse the island year-round, grazing as they please.

Cumberland Island is home to some creepy-crawlies, including mosquitoes, gnats, and, yes, ticks, the latter of which are especially prevalent throughout the maritime forest as you work your way north. Bring high-strength insect repellent with you, or buy some at the camp store. Rangers recommend you do a frequent "tick check" on yourself and your companions.

## Accommodations

The only "civilized" lodging on Cumberland is the 13-room ★ **Greyfield Inn** (Grand Ave., 904/261-6408, www.greyfieldinn. com, $475), ranked by the American Inn Association as one of the country's "Ten Most Romantic Inns." Opened in 1962 as a hotel, the Greyfield was built in 1900 as the home of the Carnegies. The room rates include meals, transportation, tours, and bicycle usage.

Many visitors opt to camp on Cumberland (reservations 877/860-6787, limit of seven nights, $4) in one of three basic ways: at the **Sea Camp,** which has restrooms and shower facilities and allows fires; the remote but pleasant **Stafford Beach,** a vigorous three-mile hike from the docks and with a basic restroom and shower; and pure wilderness camping farther north at **Hickory Hill, Yankee Paradise,** and **Brickman Bluff,** all of which are a several-mile hike away, do not permit fires, and have no facilities of any kind. Reservations are required for camping. All trash must be packed out on departure, as there are no refuse facilities on the island. Responsible alcohol consumption is limited to those 21 and over.

Insect life is abundant. Bring heavy-duty repellent or purchase some at the camp store.

## Transportation and Services

The most vital information about Cumberland is how to get ashore in the first place. Most visitors do this by purchasing a ticket on the *Cumberland Queen* at the **Cumberland Island Visitor Center** (113 St. Marys St., St. Marys, 877/860-6787, daily 8am-4:30pm, $20 adults, $18 seniors, $12 under age 13) on the waterfront in St. Marys. I strongly suggest calling or faxing ahead. Be aware that there are often very long hold times by phone.

The ferry ride is 45 minutes each way. You can call for reservations Monday-Friday 10am-4pm. The ferry does not transport pets, bicycles, kayaks, or cars. However, you can rent bicycles at the Sea Camp dock once you're there. Every visitor to Cumberland over age 16 must pay a $4 entry fee, including campers.

March 1-November 30, the ferry leaves St. Marys daily at 9am and 11:45am, returning from Cumberland at 10:15am and 4:45pm. March 1-September 30 Wednesday-Saturday, there's an additional 2:45pm departure from Cumberland back to St. Marys. December 1-February 28 the ferry operates only Thursday-Monday. Make sure you arrive and check in at least 30 minutes before your ferry leaves.

One of the quirks of Cumberland, resulting from the unusual way in which it passed into federal hands, is the existence of some private property on which you mustn't trespass, except where trails specifically allow it. Also, unlike the general public, these private landowners are allowed to use vehicles. For these reasons, it's best to make sure you have a map of the island, which you can get before you board the ferry at St. Marys or at the ranger station at the Sea Camp dock.

There are no real stores and very few facilities on Cumberland. *Bring whatever you think you'll need,* whether it be food, water, medicine, suntan lotion, insect repellent, toilet paper, or otherwise.

# Background

# The Landscape

## GEOGRAPHY

The Carolinas and Georgia are linked by more than history and shared experience. All three states are made up of the same three distinct geographical regions. The most easily identified is the **mountain region,** which forms the western edge of North and South Carolina and the extreme northern portion of Georgia.

The ridges of the Blue Ridge and Great Smoky Mountains run in a general northeast-southwest configuration, from the Virginia line to the far southwestern corner where the toe of North Carolina tickles Georgia and Tennessee. Six of the 10 highest mountains in the eastern United States are found in North Carolina, including the very highest, 6,684-foot Mount Mitchell.

Since the mid-19th century, the **Piedmont** has been the primary locus of population and industry in all three states. Most of the major cities are in the Piedmont, including Atlanta, Augusta, and Athens in Georgia; the Raleigh-Durham metro area, Charlotte, Winston-Salem, and Greensboro in North Carolina; and the Greenville-Spartanburg metro area and Columbia in South Carolina.

The **Coastal Plain** is the third region, with a name that's fairly self-explanatory. Generally speaking, the basic western edge of the Coastal Plain runs roughly parallel to I-95, a major traffic artery through all three states.

The region's big **alluvial,** or sediment-bearing, rivers originate in the Appalachian mountain chain. Key examples are the Savannah River, the Cape Fear River, and the Pee Dee River. The **blackwater river** is a particularly interesting Southern phenomenon, duplicated elsewhere only in South America and one example each in New York and Michigan. While alluvial rivers generally originate in highlands and carry with them a large amount of sediment, blackwater rivers—the Edisto River in South Carolina being the most remarkable example—tend to originate in low-lying areas and move slowly toward the sea, carrying with them very little sediment. Their dark tea color comes from the tannic acid of decaying vegetation all along the banks, washed out by the slow, inexorable movement of the river toward the sea.

Most biologists will tell you that the Coastal Plain is where things get interesting. The place where a river interfaces with the ocean is called an **estuary,** and it's perhaps the most interesting place of all. Estuaries are heavily tidal in nature (indeed, the word derives from *aestus,* Latin for "tide"), and feature brackish water and heavy silt content.

This portion of the U.S. East Coast has about a 6- to 8-foot tidal range, and the coastal ecosystem depends on this steady ebb and flow for life itself. At high tide, shellfish open and feed. At low tide, they literally clam up, keeping saltwater inside their shells until the next tide comes.

Water birds and small mammals feed on shellfish and other animals at low tide, when their prey is exposed. High tide brings an influx of fish and nutrients from the sea, in turn drawing predators like dolphins, who often come into tidal creeks to feed.

All this water action in both directions—freshwater coming from inland, saltwater encroaching from the Atlantic—results in the phenomenon of the **salt marsh.** (Freshwater marshes are rarer, Florida's Everglades being perhaps the premier example.)

Far more than just a transitional zone between land and water, marshes are also nature's nursery. Plant and animal life in

---

**Previous:** Tryon Palace in New Bern; azaleas in bloom.

# Geographical Vocabulary

The region has some unusual landscapes and environments, and some unusual vocabulary to describe them. As you explore the area, you may encounter the following terms.

## POCOSIN

Pronounced "puh-CO-sin," the word is said to come from the Algonquin for "swamp on a hill." A pocosin is a moist peat bog of a kind unique to the Southeast. The peat layer is thinnest around the edges, and usually supports communities of pine trees. Moving toward the center of the bog, the ground becomes slightly higher, and the peat thicker, more acidic, and less welcoming of plant species. Because the soil is so poor and bereft of nutrients, carnivorous plants, who have their meals delivered rather than depending on the soil's bounty, are particularly well suited to life in pocosins.

## CAROLINA BAY

The word *bay* here refers not to an inlet on the coast but to another kind of upland swamp—sort of like an inside-out pocosin. The bays' origins are mysterious, and their regularity of form and commonness in this region are most uncanny. If you look down at eastern North and South Carolina from an airplane, or in a satellite image, the bays are unmistakable. They're oval-shaped depressions, varying in size from Lake Waccamaw to mere puddles, and are always aligned in a northeast-southwest configuration. Unlike ponds and regular swamps, Carolina bays are usually unconnected to any groundwater source and are fed solely by rainwater. Like pocosins, bays attract colonies of carnivorous plants, which love to establish their dens of iniquity in such unwholesome soil.

## SANDHILLS

If you're in Wilmington, Southport, Vidalia, or the Pee Dee region of South Carolina, or somewhere else along the Southeastern coast, take note of what the soil beneath your feet looks like. Then, turn your back to the ocean and head inland. Travel 100 miles west and then look down again. What you'll see is very similar—sandy, light-colored ground, wiry vegetation (and a few carnivorous plants), maybe even some scattered shells. About 20 million years ago, during the Miocene Epoch, parts of the modern coastal plain were sand dunes on the shores of an ocean that covered what is now North Carolina's coastal plain.

## HOLLER

Here's a term that's really more of a regional pronunciation than a unique word. A holler is what is on paper termed a "hollow"—a mountain cove. It's just that we in the South aren't much for rounding words that end in "ow." If you don't believe me, just beller out the winda to that feller wallering in yonder meada.

## BALD

An ecological mystery, the Appalachian bald is a mountaintop area on which there are no trees, even though surrounding mountaintops of the same elevation may be forested. Typically, a bald is either grassy or a heath. Heaths are more easily explicable, caused by soil conditions that don't support forest. Grassy balds, though, occur on land where logically one would expect to find trees. Some theories hold that grassy balds were caused by generations of livestock grazing, but soil studies show that they were grassy meadows before the first mountain farmer turned cattle or sheep out to pasture. Grazing may still be the answer, though. The balds may originally have been chomped and trampled down by prehistoric megafauna—ancient bison, mastodons, and mammoths. Today, in the absence of mammoths as well as free-ranging cattle, some balds are gradually sealing up in woodland, except where deliberately maintained.

marshes tends not only to be diverse but to encompass multitudes. You may not see its denizens easily, but on close inspection you'll find the marsh absolutely teeming with creatures. Visually, the main identifying feature of a salt marsh is its distinctive reedlike marsh grasses, adapted to survive in brackish water.

All three states feature distinctive island formations. The **Outer Banks** of North Carolina form a magnificent, sweeping arc from the Virginia line at the north, out to its eastern ultima Thule at Cape Hatteras, to the edge of the Croatan Forest and Bogue Banks at the south. South of Bogue Banks, a crazed margin of marshes and barrier islands shelter the coast. An ever-changing sandbar, the Outer Banks shift imperceptibly from day to day as the tides nudge them back and forth, but in a hurricane can be transformed in just a few hours.

The South Carolina and Georgia coasts boast a series of barrier islands often just called the **Sea Islands.** After the Civil War, the Sea Islands remained ancestral homes to formerly enslaved people who stayed on the islands, retaining many traditional folkways. Their somewhat isolated culture is generally referred to as **Gullah,** though in parts of Georgia you'll still hear the phrase **Geechee** used to refer to the same cultural tradition.

## CLIMATE

This is a large region of the country and therefore has a wide range of climatic conditions. While summers are generally long, hot, and humid, with winters being quite mild, a clear exception exists anywhere in the mountainous regions.

Asheville and Boone in North Carolina can get snow when the trees down in the Piedmont are already green and leafy, but the average winter temperatures in the mountains stay mostly above freezing. In the summer it can be chilly in the mountains, especially in the evening, but plenty of days hit the 80s.

The central portions of the Carolinas and most of Georgia can be incredibly hot in the summer, and plenty hot in the spring and fall. Towns like Fayetteville, North Carolina; Columbia, South Carolina; and Americus, Georgia, can feel like the hottest places on earth. The Piedmont sees snow, though not nearly so much as the mountains, and the counties east of I-95 are virtually snow-free and much likelier to have rain during winter storms.

In the Outer Banks, the warm Gulf Stream keeps the air from getting too frigid in the winter, while the circulation of sea breezes makes it ever so slightly less steamy in the summer. The difference is subtle, though, and chances are that on the coldest day in January or the hottest day in August, the relief won't be perceptible.

The coastal region of all three states is subject to **hurricanes** on a fairly regular basis. The Outer Banks in particular are terribly vulnerable. Hurricane season lasts from June through November, and it's toward the end of the summer that people really start to be watchful.

**Tornadoes,** though most common in the spring, can whip up trouble any time of year in the central portions of the states. Plain old **thunderstorms** can be dangerous too, bringing lightning, flash flooding, and difficult driving conditions. **Snowstorms** with significant accumulation are more likely in the North Carolina mountains than at lower elevations.

# Plants

In the early 1700s, John Lawson, an English explorer who would soon be the first victim of the Tuscarora War, recorded a fanciful tale he'd picked up in the very young colony of North Carolina. "I have been informed of a Tulip-Tree," he wrote, "that was ten Foot Diameter; and another, wherein a lusty Man had his Bed and Household Furniture, and liv'd in it, till his Labour got him a more fashionable Mansion. He afterwards became a noted Man, in his Country, for Wealth and Conduct." Whether there was ever really a tulip poplar large enough to serve as a furnished bachelor pad, the region's virgin forests must have seemed miraculous to the first Europeans to happen upon them.

However, contrary to Hollywood portrayals, no one ever needed a machete to tear their way through an old-growth forest. Because the high, thick tree canopy blocks the light that would allow growth on the forest floor, Native Americans and early settlers could walk through these primordial forests with ease.

Few old-growth forests exist today, after generations of logging and farming throughout the state, but those enclaves of virgin woods, like the Joyce Kilmer Forest in the Smoky Mountains or the Congaree National Monument outside Columbia, South Carolina, are a sight to behold and make Lawson's anecdote seem like it might be true. Scores of specialized ecosystems host a marvelous diversity of plant and animal life, from the cypress swamps in the east to the longleaf pine forests in the sandhills to the fragrant balsam forests of the high country.

Coastal forests are dominated by hardwoods—**oaks** of many varieties, and **gum** and **cypress,** species that thrive in wetlands. There are also vast swathes of loblolly **piney woods** along the coast.

In the Piedmont, oak and **hickory** predominate, but share their range with smaller bands of piney woods. In the mountains too, oak and hickory woods are the rule. **Pine, balsam,** and other conifers put in appearances as well.

The most iconic plant life of the coastal region is the **Southern live oak.** Named because of its evergreen nature, a live oak is technically any number of evergreens in the *Quercus* genus, but in local practice the name almost always refers to the Southern live oak. Capable of living over 1,000 years and possessing wood of legendary resilience, the Southern live oak is one of nature's most magnificent creations. The timber value of live oaks has been well known since the earliest days of the American shipbuilding industry—when the oak dominated the entire coast inland of the marsh—but their value as a canopy tree has finally been widely recognized by local and state governments.

Fittingly, the other iconic plant life of the coast grows on the branches of the live oak. Contrary to popular opinion, **Spanish moss** is neither Spanish nor moss. It's an air plant, a wholly indigenous cousin to the pineapple. Also contrary to folklore, Spanish moss is not a parasite nor does it harbor parasites while living on an oak tree—although it can after it has already fallen to the ground.

Cotton or tobacco aside, you could make the case that the most important plant in the history of the Carolinas and Georgia is the **longleaf pine,** also called the pitch pine. Though something of a rarity today, the vast stands of longleaf pine that formerly blanketed the region enabled a globally important naval stores industry in the 18th and 19th centuries, producing turpentine, pitch, tar, and lumber for the world's navies and shipping fleets. Today, what's left of the longleaf piney woods are crucial habitats for several endangered species, including the red-cockaded woodpecker and the Pine Barrens tree frog.

The acres of **smooth cordgrass** for which

the Georgia Golden Isles are named are plants of the *Spartina alterniflora* species. (A cultivated cousin, *Spartina anglica,* is considered invasive.) Besides its simple natural beauty, *Spartina* is also an important food source for marsh denizens. Playing a key environmental role on the coast is **sea oats.** This wispy, fast-growing perennial grass anchors sand dunes and hence is a protected species (it's a misdemeanor to pick sea oats).

South Carolina isn't called the Palmetto State for nothing. Palm varieties are not as common here as in Florida, but you will encounter several types along the coast. The **cabbage palm,** for which South Carolina is nicknamed, is the largest variety, up to 50-60 feet tall. Its "heart of palm" is an edible delicacy, which coastal Native Americans boiled in bear fat as porridge. In dunes and sand hills you'll find clumps of the low-lying **saw palmetto.** The **bush palmetto** has distinctive fan-shaped branches. The common **Spanish bayonet** looks like a palm, but it's actually a member of the agave family.

You've probably seen **Venus flytraps** for sale in nurseries, and maybe you've even bought one and brought it home to stuff with kitchen bugs. Venus flytraps grow in the wild only in one tiny corner of the world, and that happens to be here, in a narrow band of counties between Wilmington, North Carolina, and Myrtle Beach, South Carolina. They and their dozens of carnivorous local kin, like pitcher plants, abattoirs of the bug world, and Dr. Seussian sundews, are fondest of living in places with nutrient-starved soil, like pine savannas and pocosins, where they have little competition for space and sunlight and can feed handsomely on meals that come right to them.

There are many species of **pitcher plants** here, a familiar predator of the plant world. Shaped like tubular vases, with a graceful elfin flap shading the mouth, pitcher plants attract insects with an irresistible brew. Unsuspecting bugs pile in, thinking they've found a keg party, but instead find themselves paddling in a sticky mess from which they're unable to escape, pinned down by spiny hairs that line the inside of the pitcher. Enterprising frogs and spiders that are either strong or clever enough to come and go safely from inside the pitcher will often set up shop inside a plant and help themselves to stragglers.

## FALL FOLIAGE

Arriving as early as mid-September at the highest elevations, and gradually sliding down the mountains through late October, autumn colors bring a late-season wave of visitors to western North and South Carolina and North Georgia. The latter weeks of October tend to be the peak, however. During those weeks it can be very difficult to find lodging in the mountains, so be sure to plan ahead. Some of the best places for leaf peeping are along the Blue Ridge Parkway and in Great Smoky Mountains National Park.

# Animals

## ON LAND

Perhaps the most iconic land animal—or semi-land animal, anyway—of the South is the legendary **American alligator,** the only species of crocodilian native to the area. Contrary to their fierce reputation, locals know these massive reptiles, 6-12 feet long as adults, to be quite shy. If you come in the colder months, you won't see them at all, since alligators require an outdoor temperature over 70°F to become active and feed (indeed, the appearance of alligators was once a well-known symbol of spring in the area). Often all you'll see is a couple of eyebrow ridges sticking out of the water, and a gator lying still in a shallow creek can easily be mistaken for a floating log. But should you see one or more gators basking in the sun—a favorite activity on warm days for these cold-blooded creatures—it's best to admire them from afar. A mother alligator will destroy anything that comes near her nest. Despite the alligator's short, stubby legs, it can run amazingly fast on land—faster than you, in fact.

The region hosts large populations of playful **river otter.** Not to be confused with the larger sea otters off the West Coast, these fast-swimming members of the weasel family inhabit inland waterways and marshy areas, with dominant males sometimes ranging as much as 50 miles within a single waterway. As strict carnivores, usually of fish, otters are a key indicator of the health of their ecosystem. If they're thriving, water and habitat quality are likely to be high. If they're not, something's going wrong.

While you're unlikely to encounter an otter, if you're camping, you might easily run into the **raccoon,** an exceedingly intelligent and crafty relative of the bear, sharing that larger animal's resourcefulness in stealing your food. Though nocturnal, raccoons will feed whenever food is available. Raccoons can grow so accustomed to human presence as to almost consider themselves part of the family, but resist the temptation to get close to them. Rabies is prevalent in the raccoon population, and you should always keep your distance.

Another common campsite nuisance, the **opossum** is a shy, primitive creature that is much more easily discouraged. North America's only marsupial, an opossum's usual "defense" against predators is to play dead. That said, the opossum has an immunity to snake venom and often feeds on the reptiles, even the most poisonous ones.

## IN THE WATER

Humankind's aquatic cousin, the **Atlantic bottle-nosed dolphin** is a well-known and frequent visitor to the coast, coming far upstream into creeks and rivers to feed. Children, adults, and experienced sailors alike all delight in encounters with the mammals, sociable creatures who travel in family units. When not occupied with feeding or mating activities—both of which can get surprisingly rowdy—dolphins show great curiosity about human visitors to their habitat. They will gather near boats, surfacing often with the distinctive chuffing sound of air coming from their blowholes. Occasionally they'll even lift their heads out of the water to have a look at you; consider yourself lucky indeed to have such a close encounter. Don't be fooled by their cuteness, however. Dolphins live life with gusto and aren't scared of much. They're voracious eaters of fish, amorous and energetic lovers, and will take on an encroaching shark in a heartbeat.

Another beloved part-time marine creature of the barrier islands of the coast is the **loggerhead turtle.** Though the species prefers to stay well offshore the rest of the year, females weighing up to 300 pounds come out of the sea each May-July to dig a shallow hole in the dunes and lay more than 100 leathery eggs, returning to the ocean and leaving the eggs to hatch on their own after two months. Interestingly, the mothers prefer to nest at the same spot on the same island year after year. After hatching, the baby turtles then make a dramatic, extremely dangerous (and extremely slow) trek to the safety of the waves, at the mercy of various predators. Dedicated research and conservation efforts are working hard to protect the loggerheads' traditional nursery grounds to ensure the survival of this fascinating, lovable, and threatened species. Cape Island within the Cape Romain National Wildlife Refuge in South Carolina is the leading nesting site north of Florida. Other key sites include Kiawah, Edisto, Hilton Head, and Tybee Islands.

Of course, the coastal waters and rivers are chockablock with fish. The most abundant and sought-after recreational species in the area is the **spotted sea trout,** followed by the **red drum.** Local anglers also pursue many varieties of **bass, bream, sheepshead,** and **crappie.** It may sound strange to some accustomed to considering it a "trash" fish, but many types of **catfish** are not only plentiful here but are a common and well-regarded food source. Many species of **flounder** inhabit the silty bottoms of estuaries all along the coast. Farther offshore are game and sport fish like **marlin, swordfish, shark, grouper,** and **tuna.**

Crustaceans and shellfish have been a food staple in the area for thousands of years, with the massive shell middens of the coast being testament to Native Americans' healthy appetite for them. The beds of the local variant, the **oyster,** aren't what they used to be due to overharvesting, water pollution, and disruption of habitat. In truth, these days most local restaurants import the little filter-feeders from the Gulf of Mexico. Oysters spawn May-August, hence the old folk wisdom about eating oysters only in months with the letter *r* so as not to disrupt the breeding cycle.

Each year from April to January, shrimp boats up and down the Southeastern coast trawl for **shrimp;** two local species, the white shrimp and the brown shrimp, are the most commercially viable. Shrimp are the most popular seafood item in the United States and account for bringing hundreds of millions of dollars in revenue into the coastal economy. While consumption won't slow down anytime soon, the South Carolina shrimping industry is facing serious threats, both from species decline due to pollution and overfishing and from competition from shrimp farms and the Asian shrimp industry.

Another important commercial crop is the **blue crab,** the species used in such Lowcountry delicacies as crab cakes. You'll often see floating markers bobbing up and down in rivers throughout the region. These signal the presence directly below of a crab trap, often of an amateur crabber. A true living link to primordial times, the alien-looking **horseshoe crab** is frequently found on beaches of the coast during the spring mating season (it lives in deeper water the rest of the year). More closely related to scorpions and spiders than crabs, the horseshoe has evolved hardly a lick in hundreds of millions of years. Any trip to a local salt marsh at low tide will likely uncover hundreds of **fiddler crabs,** so-named for the way the males wave their single enlarged claws in the air to attract mates. (Their other, smaller claw is the one they eat with.) The fiddlers make distinctive burrows in the pluff mud for sanctuary during high tide, recognizable by the little balls of sediment at the entrances (the crabs spit out the balls after sifting through the sand for food).

## IN THE AIR

When enjoying the marshlands of the coast, consider yourself fortunate to see an endangered **wood stork,** although their numbers are on the increase. The only storks to breed in North America, these graceful long-lived birds (routinely living over 10 years) are usually seen on a low flight path across the marsh, although at some birding spots beginning in late summer you can find them at a **roost,** sometimes numbering over 100 birds. Resting at high tide, they fan out over the marsh to feed at low tide on foot. Old-timers sometimes call them "Spanish buzzards" or simply "the preacher." Often confused with the wood stork is the gorgeous **white ibis,** distinguishable by its orange bill and black wingtips. Like the wood stork, the ibis is a communal bird that roosts in colonies. Other similar-looking coastal denizens are the white-feathered **great egret** and **snowy egret,** the former distinguishable by its yellow bill and the latter by its black bill and the tuft of plumes on the back of its head. Egrets are in the same family as herons. The most magnificent is the **great blue heron.** Despite their imposing height—up to four feet tall—these waders are shy. Often you hear them rather than see them, a loud shriek of alarm that echoes over the marsh. So how to tell the difference between all these wading birds at a glance? It's easiest when they're in flight. Egrets and herons fly with their necks tucked in, while storks and ibis fly with their necks extended.

The chief raptor of the salt marsh is the fish-eating **osprey.** These large brown-and-white birds of prey are similar to eagles but are adapted to a maritime environment, with a reversible outer toe on each talon (the better for catching wriggly fish) and closable nostrils so they can dive into the water after prey. Very common all along the coast, they like to build big nests on top of buoys and channel markers in addition to trees. The **bald eagle** is making a comeback in the area thanks to increased federal regulation and better education of trigger-happy locals. Like the osprey, the eagles prefer fish, but unlike the osprey will settle for rodents and rabbits.

Inland among the pines you'll find the most common area woodpecker, the huge **pileated woodpecker.** Less common is the smaller, more subtly marked **red-cockaded woodpecker.** Once common in the vast primordial pine forests of the Southeast, the species is now endangered, its last real refuge being the big tracts of relatively undisturbed land on military bases and national wildlife refuges.

## INSECTS

Down here they say that God invented bugs to keep the Yankees from completely taking over the South. And insects are probably the most unpleasant fact of life in the Southeastern coastal region. The list of annoying indigenous insects must begin with the infamous **sand gnat,** scourge of the lowlands. This tiny and persistent nuisance, a member of the midge family, lacks the precision of the mosquito with its long proboscis. No, the sand gnat is more torture master than surgeon, brutally gouging and digging away its victim's skin until it hits a source of blood. Most prevalent in the spring and fall, the sand gnat is drawn to its prey by the carbon dioxide trail of

its breath. While long sleeves and long pants are one way to keep gnats at bay, that causes its own discomfort because of the region's heat and humidity. The only real antidote to the sand gnat's assault—other than never breathing—is the Avon skin-care product Skin So Soft, which has taken on a new and wholly unplanned life as the South's favorite anti-gnat lotion.

Running a close second to the sand gnat are the over three dozen species of highly aggressive **mosquito,** which breed anywhere a few drops of water lie stagnant. Not surprisingly, massive populations blossom in the rainiest months, in late spring and late summer. Like the gnat, the mosquito—the biters are always female—homes in on its victim by trailing the plume of carbon dioxide exhaled in the breath. Alas, Skin So Soft has little effect on the mosquito. Try over-the-counter sprays, anything smelling of citronella, and wearing long sleeves and long pants when weather permits.

Undoubtedly the most viscerally loathed of all pests on the Lowcountry and Georgia coasts is the so-called "palmetto bug," or **American cockroach.** These black, shiny, and sometimes grotesquely massive insects—up to two inches long—are living fossils, virtually unchanged over hundreds of millions of years. And perfectly adapted as they are to life in and among wet, decaying vegetation, they're unlikely to change a bit in 100 million more years. Popular regional use of the term *palmetto bug* undoubtedly has its roots in a desire for polite Southern society to avoid using the ugly word *roach* and its connotations of filth and unclean environments.

# History

## BEFORE THE EUROPEANS

Based on studies of artifacts found throughout the state, anthropologists know that the first humans arrived in South Carolina at least 13,000 years ago, at the tail end of the last ice age. However, a still-controversial archaeological dig in the state, the Topper Site on the Savannah River near Allendale, has found artifacts that some scientists say are about 50,000 years old.

In any case, during this **Paleo-Indian Period,** sea levels were more than 200 feet lower than present levels, and large mammals such as woolly mammoths, horses, and camels were hunted for food and skins. However, rapidly increasing temperatures, rising sea levels, and efficient hunting techniques combined to quickly kill off these large mammals, ushering in the **Archaic Period.** It's during this time that the great **shell middens** of the Georgia and South Carolina coasts trace their origins. Essentially trash heaps for discarded oyster shells, as the middens grew in size they also took on a ceremonial status, often being used as sites for important rituals and meetings.

The introduction of agriculture and improved pottery techniques about 3,000 years ago led to the **Woodland Period** of Native American settlement. Native Americans had been cremating or burying their dead for years, a practice that eventually gave rise to the construction of the first mounds during the Woodland Period.

Increased agriculture led to increased population, and with that population growth came competition over resources and a more formal notion of warfare. This period, about AD 800-1600, is termed the **Mississippian Period.** It was the Mississippians who would be the first Native Americans in what's now the continental United States to encounter European explorers and settlers after Columbus. The Native Americans who would later be called the **Creek people** were the direct descendants of the Mississippians in lineage, language, and lifestyle.

## THE SPANISH ARRIVE

The first known contact by Europeans on the Southeastern coast came in 1521, roughly concurrent with Cortés's conquest of Mexico. A party of Spanish slavers ventured into what's now Port Royal Sound in South Carolina. They kidnapped a few Native American slaves and left, ranging as far north as the Cape Fear River in present-day North Carolina, and by some accounts even farther up the coast.

The first serious exploration of the coast came in 1526, when Lucas Vázquez de Ayllón and about 600 colonists made landfall at Winyah Bay near present-day Georgetown, South Carolina. They didn't stay long, however, immediately moving down the coast and trying to put down roots in the St. Catherine's Sound area of modern-day Liberty County, Georgia. That colony—called San Miguel de Gualdape—was the first European colony in North America (the continent's oldest continuously occupied settlement, St. Augustine, Florida, wasn't founded until 1565). The colony also brought with it the seed of a future nation's dissolution: enslaved people from Africa. San Miguel lasted only six weeks due to political tension and a slave uprising.

Hernando de Soto's infamous expedition of 1539-1543 began in Florida and went through southwest Georgia before crossing the Savannah River somewhere near modern-day North Augusta, South Carolina. Long after his departure and eventual death from fever in Alabama, De Soto's legacy was felt throughout the Southeast in the form of various diseases for which the indigenous Mississippian people had no immunity whatsoever.

The next serious Spanish expedition into South Carolina began on the coast in 1566, when Juan Pardo set out from Santa Elena on

Parris Island. Pardo and his party of 125 soldiers were on a mission to explore the hinterland and scout a location for a road to the main Spanish silver mines in Mexico. Along the way Pardo established several short-lived forts in what are now the Carolinas and Tennessee. One of these forts, called San Juan, has been identified by archaeologists outside present-day Morganton, North Carolina, in a community called Worry Crossroads.

## THE LOST COLONY

The next major episode in the nonnative settlement of the region is one of the strangest mysteries in American history, that of the Lost Colonists of Roanoke. After two previous failed attempts to establish an English stronghold on the island of Roanoke, fraught by poor planning and even worse diplomacy, a third group of English colonists tried their luck.

Sometime between being dropped off in the New World in 1585, and one of their leaders returning three years later to resupply them, all of the colonists—including Virginia Dare, the first English-speaking person born in the Americas—had vanished. (North Carolina at that time was part of the colony of Virginia.) A subsequent expedition found only "CROATOAN" carved into a fence and "CRO" carved into a tree.

To this day, the fate of the 90 men, 17 women, and 11 children is unknown, although a host of fascinating theories are still debated, and probably always will be. Were they murdered by Native Americans? The Spanish? Or did they simply integrate into local Native American communities, who were much better equipped to feed themselves than the woefully prepared settlers?

## THE MISSION ERA

It's rarely mentioned as a key part of U.S. history, but the Spanish missionary presence on the Georgia coast was longer and more comprehensive than its much more widely known counterpart in California.

St. Augustine governor Pedro Menéndez de Avilés, over "biscuits with honey" on the beach at St. Catherine's Island in Georgia with a local Native American chief, negotiated for the right to establish a system of Jesuit missions in two coastal chiefdoms: the Mocama on and around Cumberland Island, and the Guale (pronounced "wallie") to the north. Those early missions, the first north of Mexico, were largely unsuccessful. But a renewed, organized effort by the Franciscan Order came to fruition during the 1580s. Missions were established all along the Georgia coast, from the mainland near St. Simons and Sapelo Islands to the Altamaha River.

Spanish power waned under the English threat, however. But even as late as 1667, right before the founding of Charleston, there were still 70 missions on the Georgia coast. Pirate raids and slave uprisings finished off the Georgia missions for good by 1684.

## THE COLONY OF CAROLINA

The Carolinas are a product of the **English Restoration,** when the monarchy returned to power after the grim 11-year tenure of Oliver Cromwell. The attitudes of the Restoration era—expansionist, confident, mercantile—are key to understanding the character of South Carolina even today. Historians dispute exactly how close-minded Cromwell was, but there's no debating the puritanical tone of his reign as English head of state. Theater was banned, as was most music, except for hymns. Hair was close-cropped, and dress was extremely conservative. Most disturbing of all for the holiday-loving English, the observation of Christmas and Easter was strongly discouraged because of their supposedly pagan origins.

Enter Charles II, son of the beheaded Charles I. His ascent to the throne in 1660 signaled a release of all the pent-up creativity and energy of the English people, stagnant under Cromwell's repression. In 1665 King Charles II gave a charter to eight **Lords Proprietors** to establish a colony, generously to be named Carolina after the monarch

# Henry Woodward, Colonial Indiana Jones

He's virtually unsung in the history books, and there are no movies made about him, but Dr. Henry Woodward, the first English settler in South Carolina, lived a life that is the stuff of novels and screenplays. Educated in medicine in London, Woodward first tried his hand in the colony of Barbados. But Barbados, crowded and run by an elite, was no place for a young man with a sense of adventure but no contacts in the sugar industry. Still in his teens, Woodward left Barbados in Captain Robert Sandford's 1664 expedition to Carolina. Landing in the Cape Fear region, Sandford's cohort made his way down to Port Royal Sound to contact the Cusabo Indians. In 1666, in what is perhaps the New World's first "cultural-exchange program," Woodward volunteered to stay behind while the rest of the expedition returned to England with a Native American named Shadoo.

Woodward learned the local language and established political relations with surrounding Native American groups, actions for which the Lords Proprietors granted him temporary "formall possession of the whole Country to hold as Tennant att Will." The Spanish had different plans, however. They came and kidnapped the young Englishman, taking him to what turned out to be a very permissive state of house arrest at the Spanish stronghold of St. Augustine in Florida. Surprising the Spanish with his request—in Latin, no less—to convert to Catholicism, Woodward was popular and well treated. An excellent student of the catechism, Woodward became a favorite of the Spanish governor and was even promoted to official surgeon. During that time, he studied Spanish government, commerce, and culture, with the same diligence with which he studied the Indians a year earlier. In 1668, Woodward was "rescued" by English privateers—pirates, really—under the command of Robert Searle, who'd come to sack St. Augustine. Woodward's sojourn with the pirates would last two years, during which he was kept on board as ship's surgeon. Was the pirate raid a coincidence? Or, as some scholars suggest, was Woodward really one of history's greatest spies? We will probably never know.

Incredibly, the plot thickens. In another coincidence, in 1670 Woodward was rescued after the pirates shipwrecked on the Caribbean island of Nevis. His rescuers were none other than the settlers on their way to found Charles Towne. On landfall, Woodward asserted his previous experience in the area to direct the colonists away from Port Royal to an area of less Spanish influence. That same year he began a series of expeditions to contact indigenous people in the Carolina interior—the first non-Spanish European to set foot in the area. Using economic espionage gained from the Spanish, Woodward's goal was to jump-start the trade in deerskins that would be the bulwark of the Charles Towne colony. Woodward's unlikely 1674 alliance with the aggressive Westo people was instrumental in this burgeoning trade. As if all this weren't enough, in 1680 Woodward, now with property of his own on Johns Island, would introduce local farmers to a certain strange crop recently imported from Madagascar: rice.

Woodward made enemies, however, of settlers who were envious of his growing affluence and suspicious of his friendship with the Westo. His outspoken disgust with the spread of Indian slavery brought a charge against him of undermining the interests of the crown. But Woodward, by now a celebrity of sorts, returned to England to plead his case directly to the Lords Proprietors. They not only pardoned him but made him their official Indian agent—with a 20 percent share of the profits. Woodward would never again see the land of his birth. He returned to the American colonies to trek inland, making alliances with groups of Creek Indians in Spanish-held territory. Hounded by Spanish troops, Woodward fell ill of a fever somewhere in the Savannah River valley. He made it to Charleston and safety but never fully recovered and died around 1690—after living the kind of life you usually only see in the movies.

himself. Remarkably, none of the Proprietors ever set foot in the colony they established for their own profit.

In 1666 explorer Robert Sandford officially claimed Carolina for the king, in a ceremony on modern-day Seabrook or Wadmalaw Island. The Proprietors then sent out a fleet of three ships from England, only one of which, the *Carolina*, would make it the whole way. After stops in the thriving English colonies of Barbados and Bermuda, the ship landed in Port Royal. The English were greeted without violence, but the fact that the local indigenous people spoke Spanish led the colonists to conclude that perhaps the site was too close for comfort to Spain's sphere of influence. A Kiawah chief, eager for allies against the fierce, slave-trading Westo people, invited the colonists north to settle there instead. So the colonists—148 of them, including three enslaved Africans—moved 80 miles up the coast and in 1670 pitched camp on the Ashley River at a place they dubbed Albemarle Point, after one of their lost ships.

A few years later some colonists from Barbados, which was beginning to suffer the effects of overpopulation, joined the Carolinians. The Barbadian influence, with an emphasis on large-scale slave labor and a caste system, would have an indelible imprint on the colony. Indeed, within a generation a majority of settlers in the new colony would be enslaved Africans. By 1680, however, Albemarle Point was feeling growing pains as well, and the Proprietors ordered the site moved to Oyster Point at the confluence of the Ashley and Cooper Rivers (the present-day Battery). Within a year, Albemarle Point was abandoned, and the walls of Charles Towne were built a few hundred yards up from Oyster Point on the banks of the Cooper River.

The English settlements quickly gained root as the burgeoning deerskin trade increased exponentially. Traders upriver, using an ancient network of trails, worked with local Native Americans, mostly Cherokee people, to exploit the massive numbers of deer in the American interior. By the mid-1700s, the deer population had been so overharvested that the Cherokees had trouble feeding themselves. This led to the need to purchase or barter for food from the English, a dependency that would lead inexorably to violence in years to come.

Around this time German and Scots-Irish settlers from Pennsylvania and Virginia came down the **Great Wagon Road** along the Appalachians to enter the interior of the Carolinas in great numbers. Although many of these independent farmers owned slaves, generally they were far less sympathetic to slavery than coastal residents, and certainly much less dependent on it.

## OGLETHORPE'S VISION

In 1712, the colony of Carolina was divided into north and south after a building period of political and economic estrangement. What would be South Carolina was increasingly identified with large rice plantations dependent on slave labor. Other than a band of plantations on its southeast coast near Wilmington, North Carolina's economy evolved to be somewhat less dependent on slavery.

In 1731, a colony to be known as Georgia, after the new English king, was carved out of the southern part of the original Carolina land grant specifically to buffer the wealthy plantations in South Carolina from the Spanish. A young general, aristocrat, and humanitarian named James Edward Oglethorpe gathered together a group of trustees to take advantage.

On February 12, 1733, after stops in Beaufort and Charleston, the ship *Anne* with its 114 passengers made its way to the highest bluff on the Savannah River. The area was controlled by the peaceful Yamacraw people. Oglethorpe struck up a treaty and eventually a genuine friendship with the elderly chief Tomochichi. In negotiations with local Native Americans, the persuasive Oglethorpe convinced the coastal Creek people to cede to the crown all Georgia land to the Altamaha River "which our Nation hath not occasion for to use" in exchange for goods.

While the trustees' utopian vision was largely economic in nature, like Carolina, the Georgia colony also emphasized religious freedom. While to modern ears Oglethorpe's original ban of Roman Catholics from Georgia might seem incompatible with this goal, the reason was a coldly pragmatic one for the time: England's two main global rivals, France and Spain, were both staunchly Roman Catholic.

The conflict came to a head on the coast in 1739 with the so-called War of Jenkins' Ear. A year later Oglethorpe cobbled together a force of settlers, Native American allies, and Carolinians to reduce the Spanish fortress at St. Augustine, Florida.

The siege failed, and Oglethorpe retreated to St. Simons Island, Georgia, to await the inevitable counterattack. In 1742 a massive Spanish force invaded the island but was eventually turned back for good with heavy casualties at the **Battle of Bloody Marsh.** That clash marked the end of Spanish overtures on England's colonies in America. The stage was set for an internal battle between England and its burgeoning colonies across the Atlantic.

# REVOLUTION AND A NEW NATION

While the New England area gets most of the press when people talk about the American Revolution, the Carolinas and Georgia were key theaters of the war.

After the battles of Lexington and Concord, Governor Martin of North Carolina removed himself from the then-capital of New Bern, the first colonial governor to buck his post. North Carolina's Mecklenburg County (the Charlotte area) also made history by passing the first colonial declaration in rejection of the crown's authority.

At war's outbreak, the British failed to take Charleston—fourth-largest city in the colonies—in June 1776. The episode gave South Carolina its "Palmetto State" moniker when redcoat cannonballs bounced off the palm tree-lined walls of Fort Moultrie on Sullivan's Island. The British successfully took the city, however, in 1780, holding it until 1782. The area's two major cities were captured—Savannah had fallen to the British in 1778—but the war raged on in the surrounding area. The struggle became a guerrilla war of colonists versus the British as well as a civil war between Patriots and Loyalists, or **Tories.** Patriots of the South Carolina Lowcountry formed a guerrilla group under legendary leaders such as Francis Marion,

"the Swamp Fox," and Thomas Sumter, "the Gamecock."

In South Carolina, militiamen would defeat Loyalist forces in two pivotal battles of the war, at Cowpens and Kings Mountain. The unexpected show of patriotism from noncoastal settlers put a dagger in General Cornwallis's ill-fated Southern Strategy and led inevitably to the British retreat through North Carolina. Cornwallis received another blow at the Battle of Guilford Courthouse, which, though technically a British victory, weakened his forces considerably, leading to his eventual final defeat at Yorktown, Virginia.

# THE GOLD RUSHES

Cotton and tobacco weren't the only money-makers in the Carolinas and Georgia in the antebellum era. Two gold rushes, one in North Carolina and one in Georgia, were America's first. In Cabarrus County, North Carolina, gold nuggets were found in large numbers in the late 1790s. By the 1830s, there was so much gold that the U.S. Mint opened a branch in Charlotte.

The North Georgia strike near Dahlonega was even bigger. By 1830 there were 4,000 miners panning for gold on one Georgia creek alone. As in North Carolina, the amount and quality of gold was so extravagant that the U.S. Mint opened a branch office in Dahlonega in 1838. Before closing at the outbreak of the Civil War, it had produced 1.5 million gold coins.

Of course, the original inhabitants of the gold rush land in both states were the Cherokee people. Writing in a Cherokee newspaper, one said of the rush, "Our neighbors who regard no law and pay no respects to the laws of humanity are now reaping a plentiful harvest. . . . We are an abused people." Those words were prophetic, and decades of government activity oriented toward removing Creek and Cherokee from the region came to a head when gold was used as an excuse to take final action.

Andrew Jackson's administration presided

# Old Hickory's Legacy

Although many histories of Andrew Jackson, seventh president of the United States, say he was born in North Carolina, don't tell that to South Carolinians. They're sure Old Hickory is one of their own. If you don't believe them, get into your time machine and ask Andrew Jackson himself. He always insisted he was born in a log house in South Carolina a couple of miles from the border with the Tar Heel State.

In any case, we know that Old Hickory was born in what's called the Waxhaws region, straddling the border of the Carolinas roughly in the area of modern-day Charlotte and its suburbs to the south. Like much of the Upstate, the area was generally immune to the charms of the Lowcountry planters, whom they thought of as a pampered elite. While owning slaves was certainly a part of the entire state's economy, it was noticeably less important in the Upstate.

This sensitivity to the needs and basic dignity of the common man would go on to inform Jackson's time in the White House. Prior to Jackson's presidency, only white male landowners could vote in the United States. Setting the stage for gradually increasing suffrage gains—such as for African American men, and later for all women—Jackson changed the system so that owning land was not a requirement to vote.

Jackson had noticeably less populist sympathy for Native Americans, however. As a product of the rough Carolina frontier, the site of generations of savage wars between settlers and local indigenous people, he grew up with a strong bias against the region's original inhabitants. This enmity would see its awful height in the Trail of Tears, a direct result of Jackson's Indian Removal Act of 1830. The most famous—and possibly apocryphal—example of Jackson's literal "my way or the highway" approach came in 1831, when the Supreme Court, under Chief Justice John Marshall, ruled against the state of Georgia's action to take Cherokee land. In response, Jackson supposedly said, "John Marshall has made his decision—now let him enforce it."

Another development that didn't necessarily have such sanguine results was his introduction of the patronage system—in other words, "to the victor go the spoils." Before Jackson, civil servants kept their jobs regardless of which team was in the White House. Afterward, bureaucrats became political appointees. While today patronage is generally thought of as leading to corruption and cronyism, at the time Jackson intended it as an antidote to what he saw as a creeping aristocracy in the government and another example of the venal self-centered nature of the Lowcountry planter elite.

One of Jackson's key philosophies, a sharp distrust of banks, did not survive his time in office. Although he fought strenuously against the undue influence of the banking industry on the American body politic, no one could say he was successful in light of their power today.

Learn more about Old Hickory when you're in the state of his birth (according to the man himself, anyway) by visiting **Andrew Jackson State Park** (196 Andrew Jackson Park Rd., 803/285-3344, www.southcarolinaparks.com, during daylight saving time daily 9am-9pm, other seasons daily 8am-6pm, $2 adults, free under age 16).

Andrew Jackson's main protégé, James K. Polk, is widely considered by historians to be the most influential and important one-term president in American history. He dramatically expanded the borders of the country to the Pacific Ocean through a Jacksonian combination of hard-nosed diplomacy and outright warfare. Outside Charlotte, North Carolina, you can visit his restored homestead and birthplace at the **James K. Polk Historic Site** (12031 Lancaster Hwy., Pineville, 704/889-7145, www.nchistoricsites.org, Tues.-Sat. 9am-5pm, free).

over the passage of the Indian Removal Act in 1830, which assigned reservations in the Indian Territory of present-day Oklahoma to the "Five Civilized Tribes" of the southeastern United States—the Cherokee, Choctaw, Creek, Chickasaw, and Seminole. Thousands of Cherokee people were forced out of western North Carolina, North Georgia, eastern Tennessee, and Alabama and marched west on the Trail of Tears. About 4,000 died along the way.

Another 1,000 or so Cherokee people,

through hiding, fighting, and negotiation, managed to win the right to stay in North Carolina—an act of resistance that was the birth of the modern Eastern Band of the Cherokee, which is still centered in and around the town of Cherokee on the Qualla Boundary in North Carolina's Great Smoky Mountains.

## SECESSION

Much of the lead-in to the Civil War focused on whether slavery would be allowed in the newest U.S. territories in the West, but there's no doubt that all figurative roads eventually led to South Carolina. During Andrew Jackson's presidency in the 1820s, his vice president, South Carolina's John C. Calhoun, became a thorn in Jackson's side with his aggressive advocacy for the concept of **nullification,** which Jackson strenuously rejected. In a nutshell, Calhoun said that if a state decided that the federal government wasn't treating it fairly—in this case with regard to tariffs that were hurting the cotton trade in the Palmetto State—it could simply nullify the federal law, superseding it with law of its own.

In 1860 the national convention of the Democratic Party, then the dominant force in U.S. politics, was held in—where else?—Charleston. Rancor over slavery and states' rights was so high that they couldn't agree on a single candidate to run to replace President James Buchanan. Reconvening in Maryland, the party split along sectional lines, with the Northern wing backing Stephen A. Douglas. The Southern wing, fervently desiring secession, deliberately chose its own candidate, John Breckinridge, in order to split the Democratic vote and throw the election to Republican Abraham Lincoln, an outspoken opponent of the expansion of slavery. During that so-called **Secession Winter** before Lincoln took office, seven states seceded from the union, first among them the Palmetto State, followed by Mississippi, Florida, Alabama, Georgia, Louisiana, and Texas.

Politically moderate compared to South Carolina and some other Southern states, and less invested economically and politically in slavery, North Carolinians were painfully divided as war approached. The state's voters rejected a ballot measure to authorize a secession convention, but North Carolina's hand was forced when fighting erupted at Fort Sumter in Charleston harbor. North Carolina seceded on May 20, 1861.

## THE CIVIL WAR

Five days after South Carolina's secession on December 21, 1860, U.S. Army major Robert Anderson moved his garrison from Fort Moultrie in Charleston Harbor to nearby Fort Sumter. Over the next few months and into the spring, Anderson would ignore many calls to surrender, and Confederate forces would prevent any Union resupply or reinforcement. Shortly before dawn on April 12, 1861, Confederate batteries around Charleston—ironically none of which were at the Battery itself—opened fire on Fort Sumter and continued for 34 straight hours, until Anderson surrendered on April 13.

Far from prodding the North to sue for peace, the fall of Fort Sumter instead caused the remaining states in the union to rally around the previously unpopular tall man from Illinois. Lincoln's skillful—some would say cunning—management of the Fort Sumter standoff meant that from then on, the South would bear history's blame for initiating the conflict that would claim over half a million American lives.

In summer 1861, the Union blockade of the Southeast coast began. New Bern, North Carolina, fell in the spring of 1862 and became a major locus of strategic operations for the Union military, as well as a thriving political base for free African Americans and escaped slaves. To the south, Fort Fisher on Cape Fear, near Wilmington, was a crucial outlet for blockade-runners. It kept the city of Wilmington in Confederate hands until nearly the end of the war, and when it finally did fall to Union forces in late February 1865, it required what would remain the largest amphibious assault in American military history until World War II.

In November 1861, a massive Union invasion armada landed in Port Royal Sound in South Carolina, effectively taking the entire Lowcountry and Sea Islands out of the war. Charleston, however, did host two battles in the conflict. The **Battle of Secessionville** came in June 1862, when a Union force attempting to take Charleston was repulsed on James Island with heavy casualties. The next battle, an unsuccessful Union landing on Morris Island in July 1863, was immortalized in the movie *Glory*. The 54th Massachusetts Regiment, an African American unit with white commanders, performed so gallantly in its failed assault on the Confederate-held Battery Wagner that it inspired the North and was cited by abolitionists as further proof that African Americans should be given freedom and full citizenship rights.

Another invasion attempt on Charleston would not come, but the city was besieged and bombarded for nearly two years (devastation made even worse by a massive fire, unrelated to the shelling, that destroyed much of the city in 1861).

Large-scale fighting didn't hit Georgia until Union troops pushed down from Chattanooga, Tennessee, in 1863. The last major Confederate victory of the war came at Chickamauga in September 1863, when Confederate general Braxton Bragg, with considerable assistance from General James Longstreet, a Georgia native, pushed Union troops under General William Rosecrans back into Tennessee after three days of brutal fighting. However, the Union Army still held Chattanooga and continued to consolidate its forces for General William T. Sherman's eventual push to capture the real prize, Atlanta, and deal a dual blow to the Confederacy by seizing a major transportation and commercial hub as well as likely guaranteeing Lincoln's reelection later in 1864.

The spring of 1864 was a fateful one for the South, as Sherman's initial forays into the area

north of Atlanta were successful. Unrest in the top Confederate ranks led to Jefferson Davis firing General Joseph Johnston and replacing him with General John B. Hood, even as Sherman's army was gathering for the final assault only five miles from the city. Hood's attacks against the Union lines were too little, too late, and by the end of the summer Hood had evacuated Atlanta and left it to its fate. Sherman telegraphed Lincoln, "Atlanta is ours and fairly won."

It was during roughly the same period that the notorious Camp Sumter POW camp operated near Andersonville, the name by which it's mostly known today. At its height of prisoner population, so many captured Union troops roasted in the sun within its unsheltered, stockaded space that it would have been the Confederacy's fifth-largest city.

After three months of occupying Atlanta, Sherman was set to begin his fabled "March to the Sea" in an attempt to break the Southern will to fight for good, by destroying its means of supporting an army. On his way out of Atlanta in November, he gave the order to burn everything in the city that might be useful to the Southern war effort. The arson extended to private residences, and the entire downtown area burned in a massive and controversial conflagration.

The March to the Sea was made easier by Hood's removal of his forces to the west in an effort to draw Sherman toward Tennessee again. Sherman didn't take the bait, and with the way clear to the coast, he broke standard protocol not only by splitting his forces, but by operating without a supply line, instead wanting his army to forage off the land and whatever supplies they could obtain from the populace.

He divided his 60,000-man army into two equal wings: one would head toward Augusta and the other toward Macon. They both met at the state capital of Milledgeville, where the statehouse was ransacked and anything of remote military value was put to the torch. A Confederate cavalry force under General Joseph Wheeler harried Union forces the whole way, but to little effect. Union "bummers" took what they wanted from local farms, and railroad-wrecking crews heated railroad tracks into twisted messes called "Sherman's neckties."

In Savannah, Sherman concluded his March to the Sea in December 1864, famously giving the city to Lincoln as a Christmas present, along with 25,000 bales of cotton.

The only military uncertainty left was in how badly Charleston, the "cradle of secession," would suffer for its sins. Historians and local wags have long debated why Sherman spared Charleston, the hated epicenter of the Civil War. Did he fall in love with the city during his brief posting there as a young lieutenant? Did he literally fall in love there, with one of its legendarily beautiful and delicate local belles? We may never know for sure, but it's likely that the Lowcountry's marshy, mucky terrain simply made it too difficult to move large numbers of men and supplies from Savannah to Charleston proper. So Sherman turned his battle-hardened army inland toward the state capital, Columbia, which would not be so lucky. Most of Charleston's oncegreat plantation homes were also put to the torch.

For the African American population of the region, however, it was not a time of sadness but the great Day of Jubilee. Soon after the Confederate surrender, black Charlestonians held one of the largest parades the city has ever seen, with one of the floats being a coffin bearing the sign "Slavery is dead."

As for the place where it all began, a plucky Confederate garrison remained underground at Fort Sumter throughout the war, as the walls above them were literally pounded into dust by the long Union siege. The garrison quietly left the fort under cover of night on February 17, 1865. Major Robert Anderson, who surrendered the fort at war's beginning, returned to Sumter in April 1865 to raise the same flag he'd lowered exactly four years earlier. Later that same night, on Good Friday, Abraham Lincoln was assassinated in Washington DC.

The last major battle of the war was fought in North Carolina, when Sherman and Confederate general Joseph Johnston engaged at Bentonville. Johnston surrendered to Sherman in Durham in April 1865.

President Jefferson Davis met with his cabinet for the last time on May 5, 1865, in Washington, Georgia, essentially dissolving the Confederate government. Five days later, still on the run, he was captured by Union cavalry near Irwinville, Georgia, in the center of the state.

# RECONSTRUCTION AND THE NEW SOUTH

The years immediately after the war were painful, as a vast population of newly free African Americans tried to make a new life for themselves economically and politically in the face of tremendous opposition, and often violence, from whites. The Ku Klux Klan was born during this era, inaugurating an era of terror for African Americans throughout the South and beyond. Federal occupation and domination of the Southern states' political and legal systems also exacerbated resentment toward the North.

For a brief time, General Sherman's benevolent dictatorship on the coast held promise for an orderly postwar future. In 1865 he issued his sweeping "40 acres and a mule" order seeking dramatic economic restitution for coastal Georgia's free blacks. Politics reared its ugly head in the wake of Lincoln's assassination, however, and the order was rescinded, ushering in the chaotic Reconstruction era, echoes of which linger to this day. Nonetheless, that period in the South Carolina and Georgia Sea Islands served as an important incubator of sorts for the indigenous African American culture of the coast—called Gullah in South Carolina and Geechee in Georgia. Largely left to their own devices, these insular farming and oystering communities held to their old folkways, many of which exist today.

The late 1800s saw large-scale investment in North Carolina's railroad system, enabling an industrial boom in the New South.

Agriculture changed in this era too, as the rise of tenancy created a new form of enslavement for many farmers—black, white, and Native American. R. J. Reynolds, Washington Duke, and other entrepreneurs built a massively lucrative empire of tobacco production from field to factory. Textile and furniture mills sprouted throughout the Piedmont of the Carolinas, creating a new cultural landscape as rural Southerners migrated to mill towns.

Atlanta was gradually rebuilt and quickly regained its status as a transportation hub. In an acknowledgment of the city's overriding importance to the state, the Georgia capital was moved there from Milledgeville in 1868, a scant four years after it was burned to the ground. By 1880, Atlanta had surpassed Savannah as Georgia's largest city. The "New South" movement, spearheaded by *Atlanta Journal-Constitution* editor Henry W. Grady, posited a region less about agriculture than about industry and progressive thought.

Despite the upheaval of Reconstruction, the Victorian era in the Carolinas and Georgia was remarkably robust, with fortunes being made and glittering downtowns and residential areas rebuilt. A number of newly minted African American millionaires gained prominence during this time as well, most notably in Atlanta. The exclusive Jekyll Island Club opened in 1886, bringing the world's wealthiest people to the Georgia coast to play. In Horry County, South Carolina, the town of Conway exploded as a commercial center for the logging industry. By 1901 the first modest resort had been built on nearby Myrtle Beach, and the area rapidly became an important vacation area—a role it serves to this day.

# THE 20TH CENTURY

The arrival of the tiny but devastating boll weevil all but wiped out the cotton trade on the coast after the turn of the 20th century, forcing the economy to diversify. Naval stores and lumbering were the order of the day at the advent of **World War I,** the patriotic effort of which did wonders in repairing the

wounds of the Civil War, still vivid in many local memories.

## The New Deal

Beginning in 1915 the old cotton-growing states of the South saw the arrival of the tiny but devastating boll weevil, which all but wiped out the cotton trade. Sharecroppers, a large percentage of the population and never far from economic disaster in the best of times, were hit especially hard. Old tensions flared as the Ku Klux Klan was revived on Stone Mountain, Georgia.

During the 1920s, then-New York governor Franklin D. Roosevelt began visiting the Warm Springs area of Georgia to seek relief for his worsening polio symptoms. He saw firsthand the struggle of rural Southerners, and these experiences would influence many domestic initiatives, such as the Rural Electrification program, after he was elected president in 1932.

The coming of the Great Depression in the early 1930s was for most Southerners just a worsening of an already bad economic situation. While FDR's New Deal programs had some positive effect, they were later in coming to the South and were less effective because of resistance on the part of state politicians such as Governor Eugene Talmadge of Georgia, who was a staunch segregationist and sought to limit any benefits of Roosevelt's largesse to white citizens only.

The cities fared a good bit better due to their transportation and manufacturing importance. Atlanta in particular weathered the Great Depression well, at the same time seeing a robust growth in the black middle class, a background that nurtured a young Martin Luther King Jr. in the then-prosperous black neighborhood called Sweet Auburn. The auto bug bit Atlanta hard (it's still felt there today), and the first car suburbs were built.

The chief legacy today of the Depression era in the region is the work of the Civilian Conservation Corps (CCC), a 10-year jobs program that resulted in the construction of many of the area's state parks, many of which feature original structures built by "Roosevelt's Tree Army" that are still very much in use today. Parts of the great Appalachian Trail were also cleared by the CCC, with many of the shelters used by through-hikers still in steady use today.

## World War II

The modern-day military importance of the Carolinas and Georgia largely dates to the era of World War II. Installations at Fort Bragg, Camp Lejeune, Fort Jackson, Parris Island, and other still-vital bases in the Carolinas were constructed or expanded.

In Georgia, the enormous Bell Bomber plant was built in Marietta, near Atlanta, producing thousands of B-29 bombers for the final air offensive against the empire of Japan. Fort Benning in Columbus became the U.S. Army's main infantry, paratrooper, and Ranger training base. The "Mighty Eighth" Air Force was founded in Savannah, and enormous Fort Stewart was built in nearby Hinesville. In shipyards in Savannah and Brunswick, hundreds of Liberty ships were built to transport cargo to the citizens and allied armies of Europe.

In Aiken, South Carolina, the construction of the sprawling Savannah River Site hydrogen-bomb plant in the early 1950s forced the relocation of thousands of citizens, mostly low-income African Americans. Although environmentally problematic, the site has continued to provide many jobs to the area.

## Civil Rights

In the 1950s and 1960s, African Americans in North Carolina, and throughout the United States, struggled against the monolithic system of segregation and racism. The Ku Klux Klan stepped up its efforts in political and physical violence—against Native Americans as well as blacks, as in the famous 1958 "Battle of Maxton" in North Carolina, in which 500 armed Lumbee people foiled a Klan rally and sent the Knights running for their lives.

Change arrived slowly. The University of North Carolina accepted its first African American graduate student in 1951, and the first black undergraduates four years later. The University of Georgia enrolled its first black students in 1961.

Lunch counter sit-ins happened all over the region, including the episode of the "Friendship Nine" in Rock Hill, South Carolina, and the "Albany Movement" in Albany, Georgia. Martin Luther King Jr. visited South Carolina in the late 1960s, speaking in Charleston in 1967 and helping reestablish the Penn Center on St. Helena Island as not only a cultural center but a center of political activism as well.

In 1965, Atlanta, "the city too busy to hate," would elect its first black alderman, and 11 African Americans were elected to the state legislature. Julian Bond, Georgia's first black congressman, was sent to Washington in 1967. Atlanta's first African American mayor, Maynard Jackson, was elected in 1969.

The civil rights era would spawn another political career when a peanut farmer in tiny Plains, Georgia, was inspired to fight for social justice and equality by running for the Georgia State Senate. Jimmy Carter would go on to be governor in 1971 and then U.S. president in 1976. In an intriguing and somewhat prophetic blend of the forces that would shape American politics into the Obama era, Carter was both the first statewide Southern officeholder to publicly embrace full civil rights as well as the first evangelical Christian president.

## CONTEMPORARY TIMES

Throughout the 1980s, the region, especially Atlanta, underwent an economic surge driven by many of the same factors contributing to similar success stories throughout the U.S. Sunbelt. When the economic boom of the 1990s came, Atlanta and Charlotte were cemented as major convention and corporate business centers. Atlanta hosted the 1996 Summer Olympics, which, though marred by a bombing in Centennial Olympic Park, were pulled off quite successfully and signaled Atlanta's emergence as a truly global city—not that there was ever really any doubt.

But outside the massive twin economic engines of Atlanta and Charlotte, global trade has been a largely destructive force in the region during the past two decades. The textile industry has collapsed. This, combined with the ongoing slow death of tobacco in North Carolina and the loss of the fishing industry to international commerce, is causing the government and people of the region to look more and more toward tourism, the biotech field, and new approaches to agriculture to define their role in a changing world.

Lured by cheap labor and generous tax incentives, Hollywood discovered the Carolinas and Georgia by turns in a big way, not only because of their beautiful scenery but also by various tax incentives. Wilmington, North Carolina, was a popular film location for decades, hosting the productions of *Blue Velvet* and the TV series *Dawson's Creek*. Savannah, Georgia, followed suit, hosting film shoots such as *Forrest Gump, Glory,* and, of course, *Midnight in the Garden of Good and Evil*. Beaufort, South Carolina, was the location of *The Great Santini* and *The Big Chill*.

More recently, Georgia's generous tax incentives have made the Peach State the largest center of TV and film industry outside Hollywood itself, with credits including *The Walking Dead* and *The Hunger Games*, with most of the action shot in metro Atlanta.

# Government and Economy

## POLITICAL LIFE

For many decades, the South was dominated by the Democratic Party. Originally the party of slavery, segregation, and Jim Crow, the Democratic Party began attracting Southern African American voters in the 1930s with the election of Franklin D. Roosevelt. The allegiance of black voters was cemented in the Truman, Kennedy, and Johnson administrations.

The region would remain solidly Democratic until a backlash against the civil rights movement of the 1960s drove many white Southerners, ironically enough, into the party of Lincoln, the Republicans. This added racial element, so confounding to Americans from other parts of the country, remains just as potent today.

The default mode in the South is that white voters are massively Republican and black voters massively Democratic. The GOP currently controls the governor's mansion and both houses of the state legislature in both Carolinas and Georgia. However, plenty of progressive enclaves exist, particularly in Atlanta, Athens, and Savannah in Georgia, Asheville and Chapel Hill in North Carolina, and to a lesser extent Charleston in South Carolina.

## ECONOMY

The industries largely responsible for the wealth and development of the region in the preceding centuries have fallen by the wayside in the new world. The **tobacco** industry dominated North Carolina's economy for generations, employing countless Carolinians from field to factory and funding an inestimable portion of the state's physical and cultural infrastructure. The gradual decline of the worldwide tobacco industry from the 1980s on has changed the state forever, particularly in the rural east.

Likewise, the **textile** industry, an industrial giant from the late 19th century until the late 20th century, and the **furniture** businesses of the Piedmont have fallen off to nearly nothing as manufacturers move their operations overseas. The once-thriving **fishing** industry is also in steep decline due to globalization and pollution.

New industries and fields have taken up where the former staples left off. **Pharmaceutical** and **high-tech** corporations are an important draw of labor and revenue to the area around the North Carolina Triangle. Charlotte is second only to New York City among the United States' largest **banking** centers. Thanks largely to Atlanta's economic importance, Georgia hosts over 25 Fortune 1,000 company headquarters, including those of Home Depot, UPS, Coca-Cola, Delta Airlines, Gulfstream Aerospace (in Savannah), and Aflac (in Columbus). Kia Motors opened its first U.S. assembly plant in West Point, near Atlanta. **Tourism** is crucial, from the cobblestones of historic Wilmington, Charleston, and Savannah, to the beach-resort locales of Nag's Head, Myrtle Beach, and Hilton Head.

One old standby remains, however. **Agriculture** continues to be very important, from the hog farms of eastern North Carolina to the chicken processing plants of North Georgia to the peanut and pecan and sweet-onion farms of South Georgia. But the Peach State isn't actually the nation's largest producer of peaches anymore—that would be South Carolina.

# People and Culture

## DEMOGRAPHICS

Georgia is the ninth most populous state in the union, with nearly 10 million people. Atlanta is by far its biggest city, its metro area accounting for half that total. Whites make up 63 percent of Georgia's population and African Americans 31 percent. While the Latino population is under 10 percent, it is the most rapidly growing demographic.

North Carolina is nearly a mirror image of the Peach State. The 10th most populous state in the union, North Carolina has nine million residents. Charlotte is easily its biggest metro area. More than two-thirds of North Carolinians are white, and not quite one-third are African American. The state's population is about 6 percent Latino, and it has the sixth-largest Native American population of any state, behind only California, Arizona, Oklahoma, New Mexico, and Texas.

South Carolina is significantly smaller than its neighbors. The 24th most populous state, South Carolina is home to just under five million people. Its largest population center is the Greenville-Spartanburg metro area, closely followed by the state capital, Columbia. Like the Tar Heel State, South Carolina is about two-thirds white, one-third black, with a smaller Latino population than either North Carolina or Georgia.

## MANNERS

The prevalence and importance of good manners is the main thing to keep in mind about the South. While it's tempting for folks from more outwardly assertive parts of the world to take this as a sign of weakness, that would be a major mistake. Bottom line: Good manners will take you a long way here. Southerners use manners, courtesy, and chivalry as a system of social interaction with one goal above all: to maintain the established order during times of stress. A relic from a time of extreme class stratification, etiquette and chivalry are ways to make sure that the elites are never threatened—and, on the other hand, that even those on the lowest rungs of society are afforded at least a basic amount of dignity. But as a practical matter, it's also true that Southerners of all classes, races, and backgrounds rely on the observation of manners as a way to sum up people quickly. To any Southerner, regardless of class or race, your use or neglect of basic manners and proper respect indicates how seriously they should take you—not in a socioeconomic sense, but in the big picture.

The typical Southern sense of humor—equal parts irony, self-deprecation, and good-natured teasing—is part of the code. Southerners are loath to criticize another individual directly, so often they'll instead take

# Local Lingo

- **Bless your heart:** a complex declaration with infinitely varied intentions, interpreted depending on context or tone, ranging from a sincere thank-you to an exclamation of affection, usually applied to children and the elderly, to a criticism framed in a charitable light.

- **buggy:** a shopping cart, as at a grocery store.

- **carry:** convey, escort, give a ride to. "I carried my mother up to the mountains for her birthday."

- **cattywompus:** topsy-turvy and mixed up. Used especially in the Piedmont and farther west.

- **Coke:** any soft drink; may be called "pop" in the mountains.

- **dinner:** the midday meal.

- **evening:** not just the twilight hours, but all the hours between about 3pm and nightfall.

- **ever-how:** however; similarly, "ever-when," "ever-what," and "ever-who."

- **fair to middling:** so-so, in response to "How you?"

- **fixing:** about to or preparing to do something. "She's fixing to have a baby any day now."

- **holler:** hollow, a mountain cove.

- **Kakalak:** Carolina (also Kakalaky, Cakalack).

- **mash:** press, as a button. "I keep mashing the button, but that elevator just won't come."

- **mess:** discombobulated, in a rut, not living right. "I was a mess until I joined the church."

- **might could/should/would:** could/should/would perhaps. "Looks like it's fixing to rain. You might should go roll up your car windows."

- **mommocked:** see *cattywompus*. Used especially on the Outer Banks and in rural southeastern North Carolina.

- **piece:** a vague measure of distance, as in, "down the road a piece" (a little ways down the road) or "a fair piece" (a long way).

- **poke:** a bag, such as a paper shopping bag. Used especially in the mountains.

- **reckon:** believe, think. Often used in interrogative statements that end with falling intonation: "Reckon what we're having for dinner" ("What do you suppose is for lunch?").

- **right:** quite, very. Variations include "right quick" (soon, hurriedly), "right much" (often), and "a right many" or "a right smart of" (a great quantity).

- **sorry:** worthless, lame, shoddy. "I wanted to play basketball in college, but I was too sorry of an athlete."

- **speck so:** "I expect so," or, "Yes, I guess that's correct."

- **supper:** the evening meal (as opposed to "dinner," meaning lunch)

- **sy-goggling:** see *cattywompus, mommocked*. Used especially in the mountains.

- **ugly:** mean or unfriendly, spiteful. The favorite Southern injunction that "God don't like ugly," for example, means that we should be nice.

- **wait on:** to wait for.

- **Y'uns:** y'all, used in the mountains.

the opportunity to make an ironic joke. Self-deprecating humor is also much more common in the South than in other areas of the country. Because of this, you're also expected to be able to take a joke yourself without being too sensitive.

## Etiquette

It's rude here to inquire about personal finances, along with the usual no-go areas of religion and politics. Here are some other specific etiquette tips:

- **Basics:** Be liberal with "please" and "thank you," or conversely, "no, thank you" if you want to decline a request or offering.

- **Eye contact:** With the exception of very elderly African Americans, eye contact is not only accepted in the South, it's encouraged. In fact, to avoid eye contact in the South means you're likely a shady character with something to hide.

- **Handshake:** Men should always shake hands with a *very* firm, confident grip and appropriate eye contact. It's OK for women to offer a handshake in professional circles, but is otherwise not required.

- **Chivalry:** When men open doors for women here—and they will—it is not thought of as a patronizing gesture but as a sign of respect. Also, if a female of any age or appearance drops an object on the floor, don't be surprised if several nearby males jump to pick it up. This is considered appropriate behavior and not at all unusual.

- **The elderly:** Senior citizens—or really anyone obviously older than you—should be called "sir" or "ma'am." Again, this is not a patronizing gesture in the South but is considered a sign of respect. Also, in any situation where you're dealing with someone in the service industry, addressing them as "sir" or "ma'am" regardless of their age will get you far.

- **Bodily contact:** Interestingly, though public displays of affection by romantic couples are generally frowned upon here, Southerners are otherwise pretty touchy-feely once they get to know you. Full-on body hugs are rare, but Southerners who are well acquainted often say hello or good-bye with a small hug.

- **Driving:** With the exception of the interstate perimeter highways around the larger cities, drivers in the South are generally less aggressive than in other regions. Cutting sharply in front of someone in traffic is taken as a personal offense. If you need to cut in front of someone, poke the nose of your car a little bit in that direction and wait for a car to slow down and wave you in front. Don't forget to wave back as a thank-you. Similarly, using a car horn can also be taken as a personal affront, so use your horn sparingly, if at all. In rural areas, don't be surprised to see the driver of an oncoming car offer a little wave. This is an old custom, sadly dying out. Just give a little wave back; they're trying to be friendly.

# Essentials

# Transportation

## AIR
### North Carolina

North Carolina's international airports are in Charlotte, Greensboro, and Raleigh-Durham (with Wilmington qualifying as a major airport with more limited service). The 10th-busiest airport in the country and 30th in the world, **Charlotte-Douglas International Airport** (CLT, 5501 Josh Birmingham Pkwy., 704/359-4000, www.clt.airport.com) has more than 600 daily departures and is served by dozens of airlines. There are direct nonstop flights to over 100 domestic destinations as well as international flights between Charlotte and many cities in Latin America and the Caribbean as well as London, Frankfurt, Munich, and Toronto. Parking is abundant and inexpensive, with parking shuttles running from 5am.

**Raleigh-Durham International Airport** (RDU, 2600 W. Terminal Blvd., Morrisville, 919/840-2123, www.rdu.com), located in Wake County about midway between Raleigh and Durham, offers service to most major domestic air hubs as well as to London, Toronto, and Cancún. Hourly and daily parking is available for reasonable rates within walking distance of the terminals, and in satellite lots linked by shuttles.

**Piedmont Triad International Airport** (GSO, 1000 A. Ted Johnson Pkwy., Greensboro, 336/665-5600, www.flyfrompti.com) serves the Greensboro and Winston-Salem area, with flights to and from many domestic destinations, particularly in the South, Midwest, and mid-Atlantic. There are several smaller airports around the state, including **Wilmington International Airport** (ILM, 1740 Airport Blvd., Wilmington, 910/341-4125, www.flyilm.com), **Asheville**

**Regional Airport** (AVL, 61 Terminal Dr., Fletcher, 828/684-2226, www.flyavl.com), and **Fayetteville Regional Airport** (FAY, 400 Airport Rd., Fayetteville, 910/433-1160, www.flyfay.com). Smaller airports with regularly scheduled passenger service are in Greenville, New Bern, and Jacksonville/Richland; you can fly Delta to any of them.

### South Carolina

There are six key airports serving South Carolina. **Charleston International Airport** (CHS, 5500 International Blvd., 843/767-1100, www.iflychs.com) is served by the major national airlines and is a primary gateway to the entire coast. **Columbia Metropolitan Airport** (CAE, 3000 Aviation Way, 803/822-5000, www.columbiaairport.com) is a good access point for the center of the state, and **Greenville-Spartanburg International Airport** (GSP, 2000 GSP Dr., Greer, 864/877-7426, www.gspairport.com) is a good point of entry for the upper half of the state.

Because of the lack of interstate highway coverage in this area, **Myrtle Beach International Airport** (MYR, 1100 Jetport Rd., 843/448-1589, www.flymyrtlebeach.com) is best used only if Myrtle Beach is your primary destination. **Savannah/Hilton Head International Airport** (SAV, 400 Airways Ave., 912/964-0514, www.savannahairport.com), off I-95 in Savannah, Georgia, is perhaps the best access point to enjoy the lower portion of the South Carolina coast, and definitely Hilton Head.

### Georgia

While some may be tempted to fly into Atlanta's Hartsfield-Jackson International

---

Airport because of the sheer number of flights into that facility, unless your destination is Atlanta, I strongly advise against it because of the massive congestion in the area. **Hartsfield-Jackson Atlanta International Airport** (ATL, 6000 North Terminal Pkwy., 404/530-6600, www.atl.com) is the world's busiest, serving nearly 100 million passengers a year. Its flagship airline is Delta, with 60 percent of the airport's traffic. In all, about two dozen airlines fly in and out to domestic destinations as well as Europe, Asia, and South America.

The state's second-most comprehensive airport is **Savannah/Hilton Head International Airport** (SAV, 400 Airways Ave., 912/964-0514, www.savannahairport.com), directly off I-95 at exit 104, about 20 minutes from downtown Savannah.

The only other major airport in Georgia is **Augusta Regional Airport** (AGS, 1501 Aviation Way, 706/798-3236, www.flyags.com). Another option for coastal and southeast Georgia is **Jacksonville International Airport** (JAX, 2400 Yankee Clipper Dr., 904/741-4902, www.jia.com), about 20 miles north of Jacksonville, Florida. While it's a two-hour drive from Savannah, this airport's proximity to the attractions south of Savannah makes it attractive for visitors to the region.

# CAR
## North Carolina

Several major interstate highways spider across North Carolina, so if you're driving here and would prefer that your trip be efficient rather than scenic, you have several convenient choices. If you're coming from most anywhere along the Eastern Seaboard, you'll likely be on I-95 for much of the trip. I-95 slices through the eastern third of the state, making for easy access to the beaches (most are 1-2 hours east of I-95) and to the Triangle area (just under an hour west via U.S. 64, U.S. 70, or I-40). If you're coming to the Triangle from the north, you might also choose to veer southwest at Richmond, Virginia, on I-85; this

is a particularly efficient route to Durham and Chapel Hill, as well as to the Triad and Charlotte regions.

I-40 starts near Los Angeles and runs east all the way to Wilmington, paring the state in half horizontally much as it does the continent. It's a fast road all the way through North Carolina, although weather (ice in the fall, winter, and spring; fog any time of year) might slow you down considerably between Knoxville, Tennessee, and Asheville.

U.S. 64 and I-77 connect North Carolina to the Midwest. I-77 cuts through the toe of Virginia, in the mountains, for a straight shot to Charlotte, while U.S. 64 meanders east through the Triangle and all the way to Roanoke Island and the Outer Banks. If you're coming from the Deep South or Texas, your best bet is probably to catch I-20 to Atlanta, and from there pick up I-85 to Charlotte (or U.S. 19 or U.S. 23 if you're going to the mountains).

## South Carolina

South Carolina is extremely well served by the U.S. interstate highway system. The main interstate arteries into the region are the north-south I-95, I-77, and I-85, and the east-west I-20 and I-26. Charleston has a perimeter interstate, I-526 (the Mark Clark Expressway). Columbia's perimeter is I-126. Greenville has two, I-185 and I-386; Spartanburg's is I-585.

Keep in mind that despite being heavily traveled, the Myrtle Beach area is not served by any interstate highway. A common landmark road through the coastal region is U.S. 17, which used to be known as the Coastal Highway and currently goes by a number of local incarnations as it winds its way along the coast.

Unfortunately, the stories you've heard about speed traps in small South Carolina towns are correct. Always strictly obey the speed limit, and if you're pulled over, always deal with the police respectfully and truthfully, whether or not you agree with their judgment.

Winter driving in South Carolina is

generally easy, since it rarely snows. During periods of heavy rainfall, however, unpaved roads can become quite muddy. Should you be unlucky enough to be on the coast during a mandatory hurricane evacuation, be aware that some roads, especially interstate highways, will become one-way westbound for all lanes to streamline the evacuation. In any case, always follow all law enforcement directions. For updates on planned slowdowns due to construction projects, go to www.dot. state.sc.us.

South Carolina's copious network of interstate highways offers numerous **rest stops.** They are often a very welcome sight, since the state's heavily rural nature means services can be hard to come by on the road. The following is a list of rest areas.

- **I-95:** Mile markers 5 (northbound near the Georgia border), 17 (Ridgeland, no facilities), 47 (south of Walterboro), 99 (Santee), 139 (south of Florence), 171 (north of Florence), and 195 (southbound at the North Carolina border).

- **I-26:** Mile markers 63 (north of Newberry), 123 (south of Columbia), 150 (eastbound at Orangeburg), 152 (westbound at Orangeburg), 202 (westbound at Summerville), and 204 (eastbound at Summerville).

- **I-85:** Mile markers 17 (northbound at Anderson), 24 (southbound at Anderson), and 89 (Gaffney).

- **I-20:** Mile marker 93 (Camden).

- **I-77:** Mile marker 66 (south of Rock Hill).

While all rest stops are clean, safe, and well equipped, remember there is no gasoline sold at any of them.

## Georgia

The road-building lobby is politically very powerful in Georgia, and as a result the state and county highways are appreciably better funded and maintained than in many other states. When possible I always choose the local highways over the interstates because they are comparatively less crowded and in many cases are of equal or better quality.

But if you prefer traveling on the interstate highway system, Georgia is very well served; it includes north-south I-95, north-south I-75 and I-85 (which combine through Atlanta), the east-west I-20 across the northern half of the state, and the least-traveled example, east-west I-16 between Savannah and Macon. Shorter connecting interstate highways include the notorious I-285 around Atlanta, I-575 through North Georgia, I-185 from Columbus to I-85 proper, the small loop of I-516 in Savannah, and two "shortcut" segments, I-675 south of Atlanta and I-475 around Macon.

A common landmark road throughout the coastal region is U.S. 17, which used to be known as the Coastal Highway and which currently goes by a number of local incarnations as it winds its way down the coast, roughly paralleling I-95.

## Car Rentals

Renting a car is easy and fairly inexpensive as long as you play by the rules, which are simple. You need either a valid driver's license from any U.S. state or a valid International Driving Permit from your home country, and you must be at least 25 years old.

If you do not either purchase insurance coverage from the rental company or already have insurance coverage through the credit card you rent the car with, you will be 100 percent responsible for any damage caused to the car during your rental period. While purchasing insurance at the time of rental is by no means mandatory, it might be worth the extra expense just to have that peace of mind.

Key rental car companies in the region include **Hertz** (www.hertz.com), **Avis** (www. avis.com), **Thrifty** (www.thrifty.com), **Enterprise** (www.enterprise.com), and **Budget** (www.budget.com). Some rental car locations are in the cities, but the vast majority of outlets are at airports, so plan accordingly. The airport locations have the bonus of generally being open for longer hours than their in-town counterparts.

# TRAIN

Passenger rail service in the car-dominated United States is far behind that in other developed nations, both in quantity and quality. Many towns and cities in the Carolinas and Georgia are served by the national rail system, **Amtrak** (www.amtrak.com), which is pretty good, if erratic at times—though it certainly pales in comparison with European rail transit.

Although it does not currently serve the mountains or the coast, Amtrak is a great way to get to and around central North Carolina. The Washington DC-Florida *Auto Train* and the two main New York-Florida routes— the *Silver Meteor* and the *Silver Star*—pass through North Carolina. The first two follow roughly the I-95 corridor, while the *Silver Star* makes a dogleg west to Raleigh before continuing south. The New York-New Orleans route, the *Crescent*, goes through both Raleigh and Charlotte. Two interstate routes serve the Carolinas as their primary destinations; the *Carolinian* runs from New York to Charlotte, by way of Raleigh, and the *Palmetto* goes from New York to Savannah, crossing the eastern third of both Carolinas.

With the notable exception of the Grand Strand, South Carolina is well served by Amtrak. You'll find stations in Camden, Charleston, Clemson, Columbia, Florence, Greenville, and Spartanburg. The closest Amtrak station to the Beaufort-Hilton Head area is in Yemassee.

Two areas of Georgia, the southeast coastal portion and the northern portion, are served by two Amtrak lines. Amtrak stations on the northern route are in Atlanta, Gainesville, and Toccoa. Stations on the southeast route are in Savannah and Jesup.

# BUS

Travel to and through the region can be accomplished easily and cheaply by bus.

**Greyhound** (800/229-9424, www.grey-hound.com) offers daily service to a long list of towns and cities. In North Carolina, Greyhound runs to Ahoskie, Asheville, Burlington, Camp Lejeune, Charlotte, Concord, Durham, Edenton, Elizabeth City, Fayetteville, Gastonia, Goldsboro, Greensboro, Greenville, Henderson, High Point, Jacksonville, Kinston, New Bern, Raleigh, Rocky Mount, Salisbury, Smithfield, Wallace, Washington, Waynesville, Williamston, Wilmington, Wilson, and Winston-Salem. There is currently no Greyhound service to the Outer Banks, or to mountain locations in North Carolina other than Asheville and Waynesville, but you can sneak around the back way by coming through one of the Tennessee cities close to the state line, like Knoxville or Johnson City.

South Carolina has Greyhound stops throughout the state, including Aiken, Anderson, Beaufort, Camden, Charleston, Columbia, Florence, Georgetown, Greenville, Myrtle Beach, Orangeburg, Spartanburg, Sumter, and Walterboro.

Georgia is the largest of the three states in this book, so keep in mind that distances are longer and so are the bus rides. There are several Greyhound stations in the Atlanta metro area, including at the airport, Marietta, Norcross, and LaGrange. Other stations are in Albany, Macon, Savannah, Columbus, Valdosta, and Hinesville (Fort Stewart).

While rates are reasonable and the vehicles are high-quality, this is by far the slowest possible way to travel, as buses stop frequently and sometimes for lengthy periods of time.

# BOAT

One of the coolest things about the South Carolina coast is the prevalence of the Intracoastal Waterway, a combined artificial and natural sheltered seaway from Miami to Maine. Many boaters enjoy touring the coast by simply meandering up or down the Intracoastal, putting in at marinas along the way.

# Recreation

## STATE PARKS AND NATURAL AREAS

The Carolinas have some of the best state park systems in the United States. Many of the older parks were built by the Civilian Conservation Corps (CCC) during FDR's New Deal and boast distinctive, rustic, and well-made architecture. In all, there are nine CCC-era parks in North Carolina, 17 in South Carolina, and 11 in Georgia.

Many state parks offer fully equipped rental cabins with modern amenities that rival a hotel's. Generally speaking, such facilities tend to book early, so make reservations as soon as you can. Keep in mind that during the high season (Mar.-Nov.) there are often minimum rental requirements. While I encourage camping in the Blue Ridge, be aware that the closer you are to the Appalachian Mountains, the higher the rainfall. Be prepared to camp wet. Dogs are allowed in state parks, but they must be leashed at all times.

Currently, only three North Carolina state parks charge an entrance fee: Falls Lake, Jordan Lake, and Kerr Lake. Entrance fees vary in South Carolina, from free to $5 per person, depending on the park. Long-term visitors can save money on frequent visits by purchasing a **State Park Passport** ($75), which covers a full year of admission from the date of purchase. Get one online at www.southcarolinaparks.com.

**Georgia State Parks** (www.gastateparks.org) charge a $5 per vehicle parking fee per day on top of whatever the camping fees are, generally around $25. However, if you plan on visiting multiple parks in one day—entirely possible in some areas with a high volume of parks, such as North Georgia—that one-day $5 pass gets you into all parks for that day. There are plenty of private campgrounds as well, but if at all possible utilize the state parks system, not only because it's great, but because increased use will help ensure adequate future funding.

## NATIONAL WILDLIFE REFUGES

There are 10 federally administered National Wildlife Refuges (NWR) in North Carolina:

- **Alligator River NWR** (www.fws.gov/alligatorriver)
- **Cedar Island NWR** (www.fws.gov/cedarisland)
- **Currituck NWR** (www.fws.gov/currituck)
- **Mackay Island NWR** (www.fws.gov/mackayisland)
- **Mattamuskeet NWR** (www.fws.gov/mattamuskeet)
- **Pea Island NWR** (www.fws.gov/peaisland)
- **Pee Dee NWR** (www.fws.gov/peedee)
- **Pocosin Lakes NWR** (www.fws.gov/pocosinlakes)
- **Roanoke River NWR** (www.fws.gov/roanokeriver)
- **Swanquarter NWR** (www.fws.gov/swanquarter)

There are seven National Wildlife Refuges in South Carolina:

- **ACE Basin NWR** (www.fws.gov/acebasin)
- **Cape Romain NWR** (www.fws.gov/caperomain)
- **Carolina Sandhills NWR** (www.fws.gov/carolinasandhills)
- **Pinckney Island NWR** (www.fws.gov/pinckneyisland)
- **Santee NWR** (www.fws.gov/santee)
- **Savannah NWR** (www.fws.gov/savannah)
- **Waccamaw NWR** (www.fws.gov/waccamaw)

There are eight National Wildlife Refuges in Georgia:

- **Banks Lake NWR** (www.fws.gov/bankslake)
- **Blackbeard Island NWR** (www.fws.gov/blackbeard)
- **Bond Swamp NWR** (www.fws.gov/bondswamp)
- **Harris Neck NWR** (www.fws.gov/harrisneck)
- **Okefenokee NWR** (www.fws.gov/okefenokee)
- **Piedmont NWR** (www.fws.gov/piedmont)
- **Wassaw NWR** (www.fws.gov/wassaw)
- **Wolf Island NWR** (www.fws.gov/wolfisland)

Admission is generally free. Access is limited to daytime hours (sunrise-sunset). Keep in mind that some hunting is allowed on some refuges.

## BEACHES

Some of the best beaches in the country are in the region covered in this guide. While the upscale amenities aren't always there and they aren't very surfer friendly, the area's beaches are outstanding for anyone looking for a relaxing scenic getaway. By law, beaches in these states are fully accessible to the public up to the high-tide mark during daylight hours,

even if the beachfronts are private property and even if the only means of public access is by boat.

It is a misdemeanor to disturb sea oats, those wispy, waving, wheat-like plants among the dunes. Their root system is vital to keeping the beach intact. Never disturb a turtle nesting area, whether it is marked or not.

### Rip Currents

More than 100 people die every year on American beaches because of rip currents. Also called riptides, these dangerous currents can occur on any beach and can be very difficult to identify by sight. In rip current conditions, channels of water flow swiftly out toward deep water, and even if you are standing in relatively shallow water, you can in a matter of moments be swept under and out into deep water. Rip current safety tips are available on the National Oceanic and Atmospheric Administration (NOAA) website (www.ripcurrents.noaa.gov). Among NOAA's advice: "Don't fight the current. Swim out of the current, and then to shore. If you can't escape, float or tread water. If you need help, call or wave for assistance." Heed riptide warnings, and try to swim within sight of a lifeguard. Even good swimmers can drown in a rip current, so if you have any doubts about your swimming abilities or beach conditions, play it safe and stay close to shore.

# Travel Tips

## WOMEN TRAVELING ALONE

Women should take the same precautions they would take anywhere else in the United States. Many women traveling to this region have to adjust to the prevalence of traditional chivalry. In the South, if a man opens a door for you, it's considered a sign of respect, not condescension.

Another adjustment is the possible assumption that two or three women who go to a bar or tavern together might be there to invite male companionship. This misunderstanding can happen anywhere, but in some parts of the South it might be more prevalent.

While small towns in the Carolinas and Georgia are generally very friendly and law-abiding, some are more economically depressed than others and hence prone to more crime. Always take commonsense precautions no matter how bucolic the setting may be.

## TRAVELERS WITH DISABILITIES

While the vast majority of attractions and accommodations make every effort to comply with federal law regarding those with disabilities, as they're obligated to do, the historic nature of much of this region means that some structures simply cannot be retrofitted for maximum accessibility. This is something you'll need to find out on a case-by-case basis, so call ahead.

Call 919/855-3500 or TTY 919/855-3579 or visit http://dvr.dhhs.state.nc.us for the current edition of *Access North Carolina,* published by the state Department of Health and Human Services. The guide is divided into Mountains, Foothills, Piedmont, Coastal Plain, and Coast divisions, and broken down by counties within each division. All sites are described, with addresses, phone numbers, websites, hours of operation, admissions costs, and other types of information, and then rated in terms of accessibility.

## GAY AND LESBIAN TRAVELERS

Despite the region's essential conservatism, many of the areas in this guide can be considered quite gay friendly, with the most obvious examples being Atlanta, Asheville, Charlotte, Savannah, and Charleston, in addition to the college towns of Athens, Chapel Hill, and Durham.

Gay, lesbian, bisexual, and transgendered travelers planning to visit North Carolina can learn a great deal online about community resources and activities. Check out **Carolina Purple Pages** (www.carolinapurplepages.com), serving Charlotte, Asheville, and the Triangle, **Gay Triad** (http://gaytriadnc.homestead.com), the **Out Wilmington Community Center** (www.outwilmington.com), and **Out in Asheville** (http://outinasheville.com).

Visit **QNotes** (www.q-notes.com) for info on South Carolina and Georgia. Atlanta in particular has a large and thriving LGBT community. The "official" guide is *GA Voice* (www.gay-atlanta.com).

## SENIOR TRAVELERS

Both because of the large proportion of retirees in the region and because of the South's traditional respect for the elderly, the area is quite friendly to senior citizens. Many accommodations and attractions offer a seniors discount, which can add up over the course of a trip. Always inquire before making a reservation, however, as check-in time is sometimes too late.

## TRAVELING WITH PETS

While the United States is very pet friendly, that friendliness rarely extends to restaurants and other indoor locations. More and more accommodations are allowing pet owners to bring pets, often for an added fee, but inquire before you arrive. In any case, keep your dog on a leash at all times. Some beaches in the area permit dog-walking at certain times of the year, but as a general rule, keep dogs off beaches unless you see signs saying otherwise.

# Health and Safety

## CRIME

While crime rates are generally above national averages in much of this region, especially in inner-city areas, incidents of crime in the more heavily touristed areas are no more common than elsewhere. In fact, these areas might be safer because of the amount of foot traffic and police attention.

By far the most common crime against visitors is simple theft, primarily from cars. (Pickpocketing, thankfully, is quite rare in the United States). Always lock your car doors. Conversely, only leave them unlocked if you're absolutely comfortable living without whatever's inside at the time. As a general rule, I try to lock valuables—such as CDs, a recent purchase, or my wife's purse—in the trunk. (Just make sure the "valet" button, allowing the trunk to be opened from the driver's area, is disabled.)

Should someone corner you and demand your wallet or purse, just give it to them. Unfortunately, the old advice to scream as loud as you can is no longer the deterrent it once was, and in fact may hasten aggressive action by the robber.

A very important general rule to remember is not to pull over for cars you do not recognize as law enforcement, no matter how urgently you might be asked to do so. This is not a common occurrence, but a possibility you should be aware of. A real police officer will know the correct steps to take to identify him or herself. If you find yourself having to guess, then do the safe thing and refuse to stop.

If you are the victim of a crime, *always call the police.* Law enforcement wants more information, not less, and at the very least you'll have an incident report in case you need to make an insurance claim for lost or stolen property.

Remember that in the United States as elsewhere, no good can come from a heated argument with a police officer. The place to prove a police officer wrong is in a court of law, perhaps with an attorney by your side, not at the scene.

For emergencies, always call 911.

## AUTO ACCIDENTS

If you're in an auto accident, you're bound by law to wait for police to respond. Failure to do so can result in a "leaving the scene of an accident" charge or worse. In the old days, cars in accidents had to be left exactly where they came to rest until police gave permission to move or tow them. However, the states in this guide have recently loosened regulations so that if a car is blocking traffic as a result of an accident, the driver is allowed to move it enough to allow traffic to flow again. That is, if the car can be moved safely; if not, you're not required to move it out of the way.

Since it's illegal to drive without auto insurance, I'll assume you have some. And because you're insured, the best course of action in a minor accident, where injuries are unlikely, is to patiently wait for the police and give them your side of the story. In my experience, police react negatively to people who are too quick to start making accusations against other people. After that, let the insurance companies deal with it; that's what they're paid for.

If you suspect any injuries, call 911 immediately.

## ILLEGAL DRUGS

Marijuana, heroin, methamphetamine, and cocaine and all its derivatives are illegal in the United States with only a few exceptions, none of which apply to the areas covered by this guide. The use of ecstasy and similar mood-elevators is also illegal.

## ALCOHOL

The drinking age in all of the United States is 21. Most restaurants that serve alcoholic beverages allow those under 21 inside. Generally speaking, if only those over 21 are allowed inside, you will be greeted at the door by someone asking to see identification. These people are often poorly trained, and anything other than a state driver's license may confuse them, so be forewarned.

Drunk driving is a problem on U.S. roads. Always drive defensively, especially late at night, and obey all posted speed limits and road signs—and never assume the other driver will do the same. You may never drive with an open alcoholic beverage in the car, even if it belongs to a passenger.

# GETTING SICK

Unlike most developed nations, the United States has no comprehensive national health care system. Visitors from other countries who need nonemergency medical attention are best served by going to freestanding medical clinics. The level of care is typically very good, but unfortunately you'll be paying out of pocket for the service.

For emergencies, however, do not hesitate to go to the closest hospital emergency room, where the level of care is generally also quite good, especially for trauma. Worry about payment later; emergency rooms in the United States are required to take true emergency cases whether or not the patient can pay for services.

## Pharmaceuticals

Unlike in many other countries, antibiotics are available in the United States only on a prescription basis and are not available over the counter. Most cold, flu, and allergy remedies are available over the counter. While homeopathic remedies are gaining popularity in the United States, they are nowhere near as prevalent as in Europe.

Medications with the active ingredient ephedrine are available in the United States without a prescription, but their purchase is now tightly regulated to cut down on the use of these products to make the illegal drug methamphetamine.

# NOT GETTING SICK
## Vaccinations

As of this writing, there are no vaccination requirements to enter the United States. Contact your embassy before coming to confirm this before arrival, however.

In the autumn, at the beginning of flu season, preventive influenza vaccinations, simply called "flu shots," often become available at easily accessible locations like clinics, health departments, and even supermarkets.

## Humidity, Heat, and Sun

There is only one way to fight the South's high heat and humidity, and that's to drink lots of fluids. A surprising number of people each year refuse to take this advice and find themselves in various states of dehydration, some of which can land you in a hospital. Remember: If you're thirsty, you're already suffering from dehydration. The thing to do is keep drinking fluids before you're thirsty, as a preventative action rather than a reaction.

Always use sunscreen, even on a cloudy day. If you do get a sunburn, get a pain relief product with aloe vera as an active ingredient. On extraordinarily sunny and hot summer days, don't even go outside between the hours of 10am and 2pm.

# HAZARDS
## Insects

Because of the recent increase in the mosquito-borne West Nile virus, the most important step to take in staying healthy in the Lowcountry and Southeast coast—especially if you have small children—is to keep mosquito bites to a minimum. Do this with a combination of mosquito repellent and long sleeves and long pants, if possible. Not every mosquito bite will give you the virus; in fact, chances are quite slim that one will. But don't take the chance if you don't have to.

The second major step in avoiding insect nastiness is to steer clear of **fire ants,** whose large gray or brown dirt nests are quite common in this area. They attack instantly and in great numbers, with little or no provocation. They don't just bite; they inject you with poison from their stingers. In short, fire ants are not to be trifled with. While the only real remedy is the preventative one of never coming in contact with them, should you find yourself being bitten by fire ants, the first thing to do is to stay calm. Take off your shoes and socks and get as many of the ants off you as you can. Unless you've had a truly large number of bites—in which case you should seek medical help immediately—the best thing to do next is wash the area to get any venom off, and then disinfect it with alcohol if you have any handy. Then a topical treatment such as calamine lotion or hydrocortisone is advised. A fire ant bite will leave a red pustule that lasts about a week. Try your best not to scratch it so that it won't get infected.

Outdoor activity, especially in woodsy, undeveloped areas, may bring you in contact with another unpleasant indigenous creature, the tiny but obnoxious **chigger,** sometimes called the redbug. The bite of a chigger can't be felt, but the enzymes it leaves behind can lead to a very itchy little red spot. Contrary to folklore, putting fingernail polish on the itchy bite will not "suffocate" the chigger, because by this point the chigger itself is long gone. All you can do is get some topical itch or pain relief and go on with your life. The itching will eventually subside.

For **bee stings,** the best approach for those who aren't allergic to them is to immediately pull the stinger out, perhaps by scraping a credit card over the bite, and apply ice if possible. A topical treatment such as hydrocortisone or calamine lotion is advised. In my experience, the old folk remedy of tearing apart a cigarette and putting the tobacco leaves directly on the sting does indeed cut the pain. But that's not a medical opinion, so do with it what you will. A minor allergic reaction can be quelled by using an over-the-counter antihistamine. If the victim is severely allergic to bee stings, go to a hospital or call 911 for an ambulance.

## Threats in the Water

While enjoying area beaches, a lot of visitors become inordinately worried about **shark attacks.** Every couple of summers there's a lot of hysteria about this, but the truth is that you're much more likely to slip and fall in a bathroom than you are even to come close to being bitten by a shark in these shallow Atlantic waters.

A far more common fate for area swimmers is to get stung by a **jellyfish,** or sea nettle. They can sting you in the water, but most often beachcombers are stung by stepping on beached jellyfish stranded on the sand by the tide. If you get stung, don't panic; wash the area with saltwater, not freshwater, and apply vinegar or baking soda.

## Lightning

The southeastern United States is home to vicious, fast-moving thunderstorms, often with an amazing amount of electrical activity. Death by lightning strike occurs often in this region and is something that should be taken quite seriously. The general rule of thumb is that if you're in the water, whether at the beach or in a swimming pool, and hear thunder, get out of the water immediately until the storm passes. If you're on dry land and see lightning flash a distance away, that's your cue to seek safety indoors. Whatever you do, do not play sports outside when lightning threatens.

# Information and Services

## MONEY

Automated teller machines (ATMs) are available in all the urban areas covered in this guide. Be aware that if the ATM is not owned by your bank, not only will that ATM likely charge you a service fee, but your bank may charge you one as well. While ATMs have made traveler's checks less essential, traveler's checks do have the important advantage of accessibility, as some rural and less-developed areas have few or no ATMs. You can purchase traveler's checks at just about any bank.

Establishments in the United States only accept the national currency, the U.S. dollar. To exchange foreign money, go to any bank.

Generally, establishments that accept credit cards will feature stickers on the front entrance with the logo of the particular cards they accept, although this is not a legal requirement. The use of debit cards has dramatically increased in the United States. Most retail establishments and many fast-food chains are now accepting them. Make sure you get a receipt whenever you use a credit card or a debit card.

### Tipping

Unlike many other countries, service workers in the United States depend on tips for the bulk of their income. In restaurants and bars, the usual tip is 15 percent of the pretax portion of the bill for acceptable service, 20 percent (or more) for excellent service. For large parties, usually six or more, a 15-18 percent gratuity is sometimes automatically added to the bill.

It's also customary to tip hotel bell staff about $2 per bag when they assist you at check-in and checkout of your hotel; some sources recommend a minimum of $5.

For taxi drivers, 15 percent is customary as long as the cab is clean, smoke-free, and you were treated with respect and taken to your destination with a minimum of fuss.

## INTERNET ACCESS

Visitors from Europe and Asia are likely to be disappointed at the quality of Internet access in the United States, particularly the area covered in this guide. Fiber-optic lines are still a rarity, and while many hotels and B&Bs now offer in-room Internet access—some charge, some don't, so make sure to ask ahead—the quality and speed of the connection might prove poor.

Wireless (Wi-Fi) networks also are less than impressive, although that situation continues to improve on a daily basis in coffeehouses, hotels, and airports. Unfortunately, many Wi-Fi access points in private establishments are for rental only.

## PHONES

Generally speaking, the United States is behind Europe and much of Asia in terms of cell phone technology. Unlike Europe, where "pay-as-you-go" refills are easy to find, most American cell phone users pay for monthly plans through a handful of providers. Still, you should have no problem with cell phone coverage in urban areas. Where it gets much less dependable is in rural areas and on beaches. Bottom line: Don't depend on having cell service everywhere you go. As with a regular landline, any time you face an emergency, call 911 on your cell phone.

All phone numbers in the United States are seven digits preceded by a three-digit area code. You may have to dial a 1 before a phone number if it's a long-distance call, even within the same area code.

# Resources

## Suggested Reading

### NONFICTION

Blythe, Will. *To Hate Like This Is to Be Happy Forever: A Thoroughly Obsessive, Intermittently Uplifting, and Occasionally Unbiased Account of the Duke-North Carolina Basketball Rivalry.* New York: Harper-Collins, 2006. Entertaining book about the hatred that exists between partisans of UNC and Duke, and how the famous basketball rivalry brings out the best and worst in people.

Bryson, Bill. *A Walk in the Woods: Rediscovering America on the Appalachian Trail.* New York: Anchor, 2006. Entertaining and affecting tales from the length of the Appalachian Trail.

Carter, Jimmy. *Keeping Faith: Memoirs of a President.* Fayetteville: University of Arkansas Press, 1995. The 39th president's own account of his time in the White House from Plains, Georgia.

Cecelski, David. *The Waterman's Song: Slavery and Freedom in Maritime North Carolina.* Chapel Hill: UNC Press, 2000. A marvelous treatment of the African American heritage of resistance in eastern North Carolina, and how the region's rivers and sounds were passages to freedom for many enslaved people.

Duncan, Barbara, and Brett Riggs. *Cherokee Heritage Trails.* Chapel Hill: UNC Press, 2003 (online companion at www. cherokeeheritage.org). A fascinating guide to both the historic and present-day home of the Eastern Band of the Cherokee in North Carolina, Tennessee, and Georgia, from ancient mounds and petroglyphs to modern-day arts co-ops and sporting events.

Ferling, John E. *Almost a Miracle: The American Victory in the War of Independence.* New York: Oxford University Press, 2007. Not only perhaps the best single volume detailing the military aspects of the Revolutionary War, but absolutely indispensable for learning about the key role of the Carolinas and Georgia in it.

Fussell, Fred, with photographs by Cedric N. Chatterley. *Blue Ridge Music Trails: Finding a Place in the Circle.* Chapel Hill: UNC Press, 2003 (http://uncpress.unc. edu, www.ncfolk.org, online companion at www.blueridgemusic.org). A guide to destinations—festivals, restaurants, oprys, church singings—in the North Carolina and Virginia mountains where great authentic bluegrass, old-time, and sacred music can be experienced by visitors.

Gray, Marcus. *It Crawled from the South: An R.E.M. Companion.* Cambridge, MA: Da Capo Press, 1997. The complete guide to the band R.E.M., from personal histories to lyrics.

Greene, Melissa Fay. *Praying for Sheetrock.* New York: Ballantine, 1992. Greene explores the racism and corruption endemic in McIntosh County, Georgia, during the civil rights movement.

Hannon, Lauretta. *The Cracker Queen: A Memoir of a Jagged, Joyful Life.* New York: Gotham, 2010. A humorous recounting of the more dysfunctional aspects of the author's life in middle Georgia and Savannah.

Jones, Bobby. *Down the Fairway.* Latham, NY: British American Publishing, 1995. Golf history, lore, and lessons from the great Atlantan who founded Augusta National Golf Club.

Kemble, Fanny. *Journal of a Residence on a Georgian Plantation in 1838-1839.* Athens: University of Georgia Press, 1984. English actress's groundbreaking account of her stay on a rice plantation in McIntosh County, Georgia.

Klein, Maury. *Days of Defiance: Sumter, Secession, and the Coming of the Civil War.* New York: Vintage, 1999. A gripping and vivid account of the lead-up to war, with Charleston as the focal point.

Ray, Janisse. *Ecology of a Cracker Childhood.* Minneapolis: Milkweed Editions, 2000. Heartfelt memoir of growing up amid the last stands of the longleaf pine ecosystem in southeast Georgia.

Robinson, Sally Ann. *Gullah Home Cooking the Daufuskie Island Way.* Chapel Hill: UNC Press, 2007. Subtitled *Smokin' Joe Butter Beans, Ol' 'Fuskie Fried Crab Rice, Sticky-Bush Blackberry Dumpling, and Other Sea Island Favorites,* this cookbook by a native Daufuskie Islander features a foreword by Pat Conroy.

Todd, Leonard. *Carolina Clay: The Life and Legend of the Slave Potter Dave.* New York: W. W. Norton, 2008. A fascinating exploration of the world of the largely anonymous African American artisans who created the now-hot genre known as Edgefield pottery. We know the story of one of them, the man simply known as Dave, because he was literate enough to sign his name to his amazing works—an extremely unusual (and dangerous) act for the time.

Washington, James Melvin, ed. *A Testament of Hope: The Essential Writings and Speeches of Martin Luther King, Jr.* New York: HarperOne, 1990. A collection of works by the Atlanta native and civil rights icon.

Woodward, C. Vann, ed. *Mary Chesnut's Civil War.* New Haven, CT: Yale University Press, 1981. The Pulitzer Prize-winning compilation of the sardonically funny and quietly heartbreaking letters of Charleston's Mary Chesnut during the Civil War.

## FICTION

Berendt, John. *Midnight in the Garden of Good and Evil.* New York: Vintage, 1994. Not exactly fiction but far from completely true, this modern crime classic reads like a novel while remaining one of the unique travelogues of recent times.

Caldwell, Erskine. *God's Little Acre.* Athens: University of Georgia Press, 1995. Scandalous in its time for its graphic sexuality, Caldwell's best-selling 1933 novel chronicles socioeconomic decay in the mill towns of South Carolina and Georgia during the Great Depression.

Caldwell, Erskine. *Tobacco Road.* Athens: University of Georgia Press, 1932. Lurid and sensationalist, this portrayal of a shockingly dysfunctional rural Georgia family during the Depression paved the way for *Deliverance.*

Conroy, Pat. *The Lords of Discipline.* New York: Bantam, 1985. For all practical purposes set at the Citadel, this novel takes you behind the scenes of the notoriously insular Charleston military college.

Conroy, Pat. *The Water Is Wide*. New York: Bantam, 1987. Immortal account of Conroy's time teaching African American children in a two-room schoolhouse on "Yamacraw" (actually Daufuskie) Island.

Dickey, James. *Deliverance*. New York: Delta, 1970. Gripping and socially important tale of a North Georgia rafting expedition gone horribly awry.

Harris, Joel Chandler. *The Complete Tales of Uncle Remus*. New York: Houghton Mifflin, 2002. The Atlanta author broke new ground in oral history by compiling these African American folk stories.

Kinsella, W. P. *Shoeless Joe*. New York: Houghton Mifflin, 1982. Magical realist novel about a man who hears a voice telling him to "build it and they will come" and constructs a baseball diamond in an Iowa cornfield. Later adapted into the hit film *Field of Dreams* starring Kevin Costner and—with a totally out-of-place New York accent—Ray Liotta as Greenville, South Carolina, native "Shoeless" Joe Jackson.

Mitchell, Margaret. *Gone with the Wind*. New York: MacMillan, 1936. The Atlanta author's immortal tale of Scarlett O'Hara and Rhett Butler. One of the most popular books of all time.

O'Connor, Flannery. *Flannery O'Connor: Collected Works*. New York: Library of America, 1988. A must-read volume for anyone wanting to understand the South and the Southern Gothic genre of literature.

Poe, Edgar Allan. *The Gold Bug*. London: Hesperus Press, 2007. Inspired by his stint there with the U.S. Army, the great American author set this classic short story on Sullivan's Island, South Carolina, near Charleston.

# Internet Resources

## TOURISM AND RECREATION

### North Carolina

**Visit North Carolina**
www.visitnc.com
The state's official tourism website.

**North Carolina State Parks**
www.ncparks.gov
Info on how to enjoy North Carolina's network of state park sites and recreation areas, including camping reservations.

### South Carolina

**Discover South Carolina**
http://discoversouthcarolina.com
The state's official tourism website.

**South Carolina State Parks**
www.southcarolinaparks.com
This site offers historical and visitor information for South Carolina's excellent network of state park sites, including camping reservations.

### Georgia

**Explore Georgia**
www.exploregeorgia.org
The state's official tourism website.

**Georgia State Parks**
http://gastateparks.org
Historical and visitor information for Georgia's underrated network of state parks and historic sites, including camping reservations.

# NATURE
## North Carolina

**North Carolina Wildlife Resources Commission**
www.ncwildlife.org
Practical information about outdoor recreation in the Tar Heel State.

**CanoeNC**
www.canoenc.org
This is a nice starting point for planning a flat-water paddling trip in eastern North Carolina.

## South Carolina

**South Carolina Department of Natural Resources**
www.dnr.sc.gov
Advice on how best to enjoy South Carolina's great outdoors, whether you're an angler, a kayaker, a bird-watcher, a hiker, or a biker.

## Georgia

**Georgia Department of
Natural Resources
Wildlife Resources Division**
www.georgiawildlife.com
Lots of specific information on hunting, fishing, and outdoor recreation in Georgia's various regions.

**Paddle Georgia**
www.garivers.org
Georgia River Network site that clues you in on guided trips and tours of the state's rivers, creeks, and marshes.

# HISTORY AND CULTURE

**Blue Ridge Heritage Area**
www.blueridgeheritage.com
A resource that not only has a huge amount of mountain-area travel information but an ever-growing directory of traditional artists of all kinds in the Carolina mountains.

**Foxfire**
www.foxfire.org
Website of the long-standing nonprofit cultural organization based in Rabun County, Georgia, that seeks to preserve Appalachian folkways.

**Lost Worlds**
www.lostworlds.org
Well-researched and readable exploration of Georgia's extensive pre-Columbian Native American history.

**New Georgia Encyclopedia**
www.georgiaencyclopedia.org
A mother lode of concise, neutral, and well-written information on the natural and human history of Georgia from prehistory to the present.

**North Carolina Folklife Institute**
www.ncfolk.org
The website will fill you in on the many organizations across the state that promote traditional music, crafts, and folkways. You'll also find a calendar of folklife-related events in North Carolina, and travel itineraries for weekends exploring Core Sound, the Seagrove potteries, and Cherokee heritage in the Smokies.

**South Carolina Information Highway**
www.sciway.net
An eclectic cornucopia of interesting South Carolina history and assorted background facts makes for an interesting Internet portal into all things Palmetto State.

**Southern Highland Craft Guild**
www.southernhighlandguild.org
An Asheville-based regional arts giant with an extensive online guide to craftspeople throughout the region.

# Index

INDEX

# List of Maps

# Photo Credits

Title page photo: dock at Moccasin Creek State Park © Jim Morekis; page 8 © Meunierd | Dreamstime.com; page 10 (top left) © Jim Morekis, (top right) © Jim Morekis, (bottom) © Awakenedeye | Dreamstime.com; page 11 (top) © Jim Morekis, (bottom left) © Glenn Nagel | Dreamstime.com, (bottom right) © Jim Morekis; page 12 © Williamwise1 | Dreamstime.com; page 13 (top) © Sparhawk4242 | Dreamstime.com, (bottom left) © Revgeo | Dreamstime.com, (bottom right) © Jim Morekis; page 14-15 © Digidreamgrafix | Dreamstime.com; page 16 (top) © Bodhichita | Dreamstime.com, (bottom) © F11photo | Dreamstime.com; page 17 © F11photo | Dreamstime.com; page 18-19 (top) © Pltphotography | Dreamstime.com, (bottom) © Sepavo | Dreamstime.com; page 20 (top) © courtesy of Pinehurst Resort, (middle) © Cfmphotographyusa | Dreamstime.com, (bottom) © Jim Morekis; page 21 © Pivariz | Dreamstime.com; page 22 © Meunierd | Dreamstime.com; page 24 © Jim Morekis; page 26 © Jim Morekis; page 27 (top left) NPS photo by E. Leonard (top right) © Fallon Oldenburg | Dreamstime.com; (bottom) © Brittanygraham | Dreamstime.com; page 28 © Jilllang | Dreamstime.com; page 29 © Jim Morekis; page 30 © Meunierd | Dreamstime.com; page 32 © Appalachianviews | Dreamstime.com; page 34 © Anthonyheflin | Dreamstime.com; page 35 © Cfmphotographyusa | Dreamstime.com; page 36 © Dehooks | Dreamstime.com; page 37 (both) © Jim Morekis; page 39 © Jim Morekis; page 42 © Jim Morekis; page 49 © Jim Morekis; page 53 (both) © Jim Morekis; page 60 © Jim Morekis; page 61 © Jim Morekis; page 67 © Jaymade | Dreamstime.com; page 70 © Jim Morekis; page 71 © Jim Morekis; page 73 © Jim Morekis; page 75 (top) © Jim Morekis, (bottom) © Jim Morekis; page 77 © Marieclaire66 | Dreamstime.com; page 81 © Marieclaire66 | Dreamstime.com; page 83 © Jim Morekis; page 84 © Tlakebluemoon | Dreamstime.com; page 89 © Jim Morekis; page 91 © Jim Morekis; page 95 © Astargirl | Dreamstime.com; page 99 © Courtesy of State Archives of North Carolina Raleigh, NC; page 105 (both) © Jim Morekis; page 107 © Kzlobastov | Dreamstime.com; page 111 © Jim Morekis; page 112 © Jim Morekis; page 118 © Jim Morekis; page 119 © Jim Morekis; page 121 © Jim Morekis; page 125 © Jim Morekis; page 129 © Jim Morekis; page 135 © Jim Morekis; page 145 © Kmm7553 | Dreamstime.com; page 148 © Jim Morekis; page 149 (top) © Jim Morekis, (bottom) © Appalachianviews | Dreamstime.com; page 157 (top) © Appalachianviews | Dreamstime.com, (bottom) © Jim Morekis; page 159 © Jim Morekis; page 165 © Jim Morekis; page 169 © Jim Morekis; page 173 (both) © Jim Morekis; page 181 © Moonborne | Dreamstime.com; page 184 © Jim Morekis; page 185 © Jim Morekis; page 186 © Jim Morekis; page 189 © Jim Morekis; page 191 © Jim Morekis; page 195 © Jim Morekis; page 199 © Wolfsnap | Dreamstime.com; page 200 © Bokdavid | Dreamstime.com; page 206 (top) © Srcromer | Dreamstime.com, (bottom) © Jim Morekis; page 207 © Jim Morekis; page 212 © Jim Morekis; page 213 © Jim Morekis; page 216 © Jim Morekis; page 217 © Betty4240 | Dreamstime.com; page 219 © Jjvallee | Dreamstime.com; page 224 © Evaulphoto | Dreamstime.com; page 230 (top) © Jim Morekis, (bottom) © Jim Morekis; page 231 © Kirkikisphoto | Dreamstime.com; page 236 © Jim Morekis; page 239 © Jim Morekis; page 241 © Jim Morekis; page 242 © Jim Morekis; page 244 (both) © Jim Morekis; page 252 © Jim Morekis; page 262 © Marynag | Dreamstime.com; page 267 © Jim Morekis; page 269 © Jim Morekis; page 274 (both) © Jim Morekis; page 275 © Jim Morekis; page 281 © Jim Morekis; page 283 © Jim Morekis; page 287 © Jim Morekis; page 288 © Wickedgood | Dreamstime.com; page 290 © Jim Morekis; page 291 © Jim Morekis; page 294 © Jim Morekis; page 295 © Jim Morekis; page 296 © Jim Morekis; page 298 © Jim Morekis; page 300 © Jim Morekis; page 304 © Tinamou | Dreamstime.com; page 309 © Jim Morekis; page 317 © Wickedgood | Dreamstime.com; page 334 © Jim Morekis; page 338 © Jim Morekis; page 344 (both) © Jim Morekis; page 345 © Jim Morekis; page 349 © Jim Morekis; page 351 © Kzlobastov | Dreamstime.com; page 357 © Jim Morekis; page 358 © Jim Morekis; page 360 © Jim Morekis; page 361 © Jim Morekis; page 363 © Jim Morekis; page 365 © Jim Morekis; page 367 © Appalachianviews | Dreamstime.com; page 370 © Jim Morekis; page 371 © Jim Morekis; page 383 © Jim Morekis; page 387 © Jim Morekis; page 390 (top) © Jim Morekis, (bottom) © Americanspirit | Dreamstime.com; page 391 © Jim Morekis; page 397 (both) © Jim Morekis; page 400 © Jim Morekis; page 405 © Jim Morekis; page 407 © Jim Morekis; page 410 © Pxlman | Dreamstime.com; page 415 © Jim Morekis; page 417 © Jim Morekis; page 418 (both) © Jim Morekis; page 419 © Jim Morekis; page 425 © Jim Morekis; page 430 © Jim Morekis; page 431 © Jim Morekis; page 433 © Jim Morekis; page 436 © Jim Morekis; page 439 © Jim Morekis; page 440 © Jim Morekis; page 442 © Jim Morekis; page 444 © Jim Morekis; page 445 (top) © Sepavo | Dreamstime.com, (bottom) © Jim Morekis; page 447 © Jim Morekis; page 449 © Jim Morekis; page 454 © Jim Morekis; page 455 © Jim Morekis;

# Also Available

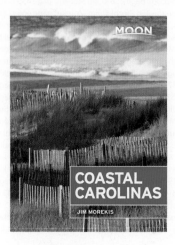

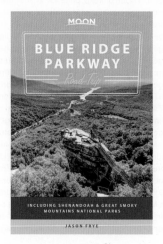

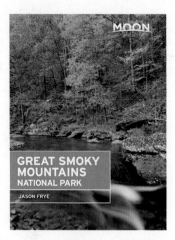

# MAP SYMBOLS

| | | | |
|---|---|---|---|
| ═════ Expressway | ○ City/Town | ✈ Airport | ⚲ Golf Course |
| ───── Primary Road | ◉ State Capital | ✗ Airfield | 🅿 Parking Area |
| ───── Secondary Road | ⊛ National Capital | ▲ Mountain | ▰ Archaeological Site |
| ─ ─ ─ ─ Unpaved Road | ★ Point of Interest | ✦ Unique Natural Feature | ⛪ Church |
| ──────── Feature Trail | • Accommodation | | ⛽ Gas Station |
| - - - - - Other Trail | ▼ Restaurant/Bar | 🗺 Waterfall | Glacier |
| ··········· Ferry | ■ Other Location | ♠ Park | Mangrove |
| ═════ Pedestrian Walkway | ▲ Campground | 🚩 Trailhead | Reef |
| ▭▭▭▭ Stairs | | ⛷ Skiing Area | Swamp |

# CONVERSION TABLES

°C = (°F - 32) / 1.8
°F = (°C x 1.8) + 32
1 inch = 2.54 centimeters (cm)
1 foot = 0.304 meters (m)
1 yard = 0.914 meters
1 mile = 1.6093 kilometers (km)
1 km = 0.6214 miles
1 fathom = 1.8288 m
1 chain = 20.1168 m
1 furlong = 201.168 m
1 acre = 0.4047 hectares
1 sq km = 100 hectares
1 sq mile = 2.59 square km
1 ounce = 28.35 grams
1 pound = 0.4536 kilograms
1 short ton = 0.90718 metric ton
1 short ton = 2,000 pounds
1 long ton = 1.016 metric tons
1 long ton = 2,240 pounds
1 metric ton = 1,000 kilograms
1 quart = 0.94635 liters
1 US gallon = 3.7854 liters
1 Imperial gallon = 4.5459 liters
1 nautical mile = 1.852 km

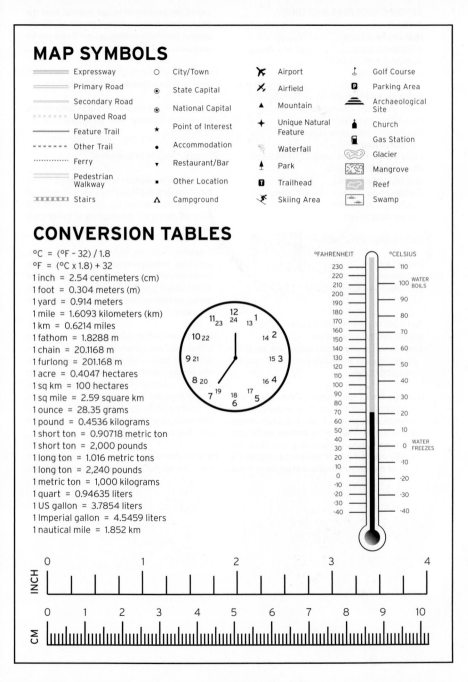

## MOON CAROLINAS & GEORGIA

Avalon Travel
Hachette Book Group
1700 Fourth Street
Berkeley, CA 94710, USA
www.moon.com

Editor: Rachel Feldman
Series Manager: Kathryn Ettinger
Copy Editor: Brett Keener
Graphics and Production Coordinator:
   Elizabeth Jang
Cover Design: Faceout Studios, Charles Brock
Moon Logo: Tim McGrath
Map Editor: Kat Bennett
Cartographers: Stephanie Poulain, Karin Dahl
Proofreader: Ann Seifert
Indexer: Greg Jewett

ISBN-13: 978-1-63121-653-4

Printing History
1st Edition — 2014
2nd Edition — December 2017
5 4 3 2 1

Front cover photo: neighborhood in Savannah, Georgia © Sean Pavone / Alamy Stock Photo

Back cover photo: autumn sunset in Great Smoky Mountains National Park © Daveallenphoto | Dreamstime

Printed in China by RR Donnelley